The Welfare Economics of Public Policy

To Vince, Brittany, Zachary, Christian, Elise, Brady, Vibeka, William,
Camila, Benjamin, Alyssa, Jaxon, Jeremy, Preston
and those yet to come

The Welfare Economics of Public Policy

A Practical Approach to Project and Policy Evaluation

Richard E. Just

Distinguished University Professor, University of Maryland, USA

Darrell L. Hueth

Professor, University of Maryland, USA and Professor Titular, Universidad de Los Andes, Colombia

Andrew Schmitz

Ben Hill Griffin Eminent Scholar and Professor, University of Florida and Research Professor, University of California, Berkeley, USA

Edward Elgar

Cheltenham, UK • Northampton, MA, USA

Published by
Edward Elgar Publishing Limited
Glensanda House
Montpellier Parade
Cheltenham
Glos GL50 1UA
UK

Edward Elgar Publishing, Inc.
136 West Street
Suite 202
Northampton
Massachusetts 01060
USA

A catalogue record for this book
is available from the British Library

Library of Congress Cataloguing in Publication Data

Just, Richard E.
The welfare economics of public policy: a practical approach to project and policy evaluation/Richard E. Just, Darrell L. Hueth, Andrew Schmitz.
p. cm.
Includes bibliographical references and index.
1. Welfare economics. 2. Economic policy. I. Hueth, Darrell L.
II. Schmitz, Andrew. III. Title
HB846.J873 2004
330.15'56—dc22

2004047151

ISBN 1 84376 688 4 (cased)

Printed and bound in Great Britain by MPG Books Ltd, Bodmin, Cornwall

Contents

Preface

This book develops economic welfare theory in the context of application to public policy questions. The authors' view is that knowledge of applied welfare theory is essential to the provision of useful and appropriate policy information. Moreover, empirical work by applied economists must be guided by the considerations of economic theory as well as the empirical possibilities suggested by econometric theory and data availability. This book provides a thorough review of economic welfare theory and illustrates how this theory can be employed to obtain policy and project evaluation information in the areas of international trade, the economics of technological change, agricultural economics, and environmental and natural resource economics, just to name a few.

The general equilibrium presentation of welfare theory emphasizes the shortcomings of the Pareto criterion as a guide to policy analysis and policy decisions. The compensation criterion, or Potential Pareto Improvement Criterion, of Kaldor and Hicks is then considered as a more promising approach to making public policy decisions. The compensation criterion is found to fall short of providing guidance to determine the optimum optimorium for society but is found to be useful in terms of identifying potential improvements in the economic well-being of society. The need for a social welfare function to enable an economist to make statements about what ought to be done in any given situation is clearly illustrated.

The emphasis of this book is on providing quantitative information on the welfare effects of alternative policy measures. After providing justification, it builds on the willingness-to-pay (WTP) measures proposed by Professor Hicks as the foundation for applied welfare economics and cost–benefit analysis. The problems that one confronts when attempting to use consumer surplus as a measure of welfare gain for the individual or household with single and multiple price changes are discussed verbally and explained graphically. Almost all chapters are followed by mathematical appendices that rigorously establish the results discussed in the chapters. Willingness-to-pay measures are developed for firms and households where households are viewed as both consumers and owners/sellers of resources.

In each case, the foremost concern is potential for applications to practical policy problems. In each case, possibilities are presented and discussed for (1) using consumer surplus as an approximation for WTP measures, (2) measuring WTP exactly (aside from econometric error) using existing econometric studies and (3) using duality theory to specify equations consistent with theory and then obtaining exact WTP measures following estimation (again aside from econometric error).

The welfare measures for individual agents are then aggregated to provide market measures of welfare gain and loss that satisfy the compensation criterion. Approaches are suggested to deal with the heterogeneity of firms and consumers based on practical data availability, which provide a way of overcoming the traditional shortcomings of representative producer or representative consumer models to the extent that data are available.

The relationship between the compensating and equivalent variation measures of Professor Hicks and the compensation criterion is explained in detail. A number of issues in applied welfare economics are treated at the market level in this book. For example, considerable emphasis is placed on the possibility of measuring welfare effects on consumers and producers in horizontally and vertically related markets to the market in which a policy change occurs. Also, the possibility of disaggregation of welfare effects for purposes of analyzing distributional issues and implications of policy decisions is investigated in detail. Some econometric considerations which arise in multimarket welfare analysis are also discussed, and suggestions are made with regard to the choice of market in which to do empirical analysis when data are sufficient to provide a choice. The conditions under which one should choose to estimate partial (or ordinary) rather than equilibrium demand and supply curves are spelled out.

Some of the later chapters cover specific areas of application and emphasize problems associated with welfare measurement when competition fails, welfare measurement under uncertainty, the welfare economics of information, nonmarket welfare measurement, dynamic issues and the welfare economics of extractive natural resources, and choice of the social rate of discount.

This book is designed to be highly flexible from the user's standpoint. The chapters are written at a level which is accessible to the upper division students in economics and related fields. The bulk of the analysis in the chapters is graphical, with simple algebra where necessary. Heuristic proofs are provided for major results whenever possible. For use as a graduate level text, full mathematical details and justification are provided in appendices and footnotes. The appendices rigorously establish the results found in the general text of the corresponding chapters and in some cases go beyond material discussed in the chapters. The proofs follow modern approaches utilizing the concepts of duality and the envelope theorem. The only mathematical tools necessarily required even for the appendices, however, are differential and integral calculus.

The topics covered by this book form a useful reference for practitioners of applied welfare economics. Government economists and engineers who are charged with providing cost effectiveness studies and with doing benefit–cost analysis will benefit by following the principles developed in this book for multimarket analysis, multiprice change analysis, and intertemporal or dynamic analysis both with and without uncertainty and risk. Natural resource economists will find Chapter 14, which deals with the economics of extractive resources, unique in that it treats the theory of intertemporal optimization in a manner understandable to students who have had only intermediate economic theory.

This book represents an expansion of an earlier book by the authors, *Applied Welfare Economics and Public Policy* (Just, Hueth and Schmitz 1982). That book, which has been used for many years as both a reference book and the text of numerous university courses across the USA and around the world, was awarded the Publication of Enduring Quality Award by the American Agricultural Economics Association in 1994. That book grew out of a course taught by Professor Andrew Schmitz at the University of California at Berkeley in the spring of 1970. The other two authors of this book were students in that course. It was there that their interest in applied welfare economics was sparked. Professor Schmitz, with two other students of a previous class, Martin Currie and John Murphy, had just published in the *Economic Journal* what subsequently became a classic survey of consumer surplus (Currie, Murphy and Schmitz 1971). In the process of the preparation of that manuscript, Professor Schmitz had uncovered a number of holes in the theory of consumer surplus, and his great enthusiasm stimulated considerable effort on the part of a number of students to fill these gaps. While the other authors have worked in a number of areas, Professor Schmitz's interest in applied welfare economics has continued unabated since that time. He has been particularly concerned with the income distributional issues that arise in applied welfare studies, which many of his less courageous contemporaries have been unwilling to address. His work with David E. Seckler in the *American Journal of Agricultural Economics* on the adoption of the tomato harvester in California has become a classic in this area (Schmitz and Seckler 1970).

This book significantly expands the scope of the material covered in its predecessor. Additionally, it provides a more modern treatment of the basic results and methods. Much of the new material was developed for use during the 1990s graduate welfare economics courses taught at the University of Maryland and the Universidad de Los Andes, Bogotá Colombia. The current book has significantly benefitted from the many comments and suggestions from students in these courses regarding the predecessor of this book and other course notes during the past ten years. Thus, the authors thank the students of welfare economics over the years at the University of Maryland, the University of California, Berkeley, the University of Florida and the Universidad de Los Andes, Bogotá, Colombia.

In addition, the authors would like to thank either individually or collectively Robert G. Chambers, Ronald G. Cummings, Steven M. Goldman, J. Arne Hallam, Harry G. Johnson, Abba P. Lerner, Juan Carlos Mendieta Lopéz, Ezra J. Mishan, Karen Mokate, Rulon D. Pope and Morris Taylor for providing inspiration and encouragement to continue pursuing this subject area and for providing various insights into welfare economics and its applications. We would also like to extend special thanks to Daniel W. Bromley, Ralph C. d'Arge, Bruce Gardner, W. Michael Hanemann, Wallace E. Oates, Rulon D. Pope, Robert D. Willig and Pan A. Yotopolos for reviewing and commenting on earlier versions of the manuscript including the original manuscript of the predecessor to this book (although any remaining errors are solely the authors' responsibility).

The authors would like to acknowledge financial support from the Experiment Stations at the University of Maryland, the Unverisity of Florida and from the Faculty of Economics at the Universidad de Los Andes. Our thanks also go to Lien Trieu for typing the manuscript, to Liesl Koch for providing copy-editing and to Katherine Faulkner for providing library assistance on countless occasions, all of the University of Maryland. Finally, we thank our wives and families for their support and sacrifice during the many hours required to complete this effort. As a meager token of our appreciation for all they have done, we dedicate this book to the grandchildren they have given us.

1. Introduction

Governments must make decisions regarding the adoption of public policies and projects. For example, the use of automobiles in the USA is recognized as being a major source of air pollution problems at the local level and as an important contributor to the accumulation of atmospheric gases and related global environmental problems. A significant increase in the federal gasoline tax has often been proposed as a mechanism to reduce this source of pollution. Such a tax would reduce domestic demand for crude oil and, possibly, crude oil prices. Given the significantly lower production costs of Middle Eastern oil producers relative to domestic oil producers, this policy would likely reduce domestic production more than oil importation.

An alternative policy that has been proposed is a significant expansion of domestic production through the opening up of now protected areas to exploration. This would reduce reliance on Middle Eastern oil imports. But onshore and offshore oil development has major environmental implications. Deterioration of air and water quality as well as damage to the beauty of the natural environment are more likely with such development. Habitat for many species is affected and some endangered species are threatened frequently with extinction. Domestic oil companies would receive windfall profits. How would consumers in the USA react to such policies? How would other countries react? What would be the effect on international trade?

Suppose you are an economist and are asked to provide expert testimony to a congressional committee regarding these policies. Which, if any, policy would you support? What would be the economic basis for your testimony? Is there an objective theoretical justification for either policy? How would you go about calculating the expected gains and losses from these proposed policies? One must bear in mind that public officials must and will make these decisions whether or not they can get objective advice.

Many developing countries also have major air pollution problems and have requested loans from international organizations such as the World Bank and the Inter-American Development Bank to finance projects such as mass transit systems, investment in less-polluting public transport fleets, and more rapid and less-polluting transportation facilities. Surveys conducted in these countries in very poor communities frequently indicate that poor households are 'willing to pay' more than their current income for improvements in air quality. Should the results of these surveys, appropriately aggregated, be used to estimate the benefits from such proposed projects?

International organizations are increasingly concerned about cost recovery, that is, the capability of a project to generate sufficient benefits to repay the loan. If the primary beneficiaries of a project have subsistence income levels, or less, should they be taxed to pay for the project? What comments could you offer in the 'cost recovery' section of the project evaluation document and what would be the economic basis for your comments?

Decisions must also be made by sovereign governments regarding import tariffs and quotas in the agricultural sector. Economic theory suggests that 'free trade' is optimal for the world as a whole assuming competitive conditions within and among trading countries. On the other hand, Japan today imposes a substantial duty on some imports from the USA (for example, beef). Similarly, US grain exports, which are partially produced from genetically modified seed, are denied full access to the European Economic Community. When asked to advise the US International Trade Commission regarding increased protection for US industries in such an economic environment, what should the position of an economist be? Would knowledge of the structure or degree of competitiveness of the industry be helpful in taking a position? Should a position be taken at all? Perhaps one should simply point out the economic ramifications of the decision.

In the context of trade policy, suppose that the decision has been made to embargo grain exports to a foreign country for political reasons and you are asked to assess the economic impacts. Do you need to consider effects other than those on the buyers and sellers of grain? If you find it necessary to consider impacts of lower grain prices on the beef sector, need you then also consider markets such as for poultry that are related to the beef market? Where does the chain of analysis end?

In natural resource industries, the major effects are frequently along the chain of markets leading from the basic resource to the eventual household consumer. Decisions regarding reductions in foreign fishing effort by a coastal nation within the 200-mile economic zone, for example, will be felt primarily in the domestic harvesting sector (by fishermen). But the seafood processing sector and the household and institutional consumers of fishing products will also be affected. With reductions in foreign effort, all these groups could gain. From a more general viewpoint, however, the public might gain more if the foreigners are allowed to continue fishing but are forced to pay taxes or fees on their catch. If so, how can the trade-off between the gains to fishermen and the losses to the public be evaluated? Should the gains and losses to these different groups be added independently of the group to whom they accrue or should the gains to one group, the lowest-income group, for example, be considered more important? Is there merit to the argument that each individual looks out for himself or herself, so the responsibility of economists is merely to put forth the *efficient* solution – which eliminates concern about income-distributional issues?

In fishing, forestry and minerals policy, and in extractive resource industries in general, the decisions made today have important consequences for future generations. This is particularly true in developing countries that obtain a large share of their income from exhaustible resource industries, such as copper in Chile and oil in Venezuela. Societies tend to use their highest valued and most accessible resources first. Hence, future production costs are increased as a result of decisions to produce today. Exhaustible resources may be eventually exhausted. What will happen when the 'well runs dry'? On the other hand, what are the chances that technological change will reduce or eliminate the demand for the resource and leave the country with large stocks of unmarketable resources?

Future generations, of course, do not have either political or 'dollar' votes in these affairs. Although the present generation tends to be willing to pay a premium for present consumption over future consumption, perhaps elected or appointed officials should act as guardians for future generations, as the famous welfare economist A.C. Pigou (1932) argued long ago. Should economic analysis for public policy evaluation consider future generations and be concerned about development policies that are sustainable? How are interests of future generations best incorporated in economic welfare analysis?

The branch of economics that deals with how economists should answer the foregoing questions, that is, evaluate proposed policies, is known as welfare economics. One objective of welfare economics is to help society make better choices. This book contains a methodology for compiling feasible economic evidence for the political process of public policy choice.

1.1 POSITIVE VERSUS NORMATIVE ECONOMICS

Positive economics is that branch of economics that is concerned with understanding and predicting economic behavior. The propositions of positive economics follow logically from axioms or assumptions about consumer and producer behavior, technology and availability of resources. What determines the prices of houses, ocean beach property and Iowa farmland, or what will happen to the output of a competitive firm when an *ad valorem* tax is imposed on each unit of its product? These are the types of questions that positive economics tries to answer. The theoretical parts of positive economics, insofar as they possess empirical implications, provide hypotheses that can be tested statistically. Rejection of the hypotheses generated by a theory suggests rejection of the underlying theory.

Moreover, while there may be controversy regarding whether or not the assumptions of a positive model conform sufficiently to reality, or whether or not they are appropriate for the circumstances where the model is proposed for application, the morality or ethics of the assumptions is not an issue in positive economics. Positive economics is only concerned with what 'is'.

Welfare economics, on the other hand, is concerned with what 'ought' to be. Welfare economics is *normative economics*. Welfare economics focuses on using resources optimally to achieve the maximum well-being for the individuals in society. But, unfortunately, agreement cannot always be reached on what is optimal. As with positive economics, the propositions of welfare economics are also logical deductions from a set of definitions and assumptions but the assumptions of welfare economics are fundamentally different from those of positive economics. They are ethical assumptions or value judgments with which economists, or for that matter any individual, may legitimately disagree.

Two of these ethical assumptions are, however, sufficiently widely accepted that they provide the foundations for a large part of applied welfare economics and policy evaluation. They are that (1) the welfare status of society must be judged solely by the members of society, which recognizes the traditional emphasis on the importance of the individual in Western society, and (2) the notion that society is better off if any member of society is made better off without making anyone else worse off. The first proposition is sometimes called the *fundamental ethical postulate* or the principle of *individualism* (Quirk and Saposnik 1968, p. 104). In determining the social preference over two possible states of the economy, this proposition demands that the only thing that counts is the preferences of the members of society. The second proposition is known as the *Pareto principle* after the founder of the principle, Vilfredo Pareto (1896). This proposition is discussed further in Chapter 2.

A second difficulty with welfare economics is that economic 'welfare' is not an observable variable like the number of machines, houses, market prices or profits. The economic welfare status of an individual is formally represented by his or her utility level, a term generally used synonymously with happiness or satisfaction.[1] A basic proposition of utility theory in positive economics is that utility increases as the amount of goods consumed increases. In welfare economics, one would like to know by how much? But one cannot measure the increase in utility, for example, by additional *utils*, obtained from consumption. Consequently, positive economics assumes that utility is only *ordinally* measurable. That is, the utility indicator of positive economics only ranks bundles in terms of whether one bundle is preferred to another and not by how much. This is not a problem for positive economics because all of the basic propositions about how consumers respond to changes in prices and income can be derived from a system where the consumer only ranks consumption bundles using preference relationships. For example, an ordinal system assumes that individuals can only rank alternatives such as whether a ski trip is preferred to staying at home or whether a concert is preferred to staying at home.

In welfare economics, one needs to measure how much a ski trip is preferred to staying at home and how much a concert is preferred to staying at home. That is, intensities of preferences matter in determining which consumers should receive which goods when goods are available in limited supply. A system where intensities of preferences can be determined is known as a *cardinal* system. A cardinal system specifies exactly how much utility each affected individual would gain or lose from a proposed policy decision. Such information would surely be helpful to those concerned with determining the maximum well-being for society and would simplify the subject of welfare economics substantially.

Measurability of utility, however, is not sufficient to determine optimal social choices. To demonstrate why this is the case, suppose two individuals visit you for the weekend and you have both ski-lift tickets and concert tickets. Suppose further that you know that one individual gets 50 utils from a ski trip, the other individual gets 30 utils from a concert and your purpose in inviting your guests was to go out together as a group. Assuming you are indifferent to concerts and ski trips and hope to maximize social welfare, what should you do? Society may well consider the concert-goer twice as important as the skier, perhaps because the skier has twice the income and ability to afford ski trips. If so, a concert is in order. The point is that, even if utility were measurable, there would still be the problem of how to weight individuals. No objective way exists for solving this problem of interpersonal comparisons.[2]

In practice, to test a welfare proposition is exceedingly difficult. In contrast to positive

1. Another fundamental proposition in welfare economics is that if an individual is observed to choose a bundle of goods *x* when a bundle *y* was available under the same conditions, then the person is 'better off' with *x* than *y*. As appealing as this proposition is, it is not generally agreed upon by philosophers, one of whom writes (Sagoff 1988, p. 57), 'There is no evidence . . . to show that people become happier, more satisfied, or better off in some substantive sense (after basic needs are met) when their income, and, therefore, the amount they can and will pay for things increases.' For example, is a smoker who is given a few cartons of free cigarettes really better off? For an earlier discussion of this issue, see I.M.D. Little (1960). As Sagoff correctly recognizes, however, it is not really important for welfare economics whether or not an individual is happier or has more utility with bundle *x* rather than *y* because neither concept is measurable. If one adopts willingness to pay for a change as the appropriate measure of benefits to the individual for the purposes of policy evaluation, then this issue is effectively avoided. A concern that arises with discussion along these lines is that if the individual does not know when he or she is better off, or at least expects to be better off, then who does?
2. The work of Sen (1979) shows that the fundamental problem in making social choices is the inability to make interpersonal comparisons rather than the lack of cardinality. In particular, he shows that the Arrow impossibility theorem holds under cardinality as well as ordinality if interpersonal noncomparability is maintained. The Arrow impossibility theorem (Arrow 1951) proves that no reasonable rule exists for combining rankings of various states of society by individuals into a societal ranking. Sen further finds that 'Interpersonal comparability without cardinality is, however, a way out of impossibility' (Sen 1979, p. 546).

economics, where the normal way of testing a theory is to test its conclusions, the procedure used to test a welfare proposition is to examine its assumptions. As J. de V. Graaff (1953, p. 3) has noted with respect to positive economics, 'the proof of the pudding is indeed in the eating. The welfare cake, on the other hand, is so difficult to taste that we must sample its ingredients before baking.' Therefore, assumptions take on increased importance in economic welfare analysis.

One view of welfare economics (especially in relationship to policy and project evaluation) is to consider it as a branch of economics that carries positive economics one step further. For example, studies have been done in energy economics to forecast the future prices of major petroleum products. These forecasts are based upon complex models, which are positive in nature. However, given the supply and demand equations on which these forecasts are based, one can easily compute effects of various government policy changes on consumers' income and on oil company profits. One can determine, for example, the effects of industry deregulation. However, conclusions should be checked carefully by scrutinizing the assumptions used to build the positive forecasting model. Models may forecast well in some cases even when the underlying assumptions are unrealistic. Thus, the economic welfare implications of two positive economic models that forecast equally well may be vastly different.

Another often misunderstood point in welfare economics is whether economists need to talk about the 'desirability' of a policy change, such as the 'goodness' or 'badness' of technological change or whether or not tariffs 'should' be imposed. A frequent misunderstanding in performing economic welfare analysis relates to whether or not the analysis should be carried to the point of making recommendations to policy-makers concerning whether or not a bridge or dam should be built, whether or not supersonic aircraft or the mechanical lettuce harvester should be introduced, and the like. Making such recommendations may not be a necessary or appropriate role for an economist to play. Rather, pointing out the economic implications of policy changes for individual groups in society may provide the critical policy analysis needed by policy-makers, who are elected and empowered to make choices that alter income distribution.

A concrete example can serve to illustrate this point. Several studies have been done on the welfare effects of US quotas to restrict the importation of beef (see, for example, US International Trade Commission 1977). Although these studies estimate the gains to consumers and the losses to cattle producers associated with removing the restrictions, they do not necessarily use their estimates of gains and losses as a basis upon which to recommend whether or not the US government should remove quotas or increase them above current levels. To politicians representing their constituencies in policy-making, political factors such as international relations or related economic considerations such as trade deficit management may be more important. But only with adequate economic welfare analysis can policy-makers undertake informed decisions with an understanding of the extent and magnitude of their economic consequences.

1.2 SOME CONTROVERSIES IN WELFARE ECONOMICS

Welfare economics has a long history as a field of inquiry within the broad scope of the study of economics. Such concepts as economic rent or producer surplus (the area above the supply curve bounded by price) and consumer surplus (the triangle-like area under the demand curve and above price), which are very much in use today, were presented in the nineteenth century. Ricardo (1829) introduced the concept of economic rent when discussing the effects of England's corn laws. Dupuit (1844), a French engineer, used the notion of consumer surplus to analyze the effects of building a bridge. These concepts were developed more fully by Marshall (1930) in the early twentieth century and have since formed the basis for most empirical economic welfare studies.

Often, however, a distinction is made between the *old welfare economics* of Marshall and what has come to be called the *new welfare economics*. The old welfare economics based on utilitarianism, which accepted both cardinality of utility and interpersonal comparisons of utilty, found that social gains are maximized by competitive markets. Therefore, where noncompetitive interferences exist, the economist is justified in recommending policy measures that eliminate those 'distortions'. Also, the old welfare economics employs the technique of partial-equilibrium analysis in developing recommendations. Partial-equilibrium or piecemeal analysis considers the welfare effects of a change in one market, assuming the effects in other markets are negligible. Finally, from an empirical standpoint, the old welfare economics holds that the triangle-like area to the left of the demand curve and above price is a serviceable money measure of utility to the consumers in a market. The triangle-like area to the left of the supply curve and below price is similarly held to be an adequate money measure of welfare for producers in a market. Changes in these areas can then be used to measure welfare changes to society.

The principles of the old welfare economics have been attacked on several grounds by those economists associated with the *new welfare economics*, who reject both cardinality and interpersonal comparability. For example, economists such as Paul A. Samuelson (1942) demonstrated that the basic welfare measure of the old welfare economics – consumer surplus – is not well defined (see also Silberberg 1972). That is, consumer surplus is not generally a unique money measure of utility, and nonuniqueness can imply contradictions depending upon the use of empirical data. This criticism of the use of consumer surplus put applied welfare economics on somewhat shaky grounds until Willig's (1973, 1976) work appeared.

Another criticism of the old welfare economics is based upon an argument advanced over a century ago by Pareto (1896). He argued that any policy that makes any person worse off cannot be supported on objective grounds. As further elaborated upon by Kaldor (1939) and Hicks (1939), the welfare weights attached to each individual need not be the same. Hence, simply showing an increase in the sum of consumer and producer surplus across individuals is not a sufficient basis to recommend a change. Pareto argued that the only objective basis under which one can say society is better off is when some people are made better off and no one is made worse off. This criterion has come to be known as the *Pareto principle*.

In an attempt to extend the class of questions that can be addressed objectively by welfare economics, Kaldor and Hicks introduced the *compensation principle* by which a change should be made if a potential Pareto improvement can be made by some redistribution of goods or income following the change so that at least one individual is better off and no one is worse off. This *compensation criterion* has also come to be known as the *potential Pareto principle*. The associated measurement problem was addressed by Hicks (1943) who suggested that alternative money measures of welfare, while not directly related to utility gains and losses, can be given willingness-to-pay (WTP) interpretations (see also Hicks 1956). For example, one could measure how much money each individual is willing to pay for a particular policy change, which may be negative for some individuals, and then observe whether the total is positive or negative. The Hicksian willingess-to-pay measures are unique measures in any situation and are not subject to the Samuelson criticism of consumer surplus. The notion of WTP and the associated compensation criteria are key concepts and form the foundation of applied welfare economics.

The compensation principle has also not escaped criticism. Scitovsky (1941), in what has become known as the *reversal paradox*, illustrated how inconsistencies can occur when using this principle in policy analysis. Later, Gorman (1955) extended this analysis to illustrate an *intransitivity* problem associated with inconsistent rankings of three or more situations.

Yet another criticism of the old welfare economics has to do with its piecemeal approach. Using the Pareto principle, Lipsey and Lancaster (1956–57) demonstrated that, if a distortion cannot be removed in one market or economic sector, then distortions must also exist in other markets or sectors to make everyone as well off as possible. Because one can hardly argue that the total economy is free of noncompetitive interferences, this result suggests that the partial approach to welfare economics may not be appropriate.

How have applied welfare economists – the practitioners – responded to these attacks? The late John V. Krutilla (1981, p. 4) has asked and answered this question: 'Did we observe – as might be expected – hesitancy in using welfare economics in the applied area? Quite the contrary. Applied welfare economics flourished throughout this period *as though* (if not actually) innocent of the controversy.' Applied welfare economists have continued to use partial equilibrium models for policy recommendations that have been made even though there are losers as well as gainers. In some cases, this analysis has even been legislatively mandated. The Flood Control Act of 1936 required that the benefits from water resource development projects must exceed the costs 'to whomever they may accrue' (s. 701a). To measure these benefits and costs in project evaluation work, economists continue to use the areas behind supply and demand curves. Policy-makers demand economic analyses of policy decisions, and applied welfare economists have used the only tools they have had available to provide information.

Fortunately, however, some theoretical justification for feasible empirical practices has followed. For example, the piecemeal approach has been shown by Davis and Whinston (1965, 1967) to be appropriate when some markets or sectors have little economic impact on others (for example, the effect of corn price supports on the automotive industry). Where market interdependencies exist, welfare economists now have better guidance as to how far they need to look to obtain the total welfare effects of a policy change.

The Samuelsonian criticism of the use of consumer surplus was answered to the satisfaction of most economists by Willig (1973, 1976), who established firm theoretical relationships between two of the Hicksian WTP measures and consumer surplus, and Hausman (1981), who showed how these Hicksian measures could be measured exactly using market price and quantity data.

Similar advances have been made in other areas and under other assumptions. One of the objectives of this book is to show how these many advances fit together to constitute a complete methodology for applied economic welfare analysis.

1.3 COMPENSATION IN WELFARE ECONOMICS

In its original Kaldor/Hicks form, the *compensation principle* states that policy *B* is preferred to policy *A* if, in the move from policy *A* to policy *B*, everyone can potentially be made better off. The reversal paradox pointed out by Tibor Scitovsky (1941) is that cases exist in which (1) the gainers can compensate the losers when going from policy *A* to policy *B* by using the initial prices and income distribution to evaluate the change, but (2) the losers can compensate the gainers when going back from policy *B* to policy *A* starting from the subsequent prices and income distribution. Thus, cases can occur where policy *B* is preferred to policy *A* and policy *A* is preferred to policy *B*. This was resolved by the adoption of the double criterion of Scitovsky which stated that policy *B* is preferred to policy *A* only if the gainers can compensate the losers when making the change, and the losers cannot bribe the gainers into not making the change. This potential compensation criterion was further broadened by Samuelson (1947, 1956), who compared all possible prices and income redistributions of the outcome associated with policy *A*. The word 'potential' is critical here because policy *B* is preferred to policy *A* as long as it is *possible* for the gainers to compensate the losers – not only when the gainers actually compensate the losers. The principle is based on potential compensation only.

Supporters of the principle of potential compensation argued that the actual payment of compensation (for example, by the gainers to the losers when moving from policy *A* to policy *B*) involves a value judgment. But a welfare gain occurs only when everyone is made better off or, at least, when someone is made better off and no one is made worse off. If one goes beyond making statements of potential gains and recommends that changes be made on the basis of these potential gains, then the application of the compensation principle may lead to changes that make some people worse off and others better off by a greater amount. If society has a high regard for the individual made worse off and a low regard for the individual made better off (perhaps because one is poor and the other is rich), then society as a whole may be worse off with the change. Thus, the application of the compensation principle when compensation is not actually paid also clearly involves a value judgment.

With this in mind, appropriate economic welfare analysis must investigate the effects of a policy change on both groups and leave the subjective evaluation of which distribution is better to the policy-maker who is elected to fulfill that responsibility. Economic welfare analysis of the effects of specific policies that do not indicate to a policy-maker how individual groups are affected differently represents, in effect, an attempt to usurp the policy-maker's authority to make such judgments.

An example serves to demonstrate the importance of the distinction between potential and actual compensation. Suppose that tomatoes are hand-picked so that the industry is labor intensive. Then a mechanical harvester is introduced that displaces a substantial number of workers. Under the compensation principle, the harvester is desirable if the gains are sufficient so that the gainers (for example, the landowners, producers, consumers and machinery manufacturers) could compensate the displaced workers if they desired (that is, there are potential gains for all). For the USA, this was indeed found to be the case by Schmitz and Seckler (1970) for mechanical harvesting of tomatoes. However, if compensation does not take place, then some groups lose, even though potential gains are available for all. Depending on society's valuation of changes in the distribution of real income, perhaps the tomato harvester should not have been introduced unless displaced workers were actually paid compensation. This issue should be decided by elected officials, but informed decisions are facilitated by economic welfare analysis that determines the distributional implications.

A defensible approach to determining whether or not the introduction of the tomato harvester represents a potential Pareto gain according to the compensation criterion is to sum the WTP of gainers and losers. That is, the tomato harvester represents a potential Pareto gain if the maximum amount of money that producers and other gainers are willing to pay rather than give up the harvester exceeds the minimum amount of money that farm laborers would have to be paid to tolerate the harvester.

1.4 COMPENSATING AND EQUIVALENT VARIATIONS

The two most widely used willingess-to-pay welfare measures proposed by John R. Hicks (1943, 1956) are the *compensating variation* and the *equivalent variation*. These measures can be directly employed in performing the compensation tests of the new welfare economics. Because many policy choices depend on the magnitudes by which the gainers gain and the losers lose, measurement in quantitative terms is often critical. Because utility is not measurable, an alternative measure must be chosen. The motivation for the Hicksian measures is that *an observable alternative for measuring the intensities of preferences of an individual for one situation versus another is the amount of money the individual is willing to pay or willing to accept to move from one situation to another.* This principle has become a foundation for modern applied welfare economics and, in particular, is a foundation for the methodology developed in this book.

Because these WTP measures are often approximated by consumer surplus, the triangle-like area behind the demand curve and above the price line, the subtleties of the difference in the old and new welfare economics should be clearly understood. A basic premise of some early welfare economists was that consumer surplus is the appropriate welfare measure for the consumer. The correct reasoning, however, is that the consumer surplus area has welfare significance only insofar as it approximates the true WTP measure.

The two most important WTP measures are compensating and equivalent variations. *Compensating variation* is the amount of money which, when taken away from an individual after an economic change, leaves the person just as well off as before. For a welfare gain, it is the maximum amount that the person would be willing to pay for the change. For a welfare loss, it is the negative of the minimum amount that the person would require as compensation for the change. *Equivalent variation* is the amount of money paid to an individual which, if an economic change does not happen, leaves the individual just as well off as if the change had occurred. For a welfare gain, it is the minimum compensation that the person would need to forgo the change. For a welfare loss, it is the negative of the maximum amount that the individual would be willing to pay to avoid the change.

Compensating variation and equivalent variation can also be used to measure producer welfare effects. For producers of a good, these measures are shown in Chapter 4 to coincide with more well-known welfare quantities (such as quasirents) and, in some cases, profits. However, there are still a number of empirical problems on the supply side. For example, it is not easy in today's complex environment to define the producer or the firm. Many firms are legal entities that do not own all of the factors used for production. As an example, in agriculture a great deal of farmland is leased by growers. This type of problem makes empirical welfare economics difficult but not unmanageable. One needs to split producers into groups. To illustrate this issue, consider the controversy surrounding the Soviet grain purchases in 1973, which, in turn, caused the price of US farmland to increase. Clearly, renters of farmland did not obtain the same benefits as did producers who owned the land they farmed.

1.5 EFFICIENCY AND EQUITY

Almost without exception, the great works in economics have focused on some aspect of the operation of the economy in terms of such criteria as efficiency and equity. *Economic efficiency* has to do with producing and facilitating as much consumption as possible with available resources, whereas *equity* has to do with how equitably goods are distributed among individuals. Do competitive markets lead to the most preferable state of society? What are the distributional effects of imperfect competition and monopoly power? How can the effects of monopoly power be measured? These are some of the fundamental questions of efficiency and equity that can be addressed with welfare economics.

Given an initial distribution of income and resources, one can possibly improve market efficiency and make society better off. However, a system may be very efficient but not very equitable in how the output is distributed. Efficiency can be defined only with reference to a given income distribution. If one changes the distribution, one changes the optimal or competitive output product mix. There is no objective way to determine both the ideal output and its distribution. There are many economically efficient states, each corresponding to different income distributions. The choice of income distribution, however, is a political matter that can be solved only by value judgments through the political process.

Nevertheless, welfare economic analyses can provide useful inputs in the policy-making process by pointing out the efficiency and distributional implications of policy changes. For example, the Organization of Petroleum Exporting Countries (OPEC) was formed and is an effective monopolistic device for pricing oil. The associated welfare impacts have, no doubt, been considerable. Partially as a response, there have been several proposals for forming an international grain export cartel. But how might the associated welfare impacts be evaluated? Although grain-exporting countries can gain benefits through such a cartel arrangement, what about the worldwide distributional effects? Is there a difference between a government export cartel and a producer cartel? Which groups would oppose a cartel? To form such a cartel in grains, would prices have to be set by governments and/or by marketing boards, or could pricing be done by the private grain companies, many of which are large, multinational firms? Welfare economics can and has been used to determine such effects (see, for example, Schmitz et al. 1981). Results indicate that a government-export cartel has very different effects on the welfare of producers than does a producer-export cartel (Carter, Gallini and Schmitz 1980).

1.6 WELFARE WEIGHTINGS

Because the question of optimal income distribution cannot be resolved on objective grounds, one approach has been to try to develop 'welfare weights' for various groups of individuals. In dealing with welfare analysis, some economists attach equal welfare weights to the various market groups in their models and attempt to identify potential Pareto improvements. For example, suppose that a competitive market becomes monopolistic. This change would cause a welfare loss to consumers and a gain to the producing sector. In this type of analysis, equal weighting implies that a dollar lost by the consumers exactly offsets a dollar gained by producers. A policy-maker, however, may prefer a change that gives \$10 to the poor at the expense of \$11 to the rich. A graduated income-tax scale with welfare assistance for the poor is evidence of such preferences and perhaps gives some basis for determining which weighting scheme matches revealed policy preferences.

Clearly, the choice of welfare weights is a value judgment. Some economists have tried to use 'revealed' weights of policy-makers but others have argued that assuming politicians' welfare weights are the appropriate weights for society is unjustified. Politicians have their own utility functions. Attempts to base such weights on previous policy choices are plagued by problems of frequent changes in policy-making bodies and problems associated with noneconomic forces playing a role in many policy decisions. An alternative approach in applied economic welfare analysis is to derive results under various welfare weightings. A policy-maker can then decide what action to take based on his or her choice of weights. Thus, the economic analyst need not select the weighting and, thus, a value judgment is not necessary in the economic analysis, even when compensation is not considered. When applied economic welfare studies focus on the distribution of effects across major groups of individuals, rather than only on the aggregate effects of a policy, this more detailed information can rightfully be used in augmenting information available to policy-makers who represent different constituencies. This book provides a framework for supplying such information.

Of course, this type of information may or may not be the deciding factor in specific policy choices. Policy formulation and the theory of policy choice is a much broader subject area. While economic welfare analysis should be viewed as an integral step in policy formation and evaluation, it is not the only component. A broad coverage of the theory of public choice in democracy, for example, can be found in texts such as those by Mueller (1979) and van den Doel (1979). There are also many other topics in welfare economics that focus on issues of a more esoteric nature, such as the 'ideal' society or social choice mechanism. This includes such subjects as the illusive *social welfare function* (a hypothetical function that resolves conflicts of efficiency and equity; see Bergson 1938) and theories of justice (for example, Rawls's 1971 theory of justice, which argues that analysis should be directed to helping the most miserable person). Some of these concepts are discussed briefly, but the mainstream of this book does not focus on such issues because of their limited use for applied policy and project evaluation.

1.7 OVERVIEW OF THE BOOK

The topic of this book is *applied* welfare economics. The major emphasis is on concepts that have empirical possibilities. However, before proceeding to the more applied aspects of welfare economics, Chapters 2 and 3 discuss theoretical welfare economics in a general equilibrium context. A discussion and understanding of such concepts as Pareto optimality, competitive equilibrium, optimal income distribution, the social welfare function and the compensation tests are necessary in order to meaningfully interpret the content of the later chapters, which focus on concepts of applied welfare economics.

Chapter 4 deals with producer welfare measurement and discusses concepts such as producer surplus, economic rent and profits. The appropriate use of each is analyzed. Measurement is considered in both input and output markets. Intertemporal welfare measurement for producers is considered in the presence of adjustment costs and capital investment.

Chapters 5 and 6 focus on consumer welfare measurement. Chapter 5 deals with the notion of consumer surplus and why it does not provide a unique measure of welfare change for consumers. Chapter 6 considers consumer welfare measurement within a WTP context. It discusses the various measures that have been proposed and the extent to which the triangle-like area under a demand curve can approximate these measures. Finally, the possibilities for exact measurement are explored.

Chapter 7 focuses on decision-making by factor owners and factor suppliers. Economic rent for a factor supplier is shown to have a welfare interpretation symmetrical with consumer surplus. Chapter 7 also demonstrates how WTP measures can be approximated by areas above factor supply curves. Applicability of the household production model is considered for problems where certain household activity is unobserved. The use of the dual approach for obtaining exact estimates of WTP is explained.

Chapters 8 and 9 focus on aggregation and multimarket general equilibrium considerations. In Chapter 8, aggregation is carried out for a single market. The effects of taxes, subsidies, quotas, price supports, price controls, tariffs and other trade barriers are analyzed and possibilities for estimating welfare effects are discussed. Chapter 9 shows how applied welfare analysis can be done when more than one market (either input or output) is affected. Results show that theoretical welfare analysis typically has a much broader interpretation than standard criticisms of partial analysis have recognized, and that econometric models focused on specific market prices and quantities can in some circumstances facilitate general equilibrium estimation of welfare effects.

Chapters 10 through 14 consider applications of welfare economics to a variety of specific areas. Chapter 10 discusses imperfect markets and shows the welfare effects of monopoly and monopsony practices. Antitrust economics is briefly discussed. Applications are made to welfare evaluation of labor unions and international trade arrangements. Chapter 11 investigates how to measure the welfare effects of information. Applications are made to advertising and information policy that demonstrate the welfare effects of withholding information or disseminating false information. Chapter 12 considers stochastic welfare economics and the welfare effects of stabilization policy depending on whether decision-makers are risk averse. Applications are made to problems in agricultural policy analysis. State contingent compensation is considered. Chapter 13 discusses the welfare economics of externalities and public goods and the role of property rights. Approaches for nonmarket welfare measurement are discussed. Applications are made to environmental economic policy analysis. Chapter 14 considers cost–benefit analysis with applications in natural resource economics. Dynamic methods of economic welfare analysis and social discounting of benefits and costs over time are introduced. Chapter 15 presents conclusions. It ends with a note of optimism and suggests that, despite the criticisms of classical welfare economics, today's body of applied economic welfare methodology can provide a useful input to the policy process.

2. Pareto optimality and the Pareto criterion

Determination of economic criteria for public policy evaluation has been a subject of great debate. The difficulty stems from the inability to decide on purely economic grounds how the goods and services produced in an economy should be distributed among individuals. Issues of distribution and equity are political and moral as well as economic in nature.

Classical economists such as Bentham (1961, first published 1823) long ago developed the concept of a social welfare function to measure the welfare of society as a function of the utilities of all individuals. The objective was to establish a complete *social ordering* of all possible alternative states of the world. A social ordering, in principle, permits comparison and choice among alternative states and would allow economists to determine precisely which set of policies maximize the good of society. The problem is that agreement on the form of a social welfare function cannot be reached so the use of such a concept has been clouded with controversy. Many functional forms have been proposed and defended on moral, ethical and philosophical grounds with specific considerations given to equity, liberty and justice (see Sections 3.3 and 3.4 for more details). Because of the subjectivity of these arguments, agreement is unlikely ever to be reached. Even if agreement were reached among economists, policy-makers may be unwilling to accept such judgments by economists as the basis for public policy choice.

Because use of a social welfare function is clouded by controversy, many economists have tried to maintain objectivity and the claim of their professional practice as a science by avoiding *value judgments*. A value judgment is simply a subjective statement about what is of value to society that helps to determine the social ordering of alternative states of the world. It is subjective in the sense that it cannot be totally supported by evidence. It is not a judgment of fact. The attempt to avoid value judgments led to development of the *Pareto principle*.

The Pareto criterion was introduced in the nineteenth century by the eminent Italian economist, Vilfredo Pareto (1896). Its potential for application to public policy choices, however, is still very much discussed. By this criterion, a policy change is socially desirable if, by the change, everyone can be made better off, or at least some are made better off, while no one is made worse off. If there are any who lose, the criterion is not met. In his book *The Zero-Sum Society: Distribution and the Possibilities for Economic Change*, Lester Thurow (1980) contends that many good projects do not get under way simply because project managers are unwilling to pay compensation to those who would actually be made worse off. If this is correct, perhaps policy measures should be considered that meet the Pareto criterion. That is, perhaps policy measures that include the payment of compensation, so that everyone is made better off, should be considered. For example, those who support tariffs argue that their removal results in short-term loss of jobs for which workers are not adequately compensated. Trade theory shows that there are economic gains from free trade, but the distribution of these gains is what the workers object to. This objection would probably not arise if only policies that met the Pareto criterion were considered. However, as will become clear, there are also limitations to using the Pareto criterion to rank policy choices.

A large part of theoretical welfare economics and its application is based on the Pareto principle and the concept of Pareto optimality. This chapter discusses both Pareto optimality and the Pareto criterion in a general equilibrium setting. The consideration of these concepts in a general equilibrium context enables greater understanding of the assumptions, limitations and generalizations associated with applying welfare economics to real-world problems discussed in later chapters.

2.1 PARETO OPTIMALITY AND THE PARETO CRITERION DEFINED

The *Pareto criterion* is a technique for comparing or ranking alternative states of the economy. By this criterion, if it is possible to make at least one person better off when moving from state *A* to state *B* without making anyone else worse off, state *B* is ranked higher by society than state *A*. If this is the case, a movement from state *A* to state *B* represents a *Pareto improvement*, or state *B* is *Pareto superior* to state *A*. As an example, suppose a new technology is introduced that causes lower food prices and, at the same time, does not harm anyone by (for example) causing unemployment or reduced profits. The introduction of such a technology would be a Pareto improvement.

To say that society should make movements that are Pareto improvements is, of course, a value judgment but one that enjoys widespread acceptance. Some would disagree, however, if policies continuously make the rich richer while the poor remain unaffected.

If society finds itself in a position from which there is no feasible Pareto improvement, such a state is called a *Pareto optimum*. That is, a *Pareto-optimal state is defined as a state from which it is impossible to make one person better off without making another person worse off*. It is important to stress that, even though a Pareto-optimal state is reached, this in no way implies that society is equitable in terms of income distribution. For example, as will become evident later, a Pareto-optimum position is consistent with a state of nature even where the distribution of income is highly skewed.

If the economy is not at a Pareto optimum, there is some inefficiency in the system. When output is divisible, it is always theoretically possible to make everyone better off in moving from a *Pareto-inferior* position to a *Pareto-superior* position. Hence, Pareto-optimal states are also referred to as *Pareto-efficient* states, and the Pareto criterion is referred to as an *efficiency criterion*. Efficiency in this context is associated with getting as much as possible for society from its limited resources. Note, however, that the Pareto criterion can be used to compare two inefficient states as well. That is, one inefficient state may represent a Pareto improvement over another inefficient state.

Of course, it may be politically infeasible to move from certain inefficient states to certain Pareto-superior states. If Thurow is correct, the only feasible options may be moves to positions where at least one person is made worse off. States where one person is made better off and another is made worse off are referred to as *Pareto-noncomparable states*. Note that all of these Pareto-related concepts are defined independently of societies' institutional arrangements for production, marketing and trade.

2.2 THE PURE CONSUMPTION CASE

Now consider the concepts of Pareto optimality and the Pareto criterion for the pure exchange case, that is, the optimal allocation of goods among individuals where the goods are, in fact, already produced. In this context, a set of marginal exchange conditions characterizing Pareto-efficient states can be developed. Suppose that there are two individuals, A and B, and quantities of two goods, $\bar{q}_1$ and $\bar{q}_2$, which have been produced and can be distributed between the two individuals. This situation is represented by the *Edgeworth–Bowley box* in Figure 2.1, where the width of the box measures the total amount of $\bar{q}_1$ produced and the height of the box measures the total amount of $\bar{q}_2$ produced.

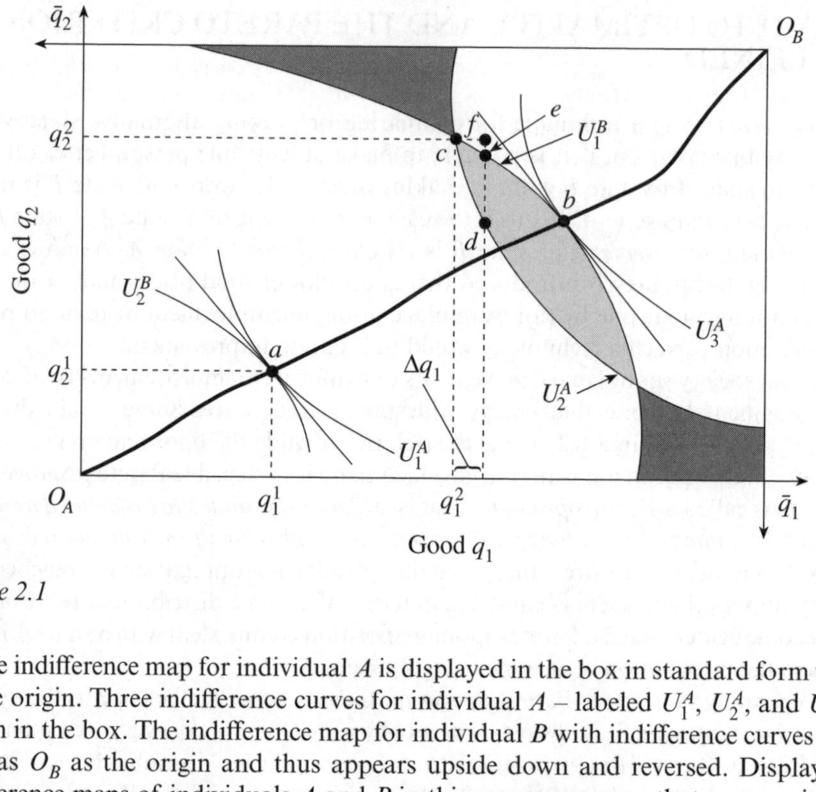

Figure 2.1

The indifference map for individual A is displayed in the box in standard form with O_A as the origin. Three indifference curves for individual A – labeled U_1^A, U_2^A, and U_3^A – are drawn in the box. The indifference map for individual B with indifference curves U_1^B and U_2^B has O_B as the origin and thus appears upside down and reversed. Displaying the indifference maps of individuals A and B in this manner ensures that every point in the box represents a particular distribution of $\bar{q}_1$ and $\bar{q}_2$ or a *state of the economy* in the pure exchange case. For example, at point a, individual A is endowed with q_1^1 of good q_1 and q_2^1 of good q_2, while the remainder of each, $\bar{q}_1 - q_1^1$ and $\bar{q}_2 - q_2^1$, respectively, is distributed to individual B.

The solid line in Figure 2.1 running from O_A to O_B through points a and b is known as the *contract curve* and is constructed by connecting all points of tangency between indifference curves for individuals A and B. At all points on this line, both consumers' indifference curves have the same slope or, in other words, both consumers have equal *marginal rates of substitution* for goods q_1 and q_2. The marginal rate of substitution measures the rate at which a consumer is willing to trade one good for another at the margin.

The marginal rate of substitution for each consumer generally varies along the contract curve for both consumers. The slope of the indifference curves at point *a*, for example, is not necessarily the same as the slope at point *b*.

Now, consider the possibility of using the Pareto criterion to compare or rank alternative states of the economy. For example, compare point *c* with other points in the Edgeworth-Bowley box. First, compare point *c* with points inside the lightly shaded area. At point *c*, the marginal rate of substitution of q_1 for q_2 for individual *A*, denoted by $MRS^A_{q_1q_2}$ is greater than the marginal rate of substitution of q_1 for q_2 for individual *B*, denoted by $MRS^B_{q_1q_2}$. This implies that the amount of q_2 that individual *A* is willing to give up to obtain an additional unit of q_1 exceeds the amount individual *B* is willing to accept to give up a unit of q_1. For the marginal increment Δq_1 in Figure 2.1, this excess corresponds to the distance *de*. That is, individual *A* is willing to pay *df* of q_2 to obtain Δq_1, whereas individual *B* requires only *ef* of q_2 to give up Δq_1. If this excess of willingness-to-pay over willingness-to-accept is not paid to individual *B*, and individual *B* is paid only the minimum amount necessary, then point *e* is Pareto superior to point *c* because individual *A* is made better off and individual *B* is no worse off. If the excess is paid to individual *B*, the movement is to point *d*, which is again Pareto superior to point *c* because individual *B* is made better off and individual *A* is no worse off. If any nontrivial portion of the excess is paid to individual *B*, both are made better off. Thus, all points, including end points, on the line *de* are Pareto superior to point *c*. Similar reasoning suggests that a movement from point *c* to any point in the lightly shaded area can be shown to be an improvement on the basis of the Pareto criterion. Thus, all points in the lightly shaded area are Pareto superior to point *c*.

Now consider comparison of point *c* with any point in the heavily shaded areas. All points in the heavily shaded areas in Figure 2.1 are on indifference curves that are lower for both individuals *A* and *B*. Hence, points in the heavily shaded regions are Pareto inferior to point *c* because at least one individual is worse off and neither individual is better off.

Finally, consider comparison of point *c* with all remaining points that are not in shaded areas in the Edgeworth–Bowley box to discover a major shortcoming of the Pareto criterion: at all these points, one person is made better off and the other person is worse off relative to point *c*. That is, at point *a*, individual *B* is better off than at point *c* but individual *A* is worse off. Hence, these points are noncomparable using the Pareto principle. *Improvements for society using the Pareto criterion can be identified only for cases where everyone gains or at least no one loses.*

Now suppose that society starts at point *c* and moves to point *e*, making a Pareto improvement. At point *e*, $MRS^A_{q_1q_2} > MRS^B_{q_1q_2}$ and, hence, further gains from trade are possible. Suppose that individuals *A* and *B* continue trading, with individual *A* giving up each time the minimum amount of q_2 necessary to obtain additional units of q_1. In this manner, the trade point moves along the indifference curve U^B_1 until point *b* is reached. At point *b*, the amount of q_2 that individual *A* is willing to give up to obtain an additional unit of q_1 is just equal to the amount of q_2 that individual *B* would demand to give up a unit of q_1. With any further movement, individual *A* would not be willing to pay the price that individual *B* would demand. In fact, a movement in any direction from point *b* must make at least one person worse off. Thus, point *b* is a Pareto optimum.

In this manner, one can verify that the marginal condition that holds at point *b*,

$$\text{MRS}^A_{q_1q_2} = \text{MRS}^B_{q_1q_2}, \tag{2.1}$$

holds at all points on the contract curve. Thus, *in the pure exchange case, any point on the contract curve is a Pareto optimum. Pareto optimality implies that the marginal rate of substitution between any two goods is the same for all consumers.* The intuition of this condition is clear because improvements for both individuals are possible (and Pareto optimality does not hold) if one individual is willing to give up more of one good to get one unit of another good than another individual is willing to accept to give up the one unit.

2.3 PRODUCTION EFFICIENCY

Efficiency in production must also be considered when discussing Pareto optimality. Consider once again Figure 2.1 – but now assume that more of good q_1, good q_2, or both can be made available by improving the efficiency with which inputs are used. This would imply that individual *B*'s origin O_B could be moved rightward, upward, or both. In any of these cases, any two indifference curves that were previously tangent on the contract curve would now be separated by a region such as the lens-shaped, lightly shaded region in Figure 2.1. Thus, individual *A*, individual *B*, or both could be made better off. If production possibilities are considered and more of q_1, q_2, or both can be produced, then the points on the contract curve in Figure 2.1 will no longer be Pareto-optimal points. Stated conversely, where alternative production possibilities exist, the points on the contract curve O_AO_B can be Pareto efficient only if the point $(\bar{q}_1, \bar{q}_2)$ is an efficient output bundle. A *Pareto-efficient output bundle* is one in which more of one good cannot be produced without producing less of another.

However, an output point can be efficient only if inputs are allocated to their most efficient uses. To see this, consider the production-efficiency frontier in the Edgeworth–Bowley box in Figure 2.2. This box is constructed by drawing the isoquant map for output q_1 as usual with isoquants q_1^1, q_1^2, and q_1^3, but with the isoquant map for q_2 upside down and reversed with origin at O_{q_2}. The total amounts of inputs x_1 and x_2 available are given by $\bar{x}_1$ and $\bar{x}_2$. Any point in this box represents an allocation of inputs to the two production processes. For example, at point *g*, x_1^1 of x_1 and x_2^1 of x_2 are allocated to the production of q_1. The remainder of inputs $\bar{x}_1 - x_1^1$ and $\bar{x}_2 - x_2^1$ are allocated to the production of q_2.

Point *g* does not represent an efficient allocation of inputs because at point *g* the *rate of technical substitution* of x_1 for x_2 in the production of q_1, denoted by $\text{RTS}^{q_2}_{x_1x_2}$, is greater than the *rate of technical substitution* of x_1 for x_2 in the production of q_2, denoted by $\text{RTS}^{q_1}_{x_1x_2}$. The rate of technical substitution measures the rate at which one input can be substituted for another while maintaining the same level of output. Thus, if an increment of x_1, say Δx_1, is shifted from the production of q_2 to q_1, then an increment of x_2, say Δx_2, could be shifted to the production of q_2 without decreasing the output of q_1 from q_1^1. But only an increment of $ab < \Delta x_2$ of x_2 is necessary to maintain the output of q_2 at the original level q_2^1. This results from the fact that the marginal rate at which x_1 substitutes for x_2 in q_2 is less than the rate at which it substitutes for x_2 in the production of q_1. If, in the exchange of Δx_1 for an increment of x_2, the output of q_2 is kept constant at q_2^1, the output

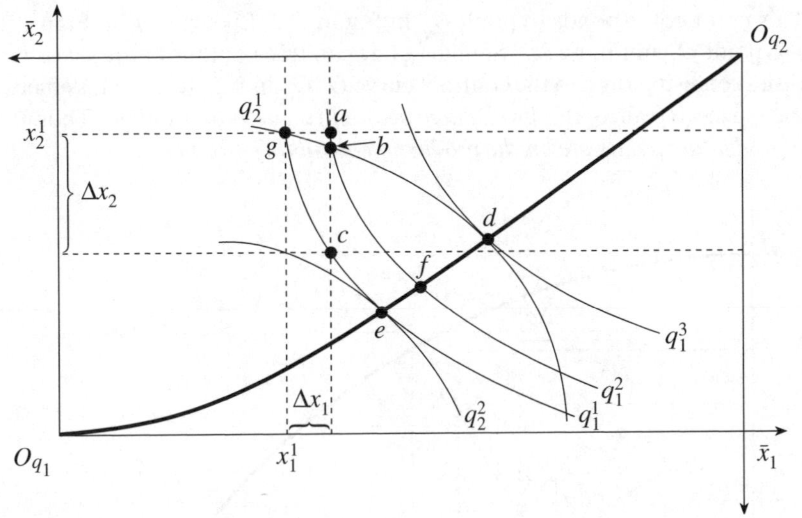

Figure 2.2

of q_1 can be increased to q_1^2. Thus, point g is an inefficient point. The output of q_2 can be increased without decreasing the output of q_1. Clearly, if any amount of x_2 on the segment bc is allocated to q_2 as Δx_1 is allocated to q_1, the outputs of both q_1 and q_2 are increased.

By identical reasoning, point b can be established as an inefficient point. The output of q_1 can again be increased, holding q_2 constant, by reallocating x_1 to q_1 and x_2 to q_2. This process can be continued until a state such as point d is reached. At point d, the amount of x_2 that can be given up in exchange for an increment of x_1, keeping q_1 constant at q_1^3, is precisely equal to the amount of x_2 needed to keep q_2 constant at q_2^1 if an increment of x_1 is removed from the production of q_2. It is impossible to increase the output of q_1 without decreasing the output of q_2. Point d is thus a Pareto-efficient output point. But it is not unique. For example, point e, a point of tangency between q_1^1 and q_2^2, is also a Pareto-efficient output point, as is point f. In fact, all points on the *efficiency locus* $O_{q_1}O_{q_2}$ are Pareto-efficient output points.

Tangency of the isoquants in Figure 2.2 implies that

$$\mathrm{RTS}^{q_1}_{x_1x_2} = \mathrm{RTS}^{q_2}_{x_1x_2}. \tag{2.2}$$

Thus, to the earlier exchange conditions, this second set of conditions for Pareto optimality can now be added. That is, *Pareto optimality in production implies that the rate of technical substitution between any two inputs is the same for all industries that use both inputs.* The intuition of this condition is clear because greater production of both goods is possible (and Pareto optimality does not hold) if one production process can give up more of one input in exchange for one unit of another input than another production process requires to give up that one unit (holding the quantities produced constant in each case).

The set of Pareto-optimal points (or the efficiency locus) $O_{q_1}O_{q_2}$ can also be represented in output space. In Figure 2.3, the curve connecting q_1^* and q_2^* corresponds to $O_{q_1}O_{q_2}$. That is, q_2^* is the maximum output possible if all factors, $\bar{x}_1$ and $\bar{x}_2$, are used in the production of q_2. This point corresponds to point O_{q_1} in Figure 2.2. Likewise, q_1^* in Figure 2.3 corresponds to point O_{q_2} in Figure 2.2. Similarly, one can trace out the entire set of production possibilities corresponding to the contract curve $O_{q_1}O_{q_2}$ in Figure 2.2. This efficiency locus in output space is called the *production possibility curve or frontier*. Thus *all Pareto-efficient production points are on the production possibility frontier.*

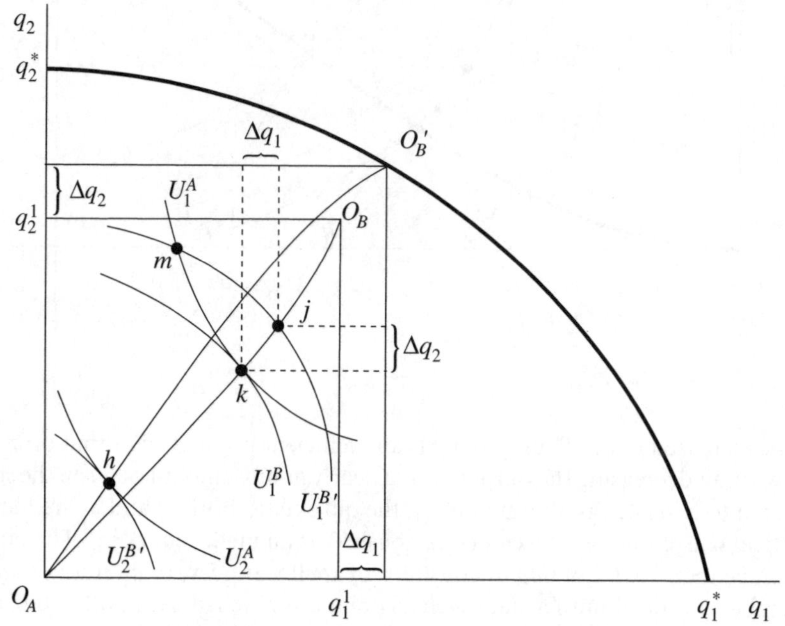

Figure 2.3

The Pareto inferiority of point *g* in Figure 2.2 is clear in Figure 2.3. The Edgeworth exchange box corresponding to output point *g* is drawn with individual *A*'s origin at O_A and individual *B*'s origin at O_B, with the output associated with point *g* in Figure 2.2 efficiently distributed at point *k*. A movement to point *f* in Figure 2.2 corresponds to providing the increments Δq_1 and Δq_2 in Figure 2.3, which shifts individual *B*'s origin to O_B'. Thus, individual *B*'s initial indifference curve U_1^B shifts to position $U_1^{B\prime}$, and his or her initial consumption point shifts to point *j*. The increase in output, $\Delta q_1 + \Delta q_2$, can then be used to make individual *A*, individual *B*, or both better off. Hence, point *g* in Figure 2.2 is not a Pareto optimum.

Although point *g* in Figure 2.2 is not a Pareto optimum, one cannot conclude that a movement from point *g* to any Pareto-efficient production point is a Pareto improvement. That is, the Pareto criterion cannot be used to compare all inefficient production points with all efficient ones. For example, a movement from O_B to O_B' in Figure 2.3 can be accompanied by a distribution of the larger output at point *h* which, although an efficient exchange and production point, results in individual *A* being made worse off and individual *B* being made better off than if output O_B is distributed at point *m*. Without a priori knowledge of the distribution of a larger bundle of goods, one cannot say whether or not a Pareto improvement occurs. *A Pareto improvement with a larger bundle of goods is attained only if it is distributed such that all individuals are made better off or no one is made worse off.* Thus, using the Pareto criterion, society cannot choose between states with more goods and states with fewer goods unless distributional information is also available.

2.4 THE PRODUCT-MIX CASE

From the foregoing, it should not be surprising that the Pareto criterion cannot be used to rank bundles of goods where one bundle has more of one good but less of another good without knowledge of how the goods are distributed. In what follows, this point is demonstrated, and the notion of Pareto optimality is discussed for the more general case where society has a choice over product mix.

First, however, the concept of the *Scitovsky indifference curve* (SIC) will be introduced. In Figure 2.4, society produces q_1^1 of good q_1 and q_2^1 of good q_2. The SIC labeled C in Figure 2.4 corresponds to point a on the contract curve, where the level of utility is represented by U_1^A for individual A and by U_1^B for individual B. To determine the SIC, hold O_A stationary, thus holding individual A's indifference curve stationary at U_1^A. At the same

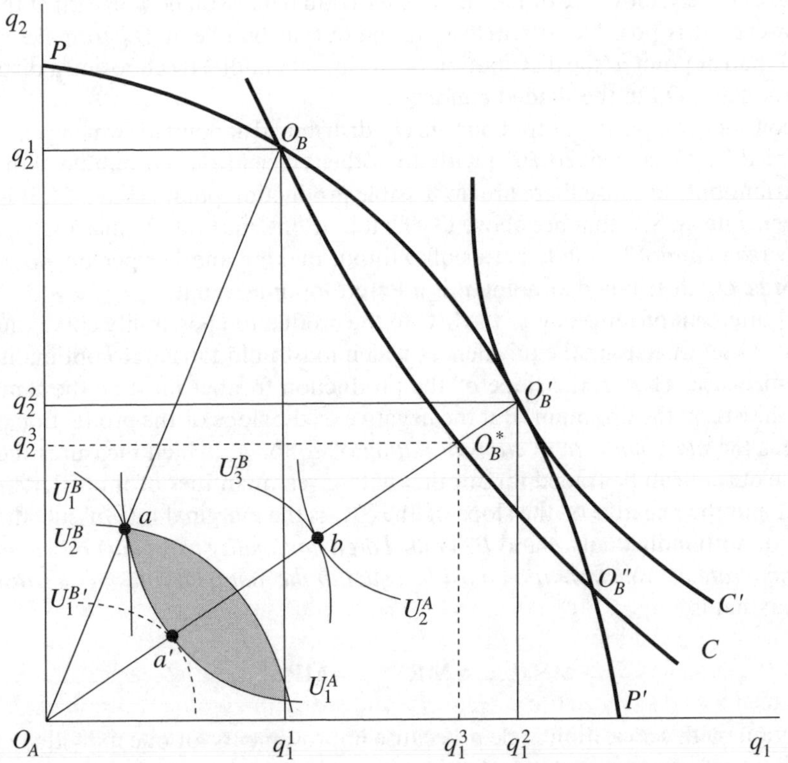

Figure 2.4

time, move O_B, thus shifting B's indifference map; but do this such that individual B's indifference curve U_1^B remains tangent to individual A's indifference curve U_1^A with axes for both goods parallel between individuals. Thus, C consists of the locus of all output bundles to which every member of society is indifferent if the bundle is initially distributed at point a.

Now consider comparing a particular distribution of one bundle of goods on the production possibility frontier with the distribution of another bundle also on the frontier. For example, in Figure 2.4 consider comparing the output bundle at O_B, which is distributed between individuals A and B at point a, with the output bundle at O_B' distributed at point a'. The Scitovsky curves corresponding to the distribution at points a and a' are C and C', respectively. Note that C is not tangent to the production possibility curve at O_B while C' is tangent at O_B'. Both individuals can be made better off by choosing the bundle at O_B' because C' lies above C and because only output at O_B^* (instead of O_B') distributed at point a' is needed to yield the same level of total utility as at O_B. The additional product $q_1^2 - q_1^3$ of q_1 and $q_2^2 - q_2^3$ of q_2 can be divided in any way desired to make both individuals better off in moving from O_B^* to O_B'.

Even though C' lies entirely above C, however, both individuals need not be made actually better off in moving from O_B to O_B' in Figure 2.4. That is, the bundle represented by O_B' may be distributed at point b, where individual A is made better off and individual B is worse off, relative to the bundle represented by O_B, distributed at point a. The SICs can lie with one entirely above the other, and one individual may still be worse off at the higher SIC. However, it is possible to redistribute the output bundle at O_B' to make everyone better off than at point a (the distribution of the initial bundle) by choosing a distribution of the product at O_B' in the shaded region.

Now consider comparing output bundle O_B' distributed at point a' (which generates the SIC denoted by C' tangent to PP') with any other efficient output bundle with all possible distributions. Because there are no feasible production points above C', it is impossible to generate an SIC that lies above C'. That is, if one starts at O_B' distributed at point a', one person cannot be made better off without making another person worse off. In other words, O_B' distributed at point a' is a Pareto-optimal point.

The requirement of tangency of the SIC to the production possibility curve thus establishes a third set of marginal equivalences which must hold for Pareto optimality in the product-mix case. That is, the slope of the production frontier must be the same as the slope of the SIC at the optimum. But the negative of the slope of the production possibility curve is the *marginal rate of transformation* of q_1 for q_2 (which measures the rate at which one output can be traded for another with given quantities of inputs), denoted by $\mathrm{MRT}_{q_1q_2}$, and the negative of the slope of the SIC is the marginal rate of substitution of q_1 for q_2 for both individuals A and B. Thus, *Pareto optimality in product mix implies that the marginal rate of transformation must be equal to the marginal rates of substitution for consumers*; that is,

$$\mathrm{MRT}_{q_1q_2} = \mathrm{MRS}^A_{q_1q_2} = \mathrm{MRS}^B_{q_1q_2}. \tag{2.3}$$

The intuition of this condition is clear because improvements for one individual are possible without affecting any other individual if production possibilities are such that the incremental amount of one output that can be produced in place of one (marginal) unit of another output is greater than the amount that some individual is willing to accept in place of that one unit. Of course, this condition does not define a Pareto optimum uniquely. *Any* point on the production possibility frontier distributed such that the corresponding SIC is tangent to the production possibility curve satisfies the condition. And, as in the pure exchange case, the Pareto criterion does not provide a basis for choosing among these points.

2.5 PARETO OPTIMALITY AND COMPETITIVE EQUILIBRIUM

Pareto optimality has thus far been examined independent of societies' institutional arrangements for organizing economic activity. However, fundamental relationships exist between the notion of Pareto optimality and the competitive market system as a mechanism for determining production, consumption, and the distribution of commodities. In particular, when a competitive equilibrium exists, it will achieve Pareto optimality. Moreover, if producers and consumers behave competitively, any Pareto optimum can be achieved by choosing an appropriate initial income distribution and appropriate price vector.

Before these relationships can be demonstrated, the concept of competitive equilibrium for a market system must be defined. Suppose that the economy consists of N traded goods, J utility-maximizing consumers and K profit-maximizing producers. Also, suppose that consumers and producers act competitively, taking prices as given. Let the demands by consumer j follow by $\mathbf{q}^j = \tilde{\mathbf{q}}^j(\mathbf{p}, m^j) = [\tilde{q}_1^j(\mathbf{p}, m^j),\ldots,\tilde{q}_N^j(\mathbf{p}, m^j)]$, which represents a vector of quantities demanded of all goods by consumer j where $\mathbf{p} = (p_1,\ldots,p_N)$ is a vector of prices for all goods and m^j is the income level of consumer j. In addition, let the supplies of consumer goods by producer k be represented by $\mathbf{q}^k = \hat{\mathbf{q}}^k(\mathbf{p}, \mathbf{w})$ and let the demands for factor inputs by producer k be represented by $\mathbf{x}^k = \hat{\mathbf{x}}^k(\mathbf{p}, \mathbf{w}) = [\hat{x}_1^k(\mathbf{p}, \mathbf{w}),\ldots,\hat{x}_L^k(\mathbf{p}, \mathbf{w})]$ where $\mathbf{w} = (w_1,\ldots,w_L)$ is a vector of all input prices. Finally, suppose factor ownership is distributed among consumers so that each consumer holds a vector of factor endowments $\tilde{\mathbf{x}}^j = (\tilde{x}_1^j,\ldots,\tilde{x}_L^j)$ and thus has income $m^j = \Sigma_{l=1}^L w_l \tilde{x}_l^j$. Then suppose there exist vectors of prices $\bar{\mathbf{p}}$ and $\bar{\mathbf{w}}$ such that the sum of quantities demanded is equal to the sum of quantities supplied in all markets,

$$\sum_{j=1}^{J} \tilde{\mathbf{q}}^j(\bar{\mathbf{p}}, m^j) = \sum_{k=1}^{K} \hat{\mathbf{q}}^k(\bar{\mathbf{p}}, \bar{\mathbf{w}}),$$

$$\sum_{k=1}^{K} \hat{\mathbf{x}}^k(\bar{\mathbf{p}}, \bar{\mathbf{w}}) = \sum_{j=1}^{J} \tilde{\mathbf{x}}^j.$$

The set of prices $\bar{\mathbf{p}}$ and $\bar{\mathbf{w}}$ then gives a competitive equilibrium.[1] Thus, *a competitive equilibrium is simply a set of prices such that all markets clear.*

1. This definition of a competitive equilibrium assumes free entry so that profits of firms are driven to zero. If profits are nonzero, then all profits must be distributed to consumers so that consumer j has income $m^j = \Sigma_{l=1}^L w_l \tilde{x}_l^j + \Sigma_{k=1}^K s_{jk}$ where s_{jk} is the share of producer k profit received by consumer j such that $\Sigma_{j=1}^J s_{jk} = \pi_k$ where π_k is the profit of firm k,

$$\pi_k = \Sigma_{n=1}^N p_n \hat{q}_n^k - \Sigma_{l=1}^L w_l \hat{x}_l^k.$$

A competitive equilibrium can be shown to exist if (1) all consumers have preferences that can be represented by indifference curves that are convex to the origin, and (2) if no increasing returns exist for any firm over a range of output that is large relative to the market.[2] Of course, *many competitive equilibria may exist depending upon the distribution of factor ownership or consumer income.*

The First Optimality Theorem

The first important relationship between competitive equilibrium and Pareto optimality is that, *when a competitive equilibrium exists, it attains Pareto optimality.*[3] This result, formally known as the first optimality theorem, is sometimes called the *invisible hand* theorem of Adam Smith (1937). In the *Wealth of Nations*, first published in 1776, Smith argued that consumers acting selfishly to maximize utility and producers concerned only with profits attain a best possible state of affairs for society, given its limited resources, without necessarily intending to do so. Although more than one best (Pareto-efficient) state of affairs generally exists, Smith was essentially correct.

To see this, first consider the case of consumer A displayed in Figure 2.5. To maximize utility, given the *budget constraint* II' associated with income m, consumer A chooses the consumption bundle $(\bar{q}_1,\bar{q}_2)$ which allows him or her to reach the highest possible indifference curve. Thus, the consumer chooses the point of tangency between II' and the indifference curve $\bar{U}^A$. At this tangency, $\text{MRS}^A_{q_1q_2}=\bar{p}_1/\bar{p}_2$ because the former is the negative of the slope of the indifference curve and the latter is the negative of the slope of the budget constraint. But under perfectly competitive conditions, all consumers face the same prices. Thus, $\text{MRS}^B_{q_1q_2}=\bar{p}_1/\bar{p}_2$ for consumer B and, hence,

$$\text{MRS}^A_{q_1q_2}=\text{MRS}^B_{q_1q_2}, \tag{2.4}$$

2. The first condition is a standard assumption of economic theory and needs no further comment. The problem that arises with increasing returns is that the average cost curve for the firm is continuously decreasing and the marginal cost curve is always below the average cost curve. With falling average costs, if it pays the firm to operate at all, then it pays the firm to expand its scale of operations indefinitely as long as output price is unaffected because the marginal revenue is greater than the marginal cost on each additional unit produced. If increasing returns exist over a large range of output, the percentage of the industry output produced by such a firm eventually reaches sufficient size to have an influence on price, and thus the firm will no longer be competitive. Hence, no profit-maximizing equilibrium exists for competitive firms in this case. As long as increasing returns are small, on the other hand, a competitive industry will consist of a great number of firms with the usual U-shaped average cost curves, and all of these profit-maximizing firms will operate at either the minimum or on the increasing portion of their average cost curve. For a rigorous development of the problem of existence and uniqueness of competitive equilibrium, see Quirk and Saposnik (1968) or Arrow and Hahn (1971).
3. Formally, this result requires that (1) *firms are technologically independent* and (2) *consumers' preferences are independent*. The first assumption implies that the output of each firm depends only on the input-use decisions it makes, and not on the production or input decisions of other firms other than quantities traded at competitive prices. The latter assumption implies that the utility function for each consumer contains as variables only items over which the consumer has a choice and not those quantities chosen by other consumers or producers other than quantities traded at competitive prices. Assumptions (1) and (2) jointly imply that no externalities exist. For a rigorous proof of this result, see Quirk and Saposnik (1968) or Arrow and Hahn (1971). A detailed discussion is also given by Arrow (1970, pp. 59–73). It is possible for a competitive equilibrium to achieve Pareto optimality in the presence of externalities if efficient markets exist for all external effects. These possibilities are discussed in Chapter 13.

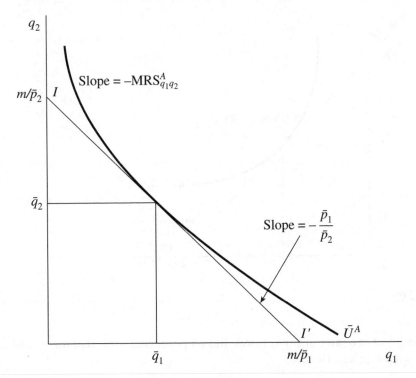

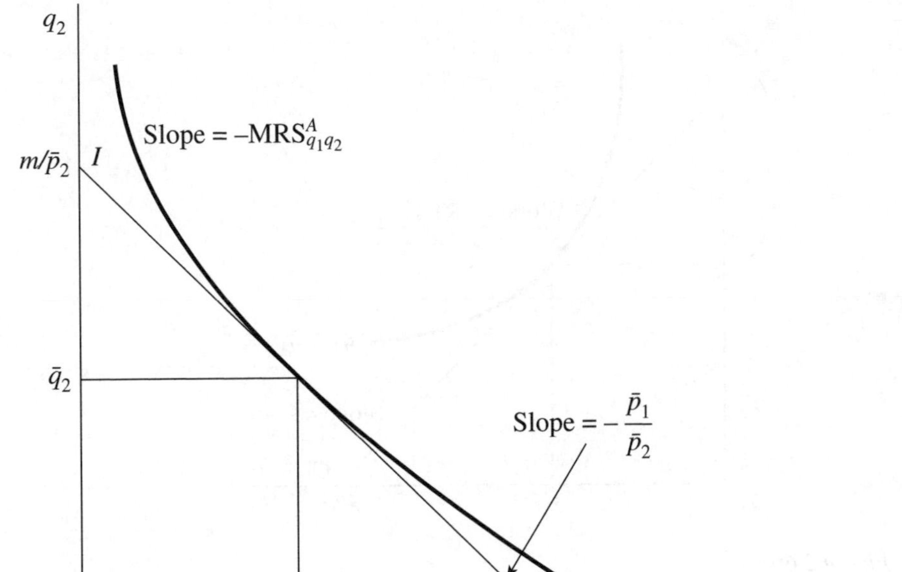

Figure 2.5

which is the Pareto-optimality exchange condition derived in equation (2.1). That is, because all consumers face the same relative prices of the two goods, their marginal evaluations must be the same in equilibrium.[4]

Now, recall that a firm cannot maximize profits for any level of output unless it is producing that output at a minimum cost. That is, profit maximization implies cost minimization. Assuming that $\bar{q}_1$ is the profit-maximizing level of output for the firm producing q_1 in Figure 2.6, the minimum cost of producing this output given input prices $\bar{w}_1$ and $\bar{w}_2$ is obtained by using $\bar{x}_1$ of x_1 and $\bar{x}_2$ of x_2. That is, the cost-minimizing input bundle is selected by finding the point of tangency of the *isocost curve* CC' (associated with cost level $\bar{c}$) with the isoquant associated with output $q_1 = \bar{q}_1$. Finding this point of tangency involves equating the slope of the isoquant, which is equal to the negative of the rate of technical substitution of x_1 for x_2, with the slope of the isocost curve, which is equal to

4. To develop this result more generally mathematically, let consumer j have utility function $U^j(\boldsymbol{q}^j)$ assumed to satisfy usual monotonicity, quasiconcavity, and differentiability properties. The consumer's budget constraint is then $m^j = \boldsymbol{p}\boldsymbol{q}^j = \Sigma_{n=1}^N p_n q_n^j$, the Lagrangian of the utility maximization problem is $U^j(\boldsymbol{q}^j) - \lambda(m^j - \boldsymbol{p}\boldsymbol{q}^j)$, and the first-order conditions are $\partial U^j/\partial q_n^j - \lambda p_n = 0$, $n = 1, \ldots, N$. Note that the demand functions $\boldsymbol{q}^j = \tilde{\boldsymbol{q}}^j(\boldsymbol{p}, m_j)$ must satisfy these first-order conditions. Taking ratios of pairs of first-order conditions implies that consumer behavior satisfies

$$\text{MRS}^j_{q_n q_{n'}} \equiv \frac{\partial U^j/\partial q_n^j}{\partial U^j/\partial q_{n'}^j} = \frac{p_n}{p_{n'}}.$$

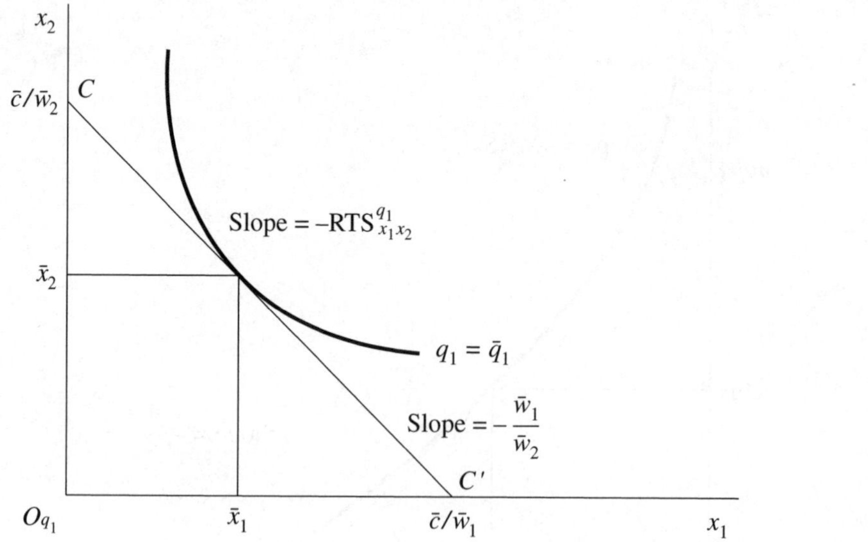

Figure 2.6

the negative of the ratio of input prices. But all producing firms that use x_1 and x_2 face the same input prices. Hence,

$$\text{RTS}^{q_2}_{x_1x_2} = \text{RTS}^{q_1}_{x_1x_2}, \tag{2.5}$$

which yields the production efficiency condition of equation (2.2).[5]

To establish that the product-mix condition of equation (2.3) is satisfied, first consider increasing the output of q_1 by Δq_1 and decreasing the output of q_2 by Δq_2 along the production possibility curve. Suppose this change is accomplished by transferring at the margin either one unit of x_1 or one unit of x_2 from production of q_2 to production of q_1. Then, the increase in output of q_1 is equal to the marginal physical product of input x_k in production of q_1. That is, $\Delta q_1 = \text{MPP}^{q_1}_{x_k}$. Similarly, the decrease in output of q_2 is $\Delta q_2 = \text{MPP}^{q_2}_{x_k}$. But the amount of q_2 that must be given up to obtain an increment of q_1 is given by the marginal rate of transformation between q_1 and q_2. Thus,[6]

5. To develop this result more generally mathematically, let producer k have short-run profit represented by $\pi^k = \boldsymbol{p}\boldsymbol{q}^k - \boldsymbol{w}\boldsymbol{x}^k = \Sigma_{n=1}^{N} p_n \hat{q}_n^k - \Sigma_{l=1}^{L} w_l x_l^k$, and implicit production function $f^k(\boldsymbol{q}^k, \boldsymbol{x}^k) = 0$ where f^k is assumed to satisfy usual monotonicity, concavity and differentiability properties. Then the Lagrangian of the profit maximization problem is $\boldsymbol{p}\boldsymbol{q}^k - \boldsymbol{w}\boldsymbol{x}^k + \mu[f^k(\boldsymbol{q}^k, \boldsymbol{x}^k)]$ and the first-order conditions are $\mu(\partial f^k/\partial q_n^k) + p_n = 0$, $n = 1, \ldots, N$, and $\mu(\partial f^k/\partial x_l^k) - w_l = 0$, $l = 1, \ldots, L$. Because all producer supplies and demands must satisfy these first-order conditions, taking appropriate ratios of pairs of first-order conditions implies

$$\text{RTS}^k_{x_l x_{l'}} \equiv \frac{\partial f^k/\partial x_l^k}{\partial f^k/\partial x_{l'}^k} = \frac{w_l}{w_{l'}}.$$

6. The first-order conditions of footnote 5 also imply

$$\text{MRT}^k_{q_n q_{n'}} \equiv \frac{\partial f^k/\partial q_{n'}^k}{\partial f^k/\partial q_n^k} = \frac{p_{n'}}{p_n},$$

which generalizes the result in equation (2.6).

$$\mathrm{MRT}_{q_1q_2} = \frac{\Delta q_2}{\Delta q_1} = \frac{\mathrm{MPP}_{x_k}^{q_2}}{\mathrm{MPP}_{x_k}^{q_1}}. \tag{2.6}$$

Now recall that cost minimization by a producer requires that producers equalize the marginal physical product per dollar spent on each input. That is, the least-cost combination $\bar{x}_1$, $\bar{x}_2$ in Figure 2.6 is characterized by the conditions

$$\frac{\mathrm{MPP}_{x_1}^{q_j}}{w_1} = \frac{\mathrm{MPP}_{x_2}^{q_j}}{w_2}, j = 1, 2. \tag{2.7}$$

But the marginal physical product of an input is equal to the increase in output Δq_j divided by the increase in input Δx_k required to obtain the increase in output. Thus, $\mathrm{MPP}_{xk}^{q_j} = \Delta q_j/\Delta x_k$. Using this result in equation (2.7) and inverting yields

$$\bar{w}_1 \frac{\Delta x_1}{\Delta q_j} = \bar{w}_2 \frac{\Delta x_2}{\Delta q_j}, j = 1, 2, \tag{2.8}$$

where $\bar{w}_k\, \Delta x_k/\Delta q_j$ is simply the marginal cost, MC_{q_j}, of obtaining an additional unit of q_j. Combining (2.7) and (2.8) thus yields

$$\mathrm{MC}_{q_j} = \frac{\bar{w}_k}{\mathrm{MPP}_{x_k}^{q_j}} j = 1, 2. \tag{2.9}$$

Finally, recall that all profit-maximizing producers equate marginal revenue, which is simply the competitive producer's output price, with marginal cost. Thus, substituting $\bar{p}_j$ for MC_{q_j} in equation (2.9) and dividing the equation with $j = 1$ by the one with $j = 2$ yields[7]

$$\frac{\bar{p}_1}{\bar{p}_2} = \frac{\mathrm{MPP}_{x_k}^{q_2}}{\mathrm{MPP}_{x_k}^{q_1}}. \tag{2.10}$$

But from equation (2.6), the right-hand side of equation (2.10) is simply $\mathrm{MRT}_{q_1q_2}$. Because consumers face these same commodity prices, the product-mix condition in equation (2.3),

$$\mathrm{MRT}_{q_1q_2} = \mathrm{MRS}_{q_1q_2}^{A} = \mathrm{MRS}_{q_1q_2}^{B}, \tag{2.11}$$

must hold with competitive market equilibrium.

Thus, under the assumptions of this chapter, competition leads to conditions (2.4), (2.5), and (2.11), which are identical to conditions (2.1)–(2.3) that define a Pareto optimum. In other words, *competitive markets are Pareto efficient, meaning that competitive markets result in an equilibrium position from which it is impossible to make a change without making someone worse off.* This conclusion is probably the single most powerful

7. To obtain equation (2.10) from equation (2.6) generally, note that comparative static analysis of the production function constraint in footnote 5 holding all but one input and all but one output constant yields

$$\frac{dq_n^k}{dx_l^k} = -\frac{\partial f^k/\partial x_l^k}{\partial f^k/\partial q_n^k}.$$

Using this and a similar relationship for $dq_{n'}^k/dx_l^k$ in the equation of footnote 6 reveals that

$$\mathrm{MRT}_{q_nq_{n'}}^k = \frac{dq_n^k/dx_l^k}{dq_{n'}^k/dx_l^k} = \frac{\partial f^k/\partial q_{n'}^k}{\partial f^k/\partial q_n^k} = \frac{p_{n'}}{p_n}.$$

The result in equation (2.11) follows because each term is equal to the same price ratio.

result in the theory of market economies and is widely used by those economists who believe that markets are competitive and, hence, that government should not intervene in economic activity. Milton Friedman and the 'Chicago School' are the best known defenders of this position (see Friedman and Friedman 1980). In addition, because of its efficiency properties, competitive equilibrium offers a useful standard for policy analysis. For this purpose, states of competitive equilibrium or Pareto optimality are called *first-best states* and the associated allocations are called *first-best bundles*. All other states or bundles are called *second-best*. Departures from competitive equilibria are called *market failures*. Examples of market failures include monopolistic behavior, taxes, and externalities. Policies that correct market failures are thus viewed as achieving competitive equilibrium and therefore attain economic efficiency.

The Second Optimality Theorem

The second optimality theorem states that *any particular Pareto optimum can be achieved through competitive markets by simply prescribing an appropriate initial distribution of factor ownership and a price vector*.[8] That is, a central planner can achieve any efficient production bundle and any distribution of consumer well-being by redistributing factor ownership and prescribing appropriate prices where consumers maximize utility subject to budget constraints and producers maximize profits. The use of the competitive mechanism in this manner is sometimes called Lange–Lerner socialism after the two economists who first recognized this possibility (see Lange 1938; Lerner 1944). This result implies that many Pareto optima exist which are competitive equilibria, each associated with different factor endowments. The potential for widely differing marginal valuations under alternative competitive equilibria illustrates the connection between efficiency and income distribution.

Many economists object to addressing efficiency and distribution in two stages where the first stage involves maximizing economic efficiency and the second stage involves distributing the product equitably. The relative value of products depends on income distribution, which depends, in turn, on the factor ownership distribution. Actually, the Lange–Lerner result suggests the opposite approach whereby distributional objectives can be achieved by first redistributing factor ownership. Then policies need to be adopted only to correct market failures in order to achieve a Pareto optimum consistent with the desired income distribution.

Figure 2.7 demonstrates this point by considering only two possible states. The two goods produced are q_1 and q_2, and PP' is the production possibility frontier. The Scitovsky indifference curve C pertains to the output bundle O_B distributed among the individuals at point a. Alternatively, the output bundle O_B' distributed at point b yields the Scitovsky indifference curve C'. As points O_B and O_B' show, both bundles and their distributions lead to Pareto-optimal states. Thus, points O_B and O_B', with corresponding distributions at points a and b, respectively, are called *first-best states*, but neither is a unique optimum because the other is also an optimum in the same sense. For example, a factor ownership distribution that produces competitive equilibrium at point a may leave the economy poorly suited to achieve a distributional objective consistent with point b. On

8. For a rigorous proof of this result, see Quirk and Saposnik (1968) or Arrow and Hahn (1971).

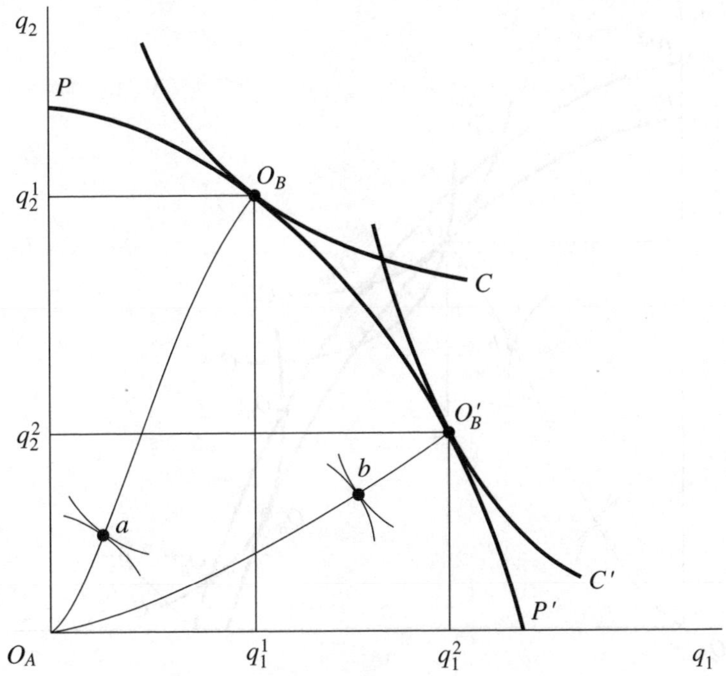

Figure 2.7

the other hand, starting from a factor ownership distribution that generates consumer incomes consistent with point *b*, the Lange–Lerner result implies that a Pareto efficient organization will be achieved automatically by the Adam Smith invisible hand in absence of market failures.

2.6 LIMITATIONS OF PARETO OPTIMALITY AND THE PARETO PRINCIPLE

Although the Pareto principle gives a plausible criterion for comparing different states of the world, its limitations are numerous. The greatest shortcoming of the Pareto principle is that many alternatives are simply not comparable. For example, in Figure 2.8, if production possibilities are represented by *PP* and production is initially O_B with distribution at point *b* corresponding to Scitovsky indifference curve *C*, then the only Pareto-preferred alternatives are in the shaded, lens-shaped area. All other production points are either infeasible, non-Pareto comparable or Pareto inferior. If production is initially at O_B with distribution at point *a* corresponding to Scitovsky indifference curve *C*′, then no other feasible alternatives are Pareto superior. In fact, once *any* competitive equilibrium is reached in the framework of this chapter, no other feasible alternatives are Pareto superior. For example, production at O_B with distribution corresponding to the Scitovsky indifference curve *C*′ is not Pareto comparable to production at O_B' with distribution corresponding to social indifference curve C^*. Thus, alternative Pareto optima are

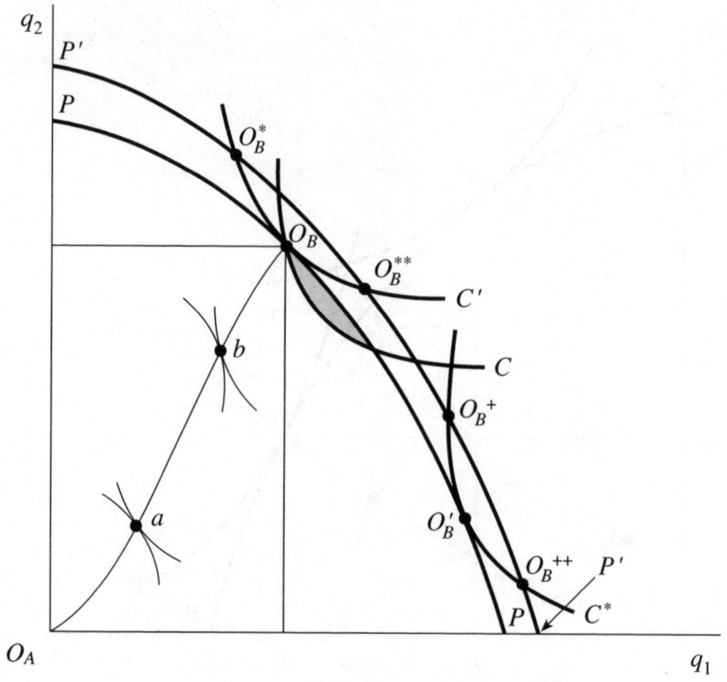

Figure 2.8

not Pareto comparable. Hence, the Pareto criterion prevents consideration of income-distributional considerations once a competitive equilibrium is attained.

Another serious problem with the Pareto principle is that no unique choice of distribution is apparent when improvements are possible. For example, suppose that a technological change takes place in Figure 2.8, shifting the production possibility frontier out to $P'P'$. If production was initially at O_B with distribution at point a corresponding to Scitovsky indifference curve C', the only points that are Pareto superior are those above C' and below or on $P'P'$. The only points that are Pareto superior and also possibly correspond to Pareto optimality with the new technology are those on the $P'P'$ frontier between $O_B{}^*$ and $O_B{}^{**}$. But the points along this interval may be associated with a wide variation in income distribution (assuming, for example, that only one distribution exists at each production point with tangency between the Scitovsky indifference curve and the new production possibility frontier). The Pareto criterion gives no basis for choosing among these alternatives. However, this problem may be viewed as an advantage because possibilities can exist for altering income distribution while fulfilling the simply appealing nature of the Pareto criterion. For example, in a rapidly growing economy (one with rapidly expanding production possibilities), the possibilities for altering income distribution while still fulfilling the Pareto criterion are many even though the Pareto criterion gives no guidance on which income distribution should be chosen.

Even with expanding production possibilities, however, the Pareto principle strongly favors the status quo. For example, if production is originally at O_B with distribution associated with Scitovsky indifference curve C', a new point of Pareto optimality is possible only at points between O_B^* and O_B^{**} on the new frontier $P'P'$ in Figure 2.8, assuming that the Pareto principle is satisfied in such a change. But if the initial production point is at O_B' with distribution associated with Scitovsky indifference curve C^*, a new Pareto optimum is possible only at points between O_B^+ and O_B^{++} on the frontier $P'P'$, again assuming the Pareto principle is satisfied in the change. In each case the set of feasible Pareto improvements does not represent a substantial departure from the initial point unless technological improvements are large. Again, alternatives with widely varying income distributions may be neither comparable nor attainable from a given initial state by strict adherence to the Pareto criterion.

In a policy context, decisions often must be made where someone is made worse off while someone else is made better off. Furthermore, some policies are directly intended to change the distribution of income (that is, narrow the gap between high- and low-income people). Hence, to evaluate such changes, a device other than the Pareto principle is needed.

2.7 CONCLUSIONS

This chapter has focused on the concept of Pareto optimality and the Pareto criterion. A Pareto improvement is a situation where a move results in at least one person becoming better off without anyone becoming worse off. Pareto optimality is achieved when it is no longer possible for a policy change to make someone better off without making someone else worse off.

From a policy point of view, the Pareto criterion favors the status quo because the range of choices that represent Pareto improvements depends critically on the initial distribution of income. The Pareto criterion cannot be used to choose among widely different income distributions. Furthermore, many Pareto-optimal policy choices may exist that correspond simply to different income distributions. Perhaps not all first-best, Pareto-optimal choices are superior to some particular second-best choice. Although it is possible to make a Pareto improvement from a second-best state, it does not follow that any Pareto-optimal state is preferred to any second-best state. For example, if a second-best and a first-best state have markedly different income distributions, the situation that is second best may not be inferior to the first-best situation. Thus, the Pareto criterion alone appears to constitute an insufficient basis for applied economic welfare analysis of public policy alternatives.

3. The compensation principle and the welfare function

In Chapter 2, emphasis was given to the Pareto criterion as a means for selecting among alternative policies. Results show that many 'first-best' bundles or many Pareto-optimal points usually exist for an economy but, unfortunately, the Pareto principle does not give a basis for selecting among them. Narrowing the range of possibilities to a single first-best bundle (which essentially requires determining the ideal income distribution) requires a more complete criterion. One such criterion, which was introduced much later than the Pareto principle in the hope that it would be a more powerful device for choosing among policies, is the *compensation principle*, sometimes called the *Kaldor–Hicks compensation test* after the two economists to which it is attributed (Kaldor 1939; Hicks 1939). The development of the compensation principle was thus an attempt to broaden the states of the world that could be compared using an accepted welfare criterion. Simply stated, state *B* is preferred to state *A* if at least one individual could be made better off without making anyone worse off at state *B* – not that all individuals are *actually* no worse off – by some feasible redistribution following the change. Unlike the Pareto principle, the compensation criterion does not require the actual payment of compensation.

The issue of compensation payments is at the heart of many policy discussions. Some argue that compensation should be paid in certain cases. According to Lester Thurow (1980, p. 208), 'If we want a world with more rapid economic change, a good system of transitional aid to individuals that does not lock us into current actions or current institutions would be desirable.' However, most policies that have been introduced have not entailed compensation. For example, bans on DDT and other pesticides have in many cases resulted in producer losses, but producers have not been compensated for their losses in revenue.

Although the compensation principle does, in fact, expand the set of comparable alternatives (at the expense of additional controversy), some states remain noncomparable. The latter part of this chapter considers the necessary features of a criterion that ranks all possible states of an economy. However, empirical possibilities for the resulting more general theoretical constructs appear bleak.

3.1 THE COMPENSATION PRINCIPLE

According to the compensation principle, state B is preferred to state A if, in making the move from state A to state B, the gainers can compensate the losers such that at least one person is better off and no one is worse off. Such states are sometimes called *potentially Pareto preferred* states. The principle is stated in terms of *potential* compensation rather than *actual* compensation because, according to those who developed the principle, the payment of compensation involves a value judgment. That is, to say that society should move to state *B* and compensate losers is a clearly subjective matter, just as recommendation for change on the basis of the Pareto criterion is a subjective matter. For example, if a Pareto improvement is undertaken, then, as demonstrated in Section 2.6, the possibilities that represent further Pareto improvements may be more restricted. Conceivably, the true optimum state of society may not be reachable by further applications of the criterion if the wrong initial Pareto improvement is undertaken. Similarly, to say that society should move to state *B* without compensating losers is also a subjective matter of perhaps a more serious nature. Thus, nonpayment of compensation also involves a value judgment. In terms of objective practice, one can only point out the potential superiority of some state *B* without actually making a recommendation that the move be made.

The Pure Consumption Case[1]

Consider the application of the compensation principle to comparing different distributions of a given bundle of goods, again using the basic model of two goods and two individuals developed in Chapter 2. In Figure 3.1, point *a* is preferred to point *b* on the basis of the Pareto principle. But how does one compare point *b* with a point such as *c*, where *c* is not inside the lens-shaped area? The compensation principle offers one possibility. For example, suppose that one redistributes the bundle such that, instead of being at point *b*, individual *A* is at point *d* and individual *B* is at point *e*. Note that the welfare of each is unchanged. However, at these points there is an excess of q_2 equal to $q_2^3 - q_2^2$ and an excess of q_1 equal to $q_1^3 - q_1^2$. Now, if the move *actually* takes place to point *c*,

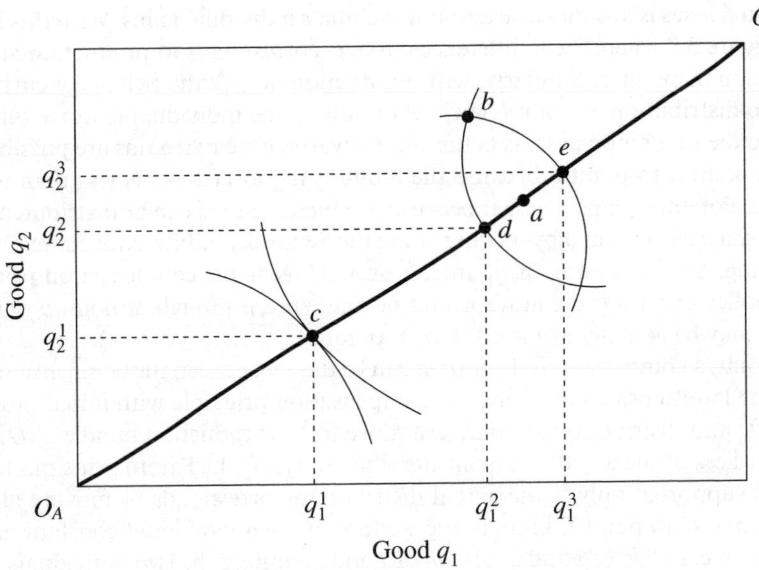

Figure 3.1

1. This section is largely based on Bailey (1954).

individual A is clearly worse off while individual B is better off. Individual A loses $q_2^2 - q_2^1$ of q_2 and $q_1^2 - q_1^1$ of q_1, but individual B gains $q_2^3 - q_2^1$ of q_2 and $q_1^3 - q_1^1$ of q_1. The amount individual B gains in physical amounts of q_1 and q_2 is greater than the loss to individual A. Hence, point c is potentially preferred to point b. *By the compensation principle, everyone is potentially better off by moving from point b to point c because the amount individual B gains is greater than the amount individual A loses.* This result holds even though compensation is not actually paid. If compensation is paid in terms of q_1 and q_2, both parties would, in effect, not agree to move to point c. Instead, a move would take place from point b only to somewhere within the lens-shaped area. But points within the lens-shaped area are comparable with point b by the Pareto principle. Thus, the application of the compensation criterion does not increase the ability to make statements about *actual* increases in welfare.

To view the problem in a different way, consider to what extent individual B would have to bribe individual A in order to make the move from point b to point c. The minimum amount is $q_2^2 - q_2^1$ of q_2 and $q_1^2 - q_1^1$ of q_1. Hence, in equilibrium, one would move from point b to point d only if compensation were paid. Individual B would gain $q_2^3 - q_2^2$ of q_2 and $q_1^3 - q_1^2$ of q_1 in the move if the minimum bribe is paid. Thus, point c is never actually reached if compensation is paid.

Distribution of Different Bundles

Consider next how the compensation principle can be used to compare different distributions of *different output bundles*. Recall from the preceding case that potential gains can be made in a move from point b to point c if, in the actual move to point c, the amount one individual loses is less than the amount the other individual gains. With this in mind, consider Figure 3.2 where the indifference curve C corresponds to production at O_B and to distribution at point a. Similarly, with production at O_B^*, the Scitovsky curve corresponding to distribution at point b is C^*. At point b, one individual is worse off than at point a, and the other individual is better off. However, potential gains are possible in the move from point a to point b because the amount the loser loses is less than what the gainer gains. Potential gains are clear because production at O_B^* can be distributed to keep welfare the same as at point a by moving along the Scitovsky indifference curve C to point f. By so doing, fh of q_2 and fg of q_1 are left over. Thus, if the compensation principle is used as a policy criterion, the move would be made (even though at point b one of the individuals may be actually worse off than at point a).

At this point, a comparison and contrast can be drawn between the compensation principle and the Pareto principle. Using the compensation principle with initial production bundle at O_B and distribution at point a, a move to the production bundle at O_B^* is supported regardless of the way it is actually distributed. Using the Pareto principle, however, the move is supported only if the actual distribution corresponds to moving along the Scitovsky curve C to point f, keeping the welfare of each individual constant and then dividing the excess of fg of good q_1 and fh of good q_2 among the two individuals in some way so that neither is worse off.

The reason that production at O_B^* is preferred to production at O_B, in either case, is that the starting point with distribution at point a is a second-best state. The corresponding Scitovsky curve C is not tangent to the production possibility frontier PP. Like the

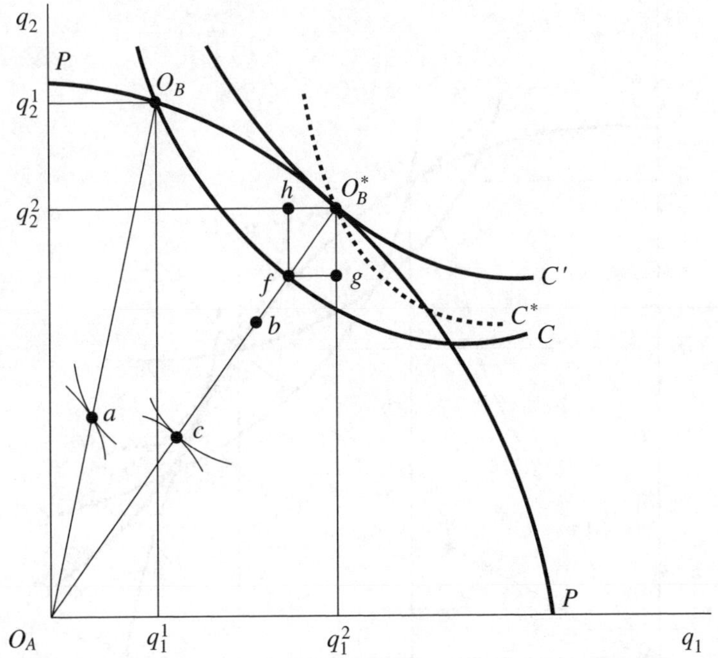

Figure 3.2

Pareto criterion, the compensation principle does not support a move away from a first-best state such as production at O_B^* with distribution point c corresponding to Scitovsky indifference curve C'. Thus, the compensation criterion, like the Pareto criterion, cannot be used to rank two first-best states. A movement from one to the other would not be supported regardless of which is used as a starting point. The compensation criterion, on the other hand, gives a means of comparing all pairs of second-best states and for comparing all second-best states with all first-best states.

The Reversal Paradox

An important class of problems in applying the compensation principle falls under the general heading of the *reversal paradox* pointed out by Scitovsky (1941). For the case where gainers can potentially compensate losers, a conclusion that one position is better than another is not always warranted. *One must ask, also, whether the losers can bribe the gainers not to make the move.* The crux of the argument is presented in Figure 3.3. The production possibility curve is PP, and the two bundles to be compared are O_B and O_B^*. Each of the bundles is distributed such that the corresponding Scitovsky indifference curves cross. In other words, both are second-best states because neither indifference curve is tangent to the production possibility curve. The curves C_1 and C_2 correspond to points a and c on the contract curves, respectively. Now, by the compensation principle, production at O_B^* with distribution at point c is better than production at O_B with distribution at point a because production at O_B^* can generally be redistributed such that all are actually

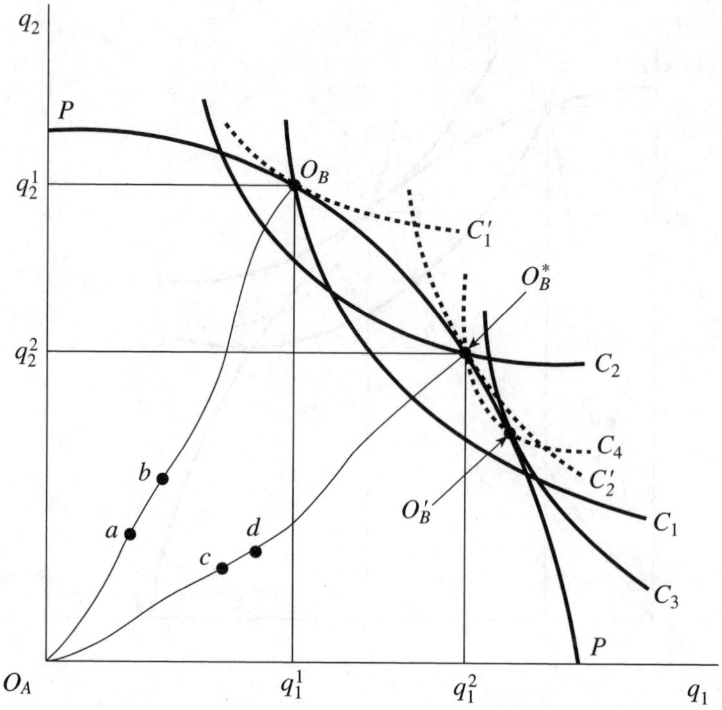

Figure 3.3

better off at point *d* (where distribution at point *d* corresponds to Scitovsky curve C_2', which lies above curve C_1 and is associated with improved welfare for both individuals). However, by this criterion, O_B^* is only potentially better off. Compensation is not actually paid. Because compensation is not actually paid, a reversal problem arises. That is, the new state with production at O_B^* and distribution at point *c* is a second-best state with Scitovsky curve C_2. Thus, according to Figure 3.3, there must be some distribution – say, at point *b* – such that production at O_B is preferred to production at O_B^* by the Scitovsky criterion (where distribution at point *b* corresponds to the Scitovsky curve C_1', which is associated with improved welfare for both individuals as compared with C_2). Thus, each is preferred to the other.

This reversal occurs because in each case a given distribution of the first bundle is compared with all possible distributions of the alternative bundle. The reversal paradox suggests that all distributions of the initial bundle should also be considered. In other words, a *reversal test* (sometimes called the *Scitovsky reversal test*) is passed if one determines, first, that gainers can bribe losers to make a change and, second, that losers cannot bribe gainers not to make the change. Unless the reversal test is passed in addition to the Kaldor–Hicks compensation test, one cannot really say that one state is even potentially preferred to another.

Some additional points that must be borne in mind with respect to the Scitovsky reversal paradox are as follows:

1. *The reversal paradox occurs only in comparing two second-best bundles.* It does not arise if one of the bundles is a first-best or Pareto-efficient bundle. For example, in Figure 3.3, if production at O_B^* with distribution corresponding to indifference curve C_2 is compared to production at O_B' with distribution corresponding to indifference curve C_3, a reversal problem does not occur.
2. *The reversal paradox does not always occur in comparing two second-best bundles even though compensation is not actually paid.* For example, in Figure 3.3, production at O_B^* with distribution corresponding to Scitovsky indifference curve C_4 does not lead to a paradox when compared to production at O_B and distribution corresponding to Scitovsky curve C_1. The paradox occurs only when the relevant Scitovsky curves cross in the interior of the feasible production region. This problem may not occur when income distributions do not change substantially.

Intransitive Rankings

If the compensation criteria (both the direct Kaldor–Hicks and Scitovsky reversal tests) are employed to rank all possible states, a further problem can arise even if the reversal problem is not encountered. That is, compensation tests can lead to intransitive welfare rankings when more than two states are compared.[2] This problem arises when, for example, one must choose among, say, *states where all the alternative policies are of a second-best nature* (that is, there is no single policy in the policy set that leads to a bundle of goods distributed with the Scitovsky community indifference curve tangent to the production possibility curve). In Figure 3.4, given the production possibility curve PP, bundle O_B^2 is preferred to O_B^1, O_B^3 is preferred to O_B^2 and bundle O_B^4 is preferred to O_B^3, using the compensation test. However, O_B^1 is also preferred to O_B^4. Hence, the Kaldor–Hicks compensation test leads to welfare rankings that are intransitive. But note that some form of distortion exists for each bundle because the Scitovsky indifference curves are not tangent to the production possibility curve in any of the four cases. All the bundles are of a second-best nature.

Suppose, on the other hand, that one policy results in a bundle of goods that is economically efficient (with the Scitovsky indifference curve tangent to the production possibility curve). For example, consider bundles O_B^1, O_B^2, O_B^3 and O_B^5. Here, O_B^5 is clearly the optimum choice. There is no desire, once at O_B^5, to return to bundles O_B^1, O_B^2 or O_B^3. As a second example, suppose that the bundles to be compared are O_B^1, O_B^2, O_B^3 and O_B^6. Again, once at O_B^6, no potential gain is generated in returning to O_B^1, O_B^2 or O_B^3. Hence, no ambiguity is encountered in choosing a top-ranked policy if the policy set contains exactly one first-best state. Thus, as with the reversal problem discussed earlier, intransitivity occurs only when all the bundles being compared are generated from second-best policies.[3]

Consider, on the other hand, one further case where the possibilities consist of O_B^1, O_B^5 and O_B^6. In this case, the Kaldor–Hicks compensation test shows that O_B^5 is preferred to

2. The results in this section are due to Gorman (1955).
3. Partly in response to the problems associated with using the compensation principle as a basis for welfare comparison, Arrow (1951) developed the impossibility theorem, which proves that no reasonable rule exists for combining rankings of various states of society by individuals into a societal ranking. See the further discussion in Section 3.4.

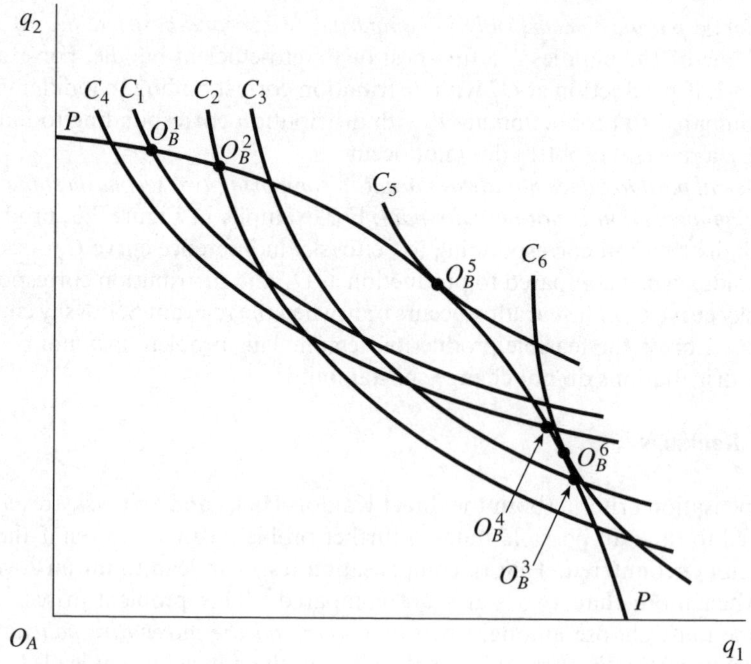

Figure 3.4

O_B^1. The possibility associated with O_B^6 is not preferred to O_B^1 even though O_B^6 is a first-best bundle. Among these three states, however, the rankings are not complete because, once at either O_B^5 or O_B^6, the compensation test does not suggest a move to either of the other states. In other words, the compensation test does not lead to a ranking of policy sets containing more than one first-best state.

3.2 UTILITY POSSIBILITY CURVES AND THE POTENTIAL WELFARE CRITERION

Another approach related to the choice of alternative income distributions and the reversal problem is based on the concept of utility possibility curves introduced by Samuelson (1947, 1956). To develop this approach, consider Figure 3.5 where the utilities of two individuals, A and B, are represented. The utility of individual B is measured on the vertical axis, while that for individual A is measured along the horizontal axis. Three utility possibility curves are represented, each of which is derived by changing the distribution of a given bundle of goods along a contract curve. For example, Q_2Q_2 shows the maximum utility both individuals can receive from a fixed production at O_B in Figure 3.3, Q_1Q_1 corresponds to a different bundle of goods, and so on.

To demonstrate the reversal paradox, consider Q_2Q_2 and Q_1Q_1. Points a and b represent particular distributions of the bundle from which Q_2Q_2 is derived. Similarly, points c and d represent particular distributions of the bundle from which Q_1Q_1 is derived.

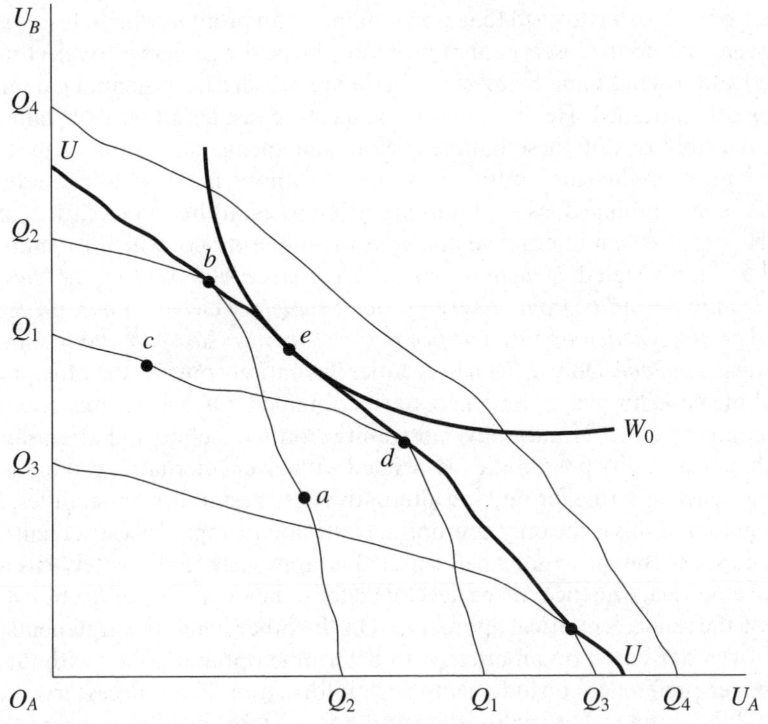

Figure 3.5

Suppose that the initial distribution is at point *c*. Then one can redistribute production when moving from Q_1Q_1 to Q_2Q_2 such that both individuals *A* and *B* would be better off at point *b* than at point *c*. Similarly, one could redistribute the other bundle so that both are better off at point *d* than at point *a*. The paradox arises because point *d* lies to the northeast of point *a*, while point *b* lies to the northeast of point *c*. Thus, one comparison implies a preference for the production bundle associated with Q_1Q_1, whereas the other comparison favors the production bundle associated with Q_2Q_2. This paradoxical situation would not arise if compensation were actually paid.

These results correspond directly with the analysis in commodity space in Figure 3.3. Points *a* and *c* in Figure 3.5 correspond to distributions that are second-best states. In other words, these points correspond to points *a* and *c* in Figure 3.3, which are also distributions giving rise to second-best states. Note that points *b* and *d* in Figure 3.5 and points *b* and *d* in Figure 3.3 correspond to first-best states.

If one considers all possible production bundles that can be obtained from a given production possibility frontier and all possible distributions of these bundles (which, in utility space, corresponds to considering utility possibility frontiers, such as Q_3Q_3, associated with all other possible production bundles), then the *grand utility possibility frontier UU* can be constructed as an envelope of the utility possibility frontiers. All points on this envelope curve correspond to first-best optima, that is, bundles distributed such that the Scitovsky curves are tangent to the production possibility curve.

Samuelson (1950) has argued that even if gainers can profitably bribe losers into accepting a movement and the losers cannot profitably bribe the gainers into rejecting it (that is, both the Kaldor–Hicks and Scitovsky criteria are satisfied), a potential gain in welfare is not necessarily attained. He argues that one has to consider all possible bundles and all possible distributions of these bundles before statements can be made about potential gains. The problem then amounts to selecting one among many first-best states for which there is no solution unless a social ranking of first-best utility possibilities can be determined. He proposes an alternative *potential welfare criterion*, which is demonstrated in Figure 3.5. Simply stated, *if there is some utility frontier such as Q_4Q_4 that lies entirely on or outside another utility frontier – Q_2Q_2, for example – owing perhaps to technological change, then any position on this new frontier is clearly at least potentially superior to any position on the old one.* Only if the new frontier lies entirely outside the other, however, are potential increases in real income necessarily obtained. Of course, this criterion can be used to compare either grand utility possibility frontiers before and after, say, a technological change or utility possibilities associated with given alternative production bundles.

In the absence of a rule for ranking alternative first-best utility possibilities, Samuelson (1950) argues that this is the only appropriate criterion to apply. In a strict sense, this argument is correct. But in a practical sense, this approach leads to few cases in which beneficial empirical evidence can be developed for policy-makers (see Section 8.3 for a discussion of the related empirical approach). On the other hand, the arguments in favor of this approach are based on an attempt to determine optimal policy without relying on policy-maker preferences or judgment. Such information is not necessary in a practical policy-making setting where political institutions exist for the express purpose of providing policy-makers to make such choices.

3.3 THE SOCIAL WELFARE FUNCTION

Because the potential welfare criterion often may not be satisfied even if utility possibility curves can be identified, economic inquiry has continued to search for a rule that can rank all states of society and thus determine which first-best state on the grand utility possibility frontier represents *the* social optimum. In theory, the social welfare function is such a concept. The *social welfare function* is simply a function – say, $W(U_A, U_B)$ – of the utility levels of all individuals such that a higher value of the function is preferred to a lower one. The assumption that the social welfare function is determined by the utilities of all individuals has been called the *fundamental ethical postulate* by Samuelson (1947) and is a cornerstone of democratic societies. Such a welfare function is called a *Bergsonian welfare function* after Abram Bergson (1938), who first used it.

The properties one would expect in such a social welfare function with respect to the utilities of individuals are much like those one would expect in an individual's utility function with respect to the quantities of commodities consumed. That is, one would expect that (1) an increase in the utility of any individual holding others constant increases social welfare (the Pareto principle); (2) if one individual is made worse off, then another individual must be made better off to retain the same level of social welfare; and (3) if some individual has a very high level of utility and another individual has a very low level of utility, then society is willing to give up some of the former individual's utility to obtain even a somewhat smaller increase in the latter individual's utility, with the intensity of this trade-off depending upon the degree of inequality.

The properties described above suggest the existence of welfare contours such as W_0 in Figure 3.5, which correspond conceptually to indifference curves for individual utility functions. By property (1), social welfare increases by moving to higher social welfare contours, either upward or to the right. By property (2), the social welfare contours have negative slope. By property (3), the welfare contours are convex to the origin.

Social welfare is maximized by moving to the highest attainable social welfare contour, which thus leads to tangency of the grand utility possibility frontier with the resulting social welfare contour such as at point *e* in Figure 3.5.[4] This tangency condition is sometimes called the *fourth optimality condition.* This condition, together with conditions in equations (2.1), (2.2) and (2.3), completely characterizes the social optimum.

3.4 LIMITATIONS OF THE SOCIAL WELFARE FUNCTION APPROACH

Although a social welfare function is a convenient and powerful concept in theory, its practical usefulness has been illusory. Many attempts have been made to specify a social welfare function sufficiently to facilitate empirical usefulness but none have been widely accepted. Apparently, little hope exists for determining a social welfare function on which general agreement can be reached. The major approaches that have been attempted include (1) the subjective approach, (2) the basic axiomatic approach and (3) the moral justice approach.

The subjective approach is represented by those who postulate a complete functional form for the social welfare function on subjective ethical grounds. Early students of the utilitarian school (for example, Bentham 1961, first published 1823) believed that changes in happiness should simply be added over individuals,

$$W = U^1 + U^2 + U^3 + \ldots \tag{3.1}$$

4. Note that the slope of the welfare contour can be represented by

$$-\frac{\partial W/\partial U_A}{\partial W/\partial U_B} \equiv -\frac{W_{U_A}}{W_{U_B}}$$

if $W(U_A, U_B)$ is continuous and first derivatives exist. The slope of the utility possibility frontier is

$$-\frac{\partial U_B/\partial q_1}{\partial U_A/\partial q_1} = -\frac{\partial U_B/\partial q_2}{\partial U_A/\partial q_2}.$$

Thus, the tangency condition can be represented mathematically by

$$\frac{W_{U_A}}{W_{U_B}} = \frac{\partial U_B/\partial q_i}{\partial U_A/\partial q_i}, \; i = 1, 2.$$

Cross-multiplying yields

$$\frac{\partial W}{\partial U_B}\left(\frac{\partial U_B}{\partial q_i}\right) = \frac{\partial W}{\partial U_A}\left(\frac{\partial U_A}{\partial q_i}\right), \; i = 1, 2,$$

which, simply stated, implies that the marginal social significance of consumption must be equated across individuals for each commodity.

where U^i represents the utility of individual i. A positive net gain is then viewed as grounds for policy implementation. This implies that the welfare contours such as W_0 in Figure 3.5 should be straight lines with slope -1. Others argue that a functional form should be used that reflects positive benefits from increases in equality consistent with 'normal' distributional judgments (see, for example, Blackorby and Donaldson 1990). One social welfare function that reflects inequality aversion is the form,

$$W = \frac{1}{1-\rho}[(U^1)^{1-\rho} + (U^2)^{1-\rho} + (U^3)^{1-\rho} + \ldots]. \qquad (3.2)$$

The problem here is that the term 'normal' is ambiguous. For example, agreement cannot be reached on the appropriate level of inequality aversion, for example, the appropriate value of ρ in equation (3.2).[5]

The axiomatic approach, on the other hand, attempts to investigate the existence and form of the social welfare function mathematically based on a set of plausible underlying axioms about individual preferences and how they count to society. The most celebrated of these efforts is Arrow's (1951) *impossibility theorem*. This theorem addresses the question of whether a general rule exists that can rank social states based only on the way these states are ranked by individual members of society. Arrow showed that no such rule exists under the following plausible requirements:

1. *The domain of decisions is unrestricted.*
2. *The Pareto principle applies.*
3. *Dictatorship is ruled out.*
4. *Rankings are independent of irrelevant alternatives.*

An example of a rule that does not work is majority voting. Arrow's (1951) results suggest that social preferences are determined by a dictator (or a group that acts as a dictator), that the intensity of preferences of individuals rather than simple rankings matters (see Kemp and Ng 1977), or that one of the other axioms such as independence of irrelevant alternatives does not apply (see Sen 1970). Accordingly, Arrow's work has spawned a voluminous literature on possibility theorems by relaxing his axioms in various ways (see Sen 1982 or Fishburn 1973 for surveys). A major practical problem with this approach is that even under weaker axioms where voting works, the transactions costs of compiling votes or rankings of all individuals on each policy issue are prohibitive.

The moral justice approach argues that basic axiomatic examinations following Arrow fail because majority groups acting selfishly will prefer to eliminate consideration of minority interests. This failure can be addressed by admitting moral considerations such as *impartiality* and *economic justice*. Suppose that society consists of three individuals and a change is considered that takes \$1000 from one individual to give \$300 to each of the other two. If the three individuals were to vote selfishly knowing who the benefactors are, the majority would favor the change. On the other hand, if the voting were done not knowing who would pay and who would receive (a *veil of ignorance*), then the change

5. To demonstrate the different inequality aversions possible with the function in equation (3.2), note that it reduces to (3.1) when $\rho = 0$, it approaches (3.4) below when ρ approaches infinity, and it approaches the multiplicative form, $W = U^1U^2U^3\ldots$ when ρ approaches 1. See Boadway and Bruce (1984, ch. 5).

would be unanimously rejected. Alternatively, moral concerns for equal treatment of individuals (*impartiality*) have led some to support value judgments whereby the social welfare function treats individuals symmetrically, for example, $W(U^A, U^B) = W(U^B, U^A)$. The contours of the social welfare function in Figure 3.5 are then symmetric about a 45° line from the origin. If all individuals have identical utility functions then the utility possibility frontier is also symmetric about the 45° line and optimality is achieved by perfect equality. On the other hand, if one individual receives proportionally more utility from consuming the same bundles of goods as another, then such a welfare function would, in effect, assign different weights to the consumption of the individuals.

Harsanyi (1953, 1955) gave the first formal treatment of moral considerations by distinguishing between an individual's personal preferences and moral preferences. In his work, moral preferences are the rankings of a rational individual given that the individual does not know which set of personal preferences he or she will have. Under a relatively weak set of assumptions, Harsanyi (1953, 1955) shows with this approach that the social welfare function is a weighted sum of individual utilities,[6]

$$W = \alpha_1 U^1 + \alpha_2 U^2 + \alpha_3 U^3 + \ldots . \tag{3.3}$$

Further imposing impartiality (symmetry), the welfare function in (3.3) reduces to the Benthamite welfare function in (3.1) with equal weights. This welfare function has been called the *just social welfare function* (see Mueller 1979).

Other moral considerations, however, tend to suggest a stronger concept of equality. Moral considerations in economic welfare issues are often called *rights* to economic justice. Various value judgments or ethical postulates representing these moral considerations include the right to consume what one produces, the right to subsistence, the right to economic liberty and the right to economic equality.[7] With these considerations, taking $1000 from a very rich individual to give $300 to each of two poor individuals may be preferred on moral grounds. The most celebrated work in this area is Rawls's (1971) *Theory of Justice*. This theory, which is really more of a philosophy than a theory, contends that policy should be evaluated by the welfare of the most miserable person in society. This implies a social welfare function of the form

$$W = \min\,(U^1, U^2, U^3, \ldots). \tag{3.4}$$

In a more general framework, Arrow (1973) and Harsanyi (1975) show that this choice would be supported by individuals' moral preferences only under infinite risk aversion about the vested interests and preferences to be assumed. With other levels of risk aversion, the welfare function in (3.2) is obtained. Arrow concludes that the possibilities of discovering a theory of justice are remote given the diversity of ethical beliefs in society.

Virtually all of these moral consideration approaches suggest a criterion of distribu-

6. The Harsanyi assumptions are that both personal and moral preferences satisfy the von Neumann–Morgenstern axioms of choice, that each individual has an equal probability of taking on any individual's personal preferences, and that two states are socially indifferent if they are indifferent for every individual. Thus, choices are made according to expected utility given uncertainty about individual preferences.
7. For a more detailed review of the theories of ethical income distribution and economic justice, see Boadway and Bruce (1984, ch. 6).

tional optimality that tends, in some sense, toward either equality or equal weighting. However, even these two simple alternatives represented by (3.1) and (3.4) differ drastically in their implications. With (3.4), the worst-off individual becomes a dictator while, with (3.1), individuals who have very small utilities (and marginal utilities) tend not to matter. Nevertheless, each of these functions can be supported by a plausible set of axioms.[8] Thus, while axiomatic developments have added to the sophistication of social welfare function specification efforts, the effect has been to shift the level of disagreement from the function itself to the axioms that support it. Agreement on the set of axioms appears to be no more possible than agreement on the form of the social welfare function.

In summary, efforts to reach a unique social welfare function have not gained widespread acceptance in spite of great effort by a host of social choice theorists and moral philosophers. Thus, no generally acceptable or objective way to make interpersonal comparisons of utility exists.[9] In spite of the lack of agreement on form, adoption of specific alternative social welfare functions is still advocated from time to time in the literature. Some observed policy choices that strictly redistribute income by, for example, taxing the rich to give to the poor, cannot be advocated or explained with other economic criteria used for policy evaluation. Even if a social welfare function is determined, however, a host of practical problems arise in any practical application. The social welfare function approach requires that individual utilities are cardinally measurable so that intensities of preferences can be compared. In contrast to this approach, Pareto and compensation criteria assume only that utility can be measured ordinally. Thus, much greater practical applicability is attained even though the associated social ordering is not sufficiently complete to identify a unique social optimum or resolve questions of income distribution.

In applied welfare economics, the notion of a social welfare function is useful conceptually but one should keep in mind that a welfare function cannot be specified for practical purposes. However, this does not mean that the study of welfare economics is impractical because the function cannot be specified. Even those who are critical of welfare economics for this reason must agree that economists can make a useful contribution by pointing out who loses and who gains, as well as the magnitude of losses and gains caused for various groups by particular policies.

To summarize the welfare function controversy, it suffices to quote a notable welfare economist, E.J. Mishan (1973, pp. 747–8):

> The social welfare function, even when it is more narrowly defined as a ranking of all conceivable combinations of individual welfare, remains but a pleasing and nebulous abstraction. It cannot be translated into practical guidance for economic policy. Even if there were no fundamental obstacles to its construction, or even if one could think up reasonable conditions under which a social welfare function could exist, there would remain the virtually impossible task of arranging for society to rank unambiguously all conceivable combinations of the individual welfares and moreover – in order to utilise this massive apparatus – to discover (without much cost)

8. For example, Maskin (1978) and Sen (1982) find that any social welfare function with unrestricted domain that satisfies independence of irrelevant alternatives, the Pareto principle, anonymity, separability of unconcerned individuals, and cardinality with interpersonal comparability must be of the form in (3.1). However, simply replacing cardinality with ordinality and adding a minimal equity assumption (the best-off individual's preferences can never be served when they conflict with all worse-off individuals' preferences) results in the Rawlsian social welfare function in (3.4).
9. For further discussion of the difficulties related to determination of a social welfare function, see Atkinson (1970) and Sen (1973).

the effect on the welfare of each person in society (in terms of utilities, goods, or money) of the introduction of alternative economic organisations. For only if we have such data can we rank all existing and future economic possibilities and pronounce some to be socially superior to others. Although one can always claim that 'useful insights' have emerged from the attempts to construct theoretical social welfare functions, the belief that they can ever by translated into useful economic advice is chimerical.

In contrast, the more pedestrian welfare criteria, although analyzed in abstract terms, can be translated into practical propositions. Modern societies do seek to rank projects or policies by some criterion of economic efficiency and to take account also of distributional consequences.

3.5 POTENTIAL VERSUS ACTUAL GAINS

Because the social welfare function is a concept upon which general agreement has not been reached and because the potential welfare criterion is one that renders many policy alternatives noncomparable, the compensation principle has emerged as the criterion that is empirically the most widely applicable. But this state of affairs underscores the controversy about whether compensation should actually be paid when adopting policy changes that satisfy the criterion. If possible, should the gainers from a new policy actually compensate the losers so that 'everyone' is actually made better off? Should a policy change be recommended only on the basis of 'potential' gains alone, given that, if the change is made, someone is actually made worse off? As an example, the United Automobile Workers (UAW) union has taken the stand that new technology that displaces workers should not be introduced unless the workers are fully compensated for their losses. This is a case where the *potential* gains criterion is not supported. But to the extent that the UAW represents displaced workers, objections from the losing groups are not surprising.

However, an economist can often analyze the distributional impacts of policy choices without getting into the issue of compensation. For example, suppose one did an analysis of the impact of removing quotas on the importation of steel into the USA. A proper analysis would show the separate effects on government revenues, producers, consumers and the like (possibly by disaggregated groups if, say, several groups of consumers are affected differently). Thus, the losers, the gainers, and the magnitudes of losses and gains would be identified. Such an analysis would be useful to government officials who are elected or appointed to decide, among other things, the issue of compensation. In fact, a welfare analysis that does not adequately indicate individual group effects may be misleading or useless to government officials who have the authority to make interpersonal comparisons. Thus, as emphasized in Chapter 1, studies on the impact of policy choices can be done using welfare economics without getting into the debate as to what 'ought to be'.

3.6 PRACTICAL APPLIED POLICY ANALYSIS: THE RELATIONSHIP OF GENERAL EQUILIBRIUM AND PARTIAL EQUILIBRIUM ANALYSIS

The practical applicability of the various criteria for policy evaluation depends on the potential for empirical implementation and on the intuitive understandability of policymakers. Both the social welfare function and potential welfare criteria suffer in both respects. First, consumer utility cannot be measured sufficiently for empirical implementation under general conditions and, second, units of measurement for utility and social welfare are abstract and not well understood by policy-makers. The Pareto and compensation criteria, however, can be implemented in terms of individuals' *willingness to pay* and *willingness to accept* the effects of policies and projects. As demonstrated throughout this book, these measures can be reported in monetary terms that are generally empirically feasible and well understood.

A second problem with the framework used thus far for practical policy analysis is that an abstract general equilibrium framework has been used to investigate possibilities for identifying potential social gains through application of compensation criteria. Such a general equilibrium framework is highly useful for understanding the nature of problems encountered in application of compensation criteria, but it is not very helpful for analyzing and quantifying the implications of specific policies or projects involving markets and prices for specific goods. Policy-makers are generally concerned with impacts on specific markets and specific types of agents in society. The remainder of this book focuses on measuring individual, market and group-specific welfare effects by first concentrating on partial equilibrium models.

To facilitate the transition from general equilibrium analysis to the analysis of specific markets and agents, consider Figure 3.6. Figure 3.6(a) illustrates a production possibility curve PP, a Scitovsky indifference curve C, and a first-best equilibrium at (q_1^*,q_2^*), which attains a tangency of the production possibility curve and Scitovsky curve at prices p_1^* and p_2^* for goods q_1 and q_2, respectively. Figure 3.6(b) illustrates the supply and demand curves for q_1, which are derived from Figure 3.6(a) by varying the price p_1. The supply curve is found by plotting the absolute value of the slope of PP for each level of q_1. In other words, it is found by varying the price p_1 holding price p_2 fixed at p_2^* and finding the corresponding tangency of the price line with slope $-p_1/p_2^*$ to the production possibility curve. This slope is the social marginal cost of q_1 in terms of q_2, that is, the value of q_2 that must be given up to gain an additional unit of q_1 at prices p_1 and p_2^*. As the amount of q_1 increases, social marginal cost increases. The demand curve in Figure 3.6(b) is the graph of the absolute value of the slope of the Scitovsky indifference curve C in Figure 3.6(a). It corresponds to varying the price p_1 holding price p_2 fixed at p_2^* and finding the corresponding tangency of the price line with slope $-p_1/p_2^*$ to the Scitovsky curve. Thus, the Scitovsky curve has a social marginal willingness-to-pay (WTP) interpretation. That is, at each point on curve C the slope is the maximum amount of q_2 society is willing to give up to gain an additional unit of q_1 at prices p_1 and p_2^*. As society has more of q_1, the social marginal WTP, or social marginal benefit (MB), declines.

At the Pareto optimal level of q_1, denoted by q_1^* in Figure 3.6, the marginal WTP is just equal to the marginal cost of q_1, so it is impossible to identify any potential economic social gains in moving from this point. In Figure 3.6(b) in particular, this result is noted by considering movements to the right and left of q_1^*. For example, for a movement to the right, say to q_1^1, the marginal cost is greater than marginal WTP and, hence, losses are associated with moving from q_1^* to q_1^1. To the left, say at q_1^2, marginal WTP exceeds marginal cost so net social benefits are possible in moving from q_1^2 to q_1^*. Finally, note that under the assumptions of Section 2.5 the competitive mechanism results in a market equilibrium at product price p_1^* and quantity q_1^*, which attains Pareto efficiency given price p_2^* for good q_2.

Chapters 4 through 7 use the approach of Figure 3.6(b) assuming the prices in other

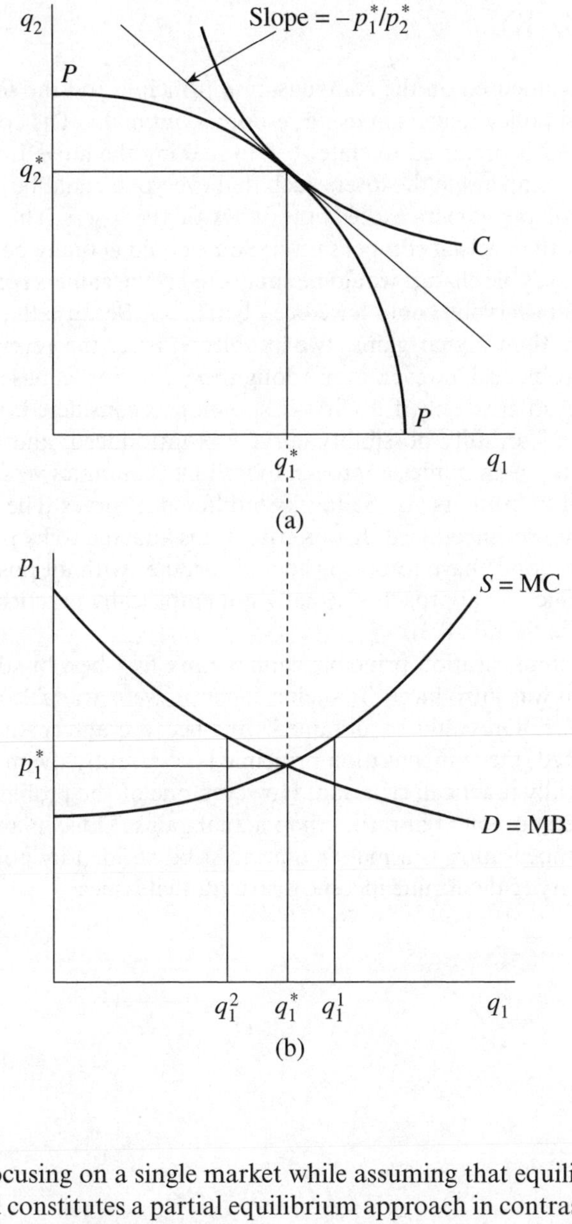

Figure 3.6

markets are fixed. Focusing on a single market while assuming that equilibrium in other markets is unaffected constitutes a partial equilibrium approach in contrast to the framework of Chapters 2 and 3, which uses a general equilibrium approach. A partial equilibrium approach is useful for illuminating how specific policies affect specific markets and groups of consumers and producers in specific markets. However, one must bear in mind that specific policies with specific effects in a given market can have additional general equilibrium implications in other markets. These are considered in Chapter 9.[10]

10. The results illustrated in the simple graphical model of Figure 3.6 are developed rigorously in the Appendix to Chapter 9 in the context of a market economy with many markets.

3.7 SUMMARY

This chapter has focused on the compensation principle and the social welfare function as devices to aid policy-makers in using resources optimally. The compensation principle states that state B is preferred to state A if, in making the move from state A to state B, the gainers can compensate the losers such that everyone could be made better off – that is, if the WTP of the gainers exceeds the WTA of the losers. The principle is based on potential rather than actual compensation. Some could actually be made worse off from a policy change, yet the change would be supported if the gainers *could* have compensated the losers so that everyone could have been better off. Because the principle is based on potential rather than actual gains, two problems arise: the reversal paradox and the intransitivity problem. However, even though the criterion is based on potential gains, these problems can arise only if no first-best bundle is considered.

The concept of a utility possibility curve was introduced, and a parallel was drawn between the utility possibilities approach to welfare economics versus that based on production possibility frontiers and Scitovsky indifference curves. The notion of a potential welfare criterion was introduced. If this criterion is adhered to by policy-makers, all possible bundles of goods have to be considered together with all possible distributions of these bundles. Such an approach is usually not empirically practical (although it is considered further in Section 8.3).

Because the compensation principle cannot rank first-best bundles, the concept of a welfare function was introduced. If such a function were available and agreed upon, the optimum organization could be obtained. But because agreement on such a function cannot be reached, the compensation principle is apparently the most widely applicable, yet also empirically practical, criterion. However, one of the problems with the principle is that it is based on potential rather than actual gains. Thus, in any policy context, the payment of compensation is a matter that must be decided by policy-makers endowed with the authority to determine income distributional issues.

4. Welfare measurement for the producer

Production is a crucial component of economic activity. Many firms produce the goods and services consumed by the general public. Some industries (for example, steel) are made up of only a few firms, whereas others are made up of many firms (for example, the US wheat-producing industry). Also, some firms are multinational in scope (that is, they manufacture and sell products in more than one country).

Increasing attention has been devoted to the question of how well producing firms and marketing firms perform. That is, do they price competitively or not? Does competitive pricing lead to economic efficiency? Do producers adequately consider the costs imposed on society by environmental pollution? Are producers affected by government policy (and, if so, by how much)? For example, what is the effect on the steel industry and on consumers of the use of import quotas?

This chapter focuses on the producer welfare measurement. Several different producer welfare measures are defined and compared. The chapter proceeds on a rather simple level, dealing with only a single competitive firm under the assumption of profit maximization. Clearly, firms may operate with more criteria in mind than only profit maximization. A vast literature exists in positive economics about firms that maximize sales, growth, market shares and the like. Although the approach developed in this chapter, and throughout the rest of this book, could be used in contexts in which firms have such objective criteria, the major emphasis is on profit maximization because it is the more popular and, perhaps, more relevant approach. The profit-maximization approach requires some generalization when price or production is random. For example, a more appropriate assumption is that producers maximize the expected utility from profits. But this distinction makes no difference when prices and production are nonrandom, as in the case of this chapter. The case with risk (random prices and production) where utility maximization may be important is introduced in Chapter 12 and considered in detail in Appendix Sections 12.A and 14.A.

Welfare analysis of an individual firm, even in a competitive industry, is often required. Examples are the analysis of effects of selective labor strikes against individual firms and the analysis of effects of antitrust litigation brought against a single processor or retailer by a single producer of a product. However, in most cases, empirical welfare analysis focuses on an entire industry. This requires aggregating producer responses and effects. This issue will be delayed until Chapter 8. The concepts derived in this chapter, however, form the basis for aggregation.

4.1 THE PROFIT-MAXIMIZING FIRM

The basic framework for the analysis of this chapter is the neoclassical model as presented in Figure 4.1. Under the assumption of profit maximization, the producer equates price and marginal cost (MC) assuming price exceeds the minimum of the average variable cost

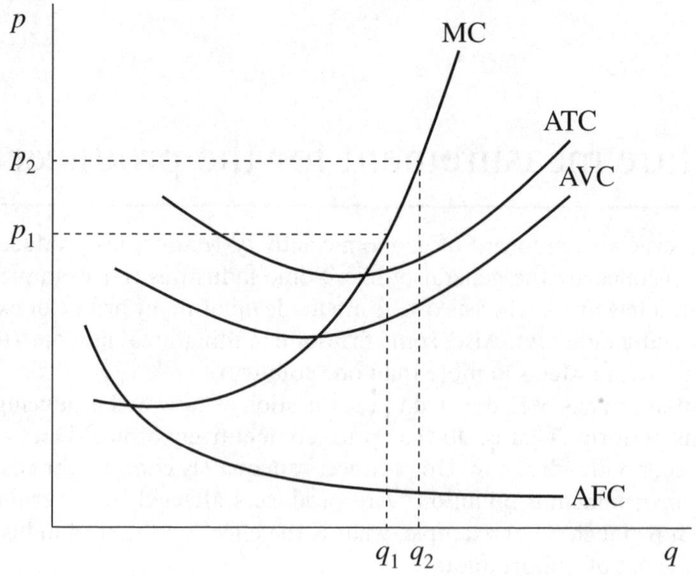

Figure 4.1

(AVC) curve. Hence, with a fixed output price of p_1, the producer chooses output level q_1. Suppose that output price is increased to p_2 because of a policy change, such as introducing a tariff or a price-support program. To maximize profits, the firm will increase output from q_1 to q_2. *Is the producer better off, and by how much?* Or, put another way, has there been an increase in revenue that may be 'taxed away' without making the firm any worse off than it was before the price change?

Alternatively, consider the case where the firm is faced with the prospect of having to discontinue production as a result of some policy decision: for example, an air quality-control board closes down factories in an urban area during a temperature-inversion period, or farmers are not allowed to harvest and market their crops because it has been found that seed treatments included a carcinogenic compound. *How would one determine the welfare loss to producers forced to shut down production?* There are some measures – profits, for example – that may be appropriate for answering questions related to changes in welfare for a producing firm but are not appropriate for questions relating to the change in welfare of a firm when it cannot produce.

A clear definition of a producer is needed to address the foregoing issues. The *producer* (that is, the firm) is defined as a legal entity that supplies either intermediate or final goods and possibly uses both variable and fixed inputs in the production process. This chapter assumes that the firm is able to purchase all the variable inputs it needs at a fixed price. That is, the supply curve for variable inputs is perfectly price elastic. With respect to the fixed factors, the analysis is appropriate for cases where the producer is either an owner and/or a renter. The fixed factors that the firm does not own are rented at a market-determined 'rental' price that is not negotiable during the period under consideration. The fixed factors owned by the firm are valued at their opportunity cost at the beginning of the period. The fixed costs associated with the fixed factors are sunken. That is, they cannot be avoided even if the firm goes out of business (for example, when a farm firm rents land and pays a cash rental at the beginning of the season). Within this framework, *the rents to primary factor owners will be unaffected by any short-run policy change imposed on the producer*.

This point is illustrated in Figure 4.2. Initially, the firm is producing output q_0 at price p_0 using x^0 of a variable factor that has a perfectly elastic supply at w^0 and R_0 of a fixed factor that has been rented at (or has an opportunity cost of) r_0. Suppose, then, that a policy change is considered that increases output price to p_1. The firm expands its level of output to q_1 and increases its variable input use from x^0 to x^1 as the derived demand for x shifts from $D_x(p_0)$ to $D_x(p_1)$ in Figure 4.2(c). Hence, in the short run, the increase in price

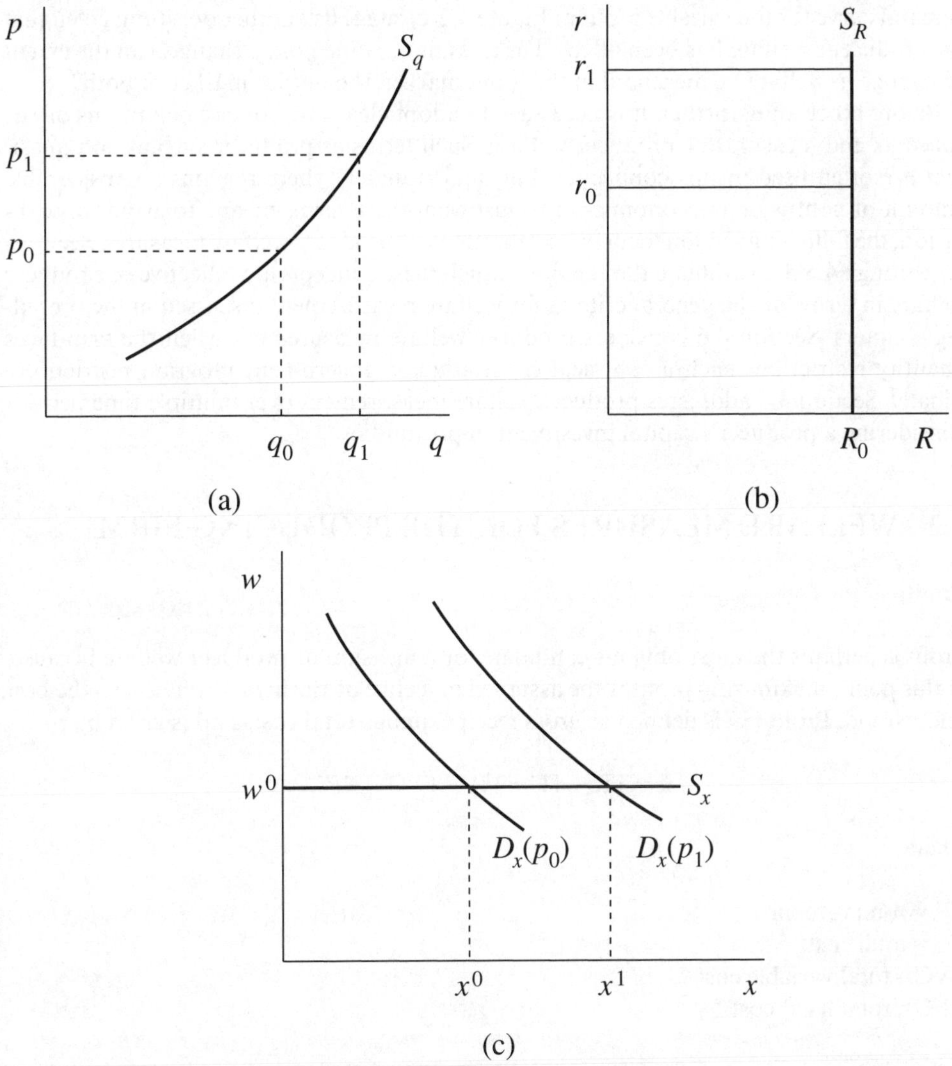

Figure 4.2

from p_0 to p_1 affects only the producing firm, not the owners of fixed factors. However, if the output price remains at p_1 and the supply of fixed factors remains perfectly elastic at w^0, rents to the fixed factor will increase under competition to, perhaps, r_1 in Figure 4.2(b) in the subsequent period. Thus, the welfare position of the firm may be reduced if the fixed factors are owned by individuals outside the firm.

This is important because firms often rent factors of production. A clear illustration is in agriculture, where many farmers rent land from landowners on a cash-lease basis. As a result, an increase in the price of farm products can improve the welfare position of the farmer in the short run. However, how long the firm can maintain this position depends upon the extent to which the owners of the fixed factor increase the rental price. Also, the observation that the increase in price in the output market in Figure 4.2(a) shifts the demand curve for the variable input in Figure 4.2(c) suggests another question: given that the producer's welfare has been affected as a result of some policy change, can the extent of change in welfare be measured in the input market, the output market or both?

Before proceeding further, it is necessary to adopt clear and concise definitions of the concepts and measures of producer welfare. Such terms as producer surplus and quasi-rent are often used in this connection but, unfortunately, there remains a considerable amount of confusion in economics as to just what these terms mean. To avoid this confusion, the following section focuses on definitions of producer welfare measures. Sections 4.3 through 4.5 then evaluate the extent to which these concepts are reflective of producer welfare in terms of the general criteria for welfare measurement discussed in the preceding chapters. Section 4.6 considers producer welfare measurement when the firm faces quantity restrictions such as physical constraints or government program restrictions. Finally, Section 4.7 addresses producer welfare measurement over multiple time periods considering a producer's capital investment opportunities.

4.2 WELFARE MEASURES FOR THE PRODUCING FIRM

Profit

Profit is perhaps the most obvious candidate for a measure of producer welfare because, at this point, maximizing profit is the assumed objective of the firm. Profit is also the best understood. Profit (π) is defined as gross receipts minus total costs and is given by

$$\pi = \text{TR} - \text{TC} = \text{TR} - \text{TVC} - \text{TFC},$$

where

TR = total revenue
TC = total cost
TVC = total variable cost
TFC = total fixed cost.

To what extent does profit measure producer welfare? To determine this, the general criteria of compensating and equivalent variation discussed in Chapters 1 and 3 are used.

First, the case is considered where the firm produces a positive level of output before and after a policy change.

The competitive firm in Figure 4.3 with supply (short-run marginal cost) curve S is faced with price p_1 and must consider the higher price p_2.[1] Profit-maximizing quantities

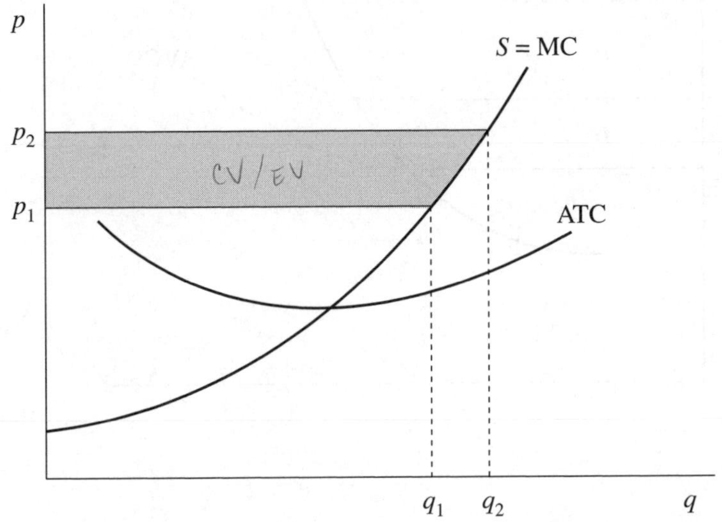

Figure 4.3

at p_1 and p_2 are q_1 and q_2, respectively. *The compensating variation associated with the price increase is the sum of money that, when taken away from the producing firm, leaves it just as well off as if the price did not change, given that it is free to adjust production (to profit-maximizing quantities) in either case.* Because profit at p_2 (and q_2) is higher than at p_1 (and q_1) by the shaded area, this area is exactly the compensating variation. *The equivalent variation associated with the price increase is the sum of money which, when given to the firm, leaves it just as well off without the price change as if the change had occurred, again assuming freedom of adjustment.* Because profit at p_1 is lower than at p_2 by the amount of the shaded area, this area must also represent the equivalent variation. Thus, the change in profit associated with such a price change provides an exact measure of both the compensating and equivalent variations.

Although profit can serve as an appropriate measure of the welfare effects of price change, it is not always appropriate in other cases. For example, consider the case where a policy change prevents a firm from producing during a period. The compensating variation of such a change is the sum of money which, when taken away from the firm, leaves the firm just as well off as if it were allowed to remain in production. This sum is generally negative. The equivalent variation is the sum of money which, when given to the firm, leaves the firm just as well off in production as if it were forced to shut down. This sum is also generally negative.

1. Again, it is assumed for convenience that the average cost curve (at its minimum) intersects marginal cost at a small output.

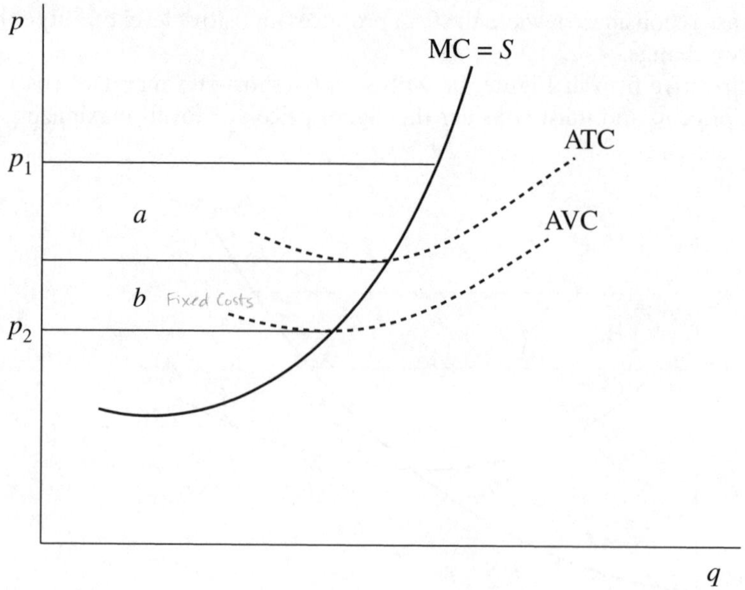

Figure 4.4

A firm with marginal cost MC, average variable cost AVC, average total cost ATC, and product price p_1 is depicted in Figure 4.4. Only by giving the firm a transfer payment in the amount of area $a+b$ is it just as well off without producing as if production had continued as usual. The firm is willing to pay more than its current profits a to remain in production because its fixed costs in the amount of area b cannot be avoided even if production is shut down. But it would be better off shutting down and absorbing fixed costs if a payment any greater than area $a+b$ were required. With any transfer payment (in lieu of production) smaller than area $a+b$, the firm would be worse off (after covering unavoidable fixed costs) than in its previous profit position. The total benefit to the producer from remaining in business is thus given by profit plus fixed cost (area $a+b$) rather than simply profit (area a). Thus, an alternative to profit is required to measure producer welfare in this case.

Producer Surplus and Quasirent

As an alternative to profit, Alfred Marshall (1930) defined a producer's net benefit as the excess of gross receipts which a producer receives for any commodities produced over their prime cost – that is, over the extra cost that the firm incurs in order to produce those things which it could have escaped if it had not produced them (see also Currie, Murphy and Schmitz 1971). This concept has been called quasirent for the firm because it is a rent on fixed factors employed by the firm but, unlike factor rent, may not persist over a long period of time. Specifically, *quasirent R is defined as the excess of gross receipts TR over total variable costs TVC*, $R = \text{TR} - \text{TVC}$. Marshall went on to suggest the area below the price line and above the supply curve – commonly called producer surplus – as a measure of this benefit. Thus, *producer surplus is defined as the area above the supply curve and below the price line of the corresponding firm or industry* (see Stigler 1952, p. 163).

Although Marshall did not emphasize the distinction between quasirent as an economic concept and producer surplus as a geometric area, more general cases (such as those in Chapter 9) suggest the need for such a distinction. For purposes of this chapter, which corresponds to Marshall's framework, however, producer surplus and quasirent are equivalent.[2]

Given the assumptions of this chapter, the welfare significance of quasirent or producer surplus can be usefully investigated by a comparison with profits. To determine the relationship among profit (π), quasirent (R), and producer surplus (P), note from above that

$$P = R = \mathrm{TR} - \mathrm{TVC}.$$

That is, the area above a competitive firm's short-run supply curve and below the price line provides a measure of the 'excess of gross receipts over prime costs' because the firm's short-run supply curve coincides with its marginal cost curve above AVC. Hence, based on the analysis of Figure 4.4, one finds that

$$R = P = \pi + \mathrm{TFC},$$

or that both quasirent and producer surplus are given by profit plus total fixed cost.[3]

Now, evaluating quasirent or producer surplus with the same criteria as for profit above (that is, by comparison with compensating and equivalent variation), one finds that the change in either is an exact measure of the compensating or equivalent variation of a price change (because the change in each is equal to the change in profit). Where the firm is forced to cease production, however, quasirent (or producer surplus) is also appropriate (whereas the profit measure is not) because quasirent exceeds profit by fixed cost. This is exactly the amount by which profit underestimates the true welfare cost of a forced shutdown.

The total benefit to the producer from remaining in business, given by profit plus fixed cost, is thus equal to quasirent, which in the present case of fixed factor prices is equivalent to producer surplus. Because profit underestimates the benefits accruing to a firm from doing business, producer surplus and quasirent are more useful focal points for economic welfare analysis.

2. The equivalence of quasirent and producer surplus has led Mishan (1968, p. 1279) to argue that the term 'producer surplus' is unnecessary jargon. Nevertheless, although producer surplus could be discarded in the context of this chapter, it is still useful to retain for measurement purposes in later chapters.
3. In a mathematical rather than graphical framework, the profit of a competitive firm might be represented by $\pi = pq - c(q) - K$ where K is fixed cost and $c(q)$ is a cost function specifying the variable cost required to produce q, with $c(0) = 0$ and derivatives $c' > 0$ and $c'' < 0$. Profit maximization yields the first-order condition $p = c'$, which equates price and marginal cost and implies c' is both the marginal cost and supply curve. If the first-order condition $p = c'$ is satisfied at $q = q^*$, then $\mathrm{TR} = pq^*$, $\mathrm{TC} = c(q^*) + K$, $\mathrm{TVC} = c(q^*)$, $\mathrm{TFC} = K$, and profit can be represented as $\pi = pq^* - c(q^*) - K = \int_0^{q^*} (p - c')dq - K$ where quasirent (or producer surplus) is $P = R = \int_0^{q^*} (p - c')dq = \pi + K$.

4.3 THE RELATIONSHIP OF PROFIT, QUASIRENT AND PRODUCER SURPLUS[4]

In various empirical and theoretical economic welfare problems, it can be advantageous to recognize the variety of ways that producer welfare gains can be computed. The most common approach in empirical and graphical theoretic work is simply to determine (according to the definition of producer surplus) the area above the short-run supply curve and below price. For a firm with marginal cost curve MC and average variable cost curve AVC in Figure 4.5, the short-run supply curve is given by $S'S$ in Figure 4.5(a) (because at any price below p_1 the firm can no longer recover any of its fixed costs and therefore ceases to operate). Hence, producer surplus or, equivalently, quasirent can be calculated as the shaded area in Figure 4.5(a).

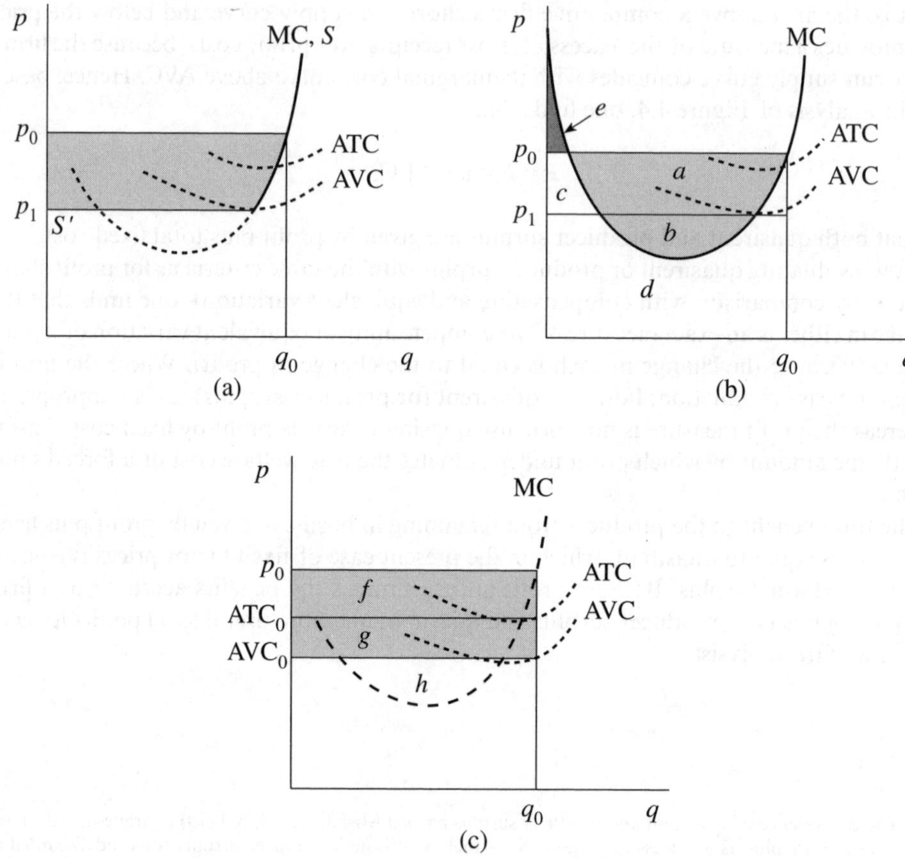

Figure 4.5

4. For a similar diagrammatic discussion, see Ferguson (1969b, p. 376). Also, note that the 'area' operator is used in this section and throughout this book without parentheses to denote the sum of areas of all terms following it. If any quantities are to be added to the area, they appear in front of the operator.

Another possibility demonstrated in Figure 4.5(b) is suggested by the definition of quasirent. At price p_0, the profit-maximizing total receipts are given by the area below p_0 and left of quantity q_0, or

$$\text{TR} = \text{area } a+b+c+d = p_0 \cdot q_0.$$

Also, one measure of total variable costs is the total area below the marginal cost curve (and left of quantity q_0):

$$\text{TVC} = \text{area } c+d+e.$$

Thus, quasirent can be calculated as the difference,

$$R = \text{TR} - \text{TVC} = \text{area } a+b-e,$$

which is the lightly shaded area minus the heavily shaded area. This is the more common theoretical approach suggested by the calculus and is the one used in the appendix of this chapter.

A third possibility, also based on the definition of quasirent, is suggested in Figure 4.5(c). Again, total receipts can be measured by the area below price p_0 and left of quantity q_0, or by

$$\text{TR} = \text{area } f+g+h = p_0 \cdot q_0.$$

Noting that, by definition,

$$\text{TVC} = \text{AVC} \cdot q,$$

it is possible to calculate total variable costs as the profit-maximizing output (q_0) multiplied by the average variable cost at that output (AVC_0), which is the area h,

$$\text{TVC} = \text{area } h = \text{AVC} \cdot q_0.$$

Hence, quasirent or, equivalently, producer surplus can also be calculated as[5]

$$R = \text{area } f+g = (p_0 - \text{AVC}_0) \cdot q_0.$$

5. To derive these various results in the mathematical framework of footnote 3, note that $\text{AVC} = c(q)/q$. Thus, quasirent can be represented as $P = R = \int_0^{q^*} (p - c')dq = pq - c(q^*) = q^*(p - \text{AVC})$. To show the equivalence of the shaded areas in Figures 4.5(a) and 4.5(b), suppose c' is first negative and then positive with $c'' > 0$ and let AVC_0 represent average variable cost at quantity q_0 where $c'(q_0) = \text{AVC}_0 = c(q_0)/q_0$. Then

$$\begin{aligned} P = R &= \int_0^{q_0} (p - c')dq \\ &= \int_0^{q_0} (p - c')dq + \int_{q_0}^{q^*} (p - c')dq \\ &= pq_0 - c(q_0) + \int_{q_0}^{q^*} (p - c')dq \\ &= q_0(p - \text{AVC}_0) + \int_{q_0}^{q^*} (p - c')dq. \end{aligned}$$

For an example of a study that uses this approach to producer welfare measurement, see Cooke and Sundquist (1993).

With this approach, determining what part of quasirent corresponds to fixed cost is a simple matter. By definition, total cost (TC) is given by the product of average total cost (ATC) and quantity,

$$TC = ATC \cdot q.$$

Hence, total fixed cost (TFC) is given by

$$TFC = TC - TVC = (ATC - AVC) \cdot q.$$

At output q_0 where average total cost is ATC_0, total fixed cost is given by area g with profit given by the remainder of the shaded area (so long as p_0 is greater than ATC_0).[6]

4.4 PRODUCER WELFARE MEASUREMENT IN THE INPUT MARKET

Measuring producer welfare effects in the output market is a useful approach in applied economic welfare analysis provided that data are available to estimate supply curves for final products. Cases arise, however, where this is not possible. Data may be sufficient only to estimate the producer's derived demand in an intermediate product market. For example, it may be possible to estimate the derived demand curve for iron ore at the firm or industry level even though the marginal cost curve for steel production for an individual firm or industry cannot be estimated. In such a case, is it possible to obtain welfare estimates by looking only at input markets? To answer this question, it is essential to understand the welfare significance of changes in areas under derived demand curves and how these relate to the quasirent or the producer surplus in the output market. This section explores these relationships. Fortunately, for the practitioner, a transition can be made from the input to the output market.

First, the possibilities for measuring the producer welfare effect of an input and/or an output price change in either the input or output markets (at the investigator's choice) are

6. This latter case suggests another algebraic approach to calculating producer welfare. That is, suppose that the firm uses quantities $x_1, x_2, \ldots, x_n$ of n respective inputs with variable input prices of $w_1, w_2, \ldots, w_n$. Then, by definition,

$$TVC = w_1 x_1 + w_2 x_2 + \cdots + w_n x_n .$$

Hence, quasirent or producer surplus is given by

$$R = TR - TVC = p_0 q_0 - w_1 x_1 - w_2 x_2 - \cdots - w_n x_n .$$

This suggests the rather simple empirical approach of using income-expense accounts for producer welfare measurement. At an aggregate economy level, such an approach suggests the use of national income accounts for measuring aggregate producer welfare as well as its distribution. The weakness of this approach is that the effects of specific policies or projects on national income accounts are difficult to estimate without a complete model of how national income accounts are affected, which is essentially the same requirement as for standard economic welfare analysis.

considered for the single-variable-factor case. These arguments are generalized to the case of evaluating a multiple price change (input and/or output) in any arbitrarily chosen market in the many-variable-factor case. In each case, an alternative sequential method of evaluation is also suggested.

The Single-Variable-Input Case

The following sections present welfare measures for cases where prices change in the input market only, when prices change in the output market only, and when both prices change together. In this simple framework, in addition to fixed factors, the firm uses only a single variable input.

Input price changes in the input market

The consideration of welfare effects of changes in factor market conditions can be made as before through application of the general willingness-to-pay welfare criteria of Chapters 1 and 3. Consider a single competitive firm (with fixed-product price) using a single variable input x. The input demand schedule D for such a firm is determined as in Figure 4.6(a) by the value of marginal product (defined as output price multiplied by the marginal physical productivity of the input). The compensating variation of a fall in input price from w^0 to w^1 is the sum of money the producer would be willing to pay to obtain the privilege of buying at the lower price (which would leave the firm just as well off at the lower price as if the price had not been lowered). The equivalent variation is the sum of money the producer would accept to forgo the privilege of buying at the lower price (which would leave the firm just as well off at the original price as if the price were lowered). But note that, at input price w^0 and corresponding profit-maximizing input use x^0, total variable cost is given by the area $b+d$ (or w^0x^0) and total receipts are area $a+b+d$.[7] Similarly, at price w^1 and input use x^1, total variable cost is area $d+e$ and total receipts are area $a+b+c+d+e$. Thus, the shaded area $b+c$ measures the change in either quasirent or profit. In keeping with the definition of producer surplus provided above, the triangle-like area below a demand curve and above a price line will be called *consumer surplus*. For this case, the compensating and equivalent variations are identical and are measured by the change in either quasirent, profit, or the change in consumer surplus in the input market. Using the same approach as in Section 4.2, it can also be shown that the compensating and equivalent variation of preventing the producer from obtaining the needed inputs is measured by quasirent or consumer surplus in the input market, rather than profit.

Input price changes measured in the output market

Interestingly, the net welfare effect on the producer of an input price change can also be measured accurately in the output market. That is, as shown in Section 4.3, producer welfare (or quasirent) is accurately measured by the producer surplus area above the short-run marginal cost curve and below price in the output market. Thus, suppose that

7. A mathematical proof of the latter claim is contained, as a special case, in Appendix Section 4.A. For those unfamiliar with the calculus, an intuitive understanding of this point may be gained by viewing the area $a+b+d$ as a discrete summation of output price multiplied by marginal product over all levels of input usage from zero to x^0.

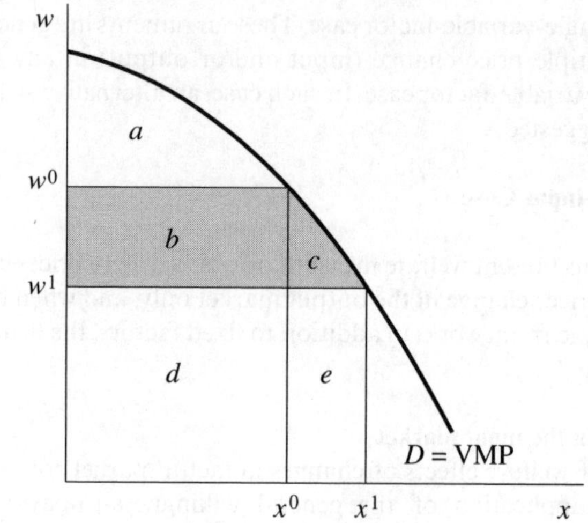

(a) Input market

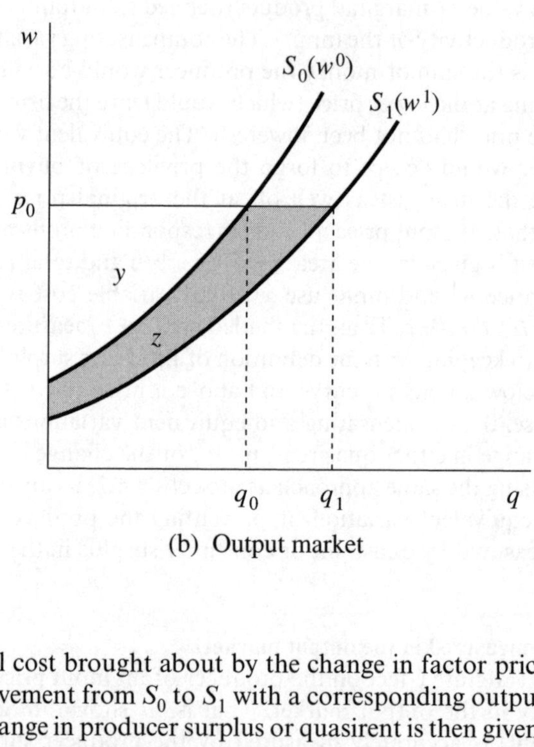

(b) Output market

Figure 4.6

the shift in marginal cost brought about by the change in factor prices is represented in Figure 4.6(b) by movement from S_0 to S_1 with a corresponding output change from q_0 to q_1.[8] The resulting change in producer surplus or quasirent is then given by the shaded area z because producer surplus is given by area y at S_0 and by area $y+z$ at S_1. This area z must also measure the change in the factor-market consumer surplus because both areas are unambiguously equivalent to quasirent.

8. Of course, depending on the magnitude and direction of the input price movement, the output market effect could be in either direction, but a rightward shift is assumed for illustrative purposes.

Output price changes measured in the input market

The preceding result suggests the additional possibility of measuring the effect of an output price change in the input market. This possibility indeed exists. That is, because the output market producer surplus, the input market consumer surplus, and quasirent are all equal in the single-variable-input case, the increase in quasirent resulting from an increase in output market price can be measured by the change in input market consumer surplus as well as by the change in output market producer surplus. Geometrically, this would imply in Figure 4.7 that the increase in producer surplus resulting from an increase in output price from p_0 to p_1 is equal to the increase in consumer surplus in the input market, where D_0 is the demand curve given output price p_0 and D_1 is the demand curve given output price p_1. Thus, where the (unchanging) input price is w^0, area a in Figure 4.7(a) is equal to area b in Figure 4.7(b).

Simultaneous changes in input and output prices

Finally, consider a simultaneous change in both input and output price, say, from w^0 to w^1 and from p_0 to p_1, respectively, in Figure 4.8. Producer surplus is given by area c at prices p_0 and w^0 and by area $a+b+c+d$ at prices p_1 and w^1. The change in producer surplus is area $a+b+d$. The input market consumer surplus, on the other hand, is given by area v at prices p_0 and w^0 and by area $v+x+y+z$ at prices p_1 and w^1. The change is area $x+y+z$. Because both producer and consumer surpluses measure quasirent in the single-input case, the change in quasirent from the multiple price change can be completely measured either in the output market (by area $a+b+d$) or in the input market (by area $x+y+z$).

Alternatively, the multiple price change can be evaluated by imposing the individual changes sequentially, say, first from p_0 to p_1 and then from w^0 to w^1. Moving from p_0 to p_1 and holding w fixed at w^0 results in a change in quasirent equal to area a. Then, holding p fixed at p_1 and moving from w^0 to w^1 results in an additional change in quasirent equal to area $y+z$. The overall change in quasirent is thus area $a+y+z$. Alternatively, the input price could be changed first with p fixed at p_0 obtaining area y. Then, changing p at $w=w^1$ obtains area $a+b$ for a total change of area $a+b+y$.

The change in quasirent associated with the dual price change from p_0 to p_1 and from w^0 to w^1 thus has at least four alternative representations in Figure 4.7:[9]

$$\Delta R = \text{area } a+b+d = \text{area } x+y+z = \text{area } a+y+z = \text{area } a+b+y.$$

It can be further noted that the four approaches outlined above are generally applicable regardless of the direction of price movements. For example, if both prices increase from, say, (p_0, w^1) to (p_1, w^0), then total evaluation in the output market implies a welfare change of area $a-d$. Evaluated completely in the input market, the change is area $x-y$. Using the sequential approach, the change is area $a+b-y-z$ or, equivalently, area $a-y$ depending on whether output price or input price is changed first.

9. Additionally, noting that area d = area y, area a = area x and area b = area z, the change in quasirent associated with the change from (p_0, w^0) to (p_1, w^1) can be represented in several other ways. As will become clear, however, the alternatives are of doubtful interest from either a theoretical or an empirical perspective.

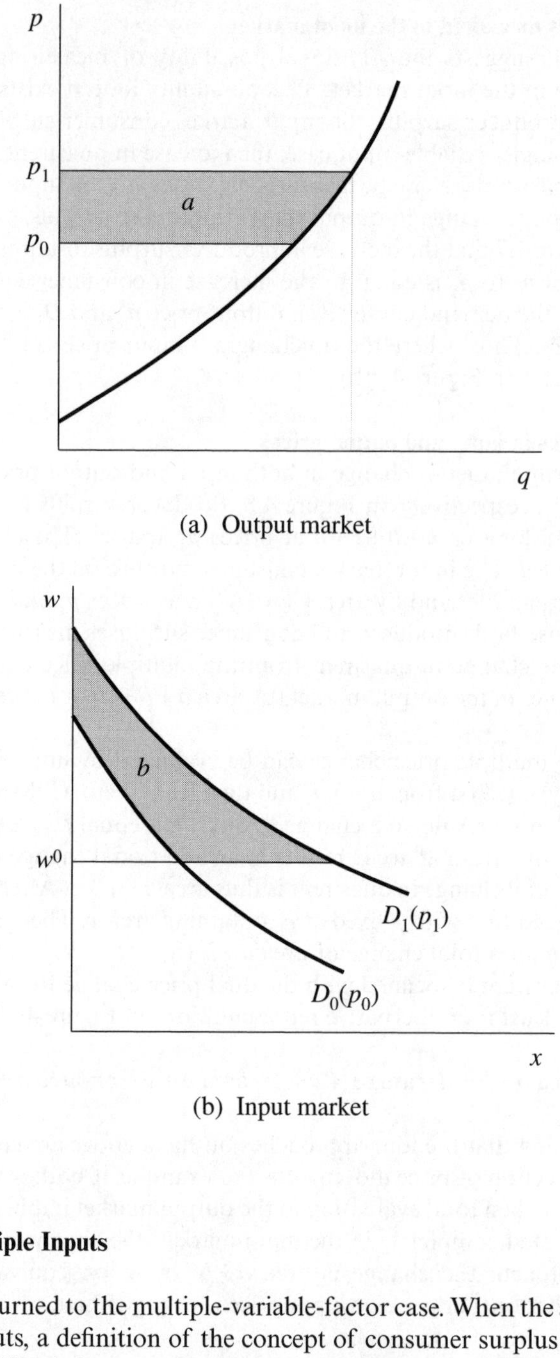

Figure 4.7

The Case of Multiple Inputs

Attention is now turned to the multiple-variable-factor case. When the analysis is extended with multiple inputs, a definition of the concept of consumer surplus in input markets is somewhat more difficult because the demand curves for inputs differ from the value-of-marginal-product curves. That is, the value-of-marginal-product curves correspond to demand for an input when uses of other inputs are held constant. Derived demand curves, on the other hand, take account of optimal adjustment in output and other input uses as

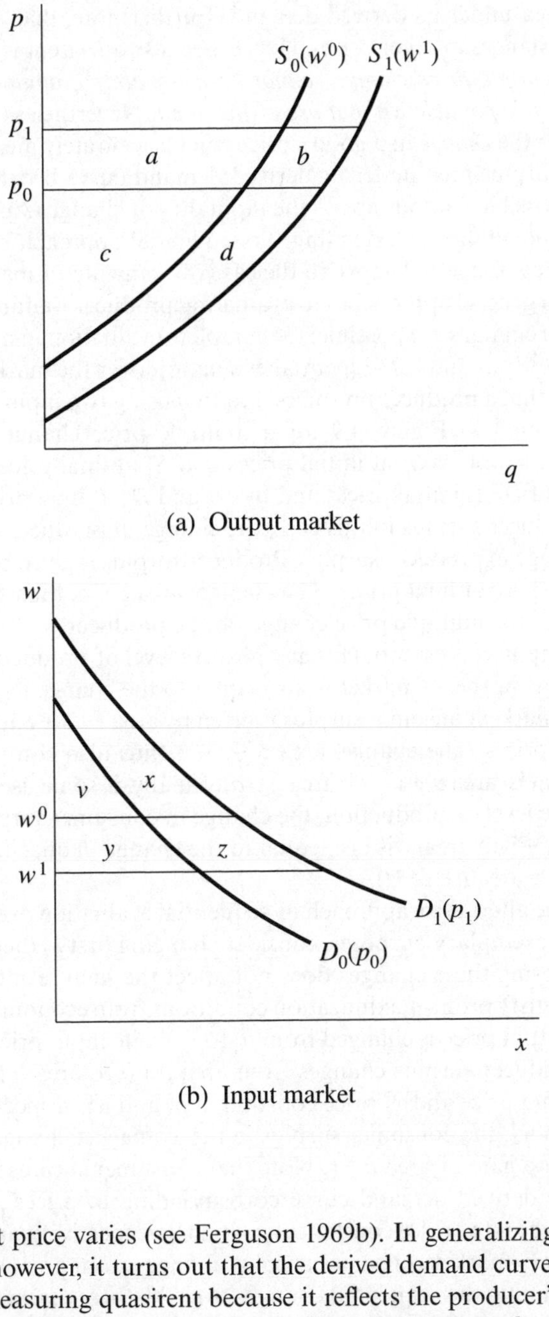

Figure 4.8

the associated input price varies (see Ferguson 1969b). In generalizing the results of the preceding section, however, it turns out that the derived demand curve is the appropriate concept to use in measuring quasirent because it reflects the producer's marginal evaluation of the input as its price and quantity vary. Hence, *the area under the derived demand curve and above price measures quasirent for the producer in the case where production requires positive use of the input, that is, where the input is essential*. This result is established rigorously in Appendix Section 4.C. If production is possible without use of the input, that part of quasirent which can be earned without use of the input would, of course, not be reflected by the area under its derived demand. Furthermore, that amount of quasirent may change with changes in other prices. Hence, because quasirent is possible without use of the input, *a multiple price change cannot be completely evaluated in the single-input market if production is possible without use of the input.* Nevertheless, the *change* in quasirent with respect to the *change* in a good's price can be accurately measured by the change in the consumer surplus area under its derived demand curve because other prices and, hence, quasirent possible without use of the input do not change (Appendix Section 4.C). This suggests the possibility of extending the sequential approach of evaluating welfare changes over markets suggested above to the case of many factor markets.

Thus, again, two general approaches to evaluating producer welfare changes associated with multiple price changes are possible: (1) complete evaluation in a single market for an essential input or output and (2) sequential evaluation over the markets where prices are changed. Suppose that a producer produces output q using two inputs, x_1 and x_2. The first approach is illustrated in Figure 4.9 for a multiple price change from (p_0,w_1^0,w_2^0) to (p_1,w_1^1,w_2^1). Product supply is S_0 at initial prices and S_1 at final prices. Derived demands are given by D_1^0 and D_2^0 at initial prices and by D_1^1 and D_2^1 at final prices. Because quasirent is equal to producer surplus in this case, the change in producer welfare or quasirent is given by the change in producer surplus. Producer surplus is given by area $a+b$ at initial prices and by area $b+c$ at final prices. The change, area $c-a$, thus completely measures the welfare effect of the multiple price change on the producer.

If some use of input x_1 is essential for any positive level of production, then the change in consumer surplus in the x_1 market is also equal to the change in producer welfare or quasirent. The x_1 market consumer surplus is given by area $r+s+t$ at initial prices and by area $r+u$ at final prices. The change, area $u-s-t$, thus also completely measures the welfare change (that is, area $u-s-t=$area $c-a$). Finally, if some use of input x_2 is essential for any positive level of production, the change in consumer surplus in the x_2 market from area $w+x+y+z$ to area w is also equal to the change in quasirent (that is, $-$area $x+y+z=$area $c-a=$area $u-s-t$).

Consider now the alternative approach of sequential evaluation over the markets where prices change. For exemplary purposes, consider changing first p, then w_1 and, finally, w_2. The order of imposing these changes does not affect the final result when demand and supply functions satisfy profit-maximization conditions from economic theory (Appendix Section 4.A). If output price is changed from p_0 to p_1 while input prices are held constant at w_1^0, w_2^0, then producer surplus changes from area $a+b$ to area b for a loss of area a. Next, holding output price and x_2 price constant at p_1 and w_2^0, respectively, and changing x_1 price from w_1^0 to w_1^1, the consumer surplus in the x_1 market changes from area $r+s$ to area $r+s+u+v$ for a gain of area $u+v$. Note that consumer surplus in this case is evaluated using D_1^*, the derived demand curve corresponding to prices p_1 and $w_2{}^0$. Finally, holding output price and x_1 price constant at p_1 and w_1^1, respectively, and changing x_2 price from w_2^0 to w_2^1, the x_2-market consumer surplus changes from area $w+y$ to area w for a loss of area y. Summing the sequential changes over the three markets obtains area $u+v-a-y$, which measures the overall gain (loss, if negative) in quasirent or producer welfare associated with the multiple price change from (p_0,w_1^0,w_2^0) to (p_1,w_1^1,w_2^1).[10]

10. In terms of Figure 4.9, one can show rigorously, on the basis of results in Appendix Sections 4.A–4.C, that area $a-c=$area $s+t-u=$area $x+y+z=$area $a+y-u-v$ so that no contradiction is implied by the results above.

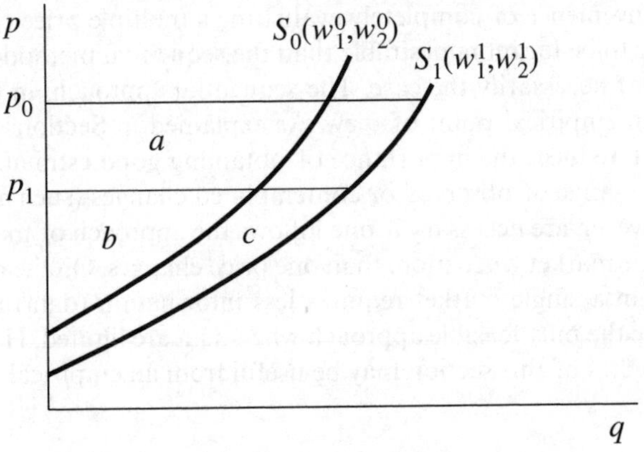

(a) Output market

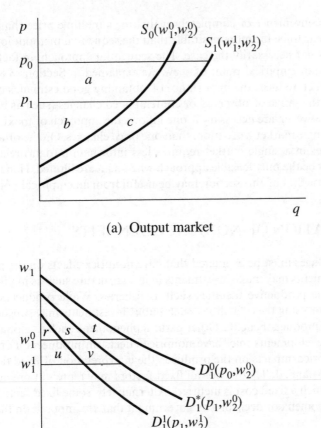

(b) Input market for x_1

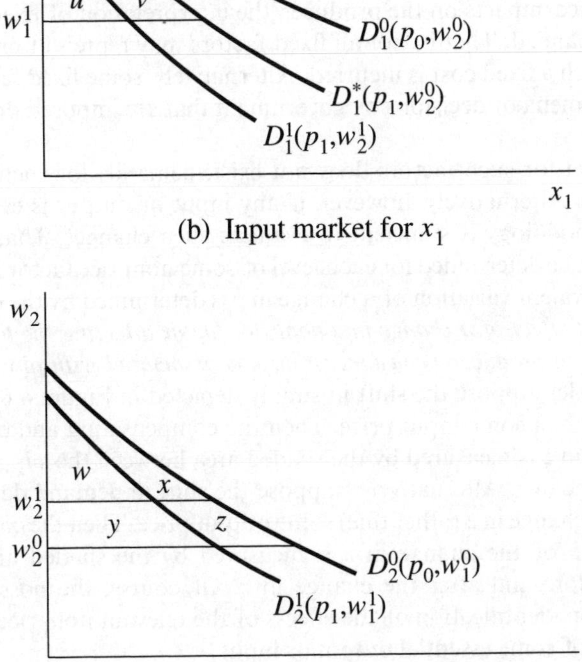

(c) Input market for x_2

Figure 4.9

Although the convenience of completely evaluating a multiple price change in a single market may appear to be far more desirable than the sequential methodology because of simplicity, this is not necessarily the case. The sequential approach, in fact, has distinct advantages from an empirical point of view. As explained in Sections 8.8 and 8.9, the sequential approach reduces the importance of obtaining good estimates of supply and demand outside the range of observed or contemplated changes (such as near the axes). Such estimates, however, are necessary if one follows the approach of making a complete evaluation in a single market when more than one price changes. On the other hand, evaluation of changes in a single market requires less information (data) relating to other markets and may be the only feasible approach when data are limited. Hence, each of the two general approaches of this section may be useful from an empirical point of view.

4.5 EVALUATION OF NONPRICE BENEFITS

Occasionally, policies must be evaluated that have nonprice effects on the producer. For example, governments may make investments in infrastructure such as highways and seaports or in public productive facilities such as fisheries. While producers may not be charged a price for using these facilities, such public investments may substantially affect productivity and producer benefits. Other natural phenomena such as global warming or environmental developments may have nonprice effects on producers. For purposes of considering nonprice impacts on the producer, the interpretation of fixed factors of production can be expanded. That is, not all fixed factors may represent previous decisions of the firm for which a fixed cost is incurred. Alternatively, some fixed factors may represent natural phenomena or decisions by government that are imposed on the firm exogenously.

Because a market for such factors does not exist, demands for such factors are not directly observable. Alternatively, however, if any input or output is essential, then the single-market methodology is sufficient to evaluate such changes. That is, suppose the firm's quasirent can be determined for each level of some nonprice factor z. Then the compensating and equivalent variation of a change in z is determined by the difference. Thus, *the producer benefit effect of a change in a nonprice factor affecting the firm can be measured by the change in producer (consumer) surplus associated with any essential output (input)*. For example, suppose the shift in supply depicted in Figure 4.6(b) is due to the change in z rather than some input price. Then the compensating and equivalent variation of the change in z is measured by the shaded area between the supply curves before and after the change in z. Alternatively, suppose the shift in demand depicted in Figure 4.7(b) is due to the change in z rather than some output price. Then the compensating and equivalent variation of the change in z is measured by the shaded area between the demand curves before and after the change in z. Of course, the possibilities for this approach depend on identification of the effects of the relevant nonprice changes on the supply or demand of some essential output or input.

4.6 INPUT QUANTITY RESTRICTIONS FOR THE COMPETITIVE FIRM

To this point, the analysis has been carried out assuming that the firm can optimally choose input quantities to maximize profits in response to price changes. This section develops welfare measures for the single-product firm when the firm faces restrictions on input choices. The case of restricted input use is common in a regulated economy. The Environmental Protection Agency, for example, continuously monitors pesticide use in agriculture and imposes restrictions on farmers through registration and use regulations. During droughts, state water agencies or water districts often restrict water quantities that growers can use. During times of national crises, industrial use of energy and other essential national resources has been restricted. The use of the environment for industrial disposal of residuals has also been increasingly restricted. In other cases, some aspect of environmental quality over which the firm has no control may directly affect the firm's profit. While environmental quality considerations are addressed in greater detail in Chapter 13, such cases may be represented as an imposed input level on the firm.

Consider the case of a single-product firm with two inputs. Profit is given by $\pi = pq(x_1,x_2) - w_1x_1 - w_2x_2 - \text{TFC}$ and quasirent is $R = pq(x_1,x_2) - w_1x_1 - w_2x_2$, where p is the output price, $q(x_1,x_2)$ is the output quantity produced by using input quantities x_1 and x_2, and w_1 and w_2 are the respective prices of inputs x_1 and x_2. Suppose that, without restrictions, profit maximization with output price p_0 and respective input prices w_1^0 and w_2^0 leads to input quantities $x_1 = x_1^0$ and $x_2 = x_2^0$ and output $q(x_1^0,x_2^0) = q_0$. Now suppose the quantity of x_2 is initially restricted to the optimum amount x_2^0. The expenditures on x_2 are thus considered fixed by the firm and the problem is to maximize profit $\pi = p_0q(x_1,x_2{}^0) - w_1^0\, x_1 - w_2^0\, x_2^0 - \text{TFC}$, where the restriction on x_2 leaves x_1 as the only variable input. With $x_2 = x_2^0$, the firm will continue to choose $x_1 = x_1^0$, yielding $q = q_0$, the same outcome as if x_2 were unrestricted.

The output supply and input demands of this firm can be depicted as in Figure 4.10. Let $S(x_2^0)$ represent the firm's supply of output and let $D_1(x_2^0)$ represent the firm's demand for x_1 when the quantity of x_2 is restricted to x_2^0 (assuming output price is p_0 and the input price for x_1 is w_1^0). From the results in Section 4.4, if $x_2 = x_2^0$ is regarded as a fixed factor, then quasirent on fixed and restricted factors can be measured by area $x+y$ in Figure 4.10(a), which is also equal to area $r+s$ in Figure 4.10(b) if x_1 is an essential input. Note, however, that quasirent in this case is $R^*(x_1^0 \mid x_2^0) = p_0q(x_1^0,x_2^0) - w_1^0x_1$, which treats the expenditure on x_2 as a fixed cost that is inapplicable in calculating quasirent. Alternatively, a more useful measure in this case is the *restricted quasirent* given by $\bar{R}\,(x_1^0 \mid x_2^0,w_2^0) = p_0q(x_1^0,x_2^0) - w_1^0x_1^0 - w_2^0x_2^0$, which differs from quasirent by the expenditure on the restricted input, $w_2^0x_2^0$. Where x_2 is an essential input and D_2 represents the firm's demand for x_2 when x_2 is unrestricted, quasirent is measured by area $a+b+c$. But this must be the same as the restricted quasirent if x_2 is restricted to its profit-maximizing level. Thus restricted quasirent is equal to area $a+b+c$ in Figure 4.10(c) when $x_2 = x_2^0$ and the price of x_2 is w_2^0. Note that the difference in quasirent and restricted quasirent in this case is $w_2^0x_2^0 =$ area $d + e$, which implies

$$\begin{aligned}\bar{R}(x_1^0 \mid x_2^0,w_2^0) &= R^*(x_1^0 \mid x_2^0) - w_2^0\, x_2^0 \\ &= \text{area } a+b+c = \text{area } x+y-d-e = \text{area } r+s-d-e. \qquad (4.1)\end{aligned}$$

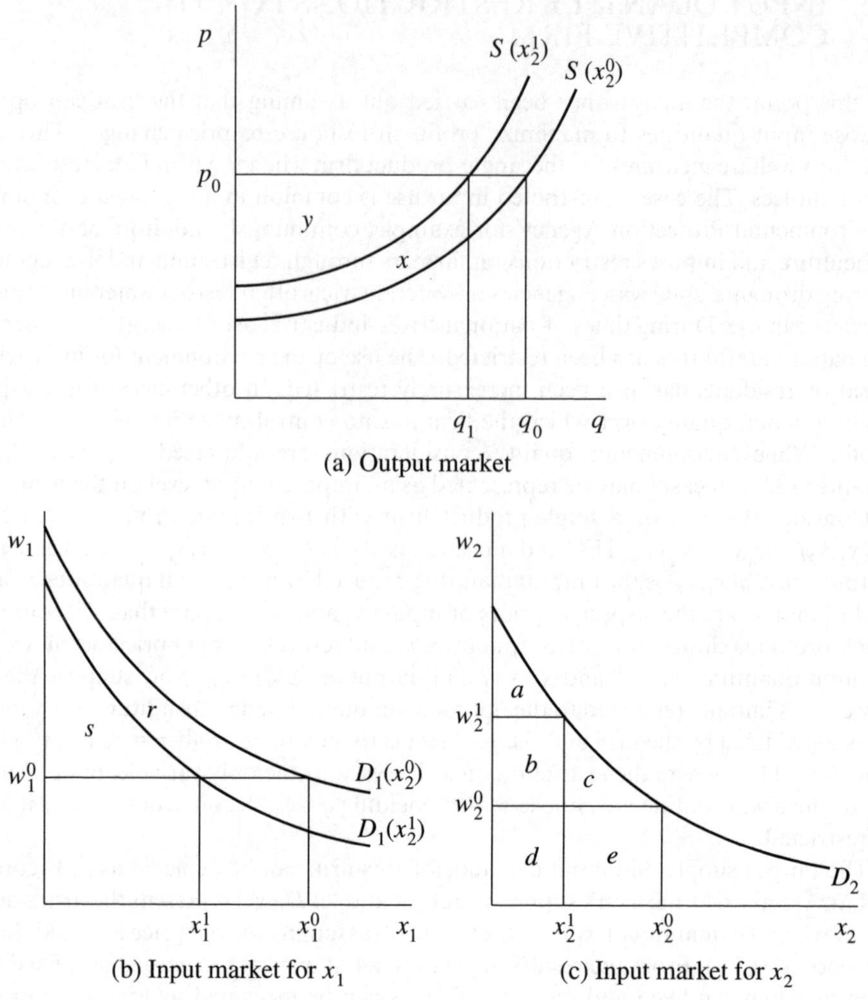

Figure 4.10

Now consider a change in the use restriction on x_2 from x_2^0 to x_2^1 given output price p^0 and input price $w_1{}^0$ for x_1. As a result, the supply curve in Figure 4.10 shifts inward from $S(x_2^0)$ to $S(x_2^1)$ and the optimal output decreases from q_0 to q_1. Also, use of input x_1 decreases from x_1^0 to x_1^1 as the demand for x_1 shifts inward from $D_1(x_2^0)$ to $D_1(x_2^1)$.

To investigate the welfare impact on the competitive firm under input use restrictions, two new welfare concepts initially introduced by John R. Hicks (1943) are necessary. These concepts, *compensating surplus* and *equivalent surplus*, have not been widely used in applied welfare economics because economic agents are generally assumed to be free in market economies to choose optimal quantities of inputs and outputs given existing market prices. In the case of government restrictions on input choice or other cases where certain input levels are determined by other agents, however, these Hicksian surplus measures are the appropriate conceptual measures of welfare change.

For the competitive firm, *compensating surplus* (C_s) *is defined as the amount of money that must be taken away from a firm (possibly negative) after a change to restore its original welfare level where quantity cannot be adjusted (from the post-change case).* Compensating surplus is represented mathematically by

$$C_s = \bar{R}(x_1^1 \mid x_2^1, w_2^0) - \bar{R}(x_1^0 \mid x_2^0, w_2^0).$$

This calculation can be made graphically in two steps. First, let w_2^1 be the price of input x_2 that would cause the same profit-maximizing use of x_2 as is imposed by the new restriction level, $x_2 = x_2^1$. Then unrestricted profit maximization at output price p_0 and respective input prices w_1^0 and $w_2{}^1$ also leads to output q^1 and input level $x_1 = x_1^1$. Thus, by analogy with results above, $\bar{R}(x_1^1 \mid x_2^1, w_2^1) = R^*(x_1^1 \mid x_2^1) - w_2^1 x_2^1 =$ area $a =$ area $y - b - d =$ area $s - b - d$. Second, the only difference between restricted profit at price w_2^1 and price w_2^0 with restriction $x_2 = x_2^1$ is the difference in expenditure on x_2 given by $x_2^1 (w_2^1 - w_2^0)$. Thus, $\bar{R}(x_1^1 \mid x_2^1, w_2^0) - \bar{R}(x_1^1 \mid x_2^1, w_2^1) = x_2^1 (w_2^1 - w_2^0) =$ area b, which implies

$$\bar{R}(x_1^1 \mid x_2^1, w_2^0) = R^*(x_1^1 \mid x_2^1) - w_2^0 x_2^1 = \text{area } a + b = \text{area } y - d = \text{area } s - d. \quad (4.2)$$

Subtracting equation (4.1) from equation (4.2) implies that compensating surplus can be measured graphically in several alternative ways,

$$C_s = \bar{R}(x_1^1 \mid x_2^1, w_2^0) - \bar{R}(x_1^0 \mid x_2^0, w_2^0) = R^*(x_1^1 \mid x_2^1) - R^*(x_1^0 \mid x_2^0) - w_2^0 (x_2^1 - x_2^0)$$
$$= -\text{area } c = \text{area } e - x = \text{area } e - r,$$

where the latter equality assumes x_1 is an essential input (q is trivially essential in the single-output case).

As in the unrestricted case of Section 4.4, welfare effects can thus be measured in alternative markets. Intuitively, with a reduction in the restricted level of x_2 from x_2^0 to x_2^1, the firm loses area x in producer surplus in the output market but saves area $e = w_2^0 (x_2^0 - x_2^1)$ in expenditures on x_2 for a net change in quasirent of area $e - x$. Alternatively, the firm loses area r in consumer surplus in the input market for x_1 while saving area $e = w_2^0 (x_2^0 - x_2^1)$ in expenditures on x_2 for a net change in quasirent of area $e - r$ (if x_1 is an essential input). Finally, the entire compensating surplus can be measured in the x_2 market by the loss in consumer surplus of area c. For the case illustrated in Figure 4.10, the compensating surplus is negative. That is, the competitive firm must be given money after the change in the quantity restriction to be made as well off as before.

Equivalent surplus (E_s) *is defined by the amount of income that must be given to the firm (possibly negative) in lieu of a change to leave it as well off as it would be with the change given that quantity cannot be adjusted from the initial situation.* Because the firm is made worse off by reducing the amount of x_2, equivalent surplus is likewise negative in the above example. Equivalent surplus is defined explicitly as

$$E_s = \bar{R}(x_1^1 \mid x_2^1, w_2^0) - \bar{R}(x_1^0 \mid x_2^0, w_2^0).$$

Thus, equivalent surplus is equal to compensating surplus for the producer. The same areas in Figure 4.10 thus measure both.

In some cases x_2 is an unpriced resource controlled by the government where in effect $w_2=0$. For example, x_2 might represent highways or other infrastructure that affects a firm's productivity. In this case, $\bar{R}(x_1 \mid x_2^0,0) = R^*(x_1 \mid x_2^0)$ so that compensating surplus and equivalent surplus in the notation of Figure 4.10 is measured by a loss of area $c+e=$ area $x=$ area r (area e is zero if $w_2=0$).

Generally, compensating and equivalent surpluses are identical for profit-maximizing producers just as compensating and equivalent variations coincide for profit-maximizing producers. Unlike the producer case, these measures will generally differ for consumers and factor owners (see Section 7.9).

4.7 INVESTMENT AND INTERTEMPORAL WELFARE MEASUREMENT

For producer welfare measurement over longer periods of time where some fixed factors become variable, the appropriate definition of the marginal cost curve vis-à-vis factor fixity requires further discussion. For example, over longer periods of time, some fixed costs become adjustable and play the role of moving the firm from one marginal cost curve to another.

Consider a firm with short-run marginal cost curve S_1 operating at initial price p_0 as in Figure 4.11. Suppose that price increases from p_0 to p_1 over two production periods. In the short run (during the first period), production increases from q_0 to q_1 along the short-run marginal cost curve. Thus, the increase in producer surplus or quasirent in the first period is given by area a. By the second period, however, the producing firm will have had time to adjust some of its fixed factors in response to the price increase. These investments

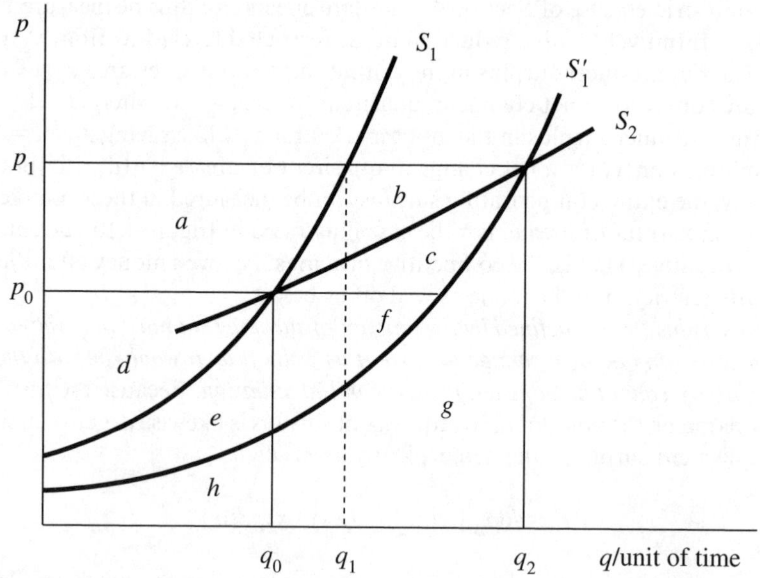

Figure 4.11

result in a rightward shift in the short-run supply curve to S_1' and a corresponding increase in production to q_2 for the second period.

The change in short-run producer surplus or quasirent for the second period can be found as follows. First, if the initial price had continued (thus inducing no adjustment), producer surplus would have been given by area *d*. With the change, however, the producer surplus area above short-run marginal cost S_1' and below price p_1 is given by area $a+b+c+d+e+f$. The change in short-run producer surplus or quasirent in the second period resulting from increased price is thus given by the difference, area $a+b+c+e+f$. Consider, however, that the movement from the initial position (p_0,q_0) to the final position (p_1,q_2) traces out an intermediate run marginal cost or supply curve S_2 corresponding to two-period production adjustment possibilities.[11] In this case, as is ordinarily true with marginal cost curves, the total adjustment costs (considered variable over two production periods) incurred to increase production from q_0 to q_2 are given by the change in area under the corresponding marginal cost curve S_2, that is, the area $c+f+g$. This implies, by the development in Section 4.3, that the correct measure of the change in producer welfare in the second time period (as viewed from the beginning of the first time period) is given by the intermediate-run producer surplus area $a+b$, that is, the increase in total receipts, area $a+b+c+f+g$, less the total adjustment costs (which are total variable costs in the two-period time horizon), area $c+f+g$. Thus, *the correct measure of the total producer welfare impact over the two time periods is not the sum of all the short-run producer surpluses over affected production periods but, rather, the sum of producer surpluses of variable lengths of run (as viewed from the initial point in time) over the affected production runs.*[12]

For example, in Figure 4.11, simply adding the change in producer surplus in the first time period (area *a*) to the simple change in short-run producer surplus for the second time period (area $a+b+c+e+f$) does not yield a correct measure of the change in producer welfare resulting from a price increase from p_0 to p_1 over the two periods. The correct change in producer welfare is the sum of the change in surplus corresponding to S_1 in the first period (that is, area *a*) and the change in surplus corresponding to S_2 in the second period (that is, area $a+b$). In general, the change in producer welfare is determined by calculating the change in producer surplus corresponding to the one-period supply curve for the first period, the two-period supply curve for the second period, the three-period supply curve for the third period, and so on.[13]

It may seem at first as though the area (or, perhaps, twice the area) above the two-period marginal cost curve and below price should appropriately measure two-period producer welfare. To understand clearly that this is *not* the case, one must note, first, that the lower axis in Figure 4.11 measures quantities for a single time period regardless of the supply

11. Although it is usually assumed in neoclassical economics that investments can be readily reversed with the same time lags as those required to bring them into productive capacity, the more general case (with varying degrees of irreversibility) would simply result in a kink in the two-period (or longer) marginal cost curve at the prevailing output level. The analysis in Figure 4.11 would not be substantively affected except that, once two-period adjustment to price p_1 is made, two-period adjustment back to q_0 would not be possible without incurring greater costs than originally (the two-period marginal cost curve to the left of q_2 would rotate upward about (p_1, q_2) owing to irreversibility).
12. These statements are made without regard to time preferences of producers at this point. The appropriate time discounting procedures for these considerations will be discussed in Chapter 14.
13. A rigorous mathematical demonstration of this procedure is given in Appendix Section 4.E. A more practical stochastic generalization accounting for imperfect anticipation of future prices is given in Appendix Section 14.A.

curve depicted and, second, that the supply curve S_2 is not attainable even when investments are begun immediately in the first period because the supply curve S_1 represents the minimum possible marginal cost attainable during the first time period. The appropriate marginal cost or supply curve that applies over the aggregate two-period time interval, on the other hand, corresponds to the horizontal summation of the supply curves S_1 and S_2 (depicted as S_{1+2}) in Figure 4.12 (note that the lower axis measures quantity over two time periods). Because the area a' is geometrically equivalent to area a, the change in the producer surplus (area $a+b+a'$) with appropriate temporal aggregation provides an accurate measurement of the producer welfare impact of the two-period price increase from p_0 to p_1. This result (and its straightforward extension) is of interest in generalizing later theoretical results over all time horizons. However, the equivalent approach with greater temporal disaggregation exemplified in Figure 4.11 is often of important practical applicability when time preferences must be considered.[14]

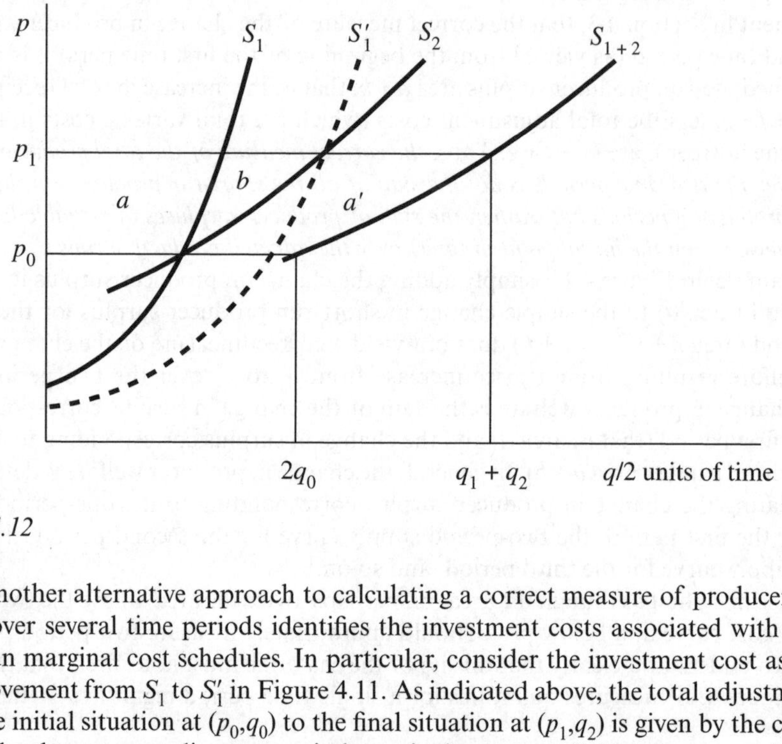

Figure 4.12

Yet another alternative approach to calculating a correct measure of producer welfare effects over several time periods identifies the investment costs associated with shifts in short-run marginal cost schedules. In particular, consider the investment cost associated with movement from S_1 to S_1' in Figure 4.11. As indicated above, the total adjustment cost from the initial situation at (p_0,q_0) to the final situation at (p_1,q_2) is given by the change in area under the corresponding two-period marginal cost curve S_2 (that is, area $c+f+g$). The total adjustment cost includes both the change in short-run variable cost and investment. But short-run total variable cost is initially area $e+h$ and, finally, area $g+h$, so the increase in total variable cost is area $g+h$ – area $e+h$, or area $g-e$. The change in investment associated with the price change must thus be the increase in total adjustment cost minus the increase in total variable cost, or area $c+f+g$ – area $g-e$ = area $c+f+e$. Alternatively, the change in investment can be viewed as the difference in the sum of short-run producer sur-

14. For a further discussion, see Section 14.1 and Appendix Section 14.A.

pluses with and without the two-period price change (area $2a+b+c+e+f$) minus the net welfare gain summed over the two periods (area $2a+b$). This implies, conversely, that the net welfare gain over the two periods is given by the sum of the changes in short-run surpluses minus the change in investment. Indeed, under certainty and with time preferences aside, Appendix Section 14.A shows that, for any general time horizon, the net producer welfare change can be accurately measured by the sum of changes in short-run producer surpluses minus the sum of changes in investment over the entire time horizon.[15] In addition, details are given in Appendix Section 14.A for calculation of investment effects of changes in price over time using standard dynamic supply equations. Similar results are also developed in Appendix Section 14.A for the case where prices cannot be anticipated perfectly and in Appendix Section 14.B for the case of temporal aggregation of consumer surplus measures considering the role of consumer durables.

4.8 SUMMARY

This chapter has dealt with the welfare analysis of a single competitive, profit-maximizing firm that may or may not own the primary factors of production.[16] A basic distinction has been made between the suppliers of primary inputs and the producing firm itself. The focus has been specifically on welfare measures for the producing firm. An exact measure of producer welfare is provided by producer surplus, quasirent or consumer surplus in any essential input market – an essential input being any input such that production without the use of some of the input is impossible. The firm's welfare can be measured in either the output or input market. The latter possibility is of particular interest when sufficient data for examining welfare impacts are available only at a primary product level. It is often easier to estimate derived demand curves for intermediate products than supply schedules for final products.

The possibility of aggregating producer welfare measures over time was also investigated. Results indicate that short-run producer surpluses, quasirents or input-market consumer surpluses cannot simply be aggregated over time but, rather, that investment costs must be subtracted from the sum of short-run surpluses or quasirents.

The results of this chapter are based on the crucial assumption that the variable factors of production used by the firm are in perfectly price-elastic supply (or else have specific quantity restrictions imposed by external influences as in Section 4.6). Because most industries contain more than one firm, however, welfare analysis at the industry level requires aggregation. Input supplies may not be perfectly elastic at the industry level. For example, the rapid worldwide rise in grain prices in 1972–75, due largely to substantial Soviet purchases, is an obvious case where it is important to recognize that input supplies can be positively sloped. During this period of phenomenal world grain price increases, to assume that the basic inputs used by producers, such as land, fertilizer, petroleum products and machinery, were in perfectly elastic supply would be unrealistic in calculating the

15. For exemplary applications of this rule, the reader is referred to Riordan (1971a, 1971b), Hirshleifer, De Haven and Milliman (1960) and Strand and Hueth (1977).
16. While these results have been derived under the assumption of simple profit maximization, Appendix Section 4.G shows that the surplus measures associated with areas behind supplies and demands have welfare significance under a broader set of behavioral criteria.

consequent welfare effects on farm producers. During this period, prices of most of these inputs more than doubled. Thus, for analyzing this case, the perfectly elastic supply assumption is unrealistic and, if used, would apparently lead to a substantial overestimate of the welfare gains to farm producers from a price rise. Chapters 8 and 9 focus on relaxing the perfect elasticity assumptions of this chapter.

Finally, the notion of consumer surplus was introduced with reference to producer derived demand curves. Hence, it was associated with producer welfare measurement. Chapter 5 focuses on welfare measurement for final consumers, where the notion of consumer surplus plays the vital but more controversial role discussed in Chapter 1.

Appendix to Chapter 4: Alternative measures of producer welfare in factor and product markets

Rigorous analysis of the question of whether or not producer welfare changes can be measured alternatively in factor input or product output markets by choice of the investigator began with the papers by Richard Schmalensee (1971, 1976), Daniel Wisecarver (1976) and James E. Anderson (1976). Although many economists had speculated or assumed that producer welfare could be measured in factor markets as well as the product market (for example, Schmitz and Seckler 1970; Hueth and Schmitz 1972; Dardis and Dennison 1969), the early works of Schmalensee (1971) and Wisecarver (1976) were interesting in that they apparently proved that this was not the case. Later, however, Schmalensee (1976) and Anderson (1976) identified errors in the earlier analyses introduced by approximations. Schmalensee has, indeed, shown that changes in producer welfare resulting from a single input price change can be accurately evaluated in either the (single) relevant input market or the output market.

Sections 4.A–4.C of this appendix show that the welfare effect of a multiple price change for profit-maximizing producers can be measured identically either by (1) the change in producer surplus in an essential output market, (2) the change in consumer surplus in an essential input market or (3) the sum over output markets of successive changes in producer surplus as the price in each respective output market changes, plus the sum over input markets of successive changes in consumer surplus as the price in each respective input market changes. Schmalensee's result is the special case of these results where the firm has one product with fixed price and the price of a single input is altered. Section 4.D demonstrates the results using a popular functional form.

Section 4.E discusses the problem whereby these theoretical results may not hold in practice if estimated supplies and demands do not incorporate proper theoretical relationships in the case of an individual producer. The advantages of dual approaches to specification and estimation of demands are discussed as a way of imposing proper theoretical relationships among supplies and demands for empirical purposes. Common second-order flexible dual specifications used empirically for such purposes are given. Results are then developed for measuring producer welfare effects in multiperiod problems involving investment in Section 4.F. Finally, Section 4.G shows that the welfare triangles behind supplies and demands can have welfare significance in some cases beyond simple profit maximization. All of the results in this appendix are developed for the case where prices do not adjust in response to producer actions (the case of a single competitive firm) and where the producer faces no risk (price changes are perfectly anticipated). The case where product prices or input prices adjust in response to the actions of many producers is considered in Chapter 8, and the case where prices in other markets are also affected is analyzed in the Appendix to Chapter 9. The case where the producer faces risk is developed in the Appendix to Chapter 12.

4.A SEQUENTIAL EVALUATION OF A MULTIPLE PRICE CHANGE

Consider a multiproduct, profit-maximizing firm facing product prices $\boldsymbol{p}=(p_1,\ldots,p_m)$ for respective outputs $\boldsymbol{q}=(q_1,\ldots,q_m)$ and variable input prices $\boldsymbol{w}=(w_1,\ldots,w_n)$ for respective input quantities $\boldsymbol{x}=(x_1,\ldots,x_n)$. Suppose that the production technology is represented by $\boldsymbol{q}=\boldsymbol{q}(\boldsymbol{x})=[q_1(\boldsymbol{x}),\ldots,q_m(\boldsymbol{x})]$ where $\boldsymbol{q}(\boldsymbol{0})=\boldsymbol{0}$, fixed production factors are assumed to exist but are not explicitly represented, and each $q_i(\boldsymbol{x})$ is assumed to be monotonically increasing ($q'_{ij}\equiv\partial q_i/\partial x_j>0$), concave, and twice differentiable in $\boldsymbol{x}$ except for some cases where certain inputs may have identically zero effects on certain outputs, $q'_{ij}\equiv 0$, but $q'_{ij}>0$ for some output i associated with each input j.[1] Thus, each input has a positive marginal productivity for at least one but perhaps many outputs.[2] The profit maximization problem is

$$\hat{\pi}(\boldsymbol{p},\boldsymbol{w})=\max_{\boldsymbol{x}}\{\pi(\boldsymbol{x})=\boldsymbol{pq}(\boldsymbol{x})-\boldsymbol{wx}-K\,|\,\boldsymbol{x}\geq 0\}$$

where $\hat{\pi}(\boldsymbol{p},\boldsymbol{w})$ is called the *profit function*, K is fixed cost and, for simplicity, $\boldsymbol{pq}(\boldsymbol{x})=\Sigma_{i=1}^m p_i q_i(\boldsymbol{x})$ and $\boldsymbol{wx}=\Sigma_{j=1}^n w_j x_j$. For inputs with internal solutions ($x_j>0$), first-order conditions for profit maximization are found by differentiating $\pi(\boldsymbol{x})$ with respect to $\boldsymbol{x}$, which yields

$$\boldsymbol{pq_x}-\boldsymbol{w}=\boldsymbol{0}, \tag{4.3}$$

where $\boldsymbol{pq_x}$ is a vector with jth element $\Sigma_{i=1}^m p_i\partial q_i/\partial x_j$. Second-order conditions are satisfied under the concavity assumptions for $\boldsymbol{q}(\boldsymbol{x})$. In principle, the first-order conditions can be solved for derived input demand functions,[3]

$$\boldsymbol{x}=\hat{\boldsymbol{x}}(\boldsymbol{p},\boldsymbol{w}),$$

1. The $\boldsymbol{x}$ vector is assumed to include possible allocations of inputs over time and space, and among subtechnologies, that is, among various individual equations in $\boldsymbol{q}=\boldsymbol{q}(\boldsymbol{x})$, so that output is determined uniquely by producer decisions. This representation of technology has been shown by Just and Pope (2002) to be more policy relevant than most common specifications because it can represent the case where policies constrain the allocation of a factor input to the production of some outputs but not others. Standard applications of dual production frameworks represent production possibilities given aggregate input vectors and thus do not admit analyses of policies that constrain allocations. More generally, dual approaches must represent allocations explicitly as in Chambers and Just (1989) to obtain similar policy relevance. In this context, the production technology can be represented more generally by $(\boldsymbol{q},\boldsymbol{x})\in T$ where $\boldsymbol{x}$ includes allocations of inputs and T is a closed convex technology set, also possibly depending on fixed production factors. The results below can be generalized accordingly. For further general discussion of the producer problem, see Fuss and McFadden (1978, ch. 4) and Takayama (1985, ch. 1, s. F).
2. The vector $\boldsymbol{x}$ is assumed to include any allocations or other decisions available to the producer that allow the product mix to be influenced with a given aggregate set of physical inputs, for example, x_1 might represent fertilizer allocated to wheat land on one date and x_2 might represent fertilizer allocated to corn land on another date. For further discussion, see Just and Pope (2002).
3. For a clear and detailed discussion of these results, the reader is referred to Henderson and Quandt (1971, p. 127).

where $\hat{\boldsymbol{x}}(\boldsymbol{p},\boldsymbol{w}) \equiv [\hat{x}_1(\boldsymbol{p},\boldsymbol{w}),\ldots,\hat{x}_n(\boldsymbol{p},\boldsymbol{w})]$, which specifies optimal input levels for given prices. Through substitution of the input demand functions, optimal output supply and quasirent functions can also be specified in terms of prices,

$$\boldsymbol{q} \equiv \boldsymbol{q}(\hat{\boldsymbol{x}}(\boldsymbol{p},\boldsymbol{w})) \equiv \hat{\boldsymbol{q}}(\boldsymbol{p},\boldsymbol{w}) = [\hat{q}_1(\boldsymbol{p},\boldsymbol{w}),\ldots,\hat{q}_m(\boldsymbol{p},\boldsymbol{w})]$$
$$R(\boldsymbol{p},\boldsymbol{w}) \equiv \boldsymbol{pq}(\hat{\boldsymbol{x}}(\boldsymbol{p},\boldsymbol{w})) - \boldsymbol{w}\hat{\boldsymbol{x}}(\boldsymbol{p},\boldsymbol{w}). \tag{4.4}$$

The *quasirent function* differs from the standard profit function, $\hat{\pi}(\boldsymbol{p},\boldsymbol{w}) \equiv \pi(\hat{\boldsymbol{x}}(\boldsymbol{p},\boldsymbol{w}))$, by the amount of fixed costs, $R(\boldsymbol{p},\boldsymbol{w}) - K = \hat{\pi}(\boldsymbol{p},\boldsymbol{w})$.[4] From these definitions of supply and quasirent functions, differentiation with respect to prices obtains (where subscripts of R denote differentiation, for example, $\boldsymbol{R_p} \equiv \partial R/\partial \boldsymbol{p}$)

$$\boldsymbol{R_p} = \hat{\boldsymbol{q}}(\boldsymbol{p},\boldsymbol{w}) + (\boldsymbol{pq_x} - \boldsymbol{w})\hat{\boldsymbol{x}}_{\boldsymbol{p}} = \hat{\boldsymbol{q}}(\boldsymbol{p},\boldsymbol{w}) \tag{4.5}$$

and

$$\boldsymbol{R_w} = -\,\hat{\boldsymbol{x}}(\boldsymbol{p},\boldsymbol{w}) + (\boldsymbol{pq_x} - \boldsymbol{w})\hat{\boldsymbol{x}}_{\boldsymbol{w}} = -\,\hat{\boldsymbol{x}}(\boldsymbol{p},\boldsymbol{w}) \tag{4.6}$$

because $\boldsymbol{pq_x} - \boldsymbol{w} = \boldsymbol{0}$ by the first-order conditions in equation (4.3).[5]

With these results, the impact of a multiple set of price changes on quasirent can be examined. The change in quasirent ΔR from initial prices $(\boldsymbol{p^0}, \boldsymbol{w^0})$ to subsequent prices $(\boldsymbol{p^1}, \boldsymbol{w^1})$ may be expressed using equations (4.5) and (4.6) as

$$\Delta R \equiv R(\boldsymbol{p}^1,\boldsymbol{w}^1) - R(\boldsymbol{p}^0,\boldsymbol{w}^0)$$
$$= \textstyle\int_L dR = \int_L(\boldsymbol{R_p}d\boldsymbol{p} + \boldsymbol{R_w}d\boldsymbol{w}) = \int_L(\hat{\boldsymbol{q}}d\boldsymbol{p} - \hat{\boldsymbol{x}}d\boldsymbol{w}), \tag{4.7}$$

where L is any path of integration from initial prices to final prices.

To evaluate welfare changes using (4.7), note that, because the integrand of (4.7) is the exact differential of R by derivation, the integral may be evaluated by choosing any particular path. For example, consider the path described by the following variations:

$$\hat{\boldsymbol{p}}_i(p_i) \equiv (p_1^1,\ldots,p_{i-1}^1,p_i,p_{i+1}^0,\ldots,p_m^0,\boldsymbol{w}^0),\ i = 1,\ \ldots,\ m,$$
$$\hat{\boldsymbol{w}}_j(w_j) \equiv (\boldsymbol{p}^1,w_1^1,\ldots,w_{j-1}^1,w_j,w_{j+1}^0,\ldots,w_n^0),\ j = 1,\ \ldots,\ n. \tag{4.8}$$

In this case, one finds that

$$\Delta R = \sum_{i=1}^{m} \int_{p_i^0}^{p_i^1} \hat{q}_i\,(\hat{\boldsymbol{p}}_i\,(p_i))dp_i - \sum_{j=1}^{n} \int_{w_j^0}^{w_j^1} \hat{x}_j\,(\hat{\boldsymbol{w}}_j\,(w_j))dw_j.$$

which is simply the sum of changes in the output market producer surpluses associated with respective changes from p_i^0 to p_i^1 (where all other output prices are fixed at p_k^1 for $k =$ 1, …, $i-1$, and at p_k^0 for $k = i+1$, …, n, and all input prices are held at initial levels), plus

4. Sometimes quasirent is called short-run profit. This terminology is used in Appendix Section 4.E consistent with the literature discussed there.
5. The results in (4.5) and (4.6) are the standard envelope theorem results that follow from Hotelling's Lemma. For further discussion, see Varian (1992) or Silberberg (1978).

the sum of changes in the input market consumer surpluses associated with changes in the respective input prices from w_j^0 to w_j^1 (where all other input prices w_k are fixed at w_k^1 for $k=1, \ldots, j-1$, and at w_k^0 for $k=j+1, \ldots, n$, and output prices are fixed at subsequent levels).

Thus, the overall change in quasirent can be evaluated by successively calculating the change in surplus over all markets for which prices change where supply or demand curves at each stage are conditioned on all previously considered changes (other prices are held at initial values) following the price path suggested by (4.8). Furthermore, because of path independence, it is a trivial extension of the foregoing results to show that the order in which price changes are considered is arbitrary and makes no difference with respect to the overall impact on rents.[6]

Another result that follows immediately is that the welfare impact of a single input price change can be completely measured in the associated factor market, or the welfare impact of a single output change can be completely measured in the associated output market even though the price change induces a shift in other output supplies and other factor demands. More generally, in the multiple-price-change case, all input markets for which prices do not change need not be considered in calculating the change in welfare.

4.B EVALUATION OF A MULTIPLE PRICE CHANGE IN THE OUTPUT MARKET

Thus far, it is clear that producer welfare effects can be unambiguously and accurately measured using surplus concepts. However, knowledge of all supply and demand schedules for which prices change appears to be required before welfare impacts can be calculated. This section, however, shows that this is not necessarily so. This is first shown from the standpoint of an output market, in which case the change in quasirent is accurately measured by the change in an output market producer surplus regardless of which prices are changed as long as the output is an essential output of the firm. An *essential output* is defined as an output for which a shutdown price exists.

Consider a general price change from $(\mathbf{p}^0,\mathbf{w}^0)$ to $(\mathbf{p}^1,\mathbf{w}^1)$. The *shutdown price* for the essential output in each case is one which is just low enough, given other prices, that the firm is induced to shut down all production.[7] Specifically and without loss of generality, suppose the first output is an essential output and define the shutdown price for q_1 as

$$\tilde{p}_1^k = \max\{p_1 | \hat{\mathbf{x}}(p_1,p_2^k,\ldots,p_m^k,\mathbf{w}^k) = 0\},\ k=0,\,1.$$

In this case, using (4.5), the producer surplus in the output market for q_1 with prices $(\mathbf{p}^k,\mathbf{w}^k)$ is

$$P_1^k = \int_{\tilde{p}_1^k}^{p_1^k} \hat{q}_1(p_1,p_2^k,\ldots,p_m^k,\mathbf{w}^k)dp_1$$

6. One should note, however, that this property will not hold empirically unless estimated relationships are specified so as to satisfy certain regularity conditions. See Appendix Section 4.E.
7. By admitting negative and possibly infinite shutdown prices, one can show that q_i is an essential output if $q_i=0$ requires $q_k=0, k=1, \ldots, m$, or $x_j=0, j=1, \ldots, n$.

$$= \int_{\tilde{p}_1^k}^{p_1^k} \frac{\partial R^k}{\partial p_1} dp_1$$

$$= \hat{R}^k(p_1^k) - \hat{R}^k(\tilde{p}_1^k) \tag{4.9}$$

$$= R(\boldsymbol{p}^k, \boldsymbol{w}^k), \tag{4.10}$$

where $\hat{R}^k(p_1) = R(p_1, p_2^k, \ldots, p_m^k, \boldsymbol{w}^k)$ and $\hat{R}^k(\tilde{p}_1^k) = 0$ by definition (that is, quasirent must be zero if all input levels and thus all output levels are zero). Thus, the welfare effect of the multiple price range is captured completely by $P_1^1 - P_1^0$, the change in producer surplus in the market for the (essential) output q_1. With this equivalence of producer surplus and quasirent, the investigator thus has alternatives as to whether to measure the impact of an input price change in the input or the output market.

While the result in (4.9) holds if $\tilde{p}_1^k$ is defined simply as the maximum price where q_1 is not produced, $\tilde{p}_1^k = \{p_1 | \hat{q}_1(p_1, p_2^k, \ldots, p_m^k, \boldsymbol{w}^k) = 0\}$, rather than the maximum price where all production ceases ($\boldsymbol{x} = \boldsymbol{0}$), the reader should note that the change in producer surplus in this case is

$$\Delta P_1 = P_1^1 - P_1^0 = R(\boldsymbol{p}^1, \boldsymbol{w}^1) - R(\boldsymbol{p}^0, \boldsymbol{w}^0) + \hat{R}^0(\tilde{p}_1^0) - \hat{R}^1(\tilde{p}_1^1)$$
$$= \Delta R + \hat{R}^0(\tilde{p}_1^0) - \hat{R}^1(\tilde{p}_1^1),$$

which does not measure the change in quasirent if $\hat{R}^0(\tilde{p}_1^0) \neq \hat{R}^1(\tilde{p}_1^1)$ In general, $\hat{R}^0(\tilde{p}_1^0) \neq \hat{R}^1(\tilde{p}_1^1)$ is likely if q_1 is not an essential output. That is, if production of other outputs occurs when production of q_1 ceases, then quasirent at prices $(\tilde{p}_1^0, p_2^0, \ldots, p_m^0, \boldsymbol{w}^0)$ given by $\hat{R}^0(\tilde{p}_1^0)$ is likely different than quasirent at prices $(\tilde{p}_1^1, p_2^1, \ldots, p_m^1, \boldsymbol{w}^1)$ given by $\hat{R}^1(\tilde{p}_1^1)$. This problem arises because all marginal adjustments are not reflected in the q_1 supply curve if the firm continues to operate when $q_1 = 0$.

4.C EVALUATION OF A MULTIPLE PRICE CHANGE IN A SINGLE-INPUT MARKET

An even wider range of alternatives is suggested by similarly integrating over quantities in input markets. In point of fact, it turns out that the impact of multiple price changes (including output prices) can also in certain cases be completely measured by using surplus concepts in any one of the input markets.

To see this, consider again a multiple price change from $(\boldsymbol{p}^0, \boldsymbol{w}^0)$ to $(\boldsymbol{p}^1, \boldsymbol{w}^1)$ and define an *essential input* as one for which a shutdown price exists. The *shutdown price* in the case of an essential input is one that is just high enough, given other prices, to induce the firm to cease all production.[8] Specifically, without loss of generality, suppose that the first input is an essential input and define the shutdown input price for x_1 as

8. By admitting possibly infinite shutdown prices, one can show that x_j is an essential input if $q_i(x_1, \ldots, x_{j-1}, 0, x_{j+1}, \ldots, x_n) = 0$ for $i = 1, \ldots, m$. Although this condition may not hold for all inputs, C.E. Ferguson (1969a, p. 61) states, 'The more reasonable assumption seems to be that a positive usage of all inputs simultaneously is required to produce a positive output.'

$$\tilde{w}_1^k = \min\{w_1 | \hat{\boldsymbol{x}}(\boldsymbol{p}^k, w_1, w_2^k, \dots, w_n^k) = 0\},\ k = 0, 1.$$

Thus, using (4.6), the consumer surplus in the input market for x_1 with prices $(\boldsymbol{p}^k, \boldsymbol{w}^k)$ is

$$\begin{aligned} C_1^k &= \int_{w_1^k}^{\tilde{w}_1^k} \hat{x}_1(\boldsymbol{p}^k, w_1, w_2^k, \dots, w_n^k) dw_1 \\ &= -\int_{w_1^k}^{\tilde{w}_1^k} \frac{\partial \tilde{R}^k}{\partial w_1} dw_1 \\ &= \tilde{R}^k(w_1^k) - \tilde{R}^k(\tilde{w}_1^k) && (4.11) \\ &= R(\boldsymbol{p}^k, \boldsymbol{w}^k), && (4.12) \end{aligned}$$

where $\tilde{R}^k(w_1) = R(\boldsymbol{p}^k, w_1, w_2^k, \dots, w_n^k)$ and $\tilde{R}^k(\tilde{w}_1^k) = 0$ by definition (because all input levels are zero at $\tilde{w}_1^k$). Thus, the welfare effect of a multiple price change is captured completely by $C_1^1 - C_1^0$, which is the change in consumer surplus in the market for an essential input.

While (4.11) holds even if x_1 is not an essential input, the reader should note as in the case of the previous section that if $\tilde{R}^k(\tilde{w}_1^k)$ is not zero, as it is when $\tilde{w}_1^k$ represents a corresponding shutdown price, then $\tilde{R}^0(\tilde{w}_1^0)$ will generally not be equal to $\tilde{R}^1(\tilde{w}_1^1)$. Rather, each would represent quasirents under different sets of prices even though $\hat{x}_1$ would be zero under each. This problem, as in the case of producer surplus, arises because not all marginal adjustments are reflected by the marginal valuations of x_1 embodied in its derived demand if the firm continues to operate when $x_1 = 0$.

4.D AN EXAMPLE

Combining the results in (4.10) and (4.12) yields

$$R^k = P_i^k = C_j^k \tag{4.13}$$

and

$$\Delta R = \Delta P_i = \Delta C_j,$$

where $\Delta R = R^1 - R^0$, $\Delta P_i = P_i^1 - P_i^0$, and $\Delta C_j = C_j^1 - C_j^0$ for all i and j such that q_i is an essential output and x_j is an essential input. The implications of these results are that the welfare impact of a policy that has possibly multiple-price effects on a price-taking, profit-maximizing producer can be completely evaluated not only in any essential output market but also in any input market for which the input is essential in the production process – whether or not the corresponding market price is among those that change. The investigator may thus have some freedom to choose a market for evaluation based on ease of measurement and data availability. Further advantages of this result from the point of view of statistical measurement are discussed in Section 8.9.

To aid in intuition and give a concrete example of this result, consider a Cobb–Douglas production function (based on implicit fixed factors),

$$q = q(x_1,x_2) = Ax_1^{\alpha_1}x_2^{\alpha_2},\ \alpha_1>0,\ \alpha_2>0,\ \alpha_1+\alpha_2<1, \tag{4.14}$$

where quasirent is

$$R = pAx_1^{\alpha_1}x_2^{\alpha_2} - w_1x_1 - w_2x_2. \tag{4.15}$$

Equation (4.14) implies that $q(0,x_2) = q(x_1,0) = 0$, so that both inputs are essential. Output is trivially an essential output in the single-product case. Solving first-order conditions, $\partial R/\partial x_i = 0$, $i = 1, 2$, for x_1 and x_2, and substituting into (4.14) yields

$$\hat{q}(p,\mathbf{w}) = A(\alpha_1 pq/w_1)^{\alpha_1}(\alpha_2 pq/w_2)^{\alpha_2} = [Ap^{\alpha_1+\alpha_2}(\alpha_1/w_1)^{\alpha_1}(\alpha_2/w_2)^{\alpha_2}]^{1/(1-\alpha_1-\alpha_2)}. \tag{4.16}$$

Further substituting for q in first-order conditions, $x_i = \alpha_i pq/w_i$, $i = 1,2$, one obtains profit-maximizing derived demands,

$$\hat{x}_i(p,\mathbf{w}) = [Ap(\alpha_i/w_i)^{1-\alpha_j}(\alpha_j/w_j)^{\alpha_j}]^{1/(1-\alpha_1-\alpha_2)},\ i = 1,2;\ j = 3-i. \tag{4.17}$$

Finally, substituting derived demands into (4.15), one obtains

$$R(p,\mathbf{w}) = (1-\alpha_1-\alpha_2)[Ap(\alpha_1/w_1)^{\alpha_1}(\alpha_2/w_2)^{\alpha_2}]^{1/(1-\alpha_1-\alpha_2)}. \tag{4.18}$$

These results can be illustrated by computing producer surplus corresponding to the supply function in (4.16) and the consumer surpluses corresponding to demand functions in (4.17). One finds that producer surplus at prices (p^0,w_1^0,w_2^0) is

$$\begin{aligned} P &= \int_0^{p_0}[Ap^{\alpha_1+\alpha_2}(\alpha_1/w_1^0)^{\alpha_1}(\alpha_2/w_2^0)^{\alpha_2}]^{1/(1-\alpha_1-\alpha_2)}dp \\ &= (1-\alpha_1-\alpha_2)[Ap(\alpha_1/w_1^0)^{\alpha_1}(\alpha_2/w_2^0)^{\alpha_2}]^{1/(1-\alpha_1-\alpha_2)}\Big|_{p=0}^{p_0} = R(p_0,w_1^0,w_2^0) \end{aligned} \tag{4.19}$$

because, from (4.16), the output shutdown price regardless of input prices is $\tilde{p}_0 = 0$. Consumer surpluses at prices (p_0,w_1^0,w_2^0) are

$$\begin{aligned} C_i &= -\int_{w_i^0}^{\infty}[Ap_0(\alpha_i/w_i)^{1-\alpha_j}(\alpha_j/w_j^0)^{\alpha_j}]^{1/(1-\alpha_1-\alpha_2)}dw_i \\ &= -(1-\alpha_1-\alpha_2)[Ap_0(\alpha_i/w_i)^{\alpha_i}(\alpha_j/w_j^0)^{\alpha_j}]^{1/(1-\alpha_1-\alpha_2)}\Big|_{wi=wi^0}^{\infty} \\ &= R(p_0,w_1^0,w_2^0),\ i = 1, 2;\ j = 3-i, \end{aligned} \tag{4.20}$$

thus verifying (4.13), because (4.17) implies that input shutdown prices are $\tilde{w}_i^0 = \infty$ regardless of other prices.

Some other useful results that can be illustrated with this example relate to the cost function. For the general (multiple-output) case, the *cost function* is defined as the minimum cost required to produce a given output vector,

$$c(\mathbf{q}) = \min_{\mathbf{x}}\{\mathbf{wx}|\mathbf{q} = \mathbf{q}(\mathbf{x})\}.$$

The cost function is useful for welfare analysis because the supply of a competitive firm follows marginal cost, $c'(\mathbf{q}) = \partial c(\mathbf{q})/\partial\mathbf{q}$, and profit-maximizing output can be found by equating price and marginal cost, $\boldsymbol{p}=c'(\boldsymbol{q})$. Producer surplus can be expressed by subtracting the cost function from total revenue as $P=\boldsymbol{pq}-c(\boldsymbol{q})$.

Using the single-output example of this section with the technology in (4.14), the cost function definition is satisfied by minimizing the Lagrangian

$$\mathcal{L}=w_1x_1+w_2x_2-\lambda(Ax_1^{\alpha_1}x_2^{\alpha_2}-q),$$

for which first-order conditions imply $x_i=\lambda\alpha_i q/w_i$, $i=1, 2$. Substituting these conditions into the production constraint represented by (4.14), solving for λ, and then substituting for λ in

$$w_1x_1+w_2x_2=\lambda\alpha_1q+\lambda\alpha_2q=\lambda(\alpha_1+\alpha_2)q,$$

as implied by first-order conditions, obtains the cost function,

$$c(q)=(\alpha_1+\alpha_2)\left[(q/A)(w_1/\alpha_1)^{\alpha_1}(w_2/\alpha_2)^{\alpha_2}\right]^{1/(\alpha_1+\alpha_2)}.$$

Equating price to the derivative of this cost function with respect to q thus obtains the supply in (4.16) and substituting (4.16) into $P=pq-c(q)$ obtains the producer surplus in (4.19).

4.E INTEGRABILITY AND UNIQUE MEASUREMENT IN PRACTICE

The results thus far suggest several alternative approaches are possible for evaluation of producer benefits when more than one price changes. According to the results in Appendix Section 4.A, the order or sequence of imposing price changes for purposes of welfare calculations should make no difference. Similarly, if welfare effects are evaluated completely in a single market, the results of Appendix Sections 4.B and 4.C imply that the choice of market should make no difference in the results obtained. From an empirical standpoint, however, one should note that the order in which price changes are considered or the choice of market for calculations will generally make a difference if product supplies and input demands are specified arbitrarily for purposes of estimation. The reason is that, once estimated, the several supplies and demands may not relate to any conceivable underlying profit-maximization problem. This problem may occur because of statistical errors of estimation but is also a result of using arbitrary specifications such as *ad hoc* linear relationships to estimate several supplies and/or demands of the same firm.

Sometimes in empirical work, the resources (time and research budgets) are not sufficient to permit econometric estimation of supply and demand relationships imposing conditions that assure all supplies and demands relate to a common underlying profit-maximization problem. Alternatively, opinions or estimates of supply and demand elasticities available from a variety of published studies are used. A prudent practice in these cases is to investigate the extent of disagreement among estimates using alternative approaches to calculation of welfare effects. This undesirable situation, where the researcher can arbitrarily influence results by choosing alternative orders of considering price changes or by choosing alternative markets as a basis for calculations, can be avoided with one of two practical approaches.[9] Both involve specifying relationships so that they necessarily relate to the same underlying profit-maximization problem upon estimation. The conditions necessary to ensure that all estimated supplies and demands integrate back to a common underlying profit maximization problem are called integrability conditions.[10]

The first approach, sometimes called the *primal approach*, is to specify a production function form that satisfies the usual properties of a production function (concavity with positive first derivatives). Then, by solving the profit-maximization problem theoretically, the implied functional forms for all supplies and demands of the firm are obtained. For example, one can start by specifying the production function in equation (4.14). Of course, one should be careful that the chosen functional form is reasonable in view of the practical aspects of the problem considered. Once this is done, one can follow the derivation of equations (4.15) through (4.17), thus producing specifications for each supply and demand equation that all relate to the same underlying profit-maximization problem. Such supplies and demands contain common parameters as in the case of equations (4.16) and (4.17). Integrability is ensured by joint estimation imposing the implied cross-equation parameter constraints so, for example, estimation of the supply in (4.16) and the demands in (4.17) yields a unique set of parameter estimates for A, α_1, and α_2. As a result, the unique implications of theory for producer quasirent are obtained, for example, as in the case of equations (4.19) and (4.20). By comparison, independent estimation of (4.16) and (4.17) ignoring the appearance of identical parameters in different equations will generally yield conflicting sets of parameter estimates for A, α_1, and α_2 because of statistical estimation errors.

While the primal approach is feasible and tractable for simple production function specifications, much greater flexibility of functional forms is tractable using the dual approach developed by Daniel McFadden.[11] Duality for the producer implies a one-to-one relationship between production functions and profit functions under the assumption of profit maximization. The *profit function* is a function of input and output prices faced by the competitive firm that gives the maximum attainable profits under those prices. If some inputs are fixed, one may use the *restricted profit function*, which is identical to the *quasirent function* in (4.4) and specifies maximum short-run profit as a function of prices of output and variable inputs, given fixed input quantities. The right-hand side of equation (4.18) is a specific example of a restricted profit function associated with the case of Appendix Section 4.D

The crux of the *dual approach* rests on the argument that starting the analysis by choosing a specification for the profit function is no more arbitrary than to start by choosing a specification for the production function. That is, a profit function under competition and nonstochastic prices characterizes a firm's technology as completely as does a production function under certain *regularity conditions* (Diewert 1974). These regularity conditions

9. A third way of avoiding this disagreement of estimates by different approaches is to impose path independence (symmetry) conditions directly in estimation, but such an approach is cumbersome and often leads to highly restricted forms when imposed on *ad hoc* specifications.
10. Integrability conditions for the producer are defined and discussed further in Appendix Section 8.B.
11. Although much of this development occurred in the late 1960s, the published work appears later in McFadden (1978). The entire two volumes by Fuss and McFadden develop and demonstrate issues related to this type of approach. See also Varian (1992) or Silberberg (1978).

require the profit (or quasirent) function to be nondecreasing in output prices, nonincreasing in input prices, and continuous, convex and homogeneous of degree 1 in all prices with $R=0$ in shutdown cases (Diewert 1974; McFadden 1978). Specifying an arbitrary functional form for a profit function that satisfies these regularity conditions guarantees that the profit function is derivable as a result of some profit-maximization process with well-behaved technology. Because profit functions so specified can be made more flexible, while allowing analytic derivation of implied supply and demand specifications, than with the primal approach, less stringent restrictions can be imposed on the related technology and market supply and demand relationships.

Once the profit function is specified, the implied specifications for supplies and demands can be easily determined using (4.5) and (4.6) by simply differentiating the profit or quasirent function with respect to the relevant output or input price. For example, if a profit or quasirent function of the form in (4.18) is arbitrarily specified as a starting point, then differentiation with respect to output price obtains the supply specification in (4.16), and differentiation with respect to respective input prices obtains the demand specifications in (4.17). Thus, using data on prices and quantities of inputs and outputs, the three equations in (4.16) and (4.17) can be estimated jointly to produce estimates of A, α_1, and α_2, which can subsequently be used for welfare calculations according to (4.18).

Several general specifications for profit functions have come into common use for these purposes because they allow second-order flexibility in approximating any profit function and because the resulting systems of supply and demand equations are estimable with simple linear estimation methods. For general notational purposes in the remainder of this section, let outputs and inputs be represented in a common netput notation so that the prices of all outputs and variable inputs are represented compactly by a single vector $\boldsymbol{p}=(p_1,\ldots,p_N)=(p_1,\ldots,p_m,w_1,\ldots,w_n)$ and the associated quantities are represented by $\boldsymbol{q}=(q_1,\ldots,q_N)=(q_1,\ldots,q_m,-x_1,\ldots,-x_n)$ where $N=m+n$ is the total number of outputs and inputs.[12] In this notation, some of the most popular second-order flexible functional forms for short-run profit functions that satisfy standard regularity conditions, along with their implied functional forms for supplies and demands, are the translog form,[13]

$$R(\boldsymbol{p})=\exp\{\alpha_0+\sum_{i=1}^{N}\alpha_i \ln p_i+\sum_{i=1}^{N}\sum_{j=1}^{N}\beta_{ij}\ln p_i \ln p_j\},\ \beta_{ij}=\beta_{ji}, \tag{4.21}$$

$$\hat{q}_i(\boldsymbol{p})=\frac{R}{p_i}\left[a_i+2\sum_{j=1}^{N}\beta_{ij}\ln p_j\right],$$

the generalized Leontief form,

$$R(\boldsymbol{p})=\sum_{i=1}^{N}\sum_{j=1}^{N}\beta_{ij}p_i^{1/2}p_j^{1/2},\ \beta_{ij}=\beta_{ji}, \tag{4.22}$$

12. Netput notation is merely a way to represent both demands and supplies in common mathematical form.
13. Note that these profit and netput specifications represent only short-run profit (otherwise called quasirent or restricted profit). That is, they reflect quantities of inputs and outputs that are variable in the short run. The amounts of fixed factors of production may be regarded as implicitly embedded in the parameters of these functions. Note also for the translog form that linear homogeneity of the profit function requires

$$\sum_{i=1}^{N}\beta_{ij}=0 \text{ and } \sum_{i=1}^{N}\alpha_i=1.$$

$$\hat{q}_i(\boldsymbol{p}) = \sum_{j=1}^{N} \beta_{ij} \left(\frac{p_j}{p_i} \right)^{1/2},$$

the generalized Cobb–Douglas form,[14]

$$R(\boldsymbol{p}) = \prod_{i=1}^{N} \prod_{j=1}^{N} \left(\frac{p_i}{2} + \frac{p_j}{2} \right)^{\beta_{ij}}, \ \beta_{ij} = \beta_{ji},$$

$$\hat{q}_i(\boldsymbol{p}) = R \sum_{j=1}^{N} \beta_{ij} \left(\frac{p_i}{2} + \frac{p_j}{2} \right)^{-1},$$

and the generalized quadratic mean form of order ρ,

$$R(\boldsymbol{p}) = \left(\sum_{i=1}^{N} \sum_{j=1}^{N} \beta_{ij} p_i^{\rho/2} p_j^{\rho/2} \right)^{1/\rho}, \ \beta_{ij} = \beta_{ji},$$

$$\hat{q}_i(\boldsymbol{p}) = \frac{R^{1-\rho}}{p_i} \sum_{j=1}^{N} \beta_{ij} (p_i p_j)^{\rho/2}.$$

Upon estimation of the associated system of supplies and demands, the compensating and equivalent variation of any general price change is found by comparing the profit function at the two different sets of prices. As is obvious from these supply/demand equations, more convenient estimable forms are obtained for the translog and generalized Cobb-Douglas cases by representing supplies and demands as quasirent shares, that is, solving for $p_i q_i / R$ before estimation. In each case, second-order flexibility is attained for the profit (or quasirent) function with little more computational difficulty than required in the primal approach with first-order flexibility.[15] These functional forms thus provide plausible and flexible ways of uniquely estimating the welfare effects of multiple price changes on a single producer.

4.F A SIMPLE INTERTEMPORAL MODEL OF PRODUCER INVESTMENT

This section provides a mathematical justification of the results exemplified in Section 4.7. The results here are not intended to be broadly applicable for analyzing real-world problems. Rather, they are intended to demonstrate that dynamic specifications for producer supplies and demands (supplies and demands with lagged prices and quantities) have specific implications for how to measure economic welfare. The more realistic case where producers are not assumed to anticipate future prices with certainty is developed in Appendix Section 14.A. Nevertheless, the case where the producing firm believes its anticipations with certainty is worth considering as a special case for several reasons. First, in some industries, future price changes may be well anticipated under government policies, particularly where the policies affect prices directly. Second, futures markets and contracts

14. For linear homogeneity of the profit function, the generalized Cobb–Douglans case requires

$$\sum_{i=1}^{N} \sum_{j=1}^{N} \beta_{ij} = 1.$$

15. For further details, see Diewert (1973, 1974).

for future delivery may exist so that future prices can be essentially locked in or guaranteed. Third, the model in this section is general enough to capture the generality allowed in some of the more popular empirical models. Finally, the limited generality of this case offers a useful intermediate step for understanding the more general case in Appendix Section 14.A.

Consider a single-product competitive firm with production function at time t given by

$$q_t = q_t(x_t, z_{t-1}^1, z_{t-2}^2, \ldots, z_{t-N}^N)$$

where x_t is a current variable input and z_t^n is the amount of fixed input n planned at time $t, n=1, \ldots, N$. Thus, z_{t-1}^1 must be planned one period in advance, z_{t-2}^2 must be planned two periods in advance, and so on. For example, in agricultural production, a factor such as land is for all intents and purposes fixed after commencement of the growing season. But fertilizer may be added at a later point in the growing season, and harvesting labor may be determined at the time of harvest. For simplicity of notation, only one input is included corresponding to each planning horizon in which a decision affecting period t must be made, but others could also be included without affecting the results below. As usual, suppose that q_t is increasing, concave and second-order differentiable in all inputs.

In attempting to determine the appropriate levels of investments to undertake in planning production for future periods, as well as to determine the appropriate production decisions for the current period, a firm maximizing its discounted stream of profits or its discounted future wealth will maximize

$$\Pi_t^T = \sum_{k=t}^{T} \pi_t^k, \tag{4.23}$$

where[16]

$$\pi_t^k = \delta^{k-t} p_k q_k - \delta^{k-t} w_k x_k - \sum_{n=1}^{k-t} \delta^{k-t-n} v_{k-n}^n z_{k-n}^n. \tag{4.24}$$

Note that $\Sigma_{n=1}^{0} y_t$ is defined to be zero for any series $\{y_t\}$ for simplicity of notation. In (4.24), p_t is the price of output in period t, w_t is the price of the variable input x_t in period t, v_t^n is the price of fixed input z_n^t in period t, δ is a discounting factor as discussed in Section 14.1 (for example, the inverse of 1 plus the rate of interest), Π_t^T represents a $(T-t+1)$-period quasirent (revenues minus costs excluding costs that have already been incurred before period t), and π_t^k represents quasirent at period k, where all inputs not yet fixed before period t are considered variable.

Because of the special separable structure of this problem (inputs affecting output in one period do not affect output in any other period), one can consider independent maximization of π_t^k for $k=t, \ldots, T$, for which first-order conditions are

$$\frac{\partial \pi_t^k}{\partial x_k} = \delta^{k-t}\left[p_k \frac{\partial q_k}{\partial x_k} - w_k\right] = 0 \tag{4.25}$$

16. Note that, in this simple problem, current decisions have no direct or indirect effects on profits beyond period T. Thus, the $T-t+1$-period planning horizon (including periods t and T) is sufficient in maximizing profits over any longer life of the firm or wealth at any period beyond period T.

$$\frac{\partial \pi_t^k}{\partial z_{k-n}^n} = \delta^{k-t} p_k \frac{\partial q_k}{\partial z_{k-n}^n} - \delta^{k-t-n} v_{k-n}^n = 0, \quad n = 1, \ldots, k-t, \tag{4.26}$$

which can be solved in principle for input demands and output supply

$$x_k = \tilde{x}_t^k(p_k, w_k, \boldsymbol{v}_t^k, \bar{\boldsymbol{z}}_t^k)$$
$$z_{k-n}^n = \tilde{z}_{k-n}^{n,t}(p_k, w_k, \boldsymbol{v}_t^k, \bar{\boldsymbol{z}}_t^k), \ n = 1, \ldots, k-t,$$
$$q_k = \tilde{q}_t^k(p_k, w_k, \boldsymbol{v}_t^k, \bar{\boldsymbol{z}}_t^k) = q_k(\tilde{x}_t^k, \tilde{z}_{k-1}^{1,t}, \ldots, \tilde{z}_t^{k-t,t}, \bar{\boldsymbol{z}}_t^k),$$

where $\boldsymbol{v}_t^k = (v_{k-1}^1, \ldots, v_t^{k-t})$ is a vector of fixed input prices affecting π_t^k, and $\bar{\boldsymbol{z}}_t^k = (z_{t-1}^{k-t+1}, z_{t-2}^{k-t+2}, \ldots, z_{k-N}^N)$ is a vector of fixed input decisions affecting q_k that were made prior to time t.

In this context, one can define quasirent functions corresponding to (4.23) and (4.24):

$$\tilde{\Pi}_t^T = \sum_{k=t}^{T} \tilde{\pi}_t^k$$

and

$$\tilde{\pi}_t^k = \delta^{k-t} p_k \tilde{q}_t^k - \delta^{k-t} w_k \tilde{x}_t^k - \sum_{n=1}^{k-t} \delta^{k-t-n} v_{k-n}^n \tilde{z}_{k-n}^{n,t},$$

for which the envelope theorem, or (4.25) and (4.26), implies that

$$\frac{\partial \tilde{\Pi}_t^T}{\partial p_k} = \frac{\partial \tilde{\pi}_t^k}{\partial p_k} = \delta^{k-t} \tilde{q}_t^k \tag{4.27}$$

$$\frac{\partial \tilde{\Pi}_t^T}{\partial w_k} = \frac{\partial \tilde{\pi}_t^k}{\partial w_k} = -\delta^{k-t} \tilde{x}_t^k. \tag{4.28}$$

Now suppose that the current variable input is an essential input for production in the sense that one can define shutdown prices

$$\tilde{p}_t^k = \max_{p_k} \{p_k | \tilde{q}_t^k(p_k, w_k, \boldsymbol{v}_t^k, \bar{\boldsymbol{z}}_t^k) = 0\}, \ k = t, \ldots, T, \tag{4.29}$$
$$\tilde{w}_t^k = \min_{w_k} \{w_k | \tilde{x}_t^k(p_k, w_k, \boldsymbol{v}_t^k, \bar{\boldsymbol{z}}_t^k) = 0\}, \ k = t, \ldots, T, \tag{4.30}$$

where $\tilde{q}_t^k = \tilde{x}_t^k = \tilde{z}_{k-1}^{1,t} = \ldots = \tilde{z}_t^{k-t,t} = 0$ in any case where at period t a production shutdown is planned for period k.

Using (4.27) and (4.29), one finds that

$$\pi_t^k = \delta^{k-t} \int_{\tilde{p}_t^k}^{p_k} \tilde{q}_t^k dp_k = \delta^{k-t} \tilde{P}_t^k,$$

where $\tilde{P}_t^k$ is the producer surplus associated with a one-period supply curve given $(k-t+1)$-period planning foresight. From this result, one finds that the welfare effect on a firm of changing the sequence of (all) prices over time periods $t, \ldots, T$ is

$$\Delta\Pi_t^T = \sum_{k=t}^{T} \Delta\tilde{\pi}_t^k = \sum_{k=t}^{T} \delta^{k-t} \Delta\tilde{P}_t^k, \tag{4.31}$$

which verifies one of the results discussed in Section 4.7 (where $\delta = 1$ is assumed). In other words, under the assumptions of this section, *the welfare effect of any change on a firm is given by the discounted sum of producer surplus changes associated with respective supply curves of all relevant lengths of run* (as viewed from the initial point in time). Similarly, one finds, using (4.28) and (4.30), that

$$\pi_t^k = \delta^{k-t} \int_{w_k}^{\tilde{w}_t^k} \tilde{x}_t^k dw_k = \delta^{k-t} \tilde{C}_t^k,$$

where $\tilde{C}_t^k$ is the consumer surplus associated with the one-period variable input-derived demand curve for a $(k-t+1)$-period planning foresight. From this result, the welfare effects of any general change in the temporal sequence of (output or input) prices facing a firm can also be measured by

$$\Delta \Pi_t^T = \sum_{k=t}^{T} \Delta \tilde{\pi}_t^k = \sum_{k=t}^{T} \delta^{k-t} \Delta \tilde{C}_t^k. \tag{4.32}$$

In other words, under the assumptions of this section, *the welfare effect of any change on a firm is given by the discounted sum of consumer surplus changes associated with variable input demand curves for an essential input of all relevant lengths of run* (as viewed from the initial point in time).

Next, consider the alternative method of measurement suggested in Section 4.7. To do this, note that the condition in (4.25) can be solved in principle for (short-run) variable input demands as a function of output price, variable input price, and all fixed input quantities,

$$x_k = \hat{x}_k(p_k, w_k, \mathbf{z}_k),$$

where $\mathbf{z}_k = (z_{k-1}^1, \ldots, z_{k-N}^N)$. Substitution into the production function yields short-run (one-period planning horizon) supply relationships,

$$q_k = \hat{q}_k(p_k, w_k, \mathbf{z}_k) \equiv q_k(\hat{x}_k, \mathbf{z}_k).$$

Using these input demand and output supply relationships, one can define short-run quasi-rent functions,

$$\hat{\pi}_k = p_k \hat{q}_k - w_k \hat{x}_k,$$

for which the envelope theorem, or use of (4.25), implies that

$$\frac{\partial \hat{\pi}_k}{\partial p_k} = \hat{q}_k$$

$$\frac{\partial \hat{\pi}_k}{\partial w_k} = -\hat{x}_k.$$

Again, assuming that the current variable input is an essential input for production regardless of earlier investment, one can define shutdown prices,

$$\tilde{p}_k = \max_{p_k} \{p_k | \hat{q}_k(p_k, w_k, z_k) = 0\},\ k = t, \ldots, T,$$

$$\tilde{w}_k = \min_{w_k} \{w_k | \hat{x}_k(p_k, w_k, z_k) = 0\},\ k = t, \ldots, T,$$

which depend on levels of all fixed inputs affecting the relevant production period (as reflected by z_k). In this context, one finds that

$$\hat{\pi}_k = \int_{\tilde{p}_k}^{p_k} \hat{q}_k \, dp_k = P_k \tag{4.33}$$

$$= \int_{w_k}^{\tilde{w}_k} \hat{x}_k \, dw_k = C_k, \tag{4.34}$$

where P_k and C_k are the producer and consumer surpluses associated with the short-run supply and variable input demand curves in period k, respectively. Note that each depends on fixed input levels represented in z_k. Returning to (4.24) and using (4.33) and (4.34) thus yields

$$\pi_t^k = \delta^{k-t}\hat{\pi}_k - \sum_{n=1}^{k-t} \delta^{k-t-n} v_{k-n}^n z_{k-n}^n$$

$$= \delta^{k-t} P_k - \sum_{n=1}^{k-t} \delta^{k-t-n} I_{k-n}^k$$

$$= \delta^{k-t} C_k - \sum_{n=1}^{k-t} \delta^{k-t-n} I_{k-n}^k,$$

so that the effect of any general change in the temporal sequence of (output or input) prices facing a firm can be measured by

$$\Delta\Pi_t^T = \sum_{k=t}^{T} \delta^{k-t} \Delta P_k - \sum_{k=t}^{T} \sum_{n=1}^{k-t} \delta^{k-t-n} \Delta I_{k-n}^k \tag{4.35}$$

$$= \sum_{k=t}^{T} \delta^{k-t} \Delta C_k - \sum_{k=1}^{T} \sum_{n=1}^{k-t} \delta^{k-t-n} \Delta I_{k-n}^k, \tag{4.36}$$

where $I_{k-n}^k = v_{k-n}^n z_{k-n}^n$ represents investment undertaken at time $k-n$ in planning for production in period k.

The result in (4.35) thus verifies and generalizes the graphical analysis of Section 4.7, which shows that *the welfare effect of any change affecting a firm over time can be measured by the (discounted) sum of changes in short-run producer surpluses minus the (discounted) sum of changes in investments*. The result in (4.36) shows that this result also holds for the demand side. Namely, *the welfare effect in terms of willingness to pay for any change affecting a firm over time can be measured by the discounted sum of changes in short-run consumer surpluses associated with an essential variable input minus the discounted sum of changes in investments.*

By comparison with (4.31) and (4.32), the advantages of the results in (4.35) and (4.36) are that they can be generalized easily for the case where the production function is not temporally separable (where each fixed input decision may affect output over several periods, including the current time period). However, the results in (4.31) and (4.32) are relatively more useful when the production function is temporally separable because changes in investments induced by a policy change may be observable only in an *ex post* sense. Thus, direct use of (4.35) or (4.36) for *ex ante* policy analysis may not be feasible.

Interestingly, however, comparison of the results in, say, (4.31) and (4.35) yields a method for estimating changes in investment induced by a policy change affecting the temporal sequence of output prices when the production function is temporally separable even though quantities of fixed inputs and/or their prices are unobservable. To see this, note from (4.31) and (4.35) that

$$\sum_{k=t}^{T} \delta^{k-t} \Delta \tilde{P}_t^k = \sum_{k=t}^{T} \delta^{k-t} \Delta P_k - \sum_{k=t}^{T} \sum_{n=1}^{k-t} \delta^{k-t-n} I_{k-n}^k.$$

Subtracting from this equation the same equation where T is replaced by $T-1$ yields

$$\delta^{T-t} \Delta P_t^T = \delta^{T-t} \Delta P_t - \sum_{n=1}^{T-t} \delta^{T-t-n} \Delta I_{T-n}^T, \tag{4.37}$$

which implies for $T=t+1$ that

$$\Delta I_t^{t+1} = \delta(\Delta P_{t+1} - \Delta \tilde{P}_t^{t+1}). \tag{4.38}$$

Advancing (4.38) one period and substituting into (4.37) with $T=t+2$ further implies that

$$\begin{aligned} \Delta I_t^{t+2} &= \delta^2(\Delta P_{t+2} - \Delta \tilde{P}_t^{t+2}) - \delta^2(\Delta P_{t+2} - \Delta \tilde{P}_{t+1}^{t+2}) \\ &= \delta^2(\Delta \tilde{P}_{t+1}^{t+2} - \Delta P_t^{t+2}). \end{aligned} \tag{4.39}$$

Noting that $\Delta P_{t+1} = \Delta \tilde{P}_{t+1}^{t+1}$ and comparing (4.38) and (4.39) thus suggests the general result

$$\Delta I_t^k = \delta^{k-t}(\Delta \tilde{P}_{t+1}^k - \Delta \tilde{P}_t^k), \tag{4.40}$$

which can be verified by continuing to substitute results such as (4.38) and (4.39) into (4.37) as T is increased.

From the result in (4.40), one can use a dynamic supply relationship to estimate amounts of investment change by time period resulting from a change in the temporal sequence of output prices over time. Thus, useful information in terms of temporally disaggregated welfare effects as well as the overall effect can be developed. Similar results can also be developed in terms of variable input demand measurements. That is, using (4.32) in (4.36), one can follow the steps in (4.37) through (4.40), simply replacing *P*s with *C*s to find

$$\Delta I_t^k = \delta^{k-t}(\Delta \tilde{C}_{t+1}^k - \Delta \tilde{C}_t^k). \tag{4.41}$$

Thus, one can also use dynamic variable input demand equations to estimate temporal effects on investment of a change in the temporal sequence of variable input prices.

An example can suffice to demonstrate how, say, a dynamic supply equation can be used to estimate temporally disaggregated effects on investment. One of the most basic supply models representing the fixity of inputs is the Koyck model, where only a fraction, β, of the difference in desired production at time t and that planned previously can be made up by an additional year of planning. That is,

$$q_t^k - q_{t-1}^k = \beta(\bar{q}_t{}^k - q_{t-1}^k), \tag{4.42}$$

where desired production for time k is given by

$$\bar{q}_t{}^k = a_0 + b_0 p_k \tag{4.43}$$

and q_t^k represents the amount of production for time k planned at period t.[17] Substitution of (4.43) into (4.42) yields

$$q_t^k - a_0\beta + b_0\beta p_k + (1-\beta)q_{t-1}^k. \tag{4.44}$$

Then further substituting (4.44) with $t=k-1$ into (4.44) with $t=k$, and so on, that is, solving the difference equation in (4.44), yields

$$q_t^k = a_t^k + b_t^k p_k \tag{4.45}$$

where

$$a_t^k + a_0\beta \sum_{j=0}^{k-t} (1-\beta)^j + (1-\beta)^{k-t+1} q_{t-1}^k$$

$$b_t^k = b_0\beta \sum_{j=0}^{k-t} (1-\beta)^j.$$

Thus, following (4.29),

$$\tilde{p}_t^k = -a_t^k / b_t^k$$

and

$$\begin{aligned} \tilde{q}_t^k &= \int_{\tilde{p}_t^k}^{p_k} (a_t^k + b_t^k p_k) dp_k \\ &= a_t^k(p_k - \tilde{p}_t^k) + \tfrac{1}{2} b_t^k [p_k^2 - (\tilde{p}_t^k)^2] \\ &= \tfrac{1}{2} b_t^k (p_k + a_t^k / b_t^k)^2. \end{aligned} \tag{4.46}$$

Calculations, such as in (4.46) for a variety of t and k, then allow computation of changes in investment over time associated with alternative output price scenarios following (4.40).

17. Although this is a somewhat unusual interpretation of the Koyck model, it is one adapted to the assumptions of this section. The more common interpretation supposes that a producer naively expects price for all future time periods to be the same as current price, and then expectations are revised each period. For the moment, however, the producer is supposed to anticipate future prices perfectly. Application in the more standard context is also accommodated by this modification, though, as shown below.

Thus, the temporal disaggregation in (4.35) is feasible even when investment quantities or prices are not directly observable.[18]

Based on the results above, one can begin to consider generalizations for cases where future prices are not perfectly anticipated. For example, consider the common interpretation of the Koyck model where a producer naively expects prices for all future time periods to be the same as current prices (with certainty) even though expectations are revised each period as new prices are observed. In this case, (4.43) is replaced by

$$\bar{q}_t^k = a_0 + b_0 p_t$$

in which case (4.45) becomes the popular form

$$\bar{q}_t^k = a_t^k + b_0 \beta \sum_{j=0}^{k-t} (1-\beta)^j p_{k-j}, \tag{4.47}$$

where a_t^k is as defined above.

Although this model has a somewhat different interpretation, the investment effects can be calculated in a similar manner. That is, if prices in this case were, by chance, to remain constant over future time periods according to naive expectations at time t, the calculations above are correct. But if that is what the producer expects, the firm will make the same investments at time t even though future prices may turn out to be different. Thus, ΔI_t^k can be calculated following (4.40), where $\tilde{P}_{t+1}^k$ and $\tilde{P}_t^k$ are calculated following (4.46) with p_k replaced by its naive expectation p_t. That is,

$$\Delta I_t^k = \delta^k (\Delta \tilde{P}_{t+1}^k - \Delta \tilde{P}_t^k) \tag{4.48}$$

where

$$\tilde{P}_{t+1}^k = \tfrac{1}{2} b_{t+i}^k (p_t + a_{t+i}^k / b_{t+i}^k)^2,\ i = 0, 1. \tag{4.49}$$

Note also that a_{t+i}^k changes if q_{t+i}^k is affected by the change in the temporal price sequence under consideration, but these changes can be determined using (4.47).

By supplementing the calculations in (4.48) and (4.49) with calculations of changes in short-run producer surpluses, $\Delta P_t \equiv \Delta \tilde{P}_t^t$, for all time periods affected by the temporal sequence of price changes, the approach in (4.35) for calculating total welfare effects becomes feasible even though calculations of $\tilde{P}_t^k$ and the related approach in (4.31) are not feasible when future price expectations are revised over time. Thus, for the general case where producers have naive expectations that all future prices will be the same as current prices, the results of this section justify a dynamic economic welfare methodology consisting of equations (4.35), (4.48) and

$$\tilde{P}_{t+i}^k = \int_{\tilde{p}_{t+i}^k}^{p_t} \tilde{q}_{t+i}^k (p_t, w_t, v_t^k, z_t^k) dp_t$$

where

18. Of course, similar results are also possible on the input side by using (4.41) if a model similar to (4.42) and (4.43) is used to represent planned variable input usage.

$$\tilde{p}_{t+i}^{k} = \max_{p_t} \{p_t | \tilde{q}_{t+i}^{k}(p_t, w_t, \mathbf{v}_t^k, \mathbf{z}_t^k) = 0\}.$$

While this section has investigated calculation of dynamic welfare effects on a producer in a rather special case, the general approach may be extended to many other cases of economic welfare analysis with other types of dynamic supply equations.

4.G ALTERNATIVE BEHAVIORAL CRITERIA AND ROBUSTNESS OF SURPLUS MEASURES

Thus far, this appendix has focused primarily on the case of profit maximization under certainty. In these cases, exact measurement of producer benefits is possible under quite general assumptions assuming competition. Producer quasirent is an accurate measure of both compensating and equivalent variation, and is reflected by standard concepts of producer surplus in output markets and consumer surplus in input markets. When quantity restrictions are imposed on the firm, the appropriate welfare measures are compensating and equivalent surplus but are still measured accurately using producer and consumer surplus areas behind supply and demand curves. When the behavioral criterion is relaxed to consider maximization of the expected utility of profits (see the Appendix to Chapter 12), many of these results remain intact although the compensating and equivalent variations no longer coincide and producer surplus is an appropriate measure only when production is nonstochastic. In general, however, the surplus areas associated with supplies and demands of nonstochastic market decision variables measure relevant willingness-to-pay measures under certain conditions.

This generality raises the question of whether surplus measures are valid under other types of behavioral criteria.[19] Some of the other behavioral hypotheses that have been employed in the literature are output constrained profit maximization, input constrained profit maximization, expenditure constrained profit maximization and sales maximization. Constraints on inputs or outputs or some combination of them may represent institutional considerations or strong behavioral preferences of the entrepreneur that cause a departure from profit maximization. Examples include constraints imposed on behavior by religious beliefs, family relationships, moral considerations or psychological factors. Expenditure constrained profit maximizing behavior may be due to imperfect capital markets or may represent financial conservatism in the entrepreneur's behavior.[20] Sales maximization may represent the behavior of entrepreneurs who have decision power but no share in profits. For example, chief executive officers of major corporations may maximize economic power and control by maximizing sales subject to an acceptable profit level (McCloskey 1982).

To consider economic surplus measures in the case of behavioral constraints on inputs and outputs, let $\boldsymbol{b}(\boldsymbol{q},\boldsymbol{x}) = \mathbf{0}$ represent a general set of constraints imposed by the entrepreneur's preferences and assume that the behavioral objective is to maximize profit subject to the behavioral constraints. In this case, the producer's problem is

19. For a discussion of alternative theories of business behavior, see McGuire (1964).
20. For an example of a study that finds empirical support for this behavioral hypothesis over unconstrained profit-maximizing behavior, see Lee and Chambers (1986).

$$\max_{x} \{\boldsymbol{pq}(\boldsymbol{x}) - \boldsymbol{wx} - K | \boldsymbol{b}(\boldsymbol{q}(\boldsymbol{x}),\boldsymbol{x}) = \boldsymbol{0},\ \boldsymbol{x} \geq \boldsymbol{0}\}.$$

To solve this problem assuming an internal solution for $\boldsymbol{x}$, consider the Lagrangian, $\mathscr{L} = \boldsymbol{pq}(\boldsymbol{x}) - \boldsymbol{wx} - K - \boldsymbol{\lambda b}(\boldsymbol{q}(\boldsymbol{x}),\boldsymbol{x})$, where $\boldsymbol{\lambda}$ is a vector of Lagrangian multipliers associated with the behavioral constraints. Assuming $\boldsymbol{b}$ is continuous, increasing in $\boldsymbol{x}$, decreasing in $\boldsymbol{q}$, and concave in $\boldsymbol{x}$ and $\boldsymbol{q}$, this problem yields unique demands and supplies, $\hat{\boldsymbol{x}}(\boldsymbol{p},\boldsymbol{w})$ and $\equiv \boldsymbol{q}(\hat{\boldsymbol{x}}(\boldsymbol{p},\boldsymbol{w}))$, respectively, that can be used to form a quasirent function, $R(\boldsymbol{p},\boldsymbol{w}) \equiv \boldsymbol{pq}(\hat{\boldsymbol{x}}(\boldsymbol{p},\boldsymbol{w})) - \boldsymbol{w}\hat{\boldsymbol{x}}(\boldsymbol{p},\boldsymbol{w})$, analogous to Appendix Section 4.A. Differentiation of the quasirent function with respect to all prices yields the same results as in equations (4.5) and (4.6) because the Lagrangian term, $\boldsymbol{\lambda b}(\boldsymbol{q},\boldsymbol{x})$, must be zero at the optimum in any solution of first-order conditions. To see this result intuitively, the technology under behavioral constraints can simply be viewed as operation of the firm under a different technology, so all conclusions follow that are associated with a fixed technology possessing the same general properties.[21] Thus, all of the results for exact welfare measurement by producer and consumer surplus apply except that now both changes in technology and behavioral constraints can cause demand or supply to shift. In particular, the surplus concepts associated with both supply and demand provide accurate measures of both compensating and equivalent variation.

Alternatively, consider an expenditure constraint in the form $\boldsymbol{wx} + K \leq c^*$ and assume that the behavioral objective is to maximize profits subject to the expenditure constraint,

$$\max_{x} \{\boldsymbol{pq}(\boldsymbol{x}) - \boldsymbol{wx} - K | \boldsymbol{wx} + K \leq c^*,\ \boldsymbol{x} \geq \boldsymbol{0}\}.$$

If the expenditure constraint is not binding, then this problem generates the same results as the problem in Appendix Section 4.A. For the case where the expenditure constraint is binding and an internal solution applies for $\boldsymbol{x}$, consider the Lagrangian $\mathscr{L} = \boldsymbol{pq}(\boldsymbol{x}) - \boldsymbol{wx} - K - \lambda(\boldsymbol{wx} + K - c^*)$, for which first-order conditions are $\boldsymbol{pq}_x - \boldsymbol{w} - \lambda \boldsymbol{w} = 0$ and $\boldsymbol{wx} + K - c^* = 0$ Solution of this problem yields demands and supplies, $\hat{\boldsymbol{x}}(\boldsymbol{p},\boldsymbol{w},K)$ and $\hat{\boldsymbol{q}}(\boldsymbol{p},\boldsymbol{w},K) \equiv \boldsymbol{q}(\hat{\boldsymbol{x}}(\boldsymbol{p},\boldsymbol{w},K))$ respectively, which depend on fixed costs because of the expenditure constraint.[22] To consider the interpretation of areas behind demand and supply curves, the quasirent function, $R(\boldsymbol{p},\boldsymbol{w},K) \equiv \boldsymbol{pq}(\hat{\boldsymbol{x}}(\boldsymbol{p},\boldsymbol{w},K)) - \boldsymbol{w}\hat{\boldsymbol{x}}(\boldsymbol{p},\boldsymbol{w},K)$, can be differentiated to obtain

$$\boldsymbol{R}_p = \hat{\boldsymbol{q}}(\boldsymbol{p},\boldsymbol{w},K) + (\boldsymbol{pq}_x - \boldsymbol{w})\hat{\boldsymbol{x}}_p = \hat{\boldsymbol{q}}(\boldsymbol{p},\boldsymbol{w},K) \tag{4.50}$$

and

$$\boldsymbol{R}_w = -\hat{\boldsymbol{x}}(\boldsymbol{p},\boldsymbol{w},K) + (\boldsymbol{pq}_x - \boldsymbol{w})\hat{\boldsymbol{x}}_w = -(1+\lambda)\hat{\boldsymbol{x}}(\boldsymbol{p},\boldsymbol{w},K). \tag{4.51}$$

Note that $\boldsymbol{pq}_x - \boldsymbol{w}$ is not zero in these expressions according to first-order conditions as in equations (4.5) and (4.6), but rather $\boldsymbol{pq}_x - \boldsymbol{w} = \lambda \boldsymbol{w}$. After substitution of this result, the

21. This simple intuition is perhaps most apparent when the technology is represented as $(\boldsymbol{q},\boldsymbol{x}) \in T$ following footnote 1. Then the behavioral constraints can be represented as $(\boldsymbol{q},\boldsymbol{x}) \in B$ and the available technology under behavioral constraints is $(\boldsymbol{q},\boldsymbol{x}) \in T \cap B$. If both T and B are closed convex sets, then $T \cap B$ is also closed and convex, which thus generates the same welfare significance of surplus measures as the case where technology is represented by $(\boldsymbol{q},\boldsymbol{x}) \in T$.
22. This quasirent function also depends on c^*, but this argument is suppressed for convenience.

second equalities follow from differentiation of the expenditure constraint $\boldsymbol{w}\hat{\boldsymbol{x}}(\boldsymbol{p},\boldsymbol{w},K) + K = c^*$) with respect to input and output prices, which yields $\boldsymbol{w}\hat{\boldsymbol{x}}_w = -\hat{\boldsymbol{x}}(\boldsymbol{p},\boldsymbol{w},K)$ and $\boldsymbol{w}\hat{\boldsymbol{x}}_p = \boldsymbol{0}$. The result in (4.50) implies that the change in the producer surplus area associated with a supply curve accurately measures the change in quasirent, that is, the compensating and equivalent variation of a change in the associated output price. On the other hand, the result in (4.51) implies that the change in consumer surplus associated with any input demand curve underestimates willingness to pay for an associated input price change by a factor of $1+\lambda$, that is, the consumer surplus change measures $\Delta R/(1+\lambda)$. Intuitively, the reason is that input adjustment is partially constrained by the expenditure constraint, so input use cannot be adjusted as much as in the unconstrained case. Because changes in producer surplus have their usual welfare significance, however, the results for an essential output hold. That is, the change in producer surplus in an essential output market accurately measures the compensating and equivalent variation of any general change in input prices, output prices, or nonprice factors affecting the firm.

A closer examination of the expenditure-constrained case, however, reveals that these conclusions only apply if compensation does not affect the expenditure constraint, as in the case where compensation is extracted or paid *ex post* when production revenues are realized. If compensation is extracted or paid *ex ante* and thus enters the expenditure constraint, then the outcome is quite different. To consider this case, redefine K as compensation paid less compensation received (where fixed cost becomes implicit and suppressed). Then totally differentiate $R-K$ with respect to $\boldsymbol{w}$ and K, $d(R-K) = \boldsymbol{R}_w d\boldsymbol{w} + (R_K - 1)dK$, and consider adjusting compensation in response to an input price change holding $R-K$ constant, $d(R-K)=0$. The change in compensation with respect to an input price change is thus

$$\frac{dK}{d\boldsymbol{w}} = -\frac{\boldsymbol{R}_w}{R_K - 1} = -\frac{(1+\lambda)\hat{\boldsymbol{x}}(\boldsymbol{p},\boldsymbol{w},K)}{1+\lambda} = -\hat{\boldsymbol{x}}(\boldsymbol{p},\boldsymbol{w},K). \tag{4.52}$$

A similar procedure for an output price change reveals

$$\frac{dK}{d\boldsymbol{p}} = -\frac{\boldsymbol{R}_p}{R_K - 1} = \frac{\hat{\boldsymbol{q}}(\boldsymbol{p},\boldsymbol{w},K)}{1+\lambda}. \tag{4.53}$$

These results follow from $R_K = (\boldsymbol{p}\boldsymbol{q}_x - \boldsymbol{w})\hat{\boldsymbol{x}}_k = -\lambda$ where the latter equality is obtained by substituting $\boldsymbol{p}\boldsymbol{q}_x - \boldsymbol{w} = \lambda\boldsymbol{w}$ and differentiating the expenditure constraint with respect to K, which implies $\boldsymbol{w}\hat{\boldsymbol{x}}_k + 1 = 0$. From (4.52), the change in the consumer surplus area associated with a demand curve accurately measures the compensating and equivalent variation of a change in the associated input price if compensation applies *ex ante*. If the input is essential and *ex ante* compensation applies, then consumer surplus can also be used to measure the compensating and equivalent variation of any general change in output prices, input prices, or nonprice factors affecting the firm. In contrast to the case of *ex post* compensation, however, equation (4.53) shows that the change in producer surplus associated with an output supply curve overestimates willingness to pay for output price changes by a factor of $1+\lambda$. Thus, in both the *ex ante* and *ex post* cases, surplus concepts are appropriate but whether compensation enters into the *ex ante* expenditure constraint or simply affects the *ex post* profit is crucial to determining which surplus concept to use.

Finally, consider the case of sales maximization subject to a minimum profit constraint. In this case, the problem is

$$\max_x \{\boldsymbol{pq}(\boldsymbol{x})|\boldsymbol{pq}(\boldsymbol{x}) - \boldsymbol{wx} - K \geq \pi^*, \boldsymbol{x} \geq \boldsymbol{0}\},$$

where K again represents fixed cost and π^* is the constrained profit level. Assuming an internal solution for $\boldsymbol{x}$ and assuming the profit constraint is binding, the Lagrangian associated with this problem is $\mathcal{L} = \boldsymbol{pq}(\boldsymbol{x}) - \lambda[\boldsymbol{pq}(\boldsymbol{x}) - \boldsymbol{wx} - K - \pi^*]$, for which first-order conditions are $(1+\lambda)\boldsymbol{pq}_x - \lambda\boldsymbol{w} = 0$ and $\boldsymbol{pq}(\boldsymbol{x}) - \boldsymbol{wx} - K - \pi^* = 0$. Solution of this problem yields demands and supplies, $\hat{\boldsymbol{x}}(\boldsymbol{p},\boldsymbol{w},K)$ and $\hat{\boldsymbol{q}}(\boldsymbol{p},\boldsymbol{w},K) \equiv \hat{\boldsymbol{q}}(\hat{\boldsymbol{x}}(\boldsymbol{p},\boldsymbol{w},K))$, respectively, which depend implicitly on the constrained profit level. Because sales revenue is what matters to the decision-maker in this case, the compensating and equivalent variation are given by the change in sales revenue. Thus, define the sales or revenue function as $R^*(\boldsymbol{p},\boldsymbol{w},K) \equiv \boldsymbol{pq}(\hat{\boldsymbol{x}}(\boldsymbol{p},\boldsymbol{w},K))$. Differentiation obtains

$$\boldsymbol{R}_p^* = \hat{\boldsymbol{q}}(\boldsymbol{p},\boldsymbol{w},K) + \boldsymbol{pq}_x\hat{\boldsymbol{x}}_p = (1+\lambda)\hat{\boldsymbol{q}}(\boldsymbol{p},\boldsymbol{w},K) \quad (4.54)$$

and

$$\boldsymbol{R}_w^* = \boldsymbol{pq}_x\hat{\boldsymbol{x}}_w = -\lambda\hat{\boldsymbol{x}}(\boldsymbol{p},\boldsymbol{w},K). \quad (4.55)$$

To derive the latter equality in (4.54), note that differentiation of the profit constraint with respect to $\boldsymbol{p}$ after substitution of $\hat{\boldsymbol{x}}(\boldsymbol{p},\boldsymbol{w},K)$ and $\hat{\boldsymbol{q}}(\boldsymbol{p},\boldsymbol{w},K)$ for $\boldsymbol{x}$ and $\boldsymbol{q}$, respectively, obtains $\hat{\boldsymbol{q}}(\boldsymbol{p},\boldsymbol{w},K) = -(\boldsymbol{pq}_x - \boldsymbol{w})\hat{\boldsymbol{x}}_p$ where the first-order condition with respect to $\boldsymbol{x}$ implies $\boldsymbol{pq}_x - \boldsymbol{w} = -\boldsymbol{p}\hat{\boldsymbol{q}}_x/\lambda$. To derive the latter equality in (4.55), similar differentiation of the profit constraint with respect to $\boldsymbol{x}$ obtains $\hat{\boldsymbol{x}}(\boldsymbol{p},\boldsymbol{w},K) = (\boldsymbol{pq}_x - \boldsymbol{w})\hat{\boldsymbol{x}}_w$ where again $\boldsymbol{pq}_x - \boldsymbol{w} = -\boldsymbol{p}\hat{\boldsymbol{q}}_x/\lambda$. Equation (4.54) implies that the change in producer surplus associated with the supply of a sales maximizing firm underestimates the compensating and equivalent variation by a factor of $1+\lambda$, that is, the producer surplus change measures $\Delta R^*/(1+\lambda)$. The same conclusion applies for attempts to measure the change in producer surplus in an essential output market associated with any general change in input prices, output prices or nonprice factors affecting the firm. Equation (4.55) implies that the consumer surplus change in an input market underestimates or overestimates the compensating and equivalent variation of a change in the associated input price depending on whether $\lambda > 1$ or $\lambda < 1$, that is, the change in consumer surplus measures $\Delta R^*/\lambda$. The same conclusion applies for attempts to measure the change in consumer surplus in an essential input market associated with any general change in input prices, output prices or nonprice factors affecting the firm. Interestingly, if both an essential input market and an essential output market are observable before and after a general change, then one can solve for the correct change in R^* as $\Delta R^* = (P_jC_i)/(P_j + C_i)$ using $\Delta R^* = -\lambda C_i$ and $\Delta R^* = (1+\lambda)P_j$ where C_i is the consumer surplus change in an essential input market and P_j is the producer surplus change in an essential output market.

The results of this section thus show that the standard surplus areas associated with supplies and demands can have welfare significance under a variety of behavioral criteria that depart from simple profit maximization, although some further modifications are required in some cases. Consumer and producer surplus have standard welfare significance when behavioral constraints apply, and either consumer or producer surplus has standard welfare significance when expenditure constraints apply depending on whether compensation is *ex ante* or *ex post*. Neither consumer nor producer surplus has direct welfare significance under sales maximization but both are qualitatively related to compensating and equivalent variation, and can be used to derive them.

These results imply that estimation of welfare effects by consumer and producer surplus is somewhat robust with respect to behavioral criteria. That is, surplus estimates may have welfare significance beyond the standard behavioral assumptions used to derive them. For example, when the parameters of supplies and demands represent not only the technology of the producer but also behavioral constraints imposed by the producer, then standard welfare conclusions hold even though the behavioral constraints are not modeled explicitly. This result demonstrates one reason why behavioral criteria are difficult empirically to distinguish from technology. On the other hand, the results for sales maximization and for expenditure-constrained profit maximization suggest some reasons why welfare measurements based on alternative markets may not agree, and suggest that comparison of alternative feasible welfare measurements may be prudent in applied economic welfare analysis.

5. Consumer surplus and consumer welfare

The definition of a measure of economic welfare for the consumer has been one of the most controversial subjects in economics. Unlike the producer's case, where observable measures of well-being, such as profit, can be clearly determined, no equally appealing *observable* measure exists for a utility-maximizing consumer. That is, the criterion of the consumer – utility – is not observable. In most practical situations, the applied welfare economist can, at best, observe income and consumption decisions at various prices and then, on the basis of these economic transactions, try to compute some money-based measure of welfare effects.

A source of confusion in deriving measures of consumer welfare lies in not distinguishing between 'cardinal' and 'ordinal' analysis. In Chapters 2 and 3, the analysis was largely ordinal in that only consumer indifference curves were used. No attempt was made to measure the intensity of change in satisfaction or utility the consumer derived when moving from one indifference curve to another. Rather, only qualitative concerns were important (for example, which indifference curve was preferred to the other). In applied welfare economics, measures of consumer welfare are generally not *cardinal* in the strict usage of the term. They are money measures of welfare change where money reflects willingness to pay (WTP) on the part of consumers, which in turn is related to the 'utility function' of the consumer. Thus, most measures do not seek to measure utility directly. Rather, they estimate a revealed WTP in terms of money.

'Consumer surplus' is the vehicle most often used in empirical work to measure consumer welfare. Unfortunately, it is at the center of the controversy surrounding consumer welfare measurement.[1] For example, one critique of consumer surplus by Pfouts (1953, p. 315) states: 'Probably no single concept in the annals of economic theory has aroused so many emphatic expressions of opinion as has consumer's surplus. Indeed, even today the biting winds of scholarly sarcasm howl around this venerable storm centre.' Indeed, the issues that arise when considering consumer surplus as a welfare measure are varied and complex, and their proper resolution requires advanced mathematical techniques. The Appendix to this chapter provides a rigorous analysis of these issues. This chapter attempts to simplify these issues without avoiding the substantive concerns. It provides heuristic developments of each issue based upon results found in the Appendix to this chapter and then resolves them in a manner that leads to a practical approach for applied welfare economics.

1. For a historical perspective on consumer surplus, see Currie, Murphy and Schmitz (1971) and Mishan (1977).

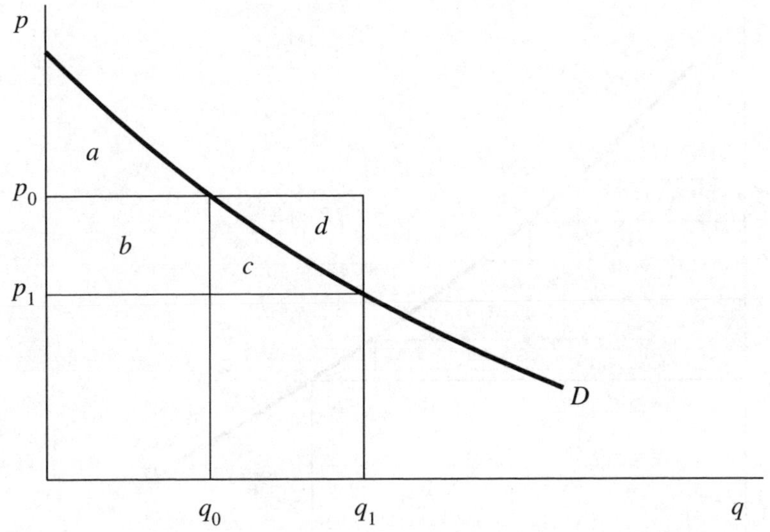

Figure 5.1

5.1 THE NOTION OF CONSUMER SURPLUS

Consider the problem of measuring the effect of a price change in terms of something that is observable (for example, dollars spent on a good). In Figure 5.1, the consumer is initially in equilibrium, consuming q_0 at price p_0 on the demand curve D. With a reduction in price to p_1, the consumer increases consumption to quantity q_1. How much better off is the consumer? Because the consumer now must spend only p_1q_0 to consume the same quantity that had required an expenditure of p_0q_0, one might argue that the consumer's gain is $(p_0 - p_1)q_0$, or area b. That is, if the consumer continued to consume q_0, there would be additional income in the amount of area b available to spend on other goods and services. This is one money measure of consumer welfare change due to a price change. As shown later, however, other money measures with perhaps better properties also exist.

Consider the alternative case of a price rise from p_1 to p_0, where the consumer is initially consuming quantity q_1. How much worse off is the consumer? In this case the consumer would require an increase in income of $(p_0 - p_1)q_1$, or area $b+c+d$, to continue buying quantity q_1.[2] This raises a paradox because the consumer apparently loses more with the price rise than is gained with the price fall. Intuition would suggest that the two changes should, on the contrary, exactly offset one another.

2. Hicks (1956) refers to the changes in area associated with expenditures as the inner cost difference if the associated quantity represents initial consumption. He defines this change in area as the outer cost difference if the quantity represents subsequent consumption. Thus, area b is the inner cost difference of the price fall and the outer cost difference associated with the price rise, and area $b+c+d$ corresponds to the converse cases. Because the inner cost difference corresponds closely with the Laspeyers index number formula where price index weights are based on initial quantities, the inner cost difference is sometimes called a Laspeyers variation. Similarly, the outer cost difference corresponds to the Paasche index number formula where price index weights are final or current quantities. Hence, the outer cost difference is sometimes called a Paasche variation. As these cases suggest, a close relationship exists between consumer surplus theory and index number theory generally, as discussed in Appendix Section 6.A.

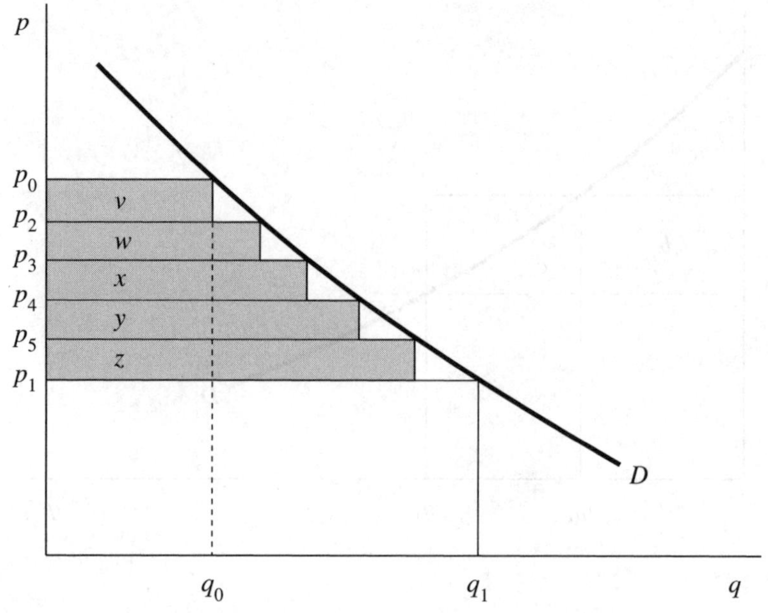

Figure 5.2

To consider one way this paradox can be resolved, suppose that the price reduction is made in a series of small steps, as in Figure 5.2, from p_0 to p_2, then from p_2 to p_3, and so on until finally reaching price p_1. The corresponding income equivalents in this context would be areas v, w, x, y, and z, respectively. Summing these effects over the entire price change, one would obtain the shaded area in Figure 5.2 as a measure of the consumer's gain. Obviously, as one divides the price change more finely, the shaded area begins to approach and become essentially synonymous with the area $b+c$ in Figure 5.1. Similarly, if one were to repeat this process in the case of a price rise, the corresponding income-equivalent measure of loss for the consumer would also approach the area $b+c$ in Figure 5.1 as the number of price increments (adding up to p_0-p_1) becomes larger. The area $b+c$ results from a summing of the cost differences in consumption bundles as price is continuously and incrementally varied from p_0 to p_1, or vice versa. Area $b+c$ is referred to as a change in consumer surplus, area $a+b+c$ is the total consumer surplus for price p_1, and area a is the consumer surplus for price p_0. That is, *consumer surplus is defined as the area under the demand curve and above the price line.*

Long ago, Jules Dupuit (1844), who actually coined the phrase 'consumer surplus', postulated that the price associated with any quantity on a consumer's demand curve is the maximum price the consumer is willing to pay for the last unit consumed. Hence, the demand curve is a marginal WTP curve. Thus, in Figure 5.3, the consumer is viewed as willing to pay p_1 for the first unit, p_2 for the second, p_3 for the third, and so on. If the consumer actually pays only p_0 for the entire quantity q_0, then the consumer gains a 'surplus' of p_1-p_0 on the first unit purchased because WTP exceeds what is actually paid by that amount. The consumer gains similar, but declining, increments of surplus on each of the units purchased up to q_0. In this context, the total area below the demand curve and left

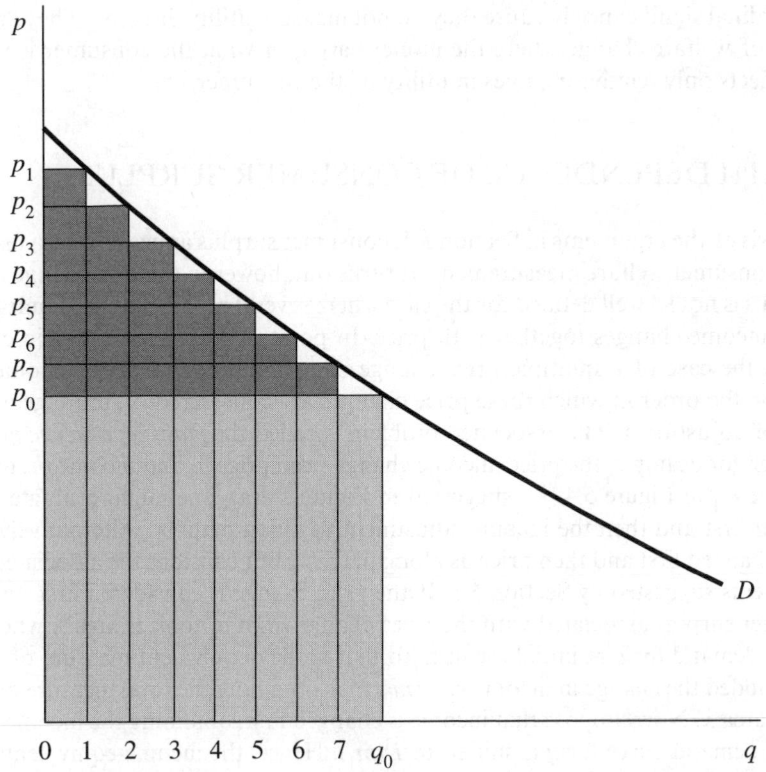

Figure 5.3

of the quantity consumed q_0 (the lightly shaded area plus the heavily shaded area) is called *gross benefits*, while the area below the demand curve and above price p_0 (the heavily shaded area), obtained by subtracting costs from gross benefits, is the net surplus accruing to the consumer from buying q_0 at p_0. Clearly, if the commodity q is perfectly divisible, the Dupuit surplus from buying q_0 at p_0 will simply be given by the triangle-like area above the price line p_0 and to the left of, or behind, the demand curve.

Referring back to Figure 5.1, the benefits to the consumer of a price reduction from p_0 to p_1, following Dupuit, would be given by area $b+c$, because this is the increase in the triangle-like area resulting from the price fall. Thus, on the surface, there are at least two reasons why the change in consumer surplus is appealing as a measure of consumer benefits: (1) it represents the sum of cost differences as price is continuously reduced from p_0 to p_1, and (2) it gives the change in what the consumer is willing to pay over that which is actually paid with the price change if the demand curve is a marginal WTP curve.

Before proceeding into the theoretical complexities of consumer surplus, however, an important point should be noted. That is, neither the cost difference approach (Figure 5.1) nor the excess of WTP over actual payments approach (Figure 5.3) claims to provide a measure of utility gains to the consumer. These approaches, except in certain cases, have only an ordinal significance because they do not measure utility directly.[3] They are money measures of welfare change where the money saved, or what the consumer is willing to spend, reflects only relative changes in utility of the consumer.

5.2 PATH DEPENDENCE OF CONSUMER SURPLUS

On the basis of the arguments in Section 5.1, consumer surplus appears to be a useful construct in consumer welfare measurement. It turns out, however, that the change in consumer surplus is not so well defined for the case where several prices change simultaneously, or where income changes together with price. In point of fact, the change in consumer surplus in the case of a multiple price change or a simultaneous price–income change depends on the order in which these price changes are considered or, more generally, on the path of adjustment. The associated problem is called the *path-dependence problem.*

Consider, for example, the price–income change from price p_0 and income m_0 to price p_1 and income m_1 in Figure 5.4. As suggested in Figure 5.4(a), one might evaluate the price adjustment first and then the income adjustment as along path L_1. Alternatively, income could be changed first and then price as along path L_2. But consider the associated welfare measurements suggested by Section 5.1. If the price change is considered first, the change in consumer surplus associated with the price change from p_0 to p_1 is area x where $D(m_0)$ represents demand for q at initial income. To that money-equivalent measure of the price change is added the change in income $m_1 - m_0$, thus obtaining the total measure of change, $m_1 - m_0 +$ area x. Now suppose that income is changed first, obtaining the income effect $m_1 - m_0$. The demand curve for q is shifted to $D(m_1)$. Hence, the income-equivalent measure of the price change in completing the path of adjustment L_2 is area $x+y$. Thus, along path L_2 the total change is $m_1 - m_0 +$ area $x+y$, which clearly differs from that obtained along path L_1.[4] The difference in these two alternatives suggests that differences can also exist among other paths of adjustment between the points (p_0,m_0) and (p_1,m_1) in Figure 5.4(a). That such differences can indeed exist is borne out by the results in Appendix Section 5.B.

A similar kind of path dependency exists for the case where several prices change even though income may be held constant. Consider the case in Figure 5.5, where the prices of q_1 and q_2 change from p_1^0 and p_2^0 to p_1^1 and p_2^1, respectively. Two possible paths of adjustment to use in consumer surplus calculations are depicted in Figure 5.5(a) by L_1 and L_2.

3. For example, two individuals with different utility functions may behave the same way and thus have identical demand curves and consumer surpluses.
4. The reader may also be concerned with whether or not the area z in Figure 5.4(b) has welfare significance because consumer surplus is defined in Section 5.1 as the total area above price and behind the demand curve. Indeed, the total change in this triangle-like area in this case is area $x+y+z$. Note, however, that the motivation for consumer surplus in Section 5.1 was developed in the case where income and prices of other goods – and thus the relevant demand curve – were held fixed. Thus, any application of the same intuition in this section would suggest breaking a price–income or price–price change into steps where the effects of individual price changes could be evaluated along a demand curve that remains stationary with respect to the individual price change.

To further investigate the meaning of area $x+y+z$, consider the case where income is first held at m_0 while increasing price from p_0 to p_2, thus creating a surplus loss of area w. Then, consider holding income at m_1 while lowering price from p_3 to p_1, thus creating a surplus gain of area $w+x+y+z$ for a net gain of area $x+y+z$. A problem exists because the intervening welfare effect of changing from price p_2 and income m_0 to price p_3 and income m_1 is ignored. In terms of Figure 5.4(a), this approach does not correspond to a complete path between (p_0, m_0) and (p_1, m_1).

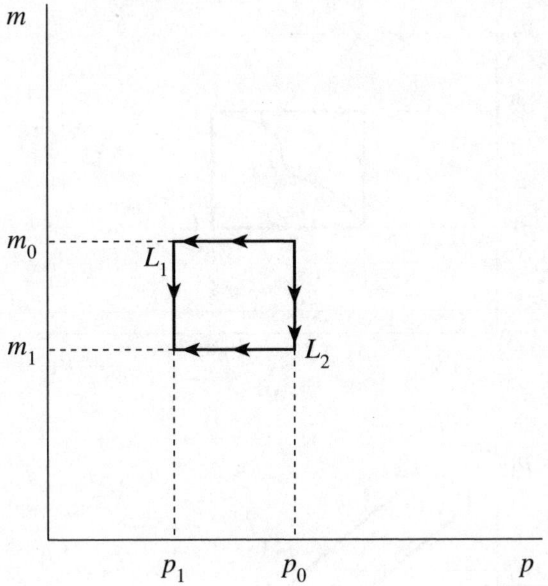

(a)

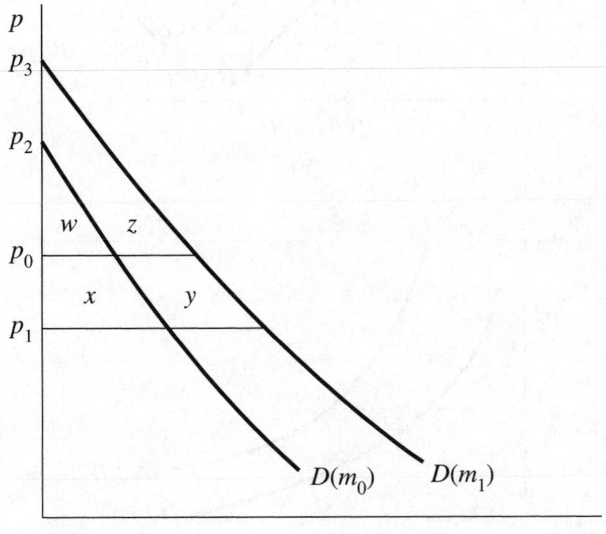

(b)

Figure 5.4

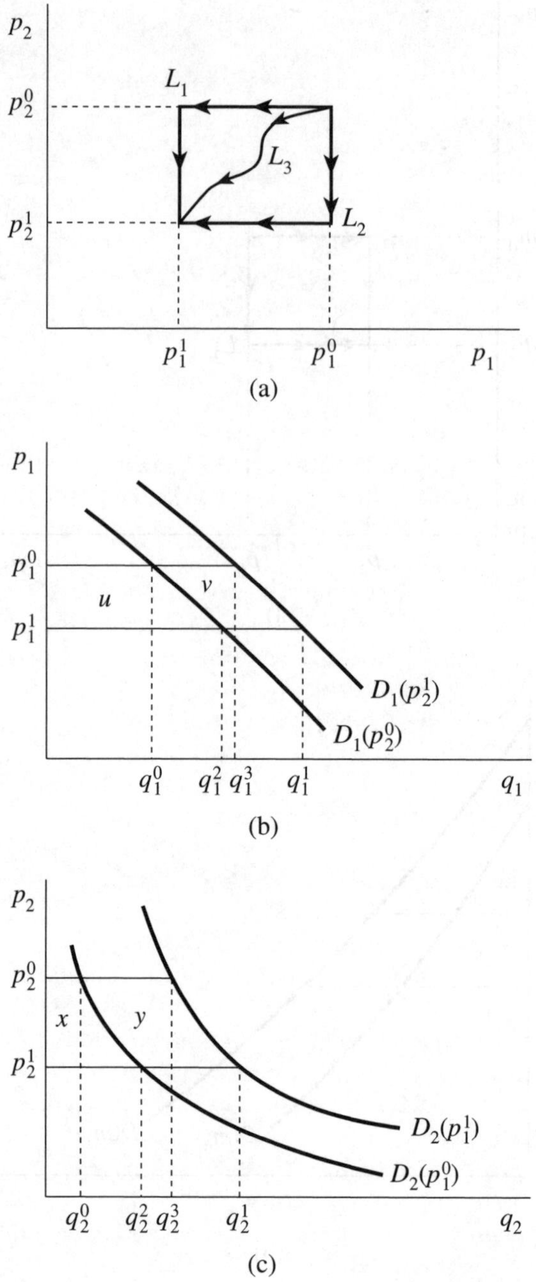
p_2
L_1
p_2^0
L_3
p_2^1
L_2
p_1^1
p_1^0
p_1
(a)
p_1
p_1^0
v
u
p_1^1
$D_1(p_2^1)$
$D_1(p_2^0)$
q_1^0
q_1^2 q_1^3
q_1^1
q_1
(b)
p_2
p_2^0
x
y
p_2^1
$D_2(p_1^1)$
$D_2(p_1^0)$
q_2^0
q_2^2 q_2^3
q_2^1
q_2
(c)

Figure 5.5

Along path L_1, the price of q_1 is first changed from p_1^0 to p_1^1, generating a gain of area u under the initial demand curve $D_1(p_2^0)$ in Figure 5.5(b). In the process, the demand curve for q_2 shifts from $D_2(p_1^0)$ to $D_2(p_1^1)$. Thus, an additional gain of area $x+y$ results in Figure 5.5(c) in subsequently moving the price of q_2 from (p_2^0 to p_2^1). Alternatively, if path L_2 is followed, a gain of area x is first generated in the q_2 market. Then a gain of area $u+v$ is obtained in the q_1 market. The resulting measures of welfare change associated with paths L_1 and L_2 – areas $u+x+y$ and $u+v+x$, respectively – need not be equal and in general will not be equal except in some special cases discussed in the following sections. Furthermore, these examples merely demonstrate the measures of welfare change resulting from two of many possible paths of price adjustment between prices (p_1^0,p_2^0) and (p_1^1,p_2^1). Many other price paths such as L_3 also exist and lead, in principle, to an endless number of measures of welfare change.

Thus, there is an ambiguity when determining the consumer surplus change associated with a multiple price and/or income change affecting consumers. (Recall that this was not generally the case with producers in Chapter 4.) The reason that the producer's case is, by comparison, unambiguous is that, under profit maximization, the owner or shareholder of the firm (producer) does not have preferences over any aspect of the firm's operation outside of its net money income (or profits). Price changes simply lead to an unambiguous expansion or contraction of the producer's or shareholder's budget constraint with no tilting of the budget surface in the space over which the producer has preferences. That is, an increase in profits to the producer is identical in effect with an increase in income to the consumer, so there is no divergence between the compensating and equivalent measures. In the consumer case, however, changes in prices lead to both income effects and substitution effects between commodities over which the interested party holds preferences.

5.3 UNIQUENESS OF CONSUMER SURPLUS

In view of the problems of path dependence, under what conditions does a *unique* money measure of welfare change exist? Of course, the problem of nonuniqueness arises only in the context of *money measurement* of welfare change (in contrast to the change in utility which is unique). But *money measurement of welfare change is the only reasonable approach for most applied economic welfare problems because consumer utility is not directly observable.* It should also be emphasized that *even though a money measure is unique, it does not necessarily follow that it measures utility change.*

Consider first the case of a simultaneous price–income change, as depicted in Figure 5.4, and the conditions under which the surplus change is unique. Examining the two particular paths L_1 and L_2, it is clear that the same result is obtained for any arbitrary price change if, and only if, the demand curves $D(m_0)$ and $D(m_1)$ coincide. Indeed, if the demand curve is uninfluenced by income changes, then the consumer surplus change in Figure 5.4(b) is the same regardless of which path may be followed between (p_0,m_0) and (p_1, m_1) in Figure 5.4(a). Thus, when both price and income change, *the consumer surplus measure is unique if, and only if, the income effect is zero* – meaning that the change in quantity consumed, Δq, associated with a change in income, Δm (that is, $\Delta q/\Delta m$), is zero. (Note that this does not imply a zero welfare effect.) Trivially, this condition is associated with zero income elasticity because income elasticity is defined by $(\Delta q/\Delta m)\cdot(m/q)$.[5] As shown in Appendix Section 5.B, this result can be generalized to the case where many prices as well as income change, in which case *uniqueness holds if, and only if, the income effects (or elasticities) of all goods for which prices possibly change along the path of adjustment are zero.* This condition cannot possibly hold if all prices and income change, because the change in income would not be offset by adjusting expenditures. Thus, the consumer's budget constraint would be violated.

It is also instructive to investigate the implications of uniqueness of the surplus measure in terms of the consumer's indifference map. The case where indifference curves lead to the same demand curve, regardless of income level, is demonstrated in Figure 5.6. The indifference curves in Figure 5.6(a) are I_1 and I_2. As income is changed from m_0 to m_1 at price p_1, the quantity consumed remains at q_1 because the associated tangencies of the budget lines with indifference curves lie directly above one another at a quantity of q_1. Thus, the demand curves for both levels of income include the point (p_1,q_1). Similarly, the budget line/indifference curve tangencies all occur at quantity q_0 when price is p_0. In other words, the same demand curve D results in Figure 5.6(b) regardless of income level. Furthermore, because the budget lines for different income levels but the same price must be parallel, it is clear that coincidence of the demand curve at different income levels is obtained if, and only if, the consumer's indifference curves are vertically parallel. In the latter case, the income-expansion path is a vertical straight line for any set of prices.

Turn now to the price–price change case depicted in Figure 5.5. In this case the two paths L_1 and L_2 lead to the same consumer surplus change if area $u+v+x=$ area $u+x+y$ (that is, if area $v=$ area y). Under what conditions would these areas be equal? To answer this question, consider arbitrary price changes, $\Delta p_1=p_1^0-p_1^1$ and $\Delta p_2=p_2^0-p_2^1$. If these price changes become small, v and y are approximately parallelograms, in which case the corresponding areas are given by the product of the price changes and the respective quantity changes, $\Delta q_1=q_1^3-q_1^0\doteq q_1^1-q_1^2$ and $\Delta q_2=q_2^3-q_2^0\doteq q_2^1-q_2^2$. Thus, the conditions of equality of areas v and y become $\Delta p_1\cdot\Delta q_1=\Delta p_2\cdot\Delta q_2$, or

$$\frac{\Delta q_1}{\Delta p_2}=\frac{\Delta q_2}{\Delta p_1}.$$

In intuitive terms, this condition implies that demand must be such that the change in consumption of the first good associated with a small unit change in the price of the second good must be the same as the change in consumption of the second good associated with a small unit change in the price of the first. If area $v=$ area y for all arbitrary sets of price changes, this condition must hold all along both sets of demand curves. As shown in a more rigorous mathematical framework in Appendix Section 5.B, this condition must hold for all pairs of goods for which prices possibly change in order to have uniqueness of consumer surplus in the general case where many prices change.

Consider, however, the economic implications of these conditions. As in the preceding case, an interesting implication can be developed by relating the conditions to a change in income. To do this, one can use the concept of *zero-degree homogeneity of demand in prices and income.* This implies that a consumer's consumption bundle choice is not altered as

5. More precisely, income elasticity of demand at a particular set of prices and income is defined as the percentage change in quantity demanded associated with a small unit percentage change in income and is given mathematically by $(\partial q/\partial m)\cdot(m/q)$, which is approximated in discrete terms by $(\Delta q/\Delta m)\cdot(m/q)$.

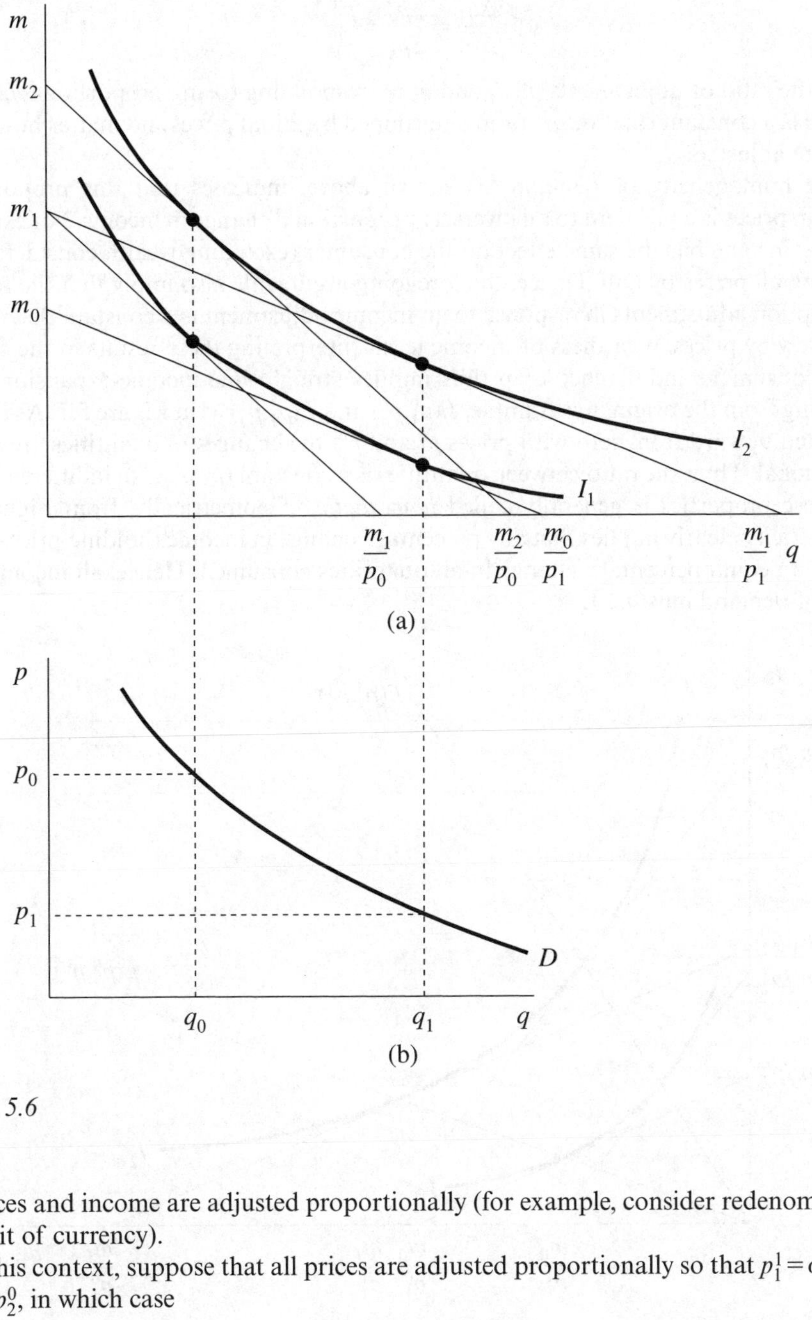

Figure 5.6

all prices and income are adjusted proportionally (for example, consider redenominating the unit of currency).

In this context, suppose that all prices are adjusted proportionally so that $p_1^1 = \alpha p_1^0$ and $p_2^1 = \alpha p_2^0$, in which case

$$\frac{\Delta p_2}{\Delta p_1} = \frac{(\alpha - 1)p_2^0}{(\alpha - 1)p_1^0} = \frac{p_2^0}{p_1^0}.$$

Using the path-independence conditions above, which correspond to equality of areas *v* and *y*, one thus finds that

$$\frac{\Delta q_1}{\Delta q_2} = \frac{\Delta p_2}{\Delta p_1} = \frac{p_2^0}{p_1^0}.$$

Hence, the ratio of adjustments of q_1 and q_2 corresponding to any proportional changes in prices is a constant (that is, the ratio determined by initial prices) no matter how much prices are adjusted.

Using homogeneity of demand, as shown above, indicates that this proportional change in prices is equivalent to an inversely proportional change in income. For example, doubling income has the same effect on the consumer (excluding wealth considerations) as cutting all prices by half. Hence, the foregoing arguments also imply that the ratio of consumption adjustments in response to an income adjustment is a constant determined completely by prices, regardless of income level. Interpreting these results in the context of the consumer's indifference map thus implies straight-line income-expansion paths emanating from the origin, for example, $E(p_1^0,p_2^0)$ and $E(p_1^1,p_2^1)$ as in Figure 5.7. As income is adjusted upward from zero with prices p_1^0 and p_2^0, the changes in quantities are always proportional. Thus, the ratio between quantities is a constant (p_2^0/p_1^0). An indifference map with these properties is generally called *homothetic*.[6] Geometrically, from Figure 5.7, homotheticity clearly implies that any percentage change in income (holding prices fixed) leads to an equal percentage change in all quantities consumed. Hence, all income elasticities of demand must be 1.

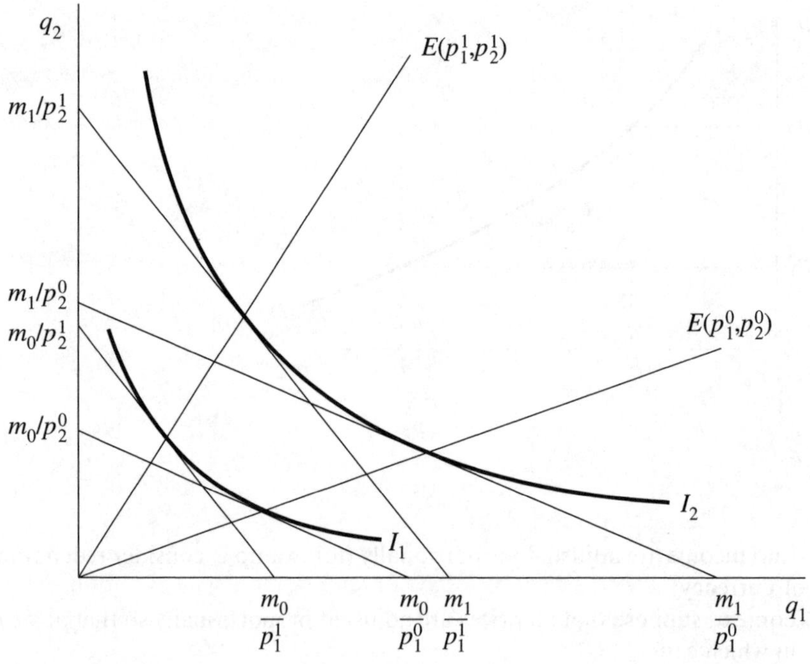

Figure 5.7

6. Mathematically, a homothetic function is any function $U(x)$ such that $U(x)=f(g(x))$, where $g(x)$ is any function such that $g(tx)=tg(x)$ for some scalar t, and $f(\cdot)$ is any monotonic function.

These results are indeed borne out by the mathematical derivation in Appendix Section 5.B. That is, *when all prices facing the consumer change, the consumer surplus change is uniquely defined if, and only if, the consumer's indifference map is homothetic, which occurs if, and only if, all income elasticities of demand are equal to 1.* However, Appendix Section 5.C further shows that if only some subset of prices change, then homotheticity is necessary with respect to merely the subset of goods for which prices change.[7] *A necessary and sufficient condition for uniqueness of consumer surplus change is that all income elasticities for the subset of goods with changing prices must be equal (but not necessarily equal to 1).*

Having determined the conditions under which the consumer surplus change is uniquely defined, one may consider the possibility of fulfilling these conditions in reality. For example, in the price–income change case, is one likely to find consumers in the real world who do not change their consumption of some goods as income changes? For a good such as salt, there may be many such consumers, but for most commodities there is overwhelming empirical evidence suggesting income effects. Similarly, in the price–price change case, one may consider the likelihood of finding consumers who adjust consumption of all or even several goods proportionally in response to income changes. For example, if a consumer receives a 10 percent increase in income, is he or she likely to increase consumption of both bread and movies by exactly 10 percent (or even by the same percentage)? Again, empirical evidence suggests different responses for many goods. Increases in income tend to be spent more on luxury goods and less on necessities at higher income levels. Thus, generally, the conditions for uniqueness of consumer surplus change may be so restrictive as to be unrealistic for many cases. Nevertheless, the applicability of the necessary conditions for applied work can be investigated empirically by estimating the associated income elasticities.

5.4 CONSTANCY OF THE MARGINAL UTILITY OF INCOME

Section 5.2 has shown that the consumer surplus measurement of the effect of a price–income or price–price change may depend on the path of adjustment followed in making the calculations. Section 5.3 has developed necessary and sufficient conditions under which the path-dependency problem vanishes and has further investigated the implications of these conditions for the preference structure of the consumer. A further important issue relates to whether or not the consumer surplus change provides a meaningful *money measure of utility change.* That is, under what conditions does a unique correspondence exist between the change in consumer surplus and the change in the consumer's actual utility?

The source of the present problem is depicted in Figure 5.8. With the utility function U_1, the same income change Δm may lead to a much different change in utility, ΔU or ΔU^*, depending on the initial income. With utility function U_2, however, the associated change in utility is the same regardless of the initial income. The utility function U_2 thus implies a constant marginal utility of income, at least with respect to income changes. As

7. Homotheticity with respect to a subset of goods implies that the budget-expansion paths in the associated subspace are straight lines through the origin where the relevant budget consists of income spent on only the subset of goods.

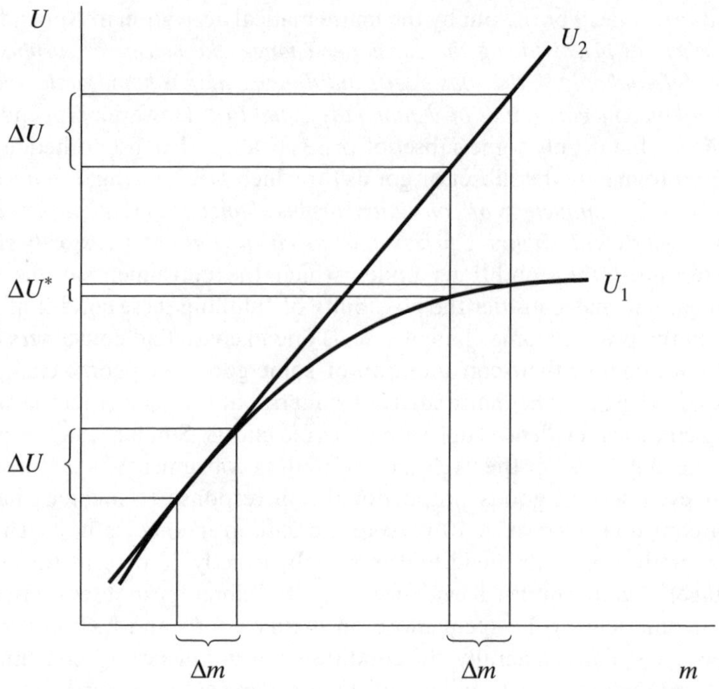

Figure 5.8

suggested by Section 5.1, the consumer surplus change is simply a money-equivalent measure of the effect of changing prices as well as, possibly, income. Hence, an unambiguous conversion of the surplus change ΔS into utility change ΔU can be made only when the slope of the utility function is constant, that is, when the marginal utility of income is constant with respect to all prices that change as well as with respect to income if it changes (note that Figure 5.8 depicts constancy of the marginal utility of income only with respect to income changes, not with respect to price changes).

Consider, for example, the price–price change case as depicted in Figure 5.9 where prices change from (p_1^0,p_2^0) to (p_1^1,p_2^1). To abstract from the problem of path dependence, consider only the path shown in Figure 5.9 and suppose that the surplus change associated with changing p_1 is ΔS_1 and the subsequent surplus change associated with changing p_2 is ΔS_2, where $\Delta S_2 = -\Delta S_1$. To examine the case where the marginal utility of income is not constant, suppose for simplicity that λ_1 is the marginal utility of income along the first segment of the path and that λ_2 is the marginal utility of income along the second segment of the path. Because ΔS_1 is the income-equivalent change along the first segment and λ_1, the change in utility per unit change in income, is constant along that segment, the surplus or income-equivalent change can be converted into utility change by multiplying by λ_1. Thus, $\Delta U_1 = \lambda_1 \Delta S_1$, where ΔU_1 is the utility change along the first segment of the path in Figure 5.9. Similarly, $\Delta U_2 = \lambda_2 \Delta S_2$, where ΔU_2 represents the utility change along the second segment of the path. The total utility change is thus $\Delta U = \Delta U_1 + \Delta U_2$.

To see the problem that can arise (even when path-independence conditions hold), note

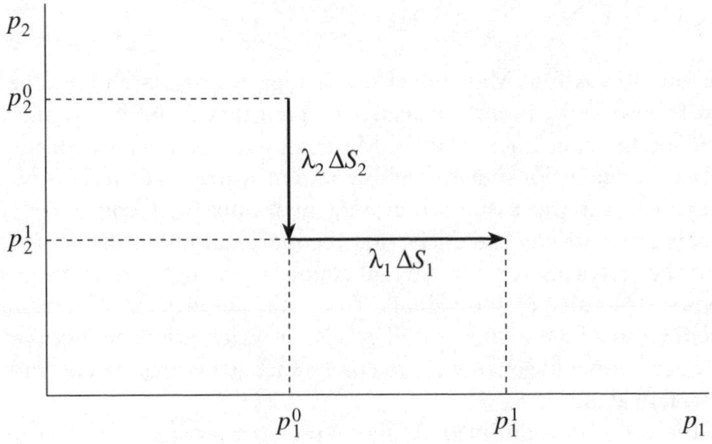

Figure 5.9

that the total surplus change is $\Delta S = \Delta S_1 + \Delta S_2 = 0$, whereas $\Delta U \neq 0$ if $\lambda_1 \neq \lambda_2$. In other words, *even with path independence, ΔS may not behave in a way qualitatively similar to ΔU. Thus, uniqueness of ΔS is not sufficient to guarantee any meaningful interpretation of ΔS as a money measure of utility change.* To be a meaningful money measure of utility change, ΔS must be at least qualitatively related to ΔU. That is, ΔS and ΔU must be of the same arithmetic sign regardless of the particular price change. As shown in Appendix Section 5.C, this relationship holds only when the factor λ, which converts income (equivalent) change into utility change, is constant over the entire set of price changes under consideration, that is, when the marginal utility of income is constant.

Appendix Section 5.C also shows that *constancy of the marginal utility of income guarantees path independence of ΔS* (but not vice versa). Hence, the condition of constancy λ is at least as restrictive as the implications of path independence outlined in Section 5.3 (in fact, more so). As indicated there, the economic implications of these conditions on the consumer indifference map are so restrictive as to prevent use of the 'money measure of utility change' approach in an *a priori* sense for essentially all practical purposes. That is, one would have little basis for estimating money measures of utility change without first carrying out considerable empirical analysis to determine, for example, whether or not all income elasticities of demand are consistent with the implications of path independence. Even then, constancy of the marginal utility of income may not hold.

It is important to stress that *constancy of the marginal utility of income guarantees path independence of ΔS, but not vice versa.* This has been a major source of confusion underlying the theory of welfare measurement. Often the phrases 'zero-income effect' and 'constancy of the marginal utility of income' have been treated as meaning the same thing. They simply do not. Once they are viewed separately, it becomes clear that, *even though one can obtain a unique measure of consumer surplus, that surplus need not measure utility change. Consumer surplus* measures utility change only when the marginal utility of income is constant.

5.5 CONCLUSIONS

The famous economist Alfred Marshall (1930) instigated the search (and the many controversies that followed) for money measures of gain that could be uniquely related to utility changes for the consumer. That is, Marshall was concerned with the conditions under which the change in consumer surplus could measure a *true surplus* of utility. This chapter has shown that the assumptions that guarantee that consumer surplus is a measure of such a *true surplus* – namely, that the marginal utility of income is constant with respect to the prices and/or income that change – are highly restrictive with respect to the preference structures of individuals. To obtain uniqueness of consumer surplus, income elasticities must be the same for all goods for which prices change and these elasticities must be zero if income changes. Such preference structures are contradicted by the bulk of empirical evidence.

Because of the conditions outlined in this chapter, the prospects for consumer welfare measurement may appear bleak at this point. However, further possibilities exist for determining whether or not given changes are in a consumer's best interest. Having determined that the original definitions and their later refinements have some serious problems from the standpoint of empirical application, Chapter 6 returns to the general concepts of willingnes to pay, as set forth in Chapters 1 and 3. These concepts, although also not having a direct correspondence with utility change, at least lead to unambiguous interpretation in empirical work.

Appendix to Chapter 5: Nonuniqueness of consumer surplus

The purpose of this appendix is to provide a rigorous mathematical analysis of consumer surplus as a measure of consumer welfare. Measurement of welfare change is considered for a single utility-maximizing consumer in a comparative static sense. Section 5.A presents a mathematical analysis of the conjectures of Marshall (1930) and Hicks (1956) discussed in Chapter 5, which began with the work by Patinkin (1963) and Samuelson (1942). Each of the latter authors was concerned with the implications and necessity of constant marginal utility of income as a condition leading to validity of consumer surplus in measuring the welfare change associated with a single price change. The problem of consumer welfare measurement with multiple price changes was introduced by Hotelling (1938) and has been examined in some detail by Harberger (1971), Silberberg (1972), Burns (1977), Richter (1974) and Chipman and Moore (1976, 1980).

Section 5.B gives a rigorous treatment of the problem of path dependence identified by these studies. Among these authors, Silberberg and Richter have cast great doubt on the usefulness of consumer surplus as a *money measure* of utility change because very stringent conditions are required to assure uniqueness of the measure irrespective of the prices and income that change. For example, Richter argued that because of path-dependence problems, construction of a broadly applicable money measure of utility change is not possible.

Section 5.C shows that, rather than path independence, the fundamental requirement for a money measure of welfare change is constancy of the marginal utility of income as originally suggested by Samuelson. Thus, the marginal utility of income needs to be constant only with respect to the prices that change (and income if it changes). Thus, the full set of path-independence conditions need not apply for most practical problems of welfare measurement. The necessary conditions are at least possible and may even be plausible for certain problems. Nevertheless, meaningful aggregation of money measures of welfare change is not possible because the marginal utility of income cannot be measured. Thus, the fatal problem for money measurement of utility change is the ultimate necessity of interpersonal comparisons in applied welfare analysis.

5.A THE PURE CONSUMER CASE

Consider a consumer with (ordinal) utility function $U(\boldsymbol{q})$, $\boldsymbol{q}=(q_1,\ldots,q_N)$, assumed to be monotonically increasing ($\partial U/\partial \boldsymbol{q}>0$), quasiconcave and twice differentiable in $\boldsymbol{q}$, where $\boldsymbol{q}$ is a vector of consumption quantities.[1] The budget constraint is given by

1. *Quasiconcavity* simply implies nonincreasing marginal rates of substitution or that indifference curves are nowhere concave to the origin. For a further explanation, see Takayama (1985, ch. 1, s. E) or Zangwill (1969, pp. 25–36).

$$m = \boldsymbol{pq} \tag{5.1}$$

where $\boldsymbol{p} = (p_1, \ldots, p_N)$ is a vector of prices corresponding to $\boldsymbol{q}$ and, for simplicity, $\boldsymbol{pq} = \Sigma_{i=1}^{N} p_i q_i$. Hence, assuming an internal solution, the consumer's utility maximization problem subject to the budget constraint,

$$\max_{\boldsymbol{q}} \{ U(\boldsymbol{q}) | m = \boldsymbol{pq}, \boldsymbol{q} \geq 0 \},$$

can be solved by maximizing the Lagrangian,[2]

$$\mathscr{L} = U(\boldsymbol{q}) + \lambda(m - \boldsymbol{pq}).$$

First-order conditions for a maximum imply that

$$\boldsymbol{U_q} = \lambda \boldsymbol{p}, \tag{5.2}$$

and (5.1) must hold at the optimum (where subscripts of U denote differentiation, that is, $\boldsymbol{U_q} \equiv \partial U / \partial \boldsymbol{q} = (\partial U / \partial q_1, \ldots, \partial U / \partial q_N)$. Second-order necessary conditions are satisfied under the quasiconcavity assumption. As pointed out by Samuelson (1942), the Lagrangian multiplier λ can be interpreted as the marginal utility of income. Furthermore, when second-order conditions hold, equations (5.1) and (5.2) can be solved for the ordinary demand functions,

$$\boldsymbol{q} = [\tilde{q}_1(\boldsymbol{p}, m), \ldots, \tilde{q}_N(\boldsymbol{p}, m)] \equiv \tilde{q}(\boldsymbol{p}, m) \tag{5.3}$$

(see Henderson and Quandt 1971, pp. 407–8 or Varian 1992, ch. 7). Substituting (5.3) into the utility function U yields

$$U \equiv U(\tilde{\boldsymbol{q}}(\boldsymbol{p}, m)) \equiv V(\boldsymbol{p}, m) \equiv V,$$

where V is the indirect utility function. To clarify notation, the tildes which appear above q and q_1, ..., q_N in this appendix denote ordinary Marshallian demands in contrast to Hicksian demands that are introduced in Chapter 6.

Using the definition of the indirect utility function, one finds that the change in utility associated with a change in prices and income from $(\boldsymbol{p}^0, m_0)$ to $(\boldsymbol{p}^1, m_1)$, where $\boldsymbol{p}^j = (p_1^j, \ldots, p_N^j)$, $j = 0, 1$, can be represented as a line integral,

$$\begin{aligned} \Delta U &= V(\boldsymbol{p}^1, m_1) - V(\boldsymbol{p}^0, m_0) \\ &= \int_L dV = \int_L [V_m dm + \boldsymbol{V_p} d\boldsymbol{p}], \end{aligned} \tag{5.4}$$

2. An internal solution means that the nonnegativity constraints on consumption, $\boldsymbol{q} \geq 0$, are not binding. While this assumption simplifies the discussion below, the more general case can be analyzed with Kuhn–Tucker conditions in which case the marginal results below apply only for goods with positive quantities. For explanation of Kuhn–Tucker conditions, see Zangwill (1969).

where $V_p dp \equiv \Sigma_{i=1}^N V_i dp_i$ (where subscripts of V represent differentiation, for example, $V_i \equiv \partial V / \partial p_i$ and $V_m \equiv \partial V / \partial m \equiv \lambda$) and L represents some path of integration in price–income space from $(\mathbf{p}^0, m_0)$ to $(\mathbf{p}^1, m_1)$. Also, substituting[3]

$$dV = dU = \mathbf{U}_q d\tilde{\mathbf{q}}$$

(where $\mathbf{U}_q d\tilde{\mathbf{q}} = \Sigma_{i=1}^N U_i d\tilde{q}_i$) into (5.4) and using (5.2) yields

$$\Delta U = \int_L \mathbf{U}_q d\tilde{\mathbf{q}} = \int_L \lambda \mathbf{p} d\tilde{\mathbf{q}}. \tag{5.5}$$

Now, using the total differential of the budget constraint,

$$dm - \tilde{\mathbf{q}} d\mathbf{p} = \mathbf{p} d\tilde{\mathbf{q}},$$

equation (5.5) becomes

$$\Delta U = \int_L \lambda [dm - \tilde{\mathbf{q}} d\mathbf{p}]. \tag{5.6}$$

This line integral gives an exact measure of utility change regardless of the path L.[4]

However, some further modification is required before (5.6) becomes useful for empirical measurement of welfare change because the marginal utility of income λ is, in general, unobservable. Consequently, the attention of economists has focused on conditions under which (5.6) can be converted to a money measure of utility change. The usual approach in this context has been to assume λ 'approximately' constant over the path L and thus divide (5.6) by λ to obtain the money measure $\Delta U / \lambda$. Alternatively, Silberberg (1972) investigates the case where λ is not necessarily constant by converting the integrand of

3. Note that $\tilde{\mathbf{q}}(\mathbf{p}, m)$ is frequently written without its arguments as $\tilde{\mathbf{q}}$ throughout this appendix for simplicity of notation.
4. A line integral between any two given points,

$$\int_L \sum_{i=1}^N g_i(z_1, \ldots, z_N) dz_i$$

is independent of the path L if

$$g_{ij} \equiv \frac{\partial g_i}{\partial z_j} = \frac{\partial g_j}{\partial z_i} \equiv g_{ji}, \quad i, j = 1, \ldots, N.$$

Equivalently, if there exists a function $f = f(z_1, \ldots, z_N)$ such that

$$g_i \equiv f_i \equiv \frac{\partial f}{\partial z_i}, \quad i, j = 1, \ldots, N.$$

then the integrability conditions (for path independence) are automatically satisfied because

$$g_{ij} = \frac{\partial^2 f}{\partial z_i \partial z_j} = \frac{\partial^2 f}{\partial z_j \partial z_j} = g_{ji}$$

always holds. Hence, the integrand is an exact differential and thus

$$\int_L \sum_{i=1}^N g_i(z_1, \ldots, z_N) dz_i = \int_L df = \Delta f.$$

Clearly, by the construction in (5.4), the integrand in (5.6) is such an exact differential. See Danese (1965, pp. 123–9).

(5.6) to money terms through division by λ. Because $1/\lambda$ can be interpreted as the marginal cost of utility or as 'the imputed marginal rent associated with the level of utility at a point along [L]', Silberberg argues that this measure, ΔS, can be regarded as the limit of a sum of marginal dollar rents associated with utility change *along a specified path.* Either way, the line integral of interest is

$$\Delta S = \int_L [dm - \tilde{\boldsymbol{q}} d\boldsymbol{p}]. \tag{5.7}$$

If λ is constant along L, then $\Delta S = \Delta U/\lambda$, whereas if λ is not constant, ΔS is not proportional to ΔU but simply measures a particular imputed dollar gain assigned by the consumer to the utility change.

One must then consider the conditions under which λ can possibly be constant along L or, at least, conditions under which ΔS is a unique measure. To do this, consider Roy's identity,[5]

$$\tilde{\boldsymbol{q}} = -\frac{\boldsymbol{V_p}}{V_m}.$$

Now, rearranging, one has

$$-\lambda\tilde{\boldsymbol{q}} = \boldsymbol{V_p}$$

because $V_m \equiv \lambda$. Thus, differentiation with respect to m yields

$$-\lambda\tilde{\boldsymbol{q}}_{\boldsymbol{m}} - \tilde{\boldsymbol{q}}\lambda_{\boldsymbol{m}} = \boldsymbol{\lambda_p} \tag{5.8}$$

(where subscripts denote differentiation in all cases) because, by definition,

$$\boldsymbol{\lambda_p} \equiv \frac{\partial V_m}{\partial \boldsymbol{p}} \equiv \frac{\partial^2 V}{\partial \boldsymbol{p}\partial m} \equiv \frac{\partial \boldsymbol{V_p}}{\partial m}.$$

5. Roy's (1947) identity can be derived by noting that, at the optimum utility level $\bar{U}$,

$$\bar{U} = U(\tilde{\boldsymbol{q}}(\boldsymbol{p},m)) = V(\boldsymbol{p},m).$$

If the marginal utility of income is always positive, $V_m > 0$, then one can solve for an inverse function V^{-1} that expresses income as a function of prices and the utility level,

$$m = V^{-1}(\boldsymbol{p},\bar{U}).$$

Now, substituting V^{-1} for m in the indirect utility function above yields the identity

$$\bar{U} = V(\boldsymbol{p}, V^{-1}(\boldsymbol{p},\bar{U})).$$

Differentiation with respect to $\boldsymbol{p}$ thus implies that

$$0 = \boldsymbol{V_p} + V_m \frac{\partial V^{-1}}{\partial \boldsymbol{p}} = \boldsymbol{V_p} + V_m \frac{\partial m}{\partial \boldsymbol{p}} = \boldsymbol{V_p} + V_m \tilde{\boldsymbol{q}}.$$

The Roy equation follows immediately. The reader might note that the inverse function $V^{-1}(\boldsymbol{p},\bar{U})$ used here is simply the expenditure functione $e(\boldsymbol{p},\bar{U})$ commonly used to describe the minimum income necessary to attain a given utility level with a given set of prices. See Appendix Section 6.A for a detailed explanation and proof that $\partial e/\partial p_j = q_j$.

It is thus evident that λ cannot be constant with respect to all prices and income because $\boldsymbol{\lambda}_p = \mathbf{0}$ and $\lambda_m = 0$ imply from (5.8) that $\tilde{\boldsymbol{q}}_m = 0$, but the budget constraint implies that

$$1 = \frac{\partial m}{\partial m} = \frac{\partial \boldsymbol{p}\tilde{\boldsymbol{q}}}{\partial m} = \boldsymbol{p}\tilde{\boldsymbol{q}}_m,$$

which cannot hold if $\tilde{\boldsymbol{q}}_m = 0$. Thus, at most, λ can be constant with respect to all prices but not income or with respect to income and $N-1$ prices. Samuelson interprets the former case as the Marshallian definition of the constancy of marginal utility of income, whereas the second case is associated with constancy of the marginal utility of 'money' where the Nth good is taken as the numeraire or money, which thus has a constant price.[6] Thus, one must carefully specify with respect to which prices (and income) the marginal utility of income is assumed to be constant. Similarly, in examining path dependence, ΔS cannot possibly be unique when all prices and income change. In fact, as shown in the following section, the various assumptions about constancy of the marginal utility of income have a very close relationship with the path-dependence problem.

5.B PATH DEPENDENCE OF CONSUMER SURPLUS

The integrand of (5.7) is not necessarily an exact differential. Hence, one must verify the path-independence conditions,[7]

$$\frac{\partial \tilde{q}_i}{\partial m} = \frac{\partial (1)}{\partial p_i} \equiv 0, \; i = 1, \ldots, N, \tag{5.9}$$

$$\frac{\partial \tilde{q}_i}{\partial p_j} = \frac{\partial \tilde{q}_j}{\partial p_i}, \; i, j = 1, \ldots, N. \tag{5.10}$$

Obviously, all these conditions cannot hold simultaneously because (as in the proof that λ cannot be constant with respect to all prices and income) $\tilde{\boldsymbol{q}}_m = 0$ as in (5.9) implies that the budget constraint would be violated with a change in income, *ceteris paribus* (because income changes while consumption and prices do not change).

Because all the conditions in (5.9) and (5.10) cannot hold simultaneously, it has been necessary in the literature to constrain price and income changes to some subset of price–income space. For example, Silberberg considers changes in all prices but holds income constant. Hence, where $dm \equiv 0$, the integral in (5.7) becomes

$$S = -\textstyle\int_L \tilde{\boldsymbol{q}} d\boldsymbol{p}. \tag{5.11}$$

The relevant path-independence conditions are given by[8]

$$\frac{\partial \tilde{q}_i}{\partial p_j} = \frac{\partial \tilde{q}_j}{\partial p_i}, \; i, j = 1, \ldots, N. \tag{5.12}$$

6. In the latter case one can easily show that the marginal utility of money and the marginal utility of income must always be the same (at equilibrium) because the first-order conditions in (5.2) imply that $U_N = \lambda$ if $p_N = 1$.
7. These conditions are derived by applying footnote 4 to equation (5.7).
8. See footnote 4.

Richter, on the other hand, considers the price of one good, q_N (the numeraire), fixed while all other prices and income may vary. In his case, (5.7) becomes

$$\Delta S = \int_L [dm - \tilde{\mathbf{q}}d\mathbf{p}], \tag{5.13}$$

where $dp_N \equiv 0$ and path-independence conditions are

$$\frac{\partial \tilde{q}_i}{\partial m} = 0, \quad i, = 1, \ldots, N-1, \tag{5.14}$$

$$\frac{\partial \tilde{q}_i}{\partial p_j} = \frac{\partial \tilde{q}_j}{\partial p_i}, \quad i, j = 1, \ldots, N-1. \tag{5.15}$$

Interestingly, the path-independence conditions in Silberberg's and Richter's cases are conditions implied by constancy of the marginal utility of income λ under the two alternative interpretations discussed by Samuelson. That is, the conditions for path independence are implied by the conditions under which λ can be factored out of (5.6) and placed in the left-hand denominator (that is, where $\Delta S = \Delta U/\lambda$), obtaining (5.11) or (5.13) if $dm \equiv 0$ or $dp_N \equiv 0$, respectively. Thus, the path-independence conditions for (5.6) can be represented generally by

$$\frac{\partial \lambda \tilde{q}_i}{\partial m} = \frac{\partial \lambda}{\partial p_i}, \quad i, = 1, \ldots, N-1, \tag{5.16}$$

$$\frac{\partial \lambda \tilde{q}_i}{\partial p_j} = \frac{\partial \lambda \tilde{q}_j}{\partial p_i}, \quad i, j = 1, \ldots, N-1, \tag{5.17}$$

which must always hold (by construction) because the integrand is an exact differential of V. Assuming $\partial \lambda / \partial p_i = 0$, $i, = 1, \ldots, N$ as in the Silberberg case, thus yields (5.12) immediately from (5.17) while assuming that $\partial \lambda / \partial m = 0$ and $\partial \lambda / \partial p_i = 0$, $i, = 1, \ldots, N-1$, as in the Richter case, yields (5.14) and (5.15) immediately from (5.16) and (5.17).[9] Conversely, however, path independence does not imply constancy of the marginal utility of income. Using the path-independence conditions in (5.14) and (5.15), for example, implies only that

$$q_i \frac{\partial \lambda}{\partial m} = \frac{\partial \lambda}{\partial p_i}, \quad i, = 1, \ldots, N-1,$$

$$q_i \frac{\partial \lambda}{\partial p_j} = q_j \frac{\partial \lambda}{\partial p_i}, \quad i, j = 1, \ldots, N-1.$$

As Mishan (1977, p. 12) has pointed out, this condition requires only that 'λ change at the same rate for each of the price changes (when connected by relative expenditures on the goods)'.

9. Although neither Silberberg nor Richter makes this relationship clear, Richter is perhaps somewhat misleading because he explicitly assumes λ constant and then belabors the derivation of conditions for path independence which, as shown above, are immediate and hold automatically with constancy of λ.

5.C MONEY MEASURES OF UTILITY CHANGE AND CONSTANCY OF THE MARGINAL UTILITY OF INCOME

The Silberberg and Richter studies attempt to develop conditions under which consumer surplus concepts can be used to measure utility change in money terms. As they find, these conditions lead to some rather restrictive and, perhaps, unrealistic utility indifference maps. Silberberg finds that, in the case where all prices can change but income does not, path-independence conditions in (5.12) hold if and only if consumer utility is homothetic, which holds if and only if all income elasticities are equal to 1 (that is, the income–consumption paths are rays emanating from the origin).[10]

In the Richter case, where one price is fixed, the conditions in (5.15) are implied by (5.14) because, by the Slutsky equation,[11]

$$\begin{aligned}\frac{\partial \tilde{q}_i}{\partial p_j} &= \frac{\partial \bar{q}_i}{\partial p_j} - \tilde{q}_j \frac{\partial \tilde{q}_i}{\partial m} = \frac{\partial \bar{q}_i}{\partial p_j} = \frac{\partial \bar{q}_j}{\partial p_i} \\ &= \frac{\partial \tilde{q}_j}{\partial p_i} - \tilde{q}_i \frac{\partial \tilde{q}_j}{\partial m} = \frac{\partial \tilde{q}_j}{\partial p_i}\end{aligned} \tag{5.18}$$

if $\partial \tilde{q}_i/\partial m = \partial \tilde{q}_j/\partial m = 0$ (where $\partial \bar{q}_i/\partial p_j$ is the partial derivative of q_i with respect to p_j holding utility rather than income constant). But (5.14) holds if and only if income elasticities are zero[12] (or, in other words, if and only if income effects are zero) for the first $N-1$ goods. Hence, all increases in income are spent entirely on one good – the numeraire q_N.

Clearly, the foregoing cases are too restrictive to provide an acceptable basis for analysis of economic welfare generally. If, however, only a subset of prices and possibly income change, the restrictions on utility surfaces and demand functions are reduced. That is,

10. To see the equivalence of path independence with the latter condition, one need merely consider the budget constraint in conjunction with the result (proved below) from path independence that income elasticities must be equal among all goods for which prices change. If all prices change and hence all income elasticities are equal, a change in income will violate the budget constraint unless all income elasticities are equal to 1. To see that path independence implies equality among income elasticities, note that (5.17) implies that

$$\tilde{q}_i \frac{\partial \lambda}{\partial p_j} + \lambda \frac{\partial \tilde{q}_i}{\partial p_j} = \tilde{q}_j \frac{\partial \lambda}{\partial p_i} + \lambda \frac{\partial \tilde{q}_j}{\partial p_i}.$$

Hence, by path independence,

$$\tilde{q}_i \frac{\partial \lambda}{\partial p_j} = \tilde{q}_j \frac{\partial \lambda}{\partial p_i}.$$

Now, multiplying both sides by $m/(\tilde{q}_i\tilde{q}_j)$ and using (5.8) yields

$$\frac{m}{\tilde{q}_j}\frac{\partial \tilde{q}_j}{\partial m} = \frac{m}{\tilde{q}_i}\frac{\partial \tilde{q}_i}{\partial m}.$$

11. The middle equality of (5.18) follows from the symmetry of the Hessian. See Henderson and Quandt (1971, p. 36) or Varian (1992, ch. 8). The derivatives that hold utility rather than income constant are the derivatives of the Hicksian demands as defined in the Appendix to Chapter 6.

12. Geometrically, the condition of zero income elasticities implies vertical income–consumption paths and is equivalent to the well-known case of *vertically parallel indifference curves*. See Figure 5.6 and the related discussion in Section 5.3 for the geometric interpretation. Preferences that generate vertically parallel indifference curves are called *quasilinear preferences* with respect to the good on the vertical axis (see Mas-Colell, Whinston and Green 1995, p. 45). When preferences are quasilinear with respect to the numeraire, then the indirect utility function is of the form $V(\mathbf{p},m) = V^*(\mathbf{p}) + m$ where $\mathbf{p}^*$ is the vector of prices with the numeraire price omitted (see Mas-Colell, Whinston and Green 1995, p. 317).

suppose (for simplicity) that only the first k prices and possibly income change with the imposition of some policy, say, from prices $(p_1^0,\ldots,p_k^0,p_{k+1}^0,\ldots,p_N^0)$ to prices $(p_1^1,\ldots,p_k^1, p_{k+1}^0,\ldots,p_N^0)$ and from income m_0 to m_1.

Because the integrand in (5.6) is an exact differential, the value of the integral is independent of the path of integration, and one may choose an arbitrary path along which to evaluate it. Consider, for example, the path where income is changed first, and then the k prices are changed in order from initial to final values. For notational convenience, let

$$\hat{\mathbf{p}}_0(m) \equiv (p_1^0,\ldots,p_N^0,m)$$

and

$$\hat{\mathbf{p}}_i(p_i) \equiv (p_1^1,\ldots,p_{i-1}^1,p_i,p_{i+1}^0,\ldots,p_N^0). \tag{5.19}$$

Then the line integral in (5.6) can be written as a sum of intermediate line integrals and, finally, as a sum of ordinary definite integrals as follows (see Danese 1965, p. 103),

$$\begin{aligned} \Delta U &= \int_L \lambda[dm - \tilde{\mathbf{q}}d\mathbf{p}] \\ &= \int_{\hat{\mathbf{p}}_0(m_0)}^{\hat{\mathbf{p}}_0(m_1)} \lambda[dm - \tilde{\mathbf{q}}d\mathbf{p}] + \sum_{j=1}^{k} \int_{\hat{\mathbf{p}}_j(p_j^0)}^{\hat{\mathbf{p}}_j(p_j^1)} \lambda[dm - \tilde{\mathbf{q}}d\mathbf{p}]\ \mathrm{p} \\ &= \int_{m_0}^{m_1} \lambda(\hat{\mathbf{p}}_0(m))dm - \sum_{j=1}^{k} \int_{p_i^0}^{p_j^1} \lambda(\hat{\mathbf{p}}_j(p_j),m_0)\tilde{q}_j(\hat{\mathbf{p}}_j(p_j),m_0)dp_j, \end{aligned} \tag{5.20}$$

where, in the latter step, λ and $\tilde{q}_j$ are written as explicitly dependent on prices and income.

From (5.20), if λ is constant only with respect to k prices that change (and income if it changes), then it can be factored out and taken to the left side, obtaining a unique money measure of utility change,

$$\Delta S = \Delta U/\lambda = \int_{m_0}^{m_1} dm - \sum_{j=1}^{k} \int_{p_j^0}^{p_j^1} \tilde{q}_j(\hat{\mathbf{p}}_j(p_j),m_0)dp_j \tag{5.21}$$

$$= \Delta m + \sum_{j=1}^{k} \Delta S_j, \tag{5.22}$$

where ΔS_j represents the change in consumer surplus in market j as a function of initial and final price vectors given by

$$\Delta S_j(\hat{\mathbf{p}}_j(p_j^0),\hat{\mathbf{p}}_j(p_j^1)) \equiv \int_{p_i^0}^{p_j^1} \tilde{q}_j(\hat{\mathbf{p}}_j(p_j),m_0)dp_j. \tag{5.23}$$

Furthermore, if income does not change from the initial to the final price–income position, the first right-hand term of equations (5.20) through (5.22) can be deleted, in which case constancy of λ with respect to income is not necessary.

The foregoing results imply that, whenever the marginal utility of income λ is constant with respect to only the prices (and income) that change, a money measure of utility change is obtained by adding (to the change in income) the changes in consumer surpluses in the markets where prices change. However, the consumer surpluses in successive markets must be evaluated along ordinary demand curves conditioned on all previously considered changes. Because the methodology leading to (5.20) and (5.22) is path independent, the order of consideration of price changes (markets) makes no difference.

These results imply that λ need be constant only with respect to the prices that change (and income if it changes) between the initial and final states. The resulting conditions, which may be useful in certain specific situations, are much less restrictive than those developed by Samuelson, Silberberg, Richter and others for their general cases. Nevertheless, some strong restrictions are required of the utility function even in this less stringent case. For example, if income and any other price p_j changes and, to attain a money measure, one assumes $\partial\lambda/\partial m = \partial\lambda/\partial p_j = 0$ for some good j, then using equation (5.8),

$$0 = \frac{\partial\lambda}{\partial p_j} = -\lambda\frac{\partial\tilde{q}_j}{\partial m} - \tilde{q}_j\frac{\partial\lambda}{\partial m} = -\lambda\frac{\partial\tilde{q}_j}{\partial m}. \tag{5.24}$$

Hence, zero income elasticities (or zero-income effects) are required for all prices that change.

If prices p_i and p_j change and, to attain a money measure, one assumes $\partial\lambda/\partial p_i = \partial\lambda/\partial p_j = 0$, then the first two equalities in (5.24) hold for both i and j, which implies

$$\frac{1}{\tilde{q}_i}\frac{\partial\tilde{q}_i}{\partial m} = -\frac{1}{\lambda}\frac{\partial\lambda}{\partial m} = \frac{1}{\tilde{q}_j}\frac{\partial\tilde{q}_j}{\partial m}.$$

Thus, (multiplying through by m) all income elasticities for prices that change must be the same although not necessarily equal to 1 or 0.

Finally, as a special case of (5.22), the early hypothesis of Marshall can be verified – specifically, if the marginal utility of income is constant with respect to the change of a single price p_j, then

$$\frac{\Delta U}{\lambda} = -\int_{p_i^0}^{p_j^1} \tilde{q}_j dp_j = \Delta S_j. \tag{5.25}$$

Thus, the change in consumer surplus in that market alone is a unique money measure of utility change.[13]

In summary, a unique money measure of utility change can be established under two conditions: (1) if $\partial\tilde{q}_i/\partial p_j = \partial\tilde{q}_j/\partial p_i$ for all pairs of prices that change[14] or (2) if λ is constant

13. Silberberg is somewhat unclear on this point because he indicates that the integral in (5.25), considered as a line integral, may be path dependent if prices p_i, $i \neq j$, change along the path of integration even though they finally attain their initial values. This is indeed true when λ is not constant with respect to the prices (income) for which final values are different from the initial values. However, by writing ΔU with an exact differential as integrand following (5.20), only constancy of λ with respect to p_j is required to obtain (5.25) as a definite integral. In effect, the ambiguity found by Silberberg results from looking for a money measure of utility change in a subspace (generated by other price movements) in which utility does not change.
14. Although not shown explicitly earlier, income cannot be held constant in case (1). As Silberberg has shown, integrating by parts yields

$$\begin{aligned}\Delta S &= \textstyle\int_L \mathbf{p}\, d\tilde{\mathbf{q}} \\ &= \mathbf{p}^1\tilde{\mathbf{q}}(\mathbf{p}^1, m_1) - \mathbf{p}^0\tilde{\mathbf{q}}(\mathbf{p}^0, m_0) - \textstyle\int_L \tilde{\mathbf{q}}\, d\mathbf{p} \\ &= m_1 - m_0 - \textstyle\int_L \tilde{\mathbf{q}}\, d\mathbf{p}.\end{aligned}$$

Thus, only the conditions in (1) are necessary for path independence in this case.

with respect to the prices that change (and income if it changes). In the former case the utility function must be homothetic with respect to the goods for which prices change, while in either case income elasticities associated with all prices that change must be the same, and these must be zero if income changes.

Unfortunately, the simple conclusions relating to (5.20) through (5.22) in the general Silberberg case, where all prices possibly change and λ is not constant, are not possible. Unless the path-independence conditions in (5.9) and (5.10) are satisfied for the prices that change (and income if it changes), an attempt to divide the integrands of (5.20) by λ turns out to correspond to only one of many possible paths in (5.11) or (5.13).

In view of these arguments, it has been suggested by Burns (1977), for example, that the class of paths considered should be restricted in some way. As pointed out by Richter (1974), however:

> various characterizations of reasonable paths of integration do not really get around the difficulty. Most importantly, the creation of a money index of utility change is a comparative statics exercise. By the very nature of such exercises one should not have to appeal to the particular adjustment path followed, reasonable or otherwise, in defining the welfare change measure. … Why in a comparative statics analysis should the actual adjustment path between the two static equilibria have any theoretical importance? Why in a comparative statics analysis should any one path be more interesting than another path?

Yet another difficulty is encountered in using money measures of utility change. Suppose that a unique money measure of utility change is obtained for each of two consumers. One must then consider what basis is gained for investigating policy actions that affect both. More restrictive assumptions are required to compare money measures among individuals. For example, suppose that a policy-maker seeks simply to maximize the sum of the two consumers' utilities. As explained in Section 6.1, this is not equivalent to maximizing the sum of their corresponding money measures of utility (unless their marginal utilities of income are identical). If their marginal utilities of income are not identically equal, no method of aggregation of the two money measures of utility change consistent with the foregoing policy-making objective is feasible unless the respective marginal utilities of income are known. But marginal utilities of income can almost certainly not be measured or even estimated in practice. For example, consider one consumer with utility function U^1 and another with utility function $\tilde{U}^2 \equiv 2U^1$. Then all observed behavior by the two consumers will be identical because the utility functions carry only an ordinal significance, while the marginal utility of income for the second consumer will always be twice that of the first. That is, as is well known, the marginal utility of money is not invariant to affine (and monotonic) transformations of the utility function, which are allowed in ordinal utility theory.

6. Willingness to pay and consumer welfare

Chapter 5 has shown that conditions under which consumers will exhibit preference structures that ensure uniqueness of the change in consumer surplus as a money measure of utility gain or loss are very stringent. Therefore, in this chapter, attention is turned to consideration of a number of alternative but less demanding money measures of consumer welfare that are partially justified on the grounds originally proposed by Dupuit (1844). In other words, attention is turned to measures of consumer welfare change that have simple but plausible willingness-to-pay (WTP) interpretations.

The welfare measures discussed and adopted in this context were originally developed by John R. Hicks (1943). Hicks suggested four measures of consumer gain or loss, but only two of these – compensating and equivalent variation – allow the consumer freedom of choice in responding to a changing economic environment.[1] Because the vast majority of policy decisions allow consumer adjustment, attention is focused on these two measures.

Compensating and equivalent variations have been generally defined in Chapter 1. This chapter focuses on price and/or income changes for the consumer. Hence, the Chapter 1 definitions imply that *compensating variation (C) is the amount of income that must be taken away from a consumer (possibly negative) after a price and/or income change to restore the consumer's original welfare level. Similarly, equivalent variation (E) is the amount of income that must be given to a consumer (again possibly negative) in lieu of price and income changes to leave the consumer as well off as with the change.*

Thus, compensating and equivalent variations are defined as income adjustments that maintain the consumer at particular levels of welfare. Compensating variation focuses on the initial level of welfare that the consumer held prior to price and/or income changes. Equivalent variation focuses on the subsequent level of welfare that the consumer would obtain with the price and/or income changes.

6.1 WILLINGNESS-TO-PAY MEASURES

To demonstrate how compensating and equivalent variation may be directly related to the consumer's ordinal preferences, consider a consumer with preferences over the good q with price p and the good y (which can be regarded as a composite of all other commodities)

1. The other two measures proposed by Hicks, compensating surplus and equivalent surplus, constrain the consumer to buy the same consumption bundle as he or she did in the subsequent and initial situations, respectively. There are, in principle, an infinite number of measures that can be generated by alternative kinds of constraints on consumer response to price and/or income change but, in most situations, only compensating and equivalent variations are consistent with competitive behavior. Hence, in applied settings, measures other than compensating and equivalent variation are seldom applicable. There are, however, nonprice change cases where compensating or equivalent surplus is the conceptually appropriate measure. An explanation of these concepts is given in Section 7.9.

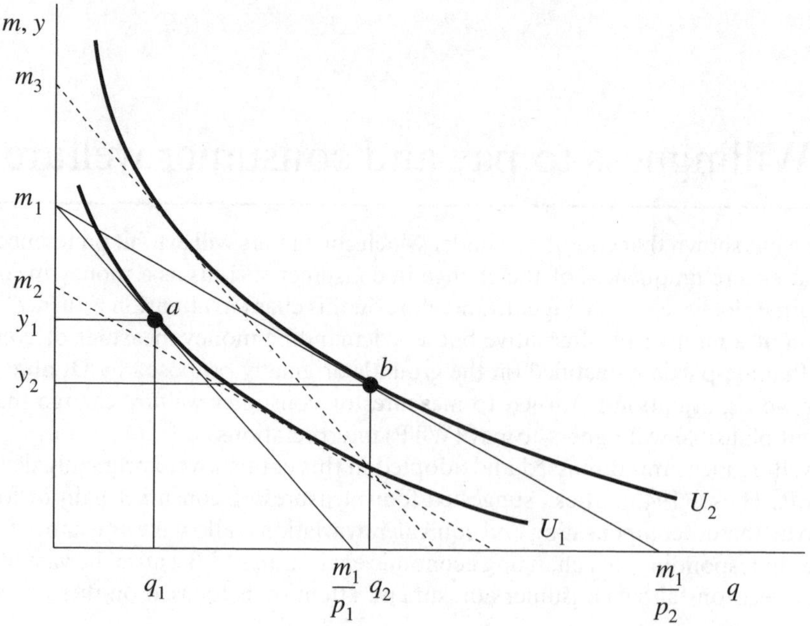

Figure 6.1

with a price of 1.[2] Faced with the budget constraint $p_1q+y=m_1$, where m_1 is initial income, the consumer chooses the optimum consumption point *a* with q_1 of *q* and y_1 of *y* in Figure 6.1. With a lower price p_2, the consumer increases the consumption of *q* to q_2 and decreases the consumption of *y* to y_2, hence moving to consumption point *b*.

Now recall that a change in income *m* results in a new budget line parallel to the old one. Hence, to find the measure of the compensating variation going from point *a* to point *b*, the budget line through point *b* is shifted downward (income is reduced) until it is just tangent to the original welfare level U_1. Thus, the compensating variation (C_{12}) associated with the price fall is given by $m_1-m_2>0$. That is, the consumer's income must be reduced by the amount m_1-m_2 after the price is reduced to p_2 for the consumer's welfare to remain unchanged.

The equivalent variation associated with the price fall (E_{12}) is found in Figure 6.1 by increasing the consumer's income, given the old price p_1, until the consumer has sufficient income to attain the utility level attained with the price fall. Thus, the budget line through point *a* is shifted upward until it is just tangent to U_2. The measure of equivalent variation is thus given by the vertical distance, $m_3-m_1>0$.

With a price rise, the amount of income that must be *taken away* to restore the consumer's original welfare level is negative. That is, the consumer in this case must be given income to maintain the same level of welfare as before the price increase. Hence, in Figure 6.1, the compensating variation associated with an increase in price from p_2 to p_1 is $m_1-m_3<0$.

Similarly, the amount of income that must be *given to* the consumer in lieu of the price

2. In this framework, good *y* serves as the numeraire, so its price serves as the accounting price.

increase is negative, or income must be taken away to make the consumer as poorly off as with the price increase. Thus, the equivalent variation in Figure 6.1 associated with an increase in price from p_2 to p_1 is given by $m_2 - m_1 < 0$.

Clearly, the compensating variation associated with a price fall is equal in magnitude but of opposite sign to the equivalent variation for the reverse movement in prices. That is, in Figure 6.1, $C_{12} = m_1 - m_2 = -(m_2 - m_1) = -E_{21}$.

Using the graphical approach described above, one can easily verify that the compensating variation for a price fall is bounded by the initial income, whereas equivalent variations may be infinite when indifference curves are asymptotic to the vertical axis. For price increases, the opposite result holds. That is, equivalent variation is bounded and compensating variation is unbounded. Moreover, both compensating variation and equivalent variation are ordinally related to utility. That is, equivalent variation varies ordinally with utility as the subsequent welfare position (point *b* in Figure 6.1) is continuously varied, and compensating variation varies ordinally as the initial welfare position (point *a* in Figure 6.1) is continuously varied.

As suggested earlier, compensating and equivalent variation can be given more strict WTP interpretations. For example, compensating variation for a price fall can be interpreted as the maximum amount of income the consumer would be *willing to pay* rather than relinquish the price reduction. For a price increase, compensating variation is the minimum amount the consumer must be paid, or is willing to accept, to tolerate the higher price. Thus, compensating variation questions measure gains or losses associated with *taking* the proposed action – in this case, changing price.

Equivalent variation, on the other hand, measures gains and losses to the consumer associated with *not taking* the proposed action. That is, equivalent variation for a price fall can be interpreted as the minimum amount of income the consumer is *willing to accept* to forgo the lower price. For a price rise, it is the maximum amount the consumer is *willing to pay* to avoid the higher price. Thus, equivalent variation is the maximum bribe the consumer is willing to pay to avoid an adverse change in economic conditions or the minimum bribe necessary to gain relinquishment of a claim on an improvement in economic conditions.[3]

To see how these concepts are related to observed quantities and prices, it is necessary to introduce the concept of the Hicksian or compensated demand curve and show how both it and the Marshallian (or ordinary) demand curve can be related to the consumer's ordinal preference map. The *Hicksian compensated demand curve* is a relationship giving quantities demanded at various prices when utility is held constant by varying only income. By contrast, the *Marshallian demand curve* is a relationship giving quantities demanded at various prices when income is held constant by varying only utility.

Consider again the consumer with budget constraint $p_1 q + y = m_1$ and preferences as given by the indifference curves in Figure 6.2(a). The consumer's optimum, initial consumption point is again point *a*, which implies the purchase of q_1 of commodity q. This

3. These interpretations underscore the attractiveness of compensating and equivalent variation for the compensation tests discussed in Chapter 3. A full discussion of how these questions naturally relate to the Kaldor–Hicks and Scitovsky compensation criteria, however, is deferred to Chapter 8 where the case of many consumers is considered because the compensation criteria make sense only in a setting with more than one individual.

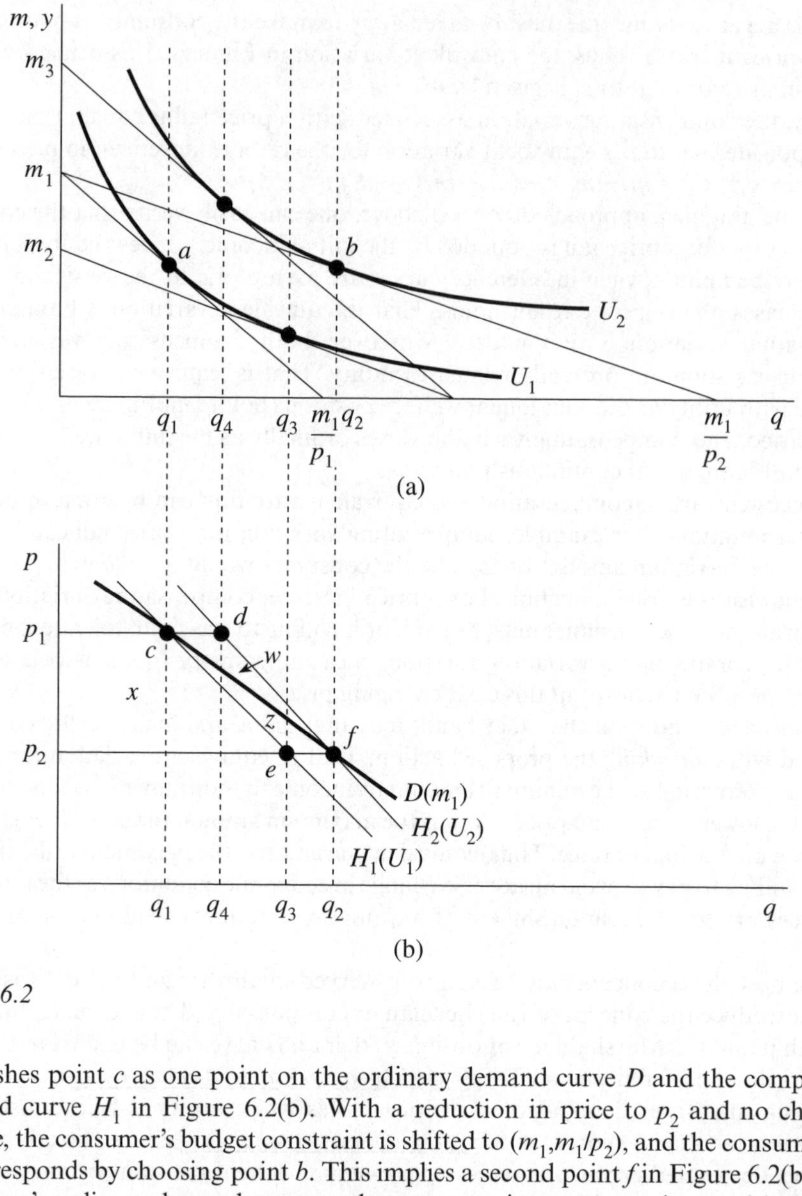

Figure 6.2

establishes point c as one point on the ordinary demand curve D and the compensated demand curve H_1 in Figure 6.2(b). With a reduction in price to p_2 and no change in income, the consumer's budget constraint is shifted to $(m_1,m_1/p_2)$, and the consumer optimally responds by choosing point b. This implies a second point f in Figure 6.2(b) on the consumer's ordinary demand curve as the consumer increases purchases with the lower price to q_2. By continuously varying price upward and downward from p_1 in Figure 6.2(a), one can, in the same manner, trace out a continuous locus of price–quantity combinations and, hence, generate the ordinary demand curve D along which income is held constant at m_1.

The Hicksian compensated demand curve going through point c in Figure 6.2(b) is generated by starting at point a in Figure 6.2(a) and determining the amounts of q purchased as price is varied but income is adjusted to maintain the consumer at utility level U_1. Thus, as price is reduced to p_2 and the compensating variation of m_1-m_2 is taken away from the consumer to restore the original welfare level, the consumption of q increases to q_3, which implies in Figure 6.2(b) a second point e on the compensated demand curve H_1. The increase in consumption from q_1 to q_3, as a result of the price fall, is due entirely to the desire to substitute q for other goods as the relative price of q falls. As long as the commodity q is a normal good (one with a positive income effect or one with an income expansion path having a positive slope), the point q_3 will lie to the left of q_2. Similar reasoning suggests that all points on the Hicksian demand curve H_1 for prices less than p_1 will lie to the left of the ordinary demand curve D.

Because the compensated demand curve considers the effects of a combined price and income change that leaves the consumer indifferent to the initial position, there will be a compensated demand curve corresponding to each level of utility, that is, to each possible initial position. For example, H_2 in Figure 6.2(b) corresponding to indifference curve U_2 in Figure 6.2(a) can be developed in a similar manner. If the consumer's initial position is point b in Figure 6.2(a) (point f in Figure 6.2(b)), a new compensated demand curve H_2 is generated, corresponding to indifference level U_2, in Figure 6.2(a) passing through point f and, for price decreases, will again lie to the left of the ordinary demand curve D.

For price increases, consider starting at point f and increasing price from p_2 to p_1. In Figure 6.2(a), the consumer must be given $m_3 - m_1$ in income (compensating variation of $m_1 - m_3$ must be taken away) to maintain the same level of welfare at the higher price. When this increase in income is combined with the higher price, the consumer optimally chooses amount q_4 of commodity q. As long as the commodity is a normal good, q_4 will lie to the right of q_1, the point on the ordinary demand curve to which the consumer would move at the higher price if income compensation were not provided. Thus, starting at any price–quantity combination on the ordinary demand curve, there exists a Hicksian compensated demand curve passing through that point which, for normal goods, will lie to the left of the Marshallian demand curve for lower prices and to the right at higher prices.

With this framework in mind, it is possible to develop compensating and equivalent variation measures in the price–quantity space of Figure 6.2(b). One can show that the compensating variation associated with a price fall from p_1 to p_2 is exactly equal to area x in Figure 6.2(b) and, hence, is equal to the vertical distance $m_1 - m_2$ in Figure 6.2(a). Similarly, the compensating variation associated with a price rise from p_2 to p_1 can be shown to be the negative of area $w+x+z$ in Figure 6.2(b), which is thus equal to $-(m_1 - m_3) = m_3 - m_1 = E_{12}$ in Figure 6.2(a). That is, the area $w+x+z$ in Figure 6.2(b) measures the equivalent variation associated with the price fall from p_1 to p_2. Thus, for a normal good, the change in consumer surplus resulting from a price fall from p_1 to p_2 is bounded from below by compensating variation and from above by equivalent variation ($C \leq \Delta S \leq E$) and differs from these two amounts by area z and area w, respectively, in Figure 6.2(b).

To begin the development of the foregoing results – that is, to show that the vertical distance measure of compensating variation in Figure 6.2(a) is equal to the change in area under the Hicksian compensated demand curve in Figure 6.2(b) – consider the consumer initially in equilibrium at point a in Figure 6.3(a). The compensating variation associated with a price fall from p_1 to p_2 is $m_1 - m_2$. To show that $m_1 - m_2 =$ area $x+w$ in Figure 6.3(b), consider the budget line $(m_3, m_3/p_2)$ passing through point a. This budget line can be determined by taking sufficient income away from the consumer at the lower price to just allow the purchase of the old bundle (y_1, q_1) at the new prices. That is, $m_1 = p_1 q_1 + y_1$

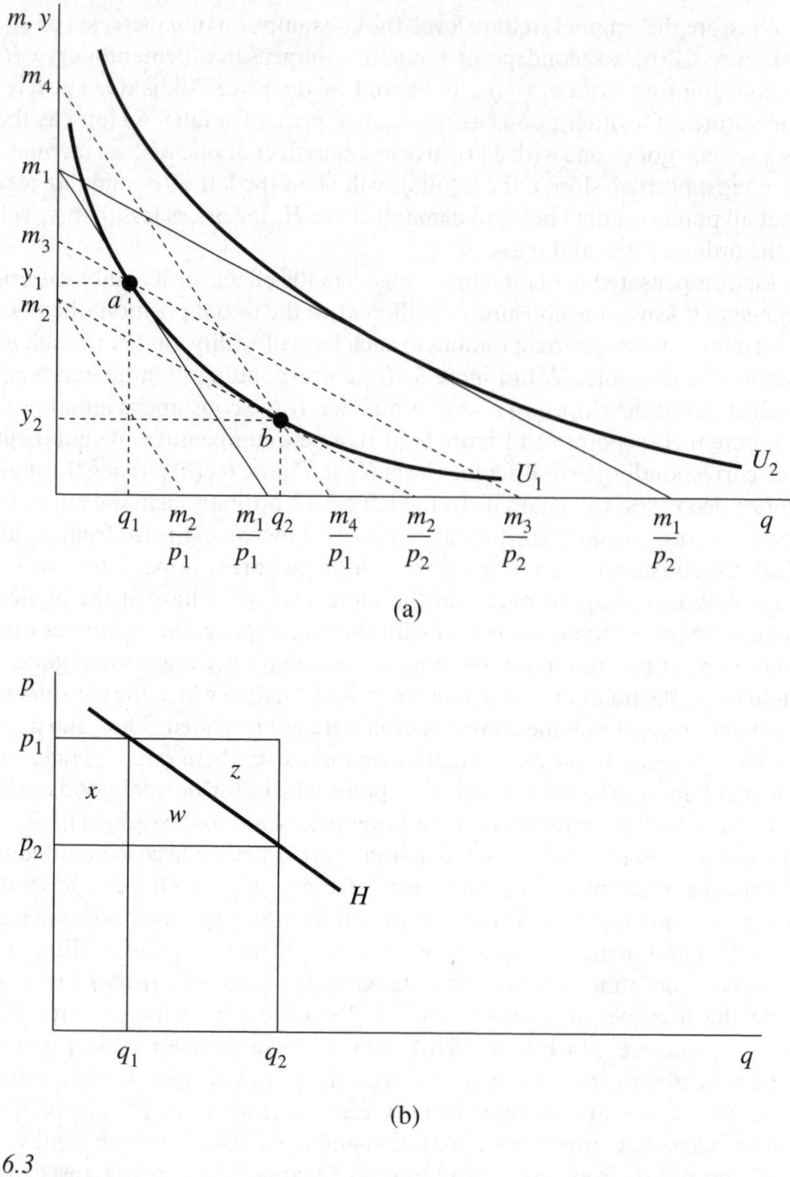

Figure 6.3

and $m_3 = p_2q_1 + y_1$. By subtracting, this implies that $m_1 - m_3 = (p_1 - p_2)q_1$, which is the inner cost difference of the original bundle of goods and is measured by area *x* in Figure 6.3(b). As long as the indifference curves in Figure 6.3(a) are convex to the origin, the inner cost differences will be less than compensating variation, or $m_2 < m_3$. That is, this cost difference is a lower bound on compensating variation in Figure 6.3(b) because at least this amount of income can be taken away after the price fall yet still leave the consumer at least as well off as before.

Now consider the possibility of establishing an upper bound on compensating variation in Figure 6.3(b). If the consumer is initially in equilibrium at point b in Figure 6.3(a) with income m_2 and price p_2, the absolute value of the compensating variation associated with a price rise from p_2 to p_1 is $m_1 - m_2$. But this is also the compensating variation determined above for the reverse price movement with initial income m_1. That is, the compensating variation for an increase in price from p_2 to p_1 with income m_2 is equal to the compensating variation for a decrease in price from p_1 to p_2 with income m_1. Thus, to place an upper bound on compensating variation beginning at point a for the price fall, consider first an upper bound on compensating variation for a price increase starting at point b. This upper bound is established by asking how much additional income must be paid to the consumer when price is increased to p_1 to enable the consumer to buy the old commodity bundle (y_2,q_2). The associated budget line with price p_1 must pass through the point b. Hence, income of $m_4 - m_2$ in Figure 6.3(a) must be paid to the consumer to make the bundle (y_2,q_2) feasible. However, $m_4 - m_2 = (p_1 - p_2)q_2$. Thus, the outer cost difference measured by area $w+x+z$ in Figure 6.3(b) is an upper bound on compensating variation.

With compensating variation now bounded in Figure 6.3(b) by area x below and by area $w+x+z$ above, the establishment of $w+x$ as the measure of compensating variation proceeds by breaking up the price change from p_1 to p_2 into a sequence of smaller and smaller price changes. For example, consider proceeding from p_1 to p_2 via the sequence p_1, p_3, p_4, …, p_2 in Figure 6.4. The lower bound on compensating variation for the first step is area v; the second, area w; and, finally, the fifth, area z. Clearly, the sum of these lower bounds (area $v+w+x+y+z$) can be made closer to the change in area under the compensated demand curve (area $x+w$ in Figure 6.3(b)) by dividing the price change into more and smaller increments. A similar approach can be used to show that an upper

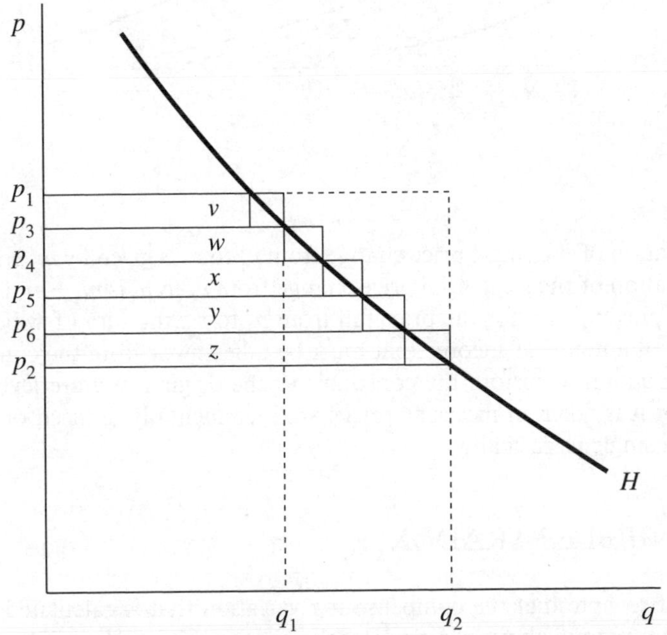

Figure 6.4

bound formed by outer cost differences for the series of small price changes also becomes equal to the area behind the compensated demand curve between the two price lines.

To obtain area $w+x+z$ in Figure 6.2 as a measure of equivalent variation, observe that area $w+x+z$ is the negative of the compensating variation for an increase in price from p_2 to p_1, and that the negative of compensating variation for a price increase is equal to equivalent variation for the corresponding price decrease.

Finally, to complete the argument, it must be shown that the compensating variation from the single price change from p_1 to p_2 is equal to the sum of the compensating variations from the sequential price changes $p_1, p_3, \ldots, p_2$. To see this, consider Figure 6.5 where the consumer is initially in equilibrium at point a with price p_1 and income m_1. The compensating variation of the single price change from p_1 to p_2 is given by $m_1 - m_2$. The compensating variation of the sequential price change from p_1 to p_2 is $m_1 - m_3$ for the change from p_1 to p_3, plus $m_3 - m_2$ for the price fall from p_3 to p_2, the sum of which is $m_1 - m_2$. That is, the total amount of income that must be taken away from the consumer with a given price reduction to restore the consumer to the original welfare level is the same whether or not it is taken in pieces as prices are incrementally reduced or taken in one amount with a single price change.

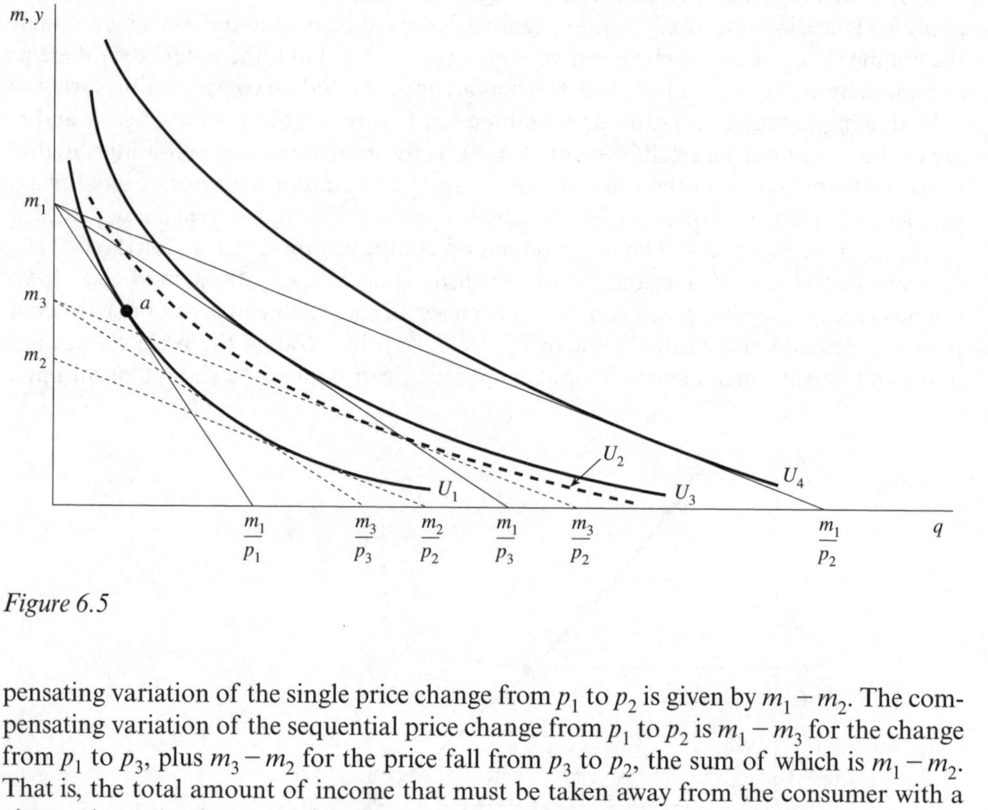

Figure 6.5

6.2 THE NIBBLE PARADOX

It is important to note that the compensating variation that is calculated for the price adjustment from p_3 to p_2 above is done after the consumer's income has been reduced by the compensating variation for the previous price adjustment from p_1 to p_3. This points out an important principle in making any stepwise computation of compensating or equivalent variation. To calculate an overall compensating (equivalent) variation in a stepwise manner (for example, imposing a change of one price, then another, and so on), one must assume that the compensating (equivalent) variation for any previous price or income change is already extracted from (paid to) the consumer before making further calculations.

The problem that arises when this principle is not adhered to is known as the *nibble paradox*. To demonstrate the nibble paradox, note that the compensating variation of the single price change from p_1 to p_4 in Figure 6.6 is given by area $a_0 + b_0 + c_0$. It appears that, if the overall price change is attained by a series of smaller changes – first, from p_1 to p_2, then from p_2 to p_3, and finally from p_3 to p_4 – the compensating variation is area a_0 for the first change, area $b_0 + b_1$ for the second change, and area $c_0 + c_1 + c_2$ for the third change, the sum of which exceeds the compensating variation for the single price change. However, if for each interval the compensating variation is extracted from the consumer before proceeding to consider the next price change (extraction of area a_0, for example, before reducing the price from p_2 to p_3), the consumer is always constrained to utility level U_1. Hence, the sum of the incremental compensating variations is properly calculated as area $a_0 + b_0 + c_0$.

6.3 EQUALITY OF COMPENSATING AND EQUIVALENT VARIATION

The focus thus far has been on two alternative WTP measures: compensating variation and equivalent variation. This raises a dilemma about which to use in any given situation. There is, however, one circumstance where these measures coincide and a choice need not

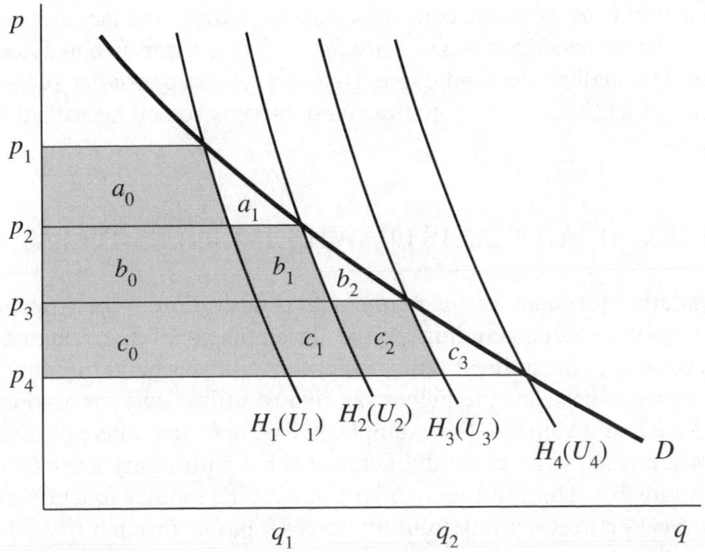

Figure 6.6

be made. This is the case of zero-income effects or vertically parallel indifference curves for the goods for which prices change (illustrated in Figure 5.6). Given a price fall, the compensated demand curve, the equivalent demand curve (the compensated demand curve for the reverse movement in price) and the ordinary Marshallian demand curve all coincide. Hence, given any single price change, $C=\Delta S=E$. Similarly, if more than one price changes and the goods for which prices change have zero-income effects, the compensated and ordinary curves will coincide in every case, so again both compensating and equivalent variation will be given by the change in consumer surplus.

Section 5.3 argues, however, that conditions for a zero-income effect, which imply that the consumer surplus measure is unique, are not likely to occur in the real world. Thus, the conditions that eliminate the dilemma of choice among WTP measures are just as stringent as those that are required to establish consumer surplus as a unique money measure of welfare gains. Indeed, there are cases where the only reasonable course of action for the applied welfare economist is to present estimates of *both* compensating and equivalent variation. In such cases, a project that is justified using one measure may not be justified using the other. In such a case, both measurements can be provided to policy-makers, and the associated value judgment of which measurement to use can be left in their hands.

A further complication that arises is how one estimates compensating and equivalent variation because the estimation of Hicksian compensated demand curves is often difficult. Fortunately, however, as long as the proportion of income spent upon the good is small, the income effect is likely to be quite small (see Hicks 1956, p. 65). Hence, in many cases, compensating variation, equivalent variation, and changes in consumer surplus are all likely to be of similar magnitude. That is, areas w and z in Figure 6.2 are likely to be quite small. Substantial progress has been made in providing a precise quantitative meaning for the word 'small'. Techniques have been developed whereby the applied welfare economist can obtain estimates of either compensating or equivalent variation with knowledge of only Marshallian consumer surplus changes and income elasticity estimates. Note that the *Marshallian consumer surplus* is the consumer surplus associated with the ordinary or Marshallian demand curve. By contrast, the consumer surplus triangle associated with a Hicksian compensated demand curve is sometimes called a *Hicksian consumer surplus*.

6.4 GRAPHICAL ANALYSIS OF WILLINGNESS TO PAY

To lay the foundation for much of the mathematical derivation in the Appendix to this chapter and to provide understanding of the development of the remainder of this chapter, this section uses the indirect utility function and the expenditure function.[4] The *indirect utility function* specifies the highest attainable utility level for a consumer as a function of price p and income m. For example, in Figure 6.7(a), where prices are p_1^0 and p_2^0, income is m_0, and U_1 denotes an indifference curve with utility level U_1, no higher utility level is attainable. Thus, in Figure 6.7(b), the indirect utility function is such that an isoutility curve V_1 corresponding to utility level U_1 passes through (p^0,m^0) where, for

4. The graphical approach in this section was developed by Zajac (1976).

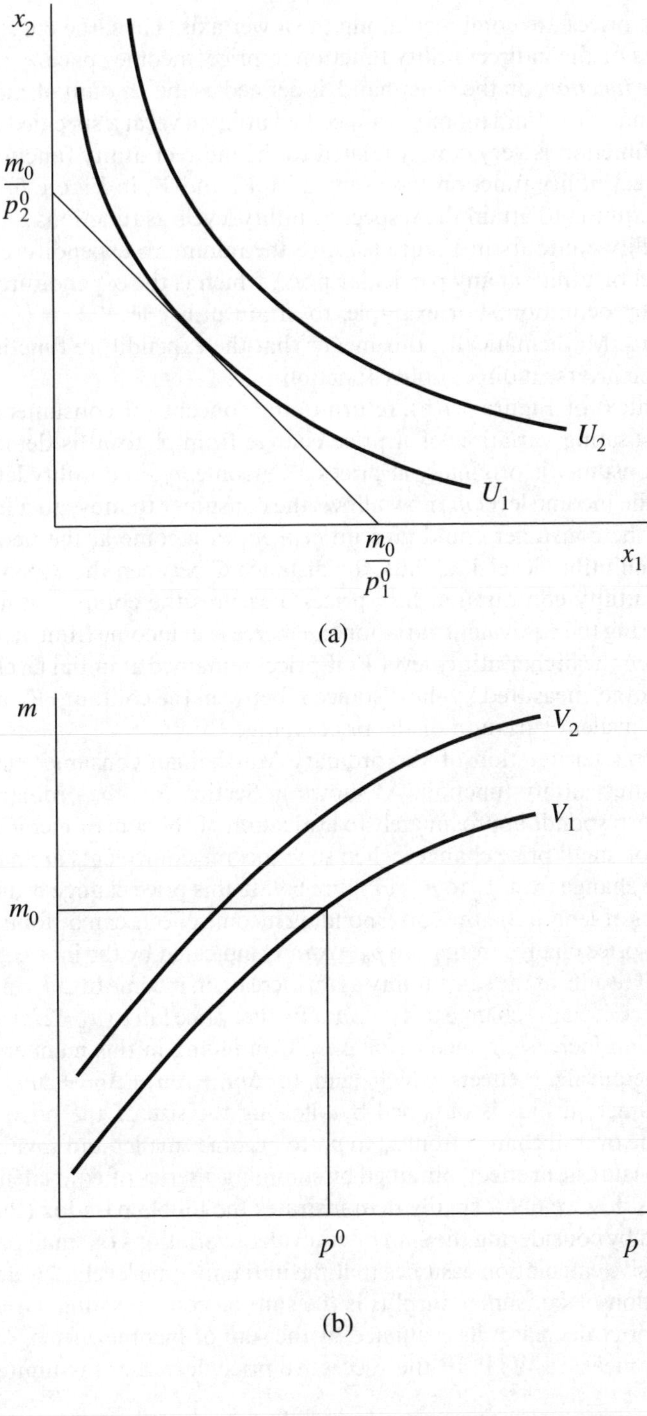

Figure 6.7

convenience, both prices are combined along the lower axis. Thus, the curves V_1 and V_2 represent contours of the indirect utility function in price–income space.

The *expenditure function*, on the other hand, is defined as the amount of money income that allows a consumer to attain (at most) a specified utility level at a specified set of prices. The expenditure function is very closely related to the indirect utility function. The contours of the indirect utility function represented by V_1 and V_2 in Figure 6.7(b) give the money incomes required to attain the respective utility levels as functions of prices. That is, the indirect utility contours in Figure 6.7 give the minimum expenditure required to attain a given level of utility at any particular price, which is the expenditure function at that utility level by definition. For example, to attain utility level $V_1 = U_1$ at prices p^0 requires income m_0. Mathematically, this means that the expenditure function in price–income space is the inverse indirect utility function.[5]

Now, in the context of Figure 6.7(b), return to the concepts of consumer surplus and WTP. The compensating variation of a price change from p^0 to p^1 is demonstrated in Figure 6.8. The consumer is originally at prices p^0, income m_0, and utility level V_1. With a price fall to p^1, the income level m_0 now allows the consumer to move to a higher utility level V_2. Clearly, the consumer could give up $m_0 - m_1$ in income at the new prices and remain at the initial utility level V_1. Thus, the distance C between the expenditure functions (or indirect utility contours) at new prices measures the compensating variation. Similarly, considering the equivalent variation, an increase in income from m_0 to m_2 would be required to reach the higher utility level V_2 if prices remained at initial levels p^0. Hence, the increase in income, measured by the distance E between the contours V_1 and V_2 at old prices p^0, is the equivalent variation of the price change.[6]

Finally, consider interpretation of the ordinary Marshallian consumer surplus in the context of the indirect utility function. As shown in Section 5.1, the ordinary consumer surplus measure corresponds approximately to evaluation of the sum of income-equivalent effects of a series of small price changes when such income equivalents are not extracted. Consider the price change from p_0 to p_1 in Figure 6.9. If this price change is divided into a series of small steps of length Δp, the corresponding income effects can be found as follows. First, consider the price change from p_0 to $p_0 - \Delta p$. As indicated by the indirect utility contours, this price fall results in the same utility as an increase in income of Δm_1 in the absence of the price change. Given the change to $p_0 - \Delta p$, a further price fall to $p_0 - 2\Delta p$ has the same effect on utility as an increase in income of Δm_2. Continuing in this manner generates a series of income-equivalent effects which sum to $\Delta m_1 + \Delta m_2 + \Delta m_3 + \Delta m_4$. The exact Marshallian consumer surplus is obtained by allowing the size of the price increments, which add up to the overall change from p_0 to p_1, to become smaller and smaller.

Because this measure is, in effect, obtained by summing a series of equivalent variations of small price falls, Figure 6.9 formally demonstrates the nibble paradox (the consumer surplus is obtained by considering the sum of equivalent variations of small price changes where each successive calculation assumes that the initial income level m_0 is unaltered). A similar interpretation of consumer surplus is the sum of compensating variations associated with small price decreases as evaluated by the sum of income effects, $\Delta m_1^* + \Delta m_2^* + \Delta m_3^* + \Delta m_4^*$, which measure WTP for the successive price decreases (assuming payments

5. This relationship is demonstrated rigorously in Appendix Section 6.A.
6. Of course, if the price change were reversed from p^1 to p^0, distance E would measure the compensating variation and distance C would measure equivalent variation.

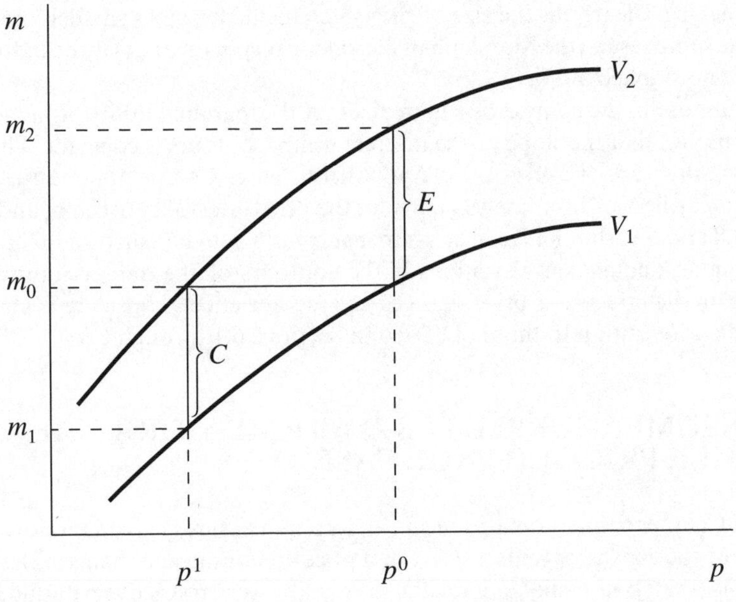

Figure 6.8

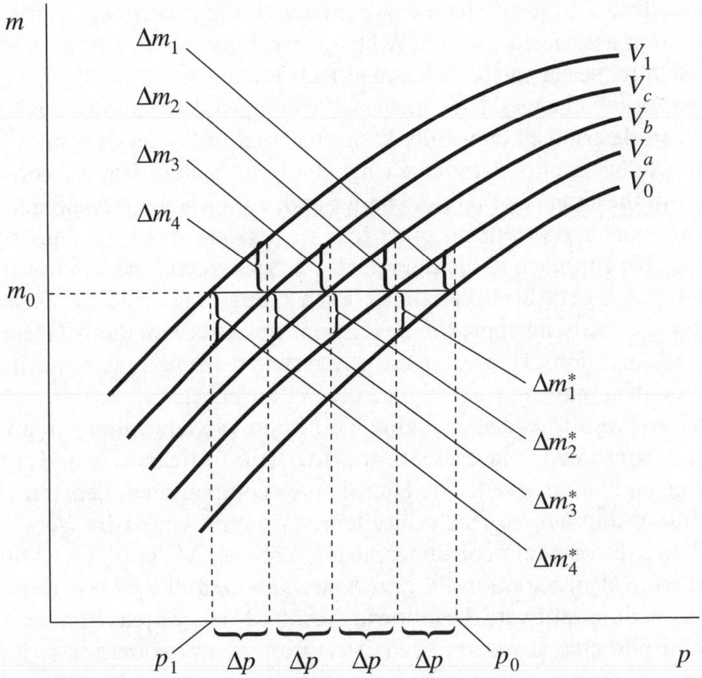

Figure 6.9

are not extracted). Clearly, as the size of price increments becomes smaller, the two sums approach the same result (the Marshallian consumer surplus change) if the indirect utility contours are not kinked at m_0.

Finally, suppose in the context of Figure 6.9 that the marginal utility of income is constant. This implies that the slope of the indirect utility contours is constant. Thus, $\Delta m_1 = \Delta m_2 = \Delta m_3 = \Delta m_4 = \Delta m_1^* = \Delta m_2^* = \Delta m_3^* = \Delta m_4^*$. In this case, $C = E = \Delta m_1 + \Delta m_2 + \ldots = \Delta m_1^* + \Delta m_2^* + \ldots$ regardless of how finely Δp divides the price interval between p_0 and p_1. Thus, in Figures 6.8 and 6.9, the change in consumer surplus would be exactly equal to both the compensating and equivalent variations if the contours of the indirect utility function were parallel in the interval of price changes and income effects considered. These results confirm and add intuition to those obtained in Sections 6.1 through 6.3.

6.5 CONSUMER SURPLUS AS A WTP MEASURE: THE SINGLE-PRICE-CHANGE CASE[7]

As shown in Chapter 5, the ordinary consumer surplus measure (1) is an intuitively appealing measure of the consumer welfare effect of a price and/or income change, (2) is generally an ambiguous (that is, nonunique) measure, (3) requires very restrictive path-independence conditions on the utility function for uniqueness and (4) requires even more restrictive conditions of constancy of the marginal utility of income to guarantee even an ordinal (qualitative) relationship with the actual utility change. For these reasons, major problems may be encountered with the use of consumer surplus and, therefore, the classical intuitive arguments are not sufficient to justify its use. Alternatively, the concepts of compensating and equivalent variation associated with the WTP approach have been advanced in the context of consumer welfare measurement as being at least unique and ordinally (or qualitatively) related to actual utility changes. Nevertheless, the compensating and equivalent variations can be difficult to determine empirically because actual utility levels cannot be observed. Generally, a researcher cannot determine what change in income leaves a consumer just as well off after or in the absence of a price change and, even when interviewed, a consumer is tempted to exaggerate one way or the other to serve personal interests. Thus, to develop an empirically tractable approach to measurement, this section considers indirectly estimating the compensating and equivalent variations. Even though the ordinary consumer surplus cannot be justified directly, an approximate relationship exists with the WTP concepts under a broad range of conditions. Hence, the use of consumer surplus may be justified indirectly or a modification of it may serve to estimate the welfare effects.

To develop these results, consider Figure 6.10 where price is initially p_0 and falls to p_1, causing quantity consumed to increase from q_0 to q_1 (the ordinary demand curve D is conditioned on a given income level). The Hicksian, or compensated, demand curves corresponding to initial and subsequent utility levels are represented by $H(U_0)$ and $H(U_1)$, respectively. Thus, the ordinary consumer surplus change, ΔS, is area $a+b$, and the compensating and equivalent variations, C and E, are areas a and $a+b+c$, respectively. Two important observations motivate the following results. First, if areas b and c are negligible, the consumer surplus change may be used directly as an approximation of both the com-

7. This section and the following section of this chapter are based on Willig (1973, 1976).

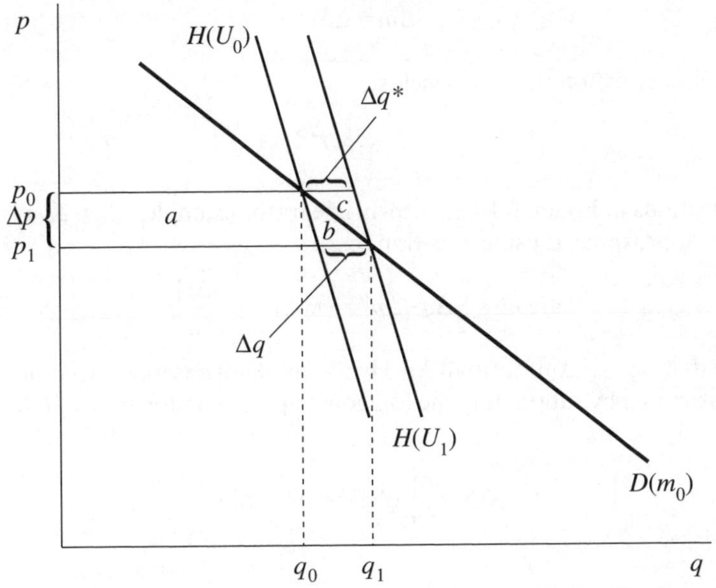

Figure 6.10

pensating and equivalent variations. Second, if areas b and c can be estimated from observable phenomena by some means, the consumer surplus change can be appropriately modified to produce approximations of the compensating and equivalent variations.

An estimate of areas b and c can be developed by noting that each is approximately a triangle for small price changes and that the height of each, Δp, is determined by the extent of the price change. Also, the base of each triangle, Δq or Δq^*, is essentially an income effect, that is, the effect of changing income by a certain amount while holding price fixed. Furthermore, the size of the income effect is related to the income elasticity of demand, which is an estimable parameter. In simple terms, the income elasticity is given by

$$\eta = \frac{\Delta q}{\Delta m}\frac{m}{q},$$

where Δm is the real income change precipitated by the price change that leads to the quantity change, Δq, when price is held constant. Thus, to determine Δq in Figure 6.10, note that the above equation implies that

$$\Delta q = \eta \cdot q \cdot \frac{\Delta m}{m}, \tag{6.1}$$

and that the income change that leads to reduction in consumption by Δq is approximately ΔS (for small Δp), that is,[8]

8. Of course, one could also consider use of $C=$ area a as the measure of the income change. Indeed, this is exactly the change in income that reduces consumption by Δq. However, C is not directly observable, whereas ΔS is. As verified by Appendix Section 6.B, the errors introduced by this approximation are not serious for the class of cases described below.

$$\Delta m \doteq \Delta S.$$

Substituting into equation (6.1) thus yields

$$\Delta q \doteq \eta \cdot q \cdot \frac{\Delta S}{m}. \tag{6.2}$$

When the functions in Figure 6.10 are nearly linear (for example, when Δp is small), area b can thus be approximated using equation (6.2):

$$\text{area } b \doteq \frac{1}{2}\Delta q \cdot |\Delta p| \doteq \frac{1}{2}\eta \cdot \Delta S \cdot q \cdot \frac{|\Delta p|}{m}.$$

Finally, note that $\Delta S \doteq q|\Delta p|$ for small Δp. Hence, the compensating variation ($C =$ area a) can be approximated by subtracting the foregoing approximation of area b from area $a+b\,(=\Delta S)$,

$$\hat{C} = \Delta S - \frac{\eta}{2m}(\Delta S)^2 = \Delta S - \hat{\varepsilon}|\Delta S| \tag{6.3}$$

where

$$\hat{\varepsilon} = \frac{\eta|s|}{2}, \; s = \frac{\Delta S}{m}. \tag{6.4}$$

A similar approximation of the equivalent variation ($E =$ area $a+b+c$) is obtained using

$$\Delta q^* \doteq -\eta \cdot q \cdot \frac{\Delta S}{m}$$

and

$$\text{area } c \doteq -\frac{1}{2}\Delta q^* |\Delta p| \doteq \frac{1}{2}\eta \cdot \Delta S \cdot q \cdot \frac{|\Delta p|}{m}.$$

That is, the equivalent variation can be approximated by

$$\hat{E} = \Delta S + \frac{\eta}{2m}(\Delta S)^2 = \Delta S + \hat{\varepsilon}|\Delta S|. \tag{6.5}$$

The approximations in (6.3) and (6.5) are useful for determining the extent of error involved in using consumer surplus change to approximate compensating and equivalent variations and for suggesting appropriate modifications of the consumer surplus change to serve as more precise estimates of the compensating and equivalent variations. First, note from (6.3) and (6.5) that $\hat{\varepsilon}$ is approximately the fraction of error in each case. Thus, using (6.4), *if the product of income elasticity and the ratio of surplus change to total income divided by 2 is less than 0.05 in absolute value, no more than about a 5 percent error* ($|\hat{\varepsilon}| = |\eta s/2| \leq 0.05$) *is made by using consumer surplus as a measure of either compensating or equivalent variation* (without modification).[9] As argued by Robert D. Willig (1976) in his seminal paper, this is a condition that is likely to hold in many cases. That is, for many goods, the change in consumer surplus or the income-equivalent change of any price

9. A precise examination of these errors in Appendix Section 6.B confirms these results.

change within reason is a very small fraction of total income. Hence, for any reasonable income elasticity, the condition will hold. For other goods, the income elasticity is small, so that the change in consumer surplus would have to be a very large fraction of total income to create a large error (which suggests a commodity for which actual expenditures may be large – at least at some intermediate prices).

For common everyday items, such as clothing and stereo sets, the percentage of income that would be spent at any relevant price is probably small enough that the condition $|\eta s/2| < 0.05$ will not be violated even if the income elasticity is 2 or 3. For items such as housing, however, the income equivalent of a large price change may represent a substantial proportion of income (for example, half). Furthermore, in some cases, the income elasticity may well be 1 or greater. Hence, this would be an instance where more than a 5 percent error may be made by using consumer surplus as a direct estimate of the compensating or equivalent variation.

If $|\eta s/2|$ is greater than 0.05 in absolute value or if more precise estimates of the WTP concepts are desired, C or E can be estimated following (6.3) or (6.5). This can be accomplished by estimating the average income elasticity η over the price-change interval and obtaining data on total income so that $\hat{\varepsilon}$ can be calculated using ΔS. Neglecting errors in statistical application, Appendix Section 6.B shows that these *modified formulas for estimating the compensating and equivalent variations lead to less than about 2 percent error when* $|\eta s/2| \leq 0.08$ *and income elasticity changes by less than 50 percent over the interval of a price change*. The latter condition is much less restrictive than that developed above for the direct use of ΔS as an estimate of C or E.

To exemplify the application of these results, suppose that a consumer's demand for beef is given by the relationship

$$q = 11 - 5p + \frac{8}{75}m, \tag{6.6}$$

where

q = quantity of beef consumed in hundred pounds per year
p = price of beef in dollars per pound
m = income in thousand dollars per year.

Assume that the initial price is $p^0 = 1$ and consumer income is $m_0 = 75/2$. Now, consider the consumer welfare effect of adding a luxury tax that increases consumer price to $p^1 = 2$. Substituting m_0 into equation (6.6) leads to the equation $q = 15 - 5p$, shown graphically in Figure 6.11. As is obvious from the graph, the change in consumer surplus is $\Delta S = -15/2$,which suggests a real income loss of \$750 per year (note that areas in Figure 6.11 are measured in hundred dollars per year). But how accurate is ΔS as a measure of the compensating or equivalent variation? If one is sure that $|\eta s/2| \leq 0.05$ and any absolute error up to about 5 percent is tolerable, then ΔS can be used directly as an estimate of C or E. If not, this question can be answered by appealing to the approximation given above.

To do this, note that the change in quantity, Δq, caused by a change in income, Δm, must always satisfy $\Delta q/\Delta m = 8/75$,according to equation (6.6). Hence, the income elasticity is

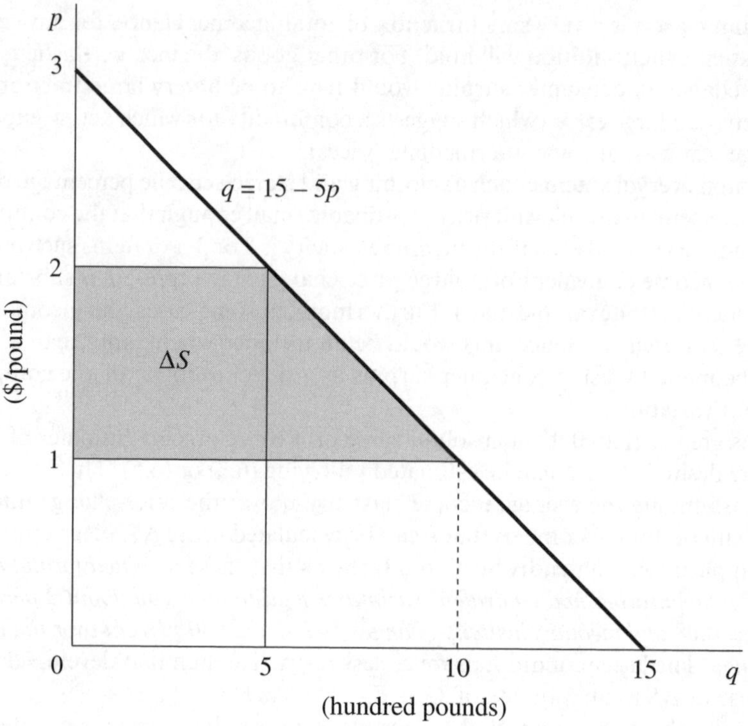

Figure 6.11

$$\eta = \frac{m}{q}\frac{\Delta q}{\Delta m} = \frac{75/2}{q}\frac{8}{75} = \frac{4}{q}.$$

Over the price interval from p^0 to p^1, the quantity q is between 5 and 10, as indicated by Figure 6.11. Hence, the income elasticity varies between $\eta_1 = 4/10$ and $\eta_2 = 4/5$. Further noting that $s = \Delta S/m = (-15/2)/(75/2) = -1/5$, one finds that $\hat{\varepsilon}$ is between $\eta_1|s|/2 = 0.04$ and $\eta_2|s|/2 = 0.08$. Following equation (6.3), this implies that ΔS overestimates the compensating variation by about 4 to 8 percent (note that both C and ΔS are negative, so the compensating variation is larger in absolute value). Similarly, equation (6.5) implies that ΔS underestimates the equivalent variation by about 4 to 8 percent.

If a 4 to 8 percent error is unacceptable,[10] equations (6.3) and (6.5) suggest a further improvement. That is, if ΔS overestimates the compensating variation by 4 to 8 percent, then increasing ΔS by 6 percent (or, in this case, reducing ΔS by 6 percent in absolute terms) will neither overestimate nor underestimate the compensating variation by more than about 2 percent. A reasonable approach amounts to choosing η equal to the average of the minimum and maximum income elasticities ($\bar{\eta} = (\eta_1 + \eta_2)/2$) for the purpose of making the calculations in equations (6.3) through (6.5). Thus, $\bar{\varepsilon} = \bar{\eta}|s|/2$ is the midpoint

10. For the purposes of the discussion in this chapter, it is assumed that the parameters of equation (6.6) are known exactly. However, an equation of the type in (6.6) would ordinarily be estimated statistically. The possible errors resulting from inaccurate estimation may make bounding the error by, say, 4 or 8 percent impossible.

of the interval generated by $\hat{\varepsilon}$ over the course of the price change – in this case the midpoint of the interval (0.04, 0.08). And substituting $\bar{\varepsilon}$ for $\hat{\varepsilon}$ in equation (6.3) obtains

$$\bar{C} = \Delta S - \bar{\varepsilon}|\Delta S| = \Delta S - 0.06|\Delta S| = 1.06(-15/2). \tag{6.7}$$

Similar reasoning suggests estimating the equivalent variation using equation (6.5) in the same way:[11]

$$\bar{E} = \Delta S + \bar{\varepsilon}|\Delta S| = \Delta S + 0.06|\Delta S| = 0.94(-15/2). \tag{6.8}$$

6.6 CONSUMER SURPLUS AS A WTP MEASURE: THE MULTIPLE-PRICE-CHANGE CASE

Section 6.5 discussed approximating WTP with consumer surplus change only in the case of a single price change. However, these results may be simply extended to the case of a multiple price change. That is, even though the consumer surplus change may be path dependent, the compensating and equivalent variations are unique. For example, compensating variation in its WTP interpretation measures the maximum amount of income the consumer is willing to pay for a change in prices, and the order in which prices are reduced

11. To exemplify the size of errors introduced by the approximation in this section, one may use Table 6.1 as explained in Appendix Section 6.B (note the symmetry about $s = 0$, which allows bounds for $s = -0.2$ to be deduced from those for $s = 0.2$) to find that

$$0.08326 \geq \frac{\Delta S - C}{|\Delta S|} \geq 0.03948$$

and

$$0.07686 \geq \frac{E - \Delta S}{|\Delta S|} \geq 0.04055.$$

Thus,

$$\Delta S - 0.08326|\Delta S| \leq C \leq \Delta S - 0.03948|\Delta S|$$

and

$$\Delta S + 0.07686|\Delta S| \geq E \geq \Delta S + 0.04055|\Delta S|.$$

Clearly, in this case $\hat{\varepsilon}$ is a good approximation of the actual percentage error (compare 0.04 to 0.03948 and 0.04055 in the case of the small income elasticity, and compare 0.08 to 0.07686 and 0.08326 in the case of the larger income elasticity). Also, using these results from Table 6.1, error bounds on the modified estimates of C and E in equations (6.3), (6.5), (6.7) or (6.8) can be developed. For example, in the context of (6.7) and (6.8), the preceding results in this footnote imply that

$$0.08326 - 0.06 = 0.02326 \geq \frac{\bar{C} - C}{|\Delta S|} \geq -0.02052 = 0.03948 - 0.06$$

and

$$0.07686 - 0.06 = 0.01686 \geq \frac{E - \bar{E}}{|\Delta S|} \geq -0.01945 = 0.04055 - 0.06.$$

Thus, only about a 2 percent error is made by using modifications of consumer surplus change for a case where the income elasticity changes by 100 percent and $|\eta s/2| \leq 0.08$ over the course of the price change.

Table 6.1 *Willig bounds on consumer surplus error*

	s							
η	*−0.10*	*−0.05*	*0.00*	*0.05*	*0.10*	*0.15*	*0.20*	*0.25*
	−0.04597	−0.02405	0.00000	−0.02660	−0.05632	−0.08993	−0.12852	−0.17374
−1.01	−0.05632	−0.02660	0.00000	−0.02405	−0.04597	−0.06609	−0.08467	−0.10190
	−0.05050	−0.02525	0.00000	−0.02525	−0.05050	−0.07575	−0.10100	−0.12625
	−0.03687	−0.01917	0.00000	−0.02091	−0.04390	−0.06938	−0.09795	−0.13042
−0.8	−0.04390	−0.02091	0.00000	−0.01917	−0.03687	−0.05328	−0.06858	−0.08290
	−0.04000	−0.02000	0.00000	−0.02000	−0.04000	−0.06000	−0.08000	−0.10000
	−0.02798	−0.01447	0.00000	−0.01557	−0.03243	−0.05079	−0.07094	−0.09327
−0.6	−0.03243	−0.01557	0.00000	−0.01447	−0.02798	−0.04065	−0.05257	−0.06383
	−0.03000	−0.01500	0.00000	−0.01500	−0.03000	−0.04500	−0.06000	−0.07500
	−0.01888	−0.00971	0.00000	−0.01031	−0.02130	−0.03307	−0.04574	−0.05946
−0.4	−0.02130	−0.01031	0.00000	−0.00971	−0.01888	−0.02758	−0.03585	−0.04372
	−0.02000	−0.01000	0.00000	−0.01000	−0.02000	−0.03000	−0.04000	−0.05000
	−0.00956	−0.00488	0.00000	−0.00512	−0.01049	−0.01616	−0.02215	−0.02850
−0.2	−0.01049	−0.00512	0.00000	−0.00488	−0.00956	−0.01404	−0.01834	−0.02248
	−0.01000	−0.00500	0.00000	−0.00500	−0.01000	−0.01500	−0.02000	−0.02500
	0.00000	0.00000	0.00000	0.00000	0.00000	0.00000	0.00000	0.00000
0.0	0.00000	0.00000	0.00000	0.00000	0.00000	0.00000	0.00000	0.00000
	0.00000	0.00000	0.00000	0.00000	0.00000	0.00000	0.00000	0.00000
	0.00980	0.00494	0.00000	0.00504	0.01020	0.01547	0.02086	0.02637
0.2	0.01020	0.00504	0.00000	0.00494	0.00980	0.01457	0.01925	0.02384
	0.01000	0.00500	0.00000	0.00500	0.01000	0.01500	0.02000	0.02500
	0.01986	0.00996	0.00000	0.01003	0.02013	0.03030	0.04055	0.05087
0.4	0.02013	0.01003	0.00000	0.00996	0.01986	0.02970	0.03948	0.04920
	0.02000	0.01000	0.00000	0.01000	0.02000	0.03000	0.04000	0.05000

	0.03019	0.01504	0.00000	0.01494	0.02979	0.04454	0.05919	0.07373
0.6	0.02979	0.01494	0.00000	0.01504	0.03019	0.04544	0.06079	0.07623
	0.03000	0.01500	0.00000	0.01500	0.03000	0.04500	0.06000	0.07500
	0.04080	0.02019	0.00000	0.01979	0.03920	0.05822	0.07686	0.09512
0.8	0.03920	0.01979	0.00000	0.02019	0.04080	0.06182	0.08326	0.10512
	0.04000	0.02000	0.00000	0.02000	0.04000	0.06000	0.08000	0.10000
	0.05231	0.02586	0.00000	0.02489	0.04889	0.07209	0.09452	0.11623
1.01	0.04889	0.02489	0.00000	0.02586	0.05231	0.07977	0.10829	0.13744
	0.05050	0.02525	0.00000	0.02525	0.05050	0.07575	0.10100	0.12625
	0.06291	0.03071	0.00000	0.02933	0.05731	0.08406	0.10964	0.13410
1.2	0.05731	0.02933	0.00000	0.03071	0.06291	0.09669	0.13216	0.16942
	0.06000	0.03000	0.00000	0.03000	0.06000	0.09000	0.12000	0.15000
	0.07444	0.03608	0.00000	0.03397	0.06602	0.09627	0.12487	0.15194
1.4	0.06602	0.03397	0.00000	0.03608	0.07444	0.11529	0.15886	0.20539
	0.07000	0.03500	0.00000	0.03500	0.07000	0.10500	0.14000	0.17500
	0.08630	0.04152	0.00000	0.03858	0.07451	0.10805	0.13942	0.16881
1.6	0.07451	0.03858	0.00000	0.04152	0.08630	0.13474	0.18726	0.24439
	0.08000	0.04000	0.00000	0.04000	0.08000	0.12000	0.16000	0.20000
	0.09852	0.04703	0.00000	0.04313	0.08281	0.11943	0.15334	0.18480
1.8	0.08281	0.04313	0.00000	0.04703	0.09852	0.15510	0.21757	0.28685
	0.09000	0.04500	0.00000	0.04500	0.09000	0.13500	0.18000	0.22500
	0.11111	0.05263	0.00000	0.04761	0.09090	0.13043	0.16666	0.20000
2.0	0.09090	0.04761	0.00000	0.05263	0.11111	0.17647	0.25000	0.33333
	0.10000	0.05000	0.00000	0.05000	0.10000	0.15000	0.20000	0.25000

Note: Each group of three numbers includes, respectively,
$\varepsilon^c = \frac{[1 + (\eta - 1)s]^{1/(1-\eta)} - 1 + s}{|s|}$, $\varepsilon^e = \frac{[1 - (\eta - 1)s]^{1/(1-\eta)} - 1 - s}{|s|}$ and $\hat{\varepsilon} = \frac{\eta|s|}{2}$.

cannot affect this amount. A time-path problem simply does not exist. Hence, if the path of price change is segmented into small steps, large errors in calculating compensating and equivalent variation can be avoided by following the procedures in Section 6.5.

In Figure 6.12, suppose that prices are p_1^0 and p_2^0 for commodities q_1 and q_2 and that prices change to p_1^1 and p_2^1, respectively. To calculate compensating or equivalent variation, the Hicksian compensated demand curves must be used rather than the ordinary demand curves. Thus, in calculating the compensating and equivalent variation in Figure 6.12, one may arbitrarily choose the path in Figure 6.12(a), changing p_1 first and then p_2. As in preceding cases, compensated demand curves are distinguished from ordinary demand curves by conditioning on utility levels rather than on income levels. Initially, income is m_0 and utility is U_0. Changing prices along the first segment of the path in Figure 6.12(a), holding the price of q_2 fixed at p_2^0, the associated change in consumer surplus, ΔS_1, is area $a+b$ in Figure 6.12(b). The compensating variation associated with this part of the path, C_1, is area a. Analogous to the single-price-change case, area b can be estimated by

$$\text{area } b \doteq \frac{1}{2}\Delta q_1 \cdot |\Delta p_1| \doteq \frac{1}{2}\,\eta^1 \cdot \Delta S_1 \cdot q_1 \cdot \frac{|\Delta p_1|}{m_0},$$

where $\Delta p_1 = p_1^1 - p_1^0$, $\Delta S_1 = \text{area } a+b$, η^1 is the income elasticity of demand for q_1 (that is, $\eta^1 = (\Delta q_1/\Delta m)/(m/q_1)$, where Δm is the income change that leads to the change in quantity demanded, Δq_1, holding prices fixed), and Δq_1 is as shown in Figure 6.12(b). Thus, following the derivation leading to equation (6.3), C_1 can be approximated by

$$\hat{C}_1 = \Delta S_1 - \frac{\eta^1}{2m_0}(\Delta S_1)^2. \tag{6.9}$$

Now consider the additional compensating variation C_2 generated by the second part of the path where p_2 is changed, holding p_1 fixed at p_1^1. Of course, the associated change in surplus, ΔS_2, is given by the area $w+x+y+z$, which is the area behind the ordinary demand curve in the q_2 market after p_1 is changed to its terminal level. Based on this surplus change, one may thus be led to estimate C_2 by

$$\tilde{C}_2 = \Delta S_2 - \frac{\eta^2}{2m_0}(\Delta S_2)^2, \tag{6.10}$$

where η^2 is the income elasticity of demand for q_2. Note, however, that $\tilde{C}_2$ is an approximation of area $w+x+y$ where area z is approximated by

$$\text{area } z \doteq \frac{1}{2}\,\Delta q_2 \cdot |\Delta p_2| \doteq \frac{1}{2}\,\eta^2 \cdot \Delta S_2 \cdot \frac{|\Delta p_2|}{m_0}.$$

where $\Delta p_2 = p_2^1 - p_2^0$. But area $w+x+y$ measures the WTP for the price change from p_2^0 to p_2^1 starting from the initial prices (p_1^1, p_2^0) rather than from (p_1^0, p_2^0). Thus, the utility level is held constant at U_1, which is the utility level corresponding to prices p_1^1 and p_2^0 and income m_0.

The compensating variation of moving from prices (p_1^0, p_2^0) to (p_1^1, p_2^1), on the other hand, must hold the utility level at U_0 along the entire path. Thus, the compensating variation of the entire price change is obtained by adding to C_1 the change in area behind $H_2(p_1^1, U_0)$, the compensated demand curve conditioned on the initial utility level (and the

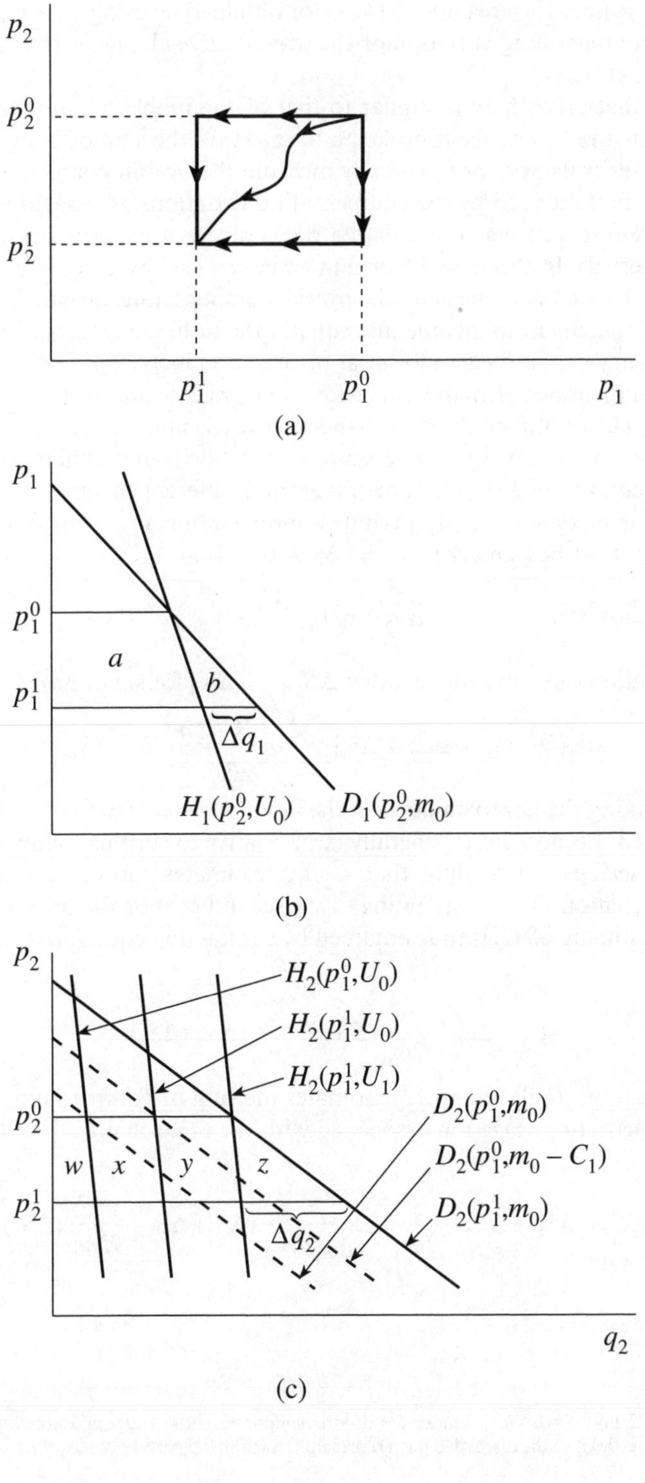
p_2
p_2^0
p_2^1
p_1^1
p_1^0
p_1
(a)
p_1
p_1^0
p_1^1
a
b
Δq_1
$H_1(p_2^0,U_0)$
$D_1(p_2^0,m_0)$
(b)
p_2
$H_2(p_1^0,U_0)$
$H_2(p_1^1,U_0)$
$H_2(p_1^1,U_1)$
$D_2(p_1^0,m_0)$
$D_2(p_1^0,m_0 - C_1)$
$D_2(p_1^1,m_0)$
p_2^0
p_2^1
w
x
y
z
Δq_2
q_2
(c)

Figure 6.12

terminal level of p_1), that is, area $w+x$. The error obtained by using $C_1+\tilde{C}_2$ as an approximation of the compensating variation of the overall price change is thus approximately area y.

The problem that arises here is similar to that of the nibble paradox. As resolved in Section 6.2, when a price change is broken into intervals, the sum of compensating variations over the intervals does not generally measure the overall compensating variation unless income is first reduced by the compensating variations associated with the previous price-change intervals when calculating the compensating variation of subsequent price-change intervals. In this case, income must be reduced by C_1 before calculating, or estimating, C_2 if C_1+C_2 is to measure the overall compensating variation.

Because that adjustment in income just equates the utility at (p_1^0,p_2^0) with the utility at (p_1^1,p_2^0), the ordinary demand curve for q_2 at price p_1^1 and income m_0-C_1 must just coincide with the compensated demand curve for q_2 at price p_1^1 and utility U_0 when $p_2=p_2^0$ (Figure 6.12(c)). Hence, for small price changes, area y is approximately a parallelogram with approximate area $|\Delta p_2|\cdot\widetilde{\Delta q_2}$ where $\widetilde{\Delta q_2}$ is the horizontal difference in ordinary demand curves conditioned on the same prices and different incomes, m_0-C_1 and m_0. Knowledge of the income elasticity permits approximating $\widetilde{\Delta q_2}$. That is, using equation (6.1) in the context of the q_2 market, where $\Delta m=C_1$, obtains

$$\widetilde{\Delta q_2}=\eta^2\cdot q_2\cdot\frac{C_1}{m_0}.$$

Thus, using equation (6.8) and the fact that $\Delta S_2\doteq q_2\,|\Delta p_2|$ for small Δp_2,

$$\text{area } y\doteq|\Delta p_2|\cdot\widetilde{\Delta q_2}\doteq|\Delta p_2|\cdot\eta^2\cdot q_2\cdot\frac{C_1}{m_0}\doteq\frac{\eta^2}{m_0}\,\Delta S_2\Delta S_1. \tag{6.11}$$

Note that, in making the approximation in the last step, a term with $(m_0)^2$ in the denominator is discarded. Because m_0 is generally large relative to surplus changes, this approximation is not serious.[12] Recalling that $\tilde{C}_2$ overestimates the correct component of compensating variation C_2 corresponding to the second part of the price path by area y, an appropriate estimate of C_2 is thus obtained by subtracting equation (6.11) from equation (6.10):

$$\hat{C}_2=\Delta S_2-\frac{\eta^2}{2m_0}(\Delta S_2)^2-\frac{\eta^2}{m_0}(\Delta S_1)(\Delta S_2). \tag{6.12}$$

Aggregating equations (6.9) and (6.12) estimates the sum of compensating variations or the overall compensating variation associated with the price change from $(p_1^0,\,p_2^0)$ to $(p_1^1,\,p_2^1)$:

$$\hat{C}_1+\hat{C}_2=\Delta S_1+\Delta S_2-\frac{\eta^1}{2m_0}(\Delta S_1)^2-\frac{\eta^2}{m_0}(\Delta S_1)(\Delta S_2)-\frac{\eta^2}{2m_0}(\Delta S_2)^2. \tag{6.13}$$

12. Actually, the discarded term is

$$\frac{\eta^1\eta^2}{2m_0^2}\,\Delta S_2(\Delta S_1)^2=\pm2\hat{\varepsilon}^1\hat{\varepsilon}^2\,\Delta S_1,$$

where $\hat{\varepsilon}=\eta^i|s_i|/2$ and $s_i=\Delta S_i/m_0$. Under conditions similar to those suggested above in the one-price-change case, $|\hat{\varepsilon}_i|\leq0.05$, so the discarded term represents less than 0.5 percent of ΔS_1 (that is, $|2\hat{\varepsilon}^1\hat{\varepsilon}^2|<0.005$).

If the income elasticities are the same in each market ($\hat{\eta}=\eta^1=\eta^2$) or are estimated by $\hat{\eta} =(\eta^1+\eta^2)/2$, then the overall compensating variation in equation (6.13) is estimated by

$$\begin{aligned}\hat{C} &= \Delta S_1 + \Delta S_2 - \frac{\hat{\eta}}{2m_0}(\Delta S_1)^2 - \frac{\hat{\eta}}{m_0}(\Delta S_1)(\Delta S_2) - \frac{\hat{\eta}}{2m_0}(\Delta S_2)^2 \\ &= \sum_{i=1}^{2} \Delta S_i - \frac{\hat{\eta}}{2m_0}\left(\sum_{i=1}^{2} \Delta S_i\right)^2 \\ &= \sum_{i=1}^{2} \Delta S_i - \hat{\varepsilon}\left|\sum_{i=1}^{2} \Delta S_i\right|,\end{aligned} \tag{6.14}$$

where

$$\hat{\varepsilon} = \frac{\hat{\eta}|s|}{2},\ s = \sum_{i=1}^{2} \frac{\Delta S_i}{m_0}.$$

Similarly, if one defines

$$\eta_1 = \min(\eta^1, \eta^2)$$

and

$$\eta_2 = \max(\eta^1, \eta^2),$$

where the minimization and maximization are performed with respect to the (arbitrary) price path as well as commodities, then approximate bounds on the true compensating variation are given by

$$\bar{C}_1 = \sum_{i=1}^{2} \Delta S_1 - \varepsilon_1\left|\sum_{i=1}^{2} \Delta S_1\right| \tag{6.15}$$

and

$$\bar{C}_2 = \sum_{i=1}^{2} \Delta S_1 - \varepsilon_2\left|\sum_{i=1}^{2} \Delta S_i\right|, \tag{6.16}$$

where

$$\varepsilon_i = \frac{\eta_i|s|}{2},\ i = 1,2.$$

As shown in Appendix Section 6.B, these approximations generalize for the case of price changes in many markets, and the associated errors of approximation are not much more serious than in the single-price-change case. A similar approximation of the equivalent variation is also possible and, as confirmed by Appendix Section 6.B, leads to the estimate

$$\hat{E} = \sum_{i=1}^{n} \Delta S_i + \hat{\varepsilon}\left|\sum_{i=1}^{n} \Delta S_i\right| \tag{6.17}$$

with approximate bounds

$$\bar{E}_1 = \sum_{i=1}^{n} \Delta S_i + \varepsilon_2 \left| \sum_{i=1}^{n} \Delta S_i \right| \tag{6.18}$$

and

$$\bar{E}_2 = \sum_{i=1}^{n} \Delta S_i + \varepsilon_1 \left| \sum_{i=1}^{n} \Delta S_i \right|. \tag{6.19}$$

Again, the errors of approximation are small for most practical cases. *If income elasticities are constant and the same in all markets for which prices change, then no more than about 1 percent error is incurred by using $\hat{C}$ or $\hat{E}$ as estimates of the associated WTP measures, as long as $|\hat{\varepsilon}| = |\hat{\eta}s/2| \leq 0.1$. If income elasticity is not constant, then no more than about 2 percent error is made by using $\hat{C}$ or $\hat{E}$ if $|\hat{\varepsilon}| = |\hat{\eta}s/2| \leq 0.08$ and income elasticity varies less than 50 percent among commodities and over the path of the price change.* As discussed earlier, these conditions are satisfied in a wide variety of (but not all) practical cases.[13]

From equations (6.14) through (6.19), it is also evident that ε_1 and ε_2 reflect the extent of error incurred by using the raw consumer surplus change, $\Sigma_{i=1}^{n} \Delta S_i$, as a direct estimate of C or E. That is, because approximate bounds are given by $\bar{C}_2 \leq C \leq \bar{C}_1$ and $\bar{E}_2 \leq E \leq \bar{E}_1$, subtraction of $\Sigma_{i=1}^{n} \Delta S_i$ and division by $|\Sigma_{i=1}^{n} \Delta S_i|$ obtains approximate bounds

$$\varepsilon_2 \geq \frac{\sum_{i=1}^{n} \Delta S_i - C}{\left| \sum_{i=1}^{n} \Delta S_i \right|} \geq \varepsilon_1 \tag{6.20}$$

and

$$\varepsilon_2 \geq \frac{E - \sum_{i=1}^{n} \Delta S_i}{\left| \sum_{i=1}^{n} \Delta S_i \right|} \geq \varepsilon_1 \tag{6.21}$$

on the respective percentage errors.

To exemplify application of the results above, consider demand relationships

$$q_i = 12 - 5p_i + 2p_j + \tfrac{3}{200} m$$

and

$$q_j = 5 - 5p_j + 3p_i + \tfrac{2}{200} m$$

for, say, beef and pork, the quantities of which are represented respectively by q_i and q_j. Suppose that respective prices change from $p_i^0 = p_j^0 = 1$ to $p_i^1 = p_j^1 = 2$ while income remains at $m_0 = 400$. First, consider the change in consumer surplus along the path where p_i is first

13. Although Willig developed an algorithm that can estimate the compensating or equivalent variations even more precisely using information about the difference in income elasticities over intervals composing the overall price change, other exact approaches are available once the convenience of Willig's rule of thumb is forgone. See Appendix Sections 6.D through 6.F.

adjusted from p_i^0 to p_i^1, then p_j is adjusted from p_j^0 to p_j^1. Holding p_j at p_j^0, the demand curve for q_i is

$$q_i = 20 - 5p_i,$$

which, as is apparent from Figure 6.13(a), generates a change in surplus of

$$\Delta S_i = -\tfrac{25}{2}$$

as p_1 moves from p_i^0 to p_i^1. Now, holding p_i at p_i^1, the demand curve for q_j is

$$q_j = 15 - 5p_j$$

which, as suggested by Figure 6.13(b), generates a surplus change of

$$\Delta S_j = -\tfrac{15}{2}$$

as p_j moves from p_i^0 to p_j^1. Thus, the consumer surplus change is

$$\Delta S_i + \Delta S_j = -20.$$

But how accurate is this figure as an estimate of the compensating or equivalent variation, and how might it be modified to obtain greater accuracy? To use equations (6.14) through (6.19) to answer these questions, one must first compute income elasticities over the path of price adjustment. Using the demand equation for q_i, one finds that

$$\frac{\Delta q_i}{\Delta m} = \tfrac{3}{200}$$

for any change in income holding prices fixed. Hence, the income elasticity is

$$\eta_i = \frac{\Delta q_i}{\Delta m}\frac{m}{q_i} = \frac{6}{q_i}.$$

Similarly,

$$\frac{\Delta q_j}{\Delta m} = \tfrac{2}{200}$$

and

$$\eta_j = \frac{4}{q_j}.$$

Noting from Figure 6.13 that $10 \le q_i \le 15$ and $5 \le q_j \le 10$ along the selected price path implies that $0.4 = 6/15 \le \eta_i \le 6/10 = 0.6$ and $0.4 = 4/10 \le \eta_j \le 4/5 = 0.8$ along the respective segments of the price path. Thus, the minimum and maximum income elasticities along the price path are $\eta_1 = 0.4$ and $\eta_2 = 0.8$, respectively, and

$$\hat{\eta} = \frac{(0.4 + 0.8)}{2} = 0.6$$

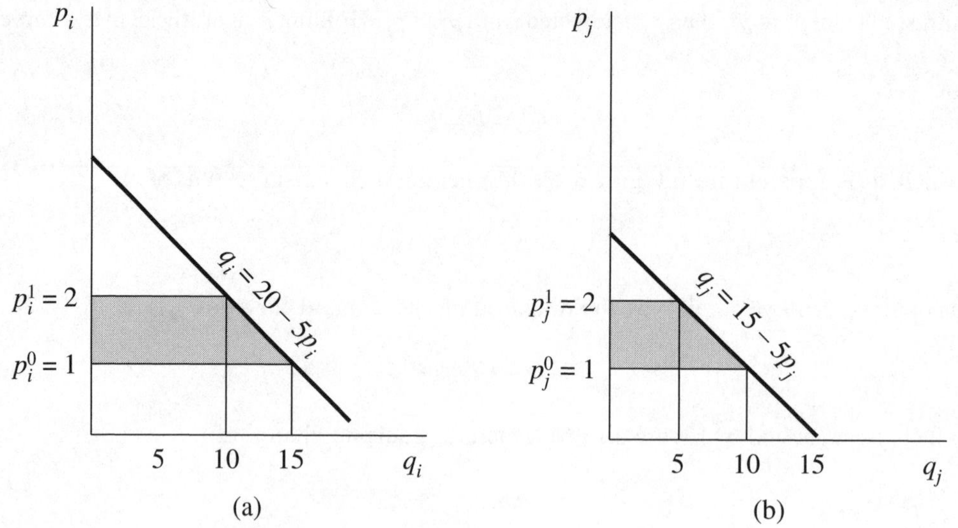

Figure 6.13

$$s = \frac{\Delta S_i + \Delta S_j}{m_0} = -\tfrac{20}{400} = -0.05$$

$$\hat{\varepsilon} = \frac{0.6|-0.05|}{2} = 0.015$$

$$\varepsilon_1 = \frac{0.4|-0.05|}{2} = 0.01$$

$$\varepsilon_2 = \frac{0.8|-0.05|}{2} = 0.02.$$

Substituting these calculations into equations (6.14) through (6.19) implies the following:

1. From equation (6.14), $\Delta S_i + \Delta S_j$ overestimates the compensating variation by about 1.5 percent ($\hat{\varepsilon} \times 100$).
2. From equation (6.17), $\Delta S_i + \Delta S_j$ underestimates the equivalent variation by about 1.5 percent.
3. Thus, using equations (6.14) and (6.17), better estimates of the compensating and equivalent variations are $\hat{C} = -20 - 0.015|-20| = -20.3$ and $\hat{E} = -20 + 0.015|-20| = -19.7$, respectively.
4. From equations (6.15) and (6.16), the compensating variation is approximately bounded by $-20.4 \leq C \leq -20.2$ and from equations (6.18) and (6.19), the equivalent variation is approximately bounded by[14] $-19.8 \leq E \leq -19.6$.

14. For cases such as this where income elasticities vary along the price path, one may use the accurate bounds from Appendix Section 6.B to determine, for example, that

$$0.02019 \geq \frac{\Delta S_i + \Delta S_j - C}{|\Delta S_i + \Delta S_j|} \geq 0.00996.$$

6.7 CONSUMER SURPLUS AS A WTP MEASURE: THE PRICE–INCOME-CHANGE CASE

One final note is necessary in using the methods of the preceding two sections when estimating WTP if income also changes. Consider, for example, changing price(s) and income according to the paths demonstrated in Figure 6.14(a), that is, either changing prices and then income (L_1), or first income and then prices (L_2). A key point to note here is that the methods for evaluating the effect of a price change in Sections 6.5 and 6.6 assume that the initial set of prices corresponds to the initial utility level. If one uses path L_1, the initial utility level on the segment where price(s) change is, indeed, the initial utility level for the overall change, so the methods of Sections 6.5 and 6.6 apply. Thus, the compensating variation corresponding to the price change must be added to the subsequent WTP for the income change, which continues to hold utility at the overall initial level. The latter effect is trivially equal to the change in income. On the other hand, if one first changes income, thus generating compensating variation equal to the change in income, the level of utility at which the price-change segment of the path begins is different from the initial utility level, and modifications in the methods to correct for this difference would be required.

The methods of Sections 6.5 and 6.6 can thus be employed directly in evaluating compensating variation for the price–income-change case only if the income change is considered after the price change(s) (merely by adding the income change to the compensating variation generated by the price change). In the case of equivalent variation, just the reverse is true because computations correspond to the terminal utility level. That is, the price change(s) must be considered after the income change, so that the terminal utility of the price–change segment of the path is the same as the terminal utility level of the overall price–income change.

Application of these arguments is considered graphically in Figure 6.14(b) for the case where income and a single price changes from (m_0,p_1^0) to (m_1,p_1^1), respectively. Initially, the ordinary and compensated demand curves are $D(m_0)$ and $H(U_0)$, respectively, and subsequently change to $D(m_1)$ and $H(U_0)$, respectively. Thus, U_0 is the initial utility level, U_1 is the subsequent utility level, and U_0^* is the utility level after the income change but before the price change. Consider, first, the case of estimating compensating variation. Of course, because $H(U_0)$ is the appropriate compensated demand curve (it is conditioned on the initial utility level), the compensating variation is

$$C=m_1-m_0+\text{area } a.$$

Area a is estimated by correcting the change in consumer surplus, area $a+b$, associated with $D(m_0)$ by an estimate of area b. If one uses the change in surplus, area $a+b+c+d$,

Substituting $\Delta S_i+\Delta S_j=-20$ thus implies that

$$-20.4038\leq C\leq -20.1992.$$

A comparison with the approximated bounds above suggests, and rightfully so, that the width in error bounds caused by income elasticity variation is great enough to make further adjustments at least when income elasticities vary to any substantial degree. For practical purposes, the bounds in (6.20) and (6.21) are close enough to accurate that the more complicated (accurate) methods of Appendix Section 6.B are not worth the additional computational burden. Furthermore, if more accuracy is desired, then the exact methods of Appendix Sections 6.D and 6.F are preferred.

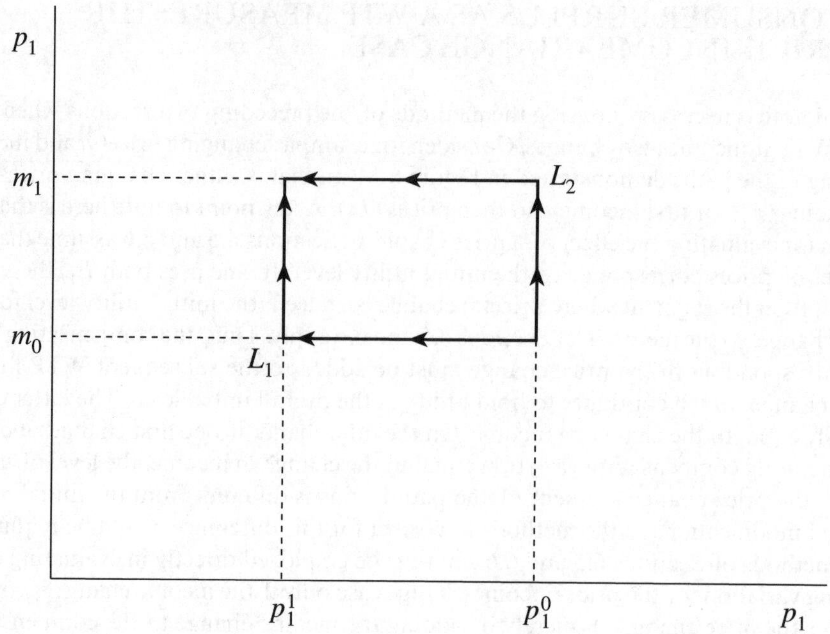

(a)

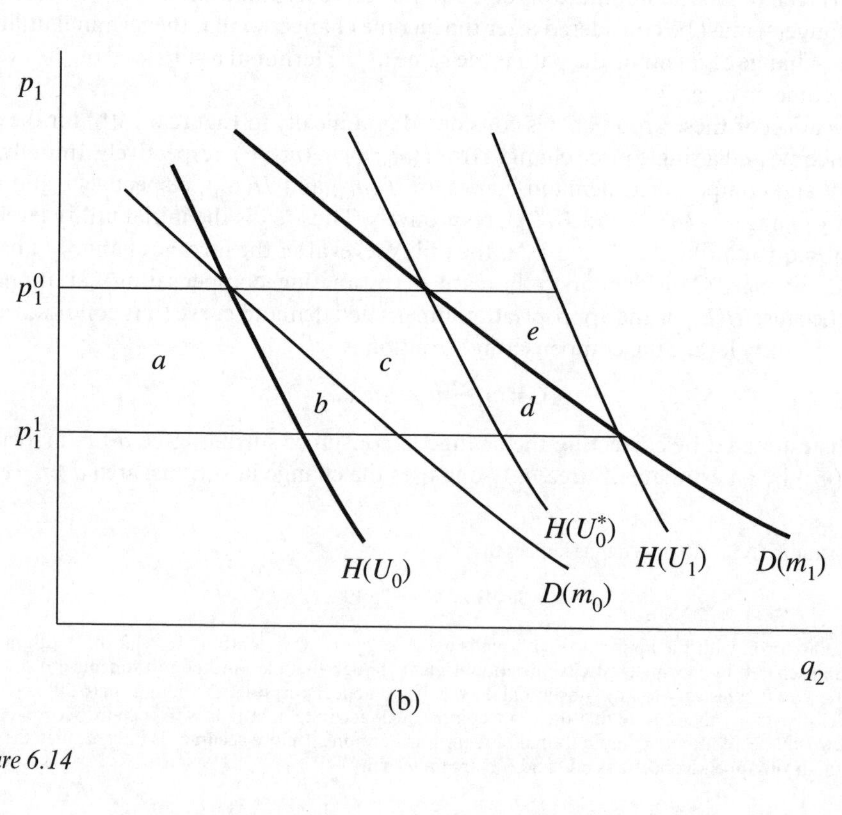

(b)

Figure 6.14

associated with $D(m_1)$, on the other hand, the correction approximates area d and gives a resulting estimate of area $a+b+c$. Hence, the associated estimate of compensating variation would approximate (area $a+b+c)+m_1-m_0$ and would be in error by approximately area $b+c$. Thus, *to estimate compensating variation using the methods of Sections 6.5 and 6.6, one must evaluate the effects of the price change at the initial income level and then add to that effect the change in income.*

Turning to estimation of equivalent variation, let U_1 represent the terminal level of utility following the price–income change. Both the price and income segments of the path of adjustment are properly evaluated at the terminal utility level. This is accomplished by evaluating the price change conditioned on the terminal income level. Thus, the change in area behind the terminal compensated demand curve, area $a+b+c+d+e$, is obtained by adding an estimate of area e to the surplus change, area $a+b+c+d$, associated with the ordinary demand curve conditioned on the terminal income. Thus, *to estimate equivalent variation, one must evaluate the effects of the price change at the terminal income level and then add that effect to the change in income.*

6.8 EXACT MEASUREMENT OF WTP

As the Willig approach suggests, ordinary demand relationships can be used to derive information about Hicksian compensated demands by using the information they contain regarding response to income changes. This information can be used to infer Hicksian demands and the related exact measurements of compensating and equivalent variation. This approach eliminates the need to rely on consumer surplus as an approximation of WTP measures.

This possibility was first suggested by Hause (1975) and later demonstrated more generally by Hausman (1981) with a somewhat different approach. To obtain estimates of the WTP measures directly from ordinary supply and demand equations, Hause recognized that the initial Hicksian demand curve $H_1(U_1)$ can be found by incrementally adjusting the income level that determines the ordinary demand curve by the compensating variation of each infinitesimal price increment beginning from the initial price as illustrated in Figure 6.6. This calculation is equivalent to calculating the income effect of moving along the initial indirect utility curve in Figure 6.9. Mathematically, this calculation turns out to be a differential equation problem. While Hause attempted to solve this problem for a multiple demand system without recognizing the restrictions implied by utility maximization, Hausman derived exact solutions for certain single-equation demand specifications. However, his approach depends on being able to find a closed-form solution to the differential equation.

In further work, Vartia (1983) developed an algorithm to solve the multiple-equation differential equation problem associated with multiple price changes numerically. His algorithm is illustrated in Figure 6.15 where a price change from p_0 to p_3 is imposed in incremental changes first to p_1, then to p_2, and finally to p_3. Initially, income is m_0 and utility is U_0 with Marshallian demand $D(m_0)$ and Hicksian demand $H(U_0)$. The compensating variation of the first price change to p_1 is given by area a_0 which, for small price changes, is approximated by the consumer surplus change, area a_0+a_1. Next, this money measure of welfare change is subtracted from initial income m_0 to obtain income m_1 and

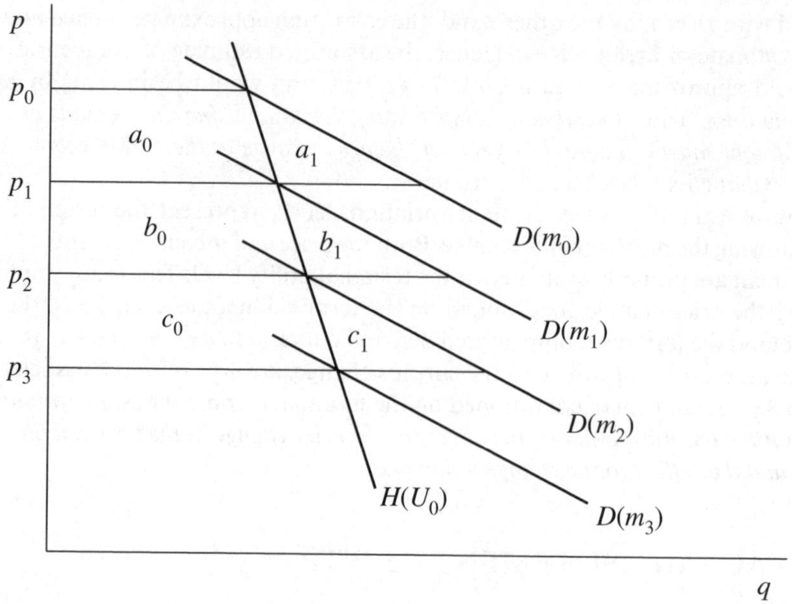

Figure 6.15

demand $D(m_1)$. Aside from the error in approximation, this obtains the demand after taking away income to attain the initial level of utility, which crosses the Hicksian compensated demand at p_1.

The same procedure is then repeated for the price increment to p_2 by subtracting area b_0+b_1 (as an approximation of area b_0) from m_1, obtaining m_2 and an approximation of $D(m_2)$, which again restores the initial utility level. The procedure is repeated again until the subsequent price p_3 is reached by subtracting area c_0+c_1 (as an approximation of area c_0) from m_2 to obtain m_3, which aside from an approximation error restores the initial utility level once more. The approximation of compensating variation for the entire price change from p_0 to p_3 is thus $m_3-m_0=$ area $a_0+a_1+b_0+b_1+c_0+c_1$. The error of approximation is $a_1+b_1+c_1$. The Vartia algorithm is to repeat this approach increasing the number of price change increments into which the overall price change is divided until the estimate of compensating variation converges. Clearly, as the overall price change is broken into many small changes the estimate converges to the true compensating variation, area $a_0+b_0+c_0$, because the error triangles become smaller.

Further details about each of these approaches are provided in Appendix Section 6.D. A related mathematical complication for multiple-price-change cases is also discussed in Appendix Section 6.D. The problem is that a set of demand equations following arbitrary specifications may not relate to any common underlying consumer utility maximization problem. All of the results in this chapter and the Appendix to this chapter, including those of Willig, Hause and Vartia, assume that the set of demand relationships for all goods under consideration is derived from a common underlying utility maximization problem.[15] The conditions that must be satisfied for a system of demands to relate to a

15. See Appendix Section 6.E for further details.

common utility maximization problem are called integrability conditions (see Appendix Section 6.E for a definition). When these conditions do not hold, the Willig bounds do not apply and the Vartia algorithm, although it may converge to a unique result, becomes arbitrary because the WTP measures become path dependent. LaFrance (1985, 1986) has shown that imposing integrability conditions on common arbitrary simple forms such as linear and log-linear demands yields an implausible and unacceptable loss of flexibility. The upshot of these results is that the most convenient way to approach empirical welfare analysis in the multiple-price-change case is to start by specifying an indirect utility function, $V(p, m)$, and then derive the demand specifications from it using results from duality. This approach is explained in Appendix Section 6.F.

6.9 CONCLUSIONS

The development of measures of gain based upon what a consumer is willing to pay for an improved situation began long ago with the French engineer Dupuit (1844). Following Alfred Marshall's (1930) shift in emphasis to money measures of utility change, Professor Hicks (1956) reestablished WTP measures as the foundation for applied welfare work. The two chief measures he proposed – compensating and equivalent variation – are directly related to the consumer's preference map, and each yields a unique measure of gain for any price path from the initial to the terminal situation. Moreover, because each can be given WTP interpretations, each can be used to perform the Kaldor–Hicks and Scitovsky compensation tests when more than one consumer is involved. That is, asking if the gainer can compensate the loser and still prefer a change is equivalent to asking if the compensating variation of the gainer (or WTP to keep the change) is greater than the compensating variation of the loser (or willingness-to-accept payment to make the change). Of course, the same questions can be asked for the reverse movement and, as Scitovsky (1941) pointed out, can lead to the paradoxical situation where the test suggests a change be made – but once made, the same test suggests the reverse movement be made. This situation arises because compensating variation is unequal to equivalent variation for each of the consumers involved. Only for the case where compensating and equivalent variation coincide are they both equal to consumer surplus so that a reversal definitely does not occur.

The definition of consumer surplus for the purpose of these comparisons is that of simply an area – the calculated dollar area behind the demand curve and above the price line. This area obtains welfare significance in the context of this chapter only insofar as it can be related to the Hicksian WTP measures of consumer welfare change. Hicks (1956) argued that, if the income effect is 'small', consumer surplus will provide a 'good' approximation of either compensating or equivalent variation. But Willig (1976) provided precise quantitative guidance as to how 'small' the income effect must be to obtain a 'good' approximation. The Willig formulas in Sections 6.5 and 6.6 can indeed be used to calculate error bounds on consumer surplus as an approximation of either welfare quantity. These empirical embellishments of Hicks's conceptual results thus provide a sound foundation for consumer welfare measurement. These results are made possible by an important dual relationship which exists between demands and preferences. That is, just as demands can be derived from preferences through utility maximization, one can, in principle, determine preferences in an ordinal context from consumer demand equations.

As an alternative to the approach of Willig, the approaches of Hause (1975), Hausman (1981) and Vartia (1983) based on these same foundations permit exact measurement of WTP (as discussed in Appendix Section 6.D). The important qualification of each of these approaches as well as that of Willig's is that demands used for welfare calculations must satisfy restrictions from consumer theory (integrability conditions) whenever multiple price changes are involved. The implication is that evaluation of the welfare effects of multiple price changes usually requires the welfare economist to estimate demands imposing proper theoretical relationships (integrability) rather than simply applying welfare calculations to estimated demands assembled from a variety of existing studies (which would almost surely fail to satisfy integrability). This approach is discussed rigorously in Appendix Section 6.F, which outlines an approach to estimation of demands based on the theory of duality. On the other hand, many applied welfare analyses involve a single price change where existing estimates of demands can be used without these problems.

Appendix to Chapter 6: Welfare measurement for consumers

Although a unique and broadly applicable money measure of utility change is seemingly impossible to develop (as demonstrated in Chapter 5), Harberger (1971) has continued to argue that consumer surplus provides a reasonable approximation as a measure of consumer welfare. Burns (1977) subsequently argued that path dependence is of little practical consequence because all reasonable paths in price–income space lead to results that are bounded by the Hicksian compensating and equivalent variations. Richter (1974), in fact, suggested abandonment of 'money measures' of utility change altogether in favor of using the well-defined willingness-to-pay (WTP) concepts of compensating and equivalent variation proposed by Hicks. He further suggested estimating the Hicksian measures directly using the expenditure function approach.

Accordingly, this chapter has turned to the alternative and less restrictive concepts of compensating and equivalent variation as measures of consumer welfare. The purpose of this appendix is fourfold. Section 6.A offers a precise justification of the alternative WTP measures of consumer welfare based on the work of Burns and Richter. This development focuses on measurement of welfare change for a single utility-maximizing consumer in a comparative static sense. Chapter 8 later generalizes the analysis to consider market aggregation.

Section 6.B turns to a precise determination of the practical applicability or accuracy of consumer surplus as a measure of the alternative Hicksian welfare concepts. Simple consumer surplus calculations as originally proposed by Marshall (1930) and supported by Harberger (1971) have continued in widespread use because of their convenience for both conceptual and empirical purposes. Thus, a precise assessment of the extent of error is needed. The work of Willig (1973, 1976) established precise error bounds on consumer surplus as an approximation of the Hicksian compensating and equivalent variations. His work shows that consumer surplus provides a useful approximation of welfare change in most cases and thus justifies the continued use of consumer surplus as an approximation.

Alternatively, Section 6.C considers circumstances under which any particular WTP measure is more appropriate than another when either can be calculated accurately. Sections 6.D through 6.F then present the approaches for accurate measurement of WTP. The approaches developed by Hause (1975), Hausman (1981) and Vartia (1983) as well as possibilities for estimating flexible and integrable system structures based on duality form the core of the methodology for accurate measurement of WTP. These approaches are based on the suggestion of estimating Hicksian measures using the expenditure function approach, or a similar approach using the indirect utility function, both of which can be inferred from estimated Marshallian demands.

6.A WTP MEASURES FOR CONSUMERS

This section defines the Hicksian concepts of compensating and equivalent variation precisely in mathematical terms. Consider the counterpart (or dual) of the standard utility-maximization problem which, rather than maximizing utility, seeks to minimize consumer expenditures subject to a given utility level $\bar{U}$:

$$e(\boldsymbol{p},\bar{U}) \equiv \min_{\boldsymbol{q}} \{\boldsymbol{pq} | U(\boldsymbol{q}) = \bar{U}, \boldsymbol{q} \geq 0\}, \tag{6.22}$$

with notation and assumptions as defined in the Appendix to Chapter 5. Solving first-order conditions of the associated Lagrangian assuming an internal solution, $\mathcal{L} = \boldsymbol{pq} + \lambda[U(\boldsymbol{q}) - \bar{U}]$, obtains the Hicksian compensated demand functions, $\boldsymbol{q}(\boldsymbol{p},\bar{U}) = [\bar{q}_1(\boldsymbol{p},\bar{U}),\ldots,\bar{q}_N(\boldsymbol{p},\bar{U})]$.The expenditure function e, defined by (6.22), which gives the minimum expenditure as a function of prices and utility level, can also be represented by substituting compensated demands into the objective function of (6.22),[1]

$$e(\boldsymbol{p},\bar{U}) = \boldsymbol{p}\bar{\boldsymbol{q}}(\boldsymbol{p},\bar{U}).$$

Setting this expenditure function equal to income m and solving for utility obtains the indirect utility function,

$$V(\boldsymbol{p},m) = e^{-1}(\boldsymbol{p},m),$$

which gives the maximum utility that can be gained with prices $\boldsymbol{p}$ and income m.

Consider now a change in prices and income from $(\boldsymbol{p}^0,m_0)$ to $(\boldsymbol{p}^1,m_1)$, which leads to a change in maximum utility from U^0 to U^1. The Hicksian compensating variation (C), that is, the amount of income that must be taken away from a consumer (possibly negative) after a price and/or income change to restore the consumer's original welfare level (where consumption adjustments are possible) is defined implicitly by

$$V(\boldsymbol{p}^1,m_1 - C) = V(\boldsymbol{p}^0,m_0) = U^0, \tag{6.23}$$

which upon solving for C yields[2]

$$C = m_1 - e(\boldsymbol{p}^1,U^0). \tag{6.24}$$

The Hicksian equivalent variation (E), that is, the amount of income that must be given to a consumer (possibly negative) in lieu of price and income changes to leave the consumer as well off as with the change (where consumption adjustments are possible), is similarly defined implicitly using the indirect utility function as

$$U^1 = V(\boldsymbol{p}^1,m_1) = V(\boldsymbol{p}^0,m_0 + E), \tag{6.25}$$

1. A clear explanation of this approach, as well as properties of the expenditure function, was given by McFadden and Winter (1968) but a more accessible reference is Varian (1992).
2. The alternative representations of compensating variation in (6.23) and (6.24) follow immediately upon noting the identity $\bar{U} = V(\boldsymbol{p},e(\boldsymbol{p},\bar{U}))$. That is, using (6.24) in the left-hand side of (6.23) yields

$$V(\boldsymbol{p}^1,m_1 + C) = V(\boldsymbol{p}^1,e(\boldsymbol{p}^1,U^0)) = V(\boldsymbol{p}^0,e(\boldsymbol{p}^0,U^0)) = V(\boldsymbol{p}^0,m_0).$$

A similar relationship holds for equivalent variation.

which upon solving for E yields

$$E = e(\mathbf{p}^0, U^1) - m_0. \tag{6.26}$$

To relate these definitions to the usual graphical analysis in quantity–quantity and price–quantity space, it can be noted that E and C correspond to the actual income change plus the areas to the left of the Hicksian compensated demand curves (and between prices) where the compensated demands are associated with final and initial utility levels, respectively.[3] To see this, note that

$$\mathbf{e_p} \equiv \partial e/\partial \mathbf{p} = \bar{\mathbf{q}}(\mathbf{p}, \bar{U}) + \mathbf{p}\bar{\mathbf{q}}_\mathbf{p},$$

where $\mathbf{p}\bar{\mathbf{q}}_\mathbf{p} \equiv \mathbf{p}\partial\bar{\mathbf{q}}/\partial\mathbf{p} \equiv \Sigma_{i=1}^N p_i\partial\bar{q}_i/\partial\mathbf{p} = [\Sigma_{i=1}^N p_i\partial\bar{q}_i/\partial p_1,\ldots,\Sigma_{i=1}^N p_i\partial\bar{q}_i/\partial p_N]$. Using (5.2) in this expression (which is basically an application of the envelope theorem) yields

$$\mathbf{p}\bar{\mathbf{q}}_\mathbf{p} = \frac{1}{\lambda}U_q\bar{\mathbf{q}}_\mathbf{p} = \frac{1}{\lambda}\frac{d\bar{U}}{d\mathbf{p}} = 0,$$

where the third equality holds because $\bar{U} \equiv U(\bar{q}(p, \bar{U}))$ is simply an identity. Hence, the partial derivatives of the expenditure function with respect to prices $\mathbf{p}$,

$$\mathbf{e_p} = \bar{\mathbf{q}}(\mathbf{p}, U), \tag{6.27}$$

are precisely the corresponding Hicksian compensated demands. Thus, using (6.27) to compute the area between prices and left of the compensated demand corresponding to utility level $\bar{U}$, one finds

$$\begin{aligned} e(\mathbf{p}^0, \bar{U}) - e(\mathbf{p}^1, \bar{U}) &= -\int_L \mathbf{e_p}(\mathbf{p}, \bar{U})d\mathbf{p} \\ &= -\int_L \bar{\mathbf{q}}(\mathbf{p}, \bar{U})d\mathbf{p}, \end{aligned} \tag{6.28}$$

where L denotes any path of integration in price space from $\mathbf{p}^0$ to $\mathbf{p}^1$ and, for example, $\mathbf{e_p}d\mathbf{p} \equiv \Sigma_{i=1}^N e_{p_i}dp_i$. Because the integrand of (6.28) is an exact differential of e with respect to $\mathbf{p}$, no path-dependence problems are encountered.[4]

3. As Bergson (1975, p. 42) has pointed out, 'the compensating and equivalent variations are nothing more than the "true" magnitudes of real income variations that we seek to approximate when we compile index numbers of real income according to the Paasche formula, on the one hand, and the Laspeyres formula, on the other'. Specifically, the Laspeyres and Paasche formulas correspond to the inner and outer cost differences, respectively, described in Section 5.1. The compensating and equivalent variations, on the other hand, correspond to the Laspeyres–Konyus and Paasche–Konyus formulas, respectively (Konyus indices are defined in terms of preferences of an individual consumer). Thus, as noted by Samuelson (1947, p. 196), the theory of consumer surplus is mathematically equivalent in many respects to the theory of index numbers. See also Wold and Jureen (1953) and Burns (1973, 1977).

   Because the Laspeyres and Paasche variations (the inner and outer cost differences, respectively) bound consumer surplus for a single-price-change case (see Section 5.1), some have argued that, in lieu of calculating consumer surplus, one can simply calculate the Paasche and Laspeyres variations and use an average of the two as a measure of welfare change if the two are acceptably close to one another. One should beware of this practice, however, because the premise does not necessarily hold for a multiple price change, as pointed out (once again) by Samuelson and Swamy (1974) in the context of index number theory. A related discussion is also found in the exchange of McKenzie (1979) and Willig (1979).
4. As is well known (Henderson and Quandt 1971, p. 36 or Varian 1992, ch. 8), $\partial\bar{q}_i/\partial p_j = \partial\bar{q}_j/\partial p_i$ holds along an indifference surface, which is exactly the condition for path independence in (6.28) when U does not change along L. See footnote 4 of the Appendix to Chapter 5.

To interpret C in (6.24) geometrically, note that the budget constraint and (6.28) implies that

$$\begin{aligned} C &= m_1 - e(\mathbf{p^1}, U^0) = m_1 - m_0 + e(\mathbf{p^0}, U^0) - e(\mathbf{p^1}, U^0) \\ &= \Delta m - \int_L \mathbf{e_p}(\mathbf{p}, U^0)\, d\mathbf{p} \end{aligned} \tag{6.29}$$

where $\Delta m = m_1 - m_0$, which upon following the same path of integration leading to (5.20) through (5.22) yields

$$C = \Delta m - \sum_{j=1}^{N} \int_{p_i^0}^{p_j^1} \bar{q}_j(\hat{\mathbf{p}}_j(p_j), U^0) dp_j.$$

where

$$\hat{\mathbf{p}}_i(p_i) \equiv (p_1^1, \ldots, p_{i-1}^1, p_i, p_{i+1}^0, \ldots, p_N^0).$$

Thus, the Hicksian compensating variation is uniquely measured by adding to the change in income all the changes left of compensated demands, where demands are all evaluated at the initial utility level but successively conditioned on previously considered price changes (conditioned on initial prices for the first good considered). Again, as in (5.22), the order of integration makes no difference.

To interpret E in (6.26) geometrically, note that the budget constraint, together with (6.28), implies that

$$\begin{aligned} E &= e(\mathbf{p^0}, U^1) - m_0 = e(\mathbf{p^0}, U^1) - e(\mathbf{p^1}, U^1) + m_1 - m_0 \\ &= -\int_L \bar{\mathbf{q}}(\mathbf{p}, U^1)\, d\mathbf{p} + \Delta m, \\ &= \Delta m - \sum_{j=1}^{N} \int_{p_j^0}^{p_j^1} \bar{q}_j(\hat{\mathbf{p}}_j(p_j), U^1) dp_j. \end{aligned} \tag{6.30}$$

Thus, the Hicksian equivalent variation is uniquely measured by adding to the actual change in income all the changes in areas left of the compensated demands where the compensated demand functions are all evaluated at the final utility level but successively conditioned on all previously considered price changes.

Clearly, the Hicksian compensating and equivalent variations are not always equal. However, from (6.29) and (6.30), one finds that

$$E - C = \sum_{j=1}^{N} \int_{p_j^0}^{p_j^1} [\bar{q}_j(\hat{\mathbf{p}}_j(p_j), U^0) - \bar{q}_j(\hat{\mathbf{p}}_j(p_j), U^1)] dp_j.$$

This difference is zero if and only if

$$\begin{aligned} &\int_{p_j^0}^{p_j^1} [\bar{q}_j(\hat{\mathbf{p}}_j(p_j), U^0) - \bar{q}_j(\hat{\mathbf{p}}_j(p_j), U^1)] dp_j \\ &= - \int_{p_j^0}^{p_j^1} \int_{U^0}^{U^1} \frac{\partial \bar{q}_j(\hat{\mathbf{p}}_j(p_j), U)}{\partial U} dU dp_j = 0 \end{aligned} \tag{6.31}$$

for each price p_j that changes. To consider when (6.31) holds, differentiate both sides of the identity $\bar{q}_j(\mathbf{p}, V(\mathbf{p}, m)) \equiv \tilde{q}_j(\mathbf{p}, m)$ with respect to m, which yields

$$\frac{\partial \bar{q}_j}{\partial m} = \frac{\partial \bar{q}_j}{\partial U}\frac{\partial V}{\partial m} = \frac{\partial \tilde{q}_j}{\partial m}. \tag{6.32}$$

Assuming nonsatiation ($\partial V/\partial m \neq 0$), equation (6.32) implies that the Hicksian demand is independent of utility if and only if the Marshallian demand is independent of income. Thus, equation (6.31) holds if and only if $\partial \tilde{q}_j/\partial m = 0$ (zero-income effects apply) for all commodities for which prices change.[5] The condition in (6.32) also implies that compensated demands $\bar{q}_j$ are independent of the utility level if and only if ordinary demands q_j are independent of income. Comparing (5.22), (5.23), (6.29) and (6.30), this implies

$$\Delta m + \sum_{j=1}^{N} \Delta S_j = E = C, \tag{6.33}$$

where ΔS_j is defined as in (5.23) if and only if income effects are zero (income elasticities are zero) for all prices that change.[6]

6.B PRACTICAL ASPECTS OF WTP MEASURES

It may appear at this point that adoption of WTP measures gains little over the money-measure-of-utility-change approach. Indeed, the conditions for equivalence of E and C are as restrictive as the conditions that lead to a unique money measure of utility change. However, in many practical cases, only one of these measures (E or C) is appropriate. Furthermore, the work of Willig (1973, 1976) has produced results that greatly enhance the WTP approach. This is accomplished by developing a general and reasonable set of conditions under which consumer surplus methodology leads to approximately the same measure of welfare change as suggested by compensating and equivalent variations – regardless of their equivalence.

The Willig results are attractive for some purposes because the estimation of consumer surplus is easier than direct estimation of compensating and equivalent variations when demands are arbitrarily specified (as in the case where a quick welfare analysis may be required on the basis of available elasticity estimates). That is, estimation of consumer surplus requires simply calculating the area under an estimated ordinary demand curve, whereas estimation of compensating and equivalent variations can involve solution of a system of partial differential equations based on estimated demand functions. See Appendix Section 6.D for further details.

The Single-Price-Change Case

Alternatively, one can use consumer surplus as a rather simple method of approximation. Errors of this approximation have been examined rigorously by Willig. This approach is

5. Again, this cannot be the case and (6.33) cannot hold if all prices change because, as shown earlier, having zero-income effects for all commodities violates the budget constraint. However, E and C may be equal in specific instances when income effects are not zero if the inner integral of (6.31) is zero. This case cannot be ruled out, because $\partial \bar{q}_j/\partial U$ may change signs over the path of integration as q_j switches from, say, a superior to an inferior good.
6. Technically, the necessity of zero-income effects requires continuous second-order differentiability of $\tilde{q}_i$ and $\tilde{q}_j$. The reader is also reminded that this is the case of quasilinear preferences. See footnote 12 of the Appendix to Chapter 5.

first demonstrated in the case of a single price change, that is, where the price change is from $\boldsymbol{p^0}=(p_1^0,\ldots,p_N^0)$ to $\boldsymbol{p^1}=(p_1^0,\ldots,p_{i-1}^0,p_i^1,p_{i+1}^0,\ldots,p_N^0), p_i^1 \neq p_i^0$. Assuming that η_1 and η_2 are lower and upper bounds on income elasticity, $\eta^i \equiv (\partial\tilde{q}_i/\partial m)(m/\tilde{q}_i)$, over the region of price and income space for which changes are considered, with $\eta_1 \neq 1 \neq \eta_2$,[7] results can be derived from the inequality[8]

$$\left(\frac{m_1}{m_0}\right)^{\eta_1} \leq \frac{\tilde{q}_i(\boldsymbol{p},m_1)}{\tilde{q}_i(\boldsymbol{p},m_0)} \leq \left(\frac{m_1}{m_0}\right)^{\eta_2}. \tag{6.34}$$

Letting $m_1 = e(\boldsymbol{p},U^0)$, the relationship in (6.34) implies that

$$\left[\frac{e(\boldsymbol{p},U^0)}{m_0}\right]^{\eta_1} \leq \frac{\tilde{q}_i[\boldsymbol{p},e(\boldsymbol{p},U^0)]}{\tilde{q}_i(\boldsymbol{p},m_0)} \leq \left[\frac{e(\boldsymbol{p},U^0)}{m_0}\right]^{\eta_2}.$$

Hence, substituting from (6.27) and rearranging implies that

$$\tilde{q}_i(\boldsymbol{p},m_0)\cdot m_0^{-\eta_1} \leq \frac{\partial e(\boldsymbol{p},U^0)}{\partial p_i}[e(\boldsymbol{p},U^0)]^{-\eta_1} = \frac{1}{1-\eta_1}\frac{\partial[e(\boldsymbol{p},U^0)^{1-\eta_1}]}{\partial p_i} \tag{6.35}$$

and

$$\frac{1}{1-\eta_2}\frac{\partial[e(\boldsymbol{p},U^0)^{1-\eta_2}]}{\partial p_i} = \frac{\partial e(\boldsymbol{p},U^0)}{\partial p_i}[e(\boldsymbol{p},U^0)]^{-\eta_2} \leq \tilde{q}_i(\boldsymbol{p},m_0)\cdot m_0^{-\eta_2}. \tag{6.36}$$

Integrating both sides of (6.35) and (6.36) then yields

$$-\Delta S_i \cdot m_0^{-\eta_1} = m_0^{-\eta_1}\int_{p_i^0}^{p_i^1} \tilde{q}_i(\boldsymbol{p},m_0)dp_i \leq \frac{[e(\boldsymbol{p^1},U^0)]^{1-\eta_1} - m_0^{1-\eta_1}}{1-\eta_1} \tag{6.37}$$

$$\frac{[e(\boldsymbol{p^1},U^0)]^{1-\eta_2} - m_0^{1-\eta_2}}{1-\eta_2} \leq m_0^{-\eta_2}\int_{p_i^0}^{p_i^1} \tilde{q}_i(\boldsymbol{p},m_0)dp_i = -\Delta S_i \cdot m_0^{-\eta_2}, \tag{6.38}$$

where ΔS_i is again the corresponding change in consumer surplus as the price of q_i changes from p_i^0 to p_i^1 (recall that $e(\boldsymbol{p^0},U^0) \equiv m_0$). From (6.38), one finds that

7. In theory, the choice of η_1 and η_2 is quite arbitrary and, of course, the width of bounds obtained depends directly on the range of income elasticities assumed. In empirical application, however, econometric estimates of income elasticity are usually obtained, and choice of η_1 and η_2 can be made objectively depending on statistical results.
8. This inequality follows from the mean value theorem upon representing m as $m \equiv e^t$. Whence, for $y(t) = \ln\tilde{q}_i(\boldsymbol{p},m)$, one has

$$\frac{dy}{dt} = \frac{dy}{dq_i}\frac{\partial\tilde{q}_i}{\partial m}\frac{dm}{dt} = \frac{1}{q_i}\frac{\partial\tilde{q}_i}{\partial m}e^t = \frac{\partial\tilde{q}_i}{\partial m}\frac{m}{q_i} = \eta^i,$$

and thus $\eta_1 \leq dy/dt \leq \eta_2$ for $\ln m_0 \leq t \leq \ln m_1$, where (m_0, m_1) is the range of income considerations. By the mean value theorem, there exists some $\tilde{t}$ such that

$$\frac{dy(\tilde{t})}{dt} = \frac{y(t_1)-y(t_0)}{t_1-t_0}.$$

Substituting the bounds on dy/dt and multiplying by $t_1 - t_0$ yields

$$\eta_1(t_1-t_0) \leq y(t_1) - y(t_0) \leq \eta_2(t_1-t_0).$$

The relationship in (6.34) follows upon noting that $t_i = \ln m_i$ and $y(t_i) = \ln\tilde{q}_i(\boldsymbol{p},m_i)$, $i=0, 1$. For more on the mean value theorem, see Danese (1965).

$$\left[\frac{e(\boldsymbol{p}^1,U^0)}{m_0}\right]^{1-\eta_2} \lesseqgtr 1-\frac{\Delta S_i}{m_0}(1-\eta_2)=1+s(\eta_2-1) \text{ as } 1-\eta_2 \lesseqgtr 0,$$

where $s \equiv \Delta S_i/m_0$. Thus, taking roots of both sides for the case where $1+s(\eta_2-1)>0$ yields

$$\frac{e(\boldsymbol{p}^1,U^0)}{m_0} \leq [1+s(\eta_2-1)]^{1/(1-\eta_2)} \tag{6.39}$$

regardless of the sign of $1-\eta_2$. A similar procedure using (6.37) also yields

$$\frac{e(\boldsymbol{p}^1,U^0)}{m_0} \geq [1+s(\eta_1-1)]^{1/(1-\eta_1)}. \tag{6.40}$$

Using (6.24) where income does not change (that is, $m_0=m_1$) and subtracting $1=m_0/m_0$ from both sides of (6.39) and (6.40) thus yields

$$[1+s(\eta_2-1)]^{1/(1-\eta_2)}-1 \geq \frac{e(\boldsymbol{p}^1,U_0)-m_0}{m_0}=\frac{-C}{m_0} \geq [1+s(\eta_1-1)]^{1/(1-\eta_1)}-1,$$

from which one can immediately conclude that

$$\varepsilon_2^c \geq \frac{\Delta S_i - C}{|\Delta S_i|} \geq \varepsilon_1^c, \tag{6.41}$$

where[9]

$$\varepsilon_k^c \equiv \frac{[1+s(\eta_k-1)]^{1/(1-\eta_k)}-1+s}{|s|},\ k=1,2. \tag{6.42}$$

Thus, error bounds are obtained on the extent to which compensating variation is approximated by the change in consumer surplus in the market where price changes.

Having derived the foregoing bounds relating to the Hicksian compensating variation, it is a simple matter to get similar bounds relating to the Hicksian equivalent variation. That is, if one simply reverses the role of $\boldsymbol{p}^0$ and $\boldsymbol{p}^1$ in (6.26), then, where $m_0=m_1$, the equivalent variation of a price change from $\boldsymbol{p}^1$ to $\boldsymbol{p}^0$ is the negative of the compensating variation of a price change from $\boldsymbol{p}^0$ to $\boldsymbol{p}^1$. When this change is made, the sign of ΔS_i and thus s is also reversed. Hence, (6.41) holds where C, ΔS_i, and s are replaced by $-E$, $-\Delta S_i$ and $-s$, respectively:

$$\varepsilon_2^e \geq \frac{E-\Delta S_i}{|\Delta S_i|} \geq \varepsilon_1^e, \tag{6.43}$$

where ε_k^e is defined similarly to ε_k^c in (6.42),

$$\varepsilon_k^e \equiv \frac{[1-s(\eta_k-1)]^{1/(1-\eta_k)}-1-s}{|s|},\ k=1,2. \tag{6.44}$$

Several interesting results are now apparent. First, bounds on the percentage error of the change in consumer surplus, as a measure of compensating or equivalent variation, can be simply calculated from information about the change in surplus (ΔS_i), income elasticity of demand (η), and base income (m_0).

9. It may be noted that some signs and directions of inequality are different here than in Willig's case because his A and C are opposite in sign to the change in consumer surplus, ΔS_i, and the compensating variation C defined here.

Second, the error bounds provide information that can be useful in improving estimates of compensating and equivalent variations over simple use of ΔS_i. For example, if both error bounds are positive (negative), it is clear from (6.41) and (6.43) that a downward (upward) adjustment of ΔS_i would better approximate the compensating variation, and an upward (downward) adjustment would better approximate the equivalent variation.

These results can be better understood using a second-order Taylor series expansion,

$$(1+t)^{1/(1-\eta)} \doteq 1 + \frac{t}{1-\eta} + \frac{\eta t^2}{2(1-\eta)^2},$$

where $t = s(\eta - 1)$ in (6.42) and $t = -s(\eta - 1)$ in (6.44). Thus,

$$\varepsilon_k^c, \varepsilon_k^e \doteq \frac{\eta_k |s|}{2} \equiv \hat{\varepsilon}_k, \; k = 1,2. \tag{6.45}$$

Using (6.45), the true bounds on percentage errors can be approximated. Furthermore, substituting these approximations into (6.41) and (6.43) leads to simple approximations of bounds on compensating and equivalent variation in terms of income elasticity, base income, and consumer surplus change. That is, where

$$\xi_2^c \equiv \Delta S_i - \varepsilon_2^c |\Delta S_i| \leq C \leq \Delta S_i - \varepsilon_1^c |\Delta S_i| \equiv \xi_1^c \tag{6.46}$$

$$\xi_2^e \equiv \Delta S_i + \varepsilon_2^e |\Delta S_i| \geq E \geq \Delta S_i + \varepsilon_1^e |\Delta S_i| \equiv \xi_1^e, \tag{6.47}$$

the approximation in (6.45) implies that

$$\xi_k^c \doteq \Delta S_i - \hat{\varepsilon}_k |\Delta S_i| = \Delta S_i - \frac{\eta_k (\Delta S_i)^2}{2m_0}, \; k = 1, 2, \tag{6.48}$$

$$\xi_k^e \doteq \Delta S_i + \hat{\varepsilon}_k |\Delta S_i| = \Delta S_i + \frac{\eta_k (\Delta S_i)^2}{2m_0}, \; k = 1, 2. \tag{6.49}$$

This implies that the second right-hand member of (6.48) or (6.49) may be a reasonable correction factor that could be added to the change in consumer surplus to estimate compensating or equivalent variation, respectively.

The question that arises is to what extent the foregoing approximations are useful and reasonably accurate. The answer is provided by Table 6.1, which is similar to that developed by Willig. This table compares the values of $\hat{\varepsilon}$, ε^c, and ε^e and gives four types of information:

1. Comparison of the entries for different values of η but the same values of s leads to observation of the width of the interval defined by the error bounds in (6.41) and (6.43).
2. Observation of the first or second entries (in their absolute levels) indicates the (relative) error made by using consumer surplus change as a measure of compensating or equivalent variation.[10]
3. Comparison of the first with the second and third entries for any given values of η

10. The first entry corresponds to a (relative) overestimate of the compensating variation. The second entry corresponds to the relative underestimate of the equivalent variation.

and s indicates the precision lost in computing error bounds by the rule of thumb in (6.45).

4. Observation of the difference in the first and the second or third entries thus also indicates the error that remains when the consumer surplus estimate of compensating and equivalent variation is modified using the factors included in (6.48) and (6.49), that is, when compensating variation is estimated by

$$\hat{C}^k \equiv \Delta S_i - \hat{\varepsilon}_k |\Delta S_i| \tag{6.50}$$

and equivalent variation is estimated by

$$\hat{E}^k \equiv \Delta S_i + \hat{\varepsilon}_k |\Delta S_i|. \tag{6.51}$$

In the latter case the respective relative errors can be bounded using (6.46) and (6.47):

$$\hat{\varepsilon}_k - \hat{\varepsilon}_2^c \le \frac{C - \hat{C}^k}{|\Delta S_i|} \le \hat{\varepsilon}_k - \varepsilon_1^c$$

$$\varepsilon_2^e - \hat{\varepsilon}_k \ge \frac{E - \hat{E}^k}{|\Delta S_i|} \ge \varepsilon_1^e - \hat{\varepsilon}_k.$$

In the case where income elasticity is not constant, however, one may prefer to work with the average income elasticity rather than the two separate bounds for simplicity. Hence, the correction factor in (6.50) and (6.51) might be based on

$$\bar{\varepsilon} \equiv \tfrac{1}{2}(\hat{\varepsilon}_1 + \hat{\varepsilon}_2)$$

rather than $\hat{\varepsilon}_k$. Then, by linearity of $\hat{\varepsilon}_k$ in η_k in (6.45), one finds that

$$\bar{C} \equiv \tfrac{1}{2}(\hat{C}^1 + \hat{C}^2) \equiv \Delta S_i - \bar{\varepsilon}|\Delta S_i| \tag{6.52}$$

$$\bar{E} \equiv \tfrac{1}{2}(\hat{E}^1 + \hat{E}^2) \equiv \Delta S_i + \bar{\varepsilon}|\Delta S_i|. \tag{6.53}$$

To use Table 6.1 in this case, note from (6.41), (6.43), (6.52), and (6.53) that

$$\varepsilon_2^c - \bar{\varepsilon} \ge \frac{\bar{C} - C}{|\Delta S_i|} \ge \varepsilon_1^c - \bar{\varepsilon} \tag{6.54}$$

$$\varepsilon_2^e - \bar{\varepsilon} \ge \frac{E - \bar{E}}{|\Delta S_i|} \ge \varepsilon_1^e - \bar{\varepsilon} \tag{6.55}$$

An example can serve to demonstrate these points. Consider, first, the case where $\eta = \eta_1 = \eta_2 = 1.01$ and $s = 0.1$ (assuming for simplicity that income elasticity is constant). In this case the change in consumer surplus (see information type 2 above) overestimates the compensating variation of a price fall by 4.889 percent but underestimates the equivalent variation by 5.231 percent. Second, and on the other hand, using the rule of thumb in (6.45) to approximate these errors (see information type 3 above) implies an approximate error of 5.049 percent in both cases, which is off by 0.160 percent in the former case and by 0.182 percent in the latter case. Finally, using Table 6.1, the modified estimates in (6.50) and (6.51) are off by 0.160 and 0.182 percent, respectively, as a percentage of the change in surplus (see information type 4 above). Of course, if ε_k^c and ε_k^e were used in (6.50) and (6.51), respectively, rather than $\hat{\varepsilon}_k$, then no error occurs in the constant-elasticity case (in this case the inequalities in (6.46) and (6.47) become equalities). Now suppose that $\eta_1 = 0.8$ and $\eta_2 = 1.2$, where $s = 0.1$. In this case (see information type 1 above), one knows that the consumer surplus change overestimates the compensating variation by between 3.920 and 5.731 percent, so that the width of the error bound is 1.811 percent. For the underestimate of equivalent variation, the respective percentages are 4.080, 6.291 and 2.211. If one uses $\bar{C}$ in (6.52) to estimate compensating variation, then (6.54) implies a percentage error (in terms of consumer surplus) of between –1.080 and 0.731 percent, that is $[0.03920 - (0.040 + 0.060)/2] \times 100$ percent and $[0.05731 - (0.040 + 0.060)/2] \times 100$ percent. Similarly (6.55) implies percentage error bounds on $\bar{E}$ as an estimate of equivalent variation of between -0.920 and 1.291 percent, that is, $[0.04080 - (0.040 + 0.060)/2] \times 100$ percent and $[0.06291 - (0.040 - 0.060)/2] \times 100$ percent.

The Multiple-Price-Change Case

Consider now the case of multiple price changes and the extent to which the sum of consumer surplus changes can be used to approximate the compensating or equivalent variations. Suppose that initial and final prices are given by $\boldsymbol{p}^0 = (p_1^0,\ldots,p_N^0)$ and $\boldsymbol{p}^N = (p_1^1,\ldots,p_N^1)$, respectively. For convenience, also let income be unchanged, $m_0 = m_1$, with initial and final utility levels given by U^0 and U^N, respectively.[11] In this case,

$$C = m_0 - e(\boldsymbol{p}^N, U^0)$$

$$E = e(\boldsymbol{p}^0, U^N) - m_0,$$

so the compensating and equivalent variations are clearly independent of the order in which the price changes are imposed (that is, are path independent). Although the sum of consumer surplus changes depends on the order in which price changes are considered, the same approach as that described above can be used to reach error bounds.

For notational purposes, let

$$\boldsymbol{p}^i \equiv (p_1^1,\ldots,p_i^1, p_{i+1}^0,\ldots,p_N^0)$$

$$\Delta S_i = -\int_{p_i^0}^{p_i^1} \tilde{q}_i(\hat{\boldsymbol{p}}_i(p_i), m_0)\,dp_i$$

and let η_1^i and η_2^i be the minimum and maximum income elasticities associated with demand for the ith good. Finally, let $\eta_1 \equiv \min(\eta_1^1,\ldots,\eta_1^N)$ and $\eta_2 = \max(\eta_2^1,\ldots,\eta_2^N)$ One can deduce immediately from equations (6.37) and (6.38) that

$$-\Delta S_i \cdot m_0^{-\eta_1} \le \frac{e(\boldsymbol{p}^i, U^0)^{1-\eta_1} - e(\boldsymbol{p}^{i-1}, U^0)^{1-\eta_1}}{1-\eta_1} \tag{6.56}$$

11. If income changes, all the results derived below would continue to hold if the sum of consumer surplus changes were simply modified by adding the change in income.

$$\frac{e(\boldsymbol{p}^{i},U^{0})^{1-\eta_2}-e(\boldsymbol{p}^{i-1},U^{0})^{1-\eta_2}}{1-\eta_2}\leq -\Delta S_i\cdot m_0^{-\eta_2}. \tag{6.57}$$

Hence, noting that $m_0 = e(\boldsymbol{p}^0, U^0)$ and summing the inequalities in (6.56) and (6.57) for $i = 1, ..., N$ yields

$$-\sum_{i=1}^{N}\Delta S_i\cdot m_0^{-\eta_1}\leq\frac{e(\boldsymbol{p}^{N},U^{0})^{1-\eta_1}-m_0^{1-\eta_1}}{1-\eta_1} \tag{6.58}$$

$$\frac{e(\boldsymbol{p}^{N},U^{0})^{1-\eta_2}-m_0^{1-\eta_2}}{1-\eta_2}\leq -\sum_{i=1}^{N}\Delta S_i\cdot m_0^{-\eta_2}. \tag{6.59}$$

Because (6.58) and (6.59) are identical to equations (6.37) and (6.38) except that ΔS_i and $\boldsymbol{p}^1$ are replaced by $\Sigma_{i=1}^{N}\Delta S_i$ and $\boldsymbol{p}^N$, respectively, the results in (6.39) through (6.55) generalize similarly, where $s = \Sigma_{i=1}^{N}\Delta S_i/m_0$. Hence,

$$\varepsilon_2^c\geq\frac{\sum_{i=1}^{N}\Delta S_i - C}{\left|\sum_{i=1}^{N}\Delta S_i\right|}\geq\varepsilon_1^c$$

$$\varepsilon_2^e\geq\frac{E-\sum_{i=1}^{N}\Delta S_i}{\left|\sum_{i=1}^{N}\Delta S_i\right|}\geq\varepsilon_1^e$$

where ε_k^c and ε_k^e are defined by (6.42) and (6.44) as before. All the information in Table 6.1 pertaining to the single-price-change case is thus also applicable with multiple price changes. That is, Table 6.1 can be used to determine error bounds on the sum of consumer surplus changes (computed sequentially) or on such modified estimates as

$$\bar{C}\equiv\sum_{i=1}^{N}\Delta S_i-\bar{\varepsilon}\left|\sum_{i=1}^{N}\Delta S_i\right|$$

$$\bar{E}\equiv\sum_{i=1}^{N}\Delta S_i+\bar{\varepsilon}\left|\sum_{i=1}^{N}\Delta S_i\right|$$

corresponding to (6.52) and (6.53) as measures of compensating and equivalent variation.[12] Using this approach, however, compensating and equivalent variation cannot be computed accurately even with constant-income elasticities unless all income elasticities are the same (that is, $\eta_1^i = \eta_2^i$, $i = 1, \ldots, N$).[13]

12. In the latter case the bounds would be computed as in (6.54) and (6.55), where the denominator $|\Delta S_i|$ is replaced by $|\Sigma_{i=1}^{N}\Delta S_i|$.
13. Following (6.46) and (6.47), where ΔS_i is replaced by $\Sigma_{i=1}^{N}\Delta S_i$, it is clear that

$$C=\sum_{i=1}^{N}\Delta S_i-\varepsilon^c\left|\sum_{i=1}^{N}\Delta S_i\right|$$

$$E=\sum_{i=1}^{N}\Delta S_i+\varepsilon^e\left|\sum_{i=1}^{N}\Delta S_i\right|$$

The foregoing bounds for multiple price changes can be useful when income elasticities do not differ greatly among the commodities for which prices change, but the bounds can be quite wide when income elasticities are quite different among the commodities for which prices change, as evidenced by Table 6.1. Fortunately, tighter bounds can be computed for such cases, although the approach for doing so is laborious and unwieldy. The improvements are possible basically because the inequalities in (6.56) and (6.57) can be made tighter by using η_1^i and η_2^i rather than η_1 and η_2, respectively, in calculations relating to market *i*, as discussed in the following section.

Computation of Tighter Error Bounds

The computation of tighter error bounds on the sum of consumer surplus changes (computed sequentially) as a measure of compensating or equivalent variation for cases of multiple price changes can be considered as follows. Suppose again that prices change from $\mathbf{p}^0$ to $\mathbf{p}^N$, where

$$\mathbf{p}^i = (p_1^1,\ldots,p_i^1,p_{i+1}^0,\ldots,p_N^0),\ i=0,\ \ldots,\ N,$$

and again the initial and final utility levels are U^0 and U^N, respectively, and income does not change ($m_0=m_1$). The change in surplus in market *i* where price changes are imposed sequentially is

$$\Delta S_i = -\int_{p_i^0}^{p_i^1} \tilde{q}_i(p_1^1,\ldots,p_{i-1}^1,p_i,p_{i+1}^0,\ldots,p_N^0,m_0)dp_i,$$

whereas the change in consumer surplus associated with a simple price change from $\mathbf{p}^{i-1}$ to $\mathbf{p}^i$ with income level $e(\mathbf{p}^{i-1},U^0)$ is

$$\Delta S_i' = -\int_{p_i^0}^{p_i^1} \tilde{q}_i(p_1^1,\ldots,p_{i-1}^1,p_i,p_{i+1}^0,\ldots,p_N^0,e(\mathbf{p}^{i-1},U^0))dp_i.$$

Now, let $\tilde{m}_i = e(\mathbf{p}^{i-1},U^0)$ and use (6.46) for the case where initial income is $\tilde{m}_i$ and prices change from $\mathbf{p}^{i-1}$ to $\mathbf{p}^i$ to find that

$$\Delta S_i' - \varepsilon_{2i}^c|\Delta S_i'| \le e(\mathbf{p}^{i-1},U^0) - e(\mathbf{p}^i,U^0) \le \Delta S_i' - \varepsilon_{1i}^c|\Delta S_i'|, \tag{6.60}$$

where

$$\varepsilon_{ki}^c \equiv \frac{[1+s_i(n_k^i-1)]^{1/(1-n_k^i)} - 1 + s_i}{|s_i|},\ k=1,2$$

and

$$s_i \equiv \frac{\Delta S_i}{\tilde{m}_i}.$$

when $\eta_1 = \eta_2$ because $\varepsilon_1^c = \varepsilon_2^c = \varepsilon^c$ and $\varepsilon_1^e = \varepsilon_2^e = \varepsilon^e$. Hence, compensating and equivalent variation can be computed accurately, and this is true regardless of the order in which price changes are imposed. Interestingly, this corresponds to the result found earlier in investigating money measures of utility change, which indicated that the order of imposing price changes (choice of path) in computing the overall change in consumer surplus makes no difference when income elasticities are identical for all prices that change.

Next, use (6.60) to find that

$$\xi_{2i}^c \le e(\mathbf{p}^{i-1},U^0) - e(\mathbf{p}^i,U^0) - \Delta S_i \le \xi_{1i}^c,$$

where

$$\xi_{ki}^c \equiv -\varepsilon_{ki}^c|\Delta S_i'| + \Delta S_i' - \Delta S_i,\ k=1,2. \tag{6.61}$$

Finally, summing over markets yields

$$\xi_2^j \equiv \sum_{i=1}^{j} \xi_{2i}^c \le m_0 - e(\mathbf{p}^j,U^0) - \sum_{i=1}^{j} \Delta S_i \le \sum_{i=1}^{j} \xi_{1i}^c \equiv \xi_1^j,\ j=1,\ldots,N, \tag{6.62}$$

which suggests

$$\xi_2^N \le C - \sum_{i=1}^{N} \Delta S_i \le \xi_1^N$$

as error bounds on the sum of consumer surplus changes as a measure of compensating variation.

The only problem with the bounds in (6.62) is that the necessary ξ_{ki}^c in (6.61) cannot be calculated on the basis of information that is normally available. One needs the unobservable demands that correspond to incomes $\tilde{m}_i = e(\mathbf{p}^{i-1},U^0)$ respectively, to obtain the $\Delta S_i'$. It is thus necessary to derive bounds on ξ_{1i}^c and ξ_{2i}^c in terms of observable information.

Such an approach has been suggested by Willig. Using the relationship in (6.34), he notes that

$$\left[\frac{e(\mathbf{p}^{i-1},U^0)}{m_0}\right]^{\eta_2^i} \Delta S_i \ge \Delta S_i' \ge \left[\frac{e(\mathbf{p}^{i-1},U^0)}{m_0}\right]^{\eta_1^i} \Delta S_i \tag{6.63}$$

for $\mathbf{p}^i > \mathbf{p}^{i-1}$ (that is, $p_i^1 > p_i^0$). Now, suppose that markets are ordered so that price increases in the first K markets but decreases in the last $N-K$ markets. Then $e(\mathbf{p}^{i-1},U^0) \ge e(\mathbf{p}^K,U^0)$ and $m_0 \ge e(\mathbf{p}^K,U^0)$ for $i=K+1,\ldots,N$. Again using (6.34), this implies that

$$\begin{aligned} &e(\mathbf{p}^K,U^0)^{\eta_2^i-\eta_1^i} e(\mathbf{p}^{i-1},U^0)^{\eta_1^i} m_0^{-\eta_2^i} \Delta S_i \ge \Delta S_i' \\ &\ge e(\mathbf{p}^K,U^0)^{\eta_1^i-\eta_2^i} e(\mathbf{p}^{i-1},U^0)^{\eta_2^i} m_0^{-\eta_1^i} \Delta S_i,\ i=K+1,\ldots,N. \end{aligned} \tag{6.64}$$

Then one can further note from (6.62) that

$$m_0 - \xi_2^j - \sum_{i=1}^{j} \Delta S_i \ge e(\mathbf{p}^j,U^0) \ge m_0 - \xi_1^j - \sum_{i=1}^{N} \Delta S_i,$$

which, together with (6.63) and (6.64), is sufficient to bound $\Delta S_i'$ for $i=1,\ldots,N$. The corresponding bounds for equivalent variation are derived similarly by noting that the equivalent variation of a change from $\mathbf{p}^N$ to $\mathbf{p}^0$ is the negative of the compensated variation of a change from $\mathbf{p}^0$ to $\mathbf{p}^N$.

Although this is the spirit of the algorithm developed by Willig, it is perhaps impractical to attempt hand calculations of these bounds or to present a detailed analytical treatment of the algorithm. But a computer program can easily handle such calculations in empirical cases.

Conclusions for the Pure Consumer Case

It is difficult to reach general conclusions from the foregoing results. Apparently, if $|\eta_1 s|$ and $|\eta_2 s|$ are close together but large, then the change in consumer surplus, ΔS_i, will not be close to C and E. Nevertheless, the modifications in (6.50) through (6.53) may be used. In fact, if $\eta_1 = \eta_2$, that is, the income elasticity for q_i is constant in the region of change, then C and E can be calculated precisely in terms of ΔS_i using (6.50) and (6.51). In general, however, the extent to which the various approximations are useful depends on the particular application and the errors the investigator is willing to accept. As Willig claims, if the investigator is willing to accept up to about a 5 percent error, then consumer surplus change can be used without modification for all cases where $|\eta s/2| < 0.05$.[14] If, on the other hand, one is not willing to accept more than a 1 percent error, one must essentially require that $|\eta s/2| \leq 0.01$ to use the (unmodified) consumer surplus change. Whereas Willig's requirement may hold for most practical problems, the latter case does not. Alternatively, with constant (and equal) income elasticity (for all commodities for which prices change), one can avoid more than about a 1 percent error by using the corrected estimates in (6.50) and (6.51) for compensating and equivalent variation, respectively, as long as $|\eta s/2| \leq 0.1$. This is a broad enough condition to include most practical single-price-change, constant-elasticity cases. Finally, if income elasticity is not constant, one can avoid more than about a 2 percent error by using the modified estimates in (6.52) and (6.53) if $|\eta s/2| \leq 0.08$ and income elasticity changes by less than 50 percent, where η is the largest income elasticity (in absolute value) associated with goods for which prices change.

6.C THE CHOICE OF MEASURE AND THE MONEY METRIC

One possibility for policy evaluation when WTP measures conflict, and in particular when they do not agree in sign, is to present estimates of *both* compensating and equivalent variation. When both measurements are provided to policy-makers, the associated value judgment of which to use is left in the hands of those who have that responsibility and authority. Furthermore, both are necessary for application of the Kaldor–Hicks–Scitovsky compensation test. Compensating variation supports the Kaldor–Hicks compensation test and equivalent variation supports the Scitovsky reversal test. In many cases, the qualitative implications of the two measures agree, as suggested by single-market analysis. Nevertheless, economists have continued to seek a complete solution to the dilemma (a complete social ordering) on economic grounds.

For example, some have considered more stringent conditions on the measure of utility change. The results of Appendix Sections 5.B and 5.C show that a unique money measure of utility change cannot be obtained except under unrealistic conditions. Alternatively, one can consider whether a money measure exists that at least ranks all alternatives ordinally the same as utility. This question was addressed by Hause (1975) who argued that the compensating variation measure does not constitute an acceptable welfare measure because it is not ordinally consistent with rankings implied by the utility function.

14. Willig also requires that $|\Delta S_i/m_0| \leq 0.9$ to ensure that $1 \pm s\,(\eta - 1) > 0$ but, as evidenced by Table 6.1, this condition holds for essentially all practical cases.

This problem can also be demonstrated in Figure 6.2(a). Suppose price and income are initially p_1 and m_1, respectively. Now consider either a price change from p_1 to p_2 or an income change from m_1 to m_3. In either case, the new ordinal utility level becomes U_2. However, the compensating variation of the price change is $m_1 - m_2$, whereas the compensating variation of the income change is $m_3 - m_1$. In general, these two measures do not agree; $m_3 - m_1$ will be larger than $m_1 - m_2$ in the normal case where income elasticity is positive. Thus, different compensating variations are generated even though the same subsequent utility level is attained. Now consider alternatively changing either price from p_1 to p_2 or income from m_1 to m_4, where m_4 is slightly less than m_3 and thus does not quite permit the indifference curve U_2 to be attained. In this case, $m_4 - m_1$ will also be larger than $m_1 - m_2$ even though the income change to m_4 yields a smaller increase in utility than the price reduction from p_1 to p_2. To see that the equivalent variation does not suffer from this problem, recall that the equivalent variation of the price fall in Figure 6.2(a) is $m_3 - m_1$ which, trivially, is the same as the equivalent variation of the income change.[15]

Because the equivalent variation does not suffer from these problems, some have supported its use over compensating variation. More specifically, equivalent variation has been justified by its direct relationship to the *money metric*. The *money metric* was defined by Samuelson (1942) as the level of expenditure required to achieve any level of utility given initial prices. Formally, the money metric is defined by $e(\mathbf{p}^0, U^1)$ and thus differs from the equivalent variation in (6.26) only by initial income.[16] Hurwicz and Uzawa (1971) have shown that the money metric is ordinally consistent with utility and McKenzie and Pearce (1976) argue that this trivially extends as a result to equivalent variation. Chipman and Moore (1976, 1980) have further shown that the conditions under which either consumer surplus or compensating variation attains general ordinal consistency with utility are the same as the conditions for path independence.

While all of these results are formally correct, one must be careful when interpreting them for policy evaluation purposes. A circumspect examination reveals that the Hurwicz–Uzawa results are directly relevant for index number theory and cost-of-living measurement where a natural basis exists for choice of base-period prices.[17] For example, a cost-of-living index is used specifically to measure how the cost of living has changed from some base period. In cases of policy evaluation, however, one must be concerned with global rankings rather than rankings relative to a base case. Making a policy change based on a positive equivalent variation and then finding a positive equivalent variation for reversing the change

15. Formally, this problem for compensating variation is demonstrated by noting that the C in (6.24) must be homogeneous of degree zero in $\mathbf{p}^1$ and m_1 if compensating variation is to be the same for all new price–income situations that attain the same utility (consider doubling all prices and income). However, this is inconsistent with the definition of $e(\mathbf{p}, U)$, which implies that C in (6.24) is linearly homogeneous in $\mathbf{p}^1$ and m_1.
16. Varying terminology subject to similar considerations can be found in the literature. For example, Hurwicz and Uzawa (1971) actually analyze the *income-compensation function* defined by $\mu(\mathbf{p},\mathbf{p}^0,m_0) \equiv e(\mathbf{p}, V(\mathbf{p}^0,m_0))$, which is called the *indirect compensation function* by Varian (1992, pp. 109–10). McKenzie (1957) proposed the concept of a *minimum-income function* defined by $M(\mathbf{p},\mathbf{q}^0) \equiv e(\mathbf{p}, U(\mathbf{q}^0))$, which is called the *direct compensation function* by Varian (1992, pp. 109–10).
17. As noted by Samuelson (1947, p. 196), the problem of finding an exact money measure of consumer welfare change is mathematically equivalent to the problem of finding a true cost-of-living index. See also Bergson (1975), Wold and Jureen (1953) and Burns (1973, 1977). A common justification for use of the money metric in welfare economics is that it measures the cost of attaining a specified standard of living (utility level) at given prices (McKenzie 1983, p. 31).

(which means the compensating variation for the original change is negative) does not lead to policy stability and, thus, is an untenable basis for policy adjustment.

In this broader policy evaluation context, the criticisms of compensating variation apply equally to equivalent variation. For example, McKenzie (1983, p. 91) argues that 'the compensation required to return the consumer to his initial level of satisfaction should always be the same irrespective of what pattern of consumption may have been taken up on a new indifference surface'. On the other hand, it should be the same irrespective of the pattern of consumption (or the set of prices that led to it) on the initial indifference surface. Requiring both means that a useful money measure can be found only when the compensating and equivalent variations (and consumer surplus change) coincide.

From another perspective, both compensating variation and equivalent variation are ordinally related to utility. Equivalent variation varies ordinally with utility as the subsequent welfare position (point *b* in Figure 6.2(a)) is continuously varied, and compensating variation varies ordinally with utility as the initial welfare position (point *a* in Figure 6.2(a)) is continuously varied. Just as compensating variation depends on the subsequent price vector, equivalent variation depends on the initial price vector. If the subsequent price vector matters as with compensating variation, then an end-point bias is admitted. But if the initial price vector matters, then a starting point bias is admitted.

Upon considering the broader requirements of consumer benefit measurement for policy evaluation purposes, arguments for using either the equivalent variation or the compensating variation over the other are not convincing. If the use of one supports a policy change, then the other must be checked to verify that the policy will not be changed back according to the same criterion after having made the first change. Alternatively, the Willig bounds give a means of characterizing circumstances where the two measures differ by insignificant amounts so that both need not be examined explicitly.

6.D ACCURATE MEASUREMENT WITH ORDINARY DEMANDS

As the Willig modified estimates hint, ordinary demand relationships can be used to derive information about Hicksian compensated demands by using the information they contain regarding response to income changes. However, this can be done with exactness so that one need not rely on consumer surplus as an approximation of WTP measures. This possibility was first suggested by Hause (1975) and later demonstrated more generally by Hausman (1981) with a somewhat different approach.

To obtain estimates of the WTP measures directly from ordinary demand equations, Hause substitutes the expenditure function into estimates of ordinary demand equations, $\tilde{q}_j(\mathbf{p},m)$, obtaining the identity

$$\bar{q}_j(\mathbf{p},\bar{U}) \equiv \tilde{q}_j(\mathbf{p},e(\mathbf{p},\bar{U})).$$

Then equation (6.27) becomes

$$\frac{\partial e(\mathbf{p},\bar{U})}{\partial p_j} = \tilde{q}_j(\mathbf{p},e(\mathbf{p},\bar{U})). \tag{6.65}$$

This gives a partial differential equation that can, in principle, be solved for the expenditure function as a function of price, given utility level $\bar{U}$. Consider a general change in prices and income from $(\mathbf{p}^0, m_0)$ to $(\mathbf{p}^1, m_1)$, which leads to a change in utility from U^0 to U^1. Then the Hicksian compensating variation is found as in (6.24) where $e(\mathbf{p}, U^0)$ is obtained by solving (6.65) with the boundary condition, $e(\mathbf{p}^0, U^0) = m_0$. The Hicksian equivalent variation is obtained from (6.26), where $e(\mathbf{p}, U^1)$ is the solution of (6.65) corresponding to the boundary condition $e(\mathbf{p}^1, U^1) = m_1$. For the case where more than one price changes, an equation (6.65) must be included for each price that changes and the system of differential equations must be solved simultaneously. Unfortunately, an exact analytical solution with this approach is often not possible even with common functional forms.

Hausman alternatively uses the differential relationship between the indirect utility function and ordinary demands following Roy's identity. Using Roy's identity, the idea is to integrate back to the indirect utility function from which compensating variation can be found as in (6.23) and equivalent variation can be found as in (6.25). While analytical solutions to this problem are possible for only certain demand specifications, a solution is possible for many demand specifications in common use. Consider, for example, a linear demand relationship given by

$$q_i = \alpha p_i + \beta m + \gamma = \tilde{q}_i(\mathbf{p}, m) \tag{6.66}$$

where α, β and γ are observable parameters estimated by econometric means and possibly depending on prices in $\mathbf{p}$ other than p_i. Holding utility and all prices except p_i constant at the initial level, comparative static analysis of $V(\mathbf{p}, m) = U^0$ yields

$$\frac{dm}{dp_i} = -\frac{\partial V / \partial p_i}{\partial V / \partial m} = \alpha p_i + \beta m + \gamma, \tag{6.67}$$

where the latter equality follows from using (6.66) in Roy's identity. The solution to the differential equation in (6.67) is[18]

$$m(p_i) = ce^{\beta p_i} - \frac{1}{\beta}\left(\alpha p_i + \frac{\alpha}{\beta} + \gamma\right), \tag{6.68}$$

where c is some constant. The indirect utility function is thus found up to a multiplicative constant by letting $U^0 = c$ and solving (6.68) for $U^0 = V(\mathbf{p}, m)$,

$$U^0 = V(\mathbf{p}, m) = \left[m + \frac{1}{\beta}\left(\alpha p_i + \frac{\alpha}{\beta} + \gamma\right)\right] e^{-\beta p_i},$$

or, equivalently, by using $m(p_i)$ in (6.68) as the expenditure function after replacing c by U^0. Substituting into (6.23) in the former case or into (6.24) in the latter case then obtains an exact expression for the compensating variation in terms of the parameters of the ordinary demand relationship,

18. To verify that $m(p_i)$ solves the differential equation, note that

$$\frac{dm(p_i)}{dp_i} = \beta c e^{\beta p_i} - \frac{\alpha}{\beta} = \alpha p_i + \beta m(p_i) + \gamma.$$

$$C=\frac{1}{\beta}\left[\tilde{q}_i(\boldsymbol{p}_i^1,m_0)+\frac{\alpha}{\beta}\right]-\frac{1}{\beta}e^{\beta(p_i^1-p_i^0)}\left[\tilde{q}_i(\boldsymbol{p}_i^0,m_0)+\frac{\alpha}{\beta}\right].$$

In the case of the log-linear demand specification,

$$\tilde{q}_i(\boldsymbol{p},m)=\Gamma p_i^{\alpha}m^{\beta}$$

Hausman similarly finds exact expressions for the indirect utility function,

$$V(\boldsymbol{p},m)=-\Gamma\frac{p_i^{1+\alpha}}{1+\alpha}+\frac{m^{1-\beta}}{1-\beta},$$

the expenditure function,

$$m(\boldsymbol{p},U^0)=\left[(1-\beta)\left(U^0+\Gamma\frac{p_i^{1+\alpha}}{1+\alpha}\right)\right]^{1/(1-\beta)}$$

and the compensating variation,

$$C=m_1-\left\{\frac{1-\beta}{(1+\alpha)m_0^{\beta}}[p_i^1\tilde{q}_i(\boldsymbol{p}_i^1,m_0)-p_i^0\tilde{q}_i(\boldsymbol{p}_i^0,m_0)]+m_0^{1-\beta}\right\}^{1/(1-\beta)}.$$

In both linear and log-linear cases, if income also changes then the change in income must be added to these compensating variation expressions. Exact expressions for the equivalent variation can be found by simply noting that equivalent variation is the negative of the compensating variation for the reverse price change. If other prices change, then this same approach can be repeated, which will have implications for how the parameters α, β and γ in the case of a change in p_i depend on other prices.

This methodology is thus superior to use of consumer surplus with Willig bounds or corrections at least for cases where the differential equations can be solved. Approximations are not necessary. But what about cases where the differential equations cannot be solved? To handle the general case, Vartia (1983) has developed an algorithm that is equivalent to solving the differential equation numerically by means of an interpolation method. Vartia's algorithm can be motivated most easily by discussing the *nibble paradox*.

The nibble paradox illustrates the difference between consumer surplus and WTP measures by breaking an overall price change into a series of small price changes. This paradox demonstrates that when compensating or equivalent variation is computed for a price change by analyzing the overall change in a series of steps, the compensating (equivalent) variation for any previous price or income change must be extracted from (paid to) the consumer before analyzing the next step. Otherwise, the net result will approximate consumer surplus (which is the seeming paradox).

The paradox is depicted in Figure 6.6. The compensating variation of the single price change from p^1 to p^4 in Figure 6.6 is given by area $a_0+b_0+c_0$. If, however, the overall price change is attained by a series of smaller changes – first, from p^1 to p^2, then from p^2 to p^3 and, finally, from p^3 to p^4 – then the compensating variation appears to be area a_0 for the first change, area b_0+b_1 for the second change, and area $c_0+c_1+c_2$ for the third change, the sum of which exceeds the compensating variation for the overall price change and approximates consumer surplus. But if, for each small change, the compensating variation is extracted from the consumer before proceeding to consider the next small price change (extraction of area a_0, for example, before reducing the price from p^2 to p^3), then the consumer is always constrained to utility level U^0, and hence the sum of the incremental compensating variations is properly calculated as area $a_0 + b_0 + c_0$.

The Vartia algorithm takes this approach where the compensating variations of the small steps are approximated by the associated consumer surpluses. The overall price interval is divided into more and more small steps until convergence occurs. Specifically, let a price change interval from $\mathbf{p}^0$ to $\mathbf{p}^1$ be represented by successive proportional and equal steps $\hat{\mathbf{p}}^0, \ldots, \hat{\mathbf{p}}^K$ and let income be $\hat{m}^0 = m_0$. Where multiple prices change from $\mathbf{p}^0$ to $\mathbf{p}^1$, these steps represent equal sized increments in all individual prices that change simultaneously. Then calculate

$$\hat{m}^k = \hat{m}^{k-1} + [\tilde{q}(\hat{p}^k, \hat{m}^{k-1}) + \tilde{q}(\hat{p}^{k-1}, \hat{m}^{k-1})]\,[\hat{p}^k - \hat{p}^{k-1}]/2,\ k = 1, \ldots, K. \qquad (6.69)$$

The estimate of compensating variation is then $\hat{C}^K = \hat{m}^0 - \hat{m}^K$. The algorithm is to increase K in this calculation until $\hat{C}^K$ converges.

To see the simple intuitive steps involved in these calculations, consider the overall price change from p^0 to p^3 in Figure 6.15. Then the compensating variation of the first price change step from p^0 to p^1 is area a_0 which is approximated by area $a_0 + a_1$. Area $a_0 + a_1$ is approximated by the second right-hand term of (6.69) where $k = 1$. Adding this 'income' to m_0 then obtains the ordinary demand curve $D(m_1)$. Then the next price step to p^2 is considered similarly. The overall Vartia estimate of compensating variation is then area $a_0 + a_1 + b_0 + b_1 + c_0 + c_1$ when $K = 3$. Clearly, as the overall price change is broken into more and more small changes, the estimate converges to the true compensating variation, area $a_0 + b_0 + c_0$. Of course, the same approach can be used to calculate equivalent variation by noting the additive inverse relationship between compensating and equivalent variation for reverse price changes.

While Figure 6.15 illustrates the accuracy attained by the Vartia algorithm for the case of a single price change, the algorithm in equation (6.69) applies for the case of multiple price changes as well. That is, the properties of equation (6.69) as an algorithm computing compensating variation apply whether the prices and quantities are scalars or vectors (transposition of vectors is omitted for convenience). This makes clear the relationship between the Vartia and Willig approaches. Whereas Willig breaks the overall price change into a series of price changes by markets, the Vartia algorithm breaks the change into arbitrarily small multivariate price changes. The accuracy follows accordingly.[19]

6.E PRACTICAL APPROXIMATION VERSUS ACCURATE MEASUREMENT

At this point, the results of Hausman and Vartia may appear to suggest that accurate calculation of compensating and equivalent variation is not a problem based on estimates of arbitrary specifications of consumer demand. If the analysis of only a single price change

19. Willig (1973) developed a procedure to compute tighter bounds and thus better correction factors for consumer surplus by further breaking price changes into smaller changes according to income elasticities. However, the approach was too unwieldy to express as a converging algorithm.

is at issue, then this is correct. However, *the results of Willig, Hausman and Vartia have an important qualification for empirical situations when more than one price change is at issue.* The qualification can be illustrated as follows. In many practical policy evaluation contexts, sufficient resources may not be available to permit econometric estimation of demand relationships associated with all prices that change. Instead, a common approach is to compile estimates of demand elasticities from previously published econometric studies or to use generally accepted elasticities. The problem with this approach is that properties that theoretically relate the demands of an individual consumer may not hold. For example, an underlying indirect utility function may not exist from which all of the demands can be found by application of Roy's identity. If so, then path independence can fail even for the utility change line integral in (5.6). Similarly, path independence can fail in practice for the compensating and equivalent variation line integrals in (6.29) and (6.30) where the compensated demands are derived from the respective ordinary demand estimates following Hausman or Vartia methods, even though in theory it should not.

To ensure that a system of ordinary demands relates to a common underlying utility maximization problem (that is, to ensure that a system of ordinary demands is *integrable*) – which is necessary for applicability of the methods of Willig, Hasuman and Vartia – the following integrability conditions must hold (assuming differentiability):[20]

1. *The budget constraint*: $\boldsymbol{p}\tilde{\boldsymbol{q}}(\boldsymbol{p},m)=m$,
2. *Homogeneity of degree zero in prices and income*: $\tilde{\boldsymbol{q}}(\boldsymbol{p},m)=\tilde{\boldsymbol{q}}(t\boldsymbol{p},tm)$,
3. *Slutsky symmetry*: $\partial\bar{q}_i/\partial p_j=\partial\bar{q}_j/\partial p_i$, where $\partial\bar{q}_i/\partial p_j=\partial\tilde{q}_i/\partial p_j+\tilde{q}_j\,\partial\tilde{q}_i/\partial m$,
4. *Negative semidefiniteness of the Slutsky matrix*:[21] $\{\partial\bar{q}_i/\partial p_j\}\le 0$.

In partial demand systems, condition 1 must be replaced by a strict inequality and condition 4 must be replaced by negative definiteness (Epstein 1982).

The likely failure of these conditions for common arbitrary demand specifications has been made evident by LaFrance (1985, 1986) who has developed necessary conditions relating linear or log-linear partial systems of demands. Linear and log-linear specifications have been the two most common arbitrary specifications used for econometric studies of demand. In the case of linear demands for a subset of goods,

$$\tilde{q}_i(\boldsymbol{p},m)=\alpha_i+\sum_{j=1}^{N}\beta_{ij}p_j+\delta_i m,$$

the necessary conditions are that either (a) all goods have zero income effects ($\delta_i=0$) and the matrix $\{\beta_{ij}\}$ is negative semidefinite or (b) all income effects must be of the same sign with $\alpha_i=\delta_i(\alpha_1+\beta_{11}/\delta_1-\beta_{1i}/\delta_i)/\delta_1$, $\beta_{ij}=\beta_{1j}\delta_i/\delta_1$ for $i\le n<N$ and $\alpha_i=-\beta_{1i}/\delta_1>0$, $\beta_{ij}=\delta_i=0$ for $i>n$ where $\beta_{11}+\delta_1 q_1\le 0$. In the case of log-linear demands for a subset of goods,

$$\ln\tilde{q}_i(\boldsymbol{p},m)=\alpha_i+\sum_{j=1}^{N}\beta_{ij}\ln p_j+\delta_i\ln m,$$

20. Integrability conditions are given, for example, by Deaton and Muellbauer (1980, p. 50).
21. The notation $\{\delta\bar{q}_i/\delta p_j\}$ represents a matrix that has $\delta\bar{q}_i/\delta p_j$ in the ith row and jth column.

the necessary conditions include either (a) that all income elasticities are identical with either $\beta_{ij}=\beta_{ji}=0$ or $\beta_{ij}=1+\beta_{jj}$, $(1+\beta_{jj})\exp(\alpha_i)=(1+\beta_{ii})\exp(\alpha_j)$, or (b) that all income elasticities are either 0 or 1 with $\beta_{ij}=0$.[22] Clearly, these conditions are not likely to hold in estimated demand systems unless imposed in estimation, and the imposition of such highly restrictive conditions appears to be unreasonable.

Whenever two or more price changes must be considered simultaneously, the failure of integrability conditions is a serious problem. When these conditions fail, the accuracy seemingly made possible by the Hausman and Vartia methods is lost and the results can become ambiguous. Apparently, when these conditions fail, one is forced back to the Willig approximations as a means of measuring consumer benefits by approximation. However, failure of these conditions also contaminates application of the Willig results. When the results in (6.57) are added together to obtain the associated overall Willig bounds for the multiple-price-change case, the expenditure function associated with each price change (each i) is assumed to be the same expenditure function. Otherwise, one does not obtain $e(\mathbf{p}^N,U^0)-e(\mathbf{p}^0,U^0)$ by adding together $e(\mathbf{p}^i,U^0)-e(\mathbf{p}^{i-1},U^0)$, $i=1, \ldots, N$.

Thus, even the Willig results do not apply when all of the ordinary demands used for surplus change calculations do not relate to a common underlying consumer utility maximization problem. One can argue that this failure is less severe in the case of the Willig results because only an approximation is claimed and because, as long as demands have been estimated for the same group of utility-maximizing consumers, the failure of demands to relate to a common underlying consumer problem is due to econometric error rather than errors in the benefit calculation methodology. This argument is perhaps sufficient to justify policy evaluation using surplus calculations when resources do not permit econometric estimation. However, one must recognize that the functional forms used to estimate demands in available econometric studies of various commodities may be inconsistent theoretically. Thus, inconsistencies in estimated demands may be imposed rather than due to errors of estimation, in which case the Willig bounds may not be applicable even theoretically. The following section discusses a methodology that yields estimated demands that satisfy integrability conditions and, thus, permits exact calculation of compensating and equivalent variation. However, integrability conditions must be imposed at the stage of estimation.

6.F EXACT MEASUREMENT WITH INTEGRABILITY

Whenever an empirical policy evaluation problem involves two or more price changes and resources are sufficient to permit econometric estimation, imposition of the assumptions of the policy evaluation methodology at the stage of estimation is desirable to ensure unambiguous calculations of compensating and equivalent variation. One way this can be done is by imposing integrability conditions (1)–(4) among arbitrarily specified

22. These results can be derived by successive application of the Hausman (1981) results and observing the conditions needed for uniqueness.

demand equations. However, as the linear and log-linear cases suggest, imposing these conditions on arbitrary specifications usually leads to implausible restrictions.[23] Alternatively, the necessary conditions can be imposed implicitly by deriving all demand specifications representing the same consumer from a single specification of a plausible underlying utility function. Upon estimation of demands, the parameter estimates can then be used to calculate exact welfare effects from the utility specification.[24] Thus, calculations of the compensating and equivalent variations are exact (aside from statistical errors in estimation) and unambiguous (regardless of statistical error).

Demand specifications can be derived from a specification of either the direct or indirect utility function but much greater functional flexibility is possible with the indirect (or dual) approach. The reason is that, with the direct (primal) approach, the utility specification must be sufficiently simple to allow solution of a system of first-order conditions that is generally nonlinear. By comparison, with the indirect (dual) approach, demand specifications are obtained by simple differentiation following Roy's identity. Roughly, only first-order approximations are possible with the primal approach whereas second-order approximations are tractable with the dual approach. In either case, the utility specification must satisfy a similarly restrictive set of regularity conditions for plausibility. Standard regularity conditions require direct utility functions to be continuous, monotonically increasing, and quasiconcave in $\boldsymbol{q}$. Alternatively, standard regularity conditions require indirect utility functions to be continuous in $\boldsymbol{p}$ and m, monotonically decreasing in $\boldsymbol{p}$, monotonically increasing in m, quasiconvex in $\boldsymbol{p}$ and m, and homogeneous of degree zero in $\boldsymbol{p}$ and m. More simply, if the indirect utility function is written as a function of $\boldsymbol{p}/m$, then the homogeneity condition is satisfied automatically and regularity conditions require only continuity, monotonicity and quasiconvexity in $\boldsymbol{p}/m$. Any functions that satisfy these properties can serve to generate integrable systems of demand equations.[25]

An example where the primal approach has been used successfully to attain first-order flexibility is the case of Houthakker's (1960) addilog utility function,

$$U(\boldsymbol{q}) = \sum_{i=1}^{N} \alpha_i q_i^{\beta_i}, \tag{6.70}$$

where α_i and β_i are unknown parameters to be estimated. The first-order conditions obtained using (6.70) cannot be solved for the direct demand equations but can be solved for the price-dependent demand equations,

23. One exception is the linear expenditure system. Originally, Klein and Rubin (1948–49) posited ordinary demand equations implicitly defined by

$$p_i \tilde{q}_i(\boldsymbol{p}, m) = \beta_i m + \sum_{j=1}^{N} \beta_{ij} p_j,\ i = 1, \ldots, N,$$

and then examined theoretical conditions relating demands. As it turns out, after imposing integrability conditions, these demands can be represented as in equation (6.71) below with the corresponding indirect utility function in (6.70) where $\Sigma_{i=1}^{N} \beta_i = 1$. As the example below illustrates, this system has greater flexibility after satisfying integrability than the linear and log-linear cases. This system was further analyzed by Stone (1954).

24. Actually, utility functions can be estimated only up to a multiplicative factor but this is all that is necessary for calculation of compensating and equivalent variation.

25. Under certain conditions, the strictness in these regularity conditions can be relaxed (for example, utility can be nondecreasing) but such generalities rarely prove useful in empirical analysis. For further discussion of regularity conditions and their role, see Blackorby, Primont and Russell (1978).

$$p_i = m\frac{\alpha_i\beta_i q_i^{\beta_i - 1}}{\sum_{j=1}^{N}\alpha_j\beta_j q_j^{\beta_j}}. \tag{6.71}$$

Using (6.71), the log of price ratios can be expressed in simple linear form to estimate the parameters of the utility function from which welfare quantities can be calculated accurately aside from statistical errors.

To exemplify the dual approach, suppose the indirect utility function follows[26]

$$V(\mathbf{p},m) = \left(1 - \sum_{j=1}^{N}\alpha_j\frac{p_j}{m}\right)\prod_{j=1}^{N}\left(\frac{m}{p_j}\right)^{\beta_j}, \quad \sum_{j=1}^{N}\beta_j = 1, \tag{6.72}$$

where β_j and α_j are parameters. The regularity conditions hold for this function so that it can serve as a valid specification of indirect utility. Application of Roy's identity obtains the ordinary demands,

$$\tilde{q}_i(\mathbf{p},m) = -\frac{\partial V/\partial p_i}{\partial V/\partial m} = \alpha_i + \beta_i\frac{m}{p_i} - \beta_i\sum_{j=1}^{N}\alpha_j\frac{p_j}{p_i}, \; i = 1, \ldots, N,$$

which can be estimated conveniently in the form of the popular linear expenditure system,[27]

$$p_i\tilde{q}_i(\mathbf{p},m) = \alpha_i p_i + \beta_i m - \sum_{j=1}^{N}\beta_i\alpha_j p_j, \; i = 1, \ldots, N. \tag{6.73}$$

Once the parameters of this system of demands are estimated, the compensating and equivalent variations of any general price–income change can be calculated according to (6.23) and (6.25). For example, solving (6.23) after substituting (6.72) obtains[28]

$$C = m_1 - \sum_{j=1}^{N}\alpha_j p_j^1 - \left(m_0 - \sum_{j=1}^{N}\alpha_j p_j^0\right)\prod_{j=1}^{N}\left(\frac{p_j^1}{p_j^0}\right)^{\beta_j}. \tag{6.74}$$

Other popular specifications have been developed that can serve as indirect utility functions with greater flexibility. In particular, several functions have been developed that attain a second-order local approximation to any arbitrary, twice-differentiable indirect utility function, and thus no a priori constraints are placed on the various price and

26. Note that Geary (1949–50) has found the direct utility function associated with this indirect utility function to be

$$U(\mathbf{q}) = \prod_{i=1}^{N}(q_i - \alpha_i)^{\beta_i},$$

where the α_i parameters are interpreted as subsistence requirements.

27. Alternatively, one can verify that the demand equations represented implicitly in (6.73) integrate uniquely to the indirect utility specification in (6.72).

28. From the result in (6.74), one can also determine by comparing with (6.24) that the expenditure function must be given by

$$e(\mathbf{p},U^0) = \sum_{j=1}^{N}\alpha_j p_j + U^0\prod_{j=1}^{N}p_j^{\beta_j}$$

because, from (6.72),

$$U^0 = \left(m_0 - \sum_{j=1}^{N}\alpha_j p_j^0\right)\prod_{j=1}^{N}(p_j^0)^{-\beta_j}.$$

income elasticities at a base point. Some common second-order-flexible functional forms used for indirect utility functions along with the associated demand specifications and compensating variation calculations facilitated by demand estimation are the translog form,[29]

$$V(\mathbf{p},m)=\exp\left[\alpha_0+\sum_{i=1}^{N}\alpha_i\ln\frac{p_i}{m}+\sum_{i=1}^{N}\sum_{j=1}^{N}\beta_{ij}\ln\frac{p_i}{m}\ln\frac{p_j}{m}\right],\ \beta_{ij}=\beta_{ji},\tag{6.75}$$

$$\tilde{q}_i(\mathbf{p},m)=\frac{m}{p_i}\frac{\alpha_i+2\sum_{j=1}^{N}\beta_{ij}\ln\frac{p_j}{m}}{\sum_{j=1}^{N}\alpha_j+2\sum_{j=1}^{N}\sum_{k=1}^{N}\beta_{jk}\ln\frac{p_k}{m}},\tag{6.76}$$

$$C=m_1-\exp\frac{\sum_{i=1}^{N}\alpha_i\ln\frac{m_0p_i^1}{p_i^0}+\sum_{i=1}^{N}\sum_{j=1}^{N}\beta_{ij}\left[\ln p_i^1\ln p_j^1-\ln\frac{p_i^0}{m_0}\ln\frac{p_j^0}{m_0}\right]}{\sum_{i=1}^{N}\alpha_i+2\sum_{i=1}^{N}\sum_{j=1}^{N}\beta_{ij}\ln p_j^1},\tag{6.77}$$

the generalized Leontief form,[30]

$$V(\mathbf{p},m)=\alpha_0+\sum_{i=1}^{N}\alpha_i\ln\frac{p_i}{m}+\sum_{i=1}^{N}\sum_{j=1}^{N}\beta_{ij}\left(\frac{p_i}{m}\right)^{1/2}\left(\frac{p_j}{m}\right)^{1/2},\ \beta_{ij}=\beta_{ji},\ \sum_{i=1}^{N}\alpha_i=0,$$

$$\tilde{q}_i(\mathbf{p},m)=\frac{m}{p_i}\frac{\sum_{j=1}^{N}\beta_{ij}(p_jp_i)^{1/2}+\alpha_i m}{\sum_{k=1}^{N}\sum_{j=1}^{N}\beta_{kj}(p_jp_k)^{1/2}},$$

$$C=m_1-\frac{\sum_{i=1}^{N}\sum_{j=1}^{N}\beta_{ij}(p_i^1p_j^1)^{1/2}}{\sum_{i=1}^{N}\alpha_i\ln\frac{p_i^0}{p_i^1}+\frac{1}{m_0}\sum_{i=1}^{N}\sum_{j=1}^{N}\beta_{ij}(p_i^0p_j^0)^{1/2}},$$

29. The derivation of compensating variation for the translog case assumes that

$$\sum_{i=1}^{N}\sum_{j=1}^{N}\beta_{ij}=0$$

which is a common normalization constraint used for the translog. For practical application, an additional constraint such as

$$\sum_{i=1}^{N}\alpha_i=1$$

is necessary for econometric identification.

30. For practical application, a constraint such as

$$\sum_{i=1}^{N}\sum_{j=1}^{N}\beta_{ij}=0$$

is necessary for econometric identification of the generalized Leontief system.

and the generalized Cobb–Douglas form,[31]

$$V(\boldsymbol{p},m)=\alpha_0+\sum_{i=1}^{N}\alpha_i\ln\frac{p_i}{m}+\prod_{i=1}^{N}\prod_{j=1}^{N}\left(\frac{p_i}{2m}+\frac{p_j}{2m}\right)^{\beta_{ij}},\ \beta_{ij}=\beta_{ji},$$

$$\tilde{q}_i(\boldsymbol{p},m)=\sum_{j=1}^{N}\beta_{ij}\left(\frac{p_i}{2m}+\frac{p_j}{2m}\right)^{-1}+\alpha_i\frac{m^2}{p_i}\prod_{j=1}^{N}\prod_{k=1}^{N}\left(\frac{p_j}{2m}+\frac{p_k}{2m}\right)^{-\beta_{ij}},$$

$$C=m_1-\frac{\prod_{i=1}^{N}\prod_{j=1}^{N}\left(\frac{p_i^1}{2}+\frac{p_j^1}{2}\right)^{\beta_{ij}}}{\sum_{i=1}^{N}\alpha_i\ln\frac{p_i^0}{p_i^1}+\frac{1}{m_0}\prod_{i=1}^{N}\prod_{j=1}^{N}\left(\frac{p_i^0}{2}+\frac{p_j^0}{2}\right)^{\beta_{ij}}}.$$

In each case, the equivalent variation can be found from these expressions simply by noting that it is the negative of the compensating variation of the reverse change. As is obvious from these demand equations, somewhat more tractable equations are obtained for estimation purposes by representing the demands implicitly in expenditure share equations, that is, solving demands for $p_i q_i/m$ before estimation.[32]

Another approach to the specification of a consistent (or integrable) set of demands is to specify a functional form for the expenditure function and then derive demand specifications as derivatives of the expenditure function. Standard regularity conditions for expenditure functions require continuity and positive monotonicity in U and $\boldsymbol{p}$ and linear homogeneity and concavity in $\boldsymbol{p}$ (Blackorby, Primont and Russell 1978). The most popular application of this approach is the almost ideal demand system (AIDS). The AIDS expenditure function is

$$e(\boldsymbol{p},U)=\exp\left[\alpha_0+\sum_{i=1}^{N}\alpha_i\ln p_i+\frac{1}{2}\sum_{i=1}^{N}\sum_{j=1}^{N}\beta_{ij}\ln p_i\ln p_j+\gamma_0 U\prod_{i=1}^{N}p_i^{\gamma_i}\right],$$

$$\sum_{i=1}^{N}\alpha_i=1,\ \sum_{i=1}^{N}\beta_{ij}=\sum_{j=1}^{N}\beta_{ij}=\sum_{i=1}^{N}\gamma_i=0,\ \beta_{ij}=\beta_{ji}$$

31. The compensating variation expression for the generalized Cobb–Douglas case assumes that

$$\sum_{i=1}^{N}\alpha_i=0,$$

which is one of two common assumptions imposed in estimation for linear homogeneity of the indirect utility function. If this assumption is not imposed, then only an implicit equation defining compensating variation can be derived. Another general form for the indirect utility function that has gained some popularity is the quadratic mean of order ρ form,

$$V(\boldsymbol{p},m)=\left[\sum_{i=1}^{N}\alpha_i\left(\frac{p_i}{m}\right)^{\rho/2}+\sum_{i=1}^{N}\sum_{j=1}^{N}\beta_{ij}\left(\frac{p_i}{m}\right)^{\rho/2}\left(\frac{p_j}{m}\right)^{\rho/2}\right]^{1/\rho},\ \beta_{ij}=\beta_{ji}.$$

In this case, one can also easily derive the demand functions using Roy's identity but only an implicit equation defining the compensating variation can be found using (6.23).

32. For further discussion and an example of application involving estimation of each of these three forms, see Berndt, Darrough and Diewert (1977).

(Deaton and Muellbauer 1980). Thus, using (6.27),

$$\frac{p_i\bar{q}_i(\mathbf{p},U)}{m}=\frac{p_i}{m}\frac{\partial e(\mathbf{p},U)}{\partial p_i}=\alpha_i+\frac{1}{2}\sum_{j=1}^{N}(\beta_{ij}+\beta_{ji})\ln p_j+\gamma_i\gamma_0U\prod_{j=1}^{N}p_j^{\gamma_j}. \qquad (6.78)$$

This equation does not facilitate estimation of demands directly because U is unobservable. However, solving $m=e(\mathbf{p},U)$ for U and substituting in (6.78) obtains[33]

$$\frac{p_i\tilde{q}_i(\mathbf{p},m)}{m}=\alpha_i+\sum_{j=1}^{N}\beta_{ij}\ln p_j+\gamma_i\left[\ln m-\alpha_0-\sum_{j=1}^{N}\alpha_j\ln p_j-\frac{1}{2}\sum_{j=1}^{N}\sum_{k=1}^{N}\beta_{ij}\ln p_j\ln p_k\right].$$

Estimation of the parameters of these equations then obtains all of the parameter estimates necessary to calculate compensating variation according to (6.24) or equivalent variation according to (6.26).

These cases demonstrate that exact calculation of consumer benefits (aside from statistical error) is possible with considerable generality in functional forms if appropriate considerations are implemented at the stage of estimation, that is, at the stage of specification of the equations to be estimated. The methodology of this section offers a coherent and defensible way of evaluating the welfare effects of multiple price changes on individual consumers without resorting to the approximating properties of consumer surplus. Because the Willig approximation properties of consumer surplus as well as the Hause, Hausman and Vartia approaches to calculating WTP from ordinary demand relationships fail in cases of multiple price changes when integrability conditions fail, the empirical approaches of this section are highly desirable and arguably necessary for evaluating welfare effects in general cases with multiple price changes.

33. To simplify estimation of demands, these equations are sometimes written as

$$\frac{p_i\tilde{q}_i(\mathbf{p},m)}{m}=\alpha_i+\sum_{j=1}^{N}\beta_{ij}\ln p_j+\gamma_i\ln(m/P),$$

where P is a price index defined by

$$\ln P=\alpha_0+\sum_{j=1}^{N}\alpha_j\ln p_j+\frac{1}{2}\sum_{j=1}^{N}\sum_{k=1}^{N}\beta_{ij}\ln p_j\ln p_k.$$

Then the price index is approximated by $P\approx\varphi P^*$ where

$$P^*=\sum_{j=1}^{N}\frac{p_jq_j}{m}\ln p_j.$$

The estimated equations thus become

$$\frac{p_i\tilde{q}_i(\mathbf{p},m)}{m}=\tilde{\alpha}_i+\sum_{j=1}^{N}\beta_{ij}\ln p_j+\gamma_i\ln(m/P^*),$$

where $\tilde{\alpha}_i=\alpha_i-\gamma_i\log\varphi$. Deaton and Muellbauer (1980) have shown that this approximation is good in widely occurring circumstances. However, this approach does not obtain estimates of the α_i, which are necessary for calculation of the compensating variation according to (6.24), nor does it attain econometric efficiency.

7. Factor supply and factor owner welfare

In the preceding two chapters, consumer welfare was analyzed in terms of the effect on consumers of changing the prices of products that consumers purchase and/or of introducing a new commodity. However, in order to purchase goods, consumers must earn income (excluding, for the moment, government welfare payments to consumers) from such sources as work, interest on savings, rental income from land holdings and the like.

The owners of factors of production, such as labor and land, derive 'economic rent' from the services provided by these factors for which there is a positive market demand (see Section 4.1). According to Mishan (1959, p. 394), economic rent has a symmetrical welfare interpretation with consumer surplus in that they are 'both measures of the change in the individual's welfare when the set of prices facing him are altered or the constraints upon him are altered'. Hence, the approach of Chapter 6 can be generalized in a straightforward fashion, although the Willig results require a somewhat different interpretation.

7.1 INITIAL CONSIDERATIONS IN FACTOR OWNER WELFARE MEASUREMENT

To use the same framework developed earlier, consider the labor supply curve in Figure 7.1, for example. Initially, the wage earner is willing to work longer hours (h) if the wage rate (w) is increased (although perhaps at higher incomes the same wage increment may lead to reduced willingness to work as explained in Section 7.4). As pointed out by Gary Becker (1965), the consumer's labor supply curve represents the mirror image of his or her demand for leisure. That is, with units of time of length τ (for example, 24-hour days), a decision to work h_1 hours automatically entails a decision to allocate $\tau - h_1$ hours to nonwork or leisure. Thus, one may further consider Figure 7.1 in the context of the demand for leisure. In point of fact, with a prevailing wage rate – say, w_1 – at which h_1 hours of labor are supplied, w_1 represents not only the marginal income from an additional hour of labor but also the marginal cost of obtaining an additional hour of leisure.

With this interpretation of the labor supply curve, consider a reduction in the wage rate to w_2 at which working hours are reduced to h_2. Following the earlier approach (Figure 5.3), the change in gross benefits from consuming leisure in Figure 7.1 is the change in area below the demand curve – area b. From this must be subtracted the costs of obtaining the additional leisure. In this case, the cost is the reduction in income resulting from the wage change and the induced change in hours worked, that is, $w_1h_1 - w_2h_2$ or area $a+b$. Subtracting this cost from the change in gross benefits obtains area a as a net loss for the consumer/labor supplier as a result of the wage reduction. Note, however, that area a is simply the change in area above the labor supply curve and below the wage rate.

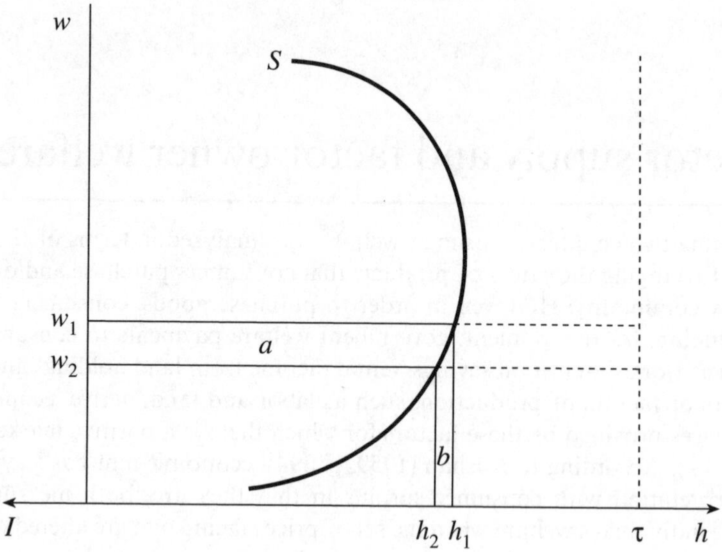

Figure 7.1

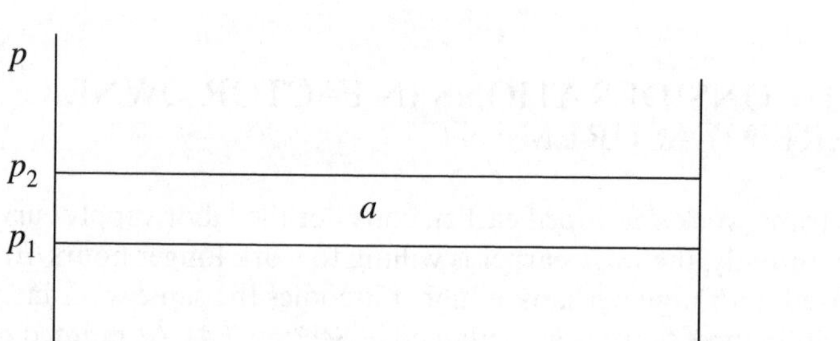

Figure 7.2

The area behind a factor supply curve is fully analogous to use of the consumer surplus area behind a consumer demand curve. To maintain symmetry of terminology with Chapter 4, however, the triangle-like area above a supply curve and below price will be called the *producer surplus* associated with the supply curve. This area is also sometimes called *economic rent* in the context of this chapter because it is a net benefit earned as a return on the factor.

However, not all factors supplied by individuals enter into their preferences (apart from the implicit purchasing power of the income they earn) as does labor. For example, suppose that in Figure 7.2 an individual owns a quantity of land q_1. As a consumer, the individual may receive no explicit benefit from using the land for himself. Thus, the landowner would be willing to rent the land to someone else who could make beneficial use of the land at the prevailing rental price p_1. If the rental price is too low, the landowner may seek to sell the land, but this would be a longer-run decision. Hence, the vertical line at q_1 may be regarded as a short-run supply curve analogous to S in Figure 7.1. For example, with an increase in rental price to p_2, the increase in producer surplus or economic rent, in the short run, is area a and is equivalent to the change in nominal rental income (the change in $p \cdot q$) on the land.

7.2 ENDOGENOUS VERSUS EXOGENOUS INCOME

The case associated with Figure 7.2 suggests yet a further distinction that becomes important from the standpoint of empirical practice, especially when applying the Willig results, to approximate willingness to pay (WTP) via the consumer or producer surplus triangles. Consider, for example, the case where the vertical supply curve in Figure 7.2 is determined in the short run strictly by the amount of a factor controlled by the individual (for example, the amount of owned land) rather than by prices of other commodities. For example, suppose that land purchases and sales require more time to implement than other consumption or factor supply decisions and, hence, short-run price variations cannot induce a shift in the supply curve of rental land. In this case, the short-run income from land rental is essentially imposed on the individual rather than determined by the individual according to personal preferences.

In economics, the term *exogenous* is used to refer to forces or variables that are determined from the outside, whereas *endogenous* variables are determined, jointly or simultaneously, from within (for example, within the consumer's decision problem) in the context of existing exogenous forces. Thus, for purposes of making the foregoing distinction, *exogenous income* will be defined as that component of income which the consumer has no ability to increase and which he or she will not voluntarily decrease in the short run. *Endogenous income*, on the other hand, will be defined as that component of income which may generally be altered by the consumer as a response to changes in prices or other exogenous forces.[1]

These concepts become important in delineating the exogenous variables that determine a factor supply curve. Conceptually, *a factor supply curve for the consumer is determined by exogenous income and the prices of consumption commodities and other factors that influence consumer behavior.* For example, a labor supply curve may be determined by consumption prices, the interest rate, and exogenous income composed of rents, dividends on shareholdings (profits) and transfer payments from government or, possibly, from private sources. That is, if the quantity of savings supplied by the consumer at a given interest rate depends on the wage rate, total interest income could not be included in exogenous income as a determinant of labor supply because interest income would itself be

1. In some earlier literature, endogenous and exogenous income have been called earned and unearned income. See, for example, Abbott and Ashenfelter (1976). Another concept that has proven to be useful in econometric work is the notion of *full income*, which is defined to be total purchasing power available to a consumer to be spent on both leisure and goods. *Full income* is exogenous plus endogenous income plus the time allocated to leisure evaluated at the wage rate or, equivalently, the total time available evaluated at the wage rate plus exogenous income.

determined or influenced by movement along the labor supply curve. The amount of land offered for rental, on the other hand, may not generally respond to changes in the wage rate at least in the short run. Hence, the income from land rental rather than the rental rate may serve as a determinant of labor supply.[2]

Consumption demand may also be treated in the same way in the context of this chapter. That is, if the consumer's decision problem is one of maximizing utility through choice of the quantities of consumer goods and factors supplied, the exogenous forces affecting the consumer are the prices of all consumer goods and factors, which are subject to variation in the short run, plus the exogenous income that results from transfers, profits and factor sales that are not subject to short-run alteration. Thus, the determinants of each consumer demand or supply curve consist of exogenous income and the prices of all other consumer goods and factors that are subject to short-run variation.

7.3 PATH DEPENDENCE AND RELATED ISSUES

Having defined an intuitive measure of welfare change for a factor owner – producer surplus – and having discussed the alternative roles of factor prices as determinants of supply and demand, consider now the applicability of such desirable properties as uniqueness and path independence when several prices and, possibly, income change. Because of the similarities between producer surplus arising from factor supply and consumer surplus arising from final consumption demand, the problems discussed in Sections 5.2 through 5.4 generalize to include the case where factor supply decisions are coupled with consumption decisions. Consider, for example, Figure 7.3 where the wage rises from w_0 to w_1, while exogenous income rises from $\bar{m}_0$ to $\bar{m}_1$. Of course, both changes entail a change in income. The former generally causes a change in endogenous income, while the latter is a change

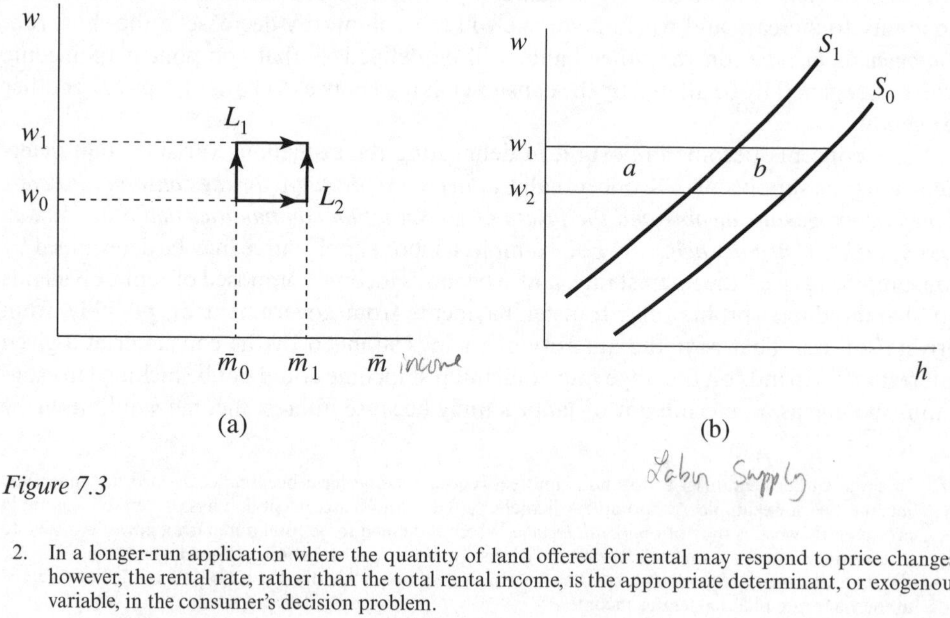

Figure 7.3

2. In a longer-run application where the quantity of land offered for rental may respond to price changes, however, the rental rate, rather than the total rental income, is the appropriate determinant, or exogenous variable, in the consumer's decision problem.

in exogenous income. Again, this distinction is important because the labor supply curve is generally determined by the level of exogenous income. For example, a change in exogenous income causes a shift in the supply curve – say, from S_0 to S_1 – whereas a change in wage rate causes movement along the labor supply curve and, thus, a change in endogenous income. As in Section 5.2, however, the surplus effect is ambiguous. Consider, for example, the two possible paths of adjustment, L_1 and L_2, depicted in Figure 7.3(a). Along path L_1, wages rise, leading to a gain of area $a+b$ along the initial supply curve S_0, with the subsequent adjustment in exogenous income $\bar{m}_1 - \bar{m}_0$. Along path L_2, income is first adjusted by the same amount, but the subsequent producer surplus change along the supply curve is a gain of only area a. The two paths, therefore, suggest the same welfare impact only if area b is zero, in which case (for arbitrary price changes) the two supply curves must coincide. Such a condition is characterized by a zero exogenous income effect. That is, a change in exogenous income does not induce a change in the associated quantity of a factor supplied when all other prices are held constant. Analogous to the Section 5.3 fixed-income case, a zero exogenous income effect also implies a zero exogenous income elasticity for the associated commodity. In simple terms, the exogenous income elasticity is the percentage change in the quantity of consumption demanded or the quantity of a factor supplied associated with a small percentage change in exogenous income.

Because these same arguments can also be developed in the consumption case, just as in the factor supply case (simply substitute the term 'exogenous income' for 'income' in the Section 5.2 and 5.3 arguments), results may be summarized as follows.[3] For arbitrary changes of prices and exogenous income, the change in surplus is unique if, and only if, exogenous income effects are zero or, equivalently, exogenous income elasticities are zero for all commodities (supplied or demanded) for which prices change.

In the case where more than one commodity price changes without a simultaneous change in exogenous income, the associated conditions for uniqueness of the surplus change are somewhat different. Consider Figure 7.4 where the wage rate changes from w_0 to w_1 and the price of a consumption commodity changes from p_0 to p_1. Initially, consumption demand is D_0 and labor supply is S_0. Following the wage–price change, demand for the consumer good is D_1 and labor supply is S_1. The change in surplus may be evaluated along any one of an infinite number of paths between initial and final wages and prices. Two possible paths, L_1 and L_2, are shown in Figure 7.4(a). Along path L_1, one obtains, first, a gain in consumer surplus of area $x+y$ and then labor supply shifts due to the consumer price change, obtaining a loss in producer surplus (or economic rent) of area a. Along path L_2, one first obtains a loss in producer surplus of area $a+b$ and, after consumption demand has shifted to D_1, a gain in consumer surplus of area x. The two surplus measures are the same if, and only if, area b is equal to area y. Following the approach of Section 5.3 and using Δ to represent changes, these areas are equal with small wage–price changes if, and only if,

$$\frac{\Delta q}{\Delta w} = \frac{\Delta h}{\Delta p}.$$

In comparison with Section 5.3, this is the same condition required for uniqueness between consumer goods with a multiple consumer price change. Thus, the same results,

3. For a rigorous derivation, see Appendix Sections 7.A and 7.B.

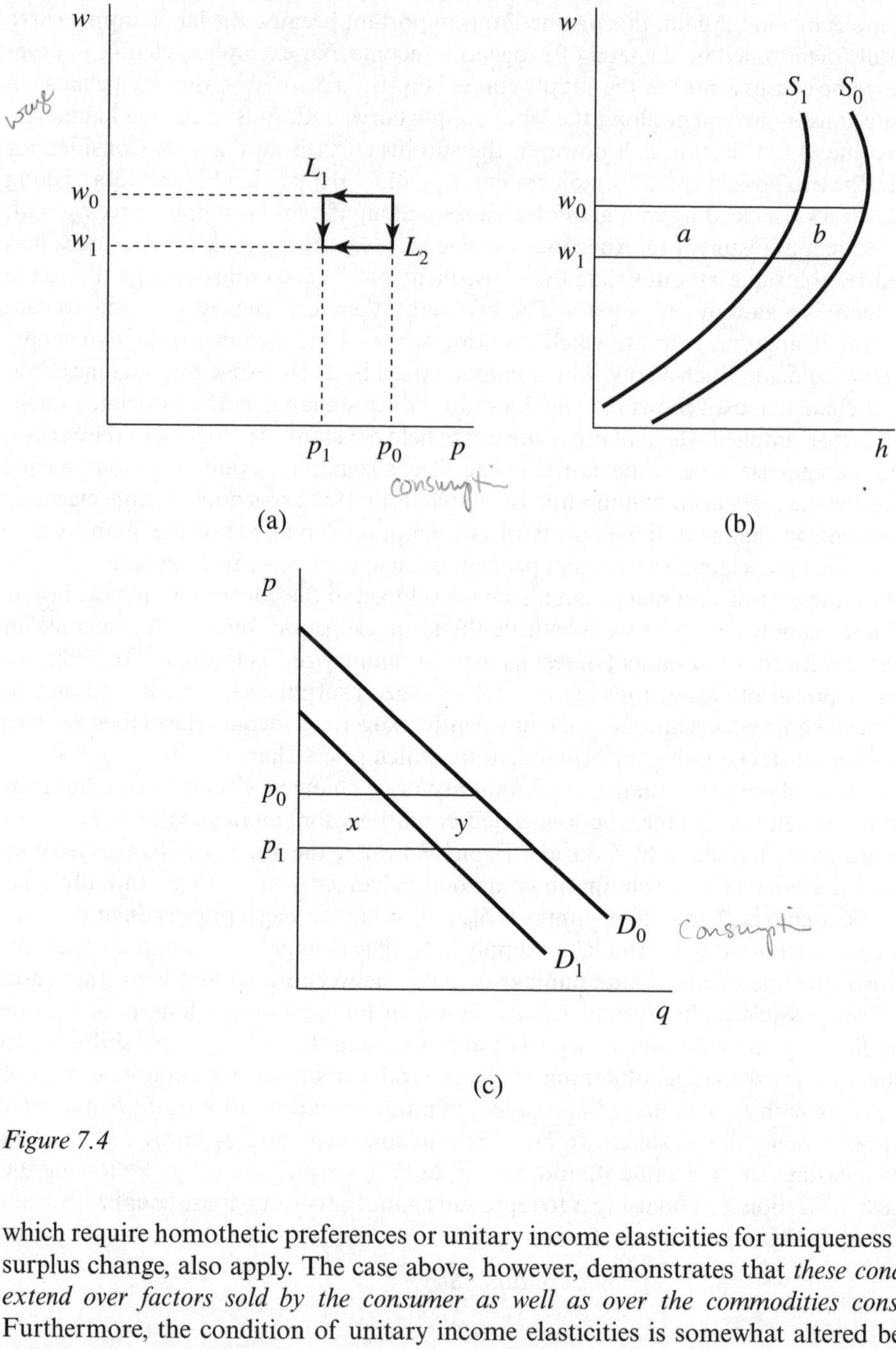

Figure 7.4

which require homothetic preferences or unitary income elasticities for uniqueness of the surplus change, also apply. The case above, however, demonstrates that *these conditions extend over factors sold by the consumer as well as over the commodities consumed.* Furthermore, the condition of unitary income elasticities is somewhat altered because only the exogenous part of income serves as the determinant of consumer demand and factor supply analogous to the income in Chapter 5. The factor prices serve as the determinants associated with endogenous income. Hence, the appropriate conclusions in the present context (verified rigorously in Appendix Section 7.B) are as follows. *The surplus change associated with a multiple change of both consumer good prices and factor prices for a single competitive consumer (holding exogenous income fixed) is unique if, and only if, preferences are homothetic or, equivalently, exogenous income elasticities are identical with respect to all commodities (subject to short-run variation) for which prices change.*

Having generalized the conclusions of Section 5.3 to the case where income is not fixed but is influenced by the consumer's decisions to sell factors, it suffices to say that the prospects of uniqueness in surplus measurement of welfare change are no brighter than the fixed-income case implies. Indeed, the same restrictiveness is implied for preferences relating to consumption, while further restrictions of a similar nature are implied with respect to factor supply.

7.4 WILLINGNESS TO PAY REVISITED

Because of problems associated with interpretation and nonuniqueness of surplus measures, a further application of WTP analysis is useful for the factor supply case. For this purpose, the definitions of compensating and equivalent variation specific to cases of price and income changes given in Chapter 6 may be used. The term 'prices', however, is interpreted more broadly to include prices of factors sold by the consumer (for example, labor) as well as prices of commodities consumed.

To develop the WTP approach with respect to factor supply, the concept of a compensated supply curve is needed. *Compensated supply* is defined by the relationship between the quantity of a factor supplied and its price for a given level of utility (holding other prices fixed). That is, by contrast with ordinary supply, it is conditioned on the level of utility rather than on the level of exogenous income. Consider the indifference map in Figure 7.5(a) between leisure (l) and income (m), where the leisure axis runs leftward. Thus, the corresponding work (h) axis runs rightward, although with a different origin. The individual can allocate total time (τ) to either leisure or work, thus implying a 'budget' line between the point τ on the leisure axis and the point $\tau \cdot w$ on the income axis where w is again the wage rate.[4] Thus, three different budget lines are obtained for wage rates w_1, w_2 and w_3, with respective optimal consumer decision points a_1, a_2 and a_3. Transferring these results to Figure 7.5(b) demonstrates the relationship of the ordinary labor supply curve S with leisure–income preferences. The ordinary supply curve, of course, is the relationship between the quantity of a factor supplied by the consumer and its price for a given level of exogenous income (holding other prices fixed). Hence, the example in Figure 7.5 clearly demonstrates that the ordinary labor supply curve may be backward bending at higher wages.

To develop a corresponding compensated supply curve, suppose that the wage rate is initially w_1 and rises successively to w_2 and w_3. The compensating variation of the change from w_1 to w_2 is the amount of income that must be taken away from the consumer to restore the original utility level I_1. Because wage w_2 leads to the higher utility level I_2, the original utility level can be obtained by imposing a lump-sum tax on the consumer without changing the wage rate. In this case, the budget line contracts to one with

4. If income is also earned from other sources, that income can be included in a nonzero origin on the income axis. The amounts $\tau \cdot w$ would then be additional income. Alternatively, the label of the income axis in Figure 7.5 can be changed from m to $m - \bar{m}$.

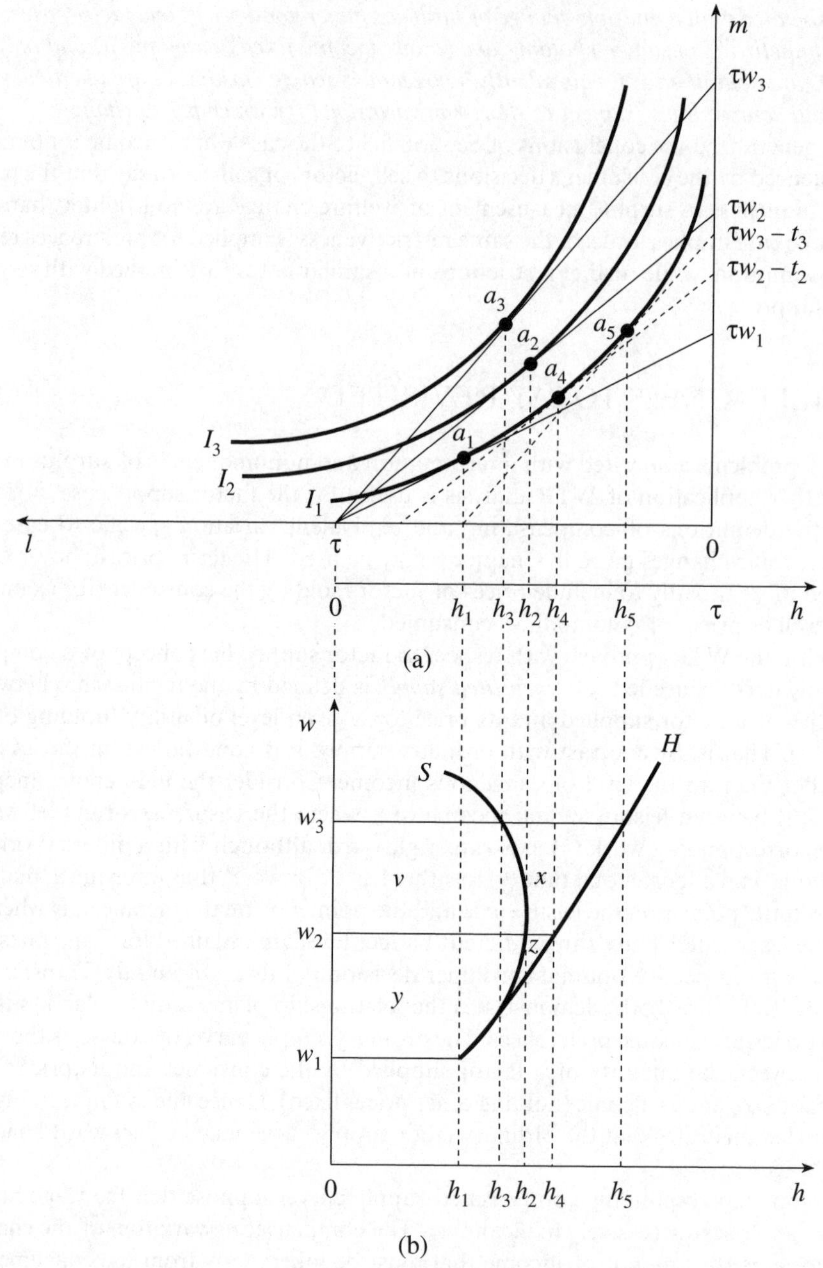
m
τw3
τw2
τw3 − t3
τw2 − t2
τw1
a3
a2
a5
a4
a1
I3
I2
I1
l
τ
0
0
h1
h3
h2
h4
h5
τ
h
(a)
w
H
S
w3
v
x
w2
z
y
w1
0
h1
h3
h2
h4
h5
h
(b)

Figure 7.5

maximum income $\tau w_2 - t_2$ and tangency with indifference curve I_1 at a_4. Hence, the compensating variation of the wage change from w_1 to w_2 is precisely t_2. Furthermore, because the utility level at a_4 with wage w_2 is the same as the utility level at a_1 with wage w_1, a pair of points on a single compensated supply curve H is obtained. A third point is obtained by changing the wage rate from w_1 to w_3 and then imposing a lump-sum tax t_3 to bring the consumer back to indifference curve I_1, with a tangency at a_5 and labor quantity h_5. By analogy, a (Hicksian) compensated labor supply curve may be constructed for any level of utility corresponding to any point on the ordinary supply curve.

One can also show in a manner analogous to results in Section 6.1 (by using inner and outer cost differences, breaking the price change into a series of small changes, and taking away the compensating or equivalent variation with each successive small change) that the income differences t_2 and t_3 are related to the change in area above the *compensated* supply curve and below price. In other words, the compensating variation of a wage change from w_1 to w_2 is given either by t_2 in Figure 7.5(a) or by area $y+z$ in Figure 7.5(b). Similarly, the compensating variation of a wage rate increase from w_1 to w_3 is measured either by the distance t_3 in Figure 7.5(a) or, equivalently, by area $v+x+y+z$ in Figure 7.5(b). In each case, the distance, or area, also measures the negative of the equivalent variation of the corresponding wage-rate reduction. Thus, the area behind a compensated factor supply curve plays an analogous role to the area behind a compensated consumption demand curve for the individual consumer.

From Figure 7.5, when indifference curves are positively sloped in the space of income and factor quantity, the corresponding compensated supply curve is positively sloped throughout, even though the ordinary supply curve may have negatively sloped portions. Under the same conditions, geometric considerations also imply that the compensated supply curve intersects the ordinary supply curve from the left unless the two curves coincide. Indeed, however, analogous to the Section 5.3 consumption case, zero exogenous income effects or, equivalently, zero exogenous income elasticities imply coincidence of the ordinary and compensated supply curves. That is, when the indifference curves in Figure 7.5(a) are vertically parallel, points a_2 and a_4 correspond to the same level of labor ($h_2 = h_4$), while a_3 and a_5 correspond to another single level of labor ($h_3 = h_5$). Given the foregoing results associated with positively sloped indifference curves, it is a simple matter to show that $C \geq \Delta S \geq E$ for increases or decreases in factor prices, where C is compensating variation, E the equivalent variation and ΔS the change in producer surplus (all three are negative in the case of wage decreases).

7.5 SURPLUS CHANGE AS AN APPROXIMATION OF WTP

Given the similarities of the results described above and those obtained in Chapter 6 for the fixed-income case, an obvious approach at this point is to attempt approximation of the empirically more difficult WTP measures using the simple surplus concepts. Because common sense suggests doubt that exogenous income effects (or elasticities) are zero in most cases, the desirable equality $C = \Delta S = E$ probably does not hold in general. Nevertheless, the approximate relationships in Sections 6.5 and 6.6 can be readily extended.

To develop these results, consider Figure 7.6, where the wage rate is initially w_0 and rises

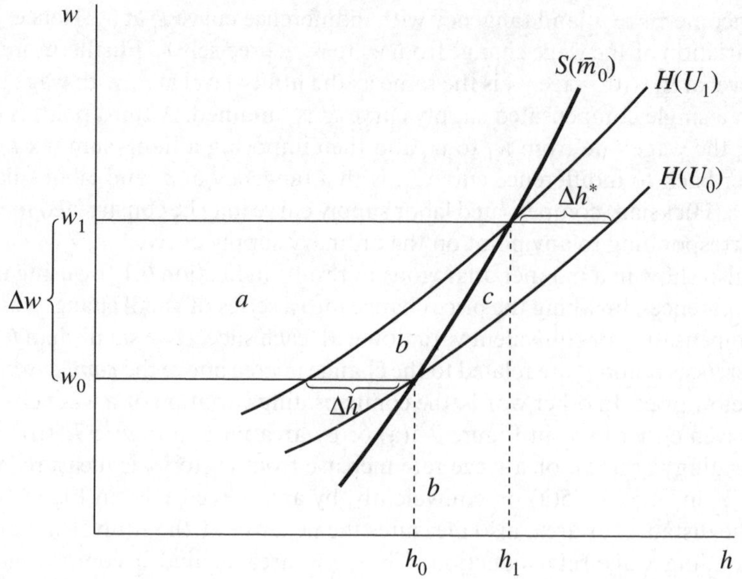

Figure 7.6

to w_1, causing the labor quantity to increase from h_0 to h_1 following the ordinary labor supply curve, $S(\bar{m}_0)$, along which the level of exogenous income, $\bar{m}_0$, and all other prices are held fixed. The compensated labor supply curves corresponding to initial and final wage rates are represented, respectively, by $H(U_0)$ and $H(U_1)$. Thus, $\Delta S=$ area $a+b$, $C=$ area $a+b+c$, and $E=$ area a.

Following the approach of Section 6.5, note that areas b and c associated with the accuracy of ΔS, as a measurement of C or E, are related to the exogenous income elasticity. That is, consider small wage changes where area $b+c$ is approximately a parallelogram with $\Delta h \doteq \Delta h^*$. Using the exogenous income elasticity definition,

$$\bar{\eta}=\frac{\Delta h}{\Delta \bar{m}}\frac{\bar{m}}{h},$$

the horizontal base of the parallelogram is obtained as an income effect of changing exogenous income,

$$\Delta h=\bar{\eta}\cdot h\cdot\frac{\Delta \bar{m}}{\bar{m}}. \tag{7.1}$$

Based on the intuitive arguments of Section 7.1, the approximate size of the change in income that induces this change is

$$\Delta \bar{m}=\Delta S. \tag{7.2}$$

Thus, substituting equation (7.2) into (7.1) and calculating areas b and c obtains

$$\text{area } b \doteq \text{area c} \doteq \tfrac{1}{2}\Delta h\cdot|\Delta w| \doteq \tfrac{1}{2}\bar{\eta}\cdot\Delta S\cdot h\cdot\frac{|\Delta w|}{\bar{m}}.$$

Finally, note that $h \cdot |\Delta w|$ in the equation above is approximately equal to ΔS for small Δw (it is a simple cost-difference approximation of ΔS). Hence, $C =$ area $a+b+c$ is approximated by adding the foregoing approximation of area c to area $a+b$ $(=\Delta S)$,

$$\hat{C} = \Delta S - \hat{\varepsilon}|\Delta S| \tag{7.3}$$

and $E =$ area a is approximated by subtracting the foregoing approximation of area b from area $a+b$,

$$\hat{E} = \Delta S + \hat{\varepsilon}|\Delta S|, \tag{7.4}$$

where

$$\hat{\varepsilon} = \frac{\bar{\eta}|\bar{s}|}{2}, \ \bar{s} = \frac{\Delta S}{\bar{m}}.$$

From these results, the conclusions of Section 6.6 generalize immediately to the case of factor supply as well as consumer demand where income has both exogenous and endogenous components (the generalization relating to consumer demand follows the derivation of Section 6.6, where the income term, m, is interpreted as only that component of income which is exogenous). That is, as suggested by equations (7.3) and (7.4), the term $\hat{\varepsilon} \times 100$ is approximately the percentage error of the surplus change as a measure of compensating or equivalent variation. Hence, if $|\hat{\varepsilon}| = |\bar{\eta}\bar{s}/2| < 0.05$, the surplus change is in error by no more than about 5 percent. Furthermore, if accurate estimates of $\bar{\eta}$ and $\bar{m}$ are available, much more precise estimation of C and E is possible on the basis of surplus changes following equations (7.3) and (7.4). Rigorous results in Appendix Sections 7.E and 7.F, which verify all of the intuitive derivations discussed above, imply that one can avoid more than about 2 percent error by using the estimates in equations (7.3) and (7.4) if $|\bar{\eta}\bar{s}/2| \leq 0.08$ and $\bar{\eta}$ changes by less than 50 percent over the course of the price change.

One must continue to bear in mind in the present context of evaluating changes in factor prices that the income elasticity $\bar{\eta}$ and relative surplus change, $\bar{s} = \Delta S/\bar{m}$, are computed with respect to exogenous rather than total income – even for consumer goods. To facilitate understanding of the implications of using exogenous income rather than total income in the cases of consumer demand for, say, q, note that

$$\hat{\varepsilon} = \frac{\bar{\eta}|\bar{s}|}{2} = \frac{1}{2}\frac{\Delta q}{\Delta \bar{m}}\frac{\bar{m}}{q}\frac{|\Delta S|}{\bar{m}} = \frac{1}{2}\frac{\Delta q}{\Delta \bar{m}}\frac{|\Delta S|}{q}. \tag{7.5}$$

If, in this case, the change in quantity demanded associated with a small change in exogenous income (that is, $\Delta q/\Delta \bar{m}$) is the same as the change in quantity demanded associated with a small but equal change in total income (that is, $\Delta q/\Delta m$), then substitution in equation (7.5) yields

$$\hat{\varepsilon} = \frac{1}{2}\frac{\Delta q}{\Delta m}\frac{|\Delta S|}{q} = \frac{1}{2}\frac{\Delta q}{\Delta m}\frac{m}{q}\frac{|\Delta S|}{m} = \frac{\eta|s|}{2}. \tag{7.6}$$

Comparing equations (7.5) and (7.6) reveals that the percentage error and associated correction factor for consumer surplus, as a measure of compensating or equivalent variation, are exactly the same as in the results of Chapter 6 for the case of consumer price changes as long as consumers do not distinguish between incomes from different sources in their marginal propensities to consume. Thus, the results of Chapter 6 relating to total income continue to hold for determining error bounds and correction factors on measurements of *consumer surplus changes*. However, an important difference also exists with respect to evaluating *income changes.* That is, the welfare effects of changes in endogenous income directly due to consumer price changes are automatically reflected in the associated consumer surplus changes (because of the consumer's ability to adjust endogenous variables to equate marginal utilities), whereas changes in exogenous income or changes in endogenous income due to changes in factor prices are not.

To see this more clearly, consider Figure 7.7(a), where q is the quantity of a consumer good and h is the quantity of labor. Initially, the wage rate is w_0, and the price of the consumer good is p_0. Also, suppose these are the only two commodities considered by the

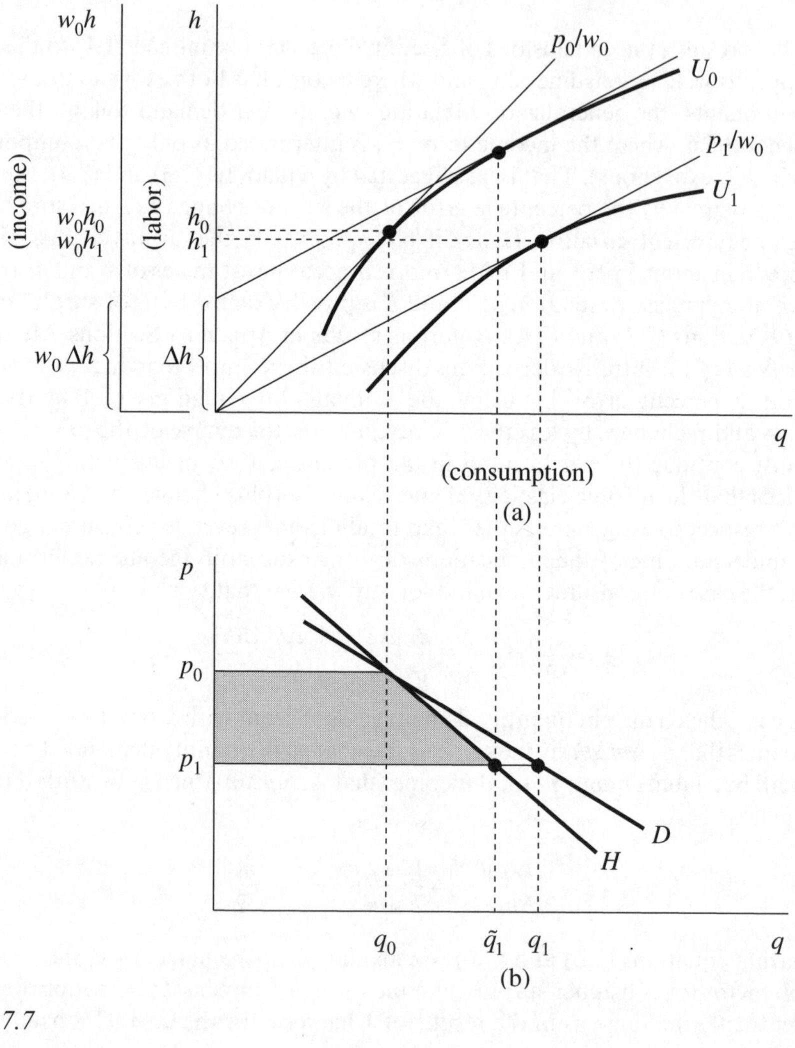

Figure 7.7

consumer and that the exogenous income is zero. With a decline in the price of the consumer good to p_1, the budget line rotates about the origin from a slope of p_0/w_0 to a slope of p_1/w_0. Utility maximization with indifference curves U_0 and U_1 thus implies an increase in consumption from q_0 to q_1 and a decrease in labor from h_0 to h_1. Transferring these results to Figure 7.7(b) yields the ordinary demand curve D. Taking away Δh (or $w_0\,\Delta h$ in terms of income at constant wage rate w_0) in order to remain on the same indifference curve implies a smaller adjustment to $\bar{q}_1$, which determines the Hicksian compensated demand curve H.

Again, recall the approach of using inner or outer cost differences, breaking the price change into small intervals, and taking away the compensating variation with each successive small price change to remain on the same compensated demand curve, to show that the shaded area behind H measures the overall compensating variation Δh (or $w_0\,\Delta h$ in money terms) of the price change. Note, however, that income has also changed as a result of the price change from w_0h_0 to w_0h_1 because of the endogenous possibilities of adjustment. Clearly, this change in income should not be subtracted from the welfare gain represented by the shaded area in arriving at a final measure of the effect. This, then, is in contrast to the case of Chapter 6 where any change in exogenous income must be considered as an additional welfare effect over and above the compensating or equivalent variations induced by accompanying price changes.

7.6 THE GENERAL PRICE CHANGE CASE FOR THE FACTOR OWNER

Having discovered the simple extension of Chapter 6 results to the case of factor supply, and the revision in approach necessary when factor quantities are influenced by consumer prices, extension to the case of multiple price changes, as in Section 6.6, or the case of multiple price changes with income changes, as in Section 6.7, is a simple matter. For exemplary purposes, this section considers only the case of a multiple price change analogous to Figure 7.4, involving one factor price and one consumer good price. Other cases may be developed as exercises, or the reader may refer to Appendix Section 7.F, which treats the general case of many factors and many consumer goods.

Suppose that, initially, the wage rate is w_0 and the price of a consumer good is p_0 with a respective change to w_1 and p_1, as in Figure 7.8. To calculate, say, the compensating variation measure of welfare change, consider first adjusting wages from w_0 to w_1 and then prices from p_0 to p_1. The choice of path is again arbitrary in evaluating WTP, as in the pure consumer case. Initially, exogenous income is $\bar{m}_0$ (and endogenous income is w_0h_0) and utility is U_0. Ordinary supplies and demands (S and D) are represented by conditioning on exogenous income, while compensated supplies and demands (HS and HD) are represented by conditioning on utilities.

To generate the compensating variation along the path holding price at p_0 and changing wages from w_0 to w_1, the results of the preceding section can be used directly. Thus,

$$\text{area } b \doteq \frac{1}{2}\,\Delta h\cdot|\Delta w| \doteq \frac{1}{2}\,\bar{\eta}_h\cdot\Delta S_h\cdot h\cdot\frac{|\Delta w|}{\bar{m}_0},$$

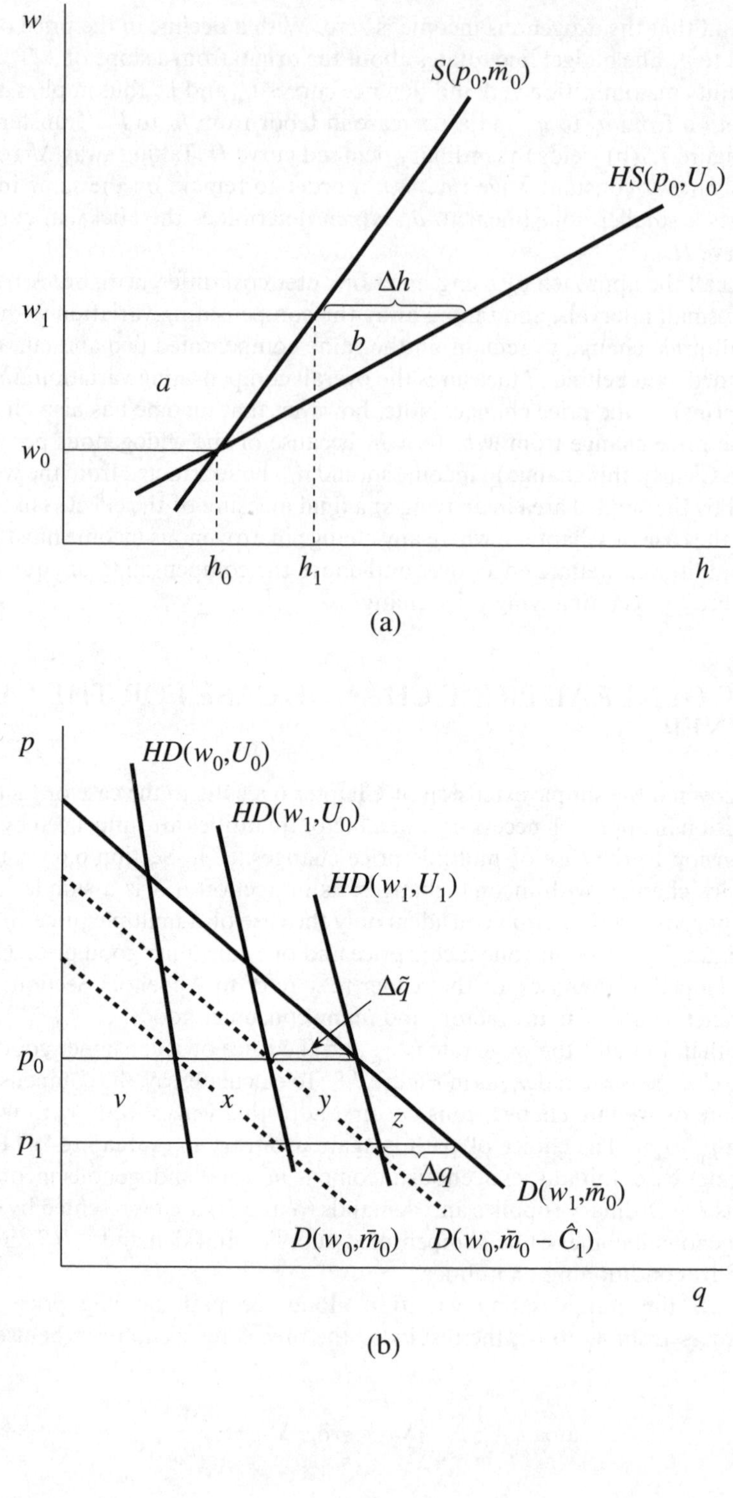

w
S(p0,m̄0)
HS(p0,U0)
Δh
w1
b
a
w0
h0
h1
h
(a)
p
HD(w0,U0)
HD(w1,U0)
HD(w1,U1)
Δq̃
p0
v
x
y
z
p1
Δq
D(w1,m̄0)
D(w0,m̄0)
D(w0,m̄0 − Ĉ1)
q
(b)

Figure 7.8

where $\Delta w = w_1 - w_0$, $\Delta S_h =$ area a, and $\bar{\eta}_h$ is the exogenous income elasticity of labor supply. Following equation (7.3), the compensating variation associated with the first part of the path is approximated by

$$\hat{C}_1 = \Delta S_h + \frac{\bar{\eta}_h}{2\bar{m}_0}(\Delta S_h)^2.$$

Now consider the additional compensating variation $\hat{C}_2$ generated by the fall in price from p_0 to p_1, holding the wage rate at w_1. Again, recalling the fundamental implication of the nibble paradox, this calculation must be made holding utility fixed at the level corresponding to the initial wage rate and initial price and not at the level afforded by the new wage rate and old price. Thus, the compensating variation along the second part of the path is the change in area behind the compensated demand curve, $HD(w_1, U_0)$ in Figure 7.8(b) (that is, area $v+x$). This contrasts with the associated change of area $v+x+y+z$ in simple consumer surplus. To determine the extent of error and to approximate the correct area, the approach of Section 6.6 may be applied almost directly. That is, area z can be approximated by

$$\text{area } z \doteq \frac{1}{2}\Delta q \cdot |\Delta p| \doteq \frac{1}{2}\bar{\eta}_q \cdot \Delta S_q \cdot q \cdot \frac{|\Delta p|}{\bar{m}_0} \doteq \frac{\bar{\eta}_q}{2\bar{m}_0}(\Delta S_q)^2,$$

and area y can be approximated by

$$\text{area } y \doteq |\Delta p| \cdot \Delta \bar{q} \doteq |\Delta p| \cdot \bar{\eta}_q \cdot q \cdot \frac{\hat{C}_1}{\bar{m}_0} \doteq \frac{\bar{\eta}_q}{\bar{m}_0}\Delta S_q \cdot \Delta S_h,$$

where $\Delta \bar{q}$ is as indicated in Figure 7.8(b), $\bar{\eta}_q$ is the exogenous income elasticity of consumption demand, and $\Delta S_q =$ area $v+x+y+z$ is the consumer surplus change along the second segment of the wage–price adjustment path. Thus, approximating area $v+x$ by subtracting the approximated areas y and z from the surplus change (area $v+x+y+z$) yields

$$\hat{C}_2 = \Delta S_q - \frac{\bar{\eta}_q}{2\bar{m}_0}(\Delta S_q)^2 - \frac{\bar{\eta}_q}{\bar{m}_0}\Delta S_q \cdot \Delta S_h.$$

Adding $\hat{C}_1$ and $\hat{C}_2$ then yields an estimate of the overall compensating variation,

$$\hat{C} = \hat{C}_1 + \hat{C}_2 = \Delta S_h + \Delta S_q + \frac{\bar{\eta}_h}{2\bar{m}_0}(\Delta S_h)^2 - \frac{\bar{\eta}_q}{\bar{m}_0}\Delta S_q \cdot \Delta S_h - \frac{\bar{\eta}_q}{2\bar{m}_0}(\Delta S_q)^2.$$

Hence, if the elasticities are additive inverses of one another ($\bar{\eta}_q = -\bar{\eta}_h = \bar{\eta}^*$) or are estimated by $\hat{\eta}_h = -\bar{\eta}^*$, $\hat{\eta}_q = \bar{\eta}^*$, $\bar{\eta}^* = (\bar{\eta}_q - \bar{\eta}_h)/2$, the overall compensating variation is estimated by

$$\hat{C} = \sum_{i=h,q} \Delta S_i - \hat{\varepsilon}\left|\sum_{i=h,q} \Delta S_i\right|$$

following the same derivation as in equation (6.14), where

$$\hat{\varepsilon} = \frac{\bar{\eta}^*|\bar{s}|}{2},\ \bar{s} = \sum_{i=h,q} \frac{\Delta S_i}{\bar{m}_0}.$$

Or, perhaps, more usefully, if one defines

$$\bar{\eta}_1 = \min(-\bar{\eta}_h, \bar{\eta}_q)$$

and

$$\bar{\eta}_2 = \max(-\bar{\eta}_h, \bar{\eta}_q)$$

where the minimization and maximization are over the arbitrary price path used in calculating s, as well as over commodities, then approximate bounds on compensating variation are given by

$$\bar{C}_1 = \sum_{i=h,q} \Delta S_i - \varepsilon_1 \left| \sum_{i=h,q} \Delta S_i \right|$$

and

$$\bar{C}_2 = \sum_{i=h,q} \Delta S_i - \varepsilon_2 \left| \sum_{i=h,q} \Delta S_i \right|,$$

where

$$\varepsilon_i = \frac{\bar{\eta}_i |\bar{s}|}{2}, \; i = 1, 2.$$

Thus, the ε_i ($\times$ 100) reflect approximate percentage bounds on the error of the surplus change ($\Sigma_i \Delta S_i$) as a measure of compensating variation. The maximum exogenous income elasticity (over the course of a particular price change) times the magnitude of surplus change relative to initial exogenous income ($\times$ 100) is about twice the maximum percentage error (in absolute terms) that can possibly be incurred.

As shown in Appendix Section 7.F, the foregoing results generalize to include the case of many consumer goods and many factors.[5] Also, similar results hold in the case of equivalent variation. To summarize the results, suppose that the consumer faces prices p_1^0, …, p_n^0 for consumer goods q_1, …, q_n and factor prices w_1^0, …, w_k^0 for factors x_1, …, x_k. Suppose that prices change to p_1^1, …, p_n^1 and w_1^1, …, w_k^1, respectively, and that the surplus change is determined by calculating first the change ΔS_1 associated with q_1 holding other prices at p_2^0, …, p_n^0, w_1^0, …, w_k^0; then calculating ΔS_2 holding other prices at p_1^1, p_3^0, …, p_n^0, w_1^0, …, w_k^0; …; then calculating ΔS_n holding other prices at p_1^1, …, p_{n-1}^1, w_1^0, …, w_k^0, then calculating ΔS_{n+1} holding other prices at p_1^1, …, p_n^1, w_2^0, …, w_k^0, …; and finally calculating ΔS_{n+k} holding other prices at p_1^1, …, p_n^1, w_1^1, …, w_{k-1}^1. Suppose that ρ^i is the exogenous income elasticity of demand for q_i and v^i is the exogenous income elasticity of the supply of x_i. Then approximate bounds on the compensating variation are given by

$$\bar{C}_1 = \sum_{i=1}^{n+k} \Delta S_i - \varepsilon_1 \left| \sum_{i=1}^{n+k} \Delta S_i \right| \tag{7.7}$$

and

$$\bar{C}_2 = \sum_{i=1}^{n+k} \Delta S_i - \varepsilon_2 \left| \sum_{i=1}^{n+k} \Delta S_i \right|, \tag{7.8}$$

5. Note, however, that in Appendix Section 7.F sales of factors are represented by negative quantities so that negative signs are not attached to the exogenous income elasticities of factor sales as they are here.

where

$$\varepsilon_i = \frac{\bar{\eta}_i|\bar{s}|}{2}, \; i=1, 2; \; \bar{s} = \sum_{i=1}^{n+k} \frac{\Delta S_i}{\bar{m}_0}$$

$$\bar{\eta}_i = \min\,(\rho^1,\ldots,\rho^n,-\nu^1,\ldots,-\nu^k)$$

and

$$\bar{\eta}_2 = \max\,(\rho^1,\ldots,\rho^n,-\nu^1,\ldots,-\nu^k).$$

Approximate bounds on the equivalent variation are given by

$$\bar{E}_1 = \sum_{i=1}^{n+k} \Delta S_i + \varepsilon_2 \left| \sum_{i=1}^{n+k} \Delta S_i \right| \tag{7.9}$$

and

$$\bar{E}_2 = \sum_{i=1}^{n+k} \Delta S_i + \varepsilon_1 \left| \sum_{i=1}^{n+k} \Delta S_i \right|. \tag{7.10}$$

Thus, the maximum error in either case of using the simple surplus change, $\Sigma_{i=1}^{n+k} \Delta S_i$, as a measure of WTP is no more than about 5 percent as long as $|\bar{\eta}_i \bar{s}/2| < 0.05, i=1, 2$. Recalling the discussion of Section 7.5, which examined the implications of using exogenous rather than total income elasticities, these conditions are just as likely fulfilled when only consumer prices change as in the pure consumer case of Chapter 6. Turning to the factor side, this condition also seems reasonable except where large changes in the wage rate, or possibly the interest rate, are involved. That is, most factor supplies such as for land rental would seem to have very small (short-run) exogenous income elasticities because the amount offered for rental is largely, if not totally, determined by ownership in the short run. With labor or savings, the response to changes in exogenous income would probably be more dramatic, but again it seems that elasticities would probably be less than 1 in absolute terms. Thus, if the change in surplus is less than 10 percent of initial exogenous income, then no more than about 5 percent error is incurred when using the surplus change as a measure of WTP. Thus, while this condition may be unlikely in some cases, there are a large number of applied economic welfare problems that fall within its bounds.

If the conditions above are not met, or more accurate estimates are desired, the bounds in equations (7.7) through (7.10) can be used to create more accurate estimates,

$$\hat{C} = \frac{(\bar{C}_1 + \bar{C}_2)}{2}$$

and

$$\hat{E} = \frac{(\bar{E}_1 + \bar{E}_2)}{2}$$

of the compensating and equivalent variations, respectively. According to the results discussed in Appendix Section 7.F, these estimates will be in error by no more than about 2 percent if $|\hat{\eta}\bar{s}/2| < 0.08$ and $\bar{\eta}_1$ and $\bar{\eta}_2$ differ by no more than 50 percent, where $\hat{\eta} = (\bar{\eta}_1 + \bar{\eta}_2)/2$. While Willig has developed an algorithm that can be adapted to find even tighter bounds and better estimates of C and E than these for the factor owner case, the exact approaches of Section 7.11 and Appendix Section 7.H are preferred when these bounds or conditions are not acceptable.

7.7 MULTIPLE PRICE CHANGES WITH CHANGES IN EXOGENOUS INCOME

Thus far in this chapter, exogenous income has been considered truly fixed. Nevertheless, because exogenous income includes such factors as profits or dividends, which may change even in the short run, an extension of the results follows immediately in a fashion analogous to that described in Section 6.7. If both prices and exogenous income change, the compensating variation can be measured by following the methods of the preceding section holding exogenous income at the initial level, and then adding the change in exogenous income to the resulting compensating variation of the price change. If the change in exogenous income is considered first, the compensating variation of the price change must be determined holding utility at the level prior to the income change. Thus, further modifications of the approach in the preceding section would be required. Similarly, the equivalent variation of a multiple price–income change can be measured by considering the change in income first and then following the methods of the preceding section to determine the additional equivalent variation associated with price movements, holding income at its terminal level. Thus, both the price and income changes can be associated with the terminal level of utility.

7.8 AN EXAMPLE

An example can serve to demonstrate the methodology of Sections 7.6 and 7.7. Consider a consumer with demand for manufactured goods represented by[6]

$$q = 11 - 5p + 2w + \frac{3}{50}\bar{m} \tag{7.11}$$

and supply of labor,

$$h = -20 + 5w + 3p - \frac{2}{50}\bar{m}, \tag{7.12}$$

where

q = quantity of manufactured goods purchased
p = price of manufactured goods
h = quantity of labor supplied
w = wage rate
$\bar{m}$ = exogenous income.

6. The possibility of estimating relationships of the type in equations (7.11) and (7.12) from observed behavior will be discussed in Section 8.8. For a discussion of several empirical studies that estimate relationships of this type, see Addison and Siebert (1979).

Suppose that the consumer initially faces prices and wages $p_0=3$ and $w_0=5$ with exogenous income $\bar{m}_0=100$. Now suppose the government establishes tight controls on production (safety and pollution standards), which cause the industry to contract and, as a result, lower wages to $w_1=4$. Also, because of reduced wages, the demand for manufactured goods falls, lowering price to $p_1=2$. In addition, suppose that the consumer's exogenous income falls to $\bar{m}_1=97$ because of reduced dividends on stockholdings in the manufactured goods industry.

In the context of Section 7.6, consider first the wage change, then the price change and, finally, the income change. At initial price and income, the consumer's labor supply curve is

$$h=-15+5w.$$

Thus, the surplus change associated with the wage reduction from $w_0=5$ to $w_1=4$ shown in Figure 7.9(a) generates a surplus loss, $\Delta S_h=-15/2$. Also, for purposes of applying the Willig results, note that the exogenous income elasticity of labor supply is

$$\eta_h=\frac{\Delta h}{\Delta \bar{m}}\frac{\bar{m}}{h}=-\frac{2}{50}\frac{100}{h}=-\frac{4}{h},$$

where $\Delta h/\Delta \bar{m}=-2/50$ is the slope or change in labor associated with a small unit change in exogenous income. Thus, the smallest exogenous income elasticity associated with the wage change is $\nu_1^h=-4/10=-0.4$ and the largest is $\nu_2^h=-4/5=-0.8$.

Next, consider the price change holding the wage rate at its new level, $w_1=4$, and exogenous income at its initial level, $\bar{m}_0=100$. Thus, the demand curve is

$$q=25-5p,$$

and the associated surplus indicated geometrically in Figure 7.9(b) is $\Delta S_q=25/2$. Again, for purposes of applying the Willig results, the exogenous income elasticity of demand is

$$\eta_q=\frac{\Delta q}{\Delta \bar{m}}\frac{\bar{m}}{q}=\frac{3}{50}\frac{100}{q}=\frac{6}{q},$$

where $\Delta q/\Delta \bar{m}$ is the change in q induced by a 1-unit change in exogenous income. The elasticity bounds associated with the price change are $\rho_1^q=6/15=0.4$ and $\rho_2^q=6/10=0.6$.

Using the simple surplus approach gives a welfare change of $\Delta S_h+\Delta S_q=-15/2+25/2=5$, to which must be added (subsequently) the change in income, $\bar{m}_1-\bar{m}_0=97-100=-3$, for a net welfare change of $\Delta S_h+\Delta S_q+\bar{m}_1-\bar{m}_0=2$. Suppose, however, that the compensating variation is of interest to a policy-maker who plans to pay compensation only if the policy is adopted. Then equations (7.7) and (7.8) can be used to develop a more precise estimate based on the estimated surplus change. The Willig approach of equations (7.7) and (7.8) would be applied only in improving the estimates $\Delta S_h+\Delta S_q$ associated with the wage–price change because the income change is an accurate measure of its money impact on WTP. One finds that

$$\bar{\eta}_1=\min(\rho^q,-\nu^h)=0.4$$
$$\bar{\eta}_2=\max(\rho^q,-\nu^h)=0.8$$

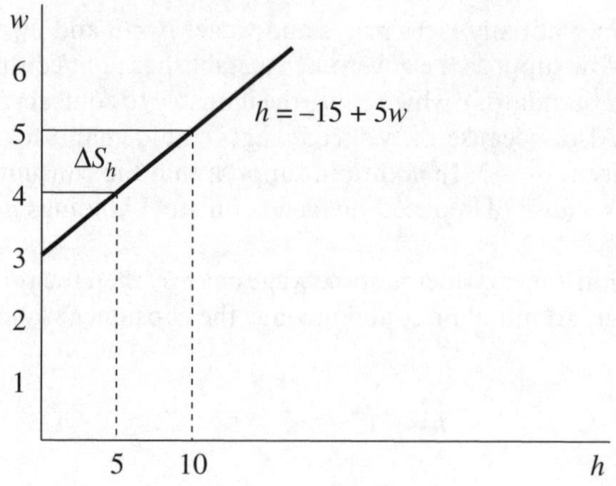

(a)

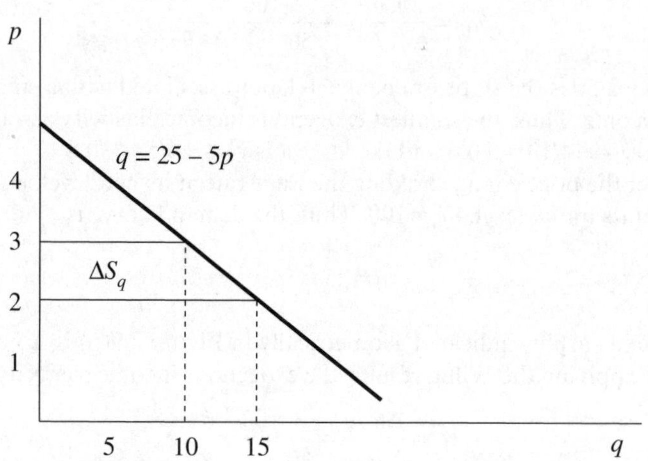

(b)

Figure 7.9

$$\bar{s} = \frac{\Delta S_q + \Delta S_h}{\bar{m}_0} = \frac{5}{100} = 0.05$$

$$\varepsilon_1 = \frac{\bar{\eta}_1 |\bar{s}|}{2} = \frac{0.4 \cdot 0.05}{2} = 0.01$$

$$\varepsilon_2 = \frac{\bar{\eta}_2 |\bar{s}|}{2} = \frac{0.8 \cdot 0.05}{2} = 0.02$$

$$\bar{C}_1 = 5 - 0.01\ |5| = 4.95$$
$$\bar{C}_2 = 5 - 0.02\ |5| = 4.90.$$

Thus, adding the change in income ($\bar{m}_1 - \bar{m}_0 = -3$) obtains bounds on the overall compensating variation of the wage–price–income change of 1.95 and 1.90. And whereas the surplus change is possibly in error by 0.1, the estimate obtained by using the average of the latter bounds (1.925) is in error by no more than 0.025. Thus, the possible percentage error is reduced from 5 percent to 1.25 percent. It may also be noted that these percentage errors of the combined wage–price–income change are greater than for the associated wage–price change because the income change is in an opposite direction and leads to comparison of the same absolute errors with a smaller surplus change.

7.9 IMPOSED QUANTITY CHANGES

Thus far this chapter has focused on evaluating welfare impacts of price changes. Proposed policies, however, often constrain amounts of production or consumption. For example, if the US Food and Drug Administration decides that some substance under its control is harmful, it may ban the substance. Hence, consumption of zero quantity is imposed. In the producer case, evaluation of such constraints poses no special problem because, in effect, compensated and ordinary supply and demand curves coincide. In the factor owner case, however, imposing quantity changes requires special consideration because the error in consumer or producer surplus as a measure of WTP may be much different.

For example, consider Figure 7.10 where the price is initially p_0 and the free-market quantity is q_0. Now suppose that a smaller quantity q_1 is imposed. From the standpoint of actual consumption, this would be equivalent to raising the price to p_1, so consumption would fall to q_1 along the ordinary demand curve D. Suppose that this price rise, in fact, accompanies the reduced quantity restriction. The compensated demand curves associated with the final and initial states are H_1 and H_0, respectively. The change in consumer surplus is a reduction of area $b+c+d$. The equivalent variation is –area $b+c$, so the associated error

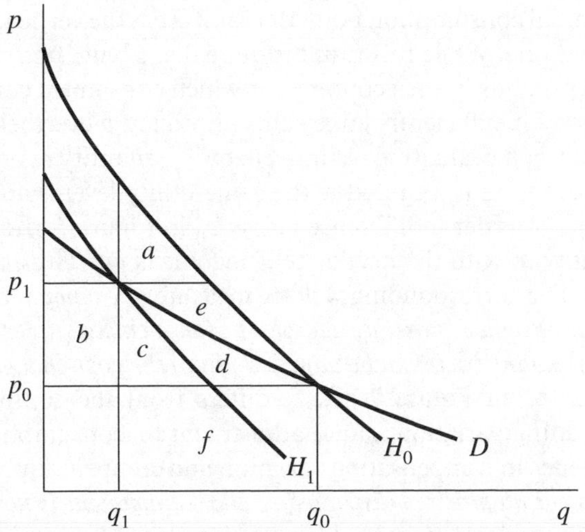

Figure 7.10

in consumer surplus change is –area d. Assuming that the price, p_1, where D crosses q_1 can be determined, the approximation of this error can follow the earlier Willig calculations. On the other hand, the compensating variation of changing price from p_0 to p_1, −area $b+c+d+e$, does not measure the WTP for the quantity restriction in the event of change. The consumer is not free to adjust q following the price change and so is worse off than otherwise. *The necessary compensation for an imposed quantity change is given by the change in area under the compensated demand curve less the change in what is actually paid* (that is, −area $a+b+c+d+e$ in this case). The consumer loses gross benefits of area $a+c+d+e+f$ but reduces expenditure by area $f-b$ for a net loss of area $a+b+c+d+e$. Thus, the error in consumer surplus change as a measure of compensating variation is not simply area e, as in the price change case, but area $a+e$. This implies that special considerations are required for measuring compensating variation when a quantity is imposed. A similar result holds for factor supply as well as for consumption demand. Similarly, special considerations are required in both factor supply and consumption demand for the equivalent welfare measure when a quantity imposition is removed. If both initial and terminal quantities are determined by binding restrictions, then Hicksian demands must be found corresponding to both consumption levels, and both variations must be determined accordingly. See Appendix Section 7.J for further details.

These considerations may be particularly bothersome because, in some cases, the area a in Figure 7.10 can be infinite. For example, some environmental amenities such as clean air or water or health services may be essential for life. This case is presented in Figure 7.11, where the price of q is initially p_0 with exogenous income $\bar{m}_0$. The ordinary demand for q induced by a utility function with indifference curves U_0 and U_1 is D. Now, imposition of quantity q_1 leads to the same actual consumption of q as raising the price from p_0 to p_1. The compensated demand curve associated with the subsequent situation is H_1 and the equivalent variation is given by −area $b+c$. What compensation is required to keep the consumer at the initial utility level U_0 if quantity q_1 is imposed? If the indifference curve U_0 does not cross a vertical line at q_1 in Figure 7.11(a), no amount of compensation can retain the initial utility level. This implies that the compensated demand curve, H_0, associated with the initial consumption point does not cross the vertical line at q_1 in Figure 7.11(b), so area a is infinite. While this result is quite disturbing, one may also argue that there are relatively few goods in the economy for which consumers could not be induced to reduce consumption for sufficiently large sums of money. Nevertheless, this possibility must be kept in mind when evaluating welfare effects of quantity restrictions.

To see what compensation is required if the same utility level is attainable at the new restricted quantity, q_1, consider indifference curve U_0' in Figure 7.11(a). This utility level is attainable at quantity q_1 with the new price if income is $\bar{m}_1$. Thus, the necessary compensation is $\bar{m}_1 - \bar{m}_0$. The corresponding welfare measure, *the amount of income that must be taken away from a consumer (possibly negative) after a change to restore his or her original welfare level where quantity cannot be adjusted (from the post-change case) is called the compensating surplus* (C_s in Figure 7.11). It differs from the compensating variation because the compensating variation allows adjustment of consumption following compensation. The difference in compensating variation and compensating surplus is given by area a. *If the subsequent quantity is restricted so that adjustment is not possible following compensation, compensating surplus should be used in place of compensating variation for welfare analysis.*

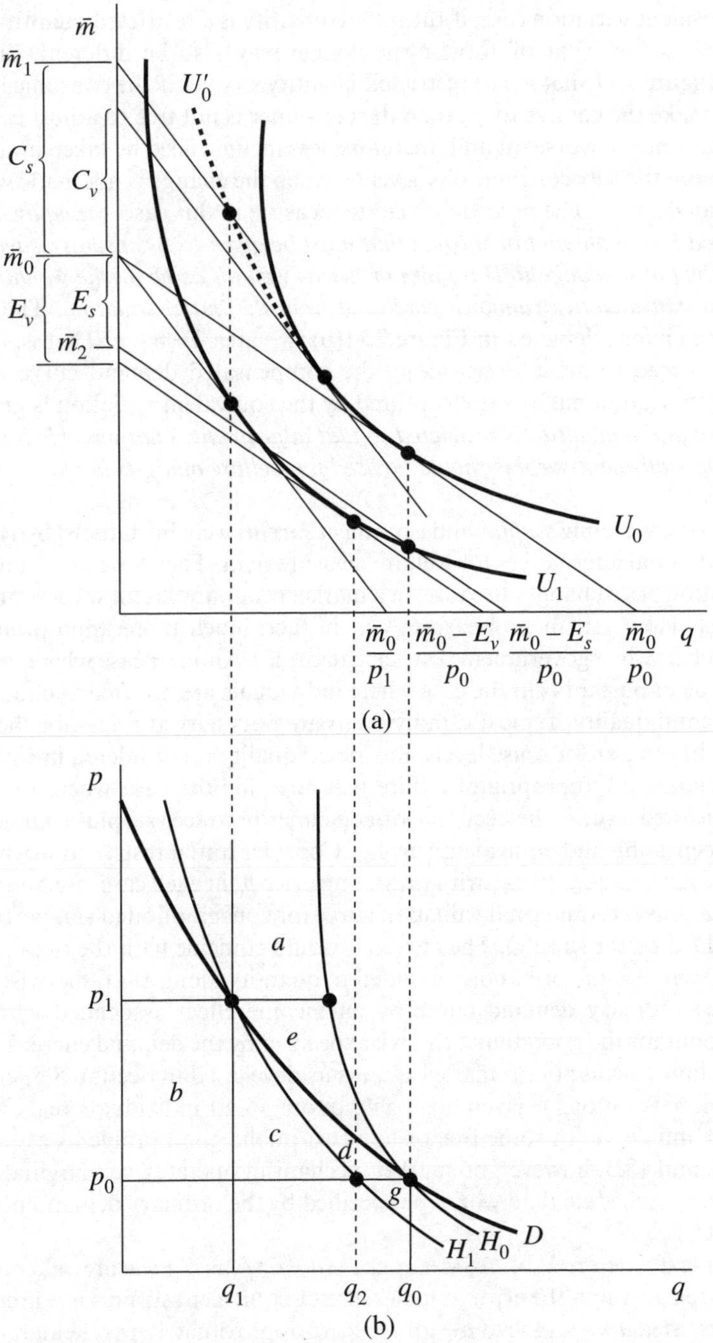

$\bar{m}$
$\bar{m}_1$
U'_0
C_s
C_v
$\bar{m}_0$
E_s
E_v
$\bar{m}_2$
U_0
U_1
$\frac{\bar{m}_0}{p_1}$
$\frac{\bar{m}_0 - E_v}{p_0}$
$\frac{\bar{m}_0 - E_s}{p_0}$
$\frac{\bar{m}_0}{p_0}$
q
(a)
p
a
p_1
e
b
c
d
p_0
g
H_1
H_0
D
q_1
q_2
q_0
q
(b)

Figure 7.11

In the equivalent variation case, if the initial quantity is a restricted quantity, necessary compensation in the event of forgoing a change may also be different. Suppose, for example, in Figure 7.11 that q_0 is a restricted quantity so that, if the consumer is compensated not to make the change to q_1, then the consumer is not free to adjust consumption to q_2. The consumer is worse off and, therefore, less income need be taken away. The consumer can attain the subsequent utility level U_1 when the change is not made with income $\bar{m}_2$ rather than $\bar{m}_0 - E_v$. The necessary welfare measure in this case, *the equivalent surplus* (E_s) *is defined by the amount of income that must be given to a consumer (again possibly negative) in lieu of a change to leave him or her as well off as he or she would be with the change, given that quantity cannot be adjusted from the initial situation.* The equivalent surplus of the change depicted in Figure 7.11(b) is $-$area $b+c-g$. That is, because the consumer is forced to move down along the compensated demand curve H_1 but still pay price p_0, the additional loss not captured by the equivalent variation is given by area g. Thus, *if the initial quantity is restricted so that adjustment is not possible in the event of compensation, equivalent surplus should be used for welfare analysis in place of equivalent variation.*

The terms *compensating surplus* and *equivalent surplus* were introduced by Hicks (1943) as simply additional alternatives for welfare measurement. They have not found common use in evaluating price changes because, in a market economy, factor owners are generally free to adjust. However, these measures are, in fact, much more appropriate in a few instances, such as when government restricts quantities. Another case where these considerations can be important is in the case where individuals are not free to choose the level of environmental quality. Typically, individuals are not charged prices for the quality of air or water they use or for noise levels. Restricted quality is considered in Chapter 11.

Having determined appropriate welfare measures for the case where quantities are restricted, a related issue is the accuracy of consumer/producer surplus changes as measures of compensating and equivalent surplus. Consider initial restricted quantity q_0 and subsequent restricted quantity q_1 with prevailing price p_0 in each case, as shown in Figure 7.12. Let D^* represent a marginal valuation curve for consumption (a similar concept can be developed for factor supply). The curve D^* would coincide with the free-market ordinary demand curve if the price corresponded to quantity along D^*. Otherwise, D^* differs from the true ordinary demand curve by an income effect associated with paying a different amount for the good than otherwise specified by the demand curve. This distinction is important because (with market quotas as developed in Section 8.5) competition among individuals rations a given aggregate quota so all individuals react along their ordinary demand curve. In some free or low-cost public good problems as presented in Sections 13.2 and 13.3, however, no market mechanism operates, so marginal valuations follow a different schedule than would be specified by the ordinary demand pertaining to a free market.

In this context, the error of $\Delta S = -$area $c+d+f+g$ as a measure of compensating surplus is $-$area $a+e$ and the error as a measure of equivalent surplus is $-$area $d+g$. For small changes, area $d+e$ and area $a+d+e+g$ are approximately parallelograms, so area $a+e \doteq$ area $d+g$. In fact, as drawn in Figure 7.12,

$$\text{area } a+e = \text{area } d+g = \frac{1}{2}\Delta\tilde{\psi}|\Delta\tilde{q}|, \qquad (7.13)$$

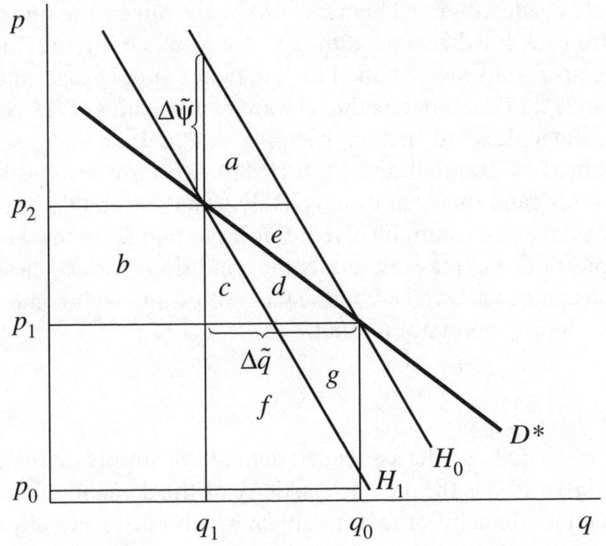

Figure 7.12

where $\Delta\tilde{q}=q_1-q_0$. To approximate this area, define price flexibility of income $\bar{\varphi}$ as

$$\bar{\varphi}=\frac{\Delta\tilde{\psi}}{\Delta\bar{m}}\frac{\bar{m}}{\tilde{\psi}}, \tag{7.14}$$

where $\tilde{\psi}$ is the vertical distance between the marginal valuation at a given utility and price p_0, and $\Delta\tilde{\psi}$ is the change in the distance associated with a change in exogenous income that causes movement from the initial welfare level to the terminal level. Solving equation (7.14) for $\Delta\tilde{\psi}$, substituting equation (7.2) – which is again applicable in the same sense as earlier where $\Delta S=-$area $c+d+f+g$ – and using equation (7.13) yields

$$\text{area } a+e=\text{area } d+g \doteq \frac{1}{2}\bar{\varphi}\cdot\tilde{\psi}\cdot\Delta S\cdot\frac{|\Delta\tilde{q}|}{\bar{m}}. \tag{7.15}$$

Next, note that $\tilde{\psi}\cdot|\Delta\tilde{q}|\doteq\Delta S$, where $\Delta S=-$area $c+d+f+g$. Hence, (7.15) becomes

$$\text{area } a+e=\text{area } d+g \doteq \bar{\varepsilon}|\Delta S|,$$

where $\bar{\varepsilon}=\bar{\varphi}|\bar{s}|/2$, $\bar{s}=\Delta S/\bar{m}$. Or, finally,

$$C_s=\Delta S-\text{area } a+e \doteq \Delta S-\bar{\varepsilon}|\Delta S| \tag{7.16}$$

and

$$E_s=\Delta S+\text{area } d+g \doteq \Delta S+\bar{\varepsilon}|\Delta S|. \tag{7.17}$$

In other words, $\bar{\varepsilon}\times 100$ approximates the percentage error of consumer surplus change as a measure of compensating and equivalent surplus.

The approximate results obtained here are also borne out by the rigorous development in Appendix Section 7.J. Furthermore, although the results in Figure 7.12 pertain to consumption, analogous results are obtained for the factor supply case, and the formulas in equations (7.16) and (7.17) summarize the relevant results. Thus, if $|\bar{\varphi}\bar{s}/2| \leq 0.05$, the errors in either the consumer demand or factor supply case will be no greater than about 5 percent. As explained by Randall and Stoll (1980), who are responsible for extending Willig's results to this case, this condition is likely to be reasonable when small quantity changes or small budget items are involved, but large budget items with strong income effects (for example, housing) may not satisfy the condition. Nevertheless, applicability of the approximation can be investigated on the basis of estimated income and price elasticities of demand or supply upon noting that

$$\bar{\varphi} = \xi \cdot \bar{\eta},$$

where ξ is the price elasticity of the associated demand or supply (defined in simple terms as $\xi = (\Delta q/\Delta p) \cdot (p/q)$) and $\bar{\eta}$ is the income elasticity of the demand or supply. Hence, estimates of any consumer demand or factor supply, which must generally include the price elasticity and income elasticity at least implicitly, provide sufficient information to determine the accuracy of consumer/producer surplus as a measure of WTP when quantities are constrained. Furthermore, if the approximation is not sufficiently accurate, equations (7.16) and (7.17) can be used to develop more accurate specific estimates of the compensating and equivalent surpluses.[7]

7.10 AREAS BETWEEN SUPPLY (OR DEMAND) CURVES AS WELFARE MEASURES FOR MULTIPLE CHANGES

Sections 7.6 through 7.8 present the sequential approach to calculating consumer welfare effects of multiple price and/or income changes. As will be discussed in Section 8.9, this approach is desirable when enough information is available to determine how all consumer demand and factor supply curves shift as multiple price changes are imposed sequentially. Often, however, computational infeasability or lack of observability of some data prevents the explicit consideration of supply and demand shifts in more than one or a few markets in any given economic welfare study. If this is true, even though prices change in many markets, the measurement of welfare effects of other price changes in the market(s) of focus is desirable and necessary. Additionally, many welfare problems require considering the effect of nonmarket variables such as environmental quality or weather on consumer demand or factor supply.

The purpose of this section is to investigate the possibility for welfare measurement of the effect of such variables through the resultant shifts in the demands and supplies of observable market goods. Two approaches are possible. First, the concept of an essential

7. Again, these results are developed in rigorous detail in Appendix Section 7.J, and results show that the same order of approximation is attained as in the case where quantities are not restricted. Also, Table 6.1 can again be used to determine accurate error bounds and, hence, to examine error bounds on the modified estimates in equations (7.16) and (7.17).

input or output from the production problem of Section 4.4 can be developed for the consumer case although its practicality is limited. Second, for the case of nonessential goods, the concept of weak complementarity can be exploited to identify a good or group of goods that eliminate the nonmarket good from the utility function when their consumption is zero.

Welfare Analysis with Essential Goods: Evaluating Multiple Price Changes in a Single Market

For the essential good case recall, as shown in Section 4.4, that the welfare effects of a multiple price change on a producer can be calculated by observing the change in a single producer surplus triangle in an output market, or the change in a single consumer surplus triangle in an input market (assuming essentiality of the respective output or input). This simplification is also possible for factor owners in some cases, at least as an approximation.

To see this, the producer's short-run problem can be stated generally as

$$\text{maximize } \pi = \sum_{i=1}^{m} p_i q_i - \sum_{j=1}^{n} w_j x_j$$

subject to

$$f(q_1,\ldots,q_m,x_1,\ldots,x_n) = 0,$$

where π is quasirent, p_i is the price of output i, q_i is the quantity produced of output i, w_j is the price of variable input j, x_j is the quantity of variable input j purchased and f represents the implicit production function.[8] One form of the factor owner's problem, on the other hand, can be written as

$$\text{minimize } \bar{m} = \sum_{j=1}^{n} w_j x_j - \sum_{i=1}^{m} p_i q_i$$

subject to

$$U(q_1,\ldots,q_m,x_1,\ldots,x_n) = U_0.$$

That is, the factor owner's problem is to minimize the exogenous income required to meet a given utility level U_0, where $\bar{m}$ is exogenous income, w_j is the price of consumer good j, x_j is the quantity consumed of good j, p_i is the price of factor i, q_i is the quantity of factor i supplied by the consumer and U represents the consumer's utility function. Upon defining

$$f(q_1,\ldots,q_m,x_1,\ldots,x_n) = U(q_1,\ldots,q_m,x_1,\ldots,x_n) - U_0$$

8. For the reader unfamiliar with implicit production functions, an ordinary single output production function that gives $q=f^*(x_1,\ldots,x_n)$ can be converted to implicit form by simply writing $f(q,x_1,\ldots,x_n) \equiv f^*(x_1,\ldots,x_n) - q = 0$.

for the factor owner, these producer and factor owner problems are mathematically equivalent.[9] Hence, any mathematical result pertaining to one problem also pertains to the other.

Mathematical equivalence of these two problems implies that areas behind firm supply and demand curves are related to the firm's quasirent exactly as areas behind a consumer's compensated supply and demand curves are related to (the negative of) expenditures necessary to attain a given utility level. That is, because the utility level is held constant in the factor owner problem, the solution of the problem gives quantities supplied or demanded at a given utility level (that is, compensated supplies and demands). Thus, the change in area behind the compensated supply or demand of any essential commodity reflects the change in welfare associated with any other price change.

While the existence of an essential good for the factor owner may seem unlikely, a common practice is to aggregate commodities into groups for analysis and to treat the individual as making a two-stage budgeting decision. The first stage is to allocate income/expenditure among the groups and then to allocate income/expenditure within the groups. For some groups such as food, the assumption of essentiality appears reasonable even though any individual food within the group may not be essential. But another important result is that the problems of choice within groups can be studied independently when the groups are weakly separable.[10] In this case, the concept of essentiality can be applied within any weakly separable group. Essentiality such as in this first-stage choice example is the subject of this subsection. Possibilities under weak separability, which might apply within separable groups, are the subject of the following subsection.

To see how this concept of essentiality allows measurement of the effects of multiple price changes in a single market in the factor owner case, consider Figure 7.13 where initial labor supply and food consumption demand for a particular consumer are S_0 and D_0, respectively. As a result of price changes from w_0 to w_1 and p_0 to p_1, the supply and demand shift to S_1 and D_1, respectively. The issue is whether areas d and x are of significance when measuring changes in economic welfare. For example, if, say, wages fall from w_0 to w_1 while food price remains at p_0, does area x reflect the welfare effect (that is, does area x = area a)? The foregoing results answer this question in the affirmative if the demand curves in Figure 7.13(b) are compensated curves associated with the same utility level and if good q is essential in the sense that it will always be consumed as long as other goods are consumed or factors (including labor) are sold. Similarly, area d is an exact measure of the welfare effect of a price change from p_0 to p_1 with wages fixed at w_1 if S_0 and S_1 are compensated supplies associated with the same utility level, and labor is essential for the con

9. Actually, one must also consider assumptions regarding slopes (monotonicity), curvature (concavity), and smoothness of f in each case, but the standard neoclassical assumptions are also the same and imply that f is strictly increasing (in the relevant range), concave and (in most studies), and twice differentiable in $(-q_1,\ldots,-q_m,x_1,\ldots,x_n)$.
10. A utility function that can be written in the form

$$U(q_1,\ldots,q_{n_1},q_{n_1+1},\ldots,q_n) = U(f_1(q_1,\ldots,q_{n_1}), f_2(q_{n_1+1},\ldots,q_n))$$

is weakly separable in the two groups determined by the functions f_1 and f_2. In this case, the marginal rates of substitution between any two goods in one group is independent of the amount of consumption of any good in the other group. For further discussion, see Deaton and Muellbauer (1980, ch. 5).

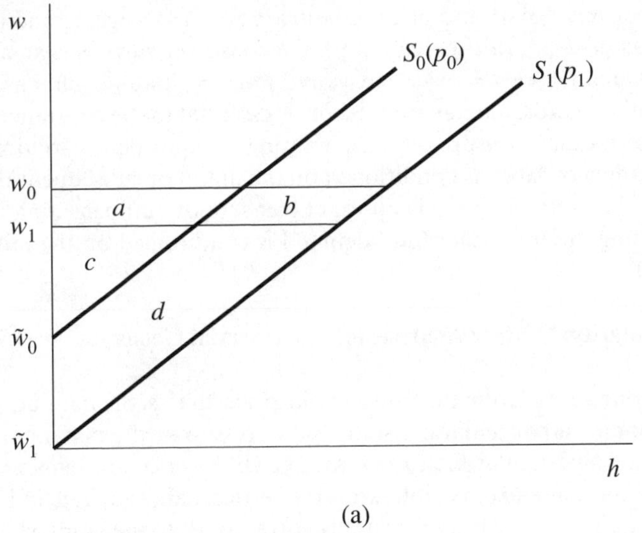

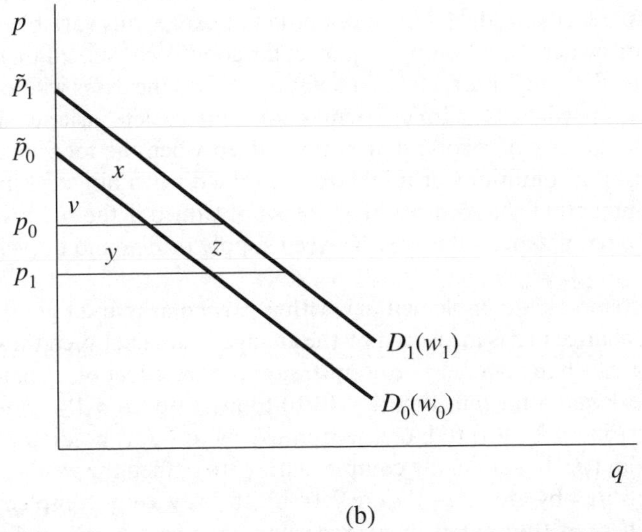

Figure 7.13

sumption process. Area d is the compensating (equivalent) variation if supplies are based on initial (final) utility.[11]

Under these essentiality assumptions, the overall welfare effect of changing both wages and prices can be measured in a single (essential) market. In Figure 7.13(a), the producer

11. Of course, labor is not essential to consumption if exogenous income is sufficiently high or economic assistance for the poor is available to a sufficient degree. Nevertheless, if the range of considerations for all other prices and exogenous incomes are such that quantities in the market of interest are never zero, the commodities are sufficiently essential so the results of this section may hold approximately.

surplus is area $a+c$ at wage w_0 and price p_0, and area $c+d$ at wage w_1 and price p_1, for a net change of area of $d-a$. In Figure 7.13(b), the consumer surplus is area v at wage w_0 and price p_0, and area $v+x+y+z$ at wage w_1 and price p_1, for a net change of area $x+y+z$. If labor (in other words, income from labor) is essential to the consumer's well-being, then area $d-a$ is an exact measure of compensating or equivalent variation, depending on whether the supply of labor is conditioned on the initial or subsequent utility level. If food is essential, then area $x+y+z$ is an exact measure of compensating or equivalent variation, depending upon whether food demand is conditioned on the initial or subsequent utility level.

Weak Complementarity: Welfare Analysis for Nonessential Goods

When a good is nonessential, one can find a choke price, that is, the minimum price under which consumption of a particular consumer good is zero or the maximum price under which the supply of a particular factor is zero. The choke price for demand corresponds to the point where the demand curve intersects the vertical axis, that is, $\tilde{p}_0$ in Figure 7.13(b) when the wage is w_0. The choke price for supply corresponds to the point where the supply curve intersects the vertical axis, for example, $\tilde{w}_0$ in Figure 7.13(a) when the price is p_0. Welfare analysis in this case can be based on use of the concept of weak complementarity. Weak complementarity holds if some nonmarket or exogenous variable, z, affects the utility of the factor owner if and only if a particular good is consumed or factor is supplied (see Appendix Section 7.I for a formal definition). Specific cases where these results are likely applicable are where (1) a luxury item is not valued when basic subsistence needs are not met, (2) the quality of a food item is not valued when the food item is not consumed, (3) the working conditions of a job are not valued when not working at that job and (4) the environmental enhancement of a site is not valued if the site is never visited. In these practical circumstances, the area between supply or demand curves has welfare significance.

If the variable z is weakly complementary with a particular market good, q_i, then the welfare effect of a change in z is measured by the change in area between the demands for q_i before and after the change in z. For example, suppose the effect of a change in z from z_0 to z_1 causes the demand for q in Figure 7.14(b) to increase from $D_0(z_0)$ to $D_1(z_1)$ and the supply of x in Figure 7.14(a) to increase from $S_0(z_0)$ to $S_1(z_1)$ holding prices at their initial levels of w_0 and p_0. If z is weakly complementary to q, then the welfare effect of the change in z is measured by area d in Figure 7.14(b). If z is weakly complementary to x, then the welfare effect of the change in z is measured by area b in Figure 7.14(a). These changes are approximate with ordinary demand and supply but are exact for compensated demand and supply.

But what if z is weakly complementary to the pair of goods, q and x, as a group? In many practical cases, the utility effects of a nonmarket variable may be eliminated only under zero consumption or production of several goods. For example, improvements in air quality in a city may increase both the supply of labor in the city (x) and the demand for recreation (q). If air quality (z) is weakly complementary with the pair of goods as a group, then z affects the utility of individuals only when the supply labor or consume recreation in the city (or both). In this case, Bockstael and Kling (1988) have shown that the calculations must be made sequentially. That is, to the area between demands for q in

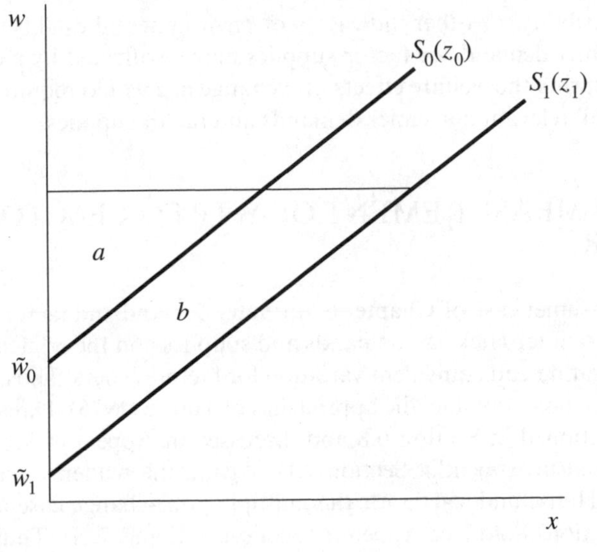

(a)

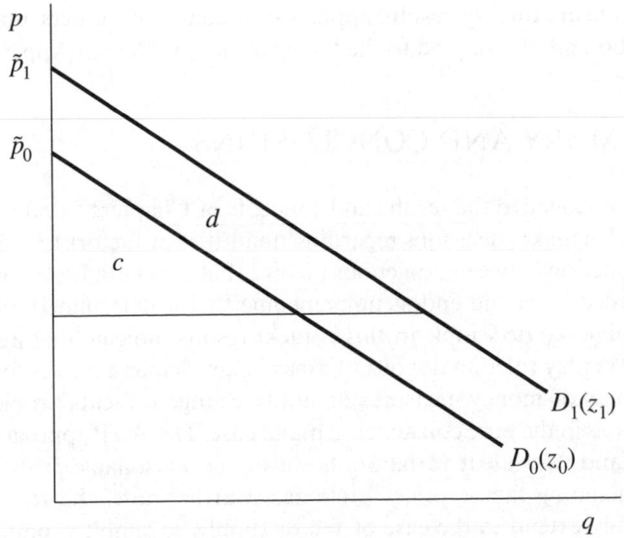

(b)

Figure 7.14

Figure 7.14, one must add the change in area between supplies of x, where the supplies of x are conditioned on $q=0$ associated with respective prices $\tilde{p}_i=0$. In this case, S_i is conditioned on z_i and $\tilde{p}_i$ rather than on z_i and p_0, $i=1,2$. With this generality, z can represent nonmarket conditions such as physical circumstances (for example, weather), social factors (for example, the educational level of society), infrastructure in the economy (for example, quality of the transportation system), or environmental attributes (for example, noise, visibility, or other indicators of environmental quality). In each case, a number of consumer demands or factor supplies may be affected by a change in z and, accordingly, measuring the welfare effects of a change in z would require sequential evaluation including all relevant consumer demands and factor supplies.

7.11 EXACT MEASUREMENT OF WTP FOR FACTOR OWNERS

As in the pure consumer case of Chapter 6, ordinary demand and factor supply relationships can be used to infer Hicksian demands and supplies and the related exact measurements of compensating and equivalent variation for factor owners. Thus, when the Willig approximations are unacceptable, the approaches of Hause (1975), Hausman (1981) and Vartia (1983) mentioned in Section 6.8 and discussed in Appendix Section 6.D can be applied as discussed in Appendix Section 7.H. Again, the reader is reminded that the results of Willig, Hause and Vartia for the multiple-price-change case apply only when integrability conditions hold (see Appendix Sections 6.E and 7.H). Thus, the most convenient approach to empirical welfare analysis in the multiple-price-change case of a single factor owner is usually to specify a complete system of consumer demands and factor supplies using duality results applied to a common indirect utility function (see Appendix Section 6.F as adapted to the factor owner problem in Appendix Section 7.H).

7.12 SUMMARY AND CONCLUSIONS

This chapter has extended the results and concepts of Chapters 5 and 6 to the case where the consumer also makes decisions regarding quantities of factors to sell. This leads to an important distinction between exogenous income that is essentially uncontrolled by short-run consumer decisions and endogenous income that is determined on the basis of the consumer's individual decisions. In this context results indicate that areas above supply curves of factors play roles analogous to areas below demand curves for consumption.

Nonuniqueness of money measures of utility change presents problems in the factor supply case just as in the pure consumer demand case. The WTP approach associated with compensating and equivalent variation, however, has reasonable properties when multiple prices – including factor prices – change. Furthermore, the results introduced in Chapter 6 readily extend to the case of factor supply, so simple producer surplus measurements associated with factor supply provide approximate measures of welfare effects.

This chapter has also introduced the concepts of compensating and equivalent surplus, which are applicable to the case where quantity changes are imposed on either pure consumers or factor owners. As for the case of free adjustment, results indicate that simple consumer and producer surplus changes provide reasonable approximations in much the same sense as do the Willig results of Sections 6.5 through 6.7. These results are applied further in determining the welfare connotations of areas between shifting supply (demand) curves, which are caused by changing prices in other markets or by changes in nonmarket variables affecting the factor owner. The possibility of welfare measurement for multiple price changes in a single market is significant because, in many cases, lack of sufficient data forces a welfare analyst to evaluate the welfare effects of many price changes within a single market. These results will be useful when dealing with instability and welfare analysis in the context of random shifts in supply and demand (see Section 12.5 and Appendix Section 14.2). The possibility of measuring welfare effects of nonmarket variables is especially important for environmental problems as illustrated further in Section 13.4.

Having now derived the possibilities for welfare measurement for the producer, the consumer and the factor owner, Chapter 8 turns to market analysis where the responses of many such decision-makers and the associated welfare effects are aggregated and then investigated on the basis of market data.

Appendix to Chapter 7: Welfare measurement for factor owners

The purpose of this appendix is to extend the concepts of consumer welfare measurement to the case where the consumer also controls and sells factors such as labor (Sections 7.A–7.B). Concepts of willingness to pay are generalized to the consumer-laborer problem in Section 7.C. Section 7.D investigates the validity of the approaches of Chapter 6 for the case where individuals make simultaneous decisions about both consumption and factor supply. Results regarding the approximating properties of consumer surplus are generalized in Section 7.E. Section 7.G shows that household production models are readily accommodated with the general methodology developed in this book. The methods of exact welfare measurement are extended to the case of factor ownership in Section 7.H. Other sections introduce additional generalizations to address consumer and factor owner welfare measurement in a variety of policy settings that arise in later chapters. These include generalization of the factor owners problem to the case of where individuals own other factors beyond labor (Section 7.F), the evaluation of welfare effects of nonprice changes such as changes in quality (Section 7.I) and the evaluation of welfare effects of imposed quantity changes (Section 7.J).

7.A THE CASE WITH CONSUMPTION AND LABOR SUPPLY

First, the mathematical analysis of Appendix Sections 5.A–5.C, 6.A, and 6.B must be extended to the case of factor ownership. The case of labor supply is considered in the first five sections of this Appendix for simplicity and clarity. The framework is then expanded to the general case of factor ownership in Appendix Section 7.F.

Owing in large part to the work of Becker (1965) and Mincer (1963), labor supply has come to be viewed as the mirror image of leisure demand. A decision to sell a marginal hour of labor in the marketplace is, in a manner of speaking, a decision not to buy the marginal hour of leisure. Viewing leisure as a consumer good, the framework of Appendix Sections 5.A and 6.A can thus be easily generalized to investigate welfare effects associated with labor and wages. At the same time, some important qualifications associated with the results in the pure consumer case relating to interdependence of consumption and labor decisions become apparent. That is, the derivation in Appendix Sections 5.A–5.C, 6.A, and 6.B is based on the assumption of fixed income. But, in fact, when a worker is faced with higher prices, he or she might react by working more – for example, becoming more willing to work overtime – in which case income would increase and partially offset the erosion of increasing prices on his or her purchasing power. For this case, the path-dependence notions of Appendix Section 5.B must be expanded to include wages as well as prices.

Consider an individual with utility function $U(l, \boldsymbol{q})$ that is monotonically increasing, quasiconcave, and twice differentiable in l and $\boldsymbol{q}$ where l is consumption of nonmarket time (leisure) and $\boldsymbol{q}$ is a consumption vector, $\boldsymbol{q}=(q_1,\ldots,q_N)$, with q_i representing consumption of commodity i per unit of time. Also, suppose that the total amount of time that can be allocated between work time (h) and leisure (l) is τ hours per unit of time (that is, $\tau=h+l$). Then the budget constraint that equates income and expenditures is

$$wl+\boldsymbol{pq}=w\tau+\bar{m}\equiv m^*,\ \tau\geq l\geq 0, \tag{7.18}$$

where $\boldsymbol{p}=(p_1,\ldots,p_N)$, $\boldsymbol{pq}=\Sigma_{i=1}^N p_i q_i$, w is the wage rate, $\bar{m}$ is exogenous income resulting from the consumer's endowment of factors that finance expenditures but do not generate utility directly through consumption and m^* is Becker's (1965) concept of *full income*, which includes the value of all consumer endowments, some of which may be partially consumed at home.[1] In this context, wl is thus interpreted as the opportunity cost of leisure time.

The individual's utility maximization problem can be formulated either in terms of full income as

$$\max_{l,\boldsymbol{q}} \{U(l,\boldsymbol{q})\,|\,wl+\boldsymbol{pq}=m^*,\ \tau\geq l\geq 0,\ \boldsymbol{q}\geq 0\},$$

or in terms of exogenous income as

$$\max_{l,\boldsymbol{q}} \{U(l,\boldsymbol{q})\,|\,w(l-\tau)+\boldsymbol{pq}=\bar{m},\ \tau\geq l\geq 0,\ \boldsymbol{q}\geq 0\}. \tag{7.19}$$

Assuming an internal solution ($\tau>l>0$, $\boldsymbol{q}>0$), the Lagrangian of the utility-maximization problem is $\mathcal{L}=U(l,\boldsymbol{q})+\lambda(wl+\boldsymbol{pq}-m^*)$ in the former case and $\mathcal{L}=U(l,\boldsymbol{q})+\lambda[\mathrm{w}(l-\tau)+\boldsymbol{pq}-\bar{m}]$ in the latter case. In either case, the associated first-order conditions for maximization imply that

$$\boldsymbol{U_q}=\lambda\boldsymbol{p}$$
$$U_l=\lambda w$$

in addition to the associated income constraint (where subscripts of U denote differentiation, for example, $\boldsymbol{U_q}\equiv\partial U/\partial\boldsymbol{q}$). Because the income constraints are compatible as in (7.18), the two problems are equivalent. Solving the first-order conditions yields the marginal utility of income, λ, the ordinary Marshallian consumption demands,

$$\boldsymbol{q}=\tilde{\boldsymbol{q}}(w,\boldsymbol{p},\bar{m}), \tag{7.20}$$

and a leisure demand equation,

$$l=\tilde{l}(w,\boldsymbol{p},\bar{m}), \tag{7.21}$$

1. Due to the work of Becker, formulations conditioned on full income are popular even though formulations conditioned on exogenous income are useful in some contexts. For a treatment of income as exogenous versus endogenous (using instead the terms 'earned' and 'unearned'), see Abbott and Ashenfelter (1976).

where $\tilde{\boldsymbol{q}}(w,\boldsymbol{p},\bar{m}) = [\tilde{q}_1(w,\boldsymbol{p},\bar{m}),\ldots,\tilde{q}_N(w,\boldsymbol{p},\bar{m})]$ compactly denotes the demands for all individual goods. The latter equation implies a labor supply function of the form

$$h = \tilde{h}(w,\boldsymbol{p},\bar{m}) \equiv \tau - \tilde{l}(w,\boldsymbol{p},\bar{m}).$$

Substituting (7.20) and (7.21) into the utility function yields the indirect utility function,

$$V = V(w,\boldsymbol{p},\bar{m}) \equiv U(\tilde{l},\tilde{\boldsymbol{q}}).$$

Alternatively, in the full income formulation, the demands in (7.20) can be written as $\boldsymbol{q} = \tilde{\boldsymbol{q}}^*(w,\boldsymbol{p},m^*) = \tilde{\boldsymbol{q}}^*(w,\boldsymbol{p},w\tau + \bar{m}) \equiv \tilde{\boldsymbol{q}}(w,\boldsymbol{p},\bar{m})$ and similarly for $l = \tilde{l}^*(w,\boldsymbol{p},m^*)$ and $\tilde{h}^*(w,\boldsymbol{p},m^*)$, in which case the indirect utility function can be written as $V = V^*(w,\boldsymbol{p},m^*) \equiv U(\tilde{l}^*,\tilde{\boldsymbol{q}}^*)$.[2]

As in the derivation of Appendix Section 5.A, the change in utility associated with a wage–price–income change from $(w^0,\boldsymbol{p}^0,\bar{m}_0)$ to $(w^1,\boldsymbol{p}^1,\bar{m}_1)$ can be represented as a line integral,

$$\begin{aligned}\Delta U &= \textstyle\int_L dU \\ &= \textstyle\int_L [U_l d\tilde{l} + \boldsymbol{U}_q d\tilde{\boldsymbol{q}}] \\ &= \textstyle\int_L \lambda[w d\tilde{l} + \boldsymbol{p} d\tilde{\boldsymbol{q}}],\end{aligned} \tag{7.22}$$

where L is some wage–price–income path between the two specified wage–price–income points.[3] Differentiating the budget constraint in (7.18) totally,

$$w d\tilde{l} + l dw + \boldsymbol{p} d\tilde{\boldsymbol{q}} + \tilde{\boldsymbol{q}} d\boldsymbol{p} = \tau dw + d\bar{m} = dm^*,$$

where $\tilde{\boldsymbol{q}}$ and $\tilde{l}$ are represented in either exogenous or full income notation, and substituting into (7.22) thus yields

$$\begin{aligned}\Delta U &= \textstyle\int_L \lambda[d\bar{m} - (\tilde{l} - \tau)dw - \tilde{\boldsymbol{q}} d\boldsymbol{p}] \\ &= \textstyle\int_L \lambda[d\bar{m} + \tilde{h} dw - \tilde{\boldsymbol{q}} d\boldsymbol{p}] \\ &= \textstyle\int_L \lambda[dm^* - \tilde{l}^* dw - \tilde{\boldsymbol{q}}^* d\boldsymbol{p}].\end{aligned} \tag{7.23}$$

Similar to the pure consumer case, (7.23) provides an exact measure of utility change regardless of path but is not meaningful for empirical measurement because the units of measurement are indeterminate in an ordinal utility world. As discussed in Appendix Section 5.A, one approach has been to assume λ is approximately constant and convert ΔU to money terms through a division by λ, the marginal utility of income, which obtains

$$\begin{aligned}\Delta S &= \textstyle\int_L [d\bar{m} + \tilde{h} dw - \tilde{\boldsymbol{q}} d\boldsymbol{p}] \\ &= \textstyle\int_L [dm^* - \tilde{l}^* dw - \tilde{\boldsymbol{q}}^* d\boldsymbol{p}].\end{aligned} \tag{7.24}$$

Choosing a particular sequential path of integration, (7.24) implies that total surplus change can be found either by adding to the change in full income the change in consu-

2. With the full income formulation, one must keep in mind that a change in the wage rate causes a change in full income but not in exogenous income.
3. For simplicity of notation, note that $\boldsymbol{U}_q d\tilde{\boldsymbol{q}} = \Sigma_{i=1}^N (\partial U/\partial \tilde{q}_i) d\tilde{q}_i$, $\tilde{\boldsymbol{q}} d\boldsymbol{p} = \Sigma_{i=1}^N \tilde{q}_i dp_i$, and $\boldsymbol{p} d\boldsymbol{q} = \Sigma_{i=1}^N p_i dq_i$.

mer surpluses associated with leisure and all consumer goods, or by adding to the change in exogenous income the change in producer surplus associated with labor supply and the change in consumer surpluses associated with all consumer goods.

The associated utility indicator in (7.24), however, possesses path-dependence problems. By analogy with the derivation in Appendix Section 5.B (e.g., let the indices in (5.9) and (5.10) range from 0 to N where $p_0 \equiv w$ and $\tilde{q}_0 = \tilde{l} = \tau - \tilde{h}$), conditions for path independence of (7.24) are[4]

$$\frac{\partial \tilde{q}_i}{\partial w} = \frac{\partial \tilde{q}_0}{\partial p_i} = -\frac{\partial \tilde{h}}{\partial p_i} = \frac{\partial \tilde{l}}{\partial p_i},\ i = 1, \ldots, N, \tag{7.25}$$

$$\frac{\partial \tilde{q}_i}{\partial p_j} = \frac{\partial \tilde{q}_j}{\partial p_i},\ i, j = 1, \ldots, N, \tag{7.26}$$

$$\frac{\partial \tilde{q}_i}{\partial \bar{m}} = 0,\ i, = 1, \ldots, N, \tag{7.27}$$

$$\frac{\partial \tilde{q}_0}{\partial \bar{m}} = -\frac{\partial \tilde{h}}{\partial \bar{m}} = \frac{\partial \tilde{l}}{\partial \bar{m}} = 0. \tag{7.28}$$

7.B MONEY MEASURES OF UTILITY CHANGE FOR LABOR SUPPLIERS

Obviously, all the path-independence conditions in (7.25)–(7.28) cannot hold simultaneously. For example, a simple change in exogenous income (or full income) holding prices and wages fixed would violate (7.18) according to (7.27), because the increase in income would not be offset by either reduced labor (increased leisure) or increased allocation to possible consumer choices. This result amounts to recognizing, as in the pure consumer case (see Appendix Section 5.A), that λ cannot be constant with respect to all prices (including wages) and income. That is, ΔS in (7.24) does not differ from ΔU in (7.23) by a multiplicative constant.

An alternative suggested by Burns (1977), for example, is to consider only those wage–

4. Under the conditions in (7.27) and (7.28),

$$\frac{\partial \tilde{q}_j}{\partial w} = \frac{\partial \tilde{q}_j^*}{\partial w} + \frac{\partial \tilde{q}_j^*}{\partial m^*}\frac{\partial m^*}{\partial w} = \frac{\partial \tilde{q}_j^*}{\partial w} + \frac{\partial \tilde{q}_j^*}{\partial m^*}\tau = \frac{\partial \tilde{q}_j^*}{\partial w}.$$

Thus, conditions similar to (7.25)–(7.28) are obtained where demands and labor supply are conditioned on full income rather than exogenous income if $\bar{m}$ is replaced by m^* in (7.25)–(7.28), and differentiation with respect to m^* holds w fixed, for example,

$$\frac{\partial \tilde{q}_j}{\partial m^*} \equiv \left.\frac{\partial \tilde{q}_j}{\partial m^*}\right|_{w\text{ const}} = \frac{\partial \tilde{q}_j}{\partial \bar{m}}.$$

Without this definition of differentiation with respect to m^*, derivation of some results using the full income formulation can be cumbersome because a change in full income has different implications depending on whether it is due to a change in exogenous income or a change in the wage rate at which the endowment of time is valued. Any change in wage rate requires consideration of the implied change in full income as well as implications in the market for leisure. For mathematical details in the general case, see Appendix Section 7.F.

price–income paths where some subset of prices, wage, and income is allowed to vary. The results of this exercise are apparent by analogy with Appendix Section 5.B. For example, if exogenous income $\bar{m}$ is held constant ($d\bar{m} \equiv 0$), then (7.25) and (7.26) constitute path-independence conditions, which, following the derivation in Appendix Section 5.C, implies unitary exogenous income elasticities for all goods, including leisure. Alternatively, if some prices are also held constant, other income elasticities need not be unitary but must be the same for all goods, including leisure.[5]

Similarly, if the price of one commodity (a numeraire) is fixed ($dp_N \equiv 0$), the path-independence conditions paralleling (5.14) and (5.15) are

$$\frac{\partial \tilde{q}_i}{\partial p_j} = \frac{\partial \tilde{q}_j}{\partial p_i},\ i, j = 0, 1, \ldots, N-1,$$

$$\frac{\partial \tilde{q}_i}{\partial \bar{m}} = 0,\ i = 0, 1, \ldots, N-1, \tag{7.29}$$

where $p_0 \equiv w$ and $\tilde{q}_0 = \tilde{l} = \tau - \tilde{h}$.[6] The Slutsky equation in (5.18) applies for $i, j = 0, 1, \ldots, N-1$ and implies that the first equation of (7.29) holds automatically if the second equation holds.[7] Hence, path independence is attained in the numeraire case when exogenous income changes if $\partial \tilde{q}_i / \partial \bar{m} = 0$ for all goods other than the numeraire. That is, the exogenous income elasticity of all goods, including labor (or leisure), is zero, and any increase in income is spent entirely on the numeraire.[8] More specifically, if other prices are also held constant, exogenous income elasticities need be zero only for goods corresponding to prices that change, and increases in income would be spent entirely on goods for which prices do not change. The exogenous income elasticity of labor (or leisure) must be zero in this case if the wage changes.

As Burns points out, the former case with fixed exogenous income requires homotheticity in the consumer's indifference map with respect to an origin determined by the amount of exogenous income (a zero origin if exogenous income is zero).[9] The latter case with changing exogenous income, on the other hand, requires zero-income effects, which imply vertically parallel indifference curves with respect to commodities for which prices change.[10]

5. The formulation based on exogenous income has a weakness for this case when exogenous income is zero because all exogenous income elasticities become zero trivially. More generally, when the first condition of (7.29) holds, the Slutsky equation implies $\tilde{q}_j(\partial \tilde{q}_i / \partial m) = \tilde{q}_i(\partial \tilde{q}_j / \partial m)$ following (5.18) whether m is exogenous or full income. Thus, dividing by $\tilde{q}_i \tilde{q}_j$ and multiplying by m on both sides implies equality of income elasticities regardless of whether the income elasticities are with respect to exogenous or full income. As these results suggest, all of the statements in the remainder of this section apply for full income elasticities as well as for exogenous income elasticities under the conditions of footnote 4.
6. Alternatively, one can define utility as a function of the amount of time given up to labor, for example, $U^*(h,\mathbf{q}) \equiv U(\tau - h,\mathbf{q}) = U(l,\mathbf{q})$. Mishan (1959) uses this approach to obtain conclusions similar to those developed here.
7. For a similar application of the Slutsky equation with respect to leisure, see Abbott and Ashenfelter (1976).
8. As Burns (1977) shows, this condition also corresponds to additive separability of the numeraire in the consumer's utility function.
9. This property is called *quasi-homotheticity*. Just as homotheticity has straight-line Engel curves running through the origin, quasi-homotheticity has straight-line Engel curves running through some point other than the origin. For further discussion, see Deaton and Muellbauer (1980, pp. 142–5).
10. This would be the case where preferences are quasilinear with respect to several goods. See footnote 12 of the Appendix to Chapter 5.

7.C WTP MEASURES FOR CONSUMER-LABORERS

Apparently, the restrictions associated with developing money measures of utility change in the labor market (where other prices may change) are quite restrictive, just as are those associated with the pure consumer case. Thus, one must conclude along with Burns (1977, p. 50) that 'appropriate conditions are ... so restrictive as to preclude operational significance'. Again, the less restrictive concepts of compensating and equivalent variation provide a possible and more applicable alternative.

Consider the consumer-laborer's utility-maximization problem from the alternative viewpoint of minimizing the exogenous income required for a particular level of utility,

$$\bar{e}(w,\boldsymbol{p},\bar{U}) = \min_{l,\boldsymbol{q}} \{w(l-\tau) + \boldsymbol{pq} \,|\, U(l,\boldsymbol{q}) = \bar{U},\ \tau \geq l \geq 0,\ \boldsymbol{q} \geq \boldsymbol{0}\}. \tag{7.30}$$

The optimum value of the objective function of this problem, $\bar{e}(w,\boldsymbol{p},\bar{U})$, is an expenditure function specifying the minimum exogenous income required to attain a given utility level with wage–price vector $(w,\boldsymbol{p})$. The problem in (7.30) thus parallels (6.22) for analytical purposes except that the commodity set has been expanded to include labor/leisure. Hence, without repeating the lengthy derivation in Appendix Sections 6.A and 6.B, a number of useful results for welfare measurement in the labor market become apparent. However, in interpreting results from Appendix Sections 6.A and 6.B in the context of this section, one must bear in mind that $\bar{e}(w,\boldsymbol{p},\bar{U})$ is not the traditional expenditure function. It specifies the amount of exogenous income rather than the amount of ordinary income required for a given utility level with a given wage–price vector $(w,\boldsymbol{p})$. Ordinary income exceeds exogenous income by wage income, wh.

By analogy with (6.27) and assuming no corner solutions, differentiation of $\bar{e}(w,\boldsymbol{p},\bar{U})$ with respect to the wage rate (where subscripts of $\bar{e}$ denote differentiation, for example, $\bar{e}_w = \partial\bar{e}/\partial w$) yields a compensated labor supply (in absolute value),[11]

$$\bar{e}_w \equiv \bar{e}_{p_0} = \bar{l}(w,\boldsymbol{p},\bar{U}) - \tau = \bar{q}_0(w,\boldsymbol{p},\bar{U}) - \tau \equiv -\bar{h}(w,\boldsymbol{p},\bar{U}), \tag{7.31}$$

which specifies the negative of the amount of labor required to attain utility level $\bar{U}$ with wage–price vector $(w,\boldsymbol{p})$.[12] As usual, differentiation with respect to other prices yields compensated demands, $\bar{\boldsymbol{e}}_{\boldsymbol{p}} = \bar{\boldsymbol{q}}(w,\boldsymbol{p},\bar{U})$.

11. For the remainder of this section, the problem in (7.30) is assumed to generate no corner solutions so that nonnegativity constraints for h, $\boldsymbol{q}$ and l are inconsequential. The case where quantity constraints are binding can be treated as in Appendix Section 7.J.
12. Note that all of these results carry through with the full income formulation if $\bar{m}$ is replaced by m^*, the minimization in (7.30) is replaced by

$$e^*(w,\boldsymbol{p},\bar{U}) = \min_{l,\boldsymbol{q}} \{wl + \boldsymbol{pq} \,|\, U(l,\boldsymbol{q}) = \bar{U},\ \tau \geq l \geq 0,\ \boldsymbol{q} \geq 0\},$$

and (7.31) is replaced by $e^*_w \equiv e^*_{p_0} = \equiv \bar{l}^*(w,\boldsymbol{p},\bar{U}) \equiv \tau - \bar{h}^*(w,\boldsymbol{p},\bar{U})$. The associated expenditure function, $e^*(w,\boldsymbol{p},\bar{U})$, gives the full income necessary for a given utility level at wage–price vector $(w, \boldsymbol{p})$. This expenditure function differs from the expenditure function defined in (7.30) by the time endowment valued at the wage rate, $e^*(w,\boldsymbol{p},\bar{U}) = \bar{e}(w,\boldsymbol{p},\bar{U}) + w\tau$. With the exogenous income approach in (7.31) derivatives of the expenditure function correspond directly to market transactions (for example, $\tau - l$ hours of labor are sold). With the full income formulation, the quantities represent amounts consumed at home (for example, l hours of leisure are consumed), which are not directly observed in typical data. Note that the ordinary income m considered in Appendix 6 differs from both exogenous income ($m = \bar{m} + wh$) and from full income ($m = m^* - wl$).

The compensating variation of a general wage–price–income change following (6.29) is

$$
\begin{aligned}
C &= \bar{m}_1 - \bar{e}(w^1,\mathbf{p}^1,U^0)\\
&= \bar{m}_1 - \bar{m}_0 + \bar{e}(w^0,\mathbf{p}^0,U^0) - \bar{e}(w^1,\mathbf{p}^1,U^0)\\
&= \Delta\bar{m} - \int_L \sum_{j=0}^{N} \bar{e}_{p_j}(w,\mathbf{p},U^0)dp_j\\
&= \Delta\bar{m} + \int_{w^0}^{w^1} \bar{h}(\hat{\mathbf{p}}_0(w),U^0)dw - \sum_{j=1}^{N}\int_{p_j^0}^{p_j^1} \bar{q}_j(\hat{\mathbf{p}}_j(p_j),U^0)dp_j \qquad (7.32)\\
&= \Delta m^* - \int_{w^0}^{w^1} \bar{l}(\hat{\mathbf{p}}_0(w),U^0)dw - \sum_{j=1}^{N}\int_{p_j^0}^{p_j^1} \bar{q}_j(\hat{\mathbf{p}}_j(p_j),U^0)dp_j
\end{aligned}
$$

where $\Delta m^* = \Delta\bar{m} + \tau(w^1 - w^0)$, L is any path from $(w^0,\mathbf{p}^0)$ to $(w^1,\mathbf{p}^1)$ and

$$
\begin{aligned}
\hat{\mathbf{p}}_j(p_j) &\equiv (p_0^1,\ldots,p_{j-1}^1,p_j,p_{j+1}^0,\ldots,p_N^0,\bar{m}_1)\\
w^0 &= p_0^0\\
w^1 &= p_0^1
\end{aligned}
$$

represents a specific path. Similarly, the equivalent variation of a wage–price–income change from $(w^0,\mathbf{p}^0,\bar{m}_0)$ to $(w^1,\mathbf{p}^1,\bar{m}_1)$ that causes a change in utility from U^0 to U^1 following (6.30) is

$$
\begin{aligned}
E &= \bar{e}(w^0,\mathbf{p}^0,U^1) - \bar{m}_0\\
&= \Delta\bar{m} - \int_L \sum_{j=0}^{N} \bar{e}_{p_j}(w,\mathbf{p},U^1)dp_j\\
&= \Delta\bar{m} + \int_{w^0}^{w^1} \bar{h}(\hat{\mathbf{p}}_0(w),U^1)dw - \sum_{j=1}^{N}\int_{p_j^0}^{p_j^1} \bar{q}_j(\hat{\mathbf{p}}_j(p_j),U^1)dp_j \qquad (7.33)\\
&= \Delta m^* - \int_{w^0}^{w^1} \bar{l}(\hat{\mathbf{p}}_0(w),U^1)dw - \sum_{j=1}^{N}\int_{p_j^0}^{p_j^1} \bar{q}_j(\hat{\mathbf{p}}_j(p_j),U^1)dp_j.
\end{aligned}
$$

The results in (7.32) and (7.33) are the basic results facilitating measurement of willingness-to-pay concepts for multiple wage–price changes. *The compensating (equivalent) variation for a general wage–price–income change is uniquely measured by adding to the change in exogenous income the change in area left of compensated labor supply plus all the changes in areas left of compensated demands for consumer goods, where each demand or supply is evaluated at the initial (final) utility level but successively conditioned on previously considered wage or price changes. Equivalently, the compensating (equivalent) variation for a general wage–price–income change is uniquely measured by adding the change in full income to the change in area left of the compensated leisure demand plus all the changes in areas left of compensated demands for consumer goods, where each demand is evaluated at the initial (final) utility level but successively conditioned on previously considered wage or price changes.* As in Appendix Section 6.A, the order of integration theoretically makes no difference.

In the special case where only the wage rate changes ($d\bar{m} \equiv 0$, $d\boldsymbol{p} \equiv 0$), these results indicate that the WTP for a wage change is completely captured by the change in area left of the compensated labor supply curve, where compensation corresponds to the initial (final) utility level in the case of compensating (equivalent) variation. There is no additional need to consider the change in income generated thereby.[13] The results are thus consistent with, but a generalization of, those by Mishan (1959).

Analogous to the derivation in (6.31)–(6.32), the possibilities for $E = C$ can be explored by differentiating both sides of the identity $\bar{q}_j(w,\boldsymbol{p},V(w,\boldsymbol{p},\bar{m})) \equiv \tilde{q}_j(w,\boldsymbol{p},\bar{m})$ with respect to $\bar{m}$, which yields

$$\frac{\partial \bar{q}_i}{\partial \bar{m}} = \frac{\partial \bar{q}_j}{\partial U}\frac{\partial V}{\partial \bar{m}} = \frac{\partial \tilde{q}_j}{\partial \bar{m}}, \tag{7.34}$$

which implies that the Hicksian demand is independent of utility if, and only if, the Marshallian demand is independent of $\bar{m}$ assuming nonsatiation ($\partial V/\partial \bar{m} \neq 0$). Thus, $E = C$ holds if and only if $\partial \tilde{q}_j/\partial \bar{m} = 0$ for all commodities for which prices change. The implication of (7.34) in this case, however, is not that zero-income effects are required for all goods but that zero *exogenous* income effects are required. This condition is needed only for those goods for which prices change. The latter situation may be more apt to occur than the former. For example, suppose that a laborer-consumer draws exogenous income from investments but, as a matter of course, reinvests all investment income, thus seeking to finance all consumption from wage and salary income. In this case, zero exogenous income effects would hold for all consumer goods (assuming a dichotomy between consumer goods and investments). If any compensation is also treated as exogenous income, the compensating and equivalent variations for any multiple price change associated only with consumer goods would be identical and would be measured exactly by the sum of changes in surpluses associated with ordinary consumption demands and labor supply.[14]

7.D SEPARABILITY OF CONSUMPTION AND FACTOR SUPPLY

While the approximating qualities of *consumer* surplus may be the same in the factor supply problem as in the pure consumption case, some important differences exist with respect to evaluating welfare effects of income changes. In particular, the welfare effects of changes in endogenous income due to adjustment of factor sales in response to consumer price changes are automatically reflected in the associated consumer surplus changes (whether Hicksian or ordinary surpluses) when demands are conditioned on factor prices and exogenous income. Such changes, if added on to the change in consumer surplus,

13. Using $l = \tau - h$, the change in producer surplus associated with the compensated labor supply is equivalent to the sum of the change in full income and the change in consumer surplus associated with the compensated leisure demand. That is, differentiating the identity $e^*(w,\boldsymbol{p},\bar{U}) = \bar{e}(w,\boldsymbol{p},\bar{U}) + w\tau$ with respect to a w yields $\bar{l}^*(\boldsymbol{\hat{p}}_0(w),\bar{U}) = \tau - \bar{h}(\boldsymbol{\hat{p}}_0(w),\bar{U})$. Integrating the latter for a specific wage change from w^0 to w^1 yields

$$\int_{w^0}^{w^1} \bar{l}^*(\boldsymbol{\hat{p}}_0(w),\bar{U})dw = \tau(w^1 - w^0) - \int_{w^0}^{w^1} \bar{h}(\boldsymbol{\hat{p}}_0(w),\bar{U})dw.$$

14. As before, however, these measurements must be successively conditioned on previously considered price changes.

result in double counting.[15] This occurs because the consumer adjusts endogenous variables to equate marginal utilities and, thus, such considerations are implicitly reflected in the demand relationships.

For example, suppose the price of beef increases, causing a reduction in beef consumption, an increase in pork consumption and an increase in labor hours to pay grocery bills. Just as WTP is captured completely by the change in beef market surplus (inaccurately by Marshallian surplus and accurately by Hicksian surplus) and requires no additional consideration of changes in pork consumption, no additional consideration of changes in labor is required either.

To see this more clearly, consider Figure 7.7(a) where q is the quantity of a consumer good and h is the quantity of labor, and a consumer/laborer has indifference curves U_0 and U_1. Initially, the wage rate is w_0 and the price of the consumer good is p_0. (Suppose these are the only two commodities considered by the consumer and that exogenous income is zero.) With a decline in the price of the consumer good to p_1, the budget line rotates about the origin from a slope of p_0/w_0 to a slope of p_1/w_0. Utility maximization with indifference curves U_0 and U_1 thus implies an increase in consumption from q_0 to q_1 and a decrease in labor from h_0 to h_1. Transferring these results to Figure 7.7(b) thus yields the ordinary demand curve D. If income is taken away from the consumer/laborer in the amount of $w_0\Delta h$ (note that the wage rate is constant) to restore the original indifference curve, then a smaller adjustment to $\tilde{q}_1$ occurs along the Hicksian compensated demand curve H.

The result in (7.32) demonstrates that the shaded area below H measures the entire compensating variation, $w_0\Delta h$, of the price change for this problem. Note, however, that ordinary income has also changed as a result of the price change from w_0h_0 to w_0h_1 because of the endogenous adjustment of labor. Clearly, this change in income should not be subtracted from the welfare gain represented by the shaded area in arriving at a final measure of the effect. This result is in contrast to the pure consumer case of Appendix Section 6.A where any change in income must be considered as an additional welfare effect over and above the compensating or equivalent variations induced by price changes. Which procedure is appropriate depends on whether income is truly exogenous, meaning factor quantities do not change with price changes.

This example raises the issue of whether the results of Appendix Section 6.A are valid for the more general problem with endogenous factor supply. To investigate this issue where $m=\bar{m}+w(\tau-l)$ is the ordinary income concept of Chapter 6, note that the condition $\partial\tilde{\mathbf{q}}/\partial\bar{m}=\partial\tilde{\mathbf{q}}/\partial m$, under which the approximation criteria are identical in the pure consumer and consumer–factor owner problems, are exactly those under which all other results for the pure consumer problem remain valid. In this case, a two-stage budgeting procedure is appropriate whereby consumption bundles can be decided for given total income and then endogenous factor supplies can be determined to meet that income and equate the marginal benefits of consumption and leisure. These requirements have been developed in the theory of separability and require that consumption commodities and factors form weakly separable groups (Blackorby, Primont and Russell 1978).

15. This is also true in the full income formulation because full income is unaffected by changes in prices of consumer goods. The change in full income must be considered additionally only when exogenous income or the wage rate changes.

To illustrate, return to the utility maximization problem in (7.19) for which first-order conditions in the case of an internal solution are

$$U_q = \lambda \boldsymbol{p},$$
$$U_l = \lambda w,$$
$$w(l - \tau) + \boldsymbol{pq} = \bar{m}.$$

Weak separability of the utility function in labor and consumer goods is defined by (Blackorby, Primont and Russell 1978, p. 52)

$$\frac{\partial}{\partial l}\left(\frac{\partial U/\partial q_i}{\partial U/\partial q_j}\right) = 0,\ i, j = 1, \ldots, N.$$

These conditions imply that substitution of consumer goods does not depend on factor consumption. But these conditions imply that the utility maximization problem can be treated as two independent problems: (1) the problem of maximizing $U(l,\boldsymbol{q})$ subject to $m = \boldsymbol{pq}$ given l, and (2) the problem of maximizing $U(l,\boldsymbol{q})$ subject to $w(\tau - l) = m - \bar{m}$ given consumption quantities in $\boldsymbol{q}$. In other words, the maximization of utility with respect to consumer good choices depends on labor supply only through ordinary income m, and maximization of utility with respect to labor supply depends on consumption choices only through the endogenous income required. Thus, for example, the consumer demands can indeed be written in the form $\boldsymbol{q} = \tilde{\boldsymbol{q}}(\boldsymbol{p},m)$, which depend on h only through m and trivially imply $\partial\tilde{\boldsymbol{q}}/\partial\bar{m} = (\partial\tilde{\boldsymbol{q}}/\partial m)(\partial m/\partial\bar{m}) = (\partial\tilde{\boldsymbol{q}}/\partial m)$. For most empirical work, leisure (labor) is assumed to be a separable commodity group at least implicitly. Hence, a strong precedent exists for assuming that the pure consumer problem is identical to the consumer-laborer problem as it relates to consumer decisions. Nevertheless, empirical work by Lopez (1984, 1986) casts doubt on the applicability of this separability assumption and suggests at least caution in so proceeding. For a further discussion and review of separability, see Blackorby, Primont and Russell (1978).

7.E APPROXIMATE MEASUREMENT OF WTP FOR CONSUMER-LABORERS

Whether or not separability applies and permits application of results in Chapter 6 to consumer-laborers, the Willig approach can be extended in a straightforward manner to the laborer-consumer case. Hence, approximate measures of WTP can be made with the consumer-surplus approach as long as exogenous income elasticities can be bounded and initial exogenous income can be measured and is not zero.[16]

Consider first a single price (wage) change from $\boldsymbol{p}^0 = (p_0^0, \ldots, p_N^0)$ to $\boldsymbol{p}^1 = (p_0^0, \ldots, p_{i-1}^0, p_i^1, p_{i+1}^0, \ldots, p_N^0)$, $p_i^1 \neq p_i^0$. Suppose that $\bar{\eta}_1$ and $\bar{\eta}_2$ are lower and upper bounds, respectively, on

16. Alternatively, and if exogenous income elasticity is zero, the results in this section carry through with the full income formulation where $q_0 \equiv l$. In this case, $\bar{m}$ is replaced by m^*, $\bar{\eta}^i$ is replaced by $\eta^{i*} = (\partial\tilde{q}_i/\partial m^*) \cdot (m^*/\tilde{q}_i)$, and the integral in (7.35) is replaced by

$$\Delta S_0 = -\int_{p_0^0}^{p_0^1} \tilde{q}_0^*(w,\boldsymbol{p},m^*)dp_0 = -\int_{w^0}^{w^1} \tilde{l}^*(w,\boldsymbol{p},m^*)dw$$

the exogenous income elasticity, $\bar{\eta}^i=(\partial\tilde{q}/q\bar{m})\cdot(\bar{m}/q_i)$, over the region of wage–price–income space for which changes are considered, $\bar{\eta}_1 \neq 1 \neq \bar{\eta}_2$. In this case the derivation of equations (6.34) through (6.55) can be repeated, simply substituting $\bar{\eta}$ for η and $\bar{m}$ for m. Note, however, in the case of a wage change ($i=0$) that

$$\begin{aligned}\Delta S_0 &= -\int_{p_0^0}^{p_0^1} \tilde{q}_0(w,\boldsymbol{p},\bar{m})dp_0 \\ &= (w^1 - w^0)\tau - \int_{w^0}^{w^1} \tilde{l}(w,\boldsymbol{p},\bar{m})dw \\ &= \int_{w^0}^{w^1} \tilde{h}(w,\boldsymbol{p},\bar{m})dw.\end{aligned} \tag{7.35}$$

That is, ΔS_0 is precisely the change in the Marshallian surplus triangle or rent associated with labor supply. Hence, letting $i=0$, the Willig results can be immediately extended to determine the usefulness of the Marshallian surplus associated with labor supply in measuring compensating and/or equivalent variation associated with a wage change.

Thus, the error bounds,

$$\bar{\varepsilon}_2^c \geq \frac{\Delta S_i - C}{|\Delta S_i|} \geq \bar{\varepsilon}_1^c \tag{7.36}$$

and

$$\bar{\varepsilon}_2^e \geq \frac{E - \Delta S_i}{|\Delta S_i|} \geq \bar{\varepsilon}_1^e \tag{7.37}$$

on consumer (factor supplier) surplus as a measure of the compensating or equivalent variation of a price (wage) change follow directly from (6.41) and (6.43) except that the bounds are based on exogenous income and exogenous income elasticities, that is,

$$\bar{\varepsilon}_k^c = \frac{[1 + \bar{s}(\bar{\eta}_k - 1)]^{1/(1-\bar{\eta}_k)} - 1 + \bar{s}}{|\bar{s}|}, \; k=1, 2,$$

and

$$\bar{\varepsilon}_k^e = \frac{[1 - \bar{s}(\bar{\eta}_k - 1)]^{1/(1-\bar{\eta}_k)} - 1 - \bar{s}}{|\bar{s}|}, \; k=1, 2,$$

where $\bar{s}=\Delta S_i/\bar{m}_0$. Similarly, (7.36) and (7.37) suggest the possibility of improving upon the surplus measure ΔS_i to obtain better estimates of compensating and equivalent variation. In point of fact, following (6.50) through (6.53) yields

$$\bar{\varepsilon}_2^c - \hat{\varepsilon} \geq \frac{\hat{C} - C}{|\Delta S_i|} \geq \bar{\varepsilon}_1^c - \hat{\varepsilon} \tag{7.38}$$

and

$$\bar{\varepsilon}_2^e - \hat{\varepsilon} \geq \frac{E - \hat{E}}{|\Delta S_i|} \geq \bar{\varepsilon}_1^e - \hat{\varepsilon}, \tag{7.39}$$

where

$$\hat{C} = \Delta S_i - \hat{\varepsilon}|\Delta S_i| \tag{7.40}$$
$$\hat{E} = \Delta S_i + \hat{\varepsilon}|\Delta S_i| \tag{7.41}$$

$$\hat{\varepsilon} = \frac{|\bar{s}|}{4}(\bar{\eta}_1 + \bar{\eta}_2). \tag{7.42}$$

Table 6.1 may again be used to investigate the magnitude of error in various cases. For example, if exogenous income elasticity is between 0 and 0.4 and the labor surplus change associated with a wage increase is 25 percent of exogenous income ($\bar{\eta}_1 = 0$, $\bar{\eta}_2 = 0.4$, $\bar{s} = 0.25$), then Table 6.1 implies that the labor surplus change overestimates the compensating variation by no more than 4.9 percent and underestimates the equivalent variation by no more than 5.1 percent.

7.F THE GENERAL FACTOR SUPPLY PROBLEM

As pointed out by Mishan (1959), supply of other factors by consumers can be treated in the same way as the labor supply. Suppose an individual holds endowments of several goods that may be partially consumed and partially sold. For this problem, the quantities consumed, $\mathbf{c} = (c_1, \ldots, c_N)$, must be differentiated from the quantities sold or purchased at market prices, $\mathbf{q} = (q_1, \ldots, q_N)$, because the two differ by the vector of factor endowments, $\mathbf{r} = (r_1, \ldots, r_N)$. Suppose the utility of consumption, $U(\mathbf{c})$, is monotonically increasing, quasiconcave, and twice differentiable in c. Then the individual's utility-maximization problem analogous to (7.19) can be represented as

$$V(\mathbf{p}, \bar{m}, \mathbf{r}) = U(\tilde{\mathbf{c}}) = \max_{\mathbf{c}} \{U(\mathbf{c}) | \mathbf{pq} = \bar{m},\ \mathbf{c} = \mathbf{q} + \mathbf{r} \geq \mathbf{0}\},$$

where the utility-maximizing consumption quantities are $\tilde{\mathbf{c}}(\mathbf{p}, \bar{m}, \mathbf{r}) = [\tilde{c}_1(\mathbf{p}, \bar{m}, \mathbf{r}), \ldots, \tilde{c}_N(\mathbf{p}, \bar{m}, \mathbf{r})]$ and the corresponding market transactions are $\tilde{\mathbf{q}}(\mathbf{p}, \bar{m}, \mathbf{r}) \equiv \tilde{\mathbf{c}}(\mathbf{p}, \bar{m}, \mathbf{r}) - \mathbf{r}$.[17] Factor endowments may be zero for many goods but are assumed to be nonnegative in any case. Because the endowment of a good may be partially sold and partially consumed (the case of net supply) or completely consumed with an additional amount purchased for consumption (the case of net demand), the market transactions in $\tilde{\mathbf{q}}(\mathbf{p}, \bar{m}, \mathbf{r})$ may be either positive (the case of net demand) or negative (the case of net supply). If good 1 is labor, then $r_1 = \tau$ represents time available for allocation between labor and leisure. The amount consumed as leisure is $c_1 = l$ and the amount sold as labor is $q_1 = c_1 - \tau = -h$ in the notation of Appendix Section 7.A. For typical consumer goods for which the consumer holds no endowments, $r_i = 0$. In the case where an endowment represents a fixed asset, r_i represents

17. Alternatively, these consumption quantities and market demands can be written in the full income approach as $\tilde{\mathbf{c}}^*(\mathbf{p}, m^*) \equiv \tilde{\mathbf{c}}(\mathbf{p}, \bar{m}, \mathbf{r})$ and $\tilde{\mathbf{q}}^*(\mathbf{p}, m^*) \equiv \tilde{\mathbf{q}}(\mathbf{p}, \bar{m}, \mathbf{r})$, respectively, where $m^* = \bar{m} + \mathbf{pr}$ because the utility-maximization problem becomes

$$\max_{\mathbf{c}} \{U(\mathbf{c}) | \mathbf{pc} = m^*,\ \mathbf{c} \geq 0\}$$

upon substitution of $\bar{m} = m^* - \mathbf{pr}$. That is, $\mathbf{r}$ affects the constraint on choice of $\mathbf{c}$ only through m^*. The consumption demands are written as explicitly depending on endowments here to emphasize empirical dependence of this approach on correctly observing endowments if they are partially consumed or not constant, and because an expenditure function corresponding to exogenous income is convenient for discussing welfare measurement for resource suppliers.

the available renewable service flow(s) that can be sold in repeated time periods as, for example, in the case where a house or plot of land is rented to others.[18] In the special case where an individual holds no other endowment than time to divide between labor and leisure, this problem reduces to (7.19) assuming an internal solution with $l \le \tau$.[19]

To determine WTP for various alternative wage–price–income situations, this utility maximization problem can be usefully considered from the point of view of minimizing the exogenous income required for a particular utility level,

$$\bar{e}(\mathbf{p},\bar{U},\mathbf{r}) = \min_{\mathbf{q}} \{\mathbf{pq} \mid U(\mathbf{c}) = \bar{U},\ \mathbf{c} = \mathbf{q} + \mathbf{r} \ge \mathbf{0}\}.$$

Solving this problem obtains the compensated market demand and supply functions, $\bar{\mathbf{q}}(\mathbf{p},\bar{U},\mathbf{r}) = [q_1(\mathbf{p},\bar{U},\mathbf{r}),\ldots,q_N(\mathbf{p},\bar{U},\mathbf{r})]$, and the associated compensated consumption functions, $\bar{\mathbf{c}}(\mathbf{p},\bar{m},\mathbf{r}) \equiv \bar{\mathbf{q}}(\mathbf{p},\bar{m},\mathbf{r}) + \mathbf{r}$. The expenditure function, which specifies the minimum amount of exogenous income necessary to attain utility level $\bar{U}$ with price vector $\mathbf{p}$ and endowment vector $\mathbf{r}$ can thus be represented as $\bar{e}(\mathbf{p},\bar{U},\mathbf{r}) = \mathbf{p}\bar{\mathbf{q}}(\mathbf{p},\bar{U},\mathbf{r}) = \mathbf{p}[\bar{\mathbf{c}}(\mathbf{p},\bar{U},\mathbf{r}) - \mathbf{r}]$.

By analogy with (6.27) and assuming no corner solutions, differentiation of $\bar{e}(\mathbf{p},\bar{U},\mathbf{r})$ with respect to the price vector yields compensated market demands (if positive) or supplies (if negative),[20]

$$\bar{e}_{\mathbf{p}} = \bar{\mathbf{q}}(\mathbf{p},\bar{U},\mathbf{r}) = \bar{\mathbf{c}}(\mathbf{p},\bar{U},\mathbf{r}) - \mathbf{r}$$

and

$$\bar{e}_{\mathbf{r}} = -\mathbf{p}.$$

Accordingly, the compensating variation of a general price–income–endowment change from $(\mathbf{p}^0,\bar{m}_0,\mathbf{r}^0)$ to $(\mathbf{p}^1,\bar{m}_1,\mathbf{r}^1)$ that changes utility from U^0 to U^1 is analogous to (7.32),

$$\begin{aligned} C &= \bar{m}_1 - \bar{e}(\mathbf{p}^1,U^0,\mathbf{r}^1) \\ &= \bar{m}_1 - \bar{m}_0 + \bar{e}(\mathbf{p}^0,U^0,\mathbf{r}^0) - \bar{e}(\mathbf{p}^1,U^0,\mathbf{r}^1) \\ &= \Delta\bar{m} - \int_{L_1} \sum_{j=1}^{N} \bar{e}_{r_j}(\mathbf{p}^0,U^0,\mathbf{r})dr_j - \int_{L_2} \sum_{j=1}^{N} \bar{e}_{p_j}(\mathbf{p},U^0,\mathbf{r}^1)dp_j \end{aligned}$$

18. Purchases and sales of consumer assets can be considered by generalizing the dynamic framework of Appendix Section 14.B to include resource endowments and sales where the sale of an asset eliminates all future service flows from the asset.
19. No upper limit on consumption is considered in this section to allow the individual to consume more than the endowed amount of goods other than time, for example, by purchasing an additional amount in the marketplace. If this is not possible (for example, if a market does not exist), then additional constraints similar to $l = -h + \tau \le \tau$ must be added where appropriate if an internal solution cannot be assumed.
20. These are envelope theorem results. Differentiation of $\bar{e}(\mathbf{p},\bar{U},\mathbf{r}) = \mathbf{p}\bar{\mathbf{q}}(\mathbf{p},\bar{U},\mathbf{r})$ with respect to $\mathbf{p}$ yields $\bar{e}_{\mathbf{p}} = \bar{\mathbf{q}}(\mathbf{p},\bar{U},\mathbf{r}) + \mathbf{p}\bar{\mathbf{q}}_{\mathbf{p}}$ where $\mathbf{p}\bar{\mathbf{q}}_{\mathbf{p}}$ is a vector with elements $\Sigma_{i=1}^{N} p_i \partial \bar{q}_i / \partial p_j, j = 1, \ldots, N$ (and similarly below). Assuming an internal solution, first-order conditions for the Lagrangian $\mathcal{L} = \mathbf{pq} - \theta[U(\mathbf{q}+\mathbf{r}) - \bar{U}]$ associated with the expenditure minimization problem require $\mathbf{p} = \theta U_{\mathbf{c}}$ so that $\mathbf{p}\bar{\mathbf{q}}_{\mathbf{p}} = \theta U_{\mathbf{c}}\bar{\mathbf{q}}_{\mathbf{p}}$ (where subscripts of U represent differentiation). But $U(\bar{\mathbf{q}}(\mathbf{p},\bar{U},\mathbf{r}) + \mathbf{r}) \equiv \bar{U}$ must hold as an identity according to the Lagrangian constraint so that its derivative with respect to $\mathbf{p}$ must be zero, that is, $U_{\mathbf{c}}\bar{\mathbf{q}}_{\mathbf{p}} = \mathbf{0}$, which proves $\bar{e}_{\mathbf{p}}, = \bar{\mathbf{q}}(\mathbf{p},\bar{U},\mathbf{r})$. Similarly, differentiation of the same identity with respect to $\mathbf{r}$ yields $U_{\mathbf{c}}\bar{\mathbf{q}}_{\mathbf{r}} + U_{\mathbf{c}} = 0$, which upon multiplying by θ and substituting first-order conditions implies $\mathbf{p}\bar{\mathbf{q}}_{\mathbf{r}} = -\mathbf{p}$. Thus, differentiation of $\bar{e}(\mathbf{p},\bar{U},\mathbf{r}) = \mathbf{p}\bar{\mathbf{q}}(\mathbf{p},\bar{U},\mathbf{r})$ with respect to $\mathbf{r}$ yields $\bar{e}_{\mathbf{r}} = \mathbf{p}\bar{\mathbf{q}}_{\mathbf{r}} = -\mathbf{p}$.

$$= \Delta \bar{m} + \boldsymbol{p}^0(\boldsymbol{r}^1 - \boldsymbol{r}^0) - \sum_{j=1}^{N} \int_{p_j^0}^{p_j^1} \bar{q}_j(\hat{\boldsymbol{p}}_j(p_j), U^0, \boldsymbol{r}^1) dp_j, \tag{7.43}$$

where

$$\hat{\boldsymbol{p}}_i(p_i) = (p_1^1, \ldots, p_{i-1}^1, p_i, p_{i+1}^0, \ldots, p_N^0),$$

and L_1 is any path from $\boldsymbol{r}^0$ to $\boldsymbol{r}^1$ holding $\boldsymbol{p}$ at $\boldsymbol{p}^0$ and L_2 is any path from $\boldsymbol{p}^0$ to $\boldsymbol{p}^1$ holding $\boldsymbol{r}$ at $\boldsymbol{r}^1$. These results show that the consumer-laborer problem generalizes in a straightforward fashion to consider sales of other factors with no further complications. The compensating variation of a general price change ($\boldsymbol{r}^0 = \boldsymbol{r}^1$) is found by adding to the change in exogenous income all the changes in areas left of compensated market supplies (where compensated supply functions are all evaluated at the initial utility level but successively conditioned on all previously considered price changes), plus all the changes in areas left of compensated market demands (where compensated demand functions are all evaluated at the initial utility level but successively conditioned on all previously considered price changes). Thus, the results in the general factor owner problem are a straightforward generalization of the results of the pure consumer problem (Appendix Section 6.A) and the consumer-laborer problem (Appendix Section 7.C).

More generally, if the consumer's endowments change ($\boldsymbol{r}^0 \neq \boldsymbol{r}^1$), then the change in exogenous income plus areas left of compensated supplies and demands can be conditioned on subsequent endowments and added to the change in endowment value evaluated at initial prices, $\boldsymbol{p}^0(\boldsymbol{r}^1 - \boldsymbol{r}^0)$. Alternatively and equivalently (not shown), the surplus changes can be conditioned on initial endowments if the change in endowment value is evaluated at subsequent prices, $\boldsymbol{p}^1(\boldsymbol{r}^1 - \boldsymbol{r}^0)$. To illustrate the importance in these calculations of evaluating the endowment value change at a given set of prices (for example, initial or subsequent prices) versus representing the endowment value change considering the change in prices, $\boldsymbol{p}^1\boldsymbol{r}^1 - \boldsymbol{p}^0\boldsymbol{r}^0$, substitute $\bar{\boldsymbol{q}}(\boldsymbol{p}, \bar{U}, \boldsymbol{r}) = \bar{\boldsymbol{c}}(\boldsymbol{p}, \bar{U}, \boldsymbol{r}) - \boldsymbol{r}$ into equation (7.43) to find

$$C = \Delta \bar{m} + \boldsymbol{p}^0(\boldsymbol{r}^1 - \boldsymbol{r}^0) - \sum_{j=1}^{N} \int_{p_j^0}^{p_j^1} [\bar{c}_j(\hat{\boldsymbol{p}}_j(p_j), U^0, \boldsymbol{r}^1) - r_j^1] dp_j$$

$$= \Delta \bar{m} + \boldsymbol{p}^1\boldsymbol{r}^1 - \boldsymbol{p}^0\boldsymbol{r}^0 - \sum_{j=1}^{N} \int_{p_j^0}^{p_j^1} \bar{c}_j(\hat{\boldsymbol{p}}_j(p_j), U^0, \boldsymbol{r}^1) dp_j$$

$$= \Delta m^* - \sum_{j=1}^{N} \int_{p_j^0}^{p_j^1} \bar{c}_j(\hat{\boldsymbol{p}}_j(p_j), U^0, \boldsymbol{r}^1) dp_j.$$

From this result, the correct surplus changes to add to the change in full income (which is the change in exogenous income plus the endowment value change considering changes in both endowments and prices) are not the surplus areas associated with compensated market supplies and demands, but rather the surplus areas associated with compensated consumption demands. The consumption demands, $\bar{\boldsymbol{c}}(\boldsymbol{p}, \bar{U}, \boldsymbol{r})$, differ from market transactions, $\bar{\boldsymbol{q}}(\boldsymbol{p}, \bar{U}, \boldsymbol{r})$, by the amount of endowments, and are nonnegative for all goods. Typically, consumption quantities are not directly observable (although they may be calculated from market transactions if data on endowments are available). Thus, a formulation based on market transactions is preferable for some welfare applications. And, in any case, one must be careful when using a full income approach to properly distinguish consumption demands from market demands in utilizing surplus areas to evaluate welfare. The two coincide only for goods of which the consumer holds no endowments.

With this caveat that applies only when endowments change, all of the additional results obtained for the pure consumer and consumer-laborer problems generalize. For example, the equivalent variation, $E=\bar{e}(\mathbf{p}^0,U^1,\mathbf{r}^0)-\bar{m}_0=\bar{e}(\mathbf{p}^0,U^1,\mathbf{r}^0)-\bar{e}(\mathbf{p}^1,U^1,\mathbf{r}^1)+\bar{m}_1-\bar{m}_0$, can be calculated similarly by replacing U^0 with U^1 in the conditions that define compensated supplies and demands. Also, Marshallian surpluses associated with the consumer's ordinary market supplies and demands serve as approximations of the surpluses associated with compensated market supplies and demands. Accordingly, error bounds on Marshallian surplus measures as a measure of compensating and equivalent variation in the single-price-change case are analogous to (7.36) and (7.37), respectively, and modified estimates such as in (7.40) and (7.41) possess the improved error bounds in (7.38) and (7.39).

Furthermore, whether or not factors besides labor are sold, the Willig results can also be extended to the multiple-price-change case. Suppose that the price vector changes from $\mathbf{p}^0=(p_1^0,\ldots,p_N^0)$ to $\mathbf{p}^1=(p_1^1,\ldots,p_N^1)$ and the resulting utility level changes from U^0 to U^1. For notational purposes, let

$$\Delta S_i=-\int_{p_i^0}^{p_i^1}\tilde{q}_i(\hat{\mathbf{p}}_i(p_i),\bar{m}_0,\mathbf{r})dp_i,$$

where, for simplicity, $\bar{m}_0=\bar{m}_1$ and $\mathbf{r}^0=\mathbf{r}^1$.[21] Finally, define $\bar{\eta}_1$ and $\bar{\eta}_2$ as the minimum and maximum exogenous income elasticities over all goods for which prices change, that is,

$$\bar{\eta}_1=\min\left\{\frac{\partial\tilde{q}_i}{\partial\bar{m}}\frac{\bar{m}}{\tilde{q}_i}\,\middle|\,\mathbf{p}\in\{\hat{\mathbf{p}}_i(p_i^0),\hat{\mathbf{p}}_i(p_i^1)\},\ \bar{m}=\bar{m}_0,\ i=1\ \ldots,N\right\}, \tag{7.44}$$

and

$$\bar{\eta}_2=\max\left\{\frac{\partial\tilde{q}_i}{\partial\bar{m}}\frac{\bar{m}}{\tilde{q}_i}\,\middle|\,\mathbf{p}\in\{\hat{\mathbf{p}}_i(p_i^0),\hat{\mathbf{p}}_i(p_i^1)\},\ \bar{m}=\bar{m}_0,\ i=1\ \ldots,N\right\}, \tag{7.45}$$

Using the definitions in (7.44) and (7.45), one can follow the derivation of (6.56) through (6.59), where η_i is replaced by $\bar{\eta}_i$ and m is replaced by $\bar{m}$ to obtain

$$\bar{\varepsilon}_2^c\geq\frac{\sum_{i=1}^{N}\Delta S_i-C}{\left|\sum_{i=1}^{N}\Delta S_i\right|}\geq\bar{\varepsilon}_1^c \tag{7.46}$$

and

$$\bar{\varepsilon}_2^e\geq\frac{E-\sum_{i=1}^{N}\Delta S_i}{\left|\sum_{i=1}^{N}\Delta S_i\right|}\geq\bar{\varepsilon}_1^e. \tag{7.47}$$

21. The approach of equation (7.43) to calculating compensating or equivalent variation is exact for evaluating a general change in endowments. Thus, the accuracy of approximations of compensating or equivalent variation by means of Marshallian surpluses need only be considered in the case of price changes.

These results also suggest the modified estimates of compensating and equivalent variation given by

$$\hat{C} = \sum_{i=1}^{N} \Delta S_i - \hat{\varepsilon} \left| \sum_{i=1}^{N} \Delta S_i \right| \tag{7.48}$$

and

$$\hat{E} = \sum_{i=1}^{N} \Delta S_i + \hat{\varepsilon} \left| \sum_{i=1}^{N} \Delta S_i \right|, \tag{7.49}$$

where $\hat{\varepsilon}$ is defined as in (7.42) with $\bar{s} = \Sigma_{i=1}^{N} \Delta S_i / \bar{m}$ and, similarly, the tighter error bounds in (7.38) and (7.39) continue to hold where ΔS_i is replaced by $\Sigma_{i=1}^{N} \Delta S_i$.

Unlike the earlier cases, however, the bounds in (7.46) and (7.47) or even the tighter bounds associated with $\hat{C}$ in (7.48) and $\hat{E}$ in (7.49) are not as satisfactory, as indicated by the Willig results discussed in Appendix Section 6.B. That is, in the case where factors are sold and consumer goods are purchased, the variation in income elasticities among commodities is likely to be much greater. For example, the exogenous income elasticity of labor may be zero (no less labor would be supplied with an increase in exogenous income), whereas the exogenous income elasticity for luxury consumer goods would be positive and greater than 1. Hence, if both wage and luxury-good prices change, then $\bar{\eta}_1 = 0$, $\bar{\eta}_2 > 1$,and the error bounds could become quite wide, as demonstrated by Table 6.1, unless the ratio of surplus change to exogenous income $\bar{s}$ is small.

Alternatively, however, reasonable error bounds can be developed according to the derivation in (6.60) through (6.64) as long as variation of income elasticities for individual commodities is not great in the range of wage–price–income considerations. In conclusion, one may reiterate the final paragraph of Appendix Section 6.B, with the minor modification that all references to income must be replaced with references to exogenous income. For example, if an investigator is willing to accept up to about a 5 percent error, then the surplus measure can be used without modification if $|\bar{\eta}\bar{s}/2| \leq 0.05$ for all goods with changing price where $\bar{\eta} = \max\ \{|\bar{\eta}_1|, |\bar{\eta}_2|\}$. One can avoid more than about a 2 percent error by using the modified estimates in (7.48) and (7.49) if $|\bar{\eta}\bar{s}/2| \leq 0.08$ for all goods with changing price, and exogenous income elasticities with respect to individual commodities vary by less than 50 percent.

Finally, consider comparison of the Willig results where all income is treated as exogenous with the more realistic case where factor sales and consumption decisions are determined simultaneously. Compared with the results in Appendix Section 6.B, the validity limits on $\bar{\eta}\bar{s}$ in this case correspond exactly to those on ηs in the pure consumer case for the same approximate validity, that is, $|\eta s| \leq 0.1$ is equivalent to $|\bar{\eta}\bar{s}| \leq 0.1$. In this context it is interesting to note that

$$\eta s = \left. \frac{\partial \tilde{q}_j}{\partial m} \frac{m}{\tilde{q}_j} \right|_{\mathbf{p} = \mathbf{p}^*, \bar{m} = \bar{m}_0, \mathbf{r} = \mathbf{r}^0} \left[\frac{\sum_{i=1}^{N} \Delta S_i}{m} \right]$$

$$= \left. \frac{\partial \tilde{q}_j}{\partial m} \frac{\bar{m}}{\tilde{q}_j} \right|_{\mathbf{p} = \mathbf{p}^*, \bar{m} = \bar{m}_0, \mathbf{r} = \mathbf{r}^0} \left[\frac{\sum_{i=1}^{N} \Delta S_i}{\bar{m}} \right], \tag{7.50}$$

where $\boldsymbol{p}^*$ is the price vector for which the maximum is reached in (7.44) if $\bar{\eta}=|\bar{\eta}_1|$ or in (7.45) if $\bar{\eta}=|\bar{\eta}_2|$. Hence, $\eta s=\bar{\eta}\bar{s}$ from (7.50) in the special case where the marginal effect of ordinary income on $\tilde{q}_j$ is the same as the marginal effect of exogenous income on $\tilde{q}_j$ (that is $\partial\tilde{q}_j/\partial m=\partial\tilde{q}_j/\partial\bar{m}$), so that the requirements for approximate application of surplus measures according to Willig's methods in Appendix Section 6.B are valid regardless of whether factor supply decisions are interdependent with consumer demand decisions.

7.G BENEFIT MEASUREMENT WITH HOUSEHOLD PRODUCTION

A common problem encountered in benefit measurement is the case where some change other than the price of a good in an observable market affects the economic well-being of a consumer or factor owner. Examples include prices of goods in unobservable markets, the amount of public goods such as highways or public recreation facilities provided by government, environmental amenities that affect market behavior, and apparent changes in tastes and preferences represented by shifts in demands. Such problems motivate the need to measure changes in welfare indirectly on the basis of behavior in observable markets. In the general case of a change in tastes and preferences, little may be said about the comparison of economic welfare before and after the change because cardinal utility cannot be measured. However, with relatively plausible assumptions, economic welfare analysis is possible. This section considers the case of unobservable prices for goods produced and consumed at home by the household. Further possibilities for indirect measurement of both price and nonprice changes are considered in Appendix Section 7.I. The framework of this section is also extended later in the Appendix to Chapter 11 to provide a way of studying the welfare effects of apparent changes in tastes and preferences for market goods when more basic underlying tastes and preferences are fixed but changes occur that affect the ability of a household to turn consumption into the goods valued by underlying tastes and preferences. Dependence of household production on environmental quality is discussed in Chapter 13.

In many cases, consumers or households do not simply consume factors directly as in the case of time (leisure) but utilize factors for home production of other commodities. For example, fertilizer and grass seed is purchased and combined with time to produce a lawn. Fuel is purchased to produce heat. In such cases, households may purchase factors that do not yield utility directly but are combined to produce commodity service flows that contribute to consumer utility. This phenomenon is represented in the household production model developed by Becker (1965) and Lancaster (1966).[22] The household production model has become popular for analysis of peasant behavior in developing countries, where households are both producers and consumers, and for analysis of environmental problems, where environmental characteristics affect a household's ability to produce 'enjoyment' from recreational activities or health of the family.

The household production model presents some unusual problems for welfare measurement because the quantities of commodity service flows produced and consumed at home are not generally observable nor are the implicit prices households must pay for

22. See also Becker and Michael (1973), Stigler and Becker (1977) and Nichols (1985).

their consumption. In general, the implicit prices of home-produced commodities depend on both the preferences and technology of the household.[23] As a result, Marshallian demands for home-produced commodities are not uniquely defined. Nevertheless, comprehensive benefit measurement for households is possible based on observations of market good transactions following results developed by Bockstael and McConnell (1983).

To consider these possibilities, suppose that the household possesses a household production technology, $\mathbf{t}(\mathbf{y},\mathbf{x})=\mathbf{0}$, consisting of relationships that are continuous, decreasing in $\mathbf{y}$, increasing in $\mathbf{x}$ and concave in $\mathbf{y}$ and $\mathbf{x}$ where $\mathbf{y}=(y_1,\ldots,y_K)$ is an unobservable vector of quantities of K nonmarket goods that are both produced and consumed at home, and $\mathbf{x}=(x_1,\ldots,x_N)$ is a vector of quantities of the N market goods where positive quantities ($x_i>0$) represent factor input use for home production and negative amounts ($x_i<0$) represent home production.[24] Suppose further that the household has a utility function $U(\mathbf{y}, \mathbf{c})$ that is monotonically increasing, quasiconcave, and twice differentiable in both $\mathbf{y}$ and $\mathbf{c}$ where $\mathbf{y}$ represents consumption of nonmarket goods (nonmarket goods are produced exclusively for home consumption) and $\mathbf{c}$ represents consumption of market goods. The key distinction between $\mathbf{y}$ and $\mathbf{x}$ and between $\mathbf{y}$ and $\mathbf{c}$ is that $\mathbf{y}$ represents distinctly different goods for which markets do not exist. Vectors $\mathbf{x}$ and $\mathbf{c}$ represent different quantities of the same market goods where the key distinction is that quantities in $\mathbf{c}$ are consumed directly by the household whereas the quantities in $\mathbf{x}$ are used as inputs or produced as outputs in household production. The vector of market demands (supplies if negative) is $\mathbf{q}=\mathbf{c}+\mathbf{x}-\mathbf{r}$ where $\mathbf{r}$ represents factor endowments as in Appendix Section 7.F.

This specification of the household production problem is general enough to represent all cases of household production for either home consumption or market sales as well as the factor sales considerations discussed earlier in this appendix. For example, the household technology may embody relationships such as $f(x_j,x_k)-y_i=0$ where two factors x_j and x_k are combined using a particular household production function $f(x_j,x_k)>0$ to produce quantity $y_i>0$ that is consumed at home. The case where a good is produced at home for sale is represented by $f(x_i,x_j)+x_k=0$ where $f(x_i,x_j)>0$ and thus $x_k<0$ representing production of x_k. Partial home consumption and partial sale can be represented by $f(x_i,x_j)+x_k=0$ where $x_k<0$, $q_k<0$, $c_k>0$ and $r_k=0$ in the net market demand equation, $\mathbf{q}=\mathbf{c}+\mathbf{x}-\mathbf{r}$. The household utilizes part of the household's endowment as a factor in home production if $x_k<r_k$ or all of the household's endowment if $x_k=r_k$, but must purchase some additional amount of the factor beyond its endowment if $x_k>r_k$. If $x_k<r_k$, then the household is assumed to derive income by selling the unused endowment at market prices.

23. Pollak and Wachter (1975) show that this is the case with either jointness or nonconstant returns to scale in household production.
24. A technology representation such as $\mathbf{y}=\mathbf{f}(\mathbf{x})$ similar to the producer case of Appendix Section 4.A could be used in place of $\mathbf{t}(\mathbf{y},\mathbf{x})=\mathbf{0}$ if the household produces no market goods. Otherwise, the $\mathbf{x}$ vector must be partitioned into an input vector $\mathbf{x}^i>0$ consisting of market goods used as factor inputs in household production, and an output vector $\mathbf{x}^o<0$ consisting of market goods produced by the household, $\mathbf{x}=(\mathbf{x}^o,\mathbf{x}^i)$, in which case the household technology can be represented by $(\mathbf{y}, -\mathbf{x}^o)=\mathbf{f}(\mathbf{x}^i)$, which is a special case of $\mathbf{t}(\mathbf{y},\mathbf{x})=\mathbf{0}$ where $(\mathbf{y},-\mathbf{x}^o)$ is a vector of outputs. Alternatively and more generally, the household production technology can be represented simply by $(\mathbf{y},\mathbf{x})\in T$, where T is a closed convex technology set. The results below can be generalized accordingly. In either case, the technology specification can be allowed to depend implicitly on durable or capital assets owned by the household.

Maximization of utility subject to both the budget constraint, $\boldsymbol{p}(\boldsymbol{c}+\boldsymbol{x}-\boldsymbol{r})=\bar{m}$, and the household production technology yields the indirect utility function,

$$V(\boldsymbol{p},\bar{m},\boldsymbol{r})\equiv U(\tilde{\boldsymbol{y}},\tilde{\boldsymbol{c}})\equiv \max_{\boldsymbol{c},\boldsymbol{x},\boldsymbol{y}}\{U(\boldsymbol{y},\boldsymbol{c})\,|\,\boldsymbol{pq}=\bar{m},\ \boldsymbol{t}(\boldsymbol{y},\boldsymbol{x})=\boldsymbol{0},\ \boldsymbol{c}=\boldsymbol{q}-\boldsymbol{x}+\boldsymbol{r}\geq\boldsymbol{0}\ \boldsymbol{y}\geq\boldsymbol{0},\},$$

where the associated utility-maximizing decision equations are represented by

$$\begin{aligned}\boldsymbol{c}&=\tilde{\boldsymbol{c}}(\boldsymbol{p},\bar{m},\boldsymbol{r}),\\ \boldsymbol{x}&=\tilde{\boldsymbol{x}}(\boldsymbol{p},\bar{m},\boldsymbol{r}),\\ \boldsymbol{y}&=\tilde{\boldsymbol{y}}(\boldsymbol{p},\bar{m},\boldsymbol{r}).\end{aligned} \tag{7.51}$$

Market demands (supplies if negative) are then defined by $\tilde{\boldsymbol{q}}(\boldsymbol{p},\bar{m},\boldsymbol{r})=\tilde{\boldsymbol{c}}(\boldsymbol{p},\bar{m},\boldsymbol{r})+\tilde{\boldsymbol{x}}(\boldsymbol{p},\bar{m},\boldsymbol{r})-\boldsymbol{r}$.[25]

Note that the relationship in (7.51) does not represent ordinary Marshallian demands for consumption of home-produced commodities because $\boldsymbol{y}$ is not a function of prices or implicit costs to the household of the nonmarket commodities included in $\boldsymbol{y}$. Rather, $\boldsymbol{y}$ is a function of the prices of market goods used to produce those commodities.[26] Fortunately, ordinary demands for nonmarket commodities are not necessary for household economic welfare analysis. Crucial duality results remain intact with respect to market transactions. For example, the Roy identity holds for market transactions,

$$-\frac{V_{\boldsymbol{p}}}{V_{\bar{m}}}=\tilde{\boldsymbol{q}} \tag{7.52}$$

(where subscripts of V denote differentiation, for example, $V_{\boldsymbol{p}}=\partial V/\partial\boldsymbol{p}$) and additionally[27]

$$-\frac{V_{\boldsymbol{r}}}{V_{\bar{m}}}=\boldsymbol{p}.$$

25. If some goods are used only as factors of home production (are not consumed) or are produced at home only for sale (not for home consumption) while other goods are consumed and not involved as factors or outputs in home production, then the $\boldsymbol{c}$ and $\boldsymbol{x}$ vectors can be characterized as representing distinct groups of goods. Alternatively, a more efficient notation is used here by letting $x_i\equiv 0$ for goods that are not used as factors, produced as outputs, or owned as endowments and $c_i\equiv 0$ for goods that are not consumed. Thus, the same price vector applies to each of $\boldsymbol{c}$, $\boldsymbol{x}$, $\boldsymbol{r}$, and $\boldsymbol{q}$.
26. Pollak and Wachter (1977) are credited with the suggestion that demands for household commodities can be modeled as a function of the prices of market goods.
27. To see this for the case of an internal solution, note that maximization of utility subject to the budget and household production technology constraints corresponds, after substitution for $\boldsymbol{c}$, to maximization of the Lagrangian $U(\boldsymbol{y},\boldsymbol{q}-\boldsymbol{x}+\boldsymbol{r})-\lambda(\boldsymbol{pq}-\bar{m})-\boldsymbol{\mu}\,\boldsymbol{t}(\boldsymbol{y},\boldsymbol{x})$ with respect to $\boldsymbol{q}$, $\boldsymbol{x}$, and $\boldsymbol{y}$, which yields first-order conditions $U_{\boldsymbol{q}}=\lambda\boldsymbol{p}$, $U_{\boldsymbol{q}}=-\boldsymbol{\mu}\boldsymbol{t}_{\boldsymbol{x}}$, and $U_{\boldsymbol{y}}=\boldsymbol{\mu}\boldsymbol{t}_{\boldsymbol{y}}$. Differentiation of the identity, $V(\boldsymbol{p},\bar{m},\boldsymbol{r})\equiv U(\tilde{\boldsymbol{y}},\tilde{\boldsymbol{q}}-\tilde{\boldsymbol{x}}+\boldsymbol{r})$ with respect to $z=(p_i,\bar{m})$ and substituting first-order conditions obtains

$$V_z=U_{\boldsymbol{y}}\frac{\partial\tilde{\boldsymbol{y}}}{\partial z}+U_{\boldsymbol{q}}\left[\frac{\partial\tilde{\boldsymbol{q}}}{\partial z}-\frac{\partial\tilde{\boldsymbol{x}}}{\partial z}\right]=\boldsymbol{\mu}\left[\boldsymbol{t}_{\boldsymbol{y}}\frac{\partial\tilde{\boldsymbol{y}}}{\partial z}+\boldsymbol{t}_{\boldsymbol{x}}\frac{\partial\tilde{\boldsymbol{x}}}{\partial z}\right]+\lambda\boldsymbol{p}\frac{\partial\tilde{\boldsymbol{q}}}{\partial z}.$$

Differentiation of the production technology constraint, $\boldsymbol{t}(\tilde{\boldsymbol{y}},\tilde{\boldsymbol{x}})=0$, with respect to $z=(p_i,\bar{m})$ yields

$$\boldsymbol{t}_{\boldsymbol{y}}\frac{\partial\tilde{\boldsymbol{y}}}{\partial z}+\boldsymbol{t}_{\boldsymbol{x}}\frac{\partial\tilde{\boldsymbol{x}}}{\partial z}=0,$$

which upon substitution in V_z reveals $V_z=\lambda\boldsymbol{p}\,\partial\tilde{\boldsymbol{q}}/\partial z$. Finally, differentiating the budget constraint, $\bar{m}=\boldsymbol{p}\tilde{\boldsymbol{q}}$, with respect to $z=(p_i,\bar{m})$ obtains $\tilde{q}_i+\boldsymbol{p}\partial\tilde{\boldsymbol{q}}/\partial p_i=0$ and $\boldsymbol{p}\partial\tilde{\boldsymbol{q}}/\partial\bar{m}=1$. The Roy identity follows immediately upon substitution of these results into $-V_{\boldsymbol{p}}/V_{\bar{m}}$. Similarly, letting $z=\boldsymbol{r}$ in this derivation reveals that $V_{\boldsymbol{r}}=\lambda\boldsymbol{p}$ and, as usual, substitution of $\boldsymbol{p}\partial\tilde{\boldsymbol{q}}/\partial\bar{m}=1$ into $V_{\bar{m}}$ obtains $V_{\bar{m}}=\lambda$.

Thus, the change in utility associated with a general price–income–endowment change from $(\boldsymbol{p}^0,\bar{m}^0,\boldsymbol{r}^0)$ to $(\boldsymbol{p}^1,\bar{m}^1,\boldsymbol{r}^1)$ can be represented as a line integral,

$$\Delta U = \int_L [V_{\bar{m}} d\bar{m} + \boldsymbol{V}_r d\boldsymbol{r} + \boldsymbol{V}_p d\boldsymbol{p}]$$
$$= \int_L \lambda[d\bar{m} + \boldsymbol{p}d\boldsymbol{r} - \tilde{\boldsymbol{q}}d\boldsymbol{p}].$$

Omitting λ from this expression as in (7.24) corresponds in the latter term to calculating the change in ordinary Marshallian surplus associated with market demands and supplies, which has the same path-dependence problems as do the price changes in equation (5.7).

Alternatively, willingness-to-pay calculations are facilitated by defining an expenditure function that minimizes the expenditure necessary to reach a required utility level using the household production technology,

$$\bar{e}(\boldsymbol{p},\bar{U},\boldsymbol{r}) = \min_{\boldsymbol{q},\boldsymbol{x},\boldsymbol{y}} \{\boldsymbol{pq} \mid U(\boldsymbol{y},\boldsymbol{c}) = \bar{U},\ \boldsymbol{t}(\boldsymbol{y},\boldsymbol{x}) = \boldsymbol{0},\ \boldsymbol{c} = \boldsymbol{q} - \boldsymbol{x} + \boldsymbol{r} \geq 0,\ \boldsymbol{y} \geq \boldsymbol{0}\}. \quad (7.53)$$

The solution of (7.53) yields Hicksian compensated decision functions $\bar{\boldsymbol{q}}(\boldsymbol{p},\bar{U},\boldsymbol{r})$, $\bar{\boldsymbol{x}}(\boldsymbol{p},\bar{U},\boldsymbol{r})$, and $\bar{\boldsymbol{y}}(\boldsymbol{p},\bar{U},\boldsymbol{r})$ where $\bar{\boldsymbol{q}}(\boldsymbol{p},\bar{U},\boldsymbol{r})$ represents compensated *market demands* (if positive) *and supplies* (if negative) of market goods, $\bar{\boldsymbol{x}}(\boldsymbol{p},\bar{U},\boldsymbol{r})$ represents compensated home production output supplies (if positive) and input demands (if negative) of market goods, $\bar{\boldsymbol{y}}(\boldsymbol{p},\bar{U},\boldsymbol{r})$ represents demands for nonmarket goods, and $\bar{\boldsymbol{c}}(\boldsymbol{p},\bar{U},\boldsymbol{r}) \equiv \bar{\boldsymbol{q}}(\boldsymbol{p},\bar{U},\boldsymbol{r}) - \bar{\boldsymbol{x}}(\boldsymbol{p},\bar{U},\boldsymbol{r}) + \boldsymbol{r}$ represents compensated *consumption demands* for market goods.

By analogy with (7.31) and assuming no corner solutions, differentiation of $\bar{e}(\boldsymbol{p},\bar{U},\boldsymbol{r})$ in (7.53) with respect to the price vector yields net compensated market demands (if positive) or supplies (if negative),[28]

$$\bar{e}_p = \bar{\boldsymbol{q}}(\boldsymbol{p},\bar{U},\boldsymbol{r})$$

and

$$\bar{e}_r = -\boldsymbol{p}.$$

Accordingly, the compensating variation of a general price–income–endowment change from $(\boldsymbol{p}^0,\bar{m}_0,\boldsymbol{r}^0)$ to $(\boldsymbol{p}^1,\bar{m}_1,\boldsymbol{r}^1)$ that changes utility from U^0 to U^1 is analogous to (7.32),

28. These are again envelope theorem results. Differentiation of $\bar{e}(\boldsymbol{p},\bar{U},\boldsymbol{r}) = \boldsymbol{p}\bar{\boldsymbol{q}}(\boldsymbol{p},\bar{U},\boldsymbol{r})$ with respect to $\boldsymbol{p}$ yields $\bar{e}_p = \bar{\boldsymbol{q}}(\boldsymbol{p},\bar{U},\boldsymbol{r}) + \boldsymbol{p}\bar{\boldsymbol{q}}_p$ where notation follows footnote 20. Assuming an internal solution, first-order conditions for the Lagrangian $\mathcal{L} = \boldsymbol{pq} - \theta[U(\boldsymbol{y},\boldsymbol{q}-\boldsymbol{x}+\boldsymbol{r}) - \bar{U}] - \boldsymbol{\mu t}(\boldsymbol{y},\boldsymbol{x})$ associated with the expenditure-minimization problem require $\boldsymbol{p} = \theta \boldsymbol{U}_c$, $\theta \boldsymbol{U}_c = \boldsymbol{\mu t}_x$, and $\theta \boldsymbol{U}_y = -\boldsymbol{\mu t}_y$ (where subscripts of both U and t represent differentiation). Because $\boldsymbol{t}(\bar{\boldsymbol{y}}(\boldsymbol{p},\bar{U},\boldsymbol{r}),\bar{\boldsymbol{x}}(\boldsymbol{p},\bar{U},\boldsymbol{r})) \equiv \boldsymbol{0}$ holds as an identity according to the second Lagrangian constraint, differentiation with respect to $\boldsymbol{p}$ yields $\boldsymbol{t}_y\bar{\boldsymbol{y}}_p + \boldsymbol{t}_x\bar{\boldsymbol{x}}_p = \boldsymbol{0}$, which upon multiplying by $\boldsymbol{\mu}/\theta$ and substituting the latter two first-order conditions implies $\boldsymbol{U}_c\bar{\boldsymbol{x}}_p = \boldsymbol{U}_y\bar{\boldsymbol{y}}_p$. Similarly, because $U(\bar{\boldsymbol{y}},\bar{\boldsymbol{q}}(\boldsymbol{p},\bar{U},\boldsymbol{r}) - \bar{\boldsymbol{x}}(\boldsymbol{p},\bar{U},\boldsymbol{r}) + \boldsymbol{r}) \equiv \bar{U}$ holds as an identity according to the first Lagrangian constraint, differentiation with respect to $\boldsymbol{p}$ yields $\boldsymbol{U}_c\bar{\boldsymbol{q}}_p - \boldsymbol{U}_c\bar{\boldsymbol{x}}_p + \boldsymbol{U}_y\bar{\boldsymbol{y}}_p = \boldsymbol{U}_c\bar{\boldsymbol{q}}_p = \boldsymbol{0}$. Using this result, the first first-order condition implies $\boldsymbol{p}\bar{\boldsymbol{q}}_p = \theta\boldsymbol{U}_c\bar{\boldsymbol{q}}_p = \boldsymbol{0}$, which proves $\bar{e}_p = \bar{\boldsymbol{q}}(\boldsymbol{p},\bar{U},\boldsymbol{r})$. To prove that $\bar{e}_r = -\boldsymbol{p}$, differentiate the latter identity with respect to $\boldsymbol{r}$ to find $\boldsymbol{U}_c\bar{\boldsymbol{q}}_r - \boldsymbol{U}_c\bar{\boldsymbol{x}}_r + \boldsymbol{U}_y\bar{\boldsymbol{y}}_r + \boldsymbol{U}_c = \boldsymbol{0}$. Differentiation of the former identity yields $\boldsymbol{t}_y\bar{\boldsymbol{y}}_r + \boldsymbol{t}_x\bar{\boldsymbol{x}}_r = \boldsymbol{0}$, which upon substituting the latter two first-order conditions shows that $\boldsymbol{U}_c\bar{\boldsymbol{x}}_r = \boldsymbol{U}_y\bar{\boldsymbol{y}}_r$. Thus, $\boldsymbol{U}_c\bar{\boldsymbol{q}}_r + \boldsymbol{U}_c = \boldsymbol{0}$, which implies $\bar{e}_r = -\boldsymbol{p}$ as in footnote 20.

$$\begin{aligned} C &= \bar{m}_1 - \bar{e}(\boldsymbol{p}^1, U^0, \boldsymbol{r}^1) \\ &= \bar{m}_1 - \bar{m}_0 + \bar{e}(\boldsymbol{p}^0, U^0, \boldsymbol{r}^0) - \bar{e}(\boldsymbol{p}^1, U^0, \boldsymbol{r}^1) \\ &= \Delta\bar{m} - \int_{L_1} \sum_{j=1}^{N} \bar{e}_{r_j}(\boldsymbol{p}^0, U^0, \boldsymbol{r}) dr_j - \int_{L_2} \sum_{j=1}^{N} \bar{e}_{p_j}(\boldsymbol{p}, U^0, \boldsymbol{r}^1) dp_j \\ &= \Delta\bar{m} + \boldsymbol{p}^0(\boldsymbol{r}^1 - \boldsymbol{r}^0) - \sum_{j=1}^{N} \int_{p_j^0}^{p_j^1} \bar{q}_j(\hat{\boldsymbol{p}}_j(p_j), U^0, \boldsymbol{r}^1) dp_j, \end{aligned} \tag{7.54}$$

where L_1 is any path from $\boldsymbol{r}^0$ to $\boldsymbol{r}^1$ holding $\boldsymbol{p}$ at $\boldsymbol{p}^0$ and L_2 is any path from $\boldsymbol{p}^0$ to $\boldsymbol{p}^1$ holding $\boldsymbol{r}$ at $\boldsymbol{r}^1$. The equivalent variation is calculated similarly after replacing U^0 with U^1. As in the calculation in Appendix Section 7.F, the same result is obtained by considering all price changes first and then all endowment changes.

Alternatively, by substituting $\bar{\boldsymbol{q}}(\boldsymbol{p}, \bar{U}, \boldsymbol{r}) \equiv \bar{\boldsymbol{c}}(\boldsymbol{p}, \bar{U}, \boldsymbol{r}) + \bar{\boldsymbol{x}}(\boldsymbol{p}, \bar{U}, \boldsymbol{r}) - \boldsymbol{r}$ in the latter expression, the proper approach for calculating compensating variation based on the change in full income is

$$\begin{aligned} C &= \Delta\bar{m} + \boldsymbol{p}^1\boldsymbol{r}^1 + \boldsymbol{p}^0\boldsymbol{r}^0 - \sum_{j=1}^{N} \int_{p_j^0}^{p_j^1} \bar{c}_j(\hat{\boldsymbol{p}}_j(p_j), U^0, \boldsymbol{r}^1) dp_j - \sum_{j=1}^{N} \int_{p_j^0}^{p_j^1} \bar{x}_j(\hat{\boldsymbol{p}}_j(p_j), U^0, \boldsymbol{r}^1) dp_j \\ &= \Delta m^* - \sum_{j=1}^{N} \int_{p_j^0}^{p_j^1} \bar{c}_j(\hat{\boldsymbol{p}}_j(p_j), U^0, \boldsymbol{r}^1) dp_j - \sum_{j=1}^{N} \int_{p_j^0}^{p_j^1} \bar{x}_j(\hat{\boldsymbol{p}}_j(p_j), U^0, \boldsymbol{r}^1) dp_j. \end{aligned}$$

From this result, the correct surplus changes to add to the change in full income (the change in exogenous income plus the endowment value change considering changes in both endowments and prices) are not the surplus areas associated with compensated market supplies and demands, but rather the surplus areas associated with compensated consumption demands plus the surpluses associated with market transactions related to household production (inputs and outputs). The sum of these two differ from market transactions, $\bar{\boldsymbol{q}}(\boldsymbol{p}, \bar{U}, \boldsymbol{r})$, by the amount of endowments. Again, the approach based on market transactions better fits typical data availability. That is, available data generally do not distinguish whether consumers use purchased goods to facilitate consumption of market goods or household production of market and nonmarket goods, nor do observed data generally distinguish whether items sold by consumers are production factors owned by the consumer or home-produced goods.

The important result of this section is that the practical implementation of the household production problem is equivalent to the general resource owner problem in Appendix Section 7.F for empirical purposes. That is, the empirical calculations set forth in equation (7.54) are identical to equation (7.43). Thus, distinction of the vectors $\bar{\boldsymbol{c}}$ and $\bar{\boldsymbol{x}}$ is not necessary for practical purpose whereas combining them with $\boldsymbol{r}$ in $\bar{\boldsymbol{q}}$ for empirical purposes makes the analysis of this section equivalent to Appendix Section 7.F. Accordingly, the change in Marshallian surplus associated with market demands and supplies of the consumer, after adding the change in exogenous income and endowment valuations (valued appropriately at a given set of prices), approximates the compensating and equivalent variation. Error bounds analogous to (7.36) and (7.37) apply while modified estimates such as in (7.40) and (7.41) possess the improved error bounds in (7.38) and (7.39). In each individual market, the ordinary surplus change is bounded by compensating and equivalent variations but the direction of inequalities depends on the income elasticity of the ordinary demand or supply relationship. However, the ordinary surplus change may not be bounded by the compensating and equivalent variations for an overall price–income–endowment change.

To understand better why welfare measurement with household production yields results identical to the case where a consumer/factor-owner simply has a utility function defined on factor and consumption decisions, suppose the technology specification, $\mathbf{t}(\mathbf{y},\mathbf{x}) = \mathbf{0}$, can be solved uniquely for $\mathbf{y}$ obtaining $\mathbf{y}=\mathbf{f}(\mathbf{x})$ where $\mathbf{f}(\mathbf{x})$ is nonnegative, increasing, concave and twice differentiable in all elements of $\mathbf{x}$ on which it depends, where $\mathbf{x}$ includes market goods used as inputs in household production positively and those sold as outputs from household production negatively. A special case is where the household does not produce market goods so that $\mathbf{x}$ is a vector consisting entirely of inputs used to produce nonmarket goods.[29] Then the household's utility maximization problem is

$$\max_{\mathbf{c},\mathbf{x},\mathbf{y}} \{ U(\mathbf{y},\mathbf{c}) \,|\, \mathbf{p}(\mathbf{c}+\mathbf{x}-\mathbf{r}) = \bar{m},\ \mathbf{y}=\mathbf{f}(\mathbf{x}),\ \mathbf{c}\geq\mathbf{0},\ \mathbf{x}\geq\mathbf{0}\}.$$

In this problem, one can simply substitute $\mathbf{y}=\mathbf{f}(\mathbf{x})$ in the utility function to express the problem as

$$\max_{\mathbf{c},\mathbf{x}} \{ U^{*}(\mathbf{x},\mathbf{c}) \,|\, \mathbf{p}(\mathbf{c}+\mathbf{x}-\mathbf{r}) = \bar{m},\ \mathbf{c}\geq\mathbf{0},\ \mathbf{x}\geq\mathbf{0}\},$$

where $U^{*}(\mathbf{x},\mathbf{c}) \equiv U(\mathbf{f}(\mathbf{x}),\mathbf{c})$ must be increasing, quasiconcave and twice differentiable in $\mathbf{x}$ because both U and $\mathbf{f}$ have those properties.

If market consumption goods and inputs used in household production represent two distinct groups of commodities, then the latter problem simply expresses utility as a function of both where the income constraint sets the sum of expenditures on both, less the value of endowments, equal to exogenous income. Thus, the latter problem is mathematically equivalent to the problem in Appendix Section 7.F where household production is ignored and purchases of inputs for household production are treated as consumption goods. Thus, household production can be considered to exist implicitly in problems represented as in Appendix Section 7.F.

As explained in Appendix Section 11.A, this possibility allows shifts in consumer supplies and demands to occur in response to a change in household technology as well as in response to changes in prices, exogenous income and endowments. Thus, shifts in consumer demands and supplies that are not explained by changes in prices, exogenous income, or endowments do not necessarily imply a change in the consumer's underlying tastes and preferences. Rather, they can represent changes in supplies and demands that occur because of actual or perceived changes in the ability of the consumer to transform market goods into nonmarket goods valued by the consumer according to a stable set of preferences. Applications of this result are discussed further in Section 11.5.

29. The technology specification thus corresponds to the producer case in Appendix Section 4.A where the usual monotonicity, concavity and differentiability properties hold with respect to some subvector of $\mathbf{x}$ representing the goods used as inputs in production, while for notational convenience other elements of $\mathbf{x}$ not involved in household production (and their effects on $\mathbf{y}$) are identically zero.

7.H EXACT MEASUREMENT AND INTEGRABILITY FOR FACTOR OWNERS

The exact welfare measurement approaches of Appendix Sections 6.D through 6.F generalize to the case of factor suppliers in a straightforward way by simply letting $\boldsymbol{q}$ represent a netput vector composed of individual elements q_i that represent consumption if positive and sales of factors if negative, and replacing ordinary income, m, by exogenous income, $\bar{m}$. Any household production is included implicitly in $\boldsymbol{q}$, positively in the case of purchases of inputs for household production and negatively in the case of sales of household production.

Following Appendix Section 6.D, WTP measures can be obtained directly from both ordinary supply and demand equations using Hause's approach. In this case, the expenditure function, $\bar{e}(\boldsymbol{p},\bar{U},\boldsymbol{r})$, which specifies the amount of exogenous income necessary to attain level $\bar{U}$ with price vector $\boldsymbol{p}$ and factor endowments $\boldsymbol{r}$, is substituted into estimates of ordinary supply or demand equations, obtaining the identity

$$\bar{\boldsymbol{q}}(\boldsymbol{p},\bar{U},\boldsymbol{r}) \equiv \tilde{\boldsymbol{q}}(\boldsymbol{p},\bar{e}(\boldsymbol{p},\bar{U},\boldsymbol{r}),\boldsymbol{r}),$$

for which differentiation of the expenditure function as in Appendix Sections 7.F or 7.G yields

$$\bar{e}_p = \bar{\boldsymbol{q}}(\boldsymbol{p},\bar{U},\boldsymbol{r}) = \tilde{\boldsymbol{q}}(\boldsymbol{p},\bar{e}(\boldsymbol{p},\bar{U},\boldsymbol{r}),\boldsymbol{r}). \tag{7.55}$$

Partial differential equations in this form representing both supplies and demands can then, in principle, be solved for the associated expenditure function. For the case of a change in prices and exogenous income from $(\boldsymbol{p}^0,\bar{m}_0)$ to $(\boldsymbol{p}^1,\bar{m}_1)$, which leads to a change in utility from U^0 to U^1 holding endowments constant at $\boldsymbol{r}^0$, the Hicksian compensating variation is found by solving (7.55) with the boundary condition, $\bar{e}(\boldsymbol{p}^0,\bar{U}_0,\boldsymbol{r}^0) = \bar{m}_0$. The Hicksian equivalent variation is obtained as the solution of (7.55) with boundary condition $\bar{e}(\boldsymbol{p}^1,\bar{U}_1,\boldsymbol{r}^0) = \bar{m}$. If endowments change, then the change in endowment values associated with the change in $\boldsymbol{r}$ from $\boldsymbol{r}^0$ (valued at prices $\boldsymbol{p}^1$) must be further added to measure compensating and equivalent variation.

Similarly, the Hausman approach can be used where the indirect utility function is expressed in terms of netput prices and exogenous income (holding $\boldsymbol{r}$ constant at $\boldsymbol{r}^0$), in which case compensating variation can be defined analogous to equation (6.23) by

$$V(\boldsymbol{p}^1,\bar{m}_1 - C,\boldsymbol{r}^0) = V(\boldsymbol{p}^0,\bar{m}_0,\boldsymbol{r}^0), \tag{7.56}$$

and equivalent variation can be defined analogous to equation (6.25) by

$$V(\boldsymbol{p}^1,\bar{m}_1,\boldsymbol{r}^0) = V(\boldsymbol{p}^0,\bar{m}_0 + E,\boldsymbol{r}^0).$$

For example, assume the labor supply relationship estimated in the consumer-laborer problem is linear as given by[30]

30. As implied by equation (7.31), this relationship corresponds to leisure demand $l = -\alpha w + \beta\bar{m} - (\gamma - 1)\tau - \delta = \tilde{l}(\boldsymbol{p},\bar{m},\boldsymbol{r})$ where the market transaction is $\tilde{l}(\boldsymbol{p},\bar{m},\boldsymbol{r}) - \tau = -\tilde{h}(\boldsymbol{p},\bar{m},\boldsymbol{r})$.

$$h = \alpha w - \beta \bar{m} + \gamma\tau + \delta = \tilde{h}(\boldsymbol{p},\bar{m},\boldsymbol{r}),$$

where the first element of the price vector is the wage rate w; the first element of the endowment vector is τ; and α, β, γ and δ are unobservable parameters estimated by econometric means. Each of the unobservable parameters may depend on other prices in $\boldsymbol{p}$ as, for example, where $\delta = \theta_1 p_1 + \ldots + \theta_N p_N$. If τ is constant, then $\gamma\tau + \delta$ can be replaced by δ alone where δ simply represents a different unknown constant, but including this term demonstrates how welfare measurement can be approached for problems where endowments change. Holding utility and all other prices in $\boldsymbol{p}$ and endowments in $\boldsymbol{r}$ constant at the initial level, comparative static analysis of $V(\boldsymbol{p},\bar{m},\boldsymbol{r}) = U^0$ implies

$$\frac{d\bar{m}}{dw} = -\frac{V_w}{V_{\bar{m}}} = -\alpha w + \beta \bar{m} - \gamma\tau - \delta,$$

where the latter equality follows from Roy's identity. The solution to this differential equation is

$$\bar{m}(w) = c e^{\beta w} + \frac{1}{\beta}\left[\frac{\alpha}{\beta} + \alpha w + \gamma\tau + \delta\right],$$

where c is some constant. The indirect utility function is found from this solution up to a multiplicative constant by letting $U^0 = c$ and solving for $U^0 = V(\boldsymbol{p},\bar{m},\boldsymbol{r})$,

$$U^0 = V(\boldsymbol{p},\bar{m},\boldsymbol{r}) = \frac{1}{\beta}\left[-\frac{\alpha}{\beta} - \alpha w + \beta\bar{m} - \gamma\tau - \delta\right] e^{-\beta w}.$$

Substituting into (7.56) thus obtains an exact expression for the compensating variation of a change in wage rate from w^0 to w^1 and a change in the time endowment from τ^0 to τ^1 using the parameters of the ordinary labor supply relationship holding other prices in $\boldsymbol{p}$ and endowment amounts in $\boldsymbol{r}$ constant,

$$C = \frac{1}{\beta}\left[\tilde{q}_0(\boldsymbol{p}^1,\bar{m}_1,\boldsymbol{r}^1) - \frac{\alpha}{\beta}\right] - \frac{1}{\beta} e^{\beta(w^1 - w^0)}\left[\tilde{q}^0(\boldsymbol{p}^0,\bar{m}_0,\boldsymbol{r}^0) - \frac{\alpha}{\beta}\right]$$

where $\boldsymbol{p}^i = (w^i, p_1, \ldots, p_N)$ and $\boldsymbol{r}^i = (\tau^i, r_1, \ldots, r_N)$, $i = 0, 1$. Similar results apply for finding the compensating variation associated with any other price, income or endowment changes, and joint estimation of such relationships can identify how unknown parameters in these relationships depend on other prices.

With this approach, systems of equations involving both demands and supplies can, in principle, be solved simultaneously for either the compensating or equivalent variation of multiple changes by noting that the equivalent variation is the negative of the compensating variation for the reverse price change. If exogenous income also changes then that change must be added to these calculations representing general netput price changes.

As in the pure consumption case, such systems of equations can be difficult or impossible to solve when they involve many equations or functional forms that do not admit closed form solutions of the relevant differential equations. Alternatively, the algorithm of Vartia can be adapted to the case where both consumer demands and factor supplies are represented in a netput system conditioned on exogenous income. Vartia's approach for this case would involve dividing a general netput price change from $\boldsymbol{p}^0$ to $\boldsymbol{p}^1$ into successive proportional and equal steps $\hat{\boldsymbol{p}}^0, \ldots, \hat{\boldsymbol{p}}^k$, and calculating

$$\hat{m}^k = \hat{m}^{k-1} + [\tilde{\boldsymbol{q}}(\hat{\boldsymbol{p}}^k, \hat{m}^{k-1}) + \tilde{\boldsymbol{q}}(\hat{\boldsymbol{p}}^{k-1}, \hat{m}^{k-1})][\hat{\boldsymbol{p}}^k - \hat{\boldsymbol{p}}^{k-1}]/2, \ k = 1, \ldots, K,$$

beginning from the initial exogenous income $\hat{m}^0 = \bar{m}^0$. The algorithm is to increase K in this calculation until the estimate of compensating variation, $\hat{C}^K = \hat{m}^0 - \bar{m}^K$, converges. Alternatively, equivalent variation can be found as the negative of the compensating variation for the reverse price change.

As in the pure consumer case of Chapter 6, both the Hausman and Vartia approaches must be qualified for cases involving more than one price change by the assumption that the systems of supplies and demands used for the calculations must satisfy integrability conditions. That is, unless the supplies and demands are consistent with a common underlying utility-maximization problem, path independence of the compensating and equivalent variation calculations may fail even though in theory it should not. The integrability conditions that must hold for the general factor supply problem are mathematically the same as for the pure consumer problem except now they include all supplies and demands included in welfare calculations and income is replaced by exogenous income. Stated in terms of netputs, the integrability conditions thus require:

1. *The budget constraint*: $\boldsymbol{p}\tilde{\boldsymbol{q}}(\boldsymbol{p},\bar{m}) = \bar{m}$,
2. *Homogeneity of degree zero in prices and exogenous income*: $\tilde{\boldsymbol{q}}(\boldsymbol{p},\bar{m}) = \tilde{\boldsymbol{q}}(t\boldsymbol{p},t\bar{m})$,
3. *Slutsky symmetry*: $\partial\bar{q}_i/\partial p_j = \partial\bar{q}_j/\partial p_i$, where $\partial\bar{q}_i/\partial p_j = \partial\tilde{q}_i/\partial p_j + \tilde{q}_j\, \partial\tilde{q}_i/\partial\bar{m}$, and
4. *Negative semidefiniteness of the Slutsky matrix*: $\{\partial\bar{q}_i/\partial p_j\} \leq 0$.

Again, in partial demand systems, condition 1 must be replaced by a strict inequality and condition 4 must be replaced by negative definiteness. In the case of factor owners, however, the quantities can be either negative or positive (negative when representing factor sales) unlike the pure consumer case where all quantities are assumed positive.

As in the pure consumer case of Chapter 6, the Willig results apply for the case of factor owners only when the supplies and demands used for calculating surplus measures satisfy these integrability conditions. For this reason, a practitioner of applied welfare economics is unlikely to find existing supply and demand estimates for use in evaluating multiple prices changes unless a single econometric study can be found that estimates a consistently specified system involving all necessary supplies and demands.

A practical methodology for estimating such systems is obtained by a slight generalization of the approach of Appendix Section 6.F whereby ordinary income, m, is replaced by exogenous income plus consumer endowments valued at applicable market prices (that is, by full income $m^* = \bar{m} + \boldsymbol{pr}$) and where the demands represent consumption demands that differ from market demands by factor endowments. That is, the quantities represented by $\boldsymbol{q}$ in the functional forms of Appendix Section 6.F correspond to the consumption quantities $\boldsymbol{c}$ in the framework of Appendix Section 7.F. The specifications for empirical purposes should thus set $\boldsymbol{q} = \boldsymbol{c} - \boldsymbol{r}$.

For example, the translog indirect utility specification in (6.75) in the factor suppliers' case becomes[31]

31. Although the generalized forms discussed in Appendix Section 6.F provide second-order approximations of any set of consumer demands and factor supplies, the approximation may be poor when boundary solutions occur (at points where inequality constraints become binding). This problem is no different than in the pure consumption case where second-order approximations are poor if some boundary conditions pre-

$$V(\mathbf{p},\bar{m},\mathbf{r}) = \exp\left[\alpha_0 + \sum_{i=1}^{N} \alpha_i \ln \frac{p_i}{\bar{m} + \mathbf{pr}} + \sum_{i=1}^{N}\sum_{j=1}^{N} \beta_{ij} \ln \frac{p_i}{\bar{m} + \mathbf{pr}} \ln \frac{p_j}{\bar{m} + \mathbf{pr}}\right], \quad (7.57)$$

where the factor endowment vector, $\mathbf{r}$, is added as an argument because the budget constraint must reflect the value of endowments. Compared to equation (6.76), applying Roy's identity as in (7.52) yields an additional term reflecting the consumer's endowment so that the equation represents the netput market transaction rather than the consumption demand, that is,[32]

$$\tilde{q}_i(\mathbf{p},\bar{m},\mathbf{r}) = -\frac{\partial V/\partial p_i}{\partial V/\partial \bar{m}} = \frac{\bar{m} + \mathbf{pr}}{p_i} \frac{\alpha_i + 2\sum_{j=1}^{N} \beta_{ij} \ln \frac{p_j}{\bar{m} + \mathbf{pr}}}{\sum_{j=1}^{N} \alpha_j + 2\sum_{j=1}^{N}\sum_{k=1}^{N} \beta_{jk} \ln \frac{p_k}{\bar{m} + \mathbf{pr}}} - r_i. \quad (7.58)$$

This equation is no more difficult to estimate than (6.76) because no unknown parameters are required to define full income. In fact, if data are available on consumption quantities, $\tilde{c}_i(\mathbf{p},\bar{m},\mathbf{r})$ rather than market transaction quantities, $\tilde{q}_i(\mathbf{p},\bar{m},\mathbf{r})$ then the $-r_i$ term can be eliminated from the right-hand side of (7.58) where the left-hand side is replaced by $\tilde{c}_i(\mathbf{p},\bar{m},\mathbf{r})$ for estimation. Having estimated such a netput system in either case, imposing coefficient restrictions $\beta_{ij} = \beta_{ji}$ and normalization constraints $\Sigma_{i=1}^{N} \Sigma_{j=1}^{N} \beta_{ij} = 0$ and $\Sigma_{i=1}^{N} \alpha_i = 1$, the integrability conditions are assured (negative semidefiniteness may require additional restrictions) so that the compensating variation of a general change in prices, exogenous income and endowments from $(\mathbf{p}^0,\bar{m}_0,\mathbf{r}^0)$ to $(\mathbf{p}^1,\bar{m}_1,\mathbf{r}^1)$ can be estimated uniquely. That is, generalizing compensating variation calculations for the case of possible changes in endowments as well as changes in prices and income, equation (7.56) becomes

$$V(\mathbf{p}^1,\bar{m}_1 - C,\mathbf{r}^1) = V(\mathbf{p}^0,\bar{m}_0,\mathbf{r}^0).$$

Solving this equation for compensating variation obtains the same result as in (6.77) where income m is replaced by full income, that is,

$$C = m_1^* - \exp\frac{\sum_{i=1}^{N} \alpha_i \ln \frac{m_0^* p_i^1}{p_i^0} + \sum_{i=1}^{N}\sum_{j=1}^{N} \beta_{ij}\left[\ln p_i^1 \ln p_j^1 - \ln \frac{p_i^0}{m_0^*} \ln \frac{p_j^0}{m_0^*}\right]}{1 + 2\sum_{i=1}^{N}\sum_{j=1}^{N} \beta_{ij} \ln p_j^1}, \quad (7.59)$$

cluding negative consumption ($q_i \equiv 0$) are effective. Thus, the generalized system forms are best applied to cases where data represent interior solutions of the factor owner's problem. If a particular good meets its boundary condition throughout the data used for estimation, then it can be eliminated for purposes of estimation (assuming its boundary condition is zero), or it can be reflected entirely in exogenous income if its boundary condition represents sales of the entire endowment of the good.

32. The additive term representing the factor endowment is obtained in (7.58) compared to the case where full income is taken as fixed in the indirect utility representation $\tilde{V}(\mathbf{p},m^*)$ because application of Roy's identity as in (7.52) must consider not only the direct dependence of indirect utility on prices but also the indirect dependence on prices through full income, that is,

$$\tilde{\mathbf{q}} = -\frac{V_{\mathbf{p}}}{V_{\bar{m}}} = -\frac{\tilde{V}_{\mathbf{p}} + \tilde{V}_{m^*}\mathbf{m}_{\mathbf{p}}^*}{\tilde{V}_{m^*}} = -\frac{\tilde{V}_{\mathbf{p}}}{\tilde{V}_{m^*}} - \mathbf{r} = \tilde{\mathbf{c}} - \mathbf{r}$$

because $\tilde{V}(\mathbf{p},m^*) = V(\mathbf{p},\bar{m},\mathbf{r})$, $\tilde{V}_{\mathbf{p}}\big|_{m^*\,\text{const}} = V_{\mathbf{p}}$, and $V_{\bar{m}} = \tilde{V}_{m^*} m^*_{\bar{m}} = \tilde{V}_{m^*}$ where $m^*_{\bar{m}} = 1$ and all subscripts represent derivatives.

where $m_1^* = \bar{m}_0 + \boldsymbol{p}^0\boldsymbol{r}^0$ and $m_1^* = \bar{m}_1 + \boldsymbol{p}^1\boldsymbol{r}^1$. Equivalent variation can be calculated similarly as the negative of the compensating variation of the reverse change.

Similar steps must be taken with the other specifications discussed in Appendix Section 6.F such as the almost ideal, generalized Leontief, and generalized Cobb-Douglas forms to appropriately reflect the role of endowments and factor supply. Thus, each of the common functional forms in Appendix Section 6.F used for analysis of consumer welfare readily extends to the case of factor owners and, in particular, to welfare analysis of labor supply.

7.I INDIRECT BENEFIT MEASUREMENT FOR PRICE AND NONPRICE CHANGES

To examine further the problem of benefit measurement in the case of some change other than the price of a good in an observable market, consider a generalization of the problem in Appendix Section 7.F where utility depends additionally on some exogenous condition represented by z. For example, z could represent the price of a good in an unobservable market or the amount or quality of some public good. That is, suppose the consumer's utility-maximization problem is

$$\max_{\boldsymbol{c}} \{ U(\boldsymbol{c},z) \mid \boldsymbol{p}(\boldsymbol{c}-\boldsymbol{r}) = \bar{m},\ \boldsymbol{c} \geq \boldsymbol{0} \}.$$

where market transactions are $\boldsymbol{q} = \boldsymbol{c} - \boldsymbol{r}$, consumption quantities are $\boldsymbol{c}$ and factor endowments are $\boldsymbol{r}$.[33]

To determine WTP for changes in z, this problem can be usefully reformulated as[34]

$$\bar{e}(\boldsymbol{p},\bar{U},z) = \min_{\boldsymbol{q}} \{ \boldsymbol{pq} \mid U(\boldsymbol{q}+\boldsymbol{r},z) = \bar{U},\ \boldsymbol{q}+\boldsymbol{r} \geq \boldsymbol{0} \}.$$

Solving this problem obtains compensated demands (if positive) or supplies (if negative), $\bar{\boldsymbol{q}}(\boldsymbol{p},\bar{U},z) = [\bar{q}_1(\boldsymbol{p},\bar{U},z),\ldots,\bar{q}_N(\boldsymbol{p},\bar{U},z)]$, such that $\bar{e}(\boldsymbol{p},\bar{U},z) = \boldsymbol{p}\bar{\boldsymbol{q}}(\boldsymbol{p},\bar{U},z)$ and $\bar{e}_{\boldsymbol{p}} = \bar{\boldsymbol{q}}(\boldsymbol{p},\bar{U},z)$ following the derivation in Appendix Section 7.F.

Now consider evaluating the WTP for a change in z from z^0 to z^1 where prices, exogenous income and endowments are held constant at $\boldsymbol{p}^0$, $\bar{m}_0$ and $\boldsymbol{r}^0$, respectively. Adapting the definition in (6.24), the compensating variation is

$$C = \bar{m}_0 - \bar{e}(\boldsymbol{p}^0,U^0,z^1) = \bar{e}(\boldsymbol{p}^0,U^0,z^0) - \bar{e}(\boldsymbol{p}^0,U^0,z^1). \qquad (7.60)$$

The approach suggested by Section 7.10 is to find choke prices $\tilde{p}_i^0$ and $\tilde{p}_i^1$ that just drive the consumption of good i to zero when $z = z^0$ and $z = z^1$, respectively, holding all other prices at their initial values, that is,

33. For the special case with no factor endowments, the reader may simply replace $\boldsymbol{c}$ with $\boldsymbol{q}$ throughout this section where $\boldsymbol{r} = \boldsymbol{0}$.

34. Note that $\boldsymbol{r}$ is suppressed as an argument of demand, supply and expenditure functions in this section for simplicity of notation because both $\boldsymbol{r}$ and $\boldsymbol{p}$ are held constant.

$$\tilde{p}_i^k = \min\,\{p_i | \bar{c}_i(\hat{\boldsymbol{p}}(p_i), \bar{U}, z^k) = 0\},\ k = 0, 1,$$

where

$$\hat{\boldsymbol{p}}(p_i), = (p_1^0,\ldots,p_{i-1}^0,p_i,p_{i+1}^0,\ldots,p_N^0).$$

Where the demands and supplies are compensated demands and supplies associated with initial utility, changes in Hicksian surplus can then be represented generally as

$$\begin{aligned} A &= \int_{p_i^0}^{\tilde{p}_i^1} \bar{q}_i(\hat{\boldsymbol{p}}(p_i), U^0, z^1)dp_i - \int_{p_i^0}^{\tilde{p}_i^0} \bar{q}_i(\hat{\boldsymbol{p}}(p_i), U^0, z^0)dp_i \\ &= \int_{p_i^0}^{\tilde{p}_i^1} \frac{\partial \bar{e}(\hat{\boldsymbol{p}}(p_i), U^0, z^1)}{\partial p_i} dp_i - \int_{p_i^0}^{\tilde{p}_i^0} \frac{\partial \bar{e}(\hat{\boldsymbol{p}}(p_i), U^0, z^1)}{\partial p_i} dp_i \qquad (7.61) \\ &= \bar{e}(\boldsymbol{p}^0, U^0, z^0) - \bar{e}(\hat{\boldsymbol{p}}(\tilde{p}_i^0), U^0, z^0) + \bar{e}(\hat{\boldsymbol{p}}(\tilde{p}_i^1), U^0, z^1) - \bar{e}(\boldsymbol{p}^0, U^0, z^1). \end{aligned}$$

Thus, the area measured by (7.61) correctly measures the compensating variation in (7.60), that is, $A = C$, if and only if

$$\bar{e}(\hat{\boldsymbol{p}}(\tilde{p}_i^1), U^0, z^1) = \bar{e}(\hat{\boldsymbol{p}}(\tilde{p}_i^0), U^0, z^0).$$

This condition does not hold in general but holds if $r_i = 0$ and

$$\frac{\partial \bar{e}(\tilde{\boldsymbol{p}}(z), U^0, z^1)}{\partial z} = 0 \text{ for } z^0 < z < z^1, \qquad (7.62)$$

where $\tilde{\boldsymbol{p}}(z) = (p_1^0,\ldots,p_{i-1}^0,\tilde{p}_i(z),p_{i+1}^0,\ldots,p_N^0)$ and gives the choke price for q_i as a function of z. Differentiating the identity

$$\bar{e}(\tilde{\boldsymbol{p}}(z), V(\tilde{\boldsymbol{p}}(z), \bar{m}, z), z) \equiv \bar{m}$$

with respect to z reveals that (7.62) holds if and only if

$$\frac{\partial V(\tilde{\boldsymbol{p}}(z), \bar{m}, z)}{\partial z} = 0 \text{ for } z^0 < z < z^1. \qquad (7.63)$$

A sufficient condition for (7.63) if the consumer has no endowment of good i ($r_i = 0$) is the condition of weak complementarity of z with respect to consumption of good i,[35]

$$\left.\frac{\partial U(\boldsymbol{q} + \boldsymbol{r}, z)}{\partial z}\right|_{c_i = q_i + r_i = 0} = 0. \qquad (7.64)$$

To see that this is the case, differentiate the identity (where $\tilde{\boldsymbol{q}}(\boldsymbol{p}, \bar{m}, z)$ are ordinary demands)

$$V(\tilde{\boldsymbol{p}}(z), \bar{m}, z) = U(\tilde{\boldsymbol{q}}(\tilde{\boldsymbol{p}}(z), \bar{m}, z) + \boldsymbol{r}, z)$$

35. Mäler (1974, p. 183) originally defined weak complementarity in the context of public environmental goods as the case where the demand for a public good is zero if the demand for a private good is zero. However, the formal mathematical condition has come to be used much more broadly in practice.

with respect to z to find

$$\frac{\partial V(\tilde{\boldsymbol{p}}(z),\bar{m},z)}{\partial z}=\sum_{j=1}^{N}\frac{\partial U}{\partial c_j}\frac{\partial \tilde{q}_j}{\partial z}+\frac{\partial U}{\partial z}, \tag{7.65}$$

where the derivatives of V and q_i with respect to z consider dependence on z both directly as well as through $\tilde{\boldsymbol{p}}(z)$. To verify (7.63), note in (7.65) that $\partial U/\partial z=0$ implies all the other right-hand terms are zero because the first-order conditions of the utility-maximization problem do not depend on z if U does not depend on z. If $c_i=q_i+r_i=0$, then (7.64) implies that the last right-hand term in (7.65) is zero, in which case (7.65) is zero, thus verifying (7.63). Note that (7.64) cannot hold in the case where z represents a good that has nonuse value independent of consumption, in which case z adds to utility whether or not any particular q_i is consumed.

The weak complementarity condition in (7.64) is useful in the case where z represents something that is of value to the consumer only if market good i is consumed. Thus, if $r_i=0$, weak complementarity of z with respect to consumption of good i is a sufficient condition for the compensating variation in (7.60) to be accurately reflected by the change in area in (7.61) behind the compensated market demand of q_i. Similarly, if U^0 is replaced by U^1 in the right-hand side of (7.60), (7.61) and (7.62), the same result applies for equivalent variation.

For the case where $r_i>0$, the above results must be altered because even with weak complementarity and zero consumption at the choke prices, the change in the choke price of good i from $\tilde{p}_i^0$ to $\tilde{p}_i^1$ changes the value of the endowment of good i so that

$$\bar{e}(\hat{\boldsymbol{p}}(\tilde{p}_i^0),U^0,z^0)-\bar{e}(\hat{\boldsymbol{p}}(\tilde{p}_i^1),U^0,z^1)=(\tilde{p}_i^1-\tilde{p}_i^0)r_i.$$

That is, where good i is not consumed and, thus, z does not matter, the exogenous expenditure function changes because the endowment vector has a different value in the budget constraint. Because only the price of good i changes, the exogenous income required for utility U^0 at price $\tilde{p}_i^1$ is lower by $(\tilde{p}_i^1-\tilde{p}_i^0)r_i$ compared to the case with price $\tilde{p}_i^0$. Noting that $\bar{\boldsymbol{q}}(\boldsymbol{p},\bar{U},z)=\bar{\boldsymbol{c}}(\boldsymbol{p},\bar{U},z)-\boldsymbol{r}$, equation (7.61) can be expressed alternatively as

$$A=\int_{p_i^0}^{\tilde{p}_i^1}\bar{c}_i(\hat{\boldsymbol{p}}(\tilde{p}_i),U^0,z^1)dp_i-\int_{p_i^0}^{\tilde{p}_i^0}\bar{c}_i(\hat{\boldsymbol{p}}(\tilde{p}_i),U^0,z^0)dp_i+[\tilde{\boldsymbol{p}}(z_1)-\tilde{\boldsymbol{p}}(z_0)]\boldsymbol{r},$$

where the latter term becomes $(\tilde{p}_i^1-\tilde{p}_i^0)r_i$ because only the price of good i changes. Thus, if z is weakly complementary with respect to consumption of good i, then

$$\begin{aligned}C&=\int_{p_i^0}^{\tilde{p}_i^1}\bar{c}_i(\hat{\boldsymbol{p}}(\tilde{p}_i),U^0,z^1)dp_i-\int_{p_i^0}^{\tilde{p}_i^0}\bar{c}_i(\hat{\boldsymbol{p}}(\tilde{p}_i),U^0,z^0)dp_i\\&=\int_{p_i^0}^{\tilde{p}_i^1}\frac{\partial\bar{e}(\hat{\boldsymbol{p}}(p_i),U^0,z^1)}{\partial p_i}dp_i-\int_{p_i^0}^{\tilde{p}_i^0}\frac{\partial\bar{e}(\hat{\boldsymbol{p}}(p_i),U^0,z^1)}{\partial p_i}dp_i-(\tilde{p}^1{}_i-\tilde{p}_i^0)r_i,\\&=\bar{e}(\boldsymbol{p}^0,U^0,z^0)-\bar{e}(\boldsymbol{p}^0,U^0,z^1)\end{aligned}$$

where $C=A-(\tilde{p}_i^1-\tilde{p}_i^0)r_i$, which implies that the compensating variation must be measured using the compensated consumption demand rather than the compensated market demand. Note also that the critical condition in (7.64) corresponds to zero consumption,

$c_i = q_i + r_i = 0$, rather than zero demand or supply, $q_i = 0$. In other words, the choke prices are prices just high enough to drive consumption to zero, at which point the consumer sells all of the corresponding endowment, $q_i = -r_i$.

These results are easily integrated into the empirical models of Appendix Section 7.H. For example, weak complementarity of good z with respect to consumption of good N can be represented by $U(c_1,\ldots,c_N,z) = \tilde{U}(c_1,\ldots,c_N f(z))$, in which z clearly has no effect if $c_N = 0$. Suppose the endowment of good N is zero, $r_N = 0$. In this case, the problem of maximizing $\tilde{U}(c_1,\ldots,c_N f(z))$ subject to $\Sigma_{i=1}^{N} p_i(c_i - r_i) = \bar{m}$ is equivalent to maximizing $\tilde{U}(c_1,\ldots,c_N^*)$ subject to $\Sigma_{i=1}^{N-1} p_i(c_i - r_i) + p_N c_N^*/f(z) = \bar{m}$ where $c_N^* = c_N f(z)$. But this is equivalent to replacing p_N by $p_N f(z)$ in the problem without $f(z)$.[36] Thus, to use standard functional forms to specify a problem under weak complementarity, one need simply replace the price of the good for which z is weakly complementary with the good's price divided by an appropriate specification for $f(z)$. For example, if $f(z) = e^{\gamma z}$ where γ is an unknown parameter, then $\ln(p_N/f(z)) = \ln p_N - \ln e^{\gamma z} = \ln p_N - \gamma z$. Thus, replacing $\ln p_N$ with $\ln p_N - \gamma z$ in the translog indirect utility specification in (7.57) obtains

$$V(\mathbf{p},\bar{m},z) = \exp\left[\alpha_0 + \sum_{i=1}^{N} \alpha_i \ln\left(\frac{p_i}{\bar{m} + \mathbf{pr}}\right) + \sum_{i=1}^{N}\sum_{j=1}^{N} \beta_{ij} \ln\left(\frac{p_i}{\bar{m} + \mathbf{pr}}\right) \ln\left(\frac{p_j}{\bar{m} + \mathbf{pr}}\right)\right.$$

$$\left. - \alpha_N \gamma z - 2\sum_{i=1}^{N} \beta_{iN} \gamma z \ln\left(\frac{p_i}{\bar{m} + \mathbf{pr}}\right) + \beta_{NN}\gamma^2 z^2\right]. \qquad (7.66)$$

The translog market demand specification implied by Roy's identity in (7.52) is then

$$\tilde{q}_i(\mathbf{p},\bar{m},z) = \frac{\bar{m} + \mathbf{pr}}{p_i} \frac{\alpha_i + 2\sum_{j=1}^{N} \beta_{ij} \ln \frac{p_j}{\bar{m} + \mathbf{pr}} - 2\beta_{iN}\gamma z}{\sum_{j=1}^{N} \alpha_j + 2\sum_{j=1}^{N}\sum_{k=1}^{N} \beta_{jk} \ln \frac{p_k}{\bar{m} + \mathbf{pr}} - 2\sum_{j=1}^{N} \beta_{jN}\gamma z} - r_i, \qquad (7.67)$$

for $i = 1, \ldots, N$ where $r_N = 0$. Thus, empirical implementation is straightforward. Estimation of netputs in (7.67) imposing coefficient restrictions $\beta_{ij} = \beta_{ji}$ and normalization constraints, $\Sigma_{i=1}^{N} \Sigma_{j=1}^{N} \beta_{ij} = 0$ and $\Sigma_{i=1}^{N} \alpha_i = 1$, yields all parameters necessary to calculate the compensating and equivalent variation of a change in z. For example, when endowments are held constant, the compensating variation of a change from $(\mathbf{p^0},\bar{m}_0,z^0)$ to $(\mathbf{p^1},\bar{m}_1,z^1)$ can be found by solving $V(\mathbf{p^1},\bar{m}_1 - C,z^1) = V(\mathbf{p^0},\bar{m}_0,z^0)$ after substituting estimated coefficients into (7.66),

$$C = m_1^* - \exp\frac{\sum_{i=1}^{N} \alpha_i \ln \frac{m_0^* p_i^1}{p_i^0} + \sum_{i=1}^{N}\sum_{j=1}^{N} \beta_{ij}\left[\ln p_i^1 \ln p_j^1 - \ln \frac{p_i^0}{m_0^*} \ln \frac{p_j^0}{m_0^*}\right] + \xi}{1 + 2\sum_{i=1}^{N}\sum_{j=1}^{N} \beta_{ij} \ln p_j^1 - 2\sum_{i=1}^{N} \beta_{iN}\gamma z^1},$$

where $m_1^* = \bar{m}_0 + \mathbf{p^0 r}$ and $m_1^* = \bar{m}_1 + \mathbf{p^1 r}$ and

36. If the endowment of good N is not zero, then replacing p_N by $p_N/f(z)$ inappropriately increases the endowment value by $[p_N/f(z) - p_N]r_N$. This increase can be corrected by simultaneously reducing exogenous income by the same amount. Corresponding adjustments would then be required in the equations that follow.

$$\xi = -\alpha_N\gamma(z^1 - z^0) - 2\sum_{i=1}^{N}\beta_{iN}\gamma\left[z^1\ln p_i^1 - z^0\ln\frac{p_i^0}{m_0^*}\right] + \beta_{NN}\gamma^2[(z^1)^2 - (z^0)^2].$$

In some practical applications, cases arise where the utility of several goods is related to some nonmarket variable. For example, the quality of water may reflect the utility of consumption, swimming and fishing. In such cases, the weak complementarity concept of (7.64) must be applied with respect to the group of related goods (q_N becomes a vector) and the choke price calculation must be expanded to drive consumption of the entire group of related goods to zero (Bockstael and Kling 1988). While this generalization is straightforward, it is notationally cumbersome and is thus left to the reader. For example, a function of z could be entered in the demand specification as a divisor of the price of each related good (possibly a different function of z for each such good). Of course, technically, this approach requires that all goods in the group must be nonessential so that choke prices exist. This requirement may be problematic depending on signs of estimated parameters unless the estimated specifications are viewed as only local approximations.

7.J APPROXIMATE WTP MEASURES WITH QUANTITY RESTRICTIONS

This section turns to the case where quantity restrictions must be considered in either consumption or factor supply (because of lumpiness, shortages, durable fixities, governmental controls, government production of public goods or exhaustion of endowments). The Willig results have been extended to consider quantity restrictions in the pure consumer case by Randall and Stoll (1980). Their work generalizes in a straightforward way to the factor owner problem. Suppose that a factor owner has a utility function $U(\mathbf{c})$ defined on consumption quantities $\mathbf{c} = \mathbf{q} + \mathbf{r}$ that is monotonically increasing, quasiconcave and twice differentiable, where $\mathbf{r}$ is an endowment vector as in Appendix Section 7.F, and the market transaction vector can be partitioned into two vectors, $\mathbf{q} = (\mathbf{q}^c, \mathbf{q}^u)$, such that $\mathbf{q}^c = (q_1, \ldots, q_n)$ is constrained to be equal to $\bar{\mathbf{q}}^c = (\bar{q}_1^c, \ldots, \bar{q}_n^c)$, and $\mathbf{q}^u = (q_{n+1}, \ldots, q_N)$ represents remaining market transaction quantities that are unconstrained except by nonnegativity, $1 < n < N$. The utility maximization problem is thus

$$\max_{\mathbf{q}} \{U(\mathbf{q} + \mathbf{r}) | \bar{m} = \mathbf{pq}, \mathbf{q}^c = \bar{\mathbf{q}}^c, \mathbf{q}^u \geq 0, \mathbf{q} = (\mathbf{q}^c, \mathbf{q}^u)\}.$$

The dual of this problem is (where $\mathbf{r}$ is suppressed in $\tilde{e}$ for convenience)

$$\tilde{e}(\mathbf{p}, \bar{U}, \bar{\mathbf{q}}^c) = \min_{\mathbf{q}} \{\mathbf{pq} | U(\mathbf{q} + \mathbf{r}) = \bar{U}, \mathbf{q}^c = \bar{\mathbf{q}}^c, \mathbf{q}^u \geq 0, \mathbf{q} = (\mathbf{q}^c, \mathbf{q}^u)\}.$$

But this problem can be further simplified to the form

$$\min_{\mathbf{q}^u} \{\mathbf{p}^u\mathbf{q}^u | U((\bar{\mathbf{q}}^c, \mathbf{q}^u) + \mathbf{r}) = \bar{U}, \mathbf{q}^u \geq 0\} \tag{7.68}$$

where $\mathbf{p}^c = (p_1, \ldots, p_n)$, $\mathbf{p}^u = (p_{n+1}, \ldots, p_N)$, $\mathbf{p} = (\mathbf{p}^c, \mathbf{p}^u)$. Obviously, for a given $\bar{\mathbf{q}}^c$, this problem is mathematically equivalent to the case of Appendix Section 7.F with respect to goods with unconstrained quantities, so evaluation of price changes in unconstrained markets follows the procedures already outlined.

To evaluate the impact of a change in the quantity restriction $\bar{\boldsymbol{q}}^c$, note that solution of either of the two expenditure-minimization problems above generates compensated demand functions, $\bar{\boldsymbol{q}}^u(\boldsymbol{p}^u,\bar{U},\bar{\boldsymbol{q}}^c)=[\bar{q}_{n+1}(\boldsymbol{p}^u,\bar{U},\bar{\boldsymbol{q}}^c),\ldots,\bar{q}_N(\boldsymbol{p}^u,\bar{U},\bar{\boldsymbol{q}}^c)]$ where $\boldsymbol{p}^u$ does not include prices of restricted quantities. The expenditure function specifying the minimum amount of exogenous income necessary to attain utility level $\bar{U}$ is

$$\tilde{e}(\boldsymbol{p},\bar{U},\bar{\boldsymbol{q}}^c)=\boldsymbol{p}^c\bar{\boldsymbol{q}}^c+\boldsymbol{p}^u\boldsymbol{q}^u(\boldsymbol{p}^u,\bar{U},\bar{\boldsymbol{q}}^c), \tag{7.69}$$

where the latter term represents the minimum of the expenditure minimization problem in (7.68). Differentiating this expenditure function with respect to $\bar{q}_j^c$ yields

$$\frac{\partial\tilde{e}}{\partial\bar{q}_j^c}=p^j+\sum_{n+1}^{N}p^i\frac{\partial\bar{q}_i}{\partial\bar{q}_j^c},\ j=1,\ldots,n. \tag{7.70}$$

Note that the Lagrangian of the first expenditure minimization problem above,

$$\mathcal{L}=\sum_{i=1}^{N}p_iq_i-\varphi[U(\boldsymbol{q})-\bar{U}]-\sum_{i=1}^{n}\psi_i(q_i-\bar{q}_i^c),$$

has first-order conditions that imply

$$p_i=\varphi\frac{\partial U}{\partial q_i}+\psi_i,\ i=1,\ldots,n,$$

$$p_i=\varphi\frac{\partial U}{\partial q_i},\ i=n+1,\ldots,N.$$

Substituting these first-order conditions into (7.70) yields[37]

$$\frac{\partial\tilde{e}}{\partial\bar{q}_j^c}=\psi_j+\varphi\sum_{i=1}^{N}\frac{\partial U}{\partial q_i}\frac{\partial\bar{q}_i}{\partial\bar{q}_j^c}=\psi_j+\varphi\frac{d\bar{U}}{d\bar{q}_j^c}=\psi_j,\ j=1,\ldots,n, \tag{7.71}$$

where, for convenience, $\partial\bar{q}_j/\partial\bar{q}_j^c=\partial\bar{q}_j^c/\partial\bar{q}_j^c=1$ and $\partial\bar{q}_k/\partial\bar{q}_j^c=0$ for $k,\ j=1,\ \ldots,\ n,\ k\neq j$. Additionally, ψ_j can be written as a function $\psi_j(\boldsymbol{p},\bar{U},\bar{\boldsymbol{q}}^c)$ and, by the usual interpretation of a Lagrangian multiplier, represents the marginal value of a change in the associated restriction, $\bar{q}_j^c$, in other words, the marginal value of consuming q_j given that price p_j must be paid for it. Because $\psi_j(\boldsymbol{p},\bar{U},\bar{\boldsymbol{q}}^c)$ gives the marginal value of consuming an additional unit of q_j over and above its price when utility is held constant, this is precisely the vertical difference in the Hicksian compensated demand of q_j in inverse form (value per unit as a function of quantity) and the price p_j.

Because of the mathematical equivalence of the expenditure-minimization problem in (7.68) above and those considered earlier, and as is directly evident from (7.69), one again finds that differentiation of the expenditure function with respect to prices of unconstrained quantities generates the associated Hicksian compensated demands, $\tilde{e}_{\boldsymbol{p}^u}(\boldsymbol{p},\bar{U},\bar{\boldsymbol{q}}^c)$

37. Note that

$$\sum_{i=1}^{N}\frac{\partial U}{\partial q_i}\frac{\partial\bar{q}_i}{\partial\bar{q}_j^c}=\frac{d\bar{U}}{d\bar{q}_j^c}=0$$

because it is the total differential of utility where quantities are adjusted to hold utility constant as $\bar{q}_j^c$ is changed.

$= \bar{\boldsymbol{q}}^u(\boldsymbol{p}^u, \bar{U}, \bar{\boldsymbol{q}}^c)$. Somewhat trivially from (7.69), differentiation of the expenditure function with respect to prices of constrained quantities generates the constrained quantities, $\tilde{e}_{\boldsymbol{p}^c}(\boldsymbol{p}, \bar{U}, \bar{\boldsymbol{q}}^c) = \bar{\boldsymbol{q}}^c$.

Next consider a change in prices, exogenous income, and quantity restrictions from $(\boldsymbol{p}^0, \bar{m}_0, \bar{\boldsymbol{q}}_0^c)$ to $(\boldsymbol{p}^1, \bar{m}_1, \bar{\boldsymbol{q}}_1^c)$, which leads to a change in maximum attainable utility from U^0 to U^1. The amount of compensation that leaves a factor supplier in the subsequent welfare position in the absence of a change is

$$E = \tilde{e}(\boldsymbol{p}^0, U^1, \bar{\boldsymbol{q}}_0^c) - \bar{m}_0. \tag{7.72}$$

Similarly, the amount of compensation that leaves a consumer in the initial welfare position following a change is

$$C = \bar{m}_1 - \tilde{e}(\boldsymbol{p}^1, U^0, \bar{\boldsymbol{q}}_1^c). \tag{7.73}$$

Note that these definitions do not strictly correspond to the Hicksian concepts of equivalent surplus or compensating surplus, because adjustment is allowed for some commodities and not for others.

In this case, one finds following the approach of Appendix Sections 6.A and 7.C, but using (7.72) and (7.73), that

$$\begin{aligned} C &= \bar{m}_1 - \bar{m}_0 + \tilde{e}(\boldsymbol{p}^0, U^0, \bar{\boldsymbol{q}}_0^c) - \tilde{e}(\boldsymbol{p}^1, U^0, \bar{\boldsymbol{q}}_1^c). \\ &= \Delta\bar{m} - \int_L \left[\sum_{i=1}^{n} \tilde{e}_{\bar{q}_i^c}(\boldsymbol{p}, U^0, \bar{\boldsymbol{q}}^c)\, d\bar{q}_i^c + \sum_{i=1}^{N} \tilde{e}_{p_i}(\boldsymbol{p}, U^0, \bar{\boldsymbol{q}}^c) dp_i \right] \\ &= \Delta\bar{m} - \int_L \left[\sum_{i=1}^{n} \bar{q}_i^c\, dp_i + \sum_{i=1}^{n} \psi_i(\boldsymbol{p}, U^0, \bar{\boldsymbol{q}}^c)\, dq_i + \sum_{i=n+1}^{N} \bar{q}_i(\boldsymbol{p}, U^0, \bar{\boldsymbol{q}}^c) dp_i \right] \\ &= \Delta\bar{m} - \sum_{i=1}^{n} q_i^1(p_i^1 - p_i^0) - \sum_{i=1}^{n} \int_{q_i^0}^{q_i^1} \psi_i(\boldsymbol{p}^0, U^0, \hat{\boldsymbol{q}}_i(q_i)) dp_i \\ &\qquad - \sum_{i=n+1}^{N} \int_{p_i^0}^{p_i^1} \bar{q}_i(\hat{\boldsymbol{p}}_i(p_i), U^0, \bar{\boldsymbol{q}}_1^c) dp_i \end{aligned} \tag{7.74}$$

and similarly that

$$\begin{aligned} E &= \tilde{e}(\boldsymbol{p}^0, U^1, \bar{\boldsymbol{q}}_0^c) - \bar{m}_0 = \tilde{e}(\boldsymbol{p}^0, U^1, \bar{\boldsymbol{q}}_0^c) - \tilde{e}(\boldsymbol{p}^1, U^1, \bar{\boldsymbol{q}}_1^c) + \bar{m}_1 - \bar{m}_0 \\ &= -\sum_{i=1}^{n} \int_{q_i^0}^{q_i^1} \psi_i(\boldsymbol{p}^1, U^1, \hat{\boldsymbol{q}}_i(q_i)) dq_i - \sum_{i=n+1}^{N} \int_{p_i^0}^{p_i^1} \bar{q}_i(\hat{\boldsymbol{p}}_i(p_i), U^1, \bar{\boldsymbol{q}}_0^c) dp_i \\ &\qquad - \sum_{i=1}^{n} q_i^0(p_i^1 - p_i^0) + \Delta\bar{m}, \end{aligned} \tag{7.75}$$

where L is any path of integration from $(\boldsymbol{p}^0, \bar{\boldsymbol{q}}_0^c)$ to $(\boldsymbol{p}^1, \bar{\boldsymbol{q}}_1^1)$, $\hat{\boldsymbol{p}}_i(p_i)$ is defined similarly to (5.19) with

$$\hat{\boldsymbol{p}}_i(p_i) = (p_{n+1}^1, \ldots, p_{i-1}^1, p_i, p_{i+1}^0, \ldots, p_N^0),$$

and

$$\hat{\boldsymbol{q}}_i(q_i) = (q_1^1, \ldots, q_{i-1}^1, q_i, q_{i+1}^0, \ldots, q_N^0).$$

The implication of (7.74) and (7.75) is that a change in a quantity restriction is evaluated by the change in area below (above) the compensated demand (supply) curve, above (below) price and left of quantity, whereas a price change for an unrestricted quantity is evaluated by the change in area below (above) the compensated demand (supply) curve and above (below) price. Any change in price for a restricted quantity acts essentially as an income change because that amount must be exactly compensated to leave the individual just as well off when adjustment is not possible. Again, these changes can be imposed sequentially along some arbitrary path from $(\boldsymbol{p}^0, \bar{\boldsymbol{q}}_0^c)$ to $(\boldsymbol{p}^1, \bar{\boldsymbol{q}}_1^c)$, but following Sections 6.7 or 7.7, the income changes and price changes that behave like income changes can be more easily imposed first in calculating the equivalent welfare measure, or last in calculating the compensating welfare measure when ordinary surplus approximations are to be used.

While these results consider only changes in the prices and quantity restrictions of restricted goods, evaluation of the welfare effects of changes in endowments of restricted quantities is straightforward. Suppose that the endowment of good i is changed from r_i^0 to r_i^1 where the corresponding quantity restriction is $\bar{q}_i^0$. Because $c_i = \bar{q}_i^0 + r_i^0$ in the initial state and $c_i = \bar{q}_i^0 + r_i^1$ in the subsequent state, the welfare effect is the same as changing the quantity restriction by the amount of the change in endowment. That is, a change in the endowment merely relaxes $(r_i^1 > r_i^0)$ or tightens $(r_i^1 < r_i^0)$ the resulting constraint on consumption. Thus, the results for changes in the quantity restriction suffice for welfare evaluation. This is true as long as the restriction is binding, that is, the shadow value of the corresponding quantity constraint is above the market price for good i.

If any change causes a restriction to become binding, then welfare evaluation can be accomplished by dividing the change into the part under which the constraint remains binding and the part where the constraint is not binding for purposes of evaluation (although utility should be properly conditioned on the overall initial level for calculating compensating variation or the overall subsequent level for calculating equivalent variation). The results of this section apply to the part where the constraint is binding while the results of Appendix Section 7.G apply to the part where the constraint is not binding.

To consider the errors associated with using a consumer or producer surplus approximation in the case of a quantity restriction (or an equivalent change in the endowment of a restricted quantity), suppose that only one quantity restriction, $\bar{q}_i^c$, is imposed while all prices remain constant. Suppose that the ordinary demand curve in implicit form (with price as a function of quantity) is represented by $\tilde{p}_i(\boldsymbol{p}, \bar{m}, q_i^c)$ and that the vertical distance between the ordinary demand curve and price is represented by

$$\tilde{\psi}_i(\boldsymbol{p}, \bar{m}, \bar{q}_i^c) \equiv \tilde{p}_i(\boldsymbol{p}, \bar{m}, q_i^c) - p_i$$

(note $\psi_i = \tilde{\psi}_i$ only for corresponding values of the variables $\boldsymbol{p}$, $\bar{m}$, q_i^c, and $\bar{U}$). Then the price flexibility of income is

$$\bar{\varphi} = \frac{\partial \tilde{\psi}_i}{\partial \bar{m}} \frac{\bar{m}}{\tilde{\psi}_i}.$$

Further defining $y(t) \equiv \ln \tilde{\psi}_i(\mathbf{p},\bar{m},\bar{q}_i^c)$ and $\bar{m}=e^t$, so that

$$\frac{dy}{dt}=\frac{dy}{d\tilde{\psi}_i}\frac{\partial\tilde{\psi}_i}{\partial\bar{m}}\frac{d\bar{m}}{dt}=\frac{1}{\tilde{\psi}_i}\frac{\partial\tilde{\psi}_i}{\partial\bar{m}}e^t=\frac{\partial\tilde{\psi}_i}{\partial\bar{m}}\frac{\bar{m}}{\tilde{\psi}_i}=\bar{\varphi},$$

and following a similar procedure as used to derive (6.34) implies that

$$\left(\frac{\bar{m}_1}{\bar{m}_0}\right)^{\bar{\varphi}_1}\leq\frac{\tilde{\psi}_i(\mathbf{p},\bar{m}_1,\bar{q}_i^c)}{\tilde{\psi}_i(\mathbf{p},\bar{m}_0,\bar{q}_i^c)}\leq\left(\frac{\bar{m}_1}{\bar{m}_0}\right)^{\bar{\varphi}_2},$$

where $\bar{\varphi}_1$ and $\bar{\varphi}_2$ are lower and upper bounds on price flexibility over the path of the imposed quantity change. Substituting $\tilde{e}(\mathbf{p},U,\bar{q}_i^c)$ for $\bar{m}_1$ and using (7.71) yields

$$\begin{aligned}\tilde{\psi}_i(\mathbf{p},\bar{m}_0,\bar{q}_i^c)\cdot(\bar{m}_0)^{-\bar{\varphi}_1}&\leq\frac{\partial\tilde{e}(\mathbf{p},U^0,\bar{q}_i^c)}{\partial\bar{q}_i^c}\,\tilde{e}(\mathbf{p},U^0,\bar{q}_i^c)^{-\bar{\varphi}_1}\\&=\frac{\partial[\tilde{e}(\mathbf{p},U^0,\bar{q}_i^c)^{1-\bar{\varphi}_1}]}{\partial\bar{q}_i^c}\end{aligned}\tag{7.76}$$

and

$$\begin{aligned}\frac{\partial[\tilde{e}(\mathbf{p},U^0,\bar{q}_i^c)^{1-\bar{\varphi}_2}]}{\partial\bar{q}_i^c}&=\frac{\partial\tilde{e}(\mathbf{p},U^0,\bar{q}_i^c)}{\partial\bar{q}_i^c}\,\tilde{e}(\mathbf{p},U^0,\bar{q}_i^c)^{-\bar{\varphi}_2}\\&\leq\tilde{\psi}_i(\mathbf{p},\bar{m}_0,\bar{q}_i^c)\cdot(\bar{m}_0)^{-\bar{\varphi}_2}.\end{aligned}\tag{7.77}$$

Integrating both sides of (7.76) and (7.77) thus yields

$$\begin{aligned}-\Delta S_i\cdot(\bar{m}_0)^{-\bar{\varphi}_1}&=(\bar{m}_0)^{-\bar{\varphi}_1}\int_{q_i^0}^{q_i^1}\tilde{\psi}_i(\mathbf{p},\bar{m}_0,\bar{q}_i^c)\,d\bar{q}_i^c\\&\leq\frac{\tilde{e}(\mathbf{p},U^0,q_i^1)^{1-\bar{\varphi}_1}-(m_0)^{1-\bar{\varphi}_1}}{1-\bar{\varphi}_1}\end{aligned}\tag{7.78}$$

and

$$\begin{aligned}\frac{\tilde{e}(\mathbf{p},U^0,q_i^1)^{1-\bar{\varphi}_2}-(\bar{m}_0)^{1-\bar{\varphi}_2}}{1-\bar{\varphi}_2}&\leq(\bar{m}_0)^{-\bar{\varphi}_2}\int_{q_i^0}^{q_i^1}\tilde{\psi}_i(\mathbf{p},\bar{m}_0,\bar{q}_i^c)\,d\bar{q}_i^c\\&=-\Delta S_i\cdot(\bar{m}_0)^{\bar{\varphi}_2},\end{aligned}\tag{7.79}$$

where ΔS_i is defined as in Section 7.9. Thus, following steps similar to those used in (6.37) through (6.40) obtains

$$[1+\bar{s}_i(\bar{\varphi}_2-1)]^{1/(1-\bar{\varphi}_2)}\geq\frac{\tilde{e}(\mathbf{p},U^0,q_i^1)}{\bar{m}_0}\geq[1+s_i(\bar{\varphi}_1-1)]^{1/(1-\bar{\varphi}_1)}$$

and

$$\varepsilon_2^c\geq\frac{\Delta S_i-C_s}{|\Delta S_i|}\geq\varepsilon_1^c,\tag{7.80}$$

where C_s represents Hicksian compensating surplus,

$$\varepsilon_k^c \equiv \frac{[1+\bar{s}_i(\bar{\varphi}_k-1)]^{1/(1-\bar{\varphi}_k)}-1+\bar{s}_i}{|\bar{s}_i|},\ k=1,2, \tag{7.81}$$

and

$$\bar{s}_i \equiv \frac{\Delta S_i}{\bar{m}_0}.$$

Similarly,

$$\varepsilon_2^e \geq \frac{E_s-\Delta S_i}{|\Delta S_i|} \geq \varepsilon_1^e, \tag{7.82}$$

where E_s represents Hicksian equivalent surplus and

$$\varepsilon_k^e \equiv \frac{[1-\bar{s}_i(\bar{\varphi}_k-1)]^{1/(1-\bar{\varphi}_k)}-1-\bar{s}_i}{|\bar{s}_i|},\ k=1,2. \tag{7.83}$$

Comparing (7.80) and (7.82) with (7.36) and (7.37), all the further approximation results in (7.38) through (7.41) hold for this case as well when $\hat{\varepsilon}=|\bar{s}_i|\cdot(\bar{\varphi}_1+\bar{\varphi}_2)/4$. Also, based on (7.81) and (7.83), Table 6.1 may again be used to investigate the magnitude of error in various cases by simply replacing η with φ. Thus, ε_k^c and ε_k^e are approximated by

$$\varepsilon_k^c,\ \varepsilon_k^e \doteq \frac{\bar{\varphi}_k|\bar{s}_i|}{2} \equiv \hat{\varepsilon}_k,\ k=1,2,$$

so that more than about a 5 percent error is avoided by using consumer surplus change in place of a WTP for changes in quantity restrictions so long as the price flexibility times the surplus change relative to income is less than 0.1 in absolute value (that is, $|\bar{\varphi}\bar{s}/2| \leq 0.05$).

These results can also be readily extended to the case of simultaneous changes in many quantity restrictions and many prices. For example, suppose that

$$\Delta S_i = -\int_{q_i^0}^{q_i^1} \tilde{\psi}_i(\boldsymbol{p}^1, \bar{m}_j, \hat{\boldsymbol{q}}_i(q_i))dq_i,\ i=1,\ldots,n,$$

$$\Delta S_i = -\int_{p_i^0}^{p_i^1} \tilde{q}_i(\hat{\boldsymbol{p}}_i(p_i), \bar{m}_j, \bar{\boldsymbol{q}}_0^c)dp_i,\ i=n+1,\ldots,N,$$

where $j=0$ in the case of compensating surplus measure and $j=1$ in the case of equivalent surplus. Thus, the total surplus change is $\Sigma_{i=1}^N \Delta S_i + \bar{m}_1 - \bar{m}_0 + \Sigma_{i=1}^n (p_i^0 - p_i^1)\cdot q_i^0$, following the methods of Sections 6.7 and 7.7, where actual income change (now also including expenditure effects of price changes for restricted quantities) is evaluated after (before) all other effects in computing compensating (equivalent) welfare measures. Here, the component $\bar{m}_1 - \bar{m}_0 + \Sigma_{i=1}^n (p_i^0 - p_i^1)\cdot q_i^0$, is without error. Bounds on the error associated with $\Sigma_{i=1}^n \Delta S_i$ follow from (7.78) and (7.79) where

$$\bar{\varphi}_1 = \min\left\{ \left.\frac{\partial\tilde{\psi}_i}{\partial\bar{m}}\frac{\bar{m}}{\tilde{\psi}_i}\right| \bar{\boldsymbol{q}}^c \in \{\hat{\boldsymbol{q}}_i(q_i^0), \hat{\boldsymbol{q}}_i(q_i^1)\}, \bar{m}=\bar{m}_j, \boldsymbol{p}=\boldsymbol{p}^1, i=1,\ldots,n \right\}, \tag{7.84}$$

$$\bar{\varphi}_2 = \max\left\{ \left.\frac{\partial\tilde{\psi}_i}{\partial\bar{m}}\frac{\bar{m}}{\tilde{\psi}_i}\right| \bar{\boldsymbol{q}}^c \in \{\hat{\boldsymbol{q}}_i(q_i^0), \hat{\boldsymbol{q}}_i(q_i^1)\}, \bar{m}=\bar{m}_j, \boldsymbol{p}=\boldsymbol{p}^1, i=1,\ldots,n \right\}. \tag{7.85}$$

Bounds on the error associated with $\Sigma_{i=n+1}^{N} \Delta S_i$ follow from (6.56) through (6.59), where $e(\mathbf{p}^i, U^0)$ is replaced by $\tilde{e}(\mathbf{p}^i, U^0, \bar{\mathbf{q}}_0^c)$, and

$$\bar{\eta}_1 = \min \left\{ \frac{\partial \tilde{q}_i}{\partial \bar{m}} \frac{\bar{m}}{\tilde{q}_i} \middle| \mathbf{p} \in \{\hat{\mathbf{p}}_i(p_i^0), \hat{\mathbf{p}}_i(p_i^1)\}, \bar{m} = \bar{m}_j, \bar{\mathbf{q}}^c = \bar{\mathbf{q}}_0^c, i = n+1 \ldots, N \right\},$$

$$\bar{\eta}_2 = \max \left\{ \frac{\partial \tilde{q}_i}{\partial \bar{m}} \frac{\bar{m}}{\tilde{q}_i} \middle| \mathbf{p} \in \{\hat{\mathbf{p}}_i(p_i^0), \hat{\mathbf{p}}_i(p_i^1)\}, \bar{m} = \bar{m}_j, \bar{\mathbf{q}}^c = \bar{\mathbf{q}}_0^c, i = n+1 \ldots, N \right\}.$$

That is, the results associated with (7.46) through (7.49) hold for the cases where some markets are affected by changes in quantity restrictions and other markets are affected by price changes.

As in the earlier case of Appendix Section 7.F, if the market transactions for unconstrained goods or the shadow prices for constrained goods include supplies as well as demands (the netput case), then these results are not as comforting as the Willig results for the pure consumption case because the bounds defined by (7.84) and (7.85) may be quite wide. Nevertheless, the approach of (6.60) through (6.64) is applicable and can lead to much narrower error bounds on the same surplus measure if the variation of income elasticities and price flexibilities of income is not great for individual commodities. In general, one can avoid an error in measurement of more than about 5 percent for $\Sigma_{i=1}^{N} \Delta S_i$ as long as $|\bar{\eta}\bar{s}/2| \leq 0.05$ for all unrestricted goods with changing price and $|\bar{\varphi}\bar{s}/2| \leq 0.05$ for all restricted goods with changing quantity restrictions.

8. Aggregation and economic welfare analysis of market-oriented policies

Chapters 4 through 7 have focused on welfare measurement for individual decision-makers: consumers, producers and factor owners. In many practical cases, however, public policies affect a large number of people, and a determination of the effects on each individual decision unit is impractical both computationally and from the standpoint of data availability. Furthermore, because of the number of people affected by most policies, a specific welfare analysis for each decision-maker is too cumbersome and incomprehensible from the point of view of presenting a policy-maker with convenient and useful information. Thus, to perform useful welfare analysis of alternative policies, some aggregation is usually necessary.

Chapters 4 through 7 are used as a basis for the aggregation discussed in this chapter. The willingness-to-pay (WTP) approach is considered first because it is apparently the most practically applicable approach in terms of analysis of individual welfare. Individual supply and demand functions are aggregated and WTP interpretations of changes in areas behind supply and demand curves apply to aggregate market groups just as for individuals. The WTP approach is attractive because market supply and demand curves can be empirically estimated. The advantages of this approach are emphasized by contrast with empirical use of money measures of utility change in the context of Samuelson's utility possibilities approach. Based on the market approach to applied welfare economics, this chapter also shows how to analyze various simple government policies, such as taxes, quotas and price controls.

8.1 AGGREGATION OF WTP: THE PRODUCER CASE

Consider the possibilities for aggregation of WTP measures of welfare change. As shown in Sections 4.2 through 4.5, the WTP for a price change by a producer (referring generally to either compensating or equivalent variation) is simply the change in area behind the firm's associated supply curve or derived demand curve, as the case may be. Consider first the aggregation of several such effects over several producers. Suppose in Figure 8.1 that the representative supply curves for firms 1 and 2 are S_1 and S_2, respectively, and that summing these supply curves horizontally over all firms in an industry obtains the supply curve S. Under competition, where all firms perceive no individual influence on price, S represents the market supply curve and specifies how much will be produced by the industry at various prices.

Now suppose that the price increases from p_0 to p_1. According to Section 4.2, the associated welfare effects are a gain of area a for firm 1 and area b for firm 2. That is, areas a and b are the compensating or equivalent variations of the price increase for firms 1 and

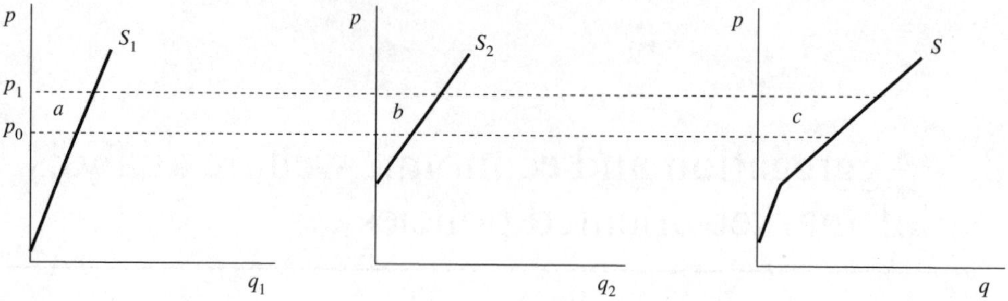

Figure 8.1

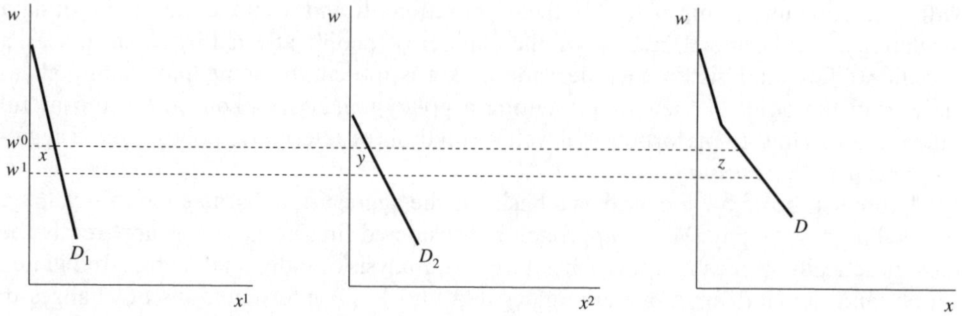

Figure 8.2

2, respectively. However, geometry verifies that area c, the change in area behind the market supply curve, is the sum of the changes in areas behind individual supply curves because all firms face the same prices and the market curve is obtained by horizontal summation of individual supply curves. Thus, the change in producer surplus associated with a market supply curve has a WTP interpretation for the market group analogous to the individual firm case of Chapter 4. Thus, area c measures the sum of compensating or equivalent variations over all firms included in the market supply.

A similar exact aggregation property holds with respect to derived demands by all firms in an industry. Where derived demands by firms 1 and 2 are represented by D_1 and D_2, respectively, in Figure 8.2, the market demand curve D under competition is obtained by summing firm demands horizontally over all firms in the industry. Thus, if price falls from w^0 to w^1, the change in market consumer surplus, area z, is the sum of changes in individual firm consumer surpluses (that is, the sum of areas x and y), because all firms face the same prices under competition. Because areas x and y are exact measures of compensating and equivalent variation for the individual firms, area z is an exact measure of the sum of compensating or equivalent variations for the industry.

Thus, based on these results, the Kaldor–Hicks and Scitovsky compensation criteria (discussed in Section 3.1) can be applied to a group of producers affected by a policy-controlled price change. *If the change in market producer (or consumer) surplus associated with a market supply (or derived demand) curve is positive, then both the Kaldor–Hicks and Scitovsky criteria are satisfied among the producing group; otherwise, neither is satisfied.*

Furthermore, if a particular policy affects several different producer market groups differently, the market surplus changes for each group can be added together to obtain the sum of compensating or equivalent variations over all affected producers. *If the sum of producer surplus changes over several markets is positive, both criteria are satisfied among all producers considered jointly; otherwise, neither is satisfied.* That is, if the criteria are met, some producers can compensate other producers so that all producers are better off with the change. Otherwise, some producers can compensate other producers so that all are better off without the change.

There are important cases, however, when different producer groups should be considered separately. Consider Figure 8.3, where long-run average total cost is ATC. Suppose

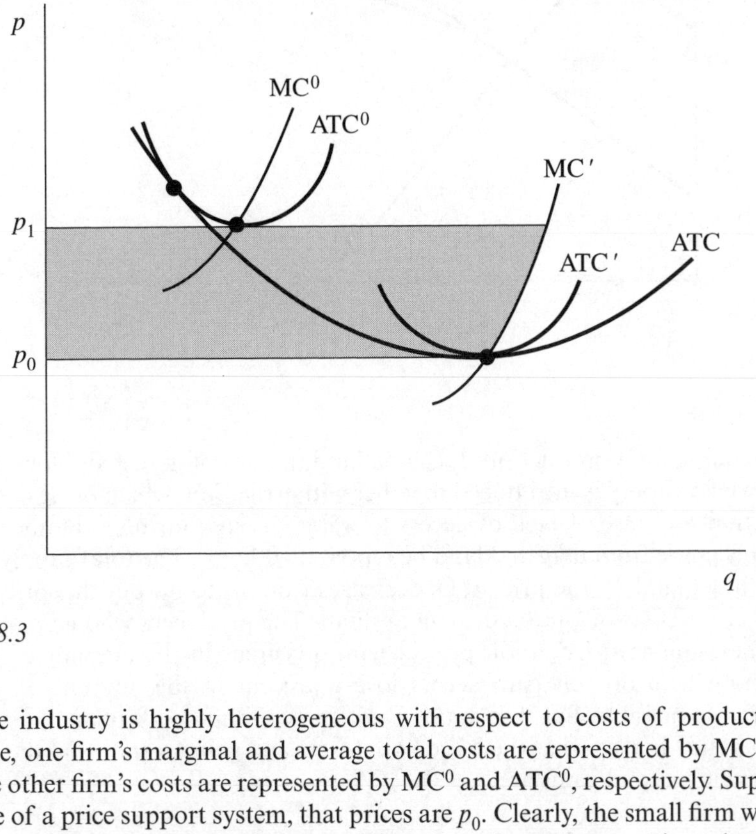

Figure 8.3

that the industry is highly heterogeneous with respect to costs of production. As an example, one firm's marginal and average total costs are represented by MC′ and ATC′ and the other firm's costs are represented by MC^0 and ATC^0, respectively. Suppose, in the absence of a price support system, that prices are p_0. Clearly, the small firm would go out of business. However, a price support system that raises price to p_1 in order to keep this firm in business helps the large firm proportionately more (the large firm gains excess profits equal to the shaded area). An example of such a support system is that in dairying. Because of the large variation in the size of dairy herds (ranging, say, from 50 cows up to several thousand cows) and, hence, differences in efficiency, the dairy price support system helps the large producer relatively more than the small one. Only welfare analysis at a disaggregated level can point out this distributional detail. In some cases, disaggregated analysis can lead to useful information even though, when changing price along a market supply curve, all producers are affected in the same direction. In the foregoing case, disaggregated analysis shows that consumers pay the cost of subsidizing a few relatively large firms that could function very well without price supports.

Another case where disaggregation is crucial is shown in Figure 8.4. Suppose that S_D

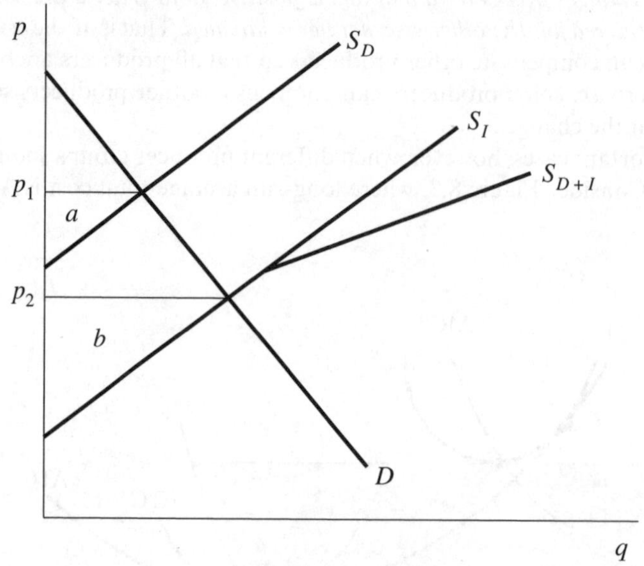

Figure 8.4

is the supply curve for a product produced on land that is not irrigated. Now suppose that a new hybrid variety is introduced together with irrigation, which brings new land into production. Because of lack of access to water, dryland farmers cannot irrigate. Let the supply curve from irrigated land be represented by S_I. The total supply is thus $S_D + S_I$. With demand D, the price thus decreases from p_1 to p_2, but this price is not sufficient to cover costs of production on dryland. The producers who gain access to the government-financed irrigation project gain quasirent in the amount of area b. However, those who do not gain access lose quasirent in the amount of area a. Compensation is possible, but if it is not paid, an economic welfare analysis should point out to policy-makers that there are both losers and gainers and what the magnitudes of those losses and gains are.

8.2 AGGREGATION OF WTP: THE CASE OF CONSUMERS AND FACTOR OWNERS

Turning to the case of consumers and factor owners, the aggregation problem is a bit more complicated because surplus changes are not, in general, accurate measures of compensating or equivalent variation unless the individual demands and supplies are compensated appropriately. Clearly, however, the derivation of Figures 8.1 and 8.2 shows that, under competition, the consumer (producer) surplus associated with a market demand (supply) curve is the same as the sum of individual consumer (producer) surpluses over all market participants. This result holds regardless of whether or not the market participants are producers, consumers or factor owners. Hence, one must consider only aggregation of the errors associated with surplus changes as measurements of compensating and equivalent variation (or as measurements of compensating and equivalent surpluses where quantity changes are imposed). But if assumptions for accuracy of surplus change hold for all individuals buying (selling) in a particular market, the same accuracy will hold for the market surplus change because, with competition, all individual surplus changes will be in the same direction.

For example, following Section 7.6, suppose that $|\eta_j^* s_j^*/2| < 0.05$ for all individuals, where η_j^* is the exogenous income elasticity of demand for individuals j and $s_j^* = \Delta S_j / m_{0j}^*$, where ΔS_j is consumer surplus change and m_{0j}^* is initial exogenous income, both for individual j. Also, suppose that market price decreases as in Figure 8.2. Then $\Delta S_j > 0$ for all individuals and, based on results from Section 7.6, approximate bounds on compensating (equivalent) variation are given by $0.95\ \Delta S_j$ and $1.05\ \Delta S_j$. That is, the consumer surplus change is no more than about 5 percent in error. Adding the lower bounds over all individuals thus obtains a lower bound on the sum of compensating (equivalent) variations, $0.95\ \Delta S$, where ΔS is the market consumer surplus change and, similarly, adding upper bounds over all individuals obtains an upper bound, $1.05\ \Delta S$. Thus, the market change in consumer surplus is no more than 5 percent in error if corresponding conditions are met that limit errors to 5 percent for all individuals.

Thus, for empirical purposes where errors in estimation are comparatively large, the simple changes in market surplus (changes in areas behind supply and demand curves) provide useful economic welfare quantities for cases where $\eta_j^* s_j^*$ is not large for any individual. Alternatively, the approach of Appendix Sections 6.D or 6.F for estimation of exact WTP measures can be used when Willig bounds are unacceptable. Again, as in the producer case, however, one must bear in mind that aggregation of all consumers into a simple market curve for welfare calculations corresponds to application of equal welfare weights. If unequal weights are considered, consumer demand or factor supply must be considered separately for each group that is to receive a different weight. Again, disaggregation into *groups* of similar consumers may be necessary to point out any serious distributional effects.

8.3 AGGREGATION OF MONEY MEASURES OF UTILITY CHANGE

Before proceeding to show how the foregoing results can be used to analyze policy changes, a short digression on money measures of utility change serves to emphasize the practicality of the WTP approach. Remember that, as discussed in Sections 5.1 through 5.3, early welfare economists sought a unique money measure of utility change. An obvious approach is then to add money measures of utility change across individuals. However, to use only the sum of individual utilities as the criterion for policy decisions implicitly assumes that a Bergsonian social welfare function is known and, in fact, equally weights utility changes for all individuals. As explained in Section 3.4, use of such a welfare function entails a value judgment any time such an objective is not explicitly mandated by the policy-maker.

In addition, maximization of the sum of money measures of utility change does not generally lead to the same policy choices as maximization of the sum of utilities. For example, suppose that one seeks to maximize the sum of utilities for two individuals with proportional utility functions, U_A and U_B, where $U_A = 2U_B$. That is, suppose that the utility of consumer *A* is twice that of consumer *B* whenever the two consume identical consumption bundles. In this case, the consumers will possess identical demand curves in identical situations (indifference maps will coincide even though indifference curves represent different utility levels for different individuals), and the corresponding money measures of utility change for any price–income change will be identical even though the utility change for one will be twice that of the other. Hence, a social welfare function that implies maximization of the sum of utilities would weight the money measure of utility change for consumer *A* twice as much as that for consumer *B*. Obviously, to maximize the simple sum (or almost any weighted sum) of consumer utilities using money measures of utility change thus requires some rather specific and generally unobtainable information about the relationship of individuals' utility functions (for example, their marginal utilities of income). Empirical aggregation of money measures of utility change in applied analysis of economic welfare is thus seemingly impossible without value judgments.

Alternatively, consider money measures of utility change in empirical economic welfare analysis along the lines suggested by Samuelson's utility possibilities approach and his potential welfare criterion (see Section 3.2). Suppose that a unique money measure of utility change with respect to a particular price change exists and can be measured for each of two individuals and that no other individuals are affected by the price change. Because the money measures of utility change are ordinally related to the respective individuals' utility levels, the approach of Section 3.2, as demonstrated in Figure 3.5, can be employed simply by making the appropriate monotonic transformation of axes. Thus, rather than using U_A and U_B on the axes, one can use the corresponding money measures ΔS_A and ΔS_B (which are ordinally related to U_A and U_B, respectively, as demonstrated in Figure 5.8). Because both ΔS_A and ΔS_B are functions of the price change, a money-measure utility possibility frontier such as Q_1Q_1 in Figure 8.5 can be generated by considering all possible levels of feasible policy controls.

Now suppose that the two consumers trade in more than one commodity and the prices of several such goods possibly change (or alternatively, consider a change in production organization as in Figure 3.5). In this case, a host of money-measure utility possibility frontiers such as Q_1Q_1, Q_2Q_2, Q_3Q_3 and Q_4Q_4 can be developed by changing one price, holding others fixed at different levels or by changing several simultaneously in specific ways. One can apply the same rules of choice developed by Samuelson for utility possibility frontiers. That is, an envelope curve or grand possibility frontier *UU* can be determined, along which any optimal policy must lie. Similarly, if the money-measure utility possibility frontier associated with one policy lies entirely outside the money-measure utility possibility frontier associated with another policy, as Q_1Q_1 lies outside Q_2Q_2, then the first policy is clearly preferable to the second. Similar comparisons may be possible using grand utility frontiers for policies that affect several prices.

Thus, using money measures of utility change, a locus of efficient points (*UU* in Figure 8.5) can be developed. Furthermore, because of the ordinal relationship of utility and money measures, these efficient points correspond to exactly the same actions that lead to

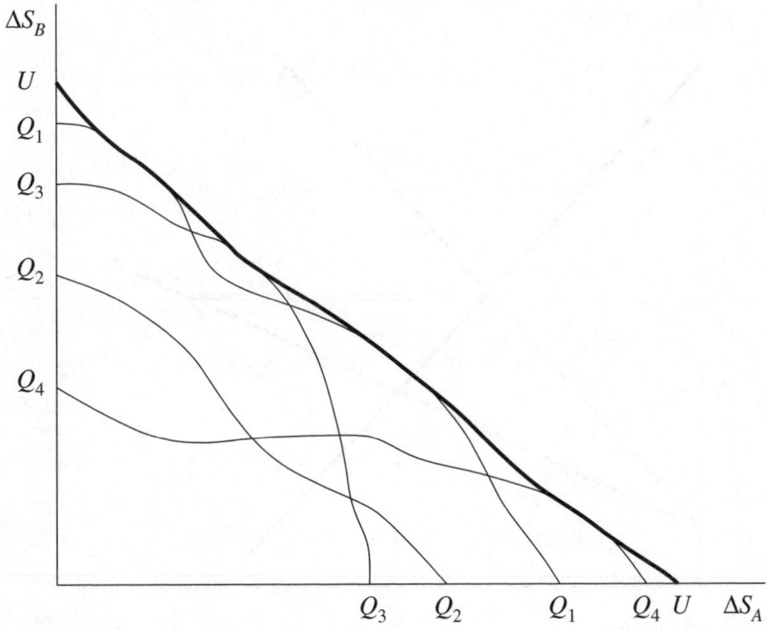

Figure 8.5

efficient points in the utility possibilities space of Figure 3.5. The problem of choosing a single point on the efficiency locus then requires a social welfare function unless one utility possibility frontier dominates all others. If a social welfare function in terms of money measures of utility is not available, the policy-maker must construct one. Without such a value judgment, ideally all a welfare economist can do is present the policy-maker with the efficient locus of points *UU* in Figure 8.5. The policy-maker must then choose a point on that locus.

In terms of empirical application of the foregoing approach, if many individuals are affected by a policy change, the diagram in Figure 8.5 takes on many dimensions, as does the empirical measurement. The problem thus becomes intractable empirically once the number of individuals gets large. In addition, because this approach introduces many dimensions, it may be impossible to comprehend from a policy-maker's standpoint even if the analysis could be carried out empirically. Furthermore, as pointed out in Section 5.3, the conditions that lead to unique money measures of utility change are likely not to be met. For these reasons, the WTP approach appears far more useful on empirical grounds.

8.4 AGGREGATION OF WTP OVER PRODUCERS AND CONSUMERS

Turning once again to WTP measures, this section demonstrates economic welfare analysis of technological change. Consider the market in Figure 8.6, with supply curve

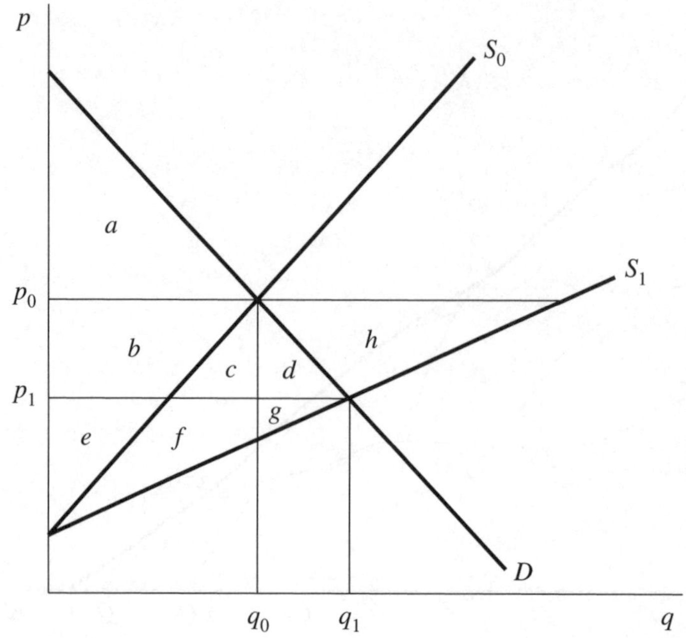

Figure 8.6

S_0, demand curve D, and equilibrium at price p_0 and quantity q_0. Consumer surplus is area a and producer surplus is area $b+e$. Now consider a policy that leads to development of a new technology such as hybrid corn. The supply curve shifts to S_1 because of accompanying cost-reducing or output-increasing possibilities. As a result, equilibrium price falls to p_1 as output is increased to q_1. But what are the welfare effects of the new technology? Consumer surplus increases from area a to area $a+b+c+d$, for a gain of area $b+c+d$. If D represents the derived demand of a producing industry that maximizes profits, then area $b+c+d$ represents the combined WTP (either compensating or equivalent variation) of that industry for the reduction in their input price. If D represents an ordinary consumer demand, then area $b+c+d$ approximates the combined WTP of all consumers under the Willig conditions discussed in Section 7.6. If D is a compensated consumer demand, then area $b+c+d$ is an exact measure of the compensating or equivalent variation, depending on the conditional utility level.

If S_0 and S_1 represent industry supply curves, the change in area behind the supply curve represents the combined WTP of the innovative industry for the new technology. Producer surplus is area $b+e$ before innovation and is area $e+f+g$ after innovation, so the gain for the innovating industry (or loss if negative) is area $f+g-b$. Note that *this welfare effect can be quite different from the usual cost-savings calculations, which would be attached by simple engineering studies of a new technology*. For example, if one were simply to consider the cost savings that could be obtained by producers under the new technology by continuing to produce the same output at the same price, the effect would be a gain of area $c+f$ (in cost savings). But with reduced marginal costs, all firms will expand output so the associated net welfare effects are in fact greater, while the producer's welfare effect may be much less or even negative. If an engineering study further considers the increase in profit-maximizing production but fails to consider product price adjustment, the producer gains would be incorrectly estimated by area $c+d+f+g+h$. But as output is increased, product prices must fall unless demand is perfectly elastic. Hence, the correct welfare effects can be assessed only by determining the shift in both equilibrium price and quantity.

As pointed out later in Chapter 9, other possible price adjustments in other markets must also be considered if present. For example, expansion of output q may entail an increase in demand for inputs used in producing q and thus the input prices may increase as a result of the technology. Or perhaps the new technology is capital intensive and displaces labor. Then wage rates for a particular type of labor may fall, and wage earners may be left unemployed. Thus, welfare effects may also be experienced by other groups not directly involved in the market in Figure 8.6. Typical engineering cost studies are sometimes deficient in considering these economic consequences, and hence this is an area in which proper economic welfare analysis can make a contribution. These latter considerations relating to other markets, however, will be introduced in Chapter 9.

To facilitate simple discussion of direct economic consequences in this chapter, prices in all other markets are assumed unaffected by changes in the market of interest. Such an assumption may be reasonable if the producing industry accounts for only a small component of each of its input markets (and thus has little price impact) and if the demand has very small cross-price elasticities or represents derived demand by an industry that is relatively unimportant in each of the other markets in which it is directly involved.

With this in mind, consider the net welfare consequences of the technological change in Figure 8.6. Adding the consumer and producer surplus gain obtains area $c+d+f+g$, which is simply the change in area above supply and below demand. What welfare connotations can be attached to this area? If the aggregate supply and demand are derived from appropriately compensated individual supplies and demands, or subject to applicability of the Willig approximation criteria in the case of aggregation of ordinary supplies and demands, this area represents the combined WTP of all producers and consumers in the marketplace. Unlike the case with area behind a market demand curve or behind a market supply curve, however, not all individuals are necessarily affected in the same direction in this case. All producers may lose while all consumers gain. In Figure 8.6, producers gain if area $f+g>$area b. Otherwise, producers lose. Thus, the combined WTP represents a net WTP after losers have just been compensated for losses. As Figure 8.6 shows, technological change generates a positive economic surplus that can be distributed in any manner whatever to attain a Pareto optimum.

If the Pareto criterion is satisfied in making such a change, however, any losers must be compensated. If some individuals lose, as producers would if area $b>$area $f+g$, then a recommendation to change (introduce the technology) without compensation involves a value judgment. That is, *some system of welfare weights must be used as a criterion to make a change unless all individuals gain or unless compensation is paid when only net gains are possible*. For example, if the producer gain is –10 and the consumer gain is 20, then – without compensation – the change is not justified unless the producer weight is no more than twice the consumer weight. Only when all welfare weights are equal can simple aggregate producer and consumer WTP be used as a criterion for change unless compensation is paid. Thus, an adequate welfare analysis of the effects of a change should generally determine the effects on each of the market groups (for example, producers and consumers) separately unless compensation is planned. Note also, however, that compensation should not always be paid. Some policies are designed with the specific objective of aiding some group even when an expense is involved for another group because of a specific problem confronting the first group. When a policy-maker has such an objective, a constraint that compensation must always be paid can severely limit the policy-maker's ability to help the former group. Section 8.5 presents several such examples.

8.5 WELFARE ANALYSIS OF SIMPLE MARKET DISTORTIONS

Given the framework developed thus far, the welfare effects of a number of government-imposed market distortions can be considered. Some common distortions imposed by governments include price ceilings/floors, support prices, taxes, subsidies and quotas. This section considers each of these possibilities and shows that such government intervention leads to a potentially Pareto-inferior state where some economic agents lose. The assumptions underlying these conclusions, however, are crucial, as shown in succeeding chapters.

Price Ceilings

Consider first the effects of price ceilings. In Figure 8.7, *D* represents demand and *S* represents supply. At market equilibrium, price is p_0 and quantity is q_0. Now, suppose that a

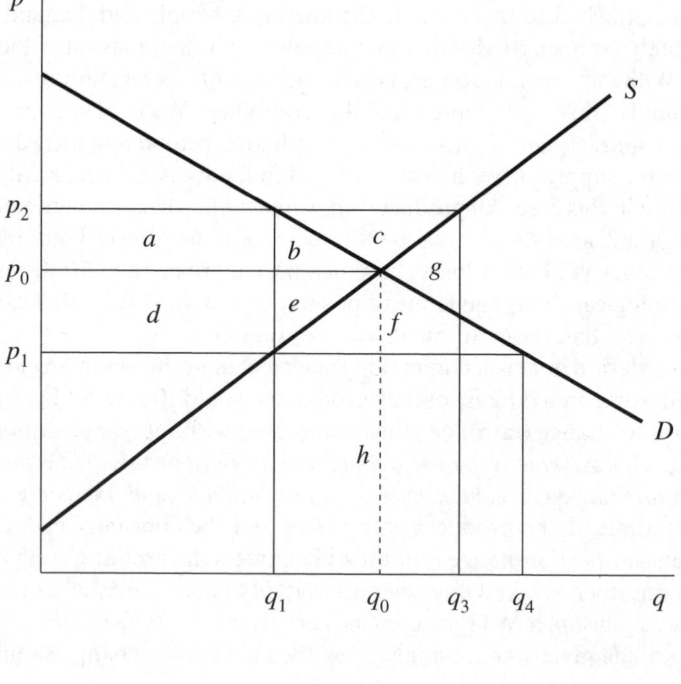

Figure 8.7

price ceiling of p_1 is imposed. At price p_1, producers are willing to supply only q_1 rather than q_0, and hence they lose area $d+e$ in producer surplus. At price p_1, however, consumers would like to buy a larger quantity q_4, but because only q_1 is produced, consumption is thus restricted. Assuming efficiency in rationing (those excluded from the market are not willing to pay more than those who are not), the effect on consumer surplus is equivalent to raising price to p_2 and then giving consumers a payment of $(p_2-p_1)\cdot q_1$. Thus, consumer surplus changes by area $d-b$. The net effect on producers plus consumers obtained by adding these two effects is thus a loss of area $b+e$. If S and D are compensated supply and demand curves wherever they represent consumers or factor owners, these areas represent exact measures of compensating or equivalent variations for each level of aggregation, depending on conditioned utility levels (otherwise, they are approximations in the Willig sense). Thus, a compensation scheme must exist such that everyone is better off without the price ceiling. For example, producers who lose area $d+e$ could instead pay only area d to consumers, and thus consumers could gain area d without giving up area b. Clearly, the adoption of a price ceiling, if either group benefits, represents an attempt to help one group at the expense of another and thus requires implicitly an unequal welfare weighting on the part of the policy-maker.

The price controls that were enacted in the US economy in the early 1970s were of this nature. The US administration was increasingly concerned about the adverse effect of inflation on consumers, and price controls or ceilings were imposed to give some short-run relief to consumers at the expense of producers. Figure 8.7 shows that such controls do indeed aid consumers (if area $d>$area b), but only at the expense of producers. Figure 8.7 also shows, however, that – with the price ceiling – a shortage of q_4-q_1 develops so that either each individual is not able to consume as much as desired at the new price or else some consumers are not able to gain access to the lower price at all. In the case of natural gas, where prices were regulated over a longer period of time, the latter effects are more apparent. When gas supplies were not sufficient, new customers were simply not allowed in some cases. This points to a possible need to disaggregate consumer welfare effects into groups that continue to have market access and those that do not (including or possibly considering another group for those who begin to desire market access at the lower price). The welfare effects on each of these groups may be different, and thus a policy-maker may wish to assign different weights to each. By this disaggregation, welfare analysis may reveal that the price ceiling actually has a severe adverse effect on at least part of the group it is intended to serve.

Price Floors

The welfare effects of a price floor can be considered similarly. If price p_2 is imposed in Figure 8.7, consumers will purchase only q_1. Once this is realized by producers, they will adjust output accordingly, because no other sales opportunities exist. Thus, consumers lose area $a+b$, while producers gain area $a-e$. The net loss due to the price ceiling is area $b+e$. Thus, without doubt, a compensation scheme exists so that everyone is better off without a price floor than with the price floor, regardless of welfare weights. For example, through a lump-sum transfer of area a from consumers to producers with equilibrium maintained at price p_0 and quantity q_0, producers would be better off by area e and consumers would be better off by area b than under the price floor. Furthermore, no one would thus be denied entrance into the market. Nevertheless, one should bear in mind that some set of welfare weights may exist such that a price floor is preferred to free market equilibrium.

A prime example of a price floor that has existed in the US economy is the minimum wage law. Under the assumptions in this chapter, where *S* represents compensated labor supply and *D* represents labor demand by industry, Figure 8.7 implies that the minimum wage reduces the quantity of labor demanded (increases unemployment). Industry is adversely affected while labor, in general, benefits. Some workers, however, are denied access to the market under the minimum wage (those represented by $q_3 - q_1$).[1] An adequate welfare analysis should point out the latter effects specifically, because the losses per individual by the unemployed may be substantial as compared with the gains per individual of those who remain in the market.

Price Supports

Sometimes price supports or controlled prices have been imposed by governments in such a way that no one is denied market access. This is accomplished by government entrance in the market to make up the difference in supply and demand. For example, suppose that p_2 in Figure 8.7 represents a price support. Government can enforce price p_2 by purchasing $q_3 - q_1$, which just makes up the difference in supply and demand at that price. The associated welfare effects are a loss of area $a+b$ for consumers and a gain of area $a+b+c$ by producers. Thus, producers and consumers jointly gain area c over the market equilibrium case. Note, however, that this gain is financed by a government expenditure of $p_2 \cdot (q_3 - q_1)$ or area $b+c+e+f+g+h$. This expenditure must be financed by taxpayers and hence leads to a net loss of area $b+e+f+g+h$ when all three groups are considered jointly. This quantity purchased by the government, however, may not be entirely worthless and may be resold on an international market or saved for periods of shortage. If this is the case, the ultimate welfare effects may be different, as shown in Sections 12.3 and 12.4.

The most common examples of price supports have been in the agricultural economy (for example, support prices for milk and grains). Price supports have been established to protect farmers from inadequate incomes due to the unstable nature of farm prices. But, from Figure 8.7, when possibilities for dumping in international markets or carrying government stocks over into periods of shortage do not exist, much better schemes of aiding producers are possible. For example, a lump-sum transfer of area a from consumers to producers and of area $b+c$ from taxpayers to producers entails as much gain for producers, with less loss for consumers and substantially less expense for taxpayers.

Taxes

The case of an *ad valorem* tax is represented in Figure 8.8. An *ad valorem* tax is a tax paid per unit of quantity, such as a sales tax. If p is the price of a good charged by the producer and t is the *ad valorem* tax that the consumer must pay on each unit of the good

1. Of course, $q_0 - q_1$ may also represent a gap in the amount of work per individual from desired levels by individuals remaining in the market, but because of the institution of a fixed-length workweek, the difference has tended to represent displacement of workers.

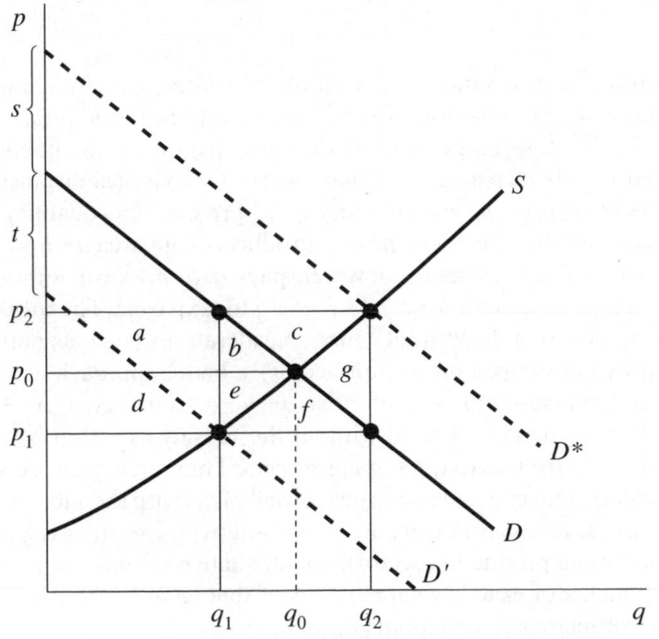

Figure 8.8

purchased, the effective price to the consumer is $p+t$. Thus, with p on the vertical axis, the effect of the tax is to lower the effective demand curve by a distance of t. Where equilibrium without the tax is at price p_0 and quantity q_0, the tax t lowers effective demand to D', thus reaching a new equilibrium at price p_1 and quantity q_1. The vertical distance between D and D' at that point, given by $p_2 - p_1$, is equal to t, so p_2 represents the effective consumer price. The welfare effects of the tax are thus a loss of area $d+e$ for producers and a loss of area $a+b$ for consumers. Both producers and consumers lose as the tax drives a wedge between supply and demand. The government, however, gains $(p_2 - p_1) \cdot q_1$, or area $a+d$, in tax revenues, which are assumed to be distributed in lump-sum form to households. Thus, the tax leads to a net welfare loss, sometimes called a *deadweight loss*, of area $b+e$.

The tax has a distorting effect because it induces producers to adjust to a different marginal price than effectively experienced by consumers. A better possibility in theory and under the simple assumptions of this chapter is to impose lump-sum taxes in the amounts of areas a and d on consumers and producers, respectively, while leaving marginal prices unaffected. In this way, market equilibrium at price p_0 and quantity q_0 can still be maintained so that area $b+e$ need not be lost. In reality, however, lump-sum taxes that truly do not affect marginal conditions are difficult to determine. Perhaps the closet approximations to a lump-sum tax that are imposed in popular practice are property and income taxes. But an income tax, for example, is by no means free of effects on marginal conditions.

Subsidies

The case of a subsidy is very similar to that of an *ad valorem* tax. Sometimes, if government wants to encourage production of some commodity or to aid failing producers in an industry, a subsidy of, say, s per unit of output is paid from the public treasury. In Figure 8.8, this effectively increases the demand curve by a vertical distance of s, so that equilibrium shifts from price p_0 and quantity q_0 to price p_1 and quantity q_2. With the subsidy, the effective producer price is thus p_2. Producers gain area $a+b+c$ while consumers gain area $d+e+f$. Government, however, pays $(p_2-p_1)\cdot q_2$ in subsidy payments, which represents a loss of area $a+b+c+d+e+f+g$ to taxpayers. The subsidy thus leads to a net welfare loss of area g. Without other considerations (such as national security associated with a well-developed production sector), a better approach in aiding producers is to make a lump-sum transfer of area $a+b+c$ from taxpayers to producers. Consumers can also be made as well off without the subsidy as with it by transferring a lump-sum area $d+e+f$ from taxpayers to consumers. Thus, area g can be saved for taxpayers while producers and consumers are just as well off as with the subsidy. On the other hand, if such factors as national security are important (where security is gained by developing a well-functioning production sector), an adequate economic welfare analysis can inform the policy-maker of exactly what the costs of that security are and how much cost must be incurred for incremental amounts of security.

Quotas and Market Rationing

Finally, consider the case of quotas imposed by government or market rationing imposed by other institutional arrangements. If a quota or limitation of q_1 is imposed in the market in Figure 8.8 such that no quantity greater than q_1 can be marketed by producers, consumers will bid up the price to p_2 in order to ration what is produced. Producers, however, incur only those costs based on the short-run supply curve S and hence, in addition to the producer surplus normally realized at price p_1, they gain $(p_2-p_1)\cdot q_1$. Thus, consumers lose area $a+b$ while producers gain area $a-e$. The quota thus leads to a net or deadweight welfare loss of area $b+e$.

In this welfare analysis, producer sales are assumed limited by the quota. Alternatively, consumer purchases could be limited by the quota. In this case, the producers would respond along their supply curve and bid the price down to p_1 in a competitive effort to capture some of the available market. Thus, producers would lose area $d+e$ while consumers would gain area $d-b$. The net effect, however, would still be a loss of area $b+e$.

These two examples suggest that quotas may be imposed in several ways. The way they are imposed may give more advantage to either producers or consumers so the area $a+d$ may be allocated in various ways between the two groups. Nevertheless, a deadweight loss from restricting the market of area $b+e$ is clear. Thus, some compensation scheme exists so that both groups are better off without the quota. However, one must also consider the fact that a policy-maker may still prefer to restrict a market if the restriction has desirable effects elsewhere in the economy, which might be the case for chemicals that are harmful to the environment. Such cases are considered in Section 13.4.

It should also be noted that the quota case is one in which quantities rather than prices are directly controlled. Hence, the compensating or equivalent surplus considerations of

Section 7.9 come into play. When the supply (demand) curve represents ordinary consumer behavior, the true welfare measure for imposing a quota is the compensating surplus rather than the compensating variation (although the equivalent variation may be applied to the question in lieu of change), and the true welfare measure for removing a quota is the equivalent surplus if the question is necessary compensation in lieu of change (although compensating variation may be used if the question is compensation in the event of change). Thus, the conditions for accuracy of the consumer/producer surplus change in assessing WTP for quotas may follow the discussion of Section 7.9 rather than Sections 7.5 through 7.7, depending on the policy question.

An Example

An example can serve to illustrate the above analyses of simple distortions. Suppose that consumer demand for wheat (and wheat equivalent in wheat products) is represented by

$$q = 18 - 2p + 2m$$

and producer supply of wheat is given by

$$q = 2 + 4p - 2w,$$

where

q = quantity of wheat in hundred million bushels per year
p = price of wheat in dollars per bushel
m = consumer disposable income in thousand dollars per capita per year
w = price of fertilizer in hundred dollars per ton.

Suppose that the best projections for consumer income and fertilizer price for next year are $m = 3$ and $w = 1$, respectively. In this case, the projected demand is represented by $q = 24 - 2p$ and projected supply is represented by $q = 4p$, as shown in Figure 8.9, with equilibrium at price $p = 4$ and quantity $q = 16$ (obtained by solving the two equations simultaneously).

Now consider the expected welfare effects of imposing a quota on wheat marketings as was done in the USA during the 1950s and early 1960s. If, say, producers are not allowed to market more than 1.2 billion bushels ($q = 12$), then consumer price will be bid up according to the demand curve to $p = 6$ (obtained by solving the demand equation for p with $q = 12$). As in the case of Figure 8.8, the producer gain is area $a - e$, and the consumer loss is area $a + b$. To calculate these effects, note that area a is $(6-4) \times 12 = 24$, and area e is a triangle with base 1 and height 4 (or vice versa) so the area is $1 \times 4 \times ½ = 2$. Similarly, area b is a triangle with base 4 and height 2 so the area is $4 \times 2 \times ½ = 4$. Thus, area $a - e = 22$, and area $a + b = 28$. Since quantity is measured in hundred million bushels and price is measured in dollars per bushel, the areas are measured in hundred million dollars. Thus, the implications of the quota in this example are a gain of \$2.2 billion for wheat producers and a loss of \$2.8 billion for wheat consumers. The deadweight loss is \$600 million.

An alternative policy control that has been used to support wheat producers' incomes

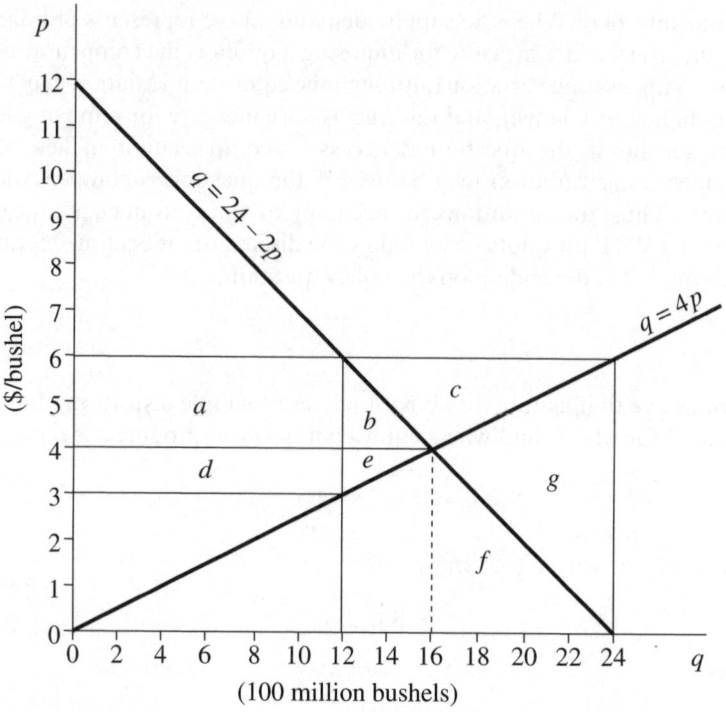

Figure 8.9

is a price support. Suppose that, instead of a quota, a price support of \$6.00 per bushel is established. The quantity produced at that price is $q=4p=24$, while the quantity demanded is $q=24-2p=12$ (Figure 8.9). Thus, with a \$6.00 per bushel price support, the model implies excess production of 1200 million bushels that would have to be purchased by the government to make the support effective (assuming no production controls). As in the analysis in Figure 8.7, producers gain area $a+b+c$, consumers lose area $a+b$ and government spends area $b+c+e+f+g$ on excess production. In terms of the present example, areas *a*, *b* and *e* are the same as above, while area *c* is a triangle of base 12 and height 2. Thus, area $c=12\times 2\times ½=12$. Area $b+c+e+f+g$ is a rectangle of dimensions 6 and 12, so the area is 72. Thus, again recalling that the areas in Figure 8.9 are measured in hundred million dollars, producers gain \$4.0 billion (area $a+b+c=40$) and consumers lose \$2.8 billion (area $a+b=28$), while government spends \$7.2 billion in accumulating 1.2 billion bushels of wheat in reserves.

Of course, the effects of other types of policies or combinations of policies can also be considered in the context of this example, but the above cases serve to demonstrate how quantitative measurements or estimates of supply and demand relationships can be used to produce meaningful quantitative information about the economic welfare consequences. One should also bear in mind in this analysis, however, the possibility that actual WTP may diverge from the ordinary consumer and producer surpluses calculated in this manner, as demonstrated in the examples in Section 6.5, 6.6 and 7.8.

8.6 LAISSEZ-FAIRE AND GOVERNMENT INTERVENTION

The cases above demonstrate that Adam Smith's 'invisible hand', associated with market competition (see Section 2.5), results in an optimal allocation of resources. That is, given the assumptions to this point, there is no way that a government can increase welfare in a Pareto-superior fashion by changing output price or quantity in either direction from the competitive equilibrium. Government intervention, however, does not always lead to net losses and Pareto suboptimality – even when compensation is not considered. Some counterexamples arise in the cases of imperfect competition (see Chapter 10), information failures (see Chapter 11), instability (see Chapter 12), externalities and public goods (see Chapter 13) and intertemporal problems where some generations are not represented (see Chapter 14). The following section demonstrates some additional exceptions where governments have separate jurisdictions and act only in the interest of concerns within their jurisdiction.

8.7 INTERNATIONAL TRADE

Thus far this book has not considered trade among countries. In effect, aggregation has been over consumers and producers within a single country allowing no trade among countries. Such a country in economics is called a closed economy. This section considers the case of an open economy where trade is possible among countries. By trade, each country can escape the limitations imposed by its own technology and resources. Gains from trade are typically possible whereby a country exports products for which the required resources are relatively abundant and imports products for which the required resources are relatively scarce. The effects of trade policies, such as tariffs, subsidies and quotas, are then considered for trading countries with emphasis on the distribution of gains from trade.

The Gains from Trade

Consider first the potential gains from trade in a general equilibrium framework. General equilibrium principles can guide meaningful application of partial equilibrium market models, yielding a useful framework for the applied welfare analysis of trade policies.

To illustrate the gains from trade in a general equilibrium framework, consider Figure 8.10. As discussed in Section 2.5, if markets exist for all goods and the production possibility curve PP' and the Scitovsky curve C_1 have their usual shapes as in Figure 8.10, then the competitive no-trade equilibrium at point a with price ratio p_1^1/p_2^1 for goods q_1 and q_2, respectively, is also Pareto optimal. Under autarky (no trade), no movement from point a can make anyone better off without making someone else worse off. No movement outside the production possibility curve is possible without either additional resources or technical change, and no movement below the Scitovsky curve will leave all consumers at least as well off.

Now suppose this country opens trade and finds that the relative world prices are p_1^2/p_2^2 rather than its domestic price ratio p_1^1/p_2^1. These differences in prices may be caused by

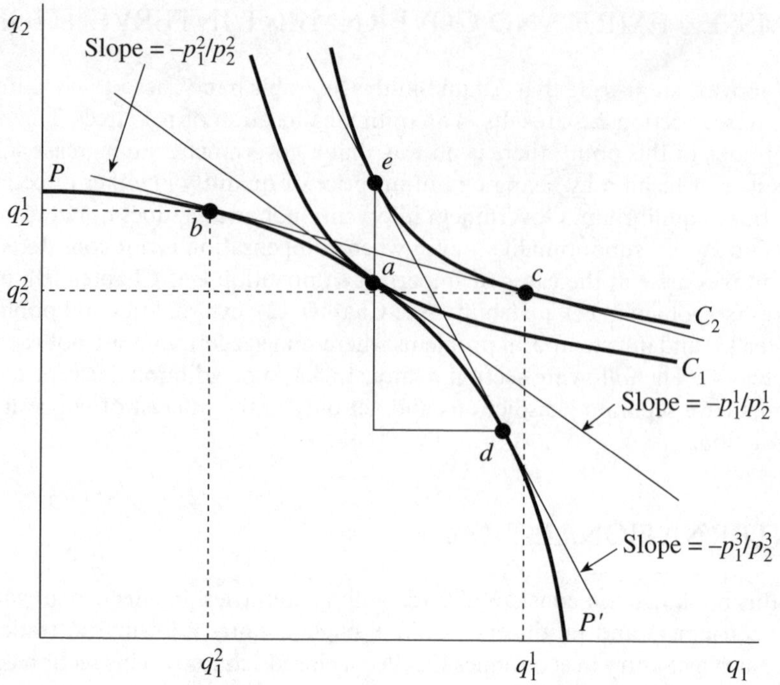

Figure 8.10

other countries having different resource endowments or different technologies. The relative world prices at which this country can buy or sell are called the terms of trade. With terms of trade p_1^2/p_2^2, this country can choose to produce at point *b* and consume at point *c*, attaining a higher Scitovsky curve C_2. This is possible by selling (exporting) quantity $q_2^1 - q_2^2$ of good q_2 and importing quantity $q_1^1 - q_1^2$ of good q_2. At terms of trade p_1^2/p_2^2 the trade balance is zero, meaning that the total cost of imports is exactly equal to the revenue received for exports. Thus, the country can consume at the point *c* outside its own production possibility curve. Consumption is thus possible at a higher Scitovsky curve, which with appropriate redistribution makes point *c* potentially Pareto superior to consumption at point *a*.

If alternatively the terms of the trade are p_1^3/p_2^3, then the country can choose to produce at the point *d* but will then trade to allow consumption at point *e*, exporting q_1 and importing q_2. Again, consumption on Scitovsky curve C_2 (at point *e*) is potentially Pareto superior to consumption under autarky at point *a*. Thus, if the terms of trade that a country faces with respect to any other country are different than it faces domestically, it can potentially increase the welfare of its citizens through trade. This is what is meant by the gains from trade.

While the above analysis is useful for demonstrating the general principle of the gains from trade, a partial equilibrium market model is more useful for examining the distribution of gains from trade. The simplest demonstration of gains from trade is given in Figure 8.11. Suppose a country produces two goods. The supply for good q_1 (oranges) is given by S_1 and the demand schedule is D_1 in Figure 8.11(a). The no-trade equilibrium

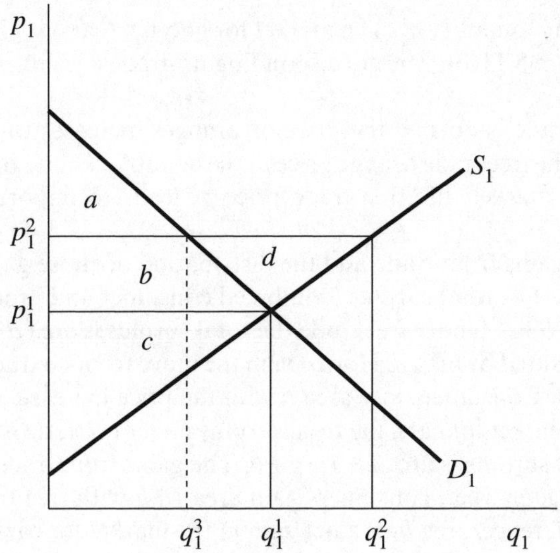

(a)

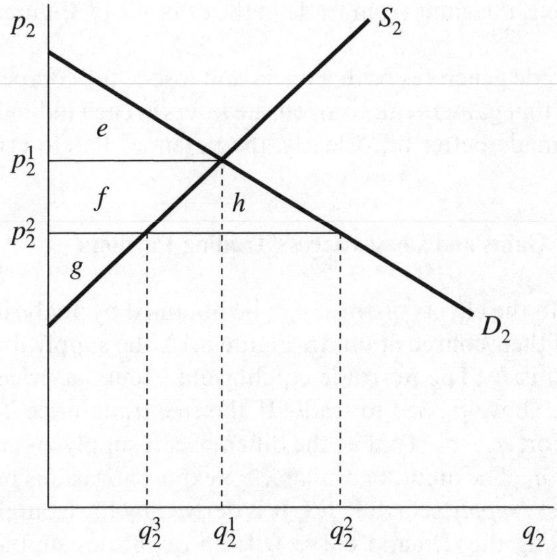

(b)

Figure 8.11

occurs at price p_1^1 and quantity q_1^1. The market for good q_2 (cars) is given by supply S_2 and demand D_2 in Figure 8.11(b). The corresponding no-trade equilibrium occurs at price p_2^1 and quantity q_2^1.

Suppose when trade is opened the price of oranges increases to p_1^2 while the price of cars falls to p_2^2. At the free trade orange price p_1^2 the country exports oranges in the amount $q_1^2 - q_1^3$. In the car market, the free trade price p_2^2 leads to importation of cars in the amount $q_2^2 - q_2^3$.

To consider the gains from trade and the distribution of those gains, consider first the market for oranges. The total surplus (combined consumer and producer surplus) under no trade is area $a+b+c$. Under free trade the total surplus is area $a+b+c+d$. The gains from trade are measured by area d. However, in the move from no trade to free trade, some lose and some gain. Consumers lose area b with the price increase, while producers gain areas $b+d$. In the market for cars, the total surplus under no trade is area $e+f+g$. Under free trade, the total surplus is area $e+f+g+h$. The gains from trade are given by area h. Unlike in the orange market, consumers gain area $f+h$ with free trade while producers lose area f. The difference, area h, is a net gain in the market for cars.

This analysis demonstrates that gains from trade occur in every market for which the price under trade is different than under no trade. Of course, markets where price is unaffected by trade would generate no effects on welfare of either producers or consumers. The net gain for the economy from trade is given by adding the gains over all markets. For example, the gains from trade in the example of Figure 8.11 would be measured by area $d+h$.

While opening trade generates both gainers and losers, the compensation criterion can be applied to verify that gainers can compensate losers in each individual market such that all are potentially made better off. Clearly, the potential Pareto criterion also supports opening trade.

The Distribution of Gains and Losses across Trading Partners

Further insights into the effects of trade can be obtained by analyzing excess supply and excess demand and their composition. In Figure 8.12, the supply for good q is S and the demand for good q is D. The no-trade equilibrium occurs at price p_1 and quantity q_1. Suppose prices rise above p_1 due to trade. If the free trade price is p_2, the country will produce q_2 and export $q_2 - q_3$. That is, the difference in supply and demand at price p_2 is $S(p_2) - D(p_2) = q_2 - q_3$. The quantity available for export at various prices above p_1 is summarized by the *excess supply* schedule ES. It is derived by horizontally subtracting quantities demanded along the demand curve D from quantities supplied along the supply curve S. For example, at price p_2 the excess supply quantity is q_4, which is equal to $q_2 - q_3$. The higher the price, the larger the quantity produced and exported, while the amount consumed is smaller. The area above the excess supply curve has an important welfare significance. That is, the area behind the excess supply curve bounded by a given price is a measure of the gains from trade. For example, area a is equal to area b, which is the excess of the producer surplus gain over the consumer surplus loss in moving from the no-trade price at p_1 to the free trade price at p_2.

The *excess demand* schedule can also be represented in Figure 8.12. Suppose opening trade causes price to fall from p_1 to p_3. The quantity consumed thus increases to q_2, the

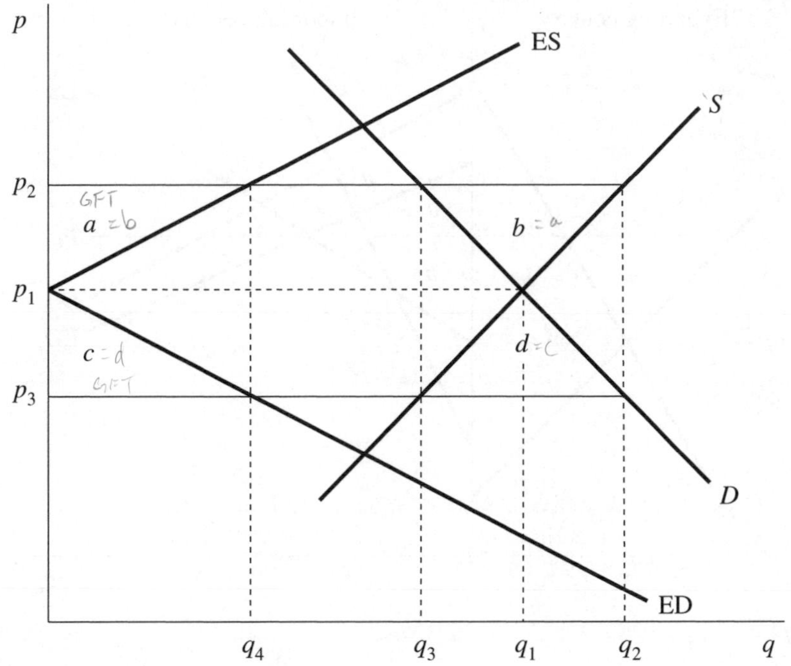

Figure 8.12

amount supplied falls to q_3, and as a result imports occur in the amount $q_2 - q_3$. Imports at various prices are summarized by the excess demand schedule ED. It is derived by horizontally subtracting quantities supplied along the supply curve *S* from quantities demanded along the demand curve *D*. For example, at price p_1 imports are zero, whereas at price p_3 imports are q_4, which is equal to $q_2 - q_3$. The area behind the excess demand curve bounded by the price is also a measure of gains from trade. For example, area *c* is equal to area *d*, which is the excess of the consumer surplus gain over the producer surplus loss in moving from price p_1 to price p_3.

To demonstrate the use of excess supply and demand curves in calculating the gains from trade and the distribution of gains and losses across groups in each country, consider Figure 8.13. Demand and supply in the importing country are given by D' and S', respectively. Demand and supply in the exporting country are represented by *D* and *S* and appear backwards in the left side of Figure 8.13. Without international trade, equilibrium prices are p_i and p_e in the two respective countries. Because price is higher in one country than in the other, there is an incentive for the first to buy from the second. The amount that the exporting country will sell at each price is given by the excess supply curve ES. Similarly, the amount that the importing country will import at each price is given by the excess demand curve ED. Equilibrium in international trade is obtained where the importer's excess demand is equal to the exporter's excess supply (that is, at international price p_t).

The welfare effects of opening trade can be examined by evaluating the effect of a price change to p_t in each country. In the exporting country, producers gain area $a+b$, and

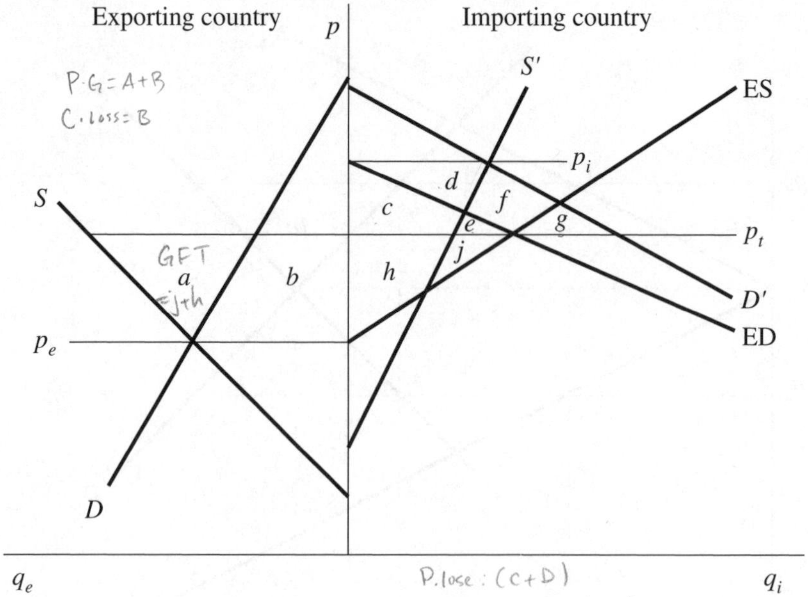

Figure 8.13

P.lose : (C+D)
C.gain : (C+D+E+F+G)
N= E+F+G = C+E
Total World C+E +H+J

consumers lose area b. The net effect in the exporting country is a gain of area a, which is equal to area $h+j$ because ES represents the horizontal difference in S and D. In the importing country, producers lose area $c+d$ while consumers gain area $c+d+e+f+g$. The net effect in the importing country is thus a gain of area $e+f+g$, which is equal to area $c+e$ because ED represents the horizontal difference in S' and D'. Thus, both countries gain from opening trade even though only one country buys from the other. The overall gain is area $c+e+h+j$, that is, the area behind excess demand and excess supply. However, the distributional effects are quite different in the two countries. In the exporting country, producers gain and consumers lose, whereas in the importing country producers lose and consumers gain. Because both countries gain, any necessary compensation can be paid from gainers to losers within countries.

The model in Figure 8.13 applies only for trade in a single good. Additional goods can be added to the analysis where the importing country becomes an exporter of a different good and the exporting country becomes an importer of the second good. The more goods and countries added to the analysis, the more the model reflects general equilibrium. Often empirical analysis is simplified by considering a two-country model where one country represents the rest of the world. Thus, the classification of a country as importer or exporter of a particular good automatically classifies the other country.

The results on the effects of free trade for a two-country, two-commodity case are summarized in Table 8.1. For both countries, the net gains from trade are positive even though distributional effects on individual groups are both positive and negative. For example, producers of the export good in country A gain from free trade while producers of the same good in country B (which is thus necessarily an importer) lose.

Table 8.1 The effects of trade with two countries and two goods

Country A		Country B	
Good X (exporter)	Good Y (importer)	Good X (importer)	Good Y (exporter)
Producers gain	Producers lose	Producers lose	Producers gain
Consumers lose	Consumers gain	Consumers gain	Consumers lose
Net gain	Net gain	Net gain	Net gain

Trade and Government Programs

Many internationally traded commodities, especially farm commodities, are regulated by government programs. The effects of such programs must be analyzed in the context of international trade. Two common farm programs are (1) production controls and (2) income support programs.

Production controls

The effects of production controls are illustrated in Figure 8.14. Suppose domestic supply of a commodity is represented by *S* and domestic demand is *D*. To introduce trade, let TD represent total demand for domestic production, which is the horizontal summation of domestic demand *D* and excess demand from the rest of the world (excess demand is not shown). With free trade the price is p_1, production is q_1, and exports are $q_1 - q_2$. Now suppose production controls are introduced so that production is restricted to q_2. As a result, the domestic and world prices rise to p_2. Due to the higher price with production controls, domestic consumers lose area *a*. On net, foreign producers and consumers combined lose area $b+c$. Domestic producers gain area $a+b$ but lose area $e+f$. If total demand is inelastic, as it is for many food commodities, then domestic producers' gain necessarily exceeds their loss.[2] On net, domestic producers and consumers gain area *b* and lose area $e+f$. This net domestic effect can be either positive or negative depending on elasticities of supply and demand, but is positive with sufficiently elastic supply (in which case area $e+f$ approaches zero). In this case, neither the compensation criterion nor the Pareto principle are met for the exporting country by removing the production quota.

Income support

Many governments subsidize farm income by artificially increasing commodity prices. In Figure 8.15, the domestic supply curve is *S*, domestic demand is *D* and total demand for domestic production (which includes foreign excess demand) is TD. As in Figure 8.14,

2. For inelastic demand, total revenue increases when the quantity is reduced. For example, if $q(p)$ specifies the quantity demanded at price *p*, then revenue is given by $pq(p)$. Use of calculus shows that the effect of a change in price on revenue is $\partial[pq(p)]/\partial p = q(p) + p\partial q(p)/\partial p$. Dividing this equation by $q(p)$ reveals that the effect on revenue of raising the price is positive or negative depending on whether $1 + \partial q(p)/\partial p\ [p/q(p)]$ is positive or negative. This expression is positive if the latter term, which is the price elasticity of demand, is less than one (inelastic demand), and is negative if the price elasticity of demand is greater than one (elastic demand). Thus, if the total demand in Figure 8.14 is inelastic for $q_2 < q < q_1$, then total revenue at q_2, which is given by p_2q_2, is less than total revenue at q_1, which is given by p_1q_1. This means that area $a+b$ is greater than area $e+f+g$, which necessarily implies that area $a+b$ is greater than area $e+f$.

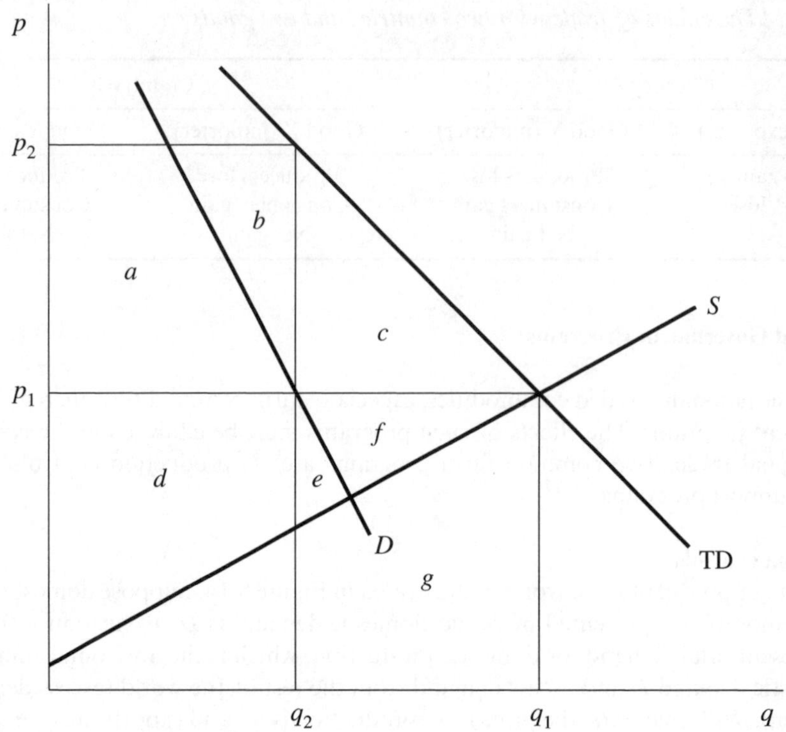

Figure 8.14

equilibrium under autarky occurs at price is p_1 and quantity q_1, while free trade has equilibrium at price p_2 and quantity q_2. Now suppose the government introduces a target price p_T for farmers that is facilitated by means of a subsidy. Price p_T will induce farmers to produce and sell quantity q_3. For farmers to receive price p_T at quantity q_3, the government must pay a subsidy of $p_T - p_3$ on each unit of output.

While the classic net gains from free trade are given by area $f+i$, the effects of trade are very different if trade is accompanied by implementation of a target price. Comparing the target price outcome to free trade, domestic consumers gain area e and foreign concerns gain area $f+g$ as the market price falls to p_3. Producers gain area $a+b+c$ because they receive the target price p_T made possible by the government subsidy in the amount of area $a+b+c+d+e+f+g$, which represents a loss to taxpayers. Thus, the net effect for both countries combined compared to free trade is (area e)+(area $f+g$)+(area $a+b+c$)−(area $a+b+c+d+e+f+g$), which amounts to a net loss of area d. However, the exporting country loses area $d+f+g$.

Comparing the target price outcome to the autarky equilibrium at price p_1 and quantity q_1, domestic consumers lose area h and producers gain area $a+b+c+e+f+h+i$. Domestic taxpayers lose area $a+b+c+d+e+f+g$, which represents subsidies paid to support the target price. The net effect for domestic concerns (which may represent the objective of domestic government) is thus (area $a+b+c+e+f+h+i$) − (area h) − (area $a+b+c+d+e+f+g$), which amounts to a net welfare effect of area $i-d-g$. This area

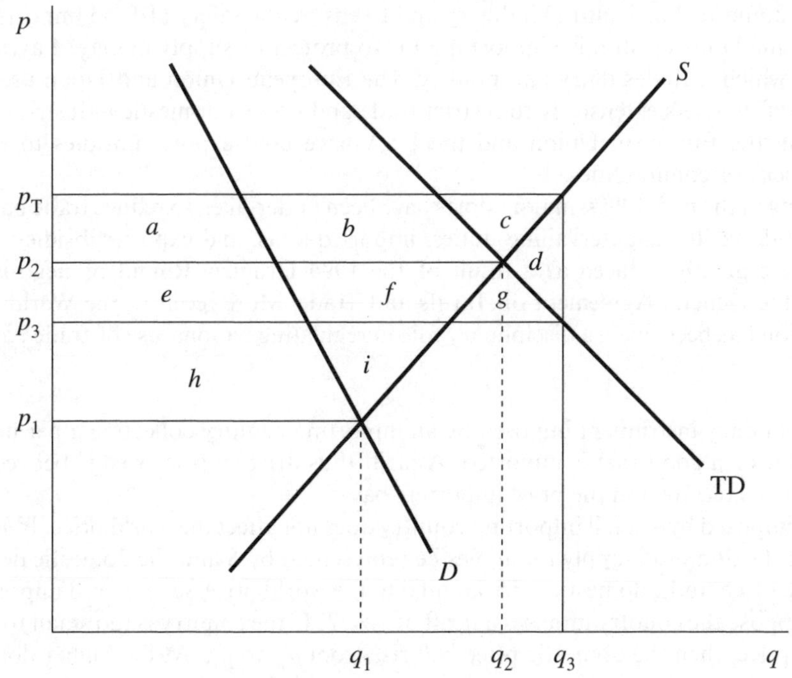

Figure 8.15

may be positive if the subsidy is small (the target price is not much greater than the free trade price) and the free trade price is sufficiently higher than the autarky price. However, the inefficiency of the subsidy can eliminate or exceed the classic gains from trade if the subsidy is large and the free trade price is not much higher than the autarky price.

Because of the adverse impact of subsidized prices on consumer and overall welfare, target prices have at times been implemented in combination with measures that limit production, such as production quotas. For example, if production quotas are established at quantities that would be free trade equilibrium quantities, then production does not increase with target prices and the total subsidy behaves more like a lump-sum transfer payment from taxpayers to producers. Because the sign of the net effect is ambiguous, the gains from trade when accompanied by a combination of target prices and quotas is an empirical question. With these considerations, actual gains from trade have been estimated to be negative for US cotton and wheat. That is, the inefficiencies of farm programs have more than negated the classic gains from trade.[3]

Tariffs, Quotas and Export Subsidies

Trade barriers restricting both agricultural and nonagricultural trade are imposed by many countries. Mexico, for example, uses an array of tariff and nontariff barriers to protect its many small farmers from foreign competition. The USA restricts imports to

3. For example, negative gains from trade have been found for US cotton and US wheat due to government programs by Schmitz, Schmitz and Dumas (1997) and Schmitz, Sigurdson and Doering (1986).

protect its domestic horticultural industry and to ensure the safety of food imports from Mexico. Canada uses restrictive import quotas to protect its supply-managed agricultural sector, which includes dairy and poultry. The European Union and Japan use tariff and nontariff barriers extensively to restrict trade and protect domestic industries. Also, in the past, the European Union and the USA have used export subsidies to reduce surplus stocks of commodities.

Beginning in the mid-1990s, major efforts have been undertaken to reduce trade barriers. These include tariffs, countervailing duties, import quotas, and export subsidies. Trade barriers were greatly reduced as a result of the 1994 Uruguay Round of negotiations related to the General Agreement on Tariffs and Trade. More recently, the World Trade Organization has been given a disciplinary role in regulating nations' use of trade barriers.

Tariffs

A tariff is a policy instrument imposed by an importing country collecting a per unit fee on each unit of a good that is imported. A tariff thus drives a price wedge between the price exporters receive and the price importers pay.

A tariff imposed by a small importing country does not affect the world price. In Figure 8.16(a), let the domestic supply for apples be represented by S and the domestic demand by D. Under free trade, domestic price is equal to the world price, say p_W, and imports are $q_2 - q_1$. Suppose the country imposes a tariff of size T. If the country is too small to affect the world price, then the domestic price will rise from p_W to p_D. At the higher domestic price, domestic production increases from q_1 to q_3 and domestic consumption declines from q_2 to q_4. Imports thus decline to $q_4 - q_3$. As a result of the tariff, producers in the importing country gain area a and consumers lose area $a+b+c+d$. The consumer loss is partially offset by an increase in government tariff revenue in the amount of area c. Adding these effects shows that the tariff makes the importing country worse off because the producer gain plus the government revenue collected from the tariff is smaller than the consumer loss due to higher prices. The net loss is area $b+d$.

For a large country, imposition of a tariff affects the world price. In this case a tariff can possibly make the importer better off because a 'terms of trade effect' causes the export price to fall. In Figure 8.16(b), the world free-trade price is p_W^1, where the excess supply quantity from the rest of the world (the excess supply schedule is shown backwards in the left side of Figure 8.16(b), which is the horizontal difference in S and D in the right side of Figure 8.16(b)) is equal to $q_2 - q_1$, which is the horizontal difference in demand D and supply S in the importing country in the right side of Figure 8.16(b) at that price. Suppose when a tariff of size T is introduced, the domestic price rises to p_D and the world price falls to p_W^2. At price p_W^2 the rest of the world supplies quantity $q_4 - q_3$ determined by the excess supply ES at that price. In this case, domestic consumers lose area $a+b+c+d$, domestic producers gain area a and tariff revenue becomes area $c+e$. The net effect on domestic welfare is thus area $e-b-d$, which can be positive if the impact on world price is sufficiently large.[4]

4. Where gains are possible by imposing a tariff, a country may seek to impose the optimal tariff that maximizes the country's net gain. The optimal tariff can be found by applying the model of Section 10.2 to the excess demand of the importer and the excess supply of the rest of the world, assuming absence of retaliation. Alternatively, a government may choose to impose the tariff that maximizes government revenue. This tariff can be found by applying the pure middleman model of Section 10.6.

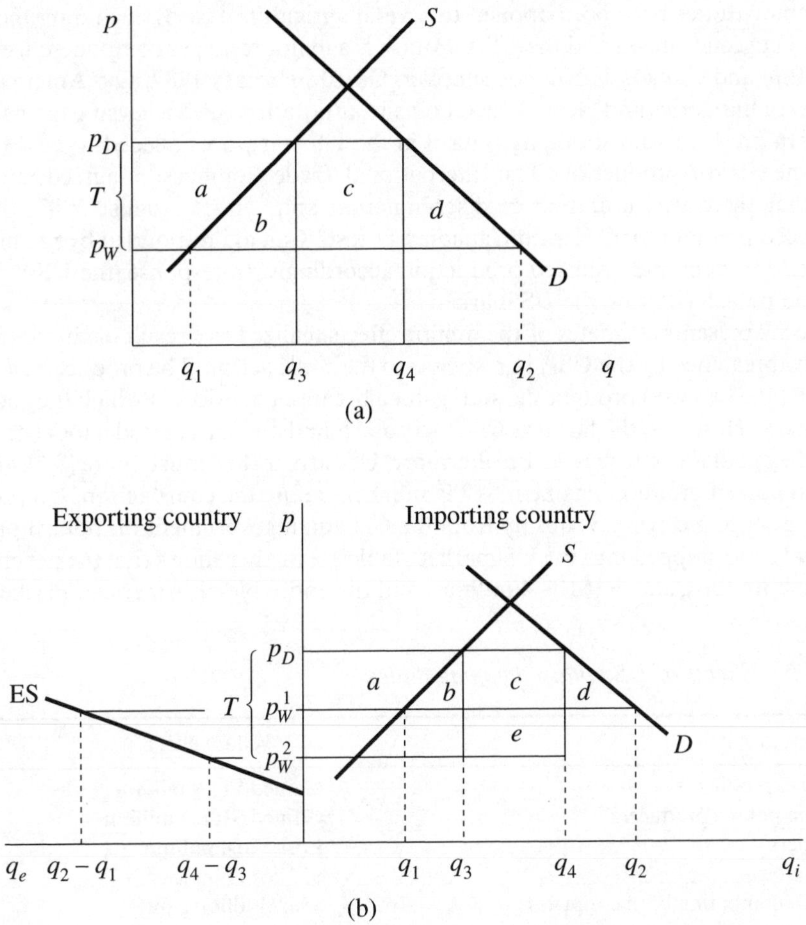

Figure 8.16

These models assume that exporters do not retaliate even though they are harmed by importers' imposition of a tariff. Comparison of these results to earlier results for closed economies (which would correspond to either autarky or a world economy under free trade) makes clear that any gain by an importing country from imposing a tariff is less than the loss suffered by exporting countries. This is why, from a global perspective, taking into account both importers and exporters, free trade is optimal.

Dumping duties

A dumping duty is a tariff imposed by the importing country in response to unfair trade practices such as export dumping, which occurs if the exporter sells below the cost of production (which can occur with subsidized production) or sells abroad at a price below that charged in the home market. Border disputes often arise over accusations of unfair trade.[5]

5. For theoretical presentations related to border disputes regarding unfair trade, see Schmitz, Firch and Hillman (1981).

Dumping duties have been applied to several agricultural cases, including the potash dispute between Canada and the USA. Potash is a major fertilizer component used in US agriculture and Canada is a major supplier. On 10 February 1987, two American firms (Lundberg Industries and New Mexico Potash Corporation) filed a lawsuit against several Canadian producers for dumping potash in the USA at prices alleged to be 43 percent below the cost of production. The International Trade Commission agreed, on 3 April 1987, that there was unfair price discrimination and, on 21 August 1987, the USA announced preliminary duties on Canadian potash. Canada responded by raising prices by over 30 percent and adjusted production accordingly. In response, the USA removed duties on potash entering the US market.

Table 8.2 presents estimates of the welfare effects realized as a result of the countervailing duty threatened by the USA in response to the court action. The producers of potash, including the two who brought the suit, gained because the prices at which they could sell potash rose. However, the farmers who use potash in the USA suffered a loss because the prices they paid for potash rose. Furthermore, US farmers lost much more ($70.4 million) than US potash producers gained ($12.9 million). Before the court action, US producers were in essence receiving a subsidy from the Canadian government on potash produced in Canada and shipped into the US market. Table 8.2 further shows that the net effect was positive both for Canada ($108.4 million) and the entire North American market ($50.9 million).

Table 8.2 Effects of US potash dumping duties

Economic group	Welfare effect
US potash producers	Gained $12.9 million
Canadian potash producers	Gained $108.4 million
US farmers	Lost $70.4 million
Net US effect	$57.5 million loss
Net effect combining both countries	$50.9 million gain

Source: Picketts, Schmitz and Schmitz (1991).

Import quotas

In internationally traded products, import quotas are common. In Figure 8.16(b), if an import quota of $q_4 - q_3$ replaces the tariff T, then the net effect of the quota for the importing country is the same as the tariff. That is, if importers are limited to buying $q_4 - q_3$ on the world market, then world price falls to p_W^2 along the excess supply ES. In this case, importers capture the welfare benefit represented by area $c + e$ because they buy at price p_W^2 but sell at price p_D. Alternatively, the government may capture part or all of these quota rents through auctioning import licenses to importers. Another possibility is that governments may award preferential trade arrangements to specific exporting countries that allow the exporters to capture quota rents by charging price p_D.

Export subsidies

During the late 1980s and early 1990s, the USA under the Export Enhancement Program and the European Union under the Export Restitutions Program spent millions of dollars

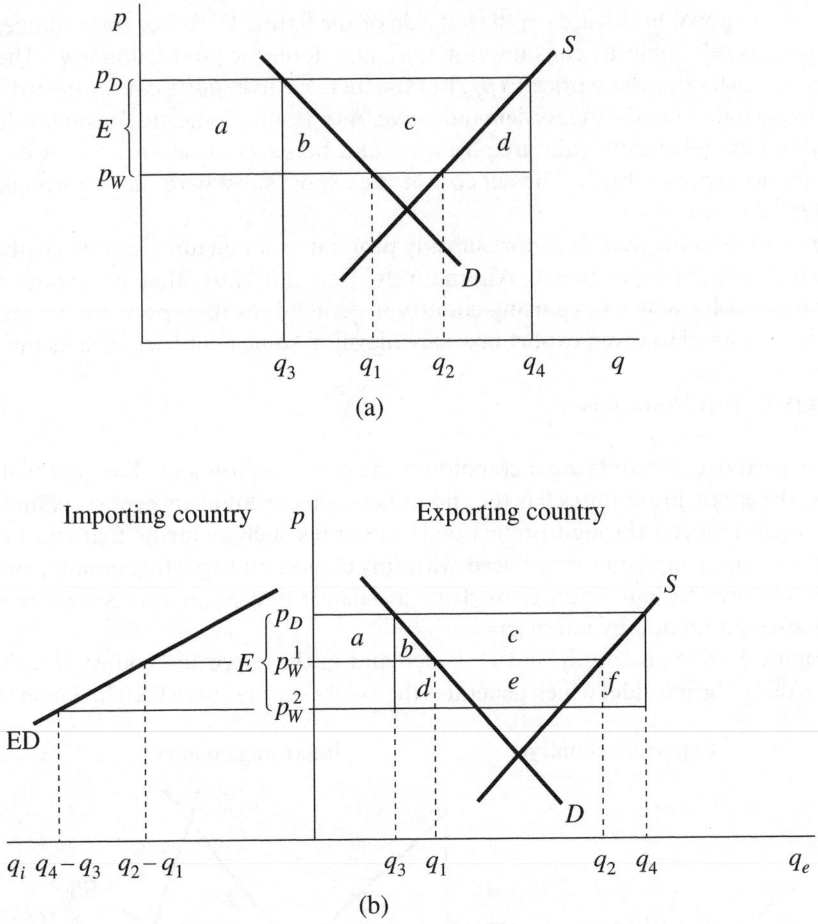

Figure 8.17

to expand international markets.[6] Two cases of export subsidies are given in Figure 8.17. The small country case where export subsidies do not influence world prices is depicted in Figure 8.17(a). Prior to the subsidy, the world price is p_W, domestic consumption is q_1, and domestic production is q_2. If an export subsidy of size E is put in place, domestic prices rise to p_D, causing production to expand from q_2 to q_4 and exports to increase from $q_2 - q_1$ to $q_4 - q_3$. The export subsidy is paid on the full amount of exports, so total government costs are $(q_4 - q_3)(p_D - p_W)$, which is equal to area $b+c+d$. Domestic producers gain area $a+b+c$ and domestic consumers lose area $a+b$. The net cost of the subsidy program for the exporting country is $b+d$.

In the large country case, export subsidies affect world prices. In Figure 8.17(b), domestic demand is given by D, domestic supply is S and excess demand from the rest of the

6. A detailed description of these export enhancement programs is given by Schmitz, Furtan and Baylis (2002).

world is ED, shown backwards in the left side of the figure. With free trade, domestic and world price is p_W^1, domestic consumption is q_1, and domestic production is q_2. The export subsidy increases domestic price to p_D, but the increase in exports causes the world price to fall to p_W^2 following the excess demand curve. As a result, domestic consumers lose area $a+b$, domestic producers gain area $a+b+c$ and taxpayers lose area $b+c+d+e+f$ in financing the export subsidy. The net cost of the export subsidy to the exporting country is area $b+d+e+f$.

These results show that an export subsidy program is an unambiguously costly way of supporting domestic producers. Alternatively, one can show that an export tax can improve the welfare of an exporting country if demand for its exports by the rest of the world is inelastic. However, export taxes are illegal in some countries such as the USA.

Voluntary Export Restraints

Voluntary export restraints are a common trade policy instrument. They are 'voluntary' because the exporting country has the choice between curtailing its exports voluntarily or having them reduced through protectionist measures such as tariffs that can be implemented by importing countries. Faced with this choice, an exporting country often voluntarily chooses to limit exports to strike a balance that improves its welfare without calling forth retaliation by importers.[7]

In Figure 8.18, S_e is supply and D_e is demand in the exporting country (both shown backwards on the left side) which generates the excess supply curve ES (shown on the right

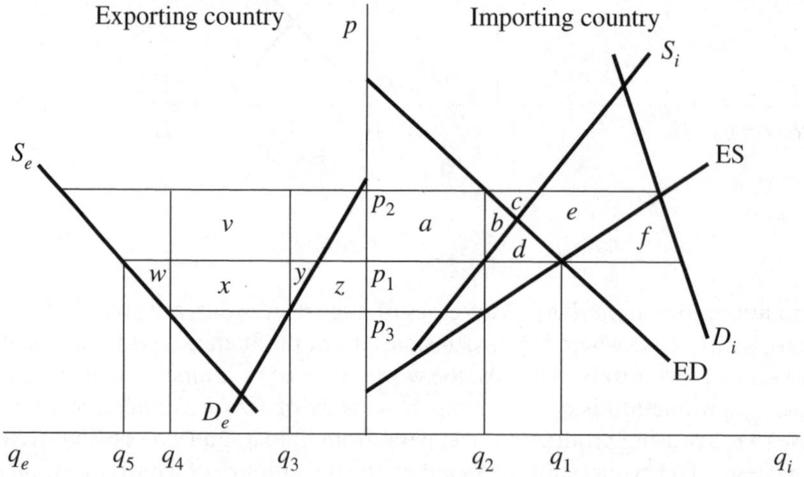

Figure 8.18

7. An excellent example of a voluntary export restraint is given by the 'Great Tomato War'. Border disputes involving Mexican tomato exports to the USA have had a long history. Historically, Florida tomato producers have brought dumping charges against Mexico and have tried to have the US government introduce tariffs on imports. In the mid-1990s, Mexico and the USA reached a cooperative agreement, whereby Mexico would not sell tomatoes into the USA below an agreed minimum price. The trade options are spelled out in Bredahl, Schmitz and Hillman (1987). The so-called Tomato Suspension Agreement is a voluntary restraint on tomato exports by Mexico.

side). Demand and supply in the importing country are D_i and S_i, respectively, leading to excess demand ED. The free trade price is p_1, at which the exported volume is q_1. Now, suppose the exporter voluntarily restricts the volume of exports to q_2. This restriction causes the excess supply to the importing country to become vertical at q_2, which drives up the trade price as well as price in the importing country to p_2 according to the importing country's excess demand.

Assuming the export restriction is imposed by the government rather than collusion among producers in the exporting country, producers in the exporting country will produce more than can be sold (for domestic consumption and export) unless production is reduced, which causes price to adjust downward.[8] Specifically, with export restriction q_2, which is equal to $q_4 - q_3$, the amount demanded in the exporting country falls from q_5 to q_4 as the amount exports falls from q_1 to q_2. Thus, the price in the exporting country falls to p_3 as producers bid down prices to fill the shrinking demand for their product. Because consumers in the exporting country enjoy a lower price, their welfare increases by area z. For producers in the exporting country, the lower domestic price generates a loss in producer surplus equal to area $w+x+y+z$, but by restricting exports the exported quantity is sold at a higher price p_2, which generates an additional revenue of area $v+x$. This additional revenue will go to exporters rather than producers if export quota rights are allocated to exporting firms by the government. But in the more typical case where the government administers export restrictions so as to provide quota rents to producers, the producers realize a net gain of area $v-w-y-z$ (which can possibly be negative but tends to be positive and large as excess demand facing the exporting country is more inelastic). The overall gain to the exporting country is thus area $v-w-y$.

With this approach, producers in the importing country also realize a gain, area $a+b+c$, while consumers in the importing country lose area $a+b+c+d+e+f$. Although importing country consumers lose more than the gain of all three other groups combined, the fact that producers in the importing country gain may be enough to establish a base of political support sufficient to prevent retaliation by the importing country (because producers are typically more organized politically than are consumers and because individual goods are typically of little importance in a consumer's overall consumption bundle). This may be particularly true if the importing country represents the rest of the world, where impacts on individual countries are small. The net loss in the importing country is thus area $e+d+f$, which by construction is equal to area $a+b+d$. Because area v and area a are the same by construction, the overall deadweight loss to both countries combined is area $b+d+w+y$.

Three points concerning voluntary export restraints are worth highlighting. First, voluntary export restraints result in a net welfare loss to the importing country. A higher import price is paid for fewer imports and the importing country does not capture any tariff or quota revenues. Second, voluntary export restraints transfer income from consumers in the importing country to producers in the importing country as well as to both producers and consumers in the exporting country. Producers benefit equally from tariffs and voluntary export restraints if the imported quantity is the same under both, but with voluntary export restraints the importing country collects no tax or tariff revenues from

8. With collusion among producers, the quantity sold both for domestic consumption and for export would be restricted, thus driving up the price on both.

which to compensate consumers. However, voluntary export restraints are more politically acceptable than tariffs because consumers generally are less aware of the price-increasing effects of exporters' voluntary restraints. Third, voluntary export restraints have the desirable quality for importing countries of protecting producers while maintaining a free-trade posture because the exporting country is the one restricting trade. An importing country cannot easily impose tariffs and also push for freer trade in its export markets.[9]

8.8 EMPIRICAL CONSIDERATIONS IN MARKET-LEVEL WELFARE ANALYSIS

Thus far, the analysis has centered on theoretical issues in welfare economics, notwithstanding that issues have been developed to lay foundations for empirical applications. This section begins to consider empirical issues surrounding the econometric applications.[10] For example, in some cases, several alternative measurements of the same welfare effect are possible. It stands to reason that more precise estimation may be possible in one case than another on econometric grounds. Thus, when data are sufficient to permit a choice among estimates of alternative welfare measures, it is important to know which estimators entail greater precision.

To estimate the welfare triangles defined by consumer or producer surplus, one must first estimate the associated demand or supply curves.[11] The science of estimating such relationships is called *econometrics* and occupies a large part of the economics literature. This book is not intended, nor could it presume, to provide a thorough discussion of all the related issues. Nevertheless, a somewhat heuristic discussion of some of the basic issues provides a sufficient foundation to discuss the related problems that frequently arise in estimating economic welfare quantities. A more detailed and general derivation of the underlying econometric results can be found in any standard econometrics text, such as those by Greene (2000) and by Judge et al. (1988). A simple but complete coverage of the properties of linear regression presented in this section is given by Draper and Smith (1966, ch. 1).

The usual approach in econometrics is to assume a particular functional form that is hoped to be sufficiently general to describe adequately the mechanism generating a par-

9. The model of voluntary export restraints in Figure 8.18 has been extended and applied to estimate the impact of increased US beef imports by Allen, Dodge and Schmitz (1983). They found that voluntary export restraints are used extensively by major beef exporters such as Australia and result in gains to exporters of roughly $8.25 million per year.
10. For the reader unfamiliar with econometrics, this is the term pertaining to the application of statistics in the estimation of economic relationships.
11. As shown in Section 4.3, producer surplus calculation may be accomplished through quasirent calculations for individual firms. Thus, estimation of supply may not be necessary. For example, if accurate data are available on costs and returns, quasirent may be calculated without error on that basis. To evaluate alternative policies, however, one must be able to estimate producers' response under the alternative policies, and this requires information about either the supply curve or the cost curves of producers. Because information on price and quantity is available more often than information on costs, this chapter focuses on estimation of supply. Similar principles apply to use of estimated cost functions in welfare economics because welfare calculations with producer supply curves are equivalent to welfare calculations with producer marginal cost curves under competition and profit maximization.

ticular set of data. For example, a supply curve may be linear and thus suggest the relationship

$$q = \alpha_0 + \alpha_1 p, \tag{8.1}$$

where q is quantity supplied and p is price; α_0 and α_1 would thus be unknown parameters that one would seek to estimate on the basis of observed price and quantity data. The price–quantity data may be generated by observing a particular market over several periods of time (for example, for several years) or by observing several firms, individuals, or groups during a given period of time.[12] The former set of data is called a *time series*, whereas the latter is called a *cross-section*.

Because, with 'real-world' data, not all of the observations thus generated are likely to fall on a straight line (or any other functional form specified prior to estimation), the usual econometric practice is to consider the relationship in equation (8.1) as stochastic (which means random) by adding a random disturbance term, say ε,

$$q = \alpha_0 + \alpha_1 p + \varepsilon,$$

where $E(\varepsilon) = 0$. That is, one expects ε to be zero on average, and in this context one usually denotes $\text{var}(\varepsilon) = E(\varepsilon^2) = \sigma^2$.[13] The parameters α_0 and α_1 are often then estimated by choosing the $\hat{\alpha}_0$ and $\hat{\alpha}_1$ that minimize the sum of squared deviations of the observed quantities from the estimated linear relationship, $\hat{\alpha}_0 + \hat{\alpha}_1 p$. Geometrically, consider Figure 8.19, where one has four observations (p_i, q_i), $i = 1, \ldots, 4$.[14] The sum of squared deviations is $a^2 + b^2 + c^2 + d^2$. The estimates that minimize this sum are called *least-squares* or *ordinary least-squares* (OLS) estimates.[15]

12. In each of these cases, the supply relationship may be affected by different sets of determinants, in which case variation in determinants should be considered in estimation as discussed below.
13. Mathematically, the expectation of a function $g(\cdot)$ of a random variable y is the associated point of central tendency and is defined by

$$E[g(y)] \equiv \int_{-\infty}^{\infty} g(y) f(y) dy,$$

where $f(y)$ is the probability density function of y (which describes the relative frequency of various values of y). The variance of a random variable measures the dispersion of the associated distribution and is defined by $\text{var}[g(y)] = E\{g(y) - E[g(y)]\}^2$.
14. Note that, in contrast to diagrams in previous chapters, Figures 8.19 and 8.20 have the price and quantity axes reversed. This is done because quantity appears as the dependent or left-hand-side variable in the regression equation in (8.1). Discussion in this context is more consistent with the econometrics literature and the notion that individual producers and consumers make quantity decisions in response to price changes following profit or utility maximization. That is, quantities are usually used as dependent or left-hand-side variables in estimating supply. The same is often true in estimating demand. The case with price as the left-hand-side variable, however, can be treated in a similar manner with analogous results for the purposes of this chapter.
15. Where one generally has, say, n observations, the sum of squared deviations can be represented algebraically as

$$SS = \sum_{i=1}^{n} (q_i - \hat{\alpha}_0 - \hat{\alpha}_1 p_i)^2.$$

Using calculus, the conditions that $\hat{\alpha}_0$ and $\hat{\alpha}_1$ must satisfy to minimize this sum are

$$\sum_{i=1}^{n} (q_i - \hat{\alpha}_0 - \hat{\alpha}_1 p_i) p_i = 0$$

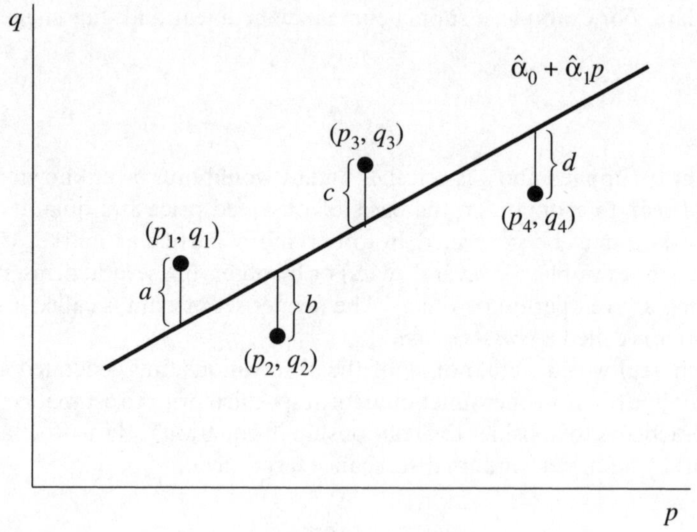

Figure 8.19

Using these estimates, one can then estimate the supply curve for various levels of p by $\hat{q} = \hat{\alpha}_0 + \hat{\alpha}_1 p$, and the corresponding estimated change in producer surplus for a particular price change from p_1 to p_2 would be[16]

$$\Delta P = \hat{\alpha}_0(p_2 - p_1) + \frac{\hat{\alpha}_1(p_2^2 - p_1^2)}{2}.$$

In statistics a key parameter that measures the accuracy of an estimate or prediction is its variance (defined by the expected value of the square of its deviation from its mean or expected average).

The variance of an estimated supply curve and its implications for the variance of estimated producer surplus are depicted in Figure 8.20. Where observed data are represented

$$\sum_{i=1}^{n} (q_i - \hat{\alpha}_0 - \hat{\alpha}_1 p_i) = 0,$$

which can be solved to find

$$\hat{\alpha}_1 = \frac{\sum_{i=1}^{n} q_i p_i - \bar{q} \sum_{i=1}^{n} p_i}{\sum_{i=1}^{n} p_i^2 - \bar{p} \sum_{i=1}^{n} \bar{p}_i} = \frac{\sum_{i=1}^{n} (q_i - \bar{q}) p_i}{\sum_{i=1}^{n} (p_i - \bar{p})^2}$$

$$\hat{\alpha}_0 = \bar{q} - \hat{\alpha}_1 \bar{p},$$

where

$$\bar{q} = \frac{1}{n} \sum_{i=1}^{n} q_i \text{ and } \bar{p} = \frac{1}{n} \sum_{i=1}^{n} p_i.$$

16. Using calculus, this is simply verified because

$$\Delta P = \int_{p_1}^{p_2} (\hat{\alpha}_0 + \hat{\alpha}_1 p) dp = \hat{\alpha}_0(p_2 - p_1) + \hat{\alpha}_1 \frac{(p_2^2 - p_1^2)}{2}.$$

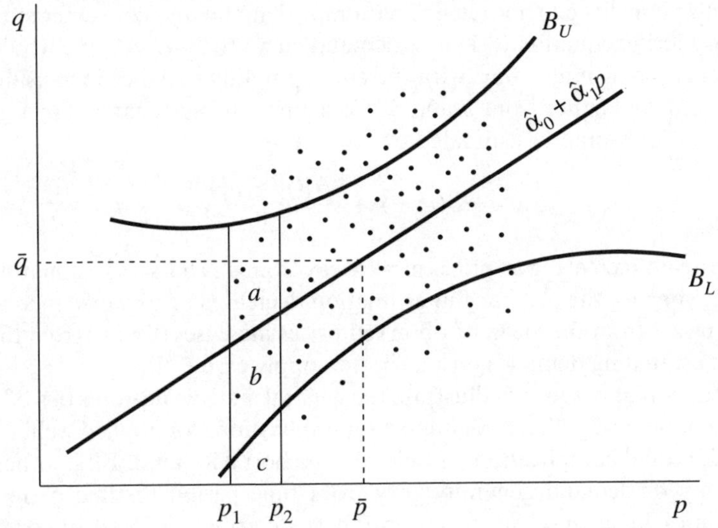

Figure 8.20

by the scatter of points around means $\bar{p}$ and $\bar{q}$, the estimated supply curve is $\hat{\alpha}_0 + \hat{\alpha}_1 p$. A general result in econometrics is that the variance of $\hat{\alpha} + \hat{\alpha}_1 p$ increases as p moves away from $\bar{p}$. Hence, the region in which one may have reasonable confidence of containing the supply curve may be represented by the area between B_L and B_U, where B_L and B_U diverge as p is farther from $\bar{p}$. Similarly, this implies that *there is an increasing loss in precision in estimating a surplus change as the corresponding price limits diverge from the mean of observed data* (that is, as p_1 or p_2 diverges from $\bar{p}$). In Figure 8.20, the estimated surplus change is area $b+c$, but at B_U it is area $a+b+c$, and at B_L it is only area c. Obviously, these areas diverge as the price interval (p_1,p_2) moves away from $\bar{p}$ and $\bar{q}$.[17] One may also

17. These results can be derived more formally as follows. Using the identity $\text{var}(y) = \Sigma_{i=1}^n k_i^2 \text{ var}(z_i)$, where $y = \Sigma_{i=1}^n k_i z_i$ and z_i and z_j are uncorrelated for all $i \neq j$, one can determine the variance of the estimated supply by noting from footnote 15 that

$$\hat{\alpha}_1 = \sum_{i=1}^n k_i q_i,\ \hat{\alpha}_0 = \sum_{i=1}^n k_i' q_i,$$

where

$$k_i = \frac{(n-1)p_i}{n\sum_{j=1}^n (p_j - \bar{p})^2},\ k_i' = \frac{1}{n} - \bar{p}k_i;\ i = 1, \ldots, n.$$

Hence, in the context of the identity, one finds a predicted quantity of

$$\hat{q} = \hat{\alpha}_0 + \hat{\alpha}_1 p = \sum_{i=1}^n k_i^* q_i,$$

where

$$k_i^* = k_i' + k_i p_i = \frac{1}{n} + k_i(p_i - \bar{p}),$$

and, similarly, using footnote 16,

$$\Delta P = \sum_{i=1}^n k_i^{**} q_i,$$

note that similar conclusions hold in estimation of demand and consumer surplus. That is, simply considering equation (8.1) as a demand curve with $\alpha_1 < 0$, one would estimate the demand curve in a similar way, with the corresponding variance increasing as prices and quantities move farther from $\bar{p}$ and $\bar{q}$, Consumer surplus change for a given price change from p_1 to p_2 would be estimated by

$$\widehat{\Delta S} = -\hat{\alpha}_0(p_2 - p_1) - \frac{\hat{\alpha}_1(p_2^2 - p_1^2)}{2},$$

with variance again increasing as prices move away from $\bar{p}$. That is, in estimating demand and consumer surplus, the accuracy in estimation decreases or variance increases as the difference of prices from the mean of observed prices increases (that is, from the mean of prices used in estimating demand), just as in the supply case.[18]

Although the foregoing results illustrate the general statistical properties of estimated supply and demand curves that have important implications for applied welfare economics, several additional complications should also be borne in mind. First, other determinants of supply or demand generally vary from time period to time period or from individual to individual or group to group. These determinants lead to corresponding movements in supply and demand that must generally be taken into account in estimation to avoid biased results. This can be done, however, simply by including the appropriate determinants as additional variables in regression. For example, one could specify a supply or demand equation as

$$q = \alpha_0 + \alpha_1 p + \alpha_2 z_1 + \alpha_3 z_2 + \ldots + \alpha_{n+1} z_n, \tag{8.2}$$

where

$$k_i^{**} \equiv k_i'(p_2 - p_1) + k_i \frac{(p_2^2 - p_1^2)}{2}.$$

Thus, assuming that the disturbance in the supply relationship (ε) is uncorrelated from observation to observation and that p is uncorrelated with ε,

$$\mathrm{var}(\hat{q}) = \sum_{i=1}^{n} (k_i^*)\,\mathrm{var}(q_i)$$

$$= \sum_{i=1}^{n} \left[\frac{1}{n^2} + \frac{1}{n} k_i(p - \bar{p}) + k_i^2(p - \bar{p})\right]\sigma^2$$

$$= \frac{\sigma^2}{n} + (p - \bar{p})\frac{\sigma^2}{n} \sum_{i=1}^{n} k_i + \sigma^2(p - \bar{p})^2 \sum_{i=1}^{n} k_i^2,$$

and, similarly,

$$\mathrm{var}(\Delta P) = \frac{\sigma^2}{n}(p_2 - p_1)^2 + \frac{\sigma^2}{n}\left[(p_2 - p_1)\frac{p_2^2 - p_1^2}{2 - \bar{p}(p_2 - p_1)^2}\right] \sum_{i=1}^{n} k_i$$

$$= \frac{\sigma^2}{n}(\Delta p)^2 + \frac{\sigma^2}{n}\left[\frac{p_1 + p_2}{2} - \bar{p}\right](\Delta p)^2 \sum_{i=1}^{n} k_i + \sigma^2 \left[\frac{p_1 + p_2}{2} - \bar{p}\right]^2 (\Delta p)^2 \sum_{i=1}^{n} k_i^2.$$

In each of these cases, it is clear that the precision of estimation falls (variance increases) as the supply curve or welfare change is estimated for prices farther from the mean of observed data. Similar results also hold when p is correlated with ε, as in a simultaneous equations problem.

18. These results follow from the mathematical framework of earlier footnotes in this chapter related to the supply case.

where $z_1, \ldots, z_n$ are the determinants of the supply or demand, respectively.[19] In this context the intercept of the supply or demand curve on the quantity axis in the price–quantity diagram in Figure 8.20 is $\alpha_0 + \alpha_2 z_1 + \ldots + \alpha_{n+1} z_n$.

Following previous chapters, $z_1, \ldots, z_n$ would include prices of other consumer goods and income. In the context of Chapter 7, $z_1, \ldots, z_n$ would include the prices of (other) consumer goods, wage rates and prices of other factors supplied by consumers, and exogenous income from other sources. In the context of Chapter 4, $z_1, \ldots, z_n$ would include the prices of other variable inputs and outputs of the firm or industry as well as quantities of fixed inputs (as indicated by Section 4.6).[20] Equations of this type can be estimated by the same general OLS approach discussed above, although the computational formulas for the coefficients (for example, α_0, α_1, and so on) are different.[21]

A second generality that must be considered in many applications is that supply and demand curves may not follow linearity. A common alternative specification, for example, follows log linearity, which implies that[22]

$$q = Ap^{\alpha_1} z_1^{\alpha_2} z_2^{\alpha_3} \ldots z_n^{\alpha_{n+1}}.$$

Such an example for the case of both supply and demand is given specifically in Appendix Section 4.D in equations (4.14) through (4.18). As is apparent from the results there, the

19. A further discussion of the choice of determinants in this context is given in Section 9.5.
20. Actually, depending on length of run, the consumer demand and factor supply equations may also be conditioned on quantities of durable consumer goods that have been purchased in the past and are thus fixed at present. That is, durable consumer goods play a somewhat analogous role to fixed inputs in producer supply. A producer seeks to maximize profit by selecting quantities of variable inputs $x_1, \ldots, x_{n_1}$, subject to given variable input prices, output prices, and quantities $\bar{x}_{n_1+1}, \ldots, \bar{x}_n$ of the fixed inputs determined by previous decisions. Thus, the resulting input demands and output supplies are functions of the variable input prices, output prices and quantities of fixed inputs. Similarly, if the consumer's decisions depend on quantities of durable goods purchased in previous decisions, then the consumer's utility-maximizing demands for nondurables are functions of *prices of nondurables* and *quantities of durables*, as well as income and prices of factors sold by the consumer. For example, if a consumer has purchased an energy-efficient refrigerator, his or her electricity consumption decision will tend to be different from that of a consumer with an energy-inefficient refrigerator, even though facing the same prices with the same preferences. The decision to replace an old durable, on the other hand, would depend on its obsolescence, cost of use relative to other durables, and quality of services produced. See Appendix Section 14.B. Another specification for using both prices and quantities as determinants of demand is given by Phlips (1974) in the context of dynamic demand where tastes and preferences depend on previous consumption.
21. For example, see Draper and Smith (1966), Greene (2000) or Judge et al. (1988).
22. The linear and log-linear functions are often used in econometrics because of their convenience. From a technical standpoint, however, one must also be concerned about whether or not specified functional forms for supply and demand make sense in terms of economic theory. For example, it can be shown that there is no utility function which, when maximized subject to a consumer budget constraint, yields demand equations that are linear in all prices and income for all goods. When a system of demand equations actually corresponds to maximizing some underlying utility function subject to a budget constraint, there are a number of conditions that must be satisfied for all possible prices and income: the budget constraint, homogeneity, Slutsky negativity and symmetry, and several aggregation conditions. These conditions and a few functional forms that are satisfactory by these criteria are discussed by Intriligator (1978, ch. 7). For a more advanced treatment, see Deaton and Muellbauer (1980), Phlips (1974) or Blackorby, Primont and Russell (1978). A similar set of issues is also of concern with respect to a producer supply function which, under competition, is equivalent to the producer's marginal cost curve (for prices above minimum average variable costs). The theory of duality implies that cost functions are, in fact, determined by the underlying production functions. Hence, concern arises about whether or not a supply (or marginal cost) curve specification corresponds to a reasonable underlying production function. A brief discussion of these issues is also given in Intriligator (1978, ch. 8) and Greene (2000, s. 15.6). At a more advanced level, see Fuss and McFadden (1978) or Blackorby, Primont and Russell (1978). See Appendix Sections 8.B and 8.C.

surplus change associated with a price change from p_1 to p_2 where determinants are held at fixed levels $\tilde{z}_1, \ldots, \tilde{z}_n$ is

$$\frac{A}{\alpha_1 + 1}(p_2^{\alpha_1+1} - p_1^{\alpha_1+1})\tilde{z}_1^{\alpha_2}\tilde{z}_2^{\alpha_3} \ldots \tilde{z}_n^{\alpha_{n+1}},$$

which represents an increase in the supply case or a decrease in the demand case (both possibly negative).

Statistical estimation in this case can be carried out in much the same way as the linear case if data are represented in logarithmic form. That is, ordinary linear least squares can be used to choose $\hat{A}$, $\hat{\alpha}_1$, $\hat{\alpha}_2$, ..., $\hat{\alpha}_{n+1}$ to minimize the sum of squares of $\log q - (\log \hat{A} + \hat{\alpha}_1 \log p + \hat{\alpha}_2 \log z_1 + \ldots + \hat{\alpha}_{n+1} \log z_n)$ over all observations. Such an approach does not lead to convenient estimates of variances for the estimator of surplus change as is the case for equation (8.2). But following the derivation in the linear case, one finds that the variance of the estimated $\log q$, given by $\log \hat{A} + \hat{\alpha}_1 \log p + \hat{\alpha}_2 \log z_1 + \ldots + \hat{\alpha}_{n+1} \log z_n$, increases as $p - \bar{p}$ increases, where $\bar{p}$ represents the mean of observed price data. Thus, the same general property of obtaining poorer estimates of supply and demand and associated surplus changes when using prices outside the range of observed prices is again suggested.

A third generality that must be considered in many cases is simultaneity of supply and demand. The problem of simultaneity must be considered unless production lags are as long as the intervals at which data are observed. That is, if the quantity supplied is determined by previous price – say, at the time of production decisions – and the price for the next period is determined subsequently when the production is actually realized, then supplies and demands are determined recursively rather than simultaneously.

If demands and supplies are determined simultaneously, the expectations for the ordinary estimators of the structural parameters α_0 and α_1 and also any corresponding surplus estimates ΔP or ΔS are biased (that is, after repeating the estimation procedure many times with different sets of data, one would *not* expect to obtain, even on average, the parameter values and welfare quantities sought). This phenomenon is referred to as *simultaneous equations bias*. Moreover, the magnitude of bias does not necessarily get small, as the number of observations gets large, and thus the resulting estimates are said to be statistically *inconsistent*. A number of alternative estimators exist that at least attain the latter criterion of consistency (that is, the magnitude of bias becomes inconsequential, and also the likely variation of estimators around the associated parameters gets small, as the number of observations gets large). The more popular of these estimation methods are two-stage least squares, three-stage least squares, indirect least squares, limited-information maximum likelihood and full-information maximum likelihood.[23]

While these estimators and other more sophisticated techniques attain desirable statistical properties, however, the resulting estimators for supply or demand or associated surplus changes have the same general properties suggested by Figure 8.20. That is, the resulting estimators become less precise as the points of evaluation are farther from the observed data used in estimation. The following section investigates the implications of these general properties of surplus estimation for applied welfare economics.

23. For a thorough coverage of these and other simultaneous equations estimation methods, see Greene (2000, ch. 16) or Judge et al. (1988, chs 14 and 15).

8.9 THE CHOICE OF MARKET FOR ESTIMATION

In Section 4.4, the results suggest that several alternatives exist for measurement of a producer welfare change associated with some (multiple) price change. These possibilities include (1) measuring the change in producer surplus associated with an essential output, (2) measuring the change in consumer surplus associated with an essential input and (3) measuring the sum of producer and consumer surplus changes obtained by sequentially imposing price changes in the respective markets. The results of the preceding section have important implications regarding which of these approaches should be used, depending on data availability. Consider, for example, evaluation of the effect of changing one particular price (which may be only a part of an overall price change). In Figure 8.21, the price change from w_1^0 to w_1^1 for input x_1 causes the derived demand by an industry for another input to increase from D_2^0 to D_2^1 and industry supply to increase from S_0 to S_1. According to the results of Section 4.4, the compensating (or equivalent) variation of this price change is given equivalently by either area a, b or c if both inputs are essential in the production process.

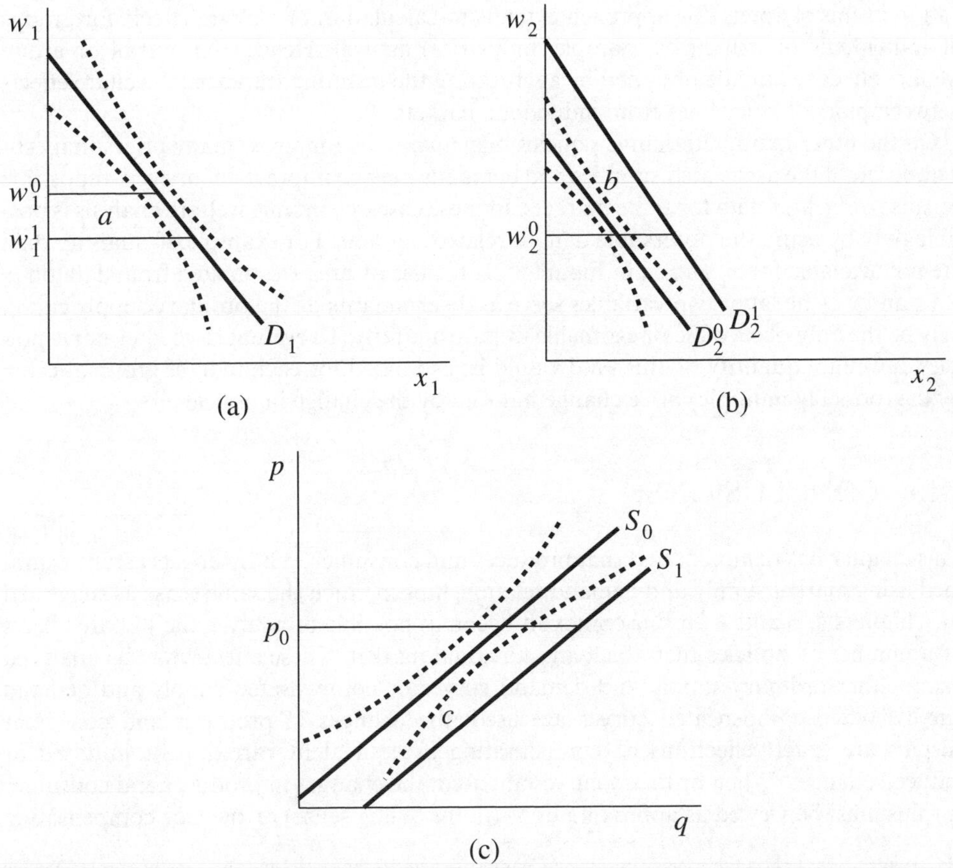

Figure 8.21

The results of Section 8.8, on the other hand, suggest that supply and demand estimates are relatively accurate only near observed prices and quantities. Thus, the precision or confidence in estimates of supply and demand prior to the change in Figure 8.21 may be limited, as represented by the broken lines on either side. Similarly, the subsequent supply and demand estimates would also be associated with less precision outside the range of normal prices and quantities. As a result, the precision in estimation of areas *b* and *c* is probably very poor compared with the precision in estimation of area *a*, because area *a* calculations rely on information about the demand curve only in the range of normal price variation. Exceptions to this rule would occur only if very imprecise estimates of the demand D_1 were obtained or if data used in estimation of D_2 or S tend to cover a broad interval of the quantity axis from zero up to the equilibrium points depicted in Figure 8.21.

These observations imply that, when data permit, the welfare effects associated with a multiple price change can be calculated more accurately by estimating supply and demand in each market for which prices change and then using the *sequential* approach, where the welfare change associated with each price change is evaluated in its respective market as illustrated in Sections 4.4 and 7.10 in Figures 4.8, 4.9 and 7.13. As implied by the aggregation in this chapter, this approach extends to calculation of welfare effects for groups of individuals or firms (for example, industries) as well. Hence, the overall or group welfare effects would be obtained by aggregating the resulting trapezoidal welfare effects between pairs of price lines from individual markets.

On the other hand, alternative policies may involve changing so many prices that estimation of all the associated supplies and demands may be impractical or even impossible because of lack of data for some markets. In these cases, economic welfare analysis is possible only by using the observable data in related markets. For example, if quantity data are not available for x_1 and x_2 in Figure 8.21, the use of area *c* estimated from data on p, q, w_1 and w_2 (the latter two variables serve as determinants of the ordinary supply curve) may be the only observable or estimable welfare quantity. To evaluate two alternative policies, a welfare quantity of this kind would be estimated for each market group affected by the (possibly multiple) price change induced by the change in policies.[24]

8.10 CONCLUSIONS

This chapter has demonstrated that producer and consumer welfare effects can be examined using market supply and demand relationships in much the same sense as suggested by Chapters 4, 6 and 7. In this context it becomes possible to analyze the welfare effects of a number of policies that affect an individual market. These effects may be analyzed using either ordinary supply and demand curves or compensated supply and demand curves. When compensated curves are used, the changes in producer and consumer surplus are exact reflections of compensating or equivalent variation of imposed or induced changes. When ordinary curves are used, the changes in producer and consumer surplus must be viewed as approximations (in the Willig sense) of the true compensating

24. It must be noted on the basis of results in Chapters 4, 6 and 7, however, that this type of surplus change has welfare meaning only in the case of commodities that are essential in the associated production or consumption processes or under weak complementarity.

or equivalent variation whenever the supply or demand curve pertains to a consumer or factor owner group.

As indicated in this chapter, two considerations are crucial in the aggregation of welfare effects. One has to do with whether or not compensation is paid when changes lead to adverse impacts on some of the individuals involved. The second has to do with appropriate interpersonal comparisons (welfare weights) for policies that may be desirable but yet do not meet the Pareto criterion. The results of this chapter indicate that, depending on a policy-maker's welfare weights, policies may be appropriate that involve gains for one group at the expense of another – even when compensation is not paid. Thus, appropriate welfare analysis should investigate the welfare impact on at least each group that is affected differently by a particular policy. On the other hand, policies may exist where compensation is considered that can make further improvements over those associated with a particular set of welfare weights without compensation. One example is when a policy-maker wishes to aid a failing industry by means of a subsidy or price support but yet can offer the same aid without as much welfare loss for other groups through a different policy, such as a lump-sum transfer that does not affect market behavior in a distorting fashion.

This chapter also explores empirical possibilities for applying the theoretical concepts developed. The associated econometric theory is not developed in rigorous fashion but is drawn upon in a semiformal sense to illuminate possibilities and potential problems in estimation of welfare quantities. Generally, the results suggest that more accurate estimation of the welfare effects associated with multiple price changes is possible by means of sequential calculations. This approach, however, necessarily involves estimation of supply and demand in all markets for which prices change. For many practical problems, such extensive estimation is not feasible. But, fortunately, estimation of the welfare effects of many price changes is often possible in a single market if estimation is not feasible by sequential evaluation across all markets with price changes.

In all the welfare analysis presented in this chapter, one must bear in mind that prices in other markets have been assumed fixed or unaffected by intervention in the market of consideration. Such an assumption is certainly unrealistic in many interesting welfare analyses. For example, when an agricultural price support is introduced, it tends to increase the price of agricultural inputs because of increased demand for inputs. These related price changes cause a further adjustment in the market of consideration as well as some additional welfare effects on the producers of inputs. Chapter 9 turns to consideration of these further adjustments and the related welfare impacts in other markets.

Appendix to Chapter 8: Measurement of aggregate market welfare

The purpose of this appendix is threefold. Section 8.A briefly formalizes the argument that the area behind a market consumer demand curve or a factor supply curve can serve as an approximate welfare measure in the context of the WTP approach. Section 8.B considers the problem of aggregation for producers under heterogeneity where aggregate supplies and demands will generally fail to satisfy integrability conditions unless heterogeneity is properly incorporated in empirical specifications. Section 8.C considers the similar problem of aggregation for consumers and factor owners under heterogeneity.

8.A AGGREGATION OF WTP FOR CONSUMER DEMAND AND FACTOR SUPPLY

Following the approach set forth by Willig (1973), suppose that bounds similar to (7.36) and (7.37) are derived for each of J consumers for a particular price change from $\mathbf{p}^0 = (p_1^0,\ldots,p_N^0)$ to $\mathbf{p}^1 = (p_1^0,\ldots,p_{i-1}^0,p_i^1,p_{i+1}^0,\ldots,p_N^0)$,

$$\bar{\varepsilon}_{2j}^c \geq \frac{\Delta S_{ij} - C_j}{|\Delta S_{ij}|} \geq \bar{\varepsilon}_{1j}^c \tag{8.3}$$

$$\bar{\varepsilon}_{2j}^e \geq \frac{E_j - \Delta S_{ij}}{|\Delta S_{ij}|} \geq \bar{\varepsilon}_{1j}^e, \tag{8.4}$$

where the j subscripts denote pertinence to consumer j, $j=1, \ldots, J$. Because the market demand (supply) curve under competition, holding all other prices constant, can be regarded as a horizontal summation of individual demand (supply) curves, it follows immediately that the area behind the market demand (supply) curve is the summation of areas behind individual demand (supply) curves over all individuals. Hence, the change in area behind the market demand (supply) curve associated with any particular price change, ΔS_i, is the sum of changes in areas behind individual demand (supply) curves, that is,

$$\Delta S_i = \sum_{j=1}^{J} \Delta S_{ij}.$$

Also, the WTP of a group of individuals is the simple summation of individuals' WTP (excluding possibilities of externalities). Hence, error bounds on changes in market surplus as a measure of compensating variation, C, or equivalent variation, E, for a group of individuals may be easily derived from (8.3) and (8.4):

$$\sum_{j=1}^{J} \bar{\varepsilon}_{2j}^{c} |\Delta S_{ij}| \geq \Delta S_i - C \geq \sum_{j=1}^{J} \bar{\varepsilon}_{1j}^{c} |\Delta S_{ij}|$$

$$\sum_{j=1}^{J} \bar{\varepsilon}_{2j}^{e} |\Delta S_{ij}| \geq E - \Delta S_i \geq \sum_{j=1}^{J} \bar{\varepsilon}_{1j}^{e} |\Delta S_{ij}|,$$

or, converting to percentage terms,

$$\sum_{j=1}^{J} \bar{\varepsilon}_{2j}^{c} \gamma_j \geq \frac{\Delta S_i - C}{|\Delta S_i|} \geq \sum_{j=1}^{J} \bar{\varepsilon}_{1j}^{c} \gamma_j \tag{8.5}$$

$$\sum_{j=1}^{J} \bar{\varepsilon}_{2j}^{e} \gamma_j \geq \frac{E - \Delta S_i}{|\Delta S_i|} \geq \sum_{j=1}^{J} \bar{\varepsilon}_{1j}^{e} \gamma_j, \tag{8.6}$$

where $\gamma_j = |\Delta S_{ij}|/|\Delta S_i|$ (note that $\Delta S_{i1}, \ldots, \Delta S_{iJ}$, and ΔS_i are all of the same sign because all consumers face the same prices). Thus, the percentage error bounds for market-level surplus change as a measure of C or E are simply weighted averages of corresponding individuals' percentage error bounds (note that $0 < \gamma_j < 1$ for $j = 1, \ldots, J$, and $\Sigma_{j=1}^{J} \gamma_j = 1$). From this, Willig (1973, p. 45) concludes that 'if consumers are similar, then we can treat their aggregate as one individual'. Furthermore, even if consumers are not similar but their individual percentage error bounds are not large (or if they are large for only an insignificant set of individuals), the market surplus measure serves a useful purpose for measuring the compensating and equivalent variation of a single price change.

Similarly, in the case of a multiple price change from $\mathbf{p^0} = (p_1^0, \ldots, p_N^0)$ to $\mathbf{p^1} = (p_1^1, \ldots, p_N^1)$, one can easily deduce from (7.46) and (7.47) that

$$\sum_{j=1}^{J} \bar{\varepsilon}_{2j}^{c} \left| \sum_{i=1}^{N} \Delta S_{ij} \right| \geq \sum_{i=1}^{N} \Delta S_i - C \geq \sum_{j=1}^{J} \bar{\varepsilon}_{1j}^{c} \left| \sum_{i=1}^{N} \Delta S_{ij} \right|$$

$$\sum_{j=1}^{J} \bar{\varepsilon}_{2j}^{e} \left| \sum_{i=1}^{N} \Delta S_{ij} \right| \geq E - \sum_{i=1}^{N} \Delta S_i \geq \sum_{j=1}^{J} \bar{\varepsilon}_{1j}^{e} \left| \sum_{i=1}^{N} \Delta S_{ij} \right|$$

or that

$$\sum_{j=1}^{J} \bar{\varepsilon}_{2j}^{c} \bar{\gamma}_j \geq \frac{\sum_{i=1}^{N} \Delta S_i - C}{\sum_{j=1}^{J} \left| \sum_{i=1}^{N} \Delta S_{ij} \right|} \geq \sum_{j=1}^{J} \bar{\varepsilon}_{1j}^{c} \bar{\gamma}_j \tag{8.7}$$

$$\sum_{j=1}^{J} \bar{\varepsilon}_{2j}^{e} \bar{\gamma}_j \geq \frac{E - \sum_{i=1}^{N} \Delta S_i}{\sum_{j=1}^{J} \left| \sum_{i=1}^{N} \Delta S_{ij} \right|} \geq \sum_{j=1}^{J} \bar{\varepsilon}_{1j}^{e} \bar{\gamma}_j, \tag{8.8}$$

where

$$\bar{\gamma}_j = \frac{\left| \sum_{i=1}^{N} \Delta S_{ij} \right|}{\sum_{j=1}^{J} \left| \sum_{i=1}^{N} \Delta S_{ij} \right|}.$$

Thus, if surpluses associated with consumer demand and/or factor supply are useful for measuring compensating and equivalent variations at the individual level of analysis, they are also reasonable at the market level of analysis. The results of Willig thus suggest that the error made by using $\Sigma_{i=1}^{N} \Delta S_i$ as a measure of compensating or equivalent variation will be no more than about 5 percent of the sum of absolute surplus changes over all individuals, as long as $|\bar{\eta}_{2j}\bar{s}_j/2| \leq 0.05$ for all individuals where $\bar{s}_j = \Sigma_{i=1}^{N} \Delta S_{ij}/\bar{m}_j$, $\bar{m}_j$ is the jth consumer's initial exogenous income, and $\bar{\eta}_{2j}$ is the jth consumer's maximum exogenous income elasticity over all goods for which prices change in the range of price changes considered. Alternatively, using the result at the end of Appendix Section 7.F, the same statement applies for endogenous income elasticities and endogenous initial income if both endogenous and exogenous income have the same marginal effects on consumer demand and factor supply decisions.

In the case that percentage errors associated with raw surpluses are too great or if additional precision is desired, the kinds of modifications in (7.48) and (7.49) can also be considered. For example, consider a single price change and suppose that $\underline{\eta s}$ and $\overline{\eta s}$ are the respective minimum and maximum values that $|\bar{\eta}_j \bar{s}_j|$ can take over all consumers in the domain of price changes to be considered. That is,

$$\underline{\eta s} = \min_j \bar{\eta}_{1j}|\bar{s}_j| \tag{8.9}$$

$$\overline{\eta s} = \max_j \bar{\eta}_{2j}|\bar{s}_j|, \tag{8.10}$$

where $\bar{\eta}_{1j}$ is the minimum exogenous income elasticity defined analogously to $\bar{\eta}_{2j}$ above. Using the approximation in (6.45) implies that

$$\min_j \bar{\varepsilon}_{1j}^c \doteq \hat{\varepsilon}_1 \doteq \min_j \bar{\varepsilon}_{1j}^e \tag{8.11}$$

$$\max_j \bar{\varepsilon}_{2j}^c \doteq \hat{\varepsilon}_2 \doteq \max_j \bar{\varepsilon}_{2j}^e \tag{8.12}$$

where $\hat{\varepsilon}_1 \equiv \underline{\eta s}/2$ and $\varepsilon_2 \equiv \overline{\eta s}/2$. Substituting into (8.5) and (8.6) then suggests that

$$\hat{\varepsilon}_2 \sum_{j=1}^{J} \gamma_j \geq \frac{\Delta S_i - C}{|\Delta S_i|} \geq \hat{\varepsilon}_1 \sum_{j=1}^{J} \gamma_j$$

$$\hat{\varepsilon}_2 \sum_{j=1}^{J} \gamma_j \geq \frac{E - \Delta S_i}{|\Delta S_i|} \geq \hat{\varepsilon}_2 \sum_{j=1}^{J} \gamma_j.$$

Multiplying by $|\Delta S_i| \,/\, \Sigma_{j=1}^{J} \gamma_j$ thus verifies that $\hat{\varepsilon}_1$ and $\hat{\varepsilon}_2$ serve as approximate lower and upper bounds, respectively, on both $(\Delta S_i - C)/|\Delta S_i|$ and $(E - \Delta S_i)/|\Delta S_i|$ (note that $|\Delta S_i| = \Sigma_{j=1}^{J} |\Delta S_{ij}|$ because all ΔS_{ij} are of the same sign).

As suggested in Appendix Section 6.B, these bounds can be fairly tight even though the magnitude of error may be sizable. Hence, improved estimates in such cases can be obtained following the approach in (7.38) to (7.42), that is, compensating variation can be estimated by

$$\bar{C}^* = \Delta S_i - \bar{\varepsilon}|\Delta S_i| \tag{8.13}$$

and equivalent variation can be estimated by

$$\bar{E}^* = \Delta S_i + \bar{\varepsilon}|\Delta S_i|, \tag{8.14}$$

where $\bar{\varepsilon} = (\hat{\varepsilon}_1 + \hat{\varepsilon}_2)/2$. The associated approximate percentage error bounds would be $\pm (\hat{\varepsilon}_1 - \hat{\varepsilon}_2)/2$. Using this procedure, one can thus avoid more than about 2 percent error if $|\bar{\eta}_{2j}\bar{s}_j/2| \leq 0.08$ and exogenous income elasticities for individual consumers change by less than 50 percent in the domain of price changes under consideration.

Unfortunately, the construction of improved estimates becomes somewhat more cumbersome in the multiple-price-change case. To examine this possibility, suppose that $\hat{\varepsilon}_1$ and $\hat{\varepsilon}_2$ are defined as in equations (8.9) to (8.12) where minimums and maximums are also taken with respect to the set of goods for which prices change. Then substitution into (8.7) and (8.8) suggests in an analogous manner that $\hat{\varepsilon}_1$ and $\hat{\varepsilon}_2$ serve as approximate lower and upper bounds, respectively, on

$$\frac{\sum_{i=1}^{N} \Delta S_i - C}{\sum_{j=1}^{J} \left| \sum_{i=1}^{N} \Delta S_{ij} \right|}$$

and

$$\frac{E - \sum_{i=1}^{N} \Delta S_i}{\sum_{j=1}^{J} \left| \sum_{i=1}^{N} \Delta S_{ij} \right|}.$$

In this case, however, modified estimates similar to (8.13) and (8.14) cannot be defined solely in terms of market-level measurements. That is, these approximate bounds would suggest modified estimates,

$$\sum_{i=1}^{N} \Delta S_i - \bar{\varepsilon} \sum_{j=1}^{J} \left| \sum_{i=1}^{N} \Delta S_{ij} \right|$$

$$\sum_{i=1}^{N} \Delta S_i + \bar{\varepsilon} \sum_{j=1}^{J} \left| \sum_{i=1}^{N} \Delta S_{ij} \right|,$$

for compensating and equivalent variation, respectively. But ΔS_{ij} can be calculated only from information about individual consumers' demand curves. Only in the case where $\Sigma_{i=1}^{N} \Delta S_{ij}$ is of the same sign for all individuals does one find that

$$\left| \sum_{i=1}^{N} \Delta S_i \right| = \sum_{j=1}^{J} \left| \sum_{i=1}^{N} \Delta S_{ij} \right|,$$

in which case the modified estimates (relying only on market surplus measurements),

$$\bar{C}^* = \sum_{i=1}^{N} \Delta S_i - \bar{\varepsilon} \left| \sum_{i=1}^{N} \Delta S_i \right| \tag{8.15}$$

$$\bar{E}^* = \sum_{i=1}^{N} \Delta S_i + \bar{\varepsilon} \left| \sum_{i=1}^{N} \Delta S_i \right|, \tag{8.16}$$

with associated approximate error bounds of $\pm (\hat{\varepsilon}_1 - \hat{\varepsilon}_2)/2$ are clearly suggested. If such is the case, application of arguments in Appendix Sections 6.B and 7.F again imply that more than about 2 percent error can be avoided even in the multiple-price-change case if $|\bar{\eta}_{2j}\bar{s}_j/2| \leq 0.08$ for $j = 1, \ldots, J$ and exogenous income elasticity varies by less than 50 percent among consumers and goods for which prices change. By application of the algorithm in (6.60) through (6.64), this requirement can be relaxed even further. That is, bounds can be computed, in effect, individually for each segment of the overall path in which exogenous income elasticities can be bounded. Also, if the marginal effects of endogenous and exogenous income on consumer decisions are the same, all requirements related to exogenous income above can be replaced by analogous requirements related to endogenous income or total income.

An important implication of the foregoing results is that disaggregation of consumer groups in measuring or estimating demand is sometimes desirable. That is, the tighter bounds associated with (8.15) and (8.16) are applicable only when all consumers in the relevant group have welfare effects in the same direction. The modifications in (8.15) and (8.16) may also lead to improvements over using raw surplus changes in most practical problems when such is not the case, but this is not necessarily so because the appropriate correction factor, $\bar{\varepsilon} \sum_{j=1}^{J} \left| \sum_{i=1}^{N} \Delta S_{ij} \right|$, may be near zero when surplus gains for some individuals offset the surplus losses for others. Thus, it behooves the practitioner of applied welfare economics to attempt measurement or estimation of demand within groups that are affected in the same direction by the set of wage–price changes under consideration, not only to increase distributional information available for policy-making purposes but also to increase accuracy. It is also intuitively clear at this point that any further possible disaggregation according to income and production elasticities is desirable, which can lead to accurate welfare measurement with the approaches of the following two sections.

8.B AGGREGATION UNDER HETEROGENEITY FOR PRODUCERS[1]

As discussed in Appendix Section 4.E, the theoretical equivalence of alternative approaches to evaluating welfare effects on producers in the case of multiple price changes depends on whether the related supplies and demands correspond to a unique producer profit-maximization problem. However, when the supplies and demands used for welfare calculations are aggregated over many producers, these properties may not hold. For example, in the simple case where all producers are of two distinct types but the number of producers of each type is changing over time, then time series data cannot be expected to relate to a single producer profit-maximization problem.

The conditions that ensure a set of supplies and demands integrate back to a common profit-maximization problem are called integrability conditions. Consider the short-run profit-maximization problem for an individual producer k to maximize $\pi_k = \boldsymbol{p}\boldsymbol{q}_k$ subject to $\boldsymbol{f}_k(\boldsymbol{q}_k) = \boldsymbol{0}$ where $\boldsymbol{q}_k = (q_{1k}, \ldots, q_{Nk})$ and q_{nk} is the quantity of good n produced by producer k (if $q_{nk} > 0$) or used as an input (if $q_{nk} < 0$), $\boldsymbol{p}$ is a vector of prices corresponding to $\boldsymbol{q}$ faced by all producers, and $\boldsymbol{f}_k$ is a possibly multivariate implicit production function

1. The discussion in this section is based on Just and Pope (1999).

(assumed to depend on fixed factors not explicitly represented) that can be expressed in an explicit form with the same properties assumed in Appendix Section 4.A.[2] Following the result of Appendix Section 4.A, the system of netputs (supplies and demands) resulting from profit maximization, $\mathbf{q}_k = \hat{\mathbf{q}}_k(\mathbf{p})$, must satisfy the following integrability conditions (Cornes 1992, pp. 117–18):

1. *Homogeneity of degree zero in prices*: $\hat{\mathbf{q}}_k(t\mathbf{p}) = \hat{\mathbf{q}}_k(\mathbf{p})$,
2. *Positive monotonicity*: $\partial \hat{q}_{nk}/\partial p_n \geq 0$,
3. *Symmetry*: $\partial \hat{q}_{ik}/\partial p_j = \partial \hat{q}_{jk}/\partial p_i$,
4. *Convexity*: $\{\partial \hat{q}_{ik}/\partial p_j\} \geq 0$,

where, for simplicity of notation, $\partial \hat{q}_{ik}/\partial p_j \equiv \partial \hat{q}_{ik}(p)/\partial p_j$. The latter condition means that the matrix with $\partial \hat{q}_{ik}/\partial p_j$ in the ith row and jth column is positive semidefinite, which is equivalent to requiring $\partial \hat{q}_{ik}/\partial p_i \cdot \partial \hat{q}_{jk}/\partial p_j - \partial \hat{q}_{ik}/\partial p_j \cdot \partial \hat{q}_{jk}/\partial p_i \geq 0$ for $i, j = 1, \ldots, N$, for in addition to monotonicity. These four properties ensure that all supplies and demands of producer k integrate to a unique and meaningful profit function.

The most common approach to imposing these conditions for the estimation of aggregate supplies and demands has been the *representative producer* approach whereby all producers are assumed to act as if they were one large producer. That is, market-level data aggregated over producers are assumed to behave as if generated by a single producer behaving competitively. Then supply and demand specifications are estimated, for example, by imposing one of the specification systems in Appendix Section 4.E such as the translog system using aggregate data instead of individual firm data.[3]

Undoubtedly, the representative producer assumption does not hold in reality when the set of producers is changing over time and space. Rather, it is employed as an approximation. Recognizing this weakness, some empirical studies have been undertaken to test statistically whether the representative producer model or the associated integrability conditions hold at the aggregate level. A predominance of such studies have rejected these hypotheses (see, for example, Shumway 1995 for a review of such studies for agricultural production). From a superficial level, rejection of integrability conditions is troubling because it implies that unique welfare measurement is not possible. In other words, under these conditions the welfare analyst would have alternative ways of measuring the same welfare impact and thus could influence measurement arbitrarily. More seriously, rejection of integrability implies that the underlying theory of producer welfare measurement does not apply.

This section first shows that aggregation, in theory, does not destroy integrability conditions and thus does not provide an explanation for the empirical rejection. More likely, failure to account for changes in the distribution of characteristics of the individual producers that are aggregated causes failure of integrability conditions. Producers may differ in many respects including size, technology, location, climate and access to input markets.

2. The technology is written in implicit form here for convenience because some elements of $\mathbf{q}_k$ are outputs (if $q_{nk} > 0$) and others are inputs (if $q_{nk} < 0$). Alternatively and more generally, the production technology can be represented simply by $q_k \equiv (q_{1k}, \ldots, q_{Nk}) \in T$, where T is a closed convex technology set (also possibly conditioned on implicit fixed inputs). The results below can be generalized accordingly.
3. Alternatively, a more cumbersome approach is to impose these conditions as constraints on estimated parameters if functional forms are sufficiently compatible. But this is also a representative producer approach with the same problems and needs for generalization discussed below.

If the distribution of these characteristics among producers changes over time and space, then rejections of integrability are to be expected if empirical specifications used for estimation do not consider them. The remainder of this section proposes two ways the distribution of producer characteristics can be incorporated depending on data availability to specify aggregate producer supplies and demands that consider heterogeneity, but yet preserve integrability at the individual firm level for welfare calculations. Thus, unique WTP welfare measures are obtained at the aggregate level.

Integrability under Aggregation

To show that integrability holds at the aggregate level if it holds at the individual firm level, define aggregate quantities $\hat{\mathbf{Q}}(\mathbf{p}) = \Sigma_{k=1}^{K} \hat{\mathbf{q}}_k(\mathbf{p})$. Then homogeneity is preserved in $\hat{\mathbf{Q}}(\mathbf{p})$ because

$$\sum_{k=1}^{K} \hat{\mathbf{q}}_k(t\mathbf{p},) = \sum_{k=1}^{K} \hat{\mathbf{q}}_k(\mathbf{p})$$

if

$$\hat{\mathbf{q}}_k(t\mathbf{p}) = \hat{\mathbf{q}}_k(\mathbf{p}) \text{ for } k = 1, \ldots, K.$$

Monotonicity is preserved because

$$\partial \hat{Q}_n / \partial p_n = \sum_{k=1}^{K} \partial \hat{q}_{nk} / \partial p_n \geq 0$$

if

$$\partial \hat{q}_{nk} / \partial p_n \geq 0 \text{ for } k = 1, \ldots, K.$$

Symmetry is preserved because

$$\partial \hat{Q}_i / \partial p_j = \sum_{k=1}^{K} \partial \hat{q}_{ik} / \partial p_j = \sum_{k=1}^{K} \partial \hat{q}_{jk} / \partial p_i = \partial \hat{Q}_j / \partial p_i$$

if

$$\partial \hat{q}_{ik} / \partial p_j = \partial \hat{q}_{jk} / \partial p_i \text{ for } k = 1, \ldots, K.$$

And convexity is preserved because

$$\{\partial \hat{q}_i / \partial p_j\} = \left\{ \sum_{k=1}^{K} \partial \hat{q}_{ik} / \partial p_j \right\} = \sum_{k=1}^{K} \{\partial \hat{q}_{ik} / \partial p_j\} \geq 0$$

if[4]

$$\{\partial \hat{q}_{ik} / \partial p_j\} \geq 0 \text{ for } k = 1, \ldots, K.$$

4. That is, addition of matrices preserves positive semidefiniteness. See, for example, Hoffman and Kunze (1971).

Thus, if all firms face the same prices and differences among firms are properly considered, then integrability conditions are preserved at the aggregate level if they hold for all individual firms.

From an empirical standpoint, however, integrability conditions may fail at the aggregate level if differences among firms are not properly considered in aggregate specifications. Such would be the case, for example, if the distribution of characteristics changes (over time or space) within the data set used for estimation but the specifications of supplies and demands are not properly conditioned on such changes in the distribution of characteristics.[5]

Modeling Producer Heterogeneity

Typically, firms differ in productive capital (plant and equipment) or other aspects of technology that cause netput structures and thus firm responses to differ. Firms also differ by constraints that may take the form of government restrictions or available amounts of allocable fixed factors of production (such as total land on a farm available for allocation among various crops). Firms may also differ in technology, know-how, information, expectations and other characteristics. Hereafter, we refer to all such attributes among firms as *firm characteristics*.

If firm characteristics are the same among all firms, then their effects can be captured in constant parameters. However, investment, technology, and know-how tend to change over time and at different rates among firms. Government restrictions change from one policy regime to another and changes at the firm level often depend on individual firm characteristics such as proximity to water resources in the case of environmental constraints. Information sources differ and expectations formed therefrom differ. The distribution of firm characteristics determines the distribution of firm-level responses to price changes. As a result, aggregate responses to changes in prices and the associated welfare effects generally depend on the distribution of characteristics among firms.

The role of firm characteristics can be represented parametrically with supplies and demands of the form $\hat{\mathbf{q}}_k(\mathbf{p}) = \hat{\mathbf{q}}(\mathbf{p},\mathbf{z}_k)$ where $\mathbf{z}_k$ is a vector characterizing capital, technology and other constraints and characteristics of firm k. If each of K firms faces the same price vector, an accurate aggregate netput specification is thus $\hat{\mathbf{Q}}(\mathbf{p},\mathbf{z}_1,\ldots,\mathbf{z}_K) = \Sigma_{k=1}^{K} \hat{\mathbf{q}}(\mathbf{p},\mathbf{z}_k)$. In other words, aggregate supplies and demands depend on the distribution of characteristics among firms.

Estimation of an aggregate equation of the form $\hat{\mathbf{Q}}(\mathbf{p},\mathbf{z}_1,\ldots,\mathbf{z}_K)$ is usually impractical both because complete firm-specific data on characteristics is typically unavailable and because too many parameters require estimation (without considerable simplifying

5. The reader should also note that integrability properties can fail at the firm level because of (1) discrete start-up/shut-down decisions, (2) imperfect capital markets, (3) temporal aggregation with discrete time measurement, (4) dynamic reality with static modeling, (5) inapplicability of profit maximization and (6) errors in the data. For example, imperfect capital markets or dynamic adjustment constraints often impose one-sided limits that can cause homogeneity to fail. Temporal aggregation can distort symmetry. Certainly, theoretical conditions may not be supported empirically if profit maximization does not hold or data are erroneous. In each of these cases except the last, steps can be taken to restore some appropriate form of integrability with proper generalizations in the theory. For example, generalizations necessary when profit maximization fails because of risk aversion are considered in the Appendix to Chapter 12, and generalizations that account for dynamic issues associated with intertemporal investment problems are considered in the Appendix of Chapter 14. For further details in each of these cases, see Just and Pope (1999).

assumptions).[6] An alternative approach is to model the statistical distribution of firm characteristics. If $G(z)$ represents the statistical probability distribution of characteristics among firms, then an accurate specification of aggregate netputs is given by[7]

$$\hat{\mathbf{Q}}(\mathbf{p},G) = K \int \hat{\mathbf{q}}(\mathbf{p},z)dG(z). \tag{8.17}$$

Note that the integrability conditions are preserved in $\hat{\mathbf{Q}}(\mathbf{p},G)$ for a given G because

$$\hat{\mathbf{Q}}(t\mathbf{p},G) = \int K\hat{\mathbf{q}}(t\mathbf{p},z)dG(z) = \int K\hat{\mathbf{q}}(\mathbf{p},z)dG(z) = \hat{\mathbf{Q}}(\mathbf{p},G),$$
$$\partial\hat{Q}_n(p,G)/\partial p_n = \partial[\int K\hat{q}_n(p,z)dG(z)]/\partial p_n = \int K[\partial\hat{q}_n(p,z)/\partial p_n]dG(z) \geq 0,$$
$$\partial\hat{Q}_i(p,G)/\partial p_j = \int K[\partial\hat{q}_i(p,z)/\partial p_j]dG(z) = \int K[\partial\hat{q}_j(p,z)/\partial p_i]dG(z) = \partial\hat{Q}_j(p,G)/\partial p_i,$$
$$\{\partial\hat{Q}_i(p,G)/\partial p_j\} = \left[\int K[\partial\hat{q}_i(p,z)/\partial p_j]dG(z)\right] = \int K\{\partial\hat{q}_i(p,z)/\partial p_j\}dG(z) \geq 0,$$

when the corresponding integrability conditions hold for individual firms.

Direct modeling of heterogeneity

The approach in equation (8.17) can be implemented in two different ways. First, one can consider direct modeling of the distribution of characteristics among firms. For example, census data or other survey data may provide an empirical distribution or permit estimation of the distribution of capital stock and financial status such as debt and equity among firms for a given time period and jurisdiction (for example, for a given county, state or nation). Such distributions of characteristics for multiple time periods can be combined with corresponding time series data on aggregate prices and quantities, or such distributions for different jurisdictions may be combined with corresponding cross-section data on aggregate prices and quantities, to estimate aggregate demands and supplies that depend on the distribution of characteristics.

For purposes of an example, suppose the supplies and demands for individual firms are specified following the generalized Leontief form in (4.22) of Appendix Section 4.E. Suppose differences among firms are explained by some firm characteristic measured by a scalar variable z. If differences are explained by several characteristics, then other variables may be added in the same form as demonstrated for z below. The netput

6. Typically, if complete firm-specific characteristic data are available then panel data (a time series of cross-section data) exist on all firms, which allows estimation of $\hat{\mathbf{q}}(\mathbf{p},z_k)$ for each firm. If such data are available, then panel estimation of firm-level netputs is preferred to aggregate netput estimation.
7. For the reader unfamiliar with this type of integral, note that

$$\hat{\mathbf{Q}}(\mathbf{p},G) = K \int \hat{\mathbf{q}}(\mathbf{p},z)dG(z).$$

represents in a single convenient way either

$$\hat{Q}_n(\mathbf{p},G) = K \int \hat{q}_n(\mathbf{p},z)g(z)dz \text{ for } n = 1, \ldots, N,$$

where $G(z)$ is a continuous distribution with probability density function $g(z)$, or

$$\hat{Q}_n(\mathbf{p},G) = K \Sigma\, \hat{q}_n(\mathbf{p},z)g(z) \text{ for } n = 1, \ldots, N,$$

where $G(z)$ is a discrete distribution with probability function $g(z)$. In each case, integration or summation is assumed to be over all possible values of z. Note that multiplying by the number of firms, K, is required to obtain aggregate production from expected production per firm.

specifications for individual firms can be conditioned on characteristics of firms by specifying some or all of the parameters of the firm-level profit functions, and the consequent netput equations, as functions of firm characteristics. For example, a second-order approximation of the effects of z on the parameters of the generalized Leontief model could be achieved by

$$\beta_{ij} = \beta_{ij}^0 + \beta_{ij}^1 z + \beta_{ij}^2 z^2. \tag{8.18}$$

Using this specification, the generalized Leontief short-run profit function in (4.22) becomes

$$R(\mathbf{p},z) = \sum_{i=1}^{N} \sum_{j=1}^{N} (\beta_{ij}^0 + \beta_{ij}^1 z + \beta_{ij}^2 z^2)(p_i)^{1/2}(p_j)^{1/2},$$

which generates netputs of the form

$$\hat{q}(\mathbf{p},z) = \sum_{j=1}^{N} (\beta_{ij}^0 + \beta_{ij}^1 z + \beta_{ij}^2 z^2)\left(\frac{p_j}{p_i}\right)^{1/2}. \tag{8.19}$$

When the system forms in Appendix Section 4.E are generalized to specify parameters as functions of firm characteristics, care must be taken to preserve regularity conditions for all possible values of z. With the symmetry conditions applicable to the generalized Leontief profit function, $\beta_{ij} = \beta_{ji}$, the generalization in (8.18) requires $\beta_{ij}^0 = \beta_{ji}^0$, $\beta_{ij}^1 = \beta_{ji}^1$, and $\beta_{ij}^2 = \beta_{ji}^2$. With other forms, more restrictions may be required.[8]

To consider direct modeling of the distribution of characteristics, suppose the individual producers are farmers and that the firm characteristic by which farms differ is farm size. The distribution of farm size in many developed countries is compiled periodically by government surveys in agricultural census data. Typically, census data are compiled in discrete form representing the number of farms in each size class such as 0–10 acres, 10–50 acres, 50–150 acres, and so on. Let g_s represent the number of farms in size class s, and let z_s represent the average farm size in size class s, $s = 1, \ldots, S$. Then an appropriate aggregate specification for netputs can be found by applying (8.17) to (8.19),

$$\hat{Q}_i(\mathbf{p},G) = \sum_{s=1}^{S} g_s \sum_{j=1}^{N} (\beta_{ij}^0 + \beta_{ij}^1 z_s + \beta_{ij}^2 z_s^2)\left(\frac{p_j}{p_i}\right)^{1/2}, \tag{8.20}$$

$$= K \sum_{j=1}^{N} (\beta_{ij}^0 + \beta_{ij}^1 \mu_1^z + \beta_{ij}^2 \mu_2^z)\left(\frac{p_j}{p_i}\right)^{1/2}$$

where

$$K = \sum_{s=1}^{S} g_s,\ \mu_1^z = \sum_{s=1}^{S} z_s g_s / K,\ \mu_2^z = \sum_{s=1}^{S} z_s^2 g_s / K.$$

Data on aggregate demand for all time periods or jurisdictions, for which agricultural census data allow estimation of the distribution of farm size, can thus be used to estimate

8. For example with the translog case in (4.21), linear homogeneity requires $\Sigma_{i=1}^N \alpha_i = 1$ and $\Sigma_{i=1}^N \beta_{ij} = 0$ (see footnote 13 of the Appendix to Chapter 4). For this case, defining, for example, $\alpha_i = \alpha_i^0 + \alpha_i^1 z$ implies $\Sigma_{i=1}^N (\alpha_i^0 + \alpha_i^1 z) = 1$, which requires $\Sigma_{i=1}^N \alpha_i^0 = 1$ and $\Sigma_{i=1}^N \alpha_i^1 = 0$; and similarly defining $\beta_{ij} = \beta_{ij}^0 + \beta_{ij}^1 z$ implies $\Sigma_{i=1}^N \beta_{ij}^0 + \beta_{ij}^1 z = 0$, which requires $\Sigma_{i=1}^N \beta_{ij}^0 = 0$ and $\Sigma_{i=1}^N \beta_{ij}^1 = 0$.

the parameters of (8.20). The result in (8.20) illustrates how exact aggregation is possible by including a small set of index numbers such as μ_1^z and μ_2^z in (8.20). The appropriate form of index numbers depends on the individual netput specifications and the specification for the distribution of characteristics.

The estimated parameters of (8.20) can be used to calculate welfare effects on individual firms with given characteristics. That is, all of the parameters of the individual netputs in (8.19) are available to calculate uniquely the welfare effects of a change in prices on a farm with given characteristic z. Unique welfare measurement for given characteristics allows unique welfare measurement at the aggregate level by aggregating welfare effects according to the distribution of characteristics at a given time period. Suppose, for example, that a generalized Leontief system of aggregate netputs such as (8.20) is estimated. Then the aggregate welfare effect (compensating or equivalent variation) of a price change from $\mathbf{p^0} = (p_0^0,\ldots,p_N^0)$ to $\mathbf{p^1} = (p_0^1,\ldots,p_N^1)$ is measured by

$$
\begin{aligned}
C &= \int K[R(\mathbf{p^1},z) - R(\mathbf{p^0},z)]dG(z) \\
&= \sum_{s=1}^{S}\sum_{i=1}^{N}\sum_{j=1}^{N} g_s\,(\beta_{ij}^0 + \beta_{ij}^1 z_s + \beta_{ij}^2 z_s^2)\,[(p_i^1)^{1/2}(p_j^1)^{1/2} - (p_i^0)^{1/2}(p_j^0)^{1/2}] \\
&= K\sum_{i=1}^{N}\sum_{j=1}^{N}(\beta_{ij}^0 + \beta_{ij}^1 \mu_s^1 + \beta_{ij}^2 \mu_2^s)\,[(p_i^1)^{1/2}(p_j^1)^{1/2} - (p_i^0)^{1/2}(p_j^0)^{1/2}].
\end{aligned}
$$

This approach can be adapted to a wide variety of circumstances including cases where firms differ in a variety of characteristics. The methodology can be as rich as the data available for estimation can identify. Also, the welfare effects of a policy that will alter the distribution of characteristics among firms can be evaluated. For example, a land reform policy in a developing country may redistribute land and thus alter the distribution of characteristics. In this case, both compensating and equivalent variation is measured by

$$
C = \int KR(\mathbf{p^1},z)dG^1(z) - \int KR(\mathbf{p^0},z)]dG^0(z)
$$

where G^0 represents the initial distribution of characteristics and G^1 represents the subsequent distribution of characteristics.

Indirect modeling of heterogeneity

When data on the distribution of characteristics are not available for each time series or cross-section observation on prices and quantities, another possibility is to model the distribution of characteristics indirectly. Data on averages or totals of important characteristics are more readily available in public data sources than are data on higher moments of the distribution of characteristics. For example, public data on agriculture typically include total land in farms, total capital stock and aggregate debt as well as total number of farms. Thus, average farm size, average capital stock and average debt are usually observable. Imposing some additional structure on the distribution of producer characteristics may be sufficient to allow these data to represent heterogeneity sufficiently.

Suppose, for example, the distribution of farm size is assumed to follow an exponential distribution, $G(z)=1-\exp(-z/\theta)$ for $z>0$, $G(z)=0$ otherwise, $\theta>0$.[9] Applying (8.17) to (8.19) under this assumption yields

$$\hat{Q}_n(\boldsymbol{p},G) = \int K\hat{q}_n(\boldsymbol{p},z)dG(z)$$

$$= \int K\sum_{j=1}^{N}(\beta_{ij}^0+\beta_{ij}^1 z+\beta_{ij}^2 z^2)\left(\frac{p_j}{p_i}\right)^{1/2}\theta^{-1}e^{-z/\theta}\,dz$$

$$= K\sum_{j=1}^{N}(\beta_{ij}^0+\beta_{ij}^1\theta+2\beta_{ij}^2\theta^2)\left(\frac{p_j}{p_i}\right)^{1/2}, \qquad (8.21)$$

using the facts that $\int_0^\infty \theta^{-1}e^{-z/\theta}dz=1$, $\int_0^\infty z\theta^{-1}e^{-z/\theta}dz=\theta$, and $\int_0^\infty z^2\theta^{-1}e^{-z/\theta}dz=2\theta^2$. Because the mean of the distribution is θ, it can be estimated by average farm size corresponding to each time series or cross-section observation on prices and quantities, thus allowing time series or cross-section estimation of aggregate netputs following (8.21). In this case, average farm size serves as the index number that permits exact aggregation.

If such data do not exist for certain characteristics, or the specified characteristic distribution has multiple parameters, another approach is to model variation in the parameters of the distribution. If the variation in the distribution of a particular characteristic over time is explained by other variables, then the dependence of the parameters of the distribution on those variables can be included explicitly for purposes of estimation. For example, if no data on farm size are available but changes in the distribution of farm size over time are specified as depending on machinery scale, then the parameters of the farm size distribution can be specified as functions of machinery scale, for example, $\theta=\theta_0+\theta_1 w$ where w is some observable time series variable representing machinery scale. Then substitution into (8.21) yields an estimable aggregate equation that preserves firm-level integrability for purposes of welfare calculations,

$$\hat{Q}_n(\boldsymbol{p},G) = K\sum_{j=1}^{N}[\beta_{ij}^0+\beta_{ij}^1(\theta_0+\theta_1 w)+2\beta_{ij}^2(\theta_0+\theta_1 w)^2]\left(\frac{p_j}{p_i}\right)^{1/2}.$$

Similar approaches can be taken when multiple characteristics differ among producers. These approaches thus allow unique welfare measurement in problems where variation in the distribution of producers within a data set would not fit any single representative producer specification. Furthermore, they facilitate examining the distribution of welfare effects as well as calculation of aggregate welfare effects. Similar approaches are applicable when all firms do not face the same prices. For this problem, it can be shown that the integrability conditions are preserved at the aggregate level for mean prices. Estimable aggregate netputs can be specified if sufficient information is available to represent the distribution of prices and how the distribution changes within the data set used for estimation. For example, transportation costs may explain the differences in prices among producers in different locations (Just and Pope 1999).

9. The exponential distribution is a special case of the Weibull distribution that is often used to model size distributions.

8.C AGGREGATION UNDER HETEROGENEITY FOR CONSUMERS AND FACTOR OWNERS

Just as in the producer problem, the most common approach to assuring path independence of WTP measures at the aggregate level has been to impose a representative consumer model on data used for estimation. Path independence of compensating and equivalent variation holds only when the integrability conditions in Appendix Sections 6.E or 7.H hold. However, most empirical tests of these conditions with aggregate data have rejected the representative consumer model (see, for example, the empirical studies reported by Jorgenson 1997). From a practical point of view, just as in the producer problem, if the composition of the aggregate is changing over time or space because of changes in the distribution of consumer characteristics, then tests involving data over time or space cannot be expected to relate to a single consumer utility-maximization problem. However, aggregation alone does not cause integrability conditions to fail in the consumer case. Theoretically, Gorman (1953) has shown that functional forms under which a representative consumer model can describe aggregate behavior are very stringent. Demand functions must be linear in income and, if demands are zero when income is zero, all consumers must have identical homothetic preferences (all income elasticities equal to 1). Thus, the representative consumer approach has greater weaknesses than the representative producer approach.

Following the notation of the Appendix to Chapter 6, suppose the aggregate netputs of consumers are given by $\tilde{\boldsymbol{Q}}(\boldsymbol{p},m_1,\ldots,m_J)=\Sigma_{j=1}^{J}\,\tilde{\boldsymbol{q}}_j(\boldsymbol{p},m_j)$, where $\tilde{\boldsymbol{q}}_j(\boldsymbol{p},m_j)$ represents the demands by consumer j given income m_j and price vector p for all goods. Assuming all consumers face the same prices, the integrability conditions in Appendix Section 6.E can be examined as follows. The budget constraint is preserved in $\tilde{\boldsymbol{Q}}(\boldsymbol{p},m_1,\ldots,m_J)$ because

$$\boldsymbol{p}\tilde{\boldsymbol{Q}}(\boldsymbol{p},m_1,\ldots,m_J) = M \equiv \sum_{j=1}^{J} m_j$$

if

$$\boldsymbol{p}\tilde{\boldsymbol{q}}(\boldsymbol{p},m_j) = m_j \text{ for } j=1,\ \ldots,\ J.$$

Homogeneity is preserved because

$$\tilde{\boldsymbol{Q}}(t\boldsymbol{p},tm_1,\ldots,tm_J) = \tilde{\boldsymbol{Q}}(\boldsymbol{p},m_1,\ldots,m_J)$$

if

$$\tilde{\boldsymbol{q}}(t\boldsymbol{p},tm_j) = \tilde{\boldsymbol{q}}(\boldsymbol{p},m_j) \text{ for } j=1,\ \ldots,\ J.$$

Slutsky symmetry is preserved because

$$\partial\tilde{Q}_i/\partial p_k = \sum_{j=1}^{J} \partial\tilde{q}_{ij}/\partial p_k = \sum_{j=1}^{J} \partial\tilde{q}_{kj}/\partial p_i = \partial\tilde{Q}_k/\partial p_i$$

if

$$\partial\tilde{q}_{ij}/\partial p_k = \partial\tilde{q}_{kj}/\partial p_i \text{ for } j=1,\ \ldots,\ J.$$

And convexity is preserved because

$$\{\partial\tilde{Q}_i/\partial p_k\} = \left\{\sum_{j=1}^{J} \partial\tilde{q}_{ij}/\partial p_k\right\} = \sum_{j=1}^{J} \{\partial\tilde{q}_{ij}/\partial p_k\} \geq 0$$

if

$$\{\partial\tilde{q}_{ij}/\partial p_k\} \geq 0 \text{ for } j=1, \ldots, J.$$

Thus, if the differences among consumers are properly considered, then integrability conditions are preserved at the aggregate level if they hold for all individuals. Similar results hold for factor owners by considering netputs $\tilde{\boldsymbol{q}}_j(\boldsymbol{p},\bar{m}_j,\boldsymbol{r}_j)$ rather than consumer demands, and replacing ordinary income with exogenous income (where the factor endowment vector $\boldsymbol{r}_j$ is not scaled in the homogeneity condition). In this case, aggregate netputs depend on the distribution of endowments as well as the distribution of exogenous income, $\tilde{\boldsymbol{Q}}(\boldsymbol{p},\bar{m}_1, \ldots, \bar{m}_J,\boldsymbol{r}_1, \ldots, \boldsymbol{r}_J) = \Sigma_{j=1}^{J} \tilde{\boldsymbol{q}}_j(\boldsymbol{p},\bar{m}_j,\boldsymbol{r}_j)$.

As in the case of producers, integrability conditions may fail at the aggregate level if differences among consumers or factor owners are not adequately considered in aggregate demand and supply specifications.[10]

Modeling Consumer and Factor Owner Heterogeneity[11]

Typically, consumers differ in income, age and other circumstances, which causes netput structures to differ. Factor owners differ in endowments. Consumers own different consumer durables. For example, the type of automobile or home heating system an individual owns will affect fuel consumption. All such differences among individuals may be called *consumer or factor owner characteristics*. Because these characteristics usually change over time and differ among individuals, aggregate responses to changes in prices and the associated welfare effects generally depend on the distribution of characteristics among individuals.

The role of these characteristics can be represented parametrically with demands of the form $\tilde{\boldsymbol{q}}_j(\boldsymbol{p},m_j) = \tilde{\boldsymbol{q}}(\boldsymbol{p},m_j,z_j)$ in the pure consumer problem or netputs of the form $\tilde{\boldsymbol{q}}_j(\boldsymbol{p},\bar{m}_j,\boldsymbol{r}_j) = \tilde{\boldsymbol{q}}(\boldsymbol{p},\bar{m}_j,\boldsymbol{r}_j,z_j)$ in the factor owner problem where z_j is a vector representing the distinct characteristics of individual j. Let $G(\bar{m},\boldsymbol{r},z)$ represent the joint statistical probability distribution of exogenous income, factor ownership, and individual characteristics among individuals. Then an accurate specification of aggregate netputs for the factor owner problem can be represented by

$$\tilde{\boldsymbol{Q}}(\boldsymbol{p},G) = \int J\, \tilde{\boldsymbol{q}}(\boldsymbol{p},\bar{m},\boldsymbol{r},z)\, dG(\bar{m},\boldsymbol{r},z). \tag{8.22}$$

Applicability of the integrability conditions can be demonstrated for (8.22) just as in the producer case except that homogeneity requires scaling the income distribution as prices

10. The reader should also note that integrability properties can fail for individual factor owners for a variety of reasons similar to those discussed for producers in footnote 5.
11. The role of heterogeneity in consumer aggregation has been studied most extensively by Werner Hildenbrand. The discussion in this section relates closely to his work. See, for example, Hildenbrand (1998).

are scaled, and aggregate exogenous income in the budget constraint is defined by $\bar{M} = \int J\,\bar{m}\,dG(\bar{m},\boldsymbol{r},\boldsymbol{z})$. Of course, the same results hold for the pure consumer problem where consideration of factor endowments is eliminated from (8.22) and exogenous income is replaced by ordinary income.

As a specific example, consider the translog indirect utility case of equation (7.57) and the associated netput forms in (7.58). To simplify notation, suppose the netputs for factor owner j are represented as functions of full income in the form

$$\tilde{q}_{nj}(\boldsymbol{p},m_j^*,\boldsymbol{r}_j) = \frac{m_j^*}{p_n} \frac{\alpha_{nj} + 2\sum_{k=1}^{N} \beta_{nk} \ln \frac{p_k}{m_j^*}}{\sum_{i=1}^{N} \alpha_{ij} + 2\sum_{i=1}^{N}\sum_{k=1}^{N} \beta_{ik} \ln \frac{p_k}{m_j^*}} - r_{nj} \tag{8.23}$$

where $\boldsymbol{r}_j = (r_{1j},\ldots,r_{Nj})$ and $m_j^* = \bar{m}_j + \boldsymbol{pr}_j$. Heterogeneity with respect to income and factor endowments is thus represented explicitly. To represent heterogeneity with respect to other characteristics, suppose $\alpha_{nj} = \alpha_n^0 + \alpha_n^1 z_j$ where the unique differences in preferences and behavior of factor owner j are captured by a scalar characteristic z_j. If differences are due to many characteristics, then α_i^1 and z_j can be regarded as vectors of corresponding dimensions for multiplication.

With the individual netputs in (8.23) for each of J individuals who face the same price vector, aggregate netputs are $\tilde{\boldsymbol{Q}}(\boldsymbol{p},\bar{m}_1,\ldots,\bar{m}_J,\boldsymbol{r}_1,\ldots,\boldsymbol{r}_J,z_1,\ldots,z_J) = \Sigma_{j=1}^{J}\tilde{\boldsymbol{q}}(\boldsymbol{p},m_j^*,\boldsymbol{r}_j,z_j)$. As in the case of producers, estimation of an aggregate equation including the characteristics of all individuals is usually impractical both because complete data on individual characteristics are unavailable and because too many parameters require estimation.[12] A more practical approach is to represent the distribution of income, factors and characteristics by aggregate indexes such as those illustrated in the producer case in (8.20). However, because factor owner netputs depend on income that must normalize prices under homogeneity conditions, finding practical forms that permit exact aggregation without highly nonlinear estimation techniques is not as simple as in the producer case. Aggregation difficulties typical of most functional forms are apparent in (8.23) because income appears in both the numerator and denominator.

Exact Aggregation

Exact aggregation of consumer demands for purposes of welfare analysis has been studied most notably by Lau (1977) and Jorgenson, Lau and Stoker (1997).[13] Their work shows that the approach to heterogeneity in (8.23) is convenient when the standard normalization constraints, $\Sigma_{i=1}^{N}\Sigma_{j=1}^{N}\beta_{ij} = 0$ and $\Sigma_{i=1}^{N}\alpha_i = 1$, are imposed. With these constraints, the denominator becomes

12. If complete data on individual incomes and characteristics are available, then usually firm-level quantity data are also available. In this case, use of a panel data approach estimating demands $\tilde{\boldsymbol{q}}(\boldsymbol{p},m_j^*,\boldsymbol{r}_j,z_j)$ for individual consumers gains econometric efficiency and thereby aids identification of the role of characteristics, particularly when many characteristics are involved. See Jorgenson and Stoker (1997). Note that Jorgenson and Stoker refer to characteristics as demographic effects.
13. Note that these studies consider only the pure consumer problem rather than the generalization involving factor supply.

$$D=\sum_{i=1}^{N}\alpha_i+2\sum_{i=1}^{N}\sum_{k=1}^{N}\beta_{ik}\ln\frac{p_k}{m_j^*}=1+2\sum_{i=1}^{N}\sum_{k=1}^{N}\beta_{ik}\ln p_k, \tag{8.24}$$

where $\Sigma_{i=1}^{N}\alpha_i=1$ requires $\Sigma_{i=1}^{N}\alpha_i^0=1$ and $\Sigma_{i=1}^{N}\alpha_i^0=0$. Aggregation is thus greatly simplified by eliminating income and individual characteristics from the denominator.

Next, note that aggregate netputs can be expressed as

$$Q_n=\sum_{j=1}^{J}\tilde{q}_{nj}(\boldsymbol{p},m_j^*,\boldsymbol{r}_j)=\frac{1}{p_nD}\sum_{j=1}^{J}m_j^*\left[\alpha_{nj}+2\sum_{k=1}^{N}\beta_{nk}\ln\frac{p_k}{m_j^*}\right]-\sum_{j=1}^{J}r_{nj}$$

$$=\frac{M^*}{p_nD}\left[\sum_{j=1}^{J}\frac{m_j^*}{M^*}\alpha_{nj}+2\sum_{k=1}^{N}\beta_{nk}\sum_{j=1}^{J}\frac{m_j^*}{M^*}\ln p_k-2\sum_{k=1}^{N}\beta_{nk}\sum_{j=1}^{J}\frac{m_j^*}{M^*}\ln m_j^*\right]-R_n$$

$$=\frac{M^*}{p_nD}\left[\alpha_n^0+\alpha_n^1\sum_{j=1}^{J}\frac{m_j^*}{M^*}z_j+2\sum_{k=1}^{N}\beta_{nk}\ln p_k-2\sum_{k=1}^{N}\beta_{nk}\sum_{j=1}^{J}\frac{m_j^*}{M^*}\ln m_j^*\right]-R_n \tag{8.25}$$

$$=\frac{M^*}{p_nD}\left[\alpha_n^0+\alpha_n^1Z+2\sum_{k=1}^{N}\beta_{nk}\ln p_k-2\sum_{k=1}^{N}\beta_{nk}\ln\bar{M}^*\right]-R_n$$

where $M^*=\Sigma_{j=1}^{J}m_j^*$ is aggregate full income, $R_n=\Sigma_{j=1}^{J}r_{nj}$ is the aggregate endowment of factor n, $Z=\Sigma_{j=1}^{J}(m_j^*/M^*)z_j$ is an index of characteristics weighted by full income shares, and $\mathrm{M}^*=\exp\{\Sigma_{j=1}^{J}(m_j^*/M^*)\ln m_j^*\}$ is a weighted index of full income. Thus, because the denominator of (8.23) as expressed in (8.24) is the same for all individuals, the aggregate netputs can be estimated as in the latter expression of (8.25) by simply using a few weighted sums (indexes) of individual variables, with weights given by full income shares.[14] Thus, estimation is no more difficult than in the case of an individual consumer once appropriate indexes are constructed.

Once the aggregate netputs in (8.25) are estimated, all of the estimated parameters are available to calculate the compensating or equivalent variation of a general change in prices, exogenous income, or factor endowments for any factor owner facing given initial and subsequent prices, income and factor endowments following equation (7.59). Using the distribution of income, factor endowments and characteristics, this permits unique estimation of the distribution as well as the aggregate compensating and equivalent variation.[15]

To make these calculations, the distribution of income, factor endowments and characteristics can be modeled either directly or indirectly. With the direct approach, the indexes required in (8.25), or more generally the integration in (8.22), would be computed directly from available data on the distribution of income, factor endowments and characteristics for each time series or cross-section observation on prices and netput quantities

14. For further discussion of special considerations in stochastic specifications for econometric estimation of aggregate netputs in the form of (8.25), see Jorgenson, Lau and Stoker (1997).
15. Jorgenson, Lau and Stoker (1997, p. 283) conclude that the translog indirect utility function associated with the specification in (8.23) provides a cardinal measure of individual welfare as well as an ordinal measure because the indirect utility is additive in functions of the attributes and total expenditure, and because this property is invariant with respect to affine transformations but not arbitrary monotonic transformations. It should be noted, however, that this is a somewhat artificial property. If one individual's utility function is U and another's is $a+bU$ for constants a and b, then they will have the same utility function up to an affine transformation. These would generate identical behavior and identical estimates of indirect utility function parameters using (8.23) even though interpersonal comparisons would be impossible without knowing a and b. As explained in Section 8.3, exploiting cardinality of utility measures in a Bergsonian welfare function requires more than invariance with respect to affine transformations.

used for estimation. With the indirect approach, a functional form may be postulated to represent this distribution parametrically and then the variation in parameters of such a distribution would be estimated either extraneously or in the process of estimating the aggregate netput equations. For example, suppose full income has an exponential distribution with parameter θ given by $G(m^*) = 1 - \exp(-m^*/\theta)$ for $m^* > 0$, $G(m^*) = 0$ otherwise, $\theta > 0$. Then θ could be estimated extraneously by average full income, which is equal to aggregate full income M^* divided by population J. Also, with this exponential distribution, the average or expected value of $m^* \ln m^*$ among factor owners is

$$E(m^* \ln m^*) = \int m^* \ln m^* \, dG(m^*) = \theta \ln \theta + \theta - \theta\gamma$$

where γ is Euler's constant (approximately 0.5772156649) so that $\ln \bar{M}^*$ can be estimated by

$$\ln \bar{M}^* = \frac{J}{M^*}(\theta \ln \theta + \theta - \theta\gamma) = \ln\left(\frac{M^*}{J}\right) + 1 - \gamma$$

upon substituting $\theta = \bar{M}^*/J$. If aggregate full income M^* and population J are observable, then these substitutions can be made into (8.25) for purposes of estimating aggregate netputs. Further assumptions would be required to represent the joint distribution of characteristics and factor endowments parametrically.

The aggregate netput estimation problem thus comes down to data availability. Data on ordinary income distribution are widely available at least in quantile form (by income classes such as \$0–10000, \$10000–20000, \$20000–40000, and so on). Data on the distribution of demographic characteristics are also widely available (for example, data on age, gender and ethnicity). Fewer data are available on the distribution of factor endowments, consumer debt, physical characteristics such as health of individuals, and so on.[16] Perhaps more seriously, the public data available on these distributions in most cases do not reflect joint distributions but only marginal distributions. The aggregate netputs in (8.25) clearly depend on the joint distribution of income and characteristics in the index Z. For example, whether those with high incomes tend to have high values of z or low values is critical. Also, the full income distribution is usually not directly observable as is the case for ordinary income. If not, determining the distribution of full income requires information on the joint distribution of exogenous income and factor endowments. For this reason, modeling demands as in the pure consumer problem may be preferable when (1) only consumer demands rather than factor supplies are required for welfare analysis and (2) the separability issues of Appendix Section 7.D are not a concern.

With the results in this appendix, many possibilities are available for relaxing the representative producer and representative consumer approaches. The major constraint thus becomes data availability for reflecting the distribution of producer and consumer characteristics over the time periods and cross-section observations used to estimate supplies and demands employed for welfare analysis.

16. The inability to aggregate meaningfully when consumer characteristics are time-variant and data are not available on characteristics is discussed by Hildenbrand (1998). He argues that many household characteristics are unobservable. However, the more common approach is simply to assume that the distribution of household characteristics is time-invariant at least within identifiable subgroups of the population (Blundell, Pashardes and Weber 1993; Jorgenson, Lau and Stoker 1997; Stoker 1993).

9. Multimarket analysis and general equilibrium considerations

The analysis of Chapter 8 is conducted under the premise that price changes occur only in the market of interest. In many policy evaluation and cost–benefit studies, however, such an assumption is unrealistic. For example, suppose that the government establishes a quota on, say, imports of Middle Eastern oil. Although this policy would clearly affect domestic crude oil prices and hence oil refinery profits, some of the increased cost would probably be passed along the marketing channel to gasoline distributors and retailers and, finally, to gasoline consumers. Similarly, increased petroleum prices can lead to higher fertilizer prices, which through competition tend to be passed along through producers to processors, retailers and consumers of agricultural products. In such cases, economic agents involved in markets other than the restricted market can obviously experience important economic welfare consequences. These consequences should be considered in any decision regarding adoption of the policy.

This chapter, accordingly, extends the framework of Chapter 8 to consider the welfare effects of price changes in markets related to the one in which some change is introduced. The analysis begins with the relationship of input markets to output markets. Alternative possibilities for discerning the welfare effects of output market price changes on input suppliers and of input market price changes on consumers are discussed. Such cases, where a clearly defined marketing channel exists – for example, the petroleum production-refining-distributing-retailing channel – are called *vertical market structures*. Consideration is then given to welfare measurement of the effects of a price change on producers or consumers of competing commodities. The situations where one industry sells different products to different industries – for example, refineries sell different petroleum derivatives to gasoline distributors and fertilizer manufacturers – or where one industry buys different inputs from several different industries are called *horizontal market structures*.

These vertical and horizontal considerations suggest a methodology for measuring the general equilibrium effects of governmental intervention, which occur, to various degrees, throughout the entire economy. Consideration and modification of this methodology is then examined for the case where these other markets are already distorted by existing taxes, subsidies, quotas, and so on. Finally, econometric considerations in the multimarket context are discussed.

9.1 WELFARE EFFECTS IN VERTICALLY RELATED MARKETS[1]

Producer Surplus Associated with Equilibrium Supply

To evaluate the welfare consequences of price changes in vertically related markets, consider a competitive final-goods industry that uses a single factor of production, where the input-producing industry is also competitive but faces perfectly elastic supplies (fixed prices) for all its factors of production. The final-goods industry, depicted in Figure 9.1(b), is initially confronted with input price p_{n-1}^0 and output price p_n^0, and thus produces output q_n^0 along its short-run supply curve $S_n(p_{n-1}^0)$. Now, suppose that the output price is decreased to p_n^l because of governmental action. Initially, the final-goods industry will attempt to adjust output along its short-run supply curve to q_n^2 because individual producers do not perceive the effects of their actions on prices. Because the industry is the sole user of its input (q_{n-1}), however, the input price will not remain at p_{n-1}^0; a decrease in output prices causes a decrease in derived demand for the input from $D_{n-1}(p_n^0)$ to $D_{n-1}(p_n^1)$. Given input supply S_{n-1}, input price thus decreases from p_{n-1}^0 to p_{n-1}^1. In turn, the lower input price leads to decreased costs for the final-goods industry. Hence, its supply shifts rightward from $S_n(p_{n-1}^0)$ to, say, $S_n(p_{n-1}^1)$ Thus, the new equilibrium output at price p_n^1 is q_n^l

Now consider the welfare implications of the output price change. First, from Section 8.1 the quasirent for an industry is given by the area above its short-run supply curve (at the associated input price) and below its product price. Hence, it is clear that quasirent in the final-goods industry changes from area $y+u$ to area $y+z$. Thus, the welfare loss (compensating or equivalent variation) for final-goods producers is area $u-z$, and this loss is obviously less than area u, the loss that would occur if input price remained at p_{n-1}^0. Also, from Section 8.1, quasirent for the final goods industry can be measured by consumer surplus associated with derived demand. In Figure 9.1(a), quasirent for the final goods industry thus changes from area $a+b$ to area $b+c$ for a loss of area $a-c$ (thus, area $y+z=$ area $b+c$, area $u+y=$ area $a+b$ and area $u-z=$ area $a-c$). As suggested by the examples in the introduction to this chapter, however, additional welfare effects from the initial price change will be experienced in related markets where prices also change – in this case by the producers of the input. From Figure 9.1(a), quasirent for the input-producing industry decreases from area $c+d+e$ to area e. Hence, their welfare effect is a loss of area $c+d$.

Determination of the net social gains from the output price change requires summing the welfare effects over the two individual industries. Collecting these effects over both industries, as reflected in the input market, yields a net social loss of area $a+d$ [$= (a-c) + (c+d)$].

Observation of the net social welfare effects in the output market is somewhat more difficult because both industries are not represented explicitly. To explore the possibilities for measurement in the output market, consider first the implications of aggregating the two industries into a single vertically integrated industry. This hypothetical industry faces perfectly elastic supplies (those in reality pertaining to the input producing industry) as

1. Results in this section were developed originally by Just and Hueth (1979).

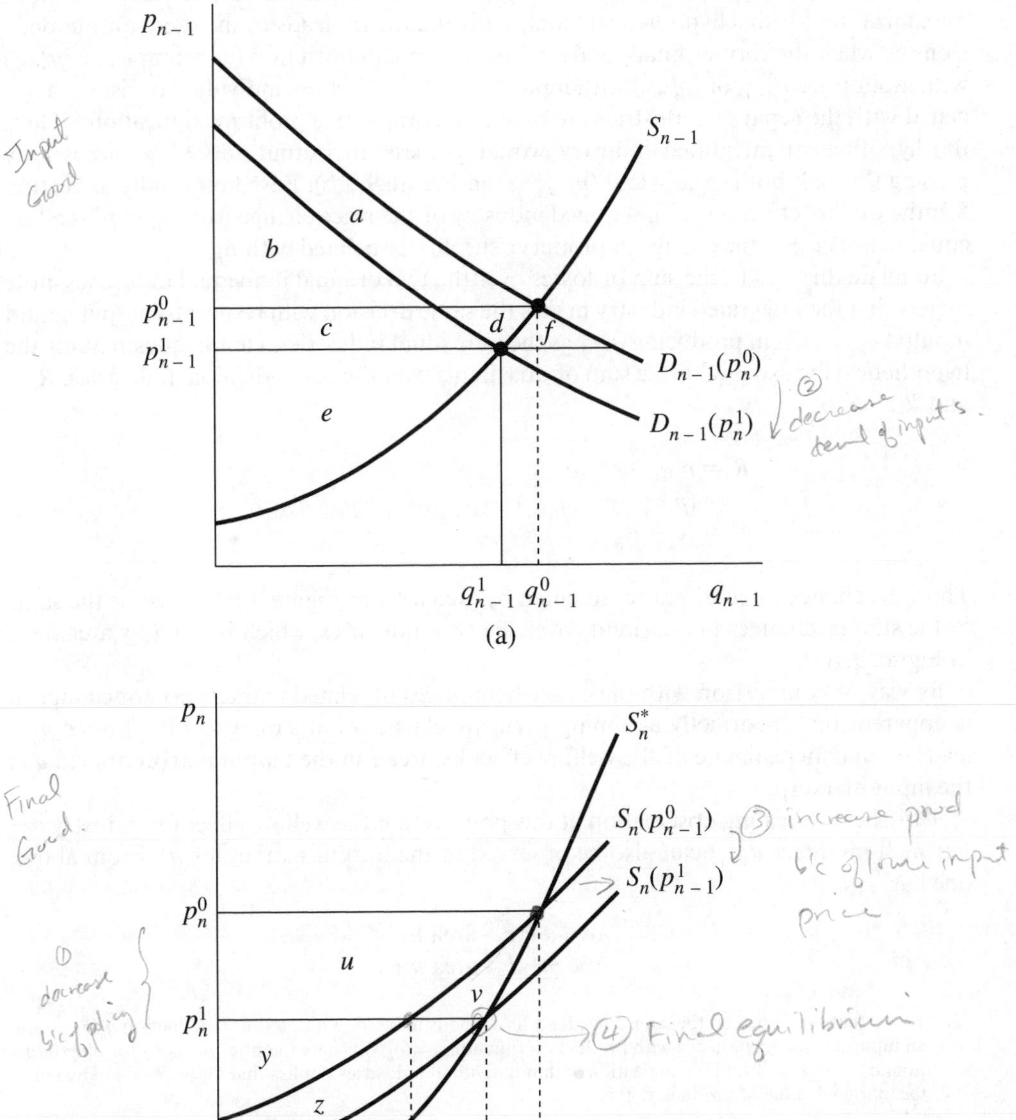

p_{n-1}
S_{n-1}
a
b
p^0_{n-1}
p^1_{n-1}
c
d
f
e
$D_{n-1}(p^0_n)$
$D_{n-1}(p^1_n)$
q^1_{n-1} q^0_{n-1}
q_{n-1}
(a)
p_n
S^*_n
$S_n(p^0_{n-1})$
$S_n(p^1_{n-1})$
p^0_n
u
v
p^1_n
y
z
q^2_n q^1_n q^0_n
q_n
(b)

Figure 9.1

well as the same output prices considered above (those facing the output industry). Profit maximization for this hypothetical (competitive) industry leads to the same output decisions as when the former final-goods industry is in equilibrium – for example, at (p_n^0,q_n^0) with input price p_{n-1}^0, or (p_n^1,q_n^1) with input price p_{n-1}^1 – because individual decisions associated with the separate industries are based on competitive profit maximization.[2] Thus, the hypothetical integrated industry would possess an output supply S_n^* necessarily passing through both (p_n^0,q_n^0) and (p_n^1,q_n^1) as in Figure 9.1(b). Based on results in Section 8.1, the welfare effect on the integrated industry of the price change from p_n^0 to p_n^1 is a loss equal to area $u+v$, the change in producer surplus associated with S_n^*.

To relate this loss to the sum of losses over the two original individual industries, note merely that the integrated industry makes the same decision with respect to output q_n and input(s) q_{n-2} used in producing q_{n-1} as the individual industries. Hence, quasirent for the hypothetical industry, R_n^* is the sum of quasirents over the two individual industries, R_{n-1} and R_n:

$$\begin{aligned} R_n^* &= p_n q_n - p_{n-2} q_{n-2} \\ &= (p_n q_n - p_{n-1} q_{n-1}) + (p_{n-1} q_{n-1} - p_{n-2} q_{n-2}) \\ &= R_n + R_{n-1}. \end{aligned}$$

Thus, the change in quasirent represented by area $u+v$ in Figure 9.1(b) must be the same as the sum of changes in quasirents over the two industries, which is given by area $a+d$ in Figure 9.1(a).

By way of comparison with the case where prices in related markets do not change, it is apparent that incorrectly assuming perfectly elastic input supply at initial price p_{n-1}^0 leads to an underestimate of the welfare effect by area v in the output market or area d in the input market.

A further interesting observation at this point is that the welfare effect for industry $n-1$ (which produces q_{n-1}) can also be observed in the output market for q_n. From above, one has

$$\begin{aligned} \text{area } a-c &= \text{area } u-z \\ \text{area } a+d &= \text{area } u+v. \end{aligned}$$

2. To see that this is indeed the case, consider a final-goods industry with production function $q_n(q_{n-1})$ and an input-producing industry with production function $q_{n-1}(q_{n-2})$, where the price of its factor of production, q_{n-2}, is p_{n-2}. Profit maximization within individual industries implies that input price is equated to the marginal value of product, that is,

$$p_{n-1} = p_n \frac{\partial q_n(q_{n-1})}{\partial q_{n-1}}, \; p_{n-2} = p_{n-1} \frac{\partial q_{n-1}(q_{n-2})}{\partial q_{n-2}}.$$

Substituting the first relationship into the second yields

$$p_{n-2} = p_n \frac{\partial q_n(q_{n-1})}{\partial q_{n-1}} \frac{\partial q_{n-1}(q_{n-2})}{\partial q_{n-2}}.$$

Now consider the hypothetical combined industry with output price p_n, input price p_{n-2}, and production function $q_n[q_{n-1}(q_{n-2})] \equiv q_n(q_{n-2})$. The associated parallel condition for profit maximization is thus (by the chain rule)

$$p_{n-2} = p_n \frac{\partial q_n(q_{n-2})}{\partial q_{n-2}} = p_n \frac{\partial q_n(q_{n-1})}{\partial q_{n-1}} \frac{\partial q_{n-1}(q_{n-2})}{\partial q_{n-2}},$$

which is identical to the implications of separate industry profit maximization.

Hence, subtracting the first equation from the second yields

$$\text{area } c+d=\text{area } v+z,$$

which is the industry $n-1$ welfare loss.

To gain practical insight into appropriate application of the principles of welfare economics, further interpretation of the meaning of the curve S_n^* in Figure 9.1(b) is useful. That is, it may be difficult to perceive how an industry resulting from a hypothetical merger might react to various parametric price changes. However, S_n^* may also be interpreted as the competitive supply curve for the final-goods industry, which takes account of equilibrium adjustments in the input market (conditioned, of course, on prices of factors used in producing the input). If the input price is intimately related to the output price, as it would be under competition, then such a supply curve may be readily discernible. After all, only the locus of points along S_n^* would be observed in response to any series of output price changes (holding p_{n-2} fixed). For this reason, a supply curve, such as S_n^*, may be called an *equilibrium supply curve*. That is, the supply curve S_n^* is different from an 'ordinary' short-run industry supply curve, such as $S_n(p_{n-1}^0)$, which indicates how the industry will respond to alternative output prices given that all input (and other output) prices are held fixed, as with perfectly elastic input supply (output demand). It is, rather, *a supply curve that allows for equilibrium adjustment of input use and input price as output price changes.* The important property of such a curve is that the change in producer surplus defined with respect to an equilibrium supply curve measures the net change in quasirent for all affected producing industries for which adjustments are considered in the supply curve. That is, where ΔP_j^* represents the change in producer surplus associated with the equilibrium supply curve in market j, and ΔR_j represents the change in quasirent in industry j (that is, the industry producing q_j), one has $\Delta P_n^*=\Delta R_n+\Delta R_{n-1}$ and $\Delta P_n^*=\Delta P_{n-1}^*+\Delta R_n$ upon noting that $\Delta R_{n-1}=\Delta P_{n-1}^*$.

Consider now the case where the factor q_{n-2} used by the input industry is also not available in perfectly elastic supply. Assume that the only use of the factor q_{n-2} is in the production of the input q_{n-1} and hence that the market for q_{n-2} bears the same relationship to the q_{n-1} market as the q_{n-1} market has previously borne to the q_n market. Even more generally, consider a sequence of competitive markets for $q_0, q_1, \ldots, q_n$, where q_{j-1} is the only input used in producing q_j and is not available in perfectly elastic supply in each stage of the marketing channel, $j=1, \ldots, n$. Hence, any change in price p_n causes a change through competition in the respective prices $p_1, \ldots, p_{n-1}$ at all intermediate stages of the marketing channel. Finally, suppose that the basic input of the sector q_0 is available in perfectly elastic supply.

On the basis of the two-good case above, one is inclined to speculate that the change in producer surplus P_n^* defined with respect to the equilibrium supply curve in the market for q_n would measure the net change in quasirent over the entire producing sector (consisting of the industries selling $q_1, \ldots, q_n$). Indeed, Appendix Section 9.A rigorously establishes for the vertically related market case that the total welfare effects over industries 1 through n of a price change in the market for q_n can be measured entirely by the change in producer surplus associated with the equilibrium supply curve in the market for q_n. That is,

$$\Delta P_n^* = \sum_{j=1}^{n} \Delta R_j, \tag{9.1}$$

from which one finds (subtracting a similar equation for ΔP^*_{n-1}) that

$$\Delta P^*_n = \Delta P^*_{n-1} + \Delta R_n. \tag{9.2}$$

Again, the intuition of the basic results in equation (9.1) can be developed much as in the two-industry case in Figure 9.1. That is, consider a hypothetical competitive industry formed by merging industries vertically throughout the marketing channel so that the hypothetical merged industry purchases input q_0 and produces output q_n. In this case the supply curve S^*_n of a hypothetical integrated industry would coincide with the actual set of equilibrium price-production points (the equilibrium supply curve) in market n (just as in Figure 9.1(b)), because profit maximization in the hypothetical industry is equivalent to profit maximization (in equilibrium) among all individual industries.

Intermediate-Market Consumer Surplus with Equilibrium Demand

As suggested earlier, the welfare effects of an input price change on an industry facing a perfectly elastic output demand (fixed output price) are reflected by the change in the consumer surplus measure associated with industry demand for the input. In the case where output price responds to a change in output supply induced by an input price change, however, equilibrium considerations can be made in a manner similar to the producer surplus case above.

Suppose that, initially, the industry producing q_{n+1} in a vertical market sector faces input price p^0_n and output demand $D_{n+1}(p_{n+2})$. Thus, the output market equilibrium depicted in Figure 9.2(b) is at price p^0_{n+1} and quantity q^0_{n+1}. If input price is raised to p^2_n through, say, a government price control, output supply shifts leftward from $S_{n+1}(p^0_n)$ to $S_{n+1}(p^2_n)$ This shift, after succeeding rounds of adjustment, induces an increase in output price from p^0_{n+1} to p^1_{n+1}; hence, the ordinary industry demand for the input increases from $D_n(p^0_{n+1})$ to $D_n(p^1_{n+1})$. The input market equilibrium thus shifts from (p^0_n, q^0_n) to (p^2_n, q^1_n) assuming that output price p_{n+2} for industry $n+2$, which purchases q_{n+1} as an input, is fixed (that is, demand for q_{n+2} is perfectly elastic). The relationship D^*_n connecting these equilibrium points as price p_n is altered is, in fact, the equilibrium demand for q_n, because it takes account of equilibrium adjustments in other affected markets.

Again, the welfare effects can be evaluated in either the input or the output market. First, in the output market, the change in quasirent is clearly a decrease of area $u+v$ for industry $n+2$ and a loss of area $y-u$ for industry $n+1$. The latter area applies because quasirent for industry $n+1$ changes from area $x+y$ to area $u+x$. The net social welfare loss from the input price change, obtained by aggregating effects over industries, is thus area $v+y$ $(=u+v+y-u)$.

Turning to evaluation in the input market, quasirent for industry $n+1$ is area $a+b$ at prices p^2_n and p^1_{n+1} and area $a+c$ at prices p^0_n and p^0_{n+1}; hence, the industry $n+1$ welfare loss is area $c-b$. To determine the net social welfare effect in the input market, it is again instructive to consider a hypothetical vertical integration of industries $n+1$ and $n+2$. Such an industry, operating under competition and facing fixed price p_{n+2} in the market for its output, would have demand D^*_n for its input q_n. Thus, the results of Section 8.1 would imply a decrease in its quasirent of area $c+d$ as the input price increases from p^0_n to p^2_n. Again, as in the previous supply case, profit maximization for the hypothetical

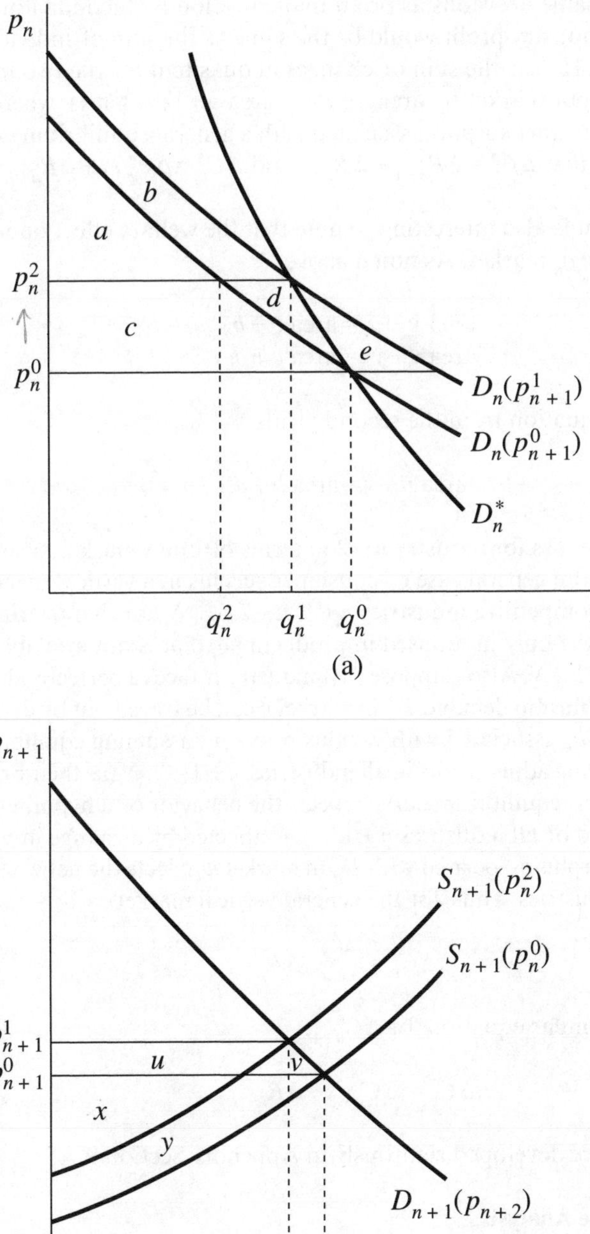

p_n
b
a
p_n^2
d
c
e
p_n^0
$D_n(p_{n+1}^1)$
$D_n(p_{n+1}^0)$
D_n^*
q_n^2 q_n^1 q_n^0
q_n
(a)
p_{n+1}
$S_{n+1}(p_n^2)$
$S_{n+1}(p_n^0)$
p_{n+1}^1
p_{n+1}^0
u
v
x
y
$D_{n+1}(p_{n+2})$
q_{n+1}^2 q_{n+1}^0
q_{n+1}
(b)

Figure 9.2

industry leads to the same decisions as profit maximization by the individual industries. Thus, the integrated industry profit would be the same as the sum of individual industry profits in equilibrium. Hence, the sum of changes in quasirent for the two industries can be measured in the input market by area $c+d$ (= area $v+y$). That is, where ΔC_j^* represents the change in consumer surplus associated with a general equilibrium demand curve in market j, one finds that $\Delta C_n^* = \Delta R_{n+1} + \Delta R_{n+2}$ and $\Delta C_n^* = \Delta C_{n+1}^* + \Delta R_{n+1}$ upon noting that $\Delta R_{n+2} = \Delta C_{n+1}^*$.

From these results, it is also interesting to note that the welfare effect on industry $n+2$ can be identified in the q_n market. As noted above,

$$\begin{aligned} \text{area } y-u &= \text{area } c-b \\ \text{area } v+y &= \text{area } c+d. \end{aligned}$$

Subtracting the first equation from the second yields

$$\text{area } u+v = \text{area } b+d,$$

which gives the welfare loss for industry $n+2$ in terms of input market measurements.

Consider now the more general case of consumer surplus in a vertical market sequence. That is, suppose that competitive industries $n+1, n+2, \ldots, N$ are characterized by a relationship where q_{j-1} is the only input used in producing q_j that is not available in perfectly elastic supply, $j=n+1, \ldots, N$. Also, suppose that industry N faces a perfectly elastic demand for q_N. Again, the equilibrium demand D_n^* in market n can be traced out by determining the equilibrium quantities q_n associated with various prices p_n, assuming equilibrium or competitive profit-maximizing adjustments in all industries, $n+1, \ldots, N$ (as their prices change). As in previous cases, this equilibrium curve reflects the behavior of a hypothetical competitive industry composed of all industries $n+1, \ldots, N$ affected by a change in p_n. Hence, the change in consumer surplus associated with D_n^* in market n reflects the net welfare effect for the entire group of industries. Thus, for the general vertical market case,

$$\Delta C_n^* = \sum_{j=n+1}^{N} \Delta R_j \tag{9.3}$$

and, subtracting the similar equation for ΔC_{n+1}^*,

$$\Delta C_n^* = \Delta C_{n+1}^* + \Delta R_{n+1}. \tag{9.4}$$

Indeed, these results are developed rigorously in Appendix Section 9.A.

Vertical-Sector Welfare Analysis

On the basis of the foregoing results, the overall social welfare effect of intervention in market n that alters either or both the supply and demand prices can be obtained by aggregating the producer and consumer surplus measures in market n,

$$\Delta P_n^* + \Delta C_n^* = \sum_{j=1}^{N} \Delta R_j, \tag{9.5}$$

assuming that industry 1 faces a perfectly elastic input supply and that industry N faces a perfectly elastic output demand. For example, consider the vertical sector depicted in Figure 9.3, where equilibrium supply and demand are represented by S_j^* and D_j^* respectively; ordinary supply and demand are represented by S_j and D_j, respectively; and equilibrium price and quantity are represented by p_j^0 and q_j^0, $j=n-1$, n, $n+1$, respectively.[3] Now suppose that an *ad valorem* tax of $p_n^2 - p_n^1$ or a quota of q_n^1 is imposed on producers in market n. The new equilibrium prices and quantities would thus be, respectively, p_{n-1}^1 and q_{n-1}^1 in market $n-1$, p_{n+1}^1 and q_{n+1}^1 in market $n+1$, and p_n^2 for consumers (p_n^1 for producers) and q_n^1 in market n. Using the analysis of Section 8.5, as modified for the sector equilibrium case by equation (9.5), the net social welfare loss is thus area $b+d$ in Figure 9.3. Using equation (9.3), the joint welfare loss for industries $n+1$, ..., N is area $a+b$. Using equation (9.1), the joint welfare effect for industries 1, ..., n is a loss of area $c+d$ in the tax case or a gain of area $a-d$ in the quota case. In the tax case, the government also collects a tax revenue gain of area $a+c$.

The specific welfare effects for various industries involved in Figure 9.3 can be determined using ordinary supplies and demands. The welfare loss for industry $n+1$ is area $z-x$ in Figure 9.3(c), which can also be determined in market n using ordinary demands $D_n(p_{n+1}^0)$ and $D_n(p_{n+1}^1)$ according to the methodology suggested by Figure 9.2, and the effect on industries $n+2$, $n+3$, ..., N is a loss of area $x+y$. The accounting for industry n, however, is somewhat different from that suggested in Figure 9.1. That is, industry n may be actually realizing output price p_n^2 after controls are imposed. Nevertheless, the resulting ordinary industry demand for q_{n-1} is not $D_{n-1}(p_n^2)$ but, rather, $D_{n-1}(p_n^1)$ because industry n is forced to act as though it were receiving price p_n^1 for its output. Hence, the welfare effect for industry n is, in fact, a gain of area $v-u$ in Figure 9.3(a) plus any additional rewards received in market n by actually receiving a price different than p_n^1. In the tax case all additional rewards above price p_n^1 are taxed away, so area $v-u$ is negative and represents a welfare loss for industry n. In the quota case the industry actually receives p_n^2 for its output, and thus receives an additional reward of $(p_n^2 - p_n^1) \cdot q_n^1 =$ area $a+c$ above that which it would have received if price p_n^1 were applicable. Hence, industry n has a welfare gain of area $a+c+v-u$. Finally, note that the joint effect on industries 1, 2, ..., $n-1$ is a loss given by area $v+w$ in Figure 9.3(a).

Extension to Factor Supply and Final Consumer Demand

Extension of the vertical market structure to include factor supply and final consumer demand is of considerable interest in many cases. For example, imposition of a quota on petroleum imports may have serious implications for petroleum industry workers as well as for consumers. Such an extension is possible *in a purely vertical framework* in the special case where the factor supply price and final product price do not affect other consumer and factor prices (including each other's price except as suggested explicitly in the vertical sector framework). In this case consumers and producers in the economy outside the vertical sector are indeed unaffected by intervention in the sector. Furthermore, all welfare

3. Here, markets $n-1$, n and $n+1$ are regarded as part of an extended vertical sector, so it is useful to define equilibrium curves in markets $n-1$ and $n+1$. If industry $n-1$ faces perfectly elastic input supply and industry $n+1$ faces perfectly elastic output demand, then S_{n-1}^* and D_{n+1}^* would, in fact, coincide with ordinary curves as in Figures 9.1 and 9.2.

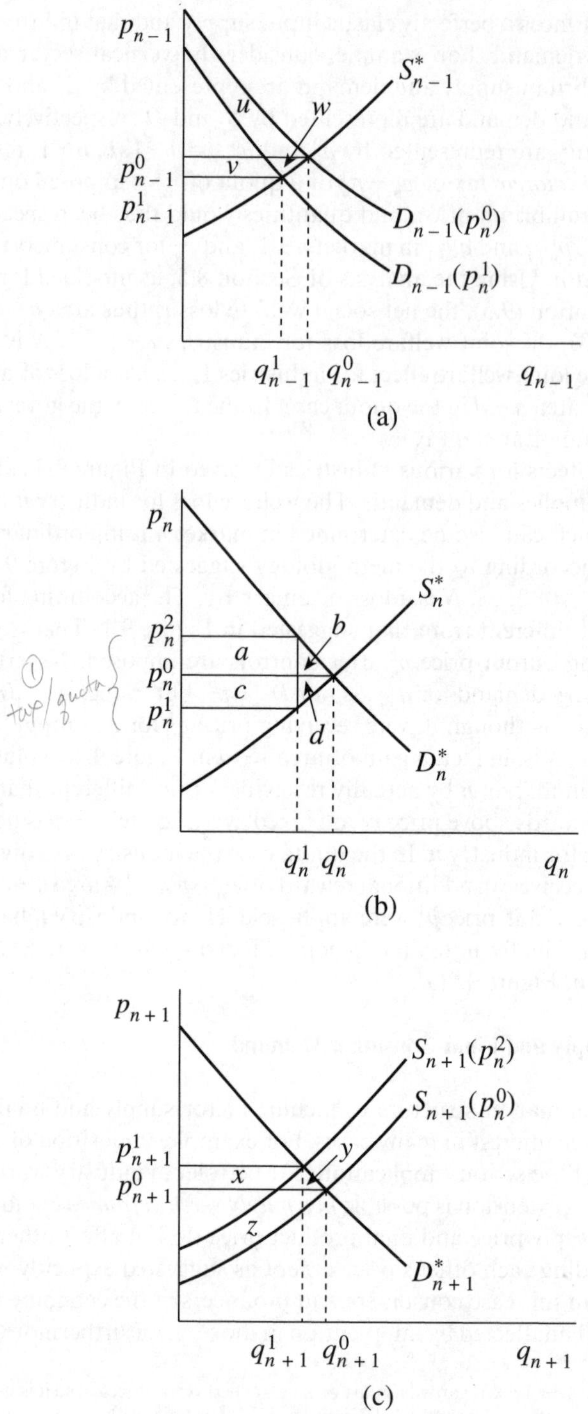

p_{n-1}
S^*_{n-1}
u
w
v
p^0_{n-1}
p^1_{n-1}
$D_{n-1}(p^0_n)$
$D_{n-1}(p^1_n)$
q^1_{n-1}
q^0_{n-1}
q_{n-1}
(a)
p_n
S^*_n
b
p^2_n
a
p^0_n
c
p^1_n
d
D^*_n
q^1_n
q^0_n
q_n
(b)
p_{n+1}
$S_{n+1}(p^2_n)$
$S_{n+1}(p^0_n)$
p^1_{n+1}
y
x
p^0_{n+1}
z
D^*_{n+1}
q^1_{n+1}
q^0_{n+1}
q_{n+1}
(c)

Figure 9.3

effects on consumers (factor suppliers) involved in the sector are reflected in the markets associated with the sector even though the quantities of goods taken in other sectors can change.

The intuition of this extension can be developed by reinterpreting Figures 9.1 and 9.2. If S_{n-1} is a factor supply curve in Figure 9.1 (consider $n=1$), then S_n^* is the equilibrium supply curve in market n, which takes account of equilibrium adjustments of factor prices as output price p_n is altered. Hence, the change in producer surplus associated with S_n^* is the sum of changes in producer surplus associated with S_{n-1} and quasirent for industry n. Where ΔP_0 represents the change in surplus associated with factor supply, the relationship in (9.1) can thus be extended using equation (9.2) for the relationships of intermediate markets, together with $\Delta P_1^* = \Delta P_0 + \Delta R_1$, to obtain

$$\Delta P_n^* = \Delta P_0 + \sum_{j=1}^{n} \Delta R_j. \tag{9.6}$$

Similarly, for the final consumer, Figure 9.2 can be reinterpreted for the case where D_{n+1} represents final consumer demand (consider $n=N-1$), in which case the change in consumer surplus associated with D_n^* includes both the change in rent for industry $n+1$ plus the change in consumer surplus associated with D_{n+1}. Denoting the surplus associated with D_N by ΔC_N, equation (9.4) implies that $\Delta C_{N-1}^* = \Delta C_N + \Delta R_n$ (ΔC_N does not have an asterisk because it represents final consumer demand which is an ordinary demand). Thus, the relationship in (9.3) can be extended using equation (9.4) (which continues to apply for intermediate markets), obtaining

$$\Delta C_n^* = \Delta C_N + \sum_{j=n+1}^{N} \Delta R_j. \tag{9.7}$$

Finally, combining equations (9.6) and (9.7) yields the welfare effect of introducing a distortion in any market n in the sector,

$$\Delta C_n^* + \Delta P_n^* = \Delta P_0 + \Delta C_N + \sum_{j=1}^{N} \Delta R_j.$$

Hence, where market 0 is a factor market and market N is a final-goods market (so that the related chain of markets, $n=0, \ldots, N$, comprises a vertical economic sector), it is found that the sum of changes in equilibrium producer and consumer surpluses from distorting some market in the sector accurately measures the change in total sector welfare to the extent that factor supply surplus and final consumer demand surplus measure welfare effects for these two groups – that is, to the extent that Willig conditions apply or exact willingness-to-pay (WTP) calculations are used for the these two groups. Furthermore, because other sectors are unaffected by this change by assumption, the change in welfare for the economy as a whole is also obtained.

Thus, it turns out that the restrictive perfect-elasticity assumptions that have been made in earlier chapters for *all* related markets are unnecessary. Surplus welfare measures (defined with respect to equilibrium curves) have validity regardless, at least in a purely vertical economic framework. More important, the equilibrium surplus measures provide an overall rather than a partial picture of welfare change. Hence, the failure of perfect-elasticity assumptions in a vertical market structure has no serious consequences as long as one is interested in aggregate welfare rather than the welfare of a particular set of producers or consumers. Furthermore, the change in welfare for a particular set of producers or consumers can still be examined using surplus measures associated with ordinary supply and demand curves to obtain distributional information.[4]

9.2 WELFARE EFFECTS IN HORIZONTALLY RELATED MARKETS

Input-Market Relationships for Industries

Consider next horizontal market relationships and the possibilities for measuring the overall social welfare effect of market intervention. Consider first a horizontal relationship of markets due to use of multiple inputs by a single industry. Suppose that inputs q_1 and q_2 are the only inputs used by some industry A facing perfectly elastic demand for its output, where q_2 is produced by an industry B facing perfectly elastic supplies of its inputs. The supply of q_2 is represented by S_2 in Figure 9.4(b), and the respective industry A demands for inputs are initially $D_1(p_2^0)$ and $D_2(p_1^0)$ in equilibrium when faced with a (controlled) price p_1^0 for q_1. Now let the price for q_1 increase from p_1^0 to p_1^1 because of some intervention in the market for q_1. Initially, the competitive industry A attempts to reduce q_1 input use from q_1^0 to q_1^2, but, because of complementarity or substitution of inputs, the higher price for q_1 causes alteration in the industry A demand for q_2 (an increase if q_1 and q_2 are substitutes or a decrease if q_1 and q_2 are complements). This shift in demand for q_2 from $D_2(p_1^0)$ to $D_2(p_1^1)$, a decline in the case of complements, thus causes a change in q_2 price from p_2^0 to p_2^1, which, in turn, leads to a shift in industry A demand for q_1 from $D_1(p_2^0)$ to $D_1(p_2^1)$. The new equilibrium finally occurs at price p_1^1 and quantity q_1^1. Thus, the demand relationship D_1^* for q_1, which takes account of equilibrium adjustments in other markets, is obtained.

To see the welfare significance of D_1^*, again consider a hypothetical merger – in this case of industries A and B – into a single competitive industry. Competitive profit maximization by the joint industry would imply behavior identical to that of the individual industries, with the same resulting aggregate quasirent. So, quasirent for the hypothetical firm decreases by area $c+d$ as q_1 price increases from p_1^0 to p_1^1. Thus, the net social welfare effect over all affected industries is a loss of area $c+d$.

Again, the welfare effects for individual industries can be determined under various assumptions by aggregating and using results shown in Section 8.1. That is, if q_1 is an essential input for industry A (meaning that industry A cannot produce without using q_1), then its quasirent changes from area $a+c$ to area $a+b$ for a net welfare loss of area $c-b$. Similarly, if input q_2 is essential for industry A production, alternative but equivalent market 2 measurements indicate a change in quasirent from area $u+v$ to area $u+x$ for a net welfare loss of area $v-x$. Industry B quasirent decreases from area $x+y+z$ to area z for a net welfare loss of area $x+y$. If both q_1 and q_2 are essential inputs for industry A, industry B welfare effects can also be measured in market 1. That is, because the overall net welfare loss for both industries taken together is area $v+y$ (= area $(v-x)+(x+y)$),

4. For an example of a study that uses a vertical market approach to differentiation of ordinary and equilibrium supplies and their implications for the distribution of welfare effects, see Cooke and Sundquist (1993).

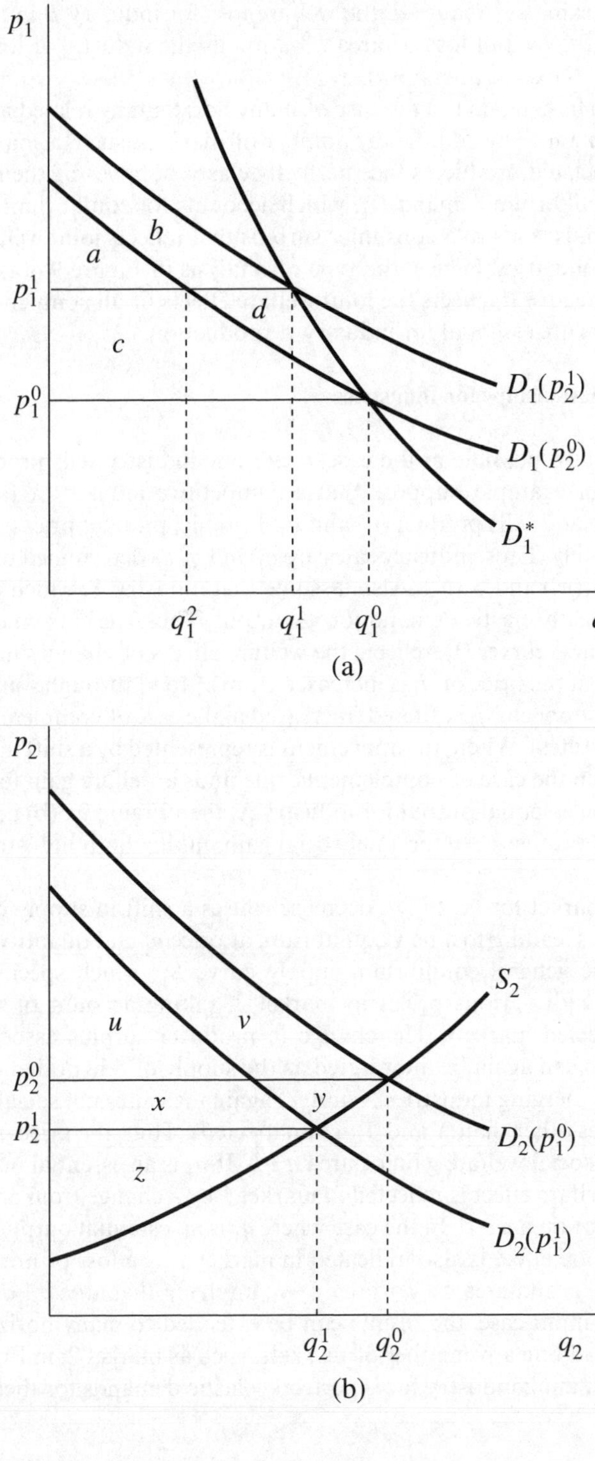

p1
a
b
p1 1
d
c
p1 0
D1(p2 1)
D1(p2 0)
D1*
q1 2
q1 1
q1 0
q1
(a)
p2
u
v
S2
p2 0
x
y
p2 1
z
D2(p1 0)
D2(p1 1)
q2 1
q2 0
q2
(b)

Figure 9.4

which must be the same as area $c+d$, the welfare loss for industry B in the q_1 market is area $b+d$ (that is, the overall loss of area $c+d$ minus the industry A loss of area $c-b$ implies an industry B loss of area $b+d$).

These results can be extended to the case of many horizontally related input markets in a straightforward manner by adding any number of markets, such as market 2 in Figure 9.4, where the associated producers face perfectly elastic supplies of their inputs. In this case the general equilibrium demand D_1^*, which accounts for equilibrium adjustments in all other markets, thus leads to a consumer surplus that reflects joint welfare effects over all the associated industries. Hence, the type of analysis in Figure 9.4(a) is again applicable, except that area $b+d$ reflects the joint welfare effects of all competing input industries if all the inputs are essential for industry A production.

Output-Market Relationships for Industries

Similar analysis is also possible in the case where one industry sells products in several output markets. For example, suppose that a competitive industry X faces a perfectly elastic input supply and sells products q_1 and q_2. Initially, product prices are p_1^0 and p_2^0 in Figure 9.5, respectively. Thus, industry sales are q_1^0 and q_2^0 as determined by the respective industry supplies $S_1(p_2^0)$ and $S_2(p_1^0)$. Also, assume that industry Y, which purchases q_2 as an input, faces perfectly elastic demand for its output. Thus, the consumer surplus associated with its demand curve, D_2, reflects the welfare effects of changes in p_2 on industry Y. Now, suppose that the price of q_1 is increased from p_1^0 to p_1^1 through some intervention. As a result, output supply of q_2 is altered (increased in the case of complements or reduced in the case of substitutes). Where this movement is represented by a shift in q_2 supply from $S_2(p_1^0)$ to $S_2(p_1^1)$, as in the case of complements, one finds a welfare gain for industry Y of area $u+v$. If q_2 is an essential output for industry X, then Figure 9.5(b) implies a welfare gain for industry X of area $y-u$ for a net social gain, taking both industries together, of area $v+y$.

Turning to the market for q_1, the p_2 decrease causes a shift in supply of q_1 from, say, $S_1(p_2^0)$ to $S_1(p_2^1)$, thus leading to a new equilibrium at price p_1^1 and quantity q_1^1. Again, it is useful to define the general equilibrium supply curve S_1^*, which specifies equilibrium output associated with various prices in market 2, taking account of all equilibrium adjustments in affected markets. The change in producer surplus associated with this supply curve (which can again be interpreted as the supply of a hypothetical competitive industry formed by merging industries X and Y) again measures net social welfare effects (assuming industries other than X and Y are unaffected). Thus, the price increase from p_1^0 to p_1^1 leads to a net social welfare gain of area $a+b$. If q_1 is an essential output for industry X, its specific welfare effect is reflected in market 1 by a change from area $c+d$ to area $a+c$ for a net gain of area $a-d$. In the case where q_1 is an essential output of industry X, the industry Y welfare effect is also indicated in market 1 by a loss of area $b+d$. That is, area $a+b=$ area $v+y$, and area $a-d=$ area $y-u$, implying that area $b+d=$ area $u+v$.

Again, as in the input case, the results can be extended to many horizontally related output markets by adding any number of markets, such as market 2, in Figure 9.5, where the associated consuming industry faces perfectly elastic demands for their outputs.

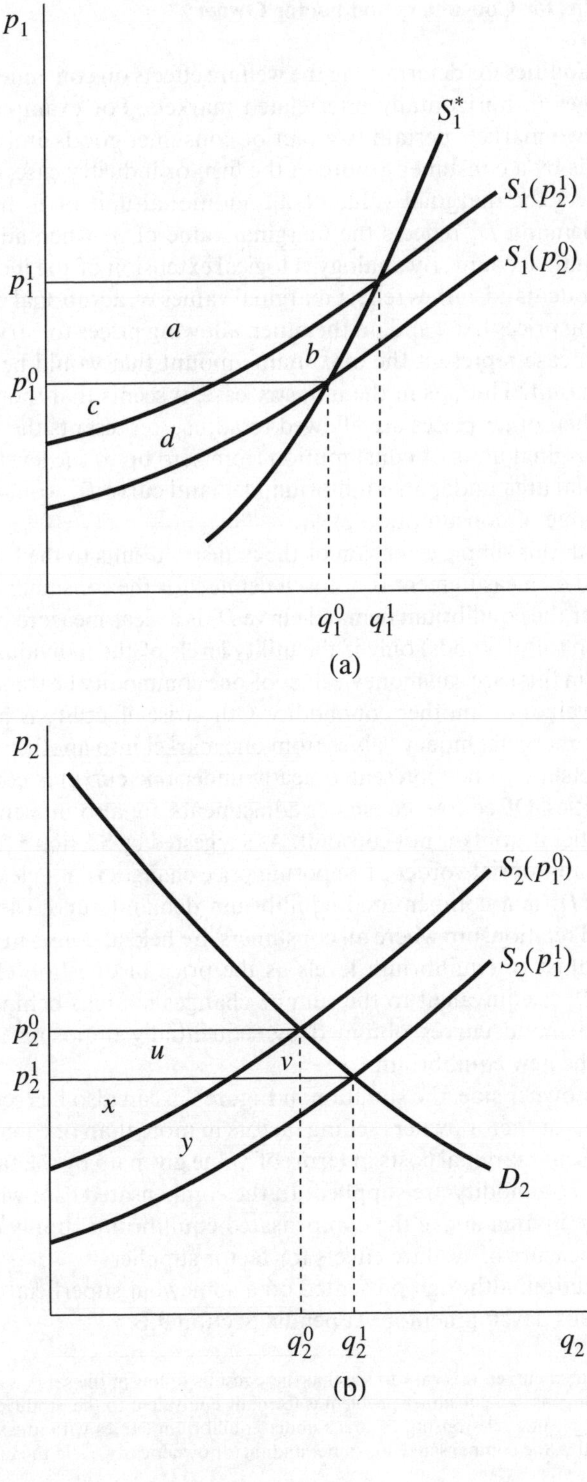

p_1
S_1^*
$S_1(p_2^1)$
$S_1(p_2^0)$
p_1^1
p_1^0
a
b
c
d
q_1^0
q_1^1
q_1
(a)
p_2
$S_2(p_1^0)$
$S_2(p_1^1)$
p_2^0
p_2^1
u
v
x
y
D_2
q_2^0
q_2^1
q_2
(b)

Figure 9.5

Horizontal Relationships for Consumers and Factor Owners

Consider next the possibilities for determining the welfare effects on consumers and factor owners of price changes in horizontally interrelated markets. For example, reconsider Figure 9.4, where the two markets pertain to a pair of consumer goods and the demands represent final demands by a consumer group. In the firm or industry case, the demands $D_1(p_2^0)$ and $D_1(p_2^1)$ reflect the marginal value of an additional unit of q_1 holding other prices fixed, and the demand D_1^* reflects the marginal value of q_1 when adjustments of other prices are taken into account. By analogy, a logical extension of the industry results suggests that consumer demand curves reflect marginal values of additional consumption – in the one case holding prices fixed and, in the other, allowing prices to vary. Indeed, the demand curves in each case represent the maximum amount that would be paid for the marginal consumption unit. Thus, as in the industry case, it seems that the area under a demand curve, even when other prices are allowed to adjust, represents the sum of marginal values over all marginal units of consumption from zero up to the level in question. If this were true, the total area under an equilibrium demand curve D_1^* would be a money measure of the total value of consumption of q_1.

The only problem with this simple extension of the industry results to the final consumer case is that the standard of measurement is not well defined for the consumer case. That is, the change in area under the equilibrium demand curve D_1^* is a clear measure of the change in value of consumption (of all goods) only if the utility levels of the individual consumers are held constant. Only in this case can money values of one commodity be translated unambiguously into money values of another commodity. Otherwise, if utility is not held constant, the translation of marginal money values from one market into another (as is needed if all money value effects are to be represented neatly under one curve) is confounded by changing marginal utilities. Of course, consumer adjustments are also influenced by these changing marginal utilities if utility is not constant. As suggested by Section 5.2, uniqueness is thus lost because the appropriate order of imposing price changes is not clear.

Nevertheless, where D_1^* is a compensated equilibrium demand curve (defined as the price–quantity demand relationship where all consumers are held at constant utility levels and all other prices adjust to equilibrium levels as the price in question changes), the change in area under D_1^* is equivalent to the sum of changes in areas behind individual market compensated demand curves obtained by sequentially imposing all the price changes suggested by the new equilibrium.[5]

Turning to the factor owner side, the situation in Figure 9.5 can also be reconsidered in the context of one group of factor owners selling factors in more than one market. Again, the supply curves represent marginal costs in terms of value given up by the factor owners as successive units of a commodity are supplied. In the compensated case where uniqueness is clear, the change in area above the compensated equilibrium supply curve represents the appropriate measure of welfare effects for factor suppliers.

The results of this section, although presented on a somewhat superficial level, follow directly from the rigorous development in Appendix Section 9.B.

5. In the case of compensated curves, it is easy to see that these results follow in the same way as the industry case because the compensated consumer problem is formally equivalent to the producer problem (see Section 7.10). Hence, the same relationship of areas under equilibrium curves with areas under market curves must be obtained in the compensated consumer and factor owner cases, as in the industry case.

9.3 GENERAL EQUILIBRIUM WELFARE MEASUREMENT

An implication of the results of the previous two sections is that net social welfare effects over the economy as a whole of intervention in any single market can be measured completely in that market using equilibrium supply and demand curves of sufficient generality. That is, Section 9.1 implies that all welfare effects extending into vertically related markets can be captured in the single market while Section 9.2 implies that all welfare effects extending into horizontally related markets can be captured in the single market. It seems a small step to extend the methodology to include effects in the rest of the economy. Although the graphical analysis becomes too cumbersome in this case for practical exposition, this generalization of the results is developed rigorously in Appendix Section 9.B using more sophisticated mathematical techniques.

Thus, a summarization of the results in their full generality is useful at this point. Consider an economy with N goods including all consumer goods and all basic factors used in production where any industry producing good j uses as inputs in their production process any subset of the N goods, $j=1, \ldots, N$. Assume all industries, factor owners and consumers operate competitively and are initially in general competitive equilibrium characterized by prices p_j^0 and quantities q_j^0, $j=1, \ldots, N$.[6] Now suppose that some intervention, such as an *ad valorem* tax in the amount of $p_n^2 - p_n^1$ or a quota of q_n^1, is imposed. Where J represents the set of all other markets, $J=\{1, \ldots, n-1, n+1, \ldots, N\}$, ordinary supply and demand (conditioned on all other prices in the economy) are initially $S_n(p_j^0, j \in J)$ and $D_n(p_j^0, j \in J)$, respectively. After intervention, ordinary supply and demand shift to $S_n(p_j^1, j \in J)$ and $D_n(p_j^1, j \in J)$, respectively, as all other prices are induced through competition to change from p_j^0 to p_j^1, $j \in J$.

The consumer surplus for industries or consumers directly consuming q_n in Figure 9.6 changes from area $b+c+f$ to area $a+b$ for a net loss of area $c+f-a$. The latter area necessarily carries welfare significance if all of q_n is purchased by industry rather than final consumers if q_n is an essential input in all industries that use it. Approximate significance holds in the consumer case under conditions discussed in Section 7.10. The producer surplus for factor suppliers or industries directly selling q_n in market n changes from area $u+v+y$ to area $y+z$ (or $y+z+c+d+u+w$ in the quota case), for a net loss of area $u+v-z$ (or a gain of area $c+d+w+z-v$ in the quota case). The net effect in this case again necessarily carries welfare significance if all of q_n is supplied by profit-maximizing industry if q_n is an essential output of all industries that sell it. Approximate significance holds for factor suppliers under conditions indicated by Section 7.10, for the multiple-price-change case.[7]

Nevertheless, regardless of whether or not the group-specific measurements above carry welfare significance, the compensated general equilibrium supply and demand

6. The assumption of competition is relaxed somewhat in Appendix Section 9.B.
7. It is also interesting to consider welfare measurement in market n for a broader set of industries. For example, suppose that the set J is reduced in size by excluding indices of markets which have, say, a vertical market relationship with market n. Then the supply and demand curves in Figure 9.6 conditioned on prices outside the vertical sector become, in a sense, sector equilibrium curves. To the extent that such industries are related by essential inputs or outputs, as the case may be, the areas discussed above carry welfare significance for the whole set of vertically related industries for which indices are excluded from the set J. Calculating these areas for all such feasible variations in the set J thus makes possible calculation of industry-specific welfare effects for all such related industries.

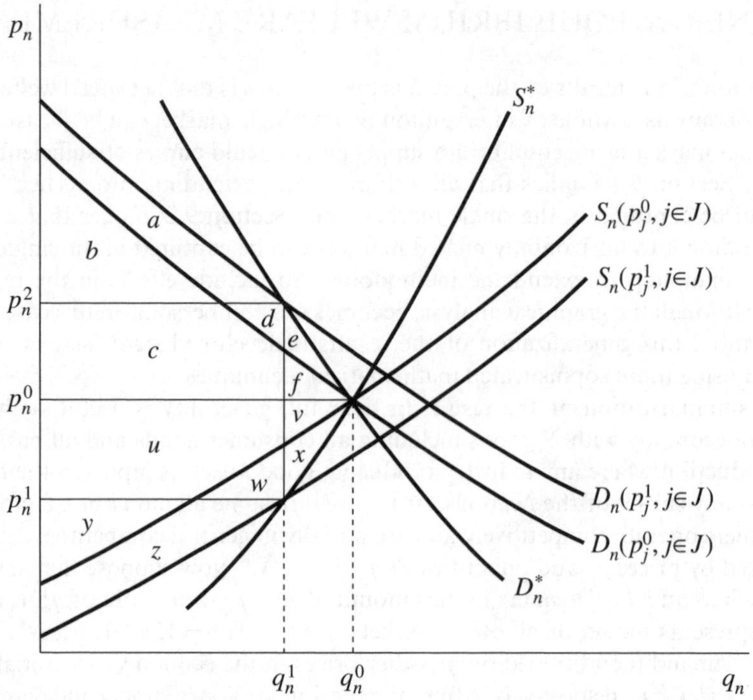

Figure 9.6

curves can be used to measure the net social welfare effects of intervention in market n. That is, suppose that S_n^* and D_n^* in Figure 9.6 are, respectively, the compensated general equilibrium supply and demand curves which specify the respective marginal cost and price that result in market n for various levels of the tax or quota assuming (1) competitive adjustments in all other markets and (2) no distortions in other markets. In this case the net social welfare effect of introducing an *ad valorem* tax of $p_n^2 - p_n^1$ or a quota of q_n^1 in market n is given by area $e+f+v+x$. This represents a loss for all producers and factor suppliers taken together in the quota case. In the tax case the area $c+d+u+w$ represents a tax gain for government, so the loss for all private parties taken together is area $c+d+e+f+u+v+w+x$.[8]

These areas apply exactly if consumers and factor owners respond along *compensated* demand/supply curves in the markets for which prices change.[9] If instead the consumers

8. The reader should bear in mind that, as demonstrated in Appendix Section 9.B, these results hold only when nondistorted markets reach equilibrium with aggregate supply equal to aggregate demand, which is the case of a closed economy where welfare is aggregated to the world level. Welfare effects of market intervention for small open economies can be also calculated essentially as demonstrated in Figure 9.6 but, in the case of a general open economy, markets with excess demand or excess supply must be considered further in order to capture all equilibrium welfare effects pertaining to a specific country. For further details, see Appendix Section 9.B.
9. In some earlier work on general equilibrium economic welfare analysis, Boadway (1974) argued that a paradox existed in that general equilibrium could no longer be maintained in the event that compensation is paid. This paradox, however, is resolved in Appendix Section 9.C by using compensated general equilibrium supply and demand concepts as opposed to the uncompensated general equilibrium concepts used by Boadway.

and factor owners make uncompensated adjustments, then the foregoing general equilibrium welfare effects are approximate to the extent that uncompensated equilibrium approximates compensated equilibrium and to the extent that uncompensated equilibrium supply and demand approximates compensated equilibrium supply and demand. The Willig results of Sections 6.5, 6.6, 7.5 and 7.6 suggest that the latter approximation is sufficiently close to be useful. The former approximation should also be close for small changes, but more investigation is needed for the case of large changes. Alternatively, the empirical approach of Appendix Section 9.D for estimating exact WTP can be used when Willig approximations are not acceptable.

One further and easily misunderstood issue relating to definition and use of single-market general equilibrium curves for welfare measurement requires discussion. That is, the usual (uncompensated) general equilibrium supply and demand curves used above are defined with respect to the variation in the *particular kind of distortion* that is being considered rather than with respect to variation in individual supply or demand prices. This is necessary because any redistribution of area $c+d+u+w$ in Figure 9.6, say, from government to factor suppliers can cause those factor suppliers to alter their consumption decisions, thus (perhaps indirectly) affecting the demand for the same good.[10] Thus, an uncompensated general equilibrium demand curve cannot be determined uniquely irrespective of the way the (effective) supply price varies in relation to demand price. The appropriate uncompensated general equilibrium curves, therefore, can be determined only in the context of a specific type of distortion.

To demonstrate an alternative distortion that can lead to different general equilibrium curves, consider Figure 9.7. Initial equilibrium is the same as in Figure 9.6, but now a price support of p_n^2 is enacted by the government such that all excess supply at that price is purchased by the government. After adjustment to equilibrium in all markets, the resulting quantity demanded in market n is q_n^2 and the quantity supplied is q_n^1. The government buys $q_n^1 - q_n^2$ at price p_n^2 at a loss of area $b+c+d+e+f$ (assuming that government acquisitions are disposed costlessly without affecting private concerns or recouping some of the loss). The net welfare effect for all private concerns taken jointly is a gain of area c. Thus, the net social welfare loss resulting from the distortion is area $b+d+e+f$.

Obviously, comparing Figure 9.7 with Figure 9.6, production takes place at a higher level under the price support than under the tax or quota case. The higher production is associated with greater use of factors at higher prices, thus creating higher incomes for consumers. Some of these increased incomes can thus percolate through the economy in the form of increased consumption, causing higher demand for q_n at prices above the free-market equilibrium. This suggests that the portion of the uncompensated general equilibrium demand curve above p_n^0 in Figure 9.7 may lie to the right of the uncompensated general equilibrium demand curve in Figure 9.6.

This problem, however, is not as severe as it might seem on the surface. In point of fact, if welfare effects are calculated on the basis of compensated general equilibrium supply and demand curves, then no such dependence on the form of distortion beyond dependence on the supply and demand prices occurs. For example, when one considers all possible redistributions of area $c+d+u+w$ in Figure 9.6, compensated supplies and

10. If (some of) the buyers are final consumers or (some of) the sellers are factor suppliers in market n, the lump-sum transfer would be equivalent to a change in their exogenous income, which would affect their marginal behavior and thus lead to different general equilibrium curves.

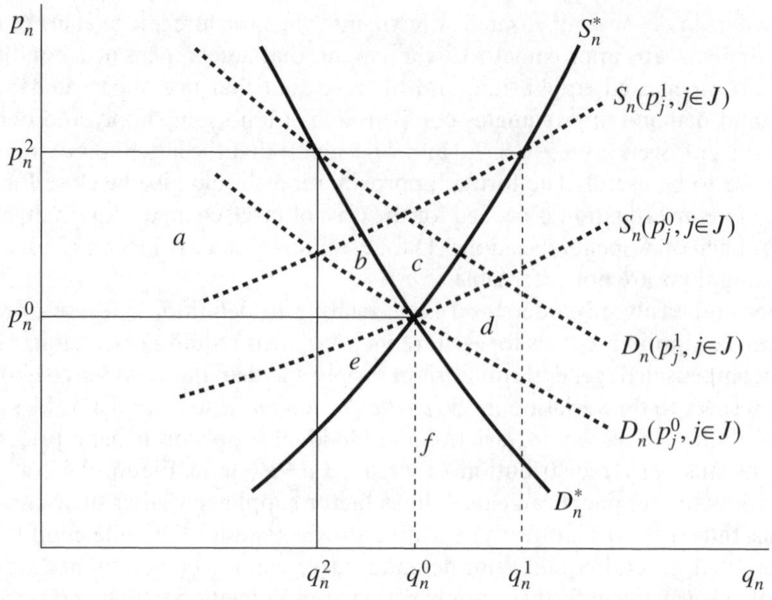

Figure 9.7

demands remain invariant. Any such lump-sum payments to (from) individuals are taken away (given back) to return them to initial utility levels (see Appendix Section 9.B). Thus, even though forms of distortions may differ for given changes in supply and demand prices, the uncompensated general equilibrium welfare measures approximate the same compensated general equilibrium welfare measures (which are the accurate measures) to the extent that ordinary supplies and demands approximate compensated supplies and demands.

In the context of the preceding discussion, however, the change in consumer surplus associated with a general equilibrium demand curve cannot necessarily be interpreted as an effect on consumer welfare and on the welfare of industries involved in transforming q_n into final consumer goods. Neither can the change in producer surplus associated with the general equilibrium supply curve be interpreted as a welfare effect on factor suppliers and those industries using various factors to produce q_n. Through competitive adjustments, *some* of the consumer surplus change may represent effects on producers and conversely.[11] Nevertheless, such conclusions may be reasonable as approximations in a variety of practical situations such as the case of a segmented economy discussed in Appendix Section 9.B.

11. For this analysis, the reader should bear in mind that this book merely defines consumer surplus as the triangle-like area behind a demand curve and above price, and producer surplus as the triangle-like area behind a supply curve and below price. The welfare significance of either, if there is any, depends on the context and definition of the associated demand or supply. For general equilibrium problems, the sum of the two can have welfare significance even though neither individually may have welfare significance for any particular group. Bullock (1993a) discusses the error that has been made in some empirical literature by inappropriately ascribing welfare significance to consumer or producer surplus quantities individually in equilibrium contexts.

9.4 WELFARE MEASUREMENT WITH EXISTING DISTORTIONS IN OTHER MARKETS

A general criticism of welfare economics has been that distortions existing elsewhere in the economy are usually not taken into account. Indeed, consideration thus far in this book has been given only to the case of introducing a single distortion in an economy otherwise completely free of distortions. In reality, however, taxes exist on many commodities (for example, a sales tax on final goods), quotas exist on some commodities (for example, some agricultural commodities), price controls or ceilings are occasionally used to control inflation or encourage development and tariffs are imposed on imports in many countries. Thus, for practical application of economic welfare analysis of any proposed additional distortion or removal of any existing distortion, the framework of Section 9.3 must be generalized to consider existing distortions.

A particularly important case is where society through its government may need to raise revenue for the financing of public goods or may simply wish to redistribute income. Since lump-sum taxes are often not feasible, commodity taxes and/or income taxes are generally used to achieve these purposes. That is, when governments try to make lump-sum transfers individuals are often able to strategically position themselves to receive greater benefits. But when changes in behavior are induced by such transfers, the lump-sum intent is undermined. As a result, a marginal tax distortion is generally associated with any project that requires public funding. An entire field of economics known as *optimal taxation* has developed to explore properties of such second-best optimal tax structures. The major objective is to identify tax structures that minimize the deadweight loss of achieving the government budget constraint. See, for example, Ramsey (1927) and Diamond and Mirrlees (1971a, 1971b).

Any policy change that affects markets in which these taxes exist must take the welfare effects of existing distortions into consideration. Some studies have tried to estimate or assess the marginal deadweight loss imposed by costly public projects that require raising additional general tax revenues or that reduce the need to raise general tax revenues. Harberger (1978) has suggested that the marginal loss associated with raising general tax revenues is no more than \$0.15 per dollar of additional taxes. Layard (1980), in a critical response to Harberger, argued that this secondary distortion is likely to be higher, particularly when it hits tax payers in high income tax brackets. Most applied studies have used marginal loss rates between \$0.15 and \$0.30 per dollar of tax financing required for a particular project. With this approach, applied welfare economists simply multiply any required public funds for a particular project by this marginal loss rate to approximate the welfare loss caused by the need to alter existing tax distortions in other markets.[12] While a complete discussion of optimal taxation is beyond the scope of this book, this section demonstrates the principles that are involved in assessing welfare effects when such distortions exist in other markets.

Consider the situation in Figure 9.8, where a vertical relationship exists between industries n, $n+1$, and $n+2$. Industry n faces perfectly elastic supplies of its inputs, thus leading

12. See Gardner (1983) for an excellent example of how such estimates of marginal tax distortions can be used to modify the estimated welfare effects of changing a policy that directly distorts a single market when the policy must be financed from general tax revenues.

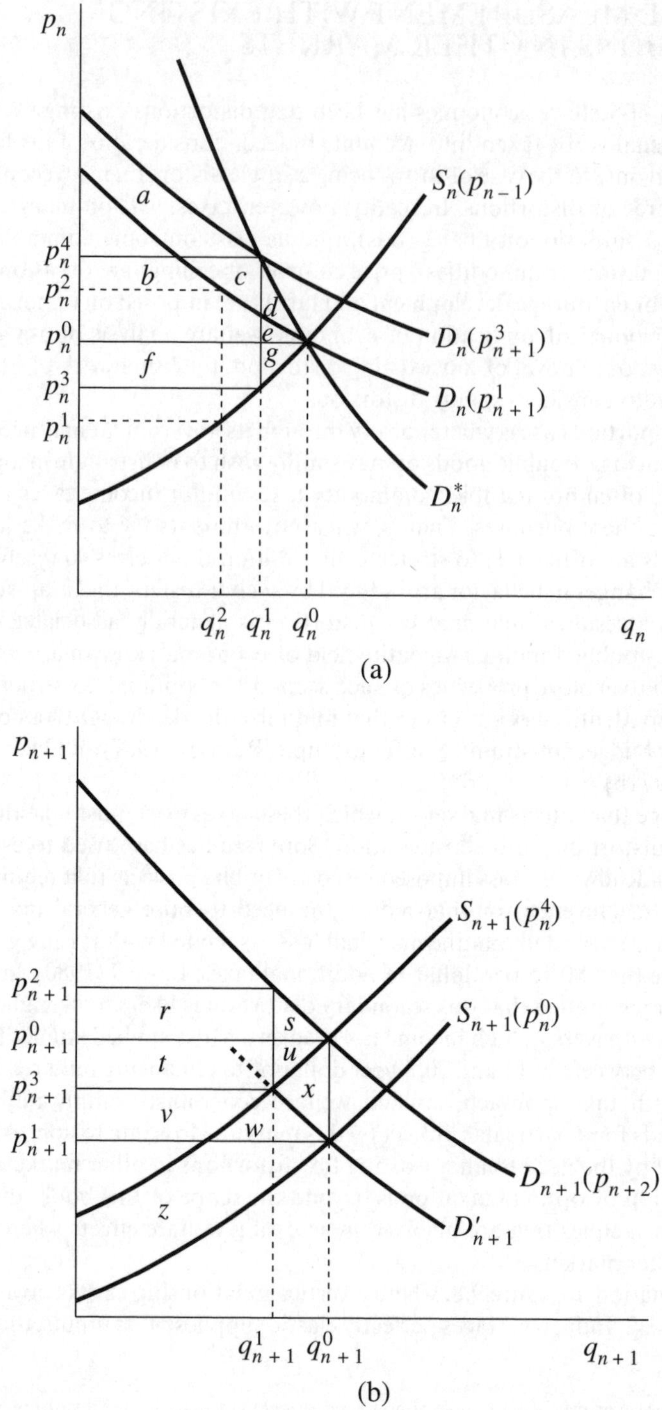

p_n
$S_n(p_{n-1})$
a
b
c
d
e
f
g
p_n^4
p_n^2
p_n^0
p_n^3
p_n^1
$D_n(p_{n+1}^3)$
$D_n(p_{n+1}^1)$
D_n^*
q_n^2 q_n^1 q_n^0
q_n
(a)
p_{n+1}
$S_{n+1}(p_n^4)$
$S_{n+1}(p_n^0)$
p_{n+1}^2
p_{n+1}^0
p_{n+1}^3
p_{n+1}^1
r
s
t
u
x
v
w
z
$D_{n+1}(p_{n+2})$
D'_{n+1}
q_{n+1}^1 q_{n+1}^0
q_{n+1}
(b)

Figure 9.8

to supply $S_n(p_{n-1})$ in market n, and industry $n+2$ faces perfectly elastic demand for its product, thus leading to demand $D_{n+1}(p_{n+2})$ in market $n+1$. Initially, an *ad valorem* tax of $p_{n+1}^0 - p_{n+1}^1$ exists in market $n+1$ that is associated with equilibrium ordinary demand $D_n(p_{n+1}^1)$ price p_n^0, and quantity q_n^0 in market n. The equilibrium ordinary supply is $S_{n+1}(p_n^0)$ in market $n+1$, the quantity transacted is q_{n+1}^0, and the price is p_{n+1}^0 or p_{n+1}^1, depending on whether or not the tax is included or excluded.

Now suppose that a tax of $p_n^2 - p_n^1$ is introduced in market n. This reduces the supply of q_{n+1}, which, in turn, raises the effective supply price (excluding tax) in market $n+1$ so that demand in market n tends to increase. As a result, a new equilibrium is achieved after sufficient adjustment at quantity q_n^1 and price p_n^4 (including tax), where $p_n^4 - p_n^3 = p_n^2 - p_n^1$. The set of equilibrium points associated with various levels of the tax in market n – for example, (p_n^0, q_n^0) and (p_n^4, q_n^1) – thus traces out an equilibrium demand curve D_n^* for q_n, *given the existing distortion.*

Now consider the welfare effects of imposing the second distortion. Given the vertical framework and elasticity assumptions above, industry $n+2$ experiences a welfare loss of area $r+s$, industry n loses area $f+g$, and industry $n+1$ loses area $b+e-a$ as measured in market n or area $z-v$ as measured in market $n+1$. In addition, the government loses area $u+v+w+x-r$ in taxes in market $n+1$ while gaining area $b+c+f$ in market n.

In this case the net social welfare effect cannot be observed in a single market except through use of the concept of equilibrium curves, and even then some changes in government tax revenues are omitted. To see this, one need merely note that all behavior and welfare effects for industries $n+1$ and $n+2$, included in the equilibrium demand curve D_n^* in this case, are exactly the same as if demand were D'_{n+1} and no distortion existed in market $n+1$ (where D'_{n+1} differs vertically from $D_{n+1}(p_{n+2})$ by the amount of the tax in market $n+1$). Hence, the welfare effect of area $r+s$ for industry $n+2$ can be equivalently measured by area $v+w$. Based on the analysis in Figure 9.2, the welfare effect for both industries $n+1$ and $n+2$ is thus reflected by the consumer surplus associated with D_n^*. These observations imply that the net social welfare effect of adding the additional distortion in market n exclusive of the reduction in tax revenue in market $n+1$ is reflected in market n by a loss of area $d+e+g$. Net private welfare loss is area $b+c+d+e+f+g$, which is partially offset by the tax revenue gain of area $b+c+f$.

Such a problem with failure to account for all social welfare effects, even those of the government, does not occur, however, when the existing distortion is a quota. Because of such differences in methodology, depending on the form of distortion, examination of at least one other case is useful before discussing general conclusions. For an alternative problem, consider the case in Figure 9.9, where industries 1 and 2 have a horizontal relationship, with both selling their output to industry 3 and facing perfectly elastic supplies of their inputs. Initially, with a quota of q_2^0 the equilibrium price in market 2 is at price p_2^0, and equilibrium in market 1 is at price p_1^0 and quantity q_1^0. Consider the introduction of an *ad valorem* tax in the amount of $p_1^2 - p_1^1$ in market 1. The tendency toward higher q_1 prices leads to reduced demand for the (complementary) input q_2, as in the case of Figure 9.4, and hence leads to the lower price p_2^1. The lower q_2 price thus leads to an increase in the ordinary demand for q_1 to $D_1(p_2^1)$, with a new equilibrium at price p_1^4 including tax or price p_1^3 excluding tax. Such variations in the q_1 tax map out an equilibrium demand curve D_1^* that is conditioned on the level of the q_2 quota.

Determination of the overall welfare effects of introducing the new distortion in this

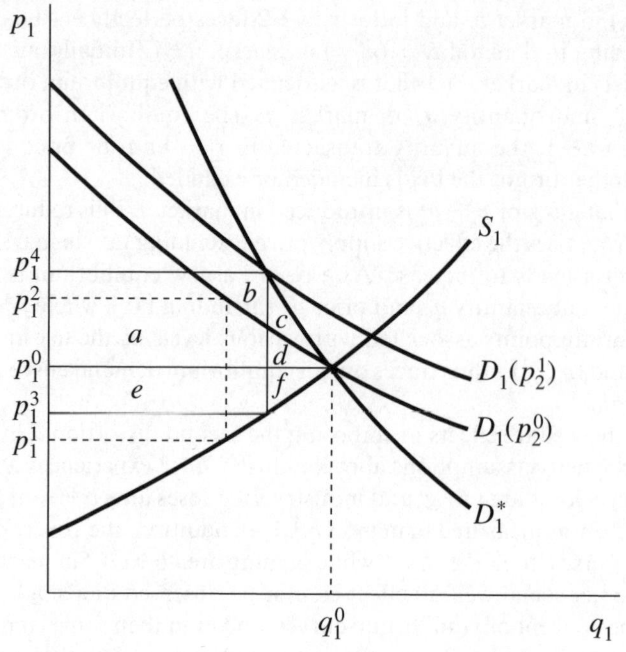

p_1
p_1^4
p_1^2
p_1^0
p_1^3
p_1^1
a
b
c
d
e
f
S_1
$D_1(p_2^1)$
$D_1(p_2^0)$
D_1^*
q_1^0
q_1

(a)

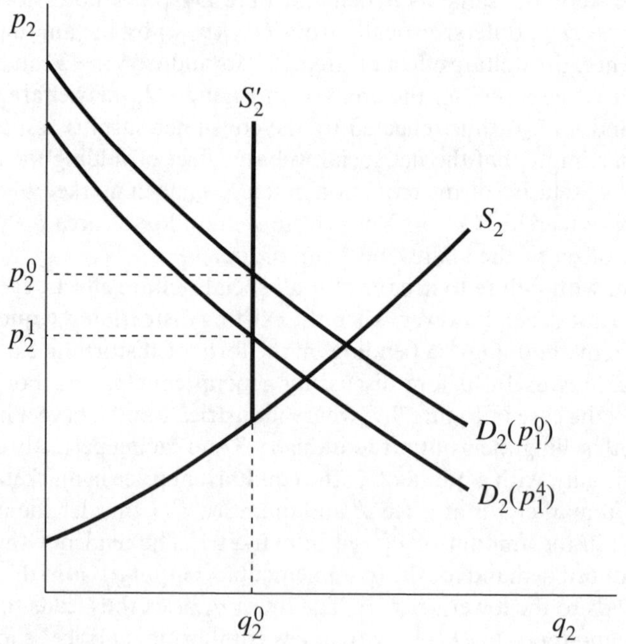

p_2
S_2'
S_2
p_2^0
p_2^1
$D_2(p_1^0)$
$D_2(p_1^4)$
q_2^0
q_2

(b)

Figure 9.9

case, given that the distortion in market 2 already exists, follows easily from the analysis in Figure 9.4. That is, imagining a hypothetical supply for industry 2 of S_2' (which coincides with S_2 at quantities below q_2^0), all of the welfare effects for industries 2 and 3 would be reflected by the change in consumer surplus associate with D_1^*. But the welfare effects on industry 1 are reflected by the producer surplus associated with S_1, which in this case is also an equilibrium supply. Thus, the net social welfare effect of introducing the tax in market 1, given the existence of the quota in market 2, is a loss of area $c+d+f$. The net private welfare loss is area $a+b+c+d+e+f$, which is offset to some extent by the gain in government tax revenues of area $a+b+e$.

Obviously, many other useful simple cases of introducing one distortion when another already exists could be examined. For example, one could consider introducing a tax, subsidy, quota, price support or some other price or production control where any one of those kinds of distortions exists in another market even in a simple two-market framework. This could be done in horizontally related input markets, horizontally related output markets, vertically related markets where the first distortion exists in the input market, or vertically related markets where the first distortion exists in the output market. Even these simple cases are too numerous to consider here, but using the framework developed thus far, the reader can investigate any additional simple cases of interest.

At this point, the general conclusions suggested by the cases above, which are developed rigorously with full generality in Appendix Section 9.B, may be summarized simply. The general conclusion is that the analysis of Chapter 8 extends directly to take account of all *private* social welfare effects (not necessarily government effects) in the entire economy of intervention in a single market if (1) the supply and demand curves used for analysis in the market of interest are conditioned on general equilibrium adjustment given all other distortions that exist in the economy, (2) all consumers and factor owners adjust along compensated demand and supply curves, (3) no existing distortions are in the form of price ceilings or floors and (4) competitive behavior prevails throughout the economy. These results also imply that one must be careful to use a consistent methodology to evaluate welfare effects. For example, if one estimates equilibrium supply and demand for the newly distorted market, then additional indirect private welfare effects in other markets with existing distortions cannot be appropriately considered additionally. On the other hand, if one estimates welfare effects in the newly distorted market using partial equilibrium supply and demand, then estimated welfare effects are not complete without considering additional indirect welfare effects in other markets. But in this case one must use a complete path of integration, that is, condition each successive change on each previous change.[13]

To be complete, several additional qualifications of these results are in order. First, to the extent that consumers and factor owners do not react along compensated demands and supplies but rather along ordinary Marshallian demands and supplies, the actual private welfare effects are approximated to the extent that compensated equilibrium prices and adjustments approximate uncompensated equilibrium prices and adjustments. Second, if distortions affect government revenues or subsidies in other distorted markets, then the effects on these revenues and subsidies must be additionally included in welfare

13. For a thorough criticism of the errors that can be made when one simply adds up (seemingly siginificant) geometric areas across markets to obtain measurements of multimarket welfare change, see Bullock (1993b).

calculations. For example, as in the cases of Figures 9.6 and 9.7, any change in government revenues or losses due to taxes, subsidies, or acquisition of commodities under price-support programs that follow directly from the new distortion under consideration can be reflected directly in the market of interest. But if the new distortion has government revenue or cost implications in other markets due to *existing distortions*, then the net social welfare effects of any new distortion can be determined only by measuring the change in aggregate government revenues (where subsidy costs are included negatively) associated with such existing distortions and adding them to the net social welfare effects reflected in the newly distorted market (which reflects aggregate net private welfare effects plus any government revenues or costs associated directly with the new distortion). Appendix Section 9.B gives additional details for cases where some markets are distorted by use of market power or by price ceilings or floors.

9.5 GENERAL EQUILIBRIUM CONSIDERATIONS IN SPECIFICATION, ESTIMATION AND INTERPRETATION

To discuss the empirical approach suggested by this chapter, an understanding of the econometric problem of multicollinearity and its relationship to specification is helpful. The problem of multicollinearity is a condition in econometrics where the variables on the right-hand side of the estimated equation in (8.2) are so closely related that statistical procedures cannot attribute changes in observed data to one variable versus another variable with very much accuracy. This condition occurs when one variable happens to be approximately a linear function of another (for example, $p=2+5z_2$) or if one variable happens to be approximately a linear function of several other variables (for example, $z_1=4+3z_2+2z_3-4z_4$) during the sample period.

Intuitively, the problem of multicollinearity can be exemplified by a situation where all observed data for, say, p and z_1 take on either values 1 and 2 or 4 and 6, respectively (thus, $z_1=2+2p$ in every observation). Suppose, also, that q is 8 in the first case and 4 in the second case. Then, observed data are not sufficient to determine whether or not the data were generated by the equation $q=12-4p+0\cdot z_1$ or by the equation $q=8-8p+2z_1$. In the first case the curve is $q=12-4p$, as represented in Figure 9.10. For the latter equation, the curve would be $q=8-8p+2\cdot 4=16-8p$ or $q=8-8p+2\cdot 6=20-8p$, depending on whether or not $p=1$, $z=4$ or $p=2$, $z=6$, respectively (again, see Figure 9.10). Thus, on the basis of observed data, if the demand equation is specified as $q=\alpha_0+\alpha_1 p+\alpha_2 z_1$, then the coefficients could be either $\alpha_0=12$, $\alpha_1=-4$, $\alpha_2=0$ or $\alpha_0=8$, $\alpha_1=-8$, $\alpha_2=2$, and no distinction is possible without additional data. Similarly, many other alternatives also exist.[14]

On the other hand, suppose that more observations are obtained where $p=1$, $z_1=5$, and the q distribution is centered on 10. Then $\alpha_0=8$, $\alpha_1=-8$, and $\alpha_2=2$ is the only set of coefficients consistent with the data. That is, $10\neq 12-4\cdot 1+0\cdot 5$, so the other alternative must now be rejected. But this distinction is possible only by obtaining more data so that p and z_1 are no longer collinear (now $z_1=2+2p$ no longer holds for all observations).

This problem of multicollinearity or near multicollinearity is one that plagues many

14. For example, let $\alpha_0=12\theta-8(1-\theta)$, $\alpha_1=-4\theta+8(1-\theta)$, and $\alpha_2=0\cdot\theta-2(1-\theta)$ for any real value of θ.

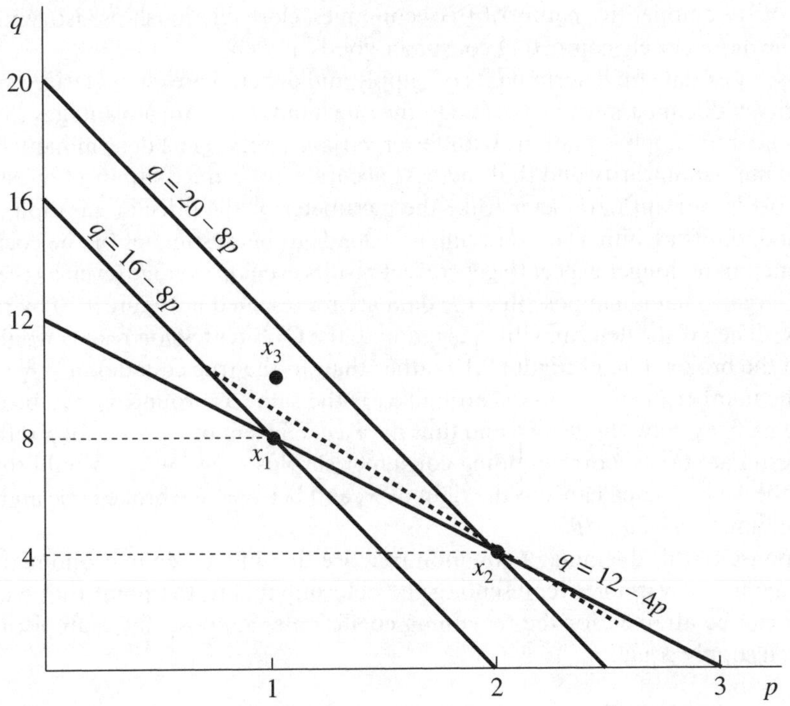

Figure 9.10

empirical studies of demand and supply. That is, appropriate practice from a theoretical point of view is to include in a demand or supply specification all the variables that serve as determinants of the demand or supply equation. Such a set of determinants generally includes a number of prices of competing consumer goods and income or of competing input prices. Because inflation tends to be reflected in all prices, these sets of variables tend to be characterized by a high degree of multicollinearity (all prices tend to rise together with time).

One possibility for avoiding these problems is to use *real* prices rather than *nominal* prices. Nominal prices reflect the actual price paid or received in terms of current dollars. Real prices, on the other hand, reflect the price level relative to some base period so that the effects of inflation tend to be removed. Real prices can be constructed by dividing observed or nominal prices by a suitable price index which reflects the level of inflation. For example, consumer prices can be deflated to real terms by dividing by the Consumer Price Index or producer prices can be deflated by dividing by the Producer Price Index, although all prices in a given problem should be deflated by the same index to maintain integrability.

Although use of real prices rather than nominal prices tends to reduce multicollinearity, bothersome and sometimes unacceptable problems may still persist. This tends to occur, for example, on the producer side, where 'booms' or 'busts' occur for particular industries relative to the rest of the economy. Hence, all the prices associated with a particular industry (which thus serve jointly as determinants in individual supply or demand equations) often increase or decrease together even relative to some overall price level.

Because of the competitive nature of free economies, close relationships also tend to exist among the more closely competing consumer goods as well.

Because most data on determinants of supply and demand are characterized by multicollinearity, a dilemma must be faced. On the one hand, there are advantages to specifying demand and supply equations with fewer variables serving as determinants in order to reduce multicollinearity and thus increase accuracy (or reduce variance) in estimation of the most important parameters (like the parameter of the price in question). On the other hand, omitting important determinants tends to bias estimates of the coefficients, so that one can no longer expect to get correct results even on average (even as the sample size gets large). That is, suppose that the data are represented in Figure 9.10 by points x_1 x_2, and x_3. Then if the determinant z_1 is ignored, the OLS regression results would correspond to the broken line in Figure 9.10 rather than to the true equation, $q=8-8p+2z$. Where the number of observations around x_1 is the same as around x_3, the broken line would lie halfway between the two and thus have a coefficient of $\alpha_1=-5$ for p rather than -8. An estimate of the corresponding consumer surplus – say, at x_1 – would thus be in error by the wedge-shaped area to the right of x_1 and between the broken line and the line corresponding to $q=20-8p$.

In response to this dilemma, a common practice that has arisen in econometrics is to shorten the list of variables representing the determinants to the point that reasonable accuracy can be attained for the remaining coefficients. Suppose, for example, that one estimates a supply equation,

$$q=\alpha_0+\alpha_1 p+\alpha_2\gamma, \tag{9.8}$$

in the market for q, where p represents the price in that market and γ represents the price of the input (or index of prices of all inputs) used in producing q. For prices $p=p^*$, $\gamma=\gamma^*$ and the corresponding quantity $q^*=\alpha_0+\alpha_1 p^*+\alpha_2\gamma^*$, the simple or ordinary surplus measure S^* which holds the input price γ fixed at γ^* is given by the area a, the area above the ordinary demand curve represented by $q=\alpha_0+\alpha_1 p+\alpha_2\gamma^*$ and below price p^*, in Figure 9.11. Because p_0, the price at which supply just falls to zero, is given by $p_0=-(\alpha_0+\alpha_2\gamma^*)/\alpha_1$ (simply set the right-hand side of equation (9.8) equal to zero and solve for p), the surplus triangle may be calculated from geometry as[15]

$$\begin{aligned} S^* &= \text{area } a = \tfrac{1}{2}(p^*-p_0)q^* \\ &= \tfrac{1}{2}(q^*/\alpha_1)q^* = (q^*)^2/(2\alpha_1). \end{aligned} \tag{9.9}$$

As implied by the results in Section 8.1, the area S^* measures quasirent only to producers selling in that market.

The equilibrium surplus, which reflects welfare effects for a broader group of producers (and consumers), is calculated on the basis of an equilibrium supply curve that is not conditioned on the input price γ. Instead, the equilibrium supply curve takes account of variation in γ induced by equilibrium adjustments in response to changes in p. For example, if cattle prices fall, cattle feeders generally respond by reducing supply through lowering the number of cattle on feed. This response, in turn, reduces demand for feed

15. Note that $\alpha_0+\alpha_2\gamma^*$ is assumed to be negative to simplify the example.

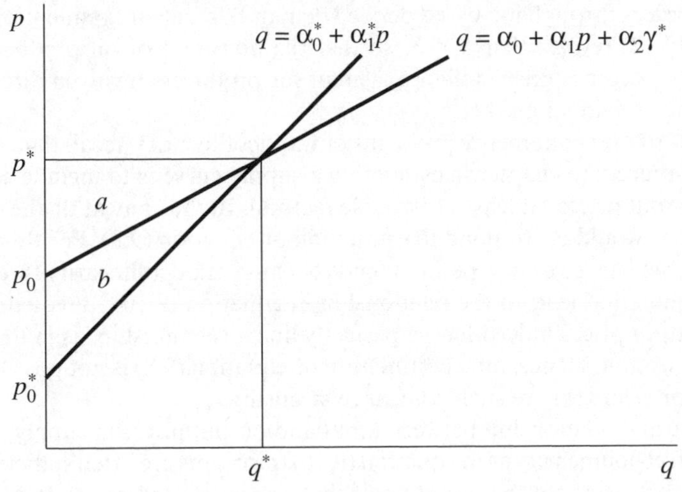

Figure 9.11

grain and causes a fall in feed price. Thus, suppose that the market in question is one of several that form a vertically related sector of the economy in the same sense as discussed in Section 9.1. Also, suppose for simplicity that the equilibrium relationship between p and γ is represented by

$$\gamma = c_0 + c_1 p. \tag{9.10}$$

Then, substituting equation (9.10) into (9.8) yields

$$\begin{aligned} q &= (\alpha_0 + \alpha_2 c_0) + (\alpha_1 + \alpha_2 c_1) p \\ &= \alpha_0^* + \alpha_1^* p \end{aligned} \tag{9.11}$$

as the equilibrium supply curve that takes account of varying input prices, where $\alpha_0^* = \alpha_0 + \alpha_2 c_0$ and $\alpha_1^* = \alpha_1 + \alpha_2 c_1$. The equilibrium surplus which reflects quasirent for all industries on the supply side of the market in the sector is given by area $a+b$ in Figure 9.11. Solving for p_0^* (setting $q=0$) implies that $p_0^* = -\alpha_0^*/\alpha_1^*$. Thus, geometric calculation of the triangular area $a+b$ implies that the equilibrium producer surplus is

$$\begin{aligned} S = \text{area } a+b &= \tfrac{1}{2}(p^* - p_0^*) q^* \\ &= \tfrac{1}{2}(q^*/\alpha_1^*) q^* \\ &= (q^*)^2/(2\alpha_1^*) \qquad (9.12) \\ &= \frac{(q^*)^2}{2(\alpha_1 + \alpha_2 c_1)}. \end{aligned}$$

Because reasonable conditions imply that both α_1 and α_1^* are positive (both ordinary and equilibrium supply are upward-sloping), that $\alpha_2 < 0$ (an increase in the price of inputs causes a reduction in supply) and that $c_1 > 0$ (an increased price of the output leads to increased input prices through increased derived demand), a casual examination of equations (9.9) and (9.12) reveals that $S^* < S$, so that the quasirent of all producers on the supply side of the sector is greater than quasirent for producers involved directly in the supply side of the individual market.

Returning now to the econometric problems of multicollinearity, recall that the general approach of the preceding chapter in estimating a supply curve is to include as determinants all of the input prices (at least of variable factors). In the context of the discussion above, this practice would correspond to estimation of equation (9.8). For this equation, however, the mere existence of competition tends to cause multicollinearity through equilibrium adjustments that lead to the relationship in equation (9.10). In equation (9.10), the input and output prices indeed have a perfectly linear relationship, as in the first case discussed in this section. Hence, direct estimation of equation (9.8) is not possible as long as observations on p and γ have such a linear relationship.

Although the usual relationship between input and output prices in supply estimation is not one of perfect collinearity as in equation (9.10), problems are often sufficiently manifest to prevent much accuracy in estimation of the associated coefficients. In practice, the severity of this condition has often led investigators to drop input prices from the supply equation specification altogether, thus estimating instead an equation of the form

$$q = \tilde{\alpha}_0 + \tilde{\alpha}_1 p. \tag{9.13}$$

But clearly, the interpretation of parameters and associated surpluses for equation (9.13) is different from that in equation (9.8). Indeed, equation (9.13) is equivalent to equation (9.11). Hence, an estimate of $\tilde{\alpha}_1$ in equation (9.13) must be interpreted as an estimate of α_1^* in equation (9.11), so the producer surplus associated with the supply in equation (9.13) is the equilibrium surplus in equation (9.12).

If, on the other hand, the relationship between p and γ is not so close as to cause problems of multicollinearity in estimating the ordinary supply equation (9.8) (say, because of a random disturbance in (9.10)), then the equilibrium supply in equation (9.11) can also be estimated in indirect fashion by computing

$$\alpha_0^* = \hat{\alpha}_0 + \hat{\alpha}_2 \hat{c}_0$$
$$\alpha_1^* = \hat{\alpha}_1 + \hat{\alpha}_2 \hat{c}_1,$$

where $\hat{\alpha}_0$, $\hat{\alpha}_1$ and $\hat{\alpha}_2$ are the estimated parameters of the ordinary supply curve in equation (9.8).

From a practical standpoint, it seems that the latter approach is the more reasonable to follow when both alternatives exist and, in fact, some generalizations can be easily considered. That is, the relationship of p and γ may not be so close as to create acute multicollinearity problems in estimation of the ordinary supply in equation (9.8) because some force elsewhere in the sector or economy (such as government intervention or prices outside the sector) may have altered equation (9.10) during the sample period. Suppose that this force is represented by z and that its effect in equation (9.10) can be represented linearly,

$$\gamma = c_0^* + c_1^* p + c_2^* z. \tag{9.14}$$

If this is the case, the appropriate equilibrium supply curve is found by substituting equation (9.14) into equation (9.8), thus obtaining

$$\begin{aligned} q &= \alpha_0 + \alpha_1 p + \alpha_2(c_0^* + c_1^* p + c_2^* z) \\ &= \bar{\alpha}_0 + \bar{\alpha}_1 p + \bar{\alpha}_2 z, \end{aligned} \tag{9.15}$$

where and $\bar{\alpha}_0 = \alpha_0 + \alpha_2 c_0^*$, $\bar{\alpha}_1 = \alpha_1 + \alpha_2 c_1^*$, and $\bar{\alpha}_2 = \alpha_2 c_2^*$.

With this type of phenomenon in mind, it seems that direct estimation of ordinary supply may be preferable to direct estimation of equilibrium supply because problems of bias due to misspecification (for example, leaving out important variables) are not likely to be so great. With the equilibrium supply equation in (9.15), on the other hand, the set of determinants corresponding to z is sometimes difficult to determine or narrow down to manageable proportions.[16] In point of fact, when one considers the context of the sector equilibrium approach given in Section 9.1, it indeed conditions results on fixed prices and incomes in the rest of the economy. These prices from the rest of the economy thus serve as determinants for the equilibrium supply and demand curves. Although the number of such prices that must be considered can be overwhelming, the approach of constructing suitable indices may serve as a reasonable means of reducing the number of variables that must be considered econometrically (the theory of separability of consumer demand and factor supply is directly applicable with respect to the prices of all goods that are not traded directly with the sector if, in fact, appropriate separable groupings exist.)[17]

In addition to the considerations raised in this section on the supply side, symmetrical arguments can be made with respect to the area under estimated demand curves for intermediate goods in a sector. That is, reinterpreting γ as the price of a product that uses q in its production process and S as a consumer surplus, all the derivation in equations (9.8) through (9.15) continues to hold.

16. Another point of interest that will be clear to a practicing econometrician has to do with the possible pitfalls of, by chance, considering as a determinant some variable z in equations (9.14) and (9.15) that does not rightfully serve as a determinant. When additional variables are considered in linear regression, they can only reduce rather than increase the sum of squares of errors. Furthermore, when one investigates a large number of variables as possibilities, chances are that some will be found that cause a significant reduction (have a t ratio greater than 2 in absolute value). With this in mind, one must consider adding variables in (9.14) that tend to take away from the explanation of γ by p, thus reducing the estimate of c_1. Substituting in the ordinary supply curve will thus lead to a smaller coefficient for p in the equilibrium estimate of supply, which thus implies more inelastic equilibrium supply. If, instead, the equilibrium relationship is turned around to estimate

$$p = \bar{c}_0 + \bar{c}_1 \gamma + \bar{c}_2 z,$$

then a smaller estimate of $\bar{c}_1$ after substitution in equation (9.8) is reflected by a more elastic estimate of equilibrium supply. Thus, one check on whether or not the right set of determinants is employed is to estimate the induced equilibrium curve both ways. One may note that direct estimation of the equilibrium curve in (9.15) will tend to yield more inelasticity if incorrectly included z terms detract from the explanation of q by p. The alternative conclusion would be reached if the supply equation were estimated with p rather than q as the left-hand-side or dependent variable.

17. For a detailed discussion of separability, see Blackorby, Primont and Russell (1978).

The General Vertical Market Approach

The essence of the general vertical market approach can be generalized to consider problems of econometric estimation and identification in the case where the equilibrium price relationships in a sector are changing because of varying prices and government policies (or determinants) imposed on the sector by the rest of the economy. That is, one can estimate an equilibrium supply curve in market j in the vertical sector case (encompassing endogenous adjustments of $(p_0,\ldots,p_{j-1},p_{j+1},\ldots,p_N)$) by regressing the quantity supplied, q_j^s, on the effective market j price for producers (for example, output price less any *ad valorem* tax, as in Figure 9.3) and all determinants γ_j^- affecting factor suppliers and industries 1, …, j,[18]

$$q_j^s = q_j^s(p_j^s, \gamma_j^-). \tag{9.16}$$

Similarly, the market j equilibrium demand can be estimated in the form

$$q_j^d = q_j^d(p_j^d, \gamma_j^+), \tag{9.17}$$

where q_j^d is quantity demanded, p_j^d is the effective market price for purchasers, and γ_j^+ a vector of all determinants associated with the rest of the economy affecting industries $j+1$, …, N and final consumer demand. If the small vertical-sector assumption applies, sector equilibrium functions are, indeed, general equilibrium curves and can be used to estimate the overall welfare effects of a distortion.

On the other hand, if one estimates (ordinary) supply and demand in the same intermediate market by considering prices in vertically related markets, that is, using a supply function of the form

$$q_j^s = \tilde{q}_j^s(p_j^s, p_{j-1}, \gamma_j) \tag{9.18}$$

and a demand function of the form

$$q_j^d = \tilde{q}_j^d(p_j^d, p_{j+1}, \gamma_{j+1}), \tag{9.19}$$

respectively, where γ_j and γ_{j+1} include only those determinants from the rest of the economy that affect industries j and $j+1$ directly, one can obtain (assuming identifiability) partial equilibrium welfare measures, that is, measures of welfare for only the producers and consumers in the market in question. If in addition one estimates the equilibrium price relationships,

$$p_{j-1} = p_{j-1}^s(p_j^s, \gamma_j^-) \tag{9.20}$$

$$p_{j+1} = p_{j+1}^d(p_j^d, \gamma_j^+), \tag{9.21}$$

then estimates of the equations (9.20) and (9.21) can be substituted into equations (9.18) and (9.19) to obtain estimates of the equilibrium functions in equations (9.16) and (9.17). Then

18. For purposes of the remainder of this chapter, the inclusion of variables in a functional form $q\,(\cdot,\cdot)$ is meant to imply which variables should be considered in the regression equation without necessarily specifying the functional form (in terms of linearity, log linearity, and so on).

equilibrium producer and consumer surplus can be calculated from the associated graphs of q_j against p_j for given values of determinants γ associated with the rest of the economy.

The General Equilibrium Approach

Turning to the general equilibrium results of Section 9.3 (which also encompass the case of Section 9.2), similar conclusions with respect to econometric practice may again be drawn. That is, one can estimate an equilibrium supply equation of the form

$$q^s = q^s(p^s, \gamma_s) \tag{9.22}$$

and an equilibrium demand equation of the form

$$q^d = q^d(p^d, \gamma_d) \tag{9.23}$$

in any particular market where q^s and q^d are quantities supplied and demanded, p^s and p^d are effective supply and demand prices, and γ_s and γ_d are determinants of the economy that affect equilibrium supply and demand, respectively. In this context all prices in the economy are viewed as being determined by the determinants of the economy. Specifically, the determinants of the economy would thus include such factors as government policy instruments (taxes, quotas, and so on), which introduce distortions in the economy, as well as all exogenous forces on the economy (weather, social and political factors, and so on), including any short-run production factor fixity or consumer durable asset fixity, and if the relevant economy does not pertain to the world as a whole, world prices of traded goods and exogenous income earned from external sources. In the latter case, conditioning of supply and demand estimates on external prices of traded goods will result in measuring equilibrium welfare for only the constituents of the economy in question, just as the sector equilibrium approach of Section 9.1 measures welfare for only the constituents of the sector in question.

From a practical standpoint, however, each of the determinants of the equilibrium supply in equation (9.22) may also affect the equilibrium demand in equation (9.23). Thus, γ_s and γ_d may be synonymous. That is, once all the effects of any exogenous force have filtered through the economy, the equilibrium adjustments brought about by competition may lead to a change in both the equilibrium supply and equilibrium demand in the market of interest because of the circular relationship among producers, consumers and factor owners in the general economy (see Section 9.3 for a similar discussion related to introducing different types of distortions).[19] An econometric problem that arises in this

19. One case in which this would not be true is where the economy can be segmented into two groups of decision-makers such that all the interaction between the two groups, direct or indirect, takes place in a single market. Thus, determinants that affect the net equilibrium supply of one group of individuals do not necessarily affect the net equilibrium demand of the other group. In particular, a change in the supply price in the single connecting market, holding the demand price fixed, does not cause adjustments within the segment of the economy associated with demand or of the resulting equilibrium demand. Similarly, a change in demand price in the connecting market, holding the supply price fixed, does not cause a shift in the equilibrium supply. Using the framework of Appendix Section 9.B, one can show in this case that the change in producer surplus associated with compensated equilibrium supply measures the net welfare effect (in terms of WTP) for the segment of the economy associated with that supply. A similar statement holds for the other segment of the economy with respect to the change in consumer surplus associated with compensated equilibrium demand. The vertical market structure is such a special case. See Appendix Section 9.B for more detailed analysis of this case.

context is that if equations (9.22) and (9.23) compose a pair of simultaneous equations (see Section 8.8), then structural identification problems can prevent estimation with reasonable properties.

For example, consider a simultaneous equations system where the same determinant affects both equations, for instance,

$$q=\alpha_0+\alpha_1 p+\alpha_2 y \tag{9.24}$$

$$q=\beta_0+\beta_1 p+\beta_2 y. \tag{9.25}$$

Solving the system for p and q implies that

$$p=a_0+a_1 y$$

$$q=b_0+b_1 y,$$

where

$$a_0=\frac{\beta_0-\alpha_0}{\alpha_1-\beta_1},\ a_1=\frac{\beta_2-\alpha_2}{\alpha_1-\beta_1}, \tag{9.26}$$

$$b_0=\frac{\alpha_0\beta_1-\alpha_1\beta_0}{\beta_1-\alpha_1},\ b_1=\frac{\alpha_2\beta_1-\alpha_1\beta_2}{\beta_1-\alpha_1}. \tag{9.27}$$

But given estimates of a_0, a_1, b_0 and b_1, there is no way to solve the corresponding four equations in (9.26) and (9.27) uniquely for the six parameters α_0, α_1, α_2, β_0, β_1 and β_2 of the structural demand and supply equations in (9.24) and (9.25). In this case, methods that can generally attain at least consistent estimators of structural equation parameters, fail.[20]

An alternative approach is to estimate conventional ordinary supply and demand equations,

$$q^s=\tilde{q}^s(p^s,p_{\bar{d}}^s,\gamma_s^*) \tag{9.28}$$

$$q^d=\tilde{q}^d(p^d,p_{\bar{d}}^d,\gamma_d^*), \tag{9.29}$$

where q^s, p^s, q^d and p^d are as defined earlier; $p_{\bar{d}}^s$ and $p_{\bar{d}}^d$ represent all prices and exogenous income in the economy that serve as determinants of ordinary supply and demand, respectively; and γ_s^* and γ_d^* represent all determinants of the economy that affect this particular ordinary supply and demand directly. With estimates of these equations, the ordinary surpluses may be calculated and used to determine welfare effects on the participants of the market from changes in policy instruments (taxes, quotas, and so on) represented in γ_s^* or γ_d^*.

Such calculations, however, require knowledge of the equilibrium adjustments of $p_{\bar{d}}^s$ and $p_{\bar{d}}^d$. These prices and incomes may, in fact, be observed both before and after a policy change so that the ordinary surpluses can be appropriately calculated on the basis of the

20. For further discussion of the identification problem and consistent estimation of equilibrium demand functions, see Thurman and Wohlgenant (1989). For a general discussion of structural identification in simultaneous equations estimation, see Greene (2000, ch. 15) or Judge et al. (1988, chs 14 and 15).

location of the ordinary supply and demand curves before and after the change as determined by the determinants. In most *ex post* policy analyses, however, it is necessary to estimate the effects of a particular policy change on equilibrium prices because the effects of many other coincidental changes must be removed in order to isolate the effects of interest.

One possible approach to estimating equilibrium price adjustments is to estimate equations that specify how prices in the economy adjust to changes in the determinants of the economy,

$$p_d^s = p_d^s(p^s, \gamma_s) \quad (9.30)$$

$$p_d^d = p_d^d(p^d, \gamma_d). \quad (9.31)$$

These equations, however, must be considered as simultaneous equations and hence may suffer from the same structural identification problems associated with equations (9.22) and (9.23).[21] Alternatively, if the functional forms in (9.30) and (9.31) are such that the equations can be rewritten as

$$\frac{p_d^s}{p^s} = \tilde{p}_d^s(\gamma_s) \quad (9.32)$$

$$\frac{p_d^d}{p^d} = \tilde{p}_d^d(\gamma_d), \quad (9.33)$$

then no such problems exist. The latter set of equations can, in principle, be estimated without structural identification problems (although stochastic identification problems associated with multicollinearity may occur).[22] Thus, substitution of estimates of equations (9.32) and (9.33) into estimates of equations (9.28) and (9.29) obtains estimates of the equilibrium supply and demand equations in (9.22) and (9.23):

$$q^s = \tilde{q}^s(p^s, p^s \cdot \tilde{p}_d^s(\gamma_s), \gamma_s^*) = q^s(p^s, \gamma_s)$$
$$q^d = \tilde{q}^d(p^d, p^d \cdot \tilde{p}_d^d(\gamma_d), \gamma_d^*) = q^d(p^d, \gamma_d),$$

21. Technically, one must also note that the prices in p^s and p^d are determined simultaneously with p_d^s and p_d^d. If this is the case, equations must also be specified for p^s and p^d and used in estimation of (9.30) and (9.31) to avoid simultaneous equations bias (see Section 8.8). Similar statements also apply to estimation of the price relationships in (9.14), (9.20) and (9.21). Also, the price variables p_d^s and p_d^d on the right-hand side of equations (9.28) and (9.29) are generally determined simultaneously with q^s, q^d, p^s and p^d. This simultaneity must also be considered in estimation. A similar statement applies to p_{j-1} and p_{j+1} in equations (9.18) and (9.19). In all these cases, however, a two-stage least squares or instrumental variables approach of first regressing the jointly dependent variables on all exogenous forces (for example, on γ) and then replacing the right-hand side jointly dependent variables by estimates suggested by these regressions can lead to an acceptable estimation procedure. Consideration of additional equations is not necessary for estimation of equations (9.11), (9.13), (9.15) through (9.17), (9.22) and (9.23), because jointly dependent variables from other markets do not appear, so simultaneity with other equations need not be considered (although some additional precision or efficiency in estimation may be possible by so doing). In econometric terms, these equations behave like (partially) reduced forms. For a discussion of related econometric issues, see Greene (2000, ch. 16).
22. The principle of separability may again suggest the use of index numbers to reflect groups of determinants of the economy so that multicollinearity problems may be circumvented. For example, a basket exchange rate may adequately reflect trade prices for an economy, so perhaps all individual trade prices may not need to be included. Again, see Blackorby, Primont and Russell (1978).

In this framework the equilibrium welfare effects of altering any policy variable in the market (reflected in γ_s^* and/or γ_d^*) can be determined following the results in Section 9.3.

Practical Aspects of Multimarket Equilibrium Welfare Analysis

The preceding material in this section provides a methodology for estimating equilibrium welfare effects, which is applicable in theory. In reality, however, one cannot expect to identify all of the determinants of an economy. Furthermore, even if all determinants of an economy could be identified and corresponding data could be collected, little hope exists for estimating equations such as (9.22) and (9.23) involving all such determinants because problems of multicollinearity become more acute as variables are added (assuming a fixed number of observations on each variable). In reality, an applied welfare economist must abstract somewhat from the true case in an effort to represent the *important* phenomena in a *tractable* model.

Early economists tried to meet this challenge by examining individual markets under the assumption that prices in all other markets remain fixed as alterations are made in the market in question. But this assumption is unacceptable for those markets that are closely related to the market in question. For example, if the price of beef is increased sharply by a tightening of import quotas, assumptions that cattle, pork and feed grain prices remain unchanged seem inappropriate.

A more acceptable yet tractable approach based on the results in this chapter is to choose a subset of markets from the entire economy that are affected in important ways by contemplated policy changes in the market in question. This subset of markets should be made as large as possible while maintaining tractability. And generally, the more important the relationship between a distant market and the market in question, the more tractable a model involving that distant market should be. That is, more important relationships are apt to generate data that make those relationships discernible.

Once such a subset of markets is determined, a reasonable approach in the context of practical possibilities is to treat that subset of markets as an economy in and of itself. Determinants of that economy would consist of prices in markets outside the designated subset of markets (which can possibly be summarized by index prices) plus government policy instruments and natural, social and political phenomena that affect the subset of markets directly. In this context, the estimated welfare quantities would capture effects for all individuals involved directly in the subset of markets and, by assumption (or econometric implication), all other welfare effects are unimportant.

Consider, for example, the problem of relaxing beef import quotas. The direct effects of such a change in policy are experienced by beef consumers and by restaurants and fast-food chains who buy imported beef (for more completeness, wholesalers and retailers could also be considered along with consumers). However, with an increased supply of foreign beef, domestic suppliers of meat may find reduced demand for their products, and these effects must also be considered. Suppose that one either postulates or determines through econometric means that the other important effects are experienced by meat packers who find reduced demand for both their beef and pork products, by feedlot operators, hog producers and cow-calf producers who find a related reduced demand for their live animals by meat packers and, finally, by feed grain producers who find the reduced demand transmitted to the feed grain market by reduced activity in feeding hogs and cattle.

This intermarket structure is represented in Figure 9.12, where each circle represents a group of decision-makers and each line segment between two circles represents a market. The circle at the top end of each line segment is the demander and the circle at the bottom end of each line segment is the supplier in the associated market. By estimating a supply and demand equation for each market, which is sensitive to the other prices faced by the relevant group of decision-makers, one obtains a system of equations that allows computation of the effects of various levels of quotas on prices, quantities traded, and ordinary consumer and producer surpluses in each market. Thus, one can determine the overall

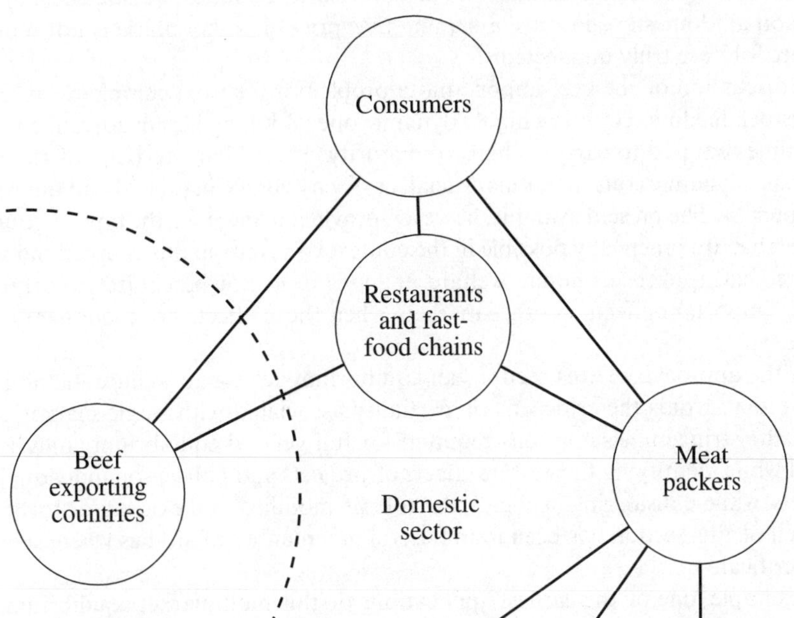

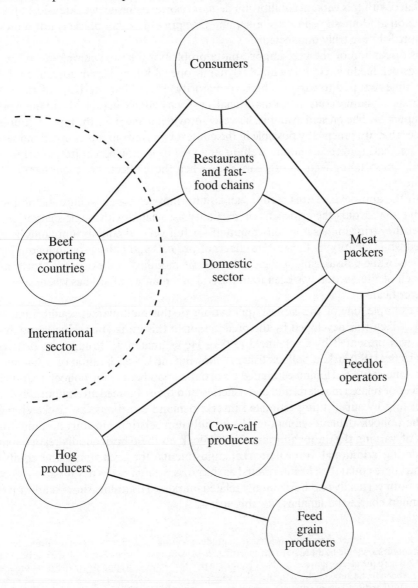

Figure 9.12

welfare effect, as well as the distribution of welfare effects, among the groups of decision-makers represented in Figure 9.12 to the extent that ordinary surpluses approximate WTP. Alternatively, one can estimate equilibrium demand for beef imports (by consumers, restaurants, and fast-food chains combined) by using as determinants those factors that are exogenous to the entire set of domestic markets represented in Figure 9.12 (such as the wage rate of labor in the meat packing industry, the price of fertilizer for feed grain producers, and so on). By the results for the case where an economy is segmented as in the last subsection of Appendix Section 9.B, the change in equilibrium consumer surplus associated with this general equilibrium demand captures the net welfare effect of a quota change on all domestic concerns, assuming that prices in other markets not represented in Figure 9.12 are truly unaffected.[23]

This discussion of the beef-import quota problem is far from complete. For example, the livestock feeding sector is a highly dynamic one with long lags in adjustment because of the time required to carry animals to maturity. These characteristics of the problem likely make dynamic considerations crucial, as discussed in Chapter 14 and the Appendix to Chapter 14. The present example, however, provides a flavor for the type of equilibrium analyses that are practically possible in the context of results in this chapter and serves to illustrate that applied economic welfare analyses need not be subject to criticisms of ignoring important effects in other markets when those effects are econometrically discernible.[24]

With the approach of this section, an equilibrium economic welfare methodology is available that avoids the criticisms of partiality associated with single-market analyses. But yet the stringent assumptions required for full general equilibrium analysis can be avoided while identifying the welfare effects of projects and policies on individual groups in society while considering explicitly the role of modified and existing distortions. The approach of this section has been found useful in a number of studies where such analyses are critical.

For example, one of the earliest applications of this multimarket equilibrium methodology, which was developed by the predecessor to this book (Just, Hueth and Schmitz 1982), was presented by Crutchfield (1983). He estimated an equilibrium demand for access to the US Alaskan pollock fishery following the US declaration of a 200 mile economic zone in 1976. He first estimated a partial demand curve for pollock that included the prices of related mackerel and cod fisheries, and then obtained an equilibrium demand relationship by substituting estimated inverse demand equations for mackerel and cod into the pollock demand equation. His equilibrium relationship thus accounts for the effects of varying the quota allowance for pollock on these horizontally related markets. Considering additional vertical market adjustments, the area under the equilibrium demand curve could then be interpreted as the gross willingness to pay for access accounting for both vertically and horizontally related markets. His results showed how much the USA might charge the Japanese for this access.

23. Incidentally, this net effect, plus the change in producer surplus associated with supply from beef exporting countries, should be the same as the sum of changes in ordinary surpluses over all the markets in Figure 9.12. This equivalence, however, will be obtained in practice only when appropriate specifications are used. See Appendix Section 9.D for a further discussion.
24. For a further discussion of empirical considerations in estimating equilibrium welfare effects, see Appendix Section 9.D.

In another study, Brännlund and Kriström (1996) estimated a system of equations for the timber and wood products sector of Sweden to calculate the welfare effects of a tax on chlorine use by the pulp industry. They assumed this multiproduct sector could be represented by a generalized Leontief restricted profit function and employed dual methodology as suggested in Appendix Section 9.D to specify output supply equations and input demand equations. Changes in quasirents for all industries were calculated for various levels of the tax. Their results showed that the deadweight loss estimated by using an ordinary chlorine demand equation was not significantly greater than the deadweight loss of using the general equilibrium demand equation although these two measures diverged as the tax level was increased.

In yet another study, Thurman and Easley (1992) estimated a general equilibrium derived demand function to evaluate the full costs of imposing commercial fishing regulations to preserve fish stock. The full costs consider not only the direct profit changes in the regulated fishery but the effects on consumers of higher priced seafood and the cost and benefit effects on nonregulated fisheries. The general equilibrium approach is used advantageously because inadequate data are available for direct estimation of the welfare effects at the retail level. The welfare effects using a partial approach are 43 per cent smaller than those estimated with the general equilibrium relationships.

Each of these studies illustrates practical application of the conceptual framework of Figure 9.12, which, based on the rigorous results of Appendix Section 9.B, provides a framework for measuring statistically identifiable welfare effects of projects and policies that have impacts beyond the market where government intervention occurs.

9.6 CONCLUSIONS

Based on the results of this chapter, rather comprehensive applied welfare analysis is possible. Depending on empirical conditions, all of the private social welfare effects of a proposed new or altered government policy can be measured completely, at least in an approximate sense, in the single market that is thereby distorted or in which a distortion is altered. If the policy introduces or alters several distortions, approximate measurement of all private effects is possible by considering the changes sequentially in the respective markets they affect directly (path independence holds in terms of the exact results relating to compensated consumer adjustments). The determination of all governmental effects is more troublesome and requires measurement in all markets in which government revenues or losses are being realized for exact results. Because changes in all prices may be induced by a single distortion, determination of the welfare effects for individual firms, industries, consumers or consumer groups generally requires measuring all of their ordinary (compensated, to be exact, in the consumer case) supply and demand curves and then calculating the sum of changes in their surpluses by imposing price changes sequentially or, in the firm or industry case, by measuring the overall change in surplus associated with their demand or supply for an essential output or input, respectively (see Appendix Section 7.I for some alternative but related possibilities).

Drawing upon both the theoretical and the econometric results outlined in this chapter, fairly accurate estimates of welfare effects can in some cases be developed by estimating supply and demand only in those markets where distortions change. In this way, welfare effects consist of areas between price lines rather than between shifting supply curves or shifting demand curves and, thus, the property of more accurate estimation suggested by Section 8.9 is apparently applicable. The discussion indicates that problems of multicollinearity will generally be less acute when this approach is taken, although problems of specification may be more severe.

This chapter has dealt with the possibilities of estimating and using equilibrium supply and demand curves. Depending on how the determinants of supplies and demands are defined, the generality of welfare effects estimated from supply and demand curves appears to depend directly on the generality with which determinants of supply and demand are specified for econometric estimation. These considerations suggest that the consumer and producer surplus areas behind demands and supplies can be construed as representing general equilibrium welfare effects in conceptual diagrammatic analyses. In empirical analyses, such surplus measures capture equilibrium welfare effects to the extent that such adjustments can be captured empirically. These interpretations are in sharp contrast to the distinctly partial equilibrium interpretation presumed in much of the classical welfare economics literature. With this discussion in mind, the results go a long way toward making the general equilibrium theoretical considerations of Chapters 2 and 3 possible at an empirical level of analysis.

Appendix to Chapter 9: Welfare measures for multimarket equilibrium

Chapters 4 through 8 of this book have focused on measuring the welfare effects of changes affecting a single market. Such approaches are called *partial equilibrium* approaches. For example, as demonstrated in Chapter 4 and the Appendix to Chapter 4, the producer surplus of a competitive supply curve conditioned on fixed input prices measures returns or quasirent on the associated fixed production factors, and the consumer surplus of a derived demand for an essential input (conditioned on fixity of other input and output prices) measures returns or quasirent on fixed production factors of the production process using the input. These results suggest that, when one estimates supply and demand in an intermediate market and calculates the associated producer and consumer surplus under the stated conditions, the welfare quantities exactly measure quasirent for the two groups of firms involved in selling and buying in that market, respectively. That is, when all other prices facing the selling and buying firms are *not* influenced by their (group) actions, the ordinary surplus quantities do not include effects on other groups (for example, final consumers), of which there would be none if all other prices were truly unaffected because of perfectly elastic supplies of inputs and perfectly elastic demands for outputs.

In contrast to this extremely partial approach, a number of authors have attempted to approach welfare measurement from a general equilibrium standpoint where all other prices in the economy are allowed to vary (see, for example, Johnson 1960 and Krauss and Winch 1971). Anderson (1974) shows that welfare changes can be determined by comparing the change in income arising from production (which, he notes, can be measured by the producer surplus triangle associated with an aggregate general equilibrium supply function for the whole economy) with the income effect of price changes in consumption (which, he notes, has been referred to as consumer surplus).

Each of these approaches has serious shortcomings in applied welfare economics. In reality, the imposition of a quota or tax in an intermediate market, such as for cattle or crude oil, may have a substantial effect on both final consumption prices and quantities, and conversely. Using partial methodology, these general equilibrium effects would be ignored. In many interesting problems, this practice is unacceptable. On the other hand, measurement with the general equilibrium approach at the aggregate economy level is not possible because of the intractability of estimating responses of *all* prices and quantities in an economy (Anderson 1974).

This appendix develops a framework for measurement of general equilibrium welfare effects that can capture the essential generality of empirical problems while maintaining tractability as well as the capability of disaggregating welfare effects. Section 9.A considers the case of a vertically structured competitive sector of an economy where each industry in the sector produces a single product using one major variable input produced within the sector and a number of other variable inputs originating in other sectors of the economy. Any number of fixed production factors may originate either from within or outside the sector. Assuming that the sector is only one of many users of inputs from outside the sector, the prices in other sectors are assumed fixed or uninfluenced by the sector in question. However, the actions of any individual industry in the sector may affect all other prices and quantities within the sector.

Section 9.B relaxes the vertical structure assumption and considers the case where prices and quantities in other sectors are also possibly altered as a result of intervention. In each case, the welfare significance of the producer and consumer surplus associated with supply and demand curves that take account of equilibrium adjustments in other markets is considered. Section 9.C considers an important paradox that arises in equilibrium welfare measurement for individuals when aggregate constraints on the economy are not adequately considered. Results show that what an individual is willing to pay for a change may be different depending on whether equilibrium adjustments caused by the compensation associated with a policy change are taken into account. As a result, aggregate compensation will be feasible only if these equilibrium adjustments are taken into account. Finally, Section 9.D considers practical matters in applying equilibrium welfare measurement given that measurement of effects in remote markets is impractical but yet some indirect market effects are substantial.

9.A THE CASE OF A SMALL VERTICALLY STRUCTURED SECTOR[1]

The development begins by building upon the results in Appendix Sections 4.B and 4.C, which show that a producing firm's welfare position is reflected in both its input and output markets when the associated input and output are essential in the production process. As noted in the introduction of the Appendix to Chapter 4, Wisecarver (1976), Schmalensee (1971, 1976), and Anderson (1976) began to investigate the relationship of surplus measures in input markets with those in output markets, but the cases considered in these papers deal only with long-run equilibrium or infinitely elastic input supply, which disregards the producer side of the problem. The earlier of these four papers contained incorrect conclusions due to approximations, but eventually Anderson (1976) showed that final market consumer surplus is the same as the input market consumer surplus when all producer quasirents are zero, and Schmalensee (1976) showed that, for a final-goods industry with nonzero quasirent but perfectly elastic supply of its input, the consumer surplus in its input market is equal to the sum of producer and consumer surplus in its output market. Both Anderson and Schmalensee assumed perfect competition, a single input, and the existence of no distortions. Although the results due to Anderson (1974) suggest extension of these propositions from the standpoint of aggregate welfare analysis, it was not made clear until the work of Just and Hueth (1979) that interpretation of the usual surplus triangles with respect to individual market groups changes with market level. In point of fact, in their framework it is possible to examine

1. The section is based on the paper by Just and Hueth (1979).

disaggregate welfare impacts on each affected market group. Nevertheless, the disaggregated results are consistent with Anderson and show that the overall impact of introducing a distortion in some intermediate market is reflected by the sum of areas behind the general equilibrium supply and demand functions in that market.

Consumer Surplus in an Intermediate Market

Consider first the welfare significance of the triangle behind demand and above price in an intermediate market of a vertically structured sector. For notational convenience, assume that the industries in a sector are competitive and can be ordered so that each industry n producing q_n and facing output price p_n uses as variable factor inputs the product q_{n-1} produced at the preceding industry level in the sector plus some subset of inputs $\boldsymbol{x}=(x_1,\ldots,x_m)$ with corresponding price vector $\boldsymbol{w}=(w_1,\ldots,w_m)$ produced in the rest of the economy, $n=1, \ldots, N$. The restricted profit (quasirent) function for the industry is, thus,

$$R_n(\boldsymbol{w},\boldsymbol{p})=p_n q_n^n(\boldsymbol{w},\boldsymbol{p})-p_{n-1}q_{n-1}^n(\boldsymbol{w},\boldsymbol{p})-\boldsymbol{w}\boldsymbol{x}^n(\boldsymbol{w},\boldsymbol{p}),$$

where $\boldsymbol{w}\boldsymbol{x}^n(\boldsymbol{w},\boldsymbol{p})=\sum_{j=1}^m w_j x_j^n(\boldsymbol{w},\boldsymbol{p})$, $\boldsymbol{p}=(p_1,\ldots,p_N)$, and profit-maximizing levels of output, input purchased within the sector and inputs purchased from outside the sector by producers at industry level n at given prices are denoted by $q_n^n(\boldsymbol{w},\boldsymbol{p})$, $q_{n-1}^n(\boldsymbol{w},\boldsymbol{p})$, and $\boldsymbol{x}^n(\boldsymbol{w},\boldsymbol{p})=[x_1^n(\boldsymbol{w},\boldsymbol{p}),\ldots,x_m^n(\boldsymbol{w},\boldsymbol{p})]$, respectively. Now suppose that prices in all industries in the sector are related through competition at the industry level so that, as price p_j is altered – perhaps by some government intervention – the entire price vector, $\boldsymbol{p}$, changes (monotonically) following $\tilde{\boldsymbol{p}}(p_j)=[\tilde{p}_1(p_j),\ldots,\tilde{p}_N(p_j)]$.[2] All inputs purchased from industries outside the sector, however, are available in elastic supply from the standpoint of the sector. Hence, their prices do not change.

As pointed out by Mishan (1968), evaluation of the welfare impact of such a distortion in this case requires looking beyond the buyers and sellers in market j. Consider first the effects on any industry n in the sector where $n>j$. By the envelope theorem, one finds that[3]

$$\frac{\partial R_n}{\partial p_j}=q_n^n\frac{\partial \tilde{p}_n}{\partial p_j}-q_{n-1}^n\frac{\partial \tilde{p}_{n-1}}{\partial p_j}.$$

Integration for a specific change from, say, p_j^0 to p_j^1 implies that

$$\Delta R_n=\int_{p_j^0}^{p_j^1}\frac{\partial R_n}{\partial p_j}dp_j=\int_{p_j^0}^{p_j^1}q_n^n\frac{\partial \tilde{p}_n}{\partial p_j}dp_j-\int_{p_j^0}^{p_j^1}q_{n-1}^n\frac{\partial \tilde{p}_{n-1}}{\partial p_j}dp_j, \tag{9.34}$$

where ΔR_n denotes the change in quasirent for industry n.

To interpret (9.34) when $n>j$, note that the first right-hand term is the negative of the change in area behind demand and above price in market n, denoted by ΔC_n^*,

$$\Delta C_n^*=-\int_{p_j^0}^{p_j^1}q_n^n\frac{\partial \tilde{p}_n}{\partial p_j}dp_j=-\int_{\tilde{p}_n(p_j^0)}^{\tilde{p}_n(p_j^1)}q_n^n\,dp_n. \tag{9.35}$$

2. The function $\tilde{\boldsymbol{p}}(p_j)$ can be determined in principle by solving the equations $q_n^n(\boldsymbol{w},\boldsymbol{p})=q_n^{n+1}(\boldsymbol{w},\boldsymbol{p})$, $n=1, \ldots, j-1, j+1, \ldots, N$, for $\boldsymbol{p}$ as a function of p_j and $\boldsymbol{w}$.
3. For more details concerning application of the envelope theorem, see Appendix Sections 4.A and 6.A.

This is clear because, with $n>j$, integration in (9.34) is along equilibrium quantities in market n as the supply curve (influenced by p_j) is shifted. It should be noted, however, that ΔC_n^* is not calculated with respect to the usual ordinary demand curve. It is, in fact, calculated according to the equilibrium demand curve, which accounts for adjustments in other industries within the sector (assuming that prices in other sectors of the economy are truly unaffected by such changes).

To interpret the remaining right-hand term of (9.34) when $n>j$, note that integration is along equilibrium quantities in market $n-1$ as input supply (influenced by p_j if $n-1>j$ or represented by p_j if $j=n-1$) is altered. Hence, the resulting integral represents the change in the area behind demand and above price in market $n-1$,

$$\Delta C_{n-1}^* = -\int_{p_j^0}^{p_j^1} q_{n-1}^n \frac{\partial \tilde{p}_{n-1}}{\partial p_j} dp_j = -\int_{\tilde{p}_{n-1}(p_j^0)}^{\tilde{p}_{n-1}(p_j^1)} q_{n-1}^n \, dp_{n-1}. \tag{9.36}$$

Again, the reader should bear in mind that the relevant demand curve for input q_{n-1} is a general equilibrium demand rather than an ordinary demand (in the same sense as above).

Substituting equations (9.35) and (9.36) into (9.34) implies that

$$\Delta R_n = \Delta C_{n-1}^* - \Delta C_n^*, \; n = j+1, \ldots, N, \tag{9.37}$$

or, upon solving these difference equations for ΔC_j^*,

$$\Delta C_j^* = \sum_{n=j+1}^{N} \Delta R_n + \Delta C_N, \tag{9.38}$$

where ΔC_N represents the change in final consumer surplus (associated with consumption of the sector's final product). Thus, the change in the 'consumer surplus' triangle in market j associated with an alteration in price p_j measures the sum of changes in final-product consumer surplus plus quasirents for all industries (related by imperfectly elastic demands) involved in transforming the commodity traded in market j into final consumption form.

Of course, the welfare significance of ΔR_n is the same as in Mishan. On the other hand, the term ΔC_N may hold welfare significance either in the context of final consumption (as in the context of Chapters 5, 6 and 7), or where some industry $N+1$ faces perfectly elastic demand for its output. In the latter case, ΔC_N measures merely the change in quasirent for that industry, and no further search (on the demand side) need be made for welfare effects of changing p_j.

Here it is interesting to note that the Schmalensee and Anderson results hold only in special cases. Anderson's derivation, assuming long-run competitive equilibrium (in which case $\Delta R_N = 0$), shows that $\Delta C_{N-1}^* = \Delta C_N$, so that consumer surplus can be measured in either the input or the output market. Schmalensee, on the other hand, assumed perfectly elastic input supply (that is, $j=N-1$) and found that $\Delta C_N + \Delta R_N = \Delta C_{N-1}^*$. Because this is the case where Mishan's results suggest that producer surplus in market N measures quasirent for industry N, equation (9.37) reduces to Schmalensee's result that the input market consumer surplus is equivalent to the sum of producer and consumer surpluses in the output market.

Producer Surplus in an Intermediate Market

To interpret the change in the triangle area behind supply and below price in an intermediate market j denoted by ΔP_j^*, consider the effect of a similar change in p_j on market n where $n \leq j$. In this case, demand rather than supply in market n is affected by the change, so integration in equation (9.34) is along equilibrium quantities supplied as demand (or output price if $j = n$) is altered. Hence,

$$\Delta P_n^* = \int_{p_j^0}^{p_j^1} q_n^n \frac{\partial \tilde{p}_n}{\partial p_j} dp_j = \int_{\tilde{p}_n(p_j^0)}^{\tilde{p}_n(p_j^1)} q_n^n dp_n,$$

and similarly for ΔP_{n-1}^*,

$$\Delta P_{n-1}^* = \int_{p_j^0}^{p_j^1} q_{n-1}^n \frac{\partial \tilde{p}_{n-1}}{\partial p_j} dp_j = \int_{\tilde{p}_{n-1}(p_j^0)}^{\tilde{p}_{n-1}(p_j^1)} q_{n-1}^n dp_{n-1},$$

which suggests that equation (9.34) can be rewritten as

$$\Delta R_n = \Delta P_n^* - \Delta P_{n-1}^*, \; n = 1, \ldots, j. \tag{9.39}$$

Solving the difference equation in (9.39), one finds that

$$\Delta P_j^* = \Delta P_0 + \sum_{n=1}^{j} \Delta R_n, \tag{9.40}$$

where ΔP_0 represents the change in the initial factor supplier's surplus. Thus, the change in the 'producer surplus' triangle in market j associated with a change in p_j measures the sum of the change in the initial factor supplier's surplus plus quasirents for all industries (related by imperfectly elastic supplies) involved in transforming the raw factor into the commodity at market level j.

Again, the welfare significance of ΔR_n is clear from Mishan (as in the context of Chapter 4). The welfare significance of ΔP_0, on the other hand, is clear from Chapter 7 in the case of a basic factor or again from Chapter 4 if there is an industry 0 facing perfectly elastic supply of *all* inputs. In the latter case, ΔP_0 measures simply the change in quasirent for industry 0, and no further search is needed (on the supply side) for welfare effects of changing p_j.

From the results in (9.37), (9.38), (9.39) and (9.40), the conclusions in Section 9.1 follow immediately. It is also a simple matter to extend this analysis to the case where distortions exist in some of the markets, but the procedure for doing so is similar to that presented in the following sections for the more general case, so no similar derivation is made here for the vertical market structure.

9.B GENERAL EQUILIBRIUM WELFARE MEASUREMENT

In this section the analysis is extended to consider the possibilities for measuring the net social welfare effects due to introduction (or alteration) of a single distortion where *all* other sectors or markets in the economy are possibly altered as a result. This subject has been examined somewhat heuristically by Harberger (1971). He argues on the basis of

Taylor series approximations to consumer surplus that all consumer effects can indeed be captured in a single market when no distortions exist in the rest of the economy. In the case where distortions exist elsewhere, he suggests that welfare effects in those markets must also be considered, although he does not make clear how this should be done.

In the development that follows, the Harberger thesis is brought more clearly into focus by developing the results rigorously without approximation (in the case of compensated consumer adjustments). It turns out that net private social welfare effects, as well as government effects, resulting directly from the new (or altered) distortion can be determined from equilibrium analysis in the market of interest. In some cases where existing distortions in the economy do not lead to market revenues or costs for government, the same results continue to hold (which is somewhat different from the implicit implications of Harberger's arguments). In any case, government effects directly associated with existing distortions in other markets must be considered, and in some cases private effects in other markets must also be considered.

Consider a competitive economy involving N goods, $q_1, \ldots, q_N$, including basic factors, intermediate good and final goods (some goods may simultaneously fall into more than one of these categories), with fixed tastes and preferences for consumers and fixed technology for producers. Suppose each of J consumers with utility function $U_j(\mathbf{c}_j)$ defined on respective personal consumption quantities $\mathbf{c}_j=(c_{ij},\ldots,c_{Nj})$,exogenous income $\bar{m}_j$, endowment vector $\mathbf{r}_j=(r_{ij},\ldots,r_{Nj})$ and common price vector $\mathbf{p}=(p_1,\ldots,p_N)$ seeks to maximize utility where U_j is strictly increasing, quasiconcave, and twice differentiable in $\mathbf{c}_j$. Alternatively, each of these J consumers may be viewed as minimizing exogenous expenditure required to attain a specific utility level $\bar{U}_j$, which, following Appendix Section 7.F, yields an expenditure function

$$\bar{e}_j(\mathbf{p},\bar{U}_j,\mathbf{r}_j)=\mathbf{p}\bar{\mathbf{q}}_j(\mathbf{p},\bar{U}_j,\mathbf{r}_j)=\Sigma_{n=1}^{N} p_n\bar{q}_{nj}(\mathbf{p},\bar{U}_j,\mathbf{r}_j)$$

such that $\bar{\mathbf{e}}_{j\mathbf{p}}\equiv\partial\bar{e}_j(\mathbf{p},\bar{U}_j,\mathbf{r}_j)/\partial\mathbf{p}=\bar{\mathbf{q}}_j(\mathbf{p},\bar{U}_j,\mathbf{r}_j)$ where $\bar{q}_{nj}(\mathbf{p},\bar{U}_j,\mathbf{r}_j)>0$ represents compensated demand and $\bar{q}_{nj}(\mathbf{p},\bar{U}_j,\mathbf{r}_j)<0$ represents compensated factor supply of good n by consumer j. Any household production activity is assumed to be included implicitly in this representation (that is, the market transactions related to household production, denoted by $\mathbf{x}$ in Appendix Section 7.G, are included in the consumption vector, $\mathbf{c}$) following results in Appendix Section 7.G so that the market transaction vector is represented simply by $\mathbf{q}=\mathbf{c}-\mathbf{r}$. If endowments are zero, then consumption quantities and market transaction quantities coincide, $\mathbf{c}=\mathbf{q}$, and $\bar{m}_j$ can represent ordinary income as in the Appendix to Chapter 6.

Suppose each of the K firms uses any subset of the N goods to produce any other subset of the N goods following an implicit production function $f_k(\mathbf{q}_k)=\mathbf{0}$ satisfying the properties assumed in Appendix Sections 4.A and 8.B, where $\mathbf{q}_k=(q_{1k},\ldots,q_{Nk})$ and each individual argument q_{nk} represents the net amount of good n produced by firm k (if $q_{nk}>0$) or the net amount of good n used as a factor input (if $q_{nk}<0$).[4] Following the results in Appendix Section 4.A, competitive maximization of profit subject to the production

4. Again, as in Appendix Section 8.B, the technology is written in implicit form for convenience because some elements of $\mathbf{q}_k$ are outputs and others are inputs. Alternatively and more generally, the production technology can be represented simply by $\mathbf{q}_k\equiv(q_{1k},\ldots,q_{Nk})\in T$, where T is a closed convex technology set. The results below can be generalized accordingly.

function and any fixed inputs (not represented explicitly) leads to a restricted profit or quasirent function R_k,

$$R_k(\boldsymbol{p}) = \boldsymbol{p}\hat{\boldsymbol{q}}_k(\boldsymbol{p}) = \Sigma_{n=1}^{N} p_n \hat{q}_{nk}(\boldsymbol{p})$$

such that $\boldsymbol{R}_{\boldsymbol{kp}} \equiv \partial R_k(\boldsymbol{p})/\partial \boldsymbol{p} = \hat{\boldsymbol{q}}_k(\boldsymbol{p})$ where $\hat{q}_{nk}(\boldsymbol{p}) > 0$ represents net output supply and $\hat{q}_{nk}(\boldsymbol{p}) < 0$ represents net input demand of good n by firm k.

Now consider the introduction of a distortion φ in market m. Depending on the type of distortion introduced, define φ as the size of the *ad valorem* tax, size of the subsidy, level of the price ceiling, level of the price floor, or so on. In the case of quotas and price controls not enforced by government buy/sell activities, assume that some *efficient rationing* procedure is employed so that those actually involved in the market transactions that take place are those willing to pay more or those willing to sell for less than those who are not. Now let the general equilibrium response of market price p_n, taking into account general equilibrium adjustments in all other markets, be represented by a differentiable function $\tilde{p}_n(\varphi)$, thus specifying price p_n as a function of the distortion in market m, $n = 1, \ldots, N$, $n \neq m$. In the case of market m, it is necessary to specify two prices. Let $p_m^s(\varphi)$ be a differentiable function specifying the price associated with marginal behavior of suppliers (for example, the price excluding tax or the supply price that would lead to the same quantity supplied in the absence of a quota), and let $p_m^d(\varphi)$ be a differentiable function specifying the price associated with marginal behavior of demanders (for example, the price including tax, and so on). Specifically, define *supply price* $p_m^s(\varphi)$ and *demand price* $p_m^d(\varphi)$ as those prices which, together with prices $\tilde{p}_n(\varphi)$, $n = 1, \ldots, N$, $n \neq$ m, lead to the same compensated equilibrium quantities supplied and demanded without distortions as are obtained in the distorted economy.[5] Of course, in other markets, which are not distorted, no such divergence in effective supply and demand prices occurs.

The existence of these two prices in market m in the case with an *ad valorem* tax or subsidy is obvious. Supply prices exclude taxes and include subsidies, whereas demand prices include taxes and exclude subsidies. Similarly, in the case of monopoly, the demand price is the market price, whereas the price associated with the marginal behavior of the producing firm is its marginal cost (see Section 10.1). Or in the case of monopsony, the supply price is the market price, whereas the price associated with the marginal behavior of the buyer is his or her marginal revenue of product (see Section 10.2).[6]

Finally, consider the case of a quota on sales or a price floor where the rationing system limits the amount that each individual can sell or, alternatively, a quota on purchases or a price ceiling where the rationing system limits the amount of the good individuals can buy. Specifically, where $q_{mk} = \hat{q}_{mk}$ is the effective limitation placed on the supply or demand of good m by firm k, the profit-maximization problem is

5. For the intuition and graphical version of these concepts of prices, see Section 9.3.
6. Generalizing this analysis to the case of dominant share price leadership oligopoly (Section 10.3) implies that the marginal behavior of all producers except those in the dominant share is also associated with the market price, whereas only the behavior of firms in the dominant share is related to their marginal cost. Or in the case of dominant-share price leadership oligopsony, the demand price for all buyers except those in the dominant share is the market price, whereas the marginal behavior of firms in the dominant share is associated with their marginal revenue of product. Although these generalizations and other noncompetitive behavior are not considered explicitly below to avoid complication in notation, they can be easily accommodated.

$$R_k^*(\boldsymbol{p},\hat{q}_{mk}) = \max_{\boldsymbol{q}_k} \{\boldsymbol{p}\boldsymbol{q}_k | \boldsymbol{f}_k(\boldsymbol{q}_k) = \boldsymbol{0},\, q_{mk} = \hat{q}_{mk}\}.$$

The associated Lagrangian is

$$\mathcal{L} = \boldsymbol{p}\boldsymbol{q}_k - \boldsymbol{\lambda}_k \boldsymbol{f}_k(\boldsymbol{q}_k) - \zeta_{mk}(q_{mk} - \hat{q}_{mk}),$$

for which first-order conditions for maximization include

$$\frac{\partial \mathcal{L}}{\partial q_{nk}} = p_n - \boldsymbol{\lambda}_k \frac{\partial \boldsymbol{f}_k}{\partial q_{nk}} = 0,\ n = 1, \ldots, N,\ n \neq m,$$

$$\frac{\partial \mathcal{L}}{\partial q_{mk}} = p_m - \boldsymbol{\lambda}_k \frac{\partial \boldsymbol{f}_k}{\partial q_{mk}} - \hat{\zeta}_{mk} = 0.$$

Comparing these conditions with the corresponding first-order conditions in the absence of the limitation, that is,

$$p_n - \boldsymbol{\lambda}_k \frac{\partial \boldsymbol{f}_k}{\partial q_{nk}} = 0,\ n = 1, \ldots, N,$$

reveals that constrained profit maximization with prices $\boldsymbol{p} = (p_1,\ldots,p_N)$ leads to the same quantities supplied and demanded as the unconstrained profit maximization problem with prices $\hat{\boldsymbol{p}}_k = (p_1,\ldots,p_{m-1},p_m - \hat{\zeta}_{mk},p_{m+1},\ldots,p_N)$, which implies $R_k^*(\boldsymbol{p},\hat{q}_{mk}) = R_k(\hat{\boldsymbol{p}}_k)$. Thus, the good m supply or demand price, as the case may be, for firm k is $p_m - \hat{\zeta}_{mk}$, which obviously exists under standard assumptions if $q_{mk} = \hat{q}_{mk}$ is within the feasible technology.

Similarly, where $q_{mj} = \bar{q}_{mj}$ is the effective limitation placed on demand or supply of good m by consumer j, the expenditure minimization problem is

$$\bar{e}_j^*(\boldsymbol{p},\bar{U}_j,\boldsymbol{r}_j,\bar{q}_{mj}) = \min_{\boldsymbol{q}_j} \{\boldsymbol{p}\boldsymbol{q}_j | U_j(\boldsymbol{q}_j) = \bar{U}_j,\, q_{mj} = \bar{q}_{mj}\}.$$

The associated Lagrangian,

$$\mathcal{L} = \boldsymbol{p}\boldsymbol{q}_j - \lambda_j(U_j - \bar{U}_j) - \zeta_{mj}(q_{mj} - \bar{q}_{mj}),$$

has first-order conditions including

$$\frac{\partial \mathcal{L}}{\partial q_{nj}} = p_n - \lambda_j \frac{\partial U_j}{\partial q_{nj}} = 0,\ n = 1, \ldots, N,\ n \neq m,$$

$$\frac{\partial \mathcal{L}}{\partial q_{mk}} = p_m - \lambda_j \frac{\partial U_j}{\partial q_{mj}} - \bar{\zeta}_{mj} = 0.$$

Comparing these conditions with the corresponding problem in the absence of the limitation, which has first-order conditions,

$$p_n - \lambda_j \frac{\partial U_j}{\partial q_{nj}} = 0,\ n = 1, \ldots, N,$$

verifies that prices $\tilde{\boldsymbol{p}}_j = (p_1,\ldots,p_{m-1},p_m - \bar{\zeta}_{mj},p_{m+1},\ldots,p_N)$ in the absence of the limitation lead to the same expenditure and thus compensated quantities supplied and demanded as prices in the presence of the limitation, for example, $\bar{e}_j^*(\boldsymbol{p},\bar{U}_j,\boldsymbol{r}_j,\bar{q}_{mj}) = \bar{e}_j(\tilde{\boldsymbol{p}}_j,\bar{U}_j,\boldsymbol{r}_j)$. Thus, the good m supply or demand price (depending on whether $\bar{q}_{mj}<0$ or $\bar{q}_{mj}>0$, respectively) for consumer j is $p_m - \bar{\zeta}_{mj}$ which obviously exists under standard assumptions if $q_{mk} = \bar{q}_{mk}$ is feasible for the consumer, for example, does not require sale of more of an endowment than the consumer holds.

For the following analysis, any quota or rationing system associated with a price ceiling or floor is assumed to be imposed or altered with *efficient rationing* in the sense that $\hat{\zeta}_{mk} = \bar{\zeta}_{mj} = \zeta^s$ for all producers with $\hat{q}_{mk}>0$ and all consumers with $\bar{q}_{mj}<0$ (that is, for all net sellers of good m) or, alternatively, that $\hat{\zeta}_{mk} = \bar{\zeta}_{mj} = \zeta^d$ for all producers with $\hat{q}_{mk}<0$ and all consumers with $\bar{q}_{mj}>0$ (that is, for all net buyers of good m). Thus, with competition, the supply price in market m is $p_m - \zeta^s$, and the demand price in market m is $p_m - \zeta^d$.These assumptions ensure that those actually involved in market transactions have equal marginal willingness to pay or marginal willingness to sell because $\hat{\zeta}_{mk}$ and $\bar{\zeta}_{mj}$ represent such marginal values. One might note that this assumption of efficiency in the allocation of a market distortion can be relaxed by retaining individualized supply and demand prices, but any associated empirical work must also be individualized in so doing.

The Equilibrium Welfare Effects of Introducing a Single Distortion

Having verified the existence of the supply and demand price concepts defined above for a variety of common distortions, the general equilibrium effect of marginally changing the distortion φ (for example, from the free-market level) on each individual firm or consumer can be determined by substituting $\hat{\boldsymbol{p}}_k$ for $\boldsymbol{p}$ in $R_k(\boldsymbol{p})$ and $\tilde{\boldsymbol{p}}_j$ for $\boldsymbol{p}$ in $\bar{e}_j(\boldsymbol{p},\bar{U}_j,\boldsymbol{r}_j)$, respectively, and then differentiating with respect to φ,

$$\frac{dR_k}{d\varphi} = \sum_{n=1}^{N} \frac{\partial R_k}{\partial \hat{p}_{nk}} \frac{\partial \hat{p}_{nk}}{\partial \varphi} = \sum_{n=1}^{N} \hat{q}_{nk}(\hat{\boldsymbol{p}}_k) \frac{\partial \hat{p}_{nk}}{\partial \varphi}, \tag{9.41}$$

$$\frac{d\bar{e}_j}{d\varphi} = \sum_{n=1}^{N} \frac{\partial \bar{e}_j}{\partial \tilde{p}_{nj}} \frac{\partial \tilde{p}_{nj}}{\partial \varphi} = \sum_{n=1}^{N} \bar{q}_{nj}(\tilde{\boldsymbol{p}}_j,\bar{U}_j,\boldsymbol{r}_j) \frac{\partial \tilde{p}_{nj}}{\partial \varphi}, \tag{9.42}$$

where for notational simplicity, $\hat{\boldsymbol{p}}_k = (\hat{p}_{1k},\ldots,\hat{p}_{Nk})$ and $\tilde{\boldsymbol{p}}_j = (\tilde{p}_{1k},\ldots,\tilde{p}_{Nk})$. Now suppose $\hat{p}_{mk} = \tilde{p}_{mj} = p_m^s(\varphi)$ for each firm k that sells good m ($\hat{q}_{mk}>0$) and each consumer j who supplies good m ($\bar{q}_{mj}<0$), and $\hat{p}_{mk} = \tilde{p}_{mj} = p_m^d(\varphi)$ for each firm k that buys good m ($\hat{q}_{mk}<0$) and each consumer j who buys good m ($\bar{q}_{mj}>0$), while $\hat{p}_{nk} = \tilde{p}_{nj} = \bar{p}_n(\varphi)$ for $n \neq m$.[7] Where φ_0 represents the level of the distortion corresponding to a free market (for example, $\varphi_0 = 0$ in the case where φ_0 is an *ad valorem* tax) and where φ_1 is the level of the distortion to be introduced, the effect of the distortion can be determined by integration of (9.41) and (9.42),

$$\Delta R_k = \int_{\varphi_0}^{\varphi_1} \sum_{n=1}^{N} \hat{q}_{nk}(\hat{\boldsymbol{p}}_k) \frac{\partial \hat{p}_{nk}}{\partial \varphi} \, d\varphi \tag{9.43}$$

7. This definition of $\hat{p}_{mk}$ and $\tilde{p}_{mj}$ may lead to a discontinuity in individual firm or consumer supplies and demands such that a marginal change in φ induces a switch from net buying to net selling, or vice versa. Nevertheless, practical examples of such cases are rare and, furthermore, in a large economy with essentially continuous income and production efficiency distributions among individuals, such a switch at the individual level is without substantive implication for the (competitive) market level of analysis. To be technically correct for all types of distortions, however, assume that production and utility functions are such that compensated changes never induce net buyers to become net sellers, or vice versa.

$$\Delta\bar{e}_j = \int_{\varphi_0}^{\varphi_1} \sum_{n=1}^{N} \bar{q}_{nj}(\tilde{p}_j, \bar{U}_j, r_j) \frac{\partial \tilde{p}_{nj}}{\partial \varphi} d\varphi. \qquad (9.44)$$

In the latter case, $\Delta\bar{e}_j$ represents the negative of the compensating or equivalent variation for consumer j, depending on whether $\bar{U}_j$ is defined as the equilibrium utility level of consumer j before or after the introduction of the distortion.

To determine the net social welfare effects ΔW of the new distortion, the individual welfare effects in (9.43) and (9.44) can be aggregated over all individuals and added to the difference in purchases and sales in market m that accrues to either producers, consumers or government, depending on the type of distortion,

$$\Delta W = \sum_{k=1}^{K} \Delta R_k - \sum_{j=1}^{J} \Delta\bar{e}_j + \Delta T_m \qquad (9.45)$$

$$= \sum_{n=1}^{N} \int_{\varphi_0}^{\varphi_1} \left[\sum_{k=1}^{K} \hat{q}_{nk} \frac{\partial \hat{p}_{nk}}{\partial \varphi} - \sum_{j=1}^{J} \bar{q}_{nj} \frac{\partial \tilde{p}_{nj}}{\partial \varphi} \right] d\varphi + \Delta T_m,$$

where

$$\Delta T_m = p_m^d(\varphi^1) q_m^d(\varphi^1) - p_m^s(\varphi^1) q_m^s(\varphi^1) - p_m^d(\varphi^0) q_m^d(\varphi^0) + p_m^s(\varphi^0) q_m^s(\varphi^0),$$

the equilibrium quantities (supplies and demands, respectively) are given by

$$q_m^s = \sum_{\substack{k=1 \\ \hat{q}_{mk}>0}}^{K} \hat{q}_{mk} - \sum_{\substack{j=1 \\ \bar{q}_{mj}<0}}^{J} \bar{q}_{mj}, \qquad (9.46)$$

$$q_m^d = \sum_{\substack{j=1 \\ \bar{q}_{mj}>0}}^{J} \bar{q}_{mj} - \sum_{\substack{k=1 \\ \hat{q}_{mk}<0}}^{K} \hat{q}_{mk}, \qquad (9.47)$$

and the arguments φ^0 and φ^1 in each case denote compensated equilibrium prices or quantities before or after alteration of the distortion in market m, respectively. Note that ΔT_m represents the change in buyer expenditures less seller receipts (evaluated at demand and supply prices as defined above) with the change in distortion. Some group in the economy (consumers, producers or government) must receive (give up, if negative) this change, as becomes clear below. For example, it may represent a government tax revenue, subsidy expense, or receipts less expenditures of a public buffer stock activity.

Changing variables of integration in (9.45) implies that[8]

$$\int_{\varphi_0}^{\varphi_1} \left[\sum_{k=1}^{K} \hat{q}_{nk} \frac{\partial \hat{p}_{nk}}{\partial \varphi} - \sum_{j=1}^{J} \bar{q}_{nj} \frac{\partial \tilde{p}_{nj}}{\partial \varphi} \right] d\varphi = \int_{\varphi_0}^{\varphi_1} \left[\sum_{k=1}^{K} \hat{q}_{nk} - \sum_{j=1}^{J} \bar{q}_{nj} \right] \frac{\partial \tilde{p}_n}{\partial \varphi} d\varphi$$

$$= \int_{\tilde{p}_n(\varphi^0)}^{\tilde{p}_n(\varphi^1)} \left[\sum_{k=1}^{K} \hat{q}_{nk} - \sum_{j=1}^{J} \bar{q}_{nj} \right] dp_n = 0, \qquad (9.48)$$

$$n = 1, \ldots, N, n \neq m,$$

8. The reader should bear in mind that the right-hand side of equation (9.48) is a line integral rather than a definite integral. The associated details of the mathematics are thus rather subtle as treated here. For a more detailed proof of (9.48), see Bullock (1993a).

because $\Sigma_{k=1}^{K} \hat{q}_{nk} - \Sigma_{j=1}^{J} \bar{q}_{nj}$ simply represents the equilibrium sum of all supplies less the equilibrium sum of all demands at a particular set of prices. The sum must be zero in equilibrium. In the case of market m, on the other hand, one finds that

$$\int_{\varphi_0}^{\varphi_1} \left[\sum_{k=1}^{K} \hat{q}_{mk} \frac{\partial \hat{p}_{mk}}{\partial \varphi} - \sum_{j=1}^{J} \bar{q}_{mj} \frac{\partial \tilde{p}_{mj}}{\partial \varphi} \right] d\varphi = \int_{\varphi_0}^{\varphi_1} \left[q_m^s \frac{\partial p_m^s}{\partial \varphi} - q_m^d \frac{\partial p_m^d}{\partial \varphi} \right] d\varphi$$

$$= \int_{p_m^s(\varphi_0)}^{p_m^s(\varphi_1)} q_m^s dp_m^s - \int_{p_m^d(\varphi_0)}^{p_m^d(\varphi_1)} q_m^d dp_m^d \qquad (9.49)$$

$$= \Delta P_m^* + \Delta C_m^*,$$

where ΔP_m^* and ΔC_m^* are the changes in producer and consumer surplus associated, respectively, with the general equilibrium supply and demand prices.

In addition, one must consider ΔT_m, which is the change in receipts minus expenditures, where receipts are calculated at the supply price and expenditures are calculated at the demand price. Specifically, ΔT_m is the change in tax revenues, subsidy expenditure, producer quasirent, or consumer expenditure not reflected by the supply and demand prices. Thus, from (9.45), (9.48) and (9.49), the total social welfare effects of a change in φ are captured completely in the distorted market by computing surpluses associated with equilibrium supply and demand curves in the distorted market that account for all associated price adjustments in the rest of the economy. The results discussed graphically in Section 9.3 thus follow immediately. From these results, it is also clear that the appropriate compensated general equilibrium curves for use in economic welfare calculations depend on the form of distortion only through its influence on the demand and supply prices.

Equilibrium Effects of a Distortion in an Otherwise Distorted Economy

The foregoing results are not of sufficient generality for practical purposes because one is not likely to encounter a problem where an economy is free of any distortions beyond the one for which change is considered. To carry the analysis to a practical level, consider the case where distortions possibly exist throughout the economy. That is, suppose that a distortion exists in principle in each market n (although possibly at a noneffective level) and can be represented by a scalar parameter φ_n, $n = 1, \ldots, N$. Also, suppose that a unique set of equilibrium prices is associated with each choice of distortions, $\boldsymbol{\varphi} = (\varphi_1,\ldots,\varphi_N)$, for each given distribution of exogenous income. That is, suppose that the supply price associated with the marginal behavior of suppliers in each market n is denoted by $p_n^s(\boldsymbol{\varphi})$ and suppose that the demand price associated with the marginal behavior of demanders in each market n is denoted by $p_n^d(\boldsymbol{\varphi})$, where both p_n^s and p_n^d are differentiable in $\boldsymbol{\varphi}$. One can demonstrate existence of such prices in the presence of several distortions following the same arguments as used above in the case where a single distortion was introduced.

Following the notation described above, one has

$$R_k(\hat{\mathbf{p}}_k) = \sum_{n=1}^{N} \hat{p}_{nk} \hat{q}_{nk}(\hat{\mathbf{p}}_k),$$

$$\bar{e}_j(\tilde{\mathbf{p}}_j, \bar{U}_j, \mathbf{r}_j) = \sum_{n=1}^{N} \tilde{p}_{nj}\bar{q}_{nj}(\tilde{\mathbf{p}}_j, \bar{U}_j, \mathbf{r}_j),$$

where $\hat{p}_{nk} = \tilde{p}_{nj} = p_n^s(\boldsymbol{\varphi})$ for each firm k and consumer j that is a net seller of good n and $\hat{p}_{nk} = \tilde{p}_{nj} = p_n^d(\boldsymbol{\varphi})$ for each firm k and consumer j that is a net buyer of good n. These definitions again presuppose efficient rationing in the case of quotas, price ceilings and price floors, so that the demanders (suppliers) gaining access to markets are those willing to pay more (receive less) at the margin than those who do not.[9]

Now suppose that the distortion in market m is altered from φ_m^0 to φ_m^1 while all other distortions remain unchanged. One finds in place of (9.41) and (9.42) that

$$\frac{\partial R_k}{\partial \varphi_m} = \sum_{n=1}^{N} \hat{q}_{nk} \frac{\partial \hat{p}_{nk}}{\partial \varphi_m}$$

$$\frac{\partial \bar{e}_j}{\partial \varphi_m} = \sum_{n=1}^{N} \bar{q}_{nj} \frac{\partial \tilde{p}_{nj}}{\partial \varphi_m}.$$

Hence, in place of (9.45) one finds a net social welfare effect,

$$\begin{aligned} \Delta W &= \sum_{k=1}^{K} \Delta R_k - \sum_{j=1}^{J} \Delta \bar{e}_j + \sum_{n=1}^{N} \Delta T_n \\ &= \int_{\varphi_m^0}^{\varphi_m^1} \left[\sum_{k=1}^{K} \frac{\partial R_k}{\partial \varphi_m} - \sum_{j=1}^{J} \frac{\partial \bar{e}_j}{\partial \varphi_m} \right] d\varphi_m + \sum_{n=1}^{N} \Delta T_n \\ &= \sum_{n=1}^{N} \int_{\varphi_m^0}^{\varphi_m^1} \left[q_n^s \frac{\partial p_n^s}{\partial \varphi_m} - q_n^d \frac{\partial p_n^d}{\partial \varphi_m} \right] d\varphi_m + \sum_{n=1}^{N} \Delta T_n \end{aligned} \tag{9.50}$$

where ΔT_n is a transfer effect associated with market n similar to the case of market m in (9.45),

$$\Delta T_n = p_n^d(\boldsymbol{\varphi}^1)q_n^d(\boldsymbol{\varphi}^1) - p_n^s(\boldsymbol{\varphi}^1)q_n^s(\boldsymbol{\varphi}^1) - p_n^d(\boldsymbol{\varphi}^0)q_n^d(\boldsymbol{\varphi}^0) + p_n^s(\boldsymbol{\varphi}^0)q_n^s(\boldsymbol{\varphi}^0),$$

but now $\boldsymbol{\varphi}^0 = (\varphi_1, \ldots, \varphi_{m-1}, \varphi_m^0, \varphi_{m+1}, \ldots, \varphi_N)$ and $\boldsymbol{\varphi}^1 = (\varphi_1, \ldots, \varphi_{m-1}, \varphi_m^1, \varphi_{m+1}, \ldots, \varphi_N)$. Note that q_n^s and q_n^d are defined as in (9.46) and (9.47) but now apply for each market n. The arguments $\boldsymbol{\varphi}^0$ and $\boldsymbol{\varphi}^1$ again determine compensated equilibrium prices or quantities in market n before or after alteration of the distortion, respectively. Specifically, ΔT_n measures the changes in receipts minus expenditures in market n, where receipts are evaluated at supply prices and expenditures are evaluated at demand prices.

The result in (9.50) can be interpreted by considering the type of distortion that exists in each market. Consider the effect

9. This assumption can be easily relaxed with respect to distortions for which changes are not considered if any inefficiency in rationing can be represented by constraints imposed on individual decision-makers. That is, individualized market access or market quotas can be represented by vectors of parameters which pertain to individual consumers or producers. Supplies, demands, quasirent functions and expenditure functions of individuals then depend on these additional vectors of parameters. If they are unchanged, however, all the results below continue to hold. The assumption of efficient rationing with a quota or price control for which change is considered can also be relaxed, but only with considerable empirical detail, as discussed earlier.

$$\Delta\tilde{S}_n = \int_{\varphi_m^0}^{\varphi_m^1} \left[q_n^s \frac{\partial p_n^s}{\partial \varphi_m} - q_n^d \frac{\partial p_n^d}{\partial \varphi_m} \right] d\varphi_m \tag{9.51}$$

in each market n of changing φ_m from φ_m^0 to φ_m^1, $n \neq m$. If distortions in any market n, $n \neq m$, are not effective, equilibrium prevails in that market, meaning that $q_n^s = q_n^d$ and $p_n^s = p_n^d = p_n$, so that $\partial p_n^s / \partial \varphi_m = \partial p_n^d / d\varphi_m = \partial p_n / d\varphi_m$ and hence

$$\Delta\tilde{S}n = \int_{\varphi_m^0}^{\varphi_m^1} (q_n^s - q_n^d) \frac{\partial p_n}{\partial \varphi_m} d\varphi_m = 0 \tag{9.52}$$

because market n attains equilibrium for each level of the distortion in market m. Note that $\Delta T_n = 0$ in this case. Thus, effects in nondistorted markets are completely captured by equilibrium measurements only in distorted markets.[10]

Next, consider the case where an *ad valorem* tax exists at an effective level in market n. Then $p_n^d = p_n^s + t_n$, where t_n is the tax rate and equilibrium prevails in the presence of the tax in the sense that $q_n^s = q_n^d$. Hence, $\partial p_n^s / \partial \varphi_m = \partial p_n^d / d\varphi_m$ if the tax rate remains fixed, so that (9.52) continues to apply. From this result, one finds that private welfare effects can be captured completely without explicit measurements in markets with taxes. However, one must note that government tax revenues in such a market increase (decrease, if negative) by

$$\Delta T_n = [q_n^s(\varphi^1) - q_n^s(\varphi^0)]t_n = [q_n^d(\varphi^1) - q_n^d(\varphi^0)]t_n.$$

Thus, whereas estimation of supply and demand in a market distorted by a tax (that does not change) is not necessary for measuring *private* welfare effects, some means of estimating the change in tax revenues is needed for measuring *social* welfare effects. One means of the latter is estimation of the effects on supply and demand in such a market.[11]

The case where a subsidy is distorting market n can be investigated similarly. In this case, $p_n^d + s_n = p_n^s$ and $q_n^s = q_n^d$ for each φ_m, where s_n is a subsidy paid by government per unit of sales in market n. Again, (9.52) applies, so *private* welfare effects are completely captured without explicit measurement in markets distorted by subsidies (for which rates do not change). However, government costs decrease (increase, if negative) by

$$\Delta T_n = [q_n^s(\varphi^0) - q_n^s(\varphi^1)]s_n = [q_n^d(\varphi^0) - q_n^d(\varphi^1)]s_n.$$

Again, one means of estimating this effect is to estimate the effects on supply and demand in market n of changing φ_m.

Consider next the case where market n is distorted by the imposition of an effective quota on sales or purchases. If such a quota does not change as φ_m changes, then q_n^s and q_n^d do not change. Hence, $\Delta\tilde{S}_n$ in (9.51) becomes

$$\Delta\tilde{S}_n = [p_n^s(\varphi^1) - p_n^s(\varphi^0)]q_n^s - [p_n^d(\varphi^1) - p_n^d(\varphi^0)]q_n^d.$$

10. This result was developed by Harberger (1971). He argued essentially that explicit measurements are required only in distorted markets. The results below carry these considerations somewhat further by determining what special considerations are needed depending on the type of distortion.
11. For empirical purposes, however, because one need measure only the effects of φ_m on the equilibrium quantity in market n, estimation of a reduced-form equation describing equilibrium quantity suffices in lieu of estimation of both supply and demand in market n.

However, because $q_n^s = q_n^d$ with a quota, one finds that $\Delta\tilde{S}_n = -\Delta T_n$, so welfare effects on participants in markets with quotas are completely captured in markets with other types of distortions. Thus, no explicit measurements are required in markets distorted by unchanged quotas to evaluate the overall social welfare change associated with altering a distortion elsewhere.

Another distortion, of particular interest in stabilization problems, is the case where a given price level is enforced by means of a buffer stock adjustment. If such an enforced price level does not change as φ_m is changed, then p_n^s and p_n^d are constant, so $\partial p_n^s/\partial\varphi_m = \partial p_n^d/\partial\varphi_m = 0$. Hence, from (9.51), $\Delta\tilde{S}_n = 0$. However,

$$\Delta T_n = [q_n^s(\varphi^0) - q_n^s(\varphi^1) + q_n^d(\varphi^1) - q_n^d(\varphi^0)]p_n,$$

which represents a net cash transaction by government in altering the buffer stock level where $p_n = p_n^s = p_n^d$. Thus, as in the case with taxes and subsidies, estimation of supply and demand in a market distorted by a government buffer stock activity is not necessary in evaluating the *private* welfare effects of altering some other distortion. However, some means of estimating quantity responses in markets distorted by government buffer stocks is necessary to evaluate the government and overall social welfare effect of any change in some other distortion.

Next, consider the case where market n has a government-imposed price floor with an efficient rationing mechanism. If the price floor does not change as φ_m changes, then $\partial p_n^d/\partial\varphi_m = 0$. Hence, $\Delta\tilde{S}_n$ in (9.51) becomes

$$\Delta\tilde{S}_n = \int_{\varphi_m^0}^{\varphi_m^1} q_n^s \frac{\partial p_n^s}{\partial\varphi_m}\, d\varphi_m = \int_{p_n^s(\varphi^0)}^{p_n^s(\varphi^1)} q_n^s\, dp_n.$$

Also, in this case, producers additionally gain

$$\Delta T_n = [p_n^d - p_n^s(\varphi^1)]q_n(\varphi^1) - [p_n^d - p_n^s(\varphi^0)]q_n(\varphi^0),$$

where $q_n(\varphi^i) = q_n^s(\varphi^i) = q_n^d(\varphi^i)$, $i = 0, 1$. The evaluation of these two effects requires measurement of the response of both equilibrium supply and demand in market n to changes in φ_m.

Similarly, in the case of a price ceiling with an efficient rationing mechanism, one has $\partial p_n^s/\partial\varphi_m = 0$ if the price ceiling is not changed as φ_m changes. Hence,

$$\Delta\tilde{S}_n = -\int_{p_n^d(\varphi^0)}^{p_n^d(\varphi^1)} q_n^d\, dp_n,$$

and consumers additionally gain

$$\Delta T_n = [p_n^s - p_n^d(\varphi^0)]q_n(\varphi^0) - [p_n^s - p_n^d(\varphi^1)]q_n(\varphi^1).$$

Again, measurement of the response of both equilibrium supply and equilibrium demand in market n to changes in φ_m is required for equilibrium social welfare analysis.

Finally, consider the case where the distortion in market n is due to market power. This case also requires explicit measurement of both equilibrium supply and equilibrium demand in market n, where the equilibrium supply and demand are defined as those that would occur with competitive behavior (for example, equilibrium supply is the equilibrium marginal cost in the case of monopoly). One finds in this case that

$$\Delta\tilde{S}_n = \int_{p_n^S(\varphi^0)}^{p_n^S(\varphi^1)} q_n^s \, dp_n - \int_{p_n^d(\varphi^0)}^{p_n^d(\varphi^1)} q_n^d \, dp_n,$$

where those exercising market power additionally gain

$$\Delta T_n = [p_n^s(\varphi^0) - p_n^d(\varphi^0)]q_n(\varphi^0) - [p_n^s(\varphi^1) - p_n^d(\varphi^1)]q_n(\varphi^1).$$

Thus, in the case of market power distortions, measurement of both equilibrium demand and equilibrium supply responses to changes in φ_m is necessary in calculating social welfare effects.

Having determined the measurements that are necessary in all markets except market m as the distortion in market m is altered, it remains to consider the necessary measurements in market m. For this case, one finds, using the notation in (9.51), that

$$\Delta\tilde{S}_m = \int_{p_m^s(\varphi^0)}^{p_m^s(\varphi^1)} q_m^s dp_m - \int_{p_m^d(\varphi^0)}^{p_m^d(\varphi^1)} q_m^d dp_m.$$

In addition, ΔT_m must be considered, which leads to the same graphical results for the market in which the distortion is changed, as described graphically in Section 9.3 and specifically in Figure 9.6.

With these results, a general equilibrium welfare methodology emerges for which the major limitation is simply the ability to measure equilibrium relationships empirically. However, some results for one further particular case are of interest in view of practical empirical possibilities.

The Case of an Open Economy

The results thus far require nondistorted markets to have aggregate supply equal to aggregate demand in equilibrium. As a consequence, the results apply only to the case of a closed economy, which applies either to measurement of welfare in a country with no trade, or measurement of world welfare.[12] For an open economy, aggregate demand exceeds aggregate supply by excess demand for imported goods and aggregate supply exceeds aggregate demand by excess supply for exported goods. To use equilibrium techniques to capture equilibrium welfare effects for an open economy, markets for traded goods where aggregate demand is not equal to aggregate supply require additional welfare considerations as in the case of other distorted markets.

To extend the results to the case of a small open economy, markets for traded goods can be analyzed beginning with the framework of equation (9.50). If no market has existing distortions other than market m in which a new distortion is to be introduced, then each term in the first right-hand summation of equation (9.50) follows (9.51). For nontraded goods, market equilibrium equates aggregate supply and aggregate demand, $q_n^s = q_n^d$ with $p_n^s = p_n^d = p_n$, so that (9.52) follows as for the nondistorted markets above. On the other hand, the prices of traded goods in a small open economy are fixed by external

12. While this point is clear implicitly, Bullock (1993a) makes this point explicitly.

conditions and do not respond to internal changes in the economy. This is, indeed, the meaning of 'small'. Thus, $\partial p_n^d/\partial\varphi_m = \partial p_n^s/\partial\varphi_m = 0$ where $\bar{p}_n = p_n^s = p_n^d$ is the world price of good n, in which case (9.51) implies $\Delta\tilde{S}_n = 0$. Thus, the first right-hand term of (9.50) reduces to consideration of $\Delta\tilde{S}_m$ alone, which can be calculated using only equilibrium relationships from the market where the distortion is introduced. To this amount must be added the transfer effect, which for nontraded goods is zero as in the case of nondistorted markets above, and for traded goods becomes

$$\Delta T_n = [q_n^d(\boldsymbol{\varphi}^1) - q_n^s(\boldsymbol{\varphi}^1) - q_n^d(\boldsymbol{\varphi}^0) + q_n^s(\boldsymbol{\varphi}^0)]\bar{p}_n.$$

Adding this transfer effect over all traded goods obtains the reduction in the aggregate trade deficit (which represents an increase if negative). The resulting implication is that the aggregate welfare effects of altering a distortion in a single market in a small open economy is completely captured using standard surplus analysis with equilibrium supply and demand in that market alone, aside from considering the additional effect of altering that distortion on the aggregate trade balance. In the case of a small open economy with balanced trade, even this aggregate trade balance effect can be safely ignored.[13]

The case of a large open economy requires a more general approach considering changes in both quantities and prices in the traded markets. That is, the additional welfare quantities in equation (9.51) simplify to

$$\Delta\tilde{S}_n = \int_{\varphi_m^0}^{\varphi_m^1} (q_n^s - q_n^d)\frac{\partial p_n^d}{\partial\varphi_m}\, d\varphi_m$$

as in (9.52) but are not zero. Again, the transfer effects simplify to

$$\Delta T_n = [q_n^d(\boldsymbol{\varphi}^1) - q_n^s(\boldsymbol{\varphi}^1) - q_n^d(\boldsymbol{\varphi}^0) + q_n^s(\boldsymbol{\varphi}^0)]\bar{p}_n,$$

assuming free trade with $p_n = p_n^s = p_n^d$, and aggregate to zero under balanced trade as in the case of the small open economy. Estimation is thus required for supplies and demands for each traded good including how those supplies and demands respond under equilibrium adjustments to changes in the distortion in question. Obviously, this approach for an open economy can become tedious and impractical at an economy-wide level if many goods are traded. In contrast, restricting focus to markets with nonnegligible effects may be more practical as discussed in the following section.

Segmenting an Economy for Purposes of Practical Economic Welfare Analysis

As discussed in Section 9.5, estimation of equilibrium welfare effects can be complicated by a combination of problems of multicollinearity and econometric identification. Multicollinearity of prices that respond to the same external forces can prevent estimation of partial (or ordinary) supply and demand relationships, whereas econometric identification of equilibrium supply and demand relationships, such as in equations (9.22) and (9.23), is not possible if the same set of determinants of the economy (that is, the same

13. This result implies that any effect of the newly altered distortion on the contribution of market m to the aggregate trade balance should also be ignored in calculating the aggregate welfare effect.

set of exogenous variables) affects both equilibrium supply and equilibrium demand. There is, however, one set of circumstances where the latter problem clearly does not occur. That is when the demand side of a market can be isolated from the supply side of a market in a general equilibrium sense or, in other words, where any change affecting one side of a market cannot filter through a series of other markets, finally affecting the other side of the market. We refer to this case as a *segmented economy*.

To develop the results in this case, suppose that the first segment of the economy is composed of consumers 1, ..., J_a and producers 1, ..., K_a whereas the second segment of the economy is composed of consumers J_b, ..., J and producers K_b, ..., K, where $J_b = J_a + 1$ and $K_b = \boldsymbol{K}_a + 1$. Suppose that all individuals possibly participate in the market for q_1 but that only consumers 1, ..., J_a and producers 1, ..., K_a participate in markets for $q_2, \ldots, q_{N_a}$; and only consumers J_b, ..., J and producers K_b, ..., K participate in markets for $q_{N_b}, \ldots,$ q_N, where $N_b = N_a + 1$. Following the notation of Appendix Section 9.B, one can thus solve the equilibrium equations

$$\sum_{k=2}^{K_a} \hat{q}_{nk}(p_1,\tilde{\boldsymbol{p}}_a) - \sum_{j=2}^{J_a} \bar{q}_{nj}(p_1,\tilde{\boldsymbol{p}}_a,\bar{U}_j,\boldsymbol{r}_{aj}) = 0 \tag{9.53}$$

for equilibrium prices $\tilde{\boldsymbol{p}}_a(p_1)$ as a function of p_1 where $\tilde{\boldsymbol{p}}_a = (\tilde{p}_2,\ldots,\tilde{p}_{N_a})$ and $\boldsymbol{r}_{aj} = (r_{1j},\ldots,r_{N_a j})$. Similarly, one can solve the equilibrium equations

$$\sum_{k=K_b}^{K} \hat{q}_{nk}(p_1,\tilde{\boldsymbol{p}}_b) - \sum_{j=J_b}^{J} \bar{q}_{nj}(p_1,\tilde{\boldsymbol{p}}_b,\bar{U}_j,\boldsymbol{r}_{bj}) = 0,\ n = N_b, \ldots, N, \tag{9.54}$$

for equilibrium prices $\tilde{\boldsymbol{p}}_b(p_1)$ as a function of p_1 where $\tilde{\boldsymbol{p}}_b = (\tilde{p}_{N_b},\ldots,\tilde{p}_N)$ and $\boldsymbol{r}_{bj} = (r_{1j},r_{N_b j},\ldots,r_{Nj})$. Thus, one finds that the equilibrium net q_1 supply (demand, if negative) of the first segment of the economy, given by

$$q_{1a}(p_1) \equiv \sum_{k=1}^{K_a} \hat{q}_{1k}(p_1,\tilde{\boldsymbol{p}}_a) - \sum_{j=1}^{J_a} \bar{q}_{1j}(p_1,\tilde{\boldsymbol{p}}_a,\bar{U}_j,\boldsymbol{r}_{ja}),$$

does not depend on phenomena in the other segment of the economy except through the price of q_1. Similarly, the equilibrium net q_1 supply of the second segment,

$$q_{1b}(p_1) \equiv \sum_{k=K_b}^{K} \hat{q}_{1k}(p_1,\tilde{\boldsymbol{p}}_b) - \sum_{j=J_b}^{J} \bar{q}_{1j}(p_1,\tilde{\boldsymbol{p}}_b,\bar{U}_j,\boldsymbol{r}_{bj}),$$

does not depend on phenomena in the first segment of the economy except through the price of q_1.

In this case, use of (9.53) implies that the overall welfare effect of changing the price of q_1 from p_{1a}^0 to p_{1a}^1 for the first segment of the economy is

$$\sum_{k=1}^{K_a} \Delta R_k - \sum_{j=1}^{J_a} \Delta \bar{e}_j = \sum_{n=1}^{N_a} \int_{p_{1a}^0}^{p_{1a}^1} \left[\sum_{k=1}^{K_a} \hat{q}_{nk} \frac{\partial \tilde{p}_n}{\partial p_1} - \sum_{j=1}^{J_a} \bar{q}_{nj} \frac{\partial \tilde{p}_n}{\partial p_1} \right] dp_1$$

$$= \int_{p_{1a}^0}^{p_{1a}^1} q_{1a} dp_1,$$

and, similarly, using (9.54), the overall welfare effect of changing the q_1 price from p_{1b}^0 to p_{1b}^1 for the second segment of the economy is

$$\sum_{k=K_b}^{K} \Delta R_k - \sum_{j=J_b}^{J} \Delta \bar{e}_j = \int_{p_{1b}^0}^{p_{1b}^1} q_{1b} dp_1,$$

where q_{1a} and q_{1b} are defined accordingly. Thus, for any policy change that causes the q_1 price associated with marginal behavior of the first (second) segment of the economy to change from p_{1a}^0 to p_{1a}^1 (p_{1b}^0 to p_{1b}^1), the overall social welfare effect is

$$\Delta W = \int_{p_{1a}^0}^{p_{1a}^1} q_{1a} dp_1 - \int_{p_{1b}^0}^{p_{1b}^1} q_{1b} dp_1 + \Delta T_1,$$

where ΔT_1 is a transfer effect to government or to one segment or the other given by,

$$\Delta T_1 = p_{1a}^0\, q_{1a}(p_{1a}^0) - p_{1a}^1\, q_{1a}(p_{1a}^1) + p_{1b}^0\, q_{1b}(p_{1b}^0) - p_{1b}^1\, q_{1b}(p_{1b}^1).$$

In other words, the change in producer (consumer) surplus for the net supplying (demanding) segment of the economy measures the net welfare effect in terms of willingness to pay over individuals in that segment.[14] These results thus make estimation of general equilibrium supply and demand and some limited distributional calculations possible in some empirical cases where multicollinearity prevents estimation of partial (or ordinary) supply and demand relationships. Further potential for using these results in practical empirical cases is discussed in Section 9.5.

9.C THE BOADWAY PARADOX

Based on simple graphical analysis, Robin W. Boadway (1974) has developed a result that apparently shows that use of compensating (or equivalent) variation leads to an implausible decision criterion when general equilibrium adjustments are considered. Mishan (1976a) later developed results that apparently resolved the conflict raised by Boadway, but pointed out another *apparent* problem with the compensating or equivalent variation criterion. Because the conclusions in each of these papers are counterintuitive and very disturbing due to the qualifications they seem to place on the use of compensating and equivalent variation in general equilibrium welfare analysis, a resolution of the conflict is needed. The results of Appendix Section 9.B are useful for this purpose because they correspond to a much more general model than that used by Boadway and Mishan.

First, consider the Boadway result in Figure A9.1 for a two-good, two-person economy with individuals A and B and goods q and m, where a fixed bundle of goods represented by O_B is available for distribution. Boadway considers the case of a purely redistributive movement along the contract curve $O_A O_B$ from point a to point b. Because both points represent Pareto optima, the results in Section 3.1 suggest that no compensation scheme exists supporting either the move from point a to point b, or vice versa. Hence, the net compensating variation of the move should be zero.

However, Boadway adds prices to the problem. Suppose that the price of m is 1 both before and after the change, whereas the price of q is p_1 in the initial state at point a and is p_2 in the subsequent state at point b. In this case, the constructs of Section 6.1 imply a

14. Of course, these results can also be generalized to consider existing distortions in other markets, as demonstrated for the general case above.

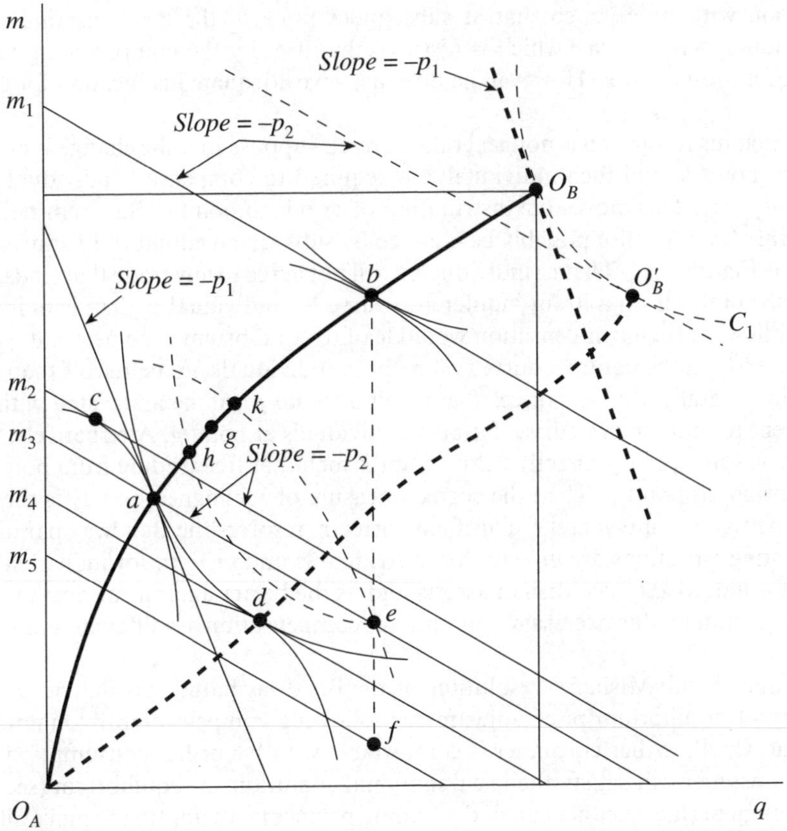

Figure A9.1

compensating variation of $m_1 - m_4$ for individual *A* and a compensating variation of $m_2 - m_1$ for individual *B* because points *c* and *d* are the subsequent choices of individuals *A* and *B*, respectively, which return both individuals to initial welfare levels by means of compensation in *m* if price remains at p_2. The sum of these compensating variations is thus $m_2 - m_4 > 0$, which contradicts the results in Section 3.1 for the pure barter economy. This seeming contradiction and apparent inconsistency in the compensating (equivalent) variation criterion is called the Boadway paradox.

Mishan (1976a) has shown that Boadway's reasoning is incorrect, however, because his subsequent compensated equilibrium where individual *A* is at point *d* and individual *B* is at point *c* does not correspond to the initial bundle of goods O_B but to some other bundle O_B' on the Scitovsky indifference curve C_1 (which holds both utility levels the same as with distribution of the initial bundle O_B at point *a*). Thus, the gain in moving from O_B to O_B' with price p_1 (or the gain in moving from O_B' to O_B with price p_2) is not surprising.

Mishan attempts to resolve this paradox by arguing that the compensating variation should be made by comparison of point *b* with a compensated point that satisfies the physical constraints associated with availability of goods (that is, a compensated point that is some allocation of O_B). He suggests that point *a* is the appropriate point for comparison with point *b*, so that at subsequent price p_2 the compensating variation for individual *A* is $m_1 - m_3$, which is just exactly offset by the compensating variation, $m_3 - m_1$, for individual *B*. However, he does not give adequate justification for choosing point *a*.

To see that his resolution is not generally correct, suppose that the change is made from point *a* to point *b*, and then individual *A* is required to compensate individual *B* by an amount $m_3 - m_1$. This moves the distribution of goods to point *e*. But from point *e*, the initial utility levels cannot possibly be attained by subsequent equilibrium adjustments in the case of Figure A9.1. That is, individual *A* will not agree to any trade that leads to point *a*, because point *a* is on a lower indifference curve for individual *A* than is point *e*. Free trading following such compensation would lead to equilibrium at some point *g* between points *h* and *k* on the contract curve (where both individuals are better off than at point *e*). And incidentally, the new prices that result at point *g* will be associated with a price line tangent to indifference curves for both individuals at point *g*. Alternatively, suppose that there is some point *f* directly below point *b* such that free trading from point *f* leads to equilibrium at point *a*. Then the correct measure of willingness to pay is the vertical distance between points *b* and *f*. This then correctly resolves the Boadway paradox. The compensating variations are $m_1 - m_5$ for individual *A* and $m_5 - m_1$ for individual *B*. The net effect is indeed zero, as Mishan asserts and as the barter analysis of Section 3.1 suggests, even though the necessary amount of compensation is different than Mishan argues.[15]

The problem with Mishan's 'resolution' of the Boadway paradox is that he ignores the possibility of equilibrium price adjustments following compensation by maintaining a price p_2 at which neither consumer is comfortable with his or her consumption bundle. Neither consumer can satisfy the usual marginal conditions of equilibrium (see Section 2.5), although perhaps neither can find a trading partner in attempting to make all desired adjustments either. And incidentally, there is no reason to assume that free trade, even at price p_2 from point *e*, will lead to point *a*. For example, individual *A* would be inclined to stop trading at some point to the right of point *a* on the *ae* segment.[16]

Two points are worth noting here. First, Mishan is correct that the appropriate measures of compensation must satisfy the physical accounting constraints, so that compensation is indeed feasible. That such physical constraints are satisfied in Appendix Section 9.B is obvious, for example, in (9.48). Second, however, compensation must be based *not* on what an individual thinks he or she is willing to pay in a partial sense where all prices (other than a directly distorted price) do not change, but on what an individual would be willing to pay if he or she could foresee all accompanying equilibrium adjustments. Mishan's analysis does not fully account for the latter point, but clearly compensation is

15. It is interesting to compare this analysis to that in Figure 3.3, which deals with the Scitovky reversal paradox. The reversal paradox arises because compensation is not actually paid (which is similar in this respect to the Boadway paradox). But clearly in Figure 3.3 compensation could be paid to make everyone *actually* better off. This is possible in Figure 3.3 because second best bundles are being compared. In the Boadway case, by definition, everyone cannot be made better off, and on further reflection, his compensation is not potentially possible because after adjustment the means for compensation do not exist.
16. The latter point is the reason why Mishan's (1976a) analysis is not correct, even when the change involves controlling prices. That is, if the change involves fixing both prices so that their ratio is p_2, equilibrium is no longer possible after compensation (given the way Figure A9.1 is drawn), and the issue of compensation cannot be decided without imposing further restrictions or incorporating a theory of disequilibrium.

based on equilibrium price adjustments in Appendix Section 9.B, because $\hat{q}_{nk}$ and $\tilde{q}_{nj}$ depend on equilibrium prices $\tilde{p}_i^s$ or $\tilde{p}_i^d$, $i = 1, \ldots, N$.

Mishan has proceeded further to point out another seeming paradox based on his misleading concept of general equilibrium compensation as depicted in Figure A9.2. Consider the case where both the distribution of goods and the bundle of goods available

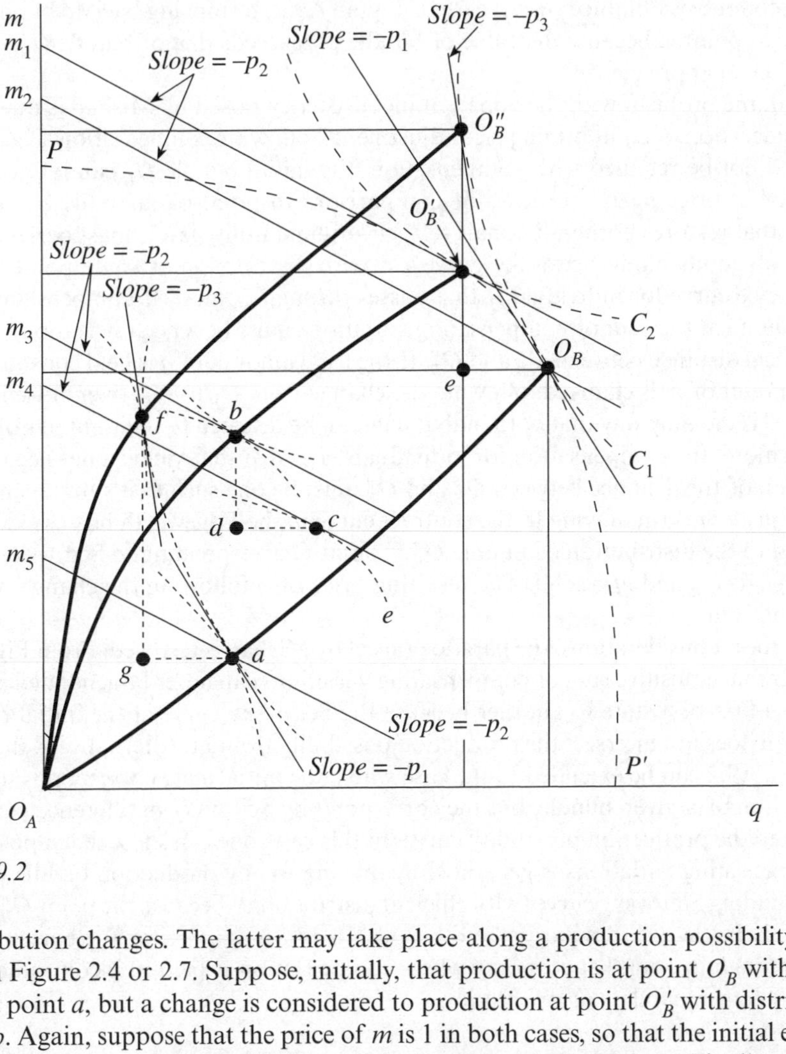

Figure A9.2

for distribution changes. The latter may take place along a production possibility curve PP' as in Figure 2.4 or 2.7. Suppose, initially, that production is at point O_B with distribution at point *a*, but a change is considered to production at point O_B' with distribution at point *b*. Again, suppose that the price of *m* is 1 in both cases, so that the initial equilibrium price of *q* is p_1 and the equilibrium price of *q* after the change is p_2. Finally, suppose that C_1 is the Scitovsky indifference curve associated with the distribution of output bundle O_B at point *a* and C_2 is the Scitovsky indifference curve associated with the distribution of output bundle O_B' at point *b*. Thus, both the initial and terminal situations represent first-best states, so that the results of Section 3.1 imply that no compensation scheme is possible such that one state is preferred to the other.

The Mishan measures, however, imply that the compensating variation for individual

A is $m_3 - m_5$, and the compensating variation for individual B is $m_5 - m_4$, for a net gain of $m_3 - m_4$. The latter compensating variation is determined by shifting point b to point d and then to point c as the origin of the indifference map for individual B is shifted from point O_B' to point e and then to point O_B. The net gain of $m_3 - m_4$ corresponds by construction to $m_1 - m_2$, which simply amounts to the difference in values of bundles O_B' and O_B evaluated at price p_2. A similar contradiction with the results of Section 3.1 for the barter economy is obtained (in the case of Figure A9.2) by moving back to bundle O_B distributed at point a, because the value of bundle O_B exceeds that of bundle O_B' when both are evaluated at price p_1.

Again, the problem with the apparent inconsistency raised by Mishan is due to a lack of consideration of equilibrium price adjustments following compensation. Because price p_2 would not be retained with compensation, the initial bundle O_B cannot generally be evaluated at price p_2 for purposes of comparison. In point of fact, any compensation scheme that restores both individuals to their original utility levels must correspond to a bundle of goods along Scitovsky curve C_1, with distribution at some point along the indifference curve for individual A that passes through point a. If compensation is paid only in m, then the sum of compensating variations must be a negative amount given by the vertical distance between O_B' and O_B''. If the total amount of q is held constant and the total amount of m is changed following the change from O_B to O_B', then movement from O_B' to O_B'' is the only way that both individuals can be restored to their initial utility levels. Furthermore, the compensation for individuals A and B that yields a net negative compensation of the distance between O_B' and O_B'' must be one such that subsequent equilibrium adjustments (in moving to the contract curve in the Edgeworth box associated with O_B'') lead to the distribution of bundle O_B'' at point f corresponding to Scitovsky curve C_1 (where $ga = eO_B$ and $gf = eO_B''$). The resulting price of q following the change with compensation is thus p_3.

With these considerations, the paradox raised by Mishan is resolved. From Figure A9.2 it is clear that a positive sum of compensating variations can never be generated in moving from one first-best state to another because the Scitovsky curve at the initial bundle by definition does not intersect the production possibility frontier. Alternatively, the analysis in Figure A9.2 can be extended to the case where the initial state corresponds to efficient distribution of a given bundle, but the corresponding Scitovsky indifference curve is not tangent to the production possibility curve. In this case, one can show that a positive sum of compensating variations is generated by moving to any production bundle above the corresponding Scitovsky curve (with efficient distribution), because the point O_B'' will then lie directly below O_B'. Similarly, the other results in Section 3.1 for the barter economy carry through in a market economy where compensation is paid in income and equilibrium adjustments follow compensation.

9.D EMPIRICAL CONSIDERATIONS

Aside from the empirical considerations discussed in Section 9.5 and Appendix Section 9.B, another important consideration suggested by the results in this appendix has to do with estimating partial market supply and demand relationships in such a way that the sum of partial welfare effects over all markets is equal to the implied general equilibrium effects. As indicated in Section 9.5, two approaches are possible in analyzing equilibrium economic welfare effects. One way is to attempt estimation of general equilibrium supply and demand in the market for which a change in policy is considered (as well as any other distorted markets for which effects of the change must be considered). In so doing, one obtains only an overall welfare effect, with no information regarding the distribution of effects or the necessary extent of compensation needed to make any indicated changes Pareto preferable. And, of course, to undertake such changes without compensation involves a value judgment in ignorance because income distribution is altered in an unknown way.

The alternative approach that can provide needed distributional information is to estimate a system of partial supply and demand relationships for all markets where substantive effects may occur. Equilibrium distributional effects can then be determined by solving the system of supply and demand equations for equilibrium prices before and after a contemplated change and then evaluating partial welfare effects on each market group using the methodology of Chapters 4 through 7 as generalized by the aggregation in Chapter 8.[17] However, when such a system of supplies and demands is estimated, one can solve for implied equilibrium supply and demand for the market in which a change is contemplated. Thus, one must be concerned that the implied equilibrium welfare effect is, indeed, the sum of the implied partial welfare effects, as the theory in Appendix Section 9.B indicates. Otherwise, the economic welfare analyst can arbitrarily influence the estimated overall welfare effects by choosing to use either the implied equilibrium welfare effect or the sum of partial effects over all included (affected) market groups. Furthermore, the added distributional information is hard to interpret if the disaggregated effects do not sum to the total effect.

This problem of inconsistency in estimated partial and general welfare effects can be avoided by ensuring that certain theoretical relationships exist among the supplies and demands that relate to common groups of decision makers. Thus, the problem here is closely related to the empirical considerations in Appendix Sections 6.E, 8.B and 8.C. That is, suppose that a single group of decision-makers is solely responsible for both the demand for q_1 and the supply of q_2. Then the estimated demand relationship for q_1 and the estimated supply relationship for q_2 must result from the same producer or consumer decision problem or must be an aggregation of such relationships that result from common underlying decision problems. If this condition is not satisfied, then even the partial effects are ambiguous, as discussed in Appendix Sections 6.E and 8.B. Thus, potential inconsistency with implied equilibrium effects is obvious.

Again, two approaches paralleling those outlined in Appendix Sections 6.F and 8.B are possible for avoiding these problems. With the primal approach, direct utility and production function forms are specified for consumers and producers, respectively. Then implied functional forms for supply and demand are generated by utility or profit maximization, as the case may be. Finally, these functions must be aggregated over consumers

17. In estimation of these supplies and demands, prices in markets among the group of markets included empirically would be considered as endogenous, whereas any prices from other markets would be considered as exogenous. The latter assumption would be appropriate if, indeed, no substantive effects of the contemplated change occur outside the group of markets considered empirically. One must be careful in this distinction, however, because a very small price effect in a distant market can have a substantive effect if it is imposed on a very large volume of trade.

and producers so that the existence of common parameters in different supplies and demands can be considered in estimation of market relationships as in Appendix Sections 8.B and 8.C. With this approach, the theoretical results of Appendix Section 9.B guarantee that partial effects will sum to the implied equilibrium effect.

With the dual approach, one begins by specifying functional forms for the indirect utility functions of consumers and the indirect profit or quasirent functions of producers. Then the implied individual supply and demand functional forms can be derived as in Appendix Sections 6.F and 8.B. Finally, these functional forms must be aggregated over producers and consumers to obtain functional forms for market supplies and demands in which the existence of common parameters is evident and can be considered in estimation.[18] Again, with this approach the theoretical results of Appendix Section 9.B guarantee that partial effects will sum to the implied overall equilibrium effect. Thus, based on these additional empirical needs and the relative tractability of the dual approach, duality offers important possibilities for specification and empirical measurement of equilibrium welfare effects in empirical policy analysis.

18. Summing functional forms over many decision-makers is impractical for empirical purposes unless some parameters are common to groups of decision-makers. Otherwise, the number of parameters requiring estimation can be econometrically intractable. For example, a common approach is to assume that all individuals in a group have the same utility or production (profit) function, where additional variables possibly are added to explain differences in tastes and preferences, and in production efficiency. Then market relationships are obtained either by multiplying individual demands and supplies by the number of individuals in the group (if efficiency or taste variables are not included) or by integrating the implied individual supply and demand relationships with respect to the distribution of efficiency or taste shifters over individuals in the group. For an application of the latter approach where differences in taste are associated with income, see Berndt, Darrough and Diewert (1977).

10. The welfare economics of market structure with applications to international trade

The theory of perfect competition and perfectly competitive markets underlies a great deal of economic thinking. To this point, this book has been based on the assumption of perfectly competitive markets. In many markets, however, the assumptions of competition break down. Market participants often do not have perfect information. More importantly, goods are often not homogeneous, and the number of buyers or sellers is not large. Sometimes entry into an industry is blocked for one reason or another. If these variations from competitive assumptions are not serious, a market may still behave essentially *as if* it were perfectly competitive. If so, the foregoing competitive theory may be a sufficient basis for welfare analysis. If such variations from competitive assumptions are serious, however, some alternative theoretical considerations are necessary. Such theories fall generally under the heading of imperfect competition. The economic welfare implications of some alternative cases of imperfect competition are examined in this chapter.

A prime example of where entry into an industry can be blocked legally is where a firm holds a patent that excludes all other firms from production or allows others to produce only if the patent-holder grants licenses to do so (for which a license fee is usually collected on the sale of each unit of the good). Patent terms vary among countries. The USA increased the term of most patents from 17 to 20 years in 1995. The purpose of a patent is to allow the firm that incurs the expense of developing a new product and bringing it to market a chance to recoup those expenses. Otherwise, competition would dissipate quasirents soon after a product has demonstrated success, so firms would have no incentive to undertake the research required to develop new products and technologies. However, once the incentive to develop new products is provided, patent expiration provides for subsequent generic entry, which leads to lower competitive prices and the associated market efficiency, and allows consumers to share in the benefits of new technology and products.

Apart from legal monopolies facilitated by patents, however, some markets have very few firms competing. In some cases, the opportunity to develop consumer loyalty to branded products while under patent makes successful entry of generic firms difficult. In addition, when small firms are successful, they are sometimes bought up by the large firms. Some economists have a growing concern that through heavy merger and acquisition activities many industries are becoming increasingly *concentrated*. An industry is more concentrated if it involves fewer competing firms. There are many examples of where the decline in the number of firms in a given industry continues almost unabated. The number of airline companies in the US has declined from the 1980s and the early 1990s. Additionally, mergers are occurring in the oil industry. The 1998 Exxon/Mobil merger took place even though Standard Oil, from which both of these companies came, was broken up into several smaller companies by a United States Supreme Court ruling in 1911 under the Sherman Antitrust Act.

In agricultural input markets, the agricultural chemical industry that consisted of 60–70 major manufacturers some 40 years ago has merged into only eight worldwide major manufacturers of mammoth proportions. A similar concentration has taken place in the agricultural seed industry as major firms like Monsanto have attempted to be the first to market with pesticide-resistant and pest-resistant seeds made possible by biotechnology. On the agricultural output side, the largest private grain company in the world, Cargill Incorporated, acquired another giant, Continental Grain, which was the fourth largest in the USA. As a result, the Continental Grain division is reducing its grain merchandising activities but is increasing its involvement in activities such as beef production, which is further increasing concentration in the beef processing industry. As a result, concerns over mergers and increased concentration in the US beef industry have triggered numerous investigations and lawsuits related to allegations of price fixing. It is estimated that the three largest beef producers, Excel, Iowa Beef, and ConAgra, control approximately 80 percent of the beef processed in the US and Canada. This concentration is partially driven by the economies of scale in beef processing.

The purpose of this chapter is to examine how markets behave when the number of firms in an industry is small, and to examine how the welfare effects of such behavior deviate from the competitive norm. Several studies have attempted to estimate the social costs from monopoly. Early estimates showed that the welfare losses from monopoly were small, amounting to only 0.1 percent of gross national product in the United States (Harberger 1954; see also Schwartzman 1960, Scherer 1970, and Worcester 1969). However, estimates of deadweight loss due to the market power of individual firms have shown welfare losses were as high as $1.8 billion for General Motors as far back as the 1960s (Cowling and Mueller 1978). The framework of this chapter demonstrates how such losses can be measured.

Throughout this and succeeding chapters, little distinction is made between the cases where supplies and demands are ordinary, compensated, equilibrium or compensated equilibrium relationships. The reason is that such distinctions needlessly complicate the discussion whereas the theoretical concepts can apply to many levels of generality. Except in a few cases as noted where the differences are important, the reader should simply bear in mind that the conclusions hold with respect to as broad a group as for which adjustments are considered in the definition of the supply or demand, and that conclusions are only approximate in cases of uncompensated curves involving consumer or factor owner responses. The related empirical considerations thus follow the discussion in Sections 8.8, 8.9 and 9.5.

10.1 THE SIMPLE MONOPOLY MODEL

The simplest and most distinctive case of imperfect competition is that of monopoly. *Pure monopoly* is a market situation in which there is a single seller of a product for which no good substitutes exist. Thus, pure monopoly is a polar case just as perfect competition is a polar case of the opposite nature.

A simple monopoly model is given in Figure 10.1. The demand for the monopolist's product is *D*. Average cost for the monopolist is AC, and marginal cost is MC. If the monopolist acts as a competitor, the industry output is q_1 and price p_1 prevails. However,

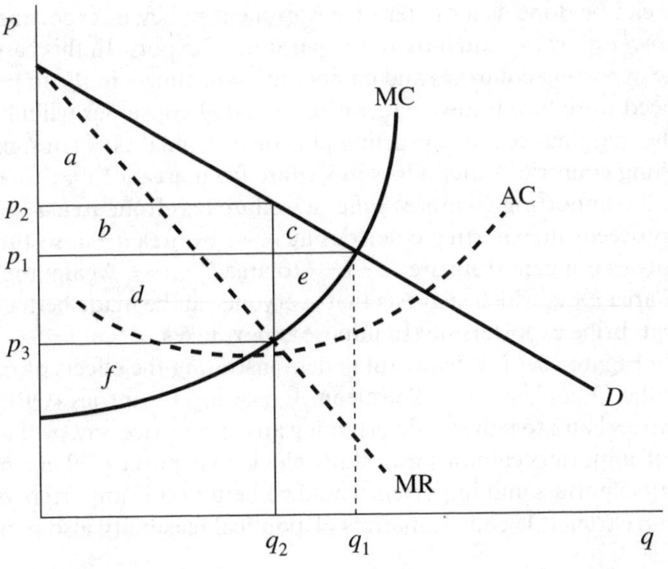

Figure 10.1

under monopoly pricing, output is less and the price is higher. The monopolist maximizes profits by equating the marginal cost MC with the marginal revenue from sales represented by MR – not the demand curve *D*.[1] The monopolist then charges price p_2 and produces output q_2. (*Note that sales volume declines when price is increased.*)

In terms of the welfare effects of moving from the competitive solution to one of monopoly, there is a gain in short-run profits or producer quasirent from area $d+e+f$ to area $d+b+f$. However, there is a loss in consumer welfare from area $a+b+c$ to area a.[2] Furthermore, there is a net loss from monopoly of area $c+e$. This area is often called the *deadweight loss* from monopoly. As in Section 8.5, the general conclusion is again that, when a distortion from the competitive solution is introduced, gainers gain less than the amount that losers lose. In the case above, if antitrust authorities could not or would not be willing to break up the monopolist, consumers would be better off banding together and bribing the monopolist to behave as a competitor.

In the model above, demand is viewed as the demand for a product in a region or country, and the industry is in private hands. However, the model in Figure 10.1 can also be viewed as a simple model of an export cartel. In this case, *D* is the aggregate demand by importing countries and MC is the aggregate supply curve of exporting countries.[3] Under free trade, the importing countries import q_1 of the good and pay price p_1.

Under a cartel arrangement, the exporters can ban together to restrict exports and raise

1. For a simple presentation of the monopoly solution, see Varian (1992).
2. This loss for consumers is an accurate approximation to the extent that Willig conditions apply, but could be measured accurately as compensating or equivalent variation if the demand in Figure 10.1 represents a Hicksian demand conditioned on initial or subsequent utility, respectively. To avoid repetition, a similar statement should be taken to apply to each consumer welfare quantity represented in this chapter.
3. As illustrated in greater detail in Section 10.9, if some of the good is produced in the importing countries, *D* can be viewed as an excess demand curve. Similarly, if some of the good is consumed in the exporting countries, the exporters' supply can be viewed as an excess supply.

the price. This can be done as a matter of government policy in exporting countries by setting an *optimal export tax* equal to $p_2 - p_3$ per unit of export. In this case, competitive suppliers in the exporting countries and competitive consumers in the importing nations would be induced to reduce trade to q_2, where marginal consumer willingness to pay is just equal to the marginal cost of exporting plus the marginal tax. Thus, market participants in exporting countries suffer a loss in welfare from area $d+e+f$ to area f. Market participants in the importing countries suffer a welfare loss from area $a+b+c$ to area a. However, tax proceeds in exporting countries increase by area $b+d$, so the net effect on exporting countries is a gain from area $d+e+f$ to area $b+d+f$. Again, the net effect is a welfare loss of area $c+e$, which suggests that everyone can be made better off if importing countries can bribe exporters not to impose export taxes.

The model in Figure 10.1 is thus useful in demonstrating the effects of cartel arrangements such as the Organization of Petroleum Exporting Countries (OPEC) where the exporting countries band together in determining an export price, say, p_2. The model demonstrates that, if importers cannot successfully block an export cartel in a major product such as oil, both exporters and importers would be better off if importers bribed exporters not to form a cartel. (Of course, matters of political feasibility also require consideration.)

While the market model in Figure 10.1 is typically considered in a partial equilibrium context, the interpretation can be generalized using the equilibrium approach of Chapter 9. In fact, if adjustments take place in other markets in response to the monopolist's price setting, then the monopolist must take account of those adjustments in maximizing profit. Specifically, the appropriate demand relationship from which to derive a marginal revenue relationship for purposes of profit maximization is the equilibrium demand that takes account of such adjustments in other markets. Similarly, the appropriate marginal cost relationship to consider in profit maximization is not the marginal cost at fixed input prices, but the monopolist's marginal cost considering the adjustments of input prices that occur as other markets adjust to the monopolist's actions. Thus, the diagrammatic analysis in Figure 10.1 applies in a general equilibrium as well as a partial equilibrium sense. Such equilibrium considerations have not been widely considered in empirical studies. Because the diagrammatic analyses of each of the cases presented in this chapter have a similar potential equilibrium interpretation, these comments are not repeated below even though the reader is encouraged to reflect on their applicability.

10.2 THE SIMPLE MONOPSONY MODEL

While the case of only one seller of a good is called a monopoly, a corresponding case with only one buyer of a good can also be considered. *Pure monopsony* is the term used to describe a market situation with one buyer of a product for which no good substitutes exist.

Consider the model in Figure 10.2, where S represents the supply curve facing a monopsonistic firm and MRP is the marginal revenue of product that the monopsonist gains from sale in its output market. The marginal outlay curve associated with the supply curve is given by MO and gives the marginal change in expenditure for good q which the monopsonist must make for successive units of q (much like a marginal revenue curve in

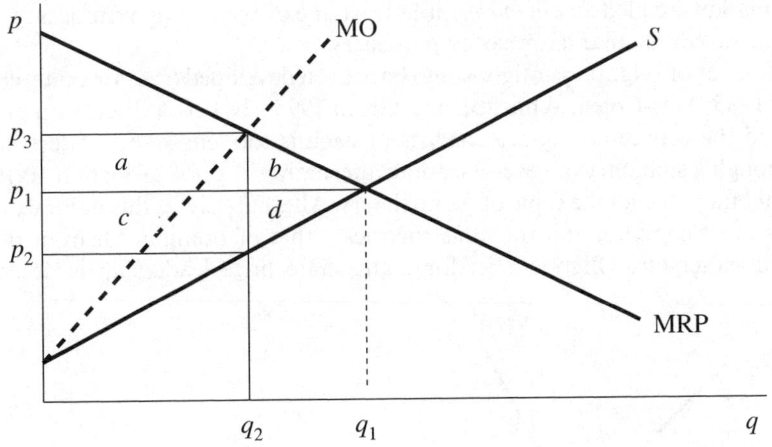

Figure 10.2

Section 10.1 gives the marginal change in total revenue for the monopolist of selling successive units of output). The monopsonist maximizes profits by equating marginal outlay and marginal revenue of product, thus purchasing quantity q_2 at price p_2. Of course, if the buyer alternatively acts competitively, then quantity q_1 is traded at price p_1. The welfare effects of monopsony are thus a loss of area $c+d$ for producers and a gain of area $c-b$ for the monopsonist for a net loss of area $b+d$. Again, the triangular area $b+d$ is referred to as a deadweight loss and suggests that producers could afford to bribe the monopsonist to act competitively and still be better off.

Similar to the simple monopoly case, the monopsony case can be viewed as a model of an importing cartel. For this case, suppose the aggregate competitive supply of all exporting countries is given by *S*, and the aggregate competitive demand among all importing countries in the cartel is given by MRP. By lowering bid prices from the competitive level p_1 to the monopsonistic level p_2 and reducing the quantity demanded to q_2, a gain for importing countries of area $c-b$ is possible.[4] The optimal import tariff is thus given by p_3-p_2 per unit according to Figure 10.2.

10.3 THE CASES OF OLIGOPOLY AND OLIGOPSONY

The monopoly and monopsony cases of the preceding sections are extreme cases where only one buyer or seller for a product exists. A more common case is where there are several buyers or sellers of a product that may or may not be homogeneous among firms. A group of firms comprising the total supply in a given market is called an *oligopoly* if at least one of the selling firms is large enough to influence the overall market price for sales and thus affect other firms single-handedly. A group of firms comprising the total demand

4. As discussed in more detail in Section 10.9, this result can be achieved in practice by means of imposing trade tariffs in importing countries. Again, as illustrated in greater detail in Section 10.9, if some of the good is produced in the importing countries, *D* can be viewed as an excess demand curve, and if some of the good is consumed in the exporting countries, the exporters' supply can be viewed as an excess supply.

in a given market is called an *oligopsony* if at least one of the buying firms is large enough to influence the overall market price for purchases.

Many theories of oligopoly (oligopsony) have been developed (see, for example, Cohen and Cyert 1965; Mas-Colell, Whinston and Green 1995, ch. 12). A discussion of all such theories and the economic welfare analysis of each is too lengthy to undertake at this point, although a summary of several leading alternatives is given in Section 10.10 of this chapter after introducing the topic of game theory. Alternatively, at this point we consider one of the most common and tractable theories – that of dominant firm or dominant share price leadership. Oligopolistic dominant share price leadership is described by

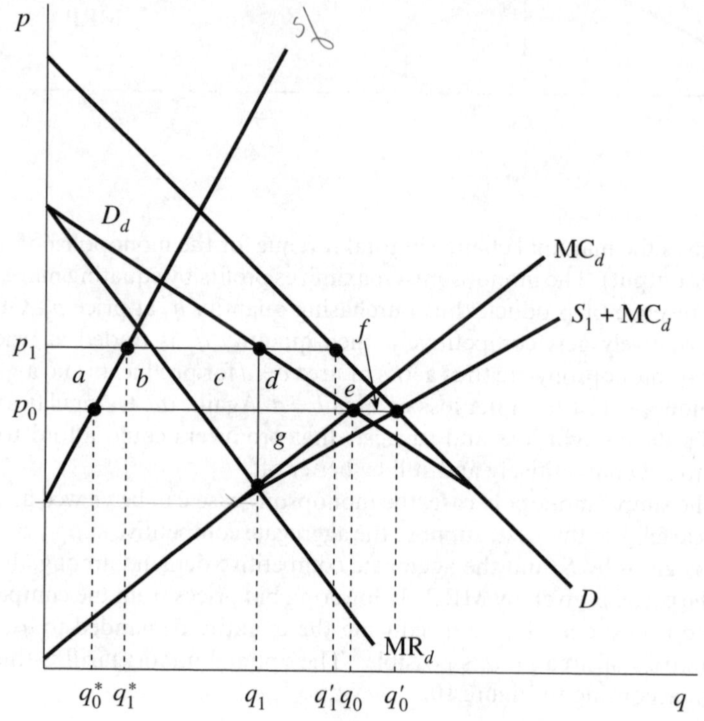

Figure 10.3

Figure 10.3, where *D* represents market demand for the product. The dominant share may be composed of one or several firms that collusively band together to raise price and restrict output to maximize their joint profits. The associated marginal cost of the dominant share is MC_d and is derived as the horizontal summation of marginal curves over firms that are part of the dominant share. In addition, there are additional firms (few or many) outside of the dominant share that do not have a direct influence on market price either because they are individually too small or because they fear retaliation by the dominant share if they attempt to affect market price directly. Hence, these firms in the *competitive fringe* (called *price followers*) act competitively, simply maximizing profits by taking the price set by the dominant share as given. The aggregate supply from all price-following firms is represented by S_f.

In this context the behavior of the dominant share is determined as follows. First, horizontally subtract the supply S_f for the price-following firms from the market demand curve D to determine the effective demand D_d facing the dominant share. Then determine the marginal revenue MR_d associated with D_d. The profit-maximizing price and quantity for the dominant share are p_1 and q_1, respectively, as determined by the intersection of MC_d and MR_d. This compares with a competitive price and quantity of p_0 and q_0, respectively, by the dominant share. The output of the price-following firms is $q_0^* = q_0' - q_0$ when the dominant share acts competitively and is $q_1^* = q_1' - q_1$ when the dominant share exercises *market power*. The welfare effects of oligopolistic pricing are thus a gain of area $a + b + c - g$ for the dominant share, a gain of area a = area $e + f$ for the price-following firms, a loss of area $a + b + c + d + e + f$ for consumers, and thus an overall net loss of area $d + g$. The case of dominant share price leadership oligopoly is thus very similar to monopoly once the excess demand curve D_d facing the dominant share is determined.

The case of oligopsony is treated similarly by simply turning the curves in Figure 10.3 upside down and reversing the supply and demand notation as well as the marginal cost and marginal revenue notation. In this way, one finds an excess supply curve facing a dominant share, and the remaining analysis becomes very similar to the case of monopsony.

Because these cases of oligopoly and oligopsony are similar to monopoly and monopsony, respectively, the remainder of this chapter focuses on monopoly and monopsony. Extension to these cases of oligopoly and oligopsony follows in a straightforward fashion.

10.4 DEMAND AND COST CONDITIONS

In studying specific industries, a crucial assumption used in the foregoing models is that both the demand and the cost conditions are the same under competition as under monopoly. The importance of this assumption has been pointed out by Williamson (1968) and is demonstrated in Figure 10.4. In Figure 10.4(a), costs under monopoly are assumed to be lower than under competition, perhaps because of lower costs of coordination or information acquisition. The marginal cost schedule under competition is MC, while MC′ is the marginal cost schedule under monopoly. Thus, in comparing monopoly to competition, the gain of area c must be considered in addition to the usual efficiency loss. Thus, if area c is greater than area b, monopoly is preferred to competition on efficiency grounds.

Suppose, on the other hand, that costs under monopoly are higher than under competition because of an increased tendency for waste with greater profits. Comanor and Leibenstein (1969) called this X-inefficiency. For example, it has been argued that costs may be higher under monopoly because a monopolist fails to minimize costs in the absence of the *competitive stick*. Thus, in Figure 10.4(a), suppose MC is the monopolist's cost curve, and MC′ is the competitive cost curve. The net loss from monopoly power is then area $a + b + c + d$.

The case where demand differs with market structure is depicted in Figure 10.4(b). Suppose, for example, that the monopolist is much more aggressive than a competitive industry in selling the product and creates demand through informative advertising (see Section 11.6). Thus, suppose that demand for the monopolist is represented by D', whereas demand is D under competition. The competitive output is q_1, which sells for a price of p_1. Under monopoly, output is q_2 and price is p_2. The welfare effects of monopoly are thus a

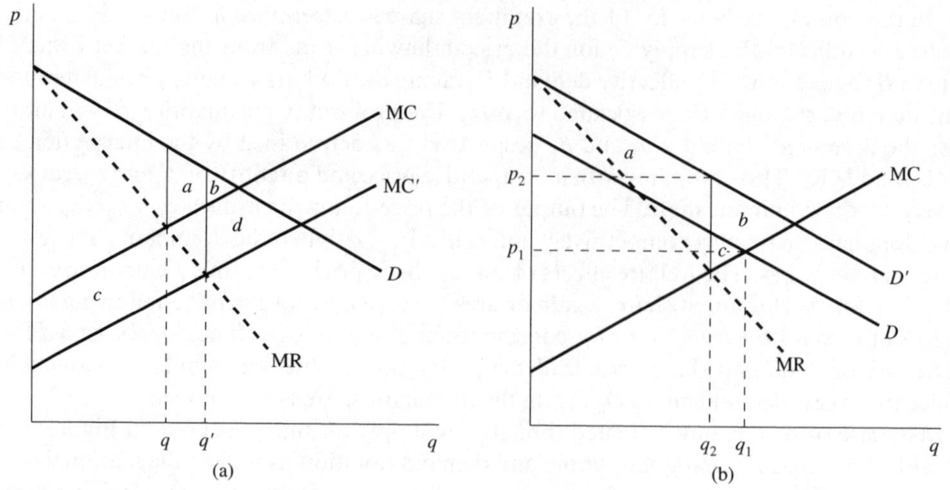

Figure 10.4

net gain for society of area $a - c$. Of course, similar considerations could be made in the case of monopsony, oligopoly, or oligopsony as well.

10.5 ECONOMIES OF SCALE

One case where monopolies tend to develop is when average costs decline substantially at larger levels of output, or in other words where economies of scale exist. Economies of scale arise from several sources, including technical (for example, economies of scale in assembly-line automobile plants) and pecuniary (for example, buying inputs in bulk rather than on a small-scale basis) sources. The extent to which economies of scale exist is industry specific. As an example, there may be large economies of scale in beef-packing plants but few economies of scale in the production of strawberries.

The importance of this issue is discussed with reference to Figure 10.5. Consider, first, the industry or firm long-run average cost curve AC. Clearly, from an efficiency standpoint, society is better off with output q_0 produced by a firm having costs AC^* and MC^* than with the same output produced by several firms having costs MC′ and AC′.

Suppose, alternatively, that a single firm produces output q^*. If the planning curve is AC, society could do better from an efficiency standpoint by 'splitting up' the firm into smaller producing units in order to produce the output under maximum efficiency. However, if the cost curve were AC^0, output q^* may be produced just as efficiently with one firm as with several. From a market power perspective, society may prefer to break up the industry into smaller units to avoid monopoly losses even though it has nothing to gain on cost-efficiency grounds.

The slope of the long-run cost curve is vital in any discussion of antitrust policy or monopoly power control. With fewer economies of scale, less social justification can be made for large firms. Another important point relates to the distinction between price surveillance policies and breaking up large businesses. In Figure 10.5, suppose that the firm

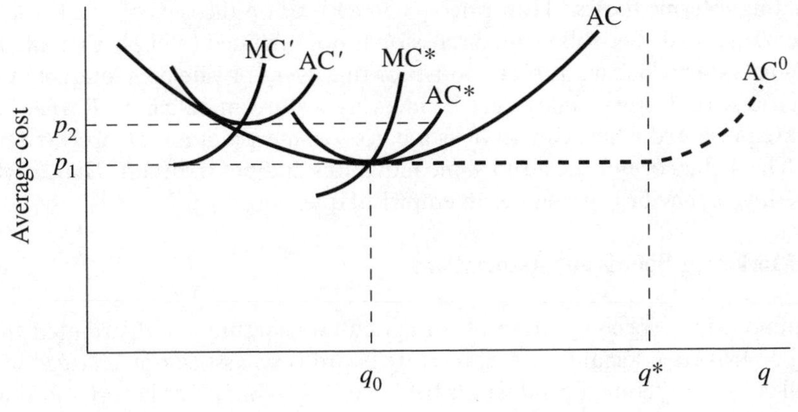

Figure 10.5

with costs MC* and AC* charges price p_2 because of its monopoly power and earns excess profits. Ideally, society should try to force the monopoly to charge price p_1 and have the industry produce output q_0 rather than keep price at p_2 and break the industry into small units with costs MC′ and AC′. Regulating monopolies in this case may involve keeping the economies of scale intact by not breaking up the industry. Rather, a competitive price may be imposed as ideally is the case in a regulated utility industry. Whether or not it is possible to prevent large companies from engaging in monopolistic practices in individual cases is another matter. In some cases, perhaps the only solution is to break up large firms into smaller units.

10.6 MARKET INTERMEDIARIES

In the equilibrium models presented in Chapters 2 and 3, the actors in the economic system are producers and consumers. Market intermediaries are not considered. However, goods seldom move directly from producers to consumers. Marketing firms (either private or public) buy the goods from producers and eventually sell them, usually in a modified form, to consumers. For example, a Kansas wheat farmer rarely sells wheat directly to consumers in Russia. The actual trade is carried out by multinational private grain companies.

In elementary monopoly theory, one views the monopolist also as the producer of the good. However, monopoly power can exist in an industry because of power in marketing a good even though producers behave competitively. As an example, in producing wheat in North America, no single producer can influence aggregate market price. However, this does not necessarily imply that the pricing of wheat to flour millers and importing countries is competitive because wheat purchased from wheat producers is sold to flour millers and importing countries through a single nationwide marketing board in Canada and primarily through a handful of large private grain traders in the USA. To understand market efficiency thus requires examining the structure, conduct, and performance of such market intermediaries.

In this section, markets are viewed as consisting of producers, consumers, government and marketing intermediaries.[5] How pricing can depend on the type of market intermediary is demonstrated. The following discussion is not intended to imply that all marketing boards necessarily behave as monopolists or that every private firm uniquely situated between groups of buyers and sellers behaves as a pure middleman. Rather, several extremes are presented which can serve as a basis for interpretation of observed market behavior. This behavior may occur in some industries and not in others. Hence, whether noncompetitive behavior is present is an empirical question.

Producer Marketing Boards and Associations

Many commodities, especially those of an agricultural nature, are distributed through marketing boards or associations. A marketing board is an association charged with the responsibility of marketing a product on behalf of a given market group – in this case, producers. In countries such as Canada, the UK and Israel, marketing boards are widespread (Hoos, 1979). A producer marketing board has many different objectives, depending on its type and the country in which it is located. Among its objectives may be price stability, equity for producers, enhancement of producer returns and the provision of tax revenue to governments. Only two alternative objectives are considered here: maximizing producer returns and providing revenue to governments.

To demonstrate the case of a producer marketing board, the demand for the product is represented by D, and the supply is represented by S in Figure 10.6(a). Suppose that the industry producing the good is perfectly competitive, and assume zero marketing costs for the board. If the board's objective is to maximize producer returns, it behaves as a monopolist and charges price p_2 to consumers instead of p_1. If the board is to be successful in this effort, it must restrict output by such devices as production quotas on producers. In doing so, the board – operating in the best interest of producers – extracts economic surplus from consumers and returns it to producers. As in the monopoly case discussed above, this leads to inefficiency because a loss of area $a+b$ must be imposed on consumers in order for producers to benefit by area $a-c$.

Suppose, instead, that the board is created by government and seeks to raise tax revenues from the producing sector in order to benefit consumers. This case is shown in Figure 10.6(b). The government, acting in the best interest of consumers (assuming that tax revenues are redistributed to consumers) will extract surplus from producers to give to consumers. The board will thus behave as a monopsonist – not as a monopolist. The board will equate its marginal outlay curve (MO) to the demand curve. It will charge consumers price p_2 and pay producers price p_3. Clearly, producers are worse off than under competition, and consumers are better off provided that the loss in consumer surplus is more than offset by the additional government revenue, which is $(p_2-p_3)q_2$. Specifically, producers lose area $c+d$, and consumers gain area $c-b$ (including benefits of redistributed taxes). The overall effect of such a marketing board, however, is a loss of area $b+d$.

In each of these cases, there is a welfare loss from the operation of a marketing board because output is restricted below the competitive level. Who gains and who loses from the operation of the board depends on the board's objective, which depends partly on the power given to it by government.

5. This characterization of market participants was suggested by Just, Schmitz and Zilberman (1979).

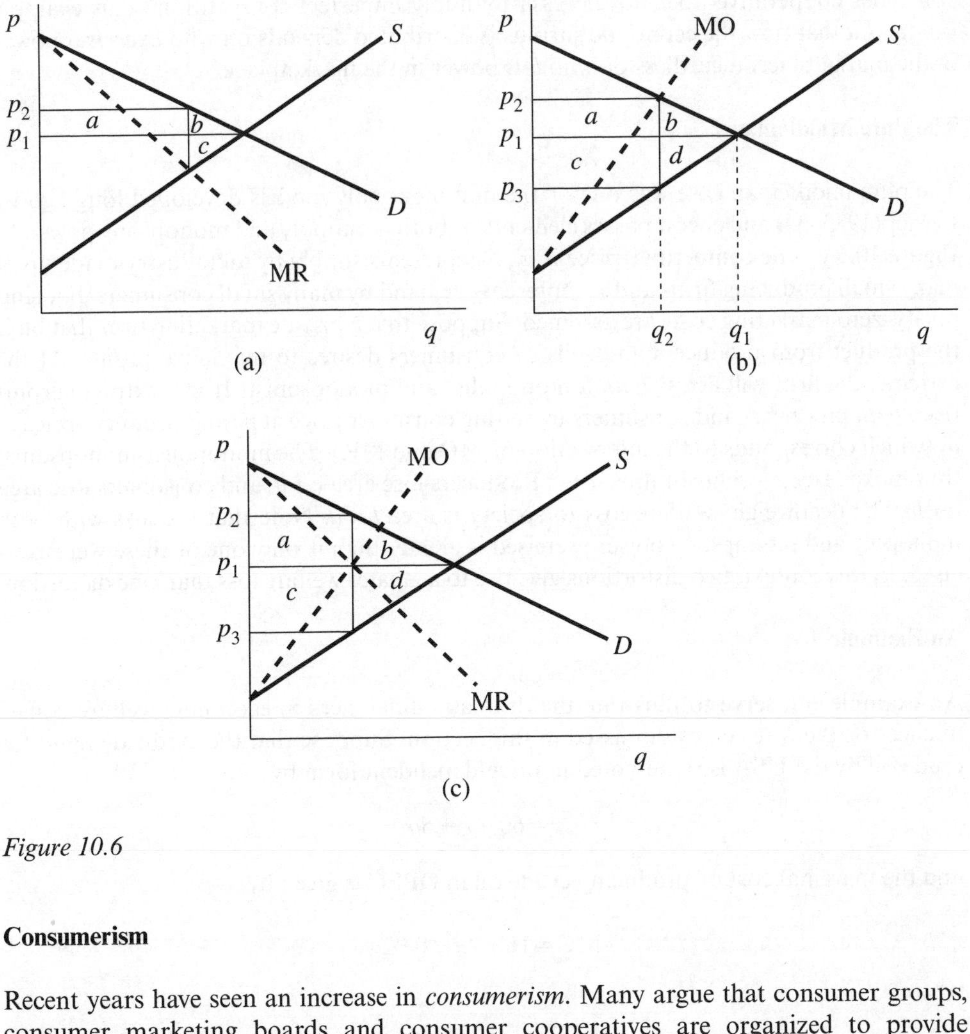

Figure 10.6

Consumerism

Recent years have seen an increase in *consumerism*. Many argue that consumer groups, consumer marketing boards and consumer cooperatives are organized to provide countervailing power to big business. This may well be the case. However, conceptually, consumerism can lead to welfare losses just as producer and government monopolies can. Consider again Figure 10.6(b). Under competition, consumers would pay price p_1 for quantity q_1. However, if they can exert monopsony power in the market by forming a cooperative or similar organization, they can be made better off than under competition. By behaving as a monopsonist, they extract surplus from producers for themselves. The cooperative, by charging its members p_2, gives rise to a loss in consumer welfare of area $a + b$. But this is more than offset by the area $a + c$, which is the difference between the amount consumers pay and the amount producers receive. Of course, the cooperative profits of area $a + c$ must be redistributed in such a way as not to affect marginal behavior in order to attain quantity q_2. If dividends are paid on the basis of purchases, consumers will buy more in order to receive a larger share of the high dividends until aggregate quantity increases to q_1 and no dividends are paid. Thus, the mere presence of a large consumer cooperative does not necessarily imply imperfect competition. This example points out that how the economic surplus is distributed depends on who *exercises* power in the marketplace, regardless of who *has* power in the marketplace.

The Pure Middleman

The pure middleman case was one of the first monopoly models developed long ago by Lerner (1933–34) and encompasses elements of both monopoly and monopsony power. In Figure 10.6(c), the competitive price is p_1, S represents supply by an industry made up of many small producing firms and D represents demand by many small consumers. For simplicity, zero marketing costs are assumed. Suppose that a private marketing firm that buys the product from producers and sells to consumers desires to maximize profits. At the extreme, the firm will act as *both* a monopolist and monopsonist. It will extract surplus from *both* producers and consumers by setting consumer price at p_2 and producer price at p_3 (which corresponds to the intersection of MO and MR). The monopolist-monopsonist thus makes excess profits of area $a+c$. Producers lose area $c+d$, and consumers lose area $a+b$. The deadweight welfare loss to society is area $b+d$. Note that the loss with both monopoly and monopsony power exercised is greater than if only one of these were exercised. In this context, two distortions give rise to a greater welfare loss than one distortion.

An Example

An example can serve to illustrate the dramatic differences in economic welfare consequences of the three cases discussed in this section. Suppose that the excess demand for crude oil by the USA is represented in price-dependent form by

$$p = 60 - q + 5m$$

and the marginal cost of producing crude oil in OPEC is given by

$$\mathrm{MC} = 16 + 2q - 0.02w$$

where

p = price of crude oil in dollars per barrel
q = quantity of crude oil in 100 million barrels
m = total disposable personal income in the USA in trillion dollars
MC = marginal cost, and
w = index of costs of oil production in OPEC countries.

For simplicity, suppose that demand by other countries and consumption in OPEC countries can be ignored. Also, suppose that $m = 2$ and $w = 300$ so that, with current levels of income and oil production costs, competitive demand and supply are given by

$$p = 70 - q$$

and

$$p = 10 + 2q,$$

respectively, as depicted in Figure 10.7. Note that MC is replaced by p to convert the marginal cost relationship to a price-dependent supply relationship under competitive conditions. With competitive trading, market equilibrium is found by solving the demand and supply equations simultaneously for p and q, which obtains $p = 50$ and $q = 20$ (see Figure 10.7).

Suppose, however, that the OPEC countries unite and sell monopolistically to the USA. Their marginal revenue[6] from sales to the USA is given by

$$MR = 70 - 2q.$$

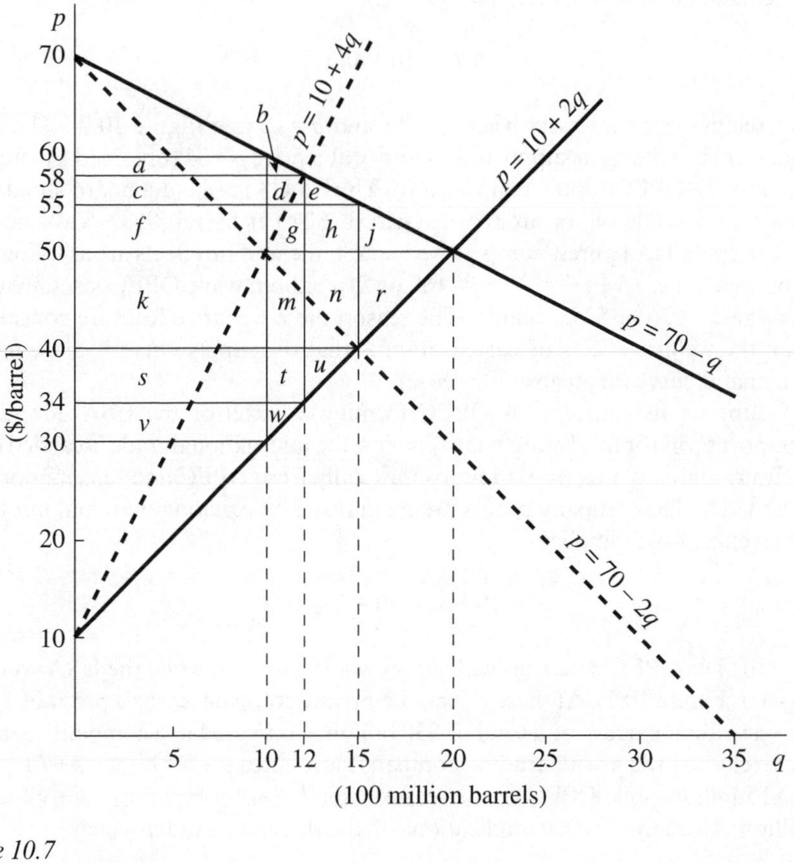

Figure 10.7

6. Marginal revenue can be found by multiplying q by the price indicated by the demand curve,

$$pq = 70q - q^2,$$

and then differentiating with respect to q,

$$MR = \frac{\partial pq}{\partial q} = 70 - 2q.$$

Equating this marginal revenue to their marginal cost given by $10+2q$ implies that $q=15$, and at $q=15$ the USA is willing to pay price $p=55$ (obtained by substituting $q=15$ into the US demand curve). At the same time, the marginal cost of production falls from 50 to 40 (obtained by substituting the respective quantities into the marginal cost relationship $10+2q$). Following Figure 10.7, the welfare effects of OPEC cartelization are as follows. The USA loses area $f+g+h+j=87.5$ or \$8.75 billion (note that areas in Figure 10.7 are measured in 100 million dollars). The OPEC countries gain area $f+g+h-r=50$ or \$5 billion.

Suppose alternatively that, instead of OPEC countries forming a cartel, the USA were to set an optimal import tariff or set up a marketing board to exercise monopsony power in crude oil purchases. Optimality for the USA occurs where the marginal outlay[7] intersects the demand curve where marginal outlay is

$$\text{MO}=10+4q.$$

These two relationships intersect where $p=58$ and $q=12$ (see Figure 10.7). The OPEC countries would be willing to supply this quantity at a price $p=34$ (obtained by substituting $q=12$ into the OPEC supply relationship). Thus, a US marketing board should offer \$34 per barrel for crude oil, or an import tariff of \$24 per barrel (\$58 − \$34) should be imposed. Compared to a purely competitive market, the welfare effects are as follows. The USA gains area $k+m+s+t-e-h-j=160$ or \$16 billion, while OPEC loses area $k+m+n+r+s+t+u=256$ or \$25.6 billion. The reason these welfare effects are considerably larger than the welfare effects of cartelization is that the supply curve is more inelastic than the demand curve (in an absolute sense).

Finally, suppose that instead of OPEC forming a cartel or the USA adopting an optimal import tariff (or marketing board) policy, the international trade is carried out by a large private company that buys monopsonistically from OPEC and sells monopolistically to the USA. The company profits are maximized by equating marginal outlay and marginal revenue, which implies

$$10+4q=70-2q,$$

that is, $q=10$. The OPEC countries will supply $q=10$ at $p=30$ while the USA will buy $q=10$ at $p=60$ (Figure 10.7). At these prices, the private company earns a profit of \$30 per barrel on one billion barrels for a total of \$30 billion. Compared to a competitive market, the USA (excluding the private trading company) loses area $a+b+c+d+e+f+g+h+j=150$ or \$15 billion while OPEC countries lose area $k+m+n+r+s+t+u+v+w=300$ or \$30 billion. Thus, the welfare implications of the three cases differ widely.

7. Marginal outlay can be found by multiplying q by the price indicated by the supply curve,

$$pq=10q+2q^2,$$

and then differentiating with respect to q,

$$\text{MO}=\frac{\partial pq}{\partial q}=10+4q.$$

10.7 LABOR UNIONS

Another area in which the theory of imperfect competition finds application is in labor negotiations. The extent to which labor is organized in the form of unions varies from country to country. For example, the percentage of the workforce in the UK belonging to unions is much greater than that in the USA. Yet, even in the USA, the numbers are significant (in 2003 about 15.8 million US workers belonged to unions). Also, there have been recent attempts to form new unions. For example, farm workers in the USA historically have not been unionized. But a serious effort has been made over the last several decades to organize laborers in this sector to bargain for higher wages and better living conditions.

A Simple Model

Consider Figure 10.8(a), where w is the wage rate, S is the supply curve of labor and q is the quantity of labor supplied. The derived demand curve for labor is represented by D. Under competitive equilibrium, w_1 is the wage rate and q_1 denotes the number of workers employed. In the simplest case, if a union were established to raise the real wage rate for the workers in this particular industry, employment would drop. If wage rate w_2 were negotiated, only q_2 would be employed in the industry, and $q_1 - q_2$ workers would have to seek employment elsewhere.[8] For the workers now represented by the union, the total wage bill increases by area a. This is desirable for the workers who remain in the industry but not for those who must seek work elsewhere. The workers who must seek employment elsewhere suffer a loss of area c.

The foregoing model can also be used to study the impact of restricted entry by unions for workers entering a profession. Suppose that a union restricts the entry of people into the medical profession, dentistry, plumbing, and the like. Restricted entry has a positive or beneficial effect for persons already in the profession and those who gain entry but not for those excluded. Also, if unions restrict entry, there is a loss to society. Area $b+c$ reflects the extent of loss where area $a+b$ consists of the loss to consumers using the service provided by the industry and area c is the loss to these workers who, because of union restrictions, cannot enter the industry.

Another possible impact of the threat or reality of unionization is to bring about technological change that displaces workers. Hence, the derived demand under unionization may be D' instead of D. If this is the case, the gains from unionization may be less than anticipated, even for those who gain entry into the unionized labor force.

Two Markets

An extension of the model described above was suggested by Rees (1971) as depicted in Figure 10.8(b). Suppose that the supply of labor is perfectly inelastic at S and that D_u, D_n and D_t represent the demand for labor in the unionized sector, the nonunionized sector and the two combined. Under competition the wage rate is w_1. If union wages increase to w_2, employment in the unionized sector declines from q_1 to q_2. As a result, employment

8. The assumption here is that the amount of work per worker remains fixed while varying the total amount of labor.

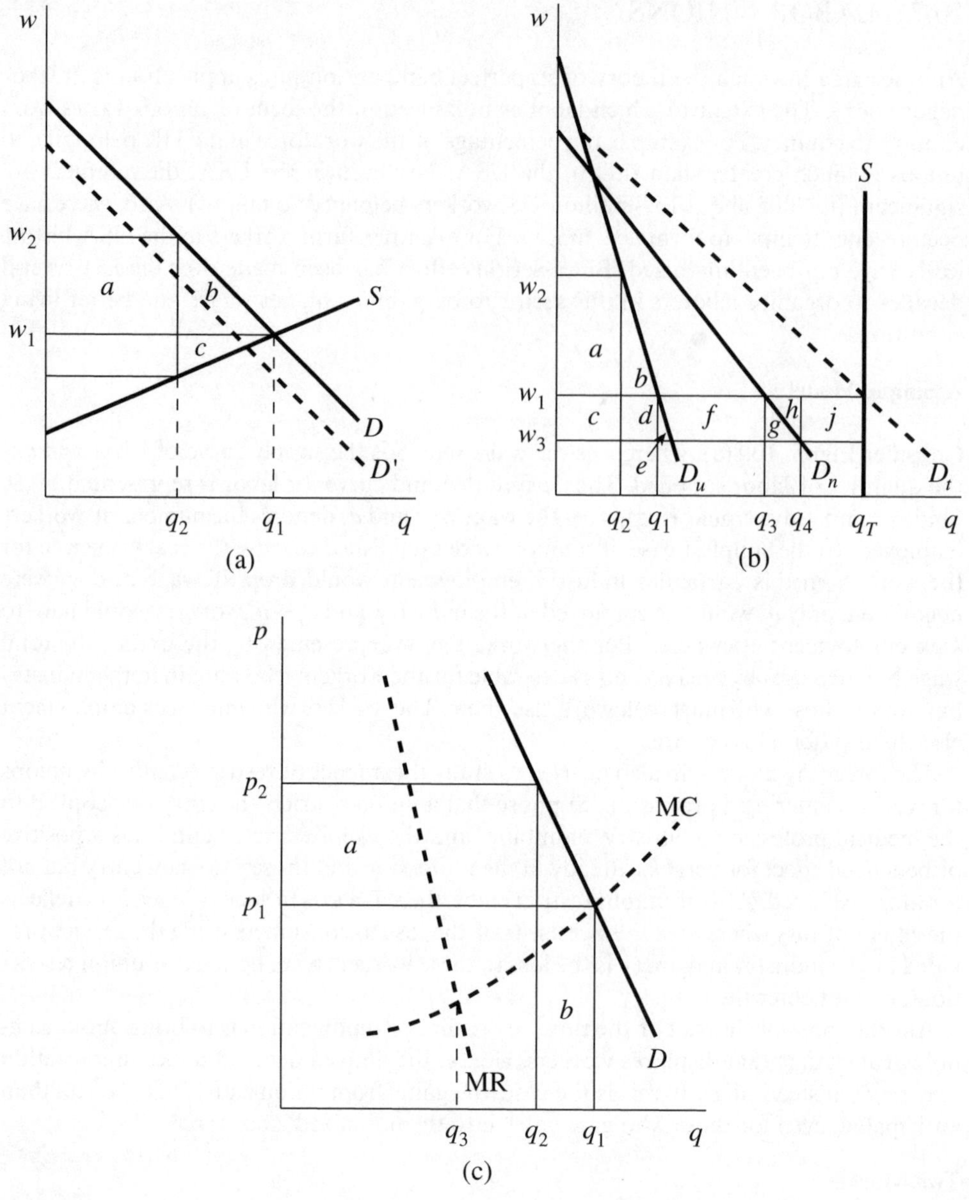

Figure 10.8

in the nonunionized sector increases from q_3 to q_4, where $q_4 - q_3 = q_1 - q_2$, so that wages drop to w_3. As a result, the total wage bill drops by area $d+e+f+g+h+j-a$, which is a welfare loss for labor as a whole in the case of perfectly inelastic labor supply even though those who remain in the unionized labor force gain area a. Producers who hire labor also lose area $a+b$ in the unionized industry but gain area $c+d+e+f+g$ in nonunionized industries. The net welfare effect is thus a loss of area $b+h$ (note that area c = area j by construction). Again, it is not surprising that the overall effect of partial unionization is an economic loss because it represents a distortion from the competitive equilibrium.

The Effective Union

Consider, finally, the simple model in Figure 10.8(c), which depicts the producers' output market rather than their labor input market. This model developed by Warren-Boulton (1977) shows that, if a union can control industrial production, it will prefer demand for the product to be inelastic. That is, if the labor union can cause a small reduction in output from, say, q_1 to q_2, that reduction will have a greater impact on price when producers' output demand is more inelastic. If the union controls production to the extent that it could close down the industry with a strike, employers will be willing to bargain with the union concerning who should get the increase in sales revenue of area $a-b$.

However, it is one thing for a union to control output to the extent of having economic power over the industry. It is quite another matter if the union cannot control output sufficiently so that the employer will bargain with the union (agriculture appears to be a case in point partly because the supply of farm workers in many labor-intensive crops is wage elastic). Note in Figure 10.8(c) that if the union can reduce output only from q_1 to q_3 due to a strike, producers become better off because the strike actually places them in a monopoly position. For the union to be effective, it has to reduce output beyond q_3. Hence, whereas an inelastic demand is desirable once the union can completely control output, it may be undesirable otherwise, because it requires the union to restrict output substantially before employers are willing to bargain with workers.[9] The analysis in Figure 10.8(c) points out the importance of considering extended market effects as suggested in Chapter 9.

10.8 ANTITRUST ECONOMICS

Another important area of application of the welfare economics of imperfect competition is in legal proceedings related to control of market power. Literally thousands of lawsuits have been brought against entire industries or certain firms within industries for price-fixing. These suits have been initiated by both the private sector and federal monopoly regulatory agencies such as the Federal Trade Commission. The number of suits appears to be growing at an exponential rate which makes the integration of law and economics an important area of inquiry. There are, in fact, some interesting contrasts, as shown earlier, between estimating the aggregate welfare effects from monopoly pricing and determining damages in individual lawsuits. For example, the amount of damages awarded in antitrust cases is often determined by seemingly arbitrary means. Figure 10.9 illustrates the problem in two different cases, which differ by whether or not the marketing firm exercises monopoly as well as monopsony power. Suppose that a group of competitive producers with supply S sues a marketing firm for *fixing price* at p_3 instead of a competitive price p_1. One could compute the competitive solution and the monopsony solution and hence the excess profits given by area $a+c$. From an economic standpoint,

9. This result was pointed out by Carter et al. (1987).

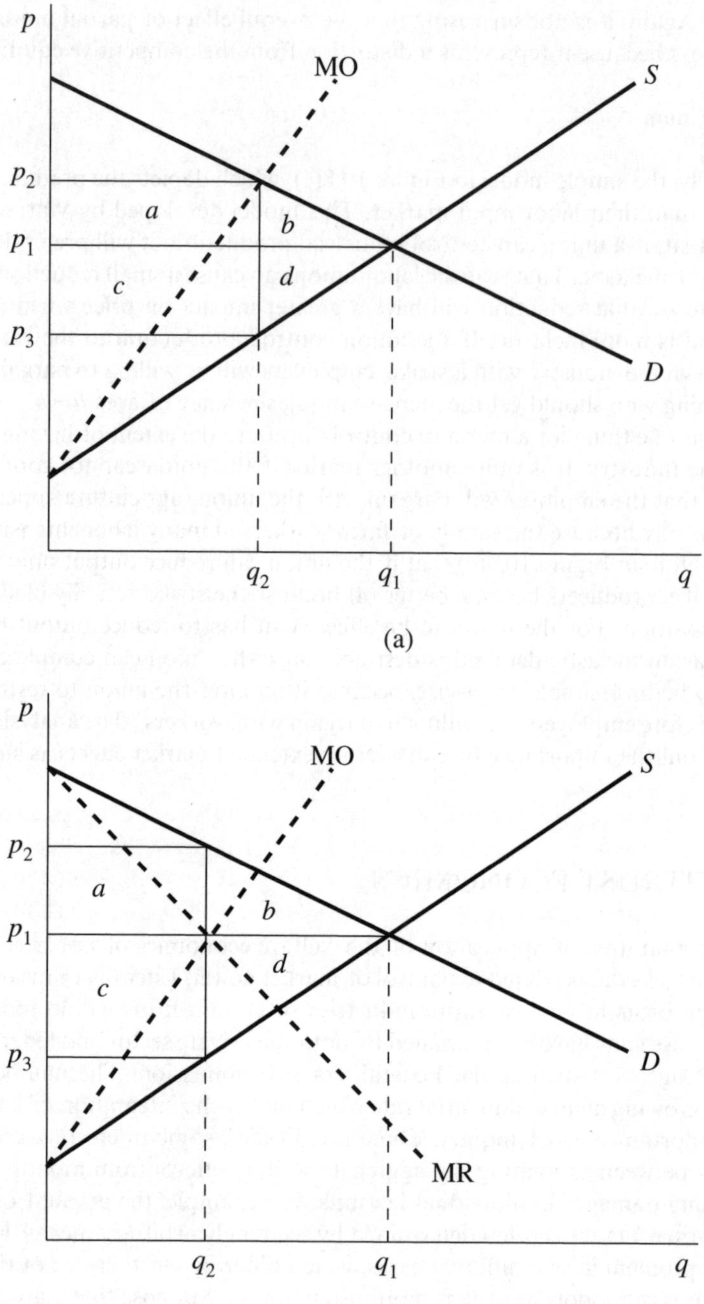

Figure 10.9

however, it is not clear that the producers should receive all the excess profits, because they lose only area $c+d$ as a result of price fixing. Part of the loss from monopsony pricing is borne by consumers (that is, the loss in consumer surplus is area $a+b$). However, the monopsonist's unfair gains are not sufficient to compensate both consumers and producers according to their losses if a court so ordered. Therefore, how the settlement should be made is unclear. Court rulings usually do not compensate consumers at all if producers win their lawsuits against a middleman. Furthermore, the comparison of Figures 10.9(a) and (b) shows that the extent of damages for producers depends on whether or not monopoly was exercised in the middleman's sales to consumers. Yet the weight of evidence in most court cases suggests that producers sue for price-fixing only in their dealings with a middleman. Any lawsuit for price-fixing in the middleman's sales to consumers must normally be brought independently by consumers (or government regulatory agencies). Thus, even though the producers' damages may be area $c+d$ in Figure 10.9(b), they may recover only the smaller area $c+d$ in Figure 10.9(a).

To consider further peculiarities, suppose that three industries exist in a chain where the middle industry acts as a monopsonist as in Figure 10.9(a). Although price-fixing in this case occurs on the input side, consumers lose area $a+b$. Thus, consumer losses are substantial even though the price-fixing is not exercised directly against them. The monopsonist is, in effect, selling competitively to consumers. However, legal precedent does not suggest the possibility of, say, consumers filing suit against middlemen or processors for their price-fixing against producers. Similar statements hold for the reverse case, where a middleman buys competitively and sells as a monopolist. Producers lose substantially even though the price-fixing is exercised against consumers, yet legal precedent does not suggest the possibility of producers filing suit against processors and retailers for their price-fixing in retail sales.

Similar problems are demonstrated by the famous *pass-through* ruling (see, for example, Schaefer 1975). Stated simply, if three market groups A, B and C are related in a chain – for example, beef producers, meat packers and retail grocery chains – then individuals in A cannot sue C for price-fixing. Neither can individuals in C sue A. Such rulings are peculiar in the context of economic theory because effects of price-fixing tend to be passed through market chains in varying degrees. Such a ruling often implies, for example, that consumers cannot sue producers for price-fixing because processing firms handle the product before it is finally sold.

To consider this case in greater detail, suppose initially that an entire economic sector is competitive (that is, only *normal profits* are being made by each industry in the sector). Now introduce monopoly pricing by industry A. If industries B and C remain competitive, a pass-through effect occurs because prices for industry C will increase because of a rise in production costs for industry B due to monopoly pricing by industry A. This effect is demonstrated in Figure 10.10, where in Figure 10.10(a), S is the supply of the input and D is the derived demand for the input and, in Figure 10.10(b), S' is the supply of the final product and D' represents final consumer demand. Under competition, the input quantity demanded is q_0 and its price is p_0. The competitive output market equilibrium price and quantity are p_0' and q_0', respectively. Now suppose that monopoly power is created in the input market. Following the framework of Section 9.1, an increase in price in the input market causes supply to decline in the output market. This results in higher price in the output market, which, in turn, causes derived demand in the input market to increase

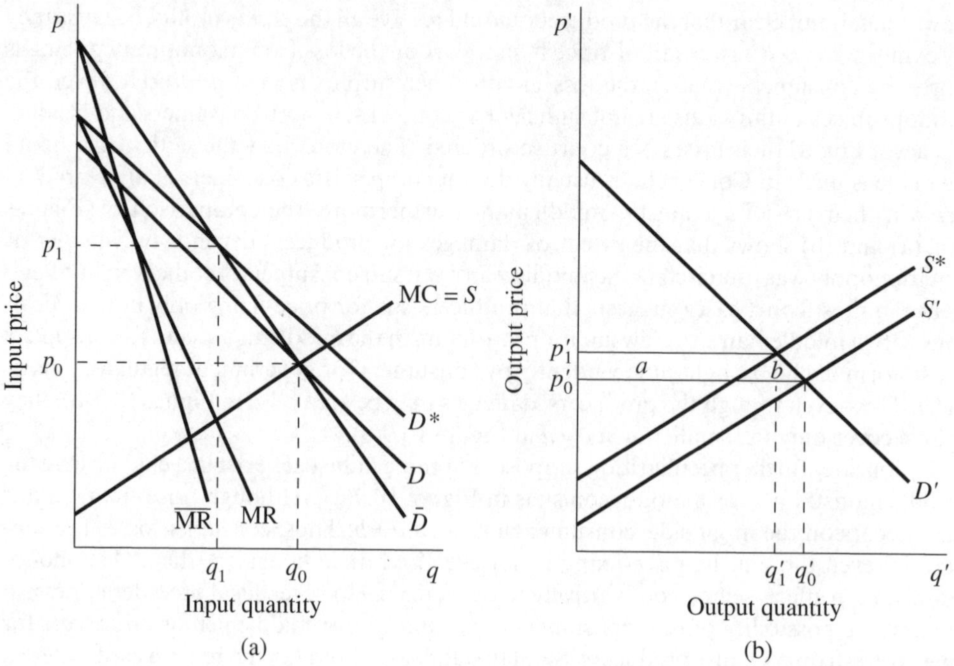

Figure 10.10

somewhat so that eventually derived demand becomes D^* and output supply becomes S^*. As a result, price in the output market increases to p_1', and consumers suffer a loss of area $a+b$ as a result of monopolization of a market in which they do not deal directly.

Note that the price and quantity in the input market in this case thus change according to an equilibrium demand curve $\bar{D}$, which takes account of adjustments in other markets. This consideration suggests that a monopolist could maximize profits naively considering the demand curve D^* and its associated marginal revenue curve MR. Alternatively, the monopolist could maximize profits with respect to the equilibrium demand curve $\bar{D}$ and its associated marginal revenue $\overline{\text{MR}}$. Of course, the latter would be appropriate for true profit maximization and would generally entail larger welfare effects. Arguments quite similar to this could also be developed where, say, a consumer cooperative exercises monopsony in the output market. In such a case it maximizes consumer welfare by equating marginal consumer benefits to an equilibrium marginal outlay curve that takes account of input market adjustments. As a result, input suppliers would suffer welfare effects even though they are not involved in the same market as the monopsonist.

These cases suggest that a wide gap yet exists between legal practice and economic theory. Such problems have arisen because empirical methods have often not been sufficiently accurate to determine whether or not price-fixing practices have been followed. Traditionally, such investigations have attempted to rely on estimation of cost functions, for which data are often unobservable or difficult to assimilate.[10] Alternatively,

10. For further discussion, see Section 10.11.

courts have attempted to verify whether formal collusive agreements have existed among firms purportedly comprising a dominant share in an industry. But as Adam Smith remarked, 'People of the same trade seldom meet together, even for merriment and diversion, but the conversation ends in a conspiracy against the public, or in some contrivance to raise prices' (Smith 1937, p. 128). In other words, social gatherings provide a vehicle by which informal gentlemen's agreements can be reached. But the consequences of such agreements can be as serious as with formal collusive agreements, even though proof in a court of law may be more difficult (Posner 1969).

In other areas, however, laws have been changed in ways that have become more consistent with economic theory. For example, historical precedent, in absence of reliable information about costs and evidence of formal collusion, has been to focus on industry concentration (number of firms with certain combined market shares) which may or may not lead to noncompetitive pricing. More recently, however, guidelines of the US Department of Justice and Federal Trade Commission issued in 1992 and revised in 1997 have focused on a firm's ability to increase profits by increasing price (specifically on whether a hypothetical 5 percent increase in price increases the profit of the firm). This gives a criterion to determine the legal presence of market power, in which case the focus turns to whether the power has been exercised. In some cases, natural experiments may be observed in practice that demonstrate profits from such a price increase. Otherwise, meeting this criterion rightfully becomes a difficult empirical exercise requiring estimation of complex multimarket effects.

10.9 INTERNATIONAL TRADE CONSIDERATIONS

Antitrust economics also has important applications in international trade. Accordingly, this section considers the economic welfare effects of noncompetitive behavior in the context of international trade. Noncompetitive behavior may occur through government intervention in the market place, collusion among producers and/or consumers in various countries, or price manipulation on the part of importers, exporters, and/or processors.

Optimal Tariffs and Export Taxes

As illustrated briefly in Sections 10.1 and 10.2, the welfare position of an individual country can be improved by monopolistic behavior in export markets and monopsonistic behavior in import markets although, when all countries are taken together in aggregate, such behavior decreases world social welfare. Three concepts of optimality may be considered from the standpoint of individual countries: an optimal welfare tariff, an optimal revenue tariff and an optimal export tax.

In Figure 10.11, the excess demand by the importing country for good q is ED and excess supply in the exporting country is ES. The free trade price is p_1, and the corresponding traded quantity is q_1. The marginal revenue for the exporter is MR, while the marginal outlay for the exporter is MO.

The optimal welfare tariff maximizes the joint welfare of all parties in the importing country. It is denoted by T_O in Figure 10.11 and is the vertical difference between excess supply and excess demand at the quantity where MO = ED. This is the case where government regulations cause the importing country to behave as the monopsonist of Section 10.2. This tariff causes price to the exporting country to decline to p_2 and the quantity imported to decline to q_2 while the price in the importing country rises to p_3. Accordingly, the tariff generates a joint welfare loss for consumers and producers combined in the importing country equal to area $b+c+d$. However, the government gains area $b+c+e+f$ in tariff revenue, yielding a net gain of area $e+f-d$ for the importing country as a whole. Also, because producers in the importing country receive the higher price p_3, they gain $p_3 - p_2$ on every unit of the good produced and consumed domestically (not shown in Figure 10.11).

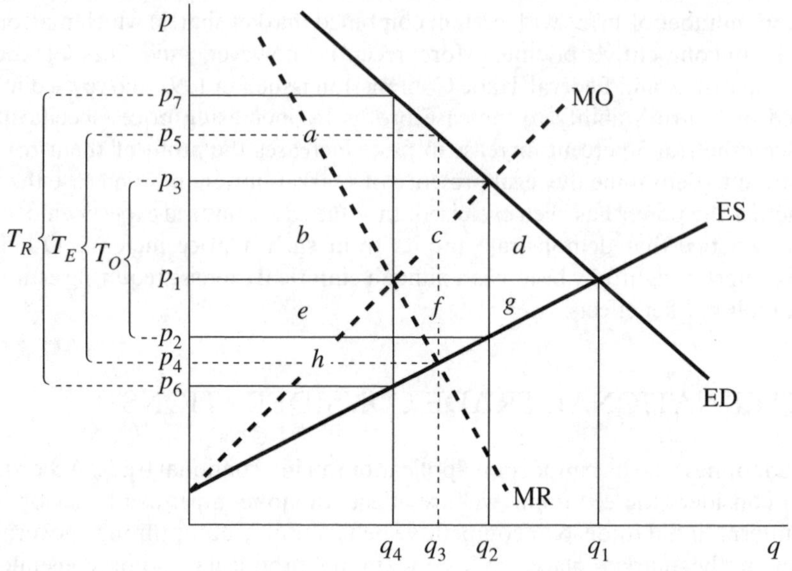

Figure 10.11

The optimal revenue tariff alternatively maximizes the tariff revenue collected by the importing country's government. It is denoted by T_R in Figure 10.11 and is the vertical difference between excess supply and excess demand at the quantity where MO = MR. In this case, the government acts essentially like the pure middleman of Section 10.6 although not taking possession of the good. This tariff causes price to the exporting country to decline further to p_6 and the quantity imported to decline further to q_4, while the price in the importing country increases further to p_7. This tariff, unlike the optimal welfare tariff, can cause overall welfare in the importing country to be lower than under free trade, even though the government maximizes the revenue collected from the tariff. Compared to the optimal welfare tariff, government revenue increases from area $b+c+e+f$ to area $a+b+e+h$.

The optimal export tax is set by the exporter to maximize welfare for the exporting country as a whole assuming the importer behaves competitively without tariffs. The optimal export tax is denoted by T_E in Figure 10.11 and is the vertical distance between excess supply and excess demand at the quantity where MR = ES. In this case, the export tax is chosen so that the exporting country behaves as the monopolist of Section 10.1. The export tax causes the price to the importing country to increase to p_5 while the price to producers and consumers in the exporting country falls to p_4. The importing country is clearly worse off than under free trade. While overall welfare in the exporting country increases, producers as well as producers and consumers combined in the exporting country are also worse off than under free trade, assuming the export tax revenue is not redistributed as a lump sum to producers and consumers.

Countries often pursue optimal protectionist strategies by imposing duties on trade. For example, the European Union is a major trading bloc in world trade and has exercised a number of protectionist policies. Studies have found that it has roughly pursued an optimal tariff strategy with its variable levy system. As theory suggests, the levies have caused losses in consumer welfare because of higher domestic prices, although this is more than offset by the gain in import tariff revenues. Carter and Schmitz (1979), for example, found for wheat that European Union gains from following a tariff strategy amounted to about \$3.7 billion. Their results, which are summarized in Table 10.1, show that the gain in tariff revenue for importers, roughly \$7.2 billion, is larger than the joint loss in welfare for producers and consumers in importing countries, \$3.5 billion, but that producers in the importing countries gain due to higher domestic prices.

Table 10.1 Welfare gains from import tariffs to wheat-importing nations

Welfare effect	Net gain (million dollars)
1. Loss in consumer surplus	−9439
2. Gain in producer surplus	5971
3. Import tariff revenue	7202
4. Net gain	3734

Source: Carter and Schmitz (1979, p. 520).

Similar concerns and controversy have arisen regarding Japanese beef policy, which has been highly restrictive with respect to imports from the USA and elsewhere. For many years, Japan restricted beef imports through the use of an import quota. On 1 April 1990, the quota was replaced by a 70 percent tariff. What is the effect of the tariff relative to free trade? First, the tariff supports beef producers' incomes in Japan. Second, Japanese beef prices are much higher than those in other trading nations. Third, the tariff allows the Japanese government to collect substantial income in the form of tariff revenues on imports. Is the beef tariff an optimal welfare tariff for Japan, or does it maximize revenue collected by the Japanese government? Interestingly, a tariff in the neighborhood of 70 to 100 percent has been found to maximize Japanese government revenue (see Wahl, Hayes and Schmitz 1992). Thus, the Japanese government's behavior is consistent with the hypothesis that the Japanese government has acted as a self-interested middleman, exercising both monopsony power over beef exporters as well as monopoly power against its own consumers.

Supply Management

As suggested by earlier sections in this chapter, industry profits are increased by raising prices above competitive levels, or equivalently, by restricting output. Unlike competitive industries, monopolies have the ability to set price and, equivalently, reduce output. However, sometimes competitive industries can achieve a similar result through cooperation in restricting output or by lobbying a government to restrict trade or sanction supply control. When an industry or firm lobbies a government or agency to manipulate regulations to its advantage, this activity is generally called *rent-seeking* because the industry or firm is trying to increase their quasirents beyond competitive levels and beyond that afforded by the status quo. While agricultural production is frequently cited as meeting the conditions of perfect competition, market outcomes may not be competitive. For example, prior to the 1996 Freedom to Farm Act, production of major US crops, such as wheat, corn and cotton, was restricted by government acreage set-aside requirements. To entice participation, the government offered price support payments or higher-than-market target prices to farmers who idled a certain percentage of their land or limited the acreage planted to a particular crop. Additionally, the Conservation Reserve Program whereby the government pays farmers to divert land into conservation activities has idled approximately 30 million acres of farmland in the USA. In other cases, tobacco allotments and dairy herd *buyouts* by the US government have been used to control production. In earlier times, producers of some crops were allowed to determine by referendum whether *marketing orders* were imposed. Such marketing orders worked much like the marketing quotas discussed in Section 8.5.

Such production controls have been used not only by the USA. For example, in Canada, supply management has been used for dairy, poultry and egg production, which has generated considerable attention and debate. Two elements of Canadian policy allow these industries to behave noncompetitively: (1) a combination of tariffs and import quotas, and (2) the legal authority to control production. The latter is authorized by the National Products Marketing Agencies Act.[11]

Figure 10.12 illustrates the theory of supply management for an importing country suggested by Vercammen and Schmitz (1992). Domestic supply is S, domestic demand is D and the world price is p_1. Under free trade, imports are $q_2 - q_1$. As long as free trade prevails, any effort to limit supply by producers will be offset by increased imports at the world price. So allowing producers to exercise some form of supply management will be to no avail unless producers are also able to persuade the government to limit imports.

Suppose producers successfully lobby the government both to impose a quota on imports and to facilitate some form of supply management. Suppose, for example, that the import quota is established at the free trade level, $q_2 - q_1$. Once the import quota is in place, the effective demand facing domestic producers becomes D', which is horizontally parallel and left of D by a distance equal to the amount of the quota. With an import quota, producers can benefit by restricting industry production, in which case the price will rise and profits will increase. The optimal solution for producers is to choose an output and thus a price where marginal revenue, MR, is equal to marginal cost, as

11. A detailed description is contained in Coffin, Saint-Louis and Rosaasen (1996). See also T.G. Schmitz (1995) and Schmitz and Schmitz (2003).

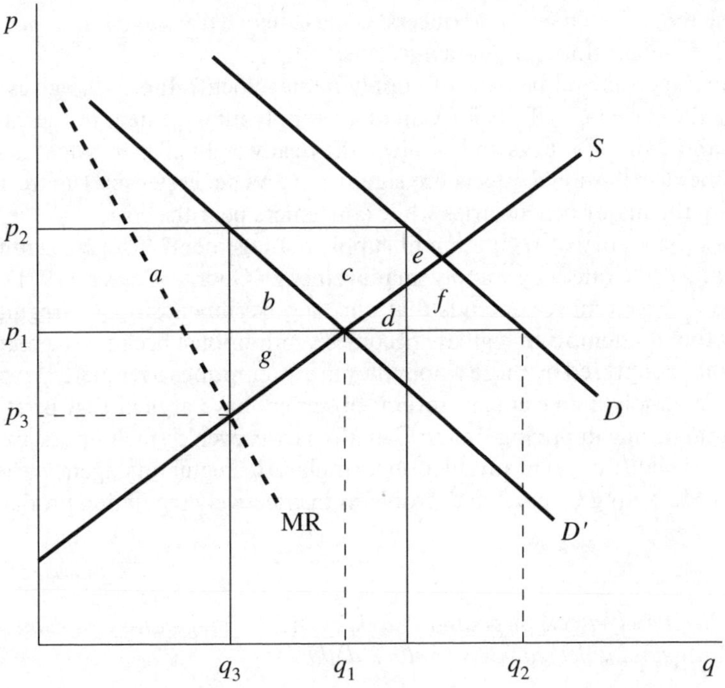

Figure 10.12

represented by S. Note that this marginal revenue curve is a marginal revenue curve associated with effective demand D' rather than total demand D. Thus, producers will limit aggregate production to quantity q_3, which yields the higher price p_2. Relative to free trade with competition, producers gain area $a-g$. Consumers lose area $a+b+c+d+e+f$. Because supply management raises both producer and consumer prices, it will also generate *quota rents* to those who hold the rights to import under the quota. These rents will amount to area $c+d+e+f$ = area $b+c+d$. This welfare effect is effectively transferred from consumers to quota holders while area a is transferred from consumers to producers. Thus, area $b+g$ is the deadweight loss of the program. Because of the transfer to quota-holders, and the likelihood that importers will receive those rights, one would expect importers and producers to combine for purposes of lobbying the government to facilitate such a program. By comparison, consumer groups are typically more diffuse and less organized, so the development of such programs is not surprising in spite of their deadweight loss.

Many questions have been raised about supply management policies:

1. Who should receive the import quota rents? Should they be given away or auctioned off by the government? Historically, importers who were in place prior to the introduction of supply management have had the right to import and, therefore, receive these rents even though this becomes a windfall gain for importers if producers are successful in organizing effective supply management. However, some have argued

that these rents should go to producers, while others have argued that they should go to the government through quota auctions.[12]

2. What are the costs and benefits of supply management? Table 10.2 gives some estimates of these welfare effects for Canadian supply management in the case of eggs, broilers and dairy. For eggs and broilers, the deadweight efficiency loss is small even though the distributional effects are significant. As suggested by Figure 10.12, producers are the major beneficiaries while consumers bear the cost.
3. How does the theory of regulation fit supply management? Why are significant producer gains generated by supply management? George Stigler (1971), a Nobel Laureate in Economics, contends that once a government imposes regulations, the industry that it attempts to regulate becomes a monopolist because the regulators are bought off or captured by those whom they are attempting to regulate.[13] Applying the concept to supply management, several observers have argued that producers have significant latitude in pricing. In the Canadian case, even though prices are supposed to be tied to realistic cost of production formulae, the regulatory agency (the National Products Marketing Council) has problems in effectively regulating producer pricing behavior.

Table 10.2 Economic effects of poultry and dairy industry regulations in Canada, farm gate level, selected years (million dollars)

	Barichello 1980	Arcus 1979	Veeman 1979	Harling and Thompson 1975–77
Eggs:				
Net domestic gain	−19	—	−0.4	−5
Producer gain	+55	+45	+38	+74
Consumer gain	−74	−56	−39	−80
Broilers:				
Net domestic gain	−13	—	−5	−11
Producer gain	+57	+71	+71	+94
Consumer gain	−73	−77	−76	−121
Importer gain	+4	—	—	—
Dairy:				
Net domestic gain	−214			
Producer gain	955			
Consumer gain	−980			
Taxpayer gain	−303			

Source: Arcus (1981), Barichello (1982), Harling and Thompson (1983), Schmitz (1996) and Veeman (1982).

12. The Canadian Minister of Agriculture ruled that existing quotas should remain with historical importers but that any expansion of import quotas should be distributed to other players such as processors.
13. For an application of Stigler's theory to agriculture, see Schmitz, Boggess and Tefertiller (1995).

Import–Export Cartels[14]

Domestic producers may seek to maximize their welfare through direct tariff and quota protection. This strategy attempts to internalize rents by limiting or excluding competing foreign producers and may enable domestic producers to obtain a noncompetitive equilibrium in the domestic market. Alternately, domestic producers may seek to maximize their welfare by forming a coalition with foreign producers to seek jointly a noncompetitive equilibrium even though trade is not restricted by formal barriers. These collusive or cooperative strategies could be successful through overt actions (bilateral agreements) or through covert collusion. The smaller the number of producers and the more concentrated is an industry, the more feasible covert and informal collusion becomes. That is, in an industry consisting of few producers, each may come to understand that they are better off with all producers limiting production to a fair share of the industry's monopoly output even though no discussions are undertaken to formalize such behavior. Also, rent-seeking activities are not limited exclusively to domestic producers. Market power can be exerted by foreign producers through, for example, voluntary export restraints of the type discussed in Section 8.7. Thus, the type and number of possible rent-seeking activities increase.

Like most other countries, the USA protects domestic producers of many agricultural commodities with both tariff and nontariff trade barriers. For example, both voluntary and legislated import quotas protect producers of products ranging from beef to cheese to sugar. But, historically, US producers of fresh winter vegetables in general, and tomatoes in particular, have not been able to generate the support necessary to protect these commodities from international competition. If domestic government will not respond, one possibility is for domestic fresh tomato producers (who are located primarily in Florida) to form a coalition with Mexican producers. Such a coalition could become an import–export cartel because the vast majority of fresh tomatoes in the USA come from one of these two sources. Such a cartel would likely pursue cooperative or collusive strategies with Mexican producers rather than competitive strategies.

Unilateral producer actions

Figure 10.13 characterizes the deep-rooted trade conflict between Mexico and the USA related to fresh winter vegetables, of which tomatoes are the dominant commodity. Mexico is a major supplier of winter vegetables to the US market. Suppose the supply curves of Mexico and the USA are S_m and S_{us}, respectively. The demand curve in the USA is D_{us}. Fresh winter vegetables are grown in Mexico almost exclusively for the export market. Therefore, a domestic demand curve is omitted for Mexico.

Initially, equilibrium equates aggregate supply, $S_{us}+S_m$, with domestic demand, D_{us}, resulting in equilibrium free-trade price p_1 and equilibrium aggregate quantity q_1. Clearly, US producers would maximize their welfare with respect to trade policy if they could successfully lobby for no trade (that is, imposition of a prohibitive tariff) since no other action can lead to larger quasirents for domestic producers. By moving from the free-trade price to the no-trade price, p_4, US producer quaisirents increase by area $a+c$ while domestic consumers would lose area $a+b+c+d$. Because the tariff is prohibitive, it generates no

14. This section is based on Bredahl, Schmitz and Hillman (1987).

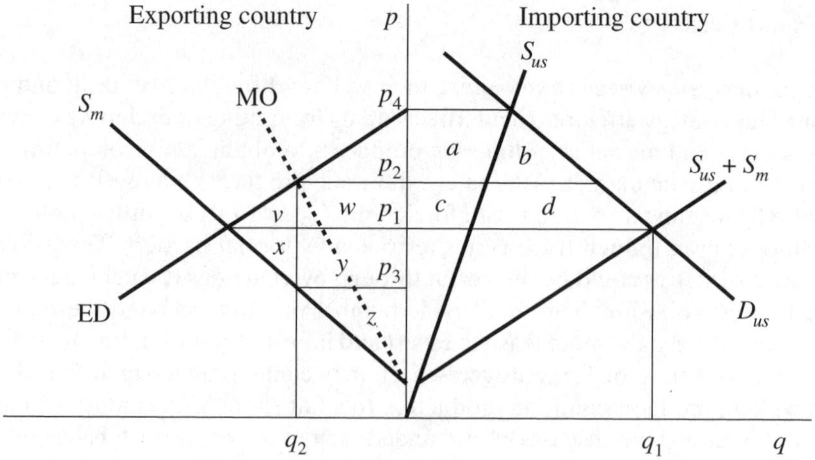

Figure 10.13

tariff revenue for the government. Thus, domestic producers are the only gainers and their gain comes at the expense of a much larger loss for consumers. The deadweight welfare loss for the importing country is area $b+d$, while producers in Mexico further lose area $x+y+z$.

Alternatively, US producers might lobby for a smaller optimal welfare tariff that improves not only domestic producer quasirents but overall domestic welfare as well. Possibilities for forming a politically feasible coalition for lobbying purposes may thus be more likely. The optimal welfare tariff yields an internal price of p_2, determined by equating the marginal outlay, MO, to excess demand, ED. The associated tariff is p_2-p_3 and the resulting Mexican price is p_3. In this case, US producer quasirents increase from the free trade case by area c, a lesser amount than under the prohibitive tariff, and overall domestic welfare increases even though consumers lose from the price increase. Specifically, the tariff revenue equal to area $w+y$ (which amounts to a tariff of p_2-p_3 on the imported quantity q_2) plus the producer gain of area c is more and possibly substantially more than the consumer loss of area $c+d$. The optimal tariff increases overall domestic welfare by area $w+y-d$.

An important point to keep in mind is that this rent-seeking by US producers through tariffs has a detrimental effect on Mexico. In spite of the US gain, the two countries combined are worse off by area $v+x$, which means that Mexican producers are worse off by area $x+y$ (note that area $d-w=$area v by construction). That is, in order for producer quasirents in the USA to increase, Mexican producer quasirents must fall by even more as both producer price and quantity in Mexico fall.

As an alternative to the adverse Mexican consequences of an optimal US tariff, Mexican producers could pursue unilateral rent-seeking activities by instituting an optimal voluntary production quota. Alternatively, Mexican producers could achieve the same welfare result by successfully lobbying their government to institute an optimal export tax with the proviso that the tax revenue would be returned to producers. The optimal export tax is derived by equating the Mexican marginal cost of production represented by S_m with the marginal revenue MR_{ed} associated with the excess demand curve ED as depicted in Figure

10.14. In this case, producer quasirents increase in both countries – by area a in the USA, and from area $y+z$ to area $x+z$ in Mexico – as the trade price increases to p_2.[15] However, consumers in the USA are worse off by area $a+b$, and the USA is worse off as a whole by area b, while the deadweight loss for the two countries combined is area $w+y$. The same welfare effects are also achieved by imposing a quota equal to q_2 on exports.

Joint producer actions

What are some possible actions that Mexican and American producers could pursue jointly to increase their welfare? The joint welfare of producers is maximized by the joint cartel solution whereby the two producers act jointly as a single monopolist.

In Figure 10.14, the cartel solution is determined by equating the marginal revenue MR_{us} associated with demand D_{us}, which is aggregate demand in this case, with the combined supply curves $S_{us}+S_m$. The corresponding cartel price is p_4. Under this solution, the US supplies quantity q_3 and Mexico exports an amount q_5 (which is equal to q_4-q_3). In this case, producer quasirents in one country do not increase from the free-trade outcome at the expense of producer quasirents in the other country. They both increase at the expense of the consuming public. In contrast to other US producer rent-seeking activities that increase US production, the cartel solution causes US production to fall from the free-trade level. But producer quasirents are greater than those under free trade. The key to the cartel solution is cooperation and agreement on market-share allocations. Failure of a cartel is due generally to the lack of agreement on market-sharing.

The theoretical model thus shows that some trade instruments yield competitive strategies while others result in cooperative strategies.[16] Table 10.3 lists some instruments used

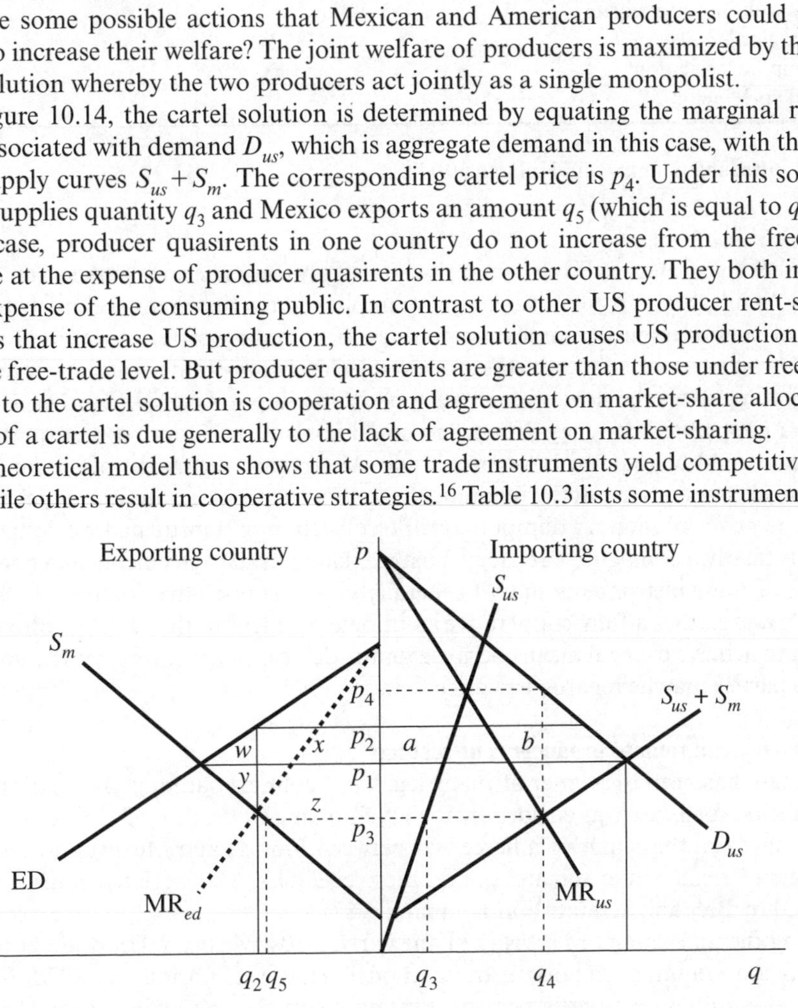

Figure 10.14

15. This is clearly the case with an optimal export tax where the tax revenue is given to producers. However, in nonoptimal cases, quasirent to Mexican producers can be below the case of free trade.
16. In this dichotomy, a competitive strategy is one where producers in the importing country lobby for tariffs to protect a border, in which case producers in the importing country gain but producers in the exporting country lose. A cooperative strategy is one where producers in both countries cooperate, for example, through voluntary export restraints, so that producers in both countries gain.

Table 10.3 Rent-seeking strategies

Trade policy instrument	Type of strategy: Competitive	Cooperative
Tariff	X	
Tariff equivalent quota (by importer)	X	
Voluntary quota (by exporter)		X
Marketing order	X	X
Antidumping legislation	X	
Bilateral agreements		X

Source: Bredahl, Schmitz and Hillman (1987).

in rent-seeking strategies. Producers seeking tariff protection clearly pursue a competitive strategy. Similarly, a tariff-equivalent quota implies competitive rent-seeking behavior on behalf of producers in the importing country. A voluntary export quota that increases quasirents to both sets of producers, however, yields a cooperative solution. A marketing order that regulates the flow of domestic goods and imports can yield either a competitive or a cooperative strategy. Importers could control the order so that quasirents to exporters would be reduced below free trade. Alternately, the marketing order could be determined cooperatively at the theoretically optimal export tax solution, which would be the cooperative solution. A dumping tariff (see Section 8.7) instigated by domestic producers is clearly a competitive strategy. Lastly, bilateral trade agreements that contain one or more of these instruments should generally yield a cooperative solution. It should be noted, however, that a fully cooperative solution equivalent to the cartel solution may be difficult to achieve by legal means because jointly determining the price of the product by the two parties may be regarded as price fixing.

US and Mexican tomato producer rent-seeking

The tomato has been the center of many legal and political battles in international trade since the first such case was decided by the US Supreme Court in 1893. More recently, the tomato has been the center of a fierce war between Florida and Mexican producers and importers of fresh winter tomatoes and other vegetables. Many related court battles are discussed by Bredahl, Schmitz and Hillman (1987).

During the marketing order years of the early 1970s, Mexican–US trade in tomatoes followed the voluntary export restraint model. However, during the 1978–84 period (called the antidumping battle period), Florida resorted to applying antidumping tariff measures but was unsuccessful. From this action, one could infer that the competitive model was in operation. Although Florida producers have failed to increase quasirents via tariff and/or nontariff barriers, the theory of rent-seeking clearly suggests other avenues for rent-seeking. Mexican and US producers could maximize quasirents by forming a coalition or cartel to limit production. Such a coalition requires that domestic and foreign producers (or the governments that represent them) jointly determine output. A second option would be to accept the voluntary export quota approach. In this case,

US output would be higher than with free trade while Mexican output would be lower. Producer surplus in both countries would be higher than with free trade.

In 1996, once again Florida tomato interests, which included the Florida Tomato Growers Exchange, filed a petition with the US Department of Commerce, International Trade Administration, and the US International Trade Commission requesting the imposition of antidumping duties on imports of fresh tomatoes from Mexico. However, instead of tariffs, the US and Mexican governments agreed to a cooperative strategy where a minimum price floor was adopted for all US imports of tomatoes. In order for this price to exceed free trade levels and benefit producers relative to free trade, Mexico and/or the USA would have to restrict the production of tomatoes.

10.10 BARGAINING, GAME THEORY AND WELFARE ECONOMICS

The 1994 Nobel Prize in Economic Science was awarded to John Harsanyi, John Nash and Reinhard Selten for their work in pioneering game theory.[17] Their work has greatly generalized the way economists consider markets with imperfect competition, strategic behavior or negotiated outcomes among groups and individuals. Game theory is intended for situations where decision-makers are affected by interactions of others' behavior with their own. Harsanyi (1986, p. 10) makes the following distinction between 'social settings' where game theory should be applied and 'private settings' where decision theory is applicable:

> Individual decision theory deals primarily with rational behavior in situations in which the outcome depends on an individual's own behavior. … The proposed basic difference between decision-theoretical situations and game situations lies in the fact that the latter involve mutually interdependent reciprocal expectations by the players about each other's behavior; the former do not.

Game theory is most applicable to problems involving contracts, cooperation, collusion, political economy and rent-seeking, and bilateral or multilateral market power – problems that inherently deal with small numbers of players or collective action.[18] Examples include landlord–tenant contracts, collective action such as by labor unions, behavior of cooperatives, insurance contracts, vertical integration, public–private research cooperation, product licensing, and issues relating to resource exploitation and environmental regulation. By comparison, the predominant approach of this book can be characterized as decision theoretic.

Relatively little economic welfare analysis and, indeed, little empirical analysis in general has been undertaken using a game-theoretic approach except for the simplest types of games. The reason is that game theory is more of a conceptual way of analyzing a problem than a way to specify a model for estimation. Many types of games have multiple equilibria. Outcomes in many cases depend on the particular strategies pursued by

17. While the Nobel Prize is offered for a lifetime contribution, representative studies include Harsanyi (1963, 1986), Nash (1950, 1953) and Selten (1965).
18. The case of international trade negotiations among sovereign countries is a prime example. See Karp and McCalla (1983).

players or the order in which actions are taken or whether games are repeated. The purpose of this section is to underscore some of the assumptions that are implicit in the specific models of market power discussed earlier in this chapter. Under certain assumptions, the outcomes of games are unique and lend themselves to empirical analysis. In these cases, economic welfare analysis is possible but the interpretation of welfare quantities and observed behavior must account for the game-theoretic strategies that are followed. In this section, we consider only a few of the simple cases amongst the now vast literature on game theory to highlight qualifications that must be placed on standard approaches in economic welfare analysis.

Bertrand versus Cournot versus Stackelberg Behavior

Perhaps the simplest way to illustrate how the behavioral strategies of players can affect the outcome of a game is to compare and contrast Bertrand (1883), Cournot (1838) and Stackelberg (1934) behavior in the case of oligopoly. *Bertrand behavior* is where each firm simultaneously names a price and then sells all the market demands at that price. *Cournot behavior* is where each firm simultaneously determines a quantity and then price adjusts to clear the market. *Stackelberg behavior* is where one firm, the leader, determines its quantity first and then other firms, the followers, choose their quantities given the choice of the leader, and finally price adjusts to clear the market.

Bertrand behavior illustrates the problem whereby the characterization of market equilibria for welfare purposes depends critically on the structure of firm cost functions. In the simple case where all firms have constant and equal marginal cost, Bertrand behavior leads to the same market outcome as competition. The reason is that (1) any firm pricing above another will sell no output, (2) only by pricing at marginal cost will firms be able to remain in the market because otherwise another firm can undercut price by an infinitesimal amount and take the entire market at almost the same profit, and (3) any firm pricing below marginal cost will incur a loss and exit the market. While this result suggests that the competitive model of previous chapters suffices whenever a market is served by more than one producer, the Bertrand equilibrium is quite different with other cost structures. Suppose, for example, that one *dominant firm* has constant marginal cost and all other *fringe firms* have increasing marginal costs such that their combined competitive output cannot satisfy all that is demanded at a price equal to the large firm's marginal cost. In this case, (1) fringe firms gain nothing by pricing above the dominant firm because all their customers would switch to the dominant firm, (2) fringe firms can sell up to the point where price is equal to their marginal cost when setting price the same as the dominant firm, and (3) fringe firms reduce their profit by pricing below the dominant firm's price because profits decline in selling a quantity beyond the point where price is equal to marginal cost. The resulting equilibrium is thus exactly as in the dominant firm price leadership model in Figure 10.3 (where the dominant firm's marginal cost curve is horizontal rather than increasing).[19] Of course, other outcomes are obtained with other structures of firm cost functions.

19. To be consistent with the definitions found in recent game theory literature, the definitions of Cournot, Stackelberg and Bertrand behavior in this section focus on whether firms choose price or quantity and on the order in which firms make choices. More generally, Cournot behavior has been defined as making decisions (whether described by quantity, price, some function relating the two, or other choices), taking the

A comparison of Cournot and Stackelberg behavior illustrates further how market observations on price and quantity may have alternative implications for welfare evaluation. To illustrate Cournot behavior, suppose consumer demand is represented by a linear relationship, $p=\alpha-\beta q$, where the market quantity is the sum of two firms' quantities, $q=q_1+q_2$, and each of the two firms has a linear marginal cost $MC=a+b_iq_i$, meaning their quasirent is $R_i=pq_i-c_i(q_i)$ where $c_i(q_i)=aq_i+bq_i^2/2$ is the short-run cost function, $i=1,2$. Taking the other firm's quantity as given as represented by $\bar{q}_j$, each firm maximizes $R_i=[\alpha-\beta(q_i+\bar{q}_j)]q_i-(aq_i+bq_i^2)$, which yields

$$q_i=\frac{\alpha-a-\beta q_j}{2\beta+b_i},\ i=1,2;j=3-i. \tag{10.1}$$

Solving the two relationships in (10.1) simultaneously yields the quantities produced by each firm,

$$q_i^C=\frac{(\beta+b_j)(\alpha-a)}{(2\beta^2+\beta b_1)(2\beta+\beta b_2)-\beta^2},\ i=1,2;j=3-i. \tag{10.2}$$

The observed *Cournot market equilibrium* quantity is the sum of the two,

$$q^C=q_1^C+q_2^C=\frac{(2\beta+b_1+b_2)(\alpha-a)}{(2\beta^2+\beta b_1)(2\beta+\beta b_2)-\beta^2}. \tag{10.3}$$

The market price is then $p^C=\alpha-\beta q^C$. The quasirent of each firm can be found by substituting equation (10.2) into the quasirent expressions and consumer surplus can be computed as $\beta(q^C)^2/2$.

In the Stackelberg case, the leader observes the behavior followed by other players and maximizes profit by strategically taking advantage of others' behavior. To illustrate Stackelberg behavior in the linear two-firm case, suppose firm 1 is the follower and firm 2 is the leader. Then firm 1's behavior follows equation (10.1). The leader, observing how the follower reacts, maximizes quasirent $R_2=[\alpha-\beta(q_1+q_2)]q_2-(aq_2+bq_2^2)$ after substituting (10.1) for q_1. This yields the Stackelberg leader's quantity,

$$q_2^S=\frac{(\beta+b_1)(\alpha-a)}{(2\beta+b_1)(2\beta+b_2)-2\beta^2}, \tag{10.4}$$

which, upon substituting into (10.1), obtains the Stackelberg follower's quantity,

$$q_1^S=\frac{[(2\beta+b_1)(\beta+b_2)-2\beta^2](\alpha-a)}{[(2\beta+b_1)(2\beta+b_2)-\beta^2](2\beta+b_1)}. \tag{10.5}$$

The observed *Stackelberg market equilibrium* quantity is thus

behavioral relationships of other firms (also possibly described more generally) as given. Accordingly, Stackelberg behavior has been defined as choosing a behavioral rule strategically taking account of the behavioral relationships of others. In this broader context, the behavior of a competitive producer is an example of Cournot behavior because the behavior of other market participants is taken as given (summarized by the prevailing market price), and the behavior of a monopolist is an example of Stackelberg behavior because the monopolist strategically maximizes profit based on the demand schedule that describes consumer behavior as in Section 10.1. In this broader context, the case of price leadership oligopoly in Section 10.3 is sometimes more commonly regarded as a special case of Stackelberg behavior where the leader strategically maximizes profit given the behavioral relationships of the competitive fringe.

$$q^S = q_1^S + q_2^S = \frac{[(2\beta + b_1)(3\beta + b_1 + b_2) - 2\beta^2](\alpha - a)}{[(2\beta + b_1)(2\beta + b_2) - 2\beta^2](2\beta + b_1)}, \tag{10.6}$$

and market price follows $p^S = \alpha - \beta q^S$. Again the quasirent of each firm can be found by substituting these results into the quasirent expressions and consumer surplus can be computed as $\beta(q^S)^2/2$.

Comparing (10.4) with (10.2) reveals that the Stackelberg leader produces more than under Cournot behavior. Also, comparing (10.3) and (10.6) reveals that the market quantity is greater under Stackelberg behavior than under Cournot behavior but less than under competitive behavior. With competitive behavior, the quantity supplied by each firm at any price p is found by equating price to marginal cost, $p = a + b_i q_i$, which yields market supply $q = (b_1 + b_2)(p - a)/(b_1 b_2)$. Solving for the competitive market equilibrium with demand $p = \alpha - \beta q$ yields the Pareto optimal market quantity

$$q^P = \frac{(b_1 + b_2)(\alpha - a)}{(\beta + b_1)(\beta + b_2) - \beta^2}, \tag{10.7}$$

where market price is $p^P = \alpha - \beta q^P$.

One can also show that each of the equilibrium quantities in (10.3), (10.6) and (10.7) is larger than if the two firms colluded to act jointly as a monopolist. That is, the marginal cost of the joint firm is given by $\mathrm{MC} = (b_1 + b_2)(p - a)/(b_1 b_2)$, which in geometric terms corresponds to horizontal addition of the firms' marginal cost curves. Equating this marginal cost with the marginal revenue associated with demand, $\mathrm{MR} = \alpha - 2\beta q$, yields the monopoly market quantity[20]

$$q^M = \frac{(b_1 + b_2)(\alpha - a)}{(2\beta + b_1)(2\beta + b_2) - 4\beta^2}, \tag{10.8}$$

where the monopoly price is $p^M = \alpha - \beta q^M$. Careful algebraic comparison of the market quantities in (10.3), (10.6), (10.7) and (10.8) reveals that $q^M < q^C < q^S < q^P$. From this ordering of market quantities, it is immediately obvious that consumer welfare as measured by consumer surplus has the same ordering as market quantities, and that market price has the inverse ordering (because price follows $\alpha - \beta q$ in each case).

While the simple strategies associated with Bertrand, Cournot and Stackelberg behavior are useful reference points for characterizing players' strategies, they represent only the simplest alternatives. Even with these simple alternatives, behavior is generally indeterminate if two or more players have market power and attempt Stackelberg behavior simultaneously. The case of *bilateral monopoly*, where a market has only one seller and one buyer, is a case in point. If the first tries to behave as a monopolist and the second tries to behave as a monopsonist, the solution is indeterminate.

Nash Bargaining

The Nash bargaining approach considers possible outcomes when two or more players attempt to exercise bargaining power simultaneously in a static cooperative game. A *coop-*

20. That is, if demand is $p = \alpha - \beta q$, then total revenue is $pq = (\alpha - \beta q)q$ and marginal revenue is $\partial(pq)/\partial q = \alpha - 2\beta q$.

erative game is a game in which the players can make binding agreements, which means that enforcement is ensured, for example, by enforceable contracts or laws.[21] Cooperative bargaining became a common technique several decades ago for modeling government action both in the case where the government acts unilaterally but is subject to political pressure from interest groups (see, for example, Beghin and Karp 1991) and where it acts multilaterally with other countries, multinational firms or centrally organized groups within its own borders (see, for example, Chan 1991).

John Nash (1950) showed that the *Nash bargaining solution*, which maximizes the product of utility gains over all players, is the unique solution of a symmetric cooperative game among a fixed group of players under a certain set of conditions called *axioms*. Specifically, the symmetric Nash bargaining solution is defined by

$$\max_x \; [U_1(x)-\bar{U}_1][U_2(x)-\bar{U}_2]\ldots[U_n(x)-\bar{U}_n], \tag{10.9}$$

where n is the number of players, U_i is the utility of player i, $\bar{U}_i$ is the reservation utility that player i can attain in absence of cooperation among the players, and x is a vector of variables that can be agreed upon in a bargaining solution. For example, in the case of bilateral monopoly where $n=2$, U_i might represent the quasirent of firm i, and $\bar{U}_i$ might represent the quasirent that firm i can attain without cooperation. For consumer problems, U_i might be measured by consumer surplus.

The axioms under which the Nash bargaining solution applies are (see, for example, Rasmusen 1989):

1. *Invariance to affine transformations*. The solution is independent of the units of utility measurement, that is, independent of a linear transformation of utility.
2. *Individual rationality*. The solution is Pareto efficient, that is, one player cannot be made better off without making another worse off.
3. *Independence of irrelevant alternatives*. Excluding possibilities for x other than the optimal choice from the feasible set does not change the solution.
4. *Symmetry* (sometimes called *anonymity*). Switching players' identities does not alter the solution.

Variations of the solution are possible by altering the axioms. For example, if the last axiom is dropped, the solution is uniquely described by the asymmetric Nash bargaining solution defined by

$$\max_x \; [U_1(x)-\bar{U}_1]^{\theta_1}[U_2(x)-\bar{U}_2]^{\theta_2}\ldots[U_n(x)-\bar{U}_n]^{\theta_n}, \tag{10.10}$$

21. Beginning with the work of Myerson (1984), many have regarded cooperative bargaining as a subset of the mechanism design and contract theory literature, which includes a broader set of problems that depend on enforcement, rather than as a part of the game theory literature, which in recent times has focused primarily on noncooperative games. The purpose of this section is not to differentiate the literature but to suggest some issues that must be considered under imperfect competition, which arise in each of these contexts. For a brief introduction to mechanism design, see Mas-Colell, Whinston and Green (1995, ch. 23).

where exponents θ_i measure the asymmetric bargaining power of player i (where the θ_is are positive and sum to one).

The appeal of the Nash bargaining solution is that it yields a unique outcome that allows analytical and empirical modeling. By using measures of individual welfare such as consumer and producer surplus to define the utilities in the Nash bargaining criterion, decision rules can be derived that enhance welfare for all individuals as a result of cooperative bargaining. However, the Nash bargaining solution also illustrates an important ambiguity that exists in many more general problems of game theory. The problem is that both the reservation utilities and the bargaining power of individuals may be unclear in specific applications whereas the Nash bargaining solution is highly sensitive to both. For example, in the problem of bilateral monopoly, should the reservation utilities represent zero profit as if a market would fail to exist in absence of striking a bargain? Or should they represent competitive profits as would be achieved if the market had not been monopolized? Or should they represent some other less than perfect level of price discrimination that might be achieved in absence of cooperation? For example, if a buyer has the ability to make a credible 'take it or leave it' offer, a market with bilateral monopoly could behave as in the case of monopsony in absence of cooperation. On the other hand, if the seller can make a credible 'take it or leave it' offer, the market may behave as in the case of monopoly in absence of cooperation, thus generating a very different set of reservation utilities. By varying the reservation utilities, virtually every possible (nonnegative) sharing of welfare among the participating firms is possible.

Similarly, the Nash bargaining solution depends heavily on the bargaining power coefficients. For example, suppose a buyer has marginal revenue of product represented by $\text{MRP}=\alpha-\beta q$ and a seller has marginal cost represented by $\text{MC}=a+bq$. If reservation utilities are zero, then the Nash bargaining problem is

$$\max_{p,q}\,[(\alpha-p)q-\beta q^2/2]^{\theta_1}[(p-a)q-bq^2/2]^{\theta_2},$$

which generates the same output as under pure competition, $q=(\alpha-a)/(\beta+b)$, and yields utilities (or surpluses) for each firm directly proportional to bargaining power, $U_i=\theta_i(\alpha-a)^2/[2(\beta+b)]$. The sum of producer and consumer surplus with competitive behavior in this case is $(\alpha-a)^2/[2(\beta+b)]$. Thus, the sum of producer and consumer surplus under the competitive market outcome is given entirely to the buyer if $\theta_1=1$ and $\theta_2=0$, entirely to the seller if $\theta_1=0$ and $\theta_2=1$, or shared in some intermediate way depending on bargaining power if $0<\theta_1<1$ and $\theta_2=1-\theta_1$. This example suggests that market behavior in terms of quantities and aggregate welfare implied by the analysis of earlier chapters in this book can be accurate when Nash bargaining is applicable even though the price among bargaining firms may be misleading if interpreted in the context of competitive models.

A critical issue in determining the welfare implications under Nash bargaining is whether surplus is transferable. Transferable surplus is the basic assumption that allows economic welfare analyses to focus on aggregate willingness to pay through application of the compensation criterion. If surplus is transferable, the Nash bargaining solution can be attained in two stages by first maximizing aggregate welfare, $\max_x \Sigma_{i=1}^n U_i(x)$, which yields the same choice for x as $\max_x \Sigma_{i=1}^n [U_i(x)-\bar{U}_i]\equiv\Delta W$, and then allocating shares of the maximum incremental welfare among players to maximize $\Pi_{i=1}^{n}(\varphi_i \Delta W)^{\theta_i}$ subject to $\Sigma_{i=1}^{n}\varphi_i = 1$.[22] This solution achieves an equal sharing of incremental welfare in the symmetric case of (10.9) where all θ_is are equal, or a sharing of incremental welfare proportional to the θ_is if the θ_is are unequal as in (10.10).

The fact that Nash bargaining leads to maximization of aggregate incremental welfare when surplus is transferable means that much of the competitive framework of previous chapters carries through when some groups have small numbers of players. While knowledge of transfer payments or other forms of compensation may be critical for measuring the effective prices among firms and the division of surplus among firms in such problems, such information may not be critical for more general welfare analysis. Typically, compensation payments or reciprocating contracts are proprietary information unavailable for most economic welfare analysis. However, based on these results for Nash bargaining with transferable surplus, groups of cooperating players may be treated as a single profit-maximizing decision-maker for purposes of economic welfare analysis in markets where the group trades with other parties.

Contestable Market Theory

Another game-related development that has implications for economic welfare evaluation in situations of market power is contestable market theory. The theory of contestable markets was developed by Baumol, Panzar and Willig (1988) and their various coauthors with the idea that announced prices (whether by a monopolist or a small group of oligopolists) are sustainable only if no output-price combinations exist for any potential entrant that can yield profits covering the cost of entry. Contestable market theory relaxes some assumptions of perfect competition to define a contestable market that achieves the same efficiency. In particular, a *perfectly contestable market* is one in which entry and exit are costless and otherwise unimpeded. Assuming no entry barriers and that all firms legally have access to the same technology and markets, the idea is that a potential competitor will enter a market if (1) a positive profit can be expected by undercutting the incumbent's price, and (2) the new entrant can costlessly exit the market without loss of investment if the incumbent subsequently cuts price below the new entrant's cost. Thus, a contestable market may contain one or a few firms but yet pricing may be competitive because of the threat of many potential entrants.

Contestable market theory underscores the importance of not only considering the number of firms involved in a market for purposes of understanding pricing and economic welfare evaluation, but also considering the ease and cost of entry of potential entrants. Contestable market theory also underscores the importance of studying cost relationships as well as supply and demand in order to identify firm strategies and behavior. For example, an important caveat in the contestability literature is that existence of sustainable equilibria (contestability) with small numbers of firms may depend heavily on the presence of flat or 'flat-bottomed' average cost curves whereas noncompetitive

22. That is, allowing transferable surplus, let $\Delta U_i = U_i(x) - \bar{U}_i + \Sigma_{j=1}^{i-1} c_{ij} - \Sigma_{j=i+1}^{n} c_{ji}$ where c_{ij} represents a transfer of surplus (possibly negative) from individual j to individual i for $j < i$ and from individual i to individual j for $j > i$. The criterion of (10.10), $\max_x \Pi_{i=1}^{n} (\Delta U_i)^{\theta_i}$, thus has first-order conditions that require $\theta_i/\Delta U_i = \theta_j/\Delta U_j$ and $\Sigma_{i=1}^{n} (\theta_i/\Delta U_i)(\partial U_i/\partial x) = 0$. Substituting the first set of conditions into the second implies $\Sigma_{i=1}^{n} (\partial U_i/\partial x) = 0$, which is the first-order condition for $\max_x \Sigma_{i=1}^{n} U_i(x)$.

behavior is evidenced by a wide difference in price and marginal cost (see Baumol, Panzar and Willig 1988, Sections 2D, 2E).

Game Theory as a Model of Lobbying and Political Economy

One of the broad areas of application of the Nash bargaining framework has been in the area of political economy and modeling the impact of lobbying efforts on policy. That is, some studies have considered the θ_is in (10.10) to represent political influence in models of political economy. In these models, the mechanism by which power is exerted is usually implicit and unclear, but policies are assumed to be chosen by a policy-maker or bureaucrat whom the other players try to influence. Players' ability to influence the policy-maker reflects their implicit political power. For example, the θ_is may be considered functions of expenditure on lobbying efforts where the chosen policy reflects a bargained outcome of negotiation among interest groups. Most models of social power assume that all groups play a continuous role in influencing political power even though social power may rise and fall as weights change. In other approaches, membership in the ruling coalition is endogenous.[23]

When policies reflect some other objective than maximizing social welfare, an interesting economic welfare problem is comparison of the political economic equilibrium with the social optimum. One simple and powerful framework that permits comparison of these two states of the economy was developed by Zusman (1976). He considers the first player in a Nash bargaining framework to be the policy-maker and allows other players to reward (or penalize) the policy-maker for adopting (or not adopting) policies favorable to their interests. He showed that policies chosen by Nash bargaining in such a political economic system are, in effect, chosen to satisfy

$$\max_x U_0(x) + \lambda_1 U_1(x) + \ldots + \lambda_n U_n(x),$$

where U_0 is the policy-maker's objective function, U_i is the objective function of interest group i, and λ_i is the marginal strength of power achieved by interest group i. Thus, policies are chosen not to maximize the policy-maker's objective function, nor the sum of producers' and consumers' welfare, but some weighted average of these that reflects the social power structure. This framework justifies the use of weighted welfare criteria in modeling observed government policies (the political economic equilibrium), which can then be compared to the social optimum.

The Generality of Game Theory

The main contribution of game theory is that it allows modeling of a wider variety of situations than does neoclassical theory alone. When a land owner and a potential renter bargain over a rental contract, game theory is needed to capture such real-world concepts as *bargaining power* and *reputation* which have no neoclassical counterpart. When an economist

23. The possibility that partial coalitions may form or that the number of players who participate is endogenous has been considered primarily in the context of games to divide a fixed surplus. See Hart and Kurz (1983), Aumann and Myerson (1988) and Thomson and Lensberg (1989). A case of endogenous coalition formation with endogenous surplus is investigated by Horowitz and Just (1995).

observes cropland rental contracts that involve revenue sharing in some cases and fixed cash payments in others, a model is needed that can predict both contract form and benefit shares for purposes of evaluating welfare consequences. Game theory provides such models. The problem for empirical purposes, however, is that game theory does not provide a unique model but many alternative models depending on strategies and conditions of the game.

The underlying assumptions of game theory are that each decision-maker behaves rationally and reasons strategically. These assumptions (see Osborne and Rubinstein 1994, p. 4) imply that a decision-maker 'is aware of his alternatives, forms expectations about any unknowns, has clear preferences, and chooses his action deliberately after some process of optimization'. Models of game theory are divided according to three broad categories: strategic games, extensive games with or without perfect information, and coalitional games. The first two categories are often called *noncooperative games* and the latter are called *cooperative games*. Nash bargaining falls in the latter category, whereas Bertrand, Cournot and Stackelberg behavior are just a few of many possible strategies for other types of games. While the framework of strategic games and extensive games is suitable for modeling players' autonomous actions, the framework of coalitional games fits situations in which actions are taken by coalitions. Public good issues can be analyzed with each of these approaches depending on the type of interaction among players.

Because, for many problems, game theory offers a host of alternatives rather than defining a unique outcome, game theoretic concepts are widely used only implicitly in much of the literature. For example, the standard moral hazard model used to model contracts is often not characterized as a game, although it clearly is one, and many papers that analyze it do not include its game-theoretic underpinnings. The corollary to this principle is that many interesting models can be analyzed without drawing on the underlying game theory. Cournot models of oligopoly are such examples. But the assumptions required for unique solutions must be borne clearly in mind in such cases.

Another likely reason for limited use of game theory for economic welfare analysis to date is the difficulty of using it as a basis for estimation. Because applied welfare economics is largely an empirical discipline, and because game theory helps in deriving conceptual models but not in specifying empirical models, it has tended not to be central to the practice of welfare economics. The purpose of this section is to help practicing welfare economists be aware that their models may be imposing determinate outcomes on data when none exist and, more constructively, to identify and clarify assumptions under which the outcomes of games are unique and lend themselves to empirical analysis. This exercise is necessarily cursory because the scope here permits considering only a few simple cases of game theory.[24]

10.11 EMPIRICAL CONSIDERATIONS IN MARKETS SUBJECT TO MARKET POWER

The possibility of multiple types of equilibria depending on the strategies of players illustrates an important problem for applied economic welfare analysis. Meaningful welfare

24. For a more complete introduction, see Rasmusen (1989) or Osborne and Rubinstein (1994) or, at a more advanced level, see Fudenberg and Tirole (1992).

analysis is possible in these cases, but the behavioral criterion of each player must be identified in order to correctly specify equations for estimation and to correctly interpret observed market behavior for welfare evaluation. For example, suppose for econometric purposes that demand is assumed to follow a linear form, $p=\gamma_0+\gamma_1 x_1+\ldots+\gamma_n x_n$, where $x_n=q$ and other x_is represent demand shifters such as consumer income. Thus, $\alpha=\gamma_0+\gamma_1 x_1+\ldots+\gamma_{n-1}x_{n-1}$ and $\beta=-\gamma_n$ in the context of equations (10.1)–(10.8). Similarly, suppose producers' marginal costs follow a linear form, $\mathrm{MC}=c_0+c_1 z_1+\ldots+c_m z_m$, where $z_m=q$ and other z_is represent supply shifters such as prices of factor inputs. Then, in the context of equations (10.1)–(10.8), $a=c_0+c_1 z_1+\ldots+c_{m-1}z_{m-1}$ where c_m, which corresponds to b_i, is the only parameter of marginal cost that varies among firms.

Now consider the problem of how to discern from the estimated relationships based on observed market prices and quantities whether market equilibrium represents the Cournot case in (10.3), the Stackelberg case in (10.6), the competitive case in (10.7) or the monopoly case in (10.8). In each case, the market equilibrium quantity and price can be expressed as

$$q^k=b^k(\alpha-a)=b^k(\gamma_0+\gamma_1 x_1+\ldots+\gamma_{n-1}x_{n-1}-c_0-c_1 z_1-\ldots-c_{m-1}z_{m-1}) \quad (10.11)$$
$$p^k=\alpha-\beta q^k=\gamma_0+\gamma_1 x_1+\ldots+\gamma_{n-1}x_{n-1}+\gamma_n q^k,$$

where $k=C, S, P$ or M (representing the four different cases), and b^k is some scalar function of b_1, b_2 and β. Because b^k is a scalar constant, estimation does not permit identifying how it depends on b_1, b_2, and β. Thus, without some other information about firms' behavioral strategies or cost functions, the underlying behavior model cannot be discerned. More explicitly, the estimated scalar b^k in (10.11) could represent

$$b^C=\frac{2\beta+b_1+b_2}{(2\beta^2+\beta b_1)(2\beta+\beta b_2)-\beta^2},$$

implying Cournot behavior (compare with equation (10.3)), or it could represent

$$b^S=\frac{(2\beta+b_1)(3\beta+b_1+b_2)-2\beta^2}{[(2\beta+b_1)(2\beta+b_2)-2\beta^2](2\beta+b_1)},$$

implying Stackelberg behavior (compare with equation (10.6)), or it could represent competitive or monopolistic behavior.

In cases such as this, estimation of cost functions can help immensely in identifying the b_1 and b_2 parameters embedded in b^k and thus permit appropriate welfare interpretations. However, cost data, particularly for industries composed of small numbers of firms, are proprietary and carefully guarded as trade secrets. Thus, cost data are generally unavailable for economic welfare analysis of concentrated industries. Another possibility is to observe behavior before and after some event that clearly alters the parameters of cost functions. Just and Chern (1980) give an example of how a major change in technology in an industry can permit such discernment. They consider adoption of the mechanical tomato harvester, which was rapid and widespread throughout the tomato processing industry. The harvester replaced the main production expense of manual harvesting labor with machinery services and thus converted variable cost to fixed cost. Due to a major change in the cost structure over a very short period of time, the variation in cost parameters was estimated by comparing data from before and after the harvester's introduction.

Thus, the underlying behavioral strategies of purported price fixing among tomato processors could be discerned, and the potential welfare gains from competitive pricing could be evaluated.

Similar problems arise in other game-theoretic settings. For example, when a group of market participants are possibly cooperating via Nash bargaining and surplus is not transferable, then a welfare economist must be careful to estimate behavior using appropriate models – decision-theoretic models based on individual optimization models such as considered in earlier chapters in this book or cooperative decision models based on the Nash bargaining solution. Surplus may not be transferable in cases where the collective actions of firms result in price fixing as precluded by law. For example, if a group of firms can gain through collective action to restrict market supply, then the formality of such action evidenced by surplus transfers (perhaps in the form of bribes) may be regarded as legally infeasible, whereas informal restriction of market quantities through unspoken gentlemen's agreements may be regarded as legally feasible. In this case, the problem is that neither the reservations utilities nor the bargaining power of individual players may be readily identifiable for empirical purposes. Determining the sharing of welfare among firms cooperating by Nash bargaining may thus be very difficult if the implicit prices, transfers and compensating agreements are unobservable.

For these reasons, how game theory might be used to provide better empirical models remains a largely unexplored research area. Games with multiple equilibria and outcomes that depend on particular players' strategies require more attention to empirical identification of behavioral strategies. A critical conclusion, which applies in principle to all types of empirical analysis, is that specification of empirical models for welfare analysis must rest on careful study of the institutional structure of decision-making if the implications are to have practical significance.

10.12 CONCLUSIONS

This chapter has focused on economic welfare analysis when markets are imperfectly competitive. The major cases considered initially were monopoly, monopsony and dominant share price leadership oligopoly or oligopsony. Later sections introduce other forms of behavior that may permit gaining market power and monopoly profits through collusion among firms, or may lead to efficient market outcomes through cooperation or contestability. While the same principles of economic welfare analysis apply in all cases, the discernment of the underlying behavioral criteria is critical to proper interpretation of observed market data for economic welfare analysis.

The economic welfare analysis in this chapter shows that, in some cases, monopoly may be preferable. This occurs if returns to scale from a large firm lead to production cost savings that outweigh the social costs of monopoly pricing. Even in this case, however, some further form of price regulation may attain both production and social efficiency. For example, government regulation of utility companies (government-sanctioned monopolies) is supposedly a case in point.

One of the plausible applications of imperfect competition relates to the role of market intermediaries. In many sectors of the economy, large marketing firms buy from many producers and sell to many consumers. The analysis shows that the distributional as well as efficiency implications of such firms depend critically on the objectives and clientele of the marketing firm. Producer cooperatives and marketing boards benefit producers at the expense of consumers. Pure middlemen adversely affect both consumers and producers and cause greater market contraction than other marketing arrangements.

Another important area of application of market power considerations is in the analysis of labor unions. Here the results show that labor union market power not only benefits labor union members at the expense of employers but also that nonunionized labor may suffer substantially as well. Thus, the distributional consequences can be large even when efficiency effects are small.

Perhaps the most natural application of economic welfare analysis under imperfect competition is in the legal area of antitrust. Economic welfare analysis as well as game theory have been used and have much to say about the effects of market power on various market groups and the social inefficiency that can occur when such power is exercised. A comparison of the implications of welfare economics with legal precedent reveals some areas of broad agreement and other areas where legal practice is at odds with the implications of welfare economics, particularly in cases involving multiple markets.

This chapter presents a variety of applications of the welfare economics of imperfect competition to policy analysis in international trade. Monopolistic and monopsonistic outcomes can be achieved by imposing tariffs on imports, and taxes or supply controls on exports. However, due to potential retaliation by trading partners in the form of similar controls on other traded goods, market power is often exercised indirectly. Sometimes indirect controls take forms that are more likely to attract support from key groups in countries that would otherwise consider retaliation or are applied indirectly in the form of taxes or subsidies that can be construed as correcting domestic externalities.

In each of these applications, the principles of welfare economics can be used to say a great deal about the social benefits or costs of various behaviors, but empirical application comes down to a thorny and difficult problem of econometric identification of whether specific behaviors are present. The additional considerations added by the wider variety of equilibrium descriptions developed from bargaining and game theory only complicate these matters. To date, most empirical welfare and policy analyses of problems with imperfect competition have used the simpler models discussed in Sections 10.1 through 10.9, while the more complicated descriptions of equilibria that have been forthcoming from the game theory literature have been used mainly for conceptual analysis. As empirical analysis becomes more sophisticated, however, welfare analysis will be needed in more general circumstances. Section 10.10 demonstrates that such generalizations are straightforward once the various equilibrium and solution concepts are better empiricized.

11. The welfare economics of information with applications to advertising and information policy

Thus far in this book, decision-makers have been assumed to possess perfect information. Perfect information is a basic assumption of perfect competition that may not approximate many real-world situations. Perfect information means that all market participants have identical and correct knowledge of a good's characteristics including current prices and future prices of goods that are used in combination. In reality, producers may undertake production anticipating a different price or demand for their output than will prevail when production is completed. Consumers may purchase a consumer durable anticipating different prices of goods that are used in combination with it than will prevail during the life of the durable. For example, a consumer may purchase electric home-heating equipment and then find the price of electricity is higher than anticipated relative to other fuels during the life of the heating equipment. Or a consumer may make consumption decisions and then find that the quality of a purchased good is different than anticipated. The quality of a good may represent the flow of services from a durable good such as the efficiency of heating equipment or frequency of breakdowns such as in the case of an automobile, or it may reflect the health effects of consumption or a variety of other factors that determine the enjoyment ultimately achieved from consumption. Once the welfare effects of misperceptions of price and quality are understood, the welfare benefits of information and the welfare costs of false information can be analyzed. In particular, the paradox whereby both demand and consumer surplus increase simply due to incorrect quality information can be resolved.

The role of information in economics has been long recognized but most progress in analyzing the economics of information was not made until the last few decades. Initially, research focused on price information and errors in expected prices. However, most empirical models assumed all individuals possessed the same price information in the form of expectations. If all individuals have the same expectations (even if they are in error), the problem is one of *symmetric information*. More recently, economic research has focused on problems with *asymmetric information*, where not all individuals have the same expectations or information. When market participants have asymmetric information, market outcomes can be quite different than with symmetric information. For example, if a producer can convince buyers of its product that its product quality is higher than it really is, then more output can be sold at a higher price even though the consumers may gain no greater utility from consumption. Similarly, an employer may gain less productivity from hiring a laborer than anticipated if the laborer can shirk duties in a way that is imperceptible to the employer. In this case, the laborer knows how much effort is expended but the employer may have less information, particularly without costly monitoring. Such problems of information asymmetry have attracted great interest over the last few decades. As a result, the literature on contracting, signaling, and mechanism design has expanded dramatically. The purpose of this chapter is not to discuss these developments in the literature but to outline the welfare concepts that are critical to proper evaluation of welfare effects in such problems when information is not perfect. Based on the principles developed in this chapter, the welfare effects of asymmetric information can then be measured in a straightforward manner based on these various specific models, solution concepts or mechanisms that potentially describe observed changes in equilibrium.

11.1 THE ROLE OF PRICE EXPECTATIONS

Virtually all economic activity depends critically on the information held by decision-makers at the time of their decisions. Each time a consumer decides to buy groceries, a complete search is not performed to determine prices offered on all products in all available grocery stores. Rather, a consumer relies on past experience related to prices occasionally observed when store visits were made previously, as well as perhaps a selected set of prices advertised in various media. Past experience and advertised prices constitute the consumer's price information that is used to decide which grocery store to visit to make current purchases. After arriving at the grocery store, prices of some products may be higher or lower than expected, in which case consumption quantities may be altered accordingly. Sometimes a consumer may purchase an item and then find out from a friend that the same item was available at another store for a lower price. Perhaps a different quantity of the good would have been purchased if the lower price would have been available. How are the welfare effects of such errors in price information evaluated? What is the value of information on where to find the lowest price? What is the welfare loss from purchasing a different amount of the good than would have been purchased with full information?

Similarly, because production requires time, producers generally must decide how much to produce before the conditions determining output prices are known. If a producer determines the amount to produce and then after production finds that demand conditions have deteriorated or that a large surplus of product has come to market from other sources, the producer may be forced to lower price in order to sell what has been produced. How are the welfare effects of such errors in price expectations measured? How do incorrect price expectations affect production and the consequent welfare effects?

The Case of the Producer

Many models have been proposed to represent how producers form price expectations. The problem of determining price expectations is especially critical for modeling supply in industries with long production lags and stochastic conditions of production. Agriculture with its rather long production cycles and weather-dependent biological growing conditions is a prime example. Some of the leading models of price expectations that have been used empirically are naive expectations where last period's price is assumed to be expected this period, extrapolative expectations where the recent trend in prices is simply extended one more period, adaptive expectations where prices in all previous periods are weighted with geometrically declining weights to form current expectations and rational expectations where all available information on current or anticipated supply and demand shifters is incorporated to estimate a new point of supply–demand equilibrium.[1] From the standpoint of welfare analysis, however, the mechanism that explains price expectations is not critical to determining how to measure the welfare effects of errors in price expectations, although applied economic welfare analysis must measure price expectations before the welfare effects of errors in expectations can be measured.

In Figure 11.1, a producer's marginal cost is given by MC. Suppose all input decisions must be made before production begins and that the producer has an *ex ante* output price expectation at the time of production decisions represented by p_0. Then a competitive producer (who takes price as given) who attempts to maximize expected profit will produce

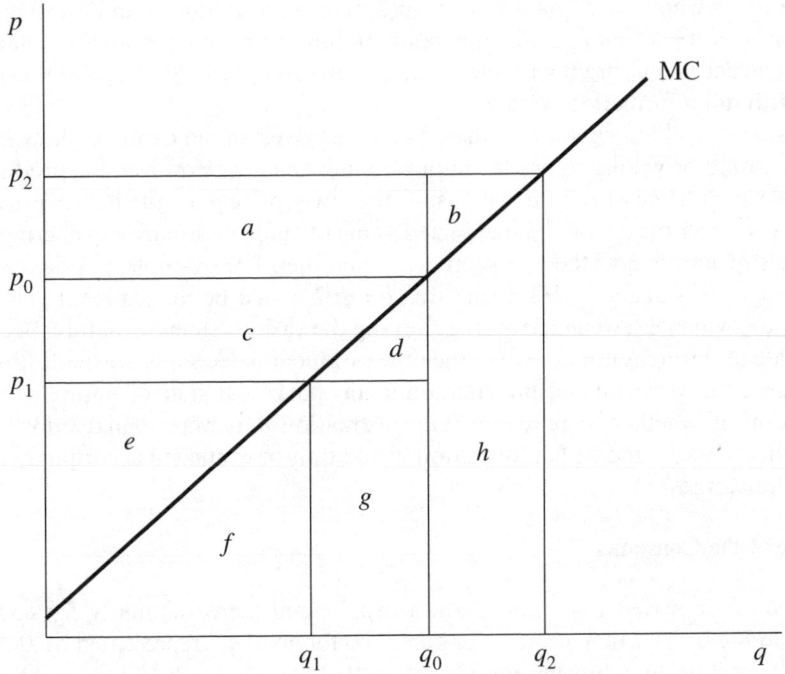

Figure 11.1

output q_0, which equates expected price and marginal cost. Now suppose the production process is completed and the *ex post* price at which production must be sold turns out to be p_1. The producer anticipates variable production cost of area $d+f+g$ and revenue of area $c+d+e+f+g$ for a consequent quasirent of area $c+e$. However, the actual *ex post* price generates a lower revenue of area $e+f+g$. Because the producer committed to produce quantity q_0 before the *ex post* price was known, the production cost is area $d+f+g$ as anticipated. So the actual *ex post* quasirent is area $e-d$. The producer is worse off

1. Various approximations of rational expectations have also been suggested that are empirically simpler to implement. For a survey of the price expectations literature, see Nerlove and Bessler (2002).

than anticipated by area $c+d$. However, with full information that allowed anticipating price p_1, the producer would have produced quantity q_1 and earned quasirent of area e. Thus, the value of full information is area d, which is the difference in actual quasirent with incorrect information, area $e-d$, and the quasirent earned with full information, area e.

Now suppose the actual *ex post* price turns out to be above the expected price at p_2. In this case, the actual *ex post* price generates a higher revenue than anticipated, area $a+c+d+e+f+g$. Because the producer committed to produce quantity q_0 before the *ex post* price was known, increasing output above q_0 in response to the higher price is not possible. Accordingly, the production cost is area $d+f+g$ as anticipated and the actual *ex post* quasirent is area $a+c+e$. The producer is better off than anticipated by area a, but worse off than if full information had allowed production decisions to be made anticipating price p_2, in which case quantity q_2 would have been produced and quasirent would have been area $a+b+c+e$. Thus, the value of full information is area b, which is the difference in actual quasirent with incorrect information, area $a+c+e$, and the quasirent earned with full information, area $a+b+c+e$.

The value of full information in these two cases gives an indication of how much the producer would be willing to pay for improved information. However, the producer does not know which 'state of nature' will result, the lower price p_1 or the higher price p_2.[2] At best, the producer must assess the expected value of information by considering all possible states of nature and their respective probabilities. For example, if prices p_1 and p_2 each occur with probability 1/2, then (area $b+d$)/2 would be the expected value of full information, which is a weighted average among the various states of nature. Because the actual state of nature is not known at the time production decisions are made, this expectation rather than the value of information in any particular state of nature would drive the decision of whether to purchase full information if it were available for sale. The welfare effects associated with information would thus be evaluated accordingly based on expected outcomes.

The Case of the Consumer

The value of improved price information can be considered similarly for consumers. Suppose in Figure 11.2 that a consumer's demand for good q is represented by D. Suppose the consumer chooses to buy the good at a store that turns out to have price p_0 and accordingly chooses by buy quantity q_0. Now suppose alternatively that the consumer subscribes to an information service such as *Consumer Reports* that gives information about an outlet with a lower price p_1. In this case, the consumer would choose to buy quantity q_1. The value of improved information is thus area $a+b$, the increase in consumer surplus from improved information. This welfare quantity would measure both the effect of finding a lower price, area a, plus the ability to adjust the consumption quantity to that lower price, area b. Area $a+b$ would measure willingness to pay accurately if the demand in Figure 11.2 is a Hicksian demand or would be an approximation if the demand is an ordinary demand. That is, the change in Hicksian surplus would measure compensating or equiv-

2. For the purposes of this discussion, a *state of nature* is a state of the economy that can possibly be observed *ex post*, that is, after decisions are made. The specific state of nature that will result is unknown *ex ante*, that is, at the time of decisions.

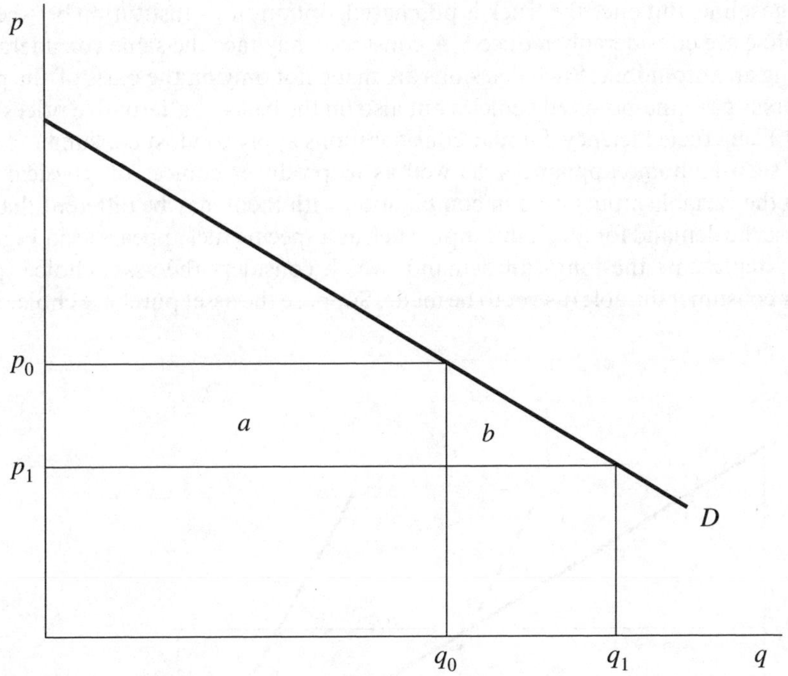

Figure 11.2

alent variation depending on whether the demand is conditioned on initial or subsequent utility, while the change in ordinary Marshallian surplus would be an approximation of either to the extent that Willig conditions apply.[3]

As in the producer case, however, the value of information is not known until a particular state of nature is observed, that is, until the consumer knows just how low the best price is. Thus, consumer decisions to acquire improved information must be based on some assessment of the expected value of information. This assessment may be based on past experience or word of mouth from friends and neighbors about the benefits of information. In such cases, accurate empirical welfare measurement depends on gaining accurate information about consumer perceptions of the value of purchased price information by direct survey or on careful modeling of mechanisms that determine consumer perceptions as well as on objective evidence that indicates how much more than minimum price is paid by various consumers.

Goods Used in Combination with Durables and Physical Capital

In many cases, both producers and consumers commit themselves to future use of certain variable inputs by their purchases of consumer durable goods and physical capital items. For example, a producer may have the option of purchasing a truck powered by either

3. Without repeating this qualification, the reader should regard a similar statement as applicable to all consumer welfare quantities discussed in this chapter except where otherwise noted.

diesel or gasoline. But once the truck is purchased, options for substitution between diesel and gasoline are considerably reduced. A consumer may face the same considerations in purchasing an automobile. Such decisions are made not only on the basis of the prices of diesel- versus gasoline-powered vehicles but also on the basis of alternative prices of fuels and their likely fuel efficiency. Similar considerations apply to most consumer choices of durables such as home appliances, as well as to producer choices of physical capital, although the variable inputs used in combination with them may be different than fuels.

Suppose the demand for a variable input such as a specific fuel appears as in Figure 11.3 where D_L represents the long-run demand, which considers the asset choice (physical capital or consumer durable) as yet to be made. Suppose the asset purchase choice is based

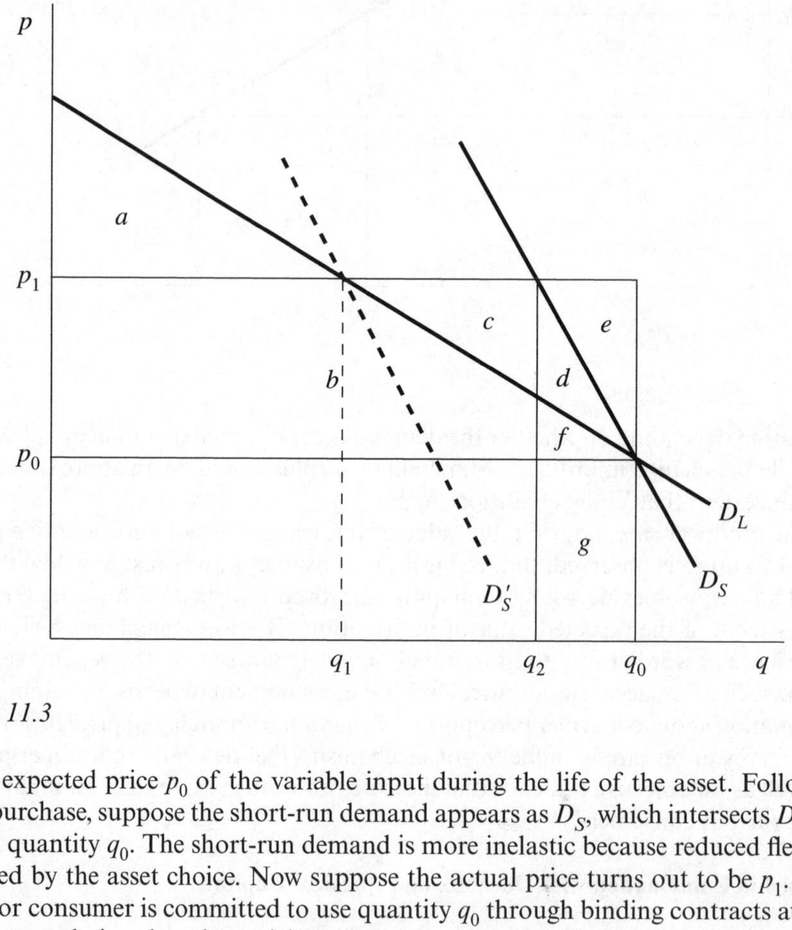

Figure 11.3

on an expected price p_0 of the variable input during the life of the asset. Following the asset purchase, suppose the short-run demand appears as D_S, which intersects D_L at price p_0 and quantity q_0. The short-run demand is more inelastic because reduced flexibility is imposed by the asset choice. Now suppose the actual price turns out to be p_1. If a producer or consumer is committed to use quantity q_0 through binding contracts at the time of the asset choice, then the anticipated consumer surplus of area $a+b+f$ turns out to be area $a-c-d-e$, which differs from the anticipated consumer surplus by the increased cost of the input, $(p_1-p_0)q_0=$ area $b+c+d+e+f$. Alternatively and more commonly, if the quantity of the variable input is not constrained following the asset purchase, then the producer or consumer can mitigate the loss from incorrect price expectations somewhat by adjusting along the short-run demand relationship to the actual price p_1. By reducing the use of the variable input from the anticipated quantity q_0 to q_2, expenditures decline by area $d+e+f+g$, but gross benefits decline by a smaller amount, area $d+f+g$, for a net gain of area e compared to the case with no adjustment. Thus, consumer surplus actually turns out to be area $a-c-d$.

This outcome can be compared to the case of full information, which would anticipate price p_1 perfectly. In this case, the asset choice would generate short-run demand D'_S and anticipated as well as actual consumer surplus would be area a. Thus, the value of full information would be area $c+d$.

Of course, the *ex post* price of the variable input might also turn out to be less than anticipated. Figure 11.3 could be drawn somewhat similarly for this case as well. By considering the relationship of actual *ex post* price to the expected price in all alternative states of nature and the probability with which each state of nature occurs, a weighted average value (expected value) of improved information can be determined. As in the producer case above, this expectation rather than the *ex post* value of information in any particular state of nature would drive the decision to purchase improved information from any service that might provide it. The welfare effects in the information market would then be evaluated accordingly.

11.2 THE ROLE OF QUALITY INFORMATION

Many goods have quality attributes that become clear to the buyer only after purchase and use. For example, automobiles and electronic equipment may have flaws that lead to unexpected repairs. Foods may have unexpected taste, spoilage, contamination or health effects. Medications may not perform as expected or have unexpected side effects. The quality of various forms of entertainment is also typically unknown until after consumption. For producers, investment in new technologies and capital equipment may have unexpected effects on production efficiency. Factor inputs may turn out to have better or worse effects on production than anticipated. Such unexpected quality has direct effects on the utility derived from consumption and on the quasirent earned by producers. In addition, when quality is not perceived correctly, both consumers and producers experience indirect welfare effects because errors are made in determining the quantities that maximize consumer utility and producer quasirent. While the graphical examples in this section are presented from the perspective of the consumer, similar principles apply in such producer problems.

Conventional welfare economic practices have confused many students with respect to the valuation of information that correctly reveals that the quality of a particular good is worse than previously understood. To illustrate, suppose in Figure 11.4 that the demand for a consumer good with *ex ante* expected quality is represented by D. At the prevailing price p_0, the consumer purchases quantity q_0. Now suppose alternatively that correct information had been released correctly indicating that the quality of the good is worse than the consumer actually realized at the time of the purchase decision. Suppose the consumer's demand with the new quality information would have been D'. In other words, D' measures the actual marginal benefits of consumption received by the consumer. If the consumer had correct information at the time of the decision, the consumption quantity would have been q_1 rather than q_0, and the consumer surplus would have been area c,

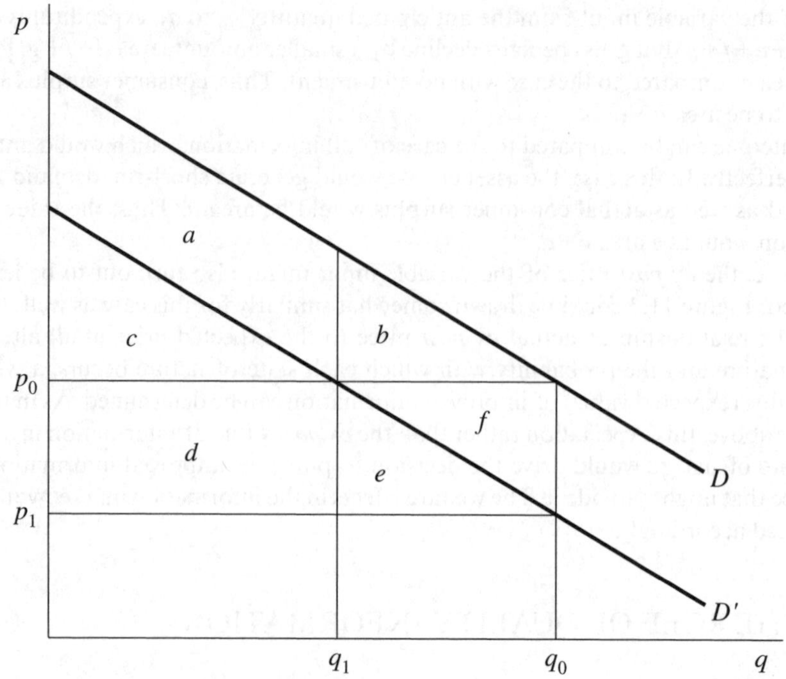

Figure 11.4

rather than the area $a+b+c$ that was anticipated when the actual consumption decision was made. By releasing correct information, consumer welfare apparently falls, implying a negative value of correct information. This paradox long prevented sensible economic welfare analysis related to changes in information.

To resolve this paradox, one must focus not only on modeling the effect of quality on consumer demand, but also on the imposition of inefficiency on consumers when information on quality is incorrect. Then the correct value of information is revealed.[4] The effect of quality on consumer demand can be modeled either by making demand a direct function of quality or by considering a household production framework whereby the quality of a good purchased as an input enhances the resulting amount of household production. According to results discussed in Appendix Section 7.G, the latter approach produces results equivalent to the former.

To correct the paradoxical analysis of Figure 11.4, suppose that after purchasing quantity q_0 the consumer discovers that the quality level is lower than expected, such as would have generated consumer demand D' if the true quality had been correctly anticipated. What is the welfare effect on the consumer of the error in quality perception? If the quality had been correctly anticipated, the consumer would have chosen quantity q_1 and consumer surplus would have been area c. However, in most cases the consumer cannot return quantity $q_0 - q_1$ to the store and get a full refund, especially in cases where consumption has exhausted the good as in the case of food. If returns are not practical, then the quan-

4. This principle was first emphasized by Foster and Just (1989).

tity of consumption is fixed at q_0 *ex post*, which essentially constrains the consumer from adjusting to optimal consumption levels.

The case of constrained consumption levels is where willingness to pay is correctly measured by compensating or equivalent surplus rather than compensating or equivalent variation because the consumer is not free to adjust to the optimum level of consumption. If the demands in Figure 11.4 represent Hicksian demands, then the compensating or equivalent surplus at price p_0 and quantity q_0 is given by area $c-f$ depending on whether demands are conditioned on initial or final utility. Alternatively, if the demands in Figure 11.4 are ordinary Marshallian demands, then the compensating and equivalent surpluses are approximated by the ordinary consumer surplus, area $c-f$, to the extent that the bounds developed in Appendix Section 7.J apply. One way to view this welfare quantity is as the consumer surplus that would be gained by unconstrained adjustment to price p_1 if the correct quality had been anticipated, area $c+d+e$, minus the additional expenditure at price p_0 compared to price p_1, $(p_0-p_1)q_0=$area $d+e+f$. Comparing the welfare quantities with and without correct information about quality, that is, area c and area $c-f$, reveals the correct and sensibly positive value of quality information, area f.

The paradox whereby correct information reveals adverse quality and causes a reduction in both demand and consumer surplus is thus resolved. With correct analysis, the poor quality causes the reduction in welfare whereas correct information about quality allows higher welfare than otherwise because of informed choice of optimal consumption quantities. An important qualification of this result is that a consumer is assumed to detect the poorer than anticipated quality in the process of consumption. Specifically, the consumer is assumed to derive the same utility from consumption as if the true quality were known at the time of purchase. This assumption presumes that the old adage 'ignorance is bliss' does not apply. If the consumer never realizes that the quality of the good is lower than anticipated, then the satisfaction derived from its consumption would be the same as anticipated. More is discussed about this possibility below.

11.3 MEASURING THE WELFARE EFFECTS OF PARTIAL AND MISLEADING INFORMATION

With the basic framework of information introduced in Sections 11.1 and 11.2, the welfare effects of partial and misleading information can be considered. Rarely can consumers and producers find sources of full information, particularly about future prices. Typically, decision-makers are faced with a variety of alternative sources of information that are each imperfect. Often the best sources of information are costly. Many information firms have been developed to produce and sell price information, for example, in the form of newsletters or market assessment reports. Some help consumers locate the lowest price currently available. Some help producers better assess the price that may prevail when current planned production comes to market.

While decision-makers can form price expectations according to the naive approach at virtually no cost, forming expectations according to the rational approach (see Section 11.1) requires costs of other information acquisition and processing, which are services typically performed by information firms who sell price forecasts and future market assessments. Some markets, such as publicly traded futures and options markets, have been developed to help buyers and sellers discover future prices. Some public agencies monitor market information and release periodic reports that such information firms use to produce their information products, some of which strongly influence futures and options markets when they are released. If all individuals had the same information, then there would be no purpose in these types of firms, marketing institutions or agency reports. Evaluation of the welfare effects of such firms, institutions and government information activities depends on correctly evaluating the benefits of partial price information to consumers and producers.

Also, consumers are faced with misleading quality information in many situations. Sometimes advertisements claim greater quality for products than can be substantiated. Perhaps more often, full quality information is not known about products by their sellers. Substances such as cigarettes, drugs or alcohol may have effects on health that are unknown to the consumer when they are used. For example, the health effects of cigarettes allegedly unknown to consumers at the time of consumption decisions made many years earlier became the issue of many lawsuits by consumers against cigarette manufacturers during the 1990s. Sometimes such quality attributes become known gradually over time with experience but such information may or may not be disseminated. Also, foods purchased by consumers may be contaminated by pesticides or have other problems unknown to the consumer at the time of purchase. For example, cases are often reported where a number of individuals have been infected with salmonella poisoning or some other sickness from eating at a particular restaurant or social gathering, or where some lots of food products sold in grocery stores are found to be contaminated. Allegedly, some doctors have tended not to recommend expensive potential medical procedures because of policies of health maintenance organizations, while others have tended not to recommend high-risk medical procedures because of potential malpractice lawsuits if something goes wrong. Or automobile repair shops may claim that more repairs are needed than are actually necessary.

Welfare Benefits of Partial Price Information

The benefits of partial price information can be evaluated by extending the framework of Section 11.1. For example, Figure 11.1 can be generalized to consider partial price information as in Figure 11.5. Where MC is the producer's marginal cost and initial *ex ante* information leads the producer to expect price p_0, suppose improved but imperfect information is purchased that leads to expected price p_2. Again assuming all input decisions must be made before production begins, in absence of improved information a competitive profit-maximizing producer produces output q_0. If the *ex post* price turns out to be p_1, the producer receives revenue equal to area $e+f+g$, incurs variable cost equal to area $c+d+f+g$ as anticipated, and gains quasirent equal to area $e-c-d$. The loss from incorrect price information is area $c+d$.

Alternatively, if the producer purchases information that leads to *ex ante* price expectation p_2, the producer attempts to maximize profit by producing output q_2 where expected price is equal to marginal cost. The improved price information allows the producer to avoid production cost of area $d+g$ and incur a cost of only area $c+f$. When *ex post* price turns out to be p_1, revenue will thus be area $e+f$ and quasirent will be area $e-c$. The *ex post* value of improved information to the producer is thus area d.

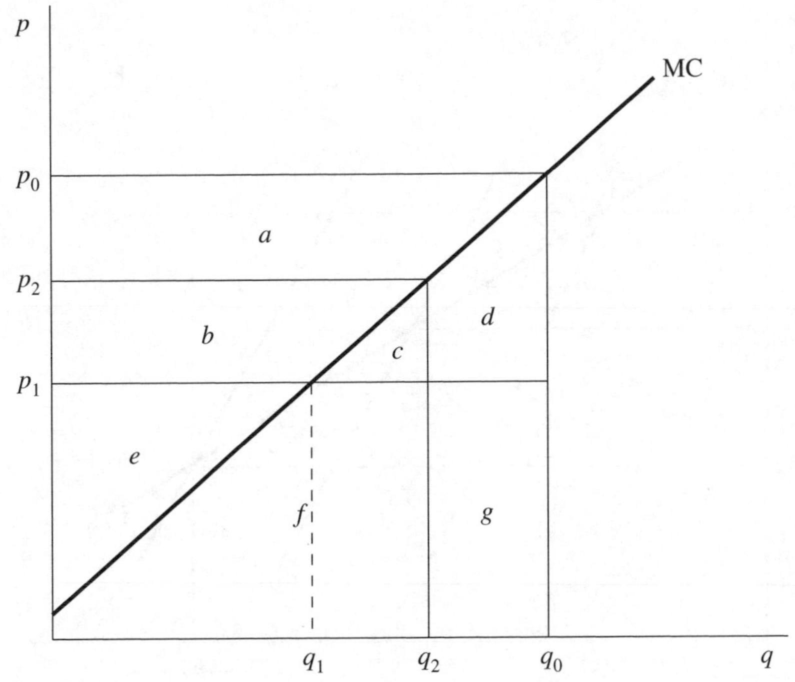

Figure 11.5

As explained in Section 11.1, this is the value of improved information only in one state of nature. To correctly value *ex ante* improved information, this type of welfare analysis should be performed for every state of nature and the consequent value of improved information must be weighted by the probability of each state of nature to determine the expected value of improved information. For purposes of this analysis, a state of nature is defined by the threesome (p_0,p_1,p_2). These three prices may have any particular order depending on unanticipated price variation and the quality of information. For example, the case where p_0 lies between p_1 and p_2 would be a state where the improved information causes a greater error than without it, which would happen only rarely if the information is really improved, while a state where p_1 lies between p_0 and p_2 would be a state where improved information overshoots. The expected value of improved information that weights all alternative possible values of this threesome by the probabilities with which each occurs would determine how much the producer would be willing to pay for improved information. The producer's benefit from improved information would be that expected value of improved information less what is paid for the information, while the information-producing firm would gain welfare equal to the price paid for the information less the cost of producing the information.

Similar principles apply to evaluating the benefits of improved but partial information in the consumer case and in the case of goods used in combination with assets. For example, generalizing the framework of Figure 11.3 to the case of partial information, suppose in Figure 11.6 that D_L represents the long-run demand for a good where the

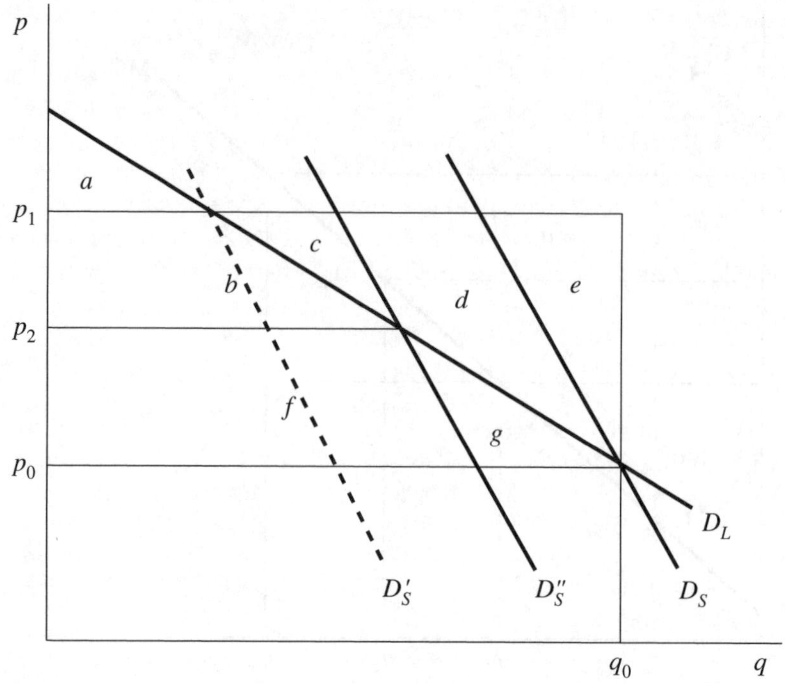

Figure 11.6

choice of assets is not yet made. Suppose in the absence of improved information that price p_0 is expected during the life of the assets for a good such as fuel that is used by the assets, and that D_S represents the short-run demand for the variable input after expected profit-maximizing asset purchases are made based on price expectation p_0. If the actual price during the life of the asset turns out to be p_1, the correct evaluation of consumer surplus is area $a-c-d$. If, however, improved information were available that generates *ex ante* price expectation p_2, then assets are chosen that generate a short-run demand for the variable input such as D_S'', which intersects D_L at p_2. While this choice would anticipate consumer surplus equal to area $a+b$, the actual surplus achieved after short-run adjustment along D_S'' to the actual price p_1 would be area $a-c$. Thus, the value of improved information would be the difference between the cases of unimproved and improved information, area d.

Of course, area d would represent the value of improved information in only one state of nature. Figure 11.6 could be drawn similarly for different orderings of the threesome (p_0,p_1,p_2). By considering this threesome in all alternative states of nature and the probability with which each state of nature occurs, the weighted average value (expected value) of improved information could be determined. This expected value of information would represent an *ex ante* willingness to pay for improved information. The net surplus equal to this expected value minus the cost of producing such information would be shared with the firm producing the information depending on the price charged by the information firm for the improved information.

Welfare Benefits of Partial Quality Information

Now consider the case where the consumer can acquire improved but imperfect information about quality. Suppose in Figure 11.7 where demand D' is based on false information that the consumer's demand with the improved information leads to *ex ante* demand D'', but true quality perceptions yield demand D. Then with improved information the consumer will purchase a smaller quantity q_2, which reduces the welfare loss from poor quality perceptions. In this case, consumer surplus is area $a-c$ compared to area $a-c-d$, which is the true consumer surplus for the case with unimproved information. The value of the improved but imperfect information is area d.

Figure 11.7 could be drawn similarly for different relationships among D, D' and D''. For example, in some states of nature the improved information may have D' between D and D'', even though on balance it would not. By considering all alternative states of nature and the probability with which each state of nature occurs, the weighted average value (expected value) of improved information could be determined for each consumer. Each consumer would be willing to pay any amount up to this expected value for improved information. The net *ex ante* social benefit would be the expected value of information for all consumers receiving it minus the cost of generating the improved information. The net benefit for each consumer would be the consumer's expected value of improved information minus the price charged for the improved information, and the net benefit for a firm producing improved information would be the amount of revenues received for improved information minus the cost of producing improved information.

Welfare Costs of False and Misleading Quality Information

A companion paradox associated with the one discussed in Section 11.2 is the case where providing false quality information to a consumer that increases demand for a product, and thus increases consumer surplus, apparently suggests a positive welfare effect of false information. For example, in Figure 11.7, suppose the consumer has *ex ante* demand D based on a correct initial perception of quality. The consumer thus purchases quantity q_0 at price p_0 and gains consumer surplus of area a. Alternatively, suppose the seller convinces the consumer that quality is greater than it really is, in which case demand increases to D'. The consumer thus purchases a larger quantity q_1, at which the consumer surplus associated with demand D' is area $a+b$. By providing false information to the consumer, consumer surplus increases, suggesting a positive value of false information.

Again, the paradox is resolved by considering how false information, in effect, constrains the consumer from making optimal adjustments to full quality information. Because the consumer is, in effect, constrained from making optimal adjustments by providing false information, welfare is correctly evaluated by compensating or equivalent surplus rather than compensating or equivalent variation. The welfare actually realized by the consumer, assuming demand D measures the true marginal benefits the consumer will receive from consumption, is area $a-c-d$. The paradox is thus resolved. Area $c+d$ measures the adverse welfare consequences of imposing false information on the consumer. The apparent welfare gain in area b turns out to be no gain at all assuming the consumer discovers the information was misleading.

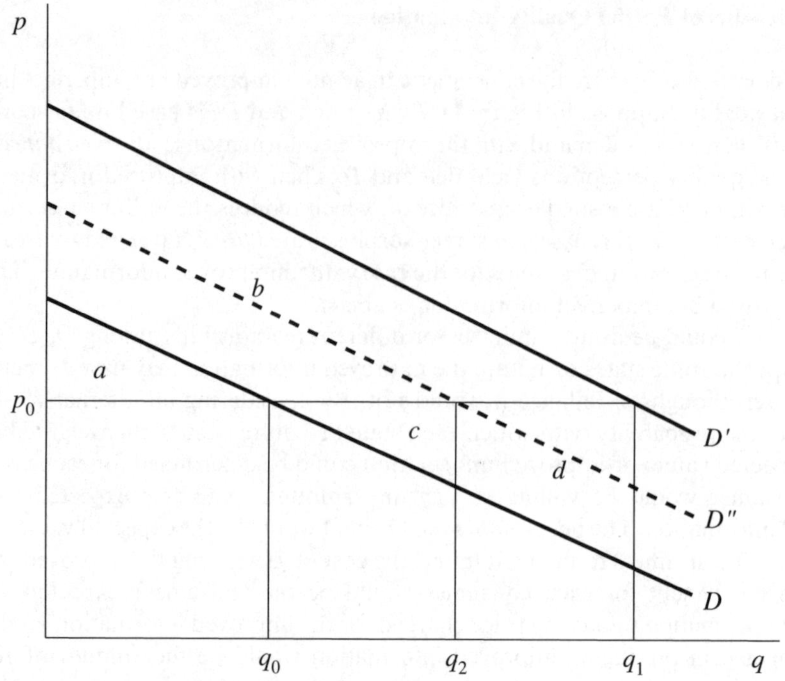

Figure 11.7

Dependence on the Timing of Obtaining Correct Information

The assumption that the consumer discovers the true quality of a good in the process of consumption deserves some additional discussion. The analyses above assume that the true quality of a good becomes immediately evident upon consumption. Examples may be the true enjoyment received from entertainment, or the true taste enjoyment received from eating at a restaurant. In other cases, the quality may become evident only after time or additional information is released to the public. Examples are delayed health effects of consuming contaminated foods or uncertain side effects of medications. If one chose to consume cigarettes at a time when the adverse health consequences were less well known, then the same risk of adverse consequences such as contracting lung cancer was faced as if the full potential health consequences and their probabilities were known and consumption was undertaken anyway. For these cases, some stronger assumptions may be needed to measure welfare effects.

For example, one can assume that the same adverse health effects bring the same ultimate disutility on an informed consumer as on an uninformed consumer who makes the same consumption choices. These adverse health effects may consist of contracting lung cancer or other adverse health effects of smoking, the cost of medical treatments, income lost due to adverse health consequences, and the associated pain and suffering. Some of these adverse welfare effects might also be estimated by using scientific information on morbidity rates of various diseases related to smoking and related data on medical treatment costs and associated lost work days. However, such direct *ex post* evaluation of the adverse consequences would not consider the disutility of pain and suffering. Alternatively, the area $b+c+d$ in Figure 11.7 may represent the utility loss due to the ultimate pain and suffering (weighted by the probability of occurrence) from lung cancer and other consequences of smoking as well as the medical expenses and lost income incurred thereby (where demand D is assumed to represent demand with full information). If this is the case, then the welfare effects of misperceived quality can be measured by comparing choices between groups of individuals with false and correct information.

Additionally, however, news of contamination may generate psychological costs of worry and concern when news of contamination is released only after consumption but before the final consequences of contaminated consumption become apparent.[5] For example, if consumers are informed that foods consumed recently were, unbeknownst to them, contaminated with a cancer-causing agent, then consumers may suffer from worry and concern even if they are lucky enough to never experience the potential adverse consequences of consumption. That is, uncertainty about health effects can have a distinct welfare effect whether or not the worst fears are realized because (1) decisions are consciously altered to avoid such uncertainty, (2) psychological costs of uncertainty may be incurred even if consumer awareness occurs after consumption of a contaminated good, and (3) an individual may prefer a more certain situation in lieu of the uncertain alternative even if something must be given up to obtain it. Such psychological costs would also be included in the area $b+c+d$ in Figure 11.7.

When the welfare effects of correct information involve psychological costs, the magnitude of welfare effects may depend on when the contamination information is released. For example, if a consumer never becomes aware of a contamination problem before the worst adverse health effect is experienced, then there is no psychological cost of worry and concern beyond the actual pain and suffering of the adverse outcome and the associated medical expenses and lost income. Furthermore, if a consumer never becomes aware of the contamination problem and is lucky enough to never experience the potential adverse outcomes, then no psychological costs of worry and concern are incurred.

For problems such as this, the welfare analyst must use judgment and reason. For example, a serious contamination problem is unlikely to remain undetected permanently because a few consumers will start experiencing the adverse consequences at some point. When this happens, the attention of the news media may generate roughly the same psychological costs of worry and concern on other consumers regardless of how much time has expired before the contamination issue becomes public.[6] If this is the case, then the welfare effects of contamination information can still be measured by comparing demands with false and full information. Alternatively, if the psychological consequences are less with delayed dissemination because of normal mortality rates of the population, then such factors must also be considered.

5. For example, Weinstein and Quinn (1983) have argued that health risks are context-dependent because *ex post* measures of consumer loss ignore the welfare loss associated with uncertainty, for example, the psychological costs of worrying about the possibility of contracting cancer, defective childbirth, and so on.
6. In fact, some studies have attempted to measure the extent of welfare effects of contamination problems by estimating consumer response to newspaper accounts measured, for example, by column inches of coverage. See, for example, Shulstad and Stoevener (1978) and Swartz and Strand (1981).

Another and perhaps more common situation is where only partial information becomes known and is released as it becomes known. In this case, demand models must be estimated that allow inferring consumer adjustment to full information if and when it becomes available, and the welfare analyst must have some way of conjecturing what full information is before the potential welfare consequences of imperfect information can be evaluated. For problems such as this, the partial information models such as in Figures 11.5 through 11.7 are useful, but welfare analyses may need to be performed based on conditional conjectures of true information.

Producer Technology Adoption with Errors in Productivity Perceptions

The benefits of producer adoption of new technology are usually evaluated on the basis of producer surplus in the output market as in Section 8.4. However, when the producer adopts technology on the basis of perceived changes in productivity that may not turn out to be correct, the errors in perceptions have distinct welfare effects. In Figure 11.8, suppose MC represents the existing marginal cost schedule and that based on advertisements and word of mouth a producer expects a new technology (implemented by means of related capital expenditures) to have marginal cost MC′. If the producer views the output price p_0 as unaffected by adoption, then anticipated quasirent increases from area d to area $d+e+f+g$. Suppose the producer decides to undertake investment and, based on anticipated productivity, makes binding commitments to produce output quantity q_0 but then discovers the increased productivity is less than expected. If actual marginal cost turns out to

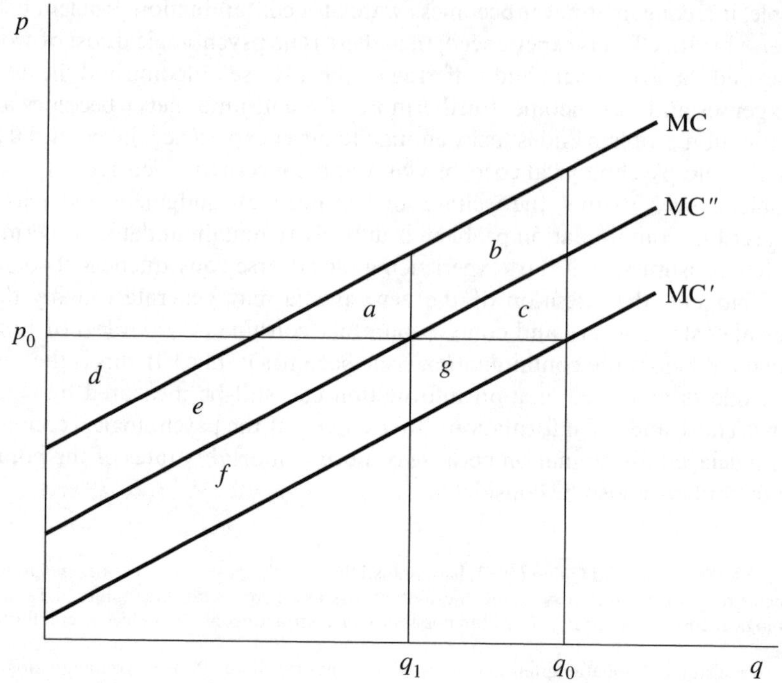

Figure 11.8

follow MC″, the producer's actual quasirent turns out to be area $d+e-c$. If the producer had correctly anticipated productivity, then commitments would have been undertaken to produce only quantity q_1 and quasirent would have been area $d+e$. The value of information to the producer that would have enabled correct anticipation of productivity is thus area c.

Several additional considerations, however, can affect welfare evaluation in the case of producer technology adoption. First, the producer may discover reduced productivity in the process of production and before sales commitments are made, in which case the producer may have flexibility to cut production to q_1 immediately. Second, even if reduced productivity is not discovered until the first production cycle is completed, the level of production can be cut to q_1 for future time periods so the loss of area c can be avoided in future time periods. Third, one must note that Figure 11.8 depicts only short-run welfare effects. If the producer undertakes capital expenditures larger than area e multiplied by the number of time periods over which that capital will be productive, then the producer will incur a welfare loss from investing in new technology. Thus, the welfare analysis in Figure 11.8 must be completed by comparing capital investment costs to the increase in quasirent over the life of the investment. This topic and possible time discounting associated with it are discussed further in Section 14.2 and Appendix Section 14.A.

Another important aspect of adoption of new technology is producer 'know-how' and learning by doing. It may be that a producer without experience cannot achieve the full benefits of a new technology without acquiring information represented by experience. For example, in Figure 11.8, a producer who has no experience with a new technology may only be able to lower marginal cost from MC to MC″ whereas after learning by doing a marginal cost of MC′ can be achieved. The point of these various examples is that information may take many forms. Careful economic welfare analysis of related information must take into account how lack or asymmetry of information causes errors or inefficiency in decision making and how such errors affect the welfare of individuals.

11.4 AN EXAMPLE OF GOVERNMENT DELAY IN DISSEMINATING CONTAMINATION INFORMATION[7]

Cases of accidental chemical contamination of food sources and environments have increasingly become a problem of public concern in recent decades. Using questionnaires as a means of measuring adverse welfare consequences has been criticized because respondents may perceive an incentive to overstate effects and because the information upon which assessments are based may be unclear. Thus, welfare evaluation based on actual revealed preference choices of decision-makers, for example, estimated supplies and demands, is preferred by many. This section outlines an application of the principles in this chapter for this purpose.

7. This section reports the empirical analysis given by Foster and Just (1989). In recognition that revealed preference data can make new information appear to have an inappropriate negative effect on household welfare, the US Environmental Protection Agency (2000, ch. 5, p. 29) has revised its guidelines for economic analysis to incorporate the methodology of this paper, explicitly stating that the Foster–Just paper 'describes this approach more fully, demonstrating that compensating surplus is an appropriate measure of willingness-to-pay under these conditions'.

Specifically, this section gives a brief description of an analysis of a particular contamination problem that arose in Hawaii in 1982 when the presence of heptachlor was discovered in the milk supply. Heptachlor is a highly toxic pesticide and carcinogen used in the production of pineapple. Dairies used pineapple leaves and stems as a cheap substitute for cattle feed otherwise imported from the mainland. Prior to 1982, the residues of heptachlor thus consumed by dairy cattle were passed on to humans through the consumption of local dairy products. Essentially the entire population of Oahu (approximately 800000 people) was exposed to heptachlor-contaminated milk because no milk was imported. The Department of Health of the State of Hawaii estimated that dairy products contained about 15 times the official acceptable level of the pesticide for adults.

The public first became aware of the contamination problem on 18 March 1982, when the state's Department of Health announced preparation to confront the rise in pesticide levels in milk. Throughout the next several months, the press offered consumers spectacular and troubling headlines and sometimes bewildering information on the safety of available milk supplies. As a result, daily fresh milk consumption dropped from 32259 gallons in February to 5404 gallons in April, a decline of over 80 percent. With little doubt, the consumer reaction indicated concern about the milk that had been consumed during ignorance of the contamination problem.

By the beginning of May, the number of headlines in Honolulu's two major newspapers regarding milk contamination had declined from approximately 20 per week to approximately four per week and thereafter little or no information was found in newspapers suggesting continued contamination. Reports in late May and later in September indicated that available milk was safe and that quality restrictions had been appropriately tightened.[8] Consumers, however, remained wary throughout the balance of 1982 and consumption returned only slowly to normal levels. By the end of August 1982, the *Honolulu Advertiser* reported that 40 percent of residents were still uncertain about the quality of milk.

One of the more disturbing aspects of this episode was the evident hesitation of state authorities to disclose information before the public became aware of the possibility of contamination. The state's Senate Committee on Health criticized the Department of Health for delaying the release of information to consumers and substantial political acrimony arose over this issue.[9]

The Hawaii heptachlor problem presents a useful example because it apparently involves the four distinct stages of a typical contamination problem: (1) contamination with continued consumption in ignorance, (2) dissemination of information about contamination involving an initial 'scare' with consumer adjustment to current information, (3) ensuing psychological costs of worry and concern about the ultimate health effects of consumption (including that undertaken in ignorance), and (4) eventual adverse health effects on a portion of the population associated with mortality or morbidity rates of the contaminant. While the effects in the fourth stage may occur much later and may never be fully accounted for because of the difficulty in tracing, say, a particular case of cancer to heptachlor contamination that occurred many years earlier, the typical need for welfare

8. See the *Honolulu Star-Bulletin*, 20 May 1982, p. A1; and the *Honolulu Advertiser*, 24 September 1982, p. A1.
9. *Honolulu Advertiser*, 1 April 1982, p. A1; *Honolulu Advertiser*, 24 July 1982, p. A3; *Honolulu Star-Bulletin*, 29 July 1982, p. A3, and 5 August 1982, p. A1.

analysis occurs in the second and third stages. The third stage is particularly important because it fully reflects the *ex ante* psychological costs of worry and concern that would be excluded in an *ex post* evaluation based strictly on fourth stage events.

To examine welfare effects, the demand for Hawaii milk was estimated in the form

$$q_t = \tilde{q}_t(p_t, m_t, \boldsymbol{\theta}_t) = f(\boldsymbol{\theta}_t)e^{\gamma m_t - \alpha p_t},$$

where q_t is per capita milk consumption in month t, p_t is milk price in month t, m_t is per capita consumer income in month t and $\boldsymbol{\theta}_t$ is a vector of variables reflecting consumer perceptions of quality.[10] In this application, the information function was represented by a set of dummy variables in months where information was changing with a geometric decay function for following months reflecting the gradual decline in consumer uncertainty. Evaluating welfare effects based on this single demand equation invokes the weak separability assumption discussed in Section 7.10 whereby milk contamination does not affect the consumers if no milk is consumed.

Table 11.1 gives the estimates of compensating and equivalent variation and of Marshallian consumer surplus change associated with a change from the actual case of contamination (assuming correct consumer perceptions in each month following disclosure) to the hypothetical case of no contamination (reflected by no news of contamination). These welfare quantities correspond to comparing area a with area $a+b$ in Figure 11.7. Compensating and equivalent measures are appropriate in these months because consumers were free to adjust to the information. The estimates are striking because the

Table 11.1 Per capita consumer welfare effects of Hawaii milk contamination, March 1982 to September 1982 (dollars per month)

Month	Compensating variation	Equivalent variation	Consumer surplus change
March	5.942	5.928	5.935
April	9.336	9.299	9.317
May	5.651	5.769	5.776
June	3.248	3.242	3.245
July	3.602	3.597	3.599
August	3.202	3.198	3.200
September	2.922	2.919	2.920

Source: Foster and Just (1989).

10. Both the price of milk and income were normalized by dividing by the price of fruit nectar, apparently the closest substitute for milk, thus satisfying appropriate homogeneity conditions. For purposes of applying the framework of the Appendix of this chapter, the associated indirect expected utility function associated with this demand is

$$V(p_t, m_t, \boldsymbol{\theta}_t) = \frac{1}{\alpha} f(\boldsymbol{\theta}_t)e^{-\alpha p_t} + K - \frac{1}{\gamma}e^{-\gamma m_t},$$

for some constant K from which the expenditure function is

$$e(p_t, U_t, \boldsymbol{\theta}_t) = \frac{1}{\gamma}\ln\left\{\gamma\left[\frac{1}{\alpha} f(\boldsymbol{\theta}_t)e^{-\alpha p_t} + K - U_t\right]\right\}.$$

loss is very high – higher than per capita milk expenditures in April 1982.[11] This is possible and plausible, however, because Hicksian demands are more inelastic than Marshallian demands, because Marshallian demands are highly inelastic (the estimated price elasticity is −0.41) and because consumption fell by such a large amount. Also, the magnitude of consumer loss increased very sharply initially followed by a rapid and then more prolonged decline as information was corrected and pineapple green chop ceased to be used in milk production.

While the results in Table 11.1 estimate the magnitude of consumer losses after information of contamination was disseminated, one of the greatest and most controllable losses apparently occurred prior to pubic awareness. Some reports indicate that public officials were aware of the contamination problem as early as April 1981, eleven months before the public was informed. This delayed political attention and the associated clean-up effort that halted the feeding of pineapple green chop to dairy cattle. Individuals who consumed milk from April 1981 to March 1982 faced the same health risks from heptachlor consumption as if they had been forced to consume normal amounts of milk with full knowledge of heptachlor contamination. Thus, the associated welfare loss from contamination can be measured by compensating surplus or equivalent surplus.

Assuming that correct information in February 1982, the month before the release of information, was the same as actually released in March 1982, and that consumer adjustments in March 1982 correctly assessed the information that was released, the appropriate compensating surplus associated with delaying the release of information by one month is[12]

$$C_s = \frac{q_0}{\alpha}[\ln f(\boldsymbol{\theta}_0) - \ln f(\boldsymbol{\theta}_1)],$$

where q_0 is the actual consumption in February 1982. This yields a compensating surplus of \$18.21 per person for each month that release of information was delayed. This large effect is consistent with the estimated hypothetical price of −\$2.28 per half gallon, which indicates that consumers would have to be paid more than they normally paid for milk to induce them to continue normal consumption with full knowledge of contamination. If consumers had full information of contamination in February 1982 and had been able to adjust to that information, the compensating variation of contamination comparable to estimates in Table 11.1 would have been \$8.33. Thus, the value of information (sometimes called the cost of ignorance) is the difference, \$9.88.

This example demonstrates that the welfare effects of contamination as well as decisions by public authorities to withhold information of contamination can exceed normal consumer expenditures.

11. Mean monthly milk consumption over the period January 1978 to July 1983 was 0.87 half gallon units at a mean price of \$0.62 per half gallon (in 1967 dollars).
12. Using the methodology of the Appendix to this chapter, compensating surplus is found as

$$C_s = e(p_1, U_0, \boldsymbol{\theta}_1) - m_0 + (p_0 - p_1)q_0,$$

where p_1 is the hypothetical price that would have generated the observed February 1982 consumption if information had already been released, U_0 represents the *ex ante* perceived utility in February 1982, $\boldsymbol{\theta}_1$ represents correct information, and p_0 and q_0 are the actual price and quantity from February 1982.

11.5 APPARENT VERSUS ACTUAL CHANGES IN TASTES AND PREFERENCES

To this point in this book, consumers have been assumed to possess constant preferences. Welfare economists have often argued that the social welfare of two states cannot be compared with ordinal concepts if preferences differ between the states. Thus, economic welfare analysis has sometimes been regarded as inapplicable when shifts in consumer demands could not be attributed to changes in prices and/or income. However, changes in information can cause consumer demands (and factor owner supplies) to shift even with no change in prices or income. If such changes in information are ignored, an observer may falsely conclude that a consumer's preferences have changed.

Two alternative approaches can be taken in such cases depending on whether changes in preferences are true changes or apparent changes. If the preferences of consumers truly change, then the comparison of economic states must be clearly conditioned on a single specific set of preferences, for example, either *ex ante* or *ex post* preferences. Alternatively, the results for household production in Appendix Section 7.G often allow apparent shifts in demands and supplies to be interpreted as the result of changes in household technology under constant preferences, in which case typical approaches to economic welfare analysis are appropriate.

True Changes in Preferences

When preferences truly change, some of the typical results do not carry through because the compensating and equivalent variations cannot be evaluated practically with the same set of preferences. That is, compensating variation is the amount of income that must be taken away from a consumer (possibly negative) after a change to restore the consumer's original welfare level. The only way to be sure that the initial welfare level is restored is to evaluate welfare according to *ex ante* preferences. Alternatively, equivalent variation as the amount of income that must be given to a consumer (again possibly negative) in lieu of a change to leave the consumer as well off as with the change. The only way to be sure that the consumer is as well off as with the change is to evaluate welfare according to *ex post* preferences.

The Marshallian consumer surplus areas behind demand curves, on the other hand, can be evaluated according to either *ex ante* or *ex post* preferences. Consumer surplus evaluated at *ex ante* preferences will have the relationship to compensating variation (but not equivalent variation) derived in Chapters 6 and 7, while consumer surplus evaluated at *ex post* preferences will have the relationship to equivalent variation (but not compensating variation) derived in Chapters 6 and 7. The compensating variation evaluated at *ex ante* preferences and equivalent variation evaluated at *ex post* preferences may not have any particular relationship. While welfare economists are typically faced with discrepancies between compensating and equivalent variations in presenting welfare analyses, the discrepancies in these cases may be far more serious. The consumer surplus measured under *ex ante* preferences may not approximate equivalent variation nor will the consumer surplus measured under *ex post* preferences necessarily approximate compensating variation.

Apparent Changes in Preferences

In contrast, the case with apparent rather than true changes in preferences permits standard welfare measurement. These possibilities follow from the two sets of results related to household production and weak complementarity (developed formally in Appendix Sections 7.G and 7.I). Intuitively, consumers or households do not simply consume goods, but in many cases utilize market goods for household production of nonmarket goods or characteristics that are valued by the consumer and consumed at home. For example, food and exercise equipment are combined through household production to produce health. States of the environment exogenous to the consumer may cause changes in a household's ability to produce health because of contamination. When such changes take place in household technology or in information that affects perceived household technology (such as the likely health effects of consuming contaminated food), the observed market transactions reflect shifts in demands and supplies of market goods that appear to reflect changes in preferences because demand shifts cannot be attributed to changes in prices or income. In the household production model, perceived health and the consumer's willingness to pay for it are typically unobservable, but changes in the consumer's perceived production function of health are reflected in the demands for the goods used to produce it. In these cases, comprehensive benefit measurement for households is possible with standard welfare measures based on observed market transactions following Bockstael and McConnell (1983).[13]

To illustrate application of the household production approach to this problem, let the consumer's utility function be $U(y,q)$ where q is a normal market good and y is a nonmarket good produce at home. Suppose that x is another good purchased by the household and used to produce y and that the household production function is represented by $y=f(x,z)$ where z represents some exogenous factor such as information, perceived or actual technology, contamination, or advertising. Examples might include cases where (1) x is the quantity of a basic food item used in preparation of household meals, z measures information that permits more efficient use of the food item in meal preparation and y measures the quantity of meals produced and consumed by the household; (2) x is fuel use, z is efficiency of a household furnace and y is the amount or perceived amount of heat produced and consumed by the household; (3) x is the quantity of a food consumed, z is the level of contamination in the food and y is the health produced and enjoyed by the household; and (4) x is the quantity of a luxury item purchased by the household, z is the level of advertising that determines a product's popularity or status and y measures prestige derived by the household from consumption. If y represents the tastiness of meals, the services of household appliances, the health effects of consumption or prestige of consumption, respectively, then household behavior changes even though the utility function $U(y,q)$ is unchanged and even though prices, exogenous income and endowments are unchanged. In each of these cases, the household production framework of Appendix Section 7.G interprets an apparent shift in the market demand for goods x and q due to a change in z as a change in the household technology. Such a change in technology causes a movement along the demand curve for the nonmarket good or characteris-

13. For example, consistent with these results, a common approach is simply to represent utility as a function of product-specific advertising as well as the quantities of market goods consumed.

tic y associated with a change in its shadow price. Accordingly, the true underlying set of preferences is constant.

Note, however, that the welfare effects of a change in z in these cases must be inferred from shifts in demand or supply. That is, because the shadow price of the nonmarket good y is not observable, the welfare effect of a change in its shadow price caused by a change in z must be inferred from the shift in a demand or supply of a market good as discussed in Section 7.10. For example, using Mäler's concept of weak complementarity (see Appendix Section 7.I), if changes in z have no effect on the consumer except when nonmarket good y is consumed and good x is an essential input for household production of good y, then the welfare effect of a change in z can be measured in three steps: (1) by raising the *ex ante* price of x before the change to a choke price, then (2) changing z from initial to subsequent levels (which would have no effect on welfare at zero consumption of x) and, finally, (3) decreasing the price of x from its choke price after the change to the *ex post* price.[14] This validates the same use of consumer surplus as in the standard case of constant preferences, that is, the area between demands for good x has the same standard welfare relevance applicable under weak complementarity of z with respect to x.[15]

11.6 THE WELFARE EFFECTS OF ADVERTISING

The principles of this chapter have direct application in evaluating the welfare effects of advertising. Advertising can take multiple forms. First, advertising may truly inform potential buyers of product availability, product quality and product prices. Second, advertising may make false claims about the quality attributes of goods. Third, advertising may generate fads such that consumers derive enjoyment from knowing they are wearing the latest styles of clothing, have experienced the latest form of entertainment or are driving the most prestigious automobile. Before considering these three types of advertising, a discussion of the underlying assumptions of welfare measurement is appropriate.

Does Advertising Change Tastes and Preferences?

Advertising can be assumed either to change the true preferences of consumers, in which case economic states are compared using either *ex ante* or *ex post* preferences, or advertising can be regarded as an input in a household production framework with constant consumer preferences, in which case advertising alters the consumer's 'technology' used to produce nonmarket goods for household consumption.

The approach in which advertising fundamentally changes consumer preferences was developed by Avinash Dixit and Victor Norman (1978).[16] Preferences are assumed to

14. If the change in z also affects household production using other goods, then a similar calculation is needed for all affected goods. See, for example, the discussion of weak complementarity with respect to groups of goods at the end of Appendix Section 7.I.
15. This is the same result demonstrated by Bockstael and McConnell (1983). For further more general discussion, see Appendix Section 7.G.
16. Dixit and Norman (1978) first made the point that changing preferences should not be an excuse for abandoning analysis. For discussion of the typical requirement of time invariance of the underlying distribution of consumer attributes such as preferences, at least within population subgroups, see Stoker (1993), Jorgenson, Lau and Stoker (1997) and Blundell, Pashardes and Weber (1993).

change as a result of *pure persuasion*. Analysis of the effects of advertising must then be conducted with an explicit set of preferences, which is usually either the *ex ante* preferences before advertising or the *ex post* preferences after advertising. Because *ex ante* and *ex post* preferences are not comparable, the welfare effects of advertising are a result of the indirect effects of advertising on prices and quantities. Dixit and Norman (1978, pp. 1–2) suggest 'one would use the former if he thought the advertising was pure deception, and the latter if he thought the resulting tastes represented the consumer's true interests'.[17]

Alternatively, Becker and Murphy (1993) argue that while advertising can create wants without producing information, the associated change in demands need not be viewed as a change in tastes. That is, consistent with standard consumer theory, goods that favorably affect the demand for other goods are usually treated as complements in demand rather than shifters of utility functions. Specifically, where advertising either provides correct and useful information or adds prestige to consumption in a household production framework, weak complementarity of advertising with respect to the good it advertises permits the welfare benefits of advertising to be evaluated by the area between demand curves for the advertised good at different levels of advertising as in Section 11.5.[18]

The household production approach to advertising allows a structured analysis of a variety of advertising effects. For example, if advertising disseminates information about how to make better use of a product, then household production using the product generates more enjoyment from using the product. As consumer benefits from using the product increase, so does demand for the product. As a result, consumers allocate more of their budget to the product. Fortunately, the results for multimarket welfare analysis from Chapter 9 imply that the demands for all goods from which expenditures are diverted need not be measured to evaluate such changes if equilibrium market relationships are used to evaluate welfare effects in the advertised market. For example, if weak complementarity applies, then the benefits from advertising the product with enhancing information about how to use it can be completely captured in the market for the advertised product.

The household production approach is also advantageous for evaluation of advertising that disseminates incorrect information, that is, false advertising. In this case, following the principles of Section 11.3, consumption choices made under false advertising must be evaluated according to expected *ex post* (correct) information that consumers discover in the process of consumption, or information disseminated after purchases that affects consumers' enjoyment from having made the purchase. For example, if consumers learn of carcinogenic effects of a good that was advertised to be safe only after consumption, then previous consumption decisions are devalued, possibly through the incurrence of health care costs and related worry and concern.

17. For a clear discussion of the contrast between pure persuasion and informative advertising as well as an example of how to condition results appropriately on a single set of preferences when preferences change, see Cardon and Pope (2003). They show that socially optimal generic advertising is positive in an industry that competes horizontally with a monopoly only if it raises the monopoly's output, but socially optimal advertising is unambiguously positive if the monopolist is the distributor of the generic industry's output.
18. If advertising also applies to other commodities (for example, convinces consumers that other goods have inferior characteristics), then all affected goods must be included in the calculation. See, for example, the discussion of weak complementarity with respect to groups of goods at the end of Appendix Section 7.I.

While the assumptions required for this approach are somewhat different than for the Dixit and Norman approach, they are less controversial.[19] Thus, for the remainder of this section, shifts in consumer demands in response to advertising are assumed to reflect only apparent rather than actual changes in preferences.

Advertising that Disseminates Correct Information

One reason a firm undertakes advertising is to make consumers aware that it is offering a lower price than other firms for a particular good. Applying the framework of Figure 11.2, advertising that has only this role is clearly socially beneficial. A firm would not undertake such advertising if it did not increase profit by more than the cost of the advertising, and clearly consumers benefit by finding a lower price, as illustrated in Figure 11.2. Indeed, such advertising may force other firms to lower prices, perhaps leading to succeeding rounds of price cuts, and eventually leading to the Adam Smith benefits of competition discussed in Section 2.5.

Similarly, firms often compete in quality as well as price. For example, a firm may undertake advertising to make consumers aware that it is offering a product with higher quality than other firms. In this case, consumer demand for the good may increase from D' to D in the framework of Figure 11.4 as consumers switch to the product with superior quality. Such advertising may force other firms to increase quality similarly or to lower prices such as from p_0 to p_1 in Figure 11.4 in order to compete. Again, the results of advertising would be socially beneficial because the firm with higher quality would not undertake the advertising expense if it were not profitable to advertise, whereas consumers benefit from higher quality on existing consumption and from adjustment of consumption quantities to higher quality, or by lower prices caused by competitive forces on other firms selling the lower-quality good.

Advertising is typically not profitable for individual firms in competitive markets because the product cannot be differentiated and therefore the increased demand in response to a single firm's advertising may go mainly to other firms. Thus, most analysis of advertising is done in models of monopoly, oligopoly or monopolistic competition. Suppose in Figure 11.9 that a monopolist's marginal cost is given by MC and that consumer demand is D. A monopolist maximizing profit would set price at p_0, where marginal revenue MR is equal to marginal cost MC, and earn profit of area $g+i$, while consumer surplus is area $a+d$. Suppose, however, that consumer demand is based on incomplete information about the desirable qualities of the product. By truthful advertisement of product quality, suppose demand increases to D'. Then the monopolist maximizes profit by raising price to p_1 where the new marginal revenue MR$'$ is equal to MC. Accordingly, producer profit increases to area $d+e+f+g+h+i+j$ less the expense of advertising, and consumer surplus changes to area $a+b+c$. Assuming the expense of advertising does not exceed area $d+e+f+h+j$, the producer profits from advertising.

Evaluation of the consumer welfare effect of advertising is possible through application of the principles developed earlier in this chapter. A comparison of the consumer surplus areas with and without advertising suggests an increase of area $b+c-d$. However,

19. For example, Fisher and McGowan (1979) have criticized Dixit and Norman for including advertising in the utility function but ignoring the direct effect that advertising has on utility in their welfare analysis.

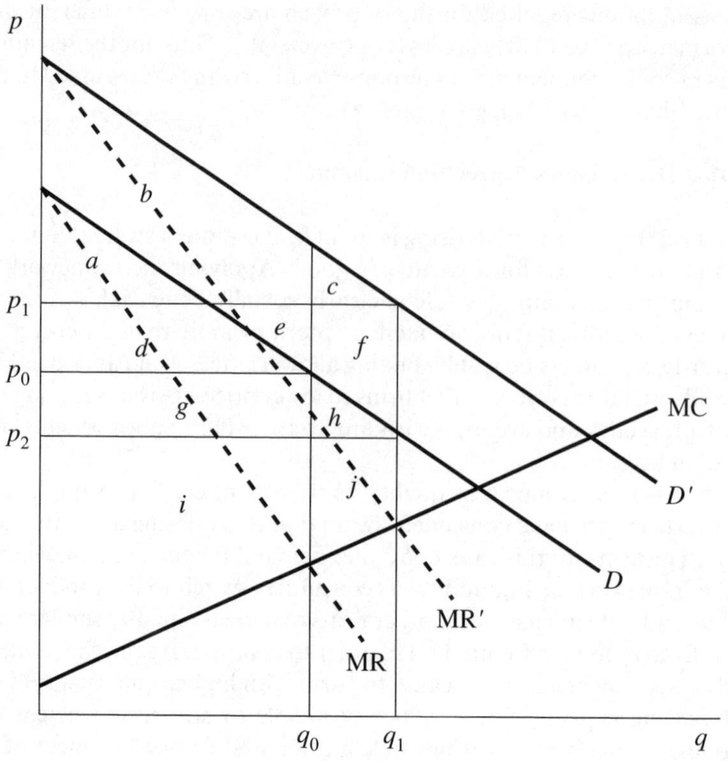

Figure 11.9

the consumer surplus area $a+d$ without advertising does not capture the true benefits received by consumers. Assuming consumers ultimately realize the benefits of quality from consumption, consumer benefits without advertising are area $a+b+d+e$. Thus, the consumer gain from advertising is area $c-d-e$, which is less than area $b+c-d$ and far more likely to be negative.

This simple analysis suggests several results that have been proven rigorously in the literature with algebraic models. First, consumers may or may not benefit from truthful advertising depending on the elasticity of demand and how it affects monopolistic behavior.[20] (Note that advertising may change not only the intercept of the demand curve as in Figure 11.9, but also the slope and curvature.) Second, because consumers may lose from advertising given monopolistic behavior, and the monopolist would be willing to incur advertising expense of any amount up to area $d+e+f+h+j$ to achieve the associated increase in demand, the advertising depicted in Figure 11.9 may or may not improve overall social welfare. That is, the monopolist's gain may be minor because of advertising expense while consumers lose.

20. For example, Butters (1977) concluded that the equilibrium level of informative advertising is socially efficient in a model with a homogeneous output and many buyers and sellers, but Stahl (1994) found that the equilibrium level of informative advertising in an oligopoly is socially suboptimal because firms cannot capture the full benefits of advertising a homogeneous output.

Advertising with False Information

Some economists have contended that consumers are capable of validating advertisers' quality claims quickly and therefore the market should immediately discipline all false advertising (see Ferguson 1974; Nelson 1974; Stigler 1961; Telser 1964). More recently, however, the evidence of false advertising has attracted frequent attention in the media, and government policing of false advertising has become a political issue especially with respect to tobacco and food products. Kotowitz and Mathewson (1979) introduced a framework with which to analyze the optimality of false advertising when consumers learn from experience but not instantaneously. Specifically, they assume a good to have quality measured in two dimensions, only one of which is affected by advertising. They find that some false advertising may be optimal in the short run. What constitutes the short run for their purposes depends on how fast consumers learn from experience. With cigarettes, where the adverse health effects of tobacco use may not be experienced for decades, profit maximization by the manufacturer may call for a substantial amount of false advertising.

Another example of false advertising is the case where a producer discovers some detrimental effect of his product but withholds the information. Failing to disclose adverse effects of consumption in advertisements is, in effect, false advertising. False advertising is effective only in cases of information asymmetry. If the seller has more quality information than the buyer, or the seller can choose which information to disclose to the buyer, then the seller faces a moral hazard incentive to take advantage of the buyer. A *moral hazard* exists when the actions or information of one economic agent are partially hidden from another in a manner that can affect the benefits of the second agent from transactions between the two.

To consider the welfare effects of false advertising, reconsider Figure 11.9 where consumer demand with full information would be D but through advertising false claims about a product a monopolistic producer is able to increase the consumer's demand to D'. Accordingly, the monopolist maximizes profit by charging price p_1 and the consumer purchases quantity q_1. In this case, assuming consumers ultimately evaluate consumption according to true quality, the consumer's actual benefit from consumption is area $a-e-f$, the same as if consumption had been constrained to be q_1 with full information, or the same as if price had been p_2 with full information and unconstrained adjustment where an additional lump sum payment of $(p_1-p_2)q_1$ had been extracted from consumers. Producer profit in this case is area $d+e+f+g+h+i+j$ less the expense of advertising.

If false advertising did not occur, then the monopolist charges price p_0, consumer surplus is correctly measured by area $a+d$, and producer profit is area $g+i$. Comparing the case of false advertising to the case without advertising, the monopolist gains area $d+e+f+h+j$ less the cost of advertising. In other words, a profit-maximizing monopolist would have a profit incentive to undertake this false advertising if the cost of advertising were any amount up to area $d+e+f+h+j$, even if consumers discover the true quality and demand returns to D in the next time period. The consumer surplus, however, changes from area $a+d$ to area $a-e-f$, which is an unambiguous loss of area $d+e+f$ from false advertising. Thus, consumers lose by an amount that is included in the producer's potential gain (depending on the cost of advertising).

Somewhat surprisingly, the social benefits of false advertising may be either positive or negative even though welfare is unambiguously transferred from consumers to the monopolist producer. The reason that false advertising can be socially beneficial is due to the monopoly distortion. If overpricing the good restricts market quantity, then false advertising can raise the quantity toward the competitive level. However, as emphasized by Dixit and Norman (1978), this is a 'third-best' approach compared to second-best policies of direct regulation of use of monopoly power.

Another type of false advertising is predatory advertising whereby false claims are made about a competitor's product. Suppose, for example, in Figure 11.9 that consumer demand with full information is D', in which case a profit-maximizing monopolist charges price p_1, earns profits of area $d+e+f+g+h+i+j$ and consumers receive consumer surplus of area $a+b+c$. Now suppose through false rumors circulated by a seller of a competing product that consumers are convinced that quality is lower than it really is, in which case demand falls to D. For example, a competing producer may convince consumers that a particular product has become contaminated or that it has adverse health effects not previously understood. With the decrease in demand, the profit-maximizing monopolist would lower price to p_0, the monopolist's profits would fall to area $g+i$, and the apparent consumer surplus would decrease to area $a+d$. Assuming that consumers ultimately gain correct information and value consumption according to the marginal benefits depicted by D', however, the true benefits received by consumers at price p_0 and quantity q_0 would be area $a+b+d+e$.

In this case, the consumers may perceive significant lost benefits from not being able to adjust consumption to correct information at price p_0. But on the other hand, the monopolist would not have priced the product at p_0 had consumers adjusted consumption to correct information. Consumers actually gain area $d+e-c$ as a result of false advertising considering the monopolist's price adjustments. The reason consumers gain in this case is that false advertising reduces the monopoly pricing distortion. The reader should note, however, that this analysis may not present the complete picture. Presumably, any advertising by a competing firm that circulates false information about this product is also designed to increase demand for the competitor's product, in which case the effects of false advertising on the competing product market must also be considered. This would be a case where Mäler's concept of weak complementarity would not apply to the individual products but possibly to the two-product group.

Advertising and Fads

The analysis of advertising that creates fads is also facilitated by the household production approach.[21] For example, if a professional sports star endorses shoes or equipment used by amateur consumers, then the fun and enjoyment derived by using such paraphernalia in household consumption may increase. If this is the case, then advertising, by creating new product characteristics such as prestige, may enhance the household production function. Consider once again Figure 11.9. In this case, the consumer demand under full information before advertising may be represented by D, in which case the profit-maximizing monopolist charges price p_0, earns profit $g+i$ and consumers receive consu-

21. See for example, Stigler and Becker (1977), Fisher and McGowan (1979), Nichols (1985) and Becker and Murphy (1993).

mer surplus of area $a+d$. After advertising, where consumers' household production functions have been boosted by a new characteristic of prestige added to use of the product, consumer demand under full information may be increased to D'. In this case, the monopolist charges price p_1, earns profit equal to area $d+e+f+g+h+i+j$ less advertising expense, and consumers' true welfare after advertising is represented by area $a+b+c$. In this case, the monopolist gains area $d+e+f+h+j$ less advertising expense, which must be positive if advertising is profitable for the monopolist, and consumers also gain area $b+c-d$. So advertising may be beneficial to all groups. If so, then this is a case where social welfare is clearly improved by advertising.

The potential flaw in this analysis has to do with applicability of weak complementarity. If the prestige factor truly influences household production involving only this one good, then the conclusion would be valid. However, the household production function of prestige may be a function involving many goods with competing prestige factors. It may be that advertising that increases the prestige associated with using golf clubs endorsed by Tiger Woods implicitly reduces the prestige associated with using golf clubs endorsed by Arnold Palmer. If so, then the welfare loss in the market for golf clubs endorsed by Arnold Palmer may offset the gains in welfare in the market for golf clubs endorsed by Tiger Woods. When increasing the prestige of one good through advertising causes an equal detraction in prestige for another good, then advertising choices among firms may become a zero-sum game in which advertising is socially wasteful. The advertising wars between Pepsi-Cola and Coca-Cola are possibly an example.

As the various cases of this section suggest, advertising can have many different alternative effects depending on the truthfulness of advertising, how it enters the household production technology, consumer preferences that determine demand elasticities and the structure of markets in which the advertised goods are produced. In some cases, the welfare effects can be completely evaluated in a single market, but in other cases weak complementarity can apply only for groups of products, in which case the effects of advertising must be evaluated accordingly.

11.7 EVALUATION OF PUBLIC INFORMATION POLICY

In the age of information, sometimes characterized by the growth of the Internet, public policy regarding information has become controversial. As cable television and electronic conveniences have given consumers the ability to filter out traditional forms of advertisement, product promotion has increasingly turned to telemarketing and the Internet. Recent policy debate has focused on limiting unwanted telemarketing and junk e-mail. Promoters have argued that they are playing a socially beneficial role of informing potential buyers. Additionally, the development of the Internet has given buyers a cheap source of price information, product descriptions and, even, quality assessments by former purchasers as well as convenient and less costly access to public information produced by government agencies and nongovernment organizations. Historically, public agencies have collected data on economic activity and sometimes processed that data into information more readily usable by the public. Other agencies have tracked and, in some cases, enforced product quality such as in meat packing, food production and pharmaceutical production. Some have focused on the truthfulness of claims in advertising. Other government agencies have been charged with ensuring that potential contaminants such as pesticides are appropriately controlled.

Should telemarketing and mass e-mail marketing be limited? Does such marketing play a socially beneficial role? Should public agencies be involved in producing data and more highly processed information for the public? How much does public data contribute to price discovery? Is the need for such efforts declining as a result of the Internet? What type and timing of reporting by public agencies will maximize social welfare when evidence of contamination is discovered? How much public effort is needed to ensure socially optimal truthfulness in advertising given that such monitoring activities are costly? The economic welfare methodology of this chapter offers principles and practices that can facilitate policy analysis that can guide public choice regarding these various policy issues. This section offers a few examples to show that private markets alone may not achieve socially optimal use of information without public intervention.

Truthfulness in Advertising Policy

Truthfulness in advertising has been an item of growing public interest over recent decades. The results in this chapter demonstrate how producers can gain from false advertising even though consumers eventually discover the falsity of claims. In some cases, social welfare is adversely affected by false advertising. In other cases, aggregate social welfare improves, but only by altering the income distribution. Thus, economic welfare analysis has much to contribute to the policy debate by identifying who gains and who loses, showing how overall social welfare can be improved and determining how much compensation may be needed to preserve the relative income distribution in doing so. Because aggregate social welfare can actually be improved by false advertising in some cases, the results also show that controlling false advertising is more critical in some cases than in others. In the cases where aggregate social welfare is improved, however, saving the public expense of controlling false advertising should be considered only as an alternative way of reducing the social cost of some other market distortion, and some compensation schemes may be needed to compensate losers from false advertising.

Public Price Information and Market Assessment

A major point from the standpoint of public policy is that the cost of information is usually independent of producer scale or consumer income, whereas the benefits are not. That is, once acquired, a particular item of information can be used on a producer's entire operation or with respect to a consumer's entire consumption quantity even though the cost of information is typically independent of the production or consumption scale to which it is applied.

The analysis in Figure 11.1 shows how much a producer would be willing to pay for improved information on output price. If without information the producer must make production decisions based on *ex ante* expected price p_0, but with information the producer can correctly anticipate price p_1 or price p_2, where each are equally probable, then the value of information to that producer is (area $b+d$)/2. Figure 11.10 expands the analysis of Figure 11.1 to show how this value of information to the producer depends on the scale of production. Suppose one producer has marginal cost MC_1 and another producer

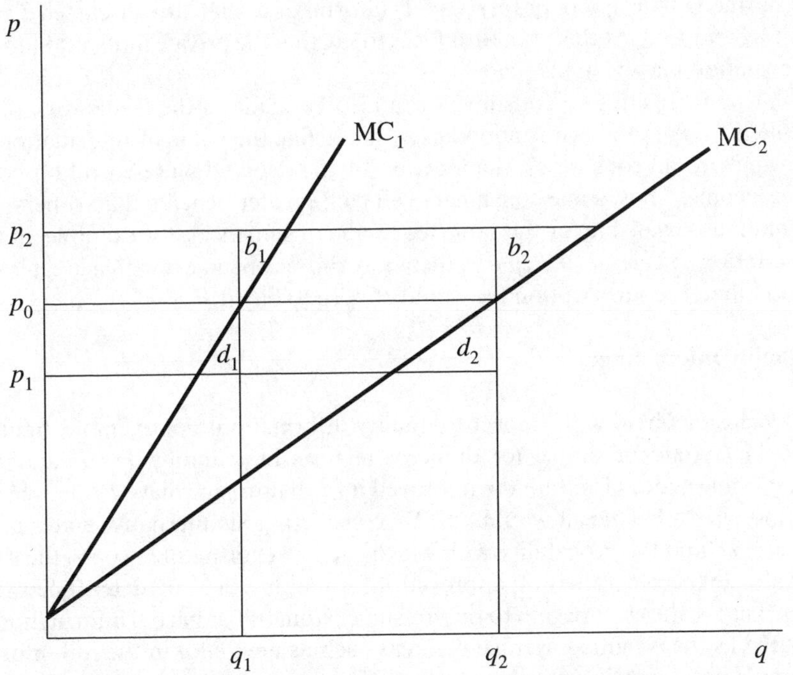

Figure 11.10

has marginal cost MC_2. To demonstrate the dependence of information benefits on producer scale, note that the gain from improved information is smaller for the producer with more rapidly rising marginal cost, which is generally the case for smaller producers. Specifically, if without information both producers must make production decisions based on *ex ante* expected price p_0, but with information they can each correctly anticipate price p_1 or price p_2, then the value of information for the producer with marginal cost MC_1 is area $(b_1 + d_1)/2$ while the value of information for the producer with marginal cost MC_2 is area $(b_2 + d_2)/2$. Area d_2 will exceed area d_1 and area b_2 will exceed area b_1 if MC_1 rises more rapidly than MC_2 for all prices between p_0 and p_1.

The implication of Figure 11.10 is that if a firm that produces and sells information charges the same fee to all subscribers, then all producers that have greater gains from improved information than the fee for the information service will buy the service and all others will not. Producers of information can be expected to set a fee for their information services to maximize profit, taking these reactions into account. Because large firms may be willing to pay high subscription fees, information-producing firms may maximize profits by setting a fee that excludes smaller producers in order to collect higher subscription fees from large producers. This outcome will constitute a market failure because the producers who do not buy the service could gain additional benefits from using it even though the information-producing firm may incur no additional costs in making it available to small producers. In fact, some information-producing firms may incur extra costs to make sure no nonsubscribers get access to the information. This market failure occurs because of the public good properties of information that are discussed further in Sections 13.2 and 13.3. At this point it suffices to say that the private motivation to provide price information may be inadequate.

A similar point relating to consumers can also be made in the framework of Figure 11.2. While the upper and lower boundaries that define the value of information, area $a+b$, may apply to all consumers, the location of the demand will depend on consumer tastes and income. Thus, some consumers will gain greater benefits than others. Thus, if the information is available for the same fee to all consumers as, for example, in the case of a subscription to *Consumer Reports*, then only those consumers with a greater value of information than the subscription fee would choose to buy it.[22]

Public Quality Information

Similar conclusions hold with respect to quality information. For example, figures such as Figure 11.7 could be drawn for different relationships among D, D' and D''. For example, in some states of nature the improved information may have D' between D and D'', even though on balance it would not. By considering all alternative states of nature of D, D' and D, and the probability with which each state of nature occurs, the weighted average value (expected value) of improved information could be determined for each consumer. That is, the welfare gain to the consumer from full or partial information would be computed as the weighted average of areas such as area $c+d$ in the full information case or area d in the partial information case. Each consumer would be willing to pay a fee of anything up to this amount for improved information. If a firm selling quality information sets the same fee to all consumers for such information, then only those consumers with a greater expected value of information would purchase it even though all consumers might benefit from it.

Public Experiment Station and Extension Programs[23]

Agriculture in the USA has often been heralded as the most productive in the world. The great success of US agriculture has been attributed to public agricultural experiment stations and public agricultural extension programs. Because of the great success of these programs, they have been imitated throughout the world. One purpose of agricultural experiment stations has been to develop and compare new technologies and then make test results publicly available to farmers. Agricultural extension programs are operated in harmony with experiment station efforts to make information developed by agricultural experiment stations available to all farmers regardless of scale and with no fees or only token fees. Because such information has scale-dependent benefits and private firms would likely be unwilling to provide such services to small farmers when higher fees can be charged to larger farmers, the results of this section suggest that public dissemination may be justified. According to the analysis in Figure 11.10, one would expect the benefits

22. As in the producer case, a market failure thus occurs because some individuals who would adjust consumption decisions in response to the information and thus benefit from it cannot, even though sharing the improved information with them may have negligible cost. One way of mitigating this market failure is for public libraries to carry subscriptions to *Consumer Reports*.
23. This section is based on historical assessments by Kerr (1987) and Rasmussen (1989).

from public information dissemination to be greater in an industry where heterogeneity is greater and, thus, the distribution of benefits of information among producers is wider. And, indeed, agriculture is a highly heterogeneous industry.

Timing of Information Release

Finally, the results of this chapter raise some important points about the timing of release of information regarding product contamination. An important dimension of public information policy in recent decades has related to full disclosure. The framework of this chapter allows evaluation of the welfare losses from delaying information dissemination, which can be substantial. However, the costs of releasing imperfect information versus releasing more certain information after a short delay must also be considered. When the consequences of contamination have not yet been determined, the psychological costs of worry and concern may be more substantial than if consequences can be more accurately determined before information dissemination. Also, more sophisticated models of how news media affect such psychological costs may be useful in structuring the release of information so that consumers better focus on the information that is known rather than unfounded speculation that can sometimes occur in an information vacuum.

11.8 CONCLUSIONS

This chapter has focused on the welfare economics of information. Information can take many forms. For purposes of discussion, this chapter divides information into two broad categories: price and quality. While the role of price information is rather clear and specific, the interpretation of quality is broad and includes almost all other product- or technology-specific information relevant to production and consumption. In cases where the economy is otherwise undistorted, better information about prices and quality enables producers and consumers to make more informed decisions that are closer to the social optimum. When other distortions exist, however, some cases exist where poor information can cause markets to come closer to a social optimum. But in such cases, better controls may be available to address other distortions.

The results of this chapter demonstrate how changes in information affect market equilibrium. A framework is provided to determine who gains and who loses with changes in information and information asymmetry. Many models have been developed in economics to represent behavior and explain contracts and equilibria that occur under information asymmetry. This chapter has not attempted to expound these various models, but rather presents the principles that are important for welfare measurement in them. The approach to welfare evaluation is to condition the consumer choice problem on information available to the consumer at the time of the choice. When initial decisions are made with imperfect information, the appropriate welfare measure for *ex post* evaluation is compensating or equivalent surplus, rather than compensating or equivalent variation, because the consumer is not free to adjust decisions already made on the basis of correct information. However, consumer preferences for this purpose must be inferred from subsequent consumer adjustments to correct or improved information, which then allows measurement of the value of information. With these concepts, a complete framework is developed to permit analysis of policies that regulate or control the production, dissemination and withholding of information, including false information.

These principles can be used to measure welfare effects in a wide variety of problems including, for example, (1) chemical contamination incidents where initial consumption is undertaken in ignorance but improved information becomes available; (2) false advertising where consumption is observed both before and after the falsity of claims becomes apparent; (3) effects of tobacco use, consumption of transgenic foods, exposure to harmful substances, or dietary considerations where early choices are made with inadequate knowledge of the likelihood of ultimate health effects; and (4) effects of economic policies that affect the benefits derived from previous durable good consumption choices such as the effects of macro or energy policies that cause changes in fuel prices following automobile or household heating appliance choices. Because these principles can be easily adapted to the producer problem in an obvious and straightforward way, many have been developed in this chapter only for the consumer problem.

Appendix to Chapter 11: Measuring the welfare effects of quality and information

This appendix considers the welfare effects of information. Cases are considered where changes in information are correctly perceived and where information is imperfect, incorrect or incorrectly perceived at the time of decisions but is later corrected either through improved information dissemination or through experience. The results are based largely on the work of William Foster and Richard E. Just (1989) who developed the approach to evaluate the effects of pesticide contamination of milk in Hawaii as described in Section 11.4. The framework of this appendix follows Bayesian decision theory in the sense that decisions are made on the basis of the subjective quality distribution held by the consumer at the time of decision-making. However, the framework also assumes that the consumer's subjective distribution is updated by receiving further information within a time frame where consumer adjustments to it are observable.[1]

For some problems such as contamination or product carcinogenicity, the ultimate harmful effects of initial consumption in ignorance may be realized only over a relatively long and, perhaps, unobservable time horizon. For example, after a consumer carcinogenicity scare, consumer perceptions about the probabilities of various levels of health loss may become reasonably accurate over a period of months whereas which specific individuals actually contract cancer may not be known for decades. For such cases, the welfare loss due to consumption in ignorance (including the psychological costs of uncertainty) can be measured on the basis of contractions in demand following the release of correct information even though the ultimate health effects for specific individuals may be determined later. That is, correct information may identify only the correct probability distribution of adverse consequences whereas the actual consequences occur beyond the observable time period. Thus, while decisions are based on subjective distributions held at the time of decision-making, the welfare effects are measured according to the consumer's evaluation of the eventual consequences and their probabilities reflected in the subsequent information.

11.A CONCEPTS OF *EX ANTE* AND *EX POST* WELFARE MEASUREMENT

To understand welfare effects of information regarding uncertain quality of consumer goods, one must distinguish between *ex ante* and *ex post* welfare evaluation. An *ex ante*

1. Graham (1983) has shown that state-dependent (quality-dependent) utility functions can be estimated only if individuals can be observed both before receiving information when choices do not affect known probabilities and after receiving information when choices can be altered to reflect probabilities.

welfare measure reflects the welfare or welfare effect for an individual as characterized prior to some release of information, whereas an *ex post welfare measure* characterizes the same welfare or welfare effect as actually realized following the release of information. The welfare measure can be producer or consumer surplus or one of the standard willingness-to-pay (WTP) measures. The relevant event for purposes of welfare evaluation is when uncertainty regarding quality is resolved or when further information about quality is obtained. For example, the cancer-causing attributes of a consumer good may be learned only after actual consumption. Or the true quality attributes of a product may be realized only after purchase and use. Or uncertain prices of related goods or conditions (such as weather) that affect the benefits of a particular consumption choice may not be realized until after a good is purchased.

At the time of the initial purchase decision, the consumer may not correctly anticipate future weather, energy prices, health effects or unknown product attributes. Thus, purchase and consumption decisions prior to the release of information are chosen to maximize *expected utility* based on anticipated *ex post conditions*, that is, based on the consumer's subjective distribution that characterizes probabilities of various *ex post outcomes* for each possible choice. Such decisions are called *ex ante decisions* and are made to maximize *ex ante welfare*. As in the case of producer decisions under risk discussed later in Appendix Sections 12.A–12.E and 14.A and consumer decisions under risk discussed later in Appendix Section 14.B, however, the actual realized welfare is determined by how well the *ex ante* decision fits the actual realized *ex post* condition, in other words, by the *ex post welfare*.

Another distinction required for the generalization in this appendix is between *ex ante* and *ex post information*. A consumer may have one set of information at the time of decision-making, which is called *ex ante information*, and another set of information by which the *ex post effects* of consumption are evaluated, called *ex post information*. The *ex ante* information may include uncertainty regarding product attributes or regarding conditions under which the product will be used. For example, a consumer may be unaware that certain foods are contaminated with pesticide residuals or have incorrect information about the likelihood that contamination will cause health effects from consumption. Or a consumer may purchase a vacation trip to the tropics and find after arrival that the accommodations are poorer than advertised or that an unexpected hurricane will severely detract from anticipated enjoyment. In other words, following the consumption decision, the consumer may become aware of product attributes, receive information about likely effects of consumption or realize specific conditions that affect the actual realized utility of consumption.

In cases where the ultimate effects of consumption are realized only over a long time horizon, such as with the actual incidence of cancer from consuming a carcinogenic product, the *ex post* information is assumed to allow the consumer to assess the probabilities of various possible consequences of consumption within the observable time period. For example, with respect to the health-linked effects of red meat consumption, consumer choice may be observable both before and after public education regarding health effects. The critical data requirement for empirical purposes is that some observed consumer decisions are based on *ex ante* information and some are based on *ex post* information.

In problems with changing information, attribution of changes in consumer choices to such changes in information is critical. Otherwise, the change in consumption can be attributed to a change in consumer preferences when, in fact, all choices are explained by a common set of preferences properly reflected by information available at the time of choice. When the choices are made by a common set of preferences, typical measures of surplus and WTP welfare measures have relevance whereas these welfare measures lose meaning if preferences change for unattributed reasons.[2]

In typical problems, four distinct stages can be identified: (1) consumption under *ex ante* information, (2) dissemination of new information, (3) consumption under *ex post* information, and (4) ultimate realization of the consequences of earlier consumption undertaken in ignorance. This appendix focuses on evaluation of welfare in the first and third stages. The second stage is assumed to be instantaneous for the conceptual development. The fourth stage is typically beyond the observable time period of analysis and, as argued below, may not generate data sufficient to evaluate the full adverse consequences. In many cases, the second and third stages become iterative processes as information is improved, in which case some or all of the fourth stage may eventually become part of the third stage. In any case, proper evaluation of welfare at the first stage depends on observing how behavior responds to information, which permits identification of true preferences from revealed preference behavior.[3] Following dissemination of new information, the welfare effects of perceived consequences of consumption as well as related psychological worry and concern can be quantified on the basis of response to implied preferences for uncertainty as reflected by the information on which subsequent consumption decisions are made. Thus, welfare effects in the third stage may reflect not only the expected consequences of consumption but also the risk associated with not knowing which consequence will occur.

In cases where the actual occurrence of a specific consequence is not known until the fourth stage, consumers must use their personal assessment of the probabilities of various outcomes in an *ex ante* sense in the third stage. This accounts for the importance of uncertainty as it affects consumer decisions and valuations. In the fourth stage, the consumer may discover the exact health effects or other attributes of consumption, but has already suffered from worry and concern in the third stage regarding the possibility of future consequences as well as the loss associated with altering decisions to avoid or reduce that risk. Furthermore, these costs are based in part on what may have been consumed in ignorance.

Actual choices reveal only preferences for what the consumer thinks he or she consumes at the time of choice. For this reason, observations of choices in the first stage alone are inadequate for welfare evaluation. In the third stage, the consumer realizes that earlier

2. One way to understand that a common set of preferences may be guiding decisions that otherwise seem to manifest changes in preferences is to interpret them in the context of the household production model as explained in Section 11.5. For simplicity and to avoid repetition of Section 11.5, this appendix focuses on market transactions without developing the full background of any underlying household production. Nevertheless, the reader should bear in mind the implicit assumptions that a common and stable set of preferences underlies such household production and that weak complementarity applies for information with respect to the good to which it applies. Thus, standard welfare measurements based on market transactions have meaning. If these assumptions fail, then only the welfare results applicable under true changes in preferences as discussed in Section 11.5 are applicable.
3. When sufficient data are not available to estimate the dependence of demand on consumer information about quality using revealed preferences, some have relied either partially or wholly on stated preference methods such as contingent valuation. See Section 13.4 for a discussion of contingent valuation methods. For a study combining revealed preference and stated preference data, see Azevedo, Herriges and Kling (2003).

choices were made in ignorance and either realizes actual consequences or obtains better information for evaluating potential future consequences and their probabilities. These are the effects that have the most important political ramifications for policy-makers because they reflect preferences at the time when public concerns and political pressures are greatest (when worry and concern about future consequences are greatest).

11.B A MODEL OF CONSUMER RESPONSE TO INFORMATION

In order to examine the change in consumers' welfare associated with information, consider the behavior of an individual consumer. Suppose a representative consumer is faced with the problem of allocating a given income between a good with uncertain quality and all other goods. Suppose the utility derived from consumption depends on the actual quality of the good, which becomes apparent only after consumption. For purposes of discussion, quality may represent an unknown product attribute, unknown health effect or other consequence of consumption, or an unknown condition such as weather that will affect utility derived from the product.

Let the quality level of the good of interest be represented by z as in Appendix Section 7.I but now suppose that z is unknown rather than fixed and that the consumer characterizes various possible outcomes for z by a probability distribution with parameter vector $\boldsymbol{\theta}$. Specific values of $\boldsymbol{\theta}$ may correspond to specific information sets such as information held at different times. Suppose further that the consumer's utility function can be represented by $U(\boldsymbol{q},z)$ where $\boldsymbol{q} = (q_1,\ldots,q_N)$ and U is assumed to be strictly increasing, quasiconcave, and twice differentiable in $\boldsymbol{q}$ for all possible levels of z.[4] For purposes of discussion, suppose increases in z represent improvements in quality so that utility is increasing in z, $\partial U/\partial z>0$. Finally, suppose z affects only contamination of q_1 under weak complementarity (see Appendix Section 7.I).

The consumer's expected utility maximization problem is[5]

$$\max_{\boldsymbol{q}} E_\theta[U(\boldsymbol{q},z)|\boldsymbol{pq}=m,\ \boldsymbol{q}\geq\boldsymbol{0}], \tag{11.1}$$

where $\boldsymbol{p}=(p_1,\ldots,p_N)$ is a vector of prices corresponding to $\boldsymbol{q}$, $\boldsymbol{pq}=\Sigma_{i=1}^N p_iq_i=m$, m is consumer income and $\boldsymbol{\theta}$ represents the information set or the consumer's perceived probability distribution of z at the time of consumption decisions.[6] In other words, $E_{\boldsymbol{\theta}}$ is an expectation taken at the time of consumption decisions.

Through comparative static analysis, one can show in this model that the consumer

4. Because z is not a choice variable, quasiconcavity of the objective criterion in z is not necessary.
5. For the analysis below, an internal solution is assumed to occur for q_1. This requires that q_1 is a good rather than a bad for all levels of quality. However, the framework can be easily expanded to consider $\partial U/\partial q_1< 0$ for low z if allowance is made for the restriction $q_1\geq 0$ to become binding, for example, by considering Kuhn–Tucker conditions rather than the simple first-order conditions of calculus.
6. The consumer's problem is treated in this appendix in the pure consumer case to avoid complexity of notation associated with endowments and differentiation of consumption from market transactions. However, the generalization to cases of factor supply and resource ownership follows in a straightforward manner and allows investigation of problems where labor is supplied under hazardous conditions represented by z. Where information on z is described by $\boldsymbol{\theta}$, one can thus assess the value of information on worker safety and the welfare effects of working in unknown hazardous conditions, such as with asbestos installation work before its harmful affects were fully understood.

increases consumption of q_1 in response to an increase in expected quality and decreases consumption in response to an increase in uncertainty regarding quality.[7] These results imply that the mean and the variance of the quality distribution have distinct qualitative effects on consumer demand. Thus, contamination information may be inadequately reflected by any scalar-valued information index. For example, information may need to be summarized by at least the mean and variance of quality if not by the complete information vector $\boldsymbol{\theta}$. For example, suppose an initial 'scare' causes consumer uncertainty to increase dramatically and then decline only gradually as further information is obtained. At the same time, expected quality may decline dramatically at the time of the initial scare, but then either increase or decrease depending on subsequent information. Thus, the information measure must be at least two-dimensional, representing both expected quality and uncertainty about the level of quality.

To understand these effects, one must distinguish between the *ex ante* quality distribution, on which consumer decisions depend, and the *ex post* quality distribution, which ultimately determines consumer welfare given consumer decisions. The probability distribution of utility is conceptually induced from the probability distribution of quality, z, by consumer choices. That is, z is a random variable that determines the specific utility effect of a given quantity of consumption whereas decisions are made to maximize expected utility given the *ex ante* distribution of quality.

11.C WELFARE EFFECTS OF CORRECT INFORMATION AND CORRECTLY PERCEIVED CHANGES IN QUALITY

Similar to other welfare measurement problems, the compensating or equivalent variation

7. To illustrate, consider the case with only two goods, q and q', with respective prices, p and p', where, upon substitution of the budget constraint and assuming an internal solution, the problem becomes $\max_q E_{\boldsymbol{\theta}}(\tilde{U}(q,m))$ where $\tilde{U}(q,m) \equiv U(q,(m-pq)/p',z)$ and $q'=(m-pq)/p'$. Suppose in addition to typical assumptions of positive and decreasing marginal utility, $U_q>0$ and $U_{qq}<0$, that the marginal utility of q increases at a decreasing rate in z, $U_{qz}>0$ and $U_{qzz}<0$, and that z does not affect the utility of consumption of the other good, $U_{q'z}=0$. The first-order condition for expected utility maximization is $E_{\boldsymbol{\theta}}(\tilde{U}_q)=E_{\boldsymbol{\theta}}(U_q-U_{q'}p/p')=0$. For comparative static analysis, suppose quality is a random variable represented by $z=\mu+\sigma\varepsilon$, where $\mu=E_{\boldsymbol{\theta}}(\varepsilon)=0$, σ represents a positive mean-preserving spread parameter, and the distribution of ε represents other parameters in $\boldsymbol{\theta}$ than the mean μ. Total differentiation of the first-order condition reveals the effects of a change in the quality distribution represented by μ and σ. The effect of a change in the mean of quality is

$$\frac{dq}{d\mu}=-\frac{\partial E_{\boldsymbol{\theta}}(\tilde{U}_q)/\partial\mu}{\partial E_{\boldsymbol{\theta}}(\tilde{U}_q)/\partial q}=-\frac{E_{\boldsymbol{\theta}}(\tilde{U}_{qz})(\partial z/\partial\mu)}{E_{\boldsymbol{\theta}}(\tilde{U}_{qq})}=-\frac{E_{\boldsymbol{\theta}}(\tilde{U}_{qz})}{E_{\boldsymbol{\theta}}(\tilde{U}_{qq})},$$

where the second equality follows from moving the differentiation operator inside the expectation operator and then using the chain rule. Note that $E_{\boldsymbol{\theta}}(\tilde{U}_{qq})<0$ follows from second-order conditions of the utility maximization problem, which must hold if U is quasiconcave and prices are positive. Also, differentiating the first-order condition reveals that $\tilde{U}_{qz}=U_{qz}-U_{q'z}p/p'=U_{qz}$, which is positive by assumption. Thus, $dq/d\mu>0$, which implies that consumption responds positively to an increase in the mean of the distribution of quality. Similarly,

$$\frac{dq}{d\sigma}=-\frac{\partial E_{\boldsymbol{\theta}}(\tilde{U}_q)/\partial\sigma}{\partial E_{\boldsymbol{\theta}}(\tilde{U}_q)/\partial q}=-\frac{E_{\boldsymbol{\theta}}(\tilde{U}_{qz})(\partial z/\partial\sigma)}{E_{\boldsymbol{\theta}}(\tilde{U}_{qq})}=-\frac{E_{\boldsymbol{\theta}}(\tilde{U}_{qz}\varepsilon)}{E_{\boldsymbol{\theta}}(\tilde{U}_{qq})}.$$

In this case, $E_{\boldsymbol{\theta}}(U_{qz}\varepsilon)$is the covariance of U_{qz} and ε, which must be negative because $U_{qz\varepsilon}\sigma=U_{qzz}<0$. That is, an increase in ε causes U_{qz} to decrease so the covariance must be negative. Thus, $dq/d\sigma<0$, which implies that an increase in quality uncertainty causes a decrease in consumption.

of a change in information measures a consumer's WTP to move to a new situation where consumption decisions are made with different information, which implies a different subjective distribution of quality, when the consumer is free to adjust consumption. When information which would have induced a correct assessment of the quality distribution (and, thus, an appropriate allocation of income) is withheld or transmitted imperfectly, however, the appropriate measure of WTP is compensating or equivalent surplus because the consumer does not have the opportunity to adjust to correct information. This section illustrates the problem where consumers are free to adjust to changes in information, that is, to *ex ante* information available both before and after the change.

Suppose the solution to the consumer's problem in (11.1) is represented by ordinary demands, $\mathbf{q}=\tilde{\mathbf{q}}(\mathbf{p},m,\boldsymbol{\theta})$, which are functions of the prices of all goods, income m, and the quality distribution parameters in $\boldsymbol{\theta}$. The expected utility evaluation at optimal consumption levels can be represented by the indirect expected utility function,

$$V \equiv V(\mathbf{p},m,\boldsymbol{\theta}) \equiv E_{\theta}[U(\tilde{\mathbf{q}},z)] \equiv \bar{U}.$$

Alternatively, the dual approach to this problem can be represented by the expenditure function, $e(\mathbf{p},\bar{U},\boldsymbol{\theta})=\mathbf{p}\bar{\mathbf{q}}(\mathbf{p},\bar{U},\boldsymbol{\theta})$, where $\bar{\mathbf{q}}(\mathbf{p},\bar{U},\boldsymbol{\theta})=[\bar{q}_1(\mathbf{p},\bar{U},\boldsymbol{\theta}),\ldots,\bar{q}_N(\mathbf{p},\bar{U},\boldsymbol{\theta})]$ solves the minimum expenditure problem,

$$e(\mathbf{p},\bar{U},\boldsymbol{\theta}) \equiv \min_{\mathbf{q}}\{\mathbf{pq} \mid E_{\theta}[U(\mathbf{q},z)]=\bar{U},\mathbf{q}\geq\mathbf{0}\},$$

which minimizes the cost of attaining a given level of expected utility $\bar{U}$. From results in Appendix Section 6.A, differentiation of the expenditure function yields the Hicksian demands,

$$\mathbf{e_p}=\bar{\mathbf{q}}(\mathbf{p},\bar{U},\boldsymbol{\theta}). \tag{11.2}$$

The willingness to accept a new situation with a different probability distribution of quality can be represented using either the indirect expected utility function or the expenditure function. Consider a change in the subjective quality distribution indicated by a change from $\boldsymbol{\theta}_0$ to $\boldsymbol{\theta}_1$ where prices and income remain constant at $\mathbf{p}^0=(p_1^0,\ldots,p_N^0)$ and m_0, respectively. In terms of the indirect expected utility function, the compensating variation, C, is defined analogous to equation (6.23) by

$$V(\mathbf{p}^0,m_0-C,\boldsymbol{\theta}_1)=V(\mathbf{p}^0,m_0,\boldsymbol{\theta}_0)=\bar{U}_0, \tag{11.3}$$

where $\bar{U}_0$ is the initial expected utility level. Or, analogous to equation (6.24) in terms of the expenditure function,[8]

$$C=m_0-e(\mathbf{p}^0,\bar{U}_0,\boldsymbol{\theta}_1)=e(\mathbf{p}^0,\bar{U}_0,\boldsymbol{\theta}_0)-e(\mathbf{p}^0,\bar{U}_0,\boldsymbol{\theta}_1). \tag{11.4}$$

8. This appendix focuses only on information changes. No price or income changes are considered. For the case where prices change from p^0 to p^1 and income changes from m_0 to m_1 at the same time information changes from $\boldsymbol{\theta}_0$ to $\boldsymbol{\theta}_1$, the compensating variation is defined by $V(\mathbf{p}^1,m_1-C,\boldsymbol{\theta}_1)=V(\mathbf{p}^0,m_0,\boldsymbol{\theta}_0)$ or $C=m_1-e(\mathbf{p}^1,\bar{U}_0,\boldsymbol{\theta}_1)$.

This measure of consumer loss (gain) can be calculated as the change in area under the compensated demand curve caused by the change in information holding expected utility at the initial level. Thus, the compensating variation is a willingness to sell the original quality distribution (or WTP for the subsequent quality distribution) as revealed by actual behavior or demand choices. To illustrate calculation of the compensating variation of the information change using compensated demands, define $\hat{p}_1(\boldsymbol{\theta})$ as the choke price for good q_1 (the price where its compensated demand curve meets the price axis) as a function of $\boldsymbol{\theta}$ when all other prices are fixed at $\boldsymbol{p}_*^0 = (p_2^0,...,p_n^0)$. In other words, suppose $\hat{p}_1(\boldsymbol{\theta})$ solves $q_1(\hat{p}_1(\boldsymbol{\theta}),\boldsymbol{p}_*^0,\bar{U}_0,\boldsymbol{\theta}) = 0$ or that $\hat{p}_1(\boldsymbol{\theta})$ is infinity if no solution exists.[9] Then, one finds from (11.2) and (11.4) that

$$C = e(\boldsymbol{p}^0,\bar{U}_0,\boldsymbol{\theta}_0) - e(\hat{\boldsymbol{p}}^0,\bar{U}_0,\boldsymbol{\theta}_0) - e(\boldsymbol{p}^0,\bar{U}_0,\boldsymbol{\theta}_1) + e(\hat{\boldsymbol{p}}^0,\bar{U}_0,\boldsymbol{\theta}_1)$$

$$= -\int_{p_1^0}^{\hat{p}_1(\boldsymbol{\theta}_0)} \frac{\partial e(p,\boldsymbol{p}_*^0,\bar{U}_0,\boldsymbol{\theta}_0)}{\partial p_1}dp + \int_{p_1^0}^{\hat{p}_1(\boldsymbol{\theta}_1)} \frac{\partial e(p,\boldsymbol{p}_*^0,\bar{U}_0,\boldsymbol{\theta}_1)}{\partial p_1}dp \qquad (11.5)$$

$$= -\int_{p_1^0}^{\hat{p}_1(\boldsymbol{\theta}_0)} \bar{q}_1(p,\boldsymbol{p}_*^0,\bar{U}_0,\boldsymbol{\theta}_0)dp + \int_{p_1^0}^{\hat{p}_1(\boldsymbol{\theta}_1)} \bar{q}_1(p,\boldsymbol{p}_*^0,\bar{U}_0,\boldsymbol{\theta}_1)dp,$$

assuming no externalities. Note that the measures in (11.4) and (11.5) coincide because a change in quality does not affect expected utility if consumption of q_1 is zero under the assumption of weak complementarity, $e(\hat{\boldsymbol{p}}^0,\bar{U}_0,\boldsymbol{\theta}_0) = e(\hat{\boldsymbol{p}}^0,\bar{U}_0,\boldsymbol{\theta}_1)$. Thus, the compensating variation is given by the area left of the initial Hicksian demand less the area left of the subsequent Hicksian demand. Equivalent variation can be defined and calculated similarly by replacing initial expected utility $\bar{U}_0$ with the subsequent expected utility level $\bar{U}_1$ in equations (11.4) and (11.5).

11.D THE WELFARE EFFECTS OF IMPERFECT INFORMATION

Compensating variation is appropriate for evaluation of the welfare effects of changes in consumer information regarding quality when consumers are free to adjust to the correct or objective quality distribution. However, when consumers are not given correct information that would alter their behavior or are given incorrect information that alters their behavior, then the subjective quality distribution guiding their decisions is incorrect. As a result, consumers make errors in allocating their budgets to maximize expected utility, which results in welfare losses. For example, if consumers purchase and consume a product they believe to be safe (because adverse information is withheld) and then receive *ex post* information indicating that consumption will cause cancer, then they experience essentially the same adverse effects as if they were forced to consume the product with perfect information. Consumers thus incur a *cost of ignorance* beyond the welfare effect

9. Note that the choke price, $\hat{\boldsymbol{p}}_1(\boldsymbol{\theta})$, is also a function of the expected utility level $\bar{U}_0$, which is suppressed for notational convenience.

they would experience if free to adjust, which also represents the incremental *value of information*. The appropriate WTP measure for evaluating a welfare change relative to the initial (subsequent) situation when consumption quantities are not free to adjust is compensating (equivalent) surplus rather than compensating (equivalent) variation.

To consider measurement of compensating surplus using observed demand behavior, define the restricted expected utility maximization problem that restricts consumption of q_1,

$$\max_{\mathbf{q}} E_{\boldsymbol{\theta}}[U(\mathbf{q},z)|\mathbf{pq}=m,\ \mathbf{q}\geq\mathbf{0},\ q_1=q_1^0].$$

The corresponding minimum expenditure problem is

$$\tilde{e}(\mathbf{p},\bar{U},\boldsymbol{\theta},q_1^0)=\min_{\mathbf{q}}\ \{\mathbf{pq}|E_{\boldsymbol{\theta}}[U(\mathbf{q},z)]=\bar{U},\ \mathbf{q}\geq\mathbf{0},\ q_1=q_1^0\}.$$

Suppose the latter problem is solved by demands $q_i=\bar{q}_i(\mathbf{p},\bar{U},\boldsymbol{\theta},q_1^0)$, $i=2, \ldots, N$, for the unrestricted quantities. The restricted expenditure function thus satisfies

$$\tilde{e}(\mathbf{p},\bar{U},\boldsymbol{\theta},q_1^0)=\mathbf{p}\bar{\mathbf{q}}(\mathbf{p},\bar{U},\boldsymbol{\theta},q_1^0)$$

where for simplicity of notation $\bar{q}_1(\mathbf{p},\bar{U},\boldsymbol{\theta},q_1^0)\equiv q_1^0$. Compensating surplus associated with providing correct information $\boldsymbol{\theta}_0^*$ instead of actual *ex ante* information $\boldsymbol{\theta}_0$ is then defined by

$$C_s=m_0-\tilde{e}(\mathbf{p}^0,\bar{U}_0,\boldsymbol{\theta}_0^*,q_1^0)=\tilde{e}(\mathbf{p}^0,\bar{U}_0,\boldsymbol{\theta}_0,q_1^0)-\tilde{e}(\mathbf{p}^0,\bar{U}_0,\boldsymbol{\theta}_0^*,q_1^0). \tag{11.6}$$

Equivalent surplus is defined similarly by replacing initial expected utility $\bar{U}_0$ with the subsequent expected utility level $\bar{U}_1$.

Two caveats should be noted concerning the use of compensating surplus for cases where information is withheld. First, the compensating surplus measure in (11.6) assumes the consumer does not remain permanently in ignorance. Following the old cliché 'ignorance is bliss', if the consumer never learns of the poor quality of a product (and *never experiences potential adverse effects* that are possible from poor quality), then the welfare loss associated with having incorrect information is not realized. The assumption here is that improved information (such as the likelihood of contracting cancer) is received soon enough that expected welfare effects are evaluated accordingly, even though specific outcomes (such as actually contracting cancer) may not be realized until much later. Thus, essentially the same worry, concern and other consequences of uncertainty, in addition to the expected real costs of adverse consequences, are incurred as if consumption were forced in the case of correct information. With these considerations in mind, welfare effects must be valued according to *ex post* information. The *ex post* subjective distribution of quality is equal to the objective distribution if *ex post* information is correct. As explained in Section 11.3, this resolves what some might consider a paradox whereby the consumer has a negative WTP for information that reveals he or she is worse off than he or she thought.

A second consideration is that the consumer may not make a change simply from a state of no information to either perfect information or continued ignorance. For example, when news of contamination breaks, it may be overstated or understated initially. Contaminating industries or government agencies may (consciously or not) downplay the extent or significance of contamination, while news coverage may overstate its extent or significance. Also, consumption prior to news of contamination may have taken place in ignorance of a contamination problem that already existed. Thus, decisions at each point in time must be considered as a function of the *ex ante* information on which those decisions are based, while the welfare benefits associated with the decisions at each point in time must be evaluated as a function of the *ex post* information that will determine the ultimate consumer benefits from consumption.

Correct Initial Information and Incorrect Subsequent Information

Suppose that initial information is correct and that it implies a distribution of quality characterized by $\boldsymbol{\theta}_0$, that a quality change takes place whereby correct information regarding the subsequent quality distribution is reflected by $\boldsymbol{\theta}_1^*$, but that the quality change is only partially reflected by the information $\boldsymbol{\theta}_1$ on which the consumer's choices are based.[10] The consumer thus chooses consumption quantities associated with information $\boldsymbol{\theta}_1$ rather than what would be consumed with correct information $\boldsymbol{\theta}_1^*$. That is, quantities $\boldsymbol{q}^1 = \tilde{\boldsymbol{q}}(\boldsymbol{p}^0, m_0, \boldsymbol{\theta}_1)$ are consumed voluntarily at $(\boldsymbol{p}^0, m_0, \boldsymbol{\theta}_1)$, whereas the consumer would maximize expected utility by consuming $\tilde{\boldsymbol{q}}(\boldsymbol{p}^0, m_0, \boldsymbol{\theta}_1^*)$.

To see the welfare effect of this change in quality, suppose the consumer subsequently obtains correct information on which the ultimate benefits of consumption depend. Then WTP is measured by a compensating surplus of the change from the initial situation with correct information at $\boldsymbol{\theta}_0$ to the subsequent situation with incorrect information at $\boldsymbol{\theta}_1$ taking account of the lack of ability to adjust to correct *ex post* information at $\boldsymbol{\theta}_1^*$ following the change,

$$\begin{aligned} C_s &= e(\boldsymbol{p}^0, \bar{U}_0, \boldsymbol{\theta}_0) - e(\boldsymbol{p}^0, \bar{U}_0, \boldsymbol{\theta}_1) + \tilde{e}(\boldsymbol{p}^0, \bar{U}_0, \boldsymbol{\theta}_1, q_1^1) - \tilde{e}(\boldsymbol{p}^0, \bar{U}_0, \boldsymbol{\theta}_1^*, q_1^1) \\ &= e(\boldsymbol{p}^0, \bar{U}_0, \boldsymbol{\theta}_0) - \tilde{e}(\boldsymbol{p}^0, \bar{U}_0, \boldsymbol{\theta}_1^*, q_1^1), \end{aligned}$$

because $e(\boldsymbol{p}^0, \bar{U}_0, \boldsymbol{\theta}_1) = \tilde{e}(\boldsymbol{p}^0, \bar{U}_0, \boldsymbol{\theta}_1, q_1^1)$. In this case, consumer choices before the change are made with correct information $\boldsymbol{\theta}_0$ so that $\boldsymbol{q}^0 = \tilde{\boldsymbol{q}}(\boldsymbol{p}^0, m_0, \boldsymbol{\theta}_0)$ is freely chosen along the unrestricted compensated demand at $(\boldsymbol{p}^0, \bar{U}_0, \boldsymbol{\theta}_0)$.To the compensating variation of the perceived change in *ex ante* information, $e(\boldsymbol{p}^0, \bar{U}_0, \boldsymbol{\theta}_0) - e(\boldsymbol{p}^0, \bar{U}_0, \boldsymbol{\theta}_1)$, must be added the welfare reduction of being constrained from adjusting optimally to *ex post* information after the change. This welfare reduction, which can be called the cost of ignorance, is

$$C_I = \tilde{e}(\boldsymbol{p}^0, \bar{U}_0, \boldsymbol{\theta}_1, q_1^1) - \tilde{e}(\boldsymbol{p}^0, \bar{U}_0, \boldsymbol{\theta}_1^*, q_1^1).$$

This amount can also be called the value of information.

10. To aid reader understanding, note that the case where $\boldsymbol{\theta}_1^* = \boldsymbol{\theta}_0$ is the case where true quality does not change but information misleads the consumer to believe that quality has changed.

Incorrect Initial Information and Correct Subsequent Information

Suppose that initial consumption has been taking place under incorrect information and subsequently correct information is released to which consumers adjust and re-evaluate consumption that has already taken place. Suppose the initial *ex ante* information implies a quality distribution characterized by $\boldsymbol{\theta}_0$, that information on which subsequent consumption decisions are based is characterized by $\boldsymbol{\theta}_1$, and that this release of information causes *ex post* evaluation of initial consumption according to a subjective quality distribution reflected by $\boldsymbol{\theta}_0^*$ which may be identical to $\boldsymbol{\theta}_1$. Then the consumer initially chooses consumption quantities associated with information $\boldsymbol{\theta}_0$, which fail to maximize expected utility. That is, initial consumption follows $\boldsymbol{q}^0 = \tilde{\boldsymbol{q}}(\boldsymbol{p}^0, m_0, \boldsymbol{\theta}_0)$, whereas the consumer would have maximized the initial expected utility by consuming $\tilde{\boldsymbol{q}}(\boldsymbol{p}^0, m_0, \boldsymbol{\theta}_0^*)$.

To see the welfare effect of this change in information, suppose the subsequent information is correct so that subsequent consumer choices maximize *ex ante* expected utility. Then the WTP welfare effect of the change using initial utility as the reference point is

$$\begin{aligned} C_s &= \tilde{e}(\boldsymbol{p}^0, \bar{U}_0, \boldsymbol{\theta}_0^*, q_1^0) - \tilde{e}(\boldsymbol{p}^0, \bar{U}_0, \boldsymbol{\theta}_0, q_1^0) + e(\boldsymbol{p}^0, \bar{U}_0, \boldsymbol{\theta}_0) - e(\boldsymbol{p}^0, \bar{U}_0, \boldsymbol{\theta}_1) \\ &= \tilde{e}(\boldsymbol{p}^0, \bar{U}_0, \boldsymbol{\theta}_0^*, q_1^0) - e(\boldsymbol{p}^0, \bar{U}_0, \boldsymbol{\theta}_1) \end{aligned} \quad (11.7)$$

because $\tilde{e}(\boldsymbol{p}^0, \bar{U}_0, \boldsymbol{\theta}_0, q_1^0) = e(\boldsymbol{p}^0, \bar{U}_0, \boldsymbol{\theta}_0)$. Consumer choices are made with information $\boldsymbol{\theta}_0$ before the change so that $\boldsymbol{q}^0 = \tilde{\boldsymbol{q}}(\boldsymbol{p}^0, m_0, \boldsymbol{\theta}_0)$ is freely chosen following the compensated demand at $(\boldsymbol{p}^0, \bar{U}_0, \boldsymbol{\theta}_0)$. To the compensating variation of the change in *ex ante* information, $e(\boldsymbol{p}^0, \bar{U}_0, \boldsymbol{\theta}_0) - e(\boldsymbol{p}^0, \bar{U}_0, \boldsymbol{\theta}_1)$ must be added the WTP for optimal adjustment to *ex post* information before the change, which is the cost of ignorance in this case,

$$C_I = \tilde{e}(\boldsymbol{p}^0, \bar{U}_0, \boldsymbol{\theta}_0^*, q_1^0) - \tilde{e}(\boldsymbol{p}^0, \bar{U}_0, \boldsymbol{\theta}_0, q_1^0).$$

Incorrect Initial and Subsequent Information

Suppose alternatively that initial consumption takes place under a subjective distribution of quality characterized by $\boldsymbol{\theta}_0$, but that *ex post* information implies a quality distribution characterized by $\boldsymbol{\theta}_0^*$ for that consumption. Then, as in the above example, suppose that information about quality changes so that the consumer's subjective distribution of quality is reflected by $\boldsymbol{\theta}_1$. Finally, suppose that *ex post* information relevant to evaluation of consumption following the change is reflected by $\boldsymbol{\theta}_1^*$. In this case, the consumer is influenced to choose initial consumption at $\boldsymbol{q}^0 = \tilde{\boldsymbol{q}}(\boldsymbol{p}^0, m_0, \boldsymbol{\theta}_0)$ prior to the change, even though the expected utility maximizing choice would be $\tilde{\boldsymbol{q}}(\boldsymbol{p}^0, m_0, \boldsymbol{\theta}_0^*)$. As in the previous case, the consumer subsequently chooses consumption at $\boldsymbol{q}^1 = \tilde{\boldsymbol{q}}(\boldsymbol{p}^0, m_0, \boldsymbol{\theta}_1)$ following the change in quality whereas the expected utility maximizing subsequent choice is $\tilde{\boldsymbol{q}}(\boldsymbol{p}^0, m_0, \boldsymbol{\theta}_1^*)$.

In this case, the WTP welfare effect of the change is

$$C_s = \tilde{e}(\boldsymbol{p}^0, \bar{U}_0, \boldsymbol{\theta}_0^*, q_1^0) - \tilde{e}(\boldsymbol{p}^0, \bar{U}_0, \boldsymbol{\theta}_1^*, q_1^1). \quad (11.8)$$

This welfare effect can be decomposed into the compensating variation of the change in *ex ante* information adjusted for the cost of ignorance in both the initial and subsequent situations, $C_s = C + C_I^1 - C_I^0$, where the compensating variation is

$$C = e(\mathbf{p}^0, \bar{U}_0, \boldsymbol{\theta}_0) - e(\mathbf{p}^0, \bar{U}_0, \boldsymbol{\theta}_1),$$

the cost of ignorance in the initial situation is

$$C_I^0 = \tilde{e}(\mathbf{p}^0, \bar{U}_0, \boldsymbol{\theta}_0^*, q_1^0) - \tilde{e}(\mathbf{p}^0, \bar{U}_0, \boldsymbol{\theta}_0, q_1^0) = \tilde{e}(\mathbf{p}^0, \bar{U}_0, \boldsymbol{\theta}_0^*, q_1^0) - e(\mathbf{p}^0, \bar{U}_0, \boldsymbol{\theta}_0),$$

and the cost of ignorance in the subsequent situation is

$$C_I^1 = \tilde{e}(\mathbf{p}^0, \bar{U}_0, \boldsymbol{\theta}_1^*, q_1^1) - \tilde{e}(\mathbf{p}^0, \bar{U}_0, \boldsymbol{\theta}_1, q_1^1) = \tilde{e}(\mathbf{p}^0, \bar{U}_0, \boldsymbol{\theta}_1^*, q_1^1) - e(\mathbf{p}^0, \bar{U}_0, \boldsymbol{\theta}_1),$$

because $\tilde{e}(\mathbf{p}^0, \bar{U}_0, \boldsymbol{\theta}_0, q_1^0) = e(\mathbf{p}^0, \bar{U}_0, \boldsymbol{\theta}_0)$ and $\tilde{e}(\mathbf{p}^0, \bar{U}_0, \boldsymbol{\theta}_1, q_1^1) = e(\mathbf{p}^0, \bar{U}_0, \boldsymbol{\theta}_1)$. That is, $\mathbf{q}^0 = \tilde{\mathbf{q}}(\mathbf{p}^0, m_0, \boldsymbol{\theta}_0)$ is freely chosen following the unrestricted compensated demand at $(\mathbf{p}^0, \bar{U}_0, \boldsymbol{\theta}_0)$ and $\mathbf{q}^1 = \tilde{\mathbf{q}}(\mathbf{p}^0, m_0, \boldsymbol{\theta}_1)$ is freely chosen following the unrestricted compensated demand at $(\mathbf{p}^0, \bar{U}_0, \boldsymbol{\theta}_1)$.

The next step is to consider estimation of these welfare effects from observed market data.

11.E EMPIRICAL CONSIDERATIONS IN WELFARE MEASUREMENT OF INFORMATION EFFECTS

Data regarding changes in perceived probabilities of quality levels are usually not available in cases where changing information causes those perceptions to be altered from time to time. Available data typically include observations on consumer incomes, and prices and quantities of goods exchanged, and some variables that reflect the information on which consumers base their subjective probabilities. From these data, Marshallian demands can be estimated as a function of the information that is used by consumers to form subjective probabilities of quality. At a simple and crude level, Marshallian surpluses can be calculated directly from estimated demands so that welfare effects of changes in information can be measured by the associated changes in consumer surplus. Alternatively and more accurately, exact estimates of compensating or equivalent variation can be inferred from estimated market demands (aside from statistical error). To do so requires inferring Hicksian demands from estimated Marshallian demands. This section discusses how the approaches of Appendix Sections 6.D–6.F can be generalized to estimate exact WTP welfare measures based on observed demands before and after changes in information or perceived quality when the estimated demands are conditioned on changes in information.

Hicksian demands can be inferred from estimated Marshallian demands in either of two ways. First, one can estimate demands implied by common demand system specifications such as those discussed in Appendix Section 6.F, which identifies parameters necessary to calculate welfare effects. Second, one can infer the expenditure function or indirect expected utility function implied by arbitrary Marshallian demand specifications following the approach of Hause (1975), Hausman (1981) or Vartia (1983) discussed in Appendix Section 6.D. In either case, to represent the effects of information, some of the fixed parameters must be replaced by functions of the information represented by $\boldsymbol{\theta}$. Additionally, measuring the effects of imperfect information requires some modifications associated with measurement of compensating or equivalent surplus as opposed to measurement of compensating or equivalent variation.

The Case of Perfect Information

To begin from the case of changes between two states of perfect information where compensating or equivalent variation is appropriate, consider the case where a Marshallian demand has been estimated from an arbitrary specification that depends on information. As in the approach of Appendix Section 6.D, Roy's identity determines the relationship of the Marshallian demand to the indirect expected utility function. The only difference from the case of Appendix Section 6.D is that the indirect expected utility definition in equation (11.3) is conditioned on information. Accordingly, the implied solution for the indirect expected utility function and expenditure function also has parameters depending on information in $\boldsymbol{\theta}$.

To illustrate, consider an estimated Marshallian demand equation of the form

$$\tilde{q}_i(\mathbf{p},m,\boldsymbol{\theta}) = \alpha(\mathbf{p}_*,\boldsymbol{\theta})p_1 + \beta(\mathbf{p}_*,\boldsymbol{\theta})m + \gamma(\mathbf{p}_*,\boldsymbol{\theta}), \tag{11.9}$$

where $\alpha(\mathbf{p}_*,\boldsymbol{\theta})$, $\beta(\mathbf{p}_*,\boldsymbol{\theta})$, and $\gamma(\mathbf{p}_*,\boldsymbol{\theta})$ are estimated functions of other prices, $\mathbf{p}_*$, and information, $\boldsymbol{\theta}$. Comparative static analysis, application of Roy's identity, and solution of the resulting differential equation following Appendix Section 6.D yields the expenditure function up to a multiplicative constant,

$$e(\mathbf{p},\bar{U},\boldsymbol{\theta}) = \bar{U}e^{\beta(\mathbf{p}_*,\boldsymbol{\theta})p_1} - \frac{\alpha(\mathbf{p}_*,\boldsymbol{\theta})}{\beta(\mathbf{p}_*,\boldsymbol{\theta})}p_1 - \frac{\alpha(\mathbf{p}_*,\boldsymbol{\theta})}{[\beta(\mathbf{p}_*,\boldsymbol{\theta})]^2} - \frac{\gamma(\mathbf{p}_*,\boldsymbol{\theta})}{\beta(\mathbf{p}_*,\boldsymbol{\theta})}, \tag{11.10}$$

from which the indirect expected utility function up to a multiplicative constant is

$$\bar{U}^0 = V(\mathbf{p},m,\boldsymbol{\theta}) = \left[m + \frac{\alpha(\mathbf{p}_*,\boldsymbol{\theta})}{\beta(\mathbf{p}_*,\boldsymbol{\theta})}p_1 + \frac{\alpha(\mathbf{p}_*,\boldsymbol{\theta})}{[\beta(\mathbf{p}_*,\boldsymbol{\theta})]^2} + \frac{\gamma(\mathbf{p}_*,\boldsymbol{\theta})}{\beta(\mathbf{p}_*,\boldsymbol{\theta})}\right] e^{-\beta(\mathbf{p}_*,\boldsymbol{\theta})p_1}.$$

An exact measure of compensating variation can thus be calculated by straightforward application of (11.4) or by solving (11.3) for C. Similarly, conditioning on the subsequent expected utility U_1 rather than the initial expected utility U_0 obtains the equivalent variation. This method of deriving the expenditure function offers only a local solution but suffices because only point estimates of the expenditure function are needed. That is, the point estimates at $\boldsymbol{\theta}_0$ and $\boldsymbol{\theta}_1$ are sufficient to solve for the appropriate WTP measure.

Of course, alternative arbitrary demand specifications such as the other forms considered in Appendix Section 6.D can also be used as long as some parameters are considered to be functions of the information in $\boldsymbol{\theta}$. Similarly, estimation of any of the demand forms in Appendix Section 6.F facilitates straightforward calculation of the compensating or equivalent variation of a change in information by using the associated expenditure function in the context of equation (11.4) or by solving the defining equation (11.3) after substitution of the implied indirect expected utility function.

The Case of Imperfect Information

One of the major advantages of beginning with or retrieving a representation of the indirect expected utility function or expenditure function associated with the observed market demand schedule is the ability to estimate WTP welfare measures associated with imperfect information. As discussed in the previous section, compensating surplus and equivalent surplus are the appropriate measures of welfare effects when information is imperfect. While these measures require using an expenditure function that restricts consumption of the good with imperfect information, the necessary point estimates of the restricted expenditure function for calculation of compensating or equivalent surplus can be inferred from the unrestricted expenditure function, which as above can be inferred from estimates of Marshallian demands.

Consider inferring a point estimate of the restricted expenditure function for a particular set of prices $\boldsymbol{p^0}$, expected utility level $\bar{U}_0$, restricted consumption of q_1 at $q_1^i = \tilde{q}_1(\boldsymbol{p^0}, \bar{U}_0, \boldsymbol{\theta}_i)$ associated with *ex ante* information $\boldsymbol{\theta}_i$, and *ex post* information $\boldsymbol{\theta}_i^*$. To do so, first find a price $\tilde{p}_1^i$ such that the unrestricted compensated demand at that price with information $\boldsymbol{\theta}_i^*$ is equal to the restricted consumption level under free choice, that is, solve $q_1^i = \bar{q}_1(\tilde{p}_1^i, \boldsymbol{p_*^0}, \bar{U}_0, \boldsymbol{\theta}_i^*)$ for $\tilde{p}_1^i$. Then the only difference in expenditure required for the restricted case at $(\boldsymbol{p^0}, \bar{U}_0, \boldsymbol{\theta}_i^*, q_1^i)$ compared to the unrestricted problem at $(\tilde{p}_1^i, \boldsymbol{p_*^0}, \bar{U}_0, \boldsymbol{\theta}_i^*)$ is that expenditure is reduced by $(\tilde{p}_1^i - p_1^0)q_1^i$ in the restricted case where the first good has price p_1^0 and restricted quantity $q_1 = q_1^i$. Thus,

$$\tilde{e}(\boldsymbol{p^0}, \bar{U}_0, \boldsymbol{\theta_1^*}, q_1^i) = e(\tilde{p}_1^1, \boldsymbol{p_*^0}, \bar{U}_0, \boldsymbol{\theta}_i^*) - (\tilde{p}_1^i - p_1^0)q_1^i. \tag{11.11}$$

Of course, the same relationship holds when the initial expected utility $\bar{U}_0$ is replaced with the subsequent expected utility level $\bar{U}_1$ as long as $\tilde{p}_1^i$ is defined for the case of subsequent expected utility to satisfy $q_1^i = \bar{q}_1(\tilde{p}_1^i, \boldsymbol{p_*^0}, \bar{U}_1, \boldsymbol{\theta}_i^*)$.

To illustrate application of (11.11), suppose a Marshallian demand for q_1 linear in price p_1 is estimated following (11.9). Then for a given set of prices $\boldsymbol{p^0}$, income m_0, *ex ante* information $\boldsymbol{\theta}_i$, and *ex post* information $\boldsymbol{\theta}_i^*$, one can first solve $q_1^i = \alpha(\boldsymbol{p_*^0}, \boldsymbol{\theta}_i^*)\tilde{p}_1^i + \beta(\boldsymbol{p_*^0}, \boldsymbol{\theta}_i^*)m_0 + \gamma(\boldsymbol{p_*^0}, \boldsymbol{\theta}_i^*)$ for $\tilde{p}_1^i$, obtaining $\tilde{p}_1^i = [q_1^i - \beta(\boldsymbol{p_*^0}, \boldsymbol{\theta}_i^*)m_0 - \gamma(\boldsymbol{p_*^0}, \boldsymbol{\theta}_i^*)]/\alpha(\boldsymbol{p_*^0}, \boldsymbol{\theta}_i^*)$ where q_1^i is the unrestricted choice under *ex ante* information, $q_1^i = \alpha(\boldsymbol{p_*^0}, \boldsymbol{\theta}_i)p_1^0 + \beta(\boldsymbol{p_*^0}, \boldsymbol{\theta}_i)m_0 + \gamma(\boldsymbol{p_*^0}, \boldsymbol{\theta}_i)$. Then necessary point estimates of the restricted expenditure function in (11.11) can be found using (11.10),

$$\tilde{e}(\boldsymbol{p^0}, \bar{U}_0, \boldsymbol{\theta_1^*}, q_1^i) = \bar{U}_0 e^{\beta(\boldsymbol{p_*^0}, \boldsymbol{\theta}_i^*)\tilde{p}_1^i} - \frac{\alpha(\boldsymbol{p_*^0}, \boldsymbol{\theta}_i^*)}{\beta(\boldsymbol{p_*^0}, \boldsymbol{\theta}_i^*)}\tilde{p}_1^i - \frac{\alpha(\boldsymbol{p_*^0}, \boldsymbol{\theta}_i^*)}{[\beta(\boldsymbol{p_*^0}, \boldsymbol{\theta}_i^*)]^2} - \frac{\gamma(\boldsymbol{p_*^0}, \boldsymbol{\theta}_i^*)}{\beta(\boldsymbol{p_*^0}, \boldsymbol{\theta}_i^*)} - (\tilde{p}_1^i - p_1^0)q_1^i,$$

where $\bar{U}_0$ is found by setting the unrestricted expenditure function in (11.10) evaluated at *ex ante* information equal to m_0, which obtains

$$\bar{U}_0 = m_0\left[e^{\beta(\boldsymbol{p_*^0}, \boldsymbol{\theta}_i)p_1^0} - \frac{\alpha(\boldsymbol{p_*^0}, \boldsymbol{\theta}_i)}{\beta(\boldsymbol{p_*^0}, \boldsymbol{\theta}_i)}p_1^0 - \frac{\alpha(\boldsymbol{p_*^0}, \boldsymbol{\theta}_i)}{[\beta(\boldsymbol{p_*^0}, \boldsymbol{\theta}_i)]^2} - \frac{\gamma(\boldsymbol{p_*^0}, \boldsymbol{\theta}_i)}{\beta(\boldsymbol{p_*^0}, \boldsymbol{\theta}_i)}\right]^{-1}.$$

With this approach, or similar ones based on other demand specifications corresponding to (11.9), each of the calculations explored below can be implemented using estimated Marshallian demands conditioned on information.

Effects of Disseminating Incorrect Information

Consider empirical measurement of welfare change for the case where initial consumption is based on correct information but subsequent consumption after a change in quality is based on imperfect information. Suppose prices and income remain at initial levels, $\mathbf{p}^0$ and m_0, respectively, and the change in information is represented by a shift in parameters of the subjective distribution of quality from $\boldsymbol{\theta}_0$ to $\boldsymbol{\theta}_1$. Suppose initial information is correct but that correct information following the change, represented by $\boldsymbol{\theta}_1^*$, is obtained by the consumer only after decisions are made with information represented by $\boldsymbol{\theta}_1$. Then following (11.11), where $\tilde{p}_1^1$ is defined to satisfy $q_1^0 = \bar{q}_1(\tilde{p}_1^1, \mathbf{p}_*^0, \bar{U}_0, \boldsymbol{\theta}_1^*)$, the WTP for the change is measured by the compensating surplus,

$$\begin{aligned} C_s &= e(\mathbf{p}^0, \bar{U}_0, \boldsymbol{\theta}_0) - \tilde{e}(\mathbf{p}^0, \bar{U}_0, \boldsymbol{\theta}_1^*, q_1^1) \\ &= m_0 - e(\tilde{p}_1^1, \mathbf{p}_*^0, \bar{U}_0, \boldsymbol{\theta}_1^*) + (\tilde{p}_1^1 - p_1^0)q_1^1, \end{aligned}$$

because the only difference in the subsequent situation with price $\tilde{p}_1^1$ versus p_1^0 is the difference in expenditure required to purchase q_1^1. The cost of ignorance associated with imperfect information is thus

$$C_I = C_s - C = e(\tilde{p}_1^1, \mathbf{p}_*^0, \bar{U}_0, \boldsymbol{\theta}_1^*) - (\tilde{p}_1^1 - p_1^0)q_1^1 - e(p_1^0, \mathbf{p}_*^0, \bar{U}_0, \boldsymbol{\theta}_1^*).$$

The price difference, $\tilde{p}_1^1 - p_1^0$, can be regarded as a measure of the substitutability between good q_1 and all other goods at the initial levels of utility and consumption but with new information. As $\tilde{p}_1^1$ approaches p_1^0, the cost of ignorance approaches zero. Of course, a similar measure could be defined as the difference in equivalent variation and equivalent surplus by conditioning on *ex post* utility.

Effects of Correcting Information

Next consider empirical measurement of WTP for the case where initial consumption is based on incorrect information but correct information is released according to which subsequent consumption is adjusted. Suppose prices and income remain at initial levels, $\mathbf{p}^0$ and m_0, respectively, and the change in information is represented by a shift in parameters of the subjective distribution of quality from $\boldsymbol{\theta}_0$ to $\boldsymbol{\theta}_1$. Suppose, consistent with improved information, the benefits of initial consumption are realized according to subsequent information as characterized by $\boldsymbol{\theta}_0^*$ rather than $\boldsymbol{\theta}_0$. Then following (11.11), where $\tilde{p}_1^0$ is defined to satisfy $q_1^0 = \bar{q}_1(\tilde{p}_1^0, \mathbf{p}_*^0, \bar{U}_0, \boldsymbol{\theta}_0^*)$, the WTP for the change as measured by the compensating surplus in (11.7) can be expressed as

$$\begin{aligned} C_s &= \tilde{e}(\mathbf{p}^0, \bar{U}_0, \boldsymbol{\theta}_0^*, q_1^0) - e(\mathbf{p}^0, \bar{U}_0, \boldsymbol{\theta}_1) \\ &= e(\tilde{p}_1^0, \mathbf{p}_*^0, \bar{U}_0, \boldsymbol{\theta}_0^*) - (\tilde{p}_1^0 - p_1^0)q_1^0 - e(\mathbf{p}^0, \bar{U}_0, \boldsymbol{\theta}_1) \end{aligned}$$

because the only difference in the initial situation with price $\tilde{p}_1^0$ versus p_1^0 is the difference in expenditure required to purchase q_1^0. The cost of ignorance associated with imperfect information in the initial situation is thus

$$C_I = C_s - C = e(\tilde{p}_1^0, \mathbf{p}_*^0, \bar{U}_0, \boldsymbol{\theta}_0^*) - (\tilde{p}_1^0 - p_1^0)q_1^0 - e(p_1^0, \mathbf{p}_*^0, \bar{U}_0, \boldsymbol{\theta}_0^*).$$

Again, a similar measure could be defined as the difference in equivalent variation and equivalent surplus.

Effects of Changing Information in a World of Imperfect Information

Finally, suppose that available initial information gives the consumer an *ex ante* subjective quality distribution with parameters $\boldsymbol{\theta}_0$, that *ex post* information by which initial consumption affects welfare yields a quality distribution with parameters $\boldsymbol{\theta}_0^*$, that available *ex ante* information for making subsequent consumption choices yields a quality distribution with parameters $\boldsymbol{\theta}_1$, and that *ex post* information by which consumption affects welfare yields a quality distribution with parameters $\boldsymbol{\theta}_1^*$. Then the measurement of welfare change must take account of errors in both the initial and subsequent allocations of income. The appropriate WTP measure of welfare using initial expected utility as the reference point following (11.8) is

$$C_s = \tilde{e}(\mathbf{p}^0, \bar{U}_0, \boldsymbol{\theta}_0^*, q_1^0) - \tilde{e}(\mathbf{p}^0, \bar{U}_0, \boldsymbol{\theta}_1^*, q_1^1).$$

This WTP measure is a compensating surplus measure where consumption is restricted in both the initial and subsequent situations but at different levels in each. For practical application using (11.11), this measure requires finding a price, $\tilde{p}_1^0$, such that $q_1^0 = \tilde{q}_1(\tilde{p}_1^0, \mathbf{p}_*^0, \bar{U}_0, \boldsymbol{\theta}_0^*)$, and a similar price, $\tilde{p}_1^1$, such that $q_1^1 = \tilde{q}_1(\tilde{p}_1^1, \mathbf{p}_*^0, \bar{U}_0, \boldsymbol{\theta}_1^*)$. Then

$$C_s = e(\tilde{p}_1^0, \mathbf{p}_*^0, \bar{U}_0, \boldsymbol{\theta}_0^*) - e(\tilde{p}_1^1, \mathbf{p}_*^0, \bar{U}_0, \boldsymbol{\theta}_1^*) - (\tilde{p}_1^0 - p_1^0)q_1^0 + (\tilde{p}_1^1 - p_1^1)q_1^1.$$

For this problem, the cost of ignorance in the initial situation can be computed as

$$C_I^0 = e(\tilde{p}_1^0, \mathbf{p}_*^0, \bar{U}_0, \boldsymbol{\theta}_0^*) - (\tilde{p}_1^0 - p_1^0)q_1^0 - m_0$$

and the cost of ignorance in the subsequent situation can be computed as

$$C_I^1 = e(\tilde{p}_1^1, \mathbf{p}_*^0, \bar{U}_0, \boldsymbol{\theta}_1^*) - (\tilde{p}_1^1 - p_1^1)q_1^1 - m_0.$$

Based on this methodology, the pertinent welfare measures are thus directly accessible once Hicksian demands are inferred from Marshallian demands. Using the subsequent expected utility level as the reference point, the only change necessary to calculate equivalent surplus rather than compensating surplus is to replace initial expected utility $\bar{U}_0$ with the subsequent expected utility level $\bar{U}_1$ in each instance. If prices and income also change as a result of the perceived change in quality, they can also be incorporated in these measures in a straightforward way. By extending these methods to multiple periods, one can consider evaluation of welfare effects over an extended third stage involving multiple periods in which initial information is incorrect and choices are made in partial ignorance as information is gradually improved.

11.F CONCLUSIONS AND POTENTIAL APPLICATIONS

The approach of this appendix is to represent the effects of changes in information by changes in the parameters of the consumer's subjective distribution of quality. The definition of quality can be adapted to a broad set of problems affecting individuals' welfare in which many policy questions related to quality uncertainty of individual consumer goods can be addressed. Quality can represent contamination with pesticide residuals, carcinogenicity of consumer goods such as foods and cell phones, health effects of red meat or alcoholic beverages, false or exaggerated claims by manufacturers regarding consumer goods, false information about genetically modified organisms, unanticipated effects of economic policies on the benefits or costs of using consumer durables, continuing contamination problems of various air and water resources that affect the quality of consumer goods such as housing, recreation and fishery uses, and so on. Using the proposed welfare measures, economic implications can be analyzed for policies that affect contamination, require environmental clean-up, regulate pesticide residuals on foods, control marketing of products based on genetically modified organisms, and so on. Additionally, these welfare measures permit analysis of information policy issues that relate to whether and how much to educate consumers and when to do so. For example, such analyses might compare the welfare implications of releasing information earlier with less accuracy (and, thus, more consumer uncertainty) versus later when more information has been accumulated and can be regarded as more accurate. These questions present an interesting trade-off between the welfare effects of consumer uncertainty (including forgone consumption due to uncertainty) and the cost of continued consumption in ignorance.

12. Stochastic welfare economics with applications to agricultural policy analysis

Thus far in this book, aside from a few exceptions in Chapter 11, producers and consumers have been assumed to know all the prices that can possibly affect their decisions. Furthermore, prices have been assumed to be nonrandom or *nonstochastic*. In reality, however, prices vary with a good deal of instability. Instability is generally thought to lead to adverse effects on both producers and consumers for two reasons. First, when prices change substantially, costs of adjustment must generally be incurred to undertake new profit or utility maximization decisions. Second, when prices change, decision-makers may not anticipate the extent of price changes and, hence, may make poor decisions. The first situation might be characterized as one of instability with certainty, in which case unstable price movements are anticipated with certainty so that profit- or utility-maximizing adjustments can be made. The second situation is one of instability with uncertainty, in which case price movements are not anticipated perfectly in advance and thus full adjustment is either not possible or very costly.

Of course, reality usually presents some mixture of these two extremes. For example, a manufacturing firm might expect the price of a product it is currently producing to rise before sale, but it may not know by how much. Because the choice of government policies can affect both price stability and uncertainty, an examination of the associated welfare effects is important. Similarly, random variation in production can lead to adverse welfare effects, although policy instruments may not be as readily available for reducing these welfare effects.

This chapter first examines the effects of instability in prices on both producers and consumers in the traditional economic welfare framework of certainty (price changes are anticipated in time to make adjustments). Then the welfare measures of earlier chapters are generalized for the case of uncertainty where decisions must be made before prices are known. In this framework, some of the classical economic welfare analyses of price instability are reconsidered, and applicability of the alternative approaches for realistic problems is considered. Subsequently, the value of maintaining options when faced with uncertainty is discussed and, finally, applications to agricultural policy issues are discussed along with the accompanying problems of moral hazard and adverse selection that are often associated with problems of uncertainty and asymmetric information.

12.1 CONSUMER WELFARE WITH RANDOM PRICES AND INSTANTANEOUS ADJUSTMENT

The welfare effects of price instability were first studied by Frederick V. Waugh (1944). He concluded, contrary to popular opinion, that consumers should prefer price instability.

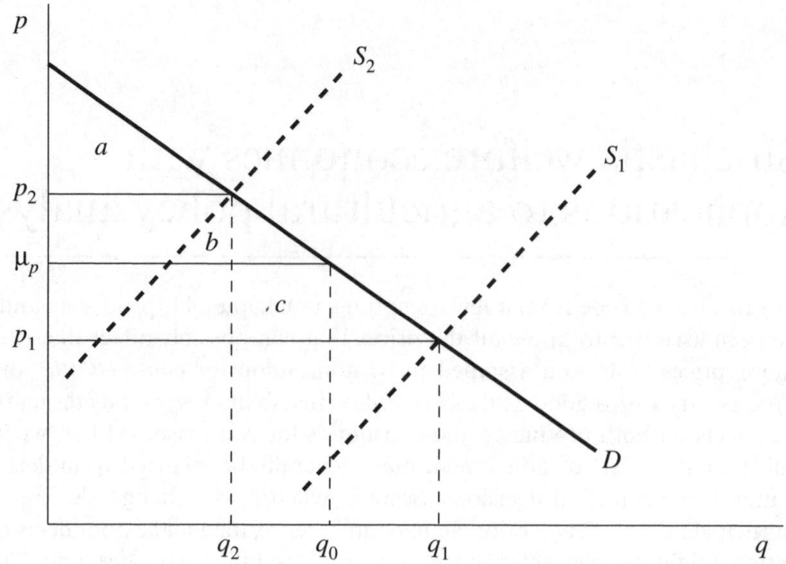

Figure 12.1

His results are developed in Figure 12.1, where *D* represents demand and consumers face prices p_1 and p_2, each of which occurs half the time (that is, with probability 0.5). These price variations may be caused by, for example, random fluctuations in supply between S_1 and S_2. When price is p_1, consumers buy q_1 so consumer surplus is area $a+b+c$. When price is p_2, consumers buy q_2 so consumer surplus is area a. If, on the other hand, prices are stabilized by means of, say, some government policy at the average price level, $\mu_p = (p_1 + p_2)/2$, then consumption takes place at q_0 with a consumer surplus of area $a+b$.

To investigate the welfare effects of price stabilization, note that half the time consumers gain area *b* as the price is lowered from p_2 to μ_p, but the other half of the time consumers lose area *c* as the price is raised from p_1 to μ_p. Because $p_2 - \mu_p = \mu_p - p_1$, the loss obviously outweighs the gain. The average loss is ½ (area $b-$ area c). This result implies that consumers prefer price instability if they can take advantage of it by buying more at low prices and less at high prices.

Although this result holds for Marshallian consumer surplus, the analysis can be applied similarly using the compensating or equivalent variation concepts. The results above with consumer surplus defined by an ordinary consumer demand curve are directly applicable if the income elasticity is zero (Section 6.3). This holds for both the single-consumer case and for a group of consumers as in the aggregate market case of Section 8.2. Alternatively, the demand curve in Figure 12.1 may be viewed as a Hicksian compensated demand curve associated with utility attained at the stabilized price μ_p. In this case, the surplus analysis above applies to the equivalent variation of moving from destabilized prices or to measuring the compensating variation of moving from stabilization to destabilization – regardless of income elasticity.

On the other hand, measuring the compensating variation of stabilization or the equivalent variation of destabilization requires use of the compensated demand curves associated with p_1 and p_2, the latter of which would lie entirely left of the former for positive income elasticities (both of which would have steeper slope than ordinary demand). The latter would be used to compare p_2 with μ_p, thus generating an area smaller than area b in Figure 12.1 (where D again represents ordinary demand). The former compensated curve would be used to compare p_1 with μ_p, thus generating an area larger than area c. Thus, the compensating variation loss from stabilization would be even greater than suggested by consumer surplus. Similarly, the equivalent variation gain from destabilization would be even greater than suggested by consumer surplus.[1]

Of course, the consumer surplus results above apply without error for measurement of compensating and equivalent variation for a profit-maximizing producer where the demand curve represents derived demand for a factor input. Similarly, the results apply to a sector equilibrium demand curve in the sense discussed in Section 9.1, although any necessary compensation may need to be distributed to groups affected only indirectly by the price changes in this particular market.

12.2 PRODUCER WELFARE WITH RANDOM BUT ANTICIPATED PRICES

The effect of stochastic output price on producers was first examined by Oi (1961). Assuming a fixed supply curve, he concluded that producers also prefer price instability when they can adjust completely to price changes. To understand his results, consider Figure 12.2, where supply is represented by S and producers are confronted with two prices – p_1 and p_2 – each of which occurs with probability 0.5. These price variations may be caused by, for example, random variation in demand between D_1 and D_2. When price is p_1, producers sell q_1 so that quasirent is given by area a. When price is p_2, producers sell q_2 so that quasirent is given by area $a+b+c$. If, on the other hand, prices are stabilized by some government policy at the average price level $\mu_p=(p_1+p_2)/2$, then production is q_0 and producer surplus is area $a+b$. When price would otherwise be p_1, producers gain area b. But when price would otherwise be p_2, producers lose area c. Because $p_2-\mu_p=\mu_p-p_1$, the latter loss is larger than the former gain. And because each occurs half the time, producers lose on average from price stabilization (unless supply is perfectly inelastic). Producers would require an average compensation of ½ (area c – area b) to be equally well off under stabilization.

Again, these producer surplus results apply directly to the case of measuring the compensating or equivalent variation associated with stabilization for one or many competitive profit-maximizing producers, to one or many consumers selling factor endowments or household production with zero exogenous income elasticities of supply, and to sector equilibrium supply curves of the type described in Section 9.1. If the supply in Figure 12.2 is regarded as a Hicksian compensated supply associated with the stabilized price, then

1. In lieu of these kinds of arguments, one can simply claim on the basis of the Willig results (Section 6.5, 6.6, 7.5 and 7.6) that areas b and c in Figure 12.1 are in error by no more than 5 percent under reasonable conditions (conditions that can be investigated empirically). However, the critical issue here is the potential benefit of price stabilization. While consumer surplus may make no more than 5 percent errors in measuring compensating or equivalent variation corresponding to areas b and c, the error in measuring ½ (area b – area c) may be considerably greater in percentage terms.

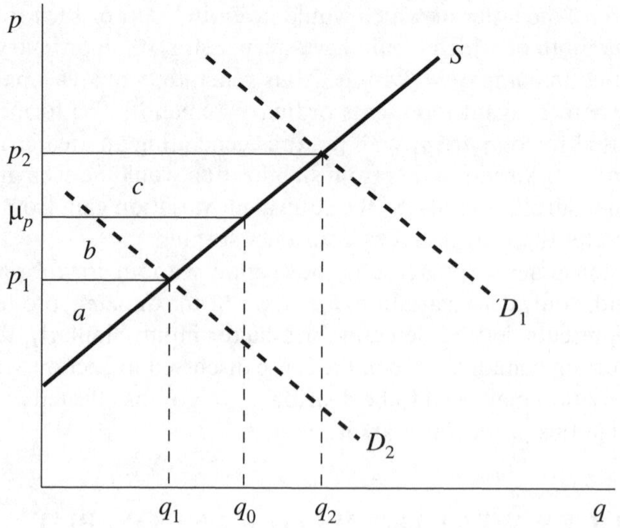

Figure 12.2

the results also apply to the equivalent variation of stabilization or the compensating variation of destabilization for a group of consumers with nonzero exogenous income elasticities selling either factor endowments or household production. Alternatively, the compensating variation of stabilization or the equivalent variation of destabilization for consumers with nonzero income elasticities requires conditioning compensated supply on utility at the random price. Because compensated factor supply curves intersect ordinary factor supply curves from the left, the compensating variation would be less than area *c* for moving from price p_2 to μ_p and would be greater than area *b* for moving from price p_1 to μ_p, so the average compensation required to move to stabilized prices would be less than ½ (area $c -$ area b).

12.3 CAN UNCERTAINTY IMPROVE WELFARE?

These two counterintuitive results favoring economic instability led economists to consider whether destabilization can really be preferred. Samuelson (1972) argued that, in fact, an economy cannot 'pull itself up by the bootstraps' simply by generating instability. Both Samuelson (1972) and Massell (1969) showed that these two results (Sections 12.1 and 12.2) cannot be simultaneously applicable and that, when effects on both sides of the market are considered, there is a net gain from stabilization. Considering the Massell approach, suppose as in Figure 12.3 that consumer demand is represented by *D* and that stochastic supply is represented by S_1 and S_2, each of which occurs with probability 0.5. Thus, equilibrium prices are p_1 and p_2, respectively, with probability 0.5 each. Now, suppose that prices are stabilized at μ_p, say, by means of a buffer stock to which excess supply, $q_1' - q_0$, is added when S_1 occurs and from which excess demand, $q_0 - q_2'$, is taken out when S_2 occurs. In the event of S_1, consumers lose area $c+d$ in consumer

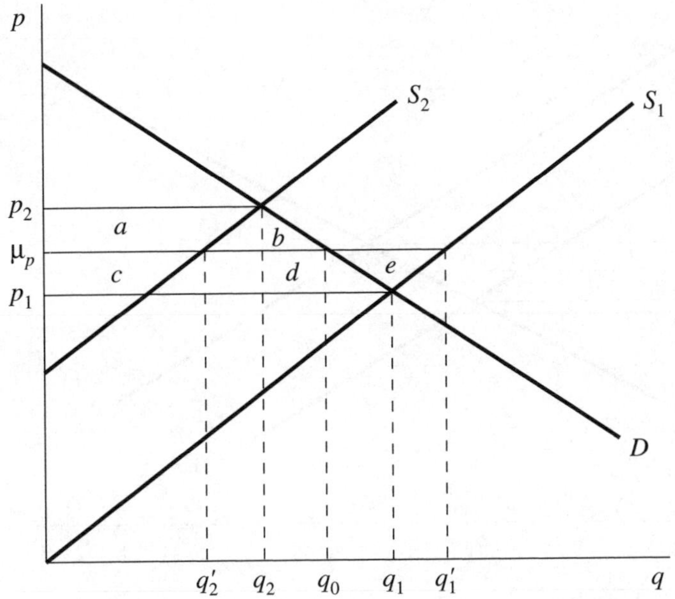

Figure 12.3

surplus while producers gain area $c+d+e$ in producer surplus for a net gain of area e. In the event of S_2, producers lose area a in producer surplus, but consumers gain area $a+b$ in consumer surplus for a net gain of area b. The average overall effect of price stabilization is thus a gain of ½ (area b + area e). This result implies that the gain from destabilization for consumers in Section 12.1 comes at the expense of the producers who are beset by instability in their production conditions (as reflected by randomly varying marginal cost). Furthermore, the effect on producers more than offsets the effect on consumers.

Similar considerations apply to the results in Section 12.2, as demonstrated in Figure 12.4. With instability represented by demand varying between D_1 and D_2 with price correspondingly varying between p_1 and p_2, price stabilization at μ_p via a buffer stock leads to a gain of area e if D_1 occurs or area c if D_2 occurs. Thus, price stabilization generates an average overall gain of ½ (area c + area e). This result implies that the gain from destabilization for producers in Section 12.2 comes at the expense of consumers who are beset by instability. On average, the producer loss from stabilization of ½ (area $a+b-d-e$) is more than offset by the consumer gain of ½ (area $a+b+c-d$).

These results may, again, be interpreted in a variety of contexts. For example, the interpretation of welfare effects for buyers in Figure 12.3 follows the discussion in Section 12.1, and the interpretation for sellers in Figure 12.4 follows the discussion in Section 12.2. The interpretation must be somewhat more careful for the sellers in Figure 12.3 and the buyers in Figure 12.4. For example, suppose that randomness in a derived demand curve is due to random output prices. Then, as shown in Section 4.4, the area behind a shifting supply or demand curve does not necessarily reflect accurately the change in quasirent for a producer unless the input is essential to the production process. If, however, the good is essential to the production process (either as an output or input) or to the well-being of a

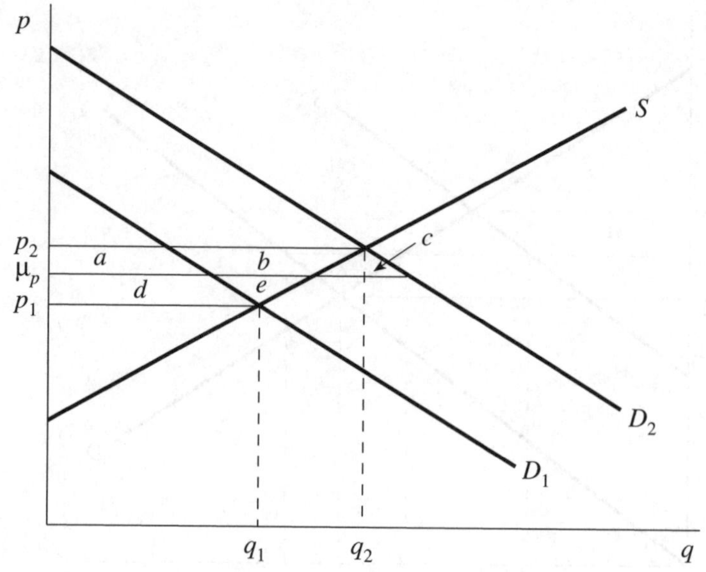

Figure 12.4

consumer or factor owner (see Section 7.10), then the area behind the associated supply or demand curve has welfare significance even when other prices (or income) are changing. Under these conditions, the area is an exact measure of quasirent for producers. For consumers and factor owners, the area is an exact measure of compensating or equivalent variation if the random supply or demand relationship is a compensated relationship, or the area is an approximation if the random supply or demand relationships are ordinary Marshallian relationships. Again, based on the aggregation results of Sections 8.1 and 8.2, these statements apply for groups of producers and consumers. And using the results of Chapter 9, these statements apply for equilibrium supplies and demands in an individual market where equilibrium variation is defined with respect to buffer stock intervention, and instability is caused by forces that are exogenous to the sector or economy (for example, external prices or weather).

The results of this section thus suggest that welfare gains for both producers and consumers are possible by stabilizing prices of storable commodities, at least beyond the case of no storage when storage costs are zero. That is, under these conditions, one group gains by more than the other loses. Thus, gainers can compensate losers so that both are better off under stabilization.[2]

Extensions to International Trade

This framework can be easily extended to consider the issue of price stabilization in international trade. For example, the supply curve in Figures 12.3 and 12.4 can be considered

2. As shown in a more general algebraic framework by Massell (1969), these conclusions may be generalized to include any joint stochastic distribution of fluctuations in supply and demand as long as supply and demand are linear and fluctuations manifest themselves in parallel shifts of the supply and demand curves.

as an excess supply by exporting countries, and the demand curve can be considered as an excess demand by importing countries. Thus, from Figure 12.3, exporters gain and importers lose from price stabilization when supply is unstable. Alternatively, from Figure 12.4, exporters lose and importers gain from stabilization when demand is unstable. In both cases, the net international effect of price stabilization is positive.

In either case, some additional implications for distribution of gains and losses within countries can be considered. For example, consider Figure 12.5, which represents supply and demand within an importing country. Prices p_1, p_2, and μ_p correspond to those in

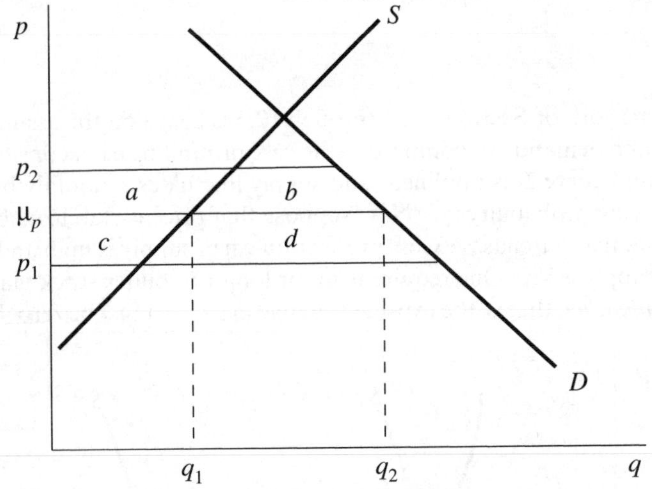

Figure 12.5

Figure 12.3 for purposes of comparing free international trade versus stabilized international trade. In this context, producers in the importing country gain area c from stabilization when exporters' excess supply is high and lose area a when exporters' excess supply is low. Consumers in the importing country, on the other hand, lose area $c+d$ when exporters' excess supply is high and gain area $a+b$ when exporters' excess supply is low. Thus, producers in the importing country suffer a net average loss of ½ (area $a-$area c), and consumers in the importing country lose on average ½ (area $c+d-a-b$). For example, if demand in an importing country is highly inelastic consumers lose relatively little, while producers may suffer substantial losses if supply is highly elastic. Effects under alternative elasticities and effects for producing and consuming groups in different countries can be analyzed similarly for alternative cases (see Hueth and Schmitz 1972 for further details).

12.4 ADDITIONAL CONSIDERATIONS REGARDING WELFARE EFFECTS OF PRICE STABILIZATION

Subsequent analysis has shown that the foregoing conclusions regarding who gains and who loses from price stabilization are highly sensitive to market structure and to shape, movement, and other aspects of specification regarding demand and supply, and that these considerations have critical implications for whether specific mechanisms governing storage are feasible. Some of the more important considerations have to do with (1) nonlinearity, (2) the form of disturbance, (3) private response to public intervention, (4) the role of market intermediaries, (5) the dependence of storage costs on stock variability and time in storage, (6) whether fluctuating prices can be anticipated, (7) the ability to make *ex post* adjustments and (8) the extent of risk aversion and risk response associated with diminishing marginal utility. The first five issues are discussed in this section and the latter three are investigated in the following three sections.

Nonlinearity

The simple framework of Sections 12.1 through 12.3 is based on the assumption of linearity in supply and demand. To compare to the case of nonlinearity, consider Figure 12.6 where the demand curve D is nonlinear and supply fluctuates randomly between S_1 and S_2 with each having probability 0.5. Now suppose that price is stabilized by some buffer stock mechanism that purchases excess production when supply is high and sells an equal amount when supply is low. One requirement for long-run buffer stock viability is that it must be *self-liquidating*, that is, the expected change in stocks must be zero. In Figure 12.6,

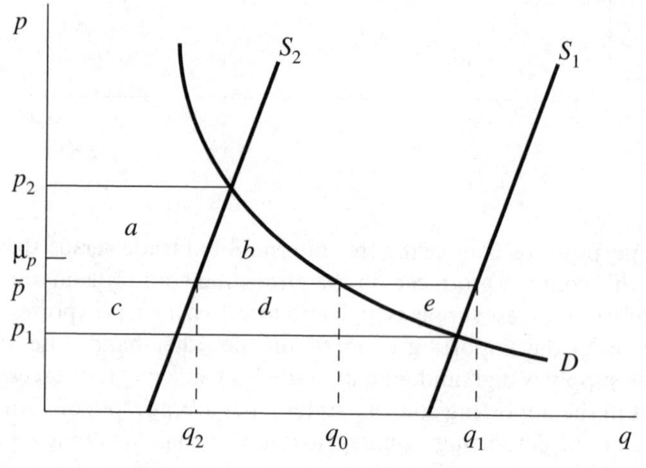

Figure 12.6

a self-liquidating buffer stock must increase stocks when supply is high by the same amount as stocks are reduced when supply is low. Otherwise the buffer stock would either tend to accumulate indefinitely until some other means of disposal is necessary, or stocks would tend to run out so that the price stabilizing mechanism could no longer be enforced. Stabilizing price with a self-liquidating stock rule implies that the stable price $\bar{p}$ in Figure 12.6 must be chosen so that the horizontal distance between S_1 and D is the same as between S_2 and D, that is, the excess supply $q_1 - q_0$ at S_1 is equal to excess demand $q_0 - q_2$ at S_2. Thus, the buffer stock's receipts in a short supply period, $\bar{p}(q_1 - q_0)$, are the same as its expenses in a long supply period, $\bar{p}(q_0 - q_2)$. Thus, the buffer stock authority is equally well off with and without the policy if storage and transaction costs are ignored. (Note that the assumptions of self-liquidation and zero storage/transaction costs are also necessary if price stabilization is implemented by a buffer stock in Figures 12.3 and 12.4 under linearity where shifts in supply or demand are parallel.)

Self-liquidation implies that the stabilized price must be lower than the average destabilized price if demand is upward-bending (convex) as in Figure 12.6. If demand is downward-bending (concave), the stabilized price must be above the average destabilized price. The welfare gains and losses for producers and consumers – in terms of areas *a*, *b*, *c*, *d* and *e* in Figure 12.6 – are exactly the same as in Figure 12.3, but now areas *a* and *b* are relatively large and areas *c*, *d* and *e* are relatively small. As a result, an average net gain of ½ (area *b* + area *e*) is still possible, but now the average consumer effect of ½ (area $a+b-c-d$) can be positive rather than negative (with sufficient nonlinearity) because the stabilized price is lower than the average destabilized price. Also, the average producer effect of ½ (area $c+d+e-a$) can become negative, thus obtaining qualitative impacts on producer groups and consumer groups exactly opposite of those in Figure 12.3.

A similar generalization of the analysis in Figure 12.4 for the case of upward-bending (convex) supply shows that sufficient nonlinearity in supply can also reverse the qualitative effects of price stabilization for individual producer and consumer groups when instability is due to fluctuations in demand. Thus, results show that the functional forms used for supply and demand in analyzing policies that affect price instability may determine to a large extent the qualitative as well as quantitative welfare effects. A simple change between the popular functional forms of linearity and log linearity with elasticities of usual magnitudes has been shown to be sufficient to induce changes in *qualitative* implications of price stabilization.[3] Thus, one must conclude that any investigation of the effects of a policy that affects price stability should be undertaken only after econometric investigation of the extent of nonlinearity in supply and demand (Just and Hallam 1978).

The Form of Disturbances

Another issue that has proven to be of importance in analyzing policies that affect price stability is the form of the disturbance in fluctuating supply or demand. In Figures 12.3, 12.4 and 12.6, random fluctuations in supply and demand take place in a parallel fashion. The form of the disturbances is additive in the sense that, if supply or demand is written with quantity q as a function of price p, say $\tilde{q}(p)$, then the actual demand or supply curves correspond to $q=\tilde{q}(p)+\varepsilon$, where ε is a random disturbance with zero expectation, $E(\varepsilon)=0$. A popular alternative form of disturbance, defended by, for example, Turnovsky (1976), is the multiplicative specification $q=\tilde{q}(p)\,\varepsilon$, $E(\varepsilon)=1$.

To demonstrate the comparative implications of these two specifications, suppose that demand is stable at D as in Figure 12.7 but that supply is unstable with multiplicative

3. This result was shown by Just et al. (1977). The role of nonlinearity has also been examined in a more elegant and advanced framework using the indirect utility function approach by Turnovsky, Shalit and Schmitz (1980). Their results show that reversal is obtained depending on the curvature of the utility function, which they measure by the Arrow–Pratt risk-aversion parameter (even though their framework is not one of risk, as the next section makes clear). Because the nonlinearity of demand is related to nonlinearity in underlying utility functions, the results of their approach are equivalent to those of the simplistic framework of Figure 12.6.

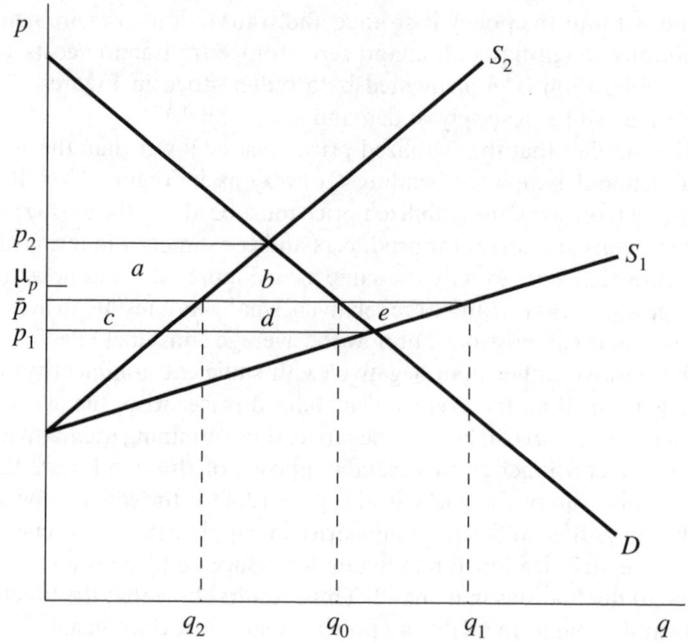

Figure 12.7

variation represented by fluctuations between S_1 and S_2, each with probability 0.5. By comparison, additive variation in supply is represented in Figure 12.3. For buffer stocks to be self-liquidating, prices must be stabilized at $\bar{p}$ such that $q_1 - q_0 = q_0 - q_2$, rather than at the average destabilized price, $\mu_p = (p_1 + p_2)/2$. Again, the welfare effects in Figure 12.7 are the same as in Figure 12.3 in terms of areas *a*, *b*, *c*, *d* and *e*. But, as with nonlinearity, areas *c*, *d* and *e* are small and areas *a* and *b* large with the multiplicative disturbance of Figure 12.7 relative to the additive disturbance case of Figure 12.3. As supplies S_1 and S_2 diverge (as the slope of S_1 falls), these results are accentuated until area $c+d+e=0$. Hence, with sufficiently strong multiplicative disturbances, net overall gains ½ (area $b+e$) are positive, but even the qualitative implications for individuals or groups may switch from the Figure 12.3 case. Producers lose if area $c+d+e-a<0$ and consumers gain if area $a+b-c-d>0$.

Results similar to those in Figure 12.7 can also be developed for the case of multiplicative disturbances in demand, in which case the qualitative implications for individual producer and consumer groups can possibly be the opposite of those in Figure 12.4, where demand disturbances are additive.[4] Again, welfare effects of price stabilization policy cannot be adequately evaluated empirically without sufficient econometric investigation of the form of disturbances (Just and Hallam 1978). For example, Turnovsky

4. The literature also implies that these conclusions carry over into models of general stochastic distributions as well as the dichotomous (two-outcome) distributions used here for illustration. This is evident by comparing the results of Massell (1969) and Hueth and Schmitz (1972) under additivity and linearity with those that pertain to the cases of nonlinearity studied by Turnovsky (1976) and multiplicative disturbances studied by Just et al. (1978).

(1976, p. 146) concluded that 'unless the policy maker has reliable information on this question, any stabilization policy may have undesirable effects on the group it is intended to assist'.

The Role of Market Intermediaries

The analysis of the instability issue is also somewhat different in the case with market intermediaries. To show the importance of market intermediaries, Bieri and Schmitz (1974) demonstrated how, in a setting of imperfect competition, certain market intermediaries can 'manufacture' price instability to their own advantage while other types of intermediaries will attempt to stabilize prices. Consider a market as in Figure 12.8(a) under linearity, where AR is the average revenue or demand curve and MR is the corresponding marginal revenue schedule. Suppose supplies S_1 and S_2 occur with probability 0.5 each, as in the earlier cases of this chapter. Note that AR for a single time period coincides with the horizontal summation of the marginal revenue schedules, ΣMR, over the two periods considered jointly. A pure middleman (one who, as defined in Section 10.6, has both monopoly and monopsony power) maximizes profits over the two periods by equating the horizontal summation of marginal costs, denoted by ΣMC, and the horizontal summation of marginal revenues, denoted by ΣMR.[5] The middleman then sets prices and quantities in each period to attain this marginal level in both buying and selling. Thus, in Figure 12.8(a), the middleman sells quantity q_0 at price p_0 in both periods but buys quantity q_1 at price p_1 in short-supply periods and quantity q_2 at price p_2 in long-supply periods. Quantity $q_2 - q_0$ is stored in long-supply periods to facilitate sale of quantity $q_0 - q_1$ in short-supply periods, $q_2 - q_0 = q_0 - q_1$. Therefore, through the use of stocks, the pure middleman stabilizes prices on the demand side but destabilizes prices on the supply side. Interestingly, a pure middleman gains an advantage by not stabilizing producer prices even though the middleman stores part of the good produced. The associated welfare effects can be calculated by comparison with the competitive solution in both stabilized and destabilized cases. These effects are not identified here explicitly because they are tedious to represent diagrammatically.

Consider alternatively the producer marketing board case in Figure 12.8(b), where the board maximizes producer returns as in Section 10.6. The producer marketing board maximizes profits for producers by equating the sum of the marginal revenue schedules, ΣMR (which is the AR schedule), with the horizontal summation of producer supply schedules over the two periods (denoted as ΣS). The marketing board also stabilizes prices to the consumer at p_0 by selling quantity q_0. However, unlike the previous case, the marketing board maximizes producer profits by stabilizing producer prices at p_1. The board then stores $q_2 - q_0$ in long-supply periods to fill the excess demand $q_0 - q_1$ in short-supply periods, $q_2 - q_0 = q_0 - q_1$. Thus, the marketing board undertakes price stabilization in the absence of a government stabilization policy, which is very different from the pure middleman case. Again, the welfare implications can be easily determined, although they are somewhat tedious to represent in Figure 12.8. An interesting issue in the marketing board case is comparison of the gains from producer price stabilization with the efficiency loss

5. Note that the marginal costs in this context are marginal costs to the intermediary, which under competitive production are marginal outlays of the intermediary as discussed in Sections 10.2 and 10.6.

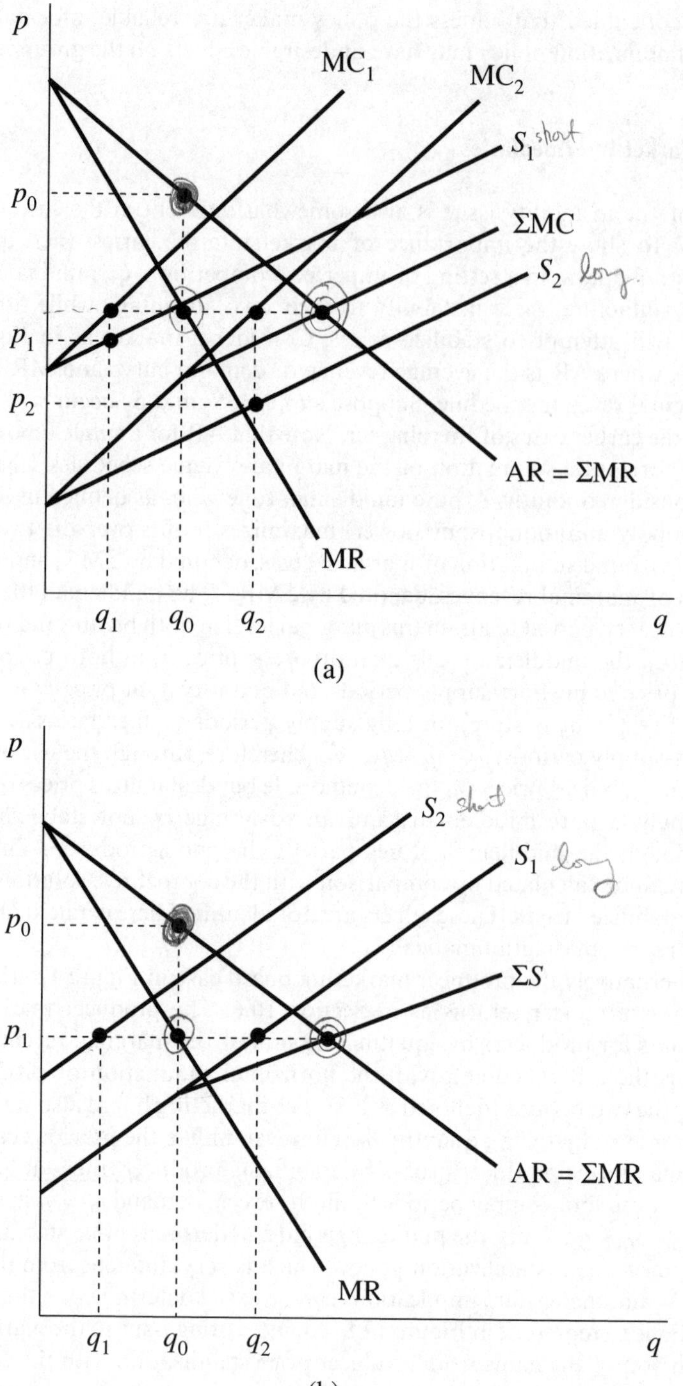
p
MC1
MC2
S1
p0
ΣMC
S2
p1
p2
AR = ΣMR
MR
q1
q0
q2
q
(a)
p
S2
S1
p0
ΣS
p1
AR = ΣMR
MR
q1
q0
q2
q
(b)

Figure 12.8

associated with monopolistic sales. It turns out that the latter loss always outweighs the former gain.[6]

While this discussion has considered the role of a specific type of market distortion that may actually generate instability, an additional principle that flows from this analysis is that any existing distortion may also affect stability or the need for price stabilization policy.

Response of Private Storage to Public Intervention

With any policy change one must consider the potential indirect reactions of private behavior. With price stabilization policy, one must consider not only the direct effect of government transactions on market price but also the indirect effect of private decision-makers' reactions to the altered prices. For example, with a government buffer stock, government stock transactions have a direct impact on market prices as reflected by market supply and demand relationships, but also an indirect effect on the incentive to hold private inventories given the reduction in future price variation.[7] If processors hold not only working stocks but also some additional stocks to avoid the contingency of inadequate product availability in periods of shortage, then the purpose of holding contingency stocks is reduced by a government buffer stock. Similarly, if some private stocks are held by speculators (on the chance that future price will be higher than present price plus storage costs), then the purpose of holding those stocks would be removed by a government policy that limits price variation to the amount of storage costs. These considerations suggest some important questions. What are the welfare effects of government stocks given the reaction of private storage to public intervention? Are private stocks held in socially optimal amounts in absence of government action, so that no public buffer stocks are needed?

Consider, for example, the diagrammatic analysis of Figure 12.3. If storage costs are negligible and producers gain from price stabilization, the same gains can be ensured if the producers undertake stock operations on their own. They need simply carry a stock of $q_1 - q_0$ from high-supply years over to periods of low supply. Alternatively, other private decision-makers would be induced to carry private stocks if they were ensured of receiving a sales price higher than their purchase price, as in Figure 12.3.

If storage costs are more than negligible, then private storage would not be induced to such a great extent. But the government also incurs storage costs. The social optimum is not necessarily different when the possibility of government stocks is added if public storage costs are the same as private storage costs. For example, consider Figure 12.9 where storage costs are $p_2' - p_1'$ per unit.[8] If price with supply S_1 is less than p_1' and price with supply S_2 is greater than p_2', profits can be made by private firms by purchasing at the low price, storing and then selling when the high price occurs. Private storage would

6. Models have also been developed to compare instability in a free-trade case with that where tariffs exist. The results concerning who gains and who loses from instability are quite different. See Bieri and Schmitz (1973).
7. The importance of considering the response of private storage to public buffer stock intervention was emphasized by Gardner (1977) and later by Gardner (1979a, ch. 5).
8. The framework of Figure 12.9 was first introduced by Massell (1969) to demonstrate that welfare gains from price stabilization can be possible even when storage costs are positive.

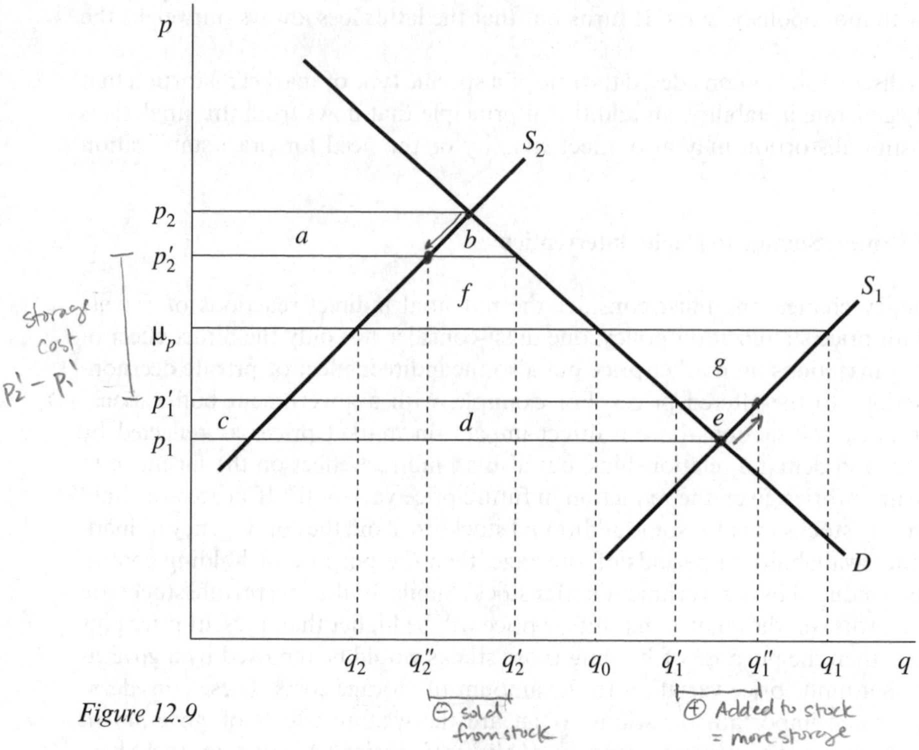

Figure 12.9

increase until price at S_1 is p_1' and price at S_2 is p_2' – in other words, to the point where the amount added to stocks at supply S_1, $q_1'' - q_1'$, is equal to the amount sold from stocks, $q_2' - q_2''$, when supply is S_2. In this case, the welfare areas *a*, *b*, *c*, *d* and *e* measure benefits for the same groups as in Figure 12.3. But, with storage costs, all welfare effects are smaller because the sales from stocks when supply is low must cover purchase and storage costs.

To demonstrate in this simple framework that an attempt to increase public storage may simply displace private storage, suppose in Figure 12.9 that a public storage program is undertaken to further stabilize prices. If the government attempts to increase total stock purchases to $q_1 - q_0$ when S_1 occurs by purchasing public stocks of $(q_1 - q_0) - (q_1'' - q_1')$ and selling an equal amount in periods of low supply, private storers can no longer cover their storage costs with the resulting price variability. Thus, they reduce private inventories until prices again vary between p_1' and p_2' or until private storage ceases.

In fact, in this simple model, any public storage beyond the private storage level $q_1'' - q_1'$ causes social inefficiency considering consumers, producers and government jointly because the increase in storage cost would be greater than the increase in net consumer plus producer surplus. In Figure 12.10, suppose both public and private storage cost per unit is $p_2' - p_1'$, and supply alternates between S_1 and S_2. With profit-maximizing private storage, quantity $q_1'' - q_1'$ is stored when supply is S_1 and released as quantity $q_2' - q_2''$ (assumed to be equal to $q_1'' - q_1'$) when supply is S_2. Now suppose the government attempts to reduce price variability marginally by increasing combined private and public stock purchases to $q_3'' - q_3'$ in high supply periods, which increases price to p_1'', and releasing

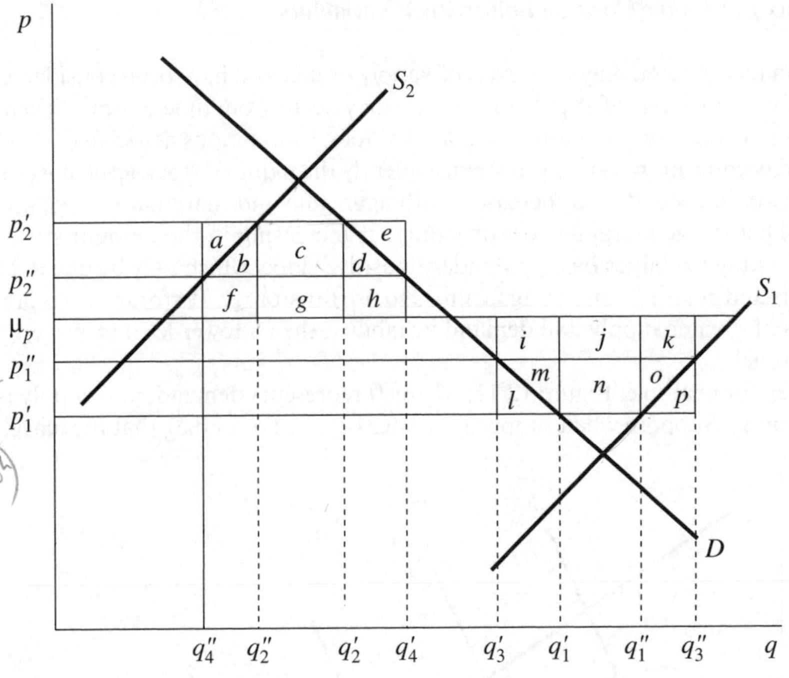

Figure 12.10

quantity $q_4' - q_4''$ (assumed to be equal to $q_3'' - q_3'$) from combined public and private stocks in low-supply periods, which reduces price to p_2'' in low supply periods. The sum of producer and consumer surplus increases by area $b+c+d$ in low supply periods and by area $m+n+o$ in high-supply periods, for an average increase of ½ area $b+c+d+m+n+o$. However, storage cost increases on average from ½ area $c+g+j+n$ to ½ area $a+b+c+d+e+f+g+h+i+j+k+l+m+n+o+p$. In addition, the revenue of selling from storage exceeds the cost of purchasing stocks by an average of ½ area $c+g+j+n$ before the increase in storage but by an average of ½ area $f+g+h+i+j+k$ after the increase. From the resulting change in net revenue, ½ area $f+h+i+k-c-n$, must be subtracted the increase in storage cost, ½ area $a+b+d+e+f+h+i+k+l+m+o+p$, which implies a net loss for government and private storers combined of ½ area $a+b+c+d+e+l+m+n+o+p$. Subtracting the net gain of producers and consumers from this loss yields a net social loss of ½ area $a+e+l+p$. Thus, if the per unit cost of both public and private storage is the same, $p_2' - p_1'$ in this case, then social welfare is reduced by increasing storage beyond the private level. With a similar analysis, one can also show that social welfare declines by moving to a lower level of storage and price stabilization through government intervention. The point is that social efficiency requires an optimal degree of price stabilization that is generally greater than no stabilization and less than complete stabilization but, unless other considerations apply, this optimal level of stabilization is achieved by private profit-maximizing storage so that no public intervention is justified.

Dependence of Storage Costs on Buffer Stock Variability

Thus far in this chapter, only two levels of supply or demand have been considered. More realistically, many levels of supply or demand may occur from time to time. When supply and demand conditions are more variable, the stock transactions associated with a given price band become more variable and consequently the required stock level must be larger. When the average stock level increases, both aggregate and marginal storage costs may increase. That is, the marginal cost of storage is increasing in the amount stored if the supply of storage facilities has the standard positive slope, which may be due to capacity constraints and costs of converting facilities to use for storage. If storage costs are higher in periods of greater supply and demand instability, then a lower level of price stabilization is optimal.

Consider, for example, Figure 12.11, where D represents demand, and supply is either S_1, S_2, S_3 or S_4. Suppose when supply alternates between S_2 and S_3 that the marginal per

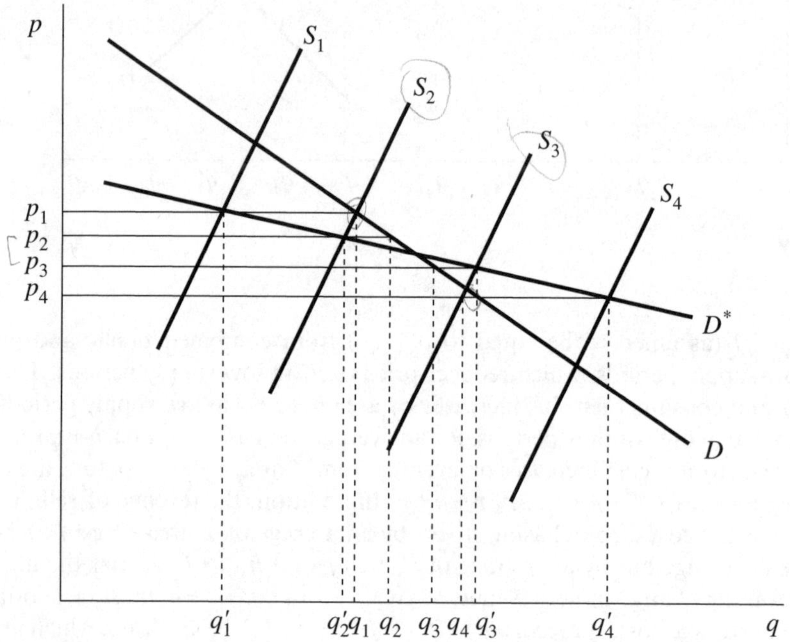

Figure 12.11

unit storage cost is $p_2 - p_3$ so that profit-maximizing private storage would carry over quantity $q_3' - q_3$ from high-supply periods to low-supply periods (where $q_3' - q_3 = q_2 - q_2'$). Alternatively, suppose when supply alternates between S_1 and S_4 that the marginal per unit storage cost is $p_1 - p_4$ so that profit-maximizing private storage would carry over quantity $q_4' - q_4$ from high-supply periods to low-supply periods (where $q_4' - q_4 = q_1 - q_1'$). Thus, greater instability is associated not only with higher marginal storage costs but also higher variability of both stock transactions and prices. This analysis suggests the existence of a function such as D^*, which prescribes the optimal regulated price and storage transaction as a function of supply variation. That is, with optimal stabilization the price is given by the intersection of D^* and supply, while the optimal storage transaction is given by the horizontal difference in D^* and D at that price.[9]

The analysis of Figures 12.10 and 12.11 implies that, when storage costs are introduced, the quantity variability of stock transactions caused by complete price stabilization significantly detracts from social benefits because a much larger buffer stock is required. Although more price stabilization may benefit producers and consumers jointly, the costs incurred for the storage necessary to achieve additional price stabilization may increase sharply. Both private storers and any government buffer stock authority are better off with quantity stabilization of buffer stock transactions. Thus, a trade-off between price stabilization and quantity stabilization must be considered. The question of economic stabilization that should properly be addressed involves finding an optimal trade-off between the two.

Dependence of Storage Costs on Time in Storage

The framework used thus far in this chapter to discuss storage policy is based on two assumptions that must be generalized for any realistic application. First, storage costs typically do not occur in the form of a one-time cost regardless of the time in storage, but as a cost proportional to the amount of time in storage (for example, storage facility rental payments), plus a transaction cost of moving the commodity in or out of storage. Second, supply or demand do not alternate with regularity between given states but rather vary randomly among many states. In a simple framework where excess supply and excess demand alternate between two states with certainty, dependence of storage costs on time in storage makes no difference because any amount placed in storage is held for only one period. More realistically, several periods of excess demand (or excess supply) can, by chance, occur consecutively. Thus, to enforce a given price band, stocks must be sufficient to meet several potentially consecutive years of excess demand. As a result, stocks are sometimes held for multiple time periods and thus incur higher storage costs accordingly.

The framework used thus far in this chapter serves merely to illustrate some of the principles that must be incorporated into any sound investigation of price stabilization or buffer stock policy. When supply and demand conditions are random with many possible states, and storage costs depend on time in storage, the welfare effects depend on how the storage mechanism responds to changes in prices and accumulated stocks, including how the mechanism operates when stocks are, by chance, depleted or accumulated in excessive quantities.[10] Such an analysis must consider the functional forms and disturbance forms in supply and demand including serial correlation, the role of any noncompetitive behavior and how private storage and international trade respond to government intervention.

While the results in this section suggest that government intervention is socially inefficient, governments may undertake such policies even with recognized inefficiencies

9. The advantages of such a stabilization rule relative to a fixed price band and other popular recommendations has been shown empirically by Cochrane and Danin (1976) for the case of wheat. A practical means of implementing such a policy is discussed by Just (1981). Gardner (1979a, ch. 5) also discusses the role of a rotated demand curve with respect to storage policy.
10. See Gardner (1979a, chs 5 and 6) for a discussion of the importance and difficulties of identifying a mechanism that deals with these various issues simultaneously, including the preferability of price bands that do not center on the mean price and the preferability of an upper limit on stock size.

for strategic purposes or as a political response to public pressure. An example is the Strategic Petroleum Reserve of the USA, the largest stockpile of government-owned emergency crude oil in the world, which was established in the aftermath of the 1973–74 oil embargo. Thus, welfare economists should be prepared to assess the social costs of such actions. In addition, a number of other issues must also be considered, such as potential differences in private and public storage costs, time preference discounting and differences in public and private discount rates (see Section 14.1), imperfections in credit markets that may limit private storage (see Appendix Section 4.G), risk preferences (see Section 12.6), and so on. Any one of these factors can cause free-market private stocks to be less than socially optimal.

12.5 INSTABILITY WITH UNCERTAINTY

Thus far in this chapter, producers and consumers have been assumed to adjust instantaneously along their supply or demand curve or, equivalently, to have *certainty* (perfect foresight) with respect to prices even though prices are *unstable*. For example, in Figure 12.4 producers can respond by producing the high quantity q_2 by correctly anticipating high demand. This approach has been criticized by, for example, Tisdell (1963) and Anderson and Riley (1976). Random prices are rarely known in advance with certainty. At best, a producer may anticipate the price to be received for its output imperfectly according to a *subjective distribution* held at the time production decisions are made. A producer's subjective distribution of prices specifies the probabilities with which each price will occur according to the producer's beliefs. Consider, for example, Figure 12.12, where prices p_1 and p_2 each have probability 0.5, but the producer must determine the quantity q before price is known. In contrast to Figure 12.2, where the producer anticipates the price with certainty, this situation is one of *instability with uncertainty*.

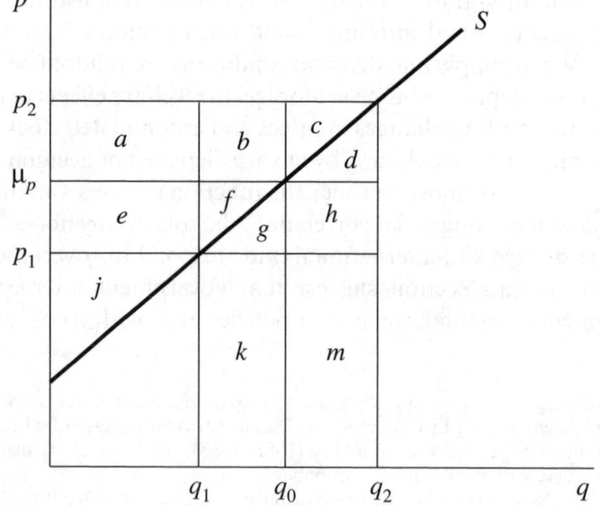

Figure 12.12

If the producer anticipates price p_1 and produces q_1, then quasirent will be area j if p_1 prevails but will be area $a+e+j$ if p_2 occurs. Costs are unchanged, but total revenue is higher by $q_1 \cdot (p_2-p_1)$ in the latter case. The average quasirent at q_1 is area $e+j$. Similarly, if production q_2 is chosen, then quasirent is area $a+b+c+e+f+j$ when price is p_2 but is area $j-d-g-h$ when price is p_1. The latter area is obtained simply by subtracting $q_2 \cdot (p_2-p_1)=$ area $a+b+c+d+e+f+g+h$ from the former. The average quasirent at q_2 is area $e+f+j-d$. Finally, in a similar manner, average quasirent at q_0 – the quantity determined by equating expected price μ_p to marginal cost – is area $e+f+j$. The optimal production decision (under expected profit maximization) is q_0, which is where average or expected quasirent is greatest.

The interesting result in Figure 12.12 is that the expected quasirent under instability is exactly the same as if prices are stabilized at their mean, in which case the certain price μ_p calls forth production q_0 and leads to a certain quasirent of area $e+f+j$. Hence, producers' welfare is unaffected by stabilization if instability is accompanied by uncertainty, unlike the case in Figure 12.2.[11]

Under uncertainty, expected welfare quantities are generally not the ones actually realized. Producers in Figure 12.12 have a statistical expectation of quasirent area $e+f+j$, but the actual price realized by producers is either p_1 or p_2. The actual quasirent thus differs from the expected quasirent in each possible outcome. To facilitate this distinction, *ex ante surplus* is defined as expected surplus at the time of decisions, and *ex post surplus* is defined as the actual surplus realized after uncertainty is resolved. In this case, *ex ante* producer surplus is defined as the area above the supply curve and below expected price while *ex post* producer surplus is further adjusted to consider actual rather than expected returns. In Figure 12.12, area $e+f+j$ is the *ex ante* producer surplus and is associated with expected returns $\mu_p \cdot q_0$. If price p_1 is realized, then costs are unchanged if production level q_0 was chosen according to expectations, but actual returns are $p_1 \cdot q_0$. Actual quasirent is thus area $j-g$, which is less than the expected quasirent by $(\mu_p-p_1) \cdot q_0$ = area $e+f+g$. Similarly, the *ex post* producer surplus associated with price p_2 is area $a+b+e+f+j$.

Thus far, only random prices have been considered. Another phenomenon that causes differences in *ex ante* and *ex post* surpluses is random production. In agriculture, for example, producers make decisions regarding planted acreage and other inputs such as fertilizer, but actual production cannot be anticipated with certainty because of random weather conditions. In Figure 12.12, producers may plan to produce q_0, but because of random yields, actual production is either q_1 or q_2. Thus, whereas *ex ante* surplus is area $e+f+j$, the *ex post* surplus would be area $j-g-k$ if p_1 and q_1 occur, area $j-g+m$ if p_1 and q_2 occur, and so on. In each case, this *ex post* surplus corresponds simply to subtracting production cost (the area below the supply or marginal cost curve and left of planned production) from the actual returns realized.

Random production introduces a further complication in the analysis because random prices are induced by random production through a demand relationship. Consider, for example, Figure 12.13, where planned production is q_0 but actual production is either q_1 or q_2, each occurring with probability 0.5, where $q_0=(q_1+q_2)/2$. With linear demand D,

11. The consumer effects of price stabilization for the case with producer uncertainty (Figure 12.12) can be investigated as in Section 12.3. But in this case, the market behaves as if supply is perfectly inelastic at q_0.

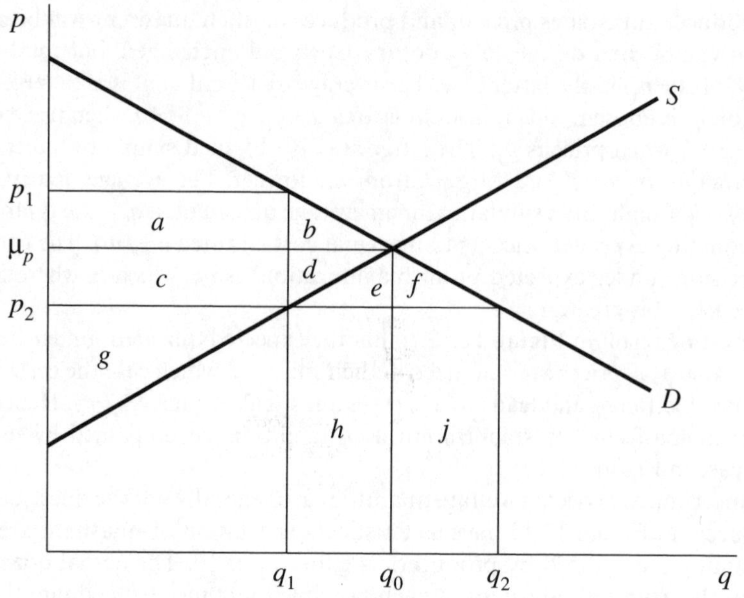

Figure 12.13

the resulting actual prices are thus p_1 at quantity q_1 and p_2 at quantity q_2. The *ex ante* producer surplus obtained by planning production q_0 to equate expected price, $\mu_p = (p_1 + p_2)/2$, and expected marginal cost is area $c+d+g$. If production is q_1, then actual returns are $p_1 \cdot q_1$ rather than $\mu_p \cdot q_0$, so that *ex post* producer surplus is area $a+c+g-e-h$. If production is q_2, then actual returns are $p_2 \cdot q_2$ instead of the planned $\mu_p \cdot q_0$, so that *ex post* producer surplus is area $g-e+j$.

The peculiar problem in this case is that the expected *ex post* producer surplus, ½ [(area $a+c+g-e-h$) + area $(g-e+j)$] = area $a+g-e$, is less than the *ex ante* producer surplus area $c+d+g$ (note that area a = area c and area j = area h assuming linearity of S and D). This result is obtained because a negative correlation of price and quantity is induced by the downward-sloping demand curve so that expected returns (price times quantity) is less than the expected price multiplied by the expected quantity.

This raises a question regarding which welfare quantity policy-makers should consider. If each individual producing firm perceives only a distribution of price and not the effect of its production on price (which is the usual competitive assumption) and makes decisions accordingly, then the producer's expected *ex ante* surplus does not reflect how well off the firm is likely to be *ex post*. When individual producers do not perceive the correlation of their production with price because of their smallness relative to the market, then the aggregate of all producers or the industry also behaves as though there is no correlation of production and price. A policy-maker who realizes this aggregate relationship can thus be faced with the question of whether to formulate policy according to what producers say they want (*ex ante* surplus) or according to what is actually in producers' best interest (expected *ex post* surplus).

This question was raised in an agricultural context by Hazell and Scandizzo (1975).

They found that if producers make decisions on the basis of expected returns rather than on the basis of expected prices and expected yields, the correlation of prices and yields is adequately considered even though the individual producers do not perceive their individual impact on prices. For example, if a producer attempts to produce q_0 in Figure 12.13 for several periods and realizes returns $p_1 \cdot q_1$ half of the time and returns $p_2 \cdot q_2$ the other half of the time, then he or she would come to expect returns $\frac{1}{2}(p_1 \cdot q_1 + p_2 \cdot q_2)$ on average even though, in Figure 12.13, the average price times average quantity, $\mu_p \cdot q_0$, is larger by area $d+e$. As shown by Hazell and Scandizzo, if producers act on the basis of expected prices and expected production (ignoring the correlation of the two) rather than on the basis of expected returns, free-market competition does not lead to Pareto optimality in this case of instability with uncertainty.[12] On the contrary, area $d+e$ must be imposed as an *ad valorem* tax (for any given q_0, (area $d+e)/q_0$ would be the per unit tax) and then redistributed as a lump-sum payment to induce producers to form the correct *ex ante* expectations of *ex post* welfare. This type of tax is called an *optimal distortion* by Hazell and Scandizzo because it is required to reach Pareto optimality assuming no other distortions exist.

Although the issue of instability with certainty versus uncertainty has been discussed in this section only from the standpoint of the producer, similar generalizations are also applicable for the consumer or factor owner, where decisions must be made before prices are known. For typical consumer items, the consumer choice problem involves deciding how much to buy or sell given prevailing market prices. Only rarely must a consumer decide upon a quantity to purchase before a price is quoted. Nevertheless, in the dynamics of the real world, a consumer must often decide how much to spend on a consumer durable before prices are known for goods that will be used in combination with the durable over its lifetime. For example, a consumer decides which automobile to buy before knowing what price of gasoline will prevail over the lifetime of the automobile. After purchasing the automobile, the consumer is free to adjust gasoline consumption decisions as gasoline prices vary, but the automobile may not be freely exchanged for a higher efficiency model if gasoline prices unexpectedly increase. The consumer problem with durables and intertemporal price instability is thus much like the producer problem with instability. In fact, the compensated consumer problem is mathematically equivalent, just as in the case of certainty discussed in Section 7.10. This point is clarified later by Appendix Sections 14.A and 14.B.

12.6 WELFARE MEASURES UNDER RISK AVERSION

Thus far in this chapter, preferences for stable versus unstable outcomes have been discussed solely in terms of gains in expected producer or consumer surplus. For individuals who neither like nor dislike random outcomes per se (that is, for risk-neutral individuals), these results are appropriate to the extent that producer and consumer surpluses measure willingness to pay (WTP). A *risk-neutral individual* is one who is indifferent to randomness in economic welfare as long as expected welfare is unaltered.

12. Assuming no producers are averse to risk, Pareto optimality among producers under instability with uncertainty is achieved by maximizing the sum of expected profit. For further discussion, see the next section.

More realistically, many individuals have an aversion to risk.[13] For example, a producer may prefer earning a profit of \$20000 year after year to earning a profit of \$10000 or \$40000 each with probability 0.5. This preference may be due to economic considerations, such as more efficient planning possibilities, as well as to purely psychological factors such as the emotional trauma of facing the unexpected. To reflect such preferences, some additional considerations are necessary for welfare measurement.

Expected Utility

This section introduces basic concepts that are used to measure welfare under risk aversion. Suppose for the case where profit, π, is risky that a producer's preferences are described by a utility function, $U(\pi)$, where the marginal utility of profit is positive and diminishing, and the producer makes decisions to maximize the expected value of this utility, $E[U(\pi)]$, when choices must be made before risk is resolved.[14] To illustrate, suppose only two states of weather are possible – good and bad. If a farmer's profit is π_g with good weather and π_b with bad weather, and if the probability of good weather is 0.6 (occurs 60 percent of the time) and the probability of bad weather is 0.4 (occurs 40 percent of the time), then expected utility is $E[U(\pi)] = 0.6U(\pi_g) + 0.4U(\pi_b)$.[15]

In this framework, a farmer faced with risky weather conditions and output prices, who must decide on seed and land inputs, x, before these actual conditions are known, makes such decisions to maximize the expected utility of profit.[16] That is, suppose profit depends on input decisions in x as represented by $\pi(x)$. Then the farmer can, at best, choose x to maximize $E[U(\pi(x))]$ because weather and output prices are not yet known. These decisions are called *ex ante decisions* because they must be made before the uncertainty is resolved. Accordingly, maximization of $E[U(\pi(x))]$ is called the *ex ante decision criterion*. The *ex ante* decision criterion generally differs from the actual *ex post* utility of profit, $U(\pi(x))$, which is realized only after actual weather conditions and output prices

13. Some individuals may also love risk. For example, participation in gambling and lotteries is sometimes regarded as risk-loving behavior because most forms of gambling and lotteries incur a loss on average. But these conclusions ignore the entertainment value of such activities. Others have argued that individuals are risk-averse over normal ranges of risk but risk-loving with respect to small risks (recreational gambling) and large risks (lotteries). See, for example, Friedman and Savage (1952). Consistent with the practical orientation of this book, risk preferences are restricted to risk neutrality and risk aversion here.
14. This type of utility is called von Neumann–Morgenstern utility. See von Neumann and Morgenstern (1944). In mathematical terms, *positive marginal utility* requires $\partial U(\pi)/\partial\pi > 0$, which is the standard *non-satiation* assumption, and *diminishing marginal utility* requires $\partial^2 U(\pi)/\partial\pi^2 < 0$, which is the definition of *risk aversion*.
15. In some analyses, the form of the utility function is also allowed to depend on the state of nature. Thus, for example, $E[U(\pi)] = 0.6U_g(\pi_g) + 0.4U_b(\pi_b)$ where U_g and U_b are distinctly different utility functions. This is the case of *state-dependent utility*. For further discussion, see Machina (1987) and Quiggin (1993). While much of the conceptual material of this chapter can be readily extended to the case of state-dependent utility, each individual is assumed to have a state-independent utility function here to simplify notation and presentation.
16. The discussion in this chapter approaches risk from the standpoint of the producer and thus focuses on the expected utility of profits. However, the same concepts apply to consumer decision-making under risk if consumers must make consumption decisions before income or some prices are known. The discussion of this section is immediately applicable to the consumer problem under risk if $E[U(\pi)]$ is replaced by the consumer's indirect expected utility function and $U(\pi)$ is replaced by the consumer's utility function evaluated at demands that maximize expected utility. Any compensation would then be subtracted from exogenous income. For further details, see Appendix Section 14.B.

along with the farmers' decisions determine production and profit at harvest time. In addition, the farmer may be able to decide on some other input quantities, such as harvest labor, after the risk of weather and output prices has been resolved. These decisions are called *ex post decisions* and are distinct from the *ex ante* decisions. These decisions would be made to maximize the actual utility of profit given actual weather, output price, and previous input decisions in x, which is the *ex post decision criterion*.[17]

Option Value as the Difference in *ex ante* and *ex post* WTP

Now suppose $\tilde{\pi}$ represents profit realized with optimal producer decisions where *ex ante* decisions maximize expected utility and *ex post* decisions maximize actual utility given *ex ante* decisions. Suppose also that the producer's profit is affected by some exogenous factor z that is determined by a project or policy choice. Then the producer's utility can be represented by $U(\tilde{\pi},z)$, which is an *indirect utility function*, and expected utility is represented by $E[U(\tilde{\pi},z)]$, which is the associated *indirect expected utility function*. Suppose policy-makers consider a policy action that changes z from z_0 to z_1. The dilemma for policy-makers is whether to consider individuals' WTP for a change based on *ex ante* welfare reflected by $E[U(\tilde{\pi},z)]$ or *ex post* welfare reflected by $U(\tilde{\pi},z)$.

To illustrate, suppose only two outcomes are possible: $\tilde{\pi}_g$ under good weather, which occurs with probability γ, and $\tilde{\pi}_b$ under bad weather, which occurs with probability $1-\gamma$. The *ex post compensating variation*, C_i^*, of the change in z in each case is defined by $U(\tilde{\pi}_i - C_i^*, z_1) = U(\tilde{\pi}_i, z_0)$, $i=g,b$.[18] In other words, C_i^* is the amount of money that must be taken away from an individual (possibly negative) after the change in z to restore the utility level the individual would have had without the change at z_0, conditioned on the actual weather, $i=g,b$. The expected *ex post* compensating variation is thus $E(C_i^*) = \gamma C_g^* + (1-\gamma)C_b^*$.

In the case where WTP is based on *ex ante* welfare reflected by $E[U(\tilde{\pi},z)]$, the corresponding *ex ante* welfare measure is defined by $E[U(\tilde{\pi}_i - O_p, z_1)] = E[U(\tilde{\pi}_i, z_0)]$, $i=g,b$, where O_p is the *ex ante compensating variation*. In other words, O_p is the amount of money that must be taken away from an individual (possibly negative) with the change in z to restore the expected utility level the individual would have had without the change at z_0. This welfare measure is denoted by O_p because it is called the *option price* in much of the

17. When the farmer has both *ex ante* and *ex post* decisions to make, the farmer essentially has a two-stage decision problem. If profit is given by $\pi(x_a,x_p,w)$ where x_a represents *ex ante* decisions, x_p represents *ex post* decisions, and w represents risky weather and output prices, then the second stage (*ex post*) problem is to choose x_p to maximize $U(\pi(x_a^*,x_p,w^*)$ where x_a^* represents the *ex ante* decisions made in the first stage and w^* is the actual realized weather and output prices. The first stage (*ex ante*) problem is to choose x_a to maximize $E[\pi(x_a,\tilde{x}_p(x_a,w),w)]$ where the expectation is with respect to w and $\tilde{x}_p(x_a,w)$ represents optimal decisions in the second-stage problem as a function of first-stage decisions in x_a and weather and output prices in w. This approach to solution of the multi-stage decision problem is an application of backward dynamic programming. For further details, see Appendix Section 14.A.
18. The *ex post* equivalent variation, E_i, could be defined similarly as $U(\tilde{\pi}_i,z_1) = U(\tilde{\pi}_i + E_i, z_0)$. For brevity, the discussion is presented here only for the case of measuring compensating variation but similar principles apply to measurement of equivalent variation as well. Also, the remainder of this chapter discusses producer welfare based on profit rather than quasirent to be more consistent with terminology found in the risk literature. The reader should simply bear in mind that profit is negative by the amount of fixed cost in the event of a shutdown. Because $\tilde{\pi}_i - C_i^*$ appears inside the utility function in this definition of compensating variation, correct welfare measurement is thus achieved when either the initial or subsequent state involves a shutdown. For example, in the risk-neutral case of a linear utility function this definition of compensating variation will coincide with the one defined in Section 4.2.

literature (see Graham 1981). The difference in expected *ex post* compensating variation and the option price, that is, the difference in expected *ex post* compensating variation and *ex ante* compensating variation, is also called *option value* (see Weisbrod 1964).[19] That is, $O_v = O_p - E(C_i^*)$ where O_v is option value.[20]

To consider option value graphically, Figure 12.14 represents compensation paid by the producer for the change in z in the case where only two states of nature are possible.

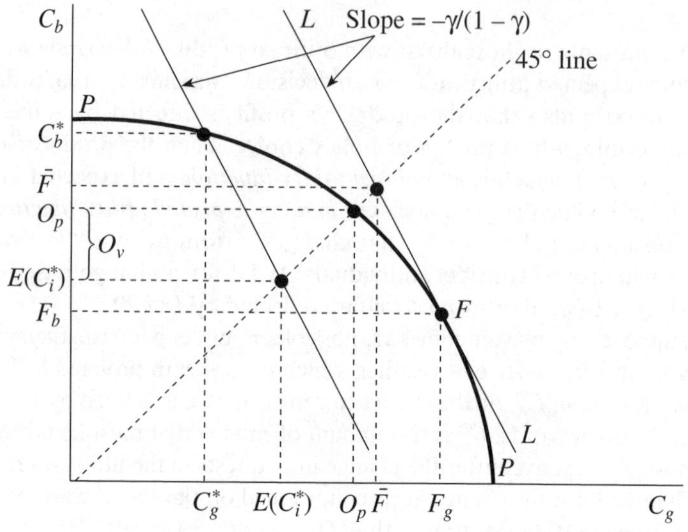

Figure 12.14

Compensation paid in the case of good weather is reflected on the horizontal axis and compensation paid in the case of bad weather is reflected on the vertical axis. The figure is drawn as though a positive amount of compensation is paid in both cases (if the origin corresponds to no compensation), but this need not be the case in either state. The frontier *PP* is the Graham *willingness-to-pay locus* (WTP locus), which consists of all the combinations of compensation in the two states of nature, (C_g, C_b), that just restore the expected utility realized by the producer in the case of no change at z_0. If the probability

19. Weisbrod argued that an 'economic man' would be willing to pay something in excess of the expected benefits he would get from visiting a park to preserve the option of being able to visit it at some future time and he termed this value 'option value'. A substantial literature ensued making his definition more precise and investigating the sign of this important nonuse value. The issue was not resolved until the work of Graham (1981). For a survey of this literature, see Freeman (2003, pp. 247–50). See Section 13.4 for a discussion of option value in the context of the measurement of nonuse environmental benefits.
20. Note that Graham (1981) uses the term 'expected surplus' rather than expected *ex post* compensating variation (along with option price) to define option value. However, the mathematical definition he uses for surplus is identical to the definition of *ex post* compensating variation. Similarly, his definition of option price is identical to the definition of *ex ante* compensating variation. Curiously, he never mentions the possibility of using *ex post* or *ex ante* equivalent variation, and accordingly his definitions of option price and option value do not consider the possible use of *ex post* or *ex ante* equivalent variation in welfare measurement.

of good weather is γ and the probability of bad weather is $1-\gamma$, then the WTP locus is described mathematically by

$$\gamma U(\tilde{\pi}_g - C_g, z_1) + (1-\gamma)U(\tilde{\pi}_b - C_b, z_1) = E[U(\tilde{\pi}_i, z_0)].$$

This locus is concave (downward-bending) if the producer is risk-averse.[21] The existence of this WTP locus demonstrates that *ex ante* and *ex post* compensating variation are merely two of many possibilities that restore the producer's initial expected utility. That is, the *ex post* compensating variation point (C_g^*, C_b^*) is the point where the producer pays compensation C_g^* with good weather and C_b^* with bad weather, while the *ex ante* compensating variation point (O_p, O_p) along the 45 degree line is the point where the producer pays the same compensation O_p regardless of the state of nature.[22] Another point on the WTP locus (not identified in Figure 12.14) corresponds to the case where $U(\tilde{\pi}_g - C_g, z_1) = U(\tilde{\pi}_b - C_b, z_1)$. This is the complete insurance point that removes all risk for the producer, that is, profit after paying compensation is the same regardless of the state of nature.

One way to analyze economic efficiency in Figure 12.14 is to consider expected compensation. Expected compensation associated with any point on the WTP locus can be found by drawing a line from that point to the 45 degree line with slope equal to the negative ratio of probabilities of the two states, $-\gamma/(1-\gamma)$. Such lines represent expected compensation contours. For example, the expected *ex post* compensating variation can be found by drawing a line with this slope from the *ex post* compensating variation point, (C_g^*, C_b^*), to the 45 degree line as shown in Figure 12.14, which reveals *expected ex post compensating variation* $E(C_i^*)$ along either axis. The highest possible expected compensation is found by drawing a line with this slope tangent to the WTP locus, as represented by LL. Graham calls the associated point of tangency, F, the *fair bet point*.

A conceptual question that has attracted considerable research is whether option value is positive or negative.[23] In Figure 12.14, $O_v = O_p - E(C_i^*) > 0$ by inspection. This result occurs if the fair bet point is on the opposite side of the 45 degree line from the *ex post* compensating variation point. If the ratio of probabilities of states is changed (that is, the slope of the expected compensation contours is changed) so that the fair bet point lies on the opposite side of the *ex post* compensating variation point from the 45 degree line, then expected *ex post* surplus exceeds the option price and option value is negative. Graham

21. To see that the WTP locus is downward-bending, totally differentiate the defining equation, which yields

$$\frac{dC_b}{dC_g} = -\frac{\gamma U'(\tilde{\pi} - C_g)}{(1-\gamma)U'(\tilde{\pi} - C_b)} < 0,$$

where $U'(\tilde{\pi} - C_i) \equiv \partial U(\tilde{\pi} - C_i, z)/\partial C_i > 0$ by assumption. Thus, an increase in C_g along the WTP locus must be accompanied by a decrease in C_b. Under the assumption of risk aversion, $U''(\tilde{\pi} - C_i) \equiv \partial^2 U(\tilde{\pi} - C_i, z)/\partial C_i^2 < 0$, it must be the case that an increase in C_g increases $U'(\tilde{\pi} - C_g)$ and the accompanying decrease in C_b decreases $U'(\tilde{\pi} - C_b)$. Thus, dC_b/dC_g must be declining in C_g along the WTP locus.

22. The reader should be very careful to interpret the points defined by *ex post* and *ex ante* compensating variation as distinct points on the WTP locus whereas all other points are merely potential compensation points under various states that leave the producer equally well off in terms of expected utility. That is, the other compensation points amount to paying a different compensation in each period than defined by either *ex post* or *ex ante* compensating variation. This distinction of the terms 'compensating variation' and 'compensation' is critical for understanding the discussion in the remainder of this section.

23. See, for example, the discussion by Freeman (2003, pp. 247–50).

(1981) argued that whether option value is positive or negative is of little consequence. A more important issue is which welfare measure is appropriate for the economic welfare analysis of particular policy issues.

Aggregation of WTP under Risk

Before determining which welfare measure is appropriate, discussion of the problem of aggregation is necessary. Figure 12.15 considers aggregation in the case where the

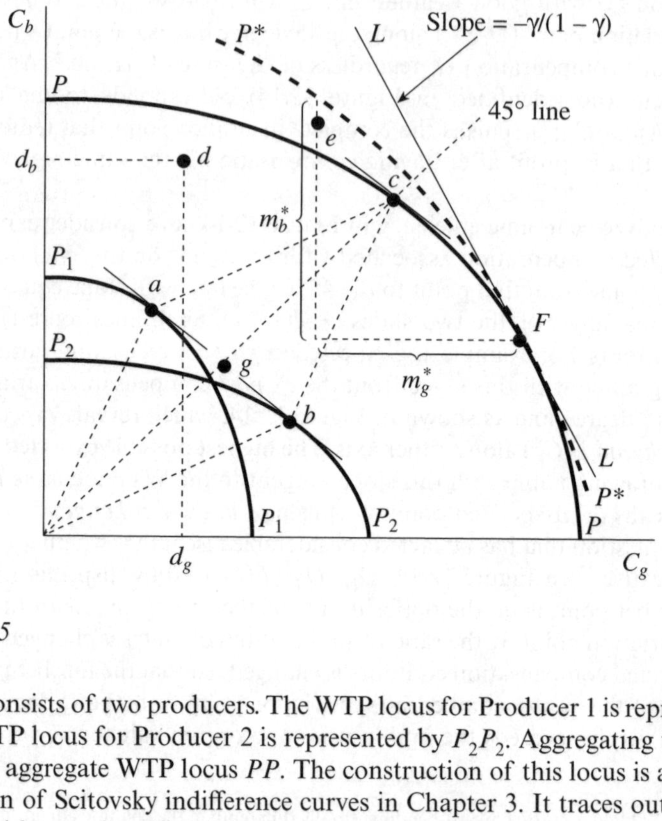

Figure 12.15

economy consists of two producers. The WTP locus for Producer 1 is represented by P_1P_1 and the WTP locus for Producer 2 is represented by P_2P_2. Aggregating these two curves obtains the aggregate WTP locus PP. The construction of this locus is analogous to the construction of Scitovsky indifference curves in Chapter 3. It traces out the WTP envelope formed by moving the origin of Producer 2's WTP locus along the WTP locus of Producer 1.

Now draw a line tangent to the aggregate WTP locus at point c on the 45 degree line, and then draw lines tangent to each producer's WTP locus with the same slope. The respective individual tangency points a and b then specify compensation amounts for each individual producer in each state of nature that add up to the aggregate compensation at point c.[24] Point c thus represents the maximum sure compensation (irrespective of the state of nature) that producers could pay to receive the change in z from z_0 to z_1. If the project has

24. In fact, another way of constructing the aggregate WTP locus is to aggregate points with the same slope from the WTP locus of all individuals for each possible slope.

a sure social cost, then the project should be adopted according to the compensation criterion if the social cost is below c on the 45 degree line (a cost that does not depend on the state of nature lies on the 45 degree line). However, as demonstrated below, cases may exist where projects with a higher social cost also meet the compensation criterion.

If the social cost of the project depends on the state of nature, then the compensation test involves comparison to points off the 45 degree line. For example, if the social cost of changing z is d_g when weather is good and d_b when weather is bad, then the state-dependent social cost is represented by point d. Since this point is inside the aggregate potential compensation frontier, reflected by the aggregate WTP locus, a Pareto improvement is possible. When social costs are state dependent but outside the WTP locus, such as at point e in Figure 12.15, application of the compensation criterion is somewhat more difficult.[25] The reason is that the extent of curvature in the aggregate WTP locus is determined by the extent of risk aversion among the producers. If contingency markets exist whereby risk can be shifted to less risk-averse individuals, then a Pareto improvement may still be possible.

Suppose, for example, that some individual, who will be called an insurance agent, is not otherwise affected by the change in z and has a utility function $U_0(\pi_0)$ with, for simplicity, constant income represented by π_0.[26] Then consider a compensation scheme where a payment of m_g is made by producers to the insurance agent if good weather occurs and a payment of m_b is received by producers from the insurance agent if bad weather occurs.[27] The insurance agent's expected utility is thus $E[U_0(\pi_0+m_i)]=\gamma U_0(\pi_0+m_g)+(1-\gamma)U_0(\pi_0-m_b)$. The insurance agent's WTP locus includes all pairs (m_g, m_b) that solve $E[U_0(\pi_0+m_i)]=E[U_0(\pi_0)]$. This locus is represented by P^*P^* in Figure 12.15 so that the origin for the insurance agent's WTP locus (where $m_g=m_b=0$) is at the aggregate fair bet point F of producers. The slope of the insurance agent's WTP locus at $m_g=m_b=0$ must be $-\gamma/(1-\gamma)$, the same as the slope of the producers' aggregate WTP locus at point F, because each individual faces the same probabilities of good and bad weather.[28] The

25. Graham (1981) concluded that, if aggregate social cost is at any point e outside the aggregate WTP locus, then a Pareto improvement is not possible. However, this is necessarily true only when individuals cannot trade their risks in contingent claims markets and the government cannot redistribute risk to those who are more willing to bear it.
26. Some authors, for example, Freeman (2003, pp. 218–32), consider state-dependent costs of a project to be imposed on a different set of individuals than those who gain the state-dependent benefits, following Hazilla and Kopp (1990). The analysis then compares the WTP locus of gainers to the required compensation locus of losers. The required compensation locus is essentially a WTP locus for those on whom costs are imposed, that is, those who have negative compensating variation. If for some state-dependent compensation scheme the gainers are able to more than compensate the losers in every state, then the compensation criterion is met. For the treatment here, individuals are not distinguished by whether they are gainers or losers, one reason being that some individuals may both gain in some states and lose in others, and thus not fit clearly into either group. If a project imposes state-dependent costs on individuals, they can simply be aggregated with other individuals who benefit, as in Figure 12.15. That is, nothing in the analysis of Figure 12.15 requires that the origin lies inside the WTP locus of every individual, or equivalently, nothing in the analysis requires all individuals' compensating variations to be positive. In Figure 12.15, the compensation criterion is thus met if the aggregate WTP locus including losers and gainers exceeds the social cost in each state. The addition of an insurance agent in Figure 12.15 is such an example.
27. To state this arrangement in the more common form of popular insurance contracts, the insurance agent may sell an insurance policy for an *ex ante* premium of m_g^* paid by producers regardless of the state of nature and then return an indemnity payment to producers equal to $m_g^*+m_b^*$ if bad weather occurs.
28. That is, totally differentiating $E[U_0(\pi_0+m_i)]=\gamma U_0(\pi_0+m_g)+(1-\gamma)U_0(\pi_0-m_b)$ with respect to m_g and m_b and evaluating at $m_g=m_b=0$ reveals $-dm_b/dm_g=-\gamma/(1-\gamma)$.

insurance agent's WTP locus is thus tangent to the producers' aggregate WTP locus at *F*. If the insurance agent's risk aversion is less than producers' risk aversion, then the insurance agent's WTP locus will lie outside the producers' WTP locus everywhere except at point *F*.[29]

Now consider application of the compensation criterion for a project that has state-dependent social cost at point *e*. The insurance agent's WTP locus includes, for example, the point (m_g^*, m_b^*) as shown in Figure 12.15. Thus, if producers pay aggregate compensation corresponding to point *F* then the insurance agent is willing to pay additional compensation m_b^* if bad weather occurs in exchange for receiving m_g^* of the compensation paid by producers if good weather occurs. Thus, aggregate compensation more than covers the state-dependent social cost. That is, because point *F* lies below the 45 degree line, it allows producers to pay greater compensation under good weather than under bad weather, while, because point *e* lies above the 45 degree line, the social costs are higher under bad weather than under good weather. The difference can be more than made up by transferring the risk of the difference to a less risk-averse agent.

This example shows that the compensation test can be met for any project with state-dependent social costs that lie inside the WTP locus P^*P^* that aggregates producers and the insurance agent. The compensation test does not limit projects according to the risk preferences of the affected producers, as does the WTP locus *PP*, if contingency markets exist. This is what is meant by the existence of a *relevant contingency market*.

To carry this analysis further, if some individuals are risk-neutral then the relevant WTP locus that determines the set of contracts for which the compensation criterion holds is the relative probability line that is tangent to the producers' aggregate WTP locus at point *F*. The compensation test can then be satisfied if social cost corresponds to any point inside this line. A relevant contingency market can also exhibit lower risk aversion than any of its individual participants due to spreading risks among individuals. For this reason, some studies simply assume that relevant contingency markets are risk-neutral. Similarly, the government is sometimes assumed to be risk-neutral due to spreading costs among many projects with stochastically independent states.

Dependence on the Specifics of Compensation

When the compensation criterion is used to determine whether a policy should be adopted but compensation is not actually paid, the resulting state is a potentially Pareto preferred state (see Chapter 3). When changes are made on this basis, little attention is typically given to identifying a compensation scheme that collects compensation from each individual commensurate with individual WTP. For risk problems, however, the compensation scheme is more critical because, as demonstrated in Figure 12.15, the compensation scheme determines the frontier of social costs that meet the compensation criterion. Only by efficient distribution of risk among producers through compensation does the aggregate WTP locus become the frontier of social costs that meet the compensation test. And only by further efficient redistribution of risk through contingency markets does the addi-

29. The insurance agent's origin where $m_g = m_b = 0$ could be placed at any point along the producers' aggregate WTP locus, but the insurance agent's WTP locus would then cut the producers' aggregate locus and lie below the case where $m_g = m_b = 0$ at *F*. Therefore, some projects that meet the compensation criterion with $m_g = m_b = 0$ at *F* would not meet the compensation criterion with such an alternative origin.

tional WTP locus P^*P^* become the frontier of social costs that meets the compensation criterion. Thus, welfare evaluation of risk redistribution must be based on how risk is actually redistributed (Chavas and Mullarkey 2002; Graham 1981; Ready 1993).

For example, suppose in Figure 12.15 that a project has a certain social cost represented by point *c* and that each producer is required to share equally in the required compensation in each state. Then each producer's required compensation is at point *g* (where $c = 2g$). But at point *g*, both producers are worse off with the project. Only if risk is allocated efficiently so that Producer 1 pays compensation at point *a* and Producer 2 pays compensation at point *b* are both producers equally well off paying the same aggregate compensation at point *c*.

Alternatively, if each producer has access to contingency markets, then the risks imposed on producers by arbitrary compensation schemes can be redistributed. But whether the compensation test can be satisfied depends on the risk aversion exhibited by available contingency markets and on how inefficiently risk is distributed by the arbitrary compensation scheme. The more inefficiently risk is distributed among producers, the more likely contingency markets will not suffice (unless the relevant contingency markets exhibit risk neutrality).

Which Welfare Measure is Appropriate?[30]

This section has defined several measures of welfare that have been used to apply the compensation test for projects or policies that affect risk. Among these are option price (or *ex ante* compensating variation), *ex post* compensating variation, expected *ex post* compensating variation, the fair bet point, and the expected fair bet point.[31] While these alternative criteria can be compared under many specific circumstances, some useful distinctions suggested by Graham (1981) are (1) whether the cost of a project or policy is certain, for example, lies on the 45 degree line in Figures 12.14 and 12.15, (2) whether producers are identical, that is, have identical utility functions and face identical risk in terms of the amounts and probabilities of payoffs, and (3) whether the risk faced by producers is collective or individual risk. If all producers are identical, then Figure 12.14 becomes a representative producer model. If producers are identical and face *pure collective risk*, then all producers receive identical payoffs in each state of nature. If producers are identical and face *pure individual risks*, then not only are the probabilities of various states the same for all producers, but the share of producers in each state at any given time also matches the probability of the state, that is, the *ex post* distribution of states among producers is the same as the *ex ante* distribution faced by each producer. For example, if the probability of good weather is 0.6 then 60 percent of producers experience good weather at any one time but all producers have the same 60 percent chance of being among those who experience good weather.

30. The literature that investigates which measure is appropriate for economic welfare analysis of alternative policies and projects is based largely on Graham's (1981) seminal work.
31. To these could be added similar measures defined with an equivalent variation approach. Such measures would correspond to applying the Scitovsky reversal test in addition to the Kaldor–Hicks compensation test. Applying both tests would be necessary only if changes are made without actually paying compensation. See Section 3.1. As explained above, however, application of the compensation test depends more heavily on paying compensation in the case of risk, in which case testing for reversals is not necessary.

The case of identical producers and certain social cost

For the case of identical producers and certain social cost, the largest sure compensation payment each producer is willing to make is given by the producer's option price (see Figure 12.14). The compensation criterion is thus satisfied if the sum of producers' option prices exceeds the certain social cost (all on the 45 degree line). With pure collective risk, all producers are in identical states simultaneously. Therefore, no redistribution of risk among producers can satisfy the compensation criterion for any greater certain social cost. Comparison of social cost to the option price or, equivalently, *ex ante* compensating variation (aggregated over producers in either case) is thus necessary and sufficient for application of the compensation test for the case of pure collective risk, identical producers and certain social cost assuming no relevant contingency market is available.

In this case, as the analysis of Figure 12.14 demonstrates, expected *ex post* compensating variation, $E(C_i^*)$, is not a useful criterion. If option value is positive, then $E(C_i^*)$ is a sufficient but weak criterion (not necessary) because the option price always identifies a larger set of possible projects that pass the compensation criterion, $O_p > E(C_i^*)$. On the other hand, when option value is negative, $E(C_i^*)$ not only exceeds the option price, but it lies on the 45 degree line outside the aggregate WTP locus of producers.[32] With certain social cost, payment of $E(C_i^*)$ by producers is feasible only if a risk-neutral contingency market will absorb variation in producers' actual *ex post* compensation without cost. But if a risk-neutral contingency market exists, then comparison of social cost to the extent of the expected fair bet point $\bar{F}$ is necessary and sufficient for the compensation test. The expected fair bet point is always higher than either $E(C_i^*)$ or option price.

Suppose alternatively that producers face pure individual risks. The fair bet point of Figure 12.14 then becomes the appropriate welfare measure assuming the *ex post* distribution among producers is the same as the *ex ante* distribution faced by each producer. That is, in Figure 12.14, each individual is willing to pay compensation for the project equal to F_g when good weather occurs and F_b when bad weather occurs. At any given time, the proportion of producers who realize good weather is γ and the proportion who realize bad weather is $1-\gamma$. Thus, producers are willing to make an average payment at any given time equal to $\bar{F} = \gamma F_g + (1-\gamma)F_b$. In Figure 12.14, $\bar{F}$ is represented by the point where the line tangent to the WTP locus at the fair bet point F crosses the 45 degree line. The compensation criterion is satisfied if $\bar{F}$ multiplied by the number of producers exceeds the certain social cost. Because point F is translated to $\bar{F}$ by a straight line with slope equal to the ratio of probabilities, further availability of contingency markets makes no difference. Thus, comparison of $\bar{F}$ (aggregated over individuals) to social cost is both necessary and sufficient for the compensation test for the case of pure individual risks, identical producers, and certain social cost regardless of contingency market considerations.

Impure individual risks

Turning to more practical cases, reality rarely presents problems where the *ex post* distribution of states among individuals is the same as the *ex ante* distribution faced by all individuals. As a result, compensation schemes that balance risks among individuals to achieve perfect aggregate certainty are usually not possible. Furthermore, public admin-

32. This can be verified by redrawing Figure 12.14 with different probabilities of states such that point F lies to the left of the *ex post* compensating variation point, that is, where the LL line has sufficiently less slope.

istration of such a scheme may be impractical even if it were conceptually possible because of the extent of individual information and transactions required. On the other hand, many problems can be described by impure individual risks, where the risks are largely independent among producers but yet generate nonnegligible aggregate risk. For example, automobile insurance companies incur relatively small but nonnegligible aggregate risk because approximately the same percentage of drivers (within a given rated category) have accidents each year, although all individuals (in the category) have about the same probability of being among those who have accidents in any given year. In this case, automobile insurance can serve as a contingency market that facilitates movement from F to $\bar{F}$ in Figure 12.14 although the insurance company presumably gains part of the benefits for providing the service.

Examples of public policies for impure individual risks include unemployment insurance, disaster assistance, and the provision of Social Security that provides income when a worker is unexpectedly disabled. By charging fees to all individuals, often in the form of general or specific taxes, such programs are designed so that aggregate compensation collected by the government is roughly sufficient to meet program expenses (unless aggregate subsidies are deliberately included). For such programs, the extent of stochastic independence of outcomes among individuals determines the extent of state-dependence of aggregate social costs. Also, the extent of variation in required aggregate compensation (relative to variation in individual compensation) determines the extent to which $\bar{F}$ rather than O_p is an appropriate comparison in the case of approximately certain social cost.

Impure collective risk

In other problems many producers experience similar although not identical adverse outcomes at the same time, for example, when market prices deteriorate due to international trade or macroeconomic conditions. Such conditions may approximate collective risk in competitive markets where all producers face the same prices (although producers' profits are not affected by equal amounts). When risk is approximately collective, the aggregate social costs of providing stability for producers can exhibit considerable state dependence. For example, provision of unemployment insurance can generate huge aggregate payouts when the economy falls into a serious recession. For these cases, determination of which welfare measure is appropriate depends on the existence of contingency markets that can absorb aggregate risk. If relevant contingency markets exist, then the critical question is whether expected social cost is less than expected WTP.[33] The highest applicable WTP for this comparison corresponds to the fair bet point.

As is well known, however, many contingency markets necessary for efficient allocation of risk do not exist.[34] If contingency markets do not exist and producer risk is largely collective, then the compensation criterion cannot be satisfied if social costs are outside the aggregate WTP locus of producers. In particular, and contrary to some of the literature, the expected fair bet point is not an appropriate welfare measure in this case (Bishop 1986; Smith 1990). The critical question in these cases is whether some practical compensation

33. If contingency markets are not risk-neutral, then this comparison should also consider discounting for risk associated with the difference in aggregate compensation and aggregate social cost according to the risk aversion inherent in contingency markets.
34. Such markets often fail to exist because of moral hazard and adverse selection. These problems are discussed in Section 12.10.

scheme can be found such that the state-dependent social cost is less than aggregate compensation in every state. Examples of practical compensation schemes are option value and *ex post* compensating variation. In either case, if the state-dependent social cost lies within the rectangles defined by these points in Figure 12.14, then the compensation test is met. But these comparisons are only sufficient, not necessary.

The general case

In the general case of policy evaluation for problems that do not approximate collective risk and/or where social costs are state-dependent, welfare analysis under risk can be difficult. In general, the problem is to find a compensation scheme $C=\{C_{ij}\}$ specifying compensation paid by each individual j in each state i such that

$$\max_{C}\left\{E\left[\sum_{j} C_{ij}-X_i\right]\middle|\sum_{j} C_{ij}\geq X_i\forall i,\ E[U_j(\tilde{\pi}_{ij}-C_{ij},z_1)]=E[U_j(\tilde{\pi}_{ij},z_0)]\forall j\right\},$$

where X_i is the state-dependent social cost of changing z from z_0 to z_1, expectations are with respect to states of nature, utility functions possibly differ by producer, and sums are over all producers.[35] The expectation conditions in this criterion define the WTP locus for producer j for the general problem with many states. This compensation problem is a nonlinear programming problem that efficiently distributes risk to maximize the excess of compensation over social cost. The excess can then be distributed among individuals in any desirable way to make at least one individual better off without making any individual worse off. Obtaining a positive value for the objective function is a necessary and sufficient condition for the compensation test when contingency markets are not available. As the complexity of this problem suggests, finding such compensation schemes when social costs are state-dependent and greater than option value (in some states) requires both considerable information about individuals and, possibly, substantial complexity in the compensation scheme. Furthermore, implementing a public compensation scheme that involves uncertain compensation payments by individuals is often politically unacceptable.

Summary

In summary, with certain social cost, the most defensible and practical approach for most economic welfare analysis under risk aversion is to compare aggregate *ex ante* compensating variation to social cost. This comparison is sufficient for the compensation test in any case but necessary only when producers are identical and a relevant contingency market is not available. If social cost is state-dependent, then one can determine whether aggregate *ex ante* compensating variation is at least equal to or greater than social cost in every state of nature, which would be sufficient for the compensation test. Otherwise, practical implementation may depend on whether the government is willing to absorb the uncertainty of spreading the difference in social cost and aggregate compensation gener-

35. Graham (1981) uses the terms 'expected value of the fair bet point' and 'expected willingness to pay' interchangeably. However, as he points out, willingness to pay has an infinite number of alternatives along the WTP locus. As a result, Graham's (1981) conclusion that 'expected willingness to pay . . . measures benefit in cases of individual risks' (p. 721) is not very helpful. To find a necessary condition for the compensation test requires examining all possible combinations of WTP along each producer's WTP locus as in this maximization problem. This is spelled out plainly by Graham (1992).

ated by this approach. Three conditions typical of many policy problems lead to these conclusions:

1. All relevant contingency markets often do not exist.
2. Administration of individual- and state-specific compensation is often impractical.
3. Public finance with uncertain compensation is often politically infeasible.

Notwithstanding these typical circumstances, policies that establish state-dependent payouts, such as federal disaster assistance or federal crop insurance, require state-dependent compensation analysis. In these cases, one can determine whether the actual *ex post* compensating variation exceeds social cost in every state, which would be sufficient for the compensation test. More generally, if aggregate compensation exceeds social cost in every state for any other specific compensation scheme, then the associated policy or project passes the compensation test. But a failure to cover social cost in some states with any specific compensation scheme does not necessarily imply a failure of the potential compensation test. The potential compensation test necessarily fails only when the general mathematical problem stated in the previous paragraph does not have a solution.

12.7 MARKET-BASED ESTIMATION OF *EX ANTE* WTP

Whereas *ex post* compensating variation can be computed as the impact of a policy or project on the profit of a producer, estimation of *ex ante* compensating variation is somewhat more difficult because it requires understanding how producers perceive and react to risk. This section considers possibilities for estimation of *ex ante* compensating variation associated with changes in market-based economic policies under risk aversion. Consider a risk-averse producer operating in a competitive market with random product price p and price expectation $\mu_p = E(p)$. Consistent with the assumption of competition, assume the firm's output has no effect on the product price distribution. Suppose that the firm makes short-run decisions by maximizing a mean-variance expected utility function,[36]

36. As shown by James Tobin (1969), expected utility follows a mean-variance specification if either the utility function is quadratic or profit is distributed normally. Kenneth Arrow (1971) has argued that a quadratic utility function is not plausible because it implies increasing absolute risk aversion. Normality of profit, however, may be a plausible assumption. This would be the case, for example, if output price is distributed normally and production and input prices are nonstochastic. With constant absolute risk aversion (CARA), $\varphi = -U''(\pi)/U'(\pi)$, the utility of profit follows $U(\pi) = \alpha - \beta \exp(-\varphi\pi)$ for positive constants α, β and φ, from which expected utility is $E[U(\pi)] = \alpha - \beta E[\exp(-\varphi\pi)] = \alpha - \beta \exp(-\varphi\mu_\pi + \varphi^2\sigma_\pi^2/2)$ if $\pi \sim N(\mu_\pi, \sigma_\pi^2)$. This expected utility is monotonically increasing in $\mu_\pi - \varphi\sigma_\pi^2/2$, which is the condition under which a linear mean-variance expected utility function is fully appropriate, that is, has equivalent implications for decision-making and welfare measurement. For a more general discussion of the von Neumann–Morgenstern utility framework underlying this analysis, see Nicholson (1978, ch. 6). Also, see Meyer (1987) for a more general justification of two-moment representations for expected utility in which this type of analysis may serve as an approximation. Some other useful and tractable specifications that can be used in place of CARA with normally distributed profits are CARA with gamma distributed revenues and constant relative risk aversion (CRRA) with log normal revenue. For further discussion, see Yassour, Zilberman and Rausser (1981) and Tsur (1993).

$$E[U(\pi)] = E(\pi) - \varphi q^2\sigma_p^2/2 \quad (12.1)$$
$$= \mu_p q - w_1x_1 - \ldots - w_nx_n - c_0 - \varphi q^2\sigma_p^2/2,$$

where U is utility, π is profit, c_0 is fixed cost, x_i is the quantity of factor input i, w_i is the input price associated with x_i, φ is the absolute risk-aversion parameter and σ_p^2 is the variance of price, $\sigma_p^2 = E(p - \mu_p)^2$. Thus, $q^2\sigma_p^2$ is the variance of profit. To simplify the discussion below, suppose that minimum cost required to produce each level of output is given by $C(q)$, so that

$$E[U(\pi)] = \mu_p q - C(q) - \varphi q\sigma_p^2/2 \quad (12.2)$$

is simply a function of q. A condition for maximization of (12.2) with respect to q (the first-order condition of calculus) is

$$\mu_p = C'(q) + \varphi q\sigma_p^2, \quad (12.3)$$

where $C'(q)$ represents marginal cost. Recall that the condition for maximization of profit from the theory of the firm under certainty is $\mu_p = C'(q)$. Thus, in the mean-variance expected utility formulation, the term $\varphi q\sigma_p^2$ represents a discounting of the expected price because of the uncertainty associated with it. Specifically, where $\varphi q^2\sigma_p^2/2$ is called a risk premium associated with output price uncertainty, the term $\varphi q\sigma_p^2$ is a marginal risk premium.

The compensating or equivalent variation associated with various parametric changes for this problem can be determined by comparing the risk-averse firm's decision problem with a risk-neutral decision problem. That is, in the case of risk neutrality, the maximand in (12.2) becomes

$$E[U^*(\pi)] = E(\pi) \quad (12.4)$$
$$= \mu_p q - C(q)$$

for which the maximization condition in (12.3) becomes

$$\mu_p = C'(q). \quad (12.5)$$

If a risk-neutral firm, which follows (12.4), faces expected price μ_p^*, and a risk-averse firm, which follows (12.2), faces expected price μ_p', then decisions are identical if the two expected prices are related by the equation

$$\mu_p^* = \mu_p' - \varphi q'\sigma_p^2, \quad (12.6)$$

where q' is the optimal output of the risk-averse firm with expected price μ_p'. This is evident upon substituting μ_p' into equation (12.3) and μ_p^* into equation (12.5) and noting that $C'(q)$ must be the same in the two cases (assuming that marginal cost is strictly upward sloping). The relationship in (12.6) allows construction and comparison of supply curves with different levels of risk as in Figure 12.16. Equation (12.6) implies that the risk-averse supply curve $S_\varphi(\sigma_p^2)$, conditioned on the risk-aversion coefficient φ, lies above the risk-neutral supply curve, $S_0(\sigma_p^2)$, at a distance $\varphi q\sigma_p^2$.

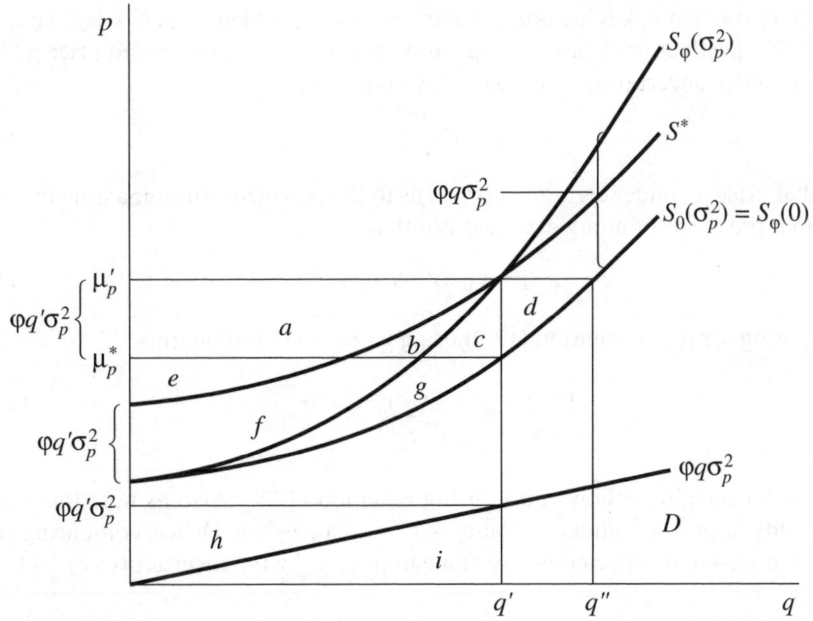

Figure 12.16

Now consider the case where the firm is risk-averse but faces no risk. Clearly, without risk, the maximand in (12.1) also reduces to

$$\begin{aligned} E[U(\pi)] &= E(\pi) \\ &= \mu_p q - C(q) \end{aligned} \tag{12.7}$$

because $\sigma_p^2 = 0$. Hence, the resulting decisions must be the same as for the maximand in (12.4), which implies that the corresponding supply curve $S_\varphi(0)$ in Figure 12.16 coincides with the risk-neutral supply curve $S_0(\sigma_p^2)$ and that the objective functions in the two cases have the same maximum. But the results of Section 4.2 and Appendix Section 4.B apply to the supply curve $S_\varphi(0)$ and show that area $e+f+g$ measures quasirent for the producer associated with expected price μ_p^*. Hence, area $e+f+g$ also provides an appropriate measure of producer welfare associated with a random price that has mean μ_p^* under risk neutrality.[37] And from Section 4.2 and Appendix Section 4.B, any change in this welfare measure under price certainty (associated with a change in any parameter affecting the firm) is an exact measure of both the compensating and equivalent variations. Thus, also under uncertainty and risk neutrality, this dual interpretation of area $e+f+g$ implies that the change in the area above the supply curve (which is now a function of the mean price) and below mean price is a measure of both compensating and equivalent variation of any change affecting the firm. This is clear because the objective criteria in equations (12.4) and (12.7) are identical.

37. This result is, in fact, a version of the result associated with Figure 12.12.

Finally, suppose that risk is introduced in the certainty problem with risk aversion. That is, suppose that product price has mean μ_p' and variance σ_p^2. Because mean price μ_p' leads to output q' under uncertainty, expected utility is given by

$$V' = \mu_p' q' - C(q') - \varphi q'^2 \sigma_p^2/2. \tag{12.8}$$

But note that price μ_p^* under certainty also leads to the expected-utility-maximizing quantity q' so that the corresponding expected utility is

$$V^* = \mu_p^* q' - C(q'), \tag{12.9}$$

and substituting for μ_p^* in equation (12.9) using equation (12.6) obtains

$$\begin{aligned} V^* &= \mu_p' q' - C(q') - \varphi q'^2 \sigma_p^2 \\ &= V' - \varphi q'^2 \sigma_p^2/2, \end{aligned} \tag{12.10}$$

where the latter equality follows upon using equation (12.8). Also as noted above, the expected utility at price μ_p^* under certainty is V^* = area $e+f+g$. Hence, comparing (12.8) and (12.10) reveals that expected utility at mean price μ_p' with uncertainty is V' = (area $e+f+g$) + $\varphi q'^2\sigma_p^2/2$.

To consider welfare measurement in the context of Figure 12.16, note that $\varphi q'^2\sigma_p^2$ = area $h+i$ = area $b+c+f+g$ where S^* is a curve constructed vertically parallel to $S_0(\sigma_p^2)$ at a distance of $\varphi q'\sigma_p^2$. Thus, by construction, $\varphi q'^2\sigma_p^2/2$ = area h = area $b+f$ and, hence, V' = area $e+f+g$ + area $b+f$. Finally, note that area $a+e$ = area $e+f+g$ by construction so that V' = area $a+b+e+f$. From this result, the expected utility under risk aversion is represented by the area below expected price and above the supply curve where the supply curve specifies the amount supplied as a function of expected price conditioned on the variance of price.

To examine the welfare effects of changing risk, consider a given mean price μ_p' but a change in the variance of price from 0 to σ^2. With variance zero, production is q'' and the expected utility in Figure 12.16 is area $a+b+c+d+e+f+g$, whereas with variance σ_p^2, expected utility is area $a+b+e+f$. The welfare effect of risk on the producer is thus a loss of area $c+d+g$. With mean-variance expected utility, a certain payment of area $c+d+g$ makes the producer just as well off under risk as with no risk. That is, area $c+d+g$ is the producer's maximum willingness to pay to totally eliminate price variation or the minimum willingness to accept the price variance σ_p^2 compared to no price variation. Hence, the area $c+d+g$ is an exact measure of both the compensating and equivalent variation of the risk.

These results thus imply that the change in producer surplus associated with a supply curve taken as a function of expected price and conditioned on respective observed levels of risk in price before and after a change gives an exact measure of both compensating and equivalent variation associated with any parametric change in the input prices or in the distribution of output price (mean or variance).[38] For example, in a mean-variance

38. Although these results have been derived in a simple mean-variance framework for intuitive purposes, they can be readily extended. The only alteration in results is that the appropriate supply curve to use for welfare calculations depends on the entire distribution of price exclusive of location (that is, on all moments about the mean) rather than simply on the variance. Also note that some important alterations are necessary when production is stochastic. See Appendix Section 12.A for further details.

framework, suppose that the mean price is changed from μ_p^0 to μ_p^1, the variance of price is changed from σ_0^2 to σ_1^2, input prices are changed from w_i^0 to w_i^1, $i=1, ..., n$, and the induced change in production is from q_0 to q_1. Suppose that the supply curve as a function of mean price μ_p conditioned on the variance of price and all input prices is represented by $S(\sigma_p^2, w_1, ..., w_n)$, as in Figure 12.17. Then both the compensating and equivalent variation of the change is given by area $b-a$.

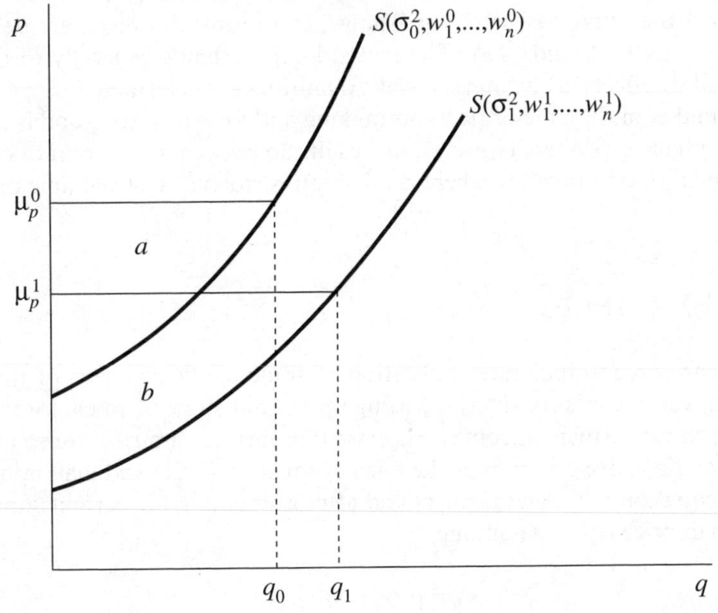

Figure 12.17

The case of risk response in factor demand may be considered similarly. For example, because of the need for advanced planning or because of lags in the production process, an industry may need to determine input quantities before output price is known. The response in derived demand to output price risk follows the same type of framework as developed in this section for supply. That is, the effects of changes in output price risk are reflected (completely) by the area under derived factor demands (for essential inputs with nonstochastic input prices). Similar statements hold for compensated consumers' demand and supply as well because their problem is equivalent to the producers' problem in the compensated case. A reasonable application in the consumer case is in the demand for durables (automobiles or appliances) where consumers face risk regarding the prices of related goods, such as fuels, that must be used over the life of the durables (see Appendix Section 14.B). Another application is the case where a firm faces the risk of technological change, which may make an adopted technology obsolete soon after investment.[39]

This section has considered the case of welfare measurement when output price is stochastic. However, in many practical problems both output prices and production are

39. See, for example, Chavas and Mullarky (2002) for a general theoretical treatment of this type of problem.

stochastic. This case is somewhat more difficult because the stochastic price is multiplied by stochastic production. Nevertheless, the results of this section can be extended to the case of stochastic production as long as welfare effects are measured in a factor input market where quantities are nonstochastic. Agriculture is a common example where both production and output price depend on stochastic future market and weather conditions at the time of decision-making, but input decisions are determined specifically by decision-makers. For a mean-variance expected utility function, these results can be shown in much the same way as above. The general results, however, are developed in Appendix Sections 12.A and 14.A. The methodology extends generally to the case of measuring welfare effects in any market where quantities are determined with certainty by the decision-maker at the time of decision-making and for which the good is essential in the related production process. However, the results do not generalize for measurement of welfare effects in output markets where production is stochastic at the time of decision-making.

12.8 AN EXAMPLE

An example can serve to illustrate application of some of the concepts of this chapter. Suppose the government is considering setting up a buffer stock of wheat for the purpose of stabilizing wheat farmers' incomes. Suppose that farmers are risk-averse and behave according to an objective criterion of the form in equation (12.1) and that, upon estimating a supply equation for wheat farmers and after accounting for current supply conditions other than price risk, one obtains

$$q = \mu_p - 1.5q\sigma_p^2,$$

where

q = quantity of wheat in billion bushels,
μ_p = expected price of wheat in dollars per bushel, and
σ_p^2 = variance of wheat price

(suppose for simplicity that wheat production is nonstochastic). Suppose that the estimated demand equation, after accounting for current levels of all determinants of demand, is

$$q = 4.5 - 0.5p + 0.5\varepsilon$$

where

p = actual price of wheat in dollars per bushel and
ε = random fluctuation in consumer preferences not known when farmers decide how much to produce.

Suppose for simplicity that $\varepsilon = 1$ or $\varepsilon = -1$, each with probability 0.5.

Solving each of these equations for implicit form (solving for p or μ_p) obtains

$$\mu_p = q + 1.5q\sigma_p^2$$

for supply and

$$p = 9 - 2q + \varepsilon$$

for demand. The supply curve is depicted in Figure 12.18 for $\sigma_p^2 = 0$ and $\sigma_p^2 = 1$, while the demand curve is shown with $\varepsilon = 1$ and $\varepsilon = -1$ and also where ε is at its expected value, $E(\varepsilon) = 0$. The latter relationship shows how expected price is determined with given quantities of production. That is, simply taking expectations in the demand equation implies

$$\mu_p = 9 - 2q + E(\varepsilon) = 9 - 2q.$$

Note that the supply equation is of the form in equation (12.3) where $C'(q) = q$ and $\varphi = 1.50$. Because equation (12.3) gives the farmers' condition for optimization, the stochastic market equilibrium is obtained by equating the supply curve with the expected price implied by the demand curve. That is,

$$q + 1.5q\sigma_p^2 = 9 - 2q,$$

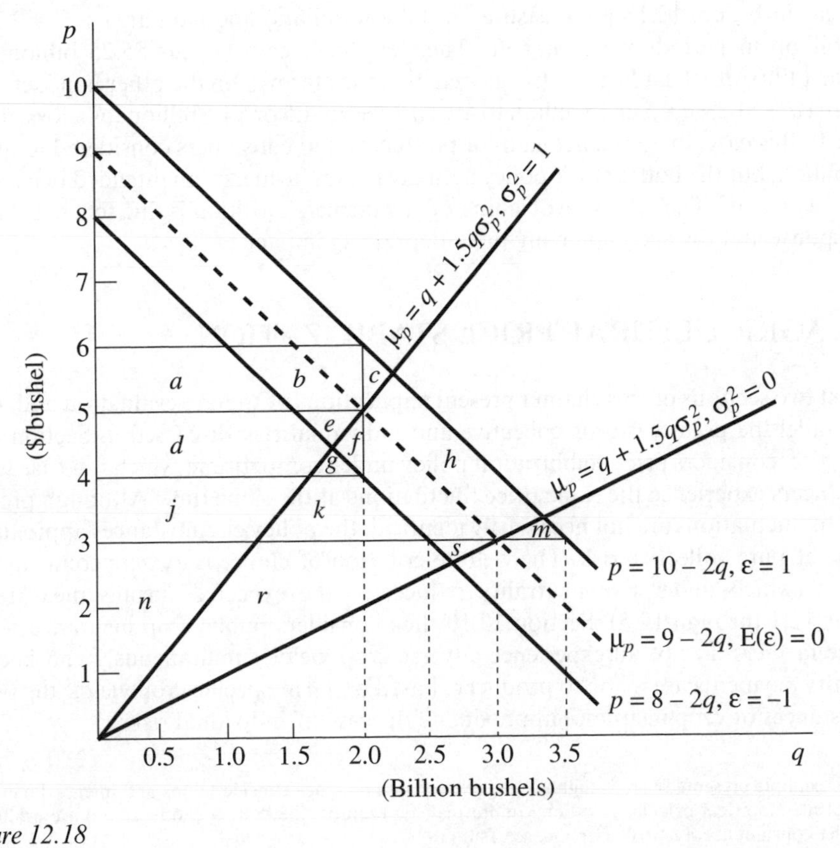

Figure 12.18

which implies

$$q=\frac{9}{3+1.5\sigma_p^2}.$$

Also, note that the variance of price if the market is freely competitive is

$$\sigma_p^2=E[(p-\mu_p)^2]=E\,\{[(9-2q+\varepsilon)-(9-2q)]^2\}=E(\varepsilon^2)=1.$$

Thus, in a free market, the equilibrium quantity is $q=9/(3+1.5\cdot 1)=2$, in which case price is $p=9-2\cdot 2+1=6$ or $p=9-2\cdot 2-1=4$, each with probability 0.5 (see Figure 12.18).

Now suppose that a buffer stock is introduced which completely stabilizes price, thus implying $\sigma_p^2=0$. In this case, the equilibrium supply is represented implicitly by $\mu_p=q$. If the government fixes a stable price at $p=3$, then the quantity produced is $q=3$. Also, following the demand curve, the quantity consumed is $q=4.5-0.5\cdot 3+0.5=3.5$ if $\varepsilon=1$, and $q=4.5-0.5\cdot 3-0.5=2.5$ if $\varepsilon=-1$. Hence, on average, the buffer stock neither grows nor declines. The expected quantity demanded is equal to the quantity supplied. Note alternatively that the buffer stock is expected to grow if stabilized price is set above $p=3$, and a decline in the buffer stock is expected if stabilized price is set below $p=3$.

The welfare effects of this buffer stock policy are thus as follows. Consumers gain area $a+b+c+d+e+f+g+h+j+k+m=8.25$ or \$8.25 billion in periods where $\varepsilon=1$ (note that areas in Figure 12.18 are measured in billion dollars) and gain area $j+k=2.25$ or \$2.25 billion in periods where $\varepsilon=-1$. Their expected gain is thus \$5.25 billion. The expected utility of wheat farmers (measured in money terms), on the other hand, changes from area $d+e+j+n=5$ or \$5 billion to area $n+r+s=4.5$ or \$4.5 billion for a loss of \$0.5 billion. In this case, there is a net gain for producers and consumers considered jointly of \$4.75 billion, but the buffer stock policy actually makes farmers – an intended beneficiary group – worse off. The relative worsening of the farmers' position is due to a substantial risk response and the accompanying price-depressing impact.[40]

12.9 AGRICULTURAL PRICE STABILIZATION

The next two sections of this chapter present applications of welfare evaluation under risk that parallel the polar cases of collective and individual risk discussed in Section 12.6. This section considers price stabilization policy under competition, which is a case where all producers experience the same price fluctuations at the same time. Although producers' profit fluctuations are not necessarily identical, the policy circumstances approximate the case of pure collective risk. The welfare criterion of choice is *ex ante* compensating variation (which under risk neutrality reduces to the expected surplus measures of Sections 12.1 through 12.5). Section 12.10 then considers public crop insurance policy. Because farmers do not all experience adverse crop yields simultaneously and because indemnity payments are made to producers based on farm-specific crop yields, the policy circumstances of crop insurance approximate the case of individual risks.

40. The example presented here is highly simplistic because of space considerations and intended merely to illustrate empirical calculations. For a more realistic example illustrating producer welfare evaluation under constant absolute risk aversion, see Tsur (1993).

Analysis of agricultural price stabilization policy is a natural application of much of the framework of this chapter. During the 1950s and 1960s, US grain policy relied mainly on price supports, sometimes augmented by marketing quotas for the purpose of supporting farm incomes. When government-owned grain stocks began to accumulate, officials realized that any rule for accumulating stocks (for example, a price support program) must be accompanied by an orderly rule for liquidating those stocks. When stock liquidation was undertaken as soon as prices exceeded price supports, the huge grain stocks caused price supports to act somewhat like price ceilings as well as price floors to the dismay of both farmers and politicians. Then the commodity boom of the mid-1970s caused unprecedented price increases for both agricultural and nonagricultural commodities (see Table 12.1 for the case of wheat), which led to consumer concerns about inflation and turned the policy focus toward price stabilization rather than simply price support. In response, the US Food and Agricultural Act of 1977 adopted a *Farmer-Owned Reserve* storage policy intended to eliminate both extreme upward and downward price fluctuations of major agricultural crops in the USA.

Table 12.1 US wheat statistics by crop year, 1970–92

Year	Price ($/bushel)	Real price (1996 $/bushel)	Acreage harvested (1000 acres)	Production	Ending farmer-owned reserve	Ending free stocks
				(million bushels)		
1970	1.33	4.54	43564	1352	0	705
1971	1.34	4.35	47685	1619	0	470
1972	1.76	5.47	47303	1546	0	628
1973	3.95	11.61	54148	1711	0	591
1974	4.09	11.06	65368	1782	0	340
1975	3.55	8.79	69499	2127	0	435
1976	2.73	6.38	70927	2149	0	666
1977	2.33	5.11	66686	2046	342	1113
1978	2.97	6.09	56495	1776	393	1130
1979	3.78	7.17	62454	2134	260	874
1980	3.91	6.81	71125	2381	360	714
1981	3.66	5.84	80642	2785	562	789
1982	3.45	5.19	77937	2765	1061	969
1983	3.51	5.07	61390	2420	611	1323
1984	3.39	4.72	66928	2595	654	1211
1985	3.08	4.16	64704	2424	433	1047
1986	2.42	3.20	60688	2091	463	1303
1987	2.57	3.30	55945	2108	467	991
1988	3.72	4.62	53189	1812	287	978
1989	3.72	4.45	62189	2037	144	511
1990	2.61	3.01	69103	2730	14	419
1991	3.00	3.34	57803	1980	50	705
1992	3.24	3.53	62761	2467	28	323

Source: US Department of Agriculture, *Agricultural Statistics* (various issues). The real price is derived using the gross domestic price deflator (1996 = 100).

The grain stock policy instituted with this Act appeared to represent an important departure from previous agricultural policy. The spread between the price support and the release price (a trigger price for incentives to liquidate stocks) provided a margin that made the Farmer-Owned Reserve policy seem something like the policy analyzed in Sections 12.1 through 12.5 of this chapter. By comparison, when only a price support is instituted, as with earlier agricultural policies, the analysis of Section 8.5 indicates an economic efficiency loss.[41] Under the policy, incentives were instituted to encourage increased farmer storage from bumper crops to prevent excessively low prices. Then, in years of shortage, incentives for stock liquidation were intended to mitigate excessively large price increases that would otherwise destabilize the industry.

Thus, in light of the extreme commodity price boom of the early 1970s and the observed price-depressing effect of stock liquidation a decade or so earlier, the Food and Agriculture Act of 1977 represented an effort to bound price variation of certain agricultural markets from both above and below, in the spirit of Figure 12.9. Unfortunately, the program did not work well in practice. Stocks tended to accumulate rather than fluctuate in a 'normal' range until 1982 when the Farmer-Owned Reserve for wheat was equal to almost 40 percent of the crop (Table 12.1). To many, these huge stocks seemed to prevent normal as well as extreme upward price fluctuations. Accordingly, the program was viewed as having a depressing effect on farmers' welfare and, accordingly, the government decided to phase out the Farmer-Owned Reserve program. The framework of Sections 12.4 through 12.7 offers several important contributing explanations for the program's lack of success.

Dependence of Who Gains on Specification

As shown in Section 12.4, the distributional impacts of a grain stock policy that limits price variation to a price band by means of a self-liquidating buffer stock are sensitive to the curvature of supply and demand and the form of disturbances in each. If demand and supply are linear and supply is highly variable because of weather, then producers gain and consumers lose, whereas if demand and supply are nonlinear (with the same price elasticities and price levels), then consumers may gain while producers lose. The same difference may apply if disturbances in supply and demand are multiplicative rather than additive. As demonstrated by Figures 12.6 and 12.7, one reason producers can be worse off is that the average stabilized price must be lower than the nonstabilized price to achieve a self-liquidating stock rule in certain cases. Thus, misspecification of functional form and disturbance structure can explain why empirical economic models could predict sustainability and gains for farmers at average prices when, in reality, farmers' welfare did not improve and buffer stocks tended to accumulate unless average prices were closer to the support price than the release price.

The analysis in Figures 12.6 and 12.7 demonstrates that any empirical economic welfare study that does not adequately investigate nonlinearity and disturbance form may determine implications of the study for estimated impacts of price stabilization (even qualita-

41. One should also note, however, that equity rather than efficiency was apparently the goal of earlier agricultural policies. But, of course, the occurrence of efficiency loss implies that some more efficient redistribution plan may have existed (apart from political feasibility considerations).

tively) through arbitrary specifications and assumptions. Such investigations were generally not undertaken in empirical stabilization studies around the time the Farmer-Owned Reserve policy was implemented nor were they easy to do.[42] Typical practice in empirical or simulation studies was to specify either a linear form with additive disturbances or a log-linear form with multiplicative disturbances, rarely even comparing the two. Hence, simplistic as the theoretical cases of this chapter may be, they lead to serious reservations about the use of empirical work with inflexible specifications for stochastic economic welfare analysis.[43]

Inability to Anticipate Favorable Demand Conditions

An obvious downfall of a price band policy in the case of agriculture is that farmers have limited ability to meet high demand with high production because of the significant time required for production. Thus, unlike the case in Figure 12.4, producers are unable to anticipate high prices and move up their supply relationship when demand is high to take advantage of favorable demand conditions unless favorable conditions persist for multiple growing seasons. In contrast, in the framework of Section 12.5 where producers are unable to anticipate favorable demand or favorable prices, the benefits of price stabilization largely vanish or become negative for producers when production is highly stochastic – a condition that characterizes agriculture.

The inability to anticipate prices is clearly evident in Table 12.1, which shows that wheat farmers actually decreased acreage and production in 1972 when the commodity boom first began, only gradually increased acreage and production through the peak of the boom in 1974, and then continued to increase acreage and production after prices had begun to decline through 1976. Again, in response to the secondary price peak in 1979, farmers increased acreage and production through 1981 even though real prices were falling. Farmers were not only unable to anticipate or respond instantaneously to the price fluctuations of the commodity boom, but then after they responded they found themselves overinvested and poorly situated for the subsequent decline in prices, which, in part, precipitated the agricultural debt crisis of the 1980s.

Time in Storage Problems

Another problem with the storage policy of the 1977 Act was that the ensuing years of excess supply were highly serially correlated. That is, grain demand conditions following the commodity boom were weak for many years rather than just for a year or two at a time. As

42. A number of studies were performed to estimate the economic welfare effects of grain price stabilization at about the time this policy was instituted, including Cochrane and Danin (1976), Sharples, Walker and Slaughter (1976), Taylor and Talpaz (1979), Zwart and Mielke (1979) and Konandreas and Schmitz (1978), the latter of which expanded analysis to the case of international trade as in Figure 12.5. These studies used essentially the Massell framework in Figures 12.3 and 12.4, although some studies considered specific nonflexible nonlinear supply and demand forms. The notable exception was Reutlinger (1976, p. 8), who in using crude, piecewise-linear demand curves, concluded that 'the storage impact on gains and losses by consumers and producers is particularly sensitive to the assumed shape of the demand function'.
43. In a retrospective study, Just and Hallam (1978) attempted to identify disturbance structure and the extent of nonlinearity using flexible specifications. They showed that, while adding joint generality with respect to functional form and disturbance structure reduces econometric accuracy, estimation can be accurate enough to make at least the qualitative distributional effects reasonably clear.

shown in Table 12.1, the real price of wheat was lower in every year from 1983 through 1992 than it had been in every year from 1972 through 1982. As a result, the stocks that were accumulated over the first few years of the program had to be carried many years, which caused high storage costs per bushel of grain stored. In the framework of Section 12.6, the incurrence of storage costs and the transfer of risk from farmers to government was thus substantially more than if demand conditions had alternated with regularity between given high and low supply as in the diagrammatic analysis of Figure 12.9. And because the risk was collective risk rather than individual risk, the aggregate risk of supporting the program with public funds became more than the government was willing to sustain.[44]

Risk Aversion and Supply Response to Stabilizing Prices

Following the framework of Section 12.6, an additional factor that must be considered in implementing a price stabilization scheme is risk aversion and risk response as price variability is reduced. In a rare empirical stabilization study considering risk response, Hazell and Scandizzo (1979, p. 378) concluded that 'the potential welfare gains to be had from optimal intervention policies are surprisingly large, in fact far greater than might be anticipated' in the case where risk response is considered. Estimation of US crop supply response has found statistically significant response of crop supply to reductions in price and yield risk (see Just 1974 and a host of studies that have followed). Although the extent to which this response is due to risk aversion is less clear (Just and Pope 2003), the framework of Section 12.7 shows that reducing risk induces an increase in supply under risk aversion. Thus, a depressing effect of price stabilization on prices should be expected as prices adjust to increased supply under stabilization. An interesting point here, however, is that farmers' welfare must be evaluated according to their risk aversion, which means that the option price (or *ex ante* compensating variation) measure of Section 12.6 is an appropriate measure of whether farmers' welfare is better or worse. Under risk aversion, stabilization may improve farmers' welfare even though expected profit (and quasirent) declines.[45] Thus, the observation that farm profits declined (even if the decline could be attributed entirely to the program rather than to a change in, say, foreign demand conditions) should not be taken as evidence that farmers' welfare declined, particularly when a major goal of the program was price stabilization.

Adaptability of Policy Controls in Stochastic Circumstances

Designing policies with optimal adjustments to unanticipated circumstances also involves dynamic issues such as are discussed later in Chapter 14. For example, a price-stabilizing

44. Table 12.1 also suggests that the Farmer-Owned Reserve, to a significant extent, displaced private storage. While storage levels of wheat were generally high in the 1980s, free stocks declined significantly during the time that the Farmer-Owned Reserve was built up, and then increased again when the Farmer-Owned Reserve was being phased down. Thus, following the discussion of private storage response to public storage in Section 12.4, the subsidies expended as Farmer-Owned Reserve storage incentives by the government may have gone to finance storage that would have otherwise taken place with private profit motives.
45. That is, in the framework of Section 12.7, where expected utility is given by $E[U(\pi)] = \mu_p q - C(q) - \varphi q^2\sigma_p^2/2$, one could have a reduction in average price causing a reduction in expected profit, $\mu_p q - C(q)$, even though the reduction in price variability, σ_p^2, causes a sufficient reduction in the risk premium, $\varphi q^2\sigma_p^2/2$, so that expected utility increases.

buffer stock might specify how price regulations should be altered depending on the accumulated stock level.[46] While optimizing policies with respect to dynamic adjustments generally requires advanced tools such as dynamic stochastic programming or stochastic control theory, the principles of stochastic welfare economics discussed in this chapter remain valid (see the Appendix to Chapter 14 for details).[47]

In summary, this section has used the Agricultural Adjustment Act of 1977 to illustrate how each of the principles of stochastic economic welfare analysis developed in this chapter can have significant implications that ultimately determine the success or failure of government policies designed to address stochastic circumstances. A major problem in implementing policies designed to deal with stochastic circumstances is that adverse consequences may begin to develop over time not only because of successive random events of one type or another, but also because the model on which the policy is based is misspecified (whether it is a formal economic model or simply the perception of a policymaker). Often policies designed for stochastic problems become unsustainable because adjustments are not specified for circumstances that can be anticipated collectively but not specifically. The Agricultural Adjustment Act of 1977 may be a case in point (although one could also argue that the goals of Congress later changed).[48] That is, a long-term rise in stocks under the program was not specifically anticipated *ex ante*, but certainly that possibility could have been anticipated as among the potential *ex post* states of nature. Similarly, sustainability of any policy designed for stochastic circumstances depends on the extent to which government actions are specified by the policy for each set of circumstances that are among the potential *ex post* states of nature, whether or not they are part of the expected outcome that motivates implementation of the policy.

12.10 FEDERAL CROP INSURANCE POLICY

Following earlier efforts to support agricultural prices by purchasing public stocks, and then efforts to stabilize prices by buffer stock manipulation, agricultural policy in the USA has gradually turned toward an emphasis on all-peril crop insurance.[49] Federal crop

46. Under the Agricultural Adjustment Act of 1977, the Secretary of Agriculture was given certain flexibility to alter some of the parameters. But the program could not function smoothly because these adjustments were not specified sufficiently to allow explicit anticipation, nor were they sufficient to keep Congress from deciding to abandon the program.
47. For an early specific application of dynamic programming to grain storage policy, see, for example, Burt, Koo and Dudley (1980). For a more recent and general discussion as well as a review of the literature, see Williams and Wright (1991, chs 12–15). In dynamic models, the possibility that stocks can become depleted and cause future shortfalls for a future generation represents an externality. Gardner (1979b) discusses the desirability of robustness of policies with respect to such externalities..
48. The unwillingness of the government to attempt further commodity storage is evidenced by the subsequent 1985 and 1990 farm bill legislation, which eliminated almost all forms of government commodity storage programs. On the other hand, a declining importance of the goal of stabilization is suggested by the 1996 farm bill, which eliminated annual acreage set-aside programs that were also argued to be stabilizing, and the 2002 farm bill, which had almost no stabilizing provisions for commodity markets. For a related discussion of the declining willingness of governments to support stabilizing commodity agreements internationally, see Gilbert (1996).
49. The discussion of this section focuses entirely on all-peril crop insurance, which insures farmers against crop loss due to all forms of risk. Specific forms of crop insurance, such as hail insurance, are not subject to the same problems and, accordingly, are offered successfully by private markets.

insurance was introduced in the USA with the Federal Crop Insurance Act of 1938 but was not an important part of the US farm program until the Federal Crop Insurance Act of 1980. Previously, participation rates were below 10 percent and, at times, few crops or cropping areas were included in the program. With the 1980 Act, coverage of both crops and geographic area was increased and a 30 percent subsidy of premiums was undertaken by the federal government. But participation rates remained below 25 percent until 1989, when participation was required as a condition for receiving retroactive drought assistance in 1988. More seriously, the loss ratio (indemnity payments divided by insurance premiums) was consistently above 1.0 and sometimes exceeded 2.0 (a loss ratio of about 0.95 is generally regarded as necessary for private insurance viability).

Since 1989 participation rates have increased but largely as a result of increased federal subsidies and mandatory participation. Annual aggregate US crop insurance subsidies were roughly doubled over 1984–89 levels with the Food, Agriculture, Conservation and Trade Act of 1990, and then were increased roughly another fourfold with the Crop Insurance Reform Act of 1994. Each of these Acts as well as the Agricultural Risk Protection Act of 2000 were intended to increase crop insurance participation by increasing subsidies. In addition, the 1994 Act instituted a low-level catastrophic coverage that for a time was mandatory for eligibility in price and income support programs.[50]

Both politicians and economists have puzzled over why such large subsidies are required to induce participation in crop insurance if farmers are risk averse. The consensus is that crop insurance in practice suffers from problems of moral hazard and adverse selection, which thus prevents efficient sharing of risk. These problems often plague schemes that involve individual risks and where payments differ among individuals and states of nature. Thus, the principles in this section supplement those in Section 12.6 in the case of individual risks.

Moral Hazard

Moral hazard is a term used to describe an asymmetric information problem involving hidden actions. Hidden actions make contracting for specific behavior impractical because it is unobservable. Or, put another way, a promise from an agent to undertake a particular action, whether spoken or implicit, involves a hazard that the agent will shirk for personal benefit such as reduced effort if the action is unobservable.[51] In crop insurance, the problem of moral hazard occurs when an insured farmer follows less costly or less time-consuming production practices when insured, thus increasing the probability or size of the indemnity payment. As a result, the insured agent is more likely to incur the insured event than if uninsured. Thus, either the insurance premium must be adjusted upward to reflect the higher and more likely payment of an indemnity or the insurer will incur losses. The alternative of higher premiums or insurer losses occurs because of endogenous changes in behavior when farmers take out insurance rather than because of inherent differences among farmers.

50. See Coble and Knight (2002) for a more complete legislative history since 1990.
51. See Mas-Colell, Whinston and Green (1995, s. 14.B) for a general treatment of the moral hazard problem in economics.

Adverse Selection

Adverse selection is a term used to describe another problem of asymmetric information where agents differ in ways not perceived by a principal who contracts for their services. For example, if workers are heterogeneous and their productivity is unobservable, then an employer may be forced to pay the same average wage to all workers. But if the more productive workers have better alternatives, then workers self-select adversely so that the employer ends up employing only the least productive workers.[52] In crop insurance, the problem of adverse selection occurs when farms and farmers differ in characteristics that affect the probability and size of indemnity payments but these characteristics are not fully reflected in the insurance premium structure. Agriculture is highly heterogeneous due to land quality, climate and farmer abilities. As a result, insurers have difficulty assessing the risk associated with individual farmers. When insurers make errors in setting premiums, the farmers who are more likely to collect indemnities or who are more likely to collect larger indemnities per unit of premium are more likely to participate. As a result, the insurer must either set the premium structure to reflect the higher risk associated with the individuals who choose to participate (thus offering less fair insurance to others) or a loss will be incurred by the insurer (for example, if the premiums reflect the average characteristics of all agents).

Decomposition of the Incentive to Participate

A useful model for decomposing the incentive to participate in crop insurance has been developed by Just, Calvin and Quiggin (1999) and extended by Coble and Knight (2002). A farmer participating in the typical US federal crop insurance contract selects a per acre yield guarantee level β representing a percentage of the normal yield, μ, and a price guarantee level, p_α. For an *ex ante* per acre premium $\gamma_{\alpha\beta}$ the farmer then receives an *ex post* indemnity payment equal to $p_\alpha(\beta\mu - y)$ whenever the farm-specific yield falls below $\beta\mu$. Because the government subsidizes the premium, the farmer pays only $(1-s)\gamma_{\alpha\beta}$, where s is the subsidy rate. The normal yield is based on an approved production history such as a 10-year moving average of farm-specific yield records filed with the government, which may or may not reflect the farmer's true normal yield when insured because the 10-year history may include some years when the farmer did not insure or where different levels of insurance were purchased. At various times, farmers have been able to choose the yield guarantee and price guarantee from only two or three specific alternatives while, at other times, ranges of possibilities have been offered. The insurance premium depends on the farmer's choice of α and β, but is also determined in part by other observable characteristics used to assess a farmer's yield distribution. For example, a risk factor based on loss experience with many farmers in the same area has typically been used in calculating the premium.

To simplify the presentation, suppose a farmer faces a certain price p and uncertain yield per acre y with a fixed crop acreage (or farm size) A. Suppose the distribution of yields that maximizes the farmer's expected utility of profit is denoted by F_0 when crop

52. See Mas-Colell, Whinston and Green (1995, s. 13.B) for a general treatment of the adverse selection problem in economics.

insurance is not chosen, by F_1 when crop insurance is chosen and moral hazard is not present (for example, where the government can observe and penalize modified behavior), and by F_2 when crop insurance is chosen and shirking actions are not observable by government. Suppose the vectors of inputs that maximize the farmer's expected utility in these cases are given by x_0, x_1 and x_2, respectively, and suppose wx_j represents the cost of input vector x_j, which is assumed to be nonstochastic. Finally, suppose the government's implicit assessment of the farmer's yield distribution under insurance, upon which the normal yield and insurance premium are based, is denoted by G.

Then the farmer's profit is[53]

$$\pi_j = \begin{cases} [py - wx_j - (1-s)\gamma_{\alpha\beta}]A \text{ if } y \geq \beta\mu \\ [py + p_\alpha(\beta\mu - y) - wx_j - (1-s)\gamma_{\alpha\beta}]A \text{ if } y < \beta\mu, \end{cases}$$

$j=1,2$, if insurance is selected, and $\pi_0(y) = [py - wx_0]A$ if not. The expected utility for an insured farmer is represented by $E(U(\pi_j)|F_j)$ where the expectation is taken with respect to the yield distribution F_j. The farmer's welfare can also be usefully described by the *certainty equivalent of profit*, which is the certain profit that gives the producer the same expected utility as does the actual stochastic profit situation, that is $U(CE(\pi_j|F_j)) = E(U(\pi_j|F_j)$.[54] Accordingly, the *risk premium*, which measures how much an uncertain payoff is discounted because of risk, is defined as the difference in the certainty equivalent of profit and expected profit, $RP(\pi_j|F_j) = CE(\pi_j|F_j) - E(U(\pi_j)|F_j)$.

The incentive to participate in crop insurance can be represented as

$$CE(\pi_2|F_2) - CE(\pi_0|F_0) = \Delta_{RA} + \Delta_{GS} + \Delta_{AS} + \Delta_{MH},$$

where Δ_{RA} is a risk aversion incentive associated with reducing the variability of profits, Δ_{GS} is a government subsidy incentive associated with government subsidization of crop insurance, Δ_{AS} is an adverse selection incentive that occurs because the government fails to correctly assess the farmer's yield distribution and Δ_{MH} is the moral hazard effect that occurs because the farmer's profit-maximizing input use is reduced when the government is unable to monitor input use. Mathematically,

$$\begin{aligned} \Delta_{RA} &= RP(\pi_2|F_2) - RP(\pi_0|F_0) \\ \Delta_{GS} &= E(U(\pi_1)|G) - E(U(\pi_0)|G) \\ \Delta_{AS} &= E(U(\pi_1)|F_1) - E(U(\pi_0)|F_0) - \{E(U(\pi_1)|G) - E(U(\pi_0)|G)\} \\ \Delta_{MH} &= E(U(\pi_2)|F_2) - E(U(\pi_1)|F_1). \end{aligned}$$

Adding these amounts with the definitions above verifies that this is an accurate decomposition of the incentive to insure.

53. If fixed costs are present, then the term 'profit' can be replaced by the term 'quasirent' throughout the remainder of this section.
54. For example, using the linear mean-variance expected utility function of Section 12.7, the certainty equivalent of profit would be $\mu_\pi - \varphi\sigma_\pi^2/2$, which in this case becomes $E(\pi_j/F_j) - \varphi V(\pi_j/F_j)/2$ where V is the variance operator. Note, however, that insurance indemnities make revenue a nonlinear function of yield, which implies that revenue cannot have a normal distribution for practical purposes. Thus, the typical motivation for a linear mean-variance utility function is not applicable. For this reason, this section represents the certainty equivalent more generally without relying on normality.

Actuarial fairness is a useful reference point for characterizing insurance premiums. A premium is actuarially fair if expected indemnity payments are equal to premiums. Based on the government's assessment of the farmer's yield distribution, the premium is actuarially fair if

$$E[p_\alpha(\beta\mu - y)\,|\,y<\beta\mu]Pr(y<\beta\mu)=\gamma_{\alpha\beta},$$

where $Pr(y<\beta\mu)$ is the probability of an indemnity. Where this is the reference point that determines the extent to which premiums are subsidized, the government subsidy can be represented simply by $\Delta_{GS}=s\gamma_{\alpha\beta}A$. Substituting into the definition of Δ_{AS}, the adverse selection incentive can be characterized as the difference in expected profit between the insured and uninsured cases (in absence of moral hazard) that is not due to the government subsidy. More specifically, if the same input vectors maximize profit in insured and uninsured cases, then the adverse selection effect reduces to the part of the actual expected indemnity in absence of moral hazard that is not due to the government subsidy. The interpretation of the remaining components of incentive, Δ_{RA} and Δ_{MH}, follow directly from the definitions. That is, the risk-aversion incentive reflects how much the farmer's risk premium is reduced by insurance and the moral hazard incentive reflects how much expected profit can be increased by shirking.

Welfare Effects of Crop Insurance

In the context of Section 12.6, crop insurance is an example of individual risks where compensation is specific to individuals. That is, individuals receive net compensation $[p_\alpha(\beta\mu - y)-(1-s)\gamma_{\alpha\beta}]A$ in low-yield years in return for paying net compensation of $(1-s)\gamma_{\alpha\beta}A$ in high-yield years. However, the compensation is not equal to compensating variation (either *ex post* or *ex ante*) because the government does not have sufficient information about individuals to calculate it. That is, the government does not know the true yield distribution F_j but has only an imperfect assessment G. If the government's assessment G were correct ($\Delta_{AS}=\Delta_{MH}=0$), then every risk-averse ($\Delta_{RA}>0$) and risk-neutral ($\Delta_{RA}=0$) expected utility-maximizing farmer would participate because of the subsidy ($\Delta_{GS}>0$).

The voluntary nature of federal crop insurance also suggests an approach that is sometimes feasible for ensuring that a program's effects on individuals are positive. Those who are adversely affected simply choose not to participate. Of course, this conclusion assumes that nonparticipants are not adversely affected by the aggregate actions of participants. In reality, if participants are risk averse, then they would likely increase supply as risk is reduced, and thus drive down market prices for nonparticipants relative to the case of no crop insurance.

Just, Calvin and Quiggin (1999) used a nationwide survey of individual farms to estimate Δ_{RA}, Δ_{GS} and Δ_{AS} for corn and soybeans. The actual yield distributions of farmers were estimated from farmers' assessments of their mean yield and the probability of yields falling below various levels. The government's assessment of individual farm yield distributions was estimated from the normal (approved production history) yields and insurance premiums assigned to individual farms by the Federal Crop Insurance Corporation. As expected, the results found positive risk-aversion incentives to participate for all farmers, which were larger for those selecting higher levels of insurance (higher α and β). The risk-aversion incentive was higher for participants than nonparticipants, with larger differences for those insuring at higher levels. More interestingly, however, the results also showed that the adverse selection effect was positive for participants and negative for nonparticipants. For example, insuring corn farmers received an average benefit of $2.18 per acre purely because of subsidized premiums and premiums that were actuarially favorable to the farmer, while the comparable incentive for noninsuring farmers was from −$0.34 to −$3.69 per acre. Because farmers received similar premium subsidies, the differences between these incentives for insuring and noninsuring farmers (from $2.52 to $5.87) were due to adverse selection.[55] By comparison, the risk-aversion incentive for participation in the most typical insurance contract was found to be only $0.65 per acre. Thus, most of the explanation for participation was found to be adverse selection, which was due to the government not being able to tailor the insurance parameters to the circumstances of individual farms very well. In effect, the crop insurance program was found to be largely a transfer program to the high-risk farmers within individual rate-making areas. The results also found that almost all farmers would not prefer crop insurance without the subsidy incentive because the normal yield used by the government is based on a history of yields that lags behind technological advancements in crop yields.

In another closely related study by Just and Calvin (1995), the magnitude of the moral hazard incentive was estimated using the same data by comparing actual yields to estimates of typical yield distributions based on farmers' survey responses. (By comparison, adverse selection is based on differences in typical yield distributions from implicit government assessments of yield distributions implied by farm-specific federal crop insurance parameters, that is, normal yields and premiums.) This study found that the difference in actual yields and typical yields was a relatively small 3.15 bushels per acre for corn but a relatively large 9.26 bushels per acre for wheat and 12.31 bushels per acre for sorghum. As a result, total annual indemnities due to moral hazard for these three crops were estimated to be $274 million.

Since the time of these studies, steps have been taken to improve the adaptation of federal crop insurance parameters to individual farms. For example, in earlier years farms without sufficient approved production histories were simply assigned normal yield levels at county averages. More recently, farmers with insufficient yield histories have been penalized and broader participation has been required at times. As a result, participation levels have risen, but participation is far from universal. If the program sets actuarially fair premiums correctly tailored to individual farms and subsidizes them heavily, then universal participation should be observed even without moral hazard incentives. The fact that increased participation has been achieved only by increasing subsidies and at times requiring participation to qualify for other subsidies suggests that significant problems remain.

55. Farmers received different rates of premium subsidies depending on their choice of β. Farmers choosing a high β received the same amount of subsidy as those choosing $\beta = 0.65$, while those choosing a low β received the same rate of subsidy, 30 percent, as those choosing $\beta = 0.65$.

12.11 CONCLUSIONS

This chapter has focused on economic welfare analysis in markets affected by random phenomena. Although much of the discussion has focused on the welfare implications of price stabilization, the principles are applicable in evaluating any policy or project that affects the underlying stochastic phenomena or individual response to such phenomena.

The framework of this chapter points out that the welfare effects of policies that affect market stability can be substantial even when decision-makers are not inherently averse to risk depending on their ability to respond quickly to developing market situations. Thus, in addition to the importance of properly determining the degree of nonlinearity and form of random variation in supply and demand, the determination of time lags required by individual decision-makers to respond is crucial from both efficiency and distributional points of view. The benefits of stability are very different for individuals who can respond relatively little than for those who can adjust quickly to take advantage of price swings. Thus, the results discussed in this chapter underscore the need for sound empirical work as a basis for applied economic welfare analysis.[56]

This chapter also investigates which measures of welfare are appropriate for policies that affect risk when individuals are risk averse. Several measures may be appropriate depending on (1) the availability of contingency markets, (2) the form in which compensation is considered, (3) whether risks are individual or collective and (4) whether social costs of policy implementation are certain. The most practical measure for most cases is *ex ante* compensating variation, which is commonly called option value in the environmental and resource economics literature. This is true particularly for problems with collective risk and certain social cost where critical contingency markets do not exist. While compensation schemes involving state and individual specific compensation can theoretically satisfy the compensation criterion in additional cases, administration of such schemes is often impractical due to moral hazard and adverse selection problems. Crop insurance is a case in point.

The issues raised in this chapter should also be considered in the analysis of policy that affects uncertainty with respect to the future. This is the subject of Appendix Sections 14.A and 14.B. Additionally, policy uncertainty itself may create substantial welfare effects (Gardner 2002). That is, when policy-makers begin to consider several alternative policies with widely different provisions, private decision-makers may become uncertain about future policies and their related impact on private markets. As a result, they may delay replacement or expansion of investments until future policy becomes clear and, so supplies are reduced. While not demonstrated explicitly here, the effects of such policy uncertainty can be examined in the framework of Section 12.7.

56. For a further survey of economic welfare implications of stability, see Turnovsky (1978).

Appendix to Chapter 12: Producer welfare measurement under risk

The purpose of this appendix is to formally develop an approach to welfare measurement in the case of stochastic prices and other stochastic factors under risk aversion (concave utility). Welfare measurement under risk was first developed by the authors of this book in its predecessor version (Just, Hueth and Schmitz 1982) and was shortly thereafter developed with a different approach but comparable results (Pope, Chavas and Just 1983). While the results are developed for the case of a producer, Appendix Section 14.B further clarifies that similar results apply for consumers who face stochastic prices but must make decisions before all relevant prices are known, for example, where adjustment costs or fixity of consumer durables limit the ability to adjust short-run consumption. Specifically, this appendix provides the mathematical results that support Section 12.6.

12.A RISK AVERSION AND EXPECTED UTILITY MAXIMIZATION

The results of Appendix Sections 4.A through 4.C can be generalized to consider the case where production and prices are stochastic. Similar results follow in most instances. To demonstrate these results, continue with the notation of Appendix Section 4.A with the corresponding assumptions regarding properties of production functions. For the moment, assume that production is nonstochastic but that both output prices $\boldsymbol{p}=(p_1,\ldots,p_m)$ and input prices $\boldsymbol{w}=(w_1,\ldots,w_n)$ prices are random with $E(\boldsymbol{p})=\bar{\boldsymbol{p}}$ and $E(\boldsymbol{w})=\bar{\boldsymbol{w}}$. To represent the producer's risk preferences following the intuition of Appendix Section 12.6, suppose that the producer possesses a utility function U defined on profit π with $U'=\partial U/\partial\pi>0$ and $U''=\partial^2U/\partial\pi^2<0$. Suppose the production technology is represented by $\boldsymbol{q}=\boldsymbol{q}(\boldsymbol{x})=[q_1(\boldsymbol{x}),\ldots,q_m(\boldsymbol{x})]$ where $q_i(0)=0$, fixed production factors may exist but are not represented explicitly, and $\boldsymbol{q}(\boldsymbol{x})$ is assumed to be concave and twice differentiable with positive marginal productivities $q_{ij}'\equiv\partial q_i/\partial x_j>0$.[1] The producer's problem is thus

$$\max_x E[U(\boldsymbol{pq}(\boldsymbol{x})-\boldsymbol{wx}-\bar{K})|\boldsymbol{x}\geq 0 \tag{12.11}$$

where $\bar{K}$ is any *ex ante* payment required of the firm, including fixed costs. The purpose and importance of $\bar{K}$ becomes apparent below.

1. Some marginal productivities can also be identically zero for some outputs as in Appendix Section 4.A as long as the $\boldsymbol{x}$ vector includes only inputs that are used in at least one of the production processes represented in $\boldsymbol{q}(\boldsymbol{x})$.

First-order conditions for expected utility maximization assuming an internal solution are

$$E[U' \cdot (\boldsymbol{p}\boldsymbol{q}' - \boldsymbol{w}) = \boldsymbol{0} \tag{12.12}$$

where the arguments of U' and $\boldsymbol{q}'$ are suppressed for notational convenience and $\boldsymbol{q}' = \{q_{ij}'\}$ is a matrix with $q_{ij}' \equiv \partial q_i/\partial x_j$ in the ith row and jth column. Second-order conditions can be verified under assumptions outlined thus far. The solution to (12.12) can be written in principle as

$$\boldsymbol{x} = \tilde{\boldsymbol{x}}(\bar{\boldsymbol{p}},\bar{\boldsymbol{w}},\boldsymbol{\alpha},\bar{K}), \tag{12.13}$$

$$\boldsymbol{q} = \boldsymbol{q}(\tilde{\boldsymbol{x}}(\bar{\boldsymbol{p}},\bar{\boldsymbol{w}},\boldsymbol{\alpha},\bar{K})) = \tilde{\boldsymbol{q}}(\bar{\boldsymbol{p}},\bar{\boldsymbol{w}},\boldsymbol{\alpha},\bar{K}) \tag{12.14}$$

where $\boldsymbol{\alpha}$ is a vector of parameters (moments about expectations) characterizing the stochastic properties of $\boldsymbol{p}$ and $\boldsymbol{w}$ other than their expectations such that $\partial\boldsymbol{\varepsilon}/\partial\bar{\boldsymbol{p}} = \boldsymbol{0}$ and $\partial\boldsymbol{\delta}/\partial\bar{\boldsymbol{w}} = \boldsymbol{0}$ where $\boldsymbol{\varepsilon} \equiv \boldsymbol{p} - \bar{\boldsymbol{p}}$ and $\boldsymbol{\delta} \equiv \boldsymbol{w} - \bar{\boldsymbol{w}}$. Substituting (12.13) and (12.14) into (12.11) obtains the *indirect expected utility function*, which specifies maximum expected utility as a function of the stochastic properties of prices (including their expectations) and the *ex ante* payment,

$$V = V(\bar{\boldsymbol{p}},\bar{\boldsymbol{w}},\boldsymbol{\alpha},\bar{K}) \equiv E[U(\boldsymbol{p}\tilde{\boldsymbol{q}} - \boldsymbol{w}\tilde{\boldsymbol{x}} - \bar{K})],$$

where the arguments of $\tilde{\boldsymbol{q}}$ and $\tilde{\boldsymbol{x}}$ are suppressed for convenience.

In this context, one finds using (12.12) or the envelope theorem that

$$\begin{aligned} \boldsymbol{V}_{\bar{\boldsymbol{p}}} \equiv \partial V/\partial\bar{\boldsymbol{p}} &= E(U' \cdot \tilde{\boldsymbol{q}}) + E\left[U' \cdot \sum_{j=1}^{n}\left(\sum_{k=1}^{m} p_k q_{kj}' - w_j\right)\partial\tilde{x}_j/\partial\bar{\boldsymbol{p}}\right] \\ &= E(U') \cdot \tilde{\boldsymbol{q}} \end{aligned} \tag{12.15}$$

and

$$\begin{aligned} \boldsymbol{V}_{\bar{\boldsymbol{w}}} \equiv \partial V/\partial\bar{\boldsymbol{w}} &= E(U' \cdot \tilde{\boldsymbol{x}}) + E\left[U' \cdot \sum_{k=1}^{n}\left(\sum_{i=1}^{m} p_i q_{ik}' - w_k\right)\partial\tilde{x}_k/\partial\bar{\boldsymbol{w}}\right] \\ &= -E(U') \cdot \tilde{\boldsymbol{x}} \end{aligned} \tag{12.16}$$

or simply $\boldsymbol{V}_{\bar{\boldsymbol{p}}} = E(U') \cdot \tilde{\boldsymbol{q}}$ and $\boldsymbol{V}_{\bar{\boldsymbol{w}}} = -E(U') \cdot \tilde{\boldsymbol{x}}$ where $\tilde{\boldsymbol{x}}$ is an *ex ante* (thus nonstochastic) decision function.

12.B EVALUATING AN EXPECTED OUTPUT PRICE CHANGE

To consider economic welfare measurement for an expected output price change, define $\hat{C}_i(\bar{p}_i^0,\bar{p}_i^1)$ as the compensating variation of a change in expected price for q_i from $\bar{p}_i^0$ to $\bar{p}_i^1$, which implies that

$$E[U(\bar{\boldsymbol{p}}^1+\boldsymbol{\varepsilon})\cdot\tilde{\boldsymbol{q}}(\bar{\boldsymbol{p}}^1,\bar{\boldsymbol{w}},\boldsymbol{\alpha},\bar{K}+\hat{C}_i)-\boldsymbol{w}\cdot\tilde{\boldsymbol{x}}(\bar{\boldsymbol{p}}^1,\bar{\boldsymbol{w}},\boldsymbol{\alpha},\bar{K}+\hat{C}_i)-\bar{K}-\hat{C}_i)] \\ =E[U((\bar{\boldsymbol{p}}^0+\boldsymbol{\varepsilon})\cdot\tilde{\boldsymbol{q}}(\bar{\boldsymbol{p}}^0,\bar{\boldsymbol{w}},\boldsymbol{\alpha},\bar{K})-\boldsymbol{w}\cdot\tilde{\boldsymbol{x}}(\bar{\boldsymbol{p}}^0,\bar{\boldsymbol{w}},\boldsymbol{\alpha},\bar{K})-\bar{K})]\equiv V_0 \tag{12.17}$$

where for convenience $\bar{\boldsymbol{p}}^i=(\bar{p}_1,\ldots,\bar{p}_{k-1},\bar{p}_k^i,\bar{p}_{k+1},\ldots,\bar{p}_m)$ for $i = 0, 1$. Differentiating both sides of (12.17) with respect to the subsequent price $\bar{p}_i^1$ and using (12.15) yields

$$E(U')\cdot\tilde{q}_i(\bar{\boldsymbol{p}}^1,\bar{\boldsymbol{w}},\boldsymbol{\alpha},\bar{K}+\hat{C}_i)-E[U'\cdot\partial\hat{C}_i/\partial\bar{p}_i^1]=0. \tag{12.18}$$

Assuming that $\hat{C}_i$ is an *ex ante* compensation, it must be nonstochastic, so that (12.18) implies that

$$\tilde{q}_i(\bar{\boldsymbol{p}}^1,\bar{\boldsymbol{w}},\boldsymbol{\alpha},\bar{K}+\hat{C}_i)=\frac{\partial C_i}{\partial\bar{p}_i^1}. \tag{12.19}$$

Also, because $\tilde{q}_i(\bar{\boldsymbol{p}}^1,\bar{\boldsymbol{w}},\boldsymbol{\alpha},\bar{K}+\hat{C}_i)$ is a supply curve that varies $\hat{C}_i$ to maintain the initial expected utility level V_0, it may be reparameterized as

$$\bar{q}_i(\bar{\boldsymbol{p}}^1,\bar{\boldsymbol{w}},\boldsymbol{\alpha},V_0)\equiv\tilde{q}_i(\bar{\boldsymbol{p}},\bar{\boldsymbol{w}},\boldsymbol{\alpha},\bar{K}+\hat{C}_i(\bar{p}_i^0,\bar{p}_i^1)). \tag{12.20}$$

Thus, using (12.19) and (12.20), and noting that $\hat{C}_i(\bar{p}_i^0,\bar{p}_i^0)=0$, *the compensating variation of a change in expected output price is given by the change in producer surplus associated with the corresponding compensated supply curve conditioned on the initial expected utility level and taken as a function of expected price,*

$$\hat{C}_i(\bar{p}_i^0,\bar{p}_i^1)=\int_{\bar{p}_i^0}^{\bar{p}_i^1}\bar{q}_i(\bar{\boldsymbol{p}},\bar{\boldsymbol{w}},\boldsymbol{\alpha},V_0)d\bar{p}_i. \tag{12.21}$$

Additionally noting that $\hat{E}_i(\bar{p}_i^1,\bar{p}_i^0)=-\hat{C}_i(\bar{p}_i^0,\bar{p}_i^1)$, where $\hat{E}_i(\bar{p}_i^1,\bar{p}_i^0)$ is the equivalent variation of an expected output price change from $\bar{p}_i^1$, to $\bar{p}_i^0$, one finds that

$$\hat{E}_i(\bar{p}_i^0,\bar{p}_i^1)=\int_{\bar{p}_i^0}^{\bar{p}_i^1}\bar{q}_i(\bar{\boldsymbol{p}},\bar{\boldsymbol{w}},\boldsymbol{\alpha},V_1)d\bar{p}_i \tag{12.22}$$

where $V_1=V(\bar{\boldsymbol{p}}^1,\bar{\boldsymbol{w}},\boldsymbol{\alpha},\bar{K})$. That is, *the equivalent variation of an expected output price change is given by the change in producer surplus associated with the corresponding compensated supply conditioned on the subsequent expected utility level and taken as a function of expected price.*

As suggested by this derivation, the compensating and equivalent variations no longer necessarily coincide in the producer case under risk, just as they do not coincide in the consumer case. The reason is that the size of the *ex ante* payment can affect the producer's aversion to risk. For example, after giving a producing firm a large amount of money, it may not be as averse to risk as before. This effect occurs because supplies and demands depend on the *ex ante* payment or compensation. If supplies and demands do not depend on the *ex ante* payment, the compensating and equivalent variations coincide. In general, the two coincide only under *constant absolute risk aversion*, in which case $r_a=-U''/U'$, the coefficient of absolute risk aversion, is constant over all levels of profit.

To see this, one can differentiate (12.12) with respect to $\bar{K}$ (which is an argument in U') and impose the condition that supplies and demands ($\boldsymbol{q}$ and $\boldsymbol{x}$) do not depend on $\bar{K}$, which implies that

$$\mathrm{E}(U''\cdot \boldsymbol{p})\boldsymbol{q}' = \mathrm{E}(U''\cdot \boldsymbol{w})$$

as compared with the direct implications of (12.12),

$$\mathrm{E}(U'\cdot \boldsymbol{p})\boldsymbol{q}' = \mathrm{E}(U'\cdot \boldsymbol{w})$$

If U'' is a scalar multiple of U', then these two conditions on decisions are the same and imply that optimal decisions do not depend on $\bar{K}$ (as under constant absolute risk aversion). Furthermore, considering all possible price distributions, it is clear that this is the only condition under which optimal decisions do not change with $\bar{K}$ generally. Thus, the compensating and equivalent variations coincide, and supplies and demands do not depend on compensation (of fixed costs), if and only if absolute risk aversion is constant.

Kenneth Arrow (1971) has argued long ago that absolute risk aversion is not constant but decreasing. Nevertheless, for empirical purposes, the assumption of constant absolute risk aversion has continued to be used in many applications because of convenience. The mean-variance expected utility methodology suggested in Chapter 12, where decisions do not depend on fixed costs or nonstochastic compensation payments, is the most common framework examined under constant absolute risk aversion. For empirical purposes, however, more general assumptions are possible. For example, if data are available on fixed costs, they give a basis for estimating the dependence of supplies and demands on payments that are fixed *ex ante*. For empirical purposes, the utility function appropriately depends on initial wealth in addition to current profits when absolute risk aversion is not constant. Changes in initial wealth enter the utility function in the same way as does an *ex ante* payment to the firm in a standard expected utility problem. Thus, necessary data must include wealth and fixed costs when the assumption of constant absolute risk aversion is relaxed. Furthermore, upon estimation, one is faced with solution of the differential equation in (12.19) with boundary condition $\hat{C}_i(\bar{p}_i^0,\bar{p}_i^0)=0$ in the case of compensating variation and $\hat{C}_i(\bar{p}_i^0,\bar{p}_i^1)=0$ in the case of equivalent variation before welfare effects can be calculated.

12.C EVALUATING AN EXPECTED INPUT PRICE CHANGE

Consider next the possibility of measuring the welfare effect of an expected input price change from, say, $\bar{w}_j^0$ to $\bar{w}_j^1$. If $\tilde{C}_i(\bar{w}_j^0,\bar{w}_j^1)$ measures the compensating variation of a change in the expectation of the jth input price, then by definition,

$$\begin{aligned} &E[U(\boldsymbol{p}\tilde{\boldsymbol{q}}(\bar{\boldsymbol{p}},\bar{\boldsymbol{w}}^1,\boldsymbol{\alpha},\bar{K}+\tilde{C}_i)-(\bar{\boldsymbol{w}}^1+\boldsymbol{\delta})\tilde{\boldsymbol{x}}(\bar{\boldsymbol{p}},\bar{\boldsymbol{w}}^1,\boldsymbol{\alpha},\bar{K}+\tilde{C}_i)-\bar{K}-\tilde{C}_i)] \\ &\quad = E[U(\boldsymbol{p}\tilde{\boldsymbol{q}}(\bar{\boldsymbol{p}},\bar{\boldsymbol{w}}^0,\boldsymbol{\alpha},\bar{K})-(\bar{\boldsymbol{w}}^0+\boldsymbol{\delta})\tilde{\boldsymbol{x}}(\bar{\boldsymbol{p}},\bar{\boldsymbol{w}}^0,\boldsymbol{\alpha},\bar{K})-\bar{K})]\equiv V_0 \end{aligned} \tag{12.23}$$

where for convenience $\bar{\boldsymbol{w}}^i=(\bar{w}_1,\ldots,\bar{w}_{j-1},\bar{w}_j^i,\bar{w}_{j+1},\ldots,\bar{w}_n)$ for $i\neq 0,1$. Differentiating both sides of (12.23) with respect to the subsequent price $\bar{w}_j^1$ and using (12.16) implies that

$$-E(U')\cdot\tilde{x}_j(\bar{\boldsymbol{p}},\bar{\boldsymbol{w}}^1,\boldsymbol{\alpha},\bar{K}+\tilde{C}_j)-E(U'\partial\tilde{C}_j/\partial\bar{w}_j^1)=0. \tag{12.24}$$

Again, if $\tilde{C}_j$ is an *ex ante* compensation and thus does not depend on randomness in prices, (12.24) implies that

$$\tilde{x}_j(\bar{\mathbf{p}},\bar{\mathbf{w}}^1,\boldsymbol{\alpha},\bar{K}+\tilde{C}_j)=\frac{\partial \tilde{C}_j}{\partial \bar{w}_j^1}. \tag{12.25}$$

Also, because $\tilde{x}_j(\bar{\mathbf{p}},\bar{\mathbf{w}}^1,\boldsymbol{\alpha},\bar{K}+\tilde{C}_j)$ is a demand curve that varies $\tilde{C}_j$ to hold expected utility at the initial level V_0, one can reparameterize as

$$\tilde{x}_j(\bar{\mathbf{p}},\bar{\mathbf{w}}^1,\boldsymbol{\alpha},V_0)\equiv\tilde{x}_j(\bar{\mathbf{p}},\bar{\mathbf{w}}^1,\boldsymbol{\alpha},\bar{K}+\tilde{C}_j) \tag{12.26}$$

Using (12.25) and (12.26) and noting that $\tilde{C}_j(\bar{w}_j^0,\bar{w}_j^0)=0$ yields

$$\tilde{C}_j(\bar{w}_j^0,\bar{w}_j^1)=-\int_{\bar{w}_j^0}^{\bar{w}_j^1}\tilde{x}_j(\bar{\mathbf{p}},\bar{\mathbf{w}},\boldsymbol{\alpha},V_0)d\bar{w}_j. \tag{12.27}$$

That is, *the compensating variation of an expected input price change is given by the change in consumer surplus associated with the corresponding compensated derived demand curve conditioned on the initial expected utility level and taken as a function of the expected input price.* Similarly, noting that $\tilde{E}_j(\bar{w}_j^1,\bar{w}_j^0)=-\tilde{C}_j(\bar{w}_j^0,\bar{w}_j^1)$, where $\tilde{E}_j(\bar{w}_j^1,\bar{w}_j^0)$ is the equivalent variation of an expected input price change from $\bar{w}_j^1$ to $\bar{w}_j^0$, one finds that

$$\tilde{E}_j(\bar{w}_j^0,\bar{w}_j^1)=-\int_{\bar{w}_j^0}^{\bar{w}_j^1}\tilde{x}_j(\bar{\mathbf{p}},\bar{\mathbf{w}},\boldsymbol{\alpha},V_1)d\bar{w}_j \tag{12.28}$$

where $V_1=V(\bar{\mathbf{p}},\bar{\mathbf{w}}^1,\boldsymbol{\alpha},\bar{K})$. That is, *the equivalent variation of an expected input price change is given by the change in consumer surplus associated with the corresponding compensated derived demand curve conditioned on the subsequent expected utility level and taken as a function of the expected input price.*

As in the consumer problem, the compensating and equivalent variations no longer coincide generally when risk is added to the producer problem. However, as shown above, optimal decisions generally do not depend on the *ex ante* payment and, thus, derived demands do not depend on $\bar{K}+\tilde{C}_j$ in (12.25) if and only if absolute risk aversion is constant. Hence, under constant absolute risk aversion, the compensating and equivalent variations associated with expected input price changes coincide. Again, comments similar to the supply estimation problem apply to empirical data needs in estimating derived demands when absolute risk aversion is not constant. Again, solution of the differential equation in (12.25) is required before welfare effects can be calculated. The appropriate boundary condition is $\tilde{C}_j(\bar{w}_j^0,\bar{w}_j^0)=0$ for calculating compensating variation and $\tilde{C}_j(\bar{w}_j^0,\bar{w}_j^1)=0$ for calculating equivalent variation.

Coupling the results in (12.27) and (12.28) with the supply results in (12.21) and (12.22) implies that any general change in some or all expected prices can be evaluated using essentially the sequential approach of Appendix Section 4.A, where each expected price change is evaluated conditionally on all preceding expected price change considerations. However, ordinary supplies and demands can be used for these calculations if and only if absolute risk aversion is constant. If absolute risk aversion is not constant, the calculations must be based on compensated supplies and demands, and each expected price change consideration must be conditioned on compensation corresponding to all preceding expected price change considerations. This approach thus becomes somewhat impractical because it involves solution of a system of differential equations composed of (12.19) and (12.25) for $i = 1, ..., m$ and $j = 1, ..., n$. Appendix Section 6.D contains a similar case related to consumer welfare measurement.

12.D EVALUATING OTHER CHANGES AFFECTING A RISK-AVERSE FIRM

Although the methodology described above gives a feasible approach in evaluating welfare change associated with expected price changes, it remains to consider the welfare effects of changes in risk or other parameters affecting the firm. To do this, suppose that output q_i is an essential output in the sense that there exists an expected price $\tilde{p}_i$ low enough to cause the firm to shut down. Specifically, for a general price-risk change from $(\bar{\mathbf{p}}^0,\bar{\mathbf{w}}^0,\boldsymbol{\alpha}^0)$ to $(\bar{\mathbf{p}}^1,\bar{\mathbf{w}}^1,\boldsymbol{\alpha}^1)$ where, without loss of generality, the first output is an essential output, define

$$\tilde{p}_1^k = \max\{\bar{p}_1 | \bar{\mathbf{x}}(\bar{p}_1,\bar{p}_2^k,...,\bar{p}_m^k,\bar{\mathbf{w}}^k,\boldsymbol{\alpha}^k,\bar{K}+C^0) = \mathbf{0}\},\ k = 0,1,$$

where C_0 denotes any compensation received in the shutdown case. Then note that the compensating variation C of the overall change is given implicitly by

$$V(\bar{\mathbf{p}}^1,\bar{\mathbf{w}}^1,\boldsymbol{\alpha}^1,\bar{K}+C) = V(\bar{\mathbf{p}}^0,\bar{\mathbf{w}}^0,\boldsymbol{\alpha}^0,\bar{K}).$$

For conceptual purposes, this change can be broken into several steps, where, first, the expected price $\bar{p}_1$ is changed from $\bar{p}_1^0$ to $\tilde{p}_1^0$, which forces a shutdown; then all parameters are changed from $(\tilde{p}_1^0,\bar{p}_2^0,...,\bar{p}_m^0,\bar{\mathbf{w}}^0,\boldsymbol{\alpha}^0)$ to $(\tilde{p}_1^1,\bar{p}_2^1,...,\bar{p}_m^1,\bar{\mathbf{w}}^1,\boldsymbol{\alpha}^1)$ which also corresponds to a shutdown; and finally, expected price $\bar{p}_1$ is changed from $\tilde{p}_1^1$ to $\bar{p}_1^1$. In this context, note that

$$\begin{aligned} V(\bar{\mathbf{p}}^1,\bar{\mathbf{w}}^1,\boldsymbol{\alpha}^1,\bar{K}+C_1+C_2) &= V(\tilde{p}_1^1,\bar{p}_2^1,...,\bar{p}_m^1,\bar{\mathbf{w}}^1,\boldsymbol{\alpha}^1,\bar{K}+C_1) \\ &= V(\tilde{p}_1^0,\bar{p}_2^0,...,\bar{p}_m^0,\bar{\mathbf{w}}_0,\boldsymbol{\alpha}^0,\bar{K}+C_1) \\ &= V(\bar{\mathbf{p}}^0,\bar{\mathbf{w}}^0,\boldsymbol{\alpha}^0,\bar{K}) = V_0 \end{aligned} \tag{12.29}$$

for some C_1, where $C = C_1 + C_2$ because the first two right-hand sides of (12.29) each represent a shutdown case with $V = U(\bar{K} + C_1) = V_0$. Following (12.17) to (12.21) with respect to the third equality in (12.29) implies that

$$C_1 = -\int_{\tilde{p}_1^0}^{\bar{p}_1^0} \bar{q}_1(\bar{p}_1,\bar{p}_2^0,...,\bar{p}_m^0,\bar{\mathbf{w}}^0,\boldsymbol{\alpha}^0,V_0)d\bar{p}_1 \tag{12.30}$$

where $V_0 = V(\bar{\mathbf{p}}^0,\bar{\mathbf{w}}^0,\boldsymbol{\alpha}^0,\bar{K})$. A similar application of (12.17) to (12.21) to the first equality in (12.29) where $\bar{K}$ is replaced by $\bar{K} + C_1$ also implies that

$$C_2 = \int_{\tilde{p}_1^1}^{\bar{p}_1^1} \bar{q}_1(\bar{p}_1,\bar{p}_2^1,...,\bar{p}_m^1,\bar{\mathbf{w}}^1,\boldsymbol{\alpha}^1,V_0)d\bar{p}_1 \tag{12.31}$$

because C_1 is the compensation that restores the initial expected utility level in the event of a shutdown following (12.29). *The overall compensating variation of the general change* *in parameters ($\bar{\boldsymbol{p}}$,$\bar{\boldsymbol{w}}$ or $\boldsymbol{\alpha}$) affecting the firm is thus given by the change in producer surplus associated with the compensated supply of an essential (nonstochastic) output conditioned on the initial level of expected utility and taken as a function of the respective expected price* (that is, $C = C_1 + C_2$).

Of course, similar results can be attained for measuring equivalent variation except that the compensated supply curve must be conditioned on the terminal level of expected utility. Again, however, the compensating and equivalent variations will generally coincide if, and only if, absolute risk aversion is constant, in which case the foregoing conclusions hold with respect to ordinary supply curves.

Turning to the demand side, similar results are possible in the case of an essential input, say x_1, for which

$$\tilde{w}_1^k = \min\{\bar{w}_1 | \bar{x}(\bar{\boldsymbol{p}}^k, \bar{w}_1, \bar{w}_2^k, \ldots, \bar{w}_n^k, \boldsymbol{\alpha}^k, \bar{K} + C_0) = 0\},\ k = 0,1,$$

where again C_0 is any compensation pertinent to the shutdown case. In this case,

$$\begin{aligned} V(\bar{\boldsymbol{p}}^1, \bar{\boldsymbol{w}}^1, \boldsymbol{\alpha}^1, \bar{K} + C_1 + C_2) &= V(\bar{\boldsymbol{p}}^1, \tilde{w}_1^1, \bar{w}_2^1, \ldots, \bar{w}_n^1, \boldsymbol{\alpha}^1, \bar{K} + C_1) \\ &= V(\bar{\boldsymbol{p}}^0, \tilde{w}_1^0, \bar{w}_2^0, \ldots, \bar{w}_n^0, \boldsymbol{\alpha}^0, \bar{K} + C_1) \\ &= V(\bar{\boldsymbol{p}}^0, \bar{\boldsymbol{w}}^0, \boldsymbol{\alpha}^0, \bar{K}) = V_0 \end{aligned} \tag{12.32}$$

where again both sides of the second equality represent a shutdown case with $V = U(\bar{K} + C_1) = V_0$. Following (12.23) to (12.27) with respect to the third equality of (12.32) yields

$$C_1 = \int_{\bar{w}_1^0}^{\tilde{w}_1^0} \bar{x}(\bar{\boldsymbol{p}}^0, \bar{w}_1, \bar{w}_2^0, \ldots, \bar{w}_n^0, \boldsymbol{\alpha}^0, V_0) d\bar{w}_1$$

and a similar application to the first equality implies that

$$C_2 = -\int_{\bar{w}_1^1}^{\tilde{w}_1^1} \bar{x}(\bar{\boldsymbol{p}}^1, \bar{w}_1, \bar{w}_2^1, \ldots, \bar{w}_n^1, \boldsymbol{\alpha}^1, V_0) d\bar{w}_1.$$

Thus, *the overall compensating variation of a general change in parameters* ($\bar{\boldsymbol{p}}$,$\bar{\boldsymbol{w}}$ or $\boldsymbol{\alpha}$) *affecting the firm is given by the change in consumer surplus associated with the compensated derived demand of an essential input conditioned on the initial level of expected utility and taken as a function of the respective expected input price* (that is, $C = C_1 + C_2$). Again, similar results apply for measuring equivalent variation where the compensated derived demand is conditioned on the subsequent level of expected utility. And again, the compensating and equivalent variations coincide generally if and only if absolute risk aversion is constant, in which case the foregoing conclusions hold for ordinary, as well as compensated, derived demands.

12.E STOCHASTIC PRODUCTION AND STATE-DEPENDENT COMPENSATION

Although the results with stochastic prices are quite similar to those with nonstochastic prices, the results are somewhat more troublesome if production is also stochastic. If production is stochastic, one can simply assume that the q_i functions are random and return to the derivation in (12.11), (12.12) and so on. The only difference that occurs is that $E(U'\cdot\tilde{q}) \neq E(U')\cdot E(\tilde{q})$ unless the producer is risk-neutral (U' is constant), so the results in (12.15), (12.18) through (12.22), and (12.30) and (12.31) do not follow. Hence, welfare calculations based on expected supply curves are not justified except in the case of risk neutrality. Alternatively, however, where $x_1, \ldots, x_n$ represent *ex ante* decisions, they must be made before observing the random components of prices or production and are thus nonstochastic from the standpoint of the decision-maker. Thus, all the results above relating to welfare calculations associated with derived demands continue to hold and give a substantial basis for economic welfare analysis of producers under both stochastic prices and stochastic production.

As another alternative, one could consider a *random* or *state-dependent compensation function* where compensation depends on the state of nature as suggested in Section 12.6. While, as demonstrated in Section 12.6, many state-dependent compensation schemes that leave the decision-maker equally well off are generally possible, one specific possibility that can demonstrate state-dependent compensation is the case of *ex post* compensating variation. Differentiating the equation

$$V(\bar{\mathbf{p}}^1,\bar{\mathbf{w}},\boldsymbol{\alpha},\bar{K}+C_i)=V(\bar{\mathbf{p}}^0,\bar{\mathbf{w}},\boldsymbol{\alpha},\bar{K})=V_0$$

with respect to $\bar{p}_i^1$ obtains

$$E\{U'[\tilde{q}_i(\bar{\mathbf{p}}^1,\bar{\mathbf{w}},\boldsymbol{\alpha},\bar{K}+C_i)-\partial C_i/\partial\bar{p}_i^1]\}=0.$$

Thus, if

$$\tilde{q}_i(\bar{\mathbf{p}}^1,\bar{\mathbf{w}},\boldsymbol{\alpha},\bar{K}+C_i)=\partial C_i/\partial\bar{p}_i^1$$

for every state of nature, then C_i determines the *ex post* compensating variation, which keeps the producer's welfare position the same with and without the change for every state of nature.

The problems associated with using *ex post* compensating variation as opposed to other *ex post* compensation schemes are discussed in Section 12.6. But an additional potential of *strategic behavior* must be considered with any type of *ex post* compensation scheme. That is, the compensation must be specified for the producer in advance (so it will affect the producer's decisions), but it must be specified as depending on the exogenous state of nature rather than some endogenous manifestation of the state of nature as represented by the producer's decisions. Otherwise, the producer may strategically alter behavior in an attempt to influence the amount of compensation received, in which case welfare calculations based on *ex post* supply may not be appropriate. For example, compensation must either be based on what *ex post* supply would be without strategic behavior or else compensation must take account of strategic behavior.

12.F DUALITY AND INTEGRABILITY

Finally, consider extension of the empirical possibilities in Appendix Section 8.B. Again, both primal and dual approaches are possible, but calculations are so tedious with the primal approach that they are practical only for very specific probability distributions and utility functions (for example, with normally distributed prices and exponential utility).[2]

Applying steps from the dual approach, however, one finds, using (12.11), (12.15) and (12.16), that

$$\frac{\partial V/\partial \bar{\boldsymbol{p}}}{\partial V/\partial \bar{K}} = -\frac{E(U')\cdot \tilde{\boldsymbol{q}}}{E(U')} = -\tilde{\boldsymbol{q}} \tag{12.33}$$

when production is nonstochastic, and

$$\frac{\partial V/\partial \bar{\boldsymbol{w}}}{\partial V/\partial \bar{K}} = +\frac{E(U')\cdot \tilde{\boldsymbol{x}}}{E(U')} = \tilde{\boldsymbol{x}} \tag{12.34}$$

whether or not production is stochastic. Thus, once an indirect expected utility function is arbitrarily specified, it is a simple matter to derive all the implied input demand specifications (and output supply specifications if production is nonstochastic) so that appropriate parameter restrictions can be applied across equations to ensure that all estimated equations relate to a common underlying expected utility maximization problem (so that implied welfare effects are unique, as implied by theory). One should note, however, that the literature to date has not developed flexible functional forms that approximate both arbitrary preferences and technology jointly.[3] Nevertheless, this approach appears to dominate arbitrary specification of supplies and demands, in which case the estimated equations may suggest nonunique welfare effects. Furthermore, this approach avoids the need to solve differential equations in computing willingness to pay for various changes when absolute risk aversion is not constant because estimates of (12.33) and (12.34) for the various outputs and inputs of the firm generally provide sufficient information to compute the necessary compensation in the context of the initial specification for V using the approach of equation (12.29). See Appendix Section 6.F for a similar example in the case of the consumer problem.

2. See, for example, the application by Freund (1956).
3. For example, flexible indirect forms for producers, such as the flexible quasirent or profit functions in Appendix Section 8.B, have not been generalized to the case of risk aversion. However, a flexible direct form for representing risk preferences has been developed by Chavas and Holt (1996).

13. Nonmarket welfare measurement with applications to environmental economic policy

Assuming perfect competition prevails throughout an economy, Section 2.5 showed that competition leads to Pareto optimality. Hence, government intervention is not needed to reach some degree of social optimality. More generally, however, the conditions of perfect competition impose a variety of specific assumptions including rivalry, excludability, appropriability, absence of externalities, competitive behavior (taking prices as given), symmetric information and complete markets. When any one of these specific assumptions fails, some form of government intervention may be required to reach Pareto optimality. Chapter 10 relaxes the assumption of competitive behavior. Chapter 11 relaxes the assumption of symmetric information. Chapters 12 relaxes the assumption of complete markets related to risks and unforeseen contingencies. Chapter 13 now turns to relaxing assumptions related to rivalry, excludability, appropriability and externalities including absence of complete markets for externalities.

With these assumptions, this book has dealt with market welfare measurement, that is, the measurement of welfare effects that are fully reflected by market phenomena. This chapter turns to nonmarket welfare measurement where individual preferences are not necessarily completely reflected in observable decisions in the marketplace. In a modern economy with large corporations, a growing government sector and increasing pollution problems, the measurement of nonmarket welfare effects is of increasing importance. For example, when an industry pollutes either air or water through its production process, it does not generally take account of those adverse effects in deciding how much to produce given the market prices of its products unless regulations require it to do so. Similarly, when a government decides to build a bridge, it may be able to determine the demand for crossing the bridge, but it may not measure in any way the utility or disutility derived by individuals from looking at the bridge. Problems of the former type are termed externalities, whereas problems of the latter type have to do with public goods, which can be viewed as a generalized externality problem. This chapter deals first in some detail with externalities and then discusses the problem of public goods. The latter part of the chapter then turns to possibilities for measuring the associated welfare effects.

13.1 EXTERNALITIES

An *externality* is defined as the case where an action of one economic agent affects the utility or production possibilities of another in a way that is not reflected in the marketplace. External effects are often classified into the effects of consumers on consumers, producers on producers, producers on consumers, and consumers on producers. Smoking is a common example of a consumer–consumer externality. When a smoker enters a restaurant and chooses to light a cigarette, it may create an unpleasant odor and cancer risk for a nonsmoker also patronizing the restaurant. Because the smoker pays for cigarettes, those actions are partially reflected in the marketplace, but the smoker does not pay the nonsmoker for the right to smoke nor does a market exist for the nonsmoker to pay the smoker to cease smoking in the restaurant! Another example of a consumer–consumer externality is the common phenomenon of 'keeping up with the Joneses'. When the family next door buys a new Lexus or Mercedes, another may become more unhappy with their Honda than previously. Again, the behavior of the family purchasing the new car is partially reflected in the marketplace by the automobile purchase, but no market exists to reflect the effect of that purchase on the neighbors. Thus, market behavior cannot possibly reflect any utility or disutility derived by one individual associated with another's consumption.

Perhaps the most widely publicized external effects are those of producers on consumers. These include the effects of industrial pollution of air and water resources. For example, when a steel plant discharges contaminants into the air, it may detract from the aesthetic qualities of the environment and may even lead to disease or other adverse effects on consumers that are not reflected in the marketplace. Similarly, if a lumber company removes all the trees from a mountainside, it may lead to flooding as well as a decrease in the aesthetic value of the mountain. The value of the lumber for building purposes will be reflected in the market for lumber, but if the lumber company does not pay for the damage due to flooding and does not compensate consumers for the loss of aesthetic pleasures in viewing the mountain, it will generally be inclined to remove too many trees from the mountainside.

With respect to external effects on producers, the effects of consumers on producers have received much less attention. Perhaps the most common external effect of consumers on producers involves theft and vandalism. The external effects of producers on producers, on the other hand, have received substantial attention and have involved a large number of legal disputes in the courts. A common agricultural producer externality involves the case where a farmer applies pesticides to his or her crop to control damaging insects but, as a result of adverse winds, kills a neighboring beekeeper's bees. The benefits of the farmer's increased production are reflected in the marketplace, but unless the beekeeper sues for damages, the farmer does not pay for the beekeeper's losses and hence will tend to overuse pesticides. Another common producer–producer externality is involved in the case where an industry pollutes a river through its production process and, as a result, the fish in the river are killed or contaminated so that fishermen suffer adverse effects.

Each of these examples involves a case where one individual is adversely affected by another's actions. External effects are not necessarily negative, however. Some consumers may be positively affected by an increase in the consumption of others. For example, a rich person may enjoy seeing the consumption of a poor person increase. Giving to charities designed to help the poor is evidence that this type of positive consumption–consumption externality can exist. In the producer–producer case, one farmer may find a pesticide application much more effective if neighboring farmers also apply the same types of pesticides, so that untreated pest populations do not immediately move into his or her fields from neighboring fields as soon as the effects of the pesticides have worn off.

Social Optimality

When externalities exist, a competitive economy will generally not attain a Pareto equilibrium (the assumptions used in Section 2.5 will not apply). To consider a concrete example, suppose that a producer–producer externality exists between two firms. Let the production function of the first firm be given by $q_1 = x_1{}^{1/2}$ and the production function of the second firm be given by $q_2 = x_2{}^{1/2} - x_0$, where x_0 is considered as a constant by the second firm. Suppose that both firms are profit maximizers with the prices of q_1, q_2, x_1 and x_2 given, respectively, by p_1, p_2, w_1, and w_2. Assume further that the second firm purchases only x_2 as an input and that $x_0 = x_1{}^{1/2}$ is imposed upon it as an externality by the first firm's input decision.

The first firm will maximize its profit $p_1q_1 - w_1x_1$, by equating its output price p_1 to its marginal cost, $2w_1q_1$, thus choosing an output quantity, $q_1 = p_1/(2w_1)$.[1] The second firm maximizes its profit, $p_2q_2 - w_2x_2$, by equating its price, p_2, with its marginal cost, $2w_2(q_2 + x_1^{1/2})$, given the amount of x_1 used by the first firm, thus obtaining the quantity $q_2 = (p_2 - 2w_2x_1^{1/2})/(2w_2)$. In other words, what constitutes optimal behavior for the second firm depends on what the first firm does.

These solutions represent a *competitive equilibrium in the presence of the externality*. Obviously, the first firm imposes a cost on the second firm in its choice of x_1 that is not reflected in the marketplace and is not considered in its profit maximization. The external effect as a function of x_1 is given by $p_2x_1^{1/2}$ and represents the damage imposed on the second firm by the input decision of the first firm. This function is called the *damage function*. The damage function gives the total external cost as a function of the amount of the pollutant (x_1 is the pollutant in this case). Social or Pareto optimality is not attained by the competitive equilibrium because this cost or damage by the first firm is not considered in its choice of action. In point of fact, the cost considered by the first firm in its profit maximization is only its *private cost*, where private cost is defined as that cost actually incurred by the individual as a result of his or her actions. The social cost that should be considered is the sum of the firm's private cost and its external cost. Social optimality for the decision of firm 1 is attained by equating its output price with its marginal social cost rather than its marginal private cost, $2w_1q_1$, used above. The social cost, $w_1x_1 + p_2x_1^{1/2}$, is obtained as the sum of private cost, w_1x_1, and external cost. Similarly, the marginal social cost of the output decision, $2w_1q_1 + p_2$, is determined by the sum of marginal private cost, $2w_1q_1$, and marginal external cost, p_2.[2] The social optimum production for firm 1 obtained by equating its product price with its marginal social cost is $q_1 = (p_1 - p_2)/(2w_1)$.

To see more clearly that this indeed represents a social optimum, consider the approach

1. The firm's marginal cost is determined here by expressing total variable cost, w_1x_1, as a function of q_1 through substitution of the inverse of the production function for x_1, that is $x_1 = q_1^2$, and then computing the derivative of total variable cost with respect to q_1.
2. The marginal cost associated with q_1 production is determined here by expressing the total external cost as a function of q_1 rather than x_1 through substitution of the production function for q_1 and then computing the derivative with respect to q_1. In this special case the analysis of externalities can be done in either the output market or the input market. More generally, producer externalities arise from emissions or residuals related to firm production or input decisions where emissions are not in fixed proportions to production or input use. In such cases, the analysis must be done in a market that considers the supply and demand for emissions reduction. Considerations are then similar to the case of pollution abatement discussed later in this section.

of *internalization*.[3] Internalization is an approach commonly used to determine social optimality in the presence of externalities by considering all of the involved economic agents jointly, as, for example, in a hypothetical merger of firms. In the preceding case, where the prices of both inputs and outputs are truly fixed for both firms, the externality can be internalized by maximizing the joint profits of the two firms as if the two firms were merged. Joint profit is given by $p_1q_1+p_2q_2-w_1x_1-w_2x_2$. Substituting for q_1 and q_2 using the respective production functions yields $p_1x_1^{1/2}+p_2x_2^{1/2}-p_2x_1^{1/2}-w_1x_1-w_2x_2$, and the associated first-order conditions of calculus for maximization require $(p_1-p_2)/(2x_1^{1/2})-w_1=0$ and $p_2/(2x_2^{1/2})-w_2=0$. Solving the first condition and substituting the first production function verifies that $q_1=(p_1-p_2)/(2w_1)$ under social optimality.

Substituting the resulting decisions in the case of competitive equilibrium in the presence of externalities leads to profit $p_1^2/(4w_1)$ for the first firm and profit $p_2^2/(4w_2)-p_2p_1/(2w_1)$ for the second firm. Using the results for the internalized solution implies joint profit for the two firms of $(p_1-p_2)^2/(4w_1)+p_2^2/(4w_2)$. The latter profit is obviously larger by $p_2^2/(4w_1)$, indicating that the competitive equilibrium in the presence of externalities is Pareto suboptimal. That is, *by moving to the internalized solution, the second firm gains more than the first firm loses and can thus compensate the first firm for its losses and still be better off.*

To understand these concepts diagrammatically and to demonstrate the general externality problem, consider Figure 13.1, where the marginal private cost of q production is represented by MPC, which is the competitive supply curve in the presence of externalities. Suppose marginal external cost is represented by MEC so that marginal social cost is represented by MSC = MPC + MEC. Note that, in general, the marginal external cost

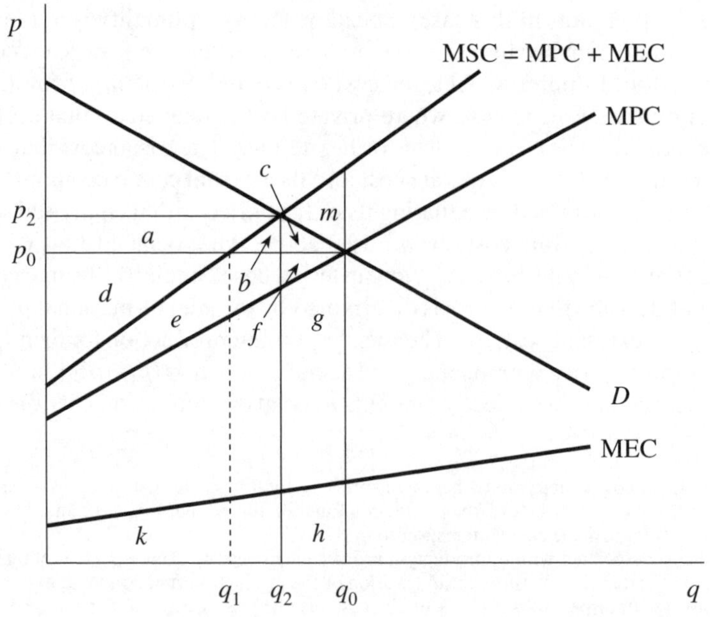

Figure 13.1

3. For a detailed discussion of externalities and the approach of internalization, see Bator (1958).

represents the change in the sum of external costs on all agents affected externally associated with a change in q. This definition is unambiguous in the case where all external effects are on profit-maximizing firms. In the case where some external effects are on consumers, external costs may be represented by willingness to pay (WTP) for increments or decrements of q (or willingness to accept increments of q). In doing so, one must bear in mind the results of Section 7.9, which discuss consumer surplus changes as approximations of WTP when quantity changes are imposed. Thus, the marginal external cost curve is a marginal WTP curve that represents either the sum of changes in compensating variations or the sum of changes in equivalent variations *over all agents* affected externally, depending on whether the associated utility levels are held at initial or final states.

If the price of q is initially p_0, then competitive production in the presence of the externality will be q_0 in Figure 13.1. External costs are represented by area $k+h$. At price p_0, social optimality is obtained by equating price and marginal social cost, which occurs at q_1. However, cutting production will, in general, lead to an increase in price along the demand curve, so that the equation of price and marginal social costs will result in equilibrium production at q_2.

Where for simplicity the ordinary and compensated demand curves coincide, the welfare effects of moving from competitive equilibrium at q_0 to social optimality at q_2 can be analyzed as follows. Production costs decrease by area $g+h$. Total revenue for producers decreases by area $f+g+h-a-b$ (which is an increase if demand is inelastic). Producers can thus be better off by area $a+b-f$ as a result of moving to social optimality. Consumers, on the other hand, lose area $a+b+c$ as a result of the increase in price and reduction in production. Finally, external agents gain area h as a reduction in external costs. The net social gain is thus area $h-c-f=$ area m because, by construction, area $h=$ area $c+f+m$.

An interesting implication of Figure 13.1 is that social optimality does not necessarily imply that externalities should be restricted to zero. In other words, if a firm is polluting the atmosphere and external effects are represented by MEC, then the optimal reduction in production from q_0 to q_2 will generally entail only a reduction in the rate of pollution rather than a complete curtailment. That is, as the rate of pollution is reduced, marginal external costs are also reduced, while marginal market benefits, as represented by the vertical difference in the demand curve and the marginal private cost curve, are increasing. With moderate reductions, the marginal private losses from reducing pollution may soon outweigh the marginal external costs. This phenomenon is ignored by some environmental groups that argue for extreme policies of environmental preservation.

The externality represented in Figure 13.1 is a negative externality. However, some positive externalities may also be derived from the production of q or its side effects. For example, in Figure 13.2 the vertical distance between MSC and MPC represents marginal external costs or the sum of changes in compensating variation (or equivalent variation as the case may be) with respect to a change in q over all those individuals (other than producers of q) affected negatively by an increase in q. The vertical distance between marginal social benefits, MSB, and marginal private benefits, MPB, represents marginal external benefits or the sum of changes in compensating variation (or equivalent variation) with respect to a change in q over all those individuals (other than consumers of q) affected positively by an increase in q. The private equilibrium for a competitive economy in the presence of externalities is attained at the intersection of MPC, which represents competitive

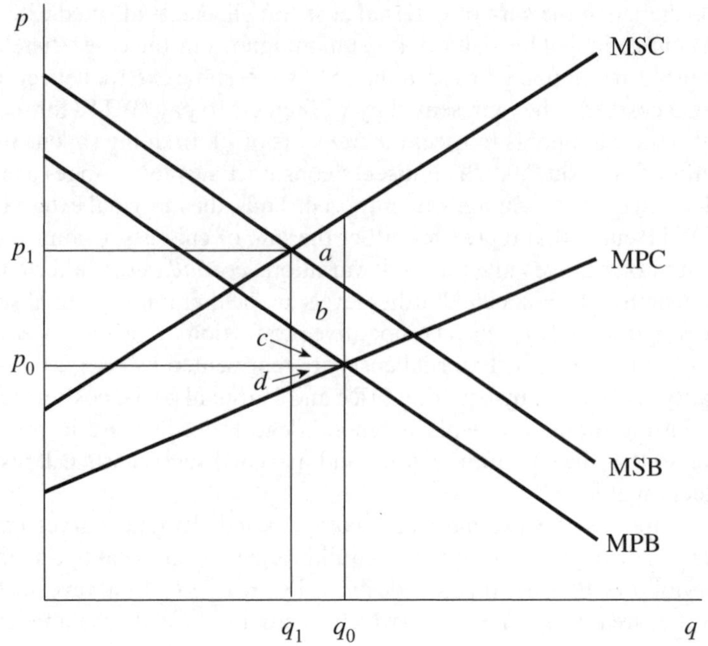

Figure 13.2

supply, with MPB, which represents competitive demand (that is, at price p_0 and quantity q_0). The social optimum, on the other hand, is obtained by equating marginal social cost and marginal social benefits (that is, at price p_1 and quantity q_1). In this case, producers and consumers jointly lose area $c+d$, those who suffer external costs gain area $a+b+c+d$, and those who derive external benefits lose area b. The net impact is thus a gain of area a. Although the case in Figure 13.2 suggests that optimum social production is smaller than optimum private production, the same methodology can be used to show that optimum social production is larger than optimum private production in the case where marginal external benefits exceed marginal external costs at the private optimum, which corresponds to a competitive equilibrium.

Another consideration in determining the social optimum relates to possibilities for pollution control and the installation of pollution abatement equipment.[4] For example, it could be that a factory can build taller smokestacks to gain more condensation within stacks and thus lead to less air pollution. Suppose that marginal external cost differs in the cases of pollution control and no control, as exemplified in Figure 13.3. Also, suppose that operation of pollution control equipment increases the marginal private cost, as indicated in Figure 13.3. In this case the marginal social cost, obtained by adding marginal external costs and marginal private costs, may fall as a result of installing pollution abatement equipment for pollution control. If so, the social optimum will result in a decrease

4. For an early exposition on corrective policies in the presence of pollution abatement equipment and a discussion of the property rights issue, see Dales (1968). For a more modern treatment, see Tietenberg (2000, ch. 15).

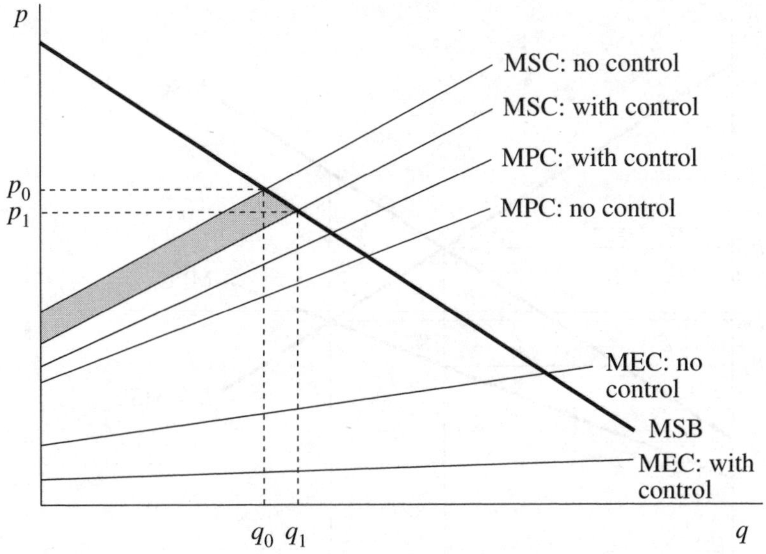

Figure 13.3

in price from p_0 to p_1 and an increase in quantity from q_0 to q_1 as pollution abatement equipment is implemented. The resulting increase in social welfare is indicated by the shaded area in Figure 13.3. However, because marginal private costs are higher with pollution abatement equipment, some incentives are required to induce profit-maximizing firms to adopt such equipment.

Policies for Obtaining Social Optimality with Externalities

Policies for dealing with externalities of the type discussed above generally include Pigouvian taxes or subsidies, standards (nontradable pollution restrictions) and assignment of property rights. Taxes, subsidies and the assignment of property rights are called *economic instruments* because they utilize economic incentives for consumers and producers to regulate the level of pollution. Standards, either on technology or the level of permissible emissions, are called *command and control* instruments because they are imposed on private actions by government. For the purpose of illustrating these three approaches, assume that only three groups are affected: producers, consumers and those affected adversely by externalities. This case seems to be the most common situation encountered in policy-making. Other cases can be handled with the same principles by considering additionally external benefits associated with production or external benefits or costs associated with consumption.

A *Pigouvian tax* is a tax named after A.C. Pigou (1932) that imposes the external cost of pollution on the generator of that pollution. For example, where marginal external cost is represented by the vertical difference in MSC and MPC in Figure 13.4, a Pigouvian tax is determined by the vertical difference in these two schedules at the chosen production level. For example, at production level q_1 the Pigouvian tax imposed on an *ad valorem* (or

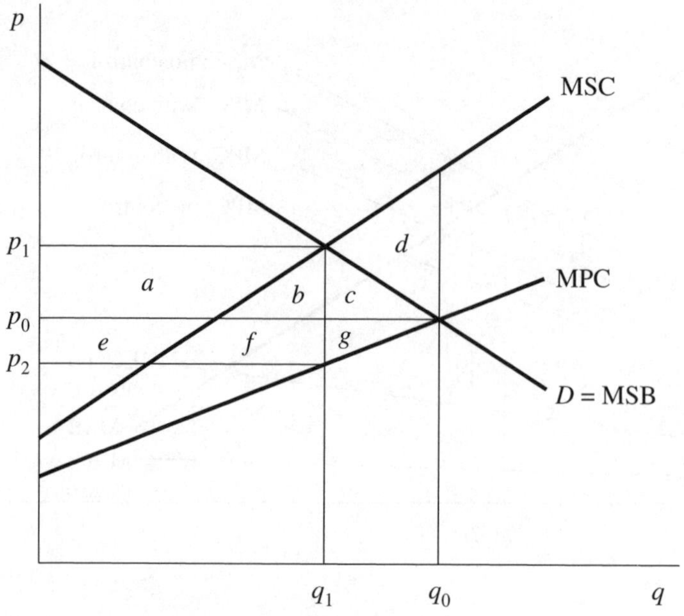

Figure 13.4

per unit) basis is $p_1 - p_2$. When the marginal tax is equal to the marginal external cost associated with the resulting output, the firm is made to bear the full marginal cost of its production, and thus its marginal private cost in the presence of the tax is equal to the marginal social cost. In a competitive economy, the imposition of a tax rate of $p_1 - p_2$ automatically induces a reduction in production from q_0 to q_1 and a consumer price adjustment from p_0 to p_1. Along the lines of the methodology in Section 8.5, the associated welfare effects are as follows. Producers lose area $e+f+g$ in producer surplus, consumers lose area $a+b+c$ in consumer surplus, government gains area $a+b+e+f$ in tax revenues, and external agents gain area $c+d+g$ as a reduction in external costs. The net effect is thus a gain of area d. Hence, with both competition and externalities, some lump-sum redistribution is possible so that all parties gain by imposing the optimal Pigouvian tax.

In the foregoing example, the relationship of pollution to production is assumed fixed, as when pollution abatement equipment is not available. If pollution can be reduced without a reduction in output (through use of pollution abatement equipment), the Pigouvian tax must be imposed directly on pollution rather than on output. Otherwise, production is excessively discouraged, and the appropriate incentive for use or installation of pollution abatement equipment is not conveyed to the polluter. Analysis similar to the above in this case implies that the Pigouvian tax per unit of pollution should be set equal to the marginal external cost of a unit of pollution at the chosen level of pollution.

The use of *standards* to control externalities can also be represented in Figure 13.4 (for the case of a fixed relationship of pollution to production). That is, because q_1 represents the socially optimal production point, the government may simply limit production to q_1.

With the imposition of such a restriction, production is thus reduced from q_0 to q_1, which induces a price increase from p_0 to p_1. The welfare effects associated with such a standard are as follows. Producers gain area $a+b-g$, consumers lose area $a+b+c$, and external agents gain area $c+d+g$. The net gain, area d, is thus the same with standards as with Pigouvian taxes. However, in the case with standards, producers are better off than under taxes, whereas other parties besides the government are equally well off under both sets of controls. Because consumers and external agents are equally well off under the two controls, whereas producers are better off, legislative lobbying interests are inclined to favor standards as opposed to taxes. This fact has been used to explain the predominance of standards or quotas in governmental policies used to deal with externalities.

Again, with quotas as with Pigouvian taxes, these considerations must be modified slightly when pollution abatement equipment is available for altering the relationship between output and pollution. To properly encourage the adoption of pollution control equipment without overly discouraging output, the standard must be imposed directly on pollution rather than on the overall production activity. Analysis of the welfare effects in this case is similar to that described above except that the pollution standard acts as a determinant of supply and simply shifts the private supply curve upward and/or rotates it counterclockwise, but not necessarily to a point of perfect inelasticity, as would a quota on production.[5]

Finally, consider the method of assigning *property rights* when externalities are present. Laws are developed to give either the polluter the right to pollute or the pollutee the right to no pollution. The permissive pollution law whereby the polluter has the right to pollute is called L law. The prohibitive pollution law that gives a pollutee the right to no pollution is called $\bar{L}$ law.

The assignment of property rights is intended to encourage the development of a market for the externality. If a polluter clearly owns the right to pollute, the pollutee may be willing to pay the polluter to either reduce or cease pollution. If the pollutee owns the right to no pollution, a potential polluter may buy the right to pollute from the pollutee. R.H. Coase (1960) was first to show in his famous *Coase theorem* that *Pareto optimality* is attained when such markets are developed. In absence of property rights, no market can form. The assignment of property rights, however, can have a profound effect on income distribution. Under one law, one agent can sell the right to pollute while, under the other law, the other agent can sell that right.

The results of assigning property rights can be demonstrated in the framework of Figure 13.4. To do this clearly, however, consider Figure 13.5, where the marginal external

5. The literature on environmental economics deals with several types of pollution problems. The controls considered explicitly here, however, are those which relate to effluents or emissions generated by individual firms, that is, those which deal with point source pollution problems. *Point source pollution* problems are those in which the amounts of pollution produced by individual firms can be identified for purposes of imposing controls. In *nonpoint source pollution* problems, where amounts of pollution generated cannot be traced to individual firms (for practical purposes), similar principles apply but controls can only relate indirectly to pollution. In such cases, controls usually take the form of taxes or quotas on production or standards on technologies used. In the latter case, the effect of imposing a technology standard is to shift cost curves and supply curves, much as discussed above where a standard is imposed on pollution. An example of standards dealing with point source pollution would be an effluent standard where effluent generation is monitored by a control agency. An example in the case of nonpoint source pollution would be ambient air quality standards, which are attained by means of emission standards imposed on the technology incorporated in automobiles.

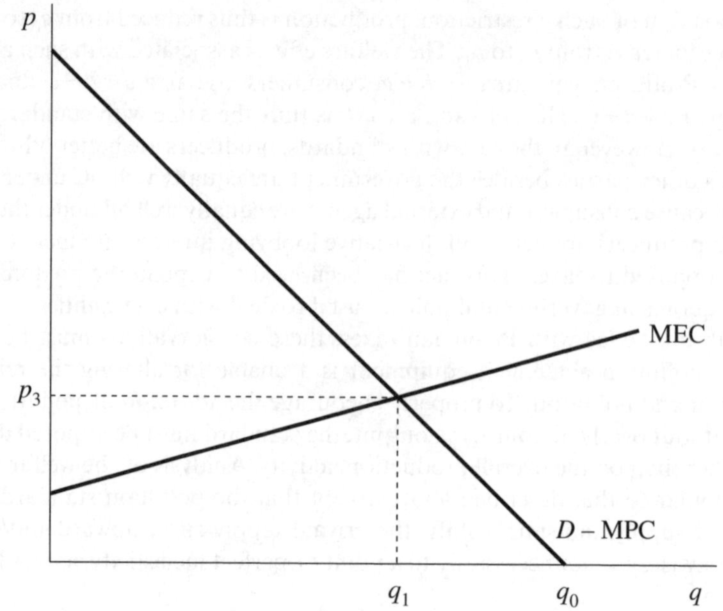

Figure 13.5

costs, MEC, represent the vertical difference in MSC and MPC in Figure 13.4 and $D-$ MPC represents the vertical difference in demand and marginal private costs in Figure 13.4. In this context, MEC represents a marginal damage function, whereas $D-$MPC represents a marginal (opportunity) *cost of control or abatement*.[6] Now suppose that the pollutee has the right to no pollution, as under $\bar{L}$ law. Then, MEC will represent the supply of pollution rights because it is simply the marginal cost to the pollutee of allowing pollution. The $D-$MPC curve, on the other hand, represents the demand by the producer for the right to pollute (with competitive behavior). Thus, if a market for the pollution right develops, the resulting price will be p_3 at a quantity of q_1. In comparison with Figure 13.4, social optimality is thus obtained where the price of pollution rights, p_3, is equal to $p_1 - p_2$, which is also the optimal Pigouvian tax.

Now suppose that the right to pollute is assigned to the polluter as under L law. In this case, the lower axis of Figure 13.5 may simply be reversed so that MEC represents the demand by the pollutee for pollution reduction. Similarly, the $D-$MPC curve will represent the supply of pollution reduction. Equilibrium will again result at price p_3 and quantity q_1, obtaining the social optimality point of Figure 13.4.

Contrasting the results under L law and $\bar{L}$ law, however, reveals substantially different

6. The *control or abatement cost function* is defined as the cost incurred by a polluter (due to reduced output and other opportunity costs in addition to direct pollution abatement costs) to reduce pollution from the level that would occur with a free market in the absence of control policies. In Figure 13.5, both the control cost function and the damage function are represented as functions of output to relate to Figure 13.4, because production and pollution are assumed to have a fixed relationship. In general, however, control cost and damage are expressed as functions of the amount of pollution, so possibilities for use of pollution abatement equipment are taken into account.

implications for income distribution. Under $\bar{L}$ law, the pollutee sells the polluter the right to pollute, associated with the quantity q_1 at price p_3, thus involving a transfer of $p_3 q_1$ from the polluter to the pollutee. Under L law, on the other hand, the polluter receives a price of p_3 per unit for reducing production from q_0 to q_1, which thus involves a transfer of $p_3(q_0 - q_1)$ from the pollutee to the polluter. In effect, the polluter's income is higher by $p_3 q_0$ under $\bar{L}$ law than under L law, while the pollutee's income is higher by the same amount in the opposite situation.

Evaluating Policies in the Presence of Distortions

In evaluating and comparing policies implemented to control externalities thus far, a critical assumption has been that only one externality is present. When other externalities or other types of distortions also exist, the conclusions can be reversed. For example, if the assumption of competition in a market is replaced by one of monopoly, then the effects of a tax in either the same or another market can be quite different from those in Figure 13.4. And, importantly, if the existence of the monopoly must be taken as given, then the optimal tax that maximizes social welfare given the monopoly is not the same as when the monopoly distortion is not present.

Multiple distortions in a single market

Consider, for example, Figure 13.6, where the monopolist's marginal private cost is given by MPC and the marginal social cost that accounts for externalities is MSC. The demand curve facing the monopolist is represented by D with the associated marginal revenue

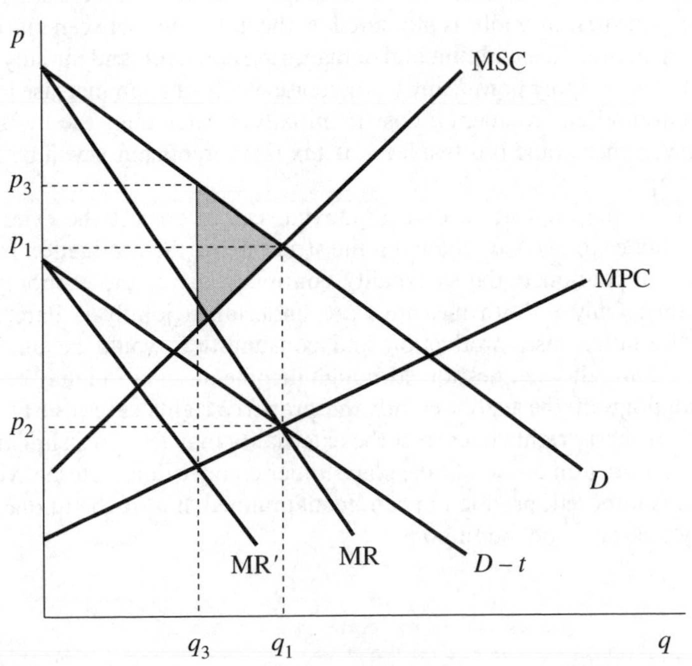

Figure 13.6

curve MR. Figure 13.6 is drawn so that the production point selected by the monopolist where marginal revenue is equal to marginal private cost at q_1 coincides with the point where marginal social cost is equal to marginal social benefits (represented by the demand curve), even though no corrective taxes, standards, or other controls are used. If the Pigouvian tax, $p_1 - p_2$, is imposed, then the free-market solution that reaches social optimality would be distorted.

With an *ad valorem* tax of $t = p_1 - p_2$, the demand curve perceived by the monopolist would shift to $D - t$ and the associated marginal revenue curve would be MR′. Thus, the production point selected by the monopolist would fall from q_1 to q_3 and raise consumer prices from p_1 to p_3. An accounting of welfare effects on individual groups in this case will demonstrate a net social loss equal to the shaded area in Figure 13.6. Of course, Figure 13.6 could be redrawn so that the monopoly solution involves either more or less production than under social optimality, but in these cases the tax that attains social optimality may be quite different and even become a subsidy when restrictive monopolistic behavior is taken into account.

The case in Figure 13.6 exemplifies the problem of *second best*.[7] The general premise of the theory of second best is that when two or more distortions exist – for example, a monopoly and an externality – then the imposition of a corrective control for one of the distortions may drive the economy further from the point of social optimality than if the distortions were allowed to (partially) offset one another. Moreover, optimal intervention in the presence of another existing distortion over which the policy-maker has no control is different than when no other distortions exist. Increasing the marginal tax rate has two effects. One is a marginal benefit through the reduction in marginal environmental damages as the monopolist reduces output in response to the tax increase. The second is a marginal cost due to monopoly as measured by the difference between market price and marginal cost. If marginal environmental damages are constant, and initially less than the marginal cost of monopoly power, any tax increase will lead to an increase in deadweight loss. If the marginal environmental cost is initially greater than the marginal cost of monopoly power, then some positive level of tax is desirable but it will be less than the Pigouvian tax.

In Figure 13.6, the imposition of a Pigouvian tax to correct the externality if the monopoly continues to exist, or changing the structure of the production industry from monopoly to competition if the externality continues, drives the economy away from social optimality. Only if both measures are undertaken jointly is Pareto optimality attained. In the latter case, production and consumption would be unchanged with respect to the commodity in question, although income distribution may be altered.

A simple analogy of the tax case with the property rights case also reveals that an assignment of property rights to correct the externality may lead to a similar problem of second best if production does not take place under competition. Alternatively, if a standard or quota is imposed, production can be maintained at q_1 if the quota corresponds to the socially optimal production point.

7. The problem of second best was introduced by Lipsey and Lancaster (1956–57) and was discussed for the particular problem presented here by Buchanan (1969).

Distortions in related markets and the possibility of the double dividend

Similar problems can arise if a corrective policy is implemented in a market when distortions exist in other related markets. A particularly important example in the environmental economics literature is known as the *double dividend.* The potential for a 'double' dividend arises because in many economies the primary means of raising revenue to fund the provision of public goods is through an income tax, which is a tax on wages that distorts the labor market.

The *double dividend hypothesis* asserts that if environmental taxes on emissions are used to reduce income taxes in a revenue-neutral manner, then the tax 'swap' yields a double dividend by reducing both the environmental externality and the income tax distortion. If so, then two distortions can be reduced with one policy instrument, and the benefits from taxing environmental degradation would be greater than partial equilibrium estimates suggest. In this case, the optimal second-best tax on emissions should be greater than the marginal environmental damages because of the marginal benefits from reducing the distortion in the related market. As Goulder (1995) has pointed out, an affirmation of this hypothesis would be highly appealing to environmentalists because it would reduce the burden of having to measure and prove the benefits of pollution reduction.

To illustrate the issues, consider Figure 13.7, where Figure 13.7(a) represents the labor market and Figure 13.7(b) represents the market for a polluting good q.[8] In the initial situation an income tax of t_L applies to labor. The demand for labor is assumed to be perfectly elastic so that important issues can be illustrated without undue complications. Given the demand for labor D_L and the supply of labor $S(p_1)$, the quantity of labor supplied is L_1 at wage rate w_1. The wage rate w_1 before taxes corresponds to wage rate $w_1 - t_L$ after taxes. Tax revenues are area $a+b$ and the deadweight loss from the income tax is area c. In the initial situation in the market for q, profit-maximizing firms ignore marginal external costs represented by MEC and produce output q_1 at price p_1 when demand is $D_q(w_1 - t_L)$, which results in a deadweight loss of area z.

Now consider evaluation of a policy that imposes a Pigouvian tax t_q equal to MEC in the market for q. The partial equilibrium analysis of Chapter 8 applied to this problem suggests a loss to consumers of area $x+y$, a gain to pollutees as a reduction of external costs of area $y+z$, a gain of area x in tax revenues (which could be redistributed to consumers as a lump sum), and thus a net social gain of area z. However, because the *ad valorem* tax t_q raises the effective price of good q to p_1+t_q, implications for the labor market must also be considered. If leisure and good q are substitutes in consumption, the increase in the price of q will cause substitution of leisure for q. As a result, labor supply shifts leftward, as represented in Figure 13.7(a) by the shift from $S(p_1)$ to $S(p_1+t_q)$, which reduces the amount of labor supplied from L_1 to L_2. As a result, tax revenues in the labor market decrease from area $a+b$ to area a for a net loss of area b. Area b is called the *tax-interaction* effect and is unambiguously negative when leisure and good q are substitutes.

8. The presentation of double dividend issues is presented here in graphical terms involving labor and a single environmental good, whereas most of the double dividend literature considers the case with labor, the environmental good and one additional good in a mathematical rather than graphical analysis. A mathematical analysis illustrates some issues that are difficult to evaluate in a graphical framework. However, invoking results from Section 9.4 and Appendix Section 9.B, the graphical analysis presented here applies regardless of how many other markets (goods) exist as long as the other markets are not distorted, labor demand is perfectly elastic and the cost of producing the environmental good is constant.

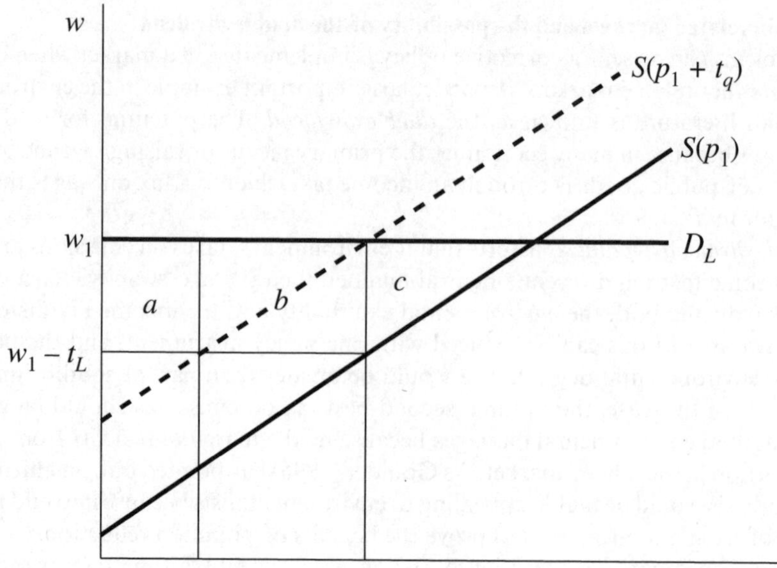
w
$S(p_1 + t_q)$
$S(p_1)$
w_1
D_L
a
b
c
$w_1 - t_L$
L_2
L_1
L
(a)

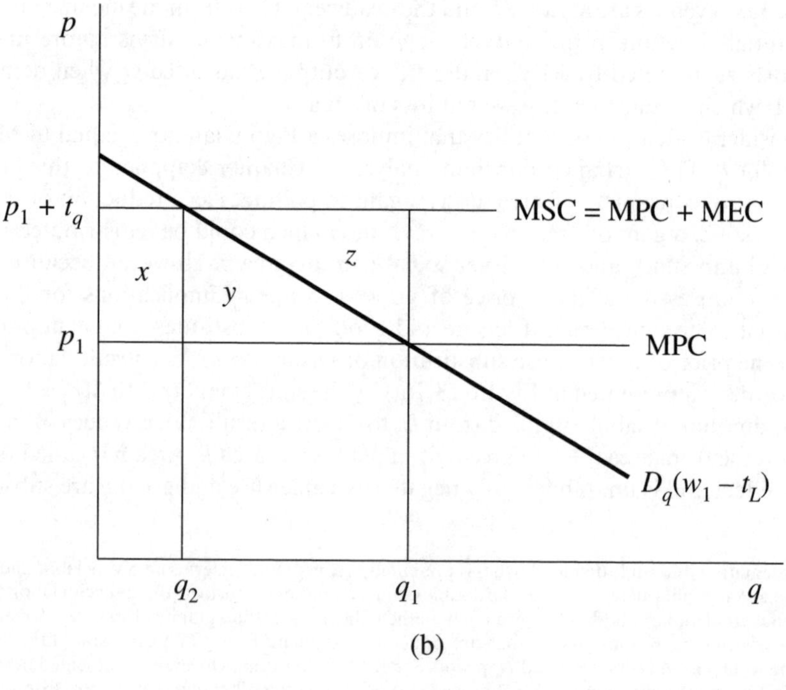
p
$p_1 + t_q$
MSC = MPC + MEC
x
y
z
p_1
MPC
$D_q(w_1 - t_L)$
q_2
q_1
q
(b)

Figure 13.7

This welfare loss at least partially offsets the positive *Pigouvian effect*, or primary effect, of the externality tax measured by area z. The general equilibrium gain from taxation of the externality tax thus appears to be less than would be anticipated on the basis of partial equilibrium analysis where the income tax distortion is ignored.[9]

To correctly evaluate the net welfare effect, the results of Section 9.4 and Appendix Section 9.B are useful. Assuming that only the two markets in Figure 13.7 are affected, if the demand curve $D_q(w_1 - t_L)$ in Figure 13.7(b) is viewed as an equilibrium demand curve conditioned on the existing distortion in the other market (on t_L), then the private welfare effects of policy intervention in the market for q can be entirely captured in the market for q. Only the government revenue effect on the tax in the labor market must be considered additionally (see Section 9.4). In the particular case of Figure 13.7, the ordinary demand for q represented by $D_q(w_1 - t_L)$, which is conditioned on $w - t_L$, must be identical to the equilibrium demand conditioned on t_L because w is fixed by the perfectly elastic demand for labor at D_L. Thus, as demonstrated in Appendix Section 9.B, all of the welfare effects of a change in t_q on sellers of labor are captured by the surplus triangles of Figure 13.7(b), aside from the tax revenue effect in the labor market. In particular, buyers of labor are unaffected when labor demand is perfectly elastic. Therefore, the net welfare effect of introducing the Pigouvian tax t_q is exactly equal to area $z - b$ in Figure 13.7.[10]

Now consider the possibilities of a tax swap, that is, the replacement of labor taxes with environmental taxes. First, note that the analysis of Figure 13.7 implicitly assumes that the welfare gain of area z is redistributed as a lump sum to consumers. Now suppose instead that this revenue is used to reduce the income tax in the labor market. Can the increase in environmental tax revenue measured by area x offset the income tax revenue of area $a + b$ so that the distortion of income taxes can be eliminated? Or, at least, can the income tax rate be reduced by a revenue-neutral policy whereby the income tax revenue in Figure 13.7(a) is reduced by the amount of increase in environmental tax revenue in Figure 13.7(b)? The effect of using environmental taxes to replace income taxes is called the *revenue-recycling effect.* What Goulder (1995) calls the *weak double dividend hypothesis* simply asserts that this revenue-recycling effect is positive – that is, a policy of taxing environmental damages and using the revenues to replace existing income taxes in a revenue-neutral manner is better than taxing environmental damages with lump-sum redistribution of the environmental tax revenues.

To explore these possibilities, consider Figure 13.8, where the income tax rate on labor is reduced from t_L to t_L^* as the Pigouvian tax t_q is imposed in such a way that total tax revenues are unaffected. When the income tax rate is reduced in the labor market, the effective wage rate after taxes will rise from $w_1 - t_L$ to $w_1 - t_L^*$. Due to substitution of good q for

9. In addition, area z may be larger where $D_q(w_1 - t_L)$ is a partial equilibrium demand holding all other prices constant than when $D_q(w_1 - t_L)$ is an equilibrium demand with respect to prices in all markets other than labor. See the discussion in Section 9.3 for details.
10. This discussion applies equilibrium analysis in the context of the two markets represented in Figure 13.7, assuming that they are related to all other markets through perfectly elastic relationships (the segmented economy case of Appendix Section 9.B). More generally, Figure 13.7 can be assumed to represent equilibrium supplies and demands that account for adjustments in all other markets. In this case, the analysis would require modification by considering shifts in D_L and MPC that occur with adjustments in other markets when t_q is altered. The equilibrium D_L and MPC relationships may not be perfectly elastic even if the ordinary ones are. Additionally, if markets other than the two depicted in Figure 13.7 are distorted, then the net welfare effect would need to include changes in government revenues associated with these other distorted markets as well.

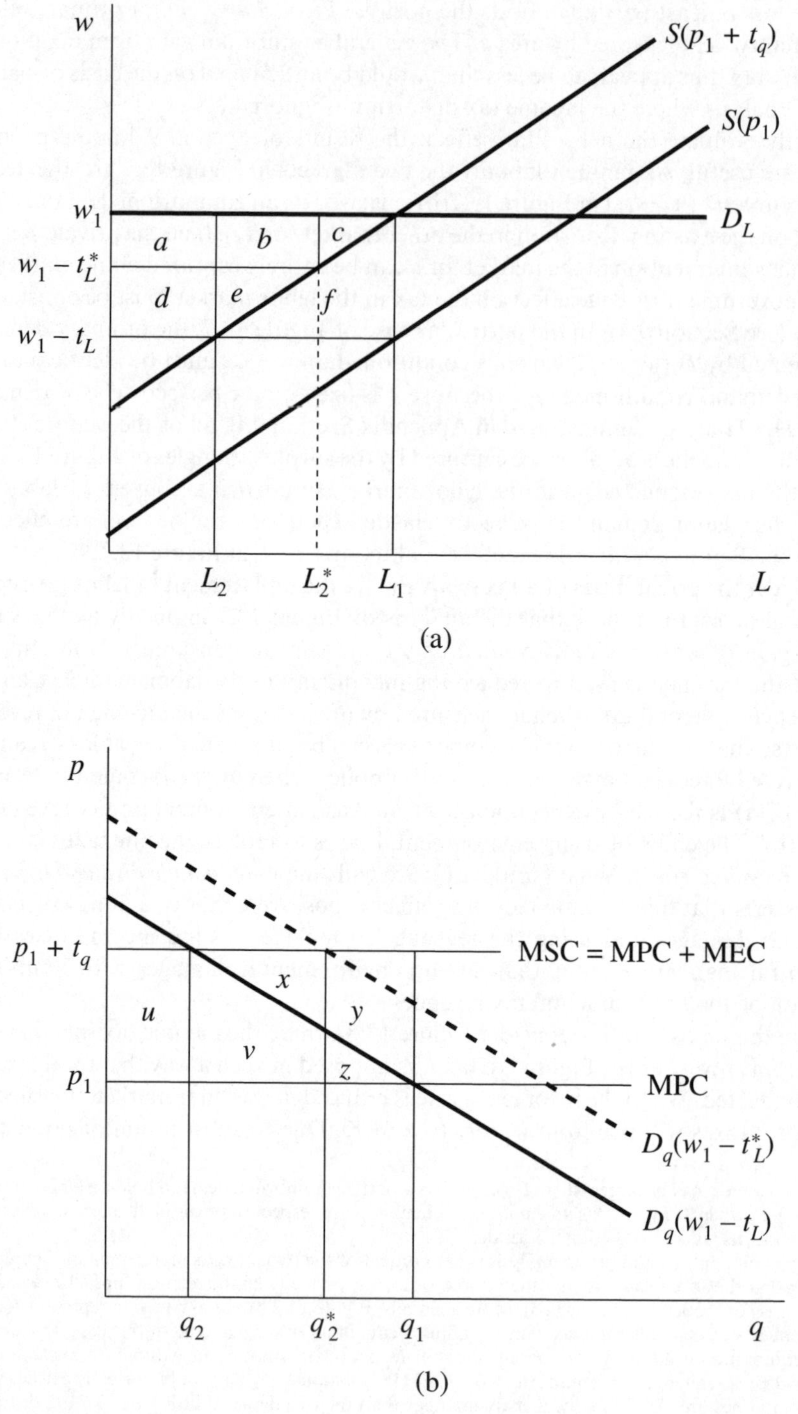
w
S(p1 + tq)
S(p1)
w1
DL
a
b
c
w1 − tL*
d
e
f
w1 − tL
L2
L2*
L1
L
(a)
p
p1 + tq
MSC = MPC + MEC
x
u
y
v
z
p1
MPC
Dq(w1 − tL*)
Dq(w1 − tL)
q2
q2*
q1
q
(b)

Figure 13.8

leisure, raising the effective price of leisure causes the ordinary demand for good q to increase to $D_q(w_1 - t_L^*)$.

To see how the welfare effects of a revenue-neutral environmental tax can be evaluated, the tax rate change can be considered in two parts, as in Figure 13.8. Considering first imposing the environmental tax rate t_q holding the income tax rate constant at its initial level t_L, from which consumers lose area $u+v+z$, pollutees gain area $v+x+y+z$, environmental tax revenue increases by area u and income tax revenue decreases by area $b+c+e+f$.[11] The net effect of imposing the environmental tax holding the income tax rate constant is thus area $x+y-b-c-e-f$.

Now consider additionally reducing the income tax rate from t_L to t_L^* holding the environmental tax rate at its subsequent level, t_q. With the environmental tax, labor supply is $S(p+t_q)$, so laborers gain area $d+e$. Income tax revenue after imposition of the environmental tax is area $a+d$ and changes to area $a+b$ for a net change of area $b-d$, which may be positive or negative. Employers are unaffected if labor demand is perfectly elastic. These changes add up to a net gain in the labor market of area $e+b$. According to the results in Appendix Section 9.B, these effects capture all of the welfare implications of a change in t_L on buyers of good q in Figure 13.8(b), aside from the environmental tax revenue effect and, of course, the environmental effect on pollutees who are not participants in the good q market. The increase in demand for good q that occurs when the income tax rate is lowered causes the environmental tax revenue to increase from area u to area $u+v+x$, for an increase of area $v+x$. Pollutees lose area $v+x$, which is equal to the constant MEC multiplied by the increase in good q quantity from q_2 to q_2^*. Because the increased environmental tax revenue is exactly equal to the pollutee welfare loss, the net effect in the good q market is zero. So the overall net effect of changing the income tax rate holding the environmental tax rate constant at t_q is equal to the net labor market effect alone, area $e+b$.

Adding the effect of changing the environmental tax rate from zero to t_q holding the income tax rate constant at its initial level t_L, area $x+y-b-c-e-f$, to the effect of reducing the income tax rate from t_L to t_L^* holding the environmental tax rate constant at its subsequent level t_q, area $e+b$, obtains the net effect of the revenue-neutral environmental tax, area $x+y-c-f$.[12] Comparing to the results in Figure 13.7 for the case of lump sum distribution of environmental tax revenue, the net effect of the environmental tax was area $z-b$, which in Figure 13.8 is analogous to area $x+y-b-c-e-f$. The difference, area $b+e$ in Figure 13.8(a), is thus gained by using the environmental tax to offset income taxes rather than using lump sums to distribute the environmental tax revenue. The positivity of this gain illustrates the existence of the weak double dividend or, in other words, shows that the revenue-recycling effect is positive.

Another question the literature has addressed is whether the revenue-recycling effect more than compensates for the negative tax-interaction effect. This is what Goulder calls the *strong double dividend hypothesis*.[13] In the context of Figure 13.8, this hypothesis would

11. Note that area $u+v+z$ in Figure 13.8(b) is analogous to area $x+y$ in Figure 13.7(b), and area $v+x+y+z$ in Figure 13.8(b) is analogous to area $y+z$ in Figure 13.7(b). Also, area $b+c+e+f$ in Figure 13.8(a) is analogous to area b in Figure 13.7(a).
12. Note that a revenue-neutral environmental tax implies that the initial income tax revenue, area $a+b+c+d+e+f$, is equal to the subsequent income tax revenue plus the environmental tax, area $a+b+u+x+v$. In other words, area $c+d+e+f=$ area $u+v+x$.
13. What Goulder calls the strong double dividend hypothesis is simply called the double dividend hypothesis in most other literature. The 'strong' adjective is used here for clarity.

mean that area $x+y-c-f$ is positive. Whether this effect is positive depends on the elasticity of q demand (which determines q_1-q_2), the elasticity of substitution (which determines $q_2^*-q_2$ and L_1-L_2) and the elasticity of labor supply (which determines $t_L-t_L^*$). Whether these effects are sufficient to lead to a strong double dividend is an empirical issue.

A strong double dividend is theoretically possible but is not supported by most studies. This conclusion, originally established by Bovenberg and de Mooij (1994) and confirmed by Parry (1995), follows basically from one major assumption and one well-known empirical fact. First, the assumption has been that the output of the polluting industry is a substitute for leisure. As Parry (1998, p. 47) points out, 'In practice it has proved difficult to estimate the overall degree of substitution between different goods and leisure.' Hence, the usual practice in these models by Parry and others has been simply to assume that the polluting sector good and leisure are average substitutes – that is, have elasticities of substitution equal to one. On the other hand, it is clear that if the output of the polluting industry and leisure are complements, then the tax-interaction effect will be positive so the strong double dividend will exist.

Second, the fact that the labor market is large and has a large marginal distortion (income tax rates are typically from 20 to 50 percent) implies that the difference in L_1 and L_2 need not be large for the tax-interaction effect to be large. Thus, if the tax-interaction effect is negative, it is likely that the double dividend does not exist. But the story does not end there.

The prospects for a strong double dividend have been shown to increase with the weakness of substitution between leisure and the polluting good, the size of the revenue-recycling effect, and the possibility of recycling environmental tax revenue for capital gains taxes rather than labor taxes. For example, Parry and Bento (2000) have shown that if tax-favored consumer goods exist, such as housing service flows, then the strong double dividend exists.[14] In summary, the likelihood of a strong double dividend is an empirical question that must be considered in the context of specific circumstances.

Fortunately, West and Williams (2002) have recently begun to rectify this deficiency in empirical work through estimation of the key parameters of a demand system for the USA. They estimate an Almost Ideal Demand System for three commodities: leisure, gasoline (the dirty goods) and all other goods. They find, in distinct contrast to the earlier assumptions and findings, that gasoline and leisure are complements. Their results suggest that the second-best optimal tax on gasoline should be \$1.16, which is significantly greater than the MEC of \$.95 taken from other studies. The sharp contrast of these results with earlier literature suggests that much more empirical work is needed in designing environmental policy in a second-best world.[15]

14. Two helpful surveys of this literature are given by Bovenberg and Goulder (1998) and Parry (1998).
15. Rather than working with economy-wide general equilibrium models, one possibility is to use the multi-market approach of Chapter 9. For example, policies regarding pesticides are unlikely to affect labor other than agricultural labor. Because identifying statistical effects beyond agricultural labor is hard to imagine, estimation of the effects of a tax on pesticides on agricultural labor alone seems empirically more sensible than estimation of effects on the national labor supply. Additionally, many policies are regional or local. Local distortions may be important to identify but effects transmitted beyond the region may be statistically imperceptible. A reasonable approach is to consider market interactions only where they can be statistically identified and make sense. Thus, for policy analysis, an intermediate approach may be advisable – that is, an approach more general than the simplistic partial equilibrium models of Pigou and Marshall but less general than the full general equilibrium models of Arrow and Debreu. The former may not account for significant interactions, while the latter may not be sufficiently estimable except under the crude assumptions regarding, for example, substitution or applicability of a representative consumer model.

Finally, an important implication of this analysis is that existence of uncorrectable distortions in related markets affects the selection of the optimal environmental tax such that the greater the negative tax-interaction effect, the less the optimal 'second-best' tax on the polluting good. In particular, where the strong double dividend does not exist, the efficient environmental tax policy is likely less than the marginal external cost, which is not a popular policy with environmentalists. Moreover, instruments that do not generate government revenue, such as standards or the granting of pollution rights in a tradable-permits market, are more likely to compare unfavorably to taxes and auctioned pollution rights when the revenue-recycling effect is considered. The practice of revenue recycling appears to be crucial in justifying environmental taxes. If revenues are kept in the agency where they are raised or distributed in lump-sum form, then Pareto gains through taxation policies appear to be difficult to find.

Other Issues in Comparing Policies

Another point to keep in mind in Figures 13.4 and 13.5 is the case where changes in income cause supply or demand curves to shift, that is, where ordinary and compensated curves do not coincide. To be accurate, all the diagrammatic analysis thus far in this chapter is assumed to be based on compensated curves. When ordinary curves do not coincide, the point of social optimality depends upon the income distributional effects of the control adopted.

Consider, for example, Figure 13.9, where the various MEC curves and $D-\text{MPC}$

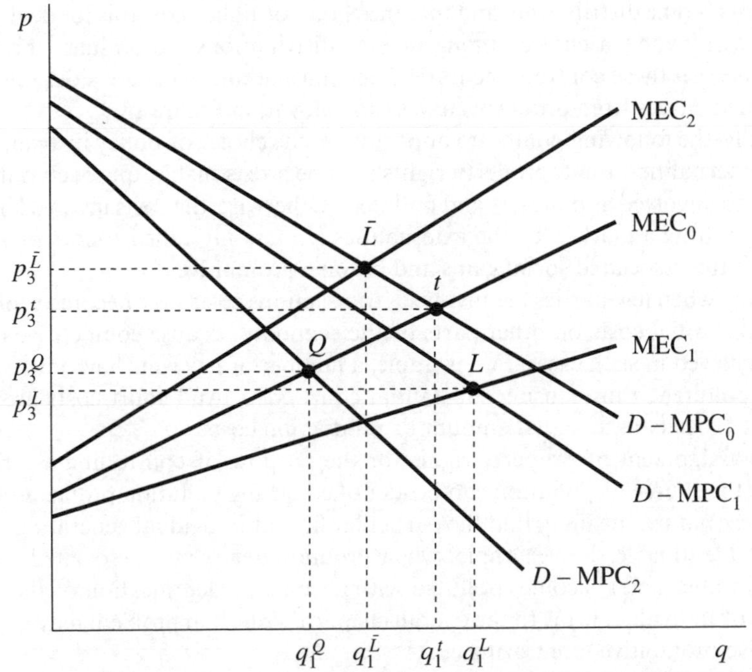

Figure 13.9

curves correspond to different income distributions. Under the case of a tax, for example, both polluters' and pollutees' incomes are not affected directly, and thus they react along their initial ordinary curves, $D-\mathrm{MPC}_0$ and MEC_0. The corresponding equilibrium is at point t with quantity q_1^t and price p_3^t. With a quota, on the other hand, external agents' income is unaffected directly, whereas the producers or sellers of q receive an additional amount, corresponding to $q_1(p_1-p_2)$ in Figure 13.4, over the amount they would ordinarily receive when reacting along their private supply curve. To examine the case in Figure 13.9, consider the marginal external cost curve MEC_0 and the pollution demand curve $D-\mathrm{MPC}_2$, which corresponds to an increase in sellers' income of $p_3^Q q_1^Q$ above the tax solution. The resulting social optimum obtained with this alternative income distribution is thus at point Q with quantity q_1^Q and price p_3^Q.

The assignment of property rights corresponds to other distributions of income. Under L law, external agents make a payment of $p_3^L(q_0-q_1^L)$ to sellers of q. With the effective reduction in income, the marginal external cost curve of external agents shifts to MEC_1, and the increase in income for sellers causes a shift of the demand for pollution to $D-\mathrm{MPC}_1$. The associated equilibrium is at point L in Figure 13.9. Finally, under $\bar{L}$ law, the income of external agents is increased by $p_3^{\bar{L}} q_1^{\bar{L}}$ thus shifting the marginal external cost curve to MEC_2, while the income of the sellers is the same as in the case without intervention. That is, turning to Figure 13.4, sellers sell at price p_1 but pay $q_1(p_1-p_2)$ to external agents, thus leaving their income the same as if price p_2 were received at quantity q_1 along their ordinary private supply curve. Thus, equilibrium under $\bar{L}$ law is at point $\bar{L}$ in Figure 13.9. The analysis in Figure 13.9 thus demonstrates along much the same lines as the pure exchange economy in Section 2.2 that the point of Pareto optimality depends critically upon income distribution, and that the choice of policy controls for dealing with externalities can involve a choice among income distributions. To evaluate the welfare differences between these controls accurately, one must additionally consider divergence of compensated curves from ordinary curves (not shown) in Figure 13.9.

Additionally, the following points are important in the choice of policy instruments for controlling externalities. First, property rights may be a reasonable approach only when a few parties are involved as polluters and pollutees. Otherwise, the costs involved in developing and operating a market for the externalities (commonly called *transactions costs*) may outweigh the associated social gains and become prohibitive.

Second, even when few parties are involved, transactions costs may become prohibitive or impose substantial costs on other parts of the economy because competitive equilibria are not achieved in such cases. For example, a number of law suits have involved pollutees suing polluters, thus causing substantial court costs. And court costs are just as much a cost to society as an equal amount of production costs.

Third, the assignment of property rights for the purpose of controlling externalities assumes that the source of pollution can be identified. Many pollution problems are of a *nonpoint-source* nature, meaning that the particular firm or individual generating the pollution is not identifiable. For example, when groundwater (water associated with the underground water table) becomes polluted with chemicals, identification of the relative contribution of individual firms to the overall chemical pollution problem may be impossible or involve prohibitive monitoring costs.

Fourth, in the assignment of property rights where few parties are involved, the individuals on one side or the other of the market in Figure 13.9 may be able to exercise market power and thus influence the price of pollution rights above or below the point of social optimality. For this reason and those cited above, the assignment of property rights found limited application in the solution of externality problems until recently, except where pollution rights and the associated damages have been decided in the courts.

A fifth consideration that can alter the conclusions of this section relates to the presence of stochastic phenomena. If pollution is stochastic and depends on, for example, wind direction or amount of rainfall, then standards can be imposed only with respect to production plans or the operation of pollution abatement equipment. Taxes, on the other hand, can be imposed either on actual pollution or on the act of production without use of abatement equipment. The risks borne by producers under these policies are quite different. For example, a standard on production technology imposes all of the risk of pollution on the pollutee, as with the case of taxes on *ex ante* production decisions. In the case of a tax on actual stochastic pollution, however, some of the risk is transferred to the polluter. The relative social benefits of one system versus the other depend upon the extent of risk aversion by polluters versus pollutees. Further research on stochastic pollution problems has also shown that a subsidy on nonpollution versus a tax on pollution can have different outcomes as well. The relative social benefits of these two controls depend upon whether the likelihood of pollution is high or low, because the degree of risk can be much different with the alternative controls in these extremes. In fact, an increase in the tax on pollution can, in some circumstances, lead to an increase in the likelihood of pollution in this case because of risk averse behavior when the probability of pollution is high (see Hochman, Zilberman and Just 1977; Just and Zilberman 1979).[16]

Even when pollution is nonstochastic, however, one control may have definite advantages over the other. For example, Baumol and Oates (1971) have shown that the optimal imposition of standards or quotas may require a substantial amount of information about individual cost curves, which, if not obtained, can imply a preference for use of taxes in controlling externalities. For example, consider the two firms exemplified in Figure 13.10, where the marginal private cost of the first firm is given by MPC_1 in Figure

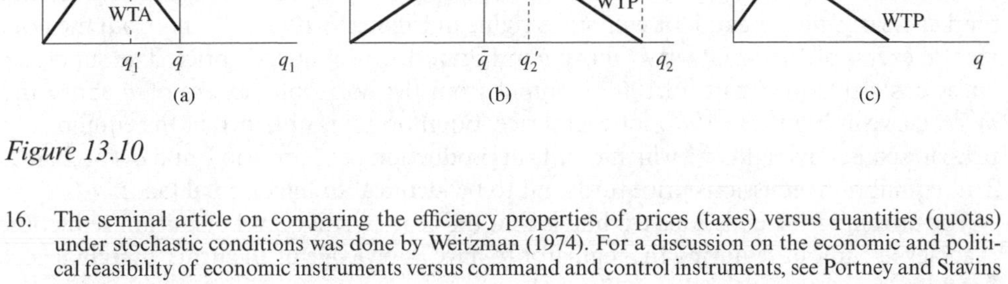

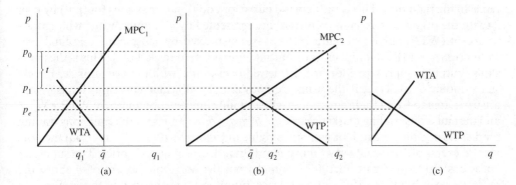

Figure 13.10

16. The seminal article on comparing the efficiency properties of prices (taxes) versus quantities (quotas) under stochastic conditions was done by Weitzman (1974). For a discussion on the economic and political feasibility of economic instruments versus command and control instruments, see Portney and Stavins (2000).

13.10(a) and the marginal private cost of the second firm is given by MPC_2 in Figure 13.10(b). Suppose that demand facing the two firms is perfectly elastic at p_0 but that a Pigouvian tax of t is imposed, thus reducing effective output price to p_1. Each firm will thus reduce its production along its marginal private cost curve to q_i', $i=1, 2$.

Now suppose alternatively that a quota is imposed on production as a means of reducing pollution. Also, suppose for simplicity that pollution occurs in constant proportions to output and that the rate of pollution is the same for both firms. In this case, if t is the appropriate tax, the quota that will achieve the same social optimality will limit production to q_1' for firm 1 and q_2' for firm 2. However, unless the regulator has knowledge of the marginal private cost curves of the individual firms, these optimal quota levels will not be known. An alternative that is employed in practice is to select an overall quota level and then allocate it among firms. In absence of information about individual cost curves, the quota level may be allocated equally among firms. For example, the quota level $\bar{q}$ may be imposed upon each firm individually so as to obtain the same overall output as if the tax t were imposed. If so, the quota will be economically inefficient because firm 1 will be producing at a higher marginal cost than firm 2 and, hence, overall costs could be reduced by increasing firm 2's production and reducing firm 1's production by an equal amount from the quota level.

If pollution is proportional to production by firm, equating marginal costs across firms can lead to the same total level of pollution with Pareto superiority. Where price is p_0 and the regulator initially allocates the quota equally across the firms at $\bar{q}$, firm 2 would be willing to pay $p_0 - MPC_2$ at $\bar{q}$ to incrementally increase output (emissions), whereas firm 1 would accept almost any positive amount to incrementally decrease output (emissions) because its marginal profit, $p_0 - MPC_1$ at $\bar{q}$, is near zero. This suggests an alternative policy option that became popular during the 1990s, namely, emissions or pollution trading. Emissions trading uses the property rights approach to regulation to achieve a cost-effective or minimum-cost solution for a given standard.

To illustrate this mechanism, consider Figure 13.10, where the WTP curve for firm 2 in Figure 13.10(b) is constructed by subtracting marginal cost from price, $p_0 - MPC_2$, for all levels to the right of $\bar{q}$. This is the demand curve for additional emissions (output) by firm 2 (with the origin of zero emissions trading represented by $\bar{q}$). Similarly, the willingness-to-accept (WTA) curve in Figure 13.10(a) is constructed by subtracting marginal cost from price, $p_0 - MPC_1$, for all units of output (emissions) to the left of $\bar{q}$. This is the emissions (output) supply curve for firm 1 (viewed backwards, with the origin of zero emissions trading at $\bar{q}$). Thus, if the firms are both initially allocated emissions levels $\bar{q}$, and are permitted to freely trade emissions rights, equilibrium will obtain where WTP = WTA and the emissions trading market clears, $\bar{q} - q_1' = q_2' - \bar{q}$. To represent the emissions trading market clearly, the demand for emissions rights in Figure 13.10(c) is found from the horizontal excess of the WTP curve above $\bar{q}$ in Figure 13.10(b) at each price. The supply of emissions rights in Figure 13.10(c) is found from the horizontal excess of $\bar{q}$ above the WTA curve in Figure 13.10(a) for each price. Equilibrium is obtained at the equilibrium price for emissions rights p_e, which results in production at q_1' for firm 1 and q_2' for firm 2. This equilibrium emissions price turns out to be identical to the optimal tax, t.

The advantage of emissions trading is that the cost-effective level of output reduction is achieved without requiring the regulator to have knowledge of the firms' marginal cost functions or of the optimal tax. Generally, the establishment of quotas with emissions trading is more popular with the private business sector than emissions taxes. A clear reason is that all producers lose compared to the unregulated case with a tax policy, whereas, under quotas with emissions trading, at least some producers gain, and all can gain if the quota is initially allocated as grants from the government.

The US Environmental Protection Agency began experimenting with emissions trading of sulfur dioxide and other air pollutants as a mechanism to help meet standards established in the Clean Air Act Amendments of 1977. These experiments were formalized and extended by the Clean Air Act Amendments of 1990. A number of evaluations of these programs have suggested positive benefits in the form of rapid compliance and significant cost savings compared to standards.

Largely on the basis of the positive outcomes from this program, the USA prevailed in securing acceptance of emissions trading of greenhouse gases among nations as a means of meeting reductions established by the 1997 Kyoto Protocol on Climate Change. The use of similar incentive-based instruments, such as deposit-refund systems, auctions, and moral suasion instruments have also gained popularity recently.[17] Challenges remain, however, including the design, implementation and enforcement of these mechanisms by regulators, particularly on an international basis.

A final point for this section is that optimal determination of the efficient tax, aggregate quota or amount of tradable pollution permits to allocate depends on equating the marginal damage function to the marginal opportunity cost of control or abatement, as illustrated in Figures 13.4 and 13.5. Unfortunately, information about the damage function associated with externally affected agents is frequently not available. Unless a market for property rights is established, information regarding damages is difficult or impossible to ascertain from market data. In fact, identification of which individuals are affected can be quite difficult. Approaches for dealing with this estimation problem are discussed later in this chapter. But first a related externality problem associated with public goods will be discussed.

13.2 PUBLIC GOODS

The goods considered thus far in this book have been private goods. A *private good* is a good that is rival and excludable. A *rival good* is one for which none of the quantity of a good consumed by one person can also be consumed by another person. Without rivalry, markets cannot be competitive because consumers do not 'compete' for consumption of goods. An *excludable good* is a good for which there exists some mechanism whereby consumption can be selectively withheld by the seller if, for example, a particular consumer does not pay the price set by the seller. If a good is rival and excludable, then its marginal benefit to an individual buyer can be appropriated by the seller. An *appropriable good* is one for which the seller is able to extract the full marginal economic benefit from the buyer.

Markets cannot allocate nonexcludable goods because a selling price cannot be enforced. Hamburgers and milkshakes are obvious examples of private goods. A consumer must pay the price required by the seller to acquire them and, once eaten, nothing is left for others. As demonstrated by the theoretical development of Section 2.5, which

17. For an international review and evaluation of these instruments, see Stavins (2000).

implicitly assumes all goods are private goods, if goods are both excludable and rival then competition leads to market allocations and prices that achieve a Pareto optimum.[18]

A *pure public good* is a good that is both nonexcludable and nonrival.[19] If any quantity of a pure public good is available for consumption by one individual, then no other individual can be excluded from also consuming it. In other words, if anyone is provided with any amount of the good, then the same amount is automatically provided to everyone else who has preferences for the good. Furthermore, each individual may derive benefit from a given quantity of the good without preventing or detracting from any other individual's enjoyment from that quantity of the good. In these conditions, a good is not appropriable. Once any quantity of the good is sold to one individual, the seller cannot appropriate the benefits received by another individual because the quantity sold to the first individual is freely available for consumption by others as well.

A public good may be nonexcludable for purely technical reasons or because imposing exclusion entails impractical costs. Examples of pure public goods are such things as national defense, the preservation of wildlife, the view of a mountain, clean air and the welfare of future generations. Similarly, environmental habitats and annual migrations of various wildlife species such as whales and geese provide visual 'sighting' benefits. Many people derive benefits simply from the knowledge that a species exists and are willing to pay for that existence even though they may never see it. Such a benefit is called *existence value*. In these cases, assignment of property rights is practically impossible, in which case appropriability fails because exclusion is impossible.[20]

The development of the Internet has had a transforming effect on the economy by reducing transaction costs through internet marketing. But an additional effect of the Internet has been to add public-good attributes to many goods that can be transferred in the form of electronic files. For example, many forms of knowledge have become freely available on the Internet, thus displacing, in part, the demand for certain kinds of books and information services. Knowledge and information is nonrival because the same information item can be used by many individuals at the same time. Once a given item of information or knowledge is made freely available on the Internet, it becomes nonexcludable as well.

Similarly, the sharing of music files and movie videos over the Internet has become highly popular as a result of such companies as Napster and its Estonian successor Kazaa. Such files are nonrival because many individuals can download and play them virtually simultaneously through internet technology. As a result, excludability has become difficult for firms that produce and sell such products. Although access can be prevented technically, music and movie companies are having great difficulty eliminating this sharing activity and are expending increasingly large amounts of funds to do so. Some have suggested that they may simply have to, in effect, give up and accept that these files are now nonexcludable as well as nonrival.

Public goods are a distinct class of externality problems. They may involve either consumers and/or producers (which are simply called individuals here) where a consumption

18. Of course, other necessary assumptions for this result include absence of distortions (as shown in Section 8.5), free trade (as shown in Section 8.7), competitive price-taking behavior (as shown in Chapter 10), full information (as shown in Chapter 11), complete markets such as markets for all risky contingencies (as shown in Chapter 12) and absence of or internalization of all externalities (as shown in Section 13.1).
19. For a seminal paper on public goods, see Samuelson (1954).
20. Ciriacy-Wantrup (1952) defines such resources as *fugitive resources*.

interdependence exists due to nonrivalry and nonexcludability, and which is therefore not reflected in the marketplace. An individual cannot be forced to pay for the good according to the benefit derived. For example, an individual can simply claim that no benefit is derived and leave it up to other individuals to make sure that the good is provided. Such an individual is often called a *free rider*. When every individual tries to be a free rider, no one wants to be the first to buy the good. As a result, no market may form, in which case no amount of the public good would be provided. On the other hand, each individual may be willing to pay a given amount for the good if assured that everyone else will pay a fair share. But in a large economy where an individual does not perceive his or her own actions as affecting the overall amount of the good, a natural inducement exists to enjoy the good without paying for it. On the other hand, because each individual likely derives a different marginal benefit at a given quantity of a public good, equality of payments among individuals is generally not a socially efficient approach.

To understand these concepts, consider Figure 13.11, where the lower axis in each case represents the amount of a public good provided and the vertical axis represents marginal valuations. The D_1 curve in Figure 13.11(a) represents the marginal WTP (or marginal benefits) derived by individual 1 from consuming the public good. Similarly, D_2 in Figure 13.11(b) represents the marginal WTP derived by individual 2. Assuming the economy is made up of two individuals, marginal social benefits associated with the public good are derived by adding the individual marginal benefit curves vertically as in Figure 13.11(c). Thus, if a quantity $\bar{q}$ of the public good is produced, the marginal benefit derived by individual 1 is p_1 as indicated in Figure 13.11(a), the marginal benefit of individual 2 is p_2 as indicated in Figure 13.11(b), and the marginal social benefit is $p_1 + p_2$ as indicated in Figure 13.11(c).[21] Social optimality is attained by equating the marginal cost of producing the good with the marginal social benefits derived by its consumption. Thus, $\bar{q}$ represents the point of social optimality.

The case of public goods is another instance in which a free competitive economy fails to reach social optimality because of market failure. For example, suppose a private firm attempts to produce the public good to maximize profit given a marginal cost curve, MC, in Figure 13.11(c). The firm will face two problems. First, if the private firm does not know the individual marginal benefit curves, it will not be able to determine the appropriate prices to charge each individual to maximize profit. Second, because the good is nonexcludable, it cannot induce one individual to pay for the good at all, given that some is produced and sold to the other individual. The firm could at best reach an agreement to produce and sell to the individual with the highest willingness to pay, which in the case of Figure 13.11 is individual 1. In this case, individual 2 is inclined to be a 'free rider' who merely benefits from the expenditure of others.

Suppose, for example, the private producer first successfully negotiates a price p^* with individual 1, a result that would equate the individual's marginal WTP with MC at quantity q^* in Figure 13.11(c).[22] In this case, individual 2 becomes a free rider able to consume

21. In economics these prices are known as *Lindahl prices*, and a competitive equilibrium where the consumers are charged these prices is called a *Lindahl equilibrium*. For a discussion of the properties of this equilibrium and the difficulties associated with discovery of these prices, see section 2.4 of Laffont (1988).
22. This case with marginal WTP equal to MC would likely not be an equilibrium because, with only one seller and one buyer, a less than competitive market quantity would likely occur as suggested by Sections 10.1 through 10.3.

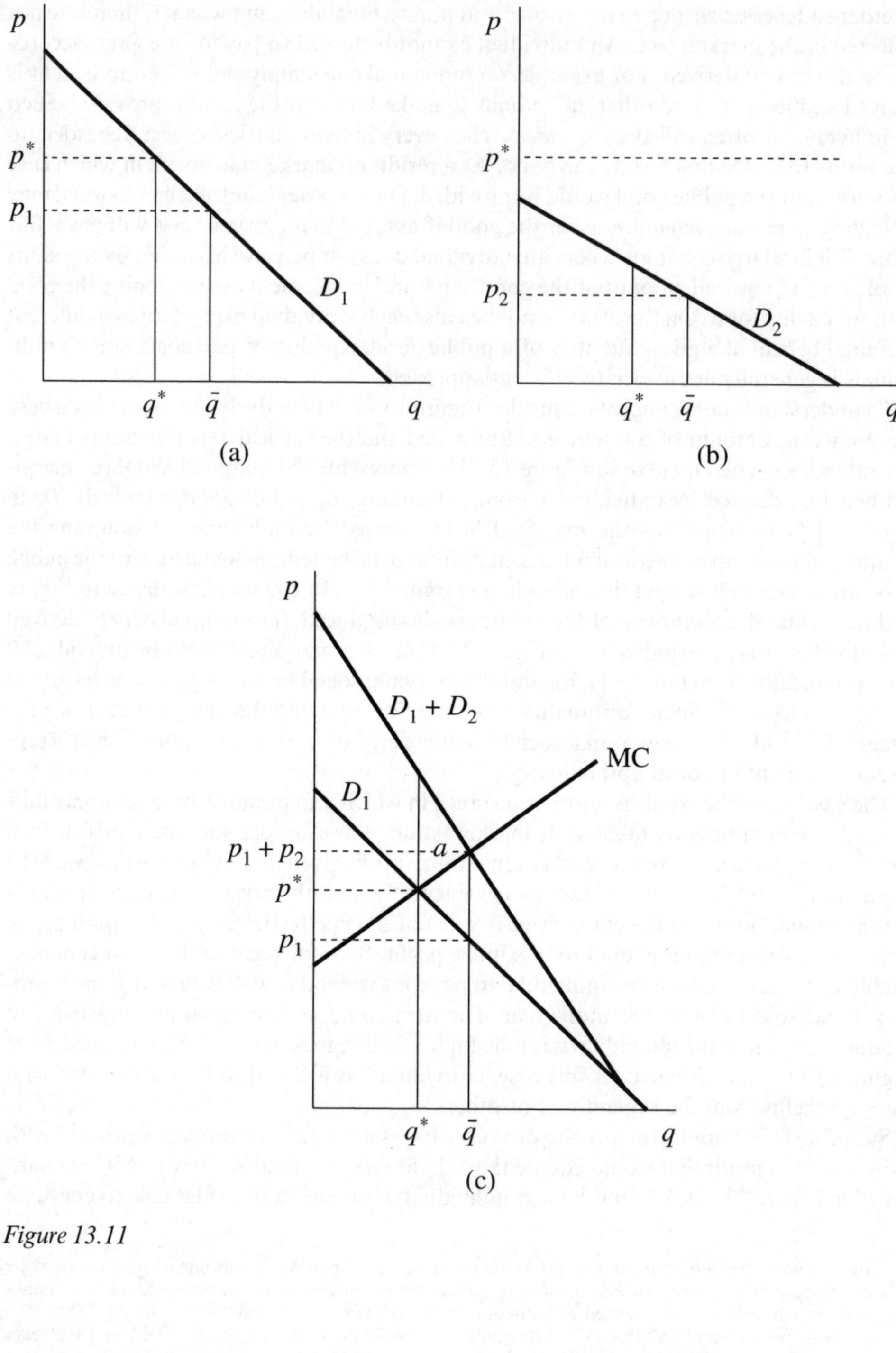

Figure 13.11

the same q^* without cost because the good is nonexcludable. The marginal WTP for individual 2 given that quantity q^* has been provided for free is only that portion of D_2 in Figure 13.11(b) to the right of q^*. Individual 2's maximum marginal WTP is thus less than the price charged to individual 1. It is less than the marginal cost of providing an additional unit of the good beyond q^*. Thus, any further negotiation with individual 2 by the producer will not result in additional sales.[23] As a result, only q^* of the good will be produced and consumed in the marketplace. Because this is less than $\bar{q}$, the public good would be under-provided to society. Social welfare could be increased by area *a* in Figure 13.11(c) by increasing production to $\bar{q}$.

Because of problems associated with pure public goods, private markets cannot attain optimality. Some form of governmental intervention is warranted. Indeed, the case of public goods presents the strongest case for government intervention of all the cases of market failure because no other mechanism can resolve the problem. The common form of intervention for providing public goods such as air quality, law enforcement and environmental preservation is for the government to play the direct role of producer or regulator, thus deciding upon $\bar{q}$. To determine the socially optimal amount of production, however, the government faces the problem of estimating the marginal social benefits in order to equate them with the marginal cost of production. And, if it wants to obtain funds for providing the public good using the benefits theory of taxation, then the government needs to know how much benefit is received by each individual. With the benefits theory of taxation, those who benefit from public provision of a good pay for it according to the marginal benefit they receive. Because information on marginal individual benefits is usually not available, governments usually determine the amounts of public goods to provide based largely upon political rather than economic criteria, which may cause significant under- or over-provision. In fact, when few individuals are involved or the variation in WTP among individuals is great, the deadweight loss of public provision of a good may be greater than what the private market could achieve (greater than area *a* in Figure 13.11).

13.3 IMPURE PUBLIC GOODS

A difficulty that must be considered in cost–benefit analysis of public goods is the fact that many so-called public goods are not pure public goods. For many goods, nonexcludability fails either partially or completely. *Partial excludability* is the case where consumption cannot be completely withheld by the seller, for example, where a consumer can derive part of the benefits of a paying customer by looking over the fence or by getting information secondhand. For other goods such as streets, highways and bridges, nonrivalry changes to partial rivalry as increased use causes congestion and exhausts capacity. *Partial rivalry* is the case where the consumption of a given amount of a good by one person reduces the amount of the good available for others to consume by only part of that amount, or reduces the benefits received by others from consuming that amount of

23. If this same exercise were carried out by the seller first negotiating with the individual with lower WTP, then both the price and the amount negotiated would be less. But, if so, the individual with higher WTP would be willing to buy an additional amount at price p^*, bringing the total quantity up to q^*. But the seller would be worse off because some of q^* would be sold to the individual with lower WTP at a lower price.

the good. For other goods such as capital investments, the service flows may produce private and public benefits jointly.[24]

Excludability, Nonrivalry and the Case of Club Goods

The class of public goods that are excludable but nonrival is large and heterogeneous. As a concrete example, consider the case of a New Hampshire farmer who has a spring on his property that is widely known for its clear, clean and fresh water. Because the spring is near a public road and the farmer does not restrict access to the spring, a well-worn path to the spring develops as people take advantage of the opportunity. Suppose the amount of water taken by one individual does not reduce that available for successive visitors. The good is fully nonrival if the amount of water is adequate for everyone who comes. But the farmer could restrict access by simply building a fence and installing a 'no trespassing' sign. Alternatively, the farmer could charge a price for access. What price should the farmer charge if he wants to maximize private benefits? What price should be charged to maximize social net benefits?

To maximize private benefits (profit), the farmer would follow the monopoly-pricing rule of Section 10.1 by setting a price that restricts access to the point where marginal revenue is equal to marginal cost. Suppose the marginal cost of providing the good is essentially zero, as in the case where the farmer suffers no damage from others using the spring. This case is illustrated in Figure 13.12, where D is the demand curve for access to the site and also represents the marginal social benefit (MSB). To maximize profit, the

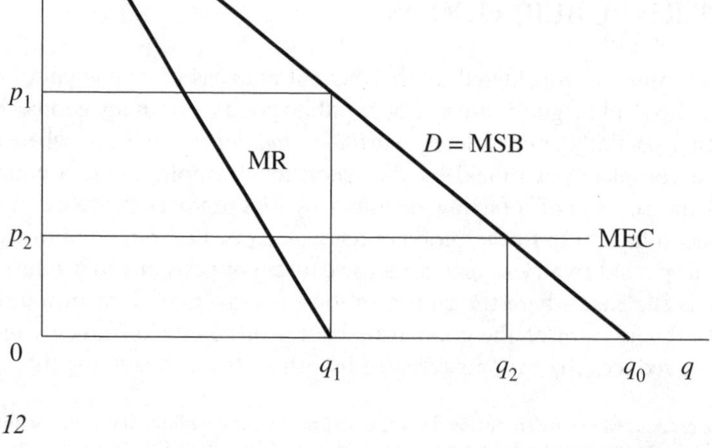

Figure 13.12

24. For a useful discussion of impure public goods, see Cornes and Sandler (1996).

farmer will set a price p_1, which restricts access to quantity q_1, and thus effectively equates marginal revenue (MR) to the zero marginal cost along the q axis. The farmer thus extracts monopoly rent in the amount p_1q_1. Social optimality, however, requires equating marginal social benefits (MSB) to marginal social cost. If marginal social cost is equal to the farmer's marginal private cost and is zero, then the price should be set at zero, which provides free access and yields quantity q_0.

The example of a New Hampshire farmer has the characteristics of many excludable nonrival goods. Namely, they tend to be tied to a specific site and they are properly viewed as a service flow associated with a natural or physical capital good. Thus, owners of such capital goods face incentives to exercise monopoly power. For this reason, most goods in this category have been called *local public goods*. Examples of local public goods are physical capital like a bridge or highway, and natural capital like a beach. When local public goods are fully excludable, the free-rider problem can be resolved by charging prices or user fees.[25] However, the socially efficient price for such nonrival service flows, once the capital good exists, is zero, aside from marginal maintenance, operation and depreciation costs.

As the New Hampshire farmer example makes clear, excludable nonrival 'public' goods can be privately owned and provided as well as publicly owned and provided. The use of the word 'public' by economists as a technical description of the consumption characteristics of such goods is probably unfortunate and certainly confusing to beginning students of economics. Consequently, the more fitting term 'club goods' has come into common use. *Club goods* are local public goods that are fully excludable but not fully rival. Public intervention is often not required to provide club goods because entry prices can be fully enforced by private owners. Even though entry fees cannot be set equal to consumers' marginal WTP, which is typically unobservable as in the case of public provision, consumers can be charged on the basis of use or number of entries, which provides an approximation.

Monopolistic pricing inefficiency can be avoided if many individuals own such capital goods and thus compete in supplying services. Physical capital can also be constructed or threatened by groups or clubs of investors to ensure socially efficient pricing and competitive access.[26] An example might be the construction of a community swimming pool or a community security system by a community organization. In the case of unique natural capital, however, public ownership may be necessary to avoid monopoly pricing and achieve social optimality. An example might be unique scenery such as in Yosemite National Park or Yellowstone National Park. With less uniqueness, however, groups or clubs may form to purchase natural capital and make it available to its members. An example might be a beach club.

While control of an excludable nonrival good by a single private company may induce monopoly pricing, one must also bear in mind that administrators of publicly provided excludable nonrival goods are also subject to the temptation to use monopoly power. For

25. Local public goods can also be nonexcludable. Examples are air quality and crime rates in a given city or locality. The analysis of these cases, however, is formally equivalent to the case of pure public goods discussed in Section 13.2 because the problem of free-ridership cannot be eliminated under nonexcludability.
26. As discussed in Section 10.10, the case where the mere threat of entry is sufficient to avoid monopoly pricing is called a contestable market. It requires costless entry and exit without other barriers to entry. For further discussion, see Baumol, Panzar and Willig (1988).

example, revenues such as entrance fees for parks, license fees for hunting and fishing, and museum tickets are seldom returned to general tax funds in any state or federal government. Administrators quickly discover that funding constraints are relaxed for their agency or department by charging fees, and that these benefits are greatest when charging monopoly prices. Sometimes this approach is easier than defending budget increases to government budget committees. For example, the Department of Fish, Wildlife, and Parks in the State of Montana has never in its history required general funds for the administration of their Fish and Wildlife Program. It operates entirely on the revenues the program produces through the sale of hunting and fishing licenses and the return of excise taxes on outdoor equipment.[27] As a result, the agency has great independence in its actions.

In conclusion, while prices can be charged for the use of excludable nonrival goods, social efficiency for services flowing from natural capital goods is usually attained by providing free access or at least minimal fees sufficient to cover marginal maintenance and operation costs. For service flows from physical capital goods, however, the longer-run question of adequate investment in the development of such goods is important. These service flows, if fully excludable, can be viewed as club goods, in which case public intervention is not necessary.

Partial Excludability and Regulation of Excludability under Nonrivalry

One of the most important types of nonrival goods that tends to be privately controlled is intellectual property and technical know-how. A research breakthrough or a technological innovation achieved in the private research laboratory of a major manufacturing company is typically nonrival or at least partially rival.[28] There may be great potential social benefits from its widespread dissemination and adoption. But to maximize profits, the company discovering the breakthrough is better off prohibiting others from using the information, or at least charging a licensing fee for use by others. Otherwise, the profit potential of using the information in its own production and sales is diminished. In fact, such profit opportunities may be necessary to induce firms to bear the expense of research and development (R&D).

Firms have two means of making nonrival R&D discoveries excludable: (1) patenting the innovation, or (2) keeping the innovation as a trade secret. A patent legally gives the firm a monopoly on the use of the innovation for a fixed period of time (currently 20 years for most US patents). While a patent may cause inefficiency due to monopoly pricing as long as it lasts, the monopoly profits offer an incentive for the private sector to continue investing in long-run, welfare-improving R&D. Patent expiration, on the other hand, eventually facilitates competition with its associated Pareto-efficient production and distribution using the new technology. Finding the optimal patent life that governments should impose to achieve a socially efficient balance between the incentive for continued innovation and the welfare-enhancing benefits of competitive use of innovations is a challenging problem.

27. Personal communication with Sue Daley, Chief Budget Officer, Montana Department of Fish, Wildlife, and Parks, January 2003.
28. Some innovations are only partially nonrival because they require additional research or adaptation before they can be used in other locations or in other production processes.

In lieu of a patent, a firm may decide to keep a new discovery as a trade secret, which allows the firm to profit from the innovation, but runs the risk that the trade secret will be stolen by an employee or that some other firm will make the same discovery and even patent it, enabling exclusive use for themselves. The trade-secret approach may be preferred to patenting if a company believes it can maintain secrecy longer than the life of a patent or if a patent is viewed as poor protection against another firm developing and patenting a similar innovation. Patenting an innovation requires making public some information about the innovation that may enhance discoverability of similar innovations that will allow other firms to appropriate some of the profits that could otherwise be earned by keeping the first innovation as a trade secret.

These examples suggest that monopolistic social inefficiency is likely to occur as a result of patents and trade secrets just as for many privately owned local public goods. They make clear that government intervention to convert excludable discoveries into nonexcludable knowledge can be important in obtaining the social benefits of competition. On the other hand, some incentive beyond competitive pricing is required to induce development of new innovations. Development of more efficient mechanisms of inducing R&D remains an interesting issue. These examples also make clear that excludability with respect to R&D has important dynamic considerations due to patent expiration as well as stochastic considerations due to the random nature of external trade secret discovery (legal or illegal) that may be important in achieving social efficiency.[29]

In some cases, making a profit from knowledge developed by R&D requires sharing that knowledge with buyers. In this case, excludability is impossible or partial at best. For example, the sellers of marketing newsletters may not be able to prevent buyers from sharing the information with other potential buyers, possibly because of high detection and enforcement costs. For such information products, the sellers can likely achieve only partial excludability. For example, the sellers of a newsletter may depend on the premium associated with timely information use. Whether the private market will adequately provide such information depends on the value of timeliness.

For other products such as genetically modified seeds, the seeds may be reproducible with a partial loss of genetically engineered properties such as pest resistance. In this case, the characteristics that command a price premium are only partially excludable. One approach to enhance excludability in this case is the contracting approach used by the Monsanto Corporation whereby buyers agree that they will not use any of the crop produced from Monsanto seeds for seeding a future crop. But enforcing such contracts requires detection and legal costs that, in effect, prevents full excludability.

Some innovations come in the form of abstract concepts that are not embodied in any particular product, material or process. Because such discoveries cannot be patented, they are typically not fully excludable and thus are not fully appropriable. Accordingly, the private sector is likely to underfund such research. Furthermore, because basic research typically has a variety of applications that remain undiscovered until results are widely disseminated, the results of basic research tend to contribute more to social welfare when they are made nonexcludable through publication in academic journals and dissemination at

29. For a further discussion of rivalry and excludability issues related to R&D and its dissemination, see Adams and Jaffe (1996), Byerlee and Traxler (1995), Evenson and Kislev (1975), Hanson and Just (2001), Henderson and Cockburn (1996), Huffman and Evenson (1993), Huffman and Just (1999a, 1999b) and Wright (1983).

meetings of learned societies. By comparison, the private sector is likely to under-disseminate such results. Thus, social welfare is often best served when the basic research that produces abstract knowledge is performed in publicly funded universities, agencies and research institutes.

In conclusion, if excludability fails at least partially then the private sector will generally under-provide because benefits are only partially appropriable. On the other hand, without profit motivations, the incentives driving public provision may be inadequate when goods are partially or mostly appropriable. For example, while a centralized government could attempt to provide all R&D publicly, the incentive for innovation of discoveries may be lower than for private firms driven by a profit motivation. The best government intervention in these cases may be to provide infrastructure or institutions that enhance excludability and thus appropriability. For example, even when a discovery is made in a public institution, selling the patent to a private firm may be necessary before any firm will undertake the expenses of developing consumer recognition and acceptance. Otherwise, other firms could enter the market and, through competition, eliminate the rewards for market development as soon as sufficient consumer acceptance was achieved. The Bayh–Dole Act of 1980 enhanced this possibility in the USA by allowing universities to sell patents generated from federally funded research in private markets. As another policy of enhancing excludability, intellectual property rights have been established and strengthened over the past several decades, for example by the US Plant Variety Protection Act of 1970 as amended in 1995, to protect the use of intellectual products that can be well defined but are not subject to patent law. As these cases demonstrate, economic welfare analysis for partially excludable nonrival goods must be carefully adapted to the specific circumstances of the good.

Partial Rivalry Due to Congestion and Physical Limitations

To extend the New Hampshire farmer example further, note that as more and more people stop to use the farmer's spring, congestion may develop. The congestion may be in the form of crowding as visitors have to stand in line at busy times. The farmer's fields may also be damaged by excessive pedestrian or automobile traffic. In these cases, the non-rivalry that exists at low levels of use becomes partial rivalry. The capacity of the spring may even become exhausted, in which case full rivalry occurs. These cases are addressed by considering congestion costs associated with use of the capital asset. Congestion costs may be zero over only a limited range of use but then increase as rivalry develops. Once rivalry develops, efficient use can be achieved by charging an appropriate admission price if the good is excludable.

Suppose, for example in Figure 13.12, that each visitor to the spring imposes a constant marginal externality cost of MEC. Then social benefits would be maximized by equating MEC with MSB. The social optimum would be achieved by charging a price equal to MEC. The social optimum would thus restrict visits to the amount q_2. Note that MEC would include both marginal damage to the farmer's fields and the marginal congestion cost imposed by visitors on other visitors. In setting a price to maximize private profit, the farmer would take demand into account but would consider only the part of MEC reflecting damage to the farmer's fields.

Another consideration for many local public goods, such as highways, bridges and beaches, is that attaining excludability may require additional capital expenditures for installation of entrance gates, toll booths and/or fences as well as additional variable costs for staffing access-control facilities. If so, then these additional costs must also be taken into account in economic welfare and efficiency analysis. The cost of capital, such as for a fence necessary to achieve excludability for the farmer, may exceed potential profit, in which case the best choice may be to not control access. Also, the marginal cost of entry control, maintenance and other operation costs, and capital depreciation add to the price charged for entry, whether in maximizing private profit or attaining a social optimum. For example, the value of the farmer's time required to collect entry fees may be worth more than he could charge. Additionally, the form of entrance control necessary for excludability may cause additional congestion costs. Such is typically the case when toll booths are installed for bridges and turnpikes because of backups caused in periods of heavy use. While a private provider may ignore such costs, the social optimum is affected and potential social benefits can possibly be negated by them. With public goods such as beaches and bridges, congestion costs are often a significant consideration in determining efficient use.

Quasipublic Goods: Joint Public and Private Service Flows[30]

Some goods have both public and private benefits, as in the case of public health and education. In other cases, capital goods, whether owned publicly or privately, produce both public and private service flows simultaneously. Such goods are called *quasipublic goods*. In many cases, these public and private service flows are technically tied so that independent production and consumption are not possible, although the mix may be varied. Consider the case of an urban development project. A low-density development project with trees, bushes, and open spaces and with a height restriction on buildings will provide apartments and parking spaces that are fully private goods. But this type of development will also provide more habitat for birds and wildlife, more ecosystem service flows and fewer restrictions on views by neighbors and passers-by than would a development composed of densely located high-rise apartments. These service flows are nonrival and likely also nonexcludable.[31] Urban planners and administrators must take into consideration benefits of both pubic service flows and private service flows when designing projects if they are to maximize the social benefits of development.[32]

As another example, consider the case of higher education. Numerous studies have

30. Burton Weisbrod first drew the distinction between pure public goods and quasipublic goods in a report to the US Congress, Joint Economic Committee (1969, pp. 177–97), which is a report that includes an impressive set of papers on practical considerations in the provision and financing of public goods.
31. The nonexcludability of public service flows from private property means that they are not appropriable. If they are not appropriable, they are not capitalized into property values even though they add to social benefits. This has led to some confusion on the part of tax appraisers. Appraisers have come to appreciate nonmarket environmental values and have attempted to adjust appraised values upward accordingly. Owners have contested these attempts, arguing that they are the beneficiaries of public service flows. In reality, the environmental capital good may have both public and private service flows. Neighbors of such a project may receive the public service flows, while the developer may receive private service flows from being able to command higher rental rates or sale prices because of the environmental characteristics incorporated in the project. For example, to the degree that landscaping and upkeep add to the marketability of a property, the appraised value would be increased.
32. For a case study of alternative development options for an urban open space, see Hueth and Mendieta (2000).

shown that college graduates earn more than noncollege graduates. Thus, the decision to invest in higher education is much like any other private investment decision. On the other hand, as the great welfare economist Pigou (1932, pp. 12–13) put it, 'a man who is attuned to the beautiful in nature or in art, whose character is simple and sincere, whose passions are controlled and sympathies developed, is in himself an important element in the ethical value of the world . . . a part of welfare'. Thus, higher education tends to produce a public return beyond the higher private income that might be earned by college graduates. Clearly, higher education has both public and private service flows. To the degree that the public service flows are not considered in the individual decision to pursue a college education, the private market would undersupply this commodity.

The case of public health education offers yet another example. Public health education and public health expenditures improve the health of individuals, which clearly offers a private return of well-being and productivity to the individuals whose health is improved. On the other hand, indirect benefits are also received as certain diseases such as smallpox are eradicated because the general public is less likely to contract diseases as a result of the improved health of the direct benefactors.[33]

As the discussion in this section illustrates, many goods have public good characteristics in various degrees. The optimal provision and regulation of these goods requires careful evaluation conditioned on the specific characteristics that apply in each case. In some cases, markets can function and can be modified by government intervention so they function efficiently, while in others they cannot. In some cases, public provision is necessary but in many cases it is not. In the case of public provision, determination of the amount to provide requires careful welfare analysis and often involves nonmarket benefit estimation.

13.4 MEASUREMENT OF EXTERNAL ENVIRONMENTAL BENEFITS AND COSTS

How does one develop a methodology for estimating marginal benefits and costs that are not reflected in the marketplace? A number of methodologies with various advantages and disadvantages exist for this purpose. As might be expected, these methodologies are more complicated and controversial in the case of evaluating consumer benefits and costs than in evaluating producer benefits and costs. The remainder of this chapter will discuss some of the more commonly used approaches.

Estimation of Producer Damage and Abatement Cost Functions

Estimation of damage and abatement cost functions follows a rather straightforward approach for the case of producer–producer externalities, as suggested by the mathematical example at the beginning of Section 13.1. For example, the demand for the product given by D in Figure 13.4 can be simply estimated along the lines suggested in Section 8.8. Similarly, for a competitive industry, the supply curve corresponds to the marginal private

33. For further discussion of this case in the context of international public health, see Sandler and Acre M (2002).

cost curve MPC in Figure 13.4 and can thus be estimated as the output supply of a competitive industry following the methodology in Section 8.8. The vertical difference in these two relationships for a given set of determinants of supply and demand can then be computed to represent the marginal (opportunity) cost of control (labeled as $D - \text{MPC}$ in Figure 13.5). This approach, of course, assumes that the level of damages has a direct relationship with the amount of production that cannot be altered, for example, by employing pollution abatement equipment.

If pollution abatement equipment exists for reducing the extent of the externality, a more extensive study of the production function of the firm or industry must be carried out. In this case, the level of production as well as the level of pollution can be estimated as functions of the productive inputs and the amount of pollution abatement equipment employed. Then under the assumption of producer profit maximization subject to the given demand curve by consumers, a demand for pollution rights or a supply of pollution can be derived by imposing various prices on pollution in profit maximization. The resulting schedule will thus correspond to $D - \text{MPC}$ in Figure 13.5 for the case where possibilities for pollution abatement are taken into account. The most common approaches for carrying out this kind of work are either to estimate the production function econometrically (much as in the methodology considered in Section 8.8) or to consider optimization directly through means of mathematical programming.

Turning to the damage function or the MEC curve in Figure 13.5, when all external agents are producers and all such agents can be identified, the estimation of damages can follow a similar methodology. That is, the production function of an external agent (or group) can be estimated with production specified as depending on the firm's (or group's) productive inputs and the pollution imposed upon it externally following the simple single-equation estimation methodology discussed in Section 8.8. Thus, damages can be calculated for varying levels of pollution using prevailing prices for inputs and output. If these inputs and output do not face perfectly elastic supplies or demand, respectively, then the associated adjustments in prices resulting from changes in pollution levels must also be considered in calculating marginal damages. Again, another approach in this case is to consider the external agent's production problem by means of mathematical programming where changes in pollution are imposed on the firm through varying pollution constraints.[34] In either case, estimation of marginal damages (that is, marginal external costs) is a rather straightforward matter, given the existence of sufficient data to estimate the associated production functions and, possibly, the input supply and output demand functions.

As evident from Section 4.3 and in contrast with Section 12.6, producer welfare measurement is greatly simplified when the objective of producers is to maximize profits, the unit of measurement for which is money. In this case of the producing firm, no distinction is necessary between the various WTP measures of welfare. They are all equal to changes in profit except in shutdown cases where fixed costs must be considered. When imposed on consumers, the problem of estimating marginal external costs (benefits) is more complicated and the appropriate welfare measure is less clear because of typical differences in compensating and equivalent surpluses.

34. A discussion of programming methods is beyond the scope of this book. The reader may, however, find a popular example of the linear programming approach in chapter 10 of Herfindahl and Kneese (1974).

Valuation of Consumer Nonmarket Benefits

Typically, the consumer has no choice over the amount of pollution to which he or she is exposed (a 'bad') or to the environmental amenities he or she enjoys at, for example, a recreational site (a 'good'). In this setting, the appropriate WTP measures are the compensating surplus and equivalent surplus measures developed in Section 7.9. That is, changes in environmental quality are conceptually equivalent to imposed quantity changes in their welfare impact because in both cases the consumer does not have control over adjustment. Thus, the theoretical results of Appendix Section 7.J apply directly where changes in imposed quantities are simply reinterpreted as changes in quantities of an environmental amenity or the quality of the environment. If a market existed for environmental quality, then the Marshallian demand and the Hicksian compensated demand for environmental quality could be reflected as in Figure 7.10. As shown in Appendix Section 7.J, as the income effect of a change in environmental quality gets small, the compensating surplus and equivalent surplus both converge to the consumer surplus change.

Unfortunately, markets do not exist for environmental quality or pollution and, hence, price and quantity data are not available to estimate the demand for environmental quality. If such data were available, an estimated Marshallian demand curve such as D in Figure 7.10 might be used as an approximation of the compensating or equivalent surplus appealing to the Willig results as in the price change case. That is, suppose there is a decrease in environmental quality (increase in pollution) in Figure 7.10 from q_0 to q_1. Then the exact compensating surplus of this change is measured in the figure by a loss of area $a+c+d+e+f$, where the price of environmental quality or pollution is zero. The change in the area under the ordinary demand curve, a loss of area $c+d+f$, is an approximation to the compensating surplus of the change. Because this curve cannot be estimated, however, efforts have focused on directly measuring the welfare quantities involved or, alternatively, trying to estimate areas in related markets that measure these gains or losses. These methods are further explained in the remainder of this section.

In the case of producer abatement cost and damage function analysis, the damage and abatement cost functions can be estimated given data availability because profit-maximizing behavior generates supplies and demands from which profit and cost effects can be inferred. For consumers or households, however, improvements in environmental quality or the preservation of a natural environment can result in both *use* and *nonuse* benefits.

Use benefits or use values include direct benefits of improved recreational experiences and aesthetic benefits received directly by the consumer from, for example, improving the water quality of a bay used for swimming, the beauty of flora and fauna of a park visited by the consumer, the fish population in a river in which the consumer fishes or the forest cover of a mountain viewed by the consumer. But use values may also represent indirect benefits such as carbon sequestration, flood control and other ecosystem service flows that contribute indirectly to the environmental, health or other benefits received by the consumer.

In addition to use values, consumers may be willing to pay for improvements in environmental quality at a site or for the preservation of a natural resource even though they never actually use the resource or visit the site. Nonmarket *nonuse values* are usually categorized as *existence values* or *option values*. Existence value is the WTP for the existence or a site or resource attributed, for example, to (1) a bequest motivation for future generations, (2) the intrinsic value of a site, (3) the 'guilt' complex resulting from environmental damage, (4) the vicarious experiences gained through giving to friends and relatives, and (5) simply knowing that a particular species continues to exist.[35]

Option value has been used alternatively to reflect uncertainty about the availability of a site at some future time when the consumer may want to use it, or the consumer is simply uncertain as to whether of not he or she will visit the site. The notion suggested by Burton A. Weisbrod (1964, p. 472) is that 'if these consumers behave as "economic men" they will be willing to pay something for the option to consume the commodity in the future'. Weisbrod characterizes this value as something in addition to the expected benefits the consumer would derive from personally visiting the site or using the resource. The concept of option value was subject to extensive economic examination by numerous economists during the 1970s and 1980s (see Freeman 2003, pp. 247–50 for a discussion) who attempted to show the conditions under which it was positive. However, the work of Schmalensee (1972) and Graham (1981) showed that *option value* is not a single well-defined measure of consumer welfare change under uncertainly. Rather, it is the difference in two justifiable measures of welfare change, namely *option price* and expected *ex post* compensating variation. The difference can be either positive or negative. Section 12.6 provides a detailed analysis of these concepts and discusses the conditions under which either of these is appropriate. While many alternative measures are possible with uncertainty, and some may be able to justify a project or policy when others cannot, the most practical measure for consumer welfare change under uncertainty is *option price*, which can also be called *ex ante* compensating variation.

We therefore agree with Freeman (1993, p. 264) who argued that, even though it has great intuitive appeal, 'it is time to expunge *option value* from the list of possible benefits associated with environmental protection'. As a result, current practice tends to calculate the total nonuse value of an environmental improvement or natural resource as the sum of existence value and expected *ex ante* WTP for future use calculated under uncertainty following the concepts of Section 12.6 as developed in Appendix Section 14.B. Nonuse value must then be added to use value to assess the total value of improvements in environmental quality.

Nonmarket use values can be estimated both by stated preference (SP) or revealed preference (RP) techniques. With SP, hypothetical markets are posed to interviewees to estimate household WTP for environmental amenities. The most frequently used SP technique, *contingent valuation*, is discussed further below. With RP, observed behavior in an observed market affected by varying amounts of a certain environmental amenity is used to estimate the benefits from improvements in environmental quality.[36] For example, a reasonable hypothesis is that deterioration in the quality and safety of publicly provided drinking water will increase the demand for bottled water in an urban area. Thus, benefits from improvements in urban water supply quality may be measurable in the bottled-water market if bottled water and clean drinking water are substitutes.

Other possibilities exist when environmental quality is complementary with a market good. For example, benefits from fishing in a stream are likely complemented by the rate of fish catch from the stream. That is, increases in the fish-catch rate will shift the demand

35. For a more comprehensive discussion of nonuse values see Freeman (2003, ch. 5).
36. Recent developments in RP techniques can be found in Herriges and Kling (1999).

curve for fishing. Thus, the benefits of policies or projects that increase the rate of fish catch in the stream might be measured by the area between the demand curves before and after the policy is implemented using one of the methodologies of Section 7.10. A rigorous approach under which the welfare effects of such policies can be evaluated is developed in Appendix Section 7.I, which extends implicitly to that case of household production of nonmarket goods based on results in Appendix 7.G. Nonuse values, however, can be estimated only with SP techniques because they generate no observed behavior from which values can be inferred. A more detailed discussion of SP or survey techniques and some of the most common RP techniques is given next.

Survey Techniques and Contingent Valuation

The first use of direct elicitation of WTP to value recreational experiences was done by Davis (1964) in Maine. Since then, elicitation has become a widely used valuation technique throughout the world and is particularly popular in developing countries where economic data are scarce and limit the use of indirect techniques. Early contingent valuation (CV) efforts used open-ended questions asking survey respondents to give their (maximum) WTP for an environmental improvement or (minimum) willingness to accept for a given increase in contamination without any particular reference point. Investigators found that respondents had difficulty responding to a hypothetical market setting without a reference point. Thus, the resulting estimates of compensating and equivalent surpluses were suspect.

Investigators next began asking respondents if they were willing to pay a small specific amount of money for a specific environmental improvement. After receiving the expected positive response they incrementally increased the amount of payment until they received a 'no' answer. For two classic examples of this approach, see Randall, Ives and Eastman (1974) and Brookshire, Ives and Schultze (1976). This approach, known as a *bidding game*, also encountered a number of methodological problems. Studies indicated that the maximum WTP by interviewees was sensitive to the initial payment specified, which is called *starting-point bias*. In addition, bidding game results were found to be sensitive to which person conducted the interview, which is called *interviewer bias*.[37]

Survey techniques have also encountered several other important problems.[38] First, the results of a survey may not be representative of the affected population. One reason is that it may be impossible to identify all affected individuals. Some visits to a polluted area or recreational facility may yet be made by individuals from other states or countries that cannot be anticipated, and their WTP for various alternatives should be properly considered. If the survey must rely on a sample rather than including all affected individuals, the sample may not be representative because of *sample selection bias*. The criteria for sample selection must be carefully scrutinized in each case. Perhaps those who satisfy criteria for being included in the survey (sample selection criteria) have good reasons for

37. An alternative approach is to give an individual a fixed hypothetical budget or set of coupons and then ask for allocation of the budget or coupons among a set of possible projects. See Pendse and Wyckoff (1974) and Strauss and Hughes (1976). The problem associated with choosing an appropriate vehicle for payment or standard of comparison in hypothetical surveys is generally called the problem of *instrument bias*.
38. Critiques of the various problems associated with bidding games can be found in Schultze, d'Arge and Brookshire (1981) and Mitchell and Carson (1989, ch. 11).

responding differently than other individuals. For example, in some surveys the individuals decide for themselves whether to be included or not. In this case, only those with a vested interest may care to participate and, thus, the sample would show greater concern than the population in general. The problem of self-selection is a serious drawback for voting schemes in general because voting participation generally varies with such characteristics as ethnicity, income and education, as well as intensity of preferences for the issues at hand.

Another problem with the survey and bidding game approach is that responses may be biased because of participants' beliefs, whether well founded or not, concerning how the information will be used. Suppose, for example, that a survey is intended to determine the optimal scale of a public goods project. If the individual believes that an additional personal cost will not be incurred regardless of scale, then he or she may be induced to claim larger benefits than actually derived. The motivation would be to enjoy a greater amount of public goods as a free-rider without bearing additional costs. When an individual responds untruthfully to such a survey because of such an attempt to influence the policy outcome, the behavior is called *strategic behavior*. On the other hand, suppose an individual expects to pay exactly what he or she reports as WTP if a project is adopted. Then the personal contribution to aggregate WTP may be viewed as insignificant because of population size. If the individual believes his or her contribution is inconsequential in aggregate WTP (derived by such survey techniques), then he or she may fail to give careful consideration to the response or fail to answer because of limited concern.

Investigators now generally acknowledge that the survey technique that minimizes response effect biases in contingent valuation surveys is the closed end survey form. W. Michael Hanemann (1992) pioneered this form, which is also known as the *referendum model*. In this framework, the respondent is simply asked to respond yes or no regarding WTP to an interviewer-specified amount, usually framed as an increase in taxes. One payment from a range of values is randomly assigned to each respondent of a sample from the relevant population. A 'yes' response to the interviewer indicates that the maximum WTP is at least as great as the specified amount. A 'no' response indicates that the specified amount is an upper bound on maximum WTP. Discrete choice econometric techniques are then used to estimate the parameters of the indirect utility function of a representative consumer, from which the mean or median compensating surplus or equivalent surplus can be calculated.[39]

The popularity of discrete choice models was greatly enhanced when a 'Blue Ribbon Panel' of experts including Nobel Laureates Kenneth Arrow and Robert Solow recommended that the discrete choice framework should be used in contingent valuation studies. This panel was convened by the US National Oceanic and Atmospheric Administration (1993) to develop guidance for the US government on the validity of CV methodology for estimating use and nonuse values in the wake of the publication of a series of studies, many critical of CV methodology, funded by the Exxon Corporation (Hausman 1993). In 1989, the grounding of the *Exxon Valdez* and the subsequent oil spill in Prince William Sound off the coast of Alaska presented clear financial peril to the Exxon Corporation if found liable for the environment damages. Moreover, because the

39. Detailed expositions of the discrete choice (referendum model) methodology can be found in the seminal papers of Hanemann (1984a, 1984b). Also, an excellent presentation of this methodology with particular application to recreation economics is given by Bockstael, McConnell and Strand (1991).

population of the immediate area was small, the majority of the damages was expected to be lost nonuse values, for which the only methodology available for measurement was CV. Hence, Exxon had an obvious reason to fund these studies in the hope that CV methodology would be discredited. The Blue Ribbon Panel found a number of troubling problems with CV, the most serious of which was consistency of the appearance of 'embedding', but in the end gave cautious endorsement to the methodology.[40] Perhaps more importantly, the panel provided a number of widely accepted guidelines for the use of CV, including the recommendation of discrete choice models.

While behavior in the hypothetical markets of CV may not be as predictable at present as behavior in real markets, the efforts of many environmental and resource economists have refined the techniques for conducting these studies and credibility has improved. Moreover, in reality, no other methodology exists for estimating nonuse values. The alternatives, such as valuing them at zero or infinity, are simply not socially or politically acceptable.[41]

Travel Cost Methods

The first attempt to value nonmarket goods indirectly resulted from a request from the Directorate of the National Park Service to several outstanding economists to consider the problem of how to value the National Park System. The directorate explained that, unlike other agencies, when defending their budgets before Congress, monetary values of the benefits and values of their programs could not be presented as justification. After giving some consideration, the famous economist (as well as mathematician and statistician) Harold Hotelling (1947) responded with a letter to the Service in which he outlined the basic idea that has become known as the *travel cost method*. Although this idea initially encountered considerable opposition, it has now become widely accepted as a nonmarket valuation technique.[42]

The travel cost method is applicable for most problems related to public provision of recreation facilities. Many public recreation areas, such as state and national parks, are provided at a zero price or a nominal entry fee. A zero entry fee is perhaps Pareto efficient because no cost is associated with admitting an additional visitor if there are no congestion externalities and no marginal operation or maintenance costs. Through entry fees, however, these areas are excludable goods (even though nonrival), and the empirical approach of estimating demand in Section 8.8 seemingly becomes applicable. However, entry fees change only rarely if at all. Often observed variation is insufficient to enable estimation of the slope of individual or group demand curves. Furthermore and more important, the entry fees, even when nonzero, are usually insignificant compared to other visitor costs, such as transportation expenses. That is, the true WTP is likely to be much greater than what visitors actually do pay. Thus, estimation of a demand equation for a recreation area based on entry fees alone would ignore the most important factors affecting use.

40. Embedding is when the value of an amenity depends upon the degree to which it is embedded in other amenities. Studies have found, for example, that respondents in CV studies have been willing to pay essentially the same amount to save 2000 birds as they would to save 200000 birds.
41. For more on the continuing debate regarding the theory and methods of CV, see Bateman and Willis (1999).
42. For an interesting historical account of the development of the travel cost method as well as other nonmarket valuation techniques, see Hanemann (1992).

Because access costs associated with transportation in most cases are large enough to make recreation areas essentially excludable goods regardless of entry fees, the travel cost method employs access costs as a 'price' for the good in applying the otherwise usual approach of Section 8.8 in estimating demand.[43] Where entry fees exist, they are added to travel costs to obtain the access costs for the site. In practice, transportation costs are determined on the basis of travel distances to and from the recreation area. Then the number of site visits is regressed on or explained by costs of transportation plus entry, as well as other determinants of demand such as income, education, site characteristics, site congestion and the like.

The travel cost methodology implicitly assumes that recreational visits are *weakly complementary* with environmental quality (or improvements in environmental quality) at a recreational site. As explained in Section 7.10, a commodity is weakly complementary with environmental quality if improvements in environmental quality cause no utility increase for a consumer who does not visit the site.[44] Thus, improved forests or stream quality at a site have no value for a recreator who is located so far away as to be excluded from visits by high transportation costs.

These results are useful for welfare analysis upon assuming that a change in the entry fee of, say, \$1 causes the same change in site visits as a \$1 change in transportation expenses. Thus, the estimated relationship can be used to easily determine the marginal benefits of, say, an increase in site availability or in the value of the site. The consumer surplus triangle is the area below the demand curve for site visits and above the access cost (access cost serves as the effective price). Errors in changes in this surplus as a measure of true WTP must be considered along the lines presented in Sections 6.5, 6.6, 7.5 and 7.6 if the quantity of site visits is a choice left in the hands of consumers. Alternatively, errors in this measure are examined following Section 7.9 if the quantity of site visits is restricted by government policy.

The travel cost approach also suffers from several problems. First, as it was originally developed, only one recreation area was assumed to be available in each region. When several recreation sites are available in each area, cross elasticities of demand for each site must be considered.[45] This problem is approached by considering demand for each site as a function of all relevant visitor costs (which entails determination of distances from each of several sites for each individual). In addition, when multiple sites are available, one must control for the quality of each site so that the list of determinants used in each estimated demand relationship may involve attributes associated with activities, facilities and aesthetic factors at a number of sites.[46] This large number of factors can, of course, complicate estimation as well as data acquisition.

Of course, if visitor data (trips) are only available for one site, then the demand for that site may be estimated as long as one properly controls for all determinants of demand for access to the site. Other sites will have other prices (travel costs) and may offer different

43. The travel cost method was originally applied by Clawson (1959), Knetsch (1964) and Clawson and Knetsch (1966).
44. The concept of weak complementarity, although used by practicing recreational economists much earlier, was first formally defined by Mäler (1974).
45. The first paper to deal with the multiple-site problem integrability conditions in the recreational literature was Burt and Brewer (1971).
46. For a paper that develops an appropriate methodology for this case, see Hanemann (1981).

activities, facilities, or aesthetic qualities that also compete and affect the number of visits to the site in question. If the determinants of demand used in estimation properly control for these factors, and if data on demand for several sites are available, this problem does not necessarily prevent application of the method.

Another difficulty with the travel cost approach is the unobservable value of time involved in site visits.[47] The greater the travel distance, the less attractive a site becomes not only because of direct monetary expense of travel but also because of time spent traveling. The travel cost method normally considers only direct monetary costs of travel. But if each $1 in travel expense also involves the loss of, say, 10 minutes of leisure time, then a $1 increase in transportation costs may reduce site visits more than a $1 increase in the entry fee. Appropriate valuation of visitor costs necessarily involves determination of the value of leisure time forgone. Otherwise, visitor costs do not adequately reflect true marginal WTP. Widely accepted methods for this purpose have not yet been developed. Some have proposed the use of shadow prices of leisure time suggested by studies of commuting models and locational preferences. But others argue that the shadow prices of leisure for recreation, travel and commuting are not the same because of different routes and perhaps modes of travel. Others have suggested using the wage rate as the marginal value of leisure, but for many workers the institution of an eight-hour workday prevents marginal adjustments between work and leisure. Many studies have used adjustments more on the order of one-fourth to one-half of the wage rate (see Cesario 1976).

Suffice it to say that, although the travel cost method is based on more objective evidence than direct surveys, treatment of questions such as leisure-time evaluation, substitute sites and other substitute activities is still in need of refinement.

Hedonic Models

The *hedonic method* is another widely used indirect method for estimating the value of improving environmental quality. Air pollution or water pollution problems can have effects on the values of surrounding property. This realization suggests using market data to explain housing values by appropriate indices of air quality or water quality as well as other common variables such as lot size, structural characteristics, age, room size, commuting distances and other neighborhood characteristics.[48]

The theory of hedonic prices, that is, explaining the price of a commodity in terms of its characteristics, is more general than suggested by its applications to environmental quality problems. Early hedonic price studies, for example, considered such cases as the effects of food appearance on food prices, the effects of automobile safety characteristics on auto prices, and the effects of soil productivity on land prices. Zvi Griliches (1971) investigated the feasibility of incorporating such effects into common price indices such as the Consumer Price Index and the Producer Price Index. Sherwin Rosen (1974) provided a general theory of hedonic price determination in a competitive market of buyers and sellers.

47. One of the first research papers to consider the opportunity cost of time used in traveling to recreational sites was McConnell (1975).
48. For studies related to air quality, see Polinsky and Rubinfeld (1977) and Polinsky and Shavell (1976). For studies related to water quality, see David (1968) and Brown and Pollakowski (1977).

Environmental economic studies have usually treated supplies, such as the supply of housing in an urban area, as fixed in the short run and focused on determining the demand for environmental characteristics. The possibilities for welfare measurement of changes in environmental quality in the housing market usually assume weak complementarity between housing and environmental characteristics such as noise and air quality. Such a welfare analysis begins with the estimation of a hedonic price function of the form

$$p_h = f(z_1,\ldots,z_i,\ldots,z_I,s_1,\ldots,s_j,\ldots,s_J,Q_1,\ldots,Q_k,\ldots,Q_K),$$

where p_h is the price of a house; the z_i are characteristics of the house such as number of bedrooms, square footage, and age; the s_j are characteristics of the neighborhood such as proximity of schools and libraries, and crime rates; and the Q_k are environmental characteristics such as air quality, noise levels, and proximity of factories generating pollution. Because this equation is a reduced-form equation reflecting both supply and demand factors, the choice of functional form is often unclear except in qualitative terms (for example, if Q_k is a 'good' then it should have a positive effect on p_h).[49]

A utility-maximizing household takes this hedonic relationship as exogenous and in equilibrium equates the marginal effect of a quality characteristic on p_h with the household's marginal WTP. Thus, the marginal effect of an environmental characteristic on the hedonic price is an implicit price of the characteristic or, in other words, a marginal WTP. That is, the hedonic price equation allows calculation of the change in housing value, Δp_h, that would result from a marginal increase in environmental quality, ΔQ_k. This information is useful for the policy process. However, many projects or policies cause large discrete changes in quality. For welfare evaluation of these changes, the household's marginal WTP function or inverse compensated demand function for environmental quality must be identified. Unfortunately, the conditions under which this can be done either require strong assumptions, such as that all consumers have identical preferences and incomes, or require extensive data that are rarely available, such as data on a number of segmented housing markets.[50]

An alternative approach is to recognize that the variation in air or water quality over individuals, groups or periods of time works much like a change in the controlled quantity of a related good. Thus, following Section 7.10, if access to housing (either rented or owned) is an essential good, which seems to be a reasonable approximation, then the welfare effects of changes in air quality, water quality, and noise, as well as other threats to health and life, can be captured in markets for real estate.[51] This is done by means of estimating supply and demand in housing markets, rented and owned, where determinants or exogenous forces explaining changes in supply and demand include variables measuring air and water quality or perhaps local life expectancy or mortality rates.

Suppose in Figure 13.13 supply and demand for housing in a particular area are estimated to be S_0 and D_0, respectively, prior to some environmental degradation that causes

49. For an argument about why concavity might be reasonable to impose on this function and an overview of the use of property value models in environmental economics, see Freeman (2003, ch. 11).
50. A discussion of the various approaches to identification of the marginal bid function as a discrete welfare measurement problem is given by Palmquist (1991).
51. This result is demonstrated in detail in the framework of Appendix Section 7.J related to quantity and quality restrictions. For a related discussion of welfare measurement with hedonic pricing, see Hanemann (1980).

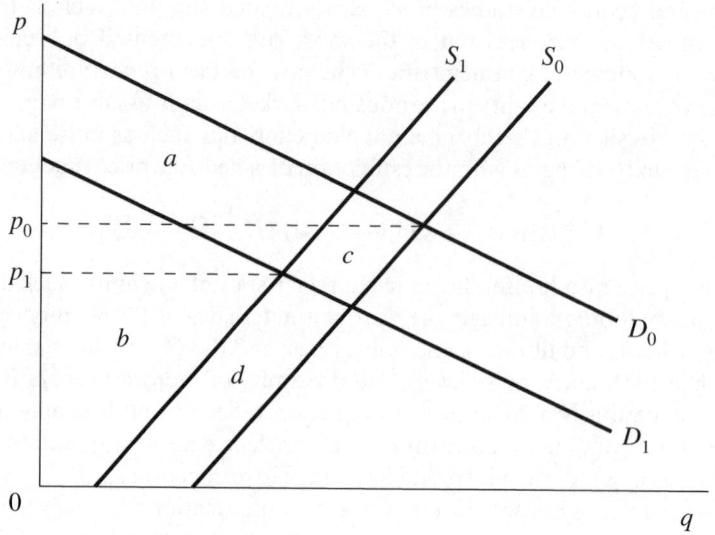

Figure 13.13

increased danger to life. Subsequently, supply and demand are estimated to be S_1 and D_1, respectively. Environmental degradation would suggest reduced demand for housing in that area because of the reluctance of consumers to willingly suffer from its effects either physically or aesthetically. The supply of housing may increase, decrease or remain unaffected, depending on the nature of the environmental degradation. Suppose, for purposes of exposition, that supply decreases. With a sufficiently small decrease in supply, rental rates would fall from, say, p_0 to p_1 in Figure 13.13. Following Section 7.10, the resulting welfare effect would be a loss from area $a+b+c+d$ to area b or a net loss of area $a+c+d$.

The major difficulty with the application of this approach is that market data are difficult to obtain. A relatively small portion of housing changes hands each year, the goods exchanged are far from homogeneous and, as a result, the data in both sales and rental markets are sparse. Furthermore, difficulties in the estimation of both supply and demand of housing are encountered when supply cannot be considered as strictly predetermined because the same exogenous forces may affect both sides of the market. Problems of econometric identification prevent estimation of supply and demand individually in this simultaneous context.[52] An alternative approach for this case has been to estimate 'reduced-form' equations that explain real estate sales or rental prices or valuations as a function of all the factors affecting either supply or demand.[53] Then the notion of equilibrium by household is employed to interpret the effect of environmental quality on housing prices as an effect on marginal WTP by each household.[54]

52. For discussion of the related problems of econometric identification, see Theil (1971, ch. 9) or Greene (2000, ch. 15).
53. The reduced-form equations are derived by solving the supply and demand equations simultaneously for price and quantity in terms of all other variables.
54. This approach, however, is only an approximation and corresponds to assuming fixed inelastic supply and vertically parallel shifts in demand in the context of Figure 13.13. Under such assumptions, simultaneous equations estimation methods need not be used. Thus the identification problem is not encountered.

13.5 CONCLUSIONS

This chapter has focused on the theory of externalities and public goods and possible approaches to measuring welfare effects in these cases. The problem in this type of analysis is that individual preferences are not completely reflected in ordinary market data. Nevertheless, interesting approaches have been used to analyze empirically the effects of externalities. Such information is important for the policy process as externality problems become more severe due to such factors as growing populations, increasing resource scarcity, and global environmental problems. While these results have been developed in the context of single markets, the principles of Chapter 9 can be applied in a straightforward manner for multimarket generalizations.

Empirical work on externality effects increased phenomenally during the 1970s because of growing problems of pollution and environmental degradation. For example, during the 1940s there was no reason to study the effects of the introduction of transgenic species into the environment because technologies to produce them did not exist. And there was little interest in controlling carbon emissions because global warming was not yet identified as a serious problem. On the other hand, with the energy crises of the late 1970s and the 1980s, new and alternative sources of energy, which resulted in undesirable side effects, became economical in the private market. As such technologies have emerged, analysis of environmental policy and its associated economic welfare effects has and will become increasingly important throughout the world. Nonmarket welfare measurement is an area of growing interest especially in the developing world.

14. Intertemporal considerations in cost–benefit analysis with applications to natural resource economics

Thus far, welfare effects have been discussed only in a static sense. That is, all the economic impacts occur during the same time period that the policy change is instituted. With many if not most policies, however, welfare effects (perhaps including both market and nonmarket effects) are realized beyond the immediate time period. For example, suppose that the government is considering building a dam with an accompanying reservoir which would generate hydroelectric power and either create or destroy recreational opportunities.[1] At the same time, those who now live where the reservoir is to be located would bear the costs of relocation. With this type of project the relocation costs must be borne during the early stages of the project, and the costs of building the dam would be incurred over the first several years of the project. However, the benefits in terms of hydroelectric power and recreational opportunities would be realized only after the construction period has ended and would extend for an indefinite period of time thereafter. Thus, a question that must be answered is, how should the benefits be weighed against the costs?

Generally, a benefit is not as valuable if it is realized later rather than earlier. For example, an individual would rather obtain \$1000 today than 10 years from now because that \$1000 can be gainfully invested during the 10-year period. Similarly, the same expense is more costly if incurred today rather than 10 years from now because, again, the associated amount of money could otherwise be employed usefully during the 10-year period or must be borrowed at the prevailing interest rate.

When a proposed policy or project generates a time series of benefits or costs over more than a single time period, the welfare effects in each individual time period can be calculated according to procedures discussed in previous chapters. However, to decide whether or not the policy is socially preferable or to evaluate the extent of overall net social benefits, the welfare effects in individual time periods must be aggregated over time, which requires some procedure for weighing benefits in one period versus another. The associated problem is referred to as social discounting.

This chapter first examines the problem of social discounting and the choice of a social discount rate. Then an approach for dynamic economic welfare analysis is set forth. The associated principles produce a framework for cost–benefit analysis of proposed public projects and policies that produce time streams of welfare effects. The remainder of the chapter then turns to the application of these principles in dealing with technological

1. The case of the proposed Hells Canyon Dam on the Snake River, for example, has been the subject of several studies of this type of problem. In this case, economic analysis played an important role in a decision not to build the dam because of the estimated future value of recreational and aesthetic opportunities that would be forgone. For further discussion, see Krutilla and Fisher (1978, ch. 6).

change and with renewable and nonrenewable natural resources. Throughout this chapter, benefits and costs are assumed to be measured appropriately in each time period involved in the analysis, so the central question is how to aggregate the benefits and costs over time.

14.1 THE SOCIAL DISCOUNT RATE

When a private, profit-maximizing firm faces a new business venture which produces a time stream of revenues and costs, one approach for deciding whether to undertake the venture is to compute the net present value (NPV) of the time stream of revenues and costs, which is sometimes called a discounted value. Suppose that the time stream of revenues or benefits is denoted by $B_0, B_1, B_2, \ldots$, and the time stream of costs is denoted by $C_0, C_1, C_2, \ldots$, where the subscript represents the time period in which the revenue or cost is incurred. In this case, the NPV of the stream of revenues and costs for the firm is given by

$$\text{PV} = B_0 - C_0 + \frac{B_1 - C_1}{1+r} + \frac{B_2 - C_2}{(1+r)^2} + \frac{B_3 - C_3}{(1+r)^3} + \ldots, \qquad (14.1)$$

where r is the interest rate that must be incurred by the firm in carrying debts from earlier periods over to later periods when net revenues are positive; or, if the firm is using its own funds to finance the project, then r represents the opportunity cost of funds that could have been invested elsewhere. In both cases, r is called the discount rate in the NPV calculation.

In private industry, many large companies coordinate investments across divisions by adopting a hurdle rate of return that represents the opportunity cost of its funds in other projects. The hurdle rate is then used as the discount rate in equation (14.1) to determine whether to undertake an individual project (if NPV>0). Suppose, for example, that a firm faces a project for which it incurs an immediate cost of \$10000 and expects a return of \$25,000 in 10 years. Then $C_0 = \$10000$ and $B_{10} = \$25000$, while all other B_t and C_t are zero, $t = 0, 1, 2, \ldots$ If the firm finances the project by borrowing \$10000 immediately with the intent of paying the accumulated interest and debt in 10 years at an interest rate of r, the payment required in year 10 would be $C_0(1+r)^{10}$. The net value of the project at year 10 thus would be $B_{10} - C_0(1+r)^{10}$. The NPV represents this amount transformed into current dollars by dividing by $(1+r)^{10}$. That is, $\text{NPV} = B_{10}/(1+r)^{10} - C_{10}$. In other words, where r is an interest rate in a perfect capital market, the NPV represents the amount of money that must be borrowed today to supply the same time stream of net returns as would be obtained through the business venture.[2] Alternatively and more typically in private industry, the NPV represents the additional amount of money that can be earned by this project over the potential return of other projects as represented by the hurdle rate r, stated in today's dollars.

The mechanism in equation (14.1) similarly provides a simple approach to determining the NPV of social benefits associated with a government policy or project. That is, where

2. A *perfect capital market* is one that carries no transactions costs or limits on amounts that can be borrowed, such as might be associated with collateral. One may either borrow or invest in any amount at the same prevailing interest rate.

B_t represents positive social benefits or aggregate willingness to pay (WTP) over all individuals affected positively in period t and C_t represents social costs or aggregate WTP over all individuals affected adversely in period t, the NPV given by equation (14.1) represents the amount of money required at time zero to finance the same stream of net benefits or WTP, given a perfect capital market with interest or discount rate r. Of course, if benefits exceed costs in every time period, a policy or project is unambiguously Pareto superior to doing nothing, and the NPV is positive for any discount rate r.

Most government investments, such as water and waste treatment plants, bridges, schools and irrigation projects, are characterized by large initial investment costs and a flow of positive benefits over long time frames of 40 to 60 years. That is, most investment projects have periods when net benefits are positive over the remaining lifetime of the project, after other periods when they are negative. In these cases, the determination of an appropriate social discount rate is crucial in determining whether the NPV is positive or negative.

In some cases, the evaluation of a project may have a time stream of net benefits that is relatively insensitive to the choice of the discount rate. In others, a long period of positive benefits may be followed by adverse costs such as the effects of environmental contamination. Consider, for example, Figure 14.1, which gives estimates of costs and benefits over time of increased CO_2 buildup in the atmosphere as a result of coal-fired electricity generation. As the diagram shows, benefits may be positive but small for a long

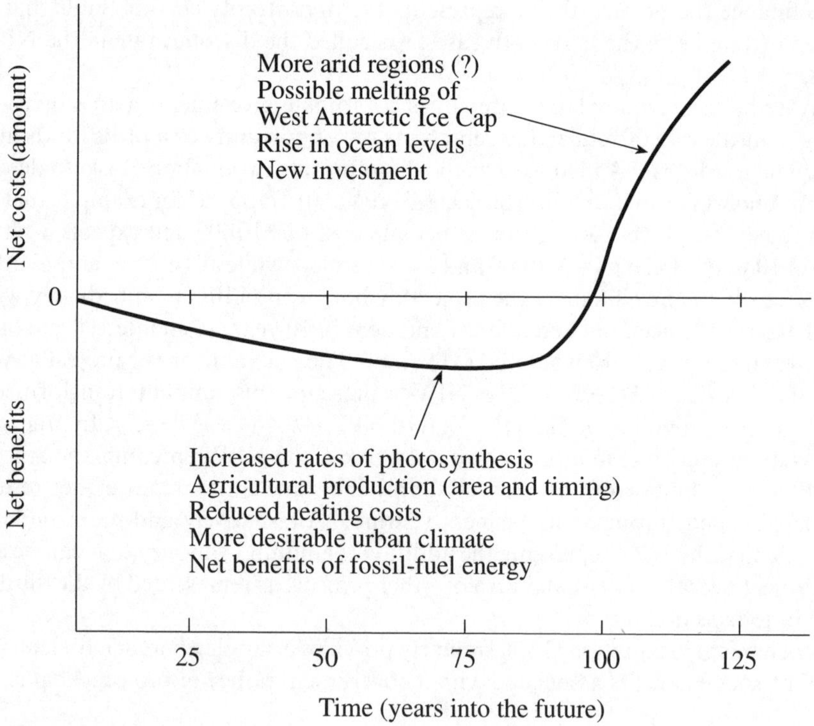

Source: d'Arge, Schultze and Brookshire (1980).

Figure 14.1

period of time and then turn negative and become large as society begins to experience global climate changes in the 'deep-future'. If these costs are far enough in the future, the NPV of the costs will be minuscule so that investments to reduce emissions of coal-fired plants cannot be justified for any reasonably positive discount rate. The hazard of discounting (the converse of the magic of compound interest) is illustrated by an example provided by Paul Portney and John Weyant (1999, p. 5):

> Assume, for example, that the gross domestic product (GDP) of the world will be \$8 quadrillion (15 zeros) in the year 2200 in current dollars. Suppose next that we want to calculate the present value of that sum using the 7% discount rate that the Office of Management and Budget recommends for such purposes. The answer we get is a surprising \$10 billion. In other words, it would not make sense for the world's present inhabitants to expend more than \$10 billion today (or about \$2 per person) on a measure that would prevent the loss of the entire GDP of the world 200 years from now.

The buildup of greenhouse gases is not the only phenomenon that has this profile of benefit and cost streams. The same holds for the disposal of radioactive wastes, losses of biodiversity and ecosystem damage.

Public concern about the appropriate discount rate to use for 'deep-discounting' led to a conference of leading scholars on the discount rate in 1996 sponsored by Resources for the Future and Stanford University's Energy Modeling Forum (see Portney and Weyant 1999 for the preceedings). These scholars generally agreed that discounting should be continued at some positive rate, even for deep-future projects involving multiple generations, but that lower rates should be used for more distant returns. In fact, empirical evidence suggests that this strategy is followed in practice (Cropper, Aydede and Portney 1994). An interesting problem presented by this approach, however, is that it leads to time-inconsistent behavior. That is, a person who at present decides to use a lower discount rate for future events will optimally have a change of mind when that future date arrives where the higher short-term discount rate is triggered.

Another interesting observation about deep-future events is the perspective of environmentalists on discounting. For cases such as global warming, radioactive waste disposal, losses of biodiversity and ecosystem damage, most environmentalists prefer to have a low or zero discount rate. However, for construction projects such as dam construction, the costs are immediate whereas the benefits occur over a long time frame. The time pattern of benefits and costs is thus just the reverse of the time pattern for most environmental issues. Environmentalists who favor free-flowing rivers and streams would prefer a high discount rate in this case. During the dam-building era of the 1950s and 1960s, environmentalists often suggested discount rates of 10 to 12 percent to evaluate proposed US Army Corps of Engineers dam proposals. Today, however, most environmental organizations support zero or negative discount rates for public investment projects with long-term environmental consequences.

These examples serve to illustrate that the choice of discount rate may have overriding importance in any cost–benefit analysis of government policy. For this reason, a major part of this chapter is devoted to the choice of discount rate.

The Rationale for Social Discounting

Several arguments have been advanced to justify the discounting of future benefits and costs. First, resources that are not used for immediate consumption can be employed in investment projects yielding a return in later periods that exceeds the value of the resources. Second, consumers are generally willing to pay more for immediate consumption than for deferred consumption. That is, they are impatient. Third, society may regard consumption by future generations as somewhat more or less important than that of the present generation. In the latter context, the problem of social discounting may become somewhat like a public goods problem. In modern terminology, the discount rate takes on a *prescriptive* nature in the latter context, whereas in the former two it is more *descriptive*. That is, the welfare of a future generation may be something for which all individuals in the current generation have concerns, regardless of their individual contributions to that welfare. Thus, as in the public goods cases of Sections 13.2 and 13.3, social efficiency may require government intervention on behalf of future generations.

The Market Rate of Interest as a Social Discount Rate

In a perfect market economy, the market rate of interest should correctly reflect the value of using resources in investment projects that do not exceed the life of existing firms. Similarly, the prevailing market rate of interest should reflect consumers' preferences toward financing current consumption through consumer debt as opposed to deferred consumption. The market rate of interest, however, may not reflect the value of using resources in investment projects that exceed the life of the present generation or in investment projects related to goods for which perfect markets do not exist (for example, public goods). In particular, the market rate of interest will not reflect society's regard for consumption by future generations. In addition, no single market rate of interest is generally agreed upon for these purposes. Consumers receive one rate of interest for savings accounts in banks and savings and loan associations, and pay other rates for home mortgages or automobile financing. Businesses pay yet another rate in financing business ventures. Furthermore, market interest rates may be altered as a result of undertaking some kinds of very large projects. Finally, interest rates are an important tool of macroeconomic policy used to control inflation and avoid recessions. Having the rule for justifying public projects depend on the cyclical activity to which macroeconomic policy responds seems unreasonable. For these reasons, the social discount rate that is appropriate for public policies may differ from the prevailing market rate of interest.[3]

Theoretical Determination of the Discount Rate: The Time Preference Approach

One conceptual approach to the problem of determining the correct social discount rate between two time periods is depicted in Figure 14.2, following essentially the same type

3. One may argue that each parent's regard for the future well-being of his or her children may lead to proper regard for future generations. Although this may lead to some regard for future generations, there is no reason why it should lead to the proper regard. For example, this line of reasoning would suggest less regard for the future generation if only one-tenth of all families had 10 children each (and other families had no children) than if every family had one child.

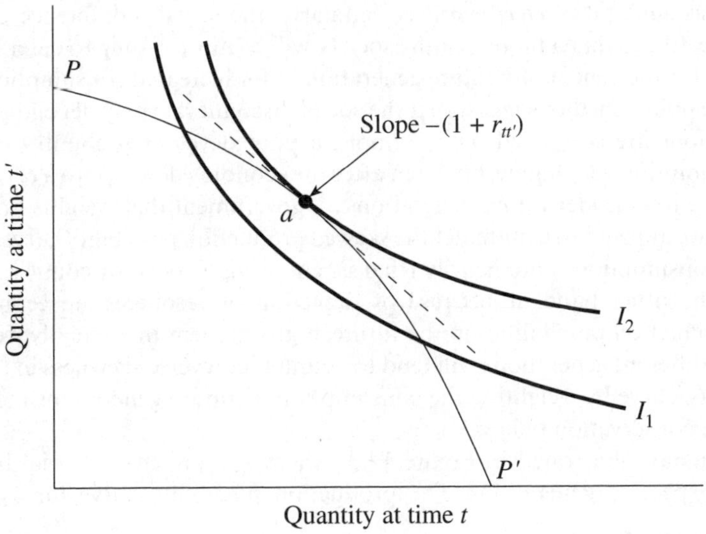

Figure 14.2

of framework as in Chapters 2 and 3. The curve PP' represents a production possibility curve depicting the trade-off between production in time period t versus production in time period t'. Production in the current period t can be given up for production in a future period t', but only at a decreasing rate. The curves I_1 and I_2 represent social indifference curves between consumption in time period t and time period t'. Social optimality is obtained where an indifference curve is exactly tangent to the production possibility curve, such as at point a. Optimality thus implies equality of the marginal rate of substitution in consumption between time periods t and t', $\text{MRS}_{tt'}$, and the marginal rate of transformation in production between time periods t and t', $\text{MRT}_{tt'}$. When markets are competitive and involve many consumers and many producers, the marginal rates of substitution and marginal rates of transformation must be the same over all individual consumers and producers. The optimal rate of substitution or transformation corresponds to the optimal social discount rate. That is, the appropriate social discount rate, $r_{tt'}$, is defined by[4]

$$\text{MRS}_{tt'} = \text{MRT}_{tt'} = 1 + r_{tt'} \tag{14.2}$$

The analysis in Figure 14.2 and equation (14.2) point out that the optimal social discount rate cannot be determined without reference to a specific economy. In point of fact, a number of underlying economic factors may influence the optimal discount rate. For example, if the size of the labor force is growing rather than declining, then the production possibility curve would be skewed toward the later time period and thus likely lead

4. For a derivation of this equation and an excellent graphical treatment of many of the issues of this chapter at the intermediate level, see Hirshleifer (1976, ch. 16).

to a lower discount rate, *ceteris paribus.* Similarly, the social indifference curves may depend on wealth, so that a more wealthy society will be more willing to defer some of its consumption for the benefit of a future generation or for increased consumption at a later period. These points further suggest that the social discount rate may depend upon which two time periods are compared. For example, a poor developing country may weight current consumption very highly, but later, after the economy develops to a certain extent, be more prone to consider future generations. A government that weights both generations equally would tend to counteract the skewed production possibility curve by weighting current consumption more heavily (that is, choosing a social discount rate near 0). Finally, on the other hand, if because of depletion of resources, an economy faces decreased production possibilities in the future, a government that equally weights consumption by different generations will tend to counteract reverse skewness in the production possibility curve by weighting the consumption of future generations more heavily, as in resource conservation policy.

These points are illustrated in Figure 14.3, where I_0 represents a social indifference curve with respect to generations. The production possibility curve for a no-growth

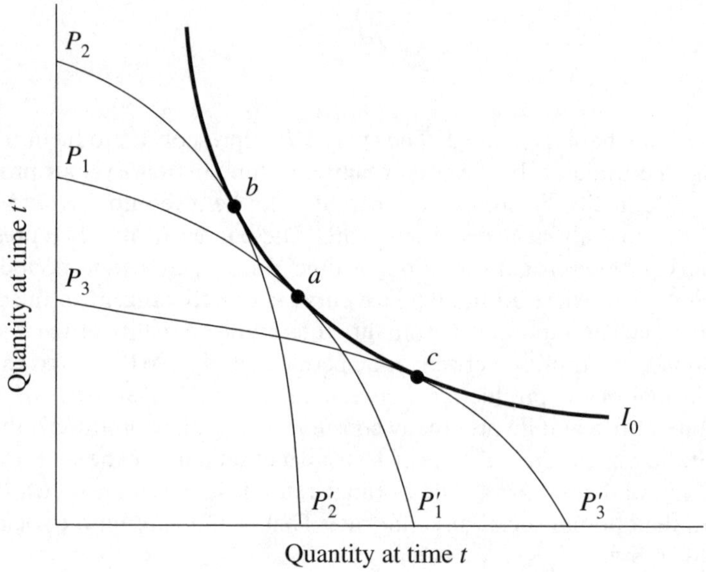

Figure 14.3

society would be symmetric with respect to generations, as in the case of P_1P_1', thus leading to social optimality at point *a*. Alternatively, in a scenario of technological progress, production possibilities may follow P_2P_2', in which case greater production is possible at time t'. Then the point of social optimality is at point *b* with greater future and less present consumption even though the implied discount rate (associated with the slope at point *b*) is higher and more in favor of present consumption. Finally, suppose production possibilities follow P_3P_3', as in the case where increasing resource scarcity implies that more can be produced now than later. Then social optimality is at point *c*.

Thus, present consumption is greater and future consumption is less even though the implied social discount rate is lower and more favorable to future consumption than at either points *a* or *b*.

Practical Determination of the Discount Rate

In a perfect economy (involving perfect markets for capital and investments with no externalities of any type, including intergenerational externalities), the correct discount rate, $r_{tt'}$, represented in Figure 14.2, would result from competition. In the absence of a perfect market economy, however, the optimal social discount rate may not be reflected by observed market phenomena. For example, some individuals or firms may have projects with a much higher rate of return than the market rate of interest but are unable to qualify for credit for other reasons. Furthermore, future generations are not involved in current markets and, hence, cannot represent their interests. The problem of determining the appropriate social discount rate is thus similar to the externality problem discussed in Section 13.1. That is, markets fail to exist for determining the appropriate interest rate. Thus, the effects of current policies and projects on future generations are external effects, and the government must take those effects into account in making policy decisions. Furthermore, the problems of measurement for this purpose are much more severe because future generations cannot be surveyed to determine their preferences. A policy-maker is thus left in the precarious situation of having to determine for them what should be in their best interest based on his or her own values.

With these considerations in mind, the choice of a social discount rate becomes a very sensitive subject. Indeed, the choice of a social discount rate is similar to one of deciding upon income distribution. In this case, income distribution is decided between different generations rather than between different groups of the same generation. Thus, as in the earlier cases of income distribution comparison in this book, perhaps the most defensible approach from the standpoint of economic welfare analysis is to determine the distributional effects of a number of discount rates and then to leave the selection of the discount rate with its accompanying implications to the choice of policy-makers who are elected or appointed for the purpose of making value judgments for society.

Other possibilities, however, are provided by either observing a policy-maker's revealed discount rate implied by previous policy choices or by comparing with opportunity costs of using the same funds in other projects. The former case would involve examining previous proposed projects and policies, some of which have been adopted and some of which have been rejected by the same policy-maker(s). *If policy-makers are consistent* in their choices, there will be a (small) range of discount rates in which all rejected policies and projects have negative NPV and all accepted ones have positive NPV. If a proposed policy or project has a positive NPV over all discount rates in this small range, it too should be accepted. If it has a negative NPV for all such discount rates, it should be rejected.

In practice, the most widely accepted approach to choice of a discount rate is the opportunity cost approach, particularly for projects of less than 100 years. This approach examines other possible uses of the same funds required for the proposed policy or project, including leaving the funds in the private sector. The question of intergenerational welfare considerations is avoided using this approach by ascribing to the discount rate the more limited role of allocating capital funds to their highest-valued use. Other social instruments are assumed to be used for ensuring fairness of income distribution among generations (see Haveman 1969). Proponents of the opportunity cost approach agree that the rate of return on a public investment should be at least as great as the rate of return that can be earned on the funds thereby displaced from the private sector. If only private investment rather than household consumption is displaced, then the highest rate of return on private investment is used as a social discount rate in the evaluation of a new proposal. If the source of funding is a general income tax, this approach leads to a weighted average of the rate of time preference and the private return to capital, where the weights are the marginal propensities to consume and save, respectively.

More recently, Robert Lind (1990) reevaluated this approach by considering the development of increased capital mobility over the past several decades and now argues that the true opportunity cost of funds is the government's borrowing rate since most funds now come from abroad. He thus concludes that the appropriate real social discount rate is between 1 and 3 percent. James Quirk and Katsuaki Terasawa (1991) take exception to this view and argue that governments operate within budgets and that the selection of an optimal portfolio of projects requires that the rate of return on each selected project should exceed the maximal internal rate of return on excluded projects. Internal rate of return (IRR) offers an alternative criterion to NPV as a means of evaluating projects. Under this methodology they suggest that the real opportunity cost rate of return exceeds 10 percent. As this discussion suggests, economists are far from general agreement on a discount rate that can serve all purposes universally.

Net Present Value versus Internal Rate of Return

Because IRR and NPV offer alternative criteria for evaluating both public and private projects, a comparison of the two approaches is useful. With NPV analysis, a discount rate r is first determined that represents the opportunity cost of funds, that is, the highest rate of return that could be earned from alternative projects available to the private or public entity considering the investment. Then NPV is calculated according to equation (14.1) using that discount rate, and only projects with $NPV > 0$ are adopted. With IRR analysis, the discount rate r is found such that $NPV = 0$ in equation (14.1). This distinct discount rate is found for each alternative project that could be adopted and is then called the IRR of the respective project. Projects are then ranked by their IRR, and projects are selected for funding beginning with the highest IRR until the budget is exhausted. Each approach has shortcomings.

With NPV analysis, a large amount of information may be required to determine the appropriate discount rate, possibly including a cost–benefit or welfare analysis of many projects or policies in addition to the one proposed. In some cases, these analyses may have been done previously, but probably not in all cases. Some previous analyses may contain errors. In addition, the revealed preference approach will often turn up inconsistencies in previous policy decisions, so that no range of discount rates is clearly applicable for future policy decisions. That is, for a given discount rate some projects with negative NPVs may have been adopted, while others with positive NPVs were rejected. Some previous projects may have been adopted for unusual reasons relating to intragenerational income distribution or noneconomic factors, such as national defense, security or political purposes. For example, a policy-maker may consider the economic considerations of one project independent of political considerations of another.

In addition, because NPV analysis involves discounting of future net returns, it requires predicting the discount rate applicable for the future. Circumstances that determine the opportunity cost of funds change, and accordingly the appropriate discount rate can be expected to change. When the discount rate is changing, equation (14.1) becomes

$$\text{PV} = B_0 - C_0 + \frac{B_1 - C_1}{1 + r_1} + \frac{B_2 - C_2}{(1 + r_1)(1 + r_2)} + \frac{B_3 - C_3}{(1 + r_1)(1 + r_2)(1 + r_3)} + \ldots,$$

where r_1 is the discount rate in period 1, r_2 is the discount rate in period 2, and so on. Also, as shown by Section 14.4 and the Appendix to this chapter, a higher discount rate is appropriate when returns are risky. Thus, NPV analysis either assumes that risks among alternative projects are equal or must use different discount rates for projects with different risks.

As serious as these shortcomings are for NPV analysis, the problems with IRR analysis can be more serious, particularly for an unsuspecting user in certain circumstances. First, the IRR of a specific series of net benefits is exactly the same as if the sign is reversed on every B_i and C_i in every time period. For example, the IRR on a project that returns \$200 in period 1 ($B_1 - C_1 = 200$) for an investment of \$100 in period 0 ($B_0 - C_0 = -100$) is the same as for a project that yields \$100 in period 0 for an obligation to pay \$200 in period 1. Both have an IRR of $r = 1$, meaning 100 percent. In the first case, one is better off with a higher IRR, for example, of 150 percent, where the return in year 1 is \$300 instead of \$200. But in the latter case, one is better off with a lower IRR, for example, 50 percent, where one has to pay back only \$150 in period 1 rather than \$200.

Second, the IRR is nonsensical for several specific cases. For example, suppose an investment of \$100 in period 0 returns \$200 in period 0 for a net return of \$100, $B_0 - C_0 = \$100$, and returns \$200 in period 1 with no further costs, $B_1 - C_1 = 200$. According to equation (14.1), the IRR that makes NPV = 0 for this project is $r = -2$, meaning -200 percent, even though the project is a clear winner in every period. In general, a nonsensical IRR is generated by any case where the net benefit or cash flow, $B_i - C_i$, is either positive in all periods or negative in all periods.

Another case where IRR analysis can generate nonsensical results is where costs and returns balance in most years but are slightly positive in one or two late periods. For example, consider comparison of the following two projects. Project *A* involves an initial cost of \$100, $B_0 - C_0 = -100$, and returns \$300 after one year, $B_1 - C_1 = 300$, and another \$400 after two years, $B_2 - C_2 = 400$. Project *B* has equal costs and benefits of \$300 each initially, $B_0 - C_0 = 0$, as well as after one year, $B_1 - C_1 = 0$, but then has costs of \$300 and benefits of \$301 two years from commencement, $B_2 - C_2 = 1$. Clearly, Project *A* appears quite attractive and indeed has an IRR of 400 percent, while Project *B* appears less attractive based on intuition. However, Project *B* has an infinite IRR and would thus be favored by an IRR ranking. If working capital requirements place a limit of \$300 on costs that can be borne in period 0, or if the costs and returns applicable to individual periods are somewhat uncertain, then Project *A* is clearly the preferred alternative, even though no project can possibly have a higher IRR than Project *B*. On the other hand, if the costs and returns of Project *B* are fully certain and the project can be duplicated many times over, then it becomes relatively attractive.

A third problem with IRR analysis is that any positive cash flows are assumed to be reinvested at a rate of return equal to the IRR, which may not be a realistic interest rate. For example, consider a project that returns \$25 in period 0, $B_0 - C_0 = 25$, costs \$100 in period 1, $B_1 - C_1 = -100$, and returns \$100 in period 2, $B_2 - C_2 = 100$. The internal rate of return for this project is 100 percent, which means that IRR analysis assumes that the \$25 return in period 0 is reinvested with a 100 percent rate of return, even though no such prospect may exist. Not only is this assumption implausible, but comparison of this project to another project that generates a different IRR presents an unfair comparison because different rates of return on positive cash flows are assumed thereby.

A fourth problem with IRR analysis is that it can rank projects inconsistent with the level of returns that would be generated at all realistic interest rate levels. Suppose Project *A* requires an investment of \$80 in period 0 to earn a return of \$140 in period 1, whereas Project *B* requires an investment of \$55 in period 0 to earn a return of \$100 in period 1. Figure 14.4 depicts the NPV of each project as a function of the discount rate, *r*. The relationship that represents NPV as a function of the discount rate is called the *NPV curve*. At

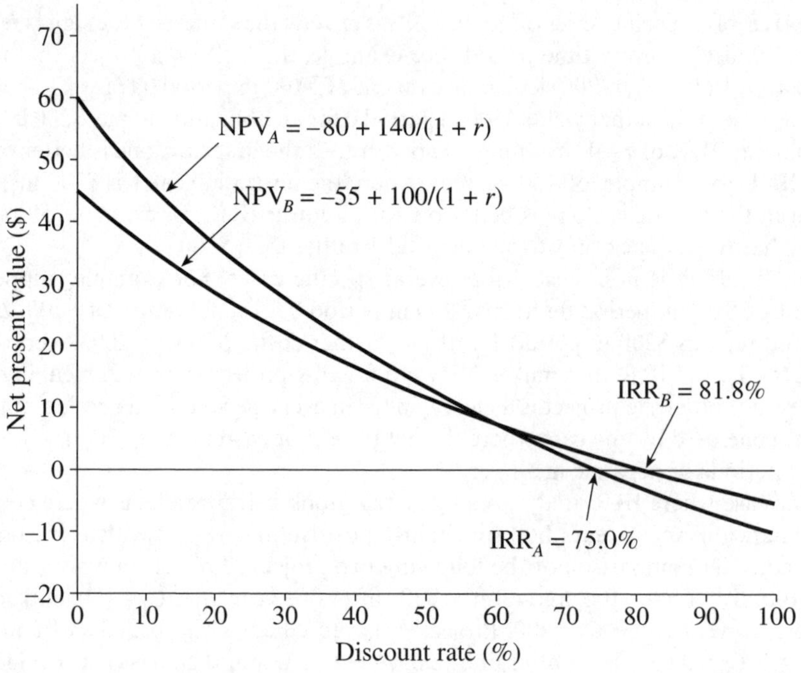

Figure 14.4

normal interest rates that one might expect to apply to actual borrowing and saving (in fact, any interest rate less than 60 percent), Project *A* generates a higher payoff than Project *B*. Yet the IRR (the point where the NPV curve intersects the horizontal axis) of Project *B* is 81.8 percent and dominates the IRR of Project *A*, which is 75.0 percent. Thus, Project *B* would be preferred by the IRR criterion but would return less than Project *A* if funds had to be borrowed at normal interest rates or diverted from other opportunities returning less than 60 percent. This type of problem is encountered whenever the NPV curves of two projects cross. When NPV curves cross, one must be careful to consider the actual (or opportunity) costs of funds that will be used for the project.

A fifth problem with IRR analysis is that the IRR may not be unique. This can occur when the stream of net benefits over time switches from negative to positive and later back to negative, or from positive to negative to positive. The first case may apply for an investment like a nuclear reactor where costs of construction are incurred first, then returns are earned through many years of electricity generation and, finally, high expenses of nuclear waste disposal are incurred when the reactor must be closed due to increased radiation. For example, suppose Project *A* requires a net investment of \$160 in period 0, $B_0 - C_0 = -160$, generates a net return of \$400 in period 1, $B_1 - C_1 = 400$, and finally requires a cost of \$245 in period 2, $B_2 - C_2 = -245$. In this case, IRRs of both 7.32 percent and 42.68 percent (rounded to two decimal places) yield NPV = 0 in equation (14.1). This case is represented by the NPV_A curve in Figure 14.5. In general, the number of IRRs that solve equation (14.1) for NPV = 0 can be as many as one less than the number of time periods in the calculation. More specifically, one can show that as many IRRs may apply for a given time series of net returns as the number of times the series switches between positive and negative values. But the number of switches is only a maximum because some of the roots of the NPV = 0 equation may not be unique. For example, if compared to Project *A* an alternative Project *B* requires the same investment in Period 0, generates the same return in Period 1, but requires a cost just \$5 higher in Period 2, $B_2 - C_2 = -250$, then the

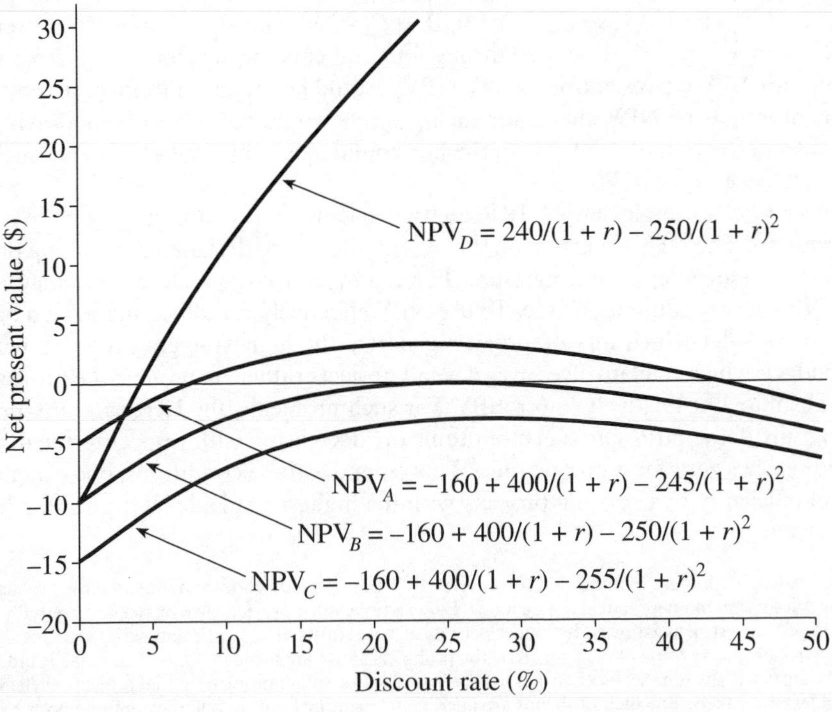

Figure 14.5

NPV_B curve touches the horizontal axis only at 25 percent, implying a unique IRR even though the series of net returns switches from negative to positive to negative.

A sixth problem is that the IRR may not exist for a project. For example, if compared to Project *A* an alternative Project *C* requires the same investment in Period 0, generates the same return in Period 1, but requires a cost just \$10 higher in Period 2, $B_2 - C_2 = -255$, then the NPV_C curve never reaches the horizontal axis, meaning that no discount rate solves the $NPV_C = 0$ equation. For cases like this, one must be careful to note whether the NPV curve is entirely above or entirely below the horizontal axis. If it is entirely below the axis, as in Figure 14.5, then no interest rate can generate a positive return from the project. If it is entirely above the axis, then the project generates a positive return for all possible interest rates.

A seventh problem is also illustrated by Figure 14.5 for the case where returns precede costs. One possibility is that a high IRR may be found for a project that is not profitable at any interest rate. For example, the NPV_B curve reveals that Project *B* at best breaks even at a 25 percent interest rate but does not earn a positive return at any interest rate. Thus, the impressive 25 percent IRR would be considered nonsensical by a wise investor. The underlying problem is that when returns precede costs in the time series of cash flows, a higher IRR is not necessarily better. For example, Project *B* generates a higher IRR than the one generated by Project *A*, where NPV_A crosses the horizontal axis from below. Yet Project *A* generates a higher NPV for every individual interest rate than Project *B*. Thus, Project *A* is clearly more advantageous than Project *B*. This problem is clearly illustrated when the time series of cash flows switches only once from positive to negative, as in the case of Project *D* in Figure 14.5. Project *D* combines the net effects of the first two periods of Project *B* into Period 1, so $B_0 - C_0 = 0$, $B_1 - C_1 = 240$, and $B_2 - C_2 = -250$. As a result, the NPV_D curve is positively sloped throughout and cuts the horizontal axis from below. Projects with NPV curves entirely above NPV_D would be preferred to Project *D* by a sensible investor, but the NPV curves for such projects would cut the horizontal axis to the left of the intersection of NPV_D with the horizontal axis, which means that all such projects would have lower IRRs.

As these brief examples imply, IRR analysis has many potential problems in specific circumstances. The NPV criterion, on the other hand, is not designed for ranking projects because it is a size-dependent measure. For example, a large-scale project may have a higher NPV just because it is large. To use NPV effectively for allocating a fixed budget, one must consider which mix of projects generate the highest aggregate NPV with the given budget, which may involve several small projects rather than one large project with higher absolute but relatively lower NPV. For such problems, the IRR can rank projects meaningfully if the NPV curve is monotonically decreasing with respect to the discount rate and reaches zero for a unique rate.[5] That is, under these conditions, one can allocate a budget efficiently by choosing projects with the highest available IRR until the budget

5. The reader should bear in mind that the adverse IRR examples are chosen to illustrate the problems and may not arise in many practical applications. For example, most projects involve net costs initially during periods of investment followed by longer periods of net returns. If the cash flow series changes sign only once from negative to positive, then all of the problems above are avoided other than possible crossing of NPV curves. If the time series of cash flows are sufficiently similar among potential projects, then even this problem is unlikely. But such problems are likely to be identified only if one is examining both NPV and IRR or examining NPV curves to compare investments.

is just exhausted. In conclusion, if a singular-valued criterion is to be used to evaluate projects, the NPV approach is preferred in spite of the problem of determining an appropriate social discount rate as long as one bears in mind that NPV provides an absolute rather than relative evaluation.[6] Alternatively, comparison of NPV curves is preferable and should be pursued whenever the IRR approach generates a different ranking than suggested by NPV analysis.

Empirical Use of Discount Rates and Sensitivity Analysis

As some of the earlier examples in this chapter suggest, empirical results of dynamic economic welfare analysis can differ substantially depending on the choice of social discount rate even in the range of those that seem reasonable. For example, many government projects involve substantial costs over the first several years of a project, with substantial benefits accruing only 20, 30 or even 100 years into the future. Suppose that a project involves investing \$1 million immediately to gain a benefit of \$50 million at the end of 50 years. With a social discount rate of 8 percent, the project will almost break even. The NPV is \$6606. With a social discount rate of 12 percent, however, the NPV is in the red by \$826990. Finally, with a social discount rate of 5 percent, the NPV is \$3360186. Obviously, the choice of discount rate is highly critical in deciding whether the project should be undertaken. By performing this kind of sensitivity analysis, the extent to which project outcomes are sensitive to the discount rate may be ascertained. In some cases, one project may remain profitable over a wide range of discount rates, while another may be highly sensitive to the discount rate. This type of sensitivity analysis amounts to examining the NPV curve at least within the range of plausible discount rates rather than relying on a single discount rate that may be open to controversy.

Social discount rates that have been employed in practice have ranged from 0 to 20 percent. For example, the US Congressional Budget Office currently uses a 2 percent rate, the US Office of Management and Budget uses a 7 percent rate and the Inter-American Development Bank mandates a 12 percent rate for evaluation of its loans. This wide range is suggestive of the great amount of controversy that has surrounded social discounting. An important distinction exists in the literature on the social discount rate, however, in that some authors concern themselves with a *real* social discount rate, whereas others use a *nominal* discount rate. The difference is, of course, associated with the rate of inflation. Where r represents the real rate of social discount, γ represents the nominal rate of social discount, and f represents the rate of inflation, the rates are related according to the following equation:

$$1+r=\frac{1+\gamma}{1+f}. \tag{14.3}$$

In this context, the formula for computation of present or discounted value of a project in equation (14.1) applies when the stream of benefits and costs is evaluated in real terms (that is, after the effects of inflation have been removed). If benefits and costs are evaluated

6. Other approaches, such as ranking proposed projects by payback period or by excess cost–benefit ratios (the ratio of discounted net benefits to discounted costs), have also been proposed but lead to similar inconsistencies. See Mishan (1976b, chs 25–37).

in nominal terms (that is, current dollars), then γ should be substituted for r in equation (14.1).

Real rates of social discount used in the literature generally fall in the range of 0 to 4 percent. Nominal rates of social discount in the literature have varied more widely but mostly fall within the range implied by a real discount rate of 0 to 4 percent as modified by the rate of inflation following equation (14.3). To point out the importance of this distinction, suppose, for example, that one chooses a nominal discount rate of 10 percent and a real discount rate of 2 percent, thus expecting a rate of inflation of slightly under 8 percent according to equation (14.3). In nominal terms, this would imply that society would prefer \$1 today in favor of \$13780 a hundred years from today. At first thought, this conclusion seems rather absurd. However, when one takes into account the effects of inflation and reduces this consideration to real terms (that is, constant dollars), one finds that society is trading \$1 today for only \$7.24 a hundred years from today. With this consideration in mind, a real discount rate in the neighborhood of 0 to 2 percent may, in fact, appear appropriate. For example, in a no-growth economy where a government weights real consumption by a future generation with the same regard it holds for consumption by the current generation, the real social discount rate would be zero. Alternatively, if because of technological advancement an economy is able to produce more goods in the future, the same government would weight current consumption more heavily by choosing a real social discount rate somewhat greater than zero. On the other hand, if an economy faces decreased production possibilities in the future because of depletion of nonrenewable resources, the same government would favor the consumption of future generations more heavily by using a negative real social discount rate and implementing stronger resource conservation policy.

The government agency discount rates cited above are all real rates and have been determined by political processes. For problems where a specific discount rate applies by regulation (projects administered by specific government agencies) or by rule (in a firm with an established hurdle rate), the welfare economist may have the luxury of considering only a single discount rate. Otherwise, some sensitivity analysis is usually advisable because no single appropriate discount rate has been agreed upon. Great care must be taken in selecting the range of discount rates appropriate for a particular study. The range of rates considered should reflect uncertainties faced by individual projects. For example, uncertainties are generally greater in deep-future settings. As one well-known resource economist once said: 'Every graduate student should spend a fair amount of time immersed in the discount rate literature, if for no other reason than to feel decidedly uncomfortable the rest of their professional career when using *any* particular discount in a cost-benefit analysis.'[7]

14.2 MEASURING WELFARE OVER TIME: COST–BENEFIT ANALYSIS

Once the choice of a (set of) social discount rate(s) is determined, the methods of previous chapters become immediately applicable in measuring welfare effects of alternative policies or changes. For example, when fixed factors remain fixed over time, the welfare

7. Personal communication to D.L. Hueth from R.G. Cummings, University of Rhode Island, 1972.

effect (that is, the discounted social welfare effect or discounted WTP) of a change beginning at time t_0 is given by

$$\Delta W_{t_0} = \sum_{t=t_0}^{\infty} \delta^{t-t_0} \sum_{i=1}^{N} C^{it} \tag{14.4}$$

or

$$\Delta W_{t_0} = \sum_{t=t_0}^{\infty} \delta^{t-t_0} \sum_{i=1}^{N} E^{it} \tag{14.5}$$

(depending on which concept of WTP is used), where $\delta = 1/(1+r)$, r is the social discount rate, C^{it} is the compensating variation of the change for individual i in period t (change in area behind the relevant short-run compensated supply or demand conditioned on the initial utility level) measured in constant dollars, E^{it} is the equivalent variation of the change for individual i in period t (change in area behind the relevant short-run compensated supply or demand conditioned on the terminal utility level) also measured in constant dollars, and N is the total number of individuals affected by the change. Following the methodology in Chapters 8 or 9, these WTP measures for groups of individuals can be determined within individual time periods by using aggregate market demand and supply curves, possibly of an equilibrium nature. Use of market or equilibrium demand and supply curves may be necessary because proposed policies or projects may be of sufficient size to alter prices in related markets. If not, simple calculations of changes in costs and benefits based on fixed prices may be sufficient.

Accounting for Changes in Investment

Although the foregoing approach is appropriate when fixed factors are indeed fixed over time, most problems of economic welfare analysis involve factors that are fixed in the short run but become variable in the longer run. As a result, short-run supply and demand curves shift from period to period and, in particular, investment costs are incurred in the process. In this case, equations (14.4) and (14.5) must be further modified. Suppose, for example, that fixed factors can be altered by producers through undertaking new investment, as suggested in Section 4.7. In this case a change in policy at time t_0 can cause a series of investments (or disinvestments). Where I_t^i represents investment made by producer i at time t and N_p is the total number of producers, the NPV or discounted value of welfare effects on producers is

$$\Delta W_p = \sum_{t=t_0}^{\infty} \delta^{t-t_0} \sum_{i=1}^{N_p} (\Delta S_t^i - \Delta I_t^i). \tag{14.6}$$

That is, ΔS_t^i represents the change in producer surplus associated with the ordinary, short-run supply curve in period t for producer i (both the supply curve and the price may differ between cases of change or no change), and ΔI_t^i is the change in investment undertaken or financed by producer i in period t.[8] Thus, ΔW_p is the NPV of changes in receipts and

8. For details on calculating ΔI_t^i from standard dynamic supply equations, see Appendix Section 4.F. Note, however, that Appendix Section 4.F applies only to the nonstochastic case where future prices are perfectly anticipated. The more realistic case of uncertainty about future prices is addressed in Appendix Section 14.A.

expenditures. If consumers make no adjustments in fixed assets as a result of the change, their welfare effect is given by

$$\Delta W_c = \sum_{t=t_0}^{\infty} \delta^{t-t_0} \sum_{i=N_p+1}^{N} \Delta S_t^i,$$

where $N - N_p$ is the number of consumers and ΔS_t^i represents the change in Hicksian consumer surplus for consumer i in period t. The net overall welfare effect on private concerns is thus $\Delta W_p + \Delta W_c$.[9]

14.3 INTERTEMPORAL ASPECTS OF THE CONSUMER PROBLEM

In some problems of economic welfare analysis, changes in consumer holdings of fixed assets are also induced. Although the dynamics of consumer adjustments in fixed assets were not considered explicitly in earlier chapters, the associated economic welfare considerations can be made in much the same framework as producer adjustments in fixed production factors using household production theory (see Appendix Section 7.G). That is, consumers can be viewed as purchasing fixed assets or durables, such as refrigerators, televisions, automobiles and houses, in order to combine them with other nondurable inputs, such as electricity, gasoline and leisure, to produce commodities such as entertainment, food, transportation and shelter from which the consumer actually derives utility. For example, suppose that each household commodity y_i is produced within the household by combining quantities of nondurables $q_1, \ldots, q_m$ with quantities of durables $q_{m+1}, \ldots, q_N$ following the household production function given by

$$y_i = f_i(q_1, \ldots, q_N).$$

Then where the consumer utility function depends on household commodities,

$$U = \bar{U}(y_1, \ldots, y_K),$$

the utility function can be rewritten through substitution as

$$U = U(q_1, \ldots, q_N),$$

where $q_{m+1}, \ldots, q_N$ are understood to be durables that are fixed in the short run, just as some inputs are fixed for producers.

Now consider the dual of the utility-maximization problem,

$$\min\, p_1 q_1 + \cdots + p_N q_N$$

subject to

9. For examples of this approach, see Crosson, Cummings and Frederick (1978), Eckstein (1961b), A. Fisher (1979), Howe and Easter (1971) and Krutilla and Eckstein (1958).

$$U^*(q_1,\ldots,q_N)=0,$$

where $p_1, \ldots, p_N$ are the prices of $q_1, \ldots, q_N$ respectively, and the constrained level of utility, $\bar{U}$ is represented in U^* by defining $U^*(q_1,\ldots,q_N)=U(q_1,\ldots,q_N)-\bar{U}$. This problem is obviously mathematically equivalent to a producer problem (by simply reversing signs of prices),

$$\max p_1q_1+\cdots+p_Nq_N$$

subject to

$$f_i(q_1,\ldots,q_N)=0,$$

where f represents an implicit production function, $q_i>0$ represents purchases for consumers and output sales for producers, and $q_i<0$ represents factor sales for consumers and input purchases for producers.[10] Because both problems can also contain the same kinds of fixities (consumer durables or fixed inputs of producers), the areas under the associated supply and demand curves with various planning horizons (various lengths of run) must also have the same interpretation. Of course, in the consumer case, the associated supply and demand curves are compensated rather than ordinary curves, because utility is constrained to a fixed level.

Hence, by analogy with the producer case, the NPV or discounted value of welfare effects on consumers is given by

$$\Delta W_c=\sum_{t=t_0}^{\infty}\delta^{t-t_0}\sum_{i=N_p+1}^{N}(\Delta S_t^i-\Delta D_t^i), \tag{14.7}$$

where ΔS_t^i is the change in consumer surplus for consumer i associated with Hicksian compensated short-run supplies or demands in period t, and ΔD_t^i represents the change in expenditures (investment) by consumer i on durables in period t. Where direct data are not available on D_t^i, durable expenditures can be estimated from the dynamics of estimated consumer demand and supply curves as explained in Appendix Section 14.B, just as in the case of calculating investment from producer supply and derived demand curves in Section 4.7 and Appendix Section 4.F, or more generally as in Appendix Section 14.A. The net overall welfare effect on private concerns is thus given by the sum of ΔW_p and ΔW_c in equations (14.6) and (14.7), respectively. Practical approximate applications of (14.7) in terms of ordinary Marshallian consumer surplus can be made through application of the Willig approximation arguments. Thus, the temporal distribution of welfare effects of any policy on both producers and consumers can be investigated empirically and aggregated with various discount rates to examine potential compensation schemes.

10. Technically, mathematical equivalence also requires the same conditions on concavity of f and U^*, which hold under usual assumptions. See Section 7.10 for a similar case of comparing the consumer and producer problems where factor fixity is not assumed.

14.4 INTERTEMPORAL WELFARE ANALYSIS OF RISKY PROJECTS AND POLICIES

In selecting an appropriate social discount rate, another consideration has to do with uncertainty regarding future time periods. For example, many policies and potential policies relate to extraction of petroleum and minerals. Although the importance of these resources in today's economy can be determined fairly accurately, their value for future generations is clouded with a great deal of uncertainty associated with adequacy of reserves and technological advancement. Exploration may yet reveal large quantities of reserves that are as yet undiscovered. Furthermore, technological changes may occur so that these resources are less important for future generations. When these kinds of uncertainties exist, society may be much less willing to trade off current consumption for future consumption. That is, as suggested by Section 12.6, private individuals may have a tendency to discount outcomes that have risky payoffs within a single time period. Similar arguments and observations suggest that decisions associated with risk over time are also discounted or valued less than if no risk existed. For example, a risk-averse individual might be more willing to pay $100 today for a certain return of $200 after 10 years than for a 50-50 chance of returns of either $50 or $350 each. This raises the question as to whether and how much policies or projects associated with risky outcomes should be discounted in making policy decisions.

Several schools of thought exist on this issue. One school argues that, because government is very large and undertakes many projects, it can spread or absorb risks easily and hence should act as a risk-neutral decision-maker and ignore risks (Samuelson 1964; Vickrey 1964). An alternative argument is that pooling risk requires negative correlation among projects (that is, when one turns out bad, another tends to turn out good). In this case, restricting consideration to negatively correlated projects may reduce the overall value of the investment. In reality, however, negative correlation of returns is not necessary for pooling. Pooling risk is possible as long as the returns on any project are independent of other components of national income (Hirshleifer 1966). But even though the government may be risk-neutral, certain risks may be imposed on individuals (for example, the risk of higher taxes), and these may adversely affect private individuals. The government should not ignore these risks if they carry private welfare effects unless they are neutralized, meaning the government actually intervenes to eliminate changes in private risk.

Neutralizing private risk, however, can carry significant transactions costs and significant moral hazards. For example, the cost of verifying the extent to which each individual must be compensated each period for imposing risks on him or her may be prohibitive. Also, individuals may be induced to 'cheat' by altering their behavior in response to the government spreading of risk. For example, if the government offers a crop insurance program to ensure profits associated with a specific crop yield level, and thus spreads risks associated with, say, a pest infestation, some farmers may use less of some (possibly unobservable) productive inputs because yields are guaranteed. Claims for damages could therefore be higher than anticipated. This type of phenomenon is called *moral hazard.* These same factors prevent the existence of perfect insurance markets, which could otherwise spread risks throughout an economy and thus reduce inefficiencies due to risk.

Another school of thought on public risk discounting argues that risk should be discounted but not at market rates. Rather, a national policy should be established on appropriate rates of discount for both expected (or average) effects and risk (Eckstein 1961a). Some have argued that the regulated public rate of discount should be determined by the desired rate of growth for an economy (Marglin 1963). These approaches are based on the assumption of market imperfections such as when externalities exist for future generations. One must again bear in mind, however, that a difference in public and private rates of discount can have serious implications for the allocation of funds between the public and private sectors. If the public discount rate is lower than the private discount rate, funds will be used in the public sector that would otherwise be used in the private sector at a higher expected rate of return. On the other hand, if the public discount rate is above the private discount rate, private individuals with access to credit at the private rate will redistribute to future time periods some of the public costs transferred to the private sector. These arguments suggest that, with sufficiently competitive capital markets, the government should regulate the private rate of return to that level deemed socially efficient so that both public and private sector investments appropriately consider future contingencies.

Finally, a third school of thought argues that public sector risks should be discounted at private rates because private individuals generally bear the risks – if not directly, then indirectly through taxes. Rarely does or can the government attempt to bear all the risks of projects that are adopted. If this is the case, any use of a public discount rate that differs from a private rate could at best reach a 'second-best' alternative. It seems that this third school of thought has been increasingly adopted by notable economists, although some of its favor may be due to the tractable approach it offers.

To understand these issues analytically, return again to the WTP criterion.[11] To consider the implications of risk, suppose that each individual i is risk averse and has, for simple but practical purposes, a mean-variance expected utility function given by

$$E[U_i(S_t^i + T_t^i)] = E(S_t^i) + E(T_t^i) - \alpha V(S_t^i + T_t^i),$$

where E is the expectation operator, V is the variance operator, U_i is the individual's utility function, S_t^i represents net benefits from market involvement as measured by Hicksian surplus at time t, T_t^i represents net benefits gained through transfers from government to individual i at time t, including commodities as well as money (possibly negative), and α is a risk-aversion coefficient. Discounting expected utility over time and aggregating over individuals obtains a welfare objective for society given by[12]

$$W = \sum_{i=1}^{N} \sum_{t=0}^{T} \delta^t E[U_i(S_t^i + T_t^i)] = \sum_{t=0}^{T} \delta^t \left[E(S_t) + E(T_t) - \alpha \sum_{i=1}^{N} V(S_t^i + T_t^i) \right]$$

$$= \sum_{t=0}^{T} \delta^t \left[E(S_t) + E(T_t) - \alpha \sum_{i=1}^{N} V(S_t^i) - \alpha \sum_{i=1}^{N} V(T_t^i) - 2\alpha \sum_{i=1}^{N} \mathrm{cov}(S_t^i, T_t^i) \right],$$

11. The results in the remainder of this section are based on Arrow and Lind (1970), although the framework used here is much more simple and heuristic.
12. This function can serve as a welfare objective for society because changes in W measure net WTP by society as a whole. Aggregation over individuals is possible in a WTP context, as in the producer case of Section 12.6, because a certain payment to any individual i is equivalent to an equal change in $E(S_t^i)$ or $E(T_t^i)$.

where $S_t=\Sigma_{i=1}^N S_t^i, T_t=\Sigma_{i=1}^N T_t^i$, $\delta=1/(1+r)$, r is the social discount rate, cov is the covariance operator, N is the total number of individuals and T is the planning horizon. Suppose, further, that benefits from government projects are divided equally among all individuals so that $T_t^i=T_t/N$. Then

$$\sum_{i=1}^{N} V(T_t^i)=\sum_{i=1}^{N}\frac{V(T_t)}{N^2}=\frac{V(T_t)}{N}$$

$$\sum_{i=1}^{N}\text{cov}(S_t^i,T_t^i)=\sum_{i=1}^{N}\frac{\text{cov}(S_t^i,T_t)}{N}=\frac{\text{cov}(S_t,T_t)}{N}.$$

Thus the welfare objective of society can be written as

$$W=\sum_{t=0}^{T}\delta^t\left[E(S_t)+E(T_t)-\alpha\sum_{i=1}^{N}V(S_t^i)-\frac{\alpha}{N}V(T_t)-\frac{2\alpha}{N}\text{cov}(S_t,T_t)\right]. \tag{14.8}$$

Now consider the spreading of government risks. If the total benefits from government are held constant as the number of individuals over which they are spread increases, the latter two terms in brackets in equation (14.8) disappear (become small as N becomes large). This result implies that government can behave in a risk-neutral manner if its actions do not affect private market risk, reflected in $V(S_t^i)$, and if the benefits of each incremental project are spread over many individuals. On the other hand, if a government project affects private risk, the effects on private risk should be used to discount expected net benefits through the risk-aversion coefficient of the private sector, α. This also implies that the appropriate risk-discounting factor may vary from project to project if different groups of individuals with different degrees of risk aversion are affected by different projects.

One must bear in mind that this result is not applicable when the government project produces a commodity with the characteristics of a public good described in Sections 13.2 and 13.3. That is, when every individual derives the full benefit of the project irrespective of how many other individuals are also involved, the total benefits from a project are necessarily proportional to the number of individuals who gain benefits. If so, then one cannot hold total benefits constant while spreading the benefits over more individuals. Instead, the total benefits may be represented by $T_t=NT_t^0$, where T_t^0 represents the size of a project. Thus, W in (14.8) becomes

$$W=\sum_{t=0}^{T}\delta^t\left[E(S_t)+NE(T_t^0)-\alpha\sum_{i=1}^{N}V(S_t^i)-\alpha NV(T_t^0)-2\alpha\text{cov}(S_t,T_t^0)\right].$$

Thus, risk on public good projects should be discounted at a much higher rate than risk in the private sector, that is, N times higher, where N is the number of individuals who benefit from the public good. This is clear because the coefficient of $V(T_t^0)$ is αN rather than α.

Even in this case, the risk considerations can become unimportant if one considers a small (additional) project that has benefits independent of other components of national income. For example, suppose that the expression in equation (14.8) corresponds to the current projected state of the economy. Now consider an additional project that generates benefits of ΔT_t^0 at time t, where Δ is the scale of the project. This consideration may be made where the new project has either the nature of a public good or not, but suppose for expositional purposes that it involves a public good so that ΔT_t^0 represents benefits enjoyed by each individual. Then, with the addition of the project, W becomes

$$W^* = \sum_{t=0}^{T} \delta^t \left[E(S_t) + E(T_t) - \Delta N E(T_t^0) - \alpha \sum_{i=1}^{N} V(S_t^i) - \frac{\alpha}{N} V(T_t) - \Delta^2 \alpha N V(T_t^0) \right.$$

$$\left. - \frac{2\alpha}{N} \text{cov}(S_t, T_t) - 2\Delta\alpha \text{cov}(S_t, T_t^0) - 2\Delta\alpha \text{cov}(T_t, T_t^0) \right].$$

Net WTP for the new project is thus

$$W^* - W = \sum_{t=0}^{T} \delta^t [\Delta N E(T_t^0) - \Delta^2 \alpha N V(T_t^0) - 2\Delta\alpha \text{cov}(S_t, T_t^0) - 2\Delta\alpha \text{cov}(T_t, T_t^0)].$$

The benefit of adding a small project is measured by the change in $W^* - W$ associated with a change in Δ at the point where $\Delta = 0$, that is, $\Sigma_{t=0}^{T} \delta^t [NE(T_t^0) - 2\alpha\text{cov}(S_t, T_t^0) - 2\alpha\text{cov}(T_t, T_t^0)]$.[13] This benefit is simply $\Sigma_{t=0}^{T} \delta^t NE(T_t^0)$ if the benefits of the new project, T_t^0, are independent of other components of national income represented by S_t and T_t.[14] Hence, if a project is of sufficiently small scale and independent of other economic phenomena, no risk discounting is necessary even on public good projects.

In summary, there are two conditions where the government can act as a risk-neutral decision-maker: (1) if the benefits (and costs) of a project are spread over a large number of individuals, the project does not affect private risk from market activities and the project does not involve public goods in the sense of Sections 13.2 and 13.3; or (2) if the project is small and has benefits that are independent of economic benefits derived from other sources. Otherwise, the government must discount risk using private risk-discounting factors associated with the individuals who actually bear the risks. Full consideration of private risk discounting presents a difficult challenge for applied economic welfare analysis. It often requires estimating revealed preferences for consumer durables as well as the role of investment in capital assets that expand production capacity. For many such problems, data are sparse or lacking. These issues are too complex to discuss without a substantial mathematical framework, and are thus treated only in the Appendix to this chapter.

14.5 INVESTING IN RESEARCH AND DEVELOPMENT

One area in which social discounting is critical for economic welfare analysis is public policy regarding research and development (R&D). Both the public and private sectors spend heavily on applied and basic R&D. Studies have concluded that some forms of public investment in R&D have generated rates of return exceeding 50 percent per year. Such studies are used to justify further public spending. In private industry, management practices often use a hurdle rate of return to determine which R&D projects should be

13. That is, differentiation of $W^* - W$ and evaluating where $\Delta = 0$ yields

$$\left. \frac{\partial (W^* - W)}{\partial \Delta} \right|_{\Delta=0} = \sum_{t=0}^{T} \delta^t [NE(T_t^0) - 2\alpha\text{cov}(S_t, T_t^0) - 2\alpha\text{cov}(T_t, T_t^0)].$$

14. In this case, only the covariance terms must vanish, but Arrow and Lind (1970) have shown in a more general framework that independence is also necessary.

undertaken. The hurdle rates used by large successful firms are often in the range of 15 to 25 percent per year. If public rates of return are higher than private rates of return, should more tax money be diverted to finance public investment? In some cases, particularly projects involving both basic and applied research, private firms have cooperated with public institutions to invest jointly in R&D. For such problems, public R&D may generate distinctly different rates of return for the private and public concerns involved. Should public projects be undertaken that raise private rates of return? These and other possibilities raise a host of questions of concern for public R&D policy.

A Basic Model of R&D Effects

Consider first a simple model where R&D is publicly financed. The basic model of R&D in Figure 14.6 was first used to estimate returns from public investments in hybrid corn research. Suppose prior to investment in R&D that supply and demand conditions are given by S and D, respectively. The equilibrium price and quantity are p_1 and q_1, respectively. Now suppose R&D shifts supply to S_1. This change is illustrated in Figure 14.6 for a closed economy with linear supply and demand curves, assuming a parallel shift in the supply curve. The new equilibrium price and quantity are p_2 and q_2, respectively. Investment has two effects: (1) an increase in consumers' real income (approximated by the increase in consumer surplus), and (2) a change in returns to fixed production factors (measured by the change in quasirent or producer surplus). Consumers clearly gain from R&D because price falls to p_2. Consumer surplus increases from area a to area $a+b+c$. Producer surplus changes from area $b+d$ to area $d+e$. One way to depict the gains from R&D is to compare the sum of producer and consumer surplus after R&D (area $a+b+c+d+e$) to the corresponding sum prior to R&D (area $a+b+d$). Comparison reveals a net gain in combined producer and consumer surplus of area $c+e$. This gain is clearly positive but must exceed the cost of undertaking the R&D to be socially preferred.

Distributional Effects of R&D

Often for political reasons, the distribution of costs and benefits caused by new technologies is a critical concern in addition to net social benefits. In Figure 14.6, consumers gain area $b+c$, which is unambiguously positive. However, producers' net welfare effect, area $e-b$, is ambiguous in sign. If supply shifts in a parallel fashion, such as to S_1, then this change is positive. But if supply shifts in a multiplicative fashion, such as to S_2, then producers may lose from the R&D even though their investment in new technology is necessary to make others better off. This adverse result for producers tends to occur when supply is more elastic and demand is more inelastic. Because the net effect of R&D (area $c+e$) is positive, consumer gain always exceeds any producer loss. Thus, the change is always preferred by the compensation criterion even though it may not be preferred by the Pareto criterion. Interestingly, if the change is not preferred by the Pareto criterion without compensation, then a Pareto preferred change would require consumers to compensate the producers who innovate the new technology. When technology development is financed by public R&D, this outcome is counterintuitive to typical consumer thinking and thus difficult to impose politically.

One may question why producers would adopt a new technology that ultimately makes

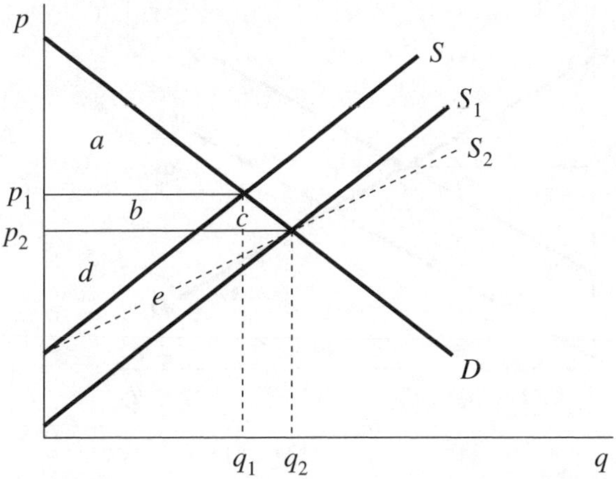

Figure 14.6

them worse off. The explanation lies in the dynamics of adoption under competition. The producers who adopt early tend to earn greater profits during the adoption phase because they achieve some combination of lower costs and higher output before prices fall to the new equilibrium. That is, aggregate supply shifts only partially because other producers are slow to adopt. But as more producers adopt, the price begins to fall and early non-adopting producers are forced to adopt to avoid losses in profit. By the time all producers adopt, they may all be worse off. Much has been written about this treadmill of technology adoption particularly in US agriculture.[15]

Distributional Effects in Related Markets

Because technology can cause major impacts in related markets, examining the welfare impacts beyond the market directly affected by new technology is also important. For example, because technology tends to be labor saving, one of the most controversial aspects of R&D, and the related technology adoption to which it leads, is the displacement of labor. Unless labor is immediately mobile, R&D can cause short-run adjustment costs that must be taken into account when calculating the net social return to R&D. The adoption of the mechanical tomato harvester is a well-known case in agriculture (Schmitz and Seckler 1970). The gross benefit from introduction of the mechanical tomato harvester in California was about $1 billion. However, the labor displacement costs were approximately $500 million, which greatly reduced the net benefits. Because only a small amount of compensation was paid to displaced workers, many individuals were adversely affected even though the gross benefits from R&D were large. Thus, the investment in R&D met the compensation test but not the Pareto test.

Figure 14.7 illustrates how new technology resulting from R&D may affect a vertically related market. Where q_a is a primary product and q_b is a product manufactured by

15. For example, the 'farm problem' has been characterized as a situation where farm incomes decline and consumers reap the benefits in the form of cheap food prices as farmers adopt more efficient production technologies. See Cochrane and Ryan (1976).

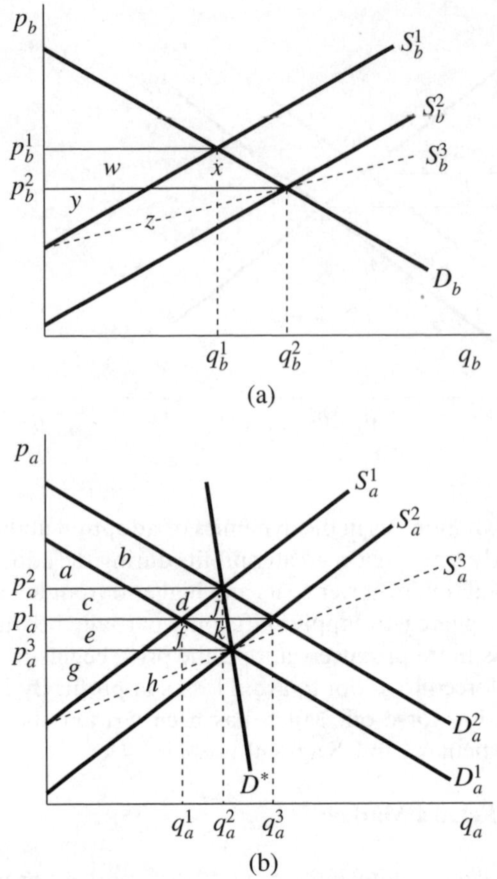

Figure 14.7

processing the primary product, suppose supply of the primary product is S_a^1, supply of the processed product is S_b^1, demand for the primary product is D_a^1 and demand for the processed product is D_b. In equilibrium, the primary product price is p_a^1 and the corresponding output is q_a^1. The price of the processed product is p_b^1 and the corresponding output is q_b^1. Now consider the effect of R&D on the processing sector where a new technique is introduced that results in less waste in processing each unit of the primary product. The effect of adoption is to increase supply of the processed product by shifting the supply curve downward and/or to the right, and to increase demand for the primary product by shifting the demand curve upward and/or to the right.

Suppose the processed product supply and primary product demand after equilibrium adjustment are represented by S_b^2 and D_a^2, respectively. Then processed product price declines to p_b^2 and primary product price increases to p_a^2. Following the discussion in Section 9.1, processed product consumers gain area $w+x$, primary product producers gain area $c+d$ and processor surplus changes from area $w+y$ to area $y+z$, which is equivalently represented by the change from area $a+c$ to area $a+b$. Again, the welfare effect on the innovating group, the processors, may be either positive or negative even though all other groups gain. If the new technology is cost-reducing and lowers marginal cost by the same amount on every unit processed (the supply curve shifts downward in vertically parallel fashion), as depicted by S_b^2, then processors gain because area z will exceed area w. If the new technology is output increasing (the supply curve shifts rightward in a horizontally multiplicative fashion), such as to S_b^3, then area w will be greater than area z if supply is sufficiently elastic and demand is sufficiently inelastic. In any case, the net welfare effect for processed product consumers and processors combined is an increase of area $x + z$, so the compensation criterion is satisfied even though the Pareto criterion may not be satisfied.

Alternatively, consider the case where R&D improves technology at the primary product level, such as an improved crop variety that raises yields for farmers. Viewing Figure 14.7 from a different perspective, suppose initial equilibrium is at price p_a^2 and quantity q_a^2 with supply S_a^1 and demand D_a^2 in the farm-level market and supply S_b^1 in the processed good market. Now consider the introduction of a new crop variety that shifts farm supply from S_a^1 to S_a^2. With increased supply, the farm-level price declines to ${p_a}^1$, calling forth an increase in production to q_a^3, assuming that the processed product price is unchanged. However, the lower primary product price causes an increase in processor supply in the processed market. The resulting reduction in the processed product price then causes a decline in demand for the farm-level product. After equilibrium adjustments, suppose the farm-level demand is represented by D_a^1, the farm-level price is p_a^3, the processed product supply is S_b^2 and the processed product price is p_b^2. The new equilibrium in the farm-level market will lie on the equilibrium demand curve D^*, which accounts for such adjustments in the processed market.

With this change, consumers of the processed product gain area $w + x$. Farm producer surplus changes from area $c + d + e + g$ to area $g + h$. If the new crop variety tends to reduce marginal costs by a constant amount across all possible output levels, then the supply shift tends to be downward in a vertically parallel fashion, in which case farm producers gain because area h will exceed area $c + d + e$. If the new crop variety tends to be output increasing (shifts farm-level supply in a horizontally multiplicative fashion), such as to S_a^3, then farm producers will lose if supply is sufficiently elastic and equilibrium demand is sufficiently inelastic. Because the equilibrium demand, D^*, tends to be more inelastic than the ordinary demand, D_a^2, a negative impact on farm producers is more likely than indicated by an analysis ignoring adjustments in related markets. Likewise, the processor welfare effect tends to be positive in this case because the change in the price of the primary product applies to every unit of the primary product purchased by processors. Thus, with elastic supply of the primary product, competitive primary producers tend to be worse off with the technological change they implement while consumers definitely gain and processors tend to gain. Again, an overall gain is clear because the area behind the equilibrium demand and ordinary supply in the primary market increases by area $f + h + j + k$. So the compensation criterion is satisfied even though the Pareto criterion is not. Again, any compensation scheme necessary for a Pareto improvement involves a transfer to the farmers, who without this understanding may be regarded by naive casual observers as the direct benefactors of the publicly financed R&D.

Open Economy Considerations

The analysis of R&D impacts is more complicated for goods that are traded internationally. Terms of trade effects and other factors such as domestic policy have to be taken into account. Consider Figure 14.8, where domestic supply and demand are given by *S* and *D*.

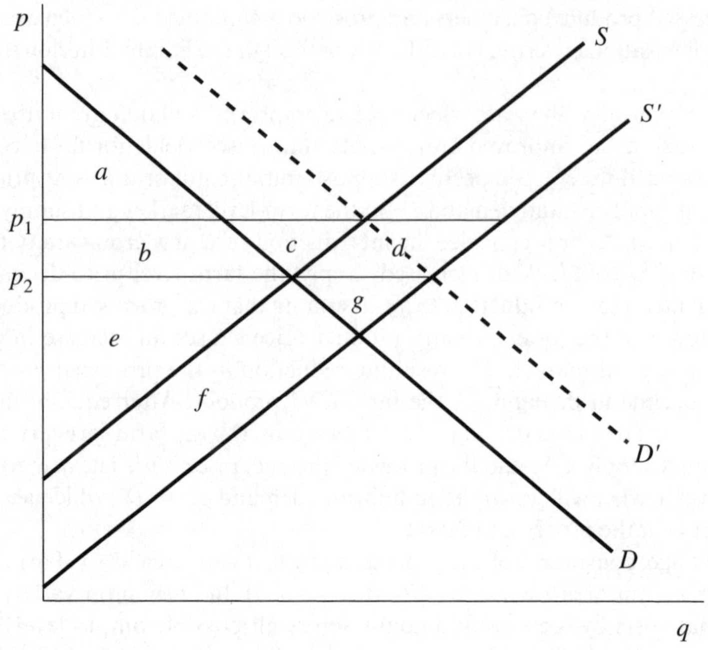

Figure 14.8

Under the small country assumption, world price is p_1 and is not affected by domestic supply shifts caused by R&D. Prior to R&D, the total surplus is area $a+b+c+e$. With R&D and adoption of the resulting technology, supply shifts to S'. Total surplus expands by area $d+f+g$. The gross gain from R&D is thus area $d+f+g$. To obtain the net gain, the gross gain must be reduced by the cost of R&D.

Consider now the large country case where R&D affects the terms of trade. In this case, R&D not only causes supply to shift to S' but also causes the world price to fall to p_2 considering total demand (for domestic consumption plus exports) D'. What is the effect? The total surplus prior to R&D is area $a+b+c+e$. With R&D, total surplus is area $a+b+e+f+g$. Thus, the gross gain from R&D is given by area $f+g$. The terms of trade effect reduces the size of R&D gains by area *d*.

Added complexities are also introduced by domestic policies such as subsidized prices and exports (Murphy, Furtan and Schmitz 1993). In Figure 14.9, domestic supply and demand of an exporting country are shown backwards in the left half of the diagram as *S* and *D*, respectively. The corresponding excess supply in the world market on the right-hand side is ES, while the excess demand curve facing the country is ED. World equilibrium occurs at free trade price p_f with export quantity q_f. The effect of supporting the

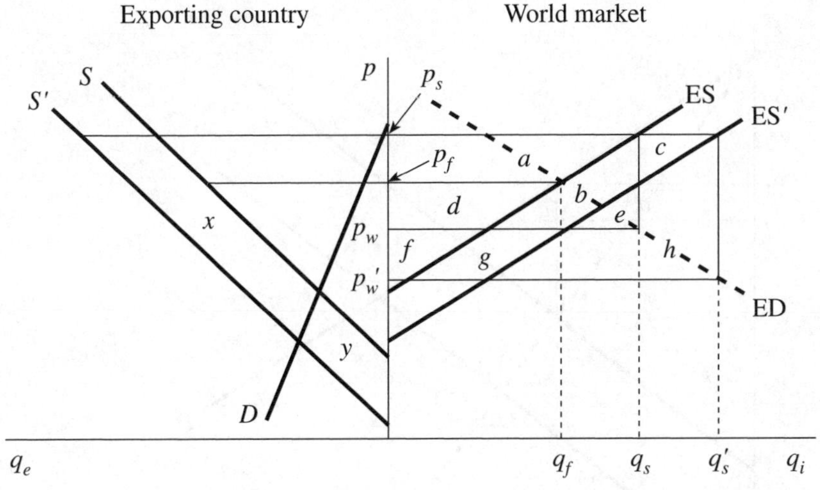

Figure 14.9

domestic price at level p_s, for example, by export refunds is to increase exports to q_s and reduce the export price to p_w. Domestic concerns (producers and consumers combined) gain area a but at a taxpayer cost of area $a+b+d+e$ in export refunds. Now suppose domestic supply shifts to S' as a result of R&D, causing the excess supply curve to shift to ES′. In the domestic market, the increase in producer surplus is area $x+y$ while domestic consumer surplus is unaffected. However, the associated increase in exports to q_s' causes the cost of export refunds to increase to area $a+b+c+d+e+f+g+h$. The increase in taxpayer costs for export refunds, area $c+f+g+h$, may exceed the increase in domestic surplus attributable to R&D if excess demand is sufficiently inelastic, particularly if the increase in supply is horizontally multiplicative rather than vertically parallel. If so, then the benefits of R&D are effectively exported to foreign consumers by means of export subsidies so that the exporting country receives a negative return on R&D.

Another possibility is that technological advances in the exporting country can spill over to (be adopted by) producers in importing countries. If so, then the excess demand will shift leftward, causing an additional negative effect on returns to R&D for the exporter. This example emphasizes once again the importance of considering all applicable distortions in the analysis of economic welfare effects.

R&D with Imperfect Competition

The benefits of R&D are also altered by imperfect competition. Investment in R&D can be examined in each of the cases of imperfect competition considered in Chapter 10. Figure 14.10 presents the monopoly case. Prior to R&D, the monopolist charges price p_1 and produces output q_1. Suppose R&D shifts the supply schedule to S'. The new equilibrium is at price p_2 and quantity q_2. Both consumers and the monopolist benefit from R&D. The consumer benefit is measured by area $a+b$. The monopolist benefit is measured by area $c+d-a$. Clearly consumer gains tend to be dominated by the monopolist's gains.

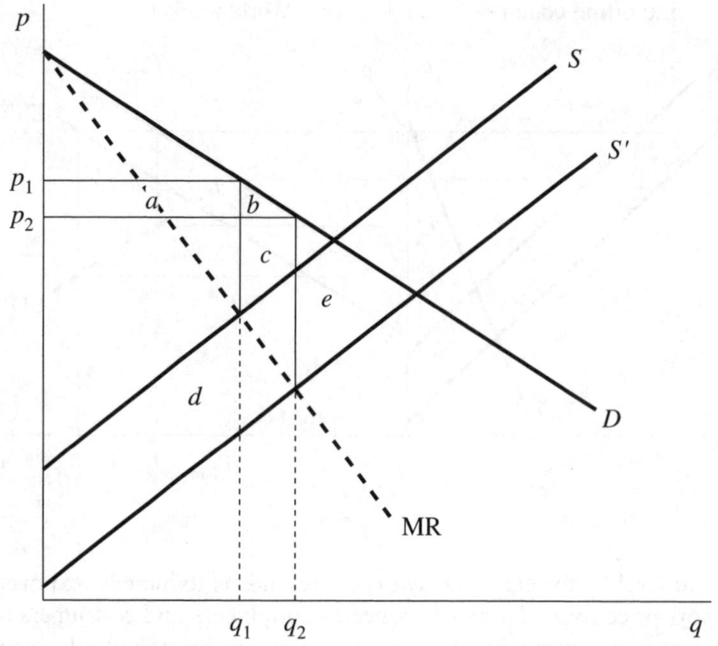

Figure 14.10

How do these results compare to the case of competition? Under competition the gross gain from R&D is area $d+e$. Under monopoly the gross gain is area $b+c+d$. The difference, area $e-b-c$, represents the additional benefit from R&D under competition as opposed to monopoly. This difference can be either positive or negative. Thus, market structure has an important effect on both the distribution of benefits of R&D and the overall social benefits of R&D.

Intertemporal Evaluation of R&D

Most research is not undertaken in a single period nor are returns realized instantaneously. Furthermore, benefits typically change over time. For example, some producers may adopt a technology early because of better information or lower risk aversion, while others adopt later. Also, market prices may decline as more producers adopt the technology, and, once adopted, the technology may decay or depreciate over time. Thus, a simple static model is not adequate for empirical research.

The simple static analysis of R&D impacts in Figure 14.6 can be extended to examine returns to R&D over time by considering the time stream of gross benefits and costs, as in equation (14.1). Applying the approach of Section 14.2, the framework of Figure 14.6 can be used to measure the welfare benefits and costs in each affected time period, and then these benefits and costs can be entered into equation (14.1) to evaluate effects over time. To use this model empirically requires estimating the benefits of R&D in each future time period. Typically, R&D involves long and uncertain lags from the time investment in R&D begins, to the time the resulting technology is finally adopted, and finally to the time when the benefits are eventually fully decayed. Also, the eventual benefits of adoption are typically uncertain before the technology has been tried and tested. For example, welfare analysis for a new crop variety requires assessing how much crop yields will increase, how many farmers will adopt the new variety, when farmers will adopt and whether or not additional inputs such as fertilizer and chemicals will be required.

Joint Public–Private Investment

Another issue raised by the introduction of the mechanical tomato harvester is related to public versus private financing of R&D. The development of the harvester was done by the private sector in conjunction with the University of California. Debate still centers around the issue of patent rights and the criteria for distribution of potential royalties from joint venture research involving a combination of private and public R&D. More recently, an increasing amount of research has been undertaken jointly by the private and public sectors as a result of the Bayh–Dole Act of 1980.

Illustration of relevant issues requires distinguishing between public and private returns and between the public and private R&D expenditures that generate them.[16] Suppose the economy is composed of J firms and K consumers, where for a particular project

I_t^p = public R&D investment at time t,
I_{jt} = private R&D investment by producer j at time t,
ΔC_{kt} = change in consumer surplus for consumer k at time t,
ΔR_{jt} = change in quasirent for producer j at time t.

Then application of equation (14.1) yields a net present social value given by

$$\mathrm{NPV}_S = \sum_{t=t_0}^{\infty}\left\{\frac{1}{(1+r_S)^{t-t_0}}\left[\sum_{k=1}^{K}\Delta C_{kt} + \sum_{j=1}^{J}\Delta R_{jt} - I_t^p - \sum_{j=1}^{J} I_{jt}\right]\right\}.$$

By comparison, the net present private value is

$$\mathrm{NPV}_P = \sum_{t=t_0}^{\infty}\left\{\frac{1}{(1+r_P)^{t-t_0}}\left[\sum_{j=1}^{J}\Delta R_{jt} - \sum_{j=1}^{J} I_{jt}\right]\right\}$$

and the net present private value for the jth producer is

$$\mathrm{NPV}_j = \sum_{t=t_0}^{\infty}\left\{\frac{1}{(1+r_j)^{t-t_0}}[\Delta R_{jt} - I_{jt}]\right\}.$$

In each case, suppose the applicable discount rate is determined as the minimum internal rate of return among projects that have been adopted. Then the social discount rate is the minimum value of r_S that makes $\mathrm{NPV}_S = 0$ among projects that have been adopted; the private rate of return is the minimum value of r_P that makes $\mathrm{NPV}_P = 0$; and the rate of return for producer j (reflecting the producer's hurdle rate) is the minimum value of r_j that makes $\mathrm{NPV}_j = 0$, assuming each exists.

16. The basic framework for this section parallels that used by Ulrich, Furtan and Schmitz (1986). They considered the case of joint public–private investment in malting barley research and found that the rates of return to private investment were significant. Also, private funding of university research funneled money away from investment in feed barley research.

Three cases of R&D may be considered:

1. Pure public investment: $I_t^p > 0$; $I_{jt} = 0$ for all j.
2. Pure private investment: $I_t^p = 0$; $I_{jt} > 0$ for some j.
3. Joint public/private investment: $I_t^p > 0$; $I_{jt} > 0$ for some j.

If investment in R&D is left to the private sector, then no private investment can be expected in projects for which $NPV_j < 0$ for all firms. On the other hand, some projects may have spillover effects because they lead to profitable possibilities for other firms after development by a first. In this case, NPV_P may be positive even though $NPV_j < 0$ for all j. Moreover, because consumers may reap some of the benefits of R&D, NPV_S may be positive even though $NPV_P < 0$ and $NPV_j < 0$ for all j.[17] The latter two cases require public investment to reach a social optimum.

Balancing investment activities when some projects involve pure private investment, some involve pure public investment, and some may require joint public–private investment is a difficult challenge. Social optimality is achieved by optimizing social welfare across all possible projects, whether public, private or joint efforts. The calculus of optimization implies that the discount rate used to determine whether a project is undertaken should be equated across all investment alternatives, whether undertaken by the public sector, private industry or by some joint arrangement. Specifically, the social optimum is characterized by undertaking all projects for which $NPV_S > 0$. If the availability of funds for public investment is limited, this problem comes down to allocating funds among projects (determining I_t^p for each project) such that public investment is undertaken at the minimum amount necessary to induce the private sector to invest in each project with $NPV_S > 0$. The social discount rate should be chosen such that this allocation just exhausts funds available for public investment. With this rule, some projects require no public investment (pure private investment), some will attract no private investment (pure public investment) and others will require joint public/private investment.

More generally, given the possibility of increasing funds available for public investment by taxation, if policy-makers use a social discount rate that differs from the private hurdle rates used to determine which private investments are undertaken, then overall investment may be socially suboptimal. For example, if the social discount rate is lower than private hurdle rates, then public projects will be undertaken that return less on average than the private projects that will be displaced by the taxation necessary to raise public funds.[18] Similarly, if private hurdle rates are lower than the social discount rate, then private investment may displace public projects that could better benefit society. A straightforward approach for a government to balance public and private investment is to regulate the private market rate of interest, for example, making it equal to the social rate of discount by regulating the money supply. However, this approach works only if unlimited credit is made available at the regulated market interest rate. Otherwise, limited borrowing capacity causes limited investment and a higher private rate of return on private investment than the market rate of interest (a second-best type of result).

17. Or alternatively, because of externalities, NPV_j could be positive for the investing firm and yet have $NPV_P < 0$ or $NPV_S < 0$, in which case the investment should not be undertaken.
18. On this point, see Hirshleifer (1966). Another possibility is that the government may increase public investment by borrowing. In this case, the cost of funds (the interest rate) is bid up, which also causes a displacement of private investment.

14.6 ECONOMIC WELFARE ANALYSIS OF NATURAL RESOURCE POLICY[19]

Another crucial area for application of social discounting and cost–benefit analysis is in natural resource economics. *Natural resource economics* is concerned with the conservation of natural resources. Whereas some environmental groups would define conservation of natural resources as the nonuse of resources, *resource conservation* is defined in economics as the optimum or efficient intertemporal use of natural resources (Ciriacy-Wantrup 1952, ch. 4).

Natural resources are often divided into two categories: renewable and nonrenewable. A *renewable resource* is one for which the stock can either increase or decrease. Increases are obtained through natural reproductive or recharging mechanisms, which can possibly be altered through resource management practices. Examples of such resources are forests and fisheries. A *nonrenewable resource* or *exhaustible resource* is one for which the stock can only decrease. Any depletion of such a resource necessarily reduces the availability of the resource for a future period. Examples are fossil fuels, iron ore and other minerals. In some cases of nonrenewable resources, the service flows can be renewed by recycling even though the resource itself cannot be renewed. For example, once iron ore is manufactured into an automobile, it cannot again be used as iron ore. But, to a large extent, the steel in an automobile can be recovered after the life of the automobile for, say, manufacturing other steel items. Such resources are sometimes called *durable* or *destructible nonrenewable resources* with renewable resource flows. Other nonrenewable resources such as natural gas and oil are immediately consumed. These nonrenewable resources are thus also *nondurable*. A third classification is that of *capital resources*, sometimes called nonrenewable resources with renewable service flows. These are resources that are available in quantities not affected by the rate at which they are exploited. Examples of such resources are solar and wind energy and land.

Social discounting is crucial in policy formulation and evaluation in each of these cases. With a nonrenewable resource, the policy questions involve intertemporal decisions about how much of the available resource should be used by the current generation and how much should be saved for use by future generations. With a renewable resource, the policy questions involve determination of resource management practices that improve the flow of goods or services from a resource over time as well as determination of optimal rates of use that appropriately balance consumption intertemporally. The use of the social discounting principle can be illustrated by its applications in policy formulation for the major natural resources in each of these categories. Some of the crucial intertemporal issues with capital resources have to do with irreversibility of resource use decisions.

Nonrenewable Resources

In the case where a resource is available in fixed supply and is destructible, meaning that once it is used it cannot be used again, the problem of temporal allocation is rather simple once the appropriate social discount rate is determined. Consider, for example, a two-

19. This section draws on the graphical analysis developed by McInnerney (1976).

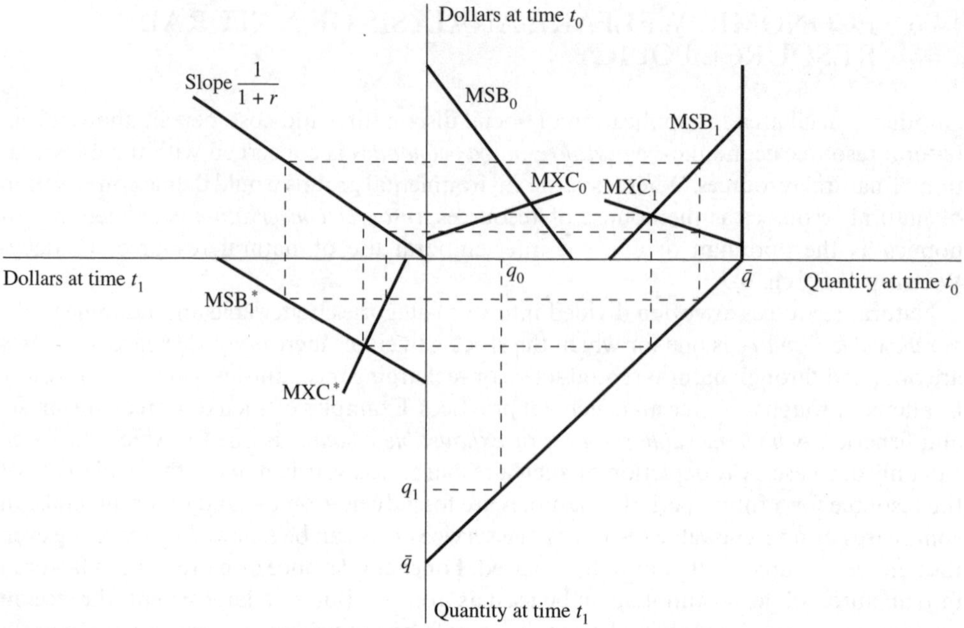

Figure 14.11

period allocation problem, as in Figure 14.11, where MSB_0 in the upper right quadrant represents marginal social benefits of using the resource in the current period, MSB_1^* in the lower left quadrant measures the marginal social benefits of using the resource in a future period, MXC_0 in the upper right quadrant represents the marginal costs of extraction for the raw material at time t_0, MXC_1^* in the lower left quadrant measures the marginal cost of extraction for the raw material at time t_1 and $\bar{q}$ represents the fixed amount of the resource available. The line $\bar{q}\bar{q}$ in the lower right quadrant simply indicates that the amount of resource can be traded between time periods in any way so that total use does not exceed $\bar{q}$. That is, if quantity q_0 is used at time t_0, then following the graph $\bar{q}\bar{q}$ from the right axis to the lower axis implies that q_1 remains for future consumption.

Now consider discounting future benefits and costs in such a way that present welfare effects may be weighed against future effects. This can be done by using the line with slope $1/(1+r)$ in the upper left quadrant, where r is the appropriate social discount rate between the two time periods (note that t_1 is not necessarily equal to t_0+1). That is, by using the lines drawn in the upper left and lower right quadrants, the MSB_1^* and MXC_1^* curves in the lower left quadrant can be transformed into the MSB_1 and MXC_1 curves in the upper right quadrant. The MSB_1 curve thus gives the *discounted* marginal social benefit of using the resource in time period t_1. The MXC_1 curve gives the *discounted* marginal extraction cost at time t_1. Both of these curves are drawn backward from quantity $\bar{q}$, representing the fact that future consumption is constrained by the amount left over from current consumption.

In this context, two cases of nonrenewable resource allocation may be depicted as in Figure 14.12. Each case corresponds to the upper right quadrant of Figure 14.11 after

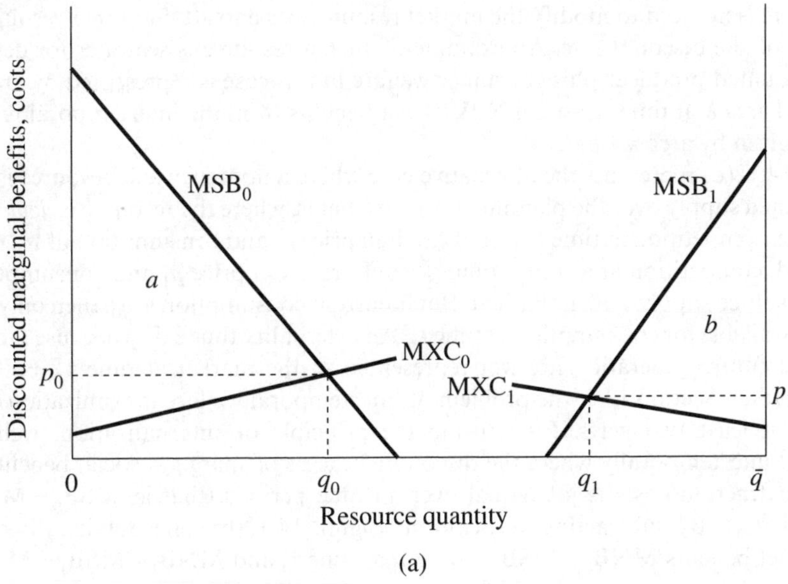

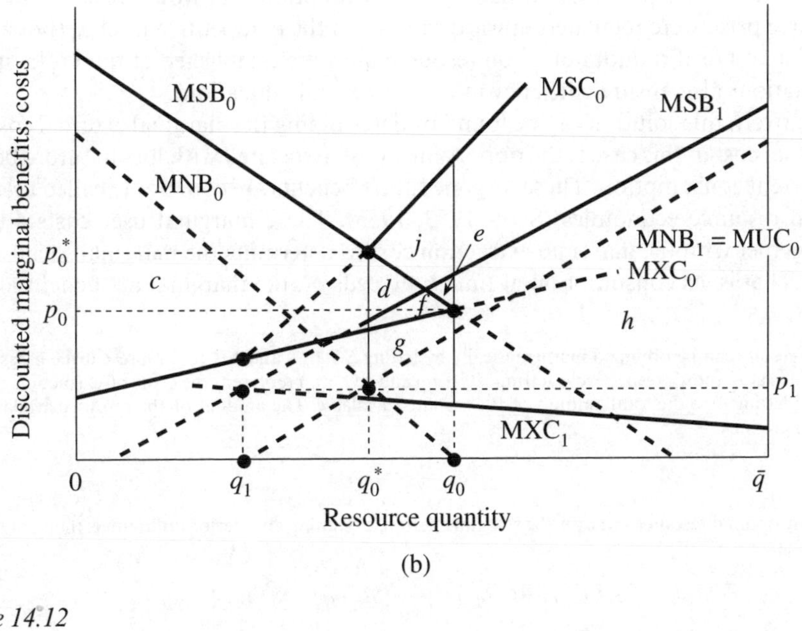

Figure 14.12

discounting. Figure 14.12(a) represents the case where a nonrenewable resource is available in unlimited quantities. The available stock exceeds the maximum that would be consumed over the planning horizon. Such resources are sometimes called *nondepletable* resources because free-market use levels do not lead to depletion. Competition at time t_0 results in price p_0 with quantity q_0 consumed at that price, and competition at time t_1 results in price p_1 with consumption of $\bar{q} - q_1$ (assuming no intratemporal externalities).

Hence, there is no need to modify the market resource price to attain proper resource use regardless of the discount rate. An example of such a resource is seawater for desalination. Discounted producer plus consumer welfare in this case is represented by area a at time t_0 and area b at time t_1, so the NPV of net benefits from the intertemporal resource market is given by area $a+b$.

Figure 14.12(b) represents the alternative case where a nonrenewable resource is available in limited supply over the planning horizon (that is, where the resource is *depletable*). In this case, competition at time t_0 would result in price p_0 and consumption of q_0. On the other hand, competition at a future time t_1 would result in price p_1 and consumption of $\bar{q}-q_1$ if resource supply were unlimited. But if current consumption is q_0, then only $\bar{q}-q_0$ would be available for consumption at time t_1. An externality thus exists because the interests of the future generation are not represented in the market at time t_0. Following the principles in Section 13.1, the problem of intertemporal welfare maximization can be solved in at least two ways. First, using the principle of internalization, welfare is maximized intertemporally where the discounted excess of marginal social benefits over marginal extraction costs is just equal over all time periods (that is, $\text{MSB}_0-\text{MXC}_0=\text{MSB}_1-\text{MXC}_1$). By subtracting vertically in Figure 14.12(b), one obtains discounted marginal net benefits $\text{MNB}_0=\text{MSB}_0-\text{MXC}_0$ at time t_0 and $\text{MNB}_1=\text{MSB}_1-\text{MXC}_1$ at time t_1. The two are equal at q_0^*, which is the consumption that would result at time t_0 if the resource price were regulated upward to p_0^* from the competitive level p_0 (possibly by means of a tax) or if a quota of q_0^* on resource use were established at time t_0 (assuming that regulations also ensure efficiency in extraction and allocation).

Alternatively, this solution can be found by determining the marginal external cost first. The external cost in this case is the opportunity cost associated with loss in future benefits due to current consumption. These forgone future benefits are commonly called *user costs* in natural resource economics (Scott 1953, 1955). These marginal user costs are then added together with the marginal extraction cost to determine the marginal social cost at time t_0.[20] That is, as consumption at time t_0 exceeds q_1, the marginal net benefit forgone

20. These results can be obtained mathematically by letting $SB_{t_0}(q_{t_0})$ and $SB_{t_1}(q_{t_1})$ represent the gross benefit functions at t_0 and t_1, respectively, letting $\text{XC}_{t_0}(q_{t_0})$ and $\text{XC}_{t_1}(q_{t_1})$ represent the costs of extraction at t_0 and t_1, and letting $\bar{q}$ be the total amount of the resource available. The amount of the resource available at t_1 is then given by

$$q_{t_1}=\bar{q}-q_{t_0}.$$

Socially optimal resource use over the two time periods assuming an interior optimum is then obtained by maximizing

$$SB_{t_0}(q_{t_0})-\text{XC}_{t_0}(q_{t_0})+\frac{1}{1+r}[SB_{t_1}(q_{t_1})-\text{XC}_{t_1}(q_{t_1})]$$

subject to resource availability. The Lagrangian expression for this problem is given by

$$\mathcal{L}=SB_{t_0}(q_{t_0})-\text{XC}_{t_0}(q_{t_0})+\frac{1}{1+r}[SB_{t_1}(q_{t_1})-\text{XC}_{t_1}(q_{t_1})]-\lambda(q_{t_1}-\bar{q}+q_{t_0}),$$

where λ is the Lagrangian multiplier. Optimizing with respect to q_{t_0} and q_{t_1} yields first-order conditions

$$\text{MSB}_{t_0}-\text{MXC}_{t_0}-\lambda=0$$

$$\frac{1}{1+r}(\text{MSB}_{t_1}-\text{MXC}_{t_1})-\lambda=0,$$

by future generations, MNB_1, becomes a marginal external cost or a *marginal user cost* at time t_0, denoted by MUC_0 in Figure 14.12(b). Adding this cost to the marginal extraction cost MXC_0 obtains marginal social cost MSC_0 at time t_0. Equating marginal social cost MSC_0 with marginal social benefits MSB_0 thus leads to the optimal consumption q_0^* of the resource at time t_0. Again, this consumption could be achieved under competition by imposing a quota of q_0^* or by imposing a price floor or regulated price of p_0^* at time t_0, assuming efficiency in extraction and allocation.[21]

To consider the welfare effects in this case, note that producer plus consumer net benefits at time t_0 are given by area $c+d+f$ if competition prevails at price p_0 and quantity q_0. If price p_0^* and quantity q_0^* are achieved as a result of regulations, then net benefits at time t_0 are given by area c. Net producer plus consumer benefits at time t_1 are given by area $e+f+g+h$ if price p_0^* and quantity q_0^* are achieved by regulation at time t_0. However, if competition prevails at time t_0, then only $\bar{q}-q_0$ of the resource remains at time t_1 and, hence, net benefits at t_1 are only area h. The effects of regulation are thus a loss of area $d+f$ at time t_0 and a gain of area $e+f+g$ at time t_1, which is equal to area $d+e+f+j$ or a net gain of area $e+g-d=$ area $e+j$. Because these welfare effects are in discounted terms, a Pareto improvement is thus possible through regulation by redistributing the net gain so that some groups are better off and no groups are worse off.

Finally, consider the case where a nonrenewable resource can be recycled. Such resources include iron, copper, lead, gold and aluminum. In this case, present consumption need not deprive future generations. However, recycling is not a costless process. The potential for recycling depends on the proportion of the extant resource services that can be recaptured, the length of time for which resource services are fixed or the rate at which they can be recycled and the costs of the recycling process.

For the purposes of diagrammatic discussion, assume that resources used at time t_0 can be recycled for use at time t_1. This case is depicted in Figure 14.13 using the approach of internalization, rather than calculating damages for the future generation and then determining a related marginal social cost curve. Figure 14.13(a) gives the marginal net benefit curve MNB_0 at time t_0, which is derived in Figure 14.12(b) by subtracting marginal extraction cost MXC_0 from marginal social benefits MSB_0. The discounted marginal net benefits from consumption MNB_1 at time t_1 in Figure 14.13(b) are derived similarly, as in Figures 14.11 and 14.12(b), by discounting and then subtracting marginal extraction cost MXC_1 from marginal social benefits MSB_1. Aggregating these two marginal net benefits horizontally thus obtains the discounted intertemporal marginal net benefit curve MNB_{0+1} depicted in Figure 14.13(c). This same principle can be extended to aggregating marginal net benefits across many time periods.

Now suppose that the total amount of the resource is given by $\bar{q}$ in Figure 14.13(c).

where $MSB_t = \partial SB_t/\partial q_t$ and $MXC_t = \partial XC_t/\partial q_t$. The latter condition implies that λ is the marginal user cost (MUC_{t_0}) at time t_0. That is, λ is the NPV of forgone marginal net benefits resulting from an incremental increase in q_{t_0}. Thus, the optimum decision rule at time t_0 is given by

$$MSB_{t_0} = MXC_{t_0} + \frac{1}{1+r}(MSB_{t_1} - MXC_{t_1}) = MXC_{t_0} + MUC_{t_0}.$$

21. One might note alternatively that the optimum consumption q_0^* could possibly result under monopoly without government intervention. In a second best type of result, the imposition of a tax in such a case may drive the economy further from Pareto optimality (see the discussion related to Figure 13.6 for a similar case).

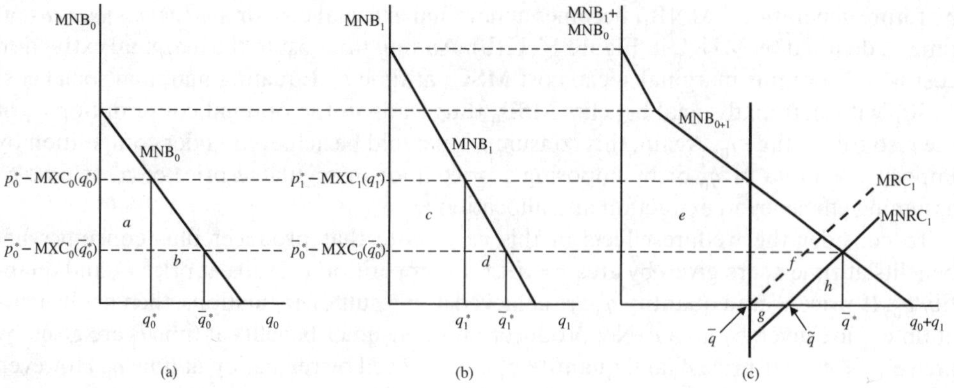

Figure 14.13

Translating the intersection of MNB_{0+1} and the vertical line at $\bar{q}$ back to Figure 14.13(a) and (b) thus obtains the appropriate discounted differential between price and marginal extraction cost for time periods t_0 and t_1, which equate discounted marginal net benefits over time when no recycling is used. This is the same solution for social optimality as obtained in Figure 14.12(b) because $\text{MNB}_0 = \text{MNB}_1$ where the total quantity of resource is exhausted between the two periods.

Consider, finally, the opportunity of recycling, which can increase total intertemporal consumption beyond $\bar{q}$. Let MRC_1 represent the *discounted* marginal cost per unit of resource recovered. With respect to recycled material, the marginal net benefits for a recovered unit of the resource would be the marginal social benefits less the marginal recovery cost, $\overline{\text{MNB}}_1 = \text{MSB}_1 - \text{MRC}_1$, whereas the marginal net benefits in Figure 14.13(c) correspond to marginal social benefits less the marginal extraction costs (for example, $\text{MNB}_1 = \text{MSB}_1 - \text{MXC}_1$ at time t_1). Thus, $\overline{\text{MNB}}_1 = \text{MNB}_1 + \text{MXC}_1 - \text{MRC}_1 = \text{MNB}_1 - \text{MNRC}_1$, where $\text{MNRC}_1 = \text{MRC}_1 - \text{MXC}_1$. The marginal net resource cost of recycling, MNRC_1, depicted in Figure 14.13(c), is the marginal recycling cost less the marginal extraction cost that would have been incurred in the absence of recycling (if the available quantity of resource were great enough). The point of social optimality is at $\bar{q}^*$ where marginal net benefit is equal to marginal net resource cost, $\text{MNB}_{0+1} = \text{MNRC}_1$, which corresponds to recycling enough of the resource used at time t_0 to support additional consumption of $\bar{q}^* - \bar{q}$. Translating back into individual time periods in Figure 14.13(a) and (b) implies optimal discounted marginal net benefits of $\bar{p}_0^* - \text{MXC}_0(\bar{q}_0^*)$ and $\bar{p}_1^* - \text{MXC}_1(\bar{q}_1^*)$, respectively, or respective discounted prices $\bar{p}_0^*$ and $\bar{p}_1^*$. Of course, price $\bar{p}_0^*$ and quantity $\bar{q}_0^*$ would not occur unless appropriate regulations were imposed as above in Figure 14.12(b).

Without recycling, net discounted consumer plus producer welfare is represented by area a at time t_0, by area c at time t_1 and by area e for both time periods considered jointly. With recycling, the NPV of benefits over both time periods increases by area $f+g$. The gain at time t_0 is represented by area b in Figure 14.13(a), assuming that recycling costs are incurred only at time t_1. The net gain at time t_1 is area $d+g-h$ because area $f+h$ is equal to area $b+d$ by construction. Hence, area f is equal to area $b+d-h$. Substituting for area f in the overall gain of area $f+g$ and subtracting the gain at time t_0, area b, thus obtains the gain at time t_1 of area $d+g-h$. Intuitively, area g represents a cost savings associated with recycling where marginal recycling costs are lower than marginal extraction costs. Area h represents the higher cost that must be incurred for consumption at time t_1 when marginal recycling costs exceed marginal extraction costs. Because the marginal net benefit curve MNB_1 in Figure 14.13(b) relates only to extraction, both of these adjustments to area d are required in calculating welfare effects of recycling at time t_1.

Of course, the solution in Figure 14.13 is valid only if the intersection of MNB_{0+1} and $MNRC_1$ is above the horizontal axis. Otherwise, recycling would be undertaken to the point of supporting consumption $\tilde{q}-\bar{q}$ at time t_1 (because recycling to this point is cheaper than extraction). Then consumption in both time periods would be expanded until marginal social benefits were equated to marginal extraction costs. In this case, resource availability would exceed free-market consumption so that the competitive market would attain social optimality. One may also note that the analysis in Figure 14.13 can be easily generalized to the case where recycling takes place in both (or many) time periods by simply replacing MRC_1 with the horizontal summation over time of all relevant discounted marginal recycling cost curves.

Renewable Resources

With renewable resources, the resource as well as the service that can be derived from it are depleted with use, but new stocks are created by a process of regeneration. Resources of this type include fisheries, forests and grasslands. In each of these cases, once an amount of the resource is used, it cannot be again added to the stock of resources. For example, a house cannot again become a tree. However, unless the resource is depleted completely, it can regenerate itself, usually at a rate that depends upon the amount of the resource left.

To consider this case, define g as the rate by which 1 unit of the resource will grow from time t_0 to time t_1 if unutilized at time t_0. Thus, if $\bar{q}$ is the total stock of the resource at the beginning of time period t_0 and q_0 of this stock is utilized for current consumption in time t_0, the stock of the resource available at time t_1 is $(\bar{q}-q_0)(1+g)$. This situation is depicted graphically in Figure 14.14, which corresponds in structure to Figure 14.11. The right axis measures quantity at time t_0, where $\bar{q}$ is the total available stock. If none of the stock is utilized at time t_0, it will grow through regeneration to a stock of $\bar{q}(1+g)$ by time t_1, as depicted on the lower axis. Any linear combination of these two extremes is also possible, as indicated by the upward-sloping line in the lower right quadrant. As in Figure 14.11, the marginal social benefits and marginal extraction costs are depicted in current dollars in the upper right quadrant for time t_0 (MSB_0 and MXC_0, respectively) and in the lower left quadrant for time t_1 (MSB_1^* and MXC_1^*, respectively).

If competition prevails, then price p_0 and utilization q_0 occurs at time t_0. Equilibrium at time t_1 would lead to price p_1^* and quantity q_1^*. However, to utilize a quantity of q_1^* at time t_1, a resource stock of at least $\bar{q}-q_1$ must remain unutilized at time t_0. This would not be the case if q_0 is utilized at time t_0. Thus, utilization at t_0 imposes an externality at time t_1. These results demonstrate that, without regulations, a fishery may be overfished, rangelands may be overgrazed or forests may be overcut at the expense of future generations. Thus, with renewable resources, user costs are associated with decisions to produce now rather than later.

To properly consider user costs in determining intertemporal marginal social cost at time t_0, one must use the appropriate social discount rate, as in Figure 14.11, but one also must consider that one unutilized unit of the resource at time t_0 supports consumption of

$1+g$ units of the resource at time t_1. This is considered by using a line of slope $(1+g)/(1+r)$ in the upper left quadrant. Thus, the marginal social benefit curve MSB_1 in the upper right quadrant is derived by deflating the marginal social benefit MSB_1^* in the lower left quadrant by a social discount rate r, but then inflating by a rate of g because nonuse of 1 unit of the resource at time t_0 supports consumption of $1+g$ units at time t_1. The marginal extraction cost MXC_1 is derived similarly and then the marginal social cost at time t_0 is obtained as $\text{MSC}_0=\text{MXC}_0+\text{MSB}_1-\text{MXC}_1$, as in Figure 14.12(b).[22] Thus, social optimality at t_0 implies that marginal social benefits at t_0 must be equal to the sum of marginal extraction cost and marginal user cost at t_0. Note that marginal user cost, in the case of renewable resources, involves two distinct components: (1) the marginal scarcity value (which is the only cost component associated with exhaustible resources), and (2) the cost imposed on future generations of reduced resource regeneration.

Social optimality in Figure 14.14 is obtained where $\text{MSB}_0=\text{MSC}_0$ or at quantity q_0^*. This quantity of resource utilization at time t_0 can be obtained by means of a tax equal to the vertical difference in MSB_0 and MXC_0 at q_0^* or by establishing a regulated price p_0^* or regulated quantity q_0^* along with some regulations to obtain efficiency in extraction and allocation. The welfare effects are a loss of area $a+c$ for market participants at time t_0 and a gain of area $b+c+d$ for market participants at time t_1, assuming that any tax revenues at time t_0 are redistributed in lump-sum payments to time t_0. The net gain from regulation is thus area $b+d-a=$ area $b+e$.

Capital Resources

A final category of resources that are neither renewable nor destructible is typified by land. Regardless of how a given area of land is utilized in one time period, the same quantity of land remains to be utilized in the succeeding time period. However, the way in which land is utilized in one period may limit the set of choices regarding use in a suc-

22. These renewable resource decision rules can be obtained mathematically as follows. Using the same notation as in footnote 20 for the nonrenewable resource case, the only change in the optimization problem is that the resource constraint becomes

$$q_{t_1}=\bar{q}-q_{t_0}+g(\bar{q}-q_{t_0})=(1+g)(\bar{q}-q_{t_0}).$$

Forming the Lagrangian with the same objective function as previously yields first-order conditions

$$\text{MSB}_{t_0}-\text{MXC}_{t_0}-\lambda(1+g)=0$$

$$\frac{1}{1+r}(\text{MSB}_{t_1}-\text{MXC}_{t_1})-\lambda=0.$$

In this case, l is the NPV of an increment of the resource at t_1, which can come from two sources: nonuse in t_0 or regeneration of the stock from t_0 to t_1. Substituting the latter condition into the former, the optimal use of the renewable resource at t_0 is given by

$$\begin{aligned}\text{MSB}_{t_0}&=\text{MXC}_{t_0}+\frac{1}{1+r}(\text{MSB}_{t_1}-\text{MXC}_{t_1})+\frac{g}{1+r}(\text{MSB}_{t_1}-\text{MXC}_{t_1})\\&=\text{MXC}_{t_0}+\frac{1+g}{1+r}(\text{MSB}_{t_1}-\text{MXC}_{t_1})\\&=\text{MXC}_{t_0}+\text{MUC}_{t_0}.\end{aligned}$$

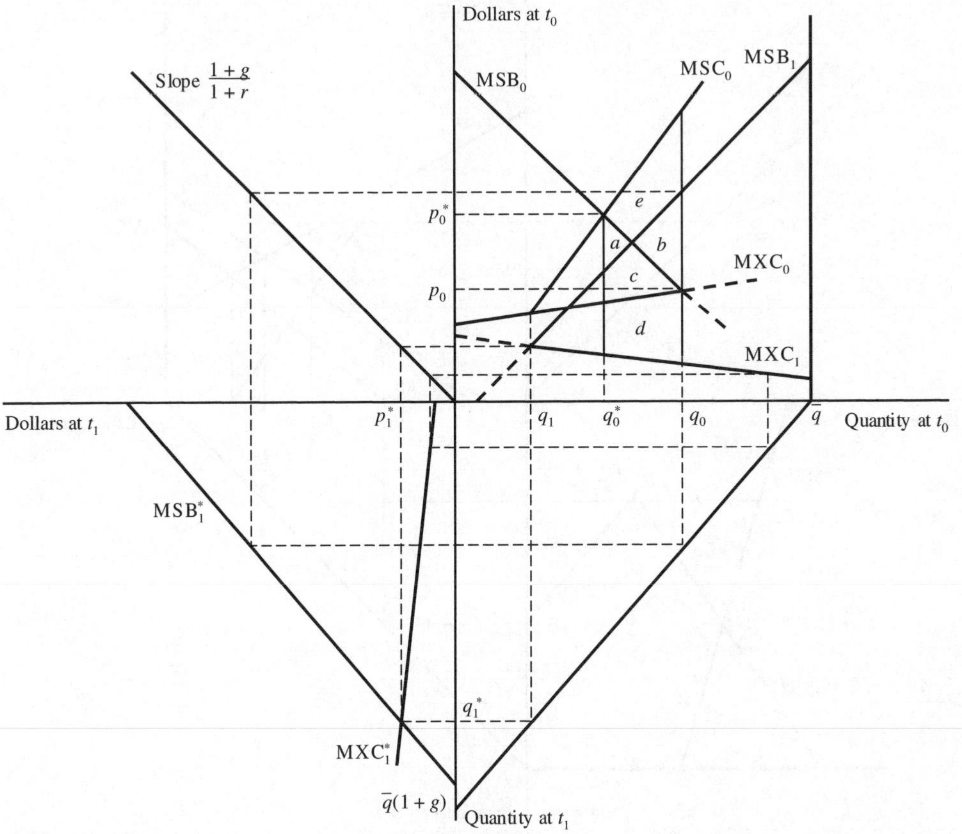

Figure 14.14

ceeding period. For example, soil mismanagement leads to fertility depletion and erosion. Nonmaintenance of housing, overpopulation of amenity areas and water pollution also affect choice sets for future generations. In these cases, regeneration may be possible in time so that a framework much like the case of renewable resources is appropriate. The more serious intertemporal decisions for land relate to uses that are irreversible (for practical purposes). For example, when land is transferred from agricultural to urban use, fields are covered by houses and streets so that reversal is impractical. The same is true when a dam is built to create a reservoir.

This problem is examined graphically in Figure 14.15, where $\bar{q}$ represents the total quantity of land. The marginal social benefits of using land for housing are given by MSB_0^H at time t_0 and by MSB_1^H at time t_1. The marginal social benefits of using land for agricultural purposes are given by MSB_0^A at time t_0 and by MSB_1^A at time t_1. If the free market prevails, equilibrium at time t_0 would occur with quantity q_0 of land in housing. But suppose that population in rural areas is declining and preferences for housing are shifting demand toward metropolitan areas so that marginal social benefits from housing in agricultural areas decline from time t_0 to time t_1. Also, suppose that increasing world demand for food causes the marginal social benefits from agricultural use to increase, as

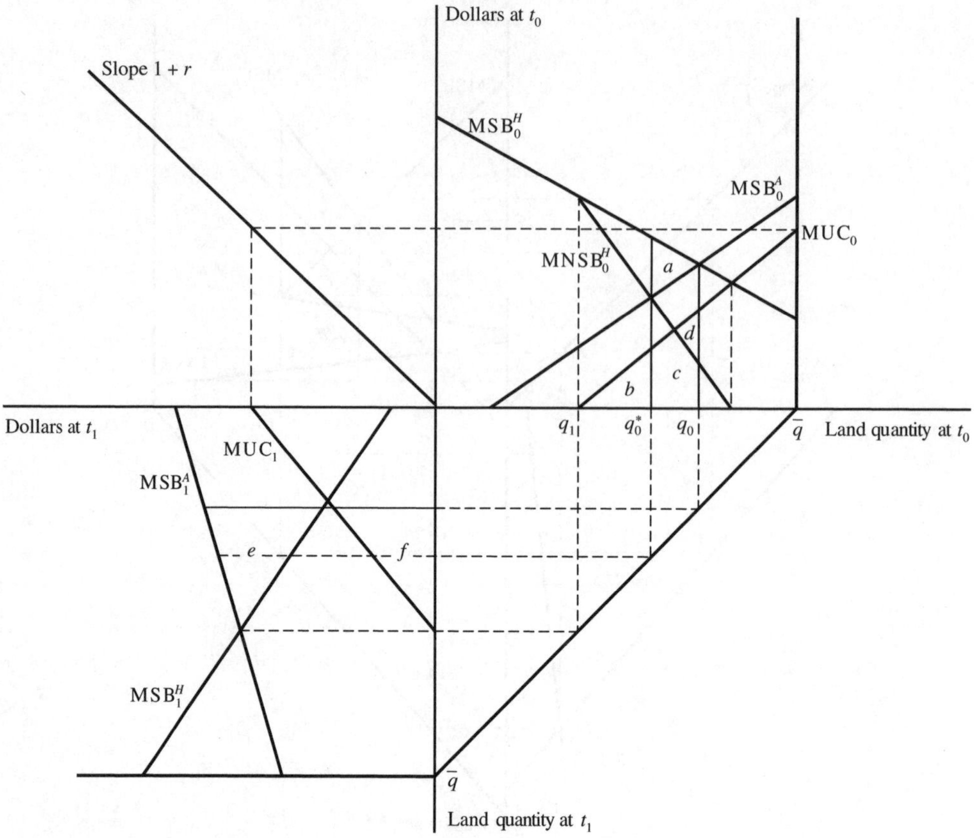

Figure 14.15

reflected in Figure 14.15. Then the desired use of land shifts so that only q_1 is used in housing (determined by the intersection of MSB_1^A and MSB_1^H in the lower left quadrant). However, if housing is irreversible, housing remains at q_0 in time t_1. The welfare effect of the reduced choice for the future generation is a loss of area *e* measured in currency at time t_1. This, of course, represents a user cost.

To determine a social optimum, first construct a marginal user cost MUC_1 by subtracting MSB_1^H from MSB_1^A in the lower left quadrant. Then area *f* is equal to area *e*, so that the area under MUC_1 measures the user cost. Next, transform this user cost curve through social discounting (in the upper left quadrant), obtaining the discounted marginal user cost curve MUC_0 in the upper right quadrant. This curve represents an external cost associated with housing because of its irreversibility. Deducting the marginal user cost from the marginal social benefit MSB_0^H obtains the marginal net social benefit curve $MNSB_0^H$ associated with housing. Equating this with the marginal social benefits from agricultural use thus determines the intertemporal social optimum at q_0^*. This optimum would be achieved by limiting the free-market growth in housing in agricultural areas at time t_0. The welfare effects of such a limitation would be a loss of area *a* for the current generation and a discounted gain of area $c + d$ for the succeeding generation.

The crucial assumptions in this analysis, of course, are the irreversibility of housing and a declining relative benefit from housing in agricultural areas. If benefits from housing continue to grow more than for agriculture or if housing were (costlessly) reversible, the free market would attain social optimality in each time period individually as well as intertemporally.

14.7 A GENERAL FRAMEWORK FOR DYNAMIC AND SUSTAINABLE ECONOMIC WELFARE ANALYSIS

Although the foregoing cases characterize some of the broad issues that can arise in intertemporal economic welfare analysis, one must bear in mind that not all problems can be categorized neatly into one of these frameworks. Some problems contain several of these aspects, as well as others such as discussed in Chapter 13. In general, the approach is to identify the economic, physical and biological processes that are affected by policy controls and economic decision-making. If private decisions are involved, the reaction of those decisions to policy controls must be considered. Then the indirect and intertemporal effects of various policies on consumer and producer welfare can be investigated.

For example, one can specify and possibly estimate a vector-valued state process,

$$\boldsymbol{X}_t = f(\boldsymbol{X}_{t-1}, \boldsymbol{Y}_t, \boldsymbol{Z}_t), \tag{14.9}$$

where $\boldsymbol{X}_t$ is a vector including such things as known reserves of a natural resource and capital accumulation in an industry at time t and possibly also at time $t-1$, $t-2$, and so on. The function f may entail search and discovery processes, technological development, natural or biological regeneration and so on; $\boldsymbol{Y}_t$ is a vector including government policy controls such as taxes, subsidies, quotas and direct involvement at time t; and $\boldsymbol{Z}_t$ is a vector including decisions made in the private sector at time t. Upon considering the influence of government controls on the private sector, one can write $\boldsymbol{Z}_t$ as a function of the other variables in the problem so that $\boldsymbol{Z}_t$ can possibly be eliminated.

The objective criteria for policy-making purposes can then be written as

$$\max_{Y_0, Y_1, \ldots, Y_T} \sum_{t=0}^{T} \left(\frac{1}{1+r}\right)^t \sum_{i=1}^{N} [S_t^i(\boldsymbol{X}_t, \boldsymbol{Y}_t, \boldsymbol{Z}_t) + E_t^i(\boldsymbol{X}_t, \boldsymbol{Y}_t, \boldsymbol{Z}_t) + T_t^i(\boldsymbol{X}_t, \boldsymbol{Y}_t, \boldsymbol{Z}_t), \tag{14.10}$$

where r is the social discount rate, S_t^i represents market effects on individual or firm i at time t in terms of (Hicksian) consumer surplus or producer surplus, E_t^i represents external effects also in terms of WTP by individual or firm i at time t, T_t^i represents transfers to individual i at time t from government (possibly negative as in the case of taxes), and T is the number of time periods in the policy planning horizon.

Maximization of (14.10) subject to (14.9) and an initial state $\boldsymbol{X}_0$ is a complicated mathematical problem but can be solved, in practice, using dynamic programming, linear or nonlinear programming, or discrete optimal control. Sometimes this type of problem is stated in terms of continuous rather than discrete time, in which case the techniques of optimal control theory are applicable.[23]

23. For a further general discussion, see Howe (1979). For some specific applications, see Burt (1964), Burt and Cummings (1973), Clark (1976), Cummings (1969), Dasgupta and Heal (1974), Hotelling (1931), Lee (1978) and Smith (1969).

The framework in (14.9) and (14.10) provides a powerful and general means of examining a wide range of problems. Because of its apparent simplicity, however, some emphasis on the importance of considering all relevant implications for related markets and external concerns is needed. The problem associated with use of public funds for R&D can serve to illustrate this need. Particularly in the area of agriculture, a large amount of public funds has been used to finance biotechnology research on seed varieties and transgenic products. The original rationale for these expenditures was that this research requires such massive expenditures that private industry was not in a position to fully undertake it. For example, in the case of developing genetically modified seed varieties, the technology has some characteristics of a public good because many producers eventually benefit by obtaining seed from neighbors if not directly from a seed company. Thus, externalities associated with the public goods cases of Sections 13.2 and 13.3 must be considered.

As more biotechnology research has led to market impacts, other objections have been raised associated with information imperfections and other externalities. First, concerns have been raised about the healthiness or safety of food produced from transgenic species. European consumers have been particularly reluctant to accept these foods and have pressured their governments to restrict the import of genetically modified foods. Second, environmental groups have argued that the genetic characteristics of these products might be transferred in the field to native plants and result in irreversible ecological damages. Third, consumer groups have argued that private industry has obtained the patent rights to some public biotechnology developments and thus have been able to exercise legal monopolies in sales, which has padded the pocketbooks of private industry at the expense of consumers. Others have argued that public funding of research has reduced incentives for private research that would otherwise have been undertaken because the likelihood of capturing rents for new technology development is reduced. Still others have argued that the effects of displacement of labor by technological advances have been undesirable and more than outweigh any benefits.

Numerous studies have been undertaken to estimate and compare the costs and benefits of R&D and the associated technological changes. Many of these studies have focused on particular aspects of the problem. For example, Mansfield et al. (1977) have focused on the private return to private investment. In so doing, they consider only the terms in (14.10) that relate to private industry (for example, agricultural seed and machinery companies), while disregarding the role of government and public expenditures. Vernon Ruttan and his coauthors have alternatively examined the returns on public investment.[24] These works generally focus only on the terms in (14.10) that relate to producers and consumers. The role of private industry and private industry's response to public expenditures has not been examined. But in both of these cases, returns to research and development have been found to be quite high, even when social costs have been taken into account.[25]

The framework in (14.9) and (14.10) serves to emphasize why, in spite of these high estimated returns, controversy still exists regarding the desirability of public expenditure for R&D. An appropriate social cost–benefit analysis of public research expenditure must

24. For a list of such studies, see Evenson, Waggoner and Ruttan (1979).
25. See, for example, Schmitz and Seckler (1970). In this case, even if workers displaced by the introduction of the harvester had been compensated, the payoff from investment in technology would still have been very high.

consider effects on all concerns (including those associated with other markets) from both public and private investment and the interactions between the two in terms of the effects of public investment on private investment decisions and the benefits captured from sales of products developed in the public sector.

A second problem that has arisen with the application of the optimization scheme suggested here is the concern for *sustainability* and *intergenerational equity*. In equation (14.10), the time frame for the analysis is fixed at T. For a private firm or an individual this may be appropriate, but an infinite planning horizon is probably more appropriate for society as a whole.[26] In the longer run, the analysis in Section 14.6 implies that many nonrenewable resources will be exhausted. The observation that a number of developing countries depend largely on income from these types of natural resources motivated publication of the Bruntland Report during the 1980s by the World Commission on Environment and Development (1987, p. 43), which called for 'development that meets the needs of the present generation without compromising the ability of future generations to meet their own needs'. The usual implementation of this concept in economics has been to investigate the conditions under which constant per capita consumption paths can be achieved through time. For a renewable resource, this is obviously possible with use at some steady-state level. For an economy based largely on exhaustible resources, however, this may not be possible.

Solow (1974) and Hartwick (1978) have investigated the conditions under which an economy dependent on exhaustible resources can achieve a constant per capita consumption path. Solow finds that sustainable consumption can be obtained under any one of three production conditions: (1) continuous-augmenting technical change, (2) Cobb-Douglas technology with a capital share greater than the share of exhaustible resources or (3) an elasticity of substitution between exhaustible resources greater than one. Views will differ on the reasonableness of meeting one or more of these conditions, but many economists agree with Weitzman (1999, p. 26), who argues that 'the research process has a sort of pattern-fitting or combinatoric feel about it. It seems that ideas build upon each other in such a way that many new ideas are essentially successful reconfigurations of already existing ideas that have not previously been combined with each other'. If this is true, continuous technological change may not be unreasonable.

Hartwick develops a simple rule for achieving sustainability in the case of a simple Cobb-Douglas economy without technical change or population growth. He finds that, if an economy invests the marginal user costs from *nonrenewable natural capital* (also called Hotelling rents) in all man-made or physical capital, then the result is a constant per capita consumption path. Thus, his rule is zero investment as measured by the increase in physical capital less the decrease in nonrenewable natural capital. The Hartwick rule has intuitive appeal because forgone future earnings from the resource (measured by the marginal user cost) are exactly recouped by the investment in physical capital. Conversely, disinvestment in natural capital (exhaustible resources) is exactly offset by the investment in

26. Dynamic optimization models for a society or an economy for an infinite planning horizon are of two types: (1) those that assume an economic agent with infinite life such as that found in Arrow and Kurz (1970), and (2) those that posit a series of overlapping generations such as those found in McCandless and Wallace (1991) or Blanchard and Fischer (1989). For an analysis of the welfare properties of dynamic competitive equilibrium of an economy with exhaustible resources in an overlapping generations model, see Olson and Knapp (1997).

physical capital so that the aggregate capital stock is kept intact.[27] Hence, the result is a solution similar to a steady-state renewable resource economy solution. In the context of the general optimization problem presented here, the Hartwick rule can be evaluated explicitly as a separate policy, as a component of the vector $\boldsymbol{Y}_t$, or as a constraint on the system when evaluating other policies.

Section 13.4 explains that households derive satisfaction not only from the consumption of material goods but also from aesthetic experiences, biodiversity and natural foods. This is evidenced by their willingness to pay for them. Thus, the focus on sustainable consumption paths may not be sufficiently robust for the analysis of the problem. One alternative approach to incorporating sustainability considerations is to put additional constraints on some of the natural capital state variables of the vector $\boldsymbol{X}_t$ in equation (14.9). For example, such constraints might not allow the oil reserves in a country, the number of hump-backed whales, or the total number of bird species to fall below certain levels.[28] The solution to the optimization problem would then indicate the opportunity cost of these restrictions on consumer and producer welfare over time as well as the shadow prices of the resources. The implementation of such a model requires data not exceptionally difficult to find.

Finally, one must bear in mind that the goal of sustainable development is fundamentally an equity rather than efficiency issue. Welfare measures for current and future generations cannot be aggregated objectively. Compensation criteria may be inapplicable because possibilities for intergenerational compensation are restricted unlike problems of intragenerational compensation. At least to date, empirical experience has shown that per capita consumption of later generations has tended to be much higher than that of earlier generations. Using the Rawlsian criterion in this context suggests focusing relatively more on the current generation than future generations. But this weighting seems to be morally unacceptable to many if not most people and corresponds to using a positive and perhaps larger discount rate than has been used in the past. Nevertheless, the current generation has an obligation to future generations as well as to itself. Perhaps intergenerational equity can be determined only by the political process, but economic welfare analysis can contribute useful information to this process even if it cannot resolve the problem.

14.8 CONCLUSIONS

This chapter expands the framework of economic welfare analysis to the case where costs and benefits accrue over a long period of time. In conclusion, some of the arguments can be briefly reviewed for clarity. Consider first the case where a perfect capital market exists through which a private decision-maker operating in a certain environment can distribute personal WTP over time in any way he or she sees fit. Then when WTP for a particular

27. The Hartwick rule has found support from Solow (2000).
28. Unfortunately, empirical guidance for natural capital or biodiversity constraints is exceptionally difficult to find. How can mosquitoes and redwoods be aggregated? What is the value of these species? What is the marginal rate of technical substitution in the ecosystem function? Even defining what is meant by biodiversity is problematical. Some key references on this subject are Simpson, Sedjo and Reid (1996), Polasky, Solow and Broadus (1993), Weitzman (1992) and Metrick and Weitzman (1998).

change (along with all its associated time stream of effects) is determined at time t_0, it will include welfare effects over all time. In this case, each individual discounts his or her own effects at his or her private discount rate (which would be the perfect capital-market rate of interest). Hence, use of the WTP criterion necessarily implies that the (implicit) social discount rate is equal to the private rate of return (assuming that all individuals face the same private rate of return as in the case of a perfect capital market).

On the other hand, suppose that markets are not perfect. If capital markets do not permit individuals to freely redistribute their welfare effects over time, then the private rate of return may not be appropriate. Rather, WTP in individual time periods would require specific determination so that necessary compensation schemes could be considered. In the event of compensation over time, as well as within time, where funds are carried forward or backward in time by government, the appropriate discount rate is the one representing the opportunity cost for government rather than the private sector (for example, the rate paid on government treasury bills). Hence, the δ in equations (14.6) and (14.7) should be associated with the public discount rate rather than respective private rates. If, however, compensation is considered only at time t_0, then the time stream of welfare effects for each individual should be discounted with the individual's private discount rate, which may differ substantially both among individuals and over time, depending on whether deficits or surpluses are being carried.

If market failure entails externalities due to unrepresented contingencies of future generations, the extent of such externalities must be estimated (as well as possible) and then a social discount rate must be used as a means of comparing relative income distributions between present and future generations. Unless a change is Pareto superior without compensation, no intratemporal compensation scheme could attain Pareto optimality. Rather, the government would be forced either to carry compensation over time or to make interpersonal comparisons between generations. In this case, the choice of a social discount rate becomes crucial in comparing welfare effects at different points in time. The theoretical analysis shows that the choice of discount rate depends on whether society anticipates an increase in production possibilities due to technological development or declining production possibilities due to natural resource depletion.

Because the crux of most natural resource problems has to do with comparing social welfare effects over very long time periods including several generations, the choice of a discount rate can be the most important issue in determining the intergenerational distribution of resource use. However, the social discounting methodology of this chapter has important applications in evaluation of *any* policy from which effects are realized over multiple time periods. Also, for practical purposes, economic welfare analysis of the future must consider the extent to which the future is unknown. Because the future is unknown, both economic decisions and economic welfare may depend on risk. Therefore, discount rates may depend on risk. This chapter presents some cases where risk implications can be simplified or ignored in cases of government risk neutrality. For more general problems where private risk discounting is critical, the reader is referred to the Appendix of this chapter.

Appendix to Chapter 14: Intertemporal welfare analysis with investment in producer capital and consumer durables

This appendix introduces a rigorous framework for dynamic economic welfare analysis for both producers and consumers. Unlike previous appendices in this book, this appendix does not offer rigorous mathematical justification of results in the text of the chapter. Rather, it goes beyond the text of the chapter to address details of dynamic welfare measurement that go beyond the scope of analysis that is feasible in relatively nonmathematical terms. Concepts of dynamic economic welfare analysis must necessarily take account of the fact that future prices cannot be anticipated with certainty. Thus, the point of departure in this appendix must be from the case of price risk introduced in Appendix Section 12.A. In this appendix, the framework considers the case where not only prices but optimal decisions in future time periods are subjectively random in the current decision-making period. Once this framework is developed for the producer (Section 14.A), generalizations follow for the dynamic case of consumer decision-making where investment decisions represent purchases of durables (Section 14.B). Section 14.C then shows how the social discount rate can, in principle, be derived by aggregating individuals' private discount rates. Finally, Section 14.D generalizes the framework of Sections 14.A–14.B for the case of equilibrium welfare measurement in the spirit of Chapter 9. One of the interesting aspects of compensation that arises in this appendix is the difference in *ex post* versus *ex ante* compensation schemes. For example, when future outcomes are unknown, policy-makers can specify not only fixed (*ex ante*) compensation schemes but also conditional (*ex post*) compensation schemes whereby the compensation received by each individual depends on the 'state of nature' realized after some uncertainty is resolved (as discussed in Section 12.6).

14.A INTERTEMPORAL ECONOMIC WELFARE ANALYSIS FOR PRODUCERS

Consider a multiple-product competitive producer with intertemporal (or dynamic) production function given in implicit form by

$$f_t^T(\mathbf{q}_t^T, \bar{\mathbf{q}}^t) = \mathbf{0},$$

where

$$\boldsymbol{q}_t^T = (\boldsymbol{q}_t^T, \boldsymbol{q}_{T-1}, \ldots, \boldsymbol{q}_t),$$
$$\boldsymbol{q}_k = (q_{1k}, \ldots, q_{Nk}),\ k = t, \ldots, T,$$
$$\bar{\boldsymbol{q}}^t = (\bar{\boldsymbol{q}}_{t-1}, \bar{\boldsymbol{q}}_{t-2}, \ldots),$$
$$\bar{\boldsymbol{q}}_k = (\bar{q}_{1k}, \ldots, \bar{q}_{Nk}),\ k = t-1, t-2, \ldots$$

Let q_{nt} (or $\bar{q}_{nt}$ if q_{nt} has already been decided) represent the quantity of good n produced (used as an input if negative) at time t, where $\bar{\boldsymbol{q}}^t$ is included to represent fixed input decisions made in previous periods. Also, assume that $\boldsymbol{f}_t^T$ is monotonically decreasing, concave and twice differentiable in $\boldsymbol{q}_t^T$ except for identities that may also be linear representing depreciation and the transition of capital among vintages (for example, machines held this year are machines held last year plus purchases minus retirements or sales). In this context, consider the producer's problem of maximizing expected utility over a planning horizon from current time t to terminal time T (which could possibly represent maximization of the expected utility of wealth at terminal time T),

$$\max_{\boldsymbol{q}_t^T} E_t[U(\pi_t - K_t, \ldots, \pi_T - K_T) | \boldsymbol{f}_t^T(\boldsymbol{q}_t^T, \bar{\boldsymbol{q}}^t) = \boldsymbol{0}] \tag{14.11}$$

where π_k is receipts less expenditures in time period k,

$$\pi_k = \boldsymbol{p}_k \boldsymbol{q}_k = \Sigma_{n=1}^N p_{nk} q_{nk};$$

$\boldsymbol{p}_k = (p_{1k}, \ldots, p_{Nk})$ is a vector of prices of goods 1, ..., N at time period k, which is subjectively random for $k \geq t$; K_k is an *ex ante* payment required of the firm in period k that includes fixed cost (similar to the static case in the Appendix to Chapter 12); U is an intertemporal utility function associated with the planning horizon and is assumed to be strictly increasing, quasiconcave and twice differentiable in $\pi_t, \ldots, \pi_T$; and E_t is the expectation operator associated with the subjective distribution at time t. The dependence of the expectation operator on time represents the learning that takes place as new information becomes available over time. Suppose the joint subjective distribution of all prices over all time, $\boldsymbol{p}_t^T = (\boldsymbol{p}_t, \ldots, \boldsymbol{p}_T)$ as of time k is characterized completely by means, $\bar{\boldsymbol{p}}_k^T = E_k(\boldsymbol{p}_t, \ldots, \boldsymbol{p}_T)$, and higher moments, $\boldsymbol{\alpha}_k^T$ where $E_k(\boldsymbol{p}_t) = (\bar{p}_{1t}^k, \ldots, \bar{p}_{Nt}^k)$ and higher moments are defined independent of means (for example, are moments about means) such that $\boldsymbol{\alpha}_k^T$ also represents the higher moments of $\boldsymbol{\varepsilon}_t^k \equiv \boldsymbol{p}_t - E_k(\boldsymbol{p}_t)$. Thus, $\partial \boldsymbol{\varepsilon}_t^k / \partial E_k(\boldsymbol{p}_t) = 0$ for all t. With the transition from time period $k-1$ to time period k, a new price vector $\boldsymbol{p}_k$ becomes known and the precision of information about prices in later time periods is updated. For added generality, suppose also that $\boldsymbol{\alpha}_k^T$ characterizes any stochastic properties of the production function, $\boldsymbol{f}_t^T$, not yet known at time k. These may include random uncontrolled conditions such as weather or lack of precision in a decision-maker's knowledge of a technology.

Intertemporal Optimization

Using Bellman's optimality principle (see, for example, Bellman and Dreyfus 1962), the problem in (14.11) can be solved by backward dynamic (stochastic) programming or, in other words, by solving the sequence of problems in each time period k, $k = T, T-1, \ldots, t$, conditioned on decisions in earlier periods (inputs fixed by the time of decisions in period

k are represented by over bars) and assuming optimal decisions in later periods (represented by tildes),[1]

$$\max_{q_k} \bar{U}_k \equiv E_k[U(\bar{\pi}_t - K_t,\ldots,\bar{\pi}_{k-1} - K_{k-1},\pi_k - K_k,\tilde{\pi}_{k+1} - K_{k+1},\ldots,\tilde{\pi}_T - K_T)] \tag{14.12}$$

subject to

$$\boldsymbol{f}_t^T(\tilde{\boldsymbol{q}}_{k+1}^T,\boldsymbol{q}_k,\bar{\boldsymbol{q}}^k) = \mathbf{0}, \tag{14.13}$$

where

$$\tilde{\boldsymbol{q}}_{k+1}^T = (\tilde{\boldsymbol{q}}_T,\tilde{\boldsymbol{q}}_{T-1},\ldots,\tilde{\boldsymbol{q}}_{k+1}), \tag{14.14}$$

$$\tilde{\pi}_h = \boldsymbol{p}_h\tilde{\boldsymbol{q}}_h \text{ for } h > k,\ \bar{\pi}_h = \boldsymbol{p}_h\bar{\boldsymbol{q}}_h \text{ for } h < k,\ \pi_k = \boldsymbol{p}_k\boldsymbol{q}_k. \tag{14.15}$$

Note in this problem that $\tilde{\boldsymbol{q}}_{k+1}^T$ represents optimal decision functions in all future time periods, $\boldsymbol{q}_k$ represents all current decisions, and $\bar{\boldsymbol{q}}^k$ represents fixed inputs resulting from all previous decisions.

The Lagrangian associated with this problem is

$$\mathcal{L}_k = E_k[U(\bar{\pi}_t - K_t,\ldots,\bar{\pi}_{k-1} - K_{k-1},\pi_k - K_k,$$
$$\tilde{\pi}_{k+1} - K_{k+1},\ldots,\tilde{\pi}_T - K_T)] - \boldsymbol{\varphi}_k \boldsymbol{f}_t^T(\tilde{\boldsymbol{q}}_{k+1}^T,\boldsymbol{q}_k,\bar{\boldsymbol{q}}^k)$$

and the associated first-order conditions for constrained optimization in addition to (14.13) are

$$\frac{\partial \mathcal{L}_k}{\partial \boldsymbol{q}_k} = \frac{\partial \bar{U}_k}{\partial \pi_k}\frac{\partial \pi_k}{\partial \boldsymbol{q}_k} - \boldsymbol{\varphi}_k \frac{\partial \boldsymbol{f}_t^T}{\partial \boldsymbol{q}_k} = \mathbf{0}, \tag{14.16}$$

where $\bar{U}_k$ is defined as in (14.12). Second-order conditions are satisfied under the assumptions above. Hence, solution of (14.13) and (14.16) leads, in principle, to decision functions (supply if positive and demand in negative) of the form

$$\boldsymbol{q}_k = \tilde{\boldsymbol{q}}_k(\bar{\boldsymbol{p}}_k^T,\boldsymbol{\alpha}_k^T,\bar{\boldsymbol{q}}^k,\boldsymbol{K}), \tag{14.17}$$

where $\boldsymbol{K} = (K_t,\ldots,K_T)$, which can be substituted into (14.12) through (14.15) to solve the problem where k is reduced by one in each successive step.

Continuing in this manner for $k = T, T-1, \ldots, t$ obtains the optimal decision functions in (14.17) for every time period in the planning horizon. Note, however, that $\tilde{\boldsymbol{q}}_k$ is generally a random vector at time t if $k > t$ because it depends on the subjective price

1. Note that one cannot simply solve the problem in (14.11) directly for $\boldsymbol{q}_t^T$ ignoring the possibility of adjusting planned decisions in later periods as more price and production information becomes available. Such an approach is appropriate only if the decision-maker proceeds naively as if the current subjective distribution of prices and production will not be modified with new information. The backward dynamic programming approach in (14.12), on the other hand, considers future optimal decisions as stochastic depending on new information that will be accumulated along the way.

distribution at time k which is not yet known at time t, and on some random components of the production function not yet known at time t, both of which become known by time k. That is, while the production function may induce a stochastic distribution on any $\boldsymbol{q}_k$, the related stochastic forces are assumed to become known by time k so that current production is subjectively nonstochastic.[2]

While tentative decision functions are formulated for all future time periods with this approach when making choices at time t, the future decision functions are updated in succeeding time periods as new information is acquired. As a result, current decisions may affect a decision-maker's ability to use future information. For example, if an irreversible decision is made or a longer-lived asset is purchased, then a decision-maker may not be able to take advantage of future information when it becomes available. The value of preserving the option to adjust to information in future time periods as it becomes available is called *quasi-option value*. It is somewhat like the option value discussed in Section 12.6 but arises in a dynamic context. The quasi-option value literature shows that decisions are inefficient if the value of this option is not considered, in which case decisions are biased toward irreversible alternatives.[3]

Intertemporal Indirect Expected Utility

Using (14.15) and (14.17), one can define an indirect expected utility function

$$V_t(\bar{\boldsymbol{p}}_t^T, \boldsymbol{\alpha}_t^T, \bar{\boldsymbol{q}}^t, \boldsymbol{K}) = E_t\left[U(\tilde{\pi}_t - K_t, \ldots, \tilde{\pi}_T - K_T) - \sum_{k=t}^{T} \boldsymbol{\varphi}_k \boldsymbol{f}_t^T(\tilde{\boldsymbol{q}}_k^T, \bar{\boldsymbol{q}}^k) \right], \tag{14.18}$$

where the last term in brackets is included for convenience below even though it is zero for every state of nature as implied by first-order conditions. That is, decisions in each period t must be made to satisfy (14.13) so that $\boldsymbol{f}_t^T = \boldsymbol{0}$.

The remaining derivation then becomes closely analogous to the general case of Appendix Section 12.A. That is, the current decisions in this problem play very much the same role as the input decisions in Appendix Section 12.A, while the future decisions are random and must thus be treated as the production variables in the random production case of Appendix Section 12.E. Specifically, by the envelope theorem (or by use of (14.16)), one obtains

$$\frac{\partial V_t}{\partial \bar{p}_{ih}^t} = E_t(U_k \cdot \tilde{q}_{ih}) + E_t\left[\sum_{k=t}^{T} \left(\frac{\partial \mathcal{L}_k}{\partial \boldsymbol{q}_k} \frac{\partial \tilde{\boldsymbol{q}}_k}{\partial \bar{p}_{ih}^t} + \left(\frac{\partial \mathcal{L}_k}{\partial \boldsymbol{\varphi}_k} \frac{\partial \boldsymbol{\varphi}_k}{\partial \bar{p}_{ih}^t} \right) \right) \right] \tag{14.19}$$

$$= E_t(U_h \cdot \tilde{q}_{ih}),\ i = 1, \ldots, N,\ h = t, \ldots, T, \tag{14.20}$$

2. This assumption is not restrictive if one assumes that some or all of the related production choices require decisions in prior periods. For example, if all input decisions in a single-product case are made in a prior period, the random disturbance in production can be viewed as becoming known in the current period, which then determines the amount of production through the production function constraint. Alternatively, one can assume at some notational expense that some current quantities are the result of other current, directly controlled decisions in a stochastic sense. In such a case, the result below in (14.19) holds for all decisions, whereas (14.20) does not hold for decisions that are not directly controlled but result stochastically from other decisions (which is analogous to Appendix Section 12.A).
3. Quasi-option value has been considered at length in the literature on environmental preservation (Arrow and Fisher 1974; Fisher and Hanemann 1987; Hanemann 1989). For a more general treatment, see Henry (1974) and Chavas and Mullarky (2002).

where $U_h \equiv \partial U/\partial \pi_h$. Note that (14.19) simplifies to (14.20) because the derivatives of $\mathcal{L}_k$ are zero for every state of nature by the first-order conditions. Also, because current decisions are nonstochastic with respect to the subjective distribution at time t, (14.20) can be written compactly as

$$\frac{\partial V_t}{\partial \bar{\boldsymbol{p}}_t^t} = E_t(U_t) \cdot \tilde{\boldsymbol{q}}_t. \tag{14.21}$$

Evaluation of Welfare Effects of Expected Price Changes

Using the result in (14.21), one can determine the compensating variation, $\hat{C}_{it}(\bar{p}_{it}^{t0}, \bar{p}_{it}^{t1})$, of any current subjective mean price change for good i from $\bar{p}_{it}^{t0}$ to $\bar{p}_{it}^{t1}$. Using the approach in Appendix Section 12.B, this compensating variation is defined by

$$V_t(\bar{\boldsymbol{p}}_t^{T1}, \boldsymbol{\alpha}_t^T, \bar{\boldsymbol{q}}^t, K_t + \hat{C}_{it}, \bar{\boldsymbol{K}}_t) = V_t(\bar{\boldsymbol{p}}_t^{T0}, \boldsymbol{\alpha}_t^T, \bar{\boldsymbol{q}}^t, K_t, \bar{\boldsymbol{K}}_t) = V_t^0, \tag{14.22}$$

where

$$\bar{\boldsymbol{p}}_t^{Tj} = E_t(\hat{\boldsymbol{p}}_t^{tj}, \boldsymbol{p}_{t+1}, \ldots, \boldsymbol{p}_t), j = 1,2,$$
$$\hat{\boldsymbol{p}}_t^{tj} = (\bar{p}_{1t}^t, \ldots, \bar{p}_{it}^{tj}, \ldots, \bar{p}_{Nt}^t), j = 1,2,$$
$$\bar{\boldsymbol{K}}_t = (K_{t+1}, \ldots, K_T).$$

Differentiating both sides of (14.22) with respect to $\bar{p}_{it}^{t1}$ and using (14.18) and (14.21) implies that

$$E_t(U_t) \cdot \tilde{q}_{it}(\bar{\boldsymbol{p}}_t^{T1}, \boldsymbol{\alpha}_t^T, \bar{\boldsymbol{q}}^t, K_t + \hat{C}_{it}, \bar{\boldsymbol{K}}_t) - E_t[U_t \cdot \partial \hat{C}_{it}/\partial \bar{p}_{it}^{t1}] = 0.$$

But if $\hat{C}_{it}$ is an *ex ante* compensation, it must be nonstochastic, and thus $\partial \hat{C}_{it}/\partial \bar{p}_{it}^{t1}$ factors out of the expectation, yielding

$$\tilde{q}_{it}(\bar{\boldsymbol{p}}_t^{T1}, \boldsymbol{\alpha}_t^T, \bar{\boldsymbol{q}}^t, K_t + \hat{C}_{it}, \bar{\boldsymbol{K}}_t) = \partial \hat{C}_{it}/\partial \bar{p}_{it}^{t1}. \tag{14.23}$$

Also, because $\hat{C}_{it}$ is determined so as to hold expected utility at its initial level, V_t^0, one may further define

$$\bar{q}_{it}(\bar{\boldsymbol{p}}_t^{T1}, \boldsymbol{\alpha}_t^T, \bar{\boldsymbol{q}}^t, V_t^0) \equiv \tilde{q}_{it}(\bar{\boldsymbol{p}}_t^{T1}, \boldsymbol{\alpha}_t^T, \bar{\boldsymbol{q}}_t^t, K_t + \hat{C}_{it}, \bar{\boldsymbol{K}}_t), \tag{14.24}$$

which is a compensated supply equation (demand if negative) for good i at time t. Thus, because $\hat{C}_{it}(\bar{p}_{it}^{t0}, \bar{p}_{it}^{t1}) = 0$, *the compensating variation of a current subjective mean price change is given by the change in producer (consumer) surplus associated with the corresponding current supply (demand) curve conditioned on initial expected utility and taken as a function of mean price*:

$$\hat{C}_{it}(\bar{p}_{it}^{t0}, \bar{p}_{it}^{t1}) = \int_{\bar{p}_{it}^{t0}}^{\bar{p}_{it}^{t1}} \bar{q}_{it}(\bar{\boldsymbol{p}}_t^T, \boldsymbol{\alpha}_t^T, \bar{\boldsymbol{q}}^t, V_t^0) dp_{it}^t.$$

Interestingly, this is true even if the good in question is an investment good that may affect production in many different production periods, possibly including the current period.[4]

Additionally noting that $\hat{E}_{it}(\bar{p}^{t1}_{it},\bar{p}^{t0}_{it}) = -\hat{C}_{it}(\bar{p}^{t0}_{it},\bar{p}^{t1}_{it})$ where $\hat{E}_{it}(\bar{p}^{t1}_{it},\bar{p}^{t0}_{it})$ is the equivalent variation of a current subjective mean price change for good i from $\bar{p}^{t1}_{it}$ to $\bar{p}^{t0}_{it}$, one finds that

$$\hat{E}_{it}(\bar{p}^{t0}_{it},\bar{p}^{t1}_{it}) = \int_{\bar{p}^{t0}_{it}}^{\bar{p}^{t1}_{it}} \bar{q}_{it}(\bar{\mathbf{p}}^{T}_{t},\boldsymbol{\alpha}^{T}_{t},\bar{\mathbf{q}}^{t},V^{1}_{t})\,dp^{t}_{it},$$

where $V^{1}_{t} = V_{t}(\bar{\mathbf{p}}^{T1}_{t},\boldsymbol{\alpha}^{T}_{t},\bar{\mathbf{q}}_{t},K_{t},\bar{\mathbf{K}})$. That is, *the equivalent variation of a current subjective mean price change is given by the change in producer (consumer) surplus associated with the corresponding current supply (demand) curve conditioned on the subsequent expected utility and taken as a function of mean price*. And this is true even though the good may be an investment good that affects many future production periods. This result thus generalizes results in Appendix Sections 12.A through 12.C.

Specification of Supplies and Demands for Purposes of Estimation

As in Appendix Section 12.A, compensating and equivalent variation generally coincide if, and only if, absolute risk aversion is constant, at least in the initial time period when compensation is paid, that is,

$$r_{at} = -\frac{U_{tt}}{U_{t}},$$

where r_{at} is a constant and $\partial^{2}U/\partial\pi^{2}_{t} \equiv U_{tt}$. If absolute risk aversion is constant, supply or demand equations can be estimated without consideration of $K_{t} + \hat{C}_{it}$ or $\bar{\mathbf{K}}$ in (14.23) or of V^{0}_{t} in (14.24). Alternatively, if risk aversion is not constant, supply or demand functions of the form on the left side of (14.23) can be estimated using data on fixed costs, any *ex ante* transfers, and initial wealth that is included implicitly (in addition to data on fixed inputs and the parameters of the subjective distribution at time t). However, in this case computation of compensating or equivalent variation involves solution of the differential equation in (14.23) with boundary condition $\hat{C}_{it}(\bar{p}^{t0}_{it},\bar{p}^{t0}_{it}) = 0$ in the former case and $\hat{C}_{it}(\bar{p}^{t0}_{it},\bar{p}^{t1}_{it}) = 0$ in the latter case.

Yet another approach is to begin with an arbitrary specification for the indirect expected utility function in (14.18) rather than an arbitrary specification of supplies and demands. Then, using the approach of Appendix Section 12.F, one can derive the implied supply and demand functions by calculating

$$\tilde{\mathbf{q}}_{t} = -\frac{\partial V_{t}/\partial\bar{\mathbf{p}}^{t}_{t}}{\partial V_{t}/\partial K_{t}},$$

which follows from (14.21) and direct calculation of $\partial V_{t}/\partial K_{t}$ using (14.18). Estimates of parameters of the resulting supplies and demands can then be used for direct calculation of compensating or equivalent variation from (14.22). With this approach, it is also a

4. The reader familiar with putty-clay production theory may note that this concept of welfare measurement is sufficiently general to consider putty-clay capital that is employed in a productive capacity for a period of years and then disposed of or replaced with random timing depending on future developments.

simple matter to consider common parameters among estimated equations so that the resulting supplies and demands all relate to a conceivable underlying producer problem.

State-Dependent Compensation for Future Welfare Effects

Although the foregoing results are quite acceptable and offer a useful generalization in evaluating the welfare effects of current expected price changes that have lingering effects (the effects of many current price changes can be evaluated using a sequential approach corresponding to Appendix Section 4.A), they are somewhat disturbing where policy changes affect prices over a number of time periods. The problem here is that future decisions are random according to the current subjective distribution. Thus, (14.20) does not simplify to (14.21). One possibility is to consider state-dependent compensation as discussed in Section 12.6. While many state-dependent compensation schemes are possible, the case of *ex post* compensating variation can serve to illustrate the general case of state-dependent compensation.

Ex post compensating variation is determined by the equation

$$V_t(\bar{\boldsymbol{p}}_t^{T1},\boldsymbol{\alpha}_t^T,\bar{\boldsymbol{q}}^t,\boldsymbol{K}+\bar{\boldsymbol{C}}_{ih}) = V_t(\bar{\boldsymbol{p}}_{th}^{T0},\boldsymbol{\alpha}_t^T,\bar{\boldsymbol{q}}^t,\boldsymbol{K}) = V_t^0, \tag{14.25}$$

where

$$\bar{\boldsymbol{p}}_{th}^{Tj} = E_t(\boldsymbol{p}_t^t,\ldots,\hat{\boldsymbol{p}}_h^{tj},\ldots,\boldsymbol{p}_T^t),\ j=1,2,$$

$$\hat{\boldsymbol{p}}_h^{tj} = (\bar{p}_{1h}^t,\ldots,\bar{p}_{ih}^{tj},\ldots,\bar{p}_{Nh}^t),\ j=1,2,$$

$$\bar{\boldsymbol{C}}_{ih} = (0,\ldots,\hat{C}_{ih},\ldots,0).$$

Differentiating both sides of (14.25) with respect to $\bar{p}_{ih}^{t1}$ using (14.18) and (14.19) yields

$$E_t\{U_h\cdot[\tilde{q}_{ih}(\bar{\boldsymbol{p}}_{th}^{T1},\boldsymbol{\alpha}_h^T,\bar{\boldsymbol{q}}^h,\boldsymbol{K}+\bar{\boldsymbol{C}}_{ih}) - \partial\hat{C}_{ih}/\partial\bar{p}_{ih}^{t1}]\} = 0,$$

which holds if

$$\tilde{q}_{ih}(\bar{\boldsymbol{p}}_{th}^{T1},\boldsymbol{\alpha}_h^T,\bar{\boldsymbol{q}}^h,\boldsymbol{K}+\bar{\boldsymbol{C}}_{ih}) = \partial\hat{C}_{ih}/\partial\bar{p}_{ih}^{t1} \tag{14.26}$$

for all states of nature. Thus, the *ex post* compensating variation for a change in the price of good *i* at time *t* is

$$\hat{C}_{it}(\bar{p}_{ih}^{t0},\bar{p}_{ih}^{t1}) = \int_{\bar{p}_{ih}^{t0}}^{\bar{p}_{ih}^{t1}} \bar{q}_{ih}(\bar{\boldsymbol{p}}_{th}^{T},\boldsymbol{\alpha}_h^T,\bar{\boldsymbol{q}}_*^h,V_h^0)d\bar{p}_{ih}^t,$$

where

$$\bar{q}_{ih}(\bar{\boldsymbol{p}}_{th}^{T},\boldsymbol{\alpha}_h^T,\bar{\boldsymbol{q}}_*^h,V_h^0) \equiv \tilde{q}_{ih}(\bar{\boldsymbol{p}}_{th}^{T},\boldsymbol{\alpha}_h^T,\bar{\boldsymbol{q}}_*^h,\boldsymbol{K}+\bar{\boldsymbol{C}}_{ih})$$

and

$$V_h^0 = V(\bar{\boldsymbol{p}}_{th}^{T0},\boldsymbol{\alpha}_h^T,\bar{\boldsymbol{q}}_*^{h0},\boldsymbol{K}).$$

Note, however, that $\bar{\boldsymbol{q}}^h$ depends on the mean price change that is anticipated at time t, $t+1$, ..., $h-1$ and thus takes into account any modifications of decisions prior to time h associated with the anticipated change. This dependence is represented by

$$\bar{\boldsymbol{q}}_*^h = (\tilde{q}_{h-1},\ldots,\tilde{q}_t,\bar{q}_{t-1},\bar{q}_{t-2},\ldots),$$

where $\bar{\boldsymbol{q}}_*^{h0}$ is the particular $\bar{\boldsymbol{q}}_*^h$ that occurs in the absence of the change.

In this context, $\bar{q}_{ih}(\bar{\boldsymbol{p}}_{th}^T,\boldsymbol{\alpha}_h^T,\bar{\boldsymbol{q}}_*^h,V_h^0)$ is clearly a supply (demand) relationship for good i in period h associated with $(h-t+1)$-period subjective foresight. Also, the associated producer (consumer) surplus is random and depends on the state of nature that occurs in period h. Thus, *the ex post compensating variation of a mean change in the period h price considered at time t is given by the period h producer (consumer) surplus change associated with compensated supply (demand) conditioned on information (expectations) as of period h and associated expected utility as of period h in the event of no change.*

Thus, the *ex post* compensating variation is determined by solving (14.26) so that the effects of a mean price change for period $h>t$ can be evaluated for each possible state of nature with compensation paid in period h depending on the state of nature that actually occurs. Of course, similar results can also be developed for evaluation of equivalent variation where the utility expectations as of period h are held at V_h^1 rather than V_h^0 where

$$V_h^1 = V(\bar{\boldsymbol{p}}_{th}^{T1},\boldsymbol{\alpha}_h^T,\bar{\boldsymbol{q}}_*^{h1},\boldsymbol{K}),$$

and $\bar{\boldsymbol{q}}_*^{h1}$ is defined as the particular $\bar{\boldsymbol{q}}_*^h$ that occurs in the event of change.

Other types of *ex post* compensation schemes could also be considered as discussed in Section 12.6. Again, as in Appendix Section 12.E, any *ex post* compensation scheme must be sensitive to the possibility of strategic behavior. Unless *ex post* compensation schemes depend on exogenous indicators of the state, rather than endogenous manifestations of the state such as represented by producer decisions, producers may alter behavior strategically to receive additional compensation. Alternatively, although less practically, if a good *ex ante* model can be developed regarding how a decision-maker reacts to proposed changes then the compensation scheme can sometimes be altered to take account of strategic behavior.

Specification and Estimation of Future Welfare Effects

As in the case of current welfare effects, future conditional compensating and equivalent variation coincide generally if and only if absolute risk aversion in period h, $r_{ah} = -U_{hh}/U_h$, is constant. In other words, with constant absolute risk aversion, the ordinary supplies and demands (with $(h-t+1)$-period foresight) coincide with the respective compensated supplies and demands in period h, and neither depends on K_h or $\hat{C}_{ih}$.

If this is not the case, estimation of compensated supplies and demands and the associated welfare measures can be accomplished in one of two ways. First, one can estimate ordinary supplies or demands with $(h-t+1)$-period foresight and then solve differential equations of the form $\bar{q}_{ih} = \partial\hat{C}_{ih}/\partial\bar{p}_{ih}^t$ for compensated supplies and demands. These equations are complicated by the fact that $\bar{q}_{ih}$ depends on $\bar{p}_{ih}^t$ not only directly but also indirectly through $\bar{\boldsymbol{q}}^h$. Alternatively one can use the dual approach to specification and estimation by specifying a functional form for $V_k = V(\bar{\boldsymbol{p}}_k^T, \boldsymbol{\alpha}_k^T, \bar{\boldsymbol{q}}^k, \boldsymbol{K})$, $k = t, \ldots, h$. Then functional forms for supplies and demands are obtained following the approach of Appendix Section 12.F,

$$\tilde{\boldsymbol{q}}_k = -\frac{\partial V_k / \partial \bar{\boldsymbol{p}}_k^k}{\partial V_k / \partial K_k},\ k = t, \ldots, h.$$

If estimation of these equations sufficiently identifies the parameters of V_k, $k = t, \ldots, h$, then $\hat{C}_{ih}$ can be calculated directly from (14.25) using estimated parameters.

Welfare Effects of Changes in Present and Future Risk

Combining the foregoing results for various combinations of changes thus gives a sequential methodology for evaluation of *any multiple mean price change* affecting a producer. However, further methodology is needed to evaluate changes in risk or other parameters in $\boldsymbol{\alpha}_t^T$. One possibility for measuring the effects of more general changes is based on the concept of essential inputs or essential outputs. To examine this case, suppose that the input of good i at time t is essential for operation of the firm in time periods $t, \ldots, T$ in the sense that a solution exists for the intertemporal shutdown price

$$\hat{p}_{it}^t = \min\{\bar{p}_{it}^t \mid \tilde{\boldsymbol{q}}_k = \boldsymbol{0} \text{ for } k = 1, \ldots, T\}, \tag{14.27}$$

where $\tilde{\boldsymbol{q}}_k \equiv \tilde{\boldsymbol{q}}_k(\bar{\boldsymbol{p}}_t^T, \boldsymbol{\alpha}_t^T, \bar{\boldsymbol{q}}^t, K_t + C_0, \bar{\boldsymbol{K}}_t) \equiv \boldsymbol{0}$ implies that $\tilde{\boldsymbol{q}}_k$ is zero for every state of nature and C_0 represents current compensation associated with the shutdown case. For an essential output, one would simply replace the 'min' in (14.27) with 'max'. Thus, one can evaluate any general change in the intertemporal distribution of prices and production (including changes in risk) from $(\bar{\boldsymbol{p}}_t^{T0}, \boldsymbol{\alpha}_t^{T0})$ to $(\bar{\boldsymbol{p}}_t^{T1}, \boldsymbol{\alpha}_t^{T1})$ by using the approach in equation (12.29),

$$\begin{aligned} V_t(\bar{\boldsymbol{p}}_t^{T1}(\bar{p}_{it}^{t1}), \boldsymbol{\alpha}_t^{T1}, \bar{\boldsymbol{q}}^t, K_t + C_1 + C_2, \bar{\boldsymbol{K}}_t) &= V_t(\bar{\boldsymbol{p}}_t^{T1}(\hat{p}_{it}^{t1}), \boldsymbol{\alpha}_t^{T1}, \bar{\boldsymbol{q}}^t, K_t + C_1, \bar{\boldsymbol{K}}_t) \\ = V_t(\bar{\boldsymbol{p}}_t^{T0}(\hat{p}_{it}^{t0}), \boldsymbol{\alpha}_t^{T0}, \bar{\boldsymbol{q}}^t, K_t + C_1, \bar{\boldsymbol{K}}_t) &= V_t(\bar{\boldsymbol{p}}_t^{T0}(\bar{p}_{it}^{t0}), \boldsymbol{\alpha}_t^{T0}, \bar{\boldsymbol{q}}^t, K_t, \bar{\boldsymbol{K}}_t) = V_t^0, \end{aligned} \tag{14.28}$$

where

$$\begin{aligned} \bar{\boldsymbol{p}}_t^{Tj}(p_{it}^{tj}) &= E_t(\hat{\boldsymbol{p}}_t(p_{it}^{tj}), \boldsymbol{p}_{t+1}, \ldots, \boldsymbol{p}_T),\ j = 1,2, \\ \hat{\boldsymbol{p}}_t(p_{it}^{tj}) &= (\bar{p}_{1t}^t, \ldots, p_{it}^{tj}, \ldots, \bar{p}_{Nt}^t),\ j = 1,2, \end{aligned}$$

$\hat{p}_{it}^{tj}$ is the shutdown mean price for good i at time t defined by (14.27) corresponding to other parameters contained in $(\bar{\boldsymbol{p}}_t^{Tj}, \boldsymbol{\alpha}_t^{Tj})$, $j = 1,2$, and C_1 is compensating variation corresponding to an intertemporal shutdown. Thus, using the approach in (14.23) and (14.24), one finds from (14.28) that

$$\begin{aligned} C = C_1 + C_2 = &-\int_{\hat{p}_{it}^{t0}}^{\bar{p}_{it}^{t0}} \bar{q}_{it}(\bar{\boldsymbol{p}}_t^{T0}(p_{it}^t), \boldsymbol{\alpha}_t^{T0}, \bar{\boldsymbol{q}}^t, V_t^0)\, dp_{it}^t \\ &+ \int_{\hat{p}_{it}^{t1}}^{\bar{p}_{it}^{t1}} \bar{q}_{it}(\bar{\boldsymbol{p}}_t^{T1}(p_{it}^t), \boldsymbol{\alpha}_t^{T1}, \bar{\boldsymbol{q}}^t, V_t^0)\, dp_{it}^t. \end{aligned} \tag{14.29}$$

In other words, *the overall compensating variation of a general change in parameters affecting the firm intertemporally is given by the change in consumer (producer) surplus associated with the compensated demand (supply) at initial time and initial expected utility for any input (output) for which purchases (sales) in the initial period are essential for operation of the firm over the planning horizon.*

Of course, similar results can be developed for measuring equivalent variation where the compensated demands or supplies are simply conditioned on the subsequent expected utility level. Again, the compensating and equivalent variations will generally coincide if and only if absolute risk aversion is constant in the initial time period, in which case the compensated supply and demand curves coincide with the ordinary supply and demand curves.

Perhaps, cases are rare where one can identify an input (or output) such that purchases (or sales) in the initial time period are essential to operation of a firm over an entire planning horizon. More likely, one can identify inputs (or outputs) such that purchases (or sales) are essential to operation of the firm in each time period individually. This observation suggests a partitioning of parameter changes affecting a firm according to groupings of commodities and time periods such that one good at one time period in each group is essential among that group (meaning that no other good in the group would be bought or sold unless the essential good were also bought or sold), and no change in a partition of parameter changes associated with one group affects any other group when the firm does not buy or sell commodities in the first group. That is, suppose that a general change in parameters affecting a firm can be broken into steps $(\bar{\mathbf{p}}_t^{Tj}, \boldsymbol{\alpha}_t^{Tj})$, $j = 0, \ldots, J$ such that $j = 0$ represents the initial situation, $j = J$ represents the final situation and each step corresponds to changing the parameters associated with one partition of the parameter set.

Suppose further that $q_{i_j h_j}$ is an essential input or output within the group of commodities associated with the *j*th change. To consider an essential input for each step, define

$$\hat{p}_{i_j h_j}^{tk} = \min\{\bar{p}_{i_j h_j}^t \mid \bar{q}_{ih}(\bar{\mathbf{p}}_h^{Tk}, \boldsymbol{\alpha}_h^{Tk}, \bar{\mathbf{q}}_*^{hk}, \mathbf{K} + \mathbf{C}_k) \equiv 0, (i,h) \in G_j\},\ k = j-1, j,$$

where G_j is the set of indices (i,h) included in group j and

$$\bar{\mathbf{q}}_*^{hk} = (\tilde{\mathbf{q}}_{h-1}^k, \ldots, \tilde{\mathbf{q}}_t^k, \bar{\mathbf{q}}_{t-1}, \bar{\mathbf{q}}_{t-2}, \ldots)$$
$$\tilde{\mathbf{q}}_\tau^k \equiv \tilde{\mathbf{q}}_\tau(\bar{\mathbf{p}}_t^{Tk}, \boldsymbol{\alpha}_t^{Tk}, \bar{\mathbf{q}}_*^{\tau k}, \mathbf{K} + \mathbf{C}_k).$$

In the case of an essential output, one can simply replace the 'min' with 'max'. Now, paralleling (14.28), note that

$$\begin{aligned} V_t(\bar{\mathbf{p}}_t^{Tj}(\bar{p}_{i_j h_j}^{tj}), \boldsymbol{\alpha}_t^{Tj}, \bar{\mathbf{q}}^t, \mathbf{K} + \mathbf{C}_j) &= V_t(\bar{\mathbf{p}}_t^{Tj}(\hat{p}_{i_j h_j}^{tj}), \boldsymbol{\alpha}_t^{Tj}, \tilde{\mathbf{q}}^t, \mathbf{K} + \mathbf{C}_{j-1} + \bar{\mathbf{C}}_j) \\ &= V_t(\bar{\mathbf{p}}^{T,j-1}(\hat{p}_{i_j h_j}^{t,j-1}), \boldsymbol{\alpha}_t^{T,j-1}, \bar{\mathbf{q}}^t, \mathbf{K} + \mathbf{C}_{j-1} + \bar{\mathbf{C}}_j) \\ &= V_t(\bar{\mathbf{p}}_t^{T,j-1}(\bar{p}_{i_j h_j}^{t,j-1}), \boldsymbol{\alpha}_t^{T,j-1}, \bar{\mathbf{q}}^t, \mathbf{K} + \mathbf{C}_{j-1}) = V_t^{j-1}, \end{aligned}$$

where

$$\bar{\mathbf{p}}_t^{Tj}(p_{ih}^{tj}) = E_t(\mathbf{p}_t, \ldots, \hat{\mathbf{p}}_h(p_{ih}^{tj}), \ldots, \mathbf{p}_T),$$
$$\hat{\mathbf{p}}_h(p_{ih}^{tj}) = (\bar{p}_{1k}^t, \ldots, p_{ih}^{tj}, \ldots, \bar{p}_{Nh}^t),$$

and $\bar{\mathbf{C}}_j = (0,\ldots,\bar{C}_{i_j h_j},\ldots,0)$ represents a period h_j compensation for losing access to markets $(i,h) \in G_j$ given parameters $(\bar{\mathbf{p}}_t^{Tj}, \boldsymbol{\alpha}_t^{Tj})$, and $\mathbf{C}_j - \mathbf{C}_{j-1} = (0,\ldots,C_{i_j h_j},\ldots,0)$ represents a period h_j compensation for the change from $(\bar{\mathbf{p}}_t^{T,j-1},\boldsymbol{\alpha}_t^{T,j-1})$ to $(\bar{\mathbf{p}}_t^{Tj},\boldsymbol{\alpha}_t^{Tj})$. Thus, paralleling (14.29) and using (14.26), one finds that

$$C_{i_j h_j} = -\int_{\hat{p}_{ijhj}^{t,j-1}}^{\bar{p}_{ijhj}^{t,j-1}} \bar{q}_{i_j h_j}(\bar{\mathbf{p}}_{\mathbf{h_j}}^{T,j-1}(p_{ijhj}^{t,j-1}),\boldsymbol{\alpha}_{\mathbf{h_j}}^{T,j-1},\bar{\mathbf{q}}_*^{h_j,j-1},V_{h_j}^0)dp_{ijhj}^{t,j-1}$$

$$+ \int_{\hat{p}_{ijhj}^{tj}}^{\bar{p}_{ijhj}^{tj}} q_{i_j h_j}(\bar{\mathbf{p}}_{\mathbf{h_j}}^{Tj}(p_{ijhj}^{tj}),\boldsymbol{\alpha}_{\mathbf{h_j}}^{Tj},\bar{\mathbf{q}}_*^{h_j,j},V_{h_j}^0)dp_{ijhj}^{tj}.$$

This represents an *ex post* compensating variation paid in period h_j depending on the state of nature both at and before period h_j. These compensating variations can then be summed over $j = 1,\ldots, J$ to determine an overall intertemporal compensating variation, C_j, which possibly involves payments in several or all time periods. A crucial requirement in this result is that

$$V_t(\bar{\mathbf{p}}_t^{tj}(\hat{p}_{ijhj}^{tj}),\boldsymbol{\alpha}_t^{Tj},\bar{\mathbf{q}}^t,K + \mathbf{C}_{j-1}) = V_t(\bar{\mathbf{p}}_t^{T,j-1}(\hat{p}_{ijhj}^{t,j-1}),\boldsymbol{\alpha}_t^{T,j-1},\bar{\mathbf{q}}^t,\mathbf{K} + \mathbf{C}_{j-1} + \bar{\mathbf{C}}_j),$$

which is satisfied as long as no change in the jth partition of parameter changes affects $\tilde{q}_{ih}$ for $(i,h) \notin G_j$ when $\tilde{q}_{i'h'} = 0$ for $(i',h') \in G_j$. For example, if a firm is induced to switch from using petroleum-powered machinery to electrical equipment because of high petroleum prices, then changes in petroleum price, the price of petroleum-using machinery and risk associated with these prices will not affect the expected utility of the producer as long as petroleum prices remain high enough to keep the firm from using petroleum-powered machinery.

Based on these results, *the overall compensating variation of a general change in parameters affecting a producer intertemporally is given by the sum of changes in producer (consumer) surplus associated with compensated supplies (demands), at expected utility in the absence of change, over all groups of goods, where the calculations for each group are made in the market of the essential good in that group considering the partition of parameter changes relevant to that group*. This result justifies one of the more common approaches in dynamic producer problems. For example, suppose that the inputs used by a single-product producer can be partitioned into groups associated with the various production periods. Then a decision not to produce in a given period will imply nonuse of inputs affecting production in that period (that are not yet fixed). Thus, the compensating variation relevant to each time period h can be determined as the change in producer surplus associated with compensated output supply in period h with $(h - t + 1)$-period foresight. Of course, the component of compensation associated with any period $h > t$ would be stochastic depending on the state of nature occurring at and before period h. Again, similar results can be developed for the case of equivalent variation, and the two coincide generally if, and only if, absolute risk aversion is constant in each time period.

The results for dynamic economic welfare analysis in the general producer case are thus partially encouraging and partially disturbing. Several approaches can be used for examining the effects of current policy changes on current plus future periods and, in particular, the empirical accuracy of the sequential approach of welfare calculations is possible if the data are available to estimate all relevant functions. However, the effects of changes in policy for future periods can, in general, be evaluated in terms of producer and consumer surpluses only if some current input is essential for operation of the firm over the planning horizon (or a similar approach can be developed if some subset of current inputs as a group is essential for operation of the firm over the planning horizon). Alternatively, stochastic compensation schemes must be considered.

14.B INTERTEMPORAL ECONOMIC WELFARE ANALYSIS FOR CONSUMERS

The general dynamic consumer case is important in empirical analyses that are related to durable choice. When a consumer makes a decision to buy a car, for example, the decision is based, in part, on expectations for gasoline prices, maintenance costs, and resale prices in future periods. Thus, the choice of a *consumer durable* – that is, a consumer good used over more than just the current period of consumption – is very much akin to the choice of a fixed input for a producer. In the context of the household production problem (see Appendix Section 7.G and Section 14.3), the consumer is viewed as producing some of his or her consumer goods at home possibly using durables as well as other goods and services. For example, warmth for a house is produced by combining, say, electricity or natural gas with a (durable) furnace. Thus, the consumer also possesses a production function, much like a producer.[5]

Consumer Welfare with Investment in Consumer Durables

To consider these various generalities, suppose that a consumer possesses a production function given in implicit form by

$$\mathbf{f}_t^T(\mathbf{q}_t^T, \bar{\mathbf{q}}^t) = \mathbf{0},$$

where $\mathbf{q}_t^T$ and $\bar{\mathbf{q}}^t$ are defined as in Appendix Section 14.A. In this case, $\bar{\mathbf{q}}^t$ represents any fixity in the household production function or carryover due to previous durable choices. Any resource endowments can also be represented in $\bar{\mathbf{q}}^t$. For example, available time to allocate to labor and leisure would be a flow resulting from a fixed 'asset' held from the initial time period. Endowments of other resources may be flows from assets that are determined by previous decisions to accumulate or sell those assets. As in the producer case, suppose that $\mathbf{f}_t^T$ is monotonically decreasing, concave, and twice differentiable in $\mathbf{q}_t^T$, except for accounting identities that may be linear where outputs are positive and inputs are negative in $\mathbf{q}_t^T$. Accounting identities may represent savings and other carrying forward of assets, aging and depreciation of durables, and the representation of consumption as the sum of purchases, resource flows from assets (endowments), and household production less input use as in Appendix Section 7.G. Suppose, also, that the consumer

5. While the framework presented here is not explicitly generalized to the case of resource endowments and resource sales, such an extension is straightforward following the approach of Appendix Section 7.F. The essential difference is that market transactions can then be negative representing supply of some goods. Negative market transactions for durables then represent asset sales by consumers where the sale of an asset eliminates all future service flows from the asset.

possesses an intertemporal utility function, $U(\boldsymbol{q}_t^T)$, corresponding to a planning horizon from period t to period T, where U is assumed to be strictly increasing, quasiconcave and twice differentiable in $\boldsymbol{q}_t^T$. The consumer's problem of maximizing expected utility over the planning horizon is thus

$$\max_{\boldsymbol{q}_t^T} E_t[U(\boldsymbol{q}_t^T) | \boldsymbol{p}_k \boldsymbol{q}_k = \bar{m}_k, k = t, ..., T, \boldsymbol{f}_t^T(\boldsymbol{q}_t^T, \bar{\boldsymbol{q}}^t) = \boldsymbol{0}]$$

where $\bar{m}_k$ is exogenous income for the consumer in period k. Again, suppose that the parameters of the subjective distribution of prices and household production at time k are denoted by $\bar{\boldsymbol{p}}_k^T$ and $\boldsymbol{\alpha}_k^T$, as in Appendix Section 14.A.

As in the producer case, this problem can be solved by backward dynamic (stochastic) programming, that is, by solving the sequence of problems conditioned on earlier decisions and assuming optimal later decisions, $k = T, T-1, ..., t$, that is,

$$\max_{\boldsymbol{q}_k} \bar{U}_k \equiv E_k[U(\bar{\boldsymbol{q}}_t, ..., \bar{\boldsymbol{q}}_{k-1}, \boldsymbol{q}_k, \tilde{\boldsymbol{q}}_{k+1}, ..., \tilde{\boldsymbol{q}}_T)] \tag{14.30}$$

subject to

$$\boldsymbol{p}_k \boldsymbol{q}_k = \bar{m}_k \tag{14.31}$$

$$\boldsymbol{f}_t^T(\tilde{\boldsymbol{q}}_{k+1}^T, \boldsymbol{q}_k, \bar{\boldsymbol{q}}^k) = \boldsymbol{0} \tag{14.32}$$

where $\tilde{\boldsymbol{q}}_{k+1}^T$ is defined as in (14.14). The Lagrangian associated with this problem is

$$\mathcal{L}_k = E_k[U(\bar{\boldsymbol{q}}_t, ..., \bar{\boldsymbol{q}}_{k-1}, \boldsymbol{q}_k, \tilde{\boldsymbol{q}}_{k+1}, ..., \tilde{\boldsymbol{q}}_T)]$$

$$- \lambda_k[\boldsymbol{p}_k \boldsymbol{q}_k - \bar{m}_k] - \boldsymbol{\varphi}_k \boldsymbol{f}_t^T(\tilde{\boldsymbol{q}}_{k+1}^T, \boldsymbol{q}_k, \bar{\boldsymbol{q}}^k),$$

so first-order conditions for constrained maximization in addition to (14.31) and (14.32) are

$$\frac{\partial \mathcal{L}_k}{\partial \boldsymbol{q}_k} = \frac{\partial \bar{U}_k}{\partial \boldsymbol{q}_k} - \lambda_k \boldsymbol{p}_k - \boldsymbol{\varphi}_k \frac{\partial \boldsymbol{f}_t^T}{\partial \boldsymbol{q}_k} = \boldsymbol{0}. \tag{14.33}$$

Note that second-order conditions are satisfied under the assumptions given above. Hence, solution of (14.31) through (14.33) leads, in principle, to demand equations (supply if negative) of the form

$$\tilde{\boldsymbol{q}}_k(\bar{\boldsymbol{p}}_k^T, \boldsymbol{\alpha}_k^T, \bar{\boldsymbol{q}}^k, \bar{\boldsymbol{m}}) \tag{14.34}$$

where $\bar{\boldsymbol{m}} = (\bar{m}_t, ..., \bar{m}_T)$. These decision functions can then be substituted into (14.30) through (14.32) to solve the problem where k is reduced by one in each successive step. Continuing in this manner for $k = T, T-1, ..., t$, thus yields the optimal decisions in (14.34) for every time period in the planning horizon, although $\boldsymbol{q}_k$ is generally a random vector at time t if $k > t$, as in the producer case, because later prices are not yet known.

At this point, one can define an indirect expected utility function for the consumer of the form

$$V_t(\bar{\boldsymbol{p}}_t^T,\boldsymbol{\alpha}_t^T,\bar{\boldsymbol{q}}^t,\bar{\boldsymbol{m}}) \equiv E_t[U(\tilde{\boldsymbol{q}}_t^T) \tag{14.35}$$

$$-\sum_{k=t}^{T}\lambda_k[\boldsymbol{p}_k\tilde{\boldsymbol{q}}_k - \bar{m}_k] - \sum_{k=t}^{T}\varphi_k f_t^T(\tilde{\boldsymbol{q}}_t^T,\bar{\boldsymbol{q}}^t)].$$

The last two terms in the brackets are included for convenience below even though they are zero for every state of nature by first-order conditions. Note, however, that λ_k, $\tilde{\boldsymbol{q}}_k$ and $\boldsymbol{\varphi}_k$ are random variables at time $t<k$. Using the envelope theorem (or (14.33)), and assuming that $E_t[E_k(z)] = E_t(z)$ for any variable z that is stochastic according to the subjective distribution at time $k>t$, one obtains

$$\frac{\partial V_t}{\partial \bar{p}_{ih}^t} = -E_t(\lambda_h\cdot\tilde{q}_{ih}) + E_t\left[\sum_{k=t}^{T}\left(\frac{\partial \mathcal{L}_k}{\partial \boldsymbol{q}_k}\frac{\partial \tilde{\boldsymbol{q}}_k}{\partial \bar{p}_{ih}^t} + \frac{\partial \mathcal{L}_k}{\partial \lambda_k}\frac{\partial \lambda_k}{\partial \bar{p}_{ih}^t} + \frac{\partial \mathcal{L}_k}{\partial \boldsymbol{\varphi}_k}\frac{\partial \boldsymbol{\varphi}_k}{\partial \bar{p}_{ih}^t}\right)\right]$$

$$= -E_t(\lambda_h\cdot\tilde{q}_{ih}),\quad i=1,\ldots,N,\ h=t,\ldots,T, \tag{14.36}$$

because the derivatives of $\mathcal{L}_k$ are zero for every state of nature by the first-order conditions (an envelope theorem result). Also, assuming that current decisions are nonstochastic with respect to the subjective distribution at time t following the assumptions of the producer case, (14.36) can be written compactly as

$$\frac{\partial V_t}{\partial \bar{\boldsymbol{p}}_t^t} = -E_t(\lambda_t)\cdot\boldsymbol{q}_t. \tag{14.37}$$

Using the result in (14.37), the compensating variation, $\tilde{C}_i(\bar{p}_{it}^{t0},\bar{p}_{it}^{t1})$, of any current subjective mean price change for good i from $\bar{p}_{it}^{t0}$ to $\bar{p}_{it}^{t1}$ can be defined by

$$V_t(\bar{\boldsymbol{p}}_t^{T1},\boldsymbol{\alpha}_t^T,\bar{\boldsymbol{q}}^t,\bar{m}_t - \tilde{C}_{it},\hat{\boldsymbol{m}}_t) = V_t(\bar{\boldsymbol{p}}_t^{T0},\boldsymbol{\alpha}_t^T,\bar{\boldsymbol{q}}^t,\bar{m}_t,\hat{\boldsymbol{m}}_t) = V_t^0 \tag{14.38}$$

where

$$\bar{\boldsymbol{p}}_t^{Tj} = E_t(\hat{\boldsymbol{p}}_t^{tj},\bar{\boldsymbol{p}}_{t+1},\ldots,\bar{\boldsymbol{p}}_T),\ j=1,2,$$

$$\hat{\boldsymbol{p}}_t^{tj} = (\bar{p}_{1t}^t,\ldots,\bar{p}_{it}^{tj},\ldots,\bar{p}_{Nt}^t),\ j=1,2,$$

and

$$\hat{\boldsymbol{m}}_t = (\bar{m}_{t+1},\ldots,\bar{m}_T).$$

Differentiating both sides of (14.38) with respect to $\bar{p}_{it}^{t1}$ and using (14.35) and (14.37) implies that

$$-E_t(\lambda_t)\cdot\tilde{q}_{it}(\bar{\boldsymbol{p}}_t^{T1},\boldsymbol{\alpha}_t^T,\bar{\boldsymbol{q}}^t,\bar{m}_t - \tilde{C}_{it},\hat{\boldsymbol{m}}_t) - E_t[\lambda_t\partial\tilde{C}_{it}/\partial\bar{p}_{it}^{t1}] = 0, \tag{14.39}$$

where $\bar{m}_t$ in (14.35) is replaced by $\bar{m}_t - \tilde{C}_{it}$ as specified in (14.38). If $\tilde{C}_{it}$ is an *ex ante* and thus nonstochastic compensation at time t, then (14.39) yields

$$\tilde{q}_{it}(\bar{\boldsymbol{p}}_t^{T1},\boldsymbol{\alpha}_t^T,\bar{\boldsymbol{q}}^t,\bar{m}_t - \tilde{C}_{it},\hat{\boldsymbol{m}}_t) = -\partial\tilde{C}_{it}/\partial\bar{p}_{it}^{t1}, \tag{14.40}$$

which can be reparameterized following (14.38) as

$$\bar{q}_{it}(\bar{\boldsymbol{p}}_t^{T1},\boldsymbol{\alpha}_t^T,\bar{\boldsymbol{q}}^t,V_t^0) \equiv \tilde{q}_{it}(\bar{\boldsymbol{p}}_t^{T1},\boldsymbol{\alpha}_t^T,\bar{\boldsymbol{q}}^t,\bar{m}_t - \tilde{C}_{it},\hat{\boldsymbol{m}}_t). \tag{14.41}$$

Thus, $\bar{q}_{it}$ is a compensated demand equation (supply if negative) for good i at time t. Because $\tilde{C}_{it}(\bar{p}_{it}^{t0},\bar{p}_{it}^{t1})=0$, *the compensating variation of a current subjective mean price change is given by the change in consumer (producer) surplus associated with the corresponding current demand (supply) curve conditioned on initial expected utility and taken as a function of mean price*,

$$\tilde{C}_{it}(\bar{p}_{it}^{t0},\bar{p}_{it}^{t1}) = -\int_{\bar{p}_{it}^{t0}}^{\bar{p}_{it}^{t1}} \bar{q}_{it}(\bar{\boldsymbol{p}}_t^T,\boldsymbol{\alpha}_t^T,\bar{\boldsymbol{q}}^t,V_t^0)\,dp_{it}^t.$$

This result significantly expands the static results of Chapters 6 and 7 because it holds not only for current consumption goods but also for durable goods that may affect many future periods.

Additionally noting that $\tilde{E}_{it}(\bar{p}_{it}^{t1},\bar{p}_{it}^{t0}) = -\tilde{C}_{it}(\bar{p}_{it}^{t0},\bar{p}_{it}^{t1})$ where $\tilde{E}_{it}(\bar{p}_{it}^{t1},\bar{p}_{it}^{t0})$ is the equivalent variation of a current subjective mean price change for good i from $\bar{p}_{it}^{t1}$ to $\bar{p}_{it}^{t0}$, the equivalent variation of a mean price change from $\bar{p}_{it}^{t0}$ to $\bar{p}_{it}^{t1}$ is

$$\tilde{E}_{it}(\bar{p}_{it}^{t0},\bar{p}_{it}^{t1}) = -\int_{\bar{p}_{it}^{t0}}^{\bar{p}_{it}^{t1}} \bar{q}_{it}(\bar{\boldsymbol{p}}_t^T,\boldsymbol{\alpha}_t^T,\bar{\boldsymbol{q}}^t,V_t^1)\,dp_{it}^t$$

where $V_t^1 = V(\bar{\boldsymbol{p}}_t^{T1},\boldsymbol{\alpha}_t^T,\bar{\boldsymbol{q}}^t,\bar{m}_t,\hat{\boldsymbol{m}}_t)$. That is, *the equivalent variation of a current subjective mean price change is given by the change in consumer (producer) surplus associated with the corresponding current demand (supply) curve conditioned on the subsequent expected utility and taken as a function of mean price*. Again, this result holds for durables as well as current consumption.

Empirical Considerations for Estimation

Clearly, from (14.40) and (14.41), the compensating and equivalent variations will coincide generally only if the current exogenous income effects on current demand are zero. In this case, welfare effects can be calculated using ordinary consumer demands and supplies that do not depend on current exogenous income. Of course, parallel to results in Appendix Section 5.B, this condition is implausible for all commodities jointly. Alternatively, the compensating and equivalent variations can be calculated by solving the differential equation in (14.40) with boundary condition $\tilde{C}_{it}(\bar{p}_{it}^{t0},\bar{p}_{it}^{t0})=0$ in the former case and $\tilde{C}_{it}(\bar{p}_{it}^{t0},\bar{p}_{it}^{t1})=0$ in the latter case. Yet another approach is to begin from an arbitrary specification for an intertemporal indirect expected utility function rather than an arbitrary specification of demands and supplies.[6] Then, using duality, one can derive the implied specifications for demands and supplies using a generalized version of Roy's identity. That is, using (14.37) and direct calculation from (14.35), one finds that

6. As in the general dynamic stochastic producer case, however, the appropriate regularity conditions, which such arbitrary specifications must satisfy for plausibility, are not well developed.

$$-\frac{\partial V_t/\partial \bar{\boldsymbol{p}}_t^t}{\partial V_t/\partial \bar{m}_t} = \frac{E_t(\lambda_t)\cdot \tilde{\boldsymbol{q}}_t}{E_t(\lambda_t)} = \tilde{\boldsymbol{q}}_t. \tag{14.42}$$

Estimates of the parameters in the resulting demand and supply specifications then allow direct calculation of the compensating and equivalent variations by an approach similar to that discussed in Appendix Section 7.H. Furthermore, with this approach, appropriate commonality of estimated parameters among estimated equations can be simply imposed so that the resulting empirical supplies and demands all relate to a conceivable underlying consumer problem.

State-Dependent Compensation for Future Welfare Effects

Turning to the problem of evaluating welfare effects of policy changes that affect future period prices, the compensation calculation is complicated by the fact that (14.36) does not simplify as in (14.37) if $h>t$ because future decisions are stochastic depending on future prices at time t. As a result, calculation of *ex ante* compensation at time t for a change in prices at time h is not a simple matter (although it is possible using an approach similar to Appendix Sections 12.A through 12.C once the consumers' intertemporal preferences are estimated). Alternatively, one can consider a stochastic compensation scheme where the compensation for a price change at time h is paid at time h according to a formula specified at time t that depends on the state of nature that occurs at (and before) time h. According to Section 12.6, many such compensation schemes can restore the consumers' initial expected welfare. One such compensation scheme is the case of *ex post* compensating variation. Suppose from the perspective at time t that the *ex post* compensating variation at time h of a subjective price change for good i at time h is represented by $\tilde{C}_{ih}(\bar{p}_{ih}^{t0},\bar{p}_{ih}^{t1})$. Then

$$V_t(\bar{\boldsymbol{p}}_t^{T1},\boldsymbol{\alpha}_t^T,\bar{\boldsymbol{q}}^t,\hat{\boldsymbol{m}}_{t-1}-\bar{\boldsymbol{C}}_i) = V_t(\bar{\boldsymbol{p}}_t^{T0},\boldsymbol{\alpha}_t^T,\bar{\boldsymbol{q}}^t,\hat{\boldsymbol{m}}_{t-1}) = V_t^0 \tag{14.43}$$

where

$$\begin{aligned}
\bar{\boldsymbol{C}}_i &= (0,\ldots,\tilde{C}_{ih},\ldots,0),\\
\bar{\boldsymbol{p}}_t^{Tj} &= E_t(\bar{\boldsymbol{p}}_t,\ldots,\hat{\boldsymbol{p}}_h^{tj},\ldots,\bar{\boldsymbol{p}}_T),\\
\hat{\boldsymbol{p}}_h^{tj} &= (\bar{p}_{1h}^t,\ldots,\bar{p}_{1h}^{tj},\ldots,\bar{p}_{Nh}^t).
\end{aligned}$$

Then differentiating (14.43) with respect to $\bar{q}_{ih}^t$ and using (14.35) and (14.36) yields

$$-E_t[E_h(\lambda_h\cdot \tilde{q}_{ih}) + E_h(\lambda_h \partial \tilde{C}_{ih}/\partial \bar{p}_{ih}^t)] = 0, \tag{14.44}$$

which simplifies to

$$-E_t[E_h(\lambda_j)(\tilde{q}_{ih} + \partial \tilde{C}_{ih}/\partial \bar{p}_{ih}^t)] = 0.$$

Thus, the *ex post* compensating variation can be determined by choosing C_{ih} so that $\tilde{q}_{ih} = \partial \tilde{C}_{ih}/\partial \bar{p}_{ih}^t$ for every state of nature, which implies that

$$\tilde{C}_{ih}(\bar{p}_{ih}^{t0},\bar{p}_{ih}^{t1}) = -\int_{\bar{p}_{ih}^{t0}}^{\bar{p}_{ih}^{t1}} \bar{q}_{ih}(\bar{\boldsymbol{p}}_h^T,\boldsymbol{\alpha}_h^T,\bar{\boldsymbol{q}}_*^h,V_h^0)dp_{ih}^t, \tag{14.45}$$

where

$$\bar{q}_{ih}(\bar{\boldsymbol{p}}_h^T,\boldsymbol{\alpha}_h^T,\bar{\boldsymbol{q}}_*^h,V_h^0) \equiv \tilde{q}_{ih}(\bar{\boldsymbol{p}}_h^T,\boldsymbol{\alpha}_h^T,\bar{\boldsymbol{q}}_*^h,\hat{\boldsymbol{m}}_{t-1}+\tilde{C}_i), \tag{14.46}$$

$$V_h^0 = V(\bar{\boldsymbol{p}}_h^{T0},\boldsymbol{\alpha}_h^T,\bar{\boldsymbol{q}}_*^{h0},\hat{\boldsymbol{m}}_{t-1}),$$

and

$$\bar{\boldsymbol{q}}_*^h = (\tilde{q}_{h-1},\ldots,\tilde{q}_t,\bar{q}_{t-1},\bar{q}_{t-2},\ldots).$$

For this case, as in the producer case of Appendix Section 14.A, $\bar{\boldsymbol{q}}^h$ depends on the mean price change that is anticipated at time t, $t+1$, ..., $h-1$, and thus takes into account any modifications of durable purchases prior to time h associated with the change in $\bar{\boldsymbol{q}}_*^h$, where, by previous definition, $\tilde{\boldsymbol{q}}_k$ depends on the subjective distribution of future prices ($\boldsymbol{p}_h$) at times $k<h$. Specifically, $\bar{\boldsymbol{q}}_*^{h0}$ is the series of decisions prior to h without the change.

The demand (supply) curve in (14.46) is clearly a one-period demand (supply) for $(h-t+1)$-period foresight. Hence, *the* ex post *compensating variation of a mean change in period h price considered at time t is given by the period h consumer (producer) surplus change associated with compensated demand (supply), conditioned on information (expectations) as of period h and the associated expected utility as of period h in the event of no change*. A similar statement also holds for evaluation of equivalent variation by simply replacing V_h^0 by V_h^1 in (14.46), where

$$V_h^1 = V(\bar{\boldsymbol{p}}_h^{T1},\boldsymbol{\alpha}_h^T,\bar{\boldsymbol{q}}_*^{h1},\hat{\boldsymbol{m}}_{t-1})$$

and $\bar{\boldsymbol{q}}_*^{h1}$ is defined as the series of decisions that would occur prior to h in the event of change.

Again, the two welfare measures coincide generally if and only if time h income effects are zero in $\tilde{q}_{ih}$, so that ordinary demands and supplies suffice for calculating welfare effects. Otherwise, as in the producer case, one must solve differential equations at time h of the form $\tilde{q}_{ih} = \partial\tilde{C}_{ih}/\partial\bar{p}_{ih}^t$ or use the dual approach to specification and estimation following application of a generalized version of Roy's identity at time h.

Consumer Welfare Effects of Future Price Risk

Combining the foregoing results for the consumer case gives a complete methodology for sequential evaluation of any *multiple mean price change* affecting a consumer over time. However, further methods are needed to evaluate changes in risk or other parameters in $\boldsymbol{\alpha}_t^T$. One possibility in this case, if the assumptions of Section 7.10 are applicable, is to define a withdrawal price by (14.27) in the case of a consumer good (or the 'min' in (14.27) is replaced by 'max' in the case of defining a withdrawal price for a factor sold by the consumer). That is, assuming that good i is a consumer good always consumed in positive amounts (or a factor always sold in positive amounts), as long as any other goods are bought or sold by the consumer, one can define a withdrawal price at which the consumer withdraws from the set of markets in the economy in question. For example, the withdrawal price could be a price at which the consumer will migrate from one economy (for example, country) to another. Thus, using (14.28), where K_t and $\bar{K}_t$ are replaced by $\bar{m}_t$ and $\hat{m}_t$, to define the compensating variation of any general change in parameters affecting the consumer, one can use (14.45) and (14.46) to derive (14.29) just as in the producer case. Thus, *the overall compensating variation of a general change in parameters affecting a consumer intertemporally is given by the change in consumer (producer) surplus associated with the compensated demand (supply) at initial time and at expected utility in absence of change for any good for which initial purchases (sales) are essential for the entire planning horizon.* A qualifying assumption in the case where a consumer is induced to migrate to another economy in the initial period is that, once moved, he or she does not consider returning within the planning horizon. Of course, similar results hold in calculating equivalent variation where compensated supply or demand is evaluated at the expected utility level occurring in the event of the change.

Alternatively, suppose that the set of changes affecting the consumer can be partitioned according to groupings of commodities and time periods so that one good at one time period in each group is essential to consumption (and factor sales) within that group (meaning that no other good in the group would be bought or sold unless the essential good in the group were also bought or sold), and no change in a partition of parameter changes associated with one group affects any other group when the consumer does not buy or sell commodities in the first group. Then the foregoing result can be generalized by considering stochastic compensation associated with later periods. Thus, just as in the producer case, *the overall compensating variation of a general change in parameters affecting a consumer intertemporally is given by the sum of changes in consumer (producer) surplus associated with compensated demands (supplies) at expected utility in the event of change over all groups of goods, where the calculations for each group are made in the market of the essential good in that group considering the partition of parameter changes relevant to that group.* For example, if the sale of labor is essential to any consumer market activity in corresponding time periods, the effect of a general change affecting the consumer that can be partitioned by the time period of effect (after compensation) would be given by the sum of changes in producer surplus associated with compensated labor supply over all time periods in the planning horizon. Of course, any supply or demand for period h used in such calculations is based on $(h-t+1)$-period foresight, and the associated change in producer or consumer surplus is viewed as a measure of the *ex post* compensating variation in period h depending on the state of nature that occurs in (and prior to) period h. Again, all these statements carry through for evaluating equivalent variation as well where all compensated supplies and demands are evaluated at the expected utility occurring in the event of change.

14.C IMPLICATIONS FOR SOCIAL DISCOUNTING

With these results, a fairly extensive methodology exists for evaluating intertemporal welfare effects on either producers or consumers. The results in Appendix Sections 14.A and 14.B, however, skirt the issue of social discounting with risk by considering stochastic compensation in each period. An issue that is crucial in determining whether a project with effects over several time periods should be undertaken is how current nonstochastic effects should be weighed against future stochastic effects.

To do this, more intertemporal structure can be considered in the problems in (14.12) and (14.30). For example, considering only current nonstochastic compensation in (14.43), one can let $\tilde{\boldsymbol{C}}_i = (\tilde{C}_{it}, 0, \ldots, 0)$, so that, in place of (14.44), one finds that

$$-E_t[E_h(\lambda_h \cdot \tilde{q}_{ih}) + \lambda_t \partial \tilde{C}_{it} / \partial \bar{p}^t_{ih}] = 0. \tag{14.47}$$

Thus, if the marginal utility of income is constant within each time period (if λ_h and λ_t are constants) but differ by a factor δ^{h-t} because of personal discounting, then (14.47) implies that

$$\delta^{h-t} E_t(\tilde{q}_{ih}) = -\partial \tilde{C}_{it} / \partial \bar{p}^t_{ih}).$$

In other words, welfare calculations can be based on consumer (producer) surpluses in later periods associated with expected demand (supply) curves, where surplus changes are discounted over time at personal discount rates.

Alternatively, a greater level of generality is possible using duality. That is, differentiating both sides of (14.22) or (14.38) with respect to $\bar{p}^{t1}_{ih}$ where $\bar{\boldsymbol{p}}^{Tj}_t$ is defined as in (14.25) or (14.43), yields

$$\frac{\partial V_t}{\partial \bar{p}^{t1}_{ih}} + \frac{\partial V_t}{\partial C_{it}} \frac{\partial C_{it}}{\partial \bar{p}^{t1}_{ih}} = 0$$

or

$$\frac{\partial C_{it}}{\partial \bar{p}^{t1}_{ih}} = -\frac{\partial V_t / \partial \bar{p}^{t1}_{ih}}{\partial V_t / \partial C_{it}}, \tag{14.48}$$

where carets and tildes on C are suppressed for simplicity. Again, once a functional form for V_t is specified, the implied functional forms for current supplies and demands follow from (14.42). If estimation of these supplies and demands identifies all the parameters of V_t involved in (14.48), the necessary calculations for a nonstochastic *ex ante* compensation can be handled easily. Whether or not this approach is possible, however, depends on the intertemporal nature of V_t and on how V_t changes over time. The latter consideration can become important in inferring the parameters of V_t related to later time periods from estimates of supplies and demands in later time periods. If this approach is feasible, one need not rely on the approximations in Section 14.4 in questions of social discounting with risk. Social risk preferences can be determined by aggregating over individuals.

14.D FURTHER GENERALIZATIONS WITH RISK

It remains to generalize the results of this appendix regarding dynamic considerations and uncertainties regarding future prices or production to consider equilibrium welfare analysis. This can be done by combining the framework of Appendix Sections 14.A and 14.B with the concept of equilibrium in (current) prices discussed in Appendix Section 9.B.

Consider a competitive economy involving N goods traded in each time period from current time t to some future time horizon T. Suppose each of J consumers possess an intertemporal utility function, $\tilde{U}_j(\tilde{\boldsymbol{q}}^T_{tj})$, have intertemporal household production function, $\tilde{\boldsymbol{f}}^T_{tj}(\tilde{\boldsymbol{q}}^T_{tj}, \bar{\boldsymbol{q}}^t_j) = \boldsymbol{0}$ and face budget constraint $\boldsymbol{p}_h \tilde{\boldsymbol{q}}_{hj} = \bar{m}_{hj}$, $h = t, \ldots, T$, where definitions are the same as in Appendix Section 14.B except that *j* subscripts are added to differentiate behavior among consumers. Similarly, suppose each of K producers possesses an intertemporal utility function, $\hat{U}_k(\pi_{tk}-K_{tk},...,\pi_{Tk}-K_{Tk})$, and an intertemporal production function, $\boldsymbol{f}_{tk}^T(\hat{\boldsymbol{q}}_{tk}^T,\bar{\boldsymbol{q}}_k^t)=\boldsymbol{0}$ where $\pi_{hk}=\boldsymbol{p}_h\hat{\boldsymbol{q}}_{hk}$ and all other definitions are the same as in Appendix Section 14.A except that k subscripts are added to refer to specific producers.

Now consider imposing a policy change that alters the subjective distribution from $(\tilde{\bar{\boldsymbol{p}}}_{tj}^0,\tilde{\boldsymbol{\alpha}}_{tj}^{T0})$ to $(\tilde{\bar{\boldsymbol{p}}}_{tj}^1,\tilde{\boldsymbol{\alpha}}_{tj}^{T1})$ for each consumer j and from $(\hat{\bar{\boldsymbol{p}}}_{tk}^0,\hat{\boldsymbol{\alpha}}_{tk}^{T0})$ to $(\hat{\bar{\boldsymbol{p}}}_{tk}^1,\hat{\boldsymbol{\alpha}}_{tk}^{T1})$ for each producer k. Under these conditions, one can in principle solve for equilibrium prices in each successive time period by equating the sum of supplies to the sum of demands in all markets (assuming the existence of short-run equilibrium).[7] Then the welfare analysis for each individual consumer or producer can be carried out following Appendix Sections 14.A and 14.B. Alternatively, welfare effects can be determined for *groups* of individuals following the results in Appendix Sections 14.A and 14.B because areas behind market supplies and demands are the sum of areas behind supplies and demands of individuals involved in the market, respectively (see Sections 8.1 and 8.2). That is, the results in Appendix Sections 14.A and 14.B hold for groups of individuals where the demands and supplies are market supplies and demands by those groups.[8] For these purposes, however, one must note that the appropriate market supply and demand relationships for such calculations are the compensated relationships. Areas behind ordinary supplies and demands have relevance only insofar as they approximate areas behind compensated supplies and demands (such as in the producer case of constant absolute risk aversion where ordinary and compensated curves coincide).

With these generalizations, the meaning of areas behind equilibrium supplies and demands is a more difficult issue. For example, one can show in a static context that the general conclusions of Appendix Section 9.B for interpretation of areas behind general equilibrium curves hold if production is nonstochastic or stochastic but predetermined and if all decision-makers are risk-neutral or risk (represented by $\boldsymbol{\alpha}_t^T$ in Appendix Sections 14.A and 14.B) is held constant for all decision-makers.[9] But in general equilibrium, the

7. If conditions are such that the equilibrium is not unique, then the welfare analysis can be performed only if one can determine from observed data which equilibrium is appropriate.
8. One must bear in mind, however, that such market supplies and demands may be sensitive to the distribution among the groups of income or fixed costs or other determinants.
9. To see this, suppose that C_i is the compensation required by individual i for some change in a policy instrument from φ_0 to φ_1 which changes expected prices from $\bar{\boldsymbol{p}}_{ti}^0$ to $\bar{\boldsymbol{p}}_{ti}^1$ and other parameters from $\boldsymbol{\alpha}_{ti}^0$ to $\boldsymbol{\alpha}_{ti}^1$. The welfare effect for the individual can be represented as

$$C_i=\int_L dC_i=\int_{\varphi_0}^{\varphi_1}\sum_{n=1}^{N}\frac{\partial C_i}{\partial \bar{p}_{nti}}\frac{\partial \bar{p}_{nti}}{\partial \varphi}d\varphi+\int_{L_\alpha} dC_i,$$

where L is any path of integration from $(\bar{\boldsymbol{p}}_{ti}^0,\boldsymbol{\alpha}_{ti}^0)$ to $(\bar{\boldsymbol{p}}_{ti}^1,\boldsymbol{\alpha}_{ti}^0)$ and L_α is any path of integration from $\boldsymbol{\alpha}_{ti}^0$ to $\boldsymbol{\alpha}_{ti}^1$. The latter term is trivially zero if $\boldsymbol{\alpha}_{ti}^0=\boldsymbol{\alpha}_{ti}^1$ or if the individual is risk-neutral, in which case C_i does not depend on $\boldsymbol{\alpha}_{ti}$. Thus, using the results in Appendix Sections 12.A, 14.A or 14.B, $\partial C_i/\partial \bar{p}_{nti}$ can be replaced by supplies or demands $\bar{q}_{nti}$ to obtain

$$C_i=\int_{\varphi_0}^{\varphi_1}\sum_{N=1}^{N}\bar{q}_{nti}\frac{\partial \bar{p}_{nti}}{\partial \varphi}d\varphi.$$

where $\bar{q}_{nti}$ is a compensated supply or demand curve such as in (14.24) or (14.41). From this point, the analysis can proceed as in Appendix Section 9.B because this result is the same as in equations (9.43) and (9.44) where C_k and $\bar{q}_{nti}$ are substituted for ΔR_k and $\hat{q}_{nk}$ for producers and C_j and $\tilde{q}_{ntj}$ are substituted for $-\Delta\tilde{e}_j$ and $\tilde{q}_{nj}$ for consumers, respectively.

assumption that risks remain fixed when altering policy is difficult to accept. And as shown in Appendix Section 12.A, not even areas behind all ordinary curves hold direct welfare significance when production is currently stochastic. Furthermore, as shown in Appendix Sections 14.A and 14.B, areas behind ordinary curves in a present time period cannot always capture future welfare effects. Thus, it is not surprising that results in Appendix Section 9.B do not generalize in a straightforward manner to provide interpretation of areas behind general equilibrium curves in all cases.

The results of this appendix also illustrate the concept of state-dependent compensation primarily for the case of measuring *ex post* compensating variation. In fact, the results suggest that estimation of *ex ante* compensating variation (as well as evaluation of many *ex post* compensation schemes) may be difficult for many dynamic problems involving intertemporal risk because of the inability and complexity of (1) assessing probabilities of future contingencies and (2) estimating intertemporal risk preferences of producers and consumers. For such problems, measurement of *ex post* compensating variation may be the only practical approach that is feasible for economic welfare analysis.

Finally, we leave to the reader to generalize the results of this appendix to the case of active learning. The framework in this appendix has been presented for the case of *passive learning* where decision-makers learn and thus update expectations from period to period in the same way regardless of the previous decisions that are made. With *active learning*, decision-makers can influence how much they learn by the decisions they make. For example, a producer may not learn about a technology without experimentation. Active learning can be incorporated in the framework of this appendix by allowing the statistical moments of price and production distributions for future periods in $\bar{\boldsymbol{p}}_k^T$ and $\boldsymbol{\alpha}_k^T$ to depend on decisions in previous periods. Active learning models become quite complex both notationally and conceptually in the many-time-period case of this appendix although the principles developed here continue to apply.[10]

10. For further information, see Chavas and Mullarky (2002) who develop the conceptual problem of welfare measurement with active learning in the two-period case. They show with active learning that not only can public information affect private decisions but private information can affect optimal public policy choice. In fact, they show that the social value of a project can be decomposed into (1) a risk-free component, (2) an individual value of learning, (3) an individual cost of risk aversion and (4) a social value of information.

15. Conclusions and further considerations

This book has presented the subject of applied welfare economics, including the theory underlying the methodology of application. Some of the basic concepts in applied welfare economics have been of a controversial nature for many years. Some economists have accepted the surplus framework as a basis for applied work, whereas others have not. However, those who are critical of the approach in this book either have not developed workable empirical alternatives or have recommended equivalent approaches (for example, index number theory). The following quotes from famous economists are presented to highlight the controversial history of the subject matter. Abba P. Lerner (1963, p. 80) argues:

> Consumer's surplus nevertheless seems to me to be of very great use not only as a heuristic device for showing students of economics the benefits from an increase in the freedom of trade, but also for indicating where one should look for indications and estimates of the social benefits or damages from many an important governmental or other policy decision.

In regard to the general usefulness of consumer surplus, Hicks (1940–41, p. 112) writes:

> The idea of consumer's surplus enables us to study in detail the effects of deviations from the optimum in a particular market. It is not merely a convenient way of showing when there will be a deviation (consumers' surplus is not necessary for that purpose, since the basic optimum conditions . . . show us at once when there will be a deviation); it also offers us a way of measuring the size of the deviation. This, if we are right in our general viewpoint, is a most important service.

Samuelson (1947, p. 197), however, states:

> My ideal *Principles* would not include consumer's surplus in the chapter on welfare economics except possibly in a footnote, although in my perfect *Primer* the concept might have a limited place, provided its antidote and the alternatives were included close at hand.

In fact, Samuelson makes the most fundamental attack on the concept of consumer surplus. In arguing that the concept is superfluous, Samuelson (1947, p. 210) writes:

> Even if consumer's surplus did give a cardinal measure of the change in utility from a given change, it is hard to see what use this could serve. Only in the contemplation of alternative movements which begin or end in the same point could this cardinal measure have any significance and then only because it is an indicator of ordinal preference.

In fairness to Samuelson, however, one should note that his attacks on consumer surplus were made prior to the development of the Willig results discussed in Chapters 6 and 7 and prior to much of the other sophistication which has led welfare economics to an equivalence with index number theory, which he supports (Samuelson and Swamy 1974). Moreover, measurement of willingness-to-pay concepts has become as accurate as current econometric methods and data allow due to (1) the development of empirical approaches to exact measurement based on the work of Hause, Hausman and Vartia, and (2) the advances in empirical methods based on duality that allow for specification and estimation of flexible systems of supplies and demands consistent with the theory of consumer and producer behavior.

Policies are continuously being introduced and modified, and it is part of the role of the economist to provide quantitative results concerning their impact. As Bhagwati (1965, p. 213) has stressed:

> Policies are maintained or changed largely for noneconomic reasons; and the (economic) 'cost' involved is a magnitude that is commonly demanded and bandied about in discussions of public policy. Whether we like it or not, this is what the policy makers do want; and the trade theorist, in consonance with the best traditions in the profession, has begun to meet this need in an attempt to bring economic analysis closer to fulfilling the objective that provides its ultimate *raison d'etre*. The result has been a definite and significant trend, in the welfare analysis of pure theory, towards measurement of welfare change.

During the heaviest period of criticism of surplus concepts and before the many subsequent generalizations, the primary force that caused continued surplus analysis in applied literature was this need for quantitative empirical analysis of alternative policies.

15.1 EMPHASIS ON APPLICATION

This book has focused on applied economic welfare analysis as facilitated by estimable market supply and demand equations. Generalizations of these methods in response to many of the classical criticisms of surplus analysis have been developed. Often in the literature, the discussion of welfare economics focuses on the validity of the concept of economic surplus as a measure of welfare change, without worrying about the additional problem of empirically estimating economic surplus. Even if, for example, consumer surplus is a valid measure of compensating or equivalent variation, how does one empirically estimate the appropriate demand curve from which the surplus is to be calculated? Even if, conceptually, the framework provided in this book is valid for applied work, errors can still be incurred in econometric estimation of these relationships. Thus, both the theory and the problems of empirical estimation must be considered together in assessing the usefulness of the methodology. For example, although this book points out some estimation problems and alternatives, in some cases there is no way of knowing whether or not the errors caused by econometric specification and estimation with some approaches are greater than or less than the errors created by using the ordinary concept of economic surplus with other approaches. Nevertheless, this book has tried to modify standard welfare analysis in the direction of making it amenable to econometric estimation at various levels of generality.

Additionally, this book recognizes the interdependence of markets in economies and the importance of considering existing unalterable distortions in related markets in modeling and policy analysis. Early concepts of economic welfare analysis were developed by

Pigou (1932) and Marshall (1930) for simplistic partial equilibrium models usually consisting of a single market. Later, full general equilibrium models were developed by Arrow and Debreu (1954) that have often been used to argue that partial equilibrium models are inappropriate for welfare analysis because the implications of policy changes may be far different after adjustments occur in related markets. We believe that what is needed for practical policy analysis is an intermediate approach – intermediate between the simplistic partial equilibrium models of Pigou and Marshall and the full general equilibrium models of Arrow and Debreu. The former may not account for significant interactions while the latter are typically not estimable (except under crude assumptions regarding, for example, substitution or applicability of a representative consumer model). The methodology of this book provides such an intermediate approach.

Theoretical Applications

The concept of economic surplus with appropriate generalizations is a very powerful one. This book has shown, for example, how the concept was used very early in economics to demonstrate the welfare loss associated with monopoly and other distortions, the gains from technological change, the notion of the optimum tariff on trade, the gains from trade, and so on. These problems were subsequently reformulated and studied along general equilibrium lines, but the basic qualitative conclusions still held. The conclusions based on the early simple surplus literature were correct. The extension of surplus concepts discussed in this book reveals why this is the case. In fact, any surplus analysis based on a simple supply and demand diagram has several levels of interpretation in theory. First, if the supply and demand schedules are interpreted as ordinary curves, the triangles represent consumer and producer surplus, which offer a basis for approximating WTP for participants in the market. Second, if the supply and demand schedules are interpreted as compensated curves, the triangles are Hicksian surpluses, the changes in which reflect exact WTP for participants in the market. Thus, with a simple interpretation of the same diagrams used early in the economics literature, the analysis becomes exact rather than approximate. Finally, if supply and demand relationships are interpreted as compensated general equilibrium curves, the triangles reflect welfare effects for the economy as a whole – not just for the participants in the individual market. Thus, the economic surplus concepts can be as general, for theoretical purposes, as many of the more sophisticated general equilibrium approaches that have been advanced. Yet the economic surplus approach is simple, intuitive and forms a useful basis for empirical work.

Empirical Applications

Although this book attempts to extend partial equilibrium analysis and models toward a more general equilibrium approach, most empirical work cannot be made completely general. For example, if the government is considering allowing more steel or cars to enter the country, the decision is usually not made even partially on the basis of the effects that steel or automobile imports might have on the real wages of farm workers. Nevertheless, the large equilibrium effects in related markets can conceivably be measured empirically because it is precisely their size which makes their effects identifiable empirically in the context of methodology advanced in Section 9.5. In fact, the frontiers of methodological development in welfare economics now seem sufficient to offer guidance for how to consider all the effects that econometric or programming models are capable of identifying.

15.2 WELFARE MAXIMIZATION AND COST–BENEFIT ANALYSIS

Cost–benefit analysis has become quite popular in public circles. A seemingly endless number of proposed government projects come before policy-making bodies. Rational public decision-making requires some understanding of the associated costs and benefits. This has led to a great demand for cost–benefit analyses of specific projects with specific specifications. Unfortunately, however, this type of approach can lead to social suboptimality. That is, the welfare effects of some general action may depend heavily on the scale of project or on some specific design parameters. Cost–benefit analyses, as they are often undertaken upon specific requests, however, generally attempt to investigate the net social benefits of a particular project with a particular scale, design, and so on. By performing a very specific cost–benefit analysis, the potential for social welfare maximization may be forgone. In some cases the adoption of a project of a particular scale may preclude any later augmentation or reduction necessary to reach a state of social efficiency or optimal scale.

For example, by one process or another, a proposed dam of a particular size and location may come before a legislative body. In many cases, preliminary costs and benefits (from perhaps electricity generation) may be based on prevailing market prices. But market prices may change as a result of project adoption. Proposed size and location may even be appropriate as a result of engineering studies – given that existing prices are not altered as a result. In many cases, however, some economic externalities may exist that, in addition to induced price changes, may invalidate initial engineering design studies. For example, recreational opportunities are benefits associated with a dam for which standard accounting prices do not exist. Congestion costs also may be experienced as externalities by surrounding residents and are generally not included in standard engineering cost studies. These considerations suggest that social welfare analysis should play an important role in determining the design or scale of a project. Otherwise, some adverse effects or possibly greater needs may be realized only after a given proposed dam is completed. But, of course, a dam is generally too costly to relocate or modify once completed.

These considerations thus emphasize the importance of applying cost–benefit analysis more generally in the context of social welfare maximization, that is, determining the best project design to adopt rather than whether or not to adopt a given project. The concept of welfare maximization is also important in deciding which set of a large group of potential projects should be adopted. Government funds are generally limited because of political factors, and so on. Hence, not all projects with positive present discounted social value can be undertaken. The set of projects to adopt should be chosen to maximize discounted net social benefits, given the funding constraint. One project may not be appropriate unless some other one is also adopted. Again, however, one should bear in mind the possibilities for improving social welfare by altering individual project designs. Also, existing prices are likely to be altered to a greater extent when many projects are undertaken than when a single project is implemented. And any cost–benefit or welfare analysis should consider the related interactions among projects where substantial cross-effects may exist. Again, the methodology of applied welfare economics is sufficiently general to lend guidance on these issues at least when a sufficient empirical base of information is available.

15.3 INCOME DISTRIBUTION

In the early chapters on general equilibrium welfare economics, the notion of a social welfare function was introduced. This was necessary both to discuss the ideal income distribution (and hence the ideal production mix in society) and to illustrate the conceptual problems of applied economic welfare analysis. The search for an 'ideal society' includes such works as those by Rawls (1971) and Nozick (1974). These studies, although belonging to the field of moral philosophy, have been studied closely by economists. Rawls offers a theory that judges the 'goodness' of the distribution of social goods according to the level of welfare provided to the least advantaged members of society. According to Rawls, society should be organized to (1) guarantee a maximal system of equal, basic liberties and (2) distribute all social goods (other than liberty) equally unless an unequal distribution of social goods benefits the least advantaged, provided that the positions and offices that foster this inequality are open to all. However, it does not follow, as Nozick points out, that equality in the distribution of income and wealth is prima facie desirable. For Nozick, the attempt by the state to pattern the distribution of income and wealth to accord with some concept of justice is a violation of basic rights. Thus, as Ordover (1979, p. 56) writes, 'utilitarians may require that the minority sacrifice itself for the sake of the majority, while a Rawlsian may demand a sacrifice by the best-off for the sake of the worst-off'.[1]

The intent of this book is much less ambitious than seeking the welfare function to define the ideal society. It provides, instead, a framework for analyzing the impacts of policy changes. The underlying view is that, at best, economists can point out the economic impact of policy changes, including distributional effects to the extent they can be empirically identified. The political process must use this along with other information and preferences of policy-makers to formulate new policy decisions. Politicians can be expected to continue to disagree on income-distributional issues because even economists or philosophers cannot reach agreement concerning an ideal distribution.

15.4 MAKING ECONOMIC WELFARE ANALYSIS USEFUL IN THE POLICY PROCESS[2]

In reality, many policies are adopted and continued contrary to the implications of economic welfare analysis. A common view among economists is that the policy process is misguided in such cases. On the other hand, those closer to the policy process argue that (welfare) economists are misguided. For example, with respect to agricultural policy,

1. Ordover (1979) offers an excellent treatment of the subject of economic justice from the viewpoint of both economics and moral philosophy.
2. This section is based largely on Just (1988).

Cochrane (1980) argued that the welfare measures derived from the economist's model of perfect competition are irrelevant to actual policy issues. With this opinion expressed in some policy circles, several questions must be raised. How can welfare economics be made more relevant to actual policy issues? Why have the principles of welfare economics played a role in some policy issues and not in others? Do cases where the principles of welfare economics are not followed represent a failing of the policy process? Or do these cases represent a failing of economic welfare analysis?

Some of the public choice literature offers some perspective on these issues. In a broad sense, the study of public choice might be regarded as a subdiscipline of welfare economics since that is where it originated (Arrow 1951; Buchanan and Tullock 1962). However, the public choice literature has diverged markedly from empirical economic welfare practices, which is the level at which practical advice is usually offered to policy-makers. In broad terms, empirical Marshallian welfare practices have followed a more normative role of evaluating the efficiency of alternative policies (suggesting at least implicitly that the most efficient policy should be adopted or evaluated based on the social cost incurred in not so doing). On the other hand, much of the public choice literature attempts a more positive approach of understanding how various policies are chosen and under what conditions those choice processes are appropriate.

Inefficiency of Competitive Equilibrium

To understand potential shortcomings of economic welfare analysis for some policy problems, consider the reasons why competitive equilibrium may fail to attain Pareto efficiency. The classical reasons include existence of public goods, indivisibilities (including natural monopolies) and externalities. In each of these cases, the standard recommendation of welfare economists is to institute some government action that corrects the distortion from competitive equilibrium. Some distortions can be corrected simply by establishing property rights or markets for externalities while others require extensive information about individual values that is difficult if not impossible to obtain. For example, externalities imposed on future generations cannot be solved by creating markets, nor are the values of future generations observable. Thus, some of the most serious problems facing society relating to research and development and environmental conservation must necessarily be evaluated on subjective grounds. Indeed, one of the least objective matters in traditional economic welfare analyses has been the choice of a discount rate in intergenerational problems. When the appropriate discount rate is not clear, even considerations of Pareto efficiency become unclear.

In addition to these traditional problems, however, a number of other difficulties with competitive equilibrium have been identified. Stiglitz (1982) among others has demonstrated that competitive equilibrium is not Pareto efficient when risk markets are incomplete or information is imperfect. Furthermore, some risk markets are apparently impossible to add due to problems of moral hazard and adverse selection with imperfect information. If some distortions are not subject to corrective action, then the problem of second best takes on a much greater significance. This book develops a methodology to evaluate welfare effects in the presence of other distortions, but many economic welfare analyses continue to be partial in nature ignoring existing distortions. Correction of a distortion may not increase Pareto efficiency when other distortions remain. Most economic welfare analyses of policy have justified continued use of the standard partial economic efficiency criterion by either arguing that other distortions should also be removed or that consideration of other distortions is not necessary if they are not closely related to the issue in question. In some important cases, however, neither of these arguments are applicable. For example, for federal crop insurance policy, the presence of risk, risk aversion, incomplete risk markets and asymmetric information prevent removal of all distortions and some of the distortions that cannot be removed are part of the immediate problem which crop insurance policy is intended to address.

Separation of Efficiency and Equity

For such problems the identity between competitive equilibrium and Pareto efficiency does not hold, which raises questions about applicability of the competitive efficiency norm. The approach of studying efficiency issues in isolation from equity concerns has often been criticized in the policy arena due to the infeasibility of defining lump-sum transfers that truly do not affect the marginal behavior of economic agents, and because lump-sum transfer schemes are often regarded as politically and administratively infeasible (Layard and Walters 1978). Lump-sum transfers can affect market equilibria simply by changing expectations about future transfers related to other policy issues even if they do not affect the intensity of efforts to maximize profits or satisfy consumptive wants.

More fundamentally, heterogeneous preferences and asymmetric information can cause situations in which lump-sum transfers necessarily affect efficiency considerations. For example, Stiglitz (1985, p. 31) finds in the case of imperfect information and incomplete risk markets that 'the separation between equity and efficiency considerations is no longer generally valid'. Furthermore, with imperfect information, the gainers and losers from a policy change may not be identifiable so the appropriate lump-sum redistribution necessary for a Pareto improvement may be impossible (Runge and Myers 1985). Certainly, redistribution can have distinct efficiency effects when individuals have heterogeneous risk or labor–leisure preferences and the set of available markets is incomplete or imperfect (Layard and Walters 1978; Stiglitz 1985).

For policy issues where these factors are important, for example, as in Section 12.6 where some contingency markets may be missing, the competitive efficiency norm may be unrealistic because the compensation scheme changes the efficient outcome. Given that policy-makers are interested in both efficiency and distribution, economists must consider whether the policies currently in effect that distort competitive equilibrium achieve their intended effects better than the policies that are socially efficient according to the competitive efficiency norm.

Without doubt, economic welfare analysis suffers from an inability to fully evaluate policy alternatives because objective means of making interpersonal comparisons are not available. Pareto (1896) argued that a change is not supported on objective grounds unless every individual is positively affected if at all. Even this level of objectivity has been questioned for cases where the rich get richer without helping the poor. Samuelson (1947) proposed a much narrower concept of objectivity where the only objective grounds upon which a change can be recommended by an economist is where the utility possibilities associated with all possible redistributions are improved for every individual. The difficulty with this level of objectivity is that it leaves economists unable to compare alternatives related to most realistic policy issues. Clearly, if economists are to remain on strictly objective grounds, they can offer few useful policy prescriptions.

The Potential Role of Welfare Economics

Faced with these problems, the welfare economics literature has evolved in several different and competing directions. The most popular approach is based on the Kaldor–Hicks–Scitovsky compensation criteria which determine whether changes should be made based on aggregate WTP. This justification has 'rehabilitated' Marshallian surplus methodology. Nevertheless, following these criteria without actually paying compensation necessarily involves a value judgment implying equal welfare weights among the individuals that are aggregated (Chipman and Moore 1978). Equal weightings may be unacceptable to policy-makers in a wide range of policy issues. On the other hand, actually paying compensation (assuming lump-sum transfers are possible), in effect, vastly reduces the domain of comparable alternatives. Specifically, it may eliminate comparability of alternatives that satisfy the distributional preferences of policy-makers.

Another body of welfare economics literature is based on the Bergsonian social welfare function. While agreement on a social welfare function is an unrealistic expectation, alternative forms have continued to be proposed in order to facilitate the interpersonal comparisons that policy evaluation demands. These include simple multiplicative forms that support income equality as well as lexicographic forms that support Rawls's (1971) notion of justice. An important point, however, is that virtually all of these forms suggest a criterion of distributional optimality (such as income equality) that is also inconsistent with some of the revealed preferences of policy-makers.[3] Even if economists (or philosophers) could agree on a social welfare function, it may not be appropriate for policy purposes because choice of a social welfare function is clearly a subjective matter. Furthermore, for cases of democratic government, the Arrow impossibility theorem implies that a social welfare function consistent with all potential social choices does not exist.

Interestingly, the Kaldor–Hicks–Scitovsky compensation approach and the Bergsonian social welfare function approach correspond, respectively, to the two economic justifications usually given for policy intervention – to improve Pareto efficiency by correcting distortions and to redistribute income. While this book has focused primarily on the former approach, only a naive view of the policy process can ignore the intent of some policies to redistribute income. Consider, for example, the gasohol subsidy program enacted in the USA in the 1980s in spite of economic studies both inside and outside of government that showed gasohol could not be justified on economic grounds. An accounting of the program showed that a single company received 54 percent of all federal subsidies while the six largest companies received about 90 percent of the subsidies. This example, among others, suggests not only that standard efficiency criteria do not play an important role in some policy issues, but also that some policies are being pursued which are biased in favor of inequity. Of course, one could argue that policy-makers do not

3. They are also obviously inconsistent with the preferences of individuals. For example, individuals do not have infinite risk aversion as shown to be necessary by Arrow (1973) and Harsanyi (1975) for Rawls's moral justice criterion (Section 3.4).

anticipate the biased effects such programs have, but that is a naive argument given the role of lobby groups in such legislation.

The results in this book justify the use of the Kaldor–Hicks–Scitovsky compensation approach when equity and efficiency are separable. Strictly speaking, the justification for using the competitive efficiency norm is based on comparing alternative distributions by the potential compensation criterion only if lump-sum transfers are possible so that any desired distribution can be achieved once the efficiency norm is reached.[4] When equity and efficiency are not separable, however, lump-sum transfers are not possible and competitive efficiency alone is not a sufficient welfare criterion for policies that redistribute income. Some have argued that efficiency analysis is still important in measuring the social cost of attaining certain distributional results. However, competitive efficiency may be inconsistent with social optimality when efficiency and distribution are not separable issues.

When equity and efficiency are not separable, the equity–efficiency tradeoff must be evaluated according to the preferences that matter. But which preferences matter? The preferences that determine which policies are adopted are the preferences of policy-makers. On the other hand, society may have a different social welfare function unknown to either economists or politicians. The appropriate norm of efficiency (not competitive efficiency in this case) is the optimum state of the economy according to those preferences. Thus, the welfare economist must consider the possibility that a competitive efficiency criterion alone may be inconsistent with both policy-maker preferences and the true but unknown preferences of society. Unless economists consider the preferences that matter for such policy questions, the scope of applicability of economic welfare analysis is limited to cases where either (1) distributional considerations are not important, (2) preferences are consistent with equal welfare weightings, (3) major factors do not prevent separation of equity and efficiency and lump-sum redistribution is politically feasible or (4) the results of economic efficiency analysis support the views that would have been held anyway. To perform welfare analysis that will be useful in this context, a careful applied welfare economist will present the results of analysis so that users of the analysis, whether politicians or the general public to whom politicians are responsible, can evaluate the distributional impacts according to their own preferences and compare those impacts to the efficiency impacts. This is accomplished by reporting economic impacts of policy alternatives in disaggregated form as well as aggregate form.

Distributional Considerations Based on Public Choice Theory

The important contribution that the theory of public choice can make to applied economic welfare analysis is that it can provide a justification for the interpersonal comparisons that make economic analyses useful to policy-makers. The public choice literature has developed a two-stage view of social decision-making whereby impartial moral and social considerations guide formulation of rules at the constitutional stage and then individuals are free to pursue their own self-interest in the later parliamentary stage subject to constitutional rules and institutions (Buchanan and Tullock 1962). This framework

4. Of course, systems of transfer payments may be attempted to approximate lump-sum transfers insofar as possible. For these cases, the competitive efficiency norm may still provide a suitable approximation if the inefficiency of the transfer system is also evaluated.

resolves the conflict between moral considerations and individual incentives. In a one-stage setting, moral considerations (or the various social welfare functions proposed by economists and philosophers) lead to equality or helping the most miserable individual which then destroys individual incentives that are necessary to attain the efficiency of competitive equilibrium because of moral hazard.

The two-stage theory of social decision-making also provides a framework that is consistent with individual rights implicit in such notions as liberty and protection from exploitation that otherwise imply impossibility of a Paretian liberal (Sen 1982). While some of the examples in the literature on the Paretian liberal (relating to such choices as reading material and sleeping positions) may appear of little real-world relevance to economists, these issues are at the heart of some environmental problems involving the right to pollute versus the right to a clean environment. The conflict of individual rights with the Pareto principle is resolved by establishing a protected sphere for individual choice or by putting in place a mechanism that can override the Pareto principle when personal liberties are involved.

A number of studies have found reasons why a representative form of democracy may be an optimal outcome of the constitutional stage. Participation by the masses in all decisions leads to high costs of decision-making for each participating individual because of transactions costs and limited information. On the other hand, representative democracy is preferred to dictatorship because of moral hazard problems associated with personal liberties and externalities associated with facilitating debate. Some studies have even shown that two-party democracy attains the same optimum welfare as an omniscient, benevolent dictator (see Mueller 1979 for a review of these results).

These results suggest that the major provisions of the constitutions of Western societies specify rules for decision-making at the parliamentary stage that are consistent with maximization of social welfare, given factors that prevent the Pareto efficiency of competitive equilibrium and that block the separation of efficiency and equity considerations – namely, transactions costs, imperfect information, moral hazard and externalities. If these rules can facilitate maximization of social welfare in the cases that cause the economist's concept of economic efficiency to break down, then the social values represented by the policy process cannot be ignored. For policy choices motivated by distributional concerns, the policy process cannot be evaluated meaningfully by comparison to competitive efficiency.

According to the literature on public choice, the process for determining society's values is set once the constitutional stage is completed (Mueller 1979). This is consistent with the political scientist's definition of the political system as 'those interactions through which values are authoritatively allocated for a society' (Easton 1965, p. 21). In this context, the social welfare function arises from the constitution and the political system it puts in place (Arrow 1951). If these are the 'authoritative values' of society, then economic welfare analyses cannot ignore them when the values based on economic efficiency fail because of the impracticality or impossibility of nondistorting lump-sum transfers and the associated lack of separation between equity and efficiency.

Implications for Economic Welfare Analysis

These observations lead to several possibilities for applied economic welfare practices depending on circumstances. When equity and efficiency are separable, the traditional focus on competitive efficiency is appropriate. Otherwise, economic welfare analysis should facilitate both equity and efficiency evaluation. In many cases, the preferences of policy-makers will not be clear. In these cases, objective practices imply that economic welfare analyses should emphasize disaggregation to the extent feasible given available data and ability to communicate results to policy-makers. Then users of economic welfare analyses can apply their own preferences or welfare weightings to the alternative policy choices. Because most Western policy processes involve representative democracy, this approach must allow each representative as well as the general public who elect them to evaluate the alternatives from the standpoint of their own individual perspectives if the information is to be used. While this approach might seem to serve the biased interests of certain individuals, the alternative of providing only aggregate welfare analyses is to reduce the relevance for individuals and, thus, indirectly to the overall policy process. Economic analyses geared to the interests of individual voting representatives as well as various individuals in society can increase the information base used in policy decisions and thus help the political system to function more effectively.

15.5 SUMMARY

The methodology developed in this book is not sufficient to provide a framework to solve all the world's problems. If they can be solved, the solutions require more than economics, let alone welfare economics. To argue that applied welfare economics has all the answers to solving real-world problems is a mistake, just as it is a mistake to argue that political science or moral philosophy has all the answers. However, this book provides a broad basis for delving into the topic of welfare economics and understanding how its constructs can be used to promote more informed public policy formulation. Welfare economists will make their greatest contribution by using the principles developed herein with judgment and understanding regarding how economic concerns fit into the overall policy process.

Bibliography

Abbott, Michael and Orley Ashenfelter (1976), 'Labour supply, commodity demand and the allocation of time', *Review of Economic Studies*, **43** (135), 389–411.

Adams, James D. and Adam B. Jaffe (1996), 'Bounding the effects of R&D: an investigation using matched establishment firm data', *RAND Journal of Economics*, **27** (4), 700–21.

Addison, John T. and W. Stanley Siebert (1979), *The Market for Labor: An Analytical Treatment*. Santa Monica, CA: Goodyear.

Allen, Roy, Claudia Dodge and Andrew Schmitz (1983), 'Voluntary export restraints as protection policy', *American Journal of Agricultural Economics*, **65** (2), 291–7.

Anderson, James and John G. Riley (1976), 'International trade with fluctuating prices', *International Economic Review*, **17** (1), 76–97.

Anderson, James E. (1974), 'A note on welfare surpluses and gains from trade in general equilibrium', *American Economic Review*, **64** (4), 758–62.

——— (1976), 'The social cost of input distortions: a comment and a generalization', *American Economic Review*, **66** (1), 235–8.

Arcus, Peter (1981), *Broilers and Eggs*, Economic Council of Canada, Technical Report No. E13, Ottawa.

Arrow, Kenneth J. (1951), *Social Choice and Individual Values*, New York: John Wiley and Sons, Inc. (revised 1963).

——— (1970), 'The organization of economic activity: issues pertinent to the choice of market versus nonmarket allocation', in J. Margolis and Robert H. Haveman (eds), *Public Expenditures and Policy Analysis*, Chicago, IL: Markham, pp. 59–73; also found in US Congress, Joint Economic Committee (1969), *The Analysis and Evaluation of Public Expenditures: The PPB System: Compendium*, 91st Congress, Session I.

——— (1971), *Essays in the Theory of Risk Bearing*, Amsterdam: North-Holland.

——— (1973), 'Some ordinalist-utilitarian notes on Rawls' theory of justice', *Journal of Philosophy*, **70** (9), 245–63.

Arrow, Kenneth J. and Gerard Debreu (1954), 'Existence of an equilibrium for a competitive economy', *Econometrica*, **22** (3), 265–90.

Arrow, Kenneth J. and Anthony C. Fisher (1974), 'Environmental preservation, uncertainty, and irreversability', *Quarterly Journal of Economics*, **88** (2), 312–19.

Arrow, Kenneth J. and Frank Hahn (1971), *Competitive Equilibrium Analysis*, San Francisco, CA: Holden-Day.

Arrow, Kenneth J. and L. Mordecai Kurz (1970), *Public Investment, the Rate of Return, and Optimal Fiscal Policy*, Baltimore, MD: Johns Hopkins University Press.

Arrow, Kenneth J. and Robert C. Lind (1970), 'Uncertainty and the evaluation of public investment decisions', *American Economic Review*, **60** (3), 364–78.

Atkinson, Anthony B. (1970), 'On the measurement of inequality', *Journal of Economic Theory*, **2** (3), 244–63.

Aumann, Robert J. and Roger B. Myerson (1988), 'Endogenous formation of links between players and of coalitions: an application of the Shapley value', in A. Roth (ed.), *The Shapley Value*, Cambridge: Cambridge University Press.

Azevedo, Christopher, Joseph A. Herriges and Catherine L. Kling (2003), 'Combining revealed and stated preferences: consistency tests and their interpretations', *American Journal of Agricultural Economics*, **85** (3), 525–37.

Bailey, Martin J. (1954), 'The interpretation and application of the compensation principle', *Economic Journal*, **64** (253), 39–52.

Barichello, Richard R. (1982), 'Government policies in support of Canadian agriculture: their costs', paper presented at the United States/Canada Agricultural Trade Research Consortium Meeting, Airlie House, VA, 16–18 December.

Bateman, Ian J. and Kenneth G. Willis (1999), *Valuing Environmental Preferences: Theory and Practice of the Contingent Valuation Method in the US, EU, and Developing Countries*, Oxford: Oxford University Press.

Bator, Francis M. (1958), 'The anatomy of market failure', *Quarterly Journal of Economics*, **72** (3), 351–79.

Baumol, William and Wallace Oates (1971), 'The use of standards and prices for protection of the environment', *Swedish Journal of Economics*, **73** (1), 42–54.

Baumol, William J., John C. Panzar, and Robert D. Willig (1988), *Contestable Markets and the Theory of Industrial Structure*, 2nd edition, New York: Harcourt Brace and Jovanovitch.

Becker, Gary S. (1965), 'A theory of the allocation of time', *Economic Journal*, **75** (299), 493–517.

Becker, Gary S. and Robert T. Michael (1973), 'On the new theory of consumer behavior', *Swedish Journal of Economics*, **75** (4), 378–96.

Becker, Gary S. and Kevin M. Murphy (1993), 'A simple theory of advertising as a good or bad', *Quarterly Journal of Economics*, **108** (4), 941–64.

Beghin, John C. and Larry S. Karp (1991), 'Estimation of price policies in Senegal', *Journal of Development Economics*, **35** (1), 49–67.

Bellman, Richard and Stuart Dreyfus (1962), *Applied Dynamic Programming*, Princeton, NJ: Princeton University Press.

Bentham, Jeremy (1961), *Principles of Morals and Legislation* (first published 1823). New York: Doubleday.

Bergson, Abram (1938), 'A reformulation of certain aspects of welfare economics', *Quarterly Journal of Economics*, **52** (2), 310–34.

——— (1975), 'A note on consumer's surplus', *Journal of Economic Literature*, **13** (1), 38–44.

Berndt, Ernst R., Masako N. Darrough and W. Erwin Diewert (1977), 'Flexible functional form and expenditure distributions: an application to Canadian consumer demand functions', *International Economic Review*, **18** (3), 651–75.

Bertrand, Joseph (1883), 'Théorie mathématique de la richesse sociale', *Journal des Savants*, **67**, 499–508.

Bhagwati, Jagdish (1965), 'The pure theory of international trade: a survey', in *American Economic Association and Royal Economic Society: Surveys of Economic Theory*, vol. 2, New York: American Economic Association/Royal Economic Society (AEA/RES), 213.

Bieri, Jurg and Andrew Schmitz (1973), 'Export instability, monopoly power and welfare', *Journal of International Economics*, **3** (4), 389–96.

——— (1974), 'Market intermediaries and price instability: some welfare implications', *American Journal of Agricultural Economics*, **56** (2), 280–5.

Bishop, Richard C. (1986), 'Resource evaluation under uncertainty: theoretical principles for empirical research', in V. Kerry Smith (ed.), *Advances in Applied Microeconomics*, vol. 4, Greenwich, CT: JAI Press.

Blackorby, Charles and David Donaldson (1990), 'A review article: the case against the use of the sum of compensating variations in cost–benefit analysis', *Canadian Journal of Economics*, **23** (3), 471–94.

Blackorby, Charles, Daniel Primont and R. Robert Russell (1978), *Duality, Separability, and Functional Structure: Theory and Economic Applications*. New York: Elsevier North-Holland.

Blanchard, Olivier J. and Stanley Fischer (1989), *Lectures on Macroeconomics*, Cambridge, MA: MIT Press.

Blundell, Richard, Panos Pashardes and Guglielmo Weber (1993), 'What do we learn about consumer demand patterns from micro data?', *American Economic Review*, **83** (3), 570–97.

Boadway, Robin W. (1974), 'The welfare foundations of cost–benefit analysis', *Economic Journal*, **84** (336), 926–39.

Boadway, Robin W. and Neil Bruce (1984), *Welfare Economics*, Cambridge, MA: Basil Blackwell.

Bockstael, Nancy E. and Catherine L. Kling (1988), 'Valuing environmental quality: weak complementarity with sets of goods', *American Journal of Agricultural Economics*, **70** (3), 654–62.

Bockstael, Nancy E. and Kenneth E. McConnell (1983), 'Welfare measurement in the household production framework', *American Economic Review*, **73** (4), 806–14.

Bockstael, Nancy E., Kenneth E. McConnell and Ivar E. Strand (1991), 'Recreation', in John B. Branden and Charles D. Kolstad (eds), *Measuring the Demand for Environmental Quality*, Amsterdam: North-Holland.

Bovenberg, A. Lans and L.H. Goulder (1998), 'Environmental taxation', in Alan J. Auerbach and Martin Feldstein (eds), *Handbook of Public Economics*, 2nd Edition, New York: Elsevier North-Holland.

Bovenberg, A. Lans and Ruud A. de Mooij (1994), 'Environmental levies and distortionary taxation', *American Economic Review*, **84** (4), 1085–9.

Brännlund, Runar and Bengt Kriström (1996), 'Welfare measurement in single and multimarket models', *American Journal of Agricultural Economics*, **78** (1), 157–65.

Bredahl, Maury, Andrew Schmitz and Jimmy S. Hillman (1987), 'Rent seeking in international trade: the great tomato war', *American Journal of Agricultural Economics*, **69** (1), 1–10.

Brookshire, David S., Berry C. Ives and William D. Schultze (1976), 'The valuation of aesthetic preferences', *Journal of Environmental Economics and Management*, **3** (4), 325–46.

Brown, Gardner M. and Henry O. Pollakowski (1977), 'Economic valuation of shoreline', *Review of Economics and Statistics*, **59** (3), 272–8.

Buchanan, James (1969), 'External diseconomies, corrective taxes, and market structure', *American Economic Review*, **59** (1), 174–7.

Buchanan, James M. and Gordon Tullock (1962), *The Calculus of Consent*, Ann Arbor: The University of Michigan Press.

Bullock, David S. (1993a), 'Welfare implications of equilibrium supply and demand curves in an open economy', *American Journal of Agricultural Economics*, **75** (1), 52–8.

——— (1993b), 'Multimarket effects of technological change: comment', *Review of Agricultural Economics*, **15** (3), 603–8.

Burns, Michael E. (1973), 'A note on the concept and measure of consumer surplus', *American Economic Review*, **63** (3), 335–44.

——— (1977), 'On the uniqueness of consumer's surplus and the invariance of economic index numbers', *The Manchester School of Economic and Social Studies*, **45** (1), 41–61.

Burt, Oscar R. (1964), 'Optimal resource use over time with an application to groundwater', *Management Science*, **11** (1), 80–93.

Burt, Oscar R. and Durward Brewer (1971), 'Estimates of net social benefits for outdoor recreation', *Econometrica*, **39** (5), 813–27.

Burt, Oscar R. and Ronald G. Cummings (1973), 'Production and investment natural resource industries', *American Economic Review*, **60** (4), 576–90.

Burt, Oscar R., Won W. Koo and Norman J. Dudley (1980), 'Optimal stochastic control of U.S. wheat stocks and exports', *American Journal of Agricultural Economics*, **62** (2), 172–87.

Butters, Gerard R. (1977), 'Equilibrium distributions of sales and advertising prices', *Review of Economic Studies*, **44** (3), 465–91.

Byerlee, Derek and Greg Traxler (1995), 'National and international wheat improvement research in the post green revolution period: evolution and impacts', *American Journal of Agricultural Economics*, **77** (2), 268–78.

Cardon, James H. and Rulon D. Pope (2003), 'Agricultural market structure, generic advertising, and welfare', *Journal of Agricultural and Resource Economics*, **28** (2), 185–200.

Carter, Colin and Andrew Schmitz (1979), 'Import tariffs and price formation in the world wheat market', *American Journal of Agricultural Economics*, **61** (3), 517–22.

Carter, Colin C., Nancy Gallini and Andrew Schmitz (1980), 'Producer-consumer trade-offs in export cartels', *American Journal of Agricultural Economics*, **62** (4), 812–18.

Carter, Colin, Darrell Hueth, John Mamer and Andrew Schmitz (1981), 'Labor strikes and the price of lettuce', *Western Journal of Agricultural Economics*, **6** (1), 1–13.

——— (1987), 'Agricultural labor strikes and farmer income', *Economic Inquiry*, **25** (1), 121–33.

Cesario, Frank J. (1976), 'Value of time in recreation benefit studies', *Land Economics*, **55** (1), 32–41.

Chambers, Robert G. and Richard E. Just (1989), 'Estimating multi-output technologies', *American Journal of Agricultural Economics*, **71** (4), 980–95.

Chan, Kenneth S. (1991), 'Bilateral trade negotiations and trade diversification', *Journal of Development Economics*, **36** (2), 243–57.

Chavas, Jean-Paul and Matthew T. Holt (1996), 'Economic behavior under uncertainty: a joint analysis of risk preferences and technology', *Review of Economics and Statistics*, **78** (2), 329–35.

Chavas, Jean-Paul and Daniel Mullarky (2002), 'On the valuation of uncertainty in welfare analysis', *American Journal of Agricultural Economics*, **84** (1), 23–38.

Chipman, John S. and James C. Moore (1976), 'The scope of consumer's surplus arguments', in Anthony M. Tang, Fred M. Westfield and James S. Worley (eds), *Evolution, Welfare, and Time in Economics: Essays in Honor of Nicholas Georgescu-Roegen*, Lexington, MA: Heath-Lexington Books, pp. 69–123.

——— (1978), 'The new welfare economics 1939–1974', *International Economic Review*, **19** (3), 547–81.

——— (1980), 'Compensating variation, consumer's surplus, and welfare', *American Economic Review*, **70** (5), 933–49.

Ciriacy-Wantrup, Siegfried V. (1952), *Resource Conservation: Economics and Policies*. Berkeley, CA: University of California Press.

Clark, Colin W. (1976), *Mathematical Bioeconomics: The Optimum Management of Renewable Resources*, New York: John Wiley and Sons.

Clawson, Marion (1959), 'Methods or measuring the demand for and value of outdoor recreation', Reprint No. 10, Washington, DC: Resources for the Future.

Clawson, Marion and Jack L. Knetsch (1966), *Economics of Outdoor Recreation*, Baltimore, MD: Johns Hopkins University Press.

Coase, Ronald H. (1960), 'The problem of social cost', *Journal of Law and Economics*, **3** (1), 1–44.

Coble, Keith H. and Thomas O. Knight (2002), 'Crop insurance as a tool for price and yield risk management', in Richard E. Just and Rulon D. Pope (eds), *A Comprehensive Assessment of the Role of Risk in U.S. Agriculture*, Norwell, MA: Kluwer.

Cochrane, Willard W. (1980), 'Some non-comformist thoughts on welfare economics and commodity stabilization policy', *American Journal of Agricultural Economics*, **62** (3), 508–11.

Cochrane, Willard W. and Yigal Danin (1976), *Reserve Stock Grain Models: The World and United States, 1975–1985*, Minnesota Agricultural Experiment Station Technical Bulletin no. 305.

Cochrane, Willard W. and Mary Ryan (1976), *American Farm Policy, 1948–1973*, Minneapolis, MN: University of Minnesota Press.

Coffin, H. Garth, Robert Saint-Louis and Kenneth A. Rosaasen (1996), 'Supply management canadian style', in Andrew Schmitz, Garth Coffin and Kenneth Rosaasen (eds), *Regulations and Protectionism Under GATT*, Boulder, CO: Westview Press, ch. 13.

Cohen, Kalman J. and Richard M. Cyert (1965), *Theory of the Firm: Resource Allocation in a Market Economy*, Englewood Cliffs, NJ: Prentice Hall.

Comanor, William S. and Harvey Leibenstein (1969), 'Allocative efficiency, x-efficiency and the measurement of welfare losses', *Economica*, **36** (143), 304–9.

Cooke, Stephen C. and W. Burt Sundquist (1993), 'The incidence of benefits from U.S. soybean productivity gains in a context of world trade', *American Journal of Agricultural Economics*, **75** (1), 169–80.

Cornes, Richard (1992), *Duality and Modern Economics*, Cambridge: Cambridge University Press.

Cornes, Richard and Todd Sandler (1996), *The Theory of Externalities, Public Goods, and Club Goods*, New York: Cambridge University Press.

Cournot, Augustin (1838), *Recherches sur les Principes Mathématiques de la Théorie des Richesses*, Paris: M. Riviére et Cie; English edition (1897), *Research into the Mathematical Principles of the Theory of Wealth*, ed. N. Bacon, London: Macmillan.

Cowling, Keith and Dennis C. Mueller (1978), 'The social costs of monopoly power', *Economic Journal*, **88** (352), 740.

Cropper, Maureen L., Sema K. Aydede and Paul R. Portney (1994), 'Preferences for life saving programs: how the public discounts time and age', *Journal of Risk and Uncertainty*, **8** (3), 243–65.

Crosson, Pierre R., Ronald G. Cummings and Kenneth D. Frederick (1978), *Selected Water Management Issues in*

Latin America, Baltimore, MD: Johns Hopkins University Press.

Crutchfield, Steven R. (1983), 'Estimation of foreign willingness to pay for U.S. fishery resources', *Land Economics*, **59** (1), 16–23.

Cummings, Ronald G. (1969), 'Some extensions of the economic theory of exhaustible resources', *Western Economic Journal*, **7** (3), 201–10.

Currie, John M., John A. Murphy and Andrew Schmitz (1971), 'The concept of economic surplus and its use in economic analysis', *Economic Journal*, **81** (324), 741–99.

Dales, John H. (1968), *Pollution, Property, and Prices*, Toronto: University of Toronto Press.

Danese, Arthur E. (1965), *Advanced Calculus*, Boston, MA: Allyn and Bacon.

Dardis, Rachel and Janet Dennison (1969), 'The welfare costs of alternative methods of protecting raw wool in the United States', *American Journal of Agricultural Economics*, **51** (2), 303–19.

d'Arge, Ralph, William Schultze and David Brookshire (1980), 'Benefit–cost evaluation of long term future effects: the case of CO', University of Wyoming Resource and Environmental Economics Laboratory Research Paper No. 13, April.

Dasgupta, Partha and Geoffrey Heal (1974), 'The optimal depletion of exhaustible resources', *The Review of Economic Studies: Symposium on the Economics of Exhaustible Resources*, **41**, 3–28.

David, Elizabeth L. (1968), 'Lake shore property values: a guide to public investment in recreation', *Water Resources Research*, **4** (4), 697–707.

Davis, Otto A. and Andrew B. Whinston (1965), 'Welfare economics and the theory of the second best', *Review of Economic Studies*, **32** (1), 1–14.

——— (1967), 'Piecemeal policy and the theory of second best', *Review of Economic Studies*, **34** (3), 323–31.

Davis, Robert K. (1964), 'The value of big game hunting in a private forest', in *Transactions of the Twenty-Ninth North American Wildlife Conference*, Washington, DC: Wildlife Management Institute.

Deaton, Angus S. and John Muellbauer (1980), *Economics and Consumer Behavior*, Cambridge: Cambridge University Press.

Diamond Peter A and James A. Mirrlees (1971a), 'Optimal taxation and public production: I – production efficiency', *American Economic Review*, **61** (1), 8–17.

——— (1971b), 'Optimal taxation and public production: II – tax rules', *American Economic Review*, **61** (3), 261–78.

Diewert, W. Erwin (1973), 'Functional forms for profit and transformation functions', *Journal of Economic Theory*, **6** (3), 284–316.

——— (1974), 'Applications of duality theory', in Michael Intriligator and David Kendrick (eds), *Frontiers of Econometrics* 2, Amsterdam: North-Holland.

Dixit, Avinash K. and Victor D. Norman (1978), 'Advertising and welfare', *Bell Journal of Economics*, **9** (1), 1–17.

Draper, Norman R. and Harry Smith (1966), *Applied Regression Analysis*, New York: John Wiley and Sons.

Dupuit, Jules (1844), 'On the measurement of utility of public works', *Annals des Ponts et Chaussees*, 2nd Series, 8.

Easton, David (1965), *A Systems Analysis of Political Life*, New York: Wiley.

Eckstein, Otto (1961a), 'A survey of the theory of public expenditure', and 'Reply', *Public Finances: Needs, Sources, and Utilization*, Princeton, NJ: National Bureau of Economic Research, pp. 493–504.

——— (1961b), *Water-Resource Development: The Economics of Project Evaluation*, Cambridge, MA: Harvard University Press.

Epstein, Larry G. (1982), 'Integrability of incomplete systems of demand functions', *Review of Economic Studies*, **49** (3), 411–25.

Evenson, Robert E. and Yoav Kislev (1975), *Agricultural Research and Productivity*, New Haven, CT: Yale University Press.

Evenson, Robert E., Paul E. Waggoner and Vernon W. Ruttan (1979) 'Economic benefit from research: an example from agriculture', *Science*, **205** (4411), 1101–7.

Ferguson, Charles E. (1969a), *The Neoclassical Theory of Production and Distribution*. Cambridge: Cambridge University Press.

——— (1969b), *Microeconomic Theory*, Homewood, IL: Richard D. Irwin.

Ferguson, James (1974), *Advertising and Competition: Theory, Measurement, Fact*, Cambridge: Ballinger.

Fishburn, Peter C. (1973), *The Theory of Social Choice*, Princeton, NJ: Princeton University Press.

Fisher, Anthony C. (1979), 'On measures of natural resource scarcity', in V. Kery Smith (ed.), *Scarcity and Growth Reconsidered*, Baltimore, MD: Johns Hopkins University Press, pp. 249–75.

Fisher, Anthony and Michael Hanemann (1987), 'Quasi-option value: some misconceptions dispelled', *Journal of Environmental Economics and Management*, **14** (2), 183–90.

Fisher, Franklin M. and John J. McGowan (1979), 'Advertising and welfare: comment', *Bell Journal of Economics*, **10** (2), 726–7.

Foster, William E. and Richard E. Just (1989), 'Measuring the welfare effects of product contamination with consumer uncertainty', *Journal of Environmental Economics and Management*, **17** (3), 266–83.

Freeman, A. Myrick III (1993), *The Measurement of Environmental and Resource Values: Theory and Methods*, Baltimore, MD: Johns Hopkins University Press.

——— (2003), *The Measurement of Environmental and Resource Values*, 2nd edn, Washington, DC: Resources for the Future.

Freund, Rudolf J. (1956), 'The introduction of risk into a programming model', *Econometrica*, **24**, 253–63.

Friedman, Milton and Rose Friedman (1980), *Free to Choose*, New York: Harcourt Brace and Jovanovich.

Friedman, Milton and L.J. Savage (1952), 'The expected-utility hypothesis and the measurability of utility', *Journal of Political Economy*, **60** (6), 463–74.

Fudenberg, Drew and Jean Tirole (1992), *Game Theory*, Cambridge, MA: MIT Press.

Fuss, Melvyn and Daniel McFadden (1978), *Production Economics: A Dual Approach to Theory and Applications*, vols 1 and 2, Amsterdam: North-Holland.

Gardner, Bruce (1977), 'Optimal stockpiling models and the effects of public on private grain storage', *Proceedings, Journal of the American Statistical Association, Business and Economic Statistics Section*, 77–83.

——— (1979a), *Optimal Stockpiling of Grain*, Lexington, MA: Lexington Books.

——— (1979b, 'Robust stabilization policies for international commodity agreements', *American Economic Review*, **69** (2), 169–72.

——— (1983), 'Efficient redistribution through commodity markets', *American Journal of Agricultural Economics*, **62** (2), 225–34.

——— (2002), 'Risk created by policy in agriculture', in Richard E. Just and Rulon D. Pope (eds), *A Comprehensive Assessment of the Role of Risk in U.S. Agriculture*, Norwell, MA: Kluwer.

Geary, Robert C. (1949–50), 'A note on "a constant utility index of the cost of living"', *Review of Economic Studies*, **18** (1), 65–6.

Gilbert, Christopher L. (1996), 'International commodity agreements: an obituary notice', *World Development*, **24** (1), 1–19.

Gorman, William M. (1953), 'Community preference fields', *Econometrica*, **21** (1), 63–80.

——— (1955), 'The intransitivity of certain criteria used in welfare economics', *Oxford Economic Papers*, New Series, **7** (1), 25–35.

Goulder, Lawrence H. (1995), 'Environmental taxation and the "double dividend": a reader's guide', *International Tax and Public Finance*, **2** (2), 157–83.

Graaff, Johann de V. (1953), *Theoretical Welfare Economics*, London: Cambridge University Press.

Graham, Daniel A. (1981), 'Cost–benefit analysis under uncertainty', *American Economic Review*, **71** (4), 715–25.

——— (1983), 'Estimating the "state dependent" utility function', *Natural Resources Journal*, **23** (3), 649–56.

——— (1992), 'Public expenditure under uncertainty: the net-benefit criteria', *American Economic Review*, **82** (4), 822–46.

Greene, William H. (2000), *Econometric Analysis*, 4th edition, Upper Saddle River, NJ: Prentice Hall.

Griliches, Zvi (1971), *Price Indexes and Quality Change*, Cambridge, MA: Harvard University Press.

Hanemann, W. Michael (1980), 'Quality changes, consumer's surplus, and hedonic price indices', Department of Agricultural and Resource Economics Working Paper No. 116, University of California, Berkeley.

——— (1981), 'Water quality and the demand for recreation', Agricultural and Resource Economics Working Paper No. 164, University of California, Berkeley, March.

——— (1984a), 'Discrete/continuous models of consumer demand', *Econometrica*, **52** (3), 541–61.

——— (1984b), 'Welfare evaluations in contingent valuation experiments with discrete responses', *American Journal of Agricultural Economics*, **66** (3), 332–41.

——— (1989), 'Information and the concept of option value', *Journal of Environmental Economics and Management*, **16** (1), 23–37.

——— (1992), 'Preface', in Stale Navrud (ed.), *Pricing the European Environment*, Oxford: Oxford University Press.

Hanson, James C. and Richard E. Just (2001), 'The potential for transition to paid extension: some guiding economic principles', *American Journal of Agricultural Economics*, **83** (3), 777–84.

Harberger, Arnold C. (1954), 'Monopoly and resource allocation', *American Economic Review, Proceedings*, **44** (2), 77–87.

——— (1971), 'Three basic postulates of applied welfare economics: an interpretative essay', *Journal of Economic Literature*, **9** (3), 785–97.

——— (1978), 'On the use of distributional weights in social cost–benefit analysis', *Journal of Political Economy*, **86** (2), Part 2, S87–S120.

Harling, Kenneth F. and Robert L. Thompson (1983), 'The economic effects of intervention in Canadian agriculture', *Canadian Journal of Agricultural Economics*, **31** (2), 153–76.

Harsanyi, John C. (1953), 'Cardinal utility

in welfare economics and in the theory of risk-taking', *Journal of Political Economy*, **61** (5), 434–5.

——— (1955), 'Cardinal welfare, individualistic ethics and interpersonal comparisons of utility', *Journal of Political Economy*, **63** (4), 309–21.

——— (1963), 'A simplified bargaining model for the n-person cooperative game', *International Economic Review*, **4** (2), 194–220.

——— (1975), 'Can the maximin principle serve as a basis for morality? A critique of John Rawls' theory', *American Political Science Review*, **69** (2), 594–606.

——— (1986), *Rational Behavior and Bargaining Equilibrium in Games and Social Situations*. Cambridge: Cambridge University Press.

Hart, Sergiu and Mordecai Kurz (1983), 'Endogenous formation of coalitions', *Econometrica*, **51** (4), 1047–64.

Hartwick, John M. (1978), 'Substitution among exhaustible resources and intergenerational equity', *Review of Economic Studies*, **45** (2), 347–543.

Hause, John C. (1975), 'The theory of welfare cost measurement', *Journal of Political Economy*, **83** (6), 1154–78.

Hausman, Jerry A. (1981), 'Exact consumer's surplus and deadweight loss', *American Economic Review*, **71** (4), 662–76.

——— (1993), *Contingent Valuation: A Critical Assessment*, Oslo: Scandinavian University Press.

Haveman, Robert H. (1969), 'The opportunity cost of displaced private spending and the social discount rate', *Water Resources Research*, **5** (5), 947–57.

Hazell, Peter B.R. and Pasquale L. Scandizzo (1975), 'Market intervention policies when production is risky', *American Journal of Agricultural Economics*, **57** (4), 641–9.

——— (1979), 'Optimal price intervention policies when production is risky', in James A. Roumasset, Jean-Marc Boussard and Inderjit Singh (eds), *Risk, Uncertainty and Agricultural Development*, Philippines: Southeast Asian Regional Center for Graduate Study and Research in Agriculture; New York: Agricultural Development Council.

Hazilla, Michael and Raymond J. Kopp (1990), 'The social cost of environmental quality regulations: a general equilibrium analysis', *Journal of Political Economy*, **98** (4), 853–73.

Henderson, James M. and Richard E. Quandt (1971), *Microeconomic Theory: A Mathematical Approach*, 2nd edition, New York: McGraw-Hill.

Henderson, Rebecca and Iain Cockburn (1996), 'Scale, scope, and spillovers: the determinants of research productivity in drug discovery', *RAND Journal of Economics*, **27** (1), 32–59.

Henry, Claude (1974), 'Investment decisions under uncertainty: the irreversabiliy effect', *American Economic Review*, **64** (6), 1006–12.

Herfindahl, Orris C. and Allen V. Kneese (1974), *Economic Theory of Natural Resources*. Columbus, OH: Charles E. Merrill.

Herriges, Joseph A. and Catherine L. Kling (1999), *Valuing Recreation and the Environment: Revealed Preference Methods in Theory and Practice*, Cheltenham, UK and Northampton, MA, USA: Edward Elgar.

Hicks, John R. (1939), 'The foundations of welfare economics', *Economic Journal*, **49** (196), 696–712.

——— (1940–41), 'The rehabilitation of consumer's surplus', *Review of Economic Studies*, **8** (1), 112.

——— (1943), 'The four consumers' surpluses', *Review of Economic Studies*, **11** (1), 31–41.

——— (1956), *A Revision of Demand Theory*, Oxford: Clarendon Press.

Hildenbrand, Werner (1998), 'How relevant are specifications of behavioral relations on the micro-level for modelling the time path of population aggregates?' *European Economic Review*, **42** (3–5), 437–58.

Hirshleifer, Jack (1966), 'Investment decision under uncertainty: applications of the state preference approach', *Quarterly Journal of Economics*, **80** (2), 270–5.

——— (1976), *Price Theory and Applications*, Englewood Cliffs, NJ: Prentice Hall.

Hirshleifer, Jack, James C. De Haven and Jerome W. Milliman (1960), *Water Supply: Economics, Technology, and Policy*, Chicago, IL: University of Chicago Press.

Hochman, Eithan, David Zilberman and Richard E. Just (1977), 'Internalization in a stochastic pollution model', *Water Resources Research*, **13** (6), 877–81.

Hoffman, Kenneth M. and Ray Kunze (1971), *Linear Algebra*, 2nd edition, Englewood Cliffs, NJ: Prentice Hall.

Hoos, Sidney (ed.) (1979), *Agricultural Marketing Boards: An International Perspective*, Cambridge, MA: Ballinger.

Horowitz, John and Richard E. Just (1995), 'Political coalition breaking and sustainability of policy reform', *Journal of Development Economics*, **47** (2), 271–86.

Honolulu Advertiser (various issues).

Honolulu Star-Bulletin (various issues).

Hotelling, Harold (1931), 'Economics of exhaustible resources', *Journal of Political Economy*, **39** (2), 137–75.

——— (1938), 'The general welfare in relation to problems of taxation and of railway and utility rates', *Econometrica*, **6** (3), 242–69; reprinted in Kenneth J. Arrow and Tibor Scitovsky (eds) (1969), *Readings in Welfare Economics*, Homewood, IL: Richard D. Irwin.

——— (1947), 'Letter to the National Park Service', reprinted in R.A. Prewitt (ed.), (1949), *The Economics of Public Recreation: The Prewitt Report*, Washington, DC: US Department of the Interior.

Houthakker, Hendrik S. (1960), 'Additive utility', *Econometrica*, **28** (2), 244–57.

Howe, Charles W. (1979), *Natural Resource Economics: Issues, Analysis, and Policy*', New York: John Wiley and Sons.

Howe, Charles W. and K. William Easter (1971), *Interbasin Transfers of Water: Economic Issues and Impacts*, Baltimore, MD: Johns Hopkins University Press.

Hueth, Darrell and Juan Carlos Mendieta (2000), 'Sobre el uso de espacio abrierto urbano: un estudio caso de las sierras del chicò', (The economics of urban open space: a case study of Las Sierras of Chico), *Desarrollo y Sociedad*, **46**, 145–95.

Hueth, Darrell and Andrew Schmitz (1972), 'International trade in intermediate and final goods: some welfare implications of destabilized prices', *Quarterly Journal of Economics*, **86** (3), 351–65.

Huffman, Wallace E. and Robert E. Evenson (1993), *Science for Agriculture: A Long Term Perspective*, Ames, IA: Iowa State University Press.

Huffman, Wallace E. and Richard E. Just (1999a), 'The organization of agricultural research in western developed countries', *Agricultural Economics*, **21** (1), 1–18.

——— (1999b), 'Agricultural research: benefits and beneficiaries of alternative funding mechanisms', *Review of Agricultural Economics*, **21** (1), 2–18.

Hurwicz, Leonid and Hirofumi Uzawa (1971), 'On the integrability of demand functions', in John S. Chipman, Leonid Hurwicz, Michael K. Richter and Hugo F. Sonnenschein (eds), *Preferences, Utility, and Demand*, New York:

Harcourt, Brace and Jonavich, pp. 114–48

Intriligator, Michael D. (1978), *Econometric Models, Techniques, and Applications*. Englewood Cliffs, NJ: Prentice Hall.

Johnson, Harry G. (1960), 'The cost of protection and the scientific tariff', *Journal of Political Economy*, **68** (4), 327–45.

Jorgenson, Dale W. (1997), *Welfare: Aggregate Consumer Behavior*, Cambridge, MA: MIT Press.

Jorgenson, Dale W. and Thomas M. Stoker (1997), 'Nonlinear three-stage least squares pooling of cross-section and time-series observations', in D.W. Jorgenson (ed.), *Welfare: Aggregate Consumer Behavior*, Cambridge, MA: MIT Press.

Jorgenson, Dale W., Lawrence J. Lau and Thomas M. Stoker (1997), 'The transcendental logarithmic model of aggregate consumer behavior', in D.W. Jorgenson (ed.), *Welfare: Aggregate Consumer Behavior*, Cambridge, MA: MIT Press.

Judge, George G., William E. Griffiths, R. Carter Hill, Helmut Lütkepohl and Tsoung Chao Lee (1988), *Introduction to the Theory and Practice of Econometrics*, 2nd edition. New York: John Wiley and Sons.

Just, Richard E. (1974), 'An investigation of the importance of risk in farmers' decisions', *American Journal of Agricultural Economics*, **56** (l), 14–25.

——— (1981), 'Theoretical and empirical considerations in agricultural buffer stock policy under the Food and Agriculture Act of 1977', report prepared for the US General Accounting Office, Washington, DC.

——— (1988), 'Making economic welfare analysis useful in the policy process: implications of the public choice literature', *American Journal of Agricultural Economics*, **70** (2), 448–53.

Just, Richard E. and Linda Calvin (1995), 'Moral hazard in U.S. crop insurance: an empirical investigation', working paper, College Park, MD: University of Maryland.

Just, Richard E. and Wen S. Chern (1980), 'Tomatoes, technology, and oligopsony', *Bell Journal of Economics*, **11** (2), 584–602.

Just, Richard E. and J. Arne Hallam (1978), 'Functional flexibility in analysis of commodity price stabilization policy', *Proceedings, Journal of the American Statistical Association, Business and Economic Statistics Section*, 177–186.

Just, Richard E. and Darrell L. Hueth (1979), 'Multimarket welfare measurement', *American Economic Review*, **69** (5), 947–54.

Just, Richard E. and Rulon D. Pope (1999), 'Implications of heterogeneity for theory and practice in production economics', *American Journal of Agricultural Economics*, **81** (2), 711–18.

——— (2002), 'The agricultural producer: theory and statistical measurement', in B. Gardner and G.C. Rausser (eds), *Handbook of Agricultural Economics*, New York: Elsevier-North-Holland.

——— (2003), 'Agricultural risk analysis: adequacy of models, data, and issues', *American Journal of Agricultural Economics*, **85** (5), 1249–56.

Just, Richard E. and David Zilberman (1979), 'Asymmetry of taxes and subsidies in regulating stochastic mishap', *Quarterly Journal of Economics*, **93** (1), 139–48.

Just, Richard E., Linda Calvin and John Quiggin (1999), 'Adverse selection in crop insurance: actuarial and asymmetric information incentives', *American Journal of Agricultural Economics*, **81** (4), 834–49.

Just, Richard E., Darrell L. Hueth and Andrew Schmitz (1982), *Applied Welfare*

Economics and Public Policy, New York: Prentice Hall.

Just, Richard E., Ernst Lutz, Andrew Schmitz and Stephen Turnovsky (1977), 'The distribution of welfare gains from international price stabilization under distortions', *American Journal of Agricultural Economics*, **59** (4), 652–61.

——— (1978), 'The distribution of welfare gains from price stabilization: an international perspective', *Journal of International Economics*, **8** (4), 511–63.

Just, Richard E., Andrew Schmitz and David Zilberman (1979), 'Price controls and optimal export policies under alternative market structures', *American Economic Review*, **69** (4), 706–14.

Kaldor, Nicholas (1939), 'Welfare propositions of economics and interpersonal comparisons of utility', *Economic Journal*, **49** (195), 549–52.

Karp, L.S. and A.F. McCalla (1983), 'Dynamic games and international trade: an application of the world corn market', *American Journal of Agricultural Economics*, **65** (4), 641–50.

Kemp, M.C. and Y.K. Ng (1977), 'More on social welfare functions: the incompatibility of individualism and ordinalism', *Economica*, **44** (173), 89–90.

Kerr, Norwood A. (1987), *The Legacy: A Centennial History of the State Agricultural Experiment Stations, 1887–1987*, Columbia, MO: Missouri Agricultural Experiment Station, University of Missouri.

Klein, Lawrence R. and H. Rubin (1948–49), 'A constant-utility index of the cost of living', *Review of Economic Studies*, **15** (2), 84–7.

Knetsch, Jack L. (1964), 'Economics of including recreation as a purpose of eastern water projects', *Journal of Farm Economics*, **46** (5), 1148–57.

Konandreas, Panos A. and Andrew Schmitz (1978), 'Welfare implications of grain price stabilization: some empirical evidence for the United States', *American Journal of Agricultural Economics*, **60** (1), 74–84.

Kotowitz, Yehuda and Frank Mathewson (1979), 'Advertising, consumer information, and product quality', *Bell Journal of Economics*, **10** (2), 566–88.

Krauss, Melvin and David Winch (1971), 'Mishan on the gains from trade: comment', *American Economic Review*, **61** (1), 199–200.

Krutilla, John V. (1981), 'Reflections of an applied welfare economist', *Journal of Environmental Economics and Management*, **8** (1), 1–10.

Krutilla, John V. and Otto Eckstein (1958), *Multiple Purpose River Development*. Baltimore, MD: Johns Hopkins University Press.

Krutilla, John V. and Anthony C. Fisher (1978), *The Economics of Natural Environments*. Baltimore, MD: Johns Hopkins University Press.

Laffont, Jean-Jacques (1988), *Fundamentals of Public Economics*. Cambridge, MA: MIT Press.

LaFrance, Jeffery T. (1985), 'Linear demand functions in theory and practice', *Journal of Economic Theory*, **37** (1), 147–66.

——— (1986), 'The structure of constant elasticity demand models', *American Journal of Agricultural Economics*, **68** (3), 543–52.

Lancaster, Kelvin J. (1966), 'A new approach to consumer theory', *Journal of Political Economy*, **74** (2), 132–57.

Lange, Oscar R. (1938), *On the Economic Theory of Socialism*, Minneapolis, MN: University of Minnesota Press.

Lau, Lawrence J. (1977), 'Existence conditions for aggregate demand functions: the case of multiple indexes', Technical Report No. 248, Stanford, CA: Institute for Mathematical Studies in the Social

Sciences, Stanford University (revised 1980 and 1982).

Layard, Richard (1980), 'On the use of distributional weights in cost–benefit analysis', *Journal of Political Economy*, **88** (5), 1041–7.

Layard, Richard and Alan A. Walters (1978), *Microeconomic Theory*, New York: McGraw-Hill.

Lee, Dwight R. (1978), 'Price controls, binding constraints, and intertemporal economic decision making', *Journal of Political Economy*, **86** (2), 293–302.

Lee, Hyunok and Robert G. Chambers (1986), 'Expenditure constraints and profit maximization in U.S. agriculture', *American Journal of Agricultural Economics*, **68** (4), 857–65.

Lerner, Abba P. (1933–34), 'The concept of monopoly and the measurement of monopoly power', *Review of Economic Studies*, **1** (1–3), 157–75.

——— (1944), *The Economics of Control*, New York: Macmillan.

——— (1963), 'Consumer's surplus and micro-macro', *Journal of Political Economy*, **71** (1), 76–81.

Lind, Robert C. (1990), 'Reassessing the government's discount rate policy in light of new theory and data in a world economy with a high degree of capital mobility', *Journal of Environmental Economics and Management*, **18** (2), Part 2, S-8 to S-28.

Lipsey, Richard G. and Kelvin Lancaster (1956–57), 'The general theory of the second best', *Review of Economic Studies*, **24** (1), 11–32.

Little, I.M.D. (1960), *A Critique of Welfare Economics*, London: Oxford University Press.

Lopez, Ramon E. (1984), 'Estimating labour supply and production decisions of self-employed farm producers', *European Economic Review*, **24** (1), 61–82.

——— (1986), 'Structural models of the farm household that allow for interdependent utility and profit maximization decisions', in Inderjit Singh, Lyn Squire and John Strauss (eds), *Agricultural Household Models: Extensions, Applications, and Policy*, Baltimore, MD: Johns Hopkins Press, pp. 306–26.

Machina, Mark J. (1987), 'Choice under uncertainty: problems solved and unsolved', *Journal of Economic Perspectives*, **1** (1), 121–54.

Mäler, Karl-Goran (1974), *Environmental Economics: A Theoretical Inquiry*, Baltimore, MD: Johns Hopkins University Press.

Mansfield, Edwin, John Rapoport, Anthony Romeo, Edmond Vallani, Samuel Wagner and Frank Husic (1977), *The Production and Application of New Industrial Technology*, New York: W.W. Norton.

Marglin, Stephen (1963), 'The social rate of discount and the optimal rate of investment', *Quarterly Journal of Economics*, **77** (1), 95–111.

Marshall, Alfred (1930), *Principles of Economics*, London: Macmillan.

Mas-Colell, Andreu, Michael D. Whinston and Jerry R. Green (1995), *Microeconomic Theory*, Oxford: Oxford University Press.

Maskin, Eric (1978), 'A theorem on utilitarianism', *Review of Economic Studies*, **45** (1), 93–6.

Massell, Benton F. (1969), 'Price stabilization and welfare', *Quarterly Journal of Economics*, **83** (2), 285–97.

McCandless, George T. and Neil Wallace (1991), *Introduction to Dynamic Macroeconomic Theory*, Cambridge, MA: Harvard University Press.

McCloskey, Donald N. (1982), *The Applied Theory of Price*, New York: Macmillan.

McConnell, Kenneth (1975), 'Some problems in estimating the demand for outdoor recreation', *American Journal of Agricultural Economics*, **57** (2), 330–4.

McFadden, Daniel (1978), 'Cost, revenue, and profit function', in Melvyn Fuss and Daniel McFadden (eds), *Production Economics: A Dual Approach to Theory and Applications*, 2 vols., Amsterdam: North-Holland.

McFadden, Daniel and Sidney G. Winter (1968), 'Lecture notes on consumer theory', University of California, Berkeley.

McGuire, Joseph W. (1964), *Theories of Business Behavior*, New York: Prentice Hall.

McInnerney, John (1976), 'The simple analytics of natural resource economics', *Journal of Agricultural Economics*, **27** (1), 31–52.

McKenzie, George and Ivor Pearce (1976), 'Exact measures of welfare and the cost of living', *Review of Economic Studies*, **43** (135), 465–8.

McKenzie, George W. (1979), 'Consumer's surplus without apology: comment', *American Economic Review*, **69** (3), 465–68.

——— (1983), *Measuring Economic Welfare: New Methods*, Cambridge: Cambridge University Press.

McKenzie, Lionel W. (1957), 'Demand theory without a utility index', *Review of Economic Studies*, **24** (3), 185–9.

Metrick, Andrew and Martin L. Weitzman (1998), 'Conflicts and choices in biodiversity preservation', *Journal of Economic Perspectives*, **12** (3), 21–34.

Meyer, Jack (1987), 'Two-moment decision models and expected utility maximization', *American Economic Review*, **77** (3), 421–30.

Mincer, Jacob (1963), 'Market prices, opportunity costs, and income effects', in Carl F. Christ, Milton Friedman and others (eds), *Measurement in Economics: Studies in Mathematical Economics and Econometrics in Memory of Yehuda Grunfeld*, Stanford, CA: Stanford University Press, pp. 368–84.

Mishan, Ezra J. (1959), 'Rent as a measure of welfare change', *American Economic Review*, **49** (3), 394.

——— (1968), 'What is producer's surplus?', *American Economic Review*, **58** (5), Part 1, 1279–82.

——— (1973), 'Welfare criteria: resolution of a paradox', *Economic Journal*, **83** (331), 747–8.

——— (1976a), 'The use of compensating and equivalent variation in cost–benefit analysis', *Economica*, **43** (170), 185–97.

——— (1976b), *Cost–Benefit Analysis*, 2nd edition, New York: Praeger.

——— (1977), 'The plain truth about consumer surplus', *Nationalokonomie Journal of Economics*, **37** (1–2), 1–24.

Mitchell, Robert C. and Richard T. Carson (1989), *Using Surveys to Value Public Goods: The Contingent Valuation Method*, Washington, DC: Resources for the Future.

Mueller, Dennis C. (1979), *Public Choice*, London: Cambridge University Press.

Murphy, John A., W. Hartley Furtan and Andrew Schmitz (1993), 'The gains from agricultural research under distorted trade', *Journal of Public Economics*, **51** (2), 161–72.

Myerson, Roger B. (1984), 'Two-person bargaining problems with incomplete information', *Econometrica*, **52** (2), 461–88.

Nash, John F. Jr (1950), 'The bargaining problem', *Econometrica*, **18** (2), 155–62.

——— (1953), 'Two-person cooperative games', *Econometrica*, **21** (1), 128–40.

Nelson, Philip (1974), 'Advertising as information', *Journal of Political Economy*, **82** (4), 729–54.

Nerlove, Marc and David A. Bessler (2002), 'Expectations, information, and dynamics', in Bruce Gardner and

Gordon C. Rausser (eds), *Handbook of Agriculural Economics*, New York: Elsevier-North-Holland.

Nichols, Len M. (1985), 'Advertising and economic welfare', *American Economic Review*, **75** (1), 213–27.

Nicholson, Walter (1978), *Microeconomic Theory: Basic Principles and Extensions*, 2nd edition, Hinsdale, IL: Dryden Press.

Nozick, Robert (1974), *Anarchy, State and Utopia*, New York: Basic Books.

Oi, Walter Y. (1961), 'The desirability of price instability under perfect competition', *Econometrica*, **27** (1), 58–64.

Olson, Lars J. and Keith C. Knapp (1997), 'Exhaustible resource allocation in an overlapping generations economy', *Journal of Environmental Economics and Management*, **32** (3), 277–92.

Ordover, Janusz A. (1979), 'Understanding economic justice: some recent developments in pure and applied welfare economics', in Maurice B. Ballabon (ed.), *Economic Perspectives*, New York: Harwood Academic, p. 56.

Osborne, Martin J. and Ariel Rubinstein (1994), *A Course in Game Theory*, Cambridge, MA: MIT Press.

Palmquist, Raymond B. (1991), 'Hedonic methods', in John B. Branden and Charles D. Kolstad (eds), *Measuring the Demand for Environmental Quality*, Amersterdam: North-Holland, pp. 77–120.

Pareto, Vilfredo (1896), *Cours d'Economie Politique*, vol. 2, Lausanne: F. Rouge.

Parry, Ian W.H. (1995), 'Pollution taxes and revenue recycling', *Journal of Environmental Economics and Management*, **29** (3), Part 2, 46–77.

——— (1998), 'The double dividend: when you get it and when you don't', *Proceedings: Ninety-First Annual Conference on Taxation*, National Tax Association, 8–10 November, pp. 46–51; see also minutes of the annual meeting of the National Tax Association (1999), Sunday, 8 November 1998, Washington, DC: National Tax Association, pp. 46–51.

Parry, Ian W.H. and Antonio M. Bento (2000), 'Tax deductions, environmental policy, and the "double dividend" hypothesis', *Journal of Environmental Economics and Management*, **39** (1), 67–96.

Patinkin, Don (1963), 'Demand curves and consumer's surplus', in Carl F. Christ, Milton Friedman and others (eds), *Measurement in Economics, Studies in Mathematical Economics and Econometrics in Memory of Yehuda Grunfeld*, Stanford, CA: Stanford University Press, pp. 83–112.

Pendse, Dilip and J.B. Wyckoff (1974), 'Scope for valuation of environmental goods', *Land Economics*, **50** (1), 89–92.

Pfouts, Ralph W. (1953), 'A critique of some recent contributions to the theory of consumer's surplus', *Southern Economic Journal*, **19** (3), 315–33.

Phlips, Louis (1974), *Applied Consumption Analysis*, Amsterdam: North-Holland.

Picketts, Valerie J., Andrew Schmitz and Troy Schmitz (1991), 'Rent seeking: the potash dispute between Canada and the United States', *American Journal of Agricultural Economics*, **73** (2), 255–65.

Pigou, Arthur C. (1932), *The Economics of Welfare*, 4th edition, London: Macmillan.

Polasky, Stephen, Andrew Solow and James Broadus (1993), 'Searching for uncertain benefits and the conservation of biological diversity', *Environmental and Resource Economics*, **3** (2), 171–81.

Polinsky, A. Mitchell and Daniel L. Rubinfeld (1977), 'Property values and the benefits of environmental improvements: theory and measurement', in Lowdon Wingo and Alan Evans (eds), *Public Economics and the Quality of Life*,

Baltimore, MD: Johns Hopkins University Press, pp. 154–80.

Polinsky, A. Mitchell and Steven Shavell (1976), 'Amenities and property values in a model of an urban area', *Journal of Public Economics*, **5** (1–2), 119–29.

Pollak, Robert A. and Michael L. Wachter (1975), 'The relevance of the household production function approach', *Journal of Political Economy*, **83** (2), 255–77.

——— (1977), 'Reply: Pollak and Wachter on the household production function approach', *Journal of Political Economy*, **85** (5), 1083–6.

Pope, Rulon, Jean Paul Chavas and Richard E. Just (1983), 'Economic welfare evaluations for producers under uncertainty', *American Journal of Agricultural Economics*, **65** (1), 98–107.

Portney, Paul R. and Robert N. Stavins (2000), *Public Policies for Environmental Protection*, Washington, DC: Resources for the Future.

Portney, Paul R. and John P. Weyant (eds) (1999), *Discounting and Intergenerational Equity*, Washington, DC: Resources for the Future.

Posner, Richard (1969), 'Oligopoly and the antitrust laws: a suggested approach', *Stanford Law Review*, **21** (6), 1562–606.

Quiggin, John (1993), *Generalized Expected Utility Theory: The Rank-dependent Model*. Boston, MA: Kluwer Academic.

Quirk, James and Rubin Saposnik (1968), *Introduction to General Equilibrium Theory and Welfare Economics*, New York: McGraw-Hill.

Quirk, James and Katsuaki Terasawa (1991), 'Choosing a government discount rate: an alternative approach', *Journal of Environmental Economics and Management*, **20** (1), 16–28.

Ramsey Frank P. (1927), 'A contribution to the theory of taxation', *Economic Journal*, **37** (145), 47–61.

Randall, Alan and John R. Stoll (1980), 'Consumer's surplus in commodity space', *American Economic Review*, **71** (3), 449–57.

Randall, Alan, Berry C. Ives and Clyde Eastman (1974), 'Bidding games for evaluation of aesthetic environmental improvement', *Journal of Environmental Economics and Management*, **1** (2), 132–49.

Rasmusen, Eric (1989), *Games and Information: An Introduction to Game Theory*, Oxford: Blackwell.

Rasmussen, Wayne D. (1989), *Taking the University to the People: Seventy-five Years of Cooperative Extension*, Ames, IA: Iowa State University Press.

Rawls, John (1971), *A Theory of Justice*, New York: Oxford University Press.

Ready, Richard C. (1993), 'The choice of a welfare measure under uncertainty', *American Journal of Agricultural Economics*, **75** (4), 896–904.

Rees, Albert (1971), 'The effects of unions on resource allocation', in John F. Burton Jr, Lee K. Benham, William M. Vaughn III and Robert J. Flanagan (eds), *Readings in Labor Market Analysis*, New York: Holt, Rinehart and Winston.

Reutlinger, Shlomo (1976), 'A simulation model for evaluating worldwide buffer stocks of wheat', *American Journal of Agricultural Economics*, **58** (1), 1–12.

Ricardo, David (1829), *The Principles of Political Economy and Taxation*, London: Macmillan.

Richter, Donald K. (1974), 'Games pythagoreans play', Department of Economics, University of Rochester Discussion Paper 74–3.

Riordan, Courtney (1971a), 'General multistage marginal cost dynamic programming model for the optimizations of investment-pricing decisions', *Water Resources Research*, **7** (2), 245–53.

——— (1971b), 'Multistage marginal cost

model of investment-pricing decisions: application to urban water supply treatment facilities', *Water Resources Research*, **7** (3), 463–78.

Rosen, Sherwin (1974), 'Hedonic prices and implicit market: product differentiation in perfect competition', *Journal of Political Economy*, **82** (1), 34–55.

Roy, René (1947), 'La distribution du revenu entre les divers biens', *Econometrica,* **15** (3), 205–25.

Runge, C. Ford and Robert J. Myers (1985), 'Shifting foundations of agricultural policy analysis: welfare economics when risk markets are incomplete', *American Journal of Agricultural Economics*, **67** (5), 1010–16.

Sagoff, Mark (1988), 'Some difficulties in the defense of environmental economics', *Environmental Ethics*, **10** (1), 55–74.

Samuelson, Paul A. (1942), 'Constancy of the marginal utility of income', in Oscar Lange, Francis McIntyre and Theodore O. Yntema (eds), *Studies in Mathematical Economics and Econometrics in Memory of Henry Schultz*, Chicago: University of Chicago Press; reprinted in J. Stiglitz (ed.) (1966), *Collected Scientific Papers of Paul A. Samuelson*, vol. 1, Cambridge, MA: MIT Press, pp. 37–53.

——— (1947), *Foundations of Economic Analysis*, Cambridge, MA: Harvard University Press.

——— (1950), 'Evaluation of real national income', *Oxford Economic Papers*, New Series, **2** (1), 1–29.

——— (1954), 'The pure theory of public expenditure', *Review of Economics and Statistics*, **36** (4), 387–9.

——— (1956), 'Social indifference curves', *Quarterly Journal of Economics*, **70** (1), 1–22; reprinted in J. Stiglitz (ed.) (1966), *Collected Scientific Papers of Paul A. Samuelson*, vol. 2, Cambridge, MA: MIT Press, pp. 1073–94.

——— (1964), 'Discussion', *American Economic Review*, *Proceedings*, **54** (3), 93–6.

——— (1972), 'The consumer does benefit from feasible price stability', *Quarterly Journal of Economics*, **86** (3), 476–93.

Samuelson, Paul A. and Subramanian Swamy (1974), 'Invariant economic index numbers and canonical duality: survey and synthesis', *American Economic Review*, **64** (4), 566–93.

Sandler, T. and Daniel G. Acre M. (2002), 'A conceptual framework for understanding global and transnational public goods for health', *Fiscal Studies*, **23** (2), 195–222.

Schaefer, Elmer (1975), 'Passing-on theory in antitrust treble damage actions: an economic and legal analysis', *William and Mary Law Review*, **16** (4), 883–936.

Scherer, Frederic M. (1970), *Industrial Market Structure and Market Performance*, Chicago, IL: Rand McNally.

Schmalensee, Richard (1971), 'Consumer's surplus and producer's goods', *American Economic Review*, **61** (4), 682–7.

——— (1972), 'Option demand and consumer's surplus: valuing price changes under uncertainty', *American Economic Review*, **62** (5), 813–24.

——— (1976), 'Another look at the social valuation of input price changes', *American Economic Review*, **66** (1), 237–43.

Schmitz, Andrew (1996), 'Introduction: trade and regulations in transition', in Andrew Schmitz, Garth Coffin and Kenneth Rosaasen, *Regulation and Protectionism Under GATT*, Boulder, CO: Westview Press.

Schmitz, Andrew and David Seckler (1970), 'Mechanized agriculture and social welfare: the case of the tomato harvester', *American Journal of Agricultural Economics*, **52** (4), 569–77.

Schmitz, Andrew, William Boggess and Kenneth Tefertiller (1995), 'Regulations: evidence from the Florida dairy industry', *American Journal of Agricultural Economics*, **77** (5), 1166–71.

Schmitz, Andrew, Robert S. Firch and Jimmy S. Hillman (1981), 'Agricultural export dumping: the case of Mexican winter vegetables in the U.S. market', *American Journal of Agricultural Economics*, **63** (4), 645–55.

Schmitz, Andrew, Hartley Furtan and Katherine Baylis (2002), *Agricultural Policy, Agribusiness, and Rent Seeking Behaviour*, Toronto: University of Toronto Press.

Schmitz, Andrew, Alex F. McCalla, Donald O. Mitchell and Colin C. Carter (1981), *Grain Export Cartels*, Cambridge, MA: Ballinger.

Schmitz, Andrew, Dale Sigurdson and Otto Doering (1986), 'Domestic farm policy and the gains from trade', *American Journal of Agricultural Economics*, **68** (4), 160–78.

Schmitz, Troy G. (1995), 'The economic effects of the general agreement on tariffs and trade on supply management in Canadian agriculture: spatial models of the Canadian broiler industry', PhD dissertation, Department of Agriculture and Resource Economics, University of California, Berkeley.

Schmitz, Troy G. and Andrew Schmitz (2003), 'Food supply management and tariffication: a game theoretic approach', *Journal of Agricultural and Food Industrial Organization*, **1** (1), 1–20.

Schmitz, Troy G., Andrew Schmitz and Chris Dumas (1997), 'Gains from trade, inefficiency of government programs, and the net economic effects of trading', *Journal of Political Economy*, **105** (3), 637–47.

Schultze, William D., Ralph C. d'Arge and David S. Brookshire (1981), 'Valuing environmental commodities: some recent experiments', *Land Economics*, **57** (2), 151–72.

Schwartzman, David (1960), 'The burden of monopoly', *Journal of Political Economy*, **68** (6), 627–30.

Scitovsky, Tibor (1941), 'A note on welfare propositions in economics', *Review of Economic Studies*, **9** (1), 77–88.

Scott, Anthony D. (1953), 'Notes on user cost', *Economic Journal*, **63** (250), 368–84.

——— (1955), *Natural Resources: The Economics of Conservation*, Canada: University of Toronto Press.

Selten, Reinhard (1965), 'Speiltheoretische behandlung eines oligopolmodells mit nachfragetragheit', *Zeitschrift fur die gesamte Staatswissenschaft*, **121**, 301–24.

Sen, Amartya K. (1970), *Collective Choice and Social Welfare*, Edinburgh: Oliver and Boyd.

——— (1973), *On Economic Inequality*, Oxford: Clarendon Press.

——— (1979), 'Personal utilities and public judgements: or what's wrong with welfare economics?', *Economic Journal*, **89** (353), 537–58.

——— (1982), *Choice, Welfare and Measurement*, Cambridge, MA: MIT Press.

Sharples, Jerry A., R.L. Walter and Rudie W. Slaughter Jr (1976), 'Buffer stock management for wheat price stabilization', Commodity Economics Division Economic Research Service, US Department of Agriculture, Washington, DC.

Shulstad, Robert N. and Herbert H. Stoevener (1978), 'The effects of mercury contamination in pheasants on the value of pheasant hunting in Oregon', *Land Economics*, **34** (1), 39–49.

Shumway, Richard (1995), 'Recent duality contributions in production economics', *Journal of Agricultural and Resource Economics*, **20** (1), 178–94.

Silberberg, Eugene (1972), 'Duality and the many consumer surpluses', *American Economic Review*, **62** (5), 942–52.

——— (1978), *The Structure of Economics: A Mathematical Analysis*, New York: McGraw-Hill.

Simpson, R. David, Roger A. Sedjo and John W. Reid (1996), 'Valuing biodiversity for use in pharmaceutical research', *Journal of Political Economy*, **104** (1), 163–85

Smith, Adam (1937), *An Inquiry into the Nature and Causes of the Wealth of Nations* (first published 1776), ed. Edwin Cannan, New York: Random House Inc.

Smith, V. Kerry (1990), 'Valuing amenity resources under uncertainty: a skeptical view of recent resolutions', *Journal of Environmental Economics and Management*, **19** (2), 193–202.

Smith, Vernon L. (1969), 'On models of commercial fishing', *Journal of Political Economy*, **77** (2), 181–98.

Solow, Robert M. (1974), 'Intergenerational equity and exhaustible resources', *Review of Economic Studies: Symposium on the Economics of Exhaustible Resources*, **41**, 29–45.

——— (2000), 'Sustainability: an economist's perspective', in R.N. Stavins (ed.), *Economics of the Environment*, 4th edition, New York: W.W. Norton, pp. 131–8.

Stackelberg, Heinrich von (1934), *Marktform und Gleichgewicht*. Berlin: J. Springer; English edition: (1952), *The Theory of the Market Economy*, ed. A. Peacock, London: William Hodge.

Stahl, Dale O. II (1994), 'Oligopolistic pricing and advertising', *Journal of Economic Theory*, **64** (1), 162–77.

Stavins, Robert N. (2000), 'Experience with market-based environmental policy instruments', in Karl-Goran Mäler and Jeffrey Vincent (eds), *Handbook of Environmental Economics*, Amsterdam: Elsevier Science.

Stigler, George J. (1952), *The Theory of Price*, New York: Macmillan.

——— (1961), 'The economics of information', in G.J. Stigler, *The Organization of Industry*, Homewood, IL: Richard D. Irwin, 171–90.

——— (1971), 'The theory of economic regulation', *Bell Journal of Economics*, **2**(1), 3–21.

Stigler, George J. and Gary S. Becker (1977), 'De gustibus non est disputandum', *American Economic Review*, **67** (1), 76–90.

Stiglitz, Joseph E. (1982), 'The inefficiency of the stock market equilibrium', *Review of Economic Studies*, **49** (2), 241–61.

——— (1985), 'Information and economic analysis: a perspective', *Economic Journal*, **95** (Conference Papers Supplement), 21–41.

Stoker, Thomas M. (1993), 'Empirical approaches to the problem of aggregation over individuals', *Journal of Economic Literature*, **31** (4), 1827–74.

Stone, J. Richard N. (1954), 'Linear expenditure systems and demand analysis: an application to the pattern of British demand', *Economic Journal*, **64** (255), 511–27.

Strand, Ivar E. and Darrell L. Hueth (1977), 'A management model for a multispecies fishery', in Lee G. Anderson (ed.), *Economic Impacts of Extended Fisheries Jurisdiction*, Ann Arbor, MI: Ann Arbor Science.

Strauss, Robert P. and G. David Hughes (1976), 'A new approach to the demand for public goods', *Journal of Public Economics*, **6** (3), 191–204.

Swartz, David G. and Ivar E. Strand (1981), 'Avoidance costs associated with imperfect information: the case of kepones', *Land Economics*, **57** (2), 139–50.

Takayama, Akira (1985), *Mathematical Economics*, Cambridge: Cambridge University Press.

Taylor, C. Robert and Hovav Talpaz (1979), 'Approximately optimal carryover levels for wheat in the United States', *American Journal of Agricultural Economics*, **61** (1), 32–40.

Telser, Lester (1964), 'Advertising and competition', *Journal of Political Economy*, **72** (6), 537–62.

Theil, Henri (1971), *Principles of Econometrics*, New York: John Wiley and Sons.

Thomson, William and Terje Lensberg (1989), *Axiomatic Theory of Bargaining with a Variable Number of Agents*, Cambridge: Cambridge University Press.

Thurman, Walter N. and J.E. Easley Jr (1992), 'Valuing changes in commercial fishery harvests: a general equilibrium derived demand analysis', *Journal of Environmental Economics and Management*, **22** (3), 226–40.

Thurman, Walter N. and Michael K. Wohlgenant (1989), 'Consistent estimation of general equilibrium welfare effects', *American Journal of Agricultural Economics*, **71** (4), 1041–5.

Thurow, Lester C. (1980), *The Zero-Sum Society: Distribution and the Possibilities for Economic Change*, New York: Basic Books.

Tietenberg, Thomas (2000), *Environmental and Natural Resource Economics*, 5th edition, New York: Addison-Wesley.

Tisdell, Clem (1963), 'Uncertainty, instability, and expected profit', *Econometrica*, **31** (1–2), 243–47.

Tobin, James (1969), 'Comment on Borch and Feldstein', *Review of Economic Studies*, **360** (105), 13–14.

Tsur, Yacov (1993), 'A simple procedure to evaluate ex ante producer welfare under price uncertainty', *American Journal of Agricultural Economics*, **75** (1), 44–51.

Turnovsky, Stephen J. (1976), 'The distribution of welfare gains from price stabilization: the case of multiplicative disturbances', *International Economic Review*, **17** (1), 133–48.

——— (1978), 'The distribution of welfare gains from price stabilization: a survey of some theoretical issues', in F. Gerard Adams and Sonia A. Klein (eds), *Stabilizing World Commodity Markets*, Lexington, MA: Heath-Lexington Books, pp. 119–48.

Turnovsky, Stephen, Haim Shalit and Andrew Schmitz (1980), 'Consumer's surplus, price instability and consumer welfare', *Econometrica*, **48** (1), 135–52.

Ulrich, Alvin, Hartley Furtan and Andrew Schmitz (1986), 'Public and private returns from join venture research: an example from agriculture', *Quarterly Journal of Economics*, **C1** (1), 103–29.

US Congress, Joint Economic Committee (1969), *The Analysis and Evaluation of Public Expenditures: The PPB System: Compendium*, 91st Congress, 1st Session I.

US Department of Agriculture (various issues), *Agricultural Statistics*, Washington, DC: US Government Printing Office.

US Environmental Protection Agency (2000), *Guidelines for Preparing Economic Analyses*, Office of the Administrator, EPA 240-R-00-003.

US International Trade Commission (1977), *Conditions of Competition in U.S. Markets between Domestic and Foreign Live Cattle and Cattle Meat Fit for Human Consumption*, **842**, 1–126.

US National Oceanic and Atmospheric Administration (1993), 'Report of the NOAA panel on contingent valuation', *Federal Register*, **58** (10), 4601–14.

van den Doel, Hans (1979), *Democracy and Welfare Economics*, London: Cambridge University Press.

Varian, Hal R. (1992), *Microeconomic Analysis*, 3rd edition, New York: W.W. Norton.

Vartia, Yrjo O. (1983), 'Efficient methods of measuring welfare change and compensated income interms of ordinary demand functions', *Econometrica*, **51** (1), 79–98.

Veeman, Michele M. (1982), 'Social cost of supply-restricting marketing boards', *Canadian Journal of Agricultural Economics*, **30** (1), 21–36.

Vercammen, James and Andrew Schmitz (1992), 'Supply management and import concessions', *Canadian Journal of Economics*, **25** (4), 951–7.

Vickrey, William (1964), 'Discussion', *American Economic Review*, Proceedings, **54** (3), 88–92.

von Neumann, John and Oscar Morgenstern (1944), *Theory of Games and Economic Behavior*, Princeton, NJ: Princeton University Press.

Wahl, Thomas, Dermot Hayes and Andrew Schmitz (1992), *Agriculture and Trade in the Pacific: Toward the Twenty-First Century*, Boulder, CO: Westview Press.

Warren-Boulton, Frederick R. (1977), 'Vertical control by labor unions', *American Economic Review*, **67** (3), 309–22.

Waugh, Frederick V. (1944), 'Does the consumer benefit from price instability?', *Quarterly Journal of Economics*, **58** (4), 602–14.

Weinstein, Milton O. and Robert J. Quinn (1983), 'Psychological considerations in valuing health risk reductions', *Natural Resources Journal*, **24** (3), 659–73.

Weisbrod, Burton A. (1964), 'Collective consumption services of individual goods', *Quarterly Journal of Economics*, **78** (3), 471–7.

Weitzman, Martin L. (1974), 'Prices vs. quantities', *Review of Economic Studies*, **41** (128), 477–91.

——— (1992), 'On Diversity', *Quarterly Journal of Economics*, **107** (2), 363–405.

——— (1999), 'Just keep discounting, but . . .', in Paul R. Portney and John P. Weyant (eds), *Discounting and Intergenerational Equity*, Washington, DC: Resources for the Future.

West, S. and R.C. Williams III (2002), 'Empirical estimates for the environmental policy making in a second-best world', Macalester College, Department of Economics Working Paper.

Williams, Jeffrey C. and Brian D. Wright (1991), *Storage and Commodity Markets*, Cambridge: Cambridge University Press.

Williamson, Oliver E. (1968), 'Economies as an antitrust defense: the welfare tradeoffs', *American Economic Review*, **58** (1), 18–36.

Willig, Robert D. (1973), *Consumer's Surplus: A Rigorous Cookbook*, Technical Report No. 98, Stanford, CA: Stanford University Press: Institute for Mathematical Studies in the Social Sciences.

——— (1976), 'Consumer's surplus without apology', *American Economic Review*, **66** (4), 589–97.

——— (1979), 'Consumer's surplus without apology: reply', *American Economic Review*, **69** (3), 469–74.

Wisecarver, Daniel (1976), 'The social cost of input distortions: a comment and a generalization', *American Economic Review*, **66** (1), 235–38.

Wold, Herman and Lars Jureen (1953), *Demand Analysis: A Study in Econometrics*, New York: John Wiley and Sons.

Worcester, Dean A. Jr (1969), 'Innovations in the calculations of welfare loss to monopoly', *Western Economic Journal*, **7** (3), 234–43.

World Commission on Environment and Development (1987), *Our Common Future* (Bruntland Report), London: Oxford University Press.

Wright, Brian (1983), 'The economics of invention incentives: patents, prizes, and research contracts', *American Economic Review*, **83** (4), 691–707.

Yassour, Joseph, David Zilberman and Gordon C. Rausser (1981), 'Optimal choices among alternative technologies with stochastic yield', *American Journal of Agricultural Economics*, **63** (4), 719–23.

Zajac, Edward E. (1976), 'An elementary road map of integrability and consumer's surplus', report, Murray Hill, NJ: Bell Telephone Laboratories, Inc.

Zangwill, Willard (1969), *Nonlinear Programming: A Unified Approach*, Englewood Cliffs, NJ: Prentice Hall.

Zusman, Pinhas (1976), 'The incorporation and measurement of social power in economic models', *International Economic Review*, **17** (2), 447–62.

Zwart, Anthony C. and Karl D. Mielke (1979), 'The influence of domestic pricing policies and buffer stocks on price stability in the world wheat industry', *American Journal of Agricultural Economics*, **61** (3), 434–47.

Name index

Subject index